The Handy Book For Genealogists

United States of America

Eighth Edition

Published by

The Everton Publishers, Inc.
P.O. Box 368, Logan, Utah 84321

FOREWORD

Eighth Edition
The Handy Book For Genealogists

The Handy Book for Genealogists has been in print since 1947. Over the years, hundreds, or even thousands of genealogists from every corner of the United States, have helped to make this book the most popular research aid available for those doing research in the United States. We thank all of you for your efforts in this regard.

In 1947 when the first edition of *The Hand Book For Genealogists* was introduced, it was through the dedicated efforts of Walter M. Everton and his wife, Pearl Knowles Everton. We owe the success of this book to the foresight, inspiration, planning, dedication, and hard work of this couple. They produced an original book, a research help that genealogical researchers needed in the early 1940's, and they continue to need today.

Other editions of *The Handy Book For Genealogists* were further improved upon and updated through the direction of George B. Everton, Sr. and his wife, Ellen Nielsen Everton.

Gunnar Rasmussen also contributed his help and expertise in preparing some of the early editions of this publication.

During the past 44 years this book has been in print we have not kept a count of the number of copies printed. However, the sixth and seventh editions had 12 printings each. We are sure that the total number of Handy Books printed since its inception would be over 750,000 copies, making it the most popular genealogical book ever printed.

Our special thanks and appreciation go out to the county officials from throughout the United States who generously responded to our request for updated data about the county records in their keeping. We have solicited their help and cooperation seven times and over 96% of these county officials have responded favorably to our appeal for help. Through the cooperation of over 3500 county officials, each edition of *The Handy Book for Genealogists* contains the most accurate and up-to-date data about county records ever compiled into a single publication.

Last of all, we must thank all of the employees of The Everton Publishing Company and our subsidiary, Global Research Systems, for their help in preparing this edition. Without their help we could not have completed our project. We know this 8th edition of *The Handy Book For Genealogists* will be more popular than any previous edition — it is new from front to back. We know you are going to enjoy it, and it will be a great help to you in your genealogical research here in the United States.

George B. Everton, Jr.
Louise Mathews Everton

CONTENTS

CONTENTS

INTRODUCTION

The Handy Book for Genealogists is a well-known, popular reference for American family historians. About 750,000 copies of the previous editions of this valuable book are in the hands of genealogists throughout the world.

The eighth edition includes many important new features, while retaining and updating the most useful aspects of previous editions. The text begins with a general section on the United States, followed by sections for each of the states and the District of Columbia, arranged in alphabetic order.

Some previous editions included short sections on foreign countries, but these have not been included in this edition. In the future we plan to publish separate books on genealogical research in each of several foreign nations.

New for this edition is a section containing color maps of each state. The map shows the state and county boundaries, county names, rivers and lakes within the state boundaries. These waterways can be extremely useful in plotting travel routes used by our ancestors as they moved from one part of the country to another.

Also new for this edition is a special section on migration routes in the eastern United States. Knowing where your ancestor may have resided prior to his current location is essential for tracking earlier records on the family. Each trail is described, and a summary of the states and counties through which the trail passed is given. Maps showing the routes of these migration trails are also included. While there is some disagreement on the exact location of each path, much effort has been put forth to assure accuracy.

As with each edition, we have requested information from every county or parish clerk on records in their custody of value to genealogists, including vital records, court proceedings, land and property records, and a variety of other record types. Approximately 95% of these county and parish officials have responded.

For those counties whose clerks have not responded, we have attempted to fill in some details with a summary of holdings by the Family History Library in Salt Lake City, Utah. This is the largest genealogical library in the world, with over 1,000 branches, known as Family History Centers. While we cannot list in detail every record available in this system for each county, we have included a summary of some major record types available for those counties whose clerks have not responded to our queries. For full information on the records available from any county, you should contact your local Family History Center.

This edition also includes the most recent, comprehensive list of archives, genealogical libraries, and societies for each state. Annual updates of this list appear in *The Genealogical Helper*. The lists of valuable printed sources have also been reviewed and updated for this edition.

State and County Information

As you seek back in time for information on your ancestors, you are certain to turn up many interesting events. This search for records to identify your ancestors requires careful attention to places where events took place. Many of these localities may have changed names, or may no longer exist. County and state boundaries may have changed. Some states were territories before attaining statehood. All of these changes affected records and the way they were kept.

This book is organized alphabetically by state, with general information on the state, its history, its records, its genealogical societies, libraries, and valuable publications on genealogy in the state. You should always consult this section first, before proceeding to the county listings that follow. Here you can find out about records and their location on a state level, possibly saving you valuable time in your search for your ancestors.

For example, the listing for Nebraska includes this information:

NEBRASKA

CAPITAL · LINCOLN — TERRITORY 1854 — STATE 1867 (37th)
State Map on Page M-25

This is followed with a brief sketch of state history.
> 1714 - the first european to enter Nebraska appears to have been Ethienne Veniard de Bourgmond, a french adventurer.
> 1803 - part of the Louisiana Purchase
> 1820 - before 1820 it was part of the Missouri Territory
> etc.

This information, supplemented with other county data, appears in alphabetic order following the general information on records in each state.

Here's a look at the listing for Nance county:

Name	Map Index	Date Created	Parent County or Territory From Which Organized	Telephone Number
* **Nance**	C4	1879	Merrick	

Nance County, PO Box 338, Fullerton, NE 68638-0338 . . . . (308)536-2331
(Co Clk has m rec from 1890, Ind rec from 1879; Co Judge has pro rec; Clk Dis Ct has div & civ ct rec from 1882)

* At least one county history has been published about this county.
† Inventory of county archives was made by the Historical Records Survey. (See Introduction)

Looking at each component separately:

Name: This is the current name of the county or parish. If the name has changed, the former name appears in alphabetic order with a reference to the current name. A county that has been discontinued is also noted.

Map Index: The grid coordinates for the county on the state map, located on page M-25.

Date Created: The year the county or parish was created or incorporated.

Parent County or Territory From Which Organized: The name or names of the county or counties from which the county was formed. Some counties were formed at the same time as the state or territory was organized ("Original Counties"), while some counties were organized from previous entities, such as a state or territory (in the eastern United States), or a Mexican municipality (in the American southwest).

To find the records of an ancestor during a specific time period, you will need to know which government office would have custody of the records for that time period. This is the reason for giving information on "parent" counties. Even if a family did not physically move their residence, the location of records on that family could have moved as jurisdictional boundaries changed.

For example, a family living in what was to become Ford County, Illinois between 1788 and 1865 may have records in the custody of nine different offices. Working backwards: Ford County was organized in 1859 from land previously belonging to Clark County. Clark County was formed in 1819 from land previously belonging to Crawford County, which was formed in 1816 from a part of Edwards County. Edwards County was organized in 1814 from parts of both Madison and Gallatin counties. Madison had been split off of St. Clair County in 1812, while Gallatin was organized from a part of Randolph County in 1812. In turn, St. Clair County was formed from the old Northwest Territory in 1790, while Randolph County was organized from the Northwest Territory in 1795. To get all of the records on your family, you would have to consult the archives of all nine of these governmental units.

* Indicates that at least one history of the county or parish has been published.

† Indicates that a survey (inventory) of county records has been published by the Historical Records Survey.

County Office: The address and phone number of the main offices of the county or parish.

Co Clk has m rec from 1890, Ind rec from 1879: The County Clerk has marriage records from 1890, land records from 1879.

Co Judge has pro rec: The County Judge has probate records.

Clk Dis Ct has dic & civ ct rec from 1882: The Clerk of the District Court has divorce and civil court records from 1882.

Census Records

Since 1790, federal censuses have been taken every ten years. Before 1850, federal census schedules listed only heads of households by full name, with the other members of the household grouped within certain age groups by sex. Beginning in 1850, federal schedules showed every member of the household, with his name, age, sex, occupation, and state or country of birth. At this time, federal census schedules for the years 1790 through 1910 are available to the general public, although the 1890 census has been almost entirely destroyed.

Although every census schedule is valuable for genealogical research, searching these censuses can be very time consuming. Fortunately, since the advent of the computer, many censuses have been indexed, and these indexes are widely available in print, on microfiche, microfilm, computer disk, or tape. Statewide indexes are available for every federal census from 1790 through 1850, and for many of the 1860 and 1870 federal censuses. Indexes are also available on microfilm from the National Archives for the 1880 and 1900 censuses, and for eleven states for the 1910 census.

For this edition of *The Handy Book for Genealogists*, we have revised the listings of available census and mortality schedules for each state, including some notes on specific schedules. However, this is not intended to be a comprehensive listing of all census records, mortality schedules, and census substitutes. For more complete information you should consult sources devoted entirely to the subject of censuses and census substitutes.

There are many sources of information on census records and indexes, including:

The United States Census Compendium, by John D. Stemmons. Everton Publishers, Logan, Utah.

Researcher's Guide to United States Census Availability, 1790-1910, by Ann B. Hamilton. Heritage Books, Bowie, MD, 1987.

Twenty Censuses: Populations and Housing Questions, 1790-1980. United States Government Printing Office, Washington, DC, 1979.

The Family History Library Catalog (FHLC), Family History Library, Salt Lake City, Utah (also available in every Family History Center).

Transcriptions, indexes, and copies of census schedules are also published every month, and many of these are reviewed in the "New on the Bookshelf" column in *The Genealogical Helper*, Everton Publishers, Box 368, Logan, Utah 84321.

Mortality Schedules

In addition to censuses, the federal government also compiled lists of persons who died in the twelve months prior to the censuses taken in 1850, 1860, 1870, and 1880. As with the population census schedules, these mortality schedules were filed geographically (by county). However, printed statewide indexes are now available for every surviving mortality schedule.

State Vital Statistics

The information included in this edition for each state was obtained from the U.S. Department of Health and Human Services, as published in the booklet *Where to Write for Vital Records*. Generally, each state will have birth, marriage, death, and divorce records for the twentieth century. Because the prices of certificates from the state offices change, we have included a phone number to call in each state for information on current prices.

Checklist of Historical Records Survey

Surveys of public record archives were conducted in most states between 1936 and 1943 by the Works Progress Administration (WPA). Many of these records are vital to genealogical research. While few WPA publications give full transcripts, they do name the records that were available in the respective archives at the time of the survey. These inventories often give the condition of the various records, where they were stored at the time of the survey, and the dates of commencement and conclusion of the records. Of course, the actual records must be consulted to extract all of the information they contain.

A checklist of these publications was originally published by the WPA as *W.P.A. Technical Series, Research and Records Bibliography Number 7*. It has been reprinted by the Genealogical Publishing Company, Baltimore, Maryland, as *Check List of Historical Records Survey Publications, Bibliography of Research Projects Reports*, by Sargent B. Child and Dorothy B. Holmes. The Family History Library in Salt Lake City has a microfilm copy, number 874,113.

Abbreviations Used in this Edition

The following abbreviations have been used to save space, making it possible for more information to be included in this edition:

appr............................ appraisement, appraisal	bur ....burial
Asr.. Assessor	cem... cemetery
Aud .... Auditor	cen ....census
b ....birth	Chan.. Chancery
bk.. book	CH ....Courthouse

City Clk	City Clerk	inc	incomplete
civ	civil	J P	Justice of the Peace
Clk	Clerk	lib	library
Clk Chan Ct	Clerk of Chancery Court	Ind	land
Clk Cir Ct	Clerk of Circuit Court	m.	marriage
Clk Cts	Clerk of Courts	Mag	Magistrate
Clk Dis Ct	Clerk of District Court	Mil Dis Rec	Military Discharge Records
Clk Mag Cts	Clerk of Magistrates Court	mtg	mortgage
Clk of Peace	Clerk of the Peace	Ord	Ordinary
Clk Sup Ct	Clerk of Superior Court	Ord Ct	Ordinary Court
Comm	Commissioner, Commissioners	Orph Ct	Orphans Court
Com Pleas Ct	Common Pleas Court	Par Clk	Parish Clerk
com	complete	pro	probate
Co	County	Pro Judge	Probate Judge
Co Asr	County Assessor	pub	public
Co Aud	County Auditor	Rcdr	Recorder
Co Clk	County Clerk	Rcdr Deeds	Recorder of Deeds
Co Health	County Health Department	rec	record, records
Co Judge	County Judge	Reg in Chan	Register in Chancery
Co Ord	County Ordinary	Reg of Wills	Register of Wills
Co Rcdr	County Recorder	Rgstr	Registrar
Ct	Court	Sup	Superior
crim	criminal	Supt	Superintendent
d	death	Surr	Surrogate
Dis Ct	District Court	Terr	Territory
div	divorce	Twn Clk	Town Clerk
FHL	Family History Library of The Church of Jesus Christ of Latter-day Saints, Salt Lake City, Utah	Treas	Treasurer
		Unorg	Unorganized
Gen Soc	Genealogical Society	Vit Stat	Vital Statistics
Hist Soc	Historical Society	War Ser	War Service

An asterisk (*) preceding a county's name indicates that at least one county history has been published for that county.

A dagger (†) preceding a county's name indicates its inclusion in the Historical Records Survey.

UNITED STATES OF AMERICA

CAPITAL - WASHINGTON, DISTRICT OF COLUMBIA

In 1607, Captain John Smith, accompanied by 105 settlers, established the English colony of Jamestown, in what is now Virginia. This started a land rush that would last for centuries. This was followed by the establishment of Plymouth Colony in 1620, Peter Minuit's purchase of Manhattan Island in 1626, the establishment of Maryland as a Roman Catholic colony in 1634, and numerous other settlements.

Over the next 150 years many people left their homes to settle in the New World. The French settled in the area of the Great Lakes, in what is now upstate New York and the province of Quebec, and along the coast of the Gulf of Mexico, in what was to become Mississippi and Louisiana. The Dutch established towns in New York, New Jersey, and Pennsylvania. Germans and other German-speaking groups fleeing religious persecution established colonies in New York, Pennsylvania, and the Carolinas. The British settled up and down the Atlantic and Gulf coasts.

The population of the new nation grew from about 4,600 in 1630 to over 100,000 in 1670 to over a quarter of a million by 1700. When space became limited on the coasts, people of all origins moved inland. Even though each settler viewed it as a land of opportunity, the various visions of opportunity, and loyalties to different political systems caused friction. Eventually, major confrontations broke out between the English colonists and the French, resulting in King George's War in 1744 and the French Indian War (the Seven Years War) in 1754. The resulting treaty, in 1763, expanded British influence in areas of Canada and the lower American Colonies.

However, as Britain's American Colony continued to grow to over two million by 1770, its citizens became increasingly uncomfortable with the absentee rule of the British Crown. A series of unpopular taxes enacted between 1764 and 1774 led to the seating of the first Continental Congress in 1774, and eventually to a Declaration of Independence by thirteen colonies in 1776, formally creating a new nation. By the time the Revolutionary War came to an end in 1781, almost 250,000 men had served the American cause, with about 34,000 casualties on the American side.

Although the colonies of the new nation had a working agreement in the Articles of Confederation, a more formal, binding document was needed to ensure that the various states would not disintegrate. At a convention in Philadelphia in 1787, a constitution was written and proposed to the individual states. That constitution was ratified and put into effect in 1789.

One of the provisions of the new constitution required a census of the population every ten years, beginning in 1790. That first census included only the names of the heads of households, and showed a population of 3,929,214. By the next federal census in 1800, the population count had risen to 5,308,483.

In 1803 the geographic size of the United States was doubled by the purchase from France of an area stretching from the Gulf Coast to what is now Montana. Total cost for the new real estate was $15 million. In 1819, Spain ceded the Florida peninsula and Gulf coastal territory west to Louisiana to the United States.

Even while the country was acquiring land to the south and west, its citizens were still fending off the British. The War of 1812 lasted until 1815, with 285,000 Americans fighting to maintain their freedom from Britain, at a cost of 7,000 casualties.

Although bonds had been raised to purchase lands from the French, the United States still had difficulty raising funds for the veterans of its wars. Instead, huge tracts of western lands were opened for exclusive use as "bounties" for those who had served in U.S. military actions. The prospect of free, open land in the west lured many veterans and their families into the new states and territories of Ohio, Indiana, Illinois, Michigan, Alabama, Mississippi, Arkansas, and Missouri.

But again, conflicts between settlers arose due to their divergent cultural backgrounds. Slavery in various states and territories was a source of conflict, and on several occasions it threatened to split the nation. Henry Clay's Missouri Compromise of 1820 set boundaries for freedom and slavery, but was only a temporary measure. In 1835 Texas declared its independence from Mexico and joined the United States in 1845. Following the war with Mexico from 1846 to 1848, Mexico ceded vast portions of the American West to the United States, including California, Arizona, New Mexico, Nevada, Utah, and part of Colorado.

The opening of these new lands with their apparently unlimited possibilities exacerbated the debate on the slavery issue, and where slavery should be allowed. Another compromise was worked out by Henry Clay in 1850, but it could not solve the problem. By the end of the 1850's several southern states had become disenchanted with the process, and openly talked of secession from the rest of the nation.

Between 1861 and 1865, the Civil War (also known as the War Between the States, or the War of the Rebellion) racked the nation. Over two million men served in the Union forces, and over a million served in the forces of the

Confederacy. By the end of the war, casualties among Union forces were about 650,000, against 130,000 suffered by the Confederacy.

Although it would take decades for the wounds of that war to heal, westward expansion in the United States continued. In 1867 Alaska was purchased from Russia for $7.2 million. To encourage settlement in new lands, the Homestead Act was passed in 1862, granting free land to those who would settle it. The first transcontinental railroad was completed in 1869, allowing easier, quicker access to frontier territories.

The effect of these developments on the population of the country was dramatic. During the decade of the Civil War, the population grew by only 7 million, from 31 million to 38 million. But the population rose to over 50 million by 1880, to almost 63 million by 1890, and to over 76 million by the turn of the century.

Between 1820 and 1920, over 30 million immigrants arrived on America's shores. The major ports for the immigrants were New York, Boston, Baltimore, Philadelphia, New Orleans, and San Francisco. But numerous other ports on the Atlantic, Pacific, and Gulf coasts also welcomed immigrants, and large numbers entered overland, crossing the Canadian and Mexican borders.

Eventually, the numbers of immigrants, and their cultural diversity from those already living in the United States created a backlash that caused the welcome mat to be removed. In 1921 Congress established a quota system limiting the amount of immigrants that would be accepted. This system did not undergo major modification until 1965, vastly reducing the number of immigrants during that 45-year span. Even so, the population of the United States grew from 106 million in 1920 to almost 180 million by 1960.

In the meantime, the United States was involved in three military actions. Its participation in the First World War lasted from 1917 to 1918, involving about 5 million American servicemen, at a cost of 320,000 casualties. The Second World War involved 16 million Americans from 1941 to 1945, with a million casualties. The United States sent 6 million men to serve in the Korean War (1950-1953), with 160,000 casualties.

In 1959 Alaska was admitted to the Union as the 49th state, with Hawaii following as the 50th state later the same year.

American military involvement in Vietnam between 1963 and 1973 involved 9 million servicemen, who suffered 200,000 casualties, while 500,000 served in the war against Iraq, with less than 400 deaths.

Valuable Printed Sources

Atlases, Maps, and Gazetteers

Adams, James Truslow. *Atlas of American History*. New York: Charles Scribner's Sons, 1943.

Bullinger's Postal and Shipping Guide for the United States and Canada. Westwood, New Jersey: Bullinger's Guides, annual.

Fanning's Illustrated Gazetteer of the United States. New York: Ensign, Bridgman, and Fanning, 1855.

Kirkham, E. Kay. *A Genealogical and Historical Atlas of the United States of America*. Logan, Utah: Everton Publishers, 1976.

Rand-McNally Commercial Atlas and Marketing Guide. New York: Rand-McNally & Co., annual.

Seltzer, Leon E. *The Columbia-Lippincott Gazetteer of the World*. Morningside Heights, New York: Columbia University Press, 1952.

United States Directory of Post Offices. Washington, DC: U.S. Postal Department, annual.

Census Records

Dubester, Henry J. *State Censuses: An Annotated Bibliography of Censuses of Population Taken After the Year 1790 by the States and Territories of the United States*. Washington, DC: Government Printing Office, 1948. Knightstown, Indiana: Bookmark, 1975 reprint.

Hamilton, Ann B. *Researcher's Guide to United States Census Availability, 1790-1910*. Bowie, Maryland: Heritage Books, 1987.

Konrad, J. *Directory of Census Information Sources*. Summit Publications, 1984.

Parker, J. Carlyle. *City, County, Town and Township Index to the 1850 Federal Census Schedules*. Detroit: Gale Research Co., 1979.

Thorndale, William. *Map Guide to the U.S. Federal Census, 1790-1910*. Baltimore: Genealogical Publishing Co., 1987.

Cemetery and Mortician Records

American Blue Book of Funeral Directors. New York: The American Funeral Director, annual.

Stemmons, Jack and Diane Stemmons. *Cemetery Record Compendium*. Logan, Utah: Everton Publishers, 1979.

Church Records

Kirkham, E. Kay. *A Survey of American Church Records*. Logan, Utah: Everton Publishers, 1978.

Mead, Frank S. *Handbook of Denominations*. New York: Arlington Press, 1965.

Directories

American Library Directory. New York: R. R. Bowker Co., annual.

Ayer Directory of Publications. Bala Cynwyd, Pennsylvania: Ayer Press, annual.

Brigham, Clarence Saunders. *History and Bibliography of American Newspapers, 1690-1820*. Hamden, Connecticut: Shoe String Press, 1962.

Encyclopedia of Associations. Detroit: Gale Research Co., annual.

Gregory, Winifred. *American Newspapers, 1821-1936: A Union List of Files Available in the United States and Canada*. New York: H. W. Wilson Co., 1937.

Library of Congress. *Newspapers in Microform, United States, 1948-1972*. Washington, DC: Catalog Publication Division Processing Department, 1976.

Milner, Anita. *Newspaper Indexes: A Location and Subject Guide for Researchers*. Metuchen, New Jersey: Scarecrow Press, 1979.

National Historical Publications and Records Commission. *Directory of Archives and Manuscript Repositories in the United States*. Washington, DC: National Archives and Records Service, 1978.

Parch, Grace D. *Directory of Newspaper Libraries in the United States and Canada*. New York: Project of the Newspaper Division, Special Libraries Association, 1976.

Genealogical Research Guides

Bentley, Elizabeth Petty. *The Genealogist's Address Book*. Baltimore: Genealogical Publishing Co., 1991.

Filby, P. William. *A Bibliography of American County Histories*. Baltimore: Genealogical Publishing Co., 1985.

Greenwood, Val D. *The Researcher's Guide to American Genealogy*. Baltimore: Genealogical Publishing Co., 1988.

Kirkham, E. Kay. *Handy Index to Record-Searching in the Larger Cities of the United States*. Logan, Utah: Everton Publishers, 1974.

————. *Index to Some of the Family Records of the Southern States*. Logan, Utah: Everton Publishers, 1979.

————. *Our Native Americans: Their Records of Genealogical Value*. Logan, Utah: Everton Publishers, 1984.

Makower, Joel and Linda Zaleskie. *The American History Sourcebook*. New York: Prentice-Hall, 1988.

Bibliographies

Filby, P. William. *American and British Genealogy and Heraldry*. Chicago: American Library Association, 1976.

Genealogical Index of the Newberry Library, Chicago. Boston: G. K. Hall, 1960.

The Greenlaw Index of the New England Historic Genealogical Society. Boston: G. K. Hall, 1979.

Herbert, Miranda C. and Barbara McNeil. *Biography and Genealogy Master Index*. Detroit: Gale Research Co., 1980.

Jacobus, Donald Lines. *Index to Genealogical Periodicals*. Baltimore: Genealogical Publishing Co., 1978.

Kaminkow, Marion J. *Genealogies in the Library of Congress: A Bibliography*. Baltimore: Magna Carta Book Co., 1972.

————. *A Complement to Genealogies in the Library of Congress*. Baltimore: Magna Carta Book Co., 1981.

————. *United States Local Histories in the Library of Congress, A Bibliography*. Baltimore: Magna Carta Book Co., 1975.

New York Public Library. *Dictionary Catalog of the Manuscript Division*. Boston: G. K. Hall, 1967.

————. *Dictionary Catalog of the Local History and Genealogy Division*. Boston: G. K. Hall, 1974.

Rider, Fremont. *The American Genealogical-Biographical Index*. Middletown, Connecticut: Godfrey Memorial Library, 1981.

Schreiner-Yantis, Netti. *Genealogical and Local History Books in Print*. Springfield, Virginia: Genealogical Books in Print, 1981.

Sperry, Kip. *Index to Genealogical Periodical Literature, 1960-1977*. Detroit: Gale Research Co., 1979.

Towle, Laird C. and Catherine M. Mayhew. *Genealogical Periodical Annual Index*. Bowie, Maryland: Heritage Books, annual.

Military Records

D.A.R. Patriot Index. Washington, DC: National Society, Daughters of the American Revolution, 1979.

Giller, Sadye, William H. Dumont and Louise M. Dumont. *Index of Revolutionary War Pension Applications*. Washington, DC: National Genealogical Society, 1966.

Groene, Bertram H. *Tracing Your Civil War Ancestor*. Winston-Salem, North Carolina: John F. Blair, 1973.

Neagles, James C. and Lila L. Neagles. *Locating Your Revolutionary War Ancestors: A Guide to the Military Records*. Logan, Utah: Everton Publishers, 1982.

National Archives

Babbel, June Andrew. *Lest We Forget: A Guide to Genealogical Research in the Nation's Capital*. Annandale, Virginia: Annandale and Oakton Stakes of The Church of Jesus Christ of Latter-day Saints, 1976.

Guide to Genealogical Research in the National Archives. Washington, DC: National Archives Trust Fund Board, 1983.

Passenger Lists and Naturalization Records

Coldham, Peter Wilson. *The Complete Book of Emigrants in Bondage, 1614-1755*. Baltimore: Genealogical Publishing Co., 1988.

Filby, P. William, et al. *Passenger and Immigration Lists Index*. Detroit: Gale Research Co., 1988.

Miller, Olga K. *Migration, Emigration, Immigration*. Logan, Utah: Everton Publishers, 1981.

Neagles, James C. and Lila Lee Neagles. *Locating Your Immigrant Ancestor*. Logan, Utah: Everton Publishers, 1975.

Newman, John J. *American Naturalization Processes and Procedures*. Indiana Historical Society, 1985.

Tepper, Michael. *American Passenger Arrival Records: A Guide to the Records of Immigrants Arriving at American Ports by Sail and Steam*. Baltimore: Genealogical Publishing Co., 1988.

Vital Records

Deputy, Marilyn. *Vital Records in the United States*. Salt Lake City: Family History Library, 1981.

Stemmons, John D. and E. Diane Stemmons. *The Vital Records Compendium*. Logan, Utah: Everton Publishers, 1979.

Where to Write for Vital Records. Hyattsville, Maryland: U.S. Department of Health and Human Services, 1987.

ALABAMA

CAPITAL · MONTGOMERY — TERRITORY 1817 — STATE 1819 (22nd)
State Map on Page M-1

The Spanish explorers, Panfilo de Narvaez and Cabeza de Vaca, were among the first white men to pass through this area in 1528. The first white settlers were Spanish and French, perhaps as early as 1699. The first community founded was Mobile in 1702, which was settled by the French. France governed the area from 1710 to 1763 when England gained control. Settlers during this period came from South Carolina and Georgia, as well as England, France, and Spain.

To avoid participation in the Revolutionary War, many British sympathizers left Georgia in 1775 to settle in the Alabama area. Planters from Georgia, Virginia, and the Carolinas followed in 1783. That same year, Britain ceded the Mobile area to Spain. The remainder of present-day Alabama was claimed by Georgia. Three years after setting the southern boundary at the 31st parallel in 1795, the Alabama region was made part of the Territory of Mississippi.

The rich Tennessee Valley district in the northern part of Alabama was settled in 1809 by Scotch-Irish from Tennessee. In the early 1800's emigrants from the Carolinas and Virginia came to the central and western parts of Alabama, especially along the Tombigbee and Black Warrior Rivers. During the War of 1812, American forces captured Mobile from the Spanish and defeated the Creek Indians. This led to the removal of the Creeks and other Indian tribes and opened the area to settlement. The influx of settlers, most of whom brought black slaves with them, resulted in the formation of the Alabama Territory in 1817. Seven counties were formed with St. Stephens becoming the capital. In November 1818, Cahaba, which existed only on paper, was made the capital, although Huntsville was used until Cahaba was built in 1820. Tuscaloosa became the capital in 1826, followed by Montgomery, the present capital, in 1846.

A convention held in Huntsville in 1819 met to prepare a state constitution. Representatives of all 22 of Alabama's counties participated in the convention. On December 14, 1819, Alabama became the 22nd state.

Alabama seceded from the Union in 1861. About 2,500 men from Alabama served in the Union forces and estimates of up to 100,000 men served in the Confederate forces. Alabama was readmitted to the Union in 1868.

The Bureau of Vital Statistics, Department of Public Health, State Office Building, Montgomery, AL 36130 (to verify current fees, call 205-261-5033), has birth and death records since 1908 and incomplete records prior to 1908. Some county clerks have pre-1908 records as well. Some counties have courthouses in cities or towns in addition to those at the county seat. Statewide registration of marriage records began in 1936. These are located at the Bureau of Vital Statistics as well. Some counties also have marriage records mixed in with Probate Court records, which generally date back to the formation of the county. Divorce records are kept by the Supreme Court of the territory and the general assembly. Most divorce proceedings were filed with local chancery courts. In 1917, the chancery courts were merged with the circuit court in each county. Entries of naturalizations are scattered throughout court minute books, especially county circuit records. Early census records for French settlements near Mobile have been published. Territorial and state censuses exist for 1816, 1818, 1820, 1831, 1844, 1850, and 1866. The state censuses are available at the Alabama Department of Archives and History, 624 Washington Avenue, Montgomery, AL 36130. A special census of Confederate Veterans was taken in 1907, which has been abstracted, indexed, and published. Microfilm copies are available at the Department of Archives and History.

Genealogical Archives, Libraries and Societies

Alabama Archives and History Dept. World War Memorial Building, Montgomery, AL 36104

Andalusia Public Library, 212 S. Three Notch St., Andalusia, AL 36420

Auburn University Library, Auburn, AL 36830

Baldwin County Genealogical Society, P. O. Box 501, Lillian, AL 36549

Birmingham Public Library, 2020 7th Ave., N. Birmingham, AL 35203

Cullman County Public Library, 200 Clarke St., NE, Cullman, AL 35055

Florence - Lauderdale Public Library, 218 N. Wood Ave., Florence, AL 35603

Huntsville Public Library, Box 443, 108 Fountain, Huntsville, AL 35804

Liles Memorial Library, Box 308, 108 E. 10th St., Anniston, AL 36201

Steward University System Library, RFD 5, Box 109, Piedmont, AL 36272

University of Alabama Library, University, AL 35486

Alabama Genealogical Society, Inc., AGS Depository & Headquarters, Samford University Library, 800 Lakeshore Drive, Birmingham, AL 35229

American College of Heraldry, Drawer CG, University of Alabama, Tuscaloosa, AL 35486-2887

Baldwin County Genealogical Society, P. O. Box 501, Lillian, AL 36549

Birmingham Genealogical Society, Inc., P. O. Box 2432, Birmingham, AL 35201

Bullock County Historical Society, P. O. Box 663, Union Springs, AL 36089

Butler County Historical Society, P. O. Box 526, Greenville, AL 36037

Central Alabama Genealogical Society, P. O. Box 125, Selma, AL 36701

Civil War Descendants Society, P. O. Box 233, Athens, AL 35611

Coosa County Historical Society, P. O. Box 5, Rockford, AL 35136

Coosa River Valley Historical and Genealogical Society, P. O. Box 295, Centre, AL 35960

Genealogical Society of East Alabama, Inc., P. O. Drawer 1351, Auburn, AL 36830

Limestone County Historical Society, P. O. Box 82, Athens, AL 35611

Marion Pioneer Territorial Genealogical Society, Northwest Regional Library, P. O. Drawer O, Winfield, AL 35594

Mobile Genealogical Society, Inc., P. O. Box 6224, Mobile, AL 36606

Montgomery Genealogical Society, Inc., P. O. Box 230194, Montgomery, AL 36123-0194

Natchez Trace Genealogical Society, P. O. Box 420, Florence, AL 35631

North Central Alabama Genealogical Society, P. O. Box 13, Cullman, AL 35056-0013

Pea River Historical and Genealogical Society, P. O. Box 628, Enterprise, AL 36331

Piedmont Historical and Genealogical Society, P. O. Box 47, Spring Garden, AL 36275

Southeast Alabama Genealogical Society P. O. Box 143, Dothan, AL 36302

Southern Society of Genealogists, Inc., P. O. Box 295, Centre, AL 35960

Tennessee Valley Genealogical Society, P. O. Box 1568 Huntsville, AL 35807

Tuscaloosa Genealogical Society, 2020 Third Court E, Tuscaloosa, AL 35401

Printed Census Records and Mortality Schedules

Federal Census 1830, 1840, 1850, 1860, 1870, 1880, 1880 (part of Perry County only), 1900, 1910
State/Territorial Census 1820 (partial)
Northern Alabama Residents 1819
Confederate Veterans 1907

Valuable Printed Sources

Atlases, Maps, and Gazetteers

Birmingham Public Library. *A List of Nineteenth Century Maps of the State of Alabama*. Birmingham, Alabama: Oxmoor University Press, 1973.

———. *A List of 16th, 17th, and 18th Century Material in the Rucker Agee Map Collection*. Birmingham, Alabama: Oxmoor University Press, 1978.

Harris, W. Stuart. *Dead Towns of Alabama*. Tuscaloosa, Alabama: University of Alabama Press, 1977.

Read, William A. *Indian Place-Names in Alabama*. Baton Rouge, Louisiana: Louisiana State University Press, 1937.

Society of Pioneers of Montgomery. *Yesterday's Faces of Alabama: A Collection of Maps, 1822-1909*. Montgomery, Alabama: Brown Printing Co., 1978.

Genealogical Research Guides

Elliott, Wendy L. *Research in Alabama*. Bountiful, Utah: American Genealogical Lending Library, 1987.

Wright, Norman Edgar. *North American Genealogical Sources - Southern States*. Provo, Utah: Brigham Young University Press, 1968.

Histories

Brewer, Willis. *Alabama: Her History, Resources, War Record, and Public Men from 1540 to 1872*. Montgomery, Alabama: Barrett & Brown, 1872.

McMillan, Malcolm C. *The Land Called Alabama*. Austin, Texas: Steck-Vaughn Co., 1968.

Owen, Thomas M. *History of Alabama and Dictionary of Alabama*. Chicago: S. J. Clarke Publishing Co., 1921. Reprinted by Reprint Publishers, Spartanburg, South Carolina, 1978.

Saunders, James Edmonds. *Early Settlers of Alabama*. Baltimore: Genealogical Publishing Co., 1977 reprint.

Summersell, Charles Grayson. *Alabama History for Schools*. Montgomery, Alabama: Viewpoint Publications, 1975.

Immigration and Naturalization Records

King, Clinton P., et al. *Naturalization Records, Mobile, Alabama, 1833-1906*. Alabama Ancestors, 1986.

Military Records

Julich, Louise. *Roster of Revolutionary Soldiers and Patriots in Alabama*. Montgomery, Alabama: Parchment Press, 1979.

Owen, Thomas. *Revolutionary Soldiers in Alabama*. Baltimore: Genealogical Publishing Co., 1967.

ALABAMA COUNTY DATA
State Map on Page M-1

Name	Map Index	Date Created	Parent County or Territory From Which Organized
* **Autauga**	E5	1818	Montgomery

Autauga County, 4th & Court Sts, Prattville, AL 36067 .... (205)365-2281
(Judge of Pro has m, pro, adpt, and land deed rec)

Baine (abolished 1867, changed to Etowah 1868)

Baker (see Chilton) Name changed to Chilton in 1874

* **Baldwin**	I3	1809	Washington, part of Fla

Baldwin County, PO Box 639, Bay Mintte, AL 36507-0639 .... (205)937-0347
[FHL has some m & lnd rec, 1855 & 1866 census, 1907 Conf soldiers census]

* **Barbour**	G6	1832	Creek Cession 1832

Barbour County, PO Box 398, Clayton, AL 36016-0398 .... (205)775-3203
(Judge of Probate has m, lnd rec from 1832 to present; plat bk 1, early lnd owners; Co Comm has div rec from 1860; civil court rec from 1912)

Benton (see Calhoun)

* **Bibb**	E4	1818	Monroe, Montgomery

Bibb County, Court Sq, Centreville, AL 35042-1244 .... (205)926-4745
(changed from Cahawba 1820) (Co Clk has m pro, lnd rec 1818 to present; Reg in Chan has div rec; Clk Cir Ct has civ ct rec)

* **Blount**	C5	1818	Cherokee Cession, Montgomery

Blount County, 220 2nd Ave E, Oneonta, AL 35121-1716 .... (205)274-9111
(Clk Cir Ct has div, pro & civ ct rec; Co Clk has m, civ ct, lnd rec from 1818 to present; pro rec 1837 to present Judge of Pro)

* **Bullock**	F6	1866	Barbour, Macon, Montgomery, Pike

Bullock County, PO Box 230, Union Springs, AL 36089-0230 .... (205)738-2280
(Cir Ct. Clk has div & civ ct rec)

* **Butler**	G4	1819	Conecuh, Monroe

Butler County, PO Box 756, Greenville, AL 36037-0756 .... (205)382-3612
(Courthouse burned April 1853 - Pro Judge has b and d rec 1894 to 1919; m pro lnd rec 1853 to present)

Cahawba (see Bibb)

* **Calhoun**	C6	1832	Creek Cession of 1832

Calhoun County, 1702 Noble St Suite 103, Anniston, AL 36201-3889 .... (205)236-3521
(Name changed from Benton Jan 29, 1858) (Pro Judge has m rec 1834 to 1979; lnd rec 1865 to 1979; Reg in Chan has div; Clk Cir Ct has civ ct rec)

* **Chambers**	E6	1832	Creek Cession of 1832

Chambers County, County Courthouse, Lafayette, AL 36862 .... (205)864-8823
[FHL has some m, cem, pro, lnd rec, 1907 Conf soldiers census]

* **Cherokee**	C6	1836	Cherokee Cession 1835

Cherokee County, Courthouse Annex Rm 303, Centre, AL 35960 .... (205)927-3079
(Rec burned in 1882)

* **Chilton**	E4	1868	Autauga, Bibb, Perry, Shelby

Chilton County, PO Box 557, Clanton, AL 35045-0557 .... (205)755-1551
(Cir Clk has pro, div rec; civ ct rec from 1868 to present; Name changed from Baker in 1874; Pro Judge has m, lnd rec)

* **Choctaw**	F2	1847	Sumter, Washington

Choctaw County, 117 S Mulberry Ave, Butler, AL 36904-2557 .... (205)459-2155
(Co Clk has m, pro & lnd rec from 1873; Clk Cir Ct has civ ct & div rec)

* **Clarke**	G3	1812	Washington

Clarke County, 117 Court St, Grove Hill, AL 36451 .... (205)275-3507
(Pro Judge has m & pro rec from 1814, lnd from 1820; Clk Cir Ct has div & civ ct rec, Health Clinic has b and d rec)

Clay	D6	1866	Randolph, Talladega

Clay County, , Ashland, AL 36251 ....
[FHL has some cem rec, 1907 Conf soldiers census]

Cleburne	C6	1866	Calhoun, Randolph, Talladega

Cleburne County, Vickery St, Heflin, AL 36264 .... (205)463-2651
[FHL has some m, cem, pro rec, 1907 soldiers census]

* **Coffee**	G6	1841	Dale

Coffee County, PO Box 402, Elba, AL 36323-0402 .... (205)897-2954
(Pro Judge has m rec 1877 to present; lnd rec early 1800's to present; Cir Clk has div, civ ct rec)

Name	Map Index	Date Created	Parent County or Territory From Which Organized

*† Colbert   B3   1867   Franklin
Colbert County, 201 N Main St, Tuscumbia, AL 35674-2060 .... (205)386-8500
(Abolished same year created, re-established 1869; Pro Judge has m, pro, Ind rec; Clk has div Rec; Co Health Dept has b, d bur rec)

*† Conecuh   G4   1818   Monroe
Conecuh County, PO Box 347, Evergreen, AL 36401-0347 .... (205)578-2095
(Pro Judge has m, pro Judge has m, pro & Ind rec)

* Coosa   E5   1832   Creek Cession of 1832
Coosa County, PO Box 218, Rockford, AL 35136-0218 .... (205)377-2420
(Pro Judge has b 1934-1941; m pro, Ind rec 1832 to present; Clk Cir Ct has civ ct rec from 1900)

Cotaco (see Morgan)

Covington   H5   1821   Henry
Covington County, County Courthouse, Andalusia, AL 36420 .... (205)222-4313
(Pro Judge has m, pro & Ind rec; Clk Cir Ct has civ ct & div rec; Rec burned 1895)

* Crenshaw   G5   1866   Butler, Coffee, Covington, Lowndes, Pike
Crenshaw County, PO Box 227, Luvern, AL 36049-0227 .... (205)335-6568
(Pro Judge has m, pro & Ind rec from 1866; Clk Cir Ct has div & civ ct rec)

*† Cullman   C4   1877   Blount, Morgan, Winston
Cullman County, 500 2nd Ave SW, Cullman, AL 35055-4155 .... (205)739-3530
(Pro Judge has m, div, pro, civ ct, Ind rec 1877 to present; final rec, wills 1877 to present; old newspapers, scattered volumes from 1880, not indexed)

* Dale   G6   1824   Covington, Henry
Dale County, PO Box 246, Ozark, AL 36361-0246 .... (205)774-6025
(Pro judge has m & pro rec from 1884, & Ind rec; Clk Cir Ct has civ ct & div rec from 1885; Co Hlth Dept has b rec)

* Dallas   F4   1818   Montgomery
Dallas County, PO Box 997, Selma, AL 36702-0997 .... (205)875-4401
(Pro Judge has m from 1818, div from 1917, pro from 1821 & Ind rec from 1820) (State of Ala has b, d and bur rec)

* Dekalb   B6   1836   Cherokee Cession of 1835
Dekalb County, 300 Grand Ave SW, Fort Payne, AL 35967-1863 .... (205)845-0404
(Pro Judge has m, div, pro, Ind rec; Health Dept has b, d, bur rec; Cir Clk has civ ct rec)

* Elmore   E5   1866   Autauga, Coosa, Montgomery, Tallapoosa
Elmore County, PO Box 338, Wetumpka, AL 36092-0338 .... (205)567-2571
[FHL has some m, cem, Ind, pro rec, 1907 Conf soldiers census]

Escambia   H4   1868   Baldwin, Conecuh
Escambia County, PO Box 848, Brewton, AL 36427-0848 .... (205)867-6261
(Co Clk has m rec from 1897, pro & Ind rec from 1869)

* Etowah   C5   1868   Blount, Calhoun, Cherokee, DeKalb, Marshall, St. Clair
Etowah County, 800 Forrest Ave, Gadsden, AL 35901-3641 .... (205)549-5313
(Pro Judge has m, div, pro & Ind rec from 1867; Organized 7 Dec 1866 as Baine Co from portions of DeKalb, Marshall, Blount, St. Clair, Calhoun and Cherokee Counties, but was abolished 3 Dec 1867, re-established 1 Dec 1868)

* Fayette   C3   1824   Marion, Pickens, Tuscaloosa
Fayette County, PO Box 819, Fayette, AL 35555-0819 .... (205)932-4510
[FHL has some m & cem rec, 1866 census, 1907 Conf soldiers census]

* Franklin   B3   1818   Cherokee & Chickasaw Cession of 1816
Franklin County, 410 N Jackson St, Russellville, AL 35653 .... (205)332-1210
(Pro Judge has m, pro & Ind rec from 1890; Clk Cir Ct has civ & crim ct rec from 1923, and div rec; Rec burned 1890)

Geneva   H6   1868   Dale, Henry, Coffee
Geneva County, PO Box 430, Geneva, AL 36340-0430 .... (205)684-2275
[FHL has some m & cem rec, 1907 Conf soldiers census]

*† Greene   E3   1819   Marengo, Tuscaloosa
Greene County, PO Box 656, Eutaw, AL 35462-0656 .... (205)372-3349
[FHL has some m, cem, pro rec, 1866 census, 1907 Conf soldiers census]

† Hale   E3   1867   Greene, Marengo, Perry, Tuscaloosa
Hale County, 1001 Main St, Greensboro, AL 36744-1510 .... (205)624-4257
(Pro Judge has m, div, pro, civ ct, deeds, and mtg rec from 1868)

Hancock (see Winston)

* Henry   G7   1819   Conecuh
Henry County, Court Sq, Abbeville, AL 36310-2135 .... (205)585-2753
[FHL has some m, cem, Ind rec, 1855 & 1866 census, 1907 Conf soldiers census]

* Houston   H7   1903   Dale, Geneva, Henry
Houston County, PO Box 6406, Dothan, AL 36302-6406 .... (205)677-4800
(Health Dept has b, d, bur rec; Pro Office has m, pro, Ind rec 1903 to present; Cir Clk has civ ct, crim rec 1903 to present; Reg in Chancery has div rec 1903 to present)

* Jackson   A6   1819   Cherokee Cession of 1816
Jackson County, PO Box 397, Scottsboro, AL 35768-0397 .... (205)574-9320
(Pro Judge has m rec from 1851, pro rec from 1850, Ind rec from 1835 & a 1900 list of Civ War vets in county; Clk Cir Ct has civ ct rec from 1920 and div rec from 1895; Co Hlth Dept has b & d rec; Pub Lib has cem rec)

Name	Map Index	Date Created	Parent County or Territory From Which Organized

* **Jefferson**   D4   1819   Blount
Jefferson County, 716 N 21st St, Birmingham, AL 35263-0001 .... (205)325-5300
[FHL has some m, cem, pro rec, 1866 census, 1907 Conf soldiers census]

Jones (see Lamar)

* **Lamar**   D2   1867   Marion, Fayette, Pickens
Lamar County, Pond St, Vernon, AL 35592 .... (205)695-7333
(Jones co formed Feb 4, 1867, abol Nov 3, 1867 & ret to parent cos. Sanford Co org Oct 8, 1868 from orig Jones, name changed to Lamar 1877. Co Clk has pro rec from 1886 and will rec from 1880)

*† **Lauderdale**   A3   1818   Cherokee & Chickasaw Cession in 1816
Lauderdale County, PO Box 1059, Florence, AL 35631-1059 .... (205)760-5700
(Pro Judge has m & pro rec)

* **Lawrence**   B4   1818   Cherokee & Chickasaw Cession in 1816
Lawrence County, 750 Main St, Moulton, AL 35650-1553 .... (205)974-0663
(Pro Judge has m, div, pro & lnd rec from 1810; Clk Cir Ct has civ ct rec)

* **Lee**   E7   1866   Chambers, Macon, Russell, Tallapoosa
Lee County, 215 S 9th St, Opelika, AL 36801-4919 .... (205)745-9767
[FHL has some m, lnd, pro rec, 1907 Conf soldiers census]

* **Limestone**   A4   1818   Cherokee & Chickasaw Cession in 1816
Limestone County, 310 W Washington St, Athens, AL 35611-2597 .... (205)233-6400
(Co Arch have b & d rec 1881-1913, m rec 1832-1900, div rec 1896-1947, pro, lnd & civ ct rec 1818-1900, tax rec 1861-1900, newspr 1868-1985; Pro Judge has m, pro & lnd rec after 1900; Clk Cir Ct has civ ct rec after 1900, and div rec after 1947; Wills begin 1823)

*† **Lowndes**   F5   1830   Butler, Dallas, Montgomery
Lowndes County, PO Box 65, Hayneville, AL 36040-0065 .... (205)548-2331
[FHL has some cem, civ ct, pro rec, 1855 & 1866 census, 1907 Conf soldiers census]

* **Macon**   F6   1832   Creek Cession of 1832
Macon County, 210 N Elm St, Tuskegee, AL 36083-1757 .... (205)727-5120
(Pro Judge has m, pro & lnd rec from 1835; Clk Cir Ct has civ ct rec from 1868)

*† **Madison**   A5   1808   Cherokee & Chichasaw Cession 1806-7
Madison County, 100 Courthouse Sq SE, Huntsville, AL 35801-4820 .... (205)532-3300
(Pro Judge has m, pro & lnd rec from 1809; Cir Ct Clk has div & civ ct rec; Co Hlth Dept has d & bur rec)

*† **Marengo**   F3   1818   Choctaw Cession of 1816
Marengo County, 101 E Coats Ave, Linden, AL 36748-1546 .... (205)295-2200
(Pro Judge has m, pro & lnd rec; Reg in Chan has div; Clk Cir Ct has civ ct rec)

* **Marion**   C3   1818   Tuscaloosa
Marion County, PO Box 1595, Hamilton, AL 35570-1595 .... (205)921-7451
(Rec burned 1883)

* **Marshall**   B5   1836   Blount, Cherokee Cession 1835, Jackson
Marshall County, 540 Ringo St, Guntersville, AL 35976 .... (205)571-7701
[FHL has some m, cem, lnd, pro rec, 1866 census, 1907 Conf soldiers census]

* **Mobile**   I2   1812   West Florida
Mobile County, 109 Government St, Mobile, AL 36602-3108 .... (205)690-8615
(Pro Judge ct has m rec from 1813, pro rec from 1809 and will books 1 to 44)

* **Monroe**   G3   1815   Creek Cession 1814, Washington
Monroe County, S Mount Plaza Ave, Monroeville, AL 36461 .... (205)743-3782
(Pro Judge has m, pro & lnd rec from 1832) (1816 census of Monroe Co pub by Monroe Journal, Monroeville, Ala) (A courthouse fire destroyed all records prior to 1833)

* **Montgomery**   F5   1816   Monroe
Montgomery County, PO Box 1667, Montgomery, AL 36192 .... (205)832-4950
(Pro Judge has m rec from 1928, pro rec from 1817, lnd rec from 1819; AL Dept of Arch & Hist has m rec from 1817-1928; Clk of Bd of Revenue has div rec from 1852, civ ct rec from 1917; State Ct has div and civ ct rec)

* **Morgan**   B4   1818   Cherokee Turkeytown Cession
Morgan County, 302 Lee St NE, Decatur, AL 35601-1999 .... (205)351-4600
(Name changed from Cotaco 1821. Pro Judge has m and pro rec from 1818)

* **Perry**   E4   1819   Montgomery
Perry County, PO Box 505, Marion, AL 36756-0505 .... (205)683-6106
(Co Clk has m, pro, lnd rec)

* **Pickens**   D2   1820   Tuscaloosa
Pickens County, PO Box 418, Carrollton, AL 35447 .... (205)367-2050
(Pro Judge has m, pro & lnd rec from 1876; Clk Cir Ct has div & civ ct rec)

* **Pike**   G6   1821   Henry, Montgomery
Pike County, 120 W Church St, Troy, AL 36081-1913 .... (205)566-6374
(Pro Judge has m, pro & lnd rec from 1830; b rec from 1881-1904, d rec from 1881-1891, 1902-1905)

* **Randolph**   D6   1832   Creek Cession 1832
Randolph County, PO Box 328, Wedowee, AL 36278-0328 .... (205)357-4551
(Courthouse burned 1897 records destroyed)

Name	Map Index	Date Created	Parent County or Territory From Which Organized
* **Russell**	F7	1832	Creek Cession 1832

Russell County, PO Box 518, Phenix, AL 36867 .... (205)298-0516
(Co Health Dept has b, d rec; Cir Ct has div, civ ct rec; Judge of Pro has m, pro, Ind rec 1833 to present) (Some rec at Seale)

* **Saint Clair**	C5	1818	Shelby

Saint Clair County, PO Box 397, Ashville, AL 35953-0397 .... (205)594-5116
(Pro Judge at Ashville has m, pro, Ind & Estate rec from 1800; Clk Cir Ct has div & civ ct rec)

Sanford (see Lamar)

* **Shelby**	D4	1818	Montgomery

Shelby County, Main St, Columbiana, AL 35051 .... (205)669-3760
(Pro Judge has m, pro & Ind rec from 1824)

*† **Sumter**	E2	1832	Choctaw Cession of 1830

Sumter County, Franklin St, Livingston, AL 35470 .... (205)652-2291
(Pro Judge has scattered b rec from 1888 to 1918; m & pro rec from 1833, Ind rec, historical, voters maps)

*† **Talladega**	D5	1832	Creek Cession of 1832

Talladega County, PO Box 755, Talladega, AL 35160-0755 .... (205)362-4175
[FHL has some m & cem rec, 1866 census, 1907 Conf soldiers census]

* **Tallapoosa**	E6	1832	Creek Cession of 1832

Tallapoosa County, 101 N Broadnax St, Dadeville, AL 36853-1395 .... (205)825-4268
(Pro Judge b rec from 1881 to 1919; m rec from 1835; d rec from 1881 to 1919; pro rec from 1835; approx 25% of total co b were put on rec; approx 10% of total co d were put on rec; div & civ ct rec kept by Cir Clk; 90 acres were swapped between Tallapoosa & Coosa Cos in 1963)

* **Tuscaloosa**	D3	1818	Cherokee & Choctaw Cession 1816

Tuscaloosa County, 714 Greensboro Ave, Tuscaloosa, AL 35401-1895 .... (205)349-3870
(Pro Judge has m & pro rec from 1823)

* **Walker**	C3	1823	Marion, Tuscaloosa

Walker County, PO Box 749, Jasper, AL 35502-0749 .... (205)384-3404
(Rec burned 1877)(Pro Judge has m & pro rec)

* **Washington**	G2	1800	Mississippi Terr., Baldwin

Washington County, PO Box 146, Chatom, AL 36518-0146 .... (205)847-2208
[FHL has some m, Ind, pro rec. 1866 census, 1907 Conf soldiers census]

† **Wilcox**	G3	1819	Monroe, Dallas

Wilcox County, PO Box 656, Camden, AL 36726-0656 .... (205)682-4126
(Pro Judge has m, pro & Ind rec from 1819)

*† **Winston**	C3	1850	Walker

Winston County, PO Box 309, Double Springs, AL 35553-0309 .... (205)489-5533
(Name changed from Hancock 1858) (Pro Judge has m, pro & Ind rec from 1891; Clk Cir Ct has div & civ ct rec)

* At least one county history has been published about this county.

† Inventory of county archives was made by the Historical Records Survey. (See Introduction)

ALASKA

CAPITAL · JUNEAU — TERRITORY 1912 — STATE 1959 (49th)
State Map on Page M-2

Russians established Alaska's first permanent white settlement at Kodiak Island in 1784. Soon thereafter, British and American traders began to enter the area. Sitka was permanently settled by the Russians in 1804 and served as the center of government until 1906. The southern and eastern boundaries of Alaska were established by treaties with the United States and Britain between 1824 and 1828. Another boundary adjustment was made in 1903 between Alaska and British Columbia.

Alaska remained under Russian control until its defeat in the Crimean War. Following this defeat, Russia sold Alaska to the United States on March 30, 1867. American settlement was sparse until the discovery of gold near Juneau in 1880. The first Organic Act, passed by Congress in 1884, provided a governor and federal courts to Alaska. The Klondike strike in 1896 resulted in an influx of settlers. Further discoveries of gold at Nome in 1898 and placer fields at Fairbanks in 1902 continued the rush of settlers.

Judicial Districts were created between 1897 and 1901, covering these areas: First Judicial District; courthouse in Juneau; covered Southeastern Alexander Archipelago and the cities of Ketchikan, Wrangell, Sitka, and Juneau. Second Judicial District; courthouse in Nome; covered northern area including Nome and Barrow. Third Judicial District; courthouse in Anchorage; covered southern area including Anchorage, Kodiak, and the Aleutian Islands. Fourth Judicial District; courthouse in Fairbanks; covered central area including Fairbanks, Bethel, and Toksook Bay.

In 1906, Juneau became the capital. The second Organic Act, passed by Congress in 1912, made Alaska a territory and provided for territorial government. Statehood was granted in 1959.

The Bureau of Vital Statistics, Department of Health and Social Services, P.O. Box H-02G, Juneau, AK 99811 (to verify current fees, call 907-465-3391), has birth, delayed birth, marriage, divorce (since 1950), and death records. State registration began in 1913 and was generally complied with by 1945. Residents of Alaska in 1867 became citizens of the United States. Naturalization records for later settlers are filed in the judicial districts. Records for some districts are at the Alaska State Archives. Old territorial records of Fairbanks, Juneau, and Nome have been transferred to the Superior Court. Naturalization records after September 1906 are at the National Archives, Seattle Branch, 6125 Sand Point Way NE, Seattle, WA 98115.

Genealogical Archives, Libraries and Societies

Alaska Division of State Libraries, Pouch G, State Capitol, Juneau, AK 99801

Alaska Historical Library and Museum, Juneau, AK 99801

University of Alaska Library, College, AK 99701

Gastineau Genealogical Society, 3270 Nowell Avenue, Juneau, AK 99801

Fairbanks, Alaska Genealogical Society, P. O. Box 60534, Fairbanks, AK 99706

Kenai Totem Tracers, Kenai Community Library, 63 Main Street Loop, Kenai, AK 99611

National Archives-Alaska Region, 654 West Third Ave. Rm 012 Anchorage, Ak 99501

Wrangell Genealogical Society, P. O. Box 928EP, Wrangell, AK 99929

Printed Census Records and Mortality Schedules

Federal Census 1900, 1910
State/Territorial Census 1904, 1905, 1906, 1907
Unalaska and Aleutian Villages 1878

Valuable Printed Sources

Atlases, Maps, and Gazetteers

Orth, Donald J. *Dictionary of Alaska Place Names*. Washington, DC: Government Printing Office, 1902.

Bibliographies

Lada-Mocarski, Valerian. *Bibliography of Books on Alaska Published Before 1868*. New Haven, Connecticut: Yale University Press, 1969.

Genealogical Sources

Dorosh, Elizabeth and John Dorosh. *Index to Baptisms, Marriages, and Deaths in the Archives of the Russian Orthodox Greek Catholic Church in Alaska, 1900-1936*. Washington, DC: Library of Congress, 1964.

Jackson, Ronald Vern and Gary Ronald Teeples. *Alaskan Records, 1870-1907*. North Salt Lake, Utah: Accelerated Indexing Systems International.

ALASKA DATA
State Map on Page M-2

Name	Map Index		
Aleutian Islands	D2		
Angoen	H3		
Bethel	E3		
Bristol Bay	F2		
Bristol Bay Borough, PO Box 189, Naknek, AK 99633-0189			(907)246-4224
Dillingham	F2		
Fairbanks	G4		
Gateway	I1		
Haines	I2		
Haines Borough, PO Box 1209, Haines, AK 99827-1209			(907)766-2711
Juneau	I2		
Juneau Borough, 155 S Seward St, Juneau, AK 99801-1332			(907)586-3300

Name	Map Index	
Kenai Peninsula	F3	
Kenai Peninsula Borough, 144 N Binkley, Soldotna, AK 99669-7520		(907)262-4441
Ketchikan	I1	
Ketchikan Borough, 344 Front St, Ketchikan, AK 99901-6494		(907)225-6151
Kodiak	F2	
Kodiak Borough, 710 Mill Bay Rd, Kodiak, AK 99615-6398		(907)486-5736
Matanuska-Susitna	G3	
Matanuska-Susitna Borough, PO Box 1608, Palmer, AK 99645-1608		(907)745-4801
Municipality of Anchorage	G3	
Municipality of Anchorage NA, PO Box 196650, Anchorage, AK 99519-6650		(907)343-4311
Nome	E5	
North Slope	G5	
North Slope Borough, PO Box 69, Barrow, AK 99723-0069		(907)852-2611
North Star	G4	
North Star Borough, 809 Pioneer Rd, Fairbanks, AK 99701-2813		(907)452-4761
Northwest Arctic	F5	
Northwest Arctic Borough, PO Box 1110, Kotzebue, AK 99752-1110		(907)442-2500
Outer Ketchikan	I1	
Prince of Wales	I1	
Sitka	I2	
Sitka Borough, 304 Lake St, Sitka, AK 99835-7563		(907)747-3294
Skagway-Yukutat	H3	
Southeast Fairbanks	H4	
Valdez Cordova	H3	
Wade Hampton	E4	
Wrangell-Petersburg	I2	
Yukon-Kuyokukuk	F4	

* At least one county history has been published about this county.
† Inventory of county archives was made by the Historical Records Survey. (See Introduction)

ARIZONA

CAPITAL — PHOENIX — TERRITORY 1863 — STATE 1912 (48th)
State Map on Page M-3

The first white people to come to Arizona were attracted by tales of the fabulous "Seven Cities of Cibola". As early as 1539, European explorers came into the region. About 150 years later, Catholic missionaries came to proselyte the Indians. The first permanent white settlement began in 1776, at the present site of Tucson. Arizona was under the control of Mexico in the section known as New Mexico in 1821. Non-Indian settlers generally came into the Gila Valley from the Sonora and Sinaloa states of Mexico.

Following the Mexican War, the portion of Arizona north of the Gila River became part of the United States. The lower portion of Arizona was purchased from Mexico in 1854 under terms of the Gadsden Purchase. Arizona was part of the territory of New Mexico which was organized in 1850. Following this organization, many Mormon families from Utah settled in Arizona. In 1863, Arizona Territory was formed with Prescott as the territorial capital. During the Civil War, Arizona had some 200 Confederate soldiers and over 6,000 from the New Mexico territory fought for the Union.

By 1870, Arizona still had under 10,000 residents. The population increased twenty-fold over the next forty years. In the next half century, the population more than tripled. Phoenix was made the capital in 1889. The foreign-born population of Arizona in descending order came from Mexico, Canada, England, Wales, Germany, Russia, Italy, Poland, Austria, Sweden, Greece, Ireland, Scotland, Yugoslavia, and Czechoslovakia.

Birth and death records are available since March 18, 1909, from Vital Records Section, Department of Health Service, P.O. Box 3887, Phoenix, AZ 85030. Similar records since 1887 are available from the county seats. Marriage records are on file with the Clerk of the Superior Court of each county. From 1891 to 1912, clerks of probate courts issued marriage licenses. Divorce actions are kept by the Clerk of the Superior Court of the county in which the license was issued. The earliest divorce records were granted by the territorial legislature and are published in the Territorial Statutes. Until 1912, the district court of each county kept these records. From 1852 to 1863, the New Mexico district, probate, and supreme courts had jurisdiction for Arizona. District courts had county-wide jurisdiction over records of chancery, criminal cases, and divorces from 1864 to 1912. After 1912, superior courts had jurisdiction for most areas. Citizenship or naturalization papers were filed in the district court of the county where the examination was conducted. From 1906 until 1912, naturalization records were recorded by the clerk of the U.S. district courts in Tucson, Tombstone, Phoenix, Prescott, and Solomonville. After 1912 (1919 for Maricopa County), naturalization records were filed in the superior courts. All real estate records are in the office of the recorder of the county where the land is located. Incomplete territorial census records for the years 1864, 1866, 1867, 1869, 1871, 1872, and 1873 are available at the Department of Libraries, Archives and Public Records, Old Capitol Building, 1700 West Washington, Phoenix, AZ 85007. Arizona was included in the New Mexico federal census for 1860.

To verify current fees, call 602-255-1080.

Genealogical Archives, Libraries and Societies

Arizona and the West Library, 318 University of Arizona, Tucson, AZ 85721

Arizona State Library, Dept. of Library, Archives and Public Records, Genealogy Library, 1700 West Washington, State Capitol, Phoenix, AZ 85007

M.H.E. Heritage Library, Circle-M Farm-Ranch, Rt. 1, Box 60-H, McNeal, AZ 85617

Tucson Public Library, 200 South 6th Ave, Tucson, AZ 85701 Mailing address P. O. Box 27470, Tucson, AZ 85726

Tucson Public Library Annex, Genealogy Room, 32 East Ochoa Street, Tucson, AZ 85701 Mailing address P. O. Box 27470, Tucson, AZ 85726

Apache Genealogy Society, P. O. Box 1084, Sierra Vista, AZ 85635

Arizona Genealogical Society, 6521 East Fayette St., Tucson, AZ 85730-2220

Arizona Jewish Historical Society, 720 West Edgewood Ave., Mesa, Arizona 85210

Arizona Jewish Historical Society, 4181 E. Pontatoc Canyon Dr., Tucson, AZ 85718

Arizona Pioneer's Historical Society, 949 East Second St., Tucson, AZ 85719

Arizona Society, Sons of the American Revolution, 1660 E. Greenway Street, Mesa, AZ 85203

Arizona State Genealogical Society, P. O. Box 42075, Tucson, AZ 85733-2075

Cherokee Family Ties, 516 N. 38th St., Mesa, AZ 85205

Cochise Genealogical Society, P. O. Box 68, Pirtleville, AZ 85626

Family History Society of Arizona, P. O. Box 310, Glendale, AZ 85311

Genealogical Society of Arizona, P. O. Box 27237, Tempe, AZ 85282

Genealogical Workshop of Mesa, Desert Station, P. O. Box 6052, Mesa, AZ 85208

Green Valley Genealogical Society, P. O. Box 1009, Green Valley, AZ 85614

Lake Havasu Genealogical Society, P. O. Box 953, Lake Havasu City, AZ 86403

Mohave County Genealogical Society, 400 West Beale Street, Kingman, AZ 86401

Northern Arizona Genealogical Society, P. O. Box 695, Prescott, AZ 86302

Northern Gila County Genealogical Society, P. O. Box 952, Payson, AZ 85547

Phoenix Genealogical Society, 4607 W. Rovey Ave., Glendale, AZ 85301

Prescott Historical Society, W. Gurley St., Prescott, AZ 86301

Sun City Genealogical Society, P. O. Box 1448, Sun City, AZ 85372-1448

Tri-State Genealogical Society, P. O. Box 6045, Mohave Valley, AZ 86440

Yuma, Arizona, Genealogical Society of, P. O. Box 2905, Yuma, AZ 85366-2905

Printed Census Records and Mortality Schedules

Federal Census 1860, 1870, 1880, 1900, 1910
Federal Mortality Schedules 1870, 1880
State/Territorial Census 1850, 1860, 1864, 1866

Valuable Printed Sources

Atlases, Maps, and Gazetteers

Barnes, William Croft. *Arizona Place Names*. Tucson: University of Arizona Press, 1960.

Theobald, John and Lillian Theobald. *Arizona Post Offices and Postmasters*. Phoenix: Arizona Historical Foundation, 1961.

Walker, Henry Pickering and Don Bufkin. *Historical Atlas of Arizona*. Norman, Oklahoma: University of Oklahoma Press, 1979.

Bibliographies

Luttrell, Estelle. *Newspapers and Periodicals of Arizona, 1859-1911*. Tucson: University of Arizona Bulletin #15, 1950.

Department of Libraries and Archives. *Newspapers of Arizona Libraries: A Union List of Newspapers Published in Arizona*. Tucson: Pioneers Historical Society, 1965.

Genealogical Research Guides

Spiros, Joyce V. Hawley. *Genealogical Guide to Arizona and Nevada*. Gallup, New Mexico: Verlene Publishing, 1983.

Histories

Bancroft, Hubert Howe. *History of Arizona and New Mexico, 1530-1888*. Albuquerque: Horn & Wallace, 1962.

Peplow, Edward Hadduck Jr. *History of Arizona*. New York: Lewis Historical Publishing Co., 1958.

Wagoner, Jay J. *Arizona Territory, 1863-1912*. Tucson: University of Arizona Press, 1970.

ARIZONA COUNTY DATA
State Map on Page M-3

Name	Map Index	Date Created	Parent County or Territory From Which Organized
Apache	C3	1879	Yavapai

Apache County, PO Box 428, Saint Johns, AZ 85936-0428 .... (602)337-4364
(Clk Sup Ct has m, div, pro, ct rec 1879 to present; Co Rcdr has Ind rec 1879 to 1979)

| **Cochise** | C7 | 1881 | Pima |

Cochise County, PO Box CK, Bisbee, AZ 85603 .... (602)432-5471
(Clk Sup Ct has m, div, pro civ ct rec; Co Recdr has Ind rec)

| * **Coconino** | E3 | 1891 | Yavapai |

Coconino County, 100 E Birch Ave Flagstaff Justice Ct, Flagstaff, AZ 86001-4696 .... (602)779-6806
(Clk Sup Ct has m, div, civ ct & pro rec from 1891; Co Rcdr has Ind rec)

| **Gila** | D5 | 1881 | Maricopa, Pinal |

Gila County, 1400 E Ash St, Globe, AZ 85501-1414 .... (602)425-3231
(Co Clk has m rec from 1881, div, pro & civ ct rec from 1914; Co Rcdr has Ind rec)

| * **Graham** | C6 | 1881 | Apache, Pima |

Graham County, 800 Main St, Safford, AZ 85546-2829 .... (602)428-3250
(Clk Sup Ct has m rec from 1881, pro rec from 1889, div & civ ct rec from 1882; Co Rcdr has Ind rec)

| **Greenlee** | C6 | 1909 | Graham |

Greenlee County, PO Box 1027, Clifton, AZ 85533-1027 .... (602)865-4242
(Clk Sup Ct has m, div, pro & civ ct rec from 1911; Co Rcdr has Ind rec)

| **La Paz** | G5 | | |

La Paz County, 1713 Kofa Suite C, Parker, AZ 85344-6477 .... (602)669-6131

| † **Maricopa** | F6 | 1871 | Yavapai, Yuma |

Maricopa County, 111 S 3rd Ave, Phoenix, AZ 85003-2225 .... (602)262-3011
(Clk Sup Ct has m from 1877, div from 1930, pro & civ ct rec from 1871, criminal from 1879; Co Rcdr has Ind rec)

| **Mohave** | G3 | 1864 | Original County |

Mohave County, 401 E Spring St, Kingman, AZ 86401-5878 .... (602)753-9141
(Clk Sup Ct has m rec 1888 to present; div, pro, civ ct 1850-1979; Co Rcdr has Ind rec)

| **Navajo** | D3 | 1895 | Apache |

Navajo County, PO Box 668, Holbrook, AZ 86025-0668 .... (602)524-6161
(Clk Sup Ct has m, div, pro, civ ct rec; Co Rcdr has Ind rec)

| † **Pima** | E7 | 1864 | Original County |

Pima County, 150 W Congress St, Tucson, AZ 85701-1333 .... (602)740-8011
(Clk Sup Ct has m, div, pro & civ ct rec from ca 1863)

| **Pinal** | E6 | 1875 | Pima |

Pinal County, 100 N Florence, Florence, AZ 85232-9742 .... (602)868-5801
(Clk Sup Ct has m, pro, civ ct rec from 1875; div rec from 1883; Co Rcdr has Ind rec)

| † **Santa Cruz** | D7 | 1899 | Pima |

Santa Cruz County, PO Box 1265, Nogales, AZ 85628-1265 .... (602)281-2047
(Clk Sup Ct has m & pro rec from 1899, div & civ ct rec from 1912)

| * **Yavapai** | F4 | 1864 | Original county |

Yavapai County, 255 E Gurley St, Prescott, AZ 86301-3868 .... (602)771-3100
(Clk Sup Ct has m, div, pro & civ ct rec; Co Rcdr has Ind rec)

| **Yuma** | G6 | 1864 | Original county |

Yuma County, 168 S 2nd Ave, Yuma, AZ 85364-2297 .... (602)782-4534
(Clk Sup Ct m, div, pro & civ ct rec from 1863)

* At least one county history has been published about this county.
† Inventory of county archives was made by the Historical Records Survey. (See Introduction)

ARKANSAS

CAPITAL · LITTLE ROCK — TERRITORY 1819 — STATE 1836 (25th)
State Map on Page M-4

In 1541, Hernando de Soto became the first European to explore the Arkansas area. Louis Joliet and Jacques Marquette in 1673 and René Robert Cavelier, sieur de la Salle, in 1682 also explored the region. La Salle claimed all the Mississippi Valley for France and named it Louisiana. This claim resulted in increased French activity in the area and the establishment of the Arkansas Post in 1686. Major Indian tribes of the area were the Quapaw, also known as the Akansa or Arkansas, the Osage, and the Caddo. In 1762, France ceded Louisiana to Spain. The Spanish opened the area to settlement by Americans in 1783, but fewer than a thousand came prior to the turn of the century. In 1801, Spain returned the area to France. The United States purchased Louisiana in 1803.

Following the Louisiana purchase, Arkansas was opened to settlement with land at very low prices. As a result, thousands of settlers from the mideast and southeast areas of the United States came to Arkansas. Many of the early settlers were English, Irish, or Scottish and came from Kentucky or Tennessee. The formation of the Missouri Territory in 1812 included Arkansas. Arkansas county was formed the following year. Additional settlers came to claim bounty land for service in the War of 1812 and to grow cotton. Many of these settlers came from Virginia and the Carolinas through Tennessee, Mississippi, or Missouri.

Arkansas territory was formed in 1819, when Missouri applied for statehood. The territory included present-day Oklahoma until June 15, 1836, when Arkansas became a state. The Panic of 1837 was a major impetus for many to leave the southern and eastern states for the new states in the west, such as Arkansas. Arkansas seceded from the Union in 1861. About 8,000 soldiers from Arkansas fought for the Union and an estimated 50,000 for the Confederacy. Arkansas was readmitted to the Union in 1868. After the Civil War, large groups of southern European immigrants came to the rich lands between the Arkansas and the White Rivers. Many Poles came directly to Pulaski County and many Italians to the northwest section of the state to raise fruit. The building of railroads in the late 19th century resulted in nearly a tripling of inhabitants from 1870 to 1900.

The Division of Vital Records, Arkansas Department of Health, 4815 West Markham Street, Little Rock, AR 72201 (to verify current fees, call 501-661-2336), has birth and death records from 1914, marriage records from 1917, and divorce records from 1921. Marriage records are also kept by county clerks. Chancery courts have county-wide jurisdiction over equity, divorce, probate, and adoption proceedings. The Arkansas State Land Office, State Capitol, Little Rock, AR 72201, has original land plats of the U.S. Government surveys of Arkansas and original entries by township and range. Naturalization records were usually filed in the circuit court in each county, although some were filed with the U.S. District Courts at Fort Smith, Little Rock, and Fort Worth, Texas. A territorial census for 1830 is available and has been indexed. The Arkansas History Commission, One Capitol Mall, Little Rock, AR 72201, has sheriffs' censuses for several counties in 1829 and for Arkansas County in 1823.

Genealogical Archives, Libraries and Societies

Arkadelphia Public Library, 609 Caddo St., Arkadelphia, AR 71923

Ashley County Library, 211 E. Lincoln, Hamburg, AR 71646

Bentonville Public Library, 125 West Central, Bentonville, AR 72712

Crowley Ridge Regional Library, 315 W. Oak, Jonesboro, AR 72401

Fayette Public Library, 217 E. Dickson St. Fayetteville, AR 72701

Ft. Smith Public Library, 61 S. 8th St., Ft. Smith, AR 72901

Garland - Montgomery Regional Library, 200 Woodbine St., Hot Springs, AR 71901

Greene County Library, S.S. Lipscomb Arkansas History and Genealogy Room, 120 N. 12th St., Paragould, AR 72450

Little Rock Public Library, 700 Louisiana St., Little Rock, AR 72201

Northeast Arkansas Regional Library, 120 N 12th Street, Paragould, AR 72450

Pike County Archives, DeWayne Gray, President, c / o Happy Valley Grocery, Murfreesboro, AR 71958

Pine Bluff and Jefferson County Public Library, 200 East Eighth Ave., Civic Center Complex, Pine Bluff, AR 71601

Pope County Library, 116 East Third Street, Russellville, AR 72801

Southwest Arkansas Regional Archives, Mary Medaris, Director, Old Washington Historic State Park, Washington, AR 71862

Texarkana Historical Museum, P. O. Box 2343 (or 219 State Line), Texarkana, AR 75501

Van Buren County Library, Clinton, AR 72031

William F. Laman Public Library, 2801 Orange, North Little Rock, AR 72114

Ark-La-Tex Genealogical Association, Inc., P. O. Box 4462, Shreveport, LA 71104

Arkansas Genealogical Society, P. O. Box 908, Hot Springs, AR 71902

Arkansas Historical Association, History Dept., Ozark Hall, 12, University of Arkansas, Fayetteville, AR 72701

Arkansas History Commission, One Capitol Mall, Little Rock, AR 72201

Arkansas Society, Sons of the American Revolution, 1119 Scenic Way, Benton, AR 72015

Ashley County Genealogical Society, P. O. Drawer R, Crossett, AR 71635

Batesville Genealogical Society, P. O. Box 3883, Batesville, AR 72503-3883

Baxter County, Arkansas Historical and Genealogical Society, 1505 Mistletoe, Mountain Home, AR 72653

Benton County Historical Society, P. O. Box 1034, Bentonville, AR 72712

Carroll County Historical Society, Berryville, AR 72616

Clay Co. Genealogy Club, Piggott Public Library, 361 West Main, Piggott, AR 72454

Crawford County Genealogical Society, P. O. Box 276, Alma, AR 72921

Crawford County Historical Society, 929 East Main St., Van Buren, AR 72956

Crowley's Ridge Genealogical Society, Box 2091, State University, AR 72467

Dallas County Arkansas Genealogical and Historical Society, Dallas County Library, Fordyce, AR 71742

Desha County Historical Society, P. O. Box 432, McGehee, AR 71654

East Arkansas Community College, Forrest City, AR 72335-9598

Faulkner County Historical Society, Conway, AR 72032

Fort Smith Historical Society, 61 South 8th Street, Fort Smith, AR 72901

Frontier Researchers Genealogical Society, P. O. Box 2123, Fort Smith, AR 72902

Grand Prairie Historical Society, P. O. Box 122, Gillett, AR 72055

Greene County Historical & Genealogical Society, 901 W. Kingshighway, Paragould, AR 72450

Hempstead County Genealogical Society, P. O. Box 1158, Hope, AR 71801

Hempstead County Historical Society, P. O. Box 1257, Hope, AR 71801

Heritage Club, The, 218 Howard, Nashville, AR 71852

Heritage Seekers Genealogical Club, 2509 South Berkley Drive, North Little Rock, AR 72118

Independence County Historical Society, Box 1412, Batesville, AR 72501

Izard County Arkansas Historical Society, Izard County Historian, P. O. Box 84, Dolph, AR 72528

Jefferson County Genealogical Society, P. O. Box 2215, Pine Bluff, AR 71613

Johnson County Historical Society, P. O. Box 505, Clarksville, AR 72830

Lafayette County Historical Society, P. O. Box 180, Bradley, AR 71826

Logan County Historical Society, P. O. Box B, Paris, AR 72855

Madison County Genealogical and Historical Society, P. O. Box 427, Huntsville, AR 72740

Marion County, Arkansas, Historical and Genealogical Society of, Marion County Library, P. O. Box 554, Yellville, AR 72687

Melting Pot Genealogical Society, P. O. Box 936, Hot Springs, AR 71902

Montgomery County Historical Society, P. O. Box 520, Mount Ida, AR 71957

Nevada County Depot Museum Association, West First Street, Prescott, AR 71857

Northwest Arkansas Genealogical Society, P. O. Box K, Rogers, AR 72756

Orphan Train Heritage Society of America, 4453 South 48th St, Springdale, AR 72764

Ouachita-Calhoun Genealogical Society, P. O. Box 2092, Camden, AR 71701

Ouachita County Historical Society, 926 Washington Northwest, Camden, AR 71701

Pike County Archives, Happy Valley Grocery, Murfreesboro, AR 71958

Polk County Genealogical Society, P. O. Box 12, Hatfield, AR 71945

Pope County Historical Association, 1120 North Detroit, Russellville, AR 72801

Professonal Genealogists of Arkansas, P. O. Box 1807, Conway, AR 72032

Pulaski County Historical Society, P. O. Box 653, Little Rock, AR 72203

Saline County History and Heritage Society, P. O. Box 221, Bryant, AR 72022-0221

Saline County Historical Commission, Gunn Museum of Saline County, 218 S. Market St., Benton, AR 72015

Sevier County Historical Society, 509 West Heynecker, DeQueen, AR 71832

Southwest Arkansas Genealogical Society, 1022 Lawton Circle, Magnolia, AR 71753

Southwest Arkansas Regional Archives, Old Washington Historic State Park, Washington, AR 71862

Stone County Genealogical Society, P. O. Box 557, Mountain View, AR 72560

Texarkana USA Genealogical Society, P. O. Box 2323, Texarkana, AR-TX 75504

Tri-County Genealogical Society, P. O. Box 580, Marvell, AR 72366

Union County Genealogical Society, Barton Library, East 5th and North Jefferson Streets, El Dorado, AR 71730

Washington County Arkansas Historical Society, 118 East Dickson Street, Fayetteville, AR 72701

Yell County Historical and Genealogical Society, Box 622, Dardanelle, AR 72834

Printed Census Records and Mortality Schedules

Federal Census 1830, 1840, 1850, 1860 (except Little River County), 1870, 1880, 1900, 1910

Valuable Printed Sources

Atlases, Maps, and Gazetteers

Baker, Russell Pierce. *Arkansas Township Atlas*. Arkansas Genealogical Society, 1984.

Genealogical Research Guides

Dillard, Tom W. and Valerie Thwing. *Researching Arkansas History: A Beginner's Guide*. Little Rock: Rose Publishing Co., 1979.

Morgan, James Logan. *A Survey of the County Records of Arkansas*. Newport, Arkansas: Arkansas Records Association, 1972.

Wagoner, Claudia. *Arkansas Researcher's Handbook*. Fayetteville, Arkansas: Research Plus, 1986.

Genealogical Sources

Christensen, Katheren. *Arkansas Military Bounty Grants (War of 1812)*. Hot Springs, Arkansas: Arkansas Ancestors, 1972.

Core, Dorothy Jones. *Abstract of Catholic Register of Arkansas, 1764-1858*. Gillett, Arkansas: Grand Prairie Historical Society, 1976.

Prudence Hall Chapter, Daughters of the American Revolution. *Index to Sources for Arkansas Cemetery Inscriptions*. Little Rock, Arkansas: Prudence Hall Chapter, DAR, 1976.

ARKANSAS COUNTY DATA
State Map on Page M-4

Name	Map Index	Date Created	Parent County or Territory From Which Organized
* **Arkansas**	F5	1813	Original county

Arkansas County, PO Box 719, Stuttgart, AR 72160-0719 .... (501)673-7311
(Co Clk has pro rec from 1809, m rec from 1838; Clk Cir Ct has div & civ ct rec from 1803, war serv discharge from 1917, & lnd rec)

| * **Ashley** | H4 | 1848 | Chicot, Union, Drew |

Ashley County, 215 E Jefferson Ave, Hamburg, AR 71646-3007 .... (501)853-5144
(Co Clk has m rec 1848; pro, lnd rec. Cir Clk has div rec)

| *† **Baxter** | C3 | 1873 | Fulton, Izard, Marion & Searcy |

Baxter County, County Courthouse, Mountain Home, AR 72653 .... (501)425-3475
[FHL has some m, cem, civ ct, pro, lnd, nat rec]

| *† **Benton** | C1 | 1836 | Washington |

Benton County, PO Box 699, Bentonville, AR 72712-0699 .... (501)271-1015
(Co Clk has m from 1861, pro from 1859; Clk Cir Ct has div, civ ct & lnd rec)

| * **Boone** | C2 | 1869 | Carrol, Madison |

Boone County, PO Box 846, Harrison, AR 72602-0846 .... (501)741-8428
(Co Clk has m & pro from 1869; Clk Cir Ct has div, civ ct & lnd rec)

| * **Bradley** | G4 | 1840 | Union |

Bradley County, County Courthouse, Warren, AR 71671 .... (501)226-3853
(Co Clk has m rec 1846 to present; pro rec 1850 to present; Cir Clk has div rec)

| **Calhoun** | G3 | 1850 | Dallas, Ouachita |

Calhoun County, Main St, Hampton, AR 71744 .... (501)798-2517
(Co Clk has m rec 1851 to present; Div, pro, civ ct, 1880 to present, lnd rec 1851 to present)

| *† **Carroll** | C2 | 1833 | Izard |

Carroll County, 210 W Church Ave, Berryville, AR 72616-4233 .... (501)423-2022
(Co Clk has m & pro rec from 1870; Clk Cir Ct has lnd, civ ct & div rec from 1870)

| **Chicot** | H5 | 1823 | Arkansas |

Chicot County, County Courthouse, Lake Village, AR 71653 .... (501)265-2208
(Co Clk has m & pro rec from 1839; Clk Cir Ct has civ ct rec from 1824, lnd & div rec)

| **Clark** | F2 | 1818 | Arkansas |

Clark County, County Courthouse Sq, Arkadelphia, AR 71923 .... (501)246-4491
(Co Clk has m from 1821, pro from 1800; Clk Cir Ct has div, civ ct & lnd rec)

| * **Clay** | C6 | 1873 | Randolph, Green |

Clay County, 2nd St, Piggott, AR 72454. Second county seat Corning, AR 72422 ...... (501)598-2813
(Records burned in 1893. Co Clk has m & pro rec from Jan 1893; Clk Cir Ct has lnd, div & civ ct rec from 1893)

| *† **Cleburne** | D4 | 1883 | White, Van Buren, Independence |

Cleburne County, 301 W Main St, Heber Springs, AR 72543-3016 .... (501)362-8141
(Co Clk has m, pro, div, civ ct, lnd rec 1883 to present)

| † **Cleveland** | F4 | 1873 | Dallas, Bradley, Jefferson, Lincoln |

Cleveland County, Main & Magnolia Sts, Rison, AR 71665 .... (501)325-6521
(Changed from Dorsey 5 March 1885) (Co Clk has m rec 1880, div, pro, civ ct rec)

| * **Columbia** | H2 | 1852 | Lafayette, Hempstead, Ouachita |

Columbia County, 1 Court Sq, Magnolia, AR 71753-3527 .... (501)234-2542
(Co Clk has m, lnd rec 1853 to present; Div, civ ct rec 1860 to present; pro rec; Co Library has cem rec)

Name	Map Index	Date Created	Parent County or Territory From Which Organized

* **Conway**   E3   1825   Pulaski
Conway County, Moose & Church Sts, Morrilton, AR 72110 .... (501)354-9621
(Co Clk has m rec from 1858 & pro rec; Cir Clk has div, civ ct & Ind rec)

* **Craighead**   D6   1859   Mississippi, Greene, Poinsett
Craighead County, 511 S Main St, Jonesboro, AR 72401-2849 .... (501)933-4500
(Co Clk has m & pro rec from 1878 & tax rec; Clk Cir Ct has civ ct & div rec from 1878 & Ind rec from 1900)

* **Crawford**   D1   1820   Pulaski
Crawford County, 3rd & Main Sts, Van Buren, AR 72956 .... (501)474-1511
(Co Clk has m & pro rec from 1877; Clk Cir Ct has civ ct & Ind rec from 1877 & div rec)

  Crittenden   D6   1825   Phillips
Crittenden County, County Courthouse, Marion, AR 72364 .... (501)739-4434
(Co Clk has m & pro rec; Clk Cir Ct has civ ct rec; Chancery Clk has div rec)

*† **Cross**   D6   1862   Crittenden, Poinsett, St. Francis
Cross County, 705 E Union Ave, Wynne, AR 72396-3039 .... (501)238-3373
(Co Clk has wills, bonds, m rec from 1863, pro, tax & county ct rec from 1865; Cir Clk has civ ct & Ind rec from 1865; Chancery Cir Clk has div rec from 1866; Co Hist Soc has newsprs from 1935, cem rec, fam hist P.O. Box 943 Wynne AR 72396; Kernodle Funeral Home, Wynne AR has bur rec from 1936)

* **Dallas**   F3   1845   Clark, Bradley
Dallas County, 3rd & Oak Sts, Fordyce, AR 71742 .... (501)352-3371
(Co Clk has m rec from 1855, Ind rec from 1845, pro, div & civ ct rec)

  Desha   G5   1838   Arkansas, Chicot
Desha County, PO Box 188, Arkansas City, AR 71630-0188 .... (501)877-2426
(Co Clk has m rec 1865 to present; pro rec; Cir Clk has div, civ ct, Ind rec)

  Dorsey (see Cleveland)

* **Drew**   G4   1846   Arkansas, Bradley
Drew County, 210 S Main St, Monticello, AR 71655-4796 .... (501)367-3574
(Co Clk has m, pro rec; Cir Clk has div, civ ct, Ind rec)

*† **Faulkner**   E3   1873   Pulaski, Conway
Faulkner County, 801 Locust St, Conway, AR 72032-5360 .... (501)450-4900
(Co Clk has m, pro, civ ct rec from 1873)

  Franklin   D1   1837   Crawford
Franklin County, Commercial St, Ozark, AR 72949 .... (501)667-3607
(Co Clk has m rec from 1850, pro rec from 1838, Ind rec from 1899)

  Fulton   C4   1842   Izard
Fulton County, PO Box 278, Salem, AR 72576-0278 .... (501)895-3341
[FHL has some cem, Ind, civ ct rec]

  Garland   F2   1873   Saline
Garland County, 501 Ouachita Ave, Hot Springs, AR 71901-5154 .... (501)321-2819
(Co Clk has m, pro rec; Cir Clk has div, civ ct, Ind rec)

  Grant   F3   1869   Jefferson, Hot Springs, Saline
Grant County, Main & Center Sts, Sheridan, AR 72150 .... (501)942-2631
(Co Clk has m, div, pro, civ ct & Ind rec from 1877)

* **Greene**   C6   1833   Lawrence
Greene County, PO Box 364, Paragould, AR 72451-0364 .... (501)239-4097
(Co Clk has m, pro, civ ct & Ind rec from 1876; Clk Cir Ct has div rec)

* **Hempstead**   G2   1818   Arkansas
Hempstead County, PO Box 1420, Hope, AR 71801-1420 .... (501)777-6164
(Co Clk has m, pro rec 1823 to present; Ind rec 1900 to present)

*† **Hot Spring**   F3   1829   Clark
Hot Spring County, 3rd & Locust St, Malvern, AR 72104 .... (501)332-2261
(Co Clk has m rec from 1825, & pro rec from 1834; Clk Cir Ct has civ ct & civ rec)

* **Howard**   F1   1873   Pike, Hempstead, Polk, Sevier
Howard County, 421 N Main St, Nashville, AR 71852-2008 .... (501)845-5916
(Co Clk has m & pro rec from 1873 & a cemetery book; Clk Cir Ct has div, civ ct & Ind rec from 1873)

* **Independence**   D5   1820   Lawrence, Arkansas
Independence County, 192 E Main St, Batesville, AR 72501-5510 .... (501)793-8800
(Co Clk has m rec from 1826 & pro rec from 1839; Clk Cir Ct has div, civ ct & Ind rec; Co Lib has bur rec)

*† **Izard**   C4   1825   Independence, Fulton
Izard County, PO Box 95, Melbourne, AR 72556-0095 .... (501)368-4316
(Line between Izard & Sharp changed 9 Mar 1877) (Co Clk has m, div, pro, civ ct, Ind rec 1889 to present)

*† **Jackson**   D5   1829   Woodruff
Jackson County, Main St, Newport, AR 72112 .... (501)523-6152
(Co Clk has m rec from 1843, pro rec from 1845; Clk Cir Ct has div & civ ct rec from 1845, & Ind rec)

* **Jefferson**   F4   1829   Arkansas, Pulaski
Jefferson County, PO Box 6317, Pine Bluff, AR 71611-6317 .... (501)541-5322
(Co Clk has m rec from 1830, pro rec from 1845; Cir Clk has div, civ ct & Ind rec)

Name	Map Index	Date Created	Parent County or Territory From Which Organized

* Johnson D2 1833 Pope
Johnson County, PO Box 278, Clarksville, AR 72830-0278 .... (501)754-2175
(Co Clk has m rec 1855 to present; pro rec 1844 to present; Cir Clk has div, civ ct, Ind rec; extension office has bur rec)

* Lafayette H2 1827 Hempstead
Lafayette County, PO Box 754, Lewisville, AR 71845-0754 .... (501)921-4858
(Co Clk has m rec 1848; pro rec; Cir Clk has div rec)

* Lawrence C5 1815 New Madrid, Mo
Lawrence County, PO Box 553, Walnut Ridge, AR 72476-0553 .... (501)886-2167
(Co Clk has m & pro rec)

* Lee E6 1873 Phillips, Monroe, Crittenden, St. Francis
Lee County, 15 E Chestnut St, Marianna, AR 72360-2330 .... (501)295-2339
(Co Clerk has m, pro rec 1883)

* Lincoln F4 1871 Arkansas, Bradley, Desha, Drew, Jefferson
Lincoln County, Drew & Wiley Sts, Star City, AR 71667 .... (501)628-4147
(Co Clk has m, pro, & Ind rec from 1871, tax rec)

* Little River G1 1867 Hempstead
Little River County, 351 N 2nd St, Ashdown, AR 71822-2753 .... (501)898-5021
(Co Clk has m & pro rec from 1880; Clk Cir Ct has div & Ind rec)

* Logan E2 1871 Pope, Franklin, Johnson, Scott, Yell
Logan County, Broadway St, Booneville, AR 72927 .... (501)675-2951
(Co Clk at Paris has m, pro rec; Co Clk at Booneville has m, pro rec 1901; Cir Clk div, civ ct, Ind rec)

* Lonoke E4 1873 Pulaski, Prairie
Lonoke County, PO Box 431, Lonoke, AR 72086-0431 .... (501)676-6403
(Co Clk has m, pro rec)

Lovely   1827 (Abolished 1828)

† Madison C2 1836 Washington
Madison County, PO Box 37, Huntsville, AR 72740-0037 .... (501)738-6721
(Co Clk has m & pro rec from 1901)

* Marion C3 1836 Izard
Marion County, Courthouse Sq, Yellville, AR 72687 .... (501)449-6231
(Co Clk has m, div, pro, civ ct, Ind rec 1888 to present; Abstractors have Ind rec)

* Miller H1 1820 Lafayette Abolished 1836 & ret to Arkansas Re-established 1874
Miller County, 4 Laurel St, Texarkana, AR 75502 .... (501)774-1500
(Co Clk has m, pro, Ind rec 1875 to present; Cir Clk has div, civ ct rec)

* Mississippi D6 1833 Crittenden
Mississippi County, Walnut & 2nd Sts, Blytheville, AR 72315 .... (501)763-3212
(Co Clk has m from 1850, pro from 1865; Clk Cir Ct has div, civ ct rec from 1866, Ind rec from 1865)

*† Monroe E5 1829 Phillips, Arkansas
Monroe County, 123 Madison St, Clarendon, AR 72029-2794 .... (501)747-3921
(Co Clk has m rec 1850 to present; pro rec 1839 to present; Cir Clk has div rec 1839 to present; civ ct rec 1830 to present; Ind rec 1829 to present; local mortuary has some bur rec)

† Montgomery F2 1842 Hot Springs
Montgomery County, PO Box 717, Mount Ida, AR 71957-0717 .... (501)867-3114
(Co Clk has m, pro, Ind, div & civ ct rec from 1845; Co Agent has bur rec at courthouse in Mt. Ida)

* Nevada G2 1871 Hempstead, Columbia, Ouachita
Nevada County, County Courthouse, Prescott, AR 71857 .... (501)887-3115
(Co Clk has m & pro rec from 1871, tombstone rec; Clk Cir Ct has div, civ ct & Ind rec from 1871)

* Newton C2 1842 Carroll
Newton County, PO Box 435, Jasper, AR 72641-0435 .... (501)446-5127
(Co Clk has m, Ind rec 1866; div rec 1820; pro civ ct rec 1880)

* Ouachita G3 1842 Union
Ouachita County, 145 Jefferson St, Camden, AR 71701 .... (501)836-4116
(Co Clk has m, pro rec Dec 1875 to present; Cir Clk has div, civ ct, Ind rec)

* Perry E3 1840 Conway
Perry County, PO Box 358, Perryville, AR 72126-0358 .... (501)889-5126
(Co Clk has m, div, pro, civ ct & Ind rec from 1882)

Phillips F6 1820 Arkansas, Hempstead
Phillips County, 626 Cherry St, Helena, AR 72342-3306 .... (501)338-5505
(Co Clk has m rec 1831 to present, pro rec 1850 to present; Cir Clk has div, civ ct, Ind rec 1820 to present)

* Pike F2 1833 Clark, Hempstead
Pike County, Washington St Courthouse Sq, Murfreesboro, AR 71958 .... (501)285-2231
(Co Clk has m, div, pro, civ ct, Ind, wills, discharge rec 1895 to present)

Poinsett D6 1838 Greene, St. Francis
Poinsett County, Courthouse Sq, Harrisburg, AR 72432 .... (501)578-5408
(Co Clk has m rec from 1873, pro rec; Clk Cir Ct has div, civ ct & Ind rec)

Name	Map Index	Date Created	Parent County or Territory From Which Organized

*† Polk   F1   1844   Sevier
Polk County, 507 Church Ave, Mena, AR 71953-3297 . . . . (501)394-6010
(Co Clk has m rec from 1885, pro rec from 1900, co ct rec from 1873; Clk Cir Ct has div rec from 1907, crim ct rec from 1873 & Ind rec from 1882)

* Pope   D3   1829   Crawford
Pope County, 100 W Main St, Russellville, AR 72801-3740 . . . . (501)968-7487
(Co Clk has m, pro, div, civ ct & Ind rec from 1830)

Prairie   E5   1846   Pulaski, Monroe
Prairie County, PO Box 278, Des Arc, AR 72040-0278 . . . . (501)256-3741
(Part of the county was taken from Monroe in 1869; Check Monroe County for records prior to this date) (Some of Lonoke County records are in Des Arc) (Co Clk in DeValls Bluff has m, div, pro, civ ct, Ind rec from 1885 to present; Naturalization rec 1907-1912; Discharge records beginning with World War I) (LDS Church has microfilmed this county's records and they are available at the Arkansas State History Commission)

Pulaski   E4   1818   Arkansas
Pulaski County, 401 W Markham St, Little Rock, AR 72201-1417 . . . . (501)372-8305
(Co Clk has m rec from 1838, pro rec from 1820, poll tax from 1892, Voter reg rec from 1952, Real estate tax rec from 1828, pers prop tax rec from 1869, minister credentials from 1884; Clk Cir Ct has civ ct, Ind & naturalization rec; Clk Chancery Ct has div rec; History Commission has pro ct files bef 1920)

* Randolph   C5   1835   Lawrence
Randolph County, 201 Marr St, Pocahontas, AR 72455 . . . . (501)892-5264
(Co Clk has m from 1836, div from 1841, pro, civ ct & Ind rec from 1836)

* Saint Francis   E6   1827   Phillips
Saint Francis County, 313 S Izard St, Forrest City, AR 72335-3856 . . . . (501)633-8640
(Co Clk has m rec from 1875, pro rec from 1910 & tax rec; Clk Cir Ct has div, civ ct & Ind rec)

*† Saline   E3   1835   Pulaski, Hempstead
Saline County, 200 N Main, Benton, AR 72015-3767 . . . . (501)778-2667
(Co Clk has m & pro rec from 1836, Ind from 1871)

*† Scott   E1   1833   Pulaski, Crawford, Pope
Scott County, PO Box 1578, Waldron, AR 72958-1578 . . . . (501)637-2155
(Co Clk has m, div, pro, civ ct rec, deeds & mortg from 1882, tax rec from 1932)

*† Searcy   C3   1838   Marion
Searcy County, PO Box 297, Marshall, AR 72650-0297 . . . . (501)448-3554
(Co Clk has m, div, pro & civ ct rec from 1881, deed rec from 1866)

* Sebastian   E1   1851   Scott, Polk, Crawford, Van Buren
Sebastian County, 6th & Rogers, Fort Smith, AR 72901 . . . . (501)783-6139
(Co Clk has m rec from 1865; pro rec 1866; Cir Clk has div, civ ct, Ind rec)

* Sevier   F1   1828   Hempstead, Miller
Sevier County, 115 N 3rd St, De Queen, AR 71832-2852 . . . . (501)642-2852
(Co Clk has m, pro rec from 1829; Cir Clk has div, civ ct, Ind rec)

* Sharp   C5   1868   Lawrence
Sharp County, County Courthouse, Ash Flat, AR 72513 . . . . (501)994-7338
(Line between Sharp & Izard changed 1877)

Stone   C4   1873   Izard, Independence, Searcy, Van Buren
Stone County, PO Box 427, Mountain View, AR 72560-0427 . . . . (501)269-3351
(Co Clk has m, div, pro, civ ct & Ind rec from 1873)

* Union   H3   1829   Hempstead, Clark
Union County, Main & Washington Sts, El Dorado, AR 71730 . . . . (501)863-6024
(Co Clk has m, pro rec from 1846; Cir Clk has div, civ ct, Ind rec)

* Van Buren   D3   1833   Independence, Conway, Izard
Van Buren County, PO Box 80, Clinton, AR 72031-0080 . . . . (501)745-4140
(Co Clk has m from 1859, div from 1874, pro from 1860, civ ct & Ind rec from 1959)

* Washington   C1   1828   Crawford
Washington County, 2 S College Ave, Fayetteville, AR 72701-5393 . . . . (501)521-8400
(Co Clk has m rec from 1845, pro rec from 1828; Clk Cir Ct has div, civ ct & Ind rec; City Lib has cem rec; Courthouse burned Civil War, but records were saved)

* White   E4   1835   Pulaski, Jackson, Independence
White County, 300 N Spruce St, Searcy, AR 72143-7720 . . . . (501)279-6200
(This county has never had a disaster in its courthouse and its records go back to the beginning of the county. Some are scattered in misc. vols. The staff does not have time to search records, but all crspd is referred to a professional researcher for answering) (Co Clk has m, div, pro, civ ct, Ind, wills, tax, misc rec)

Woodruff   E5   1862   Jackson, St. Francis
Woodruff County, PO Box 356, Augusta, AR 72006-0356 . . . . (501)347-5206
(Co Clk has m & pro rec from 1865; Clk Cir Ct has div, civ ct & Ind rec)

Name	Map Index	Date Created	Parent County or Territory From Which Organized
* **Yell**	E2	1840	Pope, Scott

Yell County, PO Box 219, Danville, AR 72833-0219 .... (501)495-2630
[FHL has some m, cem, civ ct, Ind, pro, tax rec]

* At least one county history has been published about this county.
† Inventory of county archives was made by the Historical Records Survey. (See Introduction)

CALIFORNIA

CAPITAL · SACRAMENTO — STATE 1850 (31st)
State Map on Page M-5

Juan Cabrillo discovered California in 1542. The English, due to Sir Francis Drake's visit in 1579, also laid claim to the land. The Spanish, however, were the first to establish settlements. San Diego was settled in 1769 and Monterey in 1770. Junipero Serra set up a chain of Franciscan missions throughout the state, which served not only as religious but also economic centers. The Russians built Fort Ross in 1812 to serve as a trading post, but abandoned it in 1841. After Mexican independence in 1821, California became mainly a collection of large ranches. In 1839, a Swiss, John Augustus Sutter, established the "Kingdom of New Helvetia" in the Sacramento River Valley. Two years later Americans began traveling overland to California in significant numbers. Early in the Mexican War, American forces occupied California. John C. Fremont, the American soldier and explorer, headed a short-lived Republic of California in 1846. In 1848, California was ceded to the United States. Just nine days earlier, gold was discovered at Sutter's mill. This discovery led to the California Gold Rush of 1849, which brought over 100,000 people to California from all over the United States, Asia, Australia, and Europe.

The mass migration enabled California to attain the required number of inhabitants to be admitted to the Union in 1850. During the Civil War, 15,700 soldiers fought for the Union. Thousands of Chinese were brought to the state to help build the transcontinental railroad, which was completed in 1869. A railroad rate war in 1884 and a real estate boom in 1885 led to another wave of immigration. Foreign-born Californians in descending order hail from Mexico, Canada, Italy, England, Wales, Russia, Germany, Sweden, Ireland, Scotland, Poland, Austria, France, Denmark, Norway, Switzerland, Portugal, Greece, Yugoslavia, Hungary, Netherlands, Spain, Finland, Czechoslovakia, Romania, Lithuania, and Belgium.

The Office of the State Registrar, 304 "S" Street, Sacramento, CA 95814 has records of births, deaths, and marriages since 1905. To verify current fees, call 916-445-2684.

Prior to July 1, 1905, records are available from the county recorders and from the Health Departments of many of the larger cities. County clerks have divorce, probate, civil court, and other records. Naturalization records are kept in the county offices of the Superior Courts and in the U.S. Circuit Courts in Los Angeles and San Francisco. Real estate deeds are filed in the County Recorder's office. Pre-statehood lists, termed padrons, of Spanish, Mexican, and Indian residents have been published. The California State Archives, Room 130, 1020 "O" Street, Sacramento, CA 95814, has some censuses for major California cities from 1897 to 1938.

Genealogical Archives, Libraries and Societies

Amador County Friends of the Museum-Archives, P. O. Box 913, Jackson, CA 95642

Bancroft Library, University of California, Berkeley, CA 94720

California State Archives, Rm. 200, 1020 "O" St., Sacramento, CA 95814

California State Library, California Section, Room 304, Library and Courts Building, 914 Capitol Mall, Sacramento, CA 95814 Mailing address: P. O. Box 942837, Sacramento, CA 94237-0001

California State Library (Sutro Branch), 480 Winston Dr., San Francisco, CA 94132

Federal Archives and Record Center, 1000 Commodore Dr., San Bruno, CA 94066

Florence Styles Memorial Library, c / o Paradise Genealogical Society, P. O. Box 460, Paradise, CA 95967-0460

Fremont Main Library, Alameda County Library-TS, 2450 Stevenson Blvd., Fremont, CA 94538

Friends of The Amador County Museum and Archives, P. O. Box 913, Jackson, CA 95642

Genealogy Collection of San Francisco Public Library, 480 Winston Dr., San Francisco, CA 94132

Held-Poage Memorial Home and Research Library, c / o Mendocino County Historical Society, 603 W. Perkins St., Ukiah, CA 95482

Huntington Beach Central Library, 7111 Talbert Ave., Huntington Beach, CA 92648 (Location of collection of the Orange County, California Genealogical Society).

Huntington Library, San Marino, CA 91108

Immigrant Library, 5043 Lankershim Blvd., North Hollywood, CA 91601

Library-Museum, Central California Chapter, American Historical Society of Germans from Russia, 3233 N. West, Fresno, CA 93705

Library of the Sons of the Revolution, Sons of the Revolution Building, 600 South Central Avenue, Glendale, CA 91204

Long Beach Public Library, Ocean at Pacific Ave., Long Beach, CA 90802

Los Angeles Public Library, 630 West Fifth, Los Angeles, CA 90071

Mayflower Library of California, 405 14th St., Terrace Level, Oakland, CA 94612

Mira Loma Genealogy Library, P. O. Box 527, Mira Loma, CA 91752

National Archives, Los Angeles Branch, 24000 Avila Road, Laguna Niguel, CA 92656

Native Daughters of the Golden West Library, 555 Baker St., San Francisco, CA 94117-1405

Oakland Public Library, 14th and Oak St., Oakland, CA 94612

Pasadena Public Library, 285 East Walnut St., Pasadena, CA 91101

Pomona Public Library, 625 South Garey Ave., P. O. Box 2271, Pomona, CA 91766 (Has a large collection of indexes to the U.S. Census, 210 indexes).

Riverside Public Library, Box 468, 3581 7th St., Riverside, CA 92502

San Diego Public Library, 820 "E" St., San Diego, CA 92101

San Lorenzo Library, Alameda County Library-TS, 2450 Stevenson Blvd., Fremont, CA 94538

Santa Clara County Free Library, 1095 N. 7th St., San Jose, CA 95112

Santa Cruz City-County Public Library, Central Branch, 224 Church St., Santa Cruz, CA 95060

Santa Maria Public Library, Genealogical Collection and California Room, 420 South Broadway, Santa Maria, CA 93454

Santa Rosa-Sonoma County Library, Third and E Sts., Santa Rosa, CA 95404

Shields Library, University of California, Davis, CA 95616

Siskiyou County Public Library, 719 4th St., Yreka, CA 96097

Stanislaus County Free Library, 1500 I Street, Modesto, CA 95354

Sutro Library, Branch of the California State Library, 480 Winston Dr., San Francisco, CA 94132

Triadoption Library, P. O. Box 5218, Huntington Beach, CA 90278

Tulare Public Library, 113 N. F St., Tulare, CA 93274

Ventura County Genealogical Library, E.P. Foster Library, 651 East Main, Ventura, CA 93003

Whittier College Library, Whittier, CA 90602

Amador County Genealogical Society, 322 Via Verde, Sutter Ter., Sutter Creek, CA 95685

Antelope Valley Genealogical Society, P. O. Box 1049, Lancaster, CA 93534

California Czechoslavak Club, 727 Appleberry Dr., San Rafael, CA 94903

California Genealogical Society, P. O. Box 77105, San Francisco, CA 94107-0105

California Historical Society, 2090 Jackson St., San Francisco, CA 94109

California State Genealogical Alliance, 19765 Grand Avenue, Lake Elsinore, CA 92330

Clan Diggers Genealogical Society, Inc., P. O. Box 531, Lake Isabella, CA 93240

Colorado River-Blythe Quartzsite Genealogical Society, P. O. Box 404, Blythe, CA 92226

Colusa County Genealogical Society, P. O. Box 973, Williams, CA 95987

ComputerRooters, P. O. Box 161693, Sacramento, CA 95816

Conejo Valley Genealogical Society, Inc., P. O. Box 1228, Thousand Oaks, CA 91360

Contra Costa County Genealogical Society, P. O. Box 910, Concord, CA 94522

Covina, California Chapter, DAR, 2441 SN. Cameron Ave., Covina, CA 91724

Delta Genealogical Interest Group, P. O. Box 157, Knightsen, CA 94548

Downey Historical Society, P. O. Box 554, Downey, CA 90241

East Bay Genealogical Society, P. O. Box 20417, Oakland, CA 94620-0417

El Dorado Research Society, P. O. Box 56, El Dorado, CA 95623

Escondido Genealogical Society, P. O. Box 2190, Escondido, CA 92025-0380

Fresno Genealogical Society, P. O. Box 1429, Fresno, CA 93716-1429

Genealogical Association of Sacramento, P. O. Box 28297, Sacramento, CA 95828

Genealogical Society of Coachella Valley, P.O. Box 124, Indio, CA 92202

Genealogical Society of Madera, P. O. Box 495, Madera, CA 93639

Genealogical Society of Morongo Basin, P. O. Box 234, Yucca Valley, CA 92284

Genealogical Society of Riverside, P. O. Box 2557, Riverside, CA 92516

Genealogical Society of Siskiyou County, P. O. Box 225, Yreka, CA 96097

Genealogical Society of Stanislaus County, P. O. Box 4735, Modesto, CA 95352

German Genealogical Society of America, P. O. Box 291818, Los Angeles, CA 90029

German Research Association, P. O. Box 11293, San Diego, CA 92111

Glendora Genealogy Group, P. O. Box 1141, Glendora, CA 91740

Hayward Area Genealogical Society, P. O. Box 754, Hayward, CA 94543

Hemet-San Jacinto Genealogical Society, P. O. Box 2516, Hemet, CA 92343

Hi Desert Genealogical Society, P. O. Box 1271, Victorville, CA 92392

Historical Society of Southern California, 200 E. Ave. 43, Los Angeles, CA 90031

Humboldt County Genealogical Society, 2336 G Street, Eureka, CA 95501

Immigrant Genealogical Society, P.O. Box 7369, Burbank, CA 91510-7369

Indian Wells Valley Genealogical Society, 131 Los Flores, Ridgecrest, CA 93555

Intermountain Genealogical Society, P. O. Box 399, Burney, CA 96013

Jewish Genealogical Society of Los Angeles, 4530 Woodley Avenue, Encino, CA 91436

Jewish Genealogical Society of Orange County, 11751 Cherry St., Los Alamitos, CA 90720

Jewish Genealogical Society of Sacramento, 2351 Wyda Way, Sacramento, CA 95825

Jewish Genealogical Society of San Diego, 255 South Rios Ave., Solana Beach, CA 92075

Kern County Genealogical Society, P. O. Box 2214, Bakersfield, CA 93303

Lake County Genealogical Society, P. O. Box 1323, Lakeport, CA 95453

Lake Elsinore Genealogical Society, Box 807, Lake Elsinore, CA 92330

Leisure World Genealogical Workshop, Leisure World Library, 2300 Beverly Manor Road, Seal Beach, CA 90740

Livermore-Amador Genealogical Society, P. O. Box 901, Livermore, CA 94550

Los Angeles (British Family Historical Society of), 22941 Felbar Ave., Torrance, CA 90505

Los Angeles Westside Genealogical Society, P. O. Box 10447, Marina del Rey, CA 90295

Los Banos, California Genealogical Society, P. O. Box 1106, Los Banos, CA 93635

Los Californianos, P. O. Box 5155, San Francisco, CA 94101

Marin County Genealogical Society, P. O. Box 1511, Novato, CA 94948

Mendocino Coast Genealogical Society, P. O. Box 762, Fort Bragg, CA 95437

Mendocino County Historical Society, 603 West Perkins St., Ukiah, CA 95482

Merced County Genealogical Society, P. O. Box 3061, Merced, CA 95340

Mt. Diablo Genealogical Society, P. O. Box 4654, Walnut Creek, CA 94596

Napa Valley Genealogical and Biographical Society, P. O. Box 385, Napa, CA 94550

National Archives-Pacific Sierra Region 1000 Commodore Dr., San Bruno, CA 80225

National Archives-Pacific Southwest Region 24000 Avila Rd., Laguna Niguel, CA 92677

Native Daughters of the Golden West, 555 Baker Street, San Francisco, CA 94117-1405

Native Sons of the Golden West, 414 Mason St., San Francisco, CA 94102

North San Diego County Genealogical Society, Inc., P. O. Box 581, Carlsbad, CA 92008

Orange County Genealogical Society, P. O. Box 1587, Orange, CA 92668

Pajaro Valley Genealogical Society, 53 North Drive, Freedom, CA 95019

Palatines to America, California Chapter, 1540 Danromas Way, San Jose, CA 95129

Palm Springs Genealogical Society, P. O. Box 2093, Palm Springs, CA 92263

Paradise Genealogical Society, P. O. Box 460, Paradise, CA 95967-0460

Pasadena Genealogy Society, P. O. Box 94774, Pasadena, CA 91109-4774

Patterson Genies, 525 Clover Ave., Patterson, CA 95363

Placer County Genealogical Society, P. O. Box 7385, Auburn, CA 95604-7385

Plumas County Historical Society, P. O. Box 695, Quincy, CA 95971

Pocahontas Trails Genealogical Society, 3628 Cherokee Lane, Modesto, CA 95356

Polish Genealogical Society of California, P. O. Box 713, Midway City, CA 92655

Pomona Valley Genealogical Society, P. O. Box 286, Pomona, CA 91766

Questing Heirs Genealogical Society, P. O. Box 15102, Long Beach, CA 90813

Redwood Genealogical Society, Box 645, Fortuna, CA 95540

Renegade Root Diggers, 9171 Fargo Ave., Hanford, CA 93230

Root Cellar Sacramento Genealogical Society, P. O. Box 265, Citrus Heights, CA 95611

Sacramento, Genealogical Association of, 1230 42nd Ave., Sacramento, CA 95822

Sacramento German Genealogy Society, P. O. Box 660061, Sacramento, CA 95866

San Bernardino Valley Genealogical Society, P. O. Box 26020, San Bernardino, CA 92406

San Diego Genealogical Society, 2925 Kalmia St., San Diego, CA 92104

San Francisco Bay Area Jewish Genealogical Society, 40 West 3rd Ave., San Mateo, CA 94402

San Joaquin Genealogical Society, P. O. Box 4817, Stockton, CA 95104

San Luis Obispo County Genealogical Society, Inc., P. O. Box 4, Atascadero, CA 93423-0004

San Mateo County Genealogical Society, P. O. Box 5083, San Mateo, CA 94402

San Mateo County Historical Association, San Mateo Junior College, San Mateo, CA 94402

San Ramon Valley Genealogical Society, P. O. Box 305, Diablo, CA 94528

Santa Barbara County Genealogical Society, P. O. Box 1303, Goleta, CA 93116-1303

Santa Clara County Historical and Genealogical Society, 2635 Homestead Road, Santa Clara, CA 95051

Santa Cruz County, Genealogical Society of, P. O. Box 72, Santa Cruz, CA 95063

Santa Maria Valley Genealogical Society, P. O. Box 1215, Santa Maria, CA 93456

Sequoia Genealogical Society, Inc., P. O. Box 3473, Visalia, CA 93278

Shasta Historical Society P. O. Box 277, Redding, CA 96001

Society of California Pioneers, 456 McAllister St., San Francisco, CA 94102

Society of Mayflower Descendants in the State of California, 405 Fourteenth St., Terrace Level, Oakland, CA 94612

Solano County Genealogical Society, Inc., P. O. Box 2494, Fairfield, CA 94533

Sonoma County Genealogical Society, P. O. Box 2273, Santa Rosa, CA 95405

South Bay Cities Genealogical Society, P. O. Box 6071, Torrance, CA 90504

Southern California Chapter of the Ohio Genealogical Society, P. O. Box 5057, Los Alamitos, CA 90721-5057

Southern California Genealogical Society, P. O. Box 4377, Burbank, CA 91503

Spanishtown Historical Society, Box 62, Half Moon Bay, CA 94019

Sutter-Yuba Genealogical Society, P. O. Box 1274, Yuba City, CA 95991

Taft Genealogical Society, P. O. Box 7411, Taft, CA 93268

Tehama Genealogical and Historical Society, P. O. Box 415, Red Bluff, CA 96080

TRW Genealogical Society, One Space Park S-1435, Redondo Beach, CA 90278

Tule Tree Tracers, 41 W. Thurman Ave., Porterville, CA 93257

Tuolumne County Genealogical Society, P. O. Box 3956, Sonora, CA 95370

Vandenberg Genealogical Society, P. O. Box 814, Lompoc, CA 93438

Ventura County Genealogical Society, P. O. Box 24608, Ventura, CA 93002

Whittier Area Genealogical Society, P. O. Box 4367, Whittier, CA 90607

Yorba Linda Genealogical Society, 4751 Libra Place, Yorba Linda, CA 92686

Yucaipa Valley Genealogical Society, P. O. Box 32, Yucaipa, CA 92399

Printed Census Records and Mortality Schedules

Federal Census 1850 (except Contra Costa, San Francisco, and Santa Clara counties), 1860, 1870, 1880, 1900, 1910

State Federal Census 1852

Padron Census 1790

Valuable Printed Sources

Atlases, Maps, and Gazetteers

Beck, Warren A. and Ynez D. Haase. *Historical Atlas of California*. Norman, Oklahoma: University of Oklahoma Press, 1974.

Gudde, Erwin Gustav. *California Place Names: The Origin and Etymology of Current Geographical Names*. Berkeley, California: University of California Press, 1969.

Hanna, Phil Townsend. *The Dictionary of California Land Names*. Los Angeles: Automobile Club of Southern California, 1951.

Sanchez, Nellie. *Spanish and Indian Place Names of California: Their Meaning and Romance*. San Francisco: A. M. Robertson, 1930.

Bibliographies

California Library Directory: Listings for Public, Academic, Special, State Agency, and County Law Libraries. Sacramento: California State Library, 1985.

Rocq, Margaret Miller. *California Local History: A Bibliography and Union List of Library Holdings*. Stanford: Stanford University Press, 1970.

Genealogical Research Guides

Sanders, Patricia. *Searching in California: A Reference Guide to Public and Private Records*. Costa Mesa, California: ISC Publications, 1982.

Schwartz, Mary and Luana Gilstrap. *A Guide to Reference Aids for Genealogists*. Culver City, California: Genealogy Publishing Service, 1981.

Genealogical Sources

Bancroft, Hubert Howe. *Register of Pioneer Inhabitants of California, 1542 to 1848, and Index to Information Concerning Them in Bancroft's History of California, Volumes I to V*. Los Angeles: Dawson's Book Shop, 1964 and Baltimore: Regional Publishing Co., 1964.

Northrop, Mary E. *Spanish-American Families of Early California: 1769-1850*. New Orleans: Polyanthos, 1976.

Orton, Richard H. *Records of California Men in the War of the Rebellion, 1861-1867*. Sacramento: State Office of Printing, 1890.

Parker, J. Carlyle. *An Index to the Biographies in 19th Century California Histories*. Detroit: Gale Research Co., 1979.

Rasmussen, Louis J. *California Wagon Lists*. Colma, California: San Francisco Historic Records, 1976.

――――. *Railway Passenger Lists of Overland Trains to San Francisco and the West*. Colma, California: San Francisco Historic Records, 1966.

――――. *San Francisco Ship Passenger Lists*. Baltimore: Genealogical Publishing Co., 1978.

Society of California Archivists. *Directory of Archival and Manuscript Repositories of California*. Redlands, California: Printed Beacon Printery, 1975.

CALIFORNIA COUNTY DATA
State Map on Page M-5

Name	Map Index	Date Created	Parent County or Territory From Which Organized

*† Alameda   E3   1853   Contra Costa & Santa Clara
Alameda County, 1225 Fallon St, Oakland, CA 94612-4218 .... (415)272-6790
(Co Clk has m rec from 1854; pro, div, civ ct & Ind rec from 1853, b rec 1919-1988 [some prior from 1873] d rec 1905-1988 [some prior from 1876])

Alpine   D4   1864   Eldorado, Amador, Calaveras
Alpine County, PO Box 158, Markleeville, CA 96120-0158 .... (916)694-2281
(Co Clk has b, m, d, div, pro, civ ct & Ind rec from 1900)

* Amador   D3   1854   Calaveras
Amador County, 108 Court St, Jackson, CA 95642-2379 .... (209)223-6463
(Co Clk has b, d rec from 1872; m, div, pro, civ ct, Ind rec from 1854)

Branciforte (changed to Santa Cruz 1850)

* Butte   C3   1850   Original county
Butte County, 25 County Center Dr, Oroville, CA 95965-3316 .... (916)538-7551
(Co Rcdr has m rec from 1851, b & d rec from 1859, & Ind rec; Co Clk has div, pro & civ ct rec from 1850; Meriam Lib, Calif State Univ, Chico, has div, pro, civ ct rec from 1850 to 1879, & naturalization rec 1850-1960)

* Calaveras   D3   1850   Original county
Calaveras County, 891 Mountain Ranch Rd, San Andreas, CA 95249-9713 .... (209)754-6310
(Co Rcdr has b rec from 1860, m, d & div rec from 1882, pro & civ ct rec from 1866, Ind rec from 1852, mining claims from 1850)

* Colusa   D2   1850   Original county
Colusa County, 546 Jay St, Colusa, CA 95932-2443 .... (916)458-5146
(Colusa County was created in 1850 but attached to Butte County for administration until it was organized in January, 1851. Co Clk has b rec from 1873; m rec from 1853; d rec from 1889; pro, civ ct, Ind and assessment rolls from 1851; Great Registers from 1866; mil rolls from 1879. Note: There is a fee when staff is requested to search records)

* Contra Costa   E3   1850   Original county
Contra Costa County, 725 Court St, Martinez, CA 94553-1233 .... (415)646-2950
(Co Clk has b, m, d, div, pro, civ ct, Ind rec from 1850)

* Del Norte   B1   1857   Klamath
Del Norte County, 625 6th St, Crescent City, CA 95531 .... (707)464-7205
(Co Clk has div, pro & civ ct rec from 1848; Co Rcdr has b, m & d rec from 1873, Ind rec from 1853, leases & agreements 1857-1954)

* El Dorado   D3   1850   Original county
El Dorado County, 495 Main St, Placerville, CA 95667-5699 .... (916)621-6426
(Co Clk has civ ct and pro rec; Co Rcdr has d, m, b rec)

*† Fresno   F4   1856   Merced, Mariposa
Fresno County, 2281 Tulare St Rm 300, Fresno, CA 93721-2105 .... (209)488-3531
(Co Clk has b, m, d rec 1855-1979)

Glenn   C2   1891   Colusa
Glenn County, 526 W Sycamore, Willows, CA 95988-2746 .... (916)934-3834
(Co Clk has b, m, div, pro, civ ct & Ind rec from 1891, d rec from 1905, & bur rec from 1972)

* Humboldt   B1   1853   Trinity
Humboldt County, 825 5th St, Eureka, CA 95501-1153 .... (707)445-7258
(Co Clk has div, pro & civ ct rec from 1853; Co Rcdr has b, m, d, bur & Ind rec)

* Imperial   H7   1907   San Diego
Imperial County, 852 Broadway, El Centro, CA 92243-2312 .... (619)339-4256
(Co Clk has m, div, pro & civ ct rec from 1907; Co Rcdr has b, m & d rec from 1907)

* Inyo   F5   1866   Tulare
Inyo County, 168 N Edwards St, Independence, CA 93526 .... (619)878-2411
(Co Clk has b, d rec from 1904; m, Ind rec from 1866, mining rec from 1872)

*† Kern   G5   1866   Tulare, Los Angeles
Kern County, 1415 Truxtun Ave, Bakersfield, CA 93301-5222 .... (805)861-2111
(Co Clk-Rcdr has b, m, d, & Ind rec from 1850, div, pro, civ ct & reg voting rec from 1866; An exchange of territory with San Bernardino Co took place in 1963)

* Kings   F4   1893   Tulare, Fresno
Kings County, 1400 W Lacey Blvd, Hanford, CA 93230-5925 .... (209)582-3211
(Co Clk has b, m, d, div, pro, civ ct, Ind & naturalization rec from 1893; Each cem dist has bur rec; Fed Ct in Fresno has naturalization rec from 1893 to 1957)

* Lake   D2   1861   Napa
Lake County, 255 N Forbes St., Lakeport, CA 95453-4747 .... (707)263-2372
(Co Clk has b, m, d, Ind rec from 1867; Co Clk has mining rec, misc rec; Clk Sup Ct has div, pro, civ ct rec)

* Lassen   B3   1864   Plumas, Shasta
Lassen County, 220 S Lassen St, Susanville, CA 96130-4324 .... (916)257-8311
(Co Clk has div, pro, civ ct & naturalization rec from 1864; Co Rcdr has m rec from 1864, Ind rec from 1857, b & d rec from 1907, although some prior 1907, and incomplete to 1929)

Name	Map Index	Date Created	Parent County or Territory From Which Organized

*† **Los Angeles**   G5   1850   Original county
Los Angeles County, 111 N Hill St, Los Angeles, CA 90012-3117 . . . . (213)974-6621
(Co Clk has div rec from 1880, pro & civ ct rec from 1850 & criminal rec; Co Rcdr has b, m, d & lnd rec)

* **Madera**   E4   1893   Mariposa, Fresno
Madera County, 209 W Yosemite Ave, Madera, CA 93637-3534 . . . . (209)675-7721
(Co Clk has b, m, d, div, pro, civ ct, lnd rec from 1893, some voting rec)

*† **Marin**   D2   1850   Original county
Marin County, 1501 Civic Center Dr, San Rafael, CA 94903 . . . . (415)499-6407
(Co Rcdr has b, d rec from 1863; m rec from 1856; lnd rec from 1852; Co Clk has div, civ ct rec from 1900; pro rec from 1880)

* **Mariposa**   E4   1850   Original county
Mariposa County, PO Box 247, Mariposa, CA 95338-0247 . . . . (209)966-2005
(Co Clk has div, pro & civ ct rec; Co Rcdr has b, m, d & bur rec; the dates on all these rec are indefinite)

* **Mendocino**   C1   1850   Original county
Mendocino County, State & Perkins, Ukiah, CA 95482 . . . . (707)463-4379
(Co Clk has div rec from 1858, pro from 1872, civ ct rec from 1858; Co Rcdr has b, m, d & land rec) (Some old rec in Sonoma Co)

* **Merced**   E3   1855   Mariposa
Merced County, 2222 M St, Merced, CA 95340-3780 . . . . (209)385-7434
(Co Clk has div, pro & civ ct rec from 1855; Co Rcdr has b, m, d & bur rec)

* **Modoc**   B3   1874   Siskiyou
Modoc County, PO Box 131, Alturas, CA 96101-0131 . . . . (916)233-3939
(Co Clk has div, pro, civ ct, voter registration rec from 1874; Co Rcdr has b, m, d rec)

*† **Mono**   E4   1861   Calaveras, Fresno
Mono County, PO Box 537, Bridgeport, CA 93517-0537 . . . . (619)932-7911
(Co Clk has b, m rec from 1861; d, bur, div, pro, civ ct, lnd rec from 1900)

* **Monterey**   F3   1850   Original county
Monterey County, PO Box 1819, Salinas, CA 93902-1819 . . . . (408)755-5030
[FHL has some b, m, d, cem rec]

*† **Napa**   D2   1850   Original county
Napa County, PO Box 880, Napa, CA 94559-0880 . . . . (707)253-4481
(Co Clk-Rcdr has b, m & d rec; Co Assessor has lnd rec; Ct Exec Officer has div, pro & civ ct rec from 1850)

* **Nevada**   C3   1851   Yuba
Nevada County, 201 Church St, Nevada City, CA 95959-2504 . . . . (916)265-1293
(Co Clk has b rec from 1873, m from 1856, d from 1873, div, pro, civ ct from 1880, lnd rec from 1856)

* **Orange**   H5   1889   Los Angeles
Orange County, 700 Civic Center Dr W, Santa Ana, CA 92701-4022 . . . . (714)834-2200
(Co Rcdr has b, m, d & lnd rec; Co Clk has div, pro & civ ct rec from 1964)

* **Placer**   D3   1851   Yuba, Sutter
Placer County, 11960 Heritage Oak Pl Suite 15, Auburn, CA 95604-5228 . . . . (916)889-7983
(Co Clk-Rcdr has b, m & d rec from 1873, & lnd rec from 1850; Co Clk has pro rec from 1851, & civ ct rec from 1880)

* **Plumas**   C3   1854   Butte
Plumas County, PO Box 10207, Quincy, CA 95971 . . . . (916)283-6305
(Co Clk has div rec from 1860; Co Rcdr has b, m, d, pro, civ ct, & lnd rec from 1860; Co Museum Arch has biographies and photographs)

* **Riverside**   H6   1893   San Diego, San Bernardino
Riverside County, 4050 N Main St, Riverside, CA 92501-3798 . . . . (714)275-1989
(Co Clk-Rcdr has b, m, d, & lnd rec from 1893; Sup Ct has div, pro, & civ ct rec from 1893)

* **Sacramento**   D3   1850   Original county
Sacramento County, 720 9th St, Sacramento, CA 95814-1398 . . . . (916)440-5522
(Co Clk has div, pro & civ ct rec from 1880; Co Rcdr has b, m, d & lnd rec)

*† **San Benito**   F3   1874   Monterey
San Benito County, 440 5th St, Hollister, CA 95023-3843 . . . . (408)637-3786
(Co Clk has b, m, d, div, pro civ ct, lnd rec from 1900)

*† **San Bernardino**   G6   1853   Los Angeles
San Bernardino County, 777 E Rialto Ave, San Bernardino, CA 92415-0001 . . . . (714)387-2020
(Co Clk has m lic from 1887, div and pro from 1856, civ and crim rec from 1853, insanity and inebriate rec from 1887, guardianship rec from 1856, lnd rec from 1854; Co Rcdr has b, d rec from 1853, m rec from 1857)

*† **San Diego**   H6   1850   Original county
San Diego County, 1600 Pacific Hwy, San Diego, CA 92101-2422 . . . . (619)694-3900
(Co Clk has div, pro & civ ct rec from 1855)

*† **San Francisco**   E2   1850   Original county
San Francisco County, 400 Van Ness Ave Rm 317, San Francisco, CA 94102-4607 . . . . (415)554-4114
(Co Clk has div, pro & civ ct rec from 1906; Health Officer has b, & bur rec; Co Rcdr has m rec)

* **San Joaquin**   E3   1850   Original county
San Joaquin County, 222 E Weber Ave Rm 303, Stockton, CA 95202-2709 . . . . (209)468-2355
(Co Clk has div, pro & civ ct rec from 1851; Co Rcdr has b, m, d, lnd & Clk of Board of Supervisors)

Name	Map Index	Date Created	Parent County or Territory From Which Organized

*† San Luis Obispo   G3   1850   Original county
San Luis Obispo County, 1035 Palm St Rm 385, San Luis Obispo, CA   93408-0001 .... (805)549-5245
(Co Rcdr has b, m, d & Ind rec; Co Clk has div, pro & civ ct rec from 1854)

*† San Mateo   E2   3856   San Francisco
San Mateo County, 401 Marshall St, Redwood City, CA   94063-1636 .... (415)363-4711
(Co Clk Rcdr has b, m, d rec from 1866, div, civ ct, Ind from 1880, pro from 1856)

*† Santa Barbara   G4   1850   Original county
Santa Barbara County, 1100 Anacapa St, Santa Barbara, CA   93101-2099 .... (805)568-2220
(Co Clk has b rec from 1873, d rec from 1878, m, div, pro, civ ct, & Ind rec from 1850)

*† Santa Clara   E3   1850   Original county
Santa Clara County, 70 W Hedding St 11th Fl, San Jose, CA   95110-1768 .... (408)299-2424
(Co Clk has pro rec from 1850; Co Rcdr has b, d rec from 1873, m rec from 1850 and deeds from 1846. Note: b and d rec are scattered those recorded voluntarily. On July 1, 1905 it became obligatory to record these records)

* Santa Cruz   E2   1850   Original county
Santa Cruz County, 701 Ocean St, Santa Cruz, CA   95060-4027 .... (408)425-2790
(Co Clk has b & d from 1873, m from 1852, bur from 1905, div, pro, civ ct, Ind from 1850, naturalization & voters registration rec from 1866)

* Shasta   B2   1850   Original county
Shasta County, 1500 Court St, Redding, CA   96001-1694 .... (916)225-5631
(Co Clk has div, pro & civ ct rec from 1880; Co Rcdr has b, m & d rec)

* Sierra   C3   1852   Yuba
Sierra County, PO Box D, Downieville, CA   95936-0398 .... (916)289-3295
(Co Clk-Rcdr has b, m, d, bur, div, pro, civ ct, Ind rec & reg of voters from 1852)

* Siskiyou   B2   1852   Shasta, Klamath, Oregon
Siskiyou County, 311 4th St, Yreka, CA   96097-2944 .... (916)842-8005
(Co Rcdr has b, m, d, bur, rec; Co Clk has div, pro, civ ct rec from 1853; Co Clk has election rec, board of supervisor's minutes from 1860)

* Solano   D3   1850   Original county
Solano County, 580 W Texas St, Fairfield, CA   94533-6321 .... (707)429-6218
(Co Rcdr has b, m, d, Ind rec; bur rec are maintained by cem district; Co Clk has div, pro, civ ct rec from 1850)

* Sonoma   D2   1850   Original county
Sonoma County, PO Box 11187, Santa Rosa, CA   95406-1187 .... (707)527-2611
(Co Rcdr has b, m, d, bur, Ind rec; Co Clk has div, pro, civ ct rec from 1850)

* Stanislaus   E3   1854   Tuolumne
Stanislaus County, PO Box 1098, Modesto, CA   95353-1098 .... (209)525-6416
(Co Clk-Rcdr has m rec from 1870, b & d rec from 1900; Sup Ct Clk has div, pro, & civ ct rec from 1854; Co Rcdr has Ind rec from 1854)

* Sutter   D3   1850   Original county
Sutter County, 433 2nd St, Yuba City, CA   95991-5504 .... (916)741-7120
(Co Clk has div, pro & civ ct rec from 1850)

* Tehama   C2   1856   Colusa, Butte, Shasta
Tehama County, PO Box 250, Red Bluff, CA   96080-0250 .... (916)527-4655
(Co Clk has b & d rec from 1889, m from 1856, div, pro, civ ct & Ind rec from 1856)

* Trinity   B2   1850   Original county
Trinity County, PO Box 1258, Weaverville, CA   96093-1258 .... (916)623-1222
(Co Clk has b, m, d, bur, div, pro, civ ct, Ind, misc mining, newspaper rec from 1860)

* Tulare   F4   1852   Mariposa
Tulare County, 2900 W Burrel Ave, Visalia, CA   93291-4509 .... (209)733-6266
(Co Clk has div, pro & civ ct rec; Co Rcdr has b, m, d & bur rec; Co Asr has Ind rec)

* Tuolumne   E4   1850   Original county
Tuolumne County, 2 S Green St, Sonora, CA   95370-4679 .... (209)533-5555
(Co clk Rcdr has b from 1858, m from 1850, d from 1859, bur from 1916, div, pro, civ ct & Ind from 1850, old newspapers from 1862 to 1948)

*† Ventura   G4   1872   Santa Barbara
Ventura County, 800 S Victoria Ave, Ventura, CA   93009-0001 .... (805)654-5000
(Co Clk Rcdr has b, m, & d rec from 1873, Ind rec from 1850; Sup Ct Clk has div, pro, & civ ct rec from 1873; Some land went to Kern & Los Angeles Counties in boundary change)

* Yolo   D2   1850   Original county
Yolo County, 725 Court St, Woodland, CA   95695-3436 .... (916)666-8195
(Co Clk has b, m, d & Ind rec, div, pro & civ ct rec from 1850)

* Yuba   D3   1850   Original county
Yuba County, 215 5th St, Marysville, CA   95901-5794 .... (916)741-6341
(Co Clk has m from 1865, div, pro & civ ct rec from 1850, voting rec 1866)

* At least one county history has been published about this county.
† Inventory of county archives was made by the Historical Records Survey. (See Introduction)

COLORADO

CAPITAL · DENVER — TERRITORY 1861 — STATE 1876 (38th)
State Map on Page M-6

Early Spanish explorers traveled through the Colorado area and heard exciting tales of gold and silver from the Indians. Many treasure seekers searched throughout the Southwest and Rocky Mountain areas for the elusive fortunes. Spain and France alternated control of the area until 1803, when all but the areas south and west of the Arkansas River were sold to the United States. In 1806, Zebulon Pike was sent to explore the area. Others also came such as Stephen Long in 1819 and John Fremont in 1842. The remainder of present Colorado became part of the United States in 1848. Fur traders prospered in the area, but not until 1851 was the first town, San Luis, established. In 1854, Colorado was divided among the territories of Kansas, Nebraska, Utah, and New Mexico. Settlement remained sparse until gold was discovered in 1858 and the Pikes Peak gold rush lured 50,000 people to Colorado. Denver, Golden, Boulder, and Pueblo were established as supply bases. Arapaho County of Kansas Territory was organized by the miners in 1858. The following year the residents created the Territory of Jefferson, but Congress failed to recognize it. The Territory of Colorado was finally organized in 1861, although some of its counties date their creation from 1859. The 1860 census for Colorado (then part of Kansas) shows 33,000 men and 1,500 women. During the Civil War, just under 5,000 men fought for the Union.

The completion of the transcontinental railroad linked Colorado to both coasts and provided impetus for increased migration. Colorado gained statehood in 1876. The western part of the state was officially opened to settlement in 1881, following the removal of most of the Ute Indians to reservations in Utah. By the time of the last major gold strike at Cripple Creek in 1890, the population of the state stood at more than 400,000.

Counties and towns were required to record births and deaths after January 1876. Where clerks complied, these are found with the county clerks. Statewide registration began in 1907 and records may be obtained from the Records and Statistics Sections, Colorado Department of Health, 4210 East 11th Avenue, Denver, CO 80220 (to verify current fees, call 303-320-8333). Marriage records were kept by the county clerks from the organization of the county as were divorce records in most cases. Probate records and wills are also in the offices of the county clerks, except for Denver, where there is a separate probate court. The first general land office in Colorado was established in 1863. Most land office records are at the National Archives, Denver Branch, Building 48, West 6th Avenue and Kipling, Denver Federal Center, Denver, CO 80225. Private land records were kept by county recorders. Spanish land grants prior to 1862 were processed in the New Mexico Office. The U.S. Surveyor processed claims from 1855 to 1890. An 1860 Territorial Census was taken in the four territories of which Colorado was a part. The Utah part was not yet settled. The Nebraska part is listed under "unorganized territory". The Kansas part is listed in the Arapahoe County schedules, and the New Mexico part is listed in the Taos and Mora county schedules.

Genealogical Archives, Libraries and Societies

Boulder Public Library, 1000 Canyon Blvd., Boulder, CO 80302

Carnegie Branch Library, 1125 Pine St., P. O. Drawer H, Boulder, CO 80306

Charles Leaming Tutt Library, Colorado College, Colorado Springs, CO 80903

Colorado Springs Public Library, 21 W. Kiowa St., Colorado Springs, CO 80902

Denver Public Library, 1357 Broadway, Denver, CO 80203

Friend Genealogy Library, 1448 Que Street, Penrose, CO 81240

Greeley Public Library, City Complex Bldg, 919 7th St., Greeley, CO 80631

Historical Society Library, 14th and Sherman, Denver, CO 80203

Marble Historical Museum, 412 West Main St., Marble, CO 81623 (Gunnison Count).

Montrose Public Library, City Hall, Montrose, CO 81401

Norlin Library, University of Colorado, Boulder, CO 80304

Penrose Public Library, 20 North Cascade, Colorado Springs, CO 80902

Pueblo Regional Library, 100 Abriendo Ave., Pueblo, CO 81005

Stagecoach Library, 1840 S. Wolcott Ct., Denver, CO 80219

Tutt Library, Colorado College, Colorado Springs, CO 80903

Weld County Library, 2227 23rd Ave., Greeley, CO 80631

Ancestor Seekers Genealogy Society, P. O. Box 693, Castle Rock, CO 80104

Archuleta County Genealogical Society, P. O. Box 1611, Pagosa Springs, CO 81147

Aspen Historical Society, 620 West Bleeker Street, Aspen, CO 81611

Aurora Genealogical Society of Colorado, P. O. Box 31439, Aurora, CO 80041

Boulder, Colorado Gen. Group, 856 Applewood Drive, Lafayette, CO 80026

Boulder Genealogical Society, P. O. Box 3246, Boulder, CO 80307

Brighton Genealogical Society, P. O. Box 1005, Brighton, CO 80601

Colorado Council of Genealogical Societies, P. O. Box 24379, Denver, CO 80224-0379

Colorado Historical Society, Colorado Heritage Center, 1300 Broadway, Denver, CO 80203

Colorado Genealogical Society, P. O. Box 9671, Denver, CO 80209 Organized 1924

Colorado Society, Sons of the American Revolution, 255 Moline St., Aurora, CO 80010

Columbine Genealogical and Historical Society, Inc., P. O. Box 2074, Littleton, CO 80161

Eagle County Historical Society, P. O. Box 357, Eagle, CO 81631

Eastern Colorado Historical Society, 43433 Road CC, Cheyenne Wells, CO 80810

Estes Park Genealogy Society, 2517 Longview Dr., Estes Park, CO 80517

Foothills Genealogical Society of Colorado, Inc., P. O. Box 15382, Lakewood, CO 80215

Fore-Kin Trails Genealogical Society, P. O. Box 1024, Montrose, CO 81402

Frontier Historical Society, 1001 Colorado Ave., Glenwood Springs, CO 81601

High Country Genealogical Society, 304 S. Colorado St., Gunnison, CO 81230

High Plains Heritage Genealogical Society, Princeton Court, Brush, CO 80723

Larimer County Genealogical Society, P. O. Box 8436, Fort Collins, CO 80524

Logan County Genealogical Society, P. O. Box 294, Sterling, CO 80751

Longmont Genealogical Society, P. O. Box 6081, Longmont, CO 80501

Mesa County Genealogical Society, Box 1506, Grand Junction, CO 81502

Morgan County Genealogical Society, 3 Princeton Court, Brush, CO 80723

National Archives-Rocky Mountain Region Building 48, Denver Federal Center, Denver, CO 80225

Pikes Peak Genealogical Society, P. O. Box 1262, Colorado Springs, CO 80901

Prowers County Genealogical Society, P. O. Box 175, Lamar, CO 81052-0175

San Luis Valley Genealogical Society, P. O. Box 1541, Alamosa, CO 81101

Southeastern Colorado Genealogical Society, Inc., P. O. Box 4086, Pueblo, CO 81008-0086

Weld County Genealogical Society, P. O. Box 278, Greeley, CO 80631

White River Trace Genealogical Society, 425 12th St., Meeker, CO 81641

Yuma Area Genealogical Society, P. O. Box 24, Yuma, CO 80759

Printed Census Records and Mortality Schedules

Federal Census 1860 (with Kansas), 1870, 1880, 1900, 1910
Federal Mortality Schedules 1870, 1880
State/Territorial Census 1885

Valuable Printed Sources

Atlases, Maps, and Gazetteers

Crofutt, George A. *Grip Sack Guide of Colorado*. Golden, Colorado: Cubar Associates, 1885.

Dawson, J. Frank. *Place Names in Colorado*. Lakewood, Colorado: Jefferson Records, n.d.

Biographies

Byers, William Newton. *Encyclopedia of Biography of Colorado: History of Colorado*. Chicago: Century Publishing & Engraving Co., 1901.

Colorado Families: A Territorial Heritage. Denver: Colorado Genealogical Society, 1981.

Genealogical Research Guides

Glavinick, Jacquelyn Gee. *Research Guide for Northern Colorado*. Greeley, Colorado: Genealogical Society of Weld County, 1988.

Merrill, Kay R. *Colorado Cemetery Directory*. Denver: Colorado Council of Genealogical Societies, 1985.

COLORADO COUNTY DATA
State Map on Page M-6

Name	Map Index	Date Created	Parent County or Territory From Which Organized
Adams	F5	1901	Arapahoe

Adams County, 450 S 4th Ave, Brighton, CO 80601-3196 . . . . (303)659-2120
(Co Clk has m rec from 1902, some bur rec, Ind rec from 1902, and some Ind rec from Arapahoe Co prior to 1902, school census from 1902 to 1964, military discharges; 17th Jud Dist Ct Clk has div rec; Pro Ct has pro rec; Hall of Justice has civ ct rec; New airport land annexed to Denver Co)

Name	Map Index	Date Created	Parent County or Territory From Which Organized

† **Alamosa**   E2   1913   Costilla, Conejos
Alamosa County, 402 Edison Ave, Alamosa, CO   81101-2560 .... (719)589-5887
(Co Clk has m & Ind from 1913; Clk Dis Ct has div pro & civ ct rec)

*† **Arapahoe**   F5   1861   Original county
Arapahoe County, 5334 S Prince St, Littleton, CO   80166-0001 .... (303)795-4630
(First formed in 1855 as Territorial County. For 1860 US census enumeration, see Kansas 1860. Co Clk has m & Ind rec from 1902, bur rec to 1941; Co Ct has div, pro, & civ ct rec)

Archuleta   D2   1885   Conejos
Archuleta County, PO Box 1507, Pagosa Springs, CO   81147-1507 .... (303)264-2536
(Co Clk has m & d from 1886, Ind from 1885; Clk Dis Ct has div, pro, civ ct rec & adoptions)

Baca   H2   1889   Las Animas
Baca County, 741 Main St, Springfield, CO   81073-1548 .... (719)523-4372
(Co Clk has m, Ind rec from 1889; Clk Dist Ct has div, pro, civ ct rec from 1910; Registrar of Vit Statistics as b, d rec from 1910)

*† **Bent**   G2   1874   Greenwood
Bent County, PO Box 350, Las Animas, CO   81054-0350 .... (719)456-2009
(Co Clk has m, Ind, voter reg, plat maps from 1888; Local Rgstr has b & d rec from 1910; Co Ct has div, pro & civ ct rec; bur rec may be kept by cities)

* **Boulder**   E5   1861   Original county
Boulder County, PO Box 471, Boulder, CO   80306-0471 .... (303)441-3131
(Co Clk has m & Ind rec from 1861, mil dschrg from 1918; Co Hlth Dept has b & d rec; Co Ct Clk has div, pro & civ ct rec)

Carbonate (original name of Lake Co)

Chaffee   D4   1879   Lake
Chaffee County, 132 Crestone Ave, Salida, CO   81201-1566 .... (719)539-4004
(Co Clk has m rec)

Cheyenne   G4   1889   Bent, Elbert
Cheyenne County, PO Box 67, Cheyenne Wells, CO   80810-0067 .... (719)767-5685
(Rgstr has b, d & bur rec; Co Clk has m from 1889 & Ind rec from 1888; Dis Ct has div & pro rec; Co Judge has civ ct rec)

* **Clear Creek**   E5   1861   Original county
Clear Creek County, PO Box 2000, Georgetown, CO   80444-2000 .... (303)534-5777
(Co Clk has m & Ind rec from 1862)

† **Conejos**   D2   1861   Original county
Conejos County, PO Box 157, Conejos, CO   81129-0157 .... (719)376-5772
[FHL has some cem rec]

† **Costilla**   E2   1861   Original county
Costilla County, PO Box 100, San Luis, CO   81152-0100 .... (719)672-3962
(Co Clk has m & Ind rec from 1853; Clk Dis Ct has div, pro & civ ct rec)

Crowley   G3   1911   Bent, Otero
Crowley County, 6th & Main St, Ordway, CO   81063 .... (719)267-4643
(Co Clk has m rec)

* **Custer**   E3   1877   Fremont
Custer County, 205 S 6th St, Westcliffe, CO   81252-9504 .... (719)783-2441
(Co Clk has m & bur rec)

Delta   C4   1883   Gunnison
Delta County, 501 Palmer St, Delta, CO   81416-1753 .... (303)874-7595
(Co Clk has b rec from 1920, m, d, Ind rec from 1883, school cen 1891-1964; Dist Ct has div, pro, civ ct rec)

Denver   F5   1901   Arapahoe
Denver County, City-County Bldg Rm 350, Denver, CO   80202 .... (303)575-2721
(Has annexed terr from Arapahoe, Adams & Jefferson Co on several occasions) (Co Clk has m from 1905, Ind from 1858; Clk Dis Ct has div from 1967, pro, civ ct rec from 1858)

Dolores   B2   1881   Ouray
Dolores County, 4th & Main Sts, Dove Creek, CO   81324 .... (303)677-2383
(Co Clk has b rec fro 1882, m, Ind rec from 1881, d rec from 1895)

Douglas   F4   1861   Original county
Douglas County, 301 Wilcox St, Castle Rock, CO   80104-2454 .... (303)688-6260
(Co Clk has m rec from 1867, Ind rec from 1864)

Eagle   D5   1883   Summit
Eagle County, PO Box 850, Eagle, CO   81631-0850 .... (303)328-7311
(Co Clk has b & m from 1883, d & Ind rec; Clk Dis Ct has div, pro & civ ct rec)

El Paso   F4   1861   Original county
El Paso County, 20 E Vermijo Ave, Colorado Springs, CO   80903-2214 .... (719)630-2800
(Co Clk has m, Ind rec from 1861, ser discharges 1919; District Ct has div, pro rec; Co Ct has civ ct rec; Bur Vit Statistics has b, d rec)

Elbert   F4   1874   Douglas, Greenwood
Elbert County, PO Box 37, Kiowa, CO   80117-0037 .... (303)621-2080
(Co Clk has m rec from Nov 1893, Ind rec from 1874; Clk of combined cts has div, pro, civ ct rec; Bur Vit Statistics has b, d, bur rec)

Name	Map Index	Date Created	Parent County or Territory From Which Organized

† **Fremont**   E3   1859   Original county
Fremont County, 615 Macon Rm 100, Canon City, CO 81212 . . . . (719)275-7521
(Co clk has m, Ind rec; Dis Ct has div, pro, civ ct rec; City Clks in Florence, Canon City have bur rec)

† **Garfield**   C4   1883   Summit
Garfield County, 109 8th St Suite 200, Glenwood Springs, CO 81601-3362 . . . . (303)945-2377
(Co Clk has m, Ind rec from 1892; Dis Ct has div, pro, civ ct rec; Registrar has b, d rec from 1892; City Clks for Rifle and Glenwood Springs have bur rec)

* **Gilpin**   E5   1861   Original county
Gilpin County, PO Box 366, Central City, CO 80427-0366 . . . . (303)572-0567
(Co Clk has m from 1881, Ind from 1861; Clk Dis Ct has div & pro rec)

Grand   D5   1874   Summit
Grand County, 308 Byers Ave, Hot Sulphur Springs, CO 80451-9999 . . . . (303)725-3347
(Local Rgstr has b, d & bur rec; Co & Dis Ct has div, pro & civ ct rec; Co Asr has Ind rec; Co Clk has m rec from 1874)

Greenwood (Bent and Elbert Counties formed from Greenwood)

Guadalupe (original name of Conejose Co)

* **Gunnison**   D4   1877   Lake
Gunnison County, 200 E Virginia Ave, Gunnison, CO 81230-2297 . . . . (303)641-0248
(Co Clk has m rec from 1874, Ind rec from 1879; Co Ct Clk has div & pro rec from 1877, civ ct rec from 1900; Gunnison Dept of Soc Serv has b, d & bur rec from 1910)

† **Hinsdale**   D2   1874   Conejos
Hinsdale County, PO Box 277, Lake City, CO 81235-0277 . . . . (303)944-2225
(Co Clk has m & Ind rec from 1875; Co Vital Stat has b & d rec; Co Ct has div, pro & civ ct rec)

* **Huerfano**   E2   1861   Original county
Huerfano County, 400 Main St, Walsenburg, CO 81089-2034 . . . . (719)738-2370
(Co Clk has m & Ind rec; Clk Dis Ct has div, pro & civ ct rec)

* **Jackson**   D6   1909   Grand, Larimer
Jackson County, PO Box 337, Walden, CO 80480-0337 . . . . (303)723-4334
(Co Clk has m from 1909, bur & Ind rec; Clk Dis Ct has div, pro & civ ct rec)

* **Jefferson**   E4   1861   Original county
Jefferson County, 1700 Arapahoe St, Golden, CO 80419-0001 . . . . (303)279-6511
(Co Clk has m rec from 1868, Ind rec from 1860; Co Hlth Dept has b, d & bur rec; Co Dist Ct has div rec; Co Ct has pro & civ ct rec; 1885 census taken)

* **Kiowa**   G3   1889   Cheyenne, Bent
Kiowa County, 1305 Goff St, Eads, CO 81036 . . . . (719)438-5421
(Co Clk has m & Ind rec from 1889; Clk Dis Ct has div, pro & civ ct rec)

Kit Carson   G4   1889   Elbert
Kit Carson County, PO Box 249, Burlington, CO 80807-0249 . . . . (719)346-8638
(Co Clk has m & Ind rec from 1889, & bur rec from 1902; Clk Dist Ct has b, d, div, pro, & civ ct rec)

La Plata   C2   1874   Conejos, Lake
La Plata County, 1060 E 2nd Ave, Durango, CO 81301-5157 . . . . (303)259-4000
(Co Clk has m rec from 1878, Ind rec from 1876; Co Dist Ct has div & pro rec; Co Ct has civ ct rec; San Juan Basin Hlth has b, d & bur rec)

* **Lake**   D4   1861   Original county
Lake County, PO Box 917, Leadville, CO 80461-0917 . . . . (719)486-1410
(Co Clk has m rec from 1869, Ind rec from 1861, some bur rec from 1885 to 1903; Clk Dist Ct has div, pro, & civ ct rec)

*† **Larimer**   E6   1861   Original county
Larimer County, PO Box 1190, Fort Collins, CO 80522-1190 . . . . (303)221-7000
(Co Clk has m & Ind rec from 1862; Co Hlth Dept has b & d rec)

* **Las Animas**   F2   1866   Huerfano
Las Animas County, 1st & Maple Sts, Trinidad, CO 81082 . . . . (719)846-3481
(Co Clk has m rec from 1887; Ind rec from 1883, mil discharge rec from 1918; Co Pub Health Dept has b, d rec; Clk Dis Ct has div, pro, civ ct rec; individual cemeteries have bur rec; Co Clk has bur permits)

* **Lincoln**   G4   1889   Elbert
Lincoln County, 718 3rd Ave, Hugo, CO 80821 . . . . (719)743-2444
(Co Clk has m & Ind rec from 1889; Clk Dis Ct has div, pro & civ ct rec)

*† **Logan**   G6   1887   Weld
Logan County, 315 Main St, Sterling, CO 80751-4349 . . . . (303)522-0888
(Co Clk has m, Ind, homestead, mil discharges, voter reg rec from 1887; Co Health Dept has b, d rec; Dis Ct has div, pro, civ ct rec)

* **Mesa**   B4   1883   Gunnison
Mesa County, PO Box 20000, Grand Junction, CO 81502 . . . . (303)244-1670
(Co Clk has m & Ind rec from 1883; Co Hlth Dept has b, d & bur rec; Dist Ct has div, pro & civ ct rec; Co Ct has ct rec; Co Archives have some bur rec; 1885 census taken)

Mineral   D2   1892   Hinsdale
Mineral County, Creede Ave, Creede, CO 81130 . . . . (719)658-2440
(Co Clk has m & Ind rec from 1893; Clk Dis Ct has div, pro & civ ct rec)

Name	Map Index	Date Created	Parent County or Territory From Which Organized

Moffat   C6   1911   Routt
Moffat County, 221 W Victory Way, Craig, CO 81625-2716 . . . . (303)824-5517
(Co Clk has m rec from 1911; Clk Dis Ct has div, pro & civ ct rec)

* **Montezuma**   B2   1889   La Plata
Montezuma County, 109 W Main St Suite 302, Cortez, CO 81321-3154 . . . . (303)565-8317
[FHL has some cem rec]

Montrose   B3   1883   Gunnison
Montrose County, PO Box 1289, Montrose, CO 81402-1289 . . . . (303)249-7755
(Co Clk has b & d rec from 1907, m rec from 1883, Ind rec from 1882)

† **Morgan**   G5   1889   Weld
Morgan County, 231 Ensign St, Fort Morgan, CO 80701-2307 . . . . (303)867-8202
(Co Clk has m, Ind rec from 1889; Co Health Dept has b, d rec from 1910; Clk Dis Ct has div, pro rec from 1889; Co Ct has civ ct rec from 1889)

Otero   G2   1889   Bent
Otero County, PO Box 511, La Junta, CO 81050 . . . . (719)384-8701
(Co Clk has m from 1892, Ind rec from 1889; Clk Co Ct has div & pro rec; Clk Dis Ct has civ ct rec)

Ouray   C3   1877   Hinsdale, San Juan
Ouray County, 541 4th St, Ouray, CO 81427 . . . . (303)325-4961
(Co Clk has m, div, pro, civ ct rec from 1877, discharge, unpatented mines, patented mines, transcripts from San Juan Co from 1918)

Park   E4   1861   Original county
Park County, 501 Main St, Fairplay, CO 80440 . . . . (303)838-7059
(Co Clk has m from 1893 & Ind rec; Clk Dis Ct has div, pro & cov ct rec)

*† **Phillips**   H6   1889   Logan
Phillips County, 221 S Interocean Ave, Holyoke, CO 80734-1534 . . . . (303)854-3131
(Co Clk has m & Ind rec from 1889; Dist Ct has pro rec; Co Ct has div & civ ct rec; Local registrars have b, d & bur rec)

* **Pitkin**   D4   1881   Gunnison
Pitkin County, 506 E Main St, Aspen, CO 81611-1993 . . . . (303)920-5180

† **Prowers**   H2   1889   Bent
Prowers County, 301 S Main St, Lamar, CO 81052-2857 . . . . (719)336-9001
(Co Clk has m, Ind & some d rec from 1889; Dist Ct has div & civ ct rec; Co Ct has pro & ct rec; Registrar of Vit Stat has b rec)

* **Pueblo**   F3   1861   Original county
Pueblo County, 215 W 10th St, Pueblo, CO 81003-2945 . . . . (719)543-3550
(Co Clk has m rec from 1880; Clk Dis Ct has div, pro & civ ct rec)

Rio Blanco   C5   1889   Summit
Rio Blanco County, PO Box 1067, Meeker, CO 81641-1067 . . . . (303)878-5068
(Co Clk has b, d & bur rec from 1901, m & Ind rec from 1897, also early day agriculture & stock rec, bounty books brand rec registered as Summit Co, Garfield Co & finally Rio Blanco Co; Clk Dist Ct has div, pro & civ ct rec from 1889)

Rio Grande   D2   1874   Conejos, Costilla
Rio Grande County, PO Box 160, Del Norte, CO 81132-0160 . . . . (719)657-3334

* **Routt**   D6   1877   Grand
Routt County, PO Box 773598, Steamboat Springs, CO 80477-3598 . . . . (303)879-0108
(Co Clk has m rec from 1893, Ind rec from 1885; Co Health Dept has b, d rec; Clk Dis Ct has div, pro, civ ct rec)

Saguache   D3   1866   Rio Grande
Saguache County, PO Box 655, Saguache, CO 81149-0655 . . . . (719)655-2231
(Co Clk has m rec from 1900, Ind rec from 1861)

San Juan   C2   1876   La Plata
San Juan County, PO Box 466, Silverton, CO 81433-0466 . . . . (303)387-5671
(Twn Clk has b, d & bur rec; Co Clk has m & Ind rec from 1876; Clk Dis Ct has div, pro & civ ct rec)

† **San Miguel**   B3   1883   Ouray
San Miguel County, PO Box 548, Telluride, CO 81435-0548 . . . . (303)728-3954
(Co Clk has m & Ind rec from 1883; Clk Dis Ct has div, pro & civ ct rec from 1883; some b, d & bur rec were destroyed in a recent fire so files are incomplete; Co Clk has various chattels, papers, agreements, inventories, clippings & misc, maps, some indexed)

* **Sedgwick**   H6   1889   Logan
Sedgwick County, PO Box 3, Julesburg, CO 80737-0003 . . . . (303)474-3346
(Co Clk has m & Ind rec from 1889; Clk Dis Ct has div, pro & civ ct rec)

Summit   D5   1861   Original county
Summit County, PO Box 68, Breckenridge, CO 80424-0068 . . . . (303)453-2561
(Co Clk has m & Ind rec)

Teller   E4   1899   El Paso
Teller County, PO Box 959, Cripple Creek, CO 80813-0959 . . . . (719)689-2482
(Co Clk has m, Ind rec from 1899; Ethel Pedrie, Victor, Colo has b, d rec; Clk Dis Ct has div, pro, civ ct rec)

Uncompahgre (changed to Ouray 1883)

*† **Washington**   G5   1887   Weld, Arapahoe
Washington County, 150 Ash Ave, Akron, CO 80720-1510 . . . . (303)345-2701
(Co Clk has m & Ind rec from 1887; Clk Dis Ct has div, pro & civ ct rec)

Name	Map Index	Date Created	Parent County or Territory From Which Organized
* **Weld**	F6	1861	Original county

Weld County, 915 10th St, Greeley, CO 80631-1123 .... (303)356-4000
(Co Clk has m & Ind rec; Clk Dis Ct has div, pro & civ ct rec)

| † **Yuma** | H5 | 1884 | Washington, Arapahoe |

Yuma County, PO Box 426, Wray, CO 80758-0426 .... (303)332-5809
(Co Clk has m rec from 1889, Ind rec from 1897)

* At least one county history has been published about this county.
† Inventory of county archives was made by the Historical Records Survey. (See Introduction)

CONNECTICUT

CAPITAL · HARTFORD — NINTH COLONY — STATE 1788 (5th)
State Map on Page M-7

The Dutch seafarer, Adriaen Block, was the first European in Connecticut when he sailed up the Connecticut River in 1614. In 1633, Dutch settlers from New Amsterdam built a fort and trading post at present-day Hartford. Glowing reports from John Oldham and others, combined with disgust with the intolerance of the Massachusetts Bay Colony, led to a migration from Massachusetts to Connecticut starting about 1634. Most of the settlers of Newtown (Cambridge), Watertown, and Dorchester moved to the central part of Connecticut, establishing the towns of Wethersfield, Windsor, and Suckiang (Hartford). These towns joined together in 1639 to form the Connecticut Colony, a relatively democratic colony. Meanwhile, in 1638, a party of Puritans founded New Haven, which with Milford, Stamford, and Guilford, established the New Haven Colony. The New Haven Colony was theocratic and used the Old Testament as the legal code. The decade of the 1640's saw a heavy influx of settlers from England. In 1662, John Winthrop, governor of the Connecticut Colony, was granted a charter which defined the boundaries as extending from Massachusetts to Long Island Sound and from Narragansett Bay to the Pacific Ocean. The New Haven Colony finally agreed to be absorbed into the Connecticut Colony in 1665. The next forty years were marked by migration westward, as sometimes entire towns moved to a new setting.

By 1740, Connecticut was settled and organized into incorporated towns. Towns have remained the basic governing unit and it is here that many of the records are found. Connecticut had many boundary disputes with other colonies, especially Rhode Island, Massachusetts, and New York. In 1754, Connecticut settlers colonized the Wyoming Valley in Pennsylvania. Connecticut exchanged its rights to the territory west of its present boundary for the Western Reserve in Ohio and in 1799 gave up its claims to the Wyoming Valley in Pennsylvania. In 1880, the Western Reserve was incorporated in the Northwest Territory as Trumbull County, and Connecticut's present boundaries were set.

Connecticut played an important part in the Revolutionary War. More than 40,000 of its men served in the war. In 1777, Danbury was burned, and in 1779, New Haven, Fairfield, and Norwalk were pillaged. Benedict Arnold largely destroyed New London and Groton in 1781. The 1790 Census shows a population of 223,236, most of whom came from England. Others came from Scotland, Ireland, France, and Holland.

Connecticut had more home industries than any other colony. Household gadgets invented and manufactured in the homes were carried all over the United States by "Yankee peddlars". The building of factories in the United States and the potato crop failures in Ireland brought 70,000 Irish as well as settlers from Germany, Canada, Scandinavia, Italy, Poland, Lithuania, Czechoslovakia, and Hungary. During the Civil War, Connecticut supplied about 55,000 troops to the Union.

The town clerks hold marriage licenses and records, birth and death records, and land records. Birth, death, and marriage records since July 1, 1897, are at the Connecticut State Department of Health Services, Vital Records Section, 150 Washington Street, Hartford, CT 06106 (to verify current fees, call 203-566-1124). Birth records may be searched only by the person, his parents, an attorney, or a member of a genealogical society in Connecticut. The Clerk of the Superior Court of each county holds divorce records. Naturalization records are in the office of the U.S. Circuit Court in Hartford or in the county Superior Courts. Wills, inventories, and administrations of estates are in the probate districts. The boundaries of these districts often differ from town and county boundaries. There are 118 probate districts for the 169 towns. Many probate records are now in the Connecticut State Library, 231 Capitol Avenue, Hartford, CT 06115. Almost every city in the state has printed histories, which contain much genealogical information, especially about early inhabitants. Many family histories exist in manuscript form only, but many of these have been indexed to facilitate research. Although libraries will not do research, they provide names of researchers or give information about indexes, if the request is accompanied by a self-addressed stamped envelope.

Genealogical Archives, Libraries and Societies

Abington Social Library, Abington Four Corners, Route 97, Abington, CT 06230

Archive and Resource Center, Polish Genealogical Society of Connecticut, 8 Lyle Road, New Britain, CT 06053

Beardsley and Memorial Library, Munro Place, Winsted, CT 06098

Bridgeport Public Library, 925 Broad St., Bridgeport, CT 06603

Bristol Public Library, 5 High Street, Bristol, CT 06010

Connecticut College Library, Mohegan Avenue, New London, CT 06320

Connecticut State Library, 231 Capitol Ave., Hartford, CT 06115

Cyrenius H. Booth Library, 25 Main St., Newtown, CT 06470

Danbury Public Library, 170 Main Street, P. O. Box 1160, Danbury, CT 06810

East Hartford Public Library, 840 Main Street, East Hartford, CT 06108

Fairfield Public Library, 1080 Old Post Road, Fairfield, CT 06430

Farmington Museum, 37 High Street, Farmington, CT 06032

Ferguson Library, 96 Broad Street, Stamford, CT 06901

Godfrey Memorial Library, 134 Newfield St., Middletown, CT 06457

Greenwich Library, 101 West Putnam Ave., Greenwich, CT 06830

Groton Public Library, Ft. Hill Rd., Groton, CT 06340

Hartford Public Library, 500 Main Street, Hartford, CT 06103

Indian and Colonial Research Center, Old Mystic, CT 06372

New Britain Public Library, 20 High Street, P. O. Box 1291, New Britain, CT 06050

New Haven Public Library, 133 Elm Street, New Haven, CT 06510

Noah Webster Memorial Library, 205 Main St., West Hartford, CT 06107

Otis Library, 261 Main Street, Norwich, CT 06360

Pequot Library, 720 Pequot Avenue, Southport, CT 06490

Phoebe Griffin Noyes Library, Lyme St., Lyme, CT 06371

Public Library, 63 Huntington St., New London, CT 06320

Seymour Public Library, 46 Church Street, Seymour, CT 06483

Silas Bronson Library, Public Library of the City of Waterbury, Connecticut, 267 Grand Street, Waterbury, CT 06702 Library has a separate genealogy and local history collection with considerable material on Connecticut and other New England states

Southington Public Library, 255 Main Street, Southington, CT 06489

Trinity College, Watkinson Library, 300 Summit Street, Hartford, CT 06106

Wadsworth Atheneum, 600 Main Street, Hartford, CT 06103

West Hartford Public Library, 20 South Main Street, West Hartford, CT 06107

Yale University Libraries, Box 1603A, Yale Station, New Haven, CT 06520

Aspincok Historical Society of Putnam, Inc., P. O. Box 465, Putnam, CT 06260

Brookfield, Connecticut Historical Society, 44 Hopbrook Rd., Brookfield, CT 06804

Connecticut Genealogical Society, P. O. Box 435, Glastonbury, CT 06033

Connecticut Historical Commission, 59 South Prospect Street, Hartford, CT 06106

Connecticut Historical Society, 1 Elizabeth St., Hartford, CT 06105

Connecticut League of Historical Societies, P. O. Box 906, Darien, CT 06820

Darien Historical Society, Old Kings Highway North, Darien, CT 06820

Descendants of the Founders of Ancient Windsor, The Windsor Historical Society, 96 Palisado Ave., Windsor, CT 06095

Essex Historical Society, 6 New City St., Essex, CT 06426

Fairfield Historical Society, 636 Old Post Rd., Fairfield, CT 06430

French-Canadian Genealogical Society of Connecticut, P. O. Box G-45, Tolland, CT 06084

Historical Society of Town of Greenwich, Bush-Holley House, 39 Strickland Road, Cos Cob, CT 06878

Jewish Genealogical Society of Connecticut, 25 Soneham Rd., West Hartford, CT 06117

Litchfield Historical Society, Litchfield, CT 06759

Middlesex County Historical Society, 151 Main Street, Middletown, CT 06457

Middlesex Genealogical Society, 45 Old Kings Highway, Darien, CT 06820

New Canaan Historical Society, 13 Oenoke Ridge, New Canaan, CT 06480

New Haven Colony Historical Society, 114 Whitney Ave., New Haven, CT 06510

New London County Historical Society, 11 Blinman Street, New London, CT 06320

North Haven Historical Society, 27 Broadway, North Haven, CT 06473

Polish Genealogical Society of Connecticut, Inc., 8 Lyle Road, New Britain, CT 06053

Salmon Brook Historical Society, Granby, CT 06035

Society of Mayflower Descendants, in Connecticut, 36 Arundel Avenue, Hartford, CT 06107

Southington Genealogical Society, Southington Historical Center, 239 Main Street, Southington, CT 06489

Stamford Genealogical Society, Inc., Box 249, Stamford, CT 06904

Stamford Historical Society, 1508 High Ridge Road, Stamford, CT 06903

Trumbull Historical Society, Trumbull Town Hall, Trumbull, CT 06611

Western Connecticut State College, 181 White Street, Danbury, CT 06810

Wethersfield Historical Society, 150 Main Street, Wethersfield, CT 06109

Windsor Historical Society, 96 Palisado Ave., Windsor, CT 06095

Printed Census Records and Mortality Schedules

Federal Census 1790, 1800, 1810, 1820, 1830, 1840, 1850, 1860, 1870, 1880, 1900, 1910
Census Reconstruction 1660-1673

Valuable Printed Sources

Atlases, Maps, and Gazetteers

Gannett, Henry. *A Geographic Dictionary of Connecticut and Rhode Island*. Baltimore: Genealogical Publishing Co., 1978 reprint.

Hughes, Arthur H. and Morse S. Allen. *Connecticut Place Names*. Hartford, Connecticut: Connecticut Historical Society, 1976.

Pease, John C. and John M. Niles. *A Gazetteer of the States of Connecticut and Rhode Island*. Hartford, Connecticut: William S. Marsh, 1819.

Town and City Atlas of the State of Connecticut. Boston: D. H. Hurd & Co., 1893.

Genealogical Research Guides

Claus, Robert. *Guide to Archives in the Connecticut State Library*. Hartford, Connecticut: Connecticut State Library, 1978.

Kemp, Thomas J. *Connecticut Researcher's Handbook*. Detroit: Gale Research Co., 1981.

List of Church Records in the Connecticut State Library. Hartford, Connecticut: Connecticut State Library, 1976.

Sperry, Kip. *Connecticut Sources for Family Historians and Genealogists*. Logan, Utah: Everton Publishers, 1980.

Genealogical Sources

Bailey, Frederic W. *Early Connecticut Marriages*. Baltimore: Genealogical Publishing Co., 1976 reprint.

Manwaring, Charles William. *A Digest of the Early Connecticut Probate Records*. Hartford, Connecticut, 1906.

CONNECTICUT COUNTY DATA
State Map on Page M-7

Name	Map Index	Date Created	Parent County or Territory From Which Organized
* **Fairfield**	G2	1666	Original county

Fairfield Jud Dist, 1061 Main St, Bridgeport, CT 06601 .... (203)579-6527
(Twn Clk Bridgeport has b, m & d rec from 1700, pro & lnd rec)

Towns Organized Before 1800: Brookfield 1788, Danbury 1685, Fairfield 1639, Greenwich 1640, Huntington (Shelton) 1789, New Fairfield 1740, Newtown 1711, Norwalk 1651, Redding, 1767, Ridgefield 1708, Stamford 1641, Trumbull 1798, Weston 1787

* **Hartford**	F3	1666	Original county

Hartford Jud Dist, 95 Washington St, Hartford, CT 06106-4406 .... (203)566-3170
(City Clk has b, m, d rec from 1847, bur rec from 1847 [1919-1958 missing], lnd rec from 1871, city directories from 1876)

Towns Organized Before 1800: Berlin 1785, Bristol 1785, Canton 1740, East Hartford 1783, East Windsor 1768, Enfield 1683, Farmington 1645, Glastonbury 1693, Granby 1786, Hartford 1635, Hartland 1761, Simsbury 1670, Southington 1779, Suffield 1674, Wethersfield 1634, Windsor 1633

* **Litchfield**	F2	1751	Hartford, Fairfield

Litchfield Jud Dist, 20 West St, Litchfield, CT 06759-3500 .... (203)567-0885
(Twn Clk, Litchfield has b, m & d rec from 1720, bur from 1887, lnd from 1720; Clk Sup Ct has div; Pro Judge has pro rec) (Twn Clk of Winchester has b, m & d from 1771, lnd from 1744; Clk Sup Ct has div rec; Pro Judge has pro rec; Clk Cir Ct has civ ct rec)

Towns Organized Before 1800: Barkhamsted 1799, Bethlehem 1787, Canaan 1739, Colebrook 1799, Cornwall 1740, Goshen 1739, Harwinton 1737, Kent 1739, Litchfield 1719, New Hartford 1738, New Milford 1712, Norfolk 1758, Plymouth 1795, Roxbury 1796, Salisbury 1741, Sharon 1739, Torrington 1740, Washington 1779, Warren 1768, Watertown 1780, Winchester 1771, Woodbury 1673

* **Middlesex**	G3	1785	Hartford, New London, New Haven

Middlesex Jud Dist, 265 DeKoven Dr, Middletown, CT 06457-3460 .... (203)344-2966
(Twn Clk, Middletown has b, m, d & lnd rec; Clk Sup Ct has div & civ ct rec from 1800; Pro Judge has pro rec)

Towns Organized Before 1800: Chatham 1767, Durham 1704, East Haddam 1734, Haddam 1668, Killingsworth 1667, Middletown 1651, Saybrook 1635

* **New Haven**	G3	1666	Original county

New Haven County, 200 Orange St, New Haven, CT 06510-2016 .... (203)787-8346
(Twn Clks have b, m, d, lnd rec; Co Clk has div, civ ct rec; Pro Ct has pro rec)

Towns Organized Before 1800: Branford 1639, Cheshire 1780, East Haven 1785, Guilford 1639, Hamden 1786, Meriden 1796, Millford 1639, New Haven 1638, North Haven 1786, Oxford 1798, Seymour 1672, Southbury 1787, South Derby 1675, Wallingford 1670, Waterbury 1686, Wolcott 1796, Woodbridge 1784

* **New London**	G4	1666	Original county

New London County, New London, CT 06320 ....
(Twn Clks have b, m, d rec from 1659, bur rec from 1893; Deeds and town meeting rec from 1659; Pro Judge has pro rec; Clk Sup Ct has div rec)

Towns Organized Before 1800: Bozrah 1786, Colchester 1698, Franklin 1786, Groton 1705, Lebanon 1700, Lisbon 1786, Lyme 1665, Montville 1786, New London 1646, Norwich 1659, Preston 1687, Stonington 1649, Voluntown 1721

* **Tolland**   F4   1785   Windham

Tolland Jud Dist, 69 Brooklyn St, Rockville, CT   06066-3643 . . . . (203)875-6294

(Twn Clk, Rockville has b, m, d & lnd rec; Pro Judge has pro rec; Clk Sup Ct has civ ct rec)

Towns Organized Before 1800: Bolton 1730, Coventry 1712, Ellington 1786, Hebron 1708, Mansfield 1702, Somers 1734, Stafford 1719, Tolland 1715, Union 1734, Vernon 1716, Willington 1727

* **Windham**   F4   1726   Hartford, New London

Windham Jud Dist, 155 Church St, Putnam, CT   06260-1515 . . . . (203)928-7749

(Twn Clk, Willimantic has b, m & d rec from 1692, bur rec from 1900; Pro Judge has pro rec; Clk Sup Ct has div rec)

Towns Organized Before 1800: Ashford 1714, Brooklyn 1786, Canterbury 1703, Hampton 1786, Killingly 1708, Plainfield 1699, Pomfret 1713, Sterling 1794, Thompson 1785, Windham 1692, Woodstock (New Roxbury) 1686

* At least one county history has been published about this county.
† Inventory of county archives was made by the Historical Records Survey. (See Introduction)

DELAWARE

CAPITAL · DOVER — FIRST STATE — STATE 1787 (1st)
State Map on Page M-28

Henry Hudson discovered Delaware in 1609 while in the service of the Dutch East India Company searching for the Northwest Passage. From information provided by Hudson and other Dutch navigators, the Dutch West India Company was formed in 1621. In 1629, this company adopted a charter to grant land in the new world. They bought land adjoining the Delaware River and in 1631 David Pietersen de Vries established a camp on Lewes Beach which failed. In 1638, the New Sweden Company outfitted an expedition which established the first permanent settlement in Delaware at Wilmington and called it Fort Christina. The Dutch seized Fort Christina in 1655, making it part of New Netherland. The following year, the first Finnish colonists came to Delaware. In 1664, the English conquered New Netherland. Many English settlers came shortly afterward, mainly from Virginia, Maryland, New Jersey, New York, and Europe, and mingled with the Dutch and Swedes. In 1682, Delaware was granted to William Penn, but the people in Delaware objected so strongly that they were granted their own assembly in 1703. Meanwhile, Maryland claimed the southern and western parts of Delaware from 1684 to 1763, when Mason and Dixon established the western boundary of Delaware as well as the boundary between Pennsylvania and Maryland.

Delaware was a colony of great religious diversity. The Swedes brought their religion as did the Dutch. Irish settlers brought the Presbyterian faith after 1698. Roman Catholics, as early as 1730, settled in the northern part of Delaware. French Catholics came from the West Indies in 1790.

Many of the settlers of the northern part of Delaware moved on to Pennsylvania, Maryland, and New Jersey. Delaware was on the front line of the Revolutionary War for nearly a year. This necessitated changing the capital from New Castle to Dover. Delaware became the first state to ratify the Constitution on December 7, 1787. Although Delaware was a slave state during the Civil War, it overwhelmingly supported the Union. Over 16,000 men served the Union, while only several hundred served the Confederacy.

Due to slow transportation in its early days, Delaware's counties were divided into districts, called hundreds. These correspond to townships. Emigrants came primarily from Italy, Poland, Russia, Ireland, Germany, and England.

Statewide registration of births began in 1861, stopped in 1863, and resumed in 1881. The Delaware Bureau of Vital Statistics, Jesse S. Cooper Memorial Building, William Penn Street, Dover, DE 19901 (to verify current fees, call 302-736-4721), has birth and death records from 1861. Since all records are filed by year, it is necessary to have the year before a search can be initiated. State registration of marriages began in 1847 and are also available from the Bureau of Vital Statistics. Counties began keeping marriage records as early as 1832. County recorders have deeds, mortgages, and leases from the late 1600's to the present. Probate records have been kept by the registrar of wills from 1682 to the present. Some probate records are at the Bureau of Archives and Records Management, Hall of Records, Dover, DE 19901. The Bureau also has documents from the Swedish colonial period, the Dutch settlement, the Duke of York regime, and the Penn proprietorship. Most of its records date from statehood, including probate records; state, county, and municipal records; business records; and many others. Some early colonial records are in the archives of the states of New York and Pennsylvania.

Genealogical Archives, Libraries and Societies

The Public Archives Commission, Hall of Records, Dover, DE 19901

University Library, University of Delaware, Newark, DE 19711

Wilmington Institute Free Library, Tenth and Market Sts., Wilmington, DE 19801

Delaware Genealogical Society, 505 Market Street Mall, Wilmington, New Castle County, DE 19801

Delaware Society, Sons of the American Revolution, P. O. Box 2169, Wilmington, DE 19899

Division of Historical and Cultural Affairs, Department of State, Hall of Records, Dover, DE 19901

Historical Society of Delaware, Old Town Hall, Wilmington, DE 19801

Lower Del-Mar-Va Genealogical Society, Wicomico County Library, Salisbury, MD 21801

Printed Census Records and Mortality Schedules

Federal Census 1800, 1810, 1820, 1830, 1840, 1850, 1860, 1870, 1880, 1900, 1910
Tax Lists 1790
Quit Rents 1665-1671
Residents 1675, 1677, 1693
Militia Rolls 1803-1807

Valuable Printed Sources

Atlases, Maps, and Gazetteers

Beer, D. G. *Atlas of the State of Delaware*. Sussex Prints, 1978 reprint.

Gannett, Henry. *A Gazetteer of Maryland and Delaware*. Baltimore: Genealogical Publishing Co., 1976 reprint.

Heck, L. W. *Delaware Place Names*. Washington, DC: Government Printing Office, 1966.

Bibliographies

Clay, Reed H. and Marion B. Clay. *A Bibliography of Delaware through 1960*. Newark, Delaware: University of Delaware Press, 1966.

———. *Bibliography of Delaware, 1960-1974*. Newark, Delaware: University of Delaware Press, 1976.

Genealogical Sources

Boyer, Carl. *Ship Passenger Lists, Pennsylvania and Delaware, 1641-1825*. Newhall, California: Carl Boyer, 1980.

Gehring, Charles T. *New York Historical Manuscripts: Dutch Volumes XX-XXI, Delaware Papers, 1664-1682*. Baltimore: Genealogical Publishing Co., 1977.

Weiss, Frederick Lewis. *The Colonial Clergy of Maryland, Delaware and Georgia*. Baltimore: Genealogical Publishing Co., 1978 reprint.

Histories

Ferris, Benjamin. *A History of the Original Settlements on the Delaware*. Wilmington, Delaware: Wilson & Heald, 1846.

Johnson, Amandus. *The Swedish Settlements on the Delaware*. Baltimore: Genealogical Publishing Co., 1969 reprint.

DELAWARE COUNTY DATA
State Map on Page M-28

Name	Map Index	Date Created	Parent County or Territory From Which Organized
Deale (changed to Sussex Co, 1683)			
* **Kent**	G2	1682	St. Jones, Name changed to Kent in 1682
Kent County, 414 Federal St, Dover, DE 19901-3615 . . . . (302)736-2040			
(Clk of Peace has m rec, Clk Sup Ct has div & civ ct rec; Rcdr Deeds has lnd rec from 1680)			
* **New Castle**	E2	1673	Original county
New Castle County, 800 N French St, Wilmington, DE 19801-3542 . . . . (302)571-4011			
(Clk of Peace has m rec from 1911; Prothonotary has div & civ ct rec; Reg of Wills has pro rec; Rcdr Deeds has lnd rec)			

Name	Map Index	Date Created	Parent County or Territory From Which Organized

St. Jones (changed to Kent Co, 1682)

* **Sussex**   H3   1682   Early 17th Century Horrekill District (see Deale)
    Sussex County, PO Box 609, Georgetown, DE   19947-0609 . . . . (302)856-5601
    [FHL has some cem, civ ct, lnd, nat, pro, tax rec]

* At least one county history has been published about this county.
† Inventory of county archives was made by the Historical Records Survey. (See Introduction)

DISTRICT OF COLUMBIA

TERRITORY OF WASHINGTON, D.C. — ORGANIZED 1790
SEAT OF GOVERNMENT 1800

The capital of the United States covers about seventy square miles on the northeast side of the Potomac River, about 38 miles southwest of Baltimore. Maryland ceded parts of Montgomery, including Georgetown, and Prince George's County to the United States for its capital in the late 1780's. Virginia also ceded part of Fairfax County, including Alexandria. These counties continued to govern the area until about 1801. Virginia kept permanent custody of the records from Alexandria.

Congress convened for the first time in Washington in 1800 and Thomas Jefferson's inaugural in March 1801 was its first inauguration. Growth was very slow, increasing from 8,000 in 1800 to only 75,000 in 1860. In 1801, the counties of Washington and Alexandria were established in the District. The city of Washington was incorporated in 1802. The British captured Washington during the War of 1812 and burned most of the public buildings and records. During the Civil War, Washington was again threatened, but survived unscathed. Slavery was abolished in the District of Columbia in 1862.

The land ceded by Virginia for the District was returned to Virginia in 1846. The city's status was changed to that of a federal territory in 1871. Georgetown became part of the city of Washington D.C. in 1895. Since then, the city of Washington D.C. has had the same boundaries as the District of Columbia.

Registration of birth and death records began in 1874, with general compliance by 1915 for births and 1880 for deaths, although some earlier death records exist. The Department of Human Services, Vital Records Section, Room 3007, 4265 "I" Street, N.W., Washington, DC 20001 (to verify current fees, call 202-727-5316), is the custodian for these records. The Superior Court of the District of Columbia, Marriage License Bureau, 515 Fifth Street, N.W., Washington, DC 20001, keeps the marriage records. Their registration began in 1811. Divorce proceedings prior to September 1956 are available from the Clerk of the U.S. District, Constitution Avenue and John Marshall Place, N.W., Washington, DC 20001. Divorce docket, 1803-1848, is in the National Archives at 4205 Suitland Road, Suitland, Maryland. Its mailing address is General Branch, Civil Archives Division, National Archives and Record Administration, Washington, DC 20409. The National Archives also has records for the U.S. Circuit Court for the District of Columbia and Washington County Court records. Other records include building permits for the District for 1877-1949, Internal Revenue assessment lists for 1862-1866, and other tax books for Georgetown and the city and county of Washington.

Original wills from 1801 to the present can be found at the Register of Wills and Clerk of the Probate Court, U. S. Courthouse, 500 Indiana Avenue, N.W., Washington, DC 20001. Probate records prior to 1801 were kept by the courts in Virginia and Maryland. All real estate records are in charge of the Recorder of Deeds, Sixth and D Streets, N.W., Washington, DC 20004. Prior to 1895, deeds and wills for Georgetown were registered in Montgomery County, Maryland. Some of the records for Georgetown for 1800-1879 are available from the National Archives, microfilm M605.

The National Society, Daughters of the American Revolution, 1776 D Street, N.W., Washington, DC 20004, maintains a library of over 40,000 volumes consisting of manuscripts and genealogical records, tombstone inscriptions, etc. The Genealogical Department of the Library of Congress, 1st-2nd Streets, S.E., Washington, DC 20540, and the National Archives are two of the richest sources of genealogical material for Washington D.C. and the entire United States.

Genealogical Archives, Libraries and Societies

Anderson House Library and Museum, 2118 Massachusetts Ave., N.W., Washington, DC 20008

Congressional Library, Washington, DC 20540

Genealogical Department, Library of Congress Annex, Washington, DC 20540

Library of Congress, Genealogical Room, Thomas Jefferson Annex, Washington, DC 20540

National Archives and Records Service, 8 and Pennsylvania Ave, N.W., Washington, DC 20408

Public Library, Martin Luther King Memorial Library, 901 "G" Street, N.W., Washington, DC 20001

Afro-American Historical and Genealogical Society Box 73086, Washington, DC 20009-3086

Jewish Genealogy Society of Greater Washington, P. O. Box 412, Vienna, VA 22180

National Archives, 8 and Pennsylvania Avenues, N.W., Washington, D.C. 20408

Nation Archives and Records Center, National Records Center Building Washington, D. C. 20409

National Genealogical Society, 4527 Seventeenth Street North, Arlington, VA 22207-2363

National Society Daughters of American Colonists, 2205 Massachusetts Ave., N.W., Washington, DC 20008

National Society of Daughters of the American Revolution, 1776 D. St., N.W., Washington, DC 20006

National Society of the Sons of the American Revolution, Inc., National Headquarters, 1000 South Fourth Street, Louisville, KY 40203

White House Historical Association, 740 Jackson Place, N.W., Washington, DC 20506

Printed Census Records and Mortality Schedules

Federal Census 1790 (with Maryland), 1800, 1810, 1820 (includes Alexandria County, Virginia), 1830 (includes Alexandria County, Virginia), 1840 (includes Alexandria County, Virginia), 1850, 1860, 1870, 1880, 1890, 1900, 1910

Federal Mortality Schedules 1850, 1860, 1870, 1880

Union Veterans and Widows 1890

State/Territorial Census 1867

Valuable Printed Sources

Atlases, Maps, and Gazetteers

Brown, Mary Ross. *An Illustrated Genealogy of the Counties of Maryland and District of Columbia as a Guide to Locating Records*. Baltimore: French Bay Printing, 1967.

Genealogical Research Guides

Babbel, June Andrew. *Lest We Forget: A Guide to Genealogical Research in the Nation's Capital*. Annandale, Virginia: H. Byron Hall, 1986.

Cook, Eleanor Mildred Vaughan. *Guide to the Records of Your District of Columbia Ancestors*. Silver Spring, Maryland: Family Line Publications, 1987.

Guide to Genealogical Research in the National Archives. Washington, DC: National Archives Trust Fund Board, 1983.

Histories

Crew, H. W. *History of Washington, D. C.* Dayton, Ohio: United Brethren Publishing House, 1892.

Proctor, John Clogett. *Washington, Past and Present*. New York: Lewis Historical Publishing Co., 1930.

FLORIDA

CAPITAL - TALLAHASSEE — TERRITORY 1822 — STATE 1845 (27th)
State Map on Page M-8

Ponce de Leon, the Spanish explorer, landed on the Florida coast in 1513, searching for gold and the legendary fountain of youth. Early settlements by both the Spanish and French failed, but subsequent attempts succeeded. The French settled Fort Caroline in 1564 and the Spanish settled St. Augustine in 1565. The Spanish subsequently destroyed the French settlement, making St. Augustine the first permanent white settlement in North America. Pensacola was settled in 1698. Meanwhile, the British, Scotch, and Irish were settling the colonies and slowly encroaching on Florida territory. In 1762, during the Seven Years' War, the British captured Havana, Cuba and by the Treaty of Paris in 1763, Spain agreed to trade Florida for Havana.

By proclamation in 1763, the King of England established East and West Florida, divided by the Chattahoochee and Apalachicola Rivers. The largest settlement during the next twenty years was at New Smyrna in 1767. Up to 1500 colonists from Italy, Greece, and the island of Minorca settled here. In 1783, Great Britain returned Florida to Spain in exchange for some islands in the West Indies.

In 1810 and 1812, the United States annexed portions of West Florida to Louisiana and the Mississippi Territory. Unable to govern the area, Spain ceded the remainder of west Florida and all of east Florida to the United States in 1819. Only about 5,000 white settlers lived in Florida at the time. In 1822, Florida was organized into a territory and in 1824 Tallahassee was laid out as the capital. Early settlers were predominantly Irish. Other early settlers included the Greeks from Southern Greece and the Dodecanese Islands, who worked as sponge divers and were affiliated with the Orthodox Greek Catholic Church. The middle section of Florida was settled in the 1820's by former Virginians and Carolinians.

The Seminole Wars (1835-1842) brought about by poor treatment of the Indians, resulted in removal of the Indians to present-day Oklahoma. Growth really began in the 1840's as the population grew 56 percent. Most of the growth in East Florida during this time was from Georgia, Alabama, and North and South Carolina. Florida became a state on March 3, 1845.

By 1860, the population had grown to 78,000. Half of the people were native-born while 22 percent came from Georgia, 11 percent from South Carolina and 5 percent from North Carolina. Florida seceded from the Union in 1861. Over 1000 men fought for the Union and an estimated 20,000 for the Confederacy, Florida was readmitted in 1868. A post-Civil War boom lasted to the turn of the century due to the building of railroads and resorts. Another boom occurred from 1921 to 1925 resulting in the formation of Florida's last thirteen counties.

Statewide registration of births and deaths began in 1899, with general compliance by 1920. The Office of the Bureau of Vital Statistics, P.O. Box 210, Jacksonville, FL 32231 (to verify current fees, call 904-359-6900), holds incomplete records of deaths from 1877 to 1917 and complete records since then; marriages from June 1927 to date; and divorce records. Some birth and death records are in the city or county health department. Jacksonville has birth and death records from 1893 to 1913, Pensacola from 1897 to 1916, and St. Petersburg prior to 1917. Marriage records prior to June 1927 are in the office of the County Judge of the bride's home county. County judges also have the records of wills. Divorce records prior to 1927 are filed in the Circuit Court Clerk's office where the divorce was granted. Colonial, territorial, and state censuses exist for 1783, 1786, 1790, 1793, 1814, 1825, 1837, 1845, 1855, 1865, 1868, 1875, 1885, 1895, and 1935. These are kept at the Florida State Archives, Florida Division of Archives, History, and Records Management, R. A. Gray Building, Pensacola and Bronough Streets, Tallahassee, FL 32201.

Genealogical Archives, Libraries and Societies

Bonita Springs Public Library, 26876 Pine Ave., Bonita Springs, FL 33923

Burdick International Ancestry Library, 2317 Riverbluff Pkwy. 249, Sarasota, FL 34231-5032

Cocoa Public Library, 430 Delannoy Ave., Cocoa, FL 32922

Collier County Public Library, Central Avenue, Naples, FL 33940

DeLand Public Library, 130 East Howry Ave, DeLand, FL 32724

DeSoto Correctional Institution Library, P. O. Box 1072, Arcadia, FL 33821

Fort Myers-Lee County Public Library, 2050 Lee Street, Fort Myers, FL 33901

Gainesville Public Library, 222 E. University Ave., Gainesville, FL 32601

Haydon Burns Library, 122 North Ocean Street, Jacksonville, FL 32203

Hillsborough County Historical Commission Museum Historical and Genealogical Library, County Courthouse, Tampa, FL 33602

Jackson County Florida Library, 413 No. Green St., Maryanna, FL 32446

Jacksonville Public Library, 122 N. Ocean St., Jacksonville, FL 32202

Melbourne Public Library, 540 E. Fee Ave., Melbourne, FL 32901

Miami-Dade Public Library, 1 Biscayne Blvd., No., Miami, FL 33132

Orlando Public Library, 10 N. Rosalind Ave., Orlando, FL 38201

Palatka Public Library, 216 Reid Street, Palatka, FL 32077

P. K. Yonge Library of Florida History, University of Florida, Gainesville, FL 32601

Polk County Historical and Genealogical Library, 100 E. Main St., Bartow, FL 33830

Selby Public Library, 1001 Boulevard of the Arts, Sarasota, FL 33577

Southern Genealogist's Exchange Society Library, 1580 Blanding Blvd., Jacksonville, FL 32203

State Library of Florida, R.A. Gray Building, Tallahassee, FL 32301

Tampa Public Library, 900 N. Ashley Street, Tampa, FL 33602

Volusia County Public Library, City Island, Daytona Beach, FL 32014

Alachua County Genealogical Society, P. O. Box 12078, Gainesville, FL 32604

Bay County Genealogical Society, P. O. Box 662, Panama City, FL 32401

Bonita Springs Genealogical Club, 27312 Shriver Ave., S.E., Bonita Springs, FL 33923

Brevard Genealogical Society, P. O. Box 1123, Cocoa, FL 32922

Central Florida Genealogical and Historical Society, P. O. Box 177, Orlando, FL 32802

Charlotte County Genealogical Society, P. O. Box 2682, Port Charlotte, FL 33952

Citrus County Genealogical Society, 1511 Druid Rd., Inverness, FL 32652-4507

Clay County Genealogical Society, P. O. Box 1071, Green Cove Springs, FL 32043

East Hillsborough Historical Society, Quintilla Geer Bruton Archives Center, 605 N. Collins St., Plant City, FL 33566

Florida Chapter, Ohio Genealogical Society, 2625 Johnson Point, Leesburg, FL 32748

Florida Genealogical Society, Inc., P. O. Box 18624, Tampa, FL 33679-8624

Florida Society of Genealogical Research, 8461 54th St., Pinellas Park, FL 33565

Florida State Genealogical Society, P. O. Box 10249, Tallahassee, FL 32302

Genealogical Group of Seminole County, Florida, P. O. Box 2148, Casselberry, FL 32707

Genealogical Society of Broward County, Inc., P. O. Box 485, Fort Lauderdale, FL 33302

Genealogical Society of Collier County, P. O. Box 7933, Naples, FL 33941

Genealogical Society of Greater Miami, P. O. Box 162905, Miami, FL 33116-2905

Genealogical Society of Lee County, P. O. Box 1973, Ft. Meyers, FL 33902

Genealogical Society of North Brevard, P. O. Box 897, Titusville, FL 32780

Genealogical Society of South Brevard, P. O. Box 786, Melbourne, FL 32902

Genealogical Society of Okaloosa County, P. O. Box 1175, Fort Walton Beach, FL 32549

Genealogical Society of Okeechobee, P. O. Box 371, Okeechobee, FL 33472

Genealogical Society of Sarasota, Inc., P. O. Box 1917, Sarasota, FL 33578

Genealogical Society of South Brevard County, P. O. Box 786, Melbourne, FL 32902-0786

Genealogy Society of Bay County, Florida, P. O. Box 662, Panama City, FL 32401

Genealogy Society of Hernando County, P. O. Box 1793, Brooksville, FL 34605-1793

Geneva Historical and Genealogical Society, P. O. Box 145, Geneva, FL 32732

Highlands County Genealogical Society, Avon Park Library, 116 E. Main St., Avon Park, FL 33825

Hillsborough County Historical Commission Museum Historical and Genealogical Library, County Courthouse, Tampa, FL 33602

Imperial Polk Genealogical Society, P. O. Box 10, Kathleen, FL 33849-0045

International Genealogy Fellowship of Rotarians, 5721 Antietam Dr., Sarasota, FL 34231

Jewish Genealogical Society of Broward County, 1859 N. Pine Island Road 128, Ft. Lauderdale, FL 33324

Jewish Genealogical Society of Central Florida, P. O. Box 520583, Longwood, FL 32752

Jewish Genealogical Society of Greater Miami, 9370 SW 88th Terrace, Miami, FL 33176

Keystone Genealogical Society, P. O. Box 50, Monticello, FL 32344

Lake County, Kinseekers Genealogical Society, P. O. Box 2711, Leesburg, FL 32749-2711

Lee County Genealogical Society, Cape Coral Public Library, 921 S.W. 39th Terr., Cape Coral, FL 33914

Lehigh Acres Genealogical Society, P. O. Box 965, Lehigh Acres, FL 33970-0965

Lemon Bay Historical and Genealogical Society, P. O. Box 236, Englewood, FL 33533

Martin County Genealogical Society, 1395 NE Waveland, Jensen Beach, FL 33457

Monroe County Genealogical Society, 21 Ventana Lane, Big Coppitt Key, FL 33040

Okaloosa County, Florida Genealogical Society, P. O. Drawer 1175, Fort Walton Beach, FL 32549

Osceola County Department, Genealogical Research, 326 Eastern Ave., St. Cloud, FL 32769

Palm Beach County Genealogical Society, P. O. Box 1746, West Palm Beach, FL 33402

Polk County Historical Association, P. O. Box 2749, Bartow, FL 33830-2749

Putnam County Genealogical Society, P. O. Box 418, Palatka, FL 32078

Ridge Genealogical Society, P. O. Box 477, Babson Park, FL 33827

Sarasota Genealogical Society, Inc., P. O. Box 1917, Sarasota, FL 34230-1917

South Hillsborough Genealogists, Rt. 1, Box 400, Palmetto, FL 33561

Southern Genealogist's Exchange Society, Inc., P. O. Box 2801, Jacksonville, FL 32203

St. Augustine Genealogical Society, St. Johns County Public Library, 1960 N. Ponce de Leon Blvd., St. Augustine, FL 32084

Suncoast Genealogy Society, P. O. Box 977, Crystal Beach, FL 34256-0977

Tallahassee Genealogical Society, P. O. Box 4371, Tallahassee, FL 32315

Treasure Coast Genealogical Society, P. O. Box 3401, Fort Pierce, FL 33448

Volusia Genealogical and Historical Society, Inc., P. O. Box 2039, Daytona Beach, FL 32015

West Florida Genealogical Society, P. O. Box 947, Pensacola, FL 32594

West Pasco Genealogical Society, 2225 23rd Court, New Port Richey, FL 33552

Printed Census Records and Mortality Schedules

Federal Census 1830, 1840, 1850, 1860, 1870, 1880, 1900, 1910
State/Territorial Census 1885

Valuable Printed Sources

Atlases, Maps, and Gazetteers

Ladd, Edward Johnson. *Atlas and Outline History of Southeastern United States*. Fort Payne, Alabama, 1973.

Morris, Allen Covington. *Florida Place Names*. Coral Gables, Florida: University of Miami Press, 1974.

Genealogical Research Guides

Parks, Karl E. *A Check List of Genealogical Materials in the Mease Memorial Genealogical Section of the Dunedin Public Library*. Tarpon Springs, Florida: Karl E. Parks, 1981.

Robie, Diane C. *Searching in Florida: A Reference Guide to Public and Private Records*. Costa Mesa, California: Independent Research Consultants, 1982.

Histories

Cutler, H. G. *History of Florida, Past and Present*. Chicago: Lewis Publishing Co., 1923.

Dovell, J. E. *Florida: Historic, Dramatic, Contemporary*. New York: Lewis Historical Publishing Co., 1952.

FLORIDA COUNTY DATA
State Map on Page M-8

Name	Map Index	Date Created	Parent County or Territory From Which Organized
* **Alachua**	D1	1824	Duval, St. John

Alachua County, 21 E University Ave, Gainesville, FL 32601-5348 .... (904)374-5210
(Co Clk has m rec from 1837 [m rec missing are 1856-1857, 1860-1863, 1867-1868] (Pro rec from 1840; Ind rec from 1848, civ ct rec, mortgages from 1882, plats from 1884, co minute bk from 1873; Bur Vit Statistics, Jacksonville has b rec)

| * **Baker** | C1 | 1861 | New River |

Baker County, 55 N 3rd St, Macclenny, FL 32063-2100 .... (904)259-3613
(Co Judge has m & pro rec; Clk Cir Ct has div & civ ct rec from 1880)

| **Bay** | G1 | 1913 | Calhoun, Washington |

Bay County, 300 E 4th St, Panama City, FL 32401-3073 .... (904)763-9061
(Health Dept has b, d rec; Clk Cir Ct has m, pro, div, civ ct, Ind rec from 1913)

| **Benton** | | 1843 | Alachua |

(Now Hernando)

| **Bradford** | C1 | 1861 | "New River" up to 1861 |

Bradford County, PO Box B, Starke, FL 32091-1286 .... (904)964-6280
(Co Clk has m rec from 1875, pro, civ ct rec from 1892, Ind rec from 1876; Bur Vit Statistics, Jacksonville, has b, d rec)

| * **Brevard** | B3 | 1855 | Mosquito, "St. Lucie" up to 1855 |

Brevard County, 700 S Park Ave, Titusville, FL 32780-4001 .... (407)269-8011
(Clk Cir Ct has m rec from 1868, Ind rec from 1871, div & civ ct rec from 1879, pro rec from 1917, marks and brands from 1882, mil dischg from 1919; Co Hlth Dept has d rec from 1985, & b rec; some rec prior to 1885 destroyed by fire)

| **Broward** | A6 | 1915 | Dade, Palm Beach |

Broward County, PO Box 14668, Fort Lauderdale, FL 33302 .... (305)357-7283
(Clk Cir Ct has m, pro rec from 1915, div, civ ct, Ind rec from 1915, crim ct rec from 1915)

| **Calhoun** | F1 | 1838 | Franklin, Washington, Jackson |

Calhoun County, 425 E Central Ave, Blountstown, FL 32424-2242 .... (904)674-4545
(Co Judge has m & pro rec; Co Clk has div, civ ct & Ind rec)

| † **Charlotte** | C5 | 1921 | DeSoto |

Charlotte County, 116 W Olympia Ave, Punta Gorda, FL 33950-4431 .... (813)637-2279
(Clk Cir Ct has m, div, pro, civ ct, Ind rec from 1921)

| **Citrus** | D2 | 1887 | Hernando |

Citrus County, 110 N Apopka Ave, Inverness, FL 32650-4245 .... (904)726-2881
(Clk Cir Ct has m, div, pro, civ ct rec from 1887, Ind rec from 1878, Health Dept. Inverness has b, d rec)

| *† **Clay** | C1 | 1858 | Duval |

Clay County, PO Box 698, Green Cove Springs, FL 32043-0698 .... (904)284-6300
(Clk Cir Ct has m, pro, civ ct, Ind rec from 1872, div rec from 1859; Co Health Dept has b & d rec from 1973; State Vital Statistics Bureau has b & d rec)

| *† **Collier** | B6 | 1923 | Lee, Monroe |

Collier County, 3301 Tamiami Trail E, Naples, FL 33962-4902 .... (813)774-8999
(Co Judge has m & pro rec; Clk Cir Ct has div, civ ct & Ind rec from 1923)

| * **Columbia** | D1 | 1832 | Alachua |

Columbia County, 35 N Hernando St, Lake City, FL 32055-4008 .... (904)755-4100
(Clk Cir Ct has b rec from 1943, m, Ind rec from 1875, div, civ ct rec 1892, pro rec from 1895, delayed birth certificates issued by the County Judge's Office; Co Pub Hlth Unit has b, d & bur rec)

Name	Map Index	Date Created	Parent County or Territory From Which Organized
* Dade	A6	1836	Monroe, St. Lucie (1855)

Dade County, 111 NW 1st Ave Suite 220, Miami, FL 33128-1895 .... (305)375-5124
(Co Judge has m & pro rec; Clk Cir Ct has div & lnd rec from 1890)

De Soto   C4   1887   Manatee
De Soto County, 201 E Oak St, Arcadia, FL 33821-4425 .... (813)494-3773
(Co Judge has pro rec from 1887; Clk Cir Ct has div, civ ct & lnd rec from 1887)

Dixie   D1   1921   Lafayette
Dixie County, PO Box 1206, Cross City, FL 32628-1206 .... (904)498-7021
(Clk Cir Ct has m rec from 1973, & div, pro, civ ct & lnd rec)

*† Duval   C1   1822   St. John
Duval County, 330 E Bay St, Jacksonville, FL 32202-2997 .... (904)630-2028
(Clk Cir Ct has div, cir ct rec, deeds & mtg from 1921, service rec bk from 1920; Co Judge has m & pro rec)

* Escambia   H7   1822   One of two original counties
Escambia County, 223 S Palafox Pl, Pensacola, FL 32501-5845 .... (904)436-5783
(Clk Co Ct has m, pro, civ ct, crim rec from 1821; Clk Cir Ct has civ and felony rec from 1822; Co Health Dept has b, d rec; Comptroller has lnd rec from 1821)

† Flagler   C2   1917   St. John, Volusia
Flagler County, 200 E Moody Blvd, Bunnell, FL 32110 .... (904)437-2218
(Clk Cir Ct has m, div, pro, civ ct & lnd rec from 1917)

Franklin   F1   1832   Jackson
Franklin County, Market St, Apalachicola, FL 32320 .... (904)653-8861
(Co Judge has m & pro rec; Cir Ct has div, civ ct & lnd rec)

Gadsden   F1   1823   Jackson
Gadsden County, 10 E Jefferson St, Quincy, FL 32351-2406 .... (904)875-4700
(Co Judge has m & pro rec; Clk Cir Ct has div, civ ct & lnd rec)

* Gilchrist   D1   1925   Alachua
Gilchrist County, 112 S Main St, Trenton, FL 32693 .... (904)463-2345
(Clk Cir Ct has m rec, div, pro, civ ct rec from 1926)

* Glades   B5   1921   DeSoto
Glades County, PO Box 10, Moore Haven, FL 33471-0010 .... (813)946-0949
(Co Judge has m & pro rec; Clk Cir Ct has div, civ ct & lnd rec from 1921)

Gulf   F1   1925   Calhoun
Gulf County, 1000 5th St, Port Saint Joe, FL 32456-1648 .... (904)229-6113
(Clk Cir Ct has m, pr, div, civ ct, lnd, service discharges from 1925)

Hamilton   D1   1827   Duval
Hamilton County, 207 NE 1st St, Jasper, FL 32052 .... (904)792-1288
(Co Judge has m & pro rec; Clk Cir Ct has div, civ ct rec from 1881, lnd rec from 1837)

*† Hardee   C4   1921   DeSoto
Hardee County, 412 W Orange St, Wauchula, FL 33873-2831 .... (813)773-6952
(Clk Cir Ct has m, d, div, pro, civ ct & lnd rec from 1921)

*† Hendry   B5   1923   Lee
Hendry County, Hwys 80 & 29, La Belle, FL 33935-1760 .... (813)675-5217
(Co Judge has m & pro rec; Clk Cir Ct has div, civ ct & lnd rec from 1923)

* Hernando   C3   1850   Alachua (formerly Benton)
Hernando County, 20 N Main St, Brooksville, FL 34601 .... (904)754-4000
(Clk Co Ct has m rec; Clk Cir Ct has div, pro, civ ct, lnd rec from 1877)

Highlands   B4   1921   DeSoto
Highlands County, 430 S Commerce Ave, Sebring, FL 33870-3705 .... (813)385-2581
(Clk Cir Ct has m, div, pro, civ ct, lnd rec from 1921)

* Hillsborough   C3   1834   Alachua, Monroe
Hillsborough County, 419 N Pierce St, Tampa, FL 33602-4022 .... (813)272-5000
(Co Judge has m & pro rec; Clk Cir Ct has div & lnd rec)

Holmes   G1   1848   Walton, Washington, Calhoun
Holmes County, 201 N Oklahoma St, Bonifay, FL 32425-2243 .... (904)547-2835
(Clk Cir Ct has m, pro, div, civ ct and lnd rec)

Indian River   B4   1925   St. Lucie
Indian River County, 1840 25th St, Vero Beach, FL 32960-3416 .... (407)567-8000
(Clk Cir Ct has m, div, pro, civ ct, lnd rec from 1925; County Health Dept has b, d rec)

* Jackson   F1   1822   Escambia
Jackson County, PO Box 510, Marianna, FL 32446-0510 .... (904)482-9552
(Co Judge has m & pro rec; Clk Cir Ct has div, civ ct & lnd rec from 1850)

Jefferson   E1   1827   Leon
Jefferson County, US Hwys 90 & 19 County Courthouse, Monticello, FL 32344-1498 .... (904)997-3596
(Clk Cir Ct has m rec from 1840, div rec from 1900, pro rec from 1850, civ ct rec from 1850, lnd rec from 1827; State Dept of Health, Jacksonville has b, d rec)

Name	Map Index	Date Created	Parent County or Territory From Which Organized

* **Lafayette** D1 1887 Madison
Lafayette County, Main St, Mayo, FL 32066 .... (904)294-1600
(Co Judge has m & pro rec; Clk Cir Ct has div from 1902, civ ct rec from 1907 & Ind rec from 1893)

* **Lake** C2 1856 Orange, Sumter
Lake County, 315 W Main St, Tavares, FL 32778-3878 .... (904)343-9850
(Clk Cir Ct has m, div, civ ct, & Ind rec from 1887, pro rec from 1893, & adoption rec; Co Hlth Dept has d rec)

* **Lee** C5 1887 Monroe
Lee County, 2115 2nd St, Fort Myers, FL 33901-3053 .... (813)335-2259
(Clk Cir Ct has m, div, pro, civ ct, Ind rec; Bur Vit Statistics, Jacksonville has b, d rec)

*† **Leon** E1 1824 Gadsden
Leon County, 301 S Monroe St, Tallahassee, FL 32301-1856 .... (904)488-4710
(Clk Cir Ct has m, div, pro, civ ct, Ind rec from 1825; Leon Co Health Dept has b, d, bur rec)

* **Levy** D2 1845 Alachua, Marion
Levy County, PO Box 610, Bronson, FL 32621-0610 .... (904)486-4311
(Clk Cir Ct has m, div, pro, civ ct, Ind rec from 1850)

Liberty F1 1855 Franklin, Gadsden
Liberty County, Hwy 20, Bristol, FL 32321 .... (904)643-5404
(Co Judge has m & pro rec; Clk Cir Ct has div, civ ct & Ind rec)

Madison E1 1827 Jefferson
Madison County, PO Box 237, Madison, FL 32340-0237 .... (904)973-4176
(Clk Cir Ct has m, pro, civ ct rec from 1838, Ind rec from 1831, div rec)

* **Manatee** C4 1855 Hillsboro
Manatee County, PO Box 1000, Bradenton, FL 34206-1000 .... (813)749-1800
(Clk Cir Ct has m, div, pro, civ ct, Ind rec from 1857; State Div of Health, Jacksonville, has b, d, bur rec)

* **Marion** C2 1844 Alachua, Hillsborough, Mosquito
Marion County, 601 SE 25th Ave, Ocala, FL 32671-2690 .... (904)622-0305
[FHL has some m, cem, Ind, pro rec]

Martin A4 1925 Palm Beach, St. Lucie
Martin County, 2401 SE Monterey Rd, Stuart, FL 34996-3397 .... (407)288-5400
(Clk Cir Ct has m, div, pro, civ ct, Ind rec from 1925; Martin Co Health Dept has b, d, bur rec)

* **Monroe** B6 1823 St. Johns
Monroe County, 500 Whitehead St, Key West, FL 33040-6581 .... (305)294-4641
(Clk Cir Ct has m, div, pro, civ ct, Ind rec from 1853; State Bur Vit Statistics has b, d rec)

Mosquito 1824 (changed to Orange, 1845)

Nassau C1 1824 Duval
Nassau County, 416 Centre St, Fernandina Beach, FL 32034-4243 .... (904)261-6127
(Clk Cir Ct has m, div, pro, civ ct & Ind rec from 1800s)

New River 1858 (changed to Bradford, 1861)

† **Okaloosa** H1 1915 Santa Rosa, Walton
Okaloosa County, Hwy 90, Crestview, FL 32536 .... (904)682-2711
(Co Judge has m & pro rec; Clk Cir Ct has div, civ ct & Ind rec from 1915)

* **Okeechobee** B4 1917 Osceola, Palm Beach, St Lucie
Okeechobee County, 304 NW 2nd St, Okeechobee, FL 34972-4146 .... (813)763-6441
(Clk Cir Ct has m, div, pro, civ ct rec from 1917, Ind rec from 1880s early Ind rec of those portions of Osceola and St. Lucie counties which were taken to form Okeechobee County. County Dept of Health has b, d rec)

* **Orange** B3 1824 (changed from Mosquito, 1845), Sumter (1871)
Orange County, 201 S Rosalind Ave, Orlando, FL 32801-3547 .... (407)236-7300
(Clk Cir Ct has m rec from 1890, civ, pro, ct rec from 1869; Fla Dept of Vit Statistics has b, m rec)

* **Osceola** B3 1887 Brevard, Orange
Osceola County, 12 S Vernon Ave, Kissimmee, FL 34741-5188 .... (407)847-1300
(Clk Cir Ct has m, div, pro, civ ct & Ind rec from 1887)

* **Palm Beach** A5 1909 Dade
Palm Beach County, 301 N Olive Ave, West Palm Beach, FL 33401-4705 .... (407)355-2754
(Co Judge has m & pro rec; Clk Cir Ct has div, civ ct & Ind rec)

* **Pasco** D3 1887 Hernando
Pasco County, 7530 Little Rd, New Port Richey, FL 34654-5598 .... (813)847-8190
(Clk Cir Ct has div, civ ct, Ind rec from 1887, m, pro rec)

*† **Pinellas** D4 1912 Hillsboro
Pinellas County, 315 Court St, Clearwater, FL 34616-5165 .... (813)462-3000
(Clk Cir Ct has m, div, pro, civ ct, Ind rec from 1912; Bur Vit Statistics, Jacksonville, had b, d rec)

* **Polk** C3 1861 Brevard, Hillsbourough (Boundaries changed 1871)
Polk County, 255 N Broadway Ave, Bartow, FL 33830-3912 .... (813)534-4000
(Clk Cir Ct has m, div, pro, civ ct, Ind rec from 1861)

* **Putnam** C1 1849 Alachua, Marion, Orange, St. Johns
Putnam County, 410 St Johns Ave, Palatka, FL 32177-4725 .... (904)329-0200
(Clk Cir Ct has m, div, pro, civ ct & Ind rec from 1849, naturalization rec 1849-1914, some biographical data and misc rec from 1800, cem rec survey from 19th & 20th centuries. Various cem associations have bur rec. An 1885 state census was taken)

Name	Map Index	Date Created	Parent County or Territory From Which Organized
* **Saint Johns**	C1	1822	One of two original cos

Saint Johns County, 99 Cordova St, Saint Augustine, FL 32084-4415 .... (904)824-8131
(Co Judge has m & pro rec; Clk Cir Ct has div from 1900, civ ct & Ind rec from 1821)

| **Saint Lucas** | | 1844 | (changed to Brevard, 1955) |
| * **Saint Lucie** | A4 | 1905 | Brevard |

Saint Lucie County, 221 S Indian River Dr, Fort Pierce, FL 34950-4301 .... (407)489-6900
(Clk Cir Ct has m, pro, div, civ ct, Ind rec from 1905; Co Health Dept had d rec [if recorded] and bur rec; Bur Vit Statistics, Jacksonville, has b rec)

| **Santa Rosa** | H1 | 1842 | Escambia |

Santa Rosa County, 801 Caroline St SE, Milton, FL 32570-4978 .... (904)623-0135
(Clk Cir Ct has m, div, pro, civ ct, & Ind rec from 1869; Cthouse burned in 1869)

| *† **Sarasota** | C4 | 1921 | Manatee |

Sarasota County, 2000 Main St, Sarasota, FL 34237-6036 .... (813)365-1000
(Clk Cir Ct has m, pro, civ ct & Ind rec from 1921, div rec from 1945; Co Hlth Dept has b & d rec; state census taken 1885, 1935, 1945)

| **Seminole** | B2 | 1913 | Orange |

Seminole County, 301 N Park Ave, Sanford, FL 32771-1292 .... (407)323-4482
(Co Judge has m & pro rec; Clk Cir Ct has div, civ ct, Ind rec & mtg from 1915)

| **Sumter** | C2 | 1853 | Marion |

Sumter County, 209 N Florida St, Bushnell, FL 33513-9402 .... (904)793-0200
(Clk Cir Ct has m, Ind rec from 1853, pro rec from 1856, div rec from 1900, civ ct rec from 1913; Clk Cir Ct has delayed b rec 1943-1972)

| **Suwannee** | D1 | 1858 | Columbia |

Suwannee County, 200 Ohio Ave S, Live Oak, FL 32060-3239 .... (904)362-2827
(Clk Cir Ct has m, div, pro, civ ct & Ind rec from 1859, and some bur rec for veterans; Co Hlth Dept has d rec)

| **Taylor** | E1 | 1856 | Madison |

Taylor County, PO Box 620, Perry, FL 32347-0620 .... (904)584-3531
(Co Judge has m & pro rec; Clk Cir Ct has div & Ind rec)

| **Union** | D1 | 1921 | Bradford |

Union County, 55 W Main St Rm 103, Lake Butler, FL 32054-1600 .... (904)496-3711
(Clk Cir Ct has div & civ ct rec)

| * **Volusia** | B2 | 1854 | St. Lucas |

Volusia County, 123 W Indiana Ave, De Land, FL 32720-4210 .... (904)736-5902
(Clk Cir Ct has m, div, civ ct, pro, Ind rec)

| † **Wakulla** | E1 | 1843 | Leon |

Wakulla County, PO Box 337, Crawfordville, FL 32327-0337 .... (904)926-3341
(Clk Cir Ct has m, div, pro, civ ct, & Ind rec from 1896; Co Hlth Dept has some b rec; Cthouse burned in 1896)

| * **Walton** | G1 | 1824 | Jackson |

Walton County, PO Box 1260, De Funiak Springs, FL 32433 .... (904)892-3137
(Clk Cir Ct has m rec from 1885, pro rec from 1882, div, civ ct, Ind rec; Co Hlth Dept has b, d rec; Clk Cir Ct has newspaper rec from 1905)

| **Washington** | F1 | 1825 | Jackson, Walton |

Washington County, 201 W Cypress Ave Suite B, Chipley, FL 32428 .... (904)638-6200
(Co Judge has m & pro rec; Clk Cir Ct has div, civ ct & Ind rec from 1890)

* At least one county history has been published about this county.

† Inventory of county archives was made by the Historical Records Survey. (See Introduction)

GEORGIA

CAPITAL - ATLANTA — STATE 1788 (4th)
State Map on Page M-9

From its discovery in 1540 by Hernando de Soto until 1732, the Spanish and English had sporadic disputes over the future state of Georgia. In 1732, King George II granted the land between the Savannah and Altamaha Rivers to prominent Englishmen. One of these Englishmen was James Oglethorpe, who came to Georgia to help achieve the goals of the new colony - provide a buffer between the Carolinas and Florida and establish a refuge for those who would otherwise be sent to debtors' prison. In 1733, Oglethorpe and 35 families settled Savannah. The next year Augusta was established and a group of Protestant refugees from Salzburg settled Ebenezer, in present-day Effingham County. Other settlers arrived from Switzerland, Germany, Italy, the Scottish Highlands, and Moravia in the next five years. In 1740, Georgia was divided into two counties - Savannah County, north of the Altamaha and

Frederica County, south of the Altamaha. Many of the Moravians, who had come from North Carolina, moved from Georgia to Bethlehem and Nazareth, Pennsylvania when their efforts to convert the Indians failed.

In 1752, Georgia's charter was surrendered and Georgia became a crown colony, claiming all the land between North Carolina and Florida and the Atlantic Ocean to the Mississippi. From 1758 to 1777, Georgia was divided into twelve parishes - St. James, St. Matthew, St. John, St. Paul, St George, St. Andrew, St. Philip, St. David, St. Patrick, St. Thomas, Ste. Mary, and Christ Church. These parishes were formed into seven large counties in 1777. Georgia gained statehood in 1788. In a dispute over states' rights in the 1790's, Georgia refused to carry out a Supreme Court decision against it, which led to the passage of the 11th amendment in 1798. That same year, the Territory of Mississippi, which later would become the states of Alabama and Mississippi, was created from the western half of Georgia. Georgia's present boundaries were set in 1802.

Many families were drawn to Georgia in the early 1800's by land lotteries. Families who had lived in the territory for at least one year were allowed to draw for land areas as large as 400 acres. These lotteries were held in 1803, 1806, 1819, 1827, and 1832. Lists of lottery participants are held in the office of the Secretary of State.

Georgia seceded from the Union in 1861. Well over 100,000 men fought for the Confederacy. Over 12,000 Union soldiers died as prisoners in Anderson, Georgia and are buried in a national cemetery in Sumter County. A published cemetery list by the Quartermaster General's Office entitled "Roll of Honor, Volume 3" is available.

Vital Records Service, State Department of Human Resources, 47 Trinity Avenue, S.W., Room 217-H, Atlanta, GA 30334 (to verify current fees, call 404-656-4900) has birth and death records from 1919 to the present. Certified copies of birth records are issued at county and state offices to the person, the parent, or a legal representative. The index is closed to the public. Many earlier birth records are available from county offices at Atlanta, Savannah, and Macon. Death certificates are also issued at county and state offices, but their indexes are closed to the public. Marriage records are available from County Clerks or the County Clerk of the Ordinary Court. Divorce and civil court records are kept by the Superior Court Clerk. Naturalization records are in the minutes of the Superior, District, or City Court where the hearing was held. They are also on microfilm at the Georgia Department of Archives and History, 330 Capitol Avenue, S. E., Atlanta, GA 30334. Land deeds are recorded in the office of the Court of Ordinary as well as on microfilm and printed abstract form. The Clerk of the Court of Ordinary has wills from 1777 to 1798 and after 1852, as well as records of homesteads, land warrants, licenses, indentures, pauper register, voting registers, and marriage records. State censuses taken for various years from 1786 to 1890 have survived for some counties and are located at the Georgia Department of Archives and History. Indexes to many state censuses have been published. Some county censuses are also available for the years 1827 to 1890. A published roster of Georgia Confederate infantry soldiers compiled by Lillian Henderson and entitled *Roster of the Confederate Soldiers of Georgia, 1861-65*, is available in six volumes through the Family History Library in Salt Lake City and its branches. The originals of Georgia pension records for Confederate veterans and index are at the Georgia Department of Archives and History, 330 Capitol Ave., S.E., Atlanta, GA 30334.

Genealogical Archives, Libraries and Societies

Athens Regional Library, 120 W. Dougherty St., Athens, GA 30601

Atlanta Public Library, I. Margaret Mitchell Square, corner of Carnegie Way and Forsythe, Atlanta, GA 30303

Augusta-Richmond County Public Library, 902 Greene Street, Augusta, GA 30901

Bradley Memorial Library, Bradley Dr., Columbus, GA 31906

Brunswick Regional Library, 208 Gloucester St., Brunswick, GA 31521

Chestatee Regional Library, 127 North Main, Gainesville, GA 30501

Cobb County Public Library System genealogical collection, housed in the Georgia Room, Marietta Library, 30 Atlanta Street, Marietta, GA 30060

Colquitt-Thomas Regional Library, P. O. Box 1110, Moultrie, GA 31768

Decatur-DeKalb Library, 215 Sycamore St., Decatur, GA 30030

Ellen Payne Odom Genealogy Library, c / o Moultrie-Colquitt County Library, 204 5th St., S.E., P. O. Box 1110, Moultrie, GA 31768

Genealogical Center Library, Box 71343, Marietta, GA 30007-1343

Georgia Department of Archives and History, 330 Capitol Ave., Atlanta, GA 30334

Georgia Historical Society Library, 501 Whittaker St., Savannah, GA 31401

Georgia State Library, 301 State Judicial Bldg., Capitol Hill Station, Atlanta, GA 30334

Georgia State University Archives, 104 Decatur St., S.E., Atlanta, GA 30303

Lake Blackshear Regional Library, 307 E. Lamar St., Americus, GA 31709

Lake Lanier Regional Library, Pike St., Lawrenceville, GA 30245

Murrell Memorial Library, Box 606, 207 5th Ave., N.E., Eastman, GA 31203

Oconee County Library, Watkinsville, GA 30677

Okefenokee Regional Library, Box 1669, 401 Lee Ave., Waycross, GA 31501

Piedmont Regional Library, Winder, GA 30680

Pine Mountain Regional Library, Box 508, 218 Perry St., Manchester, GA 31816

Sara Hightower Regional Library, 606 West First Street, Rome, GA 30161

Satilla Regional Library, 617 E. Ward St., Douglas, GA 31533

Savannah Public and Chatham, Effingham Liberty Regional Library, 2002 Bull Street, Savannah, GA 31401

Southwest Georgia Regional Library, Shotwell at Monroe, Bainbridge, GA 31717

Statesboro Regional Library, 124 S. Main St., Statesboro, GA 30458

Washington Memorial Library, 1180 Washington Ave., Macon, GA 31201

African-American Family History Association, P. O. Box 115268, Atlanta, GA 30310

Ancestors Unlimited, Inc., P. O. Box 1507, Jonesboro, GA 30336

Atlanta Historical Society, 3101 Andrews Dr., Atlanta, GA 30305

Augusta Genealogical Society, P. O. Box 3743, Augusta, GA 30914-3743

Bulloch County Historical Society, P. O. Box 42, Statesboro, GA 30458

Carroll County Genealogical Society, P. O. Box 576, Carrollton, GA 30117

Central Georgia Genealogical Society, P. O. Box 2024, Warner Robins, GA 31093

Chattahoochee Valley Historical Society, 1213 Fifth Avenue, West Point, GA 31833

Cherokee County, Georgia Historical Society, Haney Road, Woodstock, GA 30188

Clark-Oconee Genealogical Society of Athens, Georgia, P. O. Box 6403, Athens, GA 30604

Cobb County Genealogical Society, P. O. Box 1413, Marietta, GA 30061

Coweta Chatter Genealogical and Historical Society, Hwy. 54, Rt. 1, Sharpsburg, GA 30277

Coweta County Genealogical Society, Inc., P. O. Box 1014, Newnan, GA 30264

Delta Genealogical Society, 504 McFarland Ave., Rossville, GA 30741

Genealogical Society of Original Muscogee County, W.C. Bradley Memorial Library, 120 Bradley Drive, Columbus, GA 31906

Genealogy Unlimited, 2511 Churchill Drive, Valdosta, GA 31602

Georgia Genealogical Society, P. O. Box 38066, Atlanta, GA 30334

Georgia Society, Sons of the American Revolution, 2869 Reese Road, Columbus, GA 31907

Gwinnett Historical Society, Inc., P. O. Box 261, Lawrenceville, GA 30246

Henry County, Georgia Genealogical Society, P. O. Box 1296, 71 Macon St., McDonough, GA 30253

Huxford Genealogical Society, P. O. Box 595, Homerville, GA 31634

Lee County Historical Society, P. O. Box 393, Leesburg, GA 31763

Muscogee Genealogical Society, P. O. Box 761, Columbus, GA 31902

National Archives-Southeast Region 1557 Saint Joseph Ave., East Point, GA 30344

Northeast Cobb County, Georgia Genealogical Society, P. O. Box 1413, Marietta, GA 30060

Northeast Georgia Historical and Genealogical Society, P. O. Box 907039, Gainesville, GA 30503-0901

Northwest Georgia Historical and Genealogical Society, P. O. Box 5063, Rome, GA 30161

Savannah Area Genealogical Society, P. O. Box 15385, Savannah, GA 31416

Savannah River Valley Genealogical Society, Hart County Library, Benson St., Hartwell, GA 30643

South Georgia Genealogical Society, P. O. Box 246, Ochlocknee, GA 31773

Southwest Georgia Genealogical Society, P. O. Box 4672, Albany, GA 31706

Upson Historical Society, P. O. Box 363, Thomaston, GA 30286

West Georgia Genealogical Society, Troup County Archives, P. O. Box 1051, LaGrange, GA 30241

Whitfield-Murray Historical Society, Crown Garden and Archives, 715 Chattanooga Ave., Dalton, GA 30720

Printed Census Records and Mortality Schedules

Federal Census 1820 (except Franklin, Rabun, and Twiggs counties), 1830, 1840, 1850, 1860, 1870, 1880, 1890 (part of Muscogee County only), 1900, 1910

Federal Mortality Schedules 1850, 1860, 1870, 1880

Early Settlers 1733-1742

Land Allotments 1741-1754

Land Lottery 1805, 1820, 1821, 1827, 1832

Valuable Printed Sources

Atlases, Maps, and Gazetteers

Bonner, James C. *Atlas for Georgia History*. Milledgeville, Georgia: George College, 1969.

Hemperley, Marlon R. *Towns and Communities of Georgia Between 1847-1962: 8,500 Places and the County in Which Located*. Easley, South Carolina: Southern Historical Press, 1980.

Krakow, Kenneth K. *Georgia Place Names*. Macon, Georgia: Winship Press, 1975.

Sherwood, Adiel. *A Gazetteer of the State of Georgia*. Athens, Georgia: University of Georgia Press, 1939.

Genealogical Research Guides

Davis, Robert Scott. *A Researcher's Library of Georgia History, Genealogy, and Record Sources*. Easley, South Carolina: Southern Historical Press, 1987.

Robertson, David H. *Georgia Genealogical Research*. Stone Mountain, Georgia: David H. Robertson, 1989.

Genealogical Sources

An Index to Georgia Colonial Conveyances and Confiscated Lands Records, 1750-1804. Atlanta: R. J. Taylor Jr. Foundation, 1981.

Brooks, Ted O. *Georgia Cemetery Directory and Bibliography of Georgia Reference Sources*. Marietta, Georgia: Ted O. Brooks, 1985.

Lucas, Silas Emmett Jr. *Index to the Headright and Bounty Grants in Georgia from 1756-1909*. Easley, South Carolina: Southern Historical Press, 1981.

Maddox, Joseph T. *Early Georgia Marriages*. Irwinton, Georgia: Joseph T. Maddox, 1978.

Warren, Mary Bondurant. *Marriages and Deaths, 1763-1830, Abstracted from Extant Georgia Newspapers*. Danielsville, Georgia: Heritage Papers.

Histories

Candler, Allen D. and Clement A. Evans. *Cyclopedia of Georgia*. Atlanta: State Historical Association, 1906.

McCall, Hugh. *The History of Georgia*. Atlanta: Cherokee Publishing Co., 1969 reprint.

GEORGIA COUNTY DATA
State Map on Page M-9

Name	Map Index	Date Created	Parent County or Territory From Which Organized
Appling	G6	1818	Creek Indian Lands
Appling County, 100 N Oak St, Baxley, GA 31513-2097 .... (912)367-8100			
(Rec begin 1879; some 1859; Pro Ct has b, m, d & bur rec; Clk Sup Ct has div, pro & civ ct rec)			
Atkinson	G5	1917	Coffee, Clinch
Atkinson County, PO Box 518, Pearson, GA 31642-0518 .... (912)422-3391			
(Clk Sup Ct has div, pro & civ ct rec from 1919; Pro Ct has b & d rec from 1929, m & Ind rec from 1919)			
* **Bacon**	G6	1914	Appling, Pearce, Ware
Bacon County, 502 W 12th St, Alma, GA 31510-1957 .... (912)632-5214			
(Clk Sup Ct has div, civ ct rec & deeds from 1915; Pro Ct has b, m, d & pro rec from 1915)			
Baker	G3	1825	Early
Baker County, Courthouse Way, Newton, GA 31770 .... (912)734-3004			
[FHL has some m, civ ct, Ind, pro, tax rec]			
* **Baldwin**	E5	1803	Creek Indian Lands
Baldwin County, 201 W Hancock St, Milledgeville, GA 31061-3346 .... (912)453-4007			
(Pro Ct has b, m, d & bur rec; Co Clk has div, civ ct & Ind rec from 1861)			
* **Banks**	C4	1858	Franklin, Habersham
Banks County, PO Box 130, Homer, GA 30547-0130 .... (404)677-2320			
(Pro Ct has b & m rec; Clk ct & Ind rec from 1812)			
* **Barrow**	C4	1914	Jackson, Walton, Guinett
Barrow County, 310 S Broad St, Winder, GA 30680-1973 .... (404)867-7581			
(Pro Ct has b, m, d, bur & pro rec; Clk Sup Ct has div, civ ct & Ind rec from 1915)			
* **Bartow**	C2	1861	Changed from Cass 1861
Bartow County, PO Box 543, Cartersville, GA 30120-0543 .... (404)382-4766			
(Pro Ct has b, m & Pro rec; Clk Sup Ct has div rec from 1862, civ ct rec from 1869, Ind rec from 1837, also service discharges)			
Ben Hill	G5	1906	Irwin, Wilcox
Ben Hill County, 401 E Central Ave, Fitzgerald, GA 31750-2596 .... (912)423-2455			
(Co Clk has div, civ ct, Ind rec from 1907; Pro Judge has b, m, d, bur rec)			
Berrien	G5	1856	Lowndes, Coffee, Irwin
Berrien County, 105 E Washington Ave, Nashville, GA 31639-2256 .... (912)686-5421			
(Clk Sup Ct has div & civ ct rec from 1856; Pro Ct has b & d rec from 1919, m & pro rec from 1856)			
Bibb	E4	1822	Jones, Monroe, Twiggs, Houston
Bibb County, 601 Mulberry St, Macon, GA 31201-2672 .... (912)749-6527			
(Macon-Bibb Co Health Dept has b, d, bur rec; Pro Ct has m, pro rec; Co Clk has div, civ ct, Ind rec from 1823)			
* **Bleckley**	F4	1912	Pulaski
Bleckley County, 306 2nd St SE, Cochran, GA 31014-1633 .... (912)934-3200			
(Clk Sup Ct has div, pro, civ ct & Ind rec)			
Brantley	H6	1920	Charlton, Pierce, Wayne
Brantley County, PO Box 398, Nahunta, GA 31553-0398 .... (912)462-5256			
(Clk Sup Ct has b, div, pro & civ ct rec from 1921)			
* **Brooks**	H4	1858	Lowndes, Thomas
Brooks County, Hwy 76 & Hwy 33, Quitman, GA 31643 .... (912)263-5561			
[FHL has some m, civ ct, Ind, pro, tax rec]			

Name	Map Index	Date Created	Parent County or Territory From Which Organized

* **Bryan**   F7   1793   Effingham, Liberty
Bryan County, 401 S College St, Pembroke, GA 31321 .... (912)653-4912
(Pro Judge has m, pro, b and some d rec; Co Clk has div rec from 1920, civ ct, Ind, crim rec from 1793)

* **Bulloch**   F7   1796   Franklin
Bulloch County, N Main St, Statesboro, GA 30458 .... (912)764-9009
(Pro Ct has b & m rec; Clk Sup Ct has div, civ ct rec from 1891, Ind rec from 1876)

* **Burke**   E6   1777   St. George Parish
Burke County, 6th & Liberty St, Waynesboro, GA 30830 .... (404)554-2324
(Courthouse burned in January, 1856, all records prior to that date destroyed. Pro Ct has b, d rec from 1927, m, pro rec from 1856, b and d rec not open to public. Full time Clk available and interested in assisting with available rec)

* **Butts**   D4   1825   Henry, Monroe
Butts County, PO Box 320, Jackson, GA 30233-0320 .... (404)775-8215
(Pro Ct has b, m, d, pro rec; Clk Sup Ct has div, civ ct, Ind rec from 1825; History of Butts Co 1825-1976, copy available Clerk's office or county library)

Calhoun   G3   1854   Baker & Early
Calhoun County, Courthouse Sq, Morgan, GA 31766 .... (912)849-4835
(Co Clk has b, m, d, div, pro, civ ct, Ind rec from 1854)

* **Camden**   H7   1777   St. Mary, St. Thomas
Camden County, 4th St, Woodbine, GA 31569 .... (912)576-5601
(Fire 1870, only one book lost - Will rec "B" between years 1828-1860 - all others intact & legible) (Clk Sup Ct has div, civ ct & Ind rec; Pro Ct has b, m, d & pro rec)

Campbell   1828   Carroll, Coweta -- merged Fulton 1926 & 1932
[FHL has some m, civ ct, pro, Ind, tax rec]

Candler   F6   1914   Bulloch, Emanuel, Tattnall
Candler County, Courthouse Sq, Metter, GA 30439 .... (912)685-2835
(Co Clk has b, m, d rec from 1915, div, civ ct, Ind rec from 1914)

* **Carroll**   D2   1826   Indian Lands
Carroll County, 311 Newnan St, Carrollton, GA 30117-3124 .... (404)834-0064
(Pro Ct has b from 1827, d from 1919 & pro rec from 1827; Clk Sup Ct has div, civ ct & Ind rec from 1827)

Cass   1832   (changed to Bartow 1861)

* **Catoosa**   B2   1853   Walker, Whitfield
Catoosa County, 206 E Nashville St, Ringgold, GA 30736-1799 .... (404)935-2500
(Clk Sup Ct has civ ct rec from 1833, div rec from 1853; Pro Ct has m & pro rec from 1853)

* **Charlton**   H6   1854   Camden, Ware
Charlton County, 100 3rd St, Folkston, GA 31537 .... (912)496-2549
(Pro Judge has b, m, d, bur, pro rec; Clk Sup Ct has div, civ ct, Ind rec from 1877; Courthouse burned in 1877)

*† **Chatham**   F7   1777   St Phillip, Christ Church Parish
Chatham County, 133 Montgomery St, Savannah, GA 31401-3230 .... (912)944-4984
(Pro Ct has b, m, d, pro rec; Clk Sup Ct has div rec, civ ct rec from 1783, Ind rec from 1785; naturalization rec from 1801)

* **Chattahoochee**   F2   1854   Muscogee, Marion
Chattahoochee County, PO Box 299, Cusseta, GA 31805 .... (404)989-3602
(Pro Ct has m & pro rec from 1854, b & d rec from 1919; Clk Sup Ct has div, civ ct & Ind rec from 1854)

* **Chattooga**   B2   1838   Floyd, Walker
Chattooga County, PO Box 211, Summerville, GA 30747-0211 .... (404)857-4796
(Clk Cts has div rec from early 1900s & civ ct rec; Ord office has b, m, d, bur & pro rec)

* **Cherokee**   C3   1831   Cherokee Lands, Habersham, Hall
Cherokee County, 100 North St, Canton, GA 30114-2794 .... (404)479-1953
(Clk Sup Ct has div, civ ct rec & deeds from 1833; Pro Ct has b, m, d, bur & pro rec, deeds complete except bk Q; Wills bks A & B lost)

* **Clarke**   C4   1801   Jackson, Green
Clarke County, 325 E Washington St, Athens, GA 30601-2750 .... (404)354-2660
(Clk Sup Ct has div, deeds & civ ct rec from 1801; Pro Ct has m & pro rec from 1801)

* **Clay**   G2   1854   Early, Randolph
Clay County, PO Box 550, Fort Gaines, GA 31751-0550 .... (912)768-2631
(Clk Sup Ct has div & Ind rec)

* **Clayton**   D3   1858   Fayette, Henry
Clayton County, 121 S McDonough St, Jonesboro, GA 30236-3694 .... (404)478-9911
(Pro Ct has b, m, d & pro rec; Clk Sup Ct has div & Ind rec from 1859, civ ct rec from 1964, & crim ct rec from 1965)

*† **Clinch**   H5   1850   Ware, Lowndes
Clinch County, 100 Court Sq, Homerville, GA 31634-1400 .... (912)487-2667
(Pro Ct has b rec from 1919, m rec from 1867, d rec from 1919, pro rec from 1867; Clk Sup Ct has div, civ ct rec from 1867, Ind rec from 1868, voters list from 1890; all rec burned 1867. Previously burned 1856. Most deeds re-recorded since 1868. Clk Sup Ct has old co newspapers from 1895)

* **Cobb**   C3   1832   Cherokee
Cobb County, 10 E Park Sq, Marietta, GA 30090-0001 .... (404)429-3210
(Fire 1864; rec lost previously)

Name	Map Index	Date Created	Parent County or Territory From Which Organized

* **Coffee**   G5   1854   Clinch, Irwin, Ware, Telfair
Coffee County, 210 S Coffee Ave, Douglas, GA 31533-3815 .... (912)384-4799
(Clk Sup Ct has div, civ ct, Ind & Sup Ct rec from 1854 & some mil dischrg since WWI; Pro Ct has m & pro rec; Co Hlth Dept has b & d rec)

* **Colquitt**   H4   1856   Lowndes, Thomas
Colquitt County, Main St, Moultrie, GA 31776 .... (912)985-1324
(Pro Ct has b, m, d & pro rec; Clk Sup Ct has div, civ ct & Ind rec; fire 1881 rec lost)

* **Columbia**   D6   1790   Richmond
Columbia County, PO Box 100, Appling, GA 30802-0100 .... (404)541-1139
[FHL has some m, cem, civ ct, Ind, pro, tax rec]

† **Cook**   H4   1918   Berrien
Cook County, 212 N Hutchinson Ave, Adel, GA 31620-2400 .... (912)896-2266
(Clk Sup Ct has div, pro & civ ct rec from 1919; Pro Ct has b, m, d from 1918)

* **Coweta**   D3   1826   Indian Lands
Coweta County, PO Box 945, Newnan, GA 30264-0945 .... (404)254-2600
(Pro Ct has b rec from 1919, m from 1828, d from 1919 & pro rec from 1828; Clk Sup Ct has div, civ ct & Ind rec from 1828)

* **Crawford**   E4   1822   Houston, Marion, Talbot, Macon
Crawford County, PO Box 389, Knoxville, GA 31050-0389 .... (912)836-3782
(Clk Sup Ct has div & civ rec from 1850)

* **Crisp**   F4   1905   Dooly
Crisp County, 210 7th St S, Cordele, GA 31015-4295 .... (912)276-2672
(Clk Sup Ct has div, civ ct, Ind rec from 1905; Pro Ct has m, pro rec; Co Hlth Dept has b, m rec; Dekle Funeral Home has bur rec)

Dade   B1   1837   Walker
Dade County, PO Box 417, Trenton, GA 30752 .... (404)657-4778
(Co Clk has div, civ ct, Ind rec)

Dawson   B3   1857   Lumpkin, Gilmer
Dawson County, PO Box 192, Dawsonville, GA 30534-0192 .... (404)265-3164
(Clk Sup Ct has div, civ ct, Ind rec from 1857; Pro Ct has b, m, d, bur, pro rec from 1858)

* **Decatur**   H3   1823   Early
Decatur County, 122 W Water St, Bainbridge, GA 31717-3664 .... (912)248-3031
(Pro Ct has m from 1823, pro rec; Clk Sup Ct has div, civ ct, Ind & crim ct rec from 1823)

* **DeKalb**   D3   1822   Fayette, Gwinnett, Newton, Henry
DeKalb County, 556 N McDonough St, Decatur, GA 30030-3356 .... (404)371-2000
(Clk Sup Ct has div, civ ct & Ind rec from 1842; Pro Ct has m & pro rec from 1842; Courthouse burned 1842 & 1916)

* **Dodge**   F5   1870   Montgomery, Pulaski, Telfair
Dodge County, PO Box 818, Eastman, GA 31023-0818 .... (912)374-4361
(Pro Ct has b, m, d & pro rec; Clk Sup Ct has div, pro, civ ct & Ind rec)

* **Dooly**   F4   1821   Indian Lands
Dooly County, PO Box 322, Vienna, GA 31092-0322 .... (912)268-4228
(Clk Sup Ct has div & civ ct rec from 1846, deed rec from 1850; Pro Ct has b, m, d, bur & pro rec; fire destroyed early rec few m left 1848)

*† **Dougherty**   G3   1852   Baker
Dougherty County, PO Box 1827, Albany, GA 31703-5301 .... (912)431-2198
(Clk Sup Ct has div & civ rec from 1856, Ind rec from 1854; Pro Ct has b, m, d, & pro rec)

Douglas   D2   1870   Carroll, Campbell
Douglas County, 6754 Broad St, Douglasville, GA 30134-4501 .... (404)949-2000
(Pro Ct has b, m, d & pro rec; Clk Sup Ct has div, civ ct & Ind rec from 1870)

* **Early**   G2   1818   Creek Indian Lands
Early County, 105 Courthouse Sq, Blakely, GA 31723-1890 .... (912)723-3033
(Many rec lost; first m bk 1854)

*† **Echols**   H5   1858   Clinch, Lowndes
Echols County, PO Box 190, Statenville, GA 31648-0190 .... (912)559-6538
(Most rec burned 1897) (Clk Sup Ct has div, civ ct & Ind rec)

* **Effingham**   F7   1777   St. Mathews, St Phillips
Effingham County, 901 N Pine St, Springfield, GA 31329 .... (912)754-6071
(Pro Ct has b & d rec from 1927, m & pro rec from 1790; Clk Sup Ct has div & civ ct rec from 1777; some rec lost CW and fire 1890)

* **Elbert**   C5   1790   Wilkes
Elbert County, 14 N Oliver St, Elberton, GA 30635-1498 .... (404)283-4702
(Pro Ct has b, m, d, bur, pro rec; Clk Sup Ct has div, civ ct, Ind rec from 1790)

* **Emanuel**   E6   1812   Montgomery, Bulloch
Emanuel County, 101 N Main St, Swainsboro, GA 30401-2042 .... (912)237-3881
(Pro Ct has b, m, d & pro rec; Clk Sup Ct has div, civ ct rec, Ind rec from 1812)

* **Evans**   F7   1914   Bulloch, Tattnall
Evans County, 3 Freeman St, Claxton, GA 30417 .... (912)739-1141
(Pro Ct has b, m, d, bur, pro rec; Clk Sup Ct has div rec, civ ct, Ind rec from 1915)

Name	Map Index	Date Created	Parent County or Territory From Which Organized

* **Fannin** B3 1854 Gilmer, Union
Fannin County, PO Box 487, Blue Ridge, GA 30513-0487 .... (404)632-2203
(Pro Ct has b, m, d, rec; Clk Sup Ct has div, civ ct, Ind rec from 1854)

* **Fayette** D3 1821 Indian Lands, Henry
Fayette County, 200 Courthouse Sq, Fayetteville, GA 30214-2198 .... (404)461-6041
(Pro Ct has b, m, d & pro rec; Clk Sup Ct has div, civ ct & Ind rec)

* **Floyd** C2 1832 Cherokee, Chattooga, Palding
Floyd County, PO Box 946, Rome, GA 30162-0946 .... (404)291-5110
(Pro Ct has m & pro rec; Clk Sup Ct has div, civ ct & Ind rec from 1883)

* **Forsyth** C4 1832 Cherokee, Lumpkin
Forsyth County, PO Box 128, Cumming, GA 30130-0128 .... (404)781-2100
[FHL has some m, civ ct, Ind, pro, tax rec]

* **Franklin** C5 1784 Cherokee Lands
Franklin County, Courthouse Sq, Carnesville, GA 30521 .... (404)384-2514
(Clk Sup Ct has div & civ ct rec from 1900, Ind rec from 1860) (some rec prior to 1850 in Ga. Archives)

* **Fulton** D3 1853 DeKalb, Campbell
Fulton County, 160 Pryor St Rm 208, Atlanta, GA 30303-3405 .... (404)730-4000
(Pro Ct has m & pro rec; Clk Sup Ct has div, civ ct & Ind rec from 1854)

* **Gilmer** B3 1832 Cherokee
Gilmer County, 1 Westside Sq, Ellijay, GA 30540 .... (404)635-4361
(Pro Ct has b, m, d & bur rec; Clk Sup Ct has div from 1927, pro & civ ct from 1900 & Ind rec from 1833)

* **Glascock** D5 1857 Warren, Jefferson
Glascock County, PO Box 231, Gibson, GA 30810-0231 .... (404)598-2084
(Pro Ct has b, m, d rec; Clk Sup Ct has div, civ ct, Ind, fine, forfeits)

Glynn H7 1777 St. David, St. Patrick
Glynn County, 701 G St, Brunswick, GA 31520-6750 .... (912)267-5600
(Pro Ct has m rec from 1845, administrators, guardianship & pro rec from 1792; Clk Sup Ct has div & civ ct rec from 1792; deeds
1824-1829 burned, all rec to 1818 damaged)

* **Gordon** B2 1850 Cass, Floyd
Gordon County, 100 S Wall St Annex 1, Calhoun, GA 30701-2244 .... (404)629-3795
(Clk Sup Ct has div & civ ct rec from 1864; Pro Ct has b, m, d, bur & pro rec; rec destroyed 1864)

* **Grady** H3 1905 Decatur, Thomas
Grady County, 250 N Broad St, Cairo, GA 31728-4101 .... (912)377-1512
(Clk Sup Ct has div, civ ct, Ind rec from 1906)

* **Greene** D5 1786 Washington, Oglethorpe, Wilkes
Greene County, 201 N Main St, Greensboro, GA 30642-1109 .... (404)453-7716
(Pro Ct has m, d, pro rec; Co Health Dept has b rec from 1927; Clk Sup Ct has div rec from 1790, civ ct, Ind rec from 1785)

* **Gwinnett** C4 1818 Cherokee Lands, Jackson
Gwinnett County, 75 Langley Dr, Lawrenceville, GA 30245-6935 .... (404)822-8000
(Clk Sup Ct has div, civ ct & Ind rec; Courthouse burned 1871, few rec saved)

* **Habersham** B4 1818 Cherokee Lands, Franklin
Habersham County, PO Box 227, Clarkesville, GA 30523-0227 .... (404)754-6264
(Pro Ct has m & pro rec from 1819, b & d from 1940; Clk Sup Ct has div, civ ct, crim ct & Ind rec from 1819)

* **Hall** C4 1818 Cherokee Lands, Jackson, Franklin
Hall County, 116 Spring St E, Gainesville, GA 30501-3765 .... (404)531-7000
(Clk Sup Ct has div & civ ct rec from 1900, Ind rec from 1819; Pro Ct has m & pro rec; tornado destroyed cthouse in 1936, most
records lost, except deeds)

* **Hancock** D5 1793 Greene, Washington
Hancock County, Courthouse Sq, Sparta, GA 31087 .... (404)444-5746
(Pro Ct has b, d rec from 1927, m rec from 1805; Clk Sup Ct has div, civ ct rec from 1919, Ind rec from 1794)

* **Haralson** C2 1856 Carroll, Polk
Haralson County, PO Box 488, Buchanan, GA 30113-0488 .... (404)646-2002
(Pro Ct has b, m, d, bur, pro rec; Clk Sup Ct has div, civ ct, Ind rec)

* **Harris** E2 1827 Muscogee, Troup
Harris County, PO Box 528, Hamilton, GA 31811-0528 .... (404)628-4944
(Pro Ct has m & pro rec; Clk Sup Ct has Ind rec from 1827, div & civ ct rec from 1927; Co Hlth Dept has b & d rec)

* **Hart** C5 1853 Elbert, Franklin
Hart County, PO Box 279, Hartwell, GA 30643-0279 .... (404)376-2024
(Pro Ct has b, m, d, bur, pro rec; Clk Sup Ct has div, civ ct, Ind, plats, crim, mort rec from 1856)

* **Heard** D2 1830 Carroll, Coweta, Troup
Heard County, PO Box 40, Franklin, GA 30217-0040 .... (404)675-3821
(Pro Ct has b & d rec from 1927 and m & pro rec from 1894; fire 1894)

* **Henry** D3 1821 Indian Lands, Walton
Henry County, 345 Phillips Dr, McDonough, GA 30253-3425 .... (404)954-2400
(Clk Sup Ct has div, civ ct & Ind rec from 1821)

Name	Map Index	Date Created	Parent County or Territory From Which Organized

* **Houston**   F4   1821   Indian Lands
Houston County, 200 Carl Vinson Pkwy, Warner Robins, GA 31088-5808 .... (912)922-4471
(Pro Ct has b & d rec from 1927, m rec from 1833, pro rec from 1827; Clk Sup Ct has div, civ ct & Ind rec from 1822)

* **Irwin**   G5   1818   Indian Lands, Coffee, Telfair
Irwin County, S Irwin Ave, Ocilla, GA 31774-1098 .... (912)468-9441
(Pro Ct has b & m rec; Clk Sup Ct has div, civ ct & Ind rec from 1900)

* **Jackson**   C4   1796   Franklin
Jackson County, PO Box 68, Jefferson, GA 30549-0068 .... (404)367-1199
(Clk Sup Ct has Ind & pro rec from 1796, m rec from 1803, b rec from 1919, d rec from 1927, tax rec from 1800; early div and civ ct rec may be available elsewhere)

* **Jasper**   D4   1812   Baldwin (changed from Randolph 1812)
Jasper County, County Courthouse, Monticello, GA 31064 .... (404)468-2812
(Clk Sup Ct has div rec, civ ct, Ind & Sup Ct minutes from 1808) (Jasper Co was formed as Randolph Co in 1808 & name changed to Jasper 1812, rec go back to 1808)

Jeff Davis   G5   1905   Appling, Coffee
Jeff Davis County, Jeff Davis St, Hazlehurst, GA 31539 .... (912)375-6611
(Clk Sup Ct has div, civ ct & Ind rec from 1905)

*† **Jefferson**   E6   1796   Burke, Warren
Jefferson County, 202 E Broad St, Louisville, GA 30434-1622 .... (912)625-3332
(Rec not complete; deeds 1797-1802; 1865)

Jenkins   E6   1905   Bullock, Burke, Emanuel, Screven
Jenkins County, PO Box 797, Millen, GA 30442-0797 .... (912)982-2563
(Pro Ct has m & pro rec; Clk Sup Ct has div, civ ct & Ind rec from 1905)

Johnson   E5   1858   Emanuel, Laurens, Washington
Johnson County, PO Box 269, Wrightsville, GA 31096-0269 .... (912)864-3388
(Clk Sup Ct has div, civ ct, Ind rec from 1858)

* **Jones**   E4   1807   Baldwin, Bibb, Putnam
Jones County, PO Box 1359, Gray, GA 31032-1359 .... (912)986-6405
[FHL has some m, cem, civ ct, pro, Ind, tax rec]

Kinchafoonee   1853   Stewart (changed to Webster 1856)

* **Lamar**   E3   1920   Monroe, Pike
Lamar County, 327 Thomaston St, Barnesville, GA 30204-1616 .... (404)358-0150
(Clk Sup Ct has div, civ ct, Ind rec from 1921)

* **Lanier**   H5   1919   Berrien, Lowndes, Clinch
Lanier County, 100 W Main St, Lakeland, GA 31635-1191 .... (912)482-2088
(Clk Sup Ct has div & civ ct rec from 1921; Pro Ct has b, m, d & pro rec from 1921)

* **Laurens**   F5   1807   Montgomery, Washington, Wilkinson
Laurens County, 101 N Jefferson St, Dublin, GA 31021-6198 .... (912)272-4755
(Pro Ct has m & pro rec; Clk Sup Ct has div, civ ct & Ind rec from 1807; Co Hlth Dept has b & d rec)

*† **Lee**   G3   1826   Indian Lands
Lee County, PO Box 56, Leesburg, GA 31763-0056 .... (912)759-6000
(Clk Sup Ct has m, div & civ ct rec) (all rec lost in courthouse fire 1858)

* **Liberty**   G7   1777   St. Andrew, St. James, St Johns
Liberty County, Courthouse Sq, Hinesville, GA 31313-3240 .... (912)876-2164
(Pro Judge has m & estate rec from late 1700s, b rec from 1919, d rec from 1927; Clk of Ct has div, pro, civ ct & Ind rec from 1756; some early rec lost)

* **Lincoln**   D6   1796   Wilkes
Lincoln County, Humphrey St, Lincolnton, GA 30817 .... (404)359-4444
(Pro Ct has b rec from 1920, m rec from 1810, d rec from 1930; pro rec from 1796; Clk Sup Ct has div, civ ct rec from 1796, Ind rec from 1790)

Long   G7   1920   Liberty
Long County, McDonald St, Ludowici, GA 31316 .... (912)545-2143
(Pro Ct has b, m, d, bur & pro rec; Clk Sup Ct has div, civ ct, Ind, adoptions & Sup Ct crim rec from 1920)

* **Lowndes**   H5   1825   Irwin
Lowndes County, PO Box 1349, Valdosta, GA 31603 .... (912)333-5117
(Pro Ct has m & pro rec; Clk Sup Ct has div, civ ct & Ind rec from 1858)

* **Lumpkin**   B4   1832   Cherokee, Habersham, Hall
Lumpkin County, 280 Courthouse Cir NE, Dahlonega, GA 30533-1167 .... (404)864-3742
(Pro Ct has b, m, d, bur rec; Clk Sup Ct has div, civ ct, Ind rec from 1833)

* **Macon**   F3   1837   Houston, Marion
Macon County, Sumter St, Oglethorpe, GA 31068 .... (912)472-7021
(Courthouse burned 1857, all rec lost; Clk Sup Ct has div, civ ct, Ind rec; Pro Ct has m & pro rec from 1857, b & d rec from 1927)

Madison   C5   1811   Clarke, Elbert, Franklin, Jackson, Oglethorpe
Madison County, PO Box 147, Danielsville, GA 30633-0147 .... (404)795-3351
(Pro Ct has b, m, d, bur, pro rec; Clk Sup Ct has div, civ ct & Ind rec from 1812)

Name	Map Index	Date Created	Parent County or Territory From Which Organized

* **Marion** F3 1827 Lee, Muscogee, Stewart
Marion County, Courthouse Sq, Buena Vista, GA 31803 .... (912)649-2603
(Clk Sup Ct has div, civ ct & lnd rec; Courthouse fire 1845; all rec lost)

* **McDuffie** D6 1870 Columbia, Warren
McDuffie County, PO Box 28, Thomson, GA 30824-0028 .... (404)595-3982
(Pro Ct has b, m, d & pro rec from 1872; Clk Sup Ct has div rec from 1872, civ ct rec, lnd rec from 1870)

* **McIntosh** G7 1793 Liberty
McIntosh County, PO Box 584, Darien, GA 31305-0584 .... (912)437-6671
(Clk Sup Ct has div, civ ct, pro & lnd rec; many rec lost during CW; Courthouse fire 1931)

* **Meriwether** E3 1827 Troup
Meriwether County, PO Box 428, Greenville, GA 30222-0428 .... (404)672-1314
(Pro Ct has b rec from 1927, m rec from 1828, d rec from 1929, pro rec from 1838; Clk Sup Ct has div rec, civ ct, lnd rec from 1827, Vet discharge rec)

* **Miller** H2 1856 Baker, Early
Miller County, 155 S 1st St Suite 2, Colquitt, GA 31737-1284 .... (912)758-4104
(Courthouse fire 1873; all rec lost)

* **Mitchell** H3 1857 Baker
Mitchell County, 12 Broad St, Camilla, GA 31730 .... (912)336-2000
(Clk Sup Ct has div rec from 1857 & civ ct rec from 1847; minutes kept of civ ct rec from 1847 to present not before; Courthouse fire 1869; Sup Ct rec and some others saved; address correspondence to Clk Sup Ct together with money order in advance & stamped, addressed envelope, or no attention will be given)

* **Monroe** E4 1821 Indian Lands
Monroe County, PO Box 189, Forsyth, GA 31029-0189 .... (912)994-7000
(Pro Ct has m & pro rec from 1824, b rec from 1927, d rec from 1940; Clk Sup Ct has civ ct & lnd rec from 1821, and div rec)

* **Montgomery** F6 1793 Washington, Laurens, Tattnall, Telfair
Montgomery County, Railroad Ave, Mount Vernon, GA 30445 .... (912)583-2363
(Pro Ct has b, d rec from 1918, m rec from 1807, pro rec from 1793; Clk Sup Ct has div rec, civ ct rec from 1800, lnd rec from 1793; most original rec prior to 1890 are in State Archives)

Morgan D4 1807 Baldwin, Jasper
Morgan County, PO Box 168, Madison, GA 30650-0168 .... (404)342-0725
(Co Health Dept has b rec; Pro Ct has m, d, bur, pro rec; Clk Sup Ct has div, civ ct, lnd rec from 1807)

* **Murray** B3 1832 Cherokee
Murray County, 3rd Ave, Chatsworth, GA 30705 .... (404)695-2932
(Pro Ct has b & d rec from 1924, m rec from 1842, pro rec from 1890; Clk Sup Ct has civ ct rec from 1834)

*† **Muscogee** F2 1826 Creek Lands, Harris, Lee, Marion
Muscogee County, 100 10th St, Columbus, GA 31901-2736 .... (404)571-4860
(Clk Sup Ct has div, civ ct & lnd rec from 1838)

* **Newton** D4 1821 Henry, Jasper, Morgan, Walton
Newton County, 1113 Usher St, Covington, GA 30209 .... (404)784-2000
(Clk Sup Ct has div, civ ct & lnd rec from 1822, service rec from 1917)

Oconee C4 1875 Clarke
Oconee County, 15 Water St, Watkinsville, GA 30677-2438 .... (404)769-5120
(Pro Ct has b, m, & d rec; Clk sup Ct has div, civ ct & lnd rec from 1875)

* **Oglethorpe** C5 1793 Clarke, Wilkes
Oglethorpe County, PO Box 261, Lexington, GA 30648-0261 .... (404)743-5270
(Pro Ct has b, m, d & pro rec; Clk Sup Ct has div, civ ct & lnd rec from 1794) (Courthouse fire 1941)

* **Paulding** C2 1832 Cherokee Lands, Carroll, Cobb
Paulding County, 1 Courthouse Sq, Dallas, GA 30132-1401 .... (404)445-8871
(Clk Sup Ct has div, civ ct rec from 1876, lnd rec from 1848)

* **Peach** E4 1924 Houston, Macon
Peach County, 205 W Church St, Fort Valley, GA 31030-4155 .... (912)825-2535
(Pro Ct has b, m, d, pro rec from 1925; Clk Sup Ct has div, civ ct, lnd rec from 1925)

* **Pickens** B3 1853 Cherokee, Gilmer
Pickens County, 211-1 N Main St, Jasper, GA 30143 .... (404)692-3556
(Pro Ct has b, m, d, bur, pro rec from 1924; Clk Sup Ct has div, civ ct, lnd rec from 1854)

* **Pierce** G6 1857 Appling, Ware
Pierce County, PO Box 679, Blackshear, GA 31516-0679 .... (912)449-2022
(Pro Ct has b rec from 1926, m rec from 1875, d rec from 1924; Clk Sup Ct has div & civ ct rec from 1875; Courthouse fire 1874)

* **Pike** E3 1822 Monroe
Pike County, PO Box 377, Zebulon, GA 30295-0377 .... (404)567-3406
(Clk Sup Ct has civ ct & lnd rec from 1823)

Polk C2 1851 Paulding
Polk County, PO Box 268, Cedartown, GA 30125-0268 .... (404)749-2100
(Pro Ct has b, m & d rec; Clk Sup Ct has div, civ ct & lnd rec from 1852)

* **Pulaski** F4 1808 Laurens, Wilkinson
Pulaski County, PO Box 29, Hawkinsville, GA 31036-0029 .... (912)783-4154
(Clk Sup Ct has div, civ ct rec from 1850, lnd rec from 1810; Pro Ct has m, pro rec from 1810, b rec from 1935, d rec from 1920)

Name	Map Index	Date Created	Parent County or Territory From Which Organized
Putnam	D4	1807	Baldwin

Putnam County, 108 S Madison Ave Suite 200, Eatonton, GA 31024-1094 .... (404)485-5826
(Clk Sup Ct has div & civ ct rec from 1807; Pro Ct has b, m, d, bur & pro rec)

Quitman	G2	1858	Randolph, Stewart

Quitman County, PO Box 114, Georgetown, GA 31754-0114 .... (912)334-2159
(Courthouse burned; Clk Sup Ct has b rec from 1927, m rec from 1919, d rec, div, civ ct rec from 1923, Ind rec from 1879)

* **Rabun**	B4	1819	Cherokee Lands, Habersham

Rabun County, PO Box 925, Clayton, GA 30525-0925 .... (404)782-5271
(Pro Ct has m & pro rec; Clk Sup Ct has div, civ ct & Ind rec)

* **Randolph**	G2	1828	Baker, Lee

Randolph County, Court St, Cuthbert, GA 31740 .... (912)732-6440
(Pro Ct has m & pro rec from 1835; Clk Sup Ct has div, civ ct & Ind rec from 1835)

Randolph		1807	(changed to Jasper 1812)

*† **Richmond**	D6	1777	St. Paul Parish

Richmond County, 530 Green St, Augusta, GA 30911-0001 .... (404)821-2300
[FHL has some m, cem, civ ct, pro, Ind, tax rec]

Rockdale	D4	1870	Henry, Newton

Rockdale County, 922 Court St NE, Conyers, GA 30207-4540 .... (404)929-4000
[FHL has some m, civ ct, Ind, pro rec]

* **Schley**	F3	1857	Marion, Sumter

Schley County, PO Box 352, Ellaville, GA 31806 .... (912)937-2609
(Pro Ct has b, d, bur rec from 1927, m rec from 1858, pro rec; Clk Sup Ct has div, civ ct, Ind rec from 1857)

* **Screven**	E7	1793	Burke, Effingham

Screven County, PO Box 159, Sylvania, GA 30467-0159 .... (912)564-7535
(Pro Ct has b, d rec from 1927, m, pro rec from 1817; Clk Sup Ct has div, civ ct rec from 1816, Ind rec from 1790)

Seminole	H2	1920	Decatur, Early

Seminole County, County Courthouse, Donalsonville, GA 31745 .... (912)524-2878
(Pro Ct has b, m, d & pro rec; Clk Sup Ct has div, civ ct & Ind rec from 1921)

Spalding	D3	1851	Fayette, Henry, Pike

Spalding County, 132 W Solomon St, Griffin, GA 30223-3312 .... (404)228-9900
(Clk Sup Ct has div, civ ct & Ind rec from 1852)

* **Stephens**	B4	1905	Franklin, Habersham

Stephens County, PO Box 386, Toccoa, GA 30577 .... (404)886-9491
(Co Hlth Dept has b, d rec; Pro Ct has m, pro rec; Clk Sup Ct has div, civ ct, Ind rec from 1906)

* **Stewart**	F2	1830	Randolph

Stewart County, PO Box 157, Lumpkin, GA 31815-0157 .... (912)838-6769
(Pro Ct has b, d, bur rec from 1927, m rec from 1828, pro rec; Clk Sup Ct has div, civ ct, Ind rec from 1830)

* **Sumter**	F3	1831	Lee

Sumter County, PO Box 295, Americus, GA 31709-0295 .... (912)924-3090
(Co Hlth Dept has b, d, bur rec; Pro Ct has m, pro rec; Clk Sup Ct has div, civ ct, Ind rec from 1831)

* **Talbot**	E3	1827	Crawford, Harris, Marion, Macon, Muscogee

Talbot County, Courthouse Sq, Talbotton, GA 31827 .... (404)665-3220
(Pro Ct has b, m, d & pro rec; Clk Sup Ct has div, ct & Ind rec)

* **Taliaferro**	D5	1825	Green, Hancock, Oglethorpe, Warren, Wilkes

Taliaferro County, Courthouse Sq, Crawfordville, GA 30631 .... (404)456-2494
(Pro Ct has b rec from 1927, m & pro rec from 1826, d rec from 1920, Ind grant from 1750, church rec from 1802; Clk Sup Ct has div & civ rec 1826)

* **Tattnall**	F6	1801	Montgomery, Liberty

Tattnall County, Main & Brazell Sts, Reidsville, GA 30453 .... (912)557-4335
(Pro Ct has b, m & d rec; Clk Sup Ct has div rec from 1880, civ ct & Ind rec)

Taylor	F3	1852	Marion, Talbot

Taylor County, PO Box 278, Butler, GA 31006 .... (912)862-3336
(Pro Ct has b, m, d, bur, pro rec; Clk Sup Ct has div, civ ct, Ind rec from 1852)

* **Telfair**	F5	1807	Wilkinson, Appling

Telfair County, Courthouse Sq, McRae, GA 31055 .... (912)868-5688
(Pro Judge has m & pro rec; Clk Sup Ct has div, civ ct & Ind rec; Co Hlth Dept has b & d rec)

* **Terrell**	G3	1856	Lee, Randolph

Terrell County, 955 Forrester Dr SE, Dawson, GA 31742-2100 .... (912)995-4476
(Clk Sup Ct has div, civ ct & Ind rec from 1856)

* **Thomas**	H4	1825	Grady, Decatur, Irwin

Thomas County, PO Box 920, Thomasville, GA 31799-0920 .... (912)225-4100
(Co Hlth Dept has b, d rec; Pro Ct has m, pro rec; Clk Sup Ct has div, civ ct rec from 1919, Ind rec from 1826)

* **Tift**	G4	1905	Berrien, Irwin, Worth

Tift County, 225 N Tift Ave, Tifton, GA 31794-4463 .... (912)386-7850
(Pro Ct has m rec; Clk Sup Ct has div, pro, civ ct & Ind rec from 1905)

Name	Map Index	Date Created	Parent County or Territory From Which Organized

Toombs   F6   1905   Emanuel, Tattnall, Montgomery
Toombs County, Courthouse Sq & Hwy 280, Lyons, GA 30436 .... (912)526-3311
(Pro Ct has b, m, d, bur & pro rec from 1905; Clk Sup Ct has div, civ ct & lnd rec from 1905)

Towns   B4   1856   Rabun, Union
Towns County, PO Box 178, Hiawassee, GA 30546-0178 .... (404)896-2130
(Pro Ct has b, m, d, bur, pro rec; Clk Sup Ct has div, civ ct, lnd rec from 1856)

* **Treutlen**   F5   1917   Emanuel, Montgomery
Treutlen County, 2nd St, Soperton, GA 30457 .... (912)529-3664
(Pro Ct has b, m, d & pro rec from 1919; Clk Sup Ct has div, civ ct & lnd rec from 1919)

* **Troup**   E2   1826   Indian Lands
Troup County, PO Box 1149, La Grange, GA 30241-1149 .... (404)883-1600
(Pro Ct has b rec from 1918, m, d & pro rec; Clk Sup Ct has div & lnd rec from 1827, civ ct rec)

* **Turner**   G4   1905   Dooly, Irwin, Wilcox, Worth
Turner County, 200 E College Ave, Ashburn, GA 31714-1275 .... (912)567-2011
(Clk Sup Ct has div & civ ct rec from 1906; Pro Ct has b, m, d, bur & pro rec)

* **Twiggs**   E4   1809   Wilkinson
Twiggs County, 101 Magnolia St, Jeffersonville, GA 31044 .... (912)945-3629
[FHL has some cem, lnd, tax rec]

* **Union**   B4   1832   Cherokee Lands, Lumpkin
Union County, RR 8 Box 8005, Blairsville, GA 30512-9201 .... (404)745-2611
(Pro Ct has b, m, d & pro rec; Clk Sup Ct has div, civ ct & lnd rec)

* **Upson**   E3   1824   Crawford, Pike
Upson County, PO Box 889, Thomaston, GA 30286-0889 .... (404)647-7012
(Pro Ct has m rec from 1825, pro rec from 1920; Clk Sup Ct has div, civ ct, lnd rec, inferior ct rec from 1825, newspaper files from 1870)

* **Walker**   B2   1833   Murray
Walker County, PO Box 445, Lafayette, GA 30728-0445 .... (404)638-1437
(Clk Sup Ct has div, civ ct & lnd rec from 1883; Courthouse fire 1883; Pro Judge has m & pro rec; Co Hlth Dept has b & d rec)

* **Walton**   D4   1818   Cherokee Lands
Walton County, Court St Annex 1, Monroe, GA 30655 .... (404)267-4571
(Pro Ct has m & pro rec from 1819; Clk Sup Ct has lnd rec from 1819, div rec from 1900; Magistrate Ct has civ ct rec from 1900; Co Hlth Dept has b & d rec from 1919)

* **Ware**   H6   1824   Appling
Ware County, 800 Church St, Waycross, GA 31501-3501 .... (912)287-4300
(rec burned 1854)

* **Warren**   D5   1793   Columbia, Richmond, Wilkes
Warren County, 100 Main St, Warrenton, GA 30828 .... (404)465-2171
(Pro Ct has b, m, d & pro rec; Clk Sup Ct has div, civ ct & lnd rec)

* **Washington**   E5   1784   Indian Lands
Washington County, PO Box 271, Sandersville, GA 31082-0271 .... (912)552-2325
(Pro Ct has b & m rec; Clk Sup Ct has div, civ ct & lnd rec from 1865)

* **Wayne**   G6   1803   Indian Lands, Appling, Glynn, Camden
Wayne County, 174 N Brunswick St, Jesup, GA 31545-2808 .... (912)427-5900
(Pro Ct has b, m, d & pro rec; Clk Sup Ct has div, civ ct & lnd rec)

* **Webster**   F3   1856   Changed from Kinchafoonee 1856
Webster County, Washington St & Hwy 280, Preston, GA 31824 .... (912)828-5775
(Pro Ct has b, m, d, bur, & pro rec; Clk Sup Ct has div, civ ct & lnd rec)

Wheeler   F5   1912   Montgomery
Wheeler County, Pearl St, Alamo, GA 30411 .... (912)568-7135
(Co Hlth Dept has b, d rec from 1927; Pro Ct has m, pro rec from 1913; Clk Sup Ct has div, civ ct, lnd rec from 1913)

* **White**   B4   1857   Habersham
White County, 1657 S Main St Suite A, Cleveland, GA 30528-0185 .... (404)865-2235
(Pro Ct has b, m, d, pro rec; Clk Sup Ct has div, civ ct, lnd rec from 1858, discharges and mtg rec)

* **Whitfield**   B2   1851   Murray, Walker
Whitfield County, 300 W Crawford St, Dalton, GA 30720-4205 .... (404)278-8717
(Pro Ct has b & d rec from 1927, m & pro rec from 1852; Clk Sup Ct has div, civ ct & lnd rec from ca 1852)

* **Wilcox**   F4   1857   Dooly, Irwin, Pulaski
Wilcox County, Courthouse Sq, Abbeville, GA 31001-1099 .... (912)467-2737
(Pro Ct has b & d rec from 1927, m rec from 1857, & pro rec; Clk Sup Ct has div & civ ct rec from 1886, lnd rec from 1876)

* **Wilkes**   D5   1777   Original territory
Wilkes County, 23 E Court St Rm 222, Washington, GA 30673-1570 .... (404)678-2511
(Pro Ct has b, m, d, pro rec from 1792; Clk Sup Ct has div, civ ct rec from 1778, lnd rec from 1777, crim ct, juvenile ct, financing statements, discharge rec, medical and atty. registers)

* **Wilkinson**   E5   1803   Creek Cession
Wilkinson County, PO Box 161, Irwinton, GA 31042-0161 .... (912)946-2236
(Courthouse burned in 1852 & 1924, however property rec were not burned in 1924; Clk Sup Ct has some div rec & property rec from 1852)

Name	Map Index	Date Created	Parent County or Territory From Which Organized
* Worth	G4	1852	Dooly, Irwin

Worth County, 201 N Main St, Sylvester, GA 31791-2178 .... (912)776-8200
(Clk Sup Ct has div, civ ct & lnd rec)

* At least one county history has been published about this county.
† Inventory of county archives was made by the Historical Records Survey. (See Introduction)

HAWAII

CAPITAL - HONOLULU — TERRITORY 1900 — STATE 1959 (50th)
State Map on Page M-10

Captain James Cook discovered the Hawaiian Islands in 1778 and named them the Sandwich Islands. The 390-mile chain of islands contains eight main islands - Hawaii, Kahoolawe, Maui, Lanai, Molokai, Oahu, Kauai, and Nihau. Between 1782 and 1810, King Kamehameha extended his rule over all the islands. The dynasty he established lasted until 1872. Weakened by political strife and foreigners' desires for freedom, the kingdom finally was abolished in 1893 when Queen Liliuolalani was deposed.

Protestant missionaries from New England began arriving in Hawaii in 1820. Settlers and laborers started coming about a decade later, mostly from the Orient. Booms in sandalwood, whaling, and sugar continued the influx of foreigners to the turn of the century, when the pineapple industry exploded.

On July 4, 1894, the Republic of Hawaii was established. It continued until 1898, when it ceded itself to the United States. Two years later, the Territory of Hawaii was organized. On August 21, 1959, Hawaii became the 50th state.

State-wide registration of births began in 1842, but few records exist until 1896, and general compliance was not reached until 1929. Copies of birth, death, marriage, and divorce records are available through the Office of Research and Statistics, State Department of Health, P.O. Box 3378, 1520 Punchbowl Street, Honolulu, HI 96801 (to verify current fees, call 808-548-5819). The circuit courts have probate records from as early as the 1840's. Microfilms of probates from 1845 to 1900 are at the Hawaii State Archives, Iolani Palace Grounds, Honolulu, HI 96813. Colonial censuses exist for some parts of Hawaii for 1866, 1878, 1890, and 1896. The last three are at the Hawaii State Archives. Also at the Archives are two "census files", 1840 to 1866 and 1847 to 1896, which contain miscellaneous records such as school censuses, population lists, and vital record summaries.

Genealogical Archives, Libraries and Societies

D.A.R. Memorial Library, 1914 Makiki Hts. Dr., Honolulu, HI 96822

Library of Hawaii, King and Punchbowl Sts., Honolulu, HI 96813

Hawaii Society, Sons of the American Revolution, 1564 Piikea St., Honolulu, HI 96818

Hawaiian Historical Society, 560 Kawaiahao St., Honolulu, HI 96813

Printed Census Records and Mortality Schedules

Federal Census 1900 (incomplete), 1910
Island Census 1890

Valuable Printed Sources

Atlases, Maps, and Gazetteers

Armstrong, R. Warrick. *Atlas of Hawaii*. Honolulu: University Press of Hawaii, 1973.

Hawaii Geographic Names Information System Alphabetical List. Reston, Virginia: United States Geographic Survey, 1988.

Pukui, Mary Kawena, et al. *Place Names of Hawaii*. Honolulu: University Press of Hawaii, 1974.

Bibliographies

Alcantara, Ruben R. *The Filipinos in Hawaii: An Annotated Bibliography*. Honolulu: Social Science Research Institute, University of Hawaii, 1972.

Dickson, Diane. *World Catalog of Theses on the Pacific Islands*. Honolulu: University of Hawaii Press, 1970.

Gardner, Arthur L. *The Koreans in Hawaii: An Annotated Bibliography*. Honolulu: Social Science Institute, University of Hawaii, 1970.

Matsuda, Mitsugu. *The Japanese in Hawaii: An Annotated Bibliography*. Honolulu: University of Hawaii, 1975.

Murdock, Clare G. *Basic Hawaiiana: An Annotated Bibliography of the Basic Hawaiiana Printed Materials*. Honolulu: Hawaii State Library, 1969.

Young, Nancy Foon. *The Chinese in Hawaii: An Annotated Bibliography*. Honolulu: Social Science Research Institute, University of Hawaii, 1973.

Genealogical Research Guides

Conrad, Agnes C. *Genealogical Sources in Hawaii*. Honolulu: Hawaii Library Association, 1987.

Histories

Bradley, Harold Whitman. *The American Frontier in Hawaii: The Pioneers, 1789-1843*. Gloucester, Massachusetts: Peter Smith, 1968.

Daws, Gavan. *Shoal of Time*. New York: Macmillan, 1968.

Kuykendall, Ralph S. *The Hawaiian Kingdom, 1778-1893*. Honolulu: University Press of Hawaii, 1967.

HAWAII COUNTY DATA
State Map on Page M-10

Name	Map Index	Date Created	Parent County or Territory From Which Organized
Hawaii	H2		
Hawaii County, 25 Aupuni St, Hilo, HI 96720-4252			(808)961-8255
Honolulu	D5		
Honolulu County, 530 S King St, Honolulu, HI 96813-3014			(808)523-4141
Kauai	B6		
Kauai County, 4396 Rice St, Lihue, HI 96766-1337			(808)245-4785
Maui	F4		
Maui County, 200 S High St, Wailuku, HI 96793-2134			(808)243-7825

* At least one county history has been published about this county.

† Inventory of county archives was made by the Historical Records Survey. (See Introduction)

IDAHO

CAPITAL · BOISE — TERRITORY 1863 — STATE 1890 (43rd)
State Map on M-11

The first Americans to travel to Idaho were Lewis and Clark in 1805. Fur traders followed, building Fort Hall trading post in 1834 on the Snake River, near present-day Pocatello and Fort Boise soon after. These outposts served as important stopping points on the Oregon Trail. In 1848, Idaho became part of the Oregon Territory and in 1859, part of the Washington Territory.

The southern part of the state was settled first. Mormon immigrants from Northern Europe founded Franklin, in Cache Valley in 1860. A series of gold rushes in the river valleys of northern Idaho between 1860 and 1863 led to a mining boom. On March 3, 1863, the Idaho Territory was formed from the Washington and Dakota Territories. The Idaho Territory included all of Montana and nearly all of Wyoming in addition to Idaho. With the organization of the Montana Territory in 1864 and the Wyoming Territory in 1868, Idaho gained its present shape. Indian conflicts hampered settlement until the 1880's, when they were assigned to reservations. Another mining boom and the coming of railroads brought more settlers in the 1880's. About 1910, large irrigation systems and districts were constructed around the Snake River, opening up new areas for farming. This brought many western and mid-western farmers to the area.

Although Idaho was originally settled by Mormons, other churches, particularly Catholic and Protestant, have grown in the state. The general population is made up of mostly Caucasians, but also includes Indians, Japanese, Negroes, and some Chinese, Filipinos, and others. Foreigners mainly came from Canada, Great Britain, and Germany.

The first birth records came from midwives in the 1870's, who sent their reports to county clerks. The counties were required to keep birth and death records between January 1907 and July 1911. Since then birth and death records are kept on a statewide basis at the Bureau of Vital Statistics, Statehouse, Boise, ID 83720 (to verify current fees, call 208-334-5988). Marriages and divorces from 1947 are also kept there. County recorders have records of marriages for their county, however, no licenses were required before March 11, 1895. Wills and probate matters are filed in the county clerk's office. Land records are in the custody of the county recorder. Idaho settlers were included in censuses of the Oregon Territory in 1850, Washington Territory in 1860, and Idaho Territory in 1870 and 1880. The 1860 Census of Idaho County is located with the Spokane County, Washington enumeration. Parts of southern Idaho were included in the 1860 and 1870 censuses of Cache County, Utah. Statewide indexes and mortality schedules are available for the 1870 and 1880 censuses.

Genealogical Archives, Libraries and Societies

Boise State University Library, Boise, ID 83725

College of Idaho Library, Caldwell, ID 83605

College of St. Gertrude Library, Cottonwood, ID 83522

College of Southern Idaho Library, Twin Falls, ID 83301

Hayden Lake Area Free Library, Hayden Lake, ID 83835

Idaho Genealogical Library, 325 W. State, Boise, ID 83702

Idaho State University Library, Pocatello, ID 83209

Lewis-Clark State College Library, Lewiston, ID 83501

Lewiston-Nez Perce County Library, 533 Thain Rd., Lewiston, ID 83501

McCall City Library, McCall, ID 83638

North Idaho College Library, Coeur d' Alene, ID 83814

Northwest Nazarene College Library, Nampa, ID 83651

Ricks College Library, Rexburg, ID 83440

University of Idaho Library, Moscow, ID 83843

Upper Snake River Valley Historical Society, P. O. Box 244, Rexburg, ID 83440

Adams County Historical Society, P. O. Box 352, New Meadows, ID 83654

Bannock County Historical Society, 105 South Garfield Ave., Pocatello, ID 83201

Bonner County Genealogical Society, P. O. Box 27, Dover, ID 83825

Bonner County Historical Society, P. O. Box 1063, Sandpoint, ID 83864

Bonneville County Historical Society, P. O. Box 1784, Idaho Falls, ID 83401

Boundary County Historical Society, P. O. Box 808, Bonners Ferry, ID 83805

Caldwell, Idaho Genealogical Group, 3504 S. Illinois, Caldwell, ID 83605

Camas County Historical Society, Fairfield, ID 83327

Canyon County Historical Society, P. O. Box 595, Nampa, ID 83651

Caribou County Historical Society, County Courthouse, Soda Springs, ID 83276

Clearwater County Historical Society, P. O. Box 1454, Orofino, ID 83544

Elmore County Historical Foundation, P. O. Box 204, Mountain Home, ID 83647

Family Scanner Chapter, IGS, P. O. Box 581, Caldwell, ID 83605

Fremont County Historical Society, St. Anthony, ID 83445

Gooding County Historical Society, Gooding Museum, 134 7th Ave. W., Gooding, ID 83330-1228

Idaho County Chapter, IGS, Grangeville Centennial Library, 215 W. North, Grangeville, ID 83530

Idaho Genealogical Society, P. O. Box 326, 302 North Meadow, Grangeville, ID 83530

Idaho Genealogical Society, Inc., 4620 Overland Road, Room 204, Boise, ID 83705-2867

Idaho Historical Society, 325 State St., Boise, ID 83702

Kamiah Genealogical Society, Box 322, Kamiah, ID 83536

Kootenai County Genealogical Society, 8385 N. Government Way, Hayden Lake, ID 83835

Latah County Genealogical Society, 110 S. Adams St., Moscow, ID 83843

Latah County Historical Society, 110 Adams St., Moscow, ID 83843

Lewis County Historical Society, Rt. 2, Box 10, Kamiah, ID 83536

Luna House Historical Society, 0310 Third Street, Lewiston, ID 83501

Magic Valley Chapter, IGS, Rt. 2, 770 S. River Dr., Heyburn, ID 83336

Minidoka County Historical Society, 100 East Baseline, Rupert, ID 83350

Nez Perce Historical Society, P. O. Box 86, Nez Perce, ID 83542

Old Fort Boise Historical Society, Parma, ID 83660

Payette County Historical Society, P. O. Box 476, Payette, ID 83661

Pocatello Branch Genealogical Society, 156-1/2 South 6th Ave., Pocatello, ID 83201

Shoshone County Genealogical Society, P. O. Box 183, Kellogg, ID 83837

South Bannock County Historical Society & Museum, 8 East Main St., Lava Hot Springs, ID 83246

South Custer County Historical Society, P. O. Box 355, Mackay, ID 83251

Spirit Lake Historical Society, Spirit Lake, ID 83869

Treasure Valley Chapter, IGS, 325 W. State Street, Boise, ID 83702

Twin Rivers Genealogy Society, P. O. Box 386, Lewiston, ID 83501

Upper Snake River Valley Historical Society, P. O. Box 244, Rexburg, ID 83440

Valley County Genealogical Society, P. O. Box 697, Cascade, ID 83611

Wood River Historical Society, P. O. Box 552, Ketchum, ID 83340

Printed Census Records and Mortality Schedules

Federal Census 1870, 1880, 1900, 1910

Valuable Printed Sources

Atlases, Maps, and Gazetteers

Boone, Lalia. *Idaho Place Names: A Geographical Dictionary*. Moscow, Idaho: University of Idaho Press, 1988.

Federal Writers' Project. *The Idaho Encyclopedia*. Caldwell, Idaho: Caxton Printers, 1938.

Gazetteer of Cities, Villages, Unincorporated Communities and Landmark Sites in the State of Idaho. Idaho Department of Highways, 1966.

Maps of Early Idaho. Corvallis, Oregon: Western Guide Publishers, 1972.

Bibliographies

Etulain, Richard W. and Merwin Swanson. *Idaho History: A Bibliography*. Pocatello, Idaho: Idaho State University Press, 1979.

Nelson, Milo G. and Charles A. Webbert. *Idaho Local History: A Bibliography with a Checklist of Library Holdings*. Moscow, Idaho: University Press of Idaho, 1976.

Histories

An Illustrated History of the State of Idaho. Chicago: Lewis Publishing Co., 1899.

Beal, Merrill D. and Merle W. Wells. *History of Idaho*. New York: Lewis Historical Publishing Co., 1959.

Defenbach, Byron. *Idaho: The Place and Its People*. Chicago: The American Historical Society, 1933.

Idaho, An Illustrated History. Boise: Idaho State Historical Society, 1976.

IDAHO COUNTY DATA
State Map on Page M-11

Name	Map Index	Date Created	Parent County or Territory From Which Organized
* **Ada**	G3	1864	Boise
Ada County, 650 Main St, Boise, ID 83702-5986 .... (208)383-4417			
(Co Clk has m, div, pro, civ ct, Ind rec from 1864)			
Adams	E3	1911	Washington
Adams County, PO Box 48, Council, ID 83612-0048 .... (208)253-4561			
(Co Clk has m, div, pro, civ ct & Ind rec from 1900)			
Alturas		1863	Original county; (discontinued)
* **Bannock**	G6	1893	Oneida, Bear Lake
Bannock County, 624 E Center St, Pocatello, ID 83201-6274 .... (208)236-7210			
(Co Clk has b & d rec from 1902, m rec from 1893, div, pro & civ ct rec)			
* **Bear Lake**	H7	1875	Oneida
Bear Lake County, 7 E Center St, Paris, ID 83261 .... (208)945-2212			
(Co Clk has b rec from 1907-1911, d rec from 1907-1915, m, Ind rec from 1875, div rec from 1884)			
* **Benewah**	C3	1915	Kootenai
Benewah County, 7th & College Aves, Saint Maries, ID 83861 .... (208)245-2234			
(Co Clk has m, bur, div, pro, civ ct, Ind rec from 1915)			
*† **Bingham**	G6	1885	Oneida
Bingham County, 501 N Maple St, Blackfoot, ID 83221-1700 .... (208)785-5005			
(Co Clk has m & Ind rec from 1885, div & civ ct rec from 1900, pro rec from 1892, homestead rec from 1889; Commissioners minutes from 1855, brand and naturalization rec; school census taken 1898 to 1933)			
* **Blaine**	G4	1895	Alturas
Blaine County, PO Box 400, Hailey, ID 83333-0400 .... (208)788-4290			
(Co Clk has b & d rec from 1907 to 1911, m, div, pro, civ ct, Ind rec from 1885)			
Boise	F3	1864	Original county
Boise County, PO Box 157, Idaho City, ID 83631-0157 .... (208)392-4431			
(Co Clk has m rec from 1868, div from 1904, pro from 1865, civ ct from 1867 & Ind rec 1865, some records are not complete because of fires)			
Bonner	B3	1907	Kootenai
Bonner County, 215 S 1st Ave, Sandpoint, ID 83864-1392 .... (208)263-6841			
(Co Clk has b & d rec from 1907 to 1911, m, div & civ ct rec from 1907, pro from 1890, Ind rec from 1889)			
* **Bonneville**	G6	1911	Bingham
Bonneville County, 605 N Capital Ave, Idaho Falls, ID 83402-3582 .... (208)529-1350			
(Co Clk has m, div, pro, civ ct & Ind rec from 1911)			
*† **Boundary**	A3	1915	Bonner
Boundary County, 315 Kootnai St, Bonners Ferry, ID 83805 .... (208)267-2242			
(Co Clk has m, div, pro, civ ct, Ind, mining rec, some b, d rec from 1915; State Bur Vit Statistics has b, d rec)			

Name	Map Index	Date Created	Parent County or Territory From Which Organized

Butte   F5   1917   Bingham, Blaine, Jefferson
Butte County, PO Box 737, Arco, ID 83213-0737 .... (208)527-3021
(Co Clk has m, bur, div, pro, school rec from 1917, civ ct rec from 1895, Ind rec from 1890)

Camas   G4   1917   Blaine
Camas County, PO Box 430, Fairfield, ID 83327-0430 .... (208)764-2242
(Co Clk has m, div & civ ct rec from 1917, bur rec incomplete; Bur of Vit Stat has b & d rec from 1941; Pro Ct has pro rec from 1890)

* **Canyon**   G3   1892   Owyhee, Ada
Canyon County, 1115 Albany St, Caldwell, ID 83605-3542 .... (208)454-7300
(Bur Vit Statistics, Boise has b, d rec; Co Clk has some b, d rec from 1907-1911, m rec from 1895, Ind rec from 1892, Dist Ct has div rec from 1892, Magistrate Ct has pro, civ ct rec from 1892)

* **Caribou**   G7   1919   Bannock, Oneida
Caribou County, PO Box 775, Soda Springs, ID 83276-0775 .... (208)547-4324
(Co Clk has m rec from 1919, div, pro, civ ct & Ind rec)

Cassia   H5   1879   Oneida
Cassia County, County Courthouse, Burley, ID 83318 .... (208)678-7302
(Co Clk has b, d rec 1908-1911, m, div, civ ct, Ind rec & pro rec from 1879)

*† **Clark**   F6   1919   Fremont
Clark County, PO Box 205, Dubois, ID 83423-0205 .... (208)374-5304
(State Bur Vit Statistics, Boise has b, d rec; Co Clk has m, div, civ ct, Ind rec from 1919)

Clearwater   C3   1911   Nez Perce
Clearwater County, PO Box 586, Orofino, ID 83544-0586 .... (208)476-3615
(Co Clk has m, div, pro, civ ct & Ind rec from 1911)

* **Custer**   F4   1881   Alturas
Custer County, PO Box 597, Challis, ID 83226 .... (208)879-2325
(Co Clk has m, div, civ ct & deeds rec from 1872; Bur Vit Stat has b & d rec; Cem Dis (Challis & Big Lost River) has bur rec; Pro Ct has pro rec)

* **Elmore**   G3   1889   Alturus, Ada
Elmore County, 150 S 4th East St, Mountain Home, ID 83647-3028 .... (208)587-2129
(Co Clk has b & d rec 1907-1911, m, div, pro, civ ct & Ind rec from 1889; City of Mtn Home has bur rec)

* **Franklin**   H6   1913   Oneida
Franklin County, 39 W Oneida St, Preston, ID 83263-1234 .... (208)852-1091
(Bur Vit Statistics, Boise has b, d rec; Co Clk has m rec from 1913)

* **Fremont**   F6   1893   Bingham, Lemhi
Fremont County, 151 W 1st North, Saint Anthony, ID 83445-1403 .... (208)624-7332
(Co Clk has m, div, pro, civ ct & Ind rec)

* **Gem**   F3   1915   Boise, Canyon
Gem County, 415 E Main St, Emmett, ID 83617-3049 .... (208)365-4561
(Co Clk has m, div, civ ct rec, Ind rec from 1915; Magistrate has pro rec from 1915)

Gooding   G4   1913   Lincoln
Gooding County, PO Box 417, Gooding, ID 83330-0417 .... (208)934-4221
(Bur Vit Statistics, Boise has b, d rec; Local cem dist has bur rec; Co Clk has m, div, pro, civ ct, Ind rec from 1913)

* **Idaho**   D3   1864   Original County
Idaho County, 320 W Main St, Grangeville, ID 83530-1948 .... (208)983-2751
(Co Clk has b & d rec from 1907 to 1911, m & Ind rec from 1862, div & civ ct rec from 1888)

* **Jefferson**   F6   1913   Fremont
Jefferson County, 134 N Clark St, Rigby, ID 83442-1437 .... (208)745-9222
(Co Clk has m, div, pro, civ ct, Ind rec from 1914)

Jerome   G4   1919   Gooding, Lincoln
Jerome County, 300 N Lincoln Ave, Jerome, ID 83338-2344 .... (208)324-8811
(Co Clk has m, div, pro, civ ct, Ind rec from 1919)

* **Kootenai**   B3   1864   Nez Perce
Kootenai County, 501 N Government Way, Coeur d'Alene, ID 83814-2990 .... (208)769-4400
(Created in 1864, but not organized or staffed until 1881. Co Clk has b & d rec from 1907 to 1912, m, div, pro & civ ct rec from 1881)

* **Latah**   C3   1888   Nez Perce
Latah County, 522 S Adams St, Moscow, ID 83843-2963 .... (208)882-8580
(Created & organized by U.S. congressional enactment, said to be the only Co in the U.S. so created. Co Clk has b & d rec from 1907 to 1911, m, div & civ ct rec from 1888)

*† **Lemhi**   E4   1869   Idaho
Lemhi County, 206 Courthouse Dr, Salmon, ID 83467-3992 .... (208)756-2815
(Co Clk has b & d rec 1907-1911, m, div, pro, civ ct & Ind rec from 1869)

* **Lewis**   D3   1911   Nez Perce
Lewis County, 510 Oak St, Nezperce, ID 83543 .... (208)937-2661
(Bur Vit Statistics, Boise has b, d, rec; cem districts have bur rec; Co Clk has m, div, pro, civ ct, Ind rec from 1911)

Name	Map Index	Date Created	Parent County or Territory From Which Organized

* **Lincoln**   G4   1895   Alturas
Lincoln County, 111 W 'B' St, Shoshone, ID   83352 .... (208)886-7641
(Bur Vit Statistics, Boise has b, d rec: Bergen Funeral Home has bur rec; Co Clk has some b, d rec 1895-1913, m, div, pro, civ ct, Ind rec from 1895, some school rec)

* **Madison**   F6   1913   Fremont
Madison County, PO Box 389, Rexburg, ID   83440-0389 .... (208)356-3662
(Bur Vit Statistics, Boise has b, d rec; Co Clk has m, div, pro, civ ct, Ind rec from 1914)

*† **Minidoka**   G5   1913   Lincoln
Minidoka County, 715 G St, Rupert, ID   83350 .... (208)436-9511
(Co Clk has m, div, pro, civ ct & Ind rec from 1913)

*† **Nez Perce**   D3   1861   Original county
Nez Perce County, PO Box 896, Lewiston, ID   83501-0896 .... (208)799-3090
(Co Clk has b & d rec 1900-1911, m, div, pro, civ ct and Ind rec from 1860)

* **Oneida**   H6   1865   Original county
Oneida County, 10 Court St, Malad City, ID   83252 .... (208)766-4116
(Co Clk has b rec from 1907 to 1911, m rec from 1866, div, pro, civ ct & Ind rec)

* **Owyhee**   H3   1863   Original county
Owyhee County, PO Box 128, Murphy, ID   83650-0128 .... (208)495-2421
(Co Clk has b & d rec from 1907 to 1913, m rec from 1895, div & civ ct rec from 1864, naturalization rec 1893-1911)

   Payette   F3   1917   Canyon
Payette County, PO Box D, Payette, ID   83661-0277 .... (208)642-6000
(Co Clk has m, div, pro, civ ct & Ind rec from 1917, and mil dischrg rec from 1919)

† **Power**   G6   1913   Bingham, Blaine, Oneida
Power County, 543 Bannock Ave, American Falls, ID   83211-1200 .... (208)226-7611
(Co Clk has m rec from 1914, div rec from 1916; Pro Ct has pro rec; Mag Ct has civ ct rec; Asr Office has Ind rec)

* **Shoshone**   C3   1864   Original county
Shoshone County, PO Box 1049, Wallace, ID   83873-1049 .... (208)752-3331
(Co Clk has b & d rec from 1907 to 1911, m from 1875, div from 1887, pro from 1885, civ ct from 1884 & Ind rec from 1871)

*† **Teton**   F7   1915   Madison, Fremont, Bingham
Teton County, PO Box 756, Driggs, ID   83422-0756 .... (208)354-2905
(Co Clk has m, div, pro, civ ct & Ind rec from 1916)

   Twin Falls   H4   1907   Cassia
Twin Falls County, PO Box 126, Twin Falls, ID   83303-0126 .... (208)736-4004
(Co Clk has m, div, pro, ct & Ind rec from 1907)

* **Valley**   E3   1917   Boise, Idaho
Valley County, PO Box 737, Cascade, ID   83611-0737 .... (208)382-4297
(Co Clk has m, div, pro, civ ct, Ind rec from 1917)

   Washington   F3   1879   Boise
Washington County, PO Box 670, Weiser, ID   83672-0670 .... (208)549-2092
(Bur Vit Statistics, Boise has b, d rec after 1911; Co Clk has b, d rec 1907-1911, m, div, pro, civ ct, Ind rec from 1879)

* At least one county history has been published about this county.
† Inventory of county archives was made by the Historical Records Survey. (See Introduction)

ILLINOIS

CAPITAL · SPRINGFIELD — TERRITORY 1809 — STATE 1818 (21st)
State Map on Page M-12

In 1673, Jacques Marquette and Louis Joliet became the first to explore Illinois. The French established permanent settlements in 1699 at Cahokia and 1703 at Kaskaskia. The Illinois area was ceded to Great Britain in 1763 after the French and Indian War. Many of the French settlers fled to St. Louis, Natchez, and other towns at this time. Virginians began to move into the region about 1769. The area was attached to Quebec in 1774.

During the Revolutionary War, George Rogers Clark captured Kaskaskia and Cahokia, securing the lands north of the Ohio River for the United States. Virginia claimed all the land north of the Ohio River for itself, but ceded it to the United States in 1784. In 1787, Illinois became part of the Northwest Territory. Three years later, Illinois became part of the Indiana Territory. The Illinois Territory was formed in 1809, with the Wisconsin region being transferred to the Michigan Territory in 1818.

The first settlers came by way of the Ohio River from North Carolina, Tennessee, Virginia, Kentucky, Maryland, and Pennsylvania and settled in the southern part of the state. The first blacks came with the French in 1719, but their numbers remained few until after the Civil War. At statehood in 1818, most of the population still resided in the southern part of the state. About 1825, settlers from the New England states and New York came on the Erie Canal, the Great Lakes, or the National Road to settle the northern portion of the state. Industrial growth in the 1830's and 1840's brought thousands of Irish, southern Europeans, and Germans to man the factories around Lake Michigan. The expulsion of Sauk and Fox warriors in 1832 ended the last Indian threats to settlement. Transportation improvements between 1838 and 1856, such as the National Road which reached Vandalia in 1838; the Illinois-Michigan Canal which opened in 1848; and the Illinois Central Railroad which was completed in 1856, stimulated migration into the state. The Mormons came to Illinois in 1839 and founded Nauvoo on the Mississippi River, which at one time was the state's most populous city. Illinois sent about 255,000 men to fight the Confederacy.

Statewide registration of births and deaths began in 1916. Certified copies can be issued only to legally authorized (related) persons, however uncertified copies can be issued for genealogical purposes. They are kept at the Office of Vital Records, State Department of Public Health, 605 West Jefferson Street, Springfield, IL 62702 (to verify current fees, call 217-782-6553). Some county clerks have birth and death records from 1877 to 1916, with a few as early as 1838. Marriage records are in the custody of the county clerks. Marriage licenses were not required until 1877, but some counties have records as early as 1790. Divorces were granted by the legislature and the circuit courts in the early 1800's. The Superior Court of Cook County in Chicago has custody of divorces and the county court clerks have custody of the divorce records. Counties with a population of more than 70,000 had probate courts prior to 1960. Counties with fewer people handled probate matters in the county court. Since 1960, probate matters have been handled by the circuit court. The court recorder of deeds handles all matters pertaining to real estate. Territorial and state censuses were taken in 1810, 1818, 1820, 1825, 1835, 1840, 1845, 1855, and 1865. Some residents were also listed in the 1807 Indiana Territorial census.

The Department of Veterans Affairs, 208 West Cook Street, Springfield, IL 62706, has files with names of about 600,000 veterans buried in Illinois, in alphabetical order by war. A cemetery listing, by county, lists veteran burials. An index file on peacetime soldiers and on those with unknown service is also here. Soldiers' discharge records are available at county courthouses. The State Archivist, Archives Building, Springfield, Il 62756, also has many useful records.

Genealogical Archives, Libraries and Societies

Assumption Public Library, 131 N. Chestnut, P. O. Box 227, Assumption, IL 62510-0227

Balzekas Museum of Lithuanian Culture, 6500 S. Pulaski, Chicago, IL 60632

Bryan-Bennett Library, 402 S. Broadway, Salem, IL 62881

Carnegie Public Library, 6th and Van Buren Sts., Charleston, IL 61920

Danville Public Library, 307 N. Vermilion St., Danville, IL 61832

DuPage County Historical Museum, 103 E. Wesley St., Wheaton, IL 60187

Ellwood House Museum (DeKalb County), 509 N. First St., DeKalb, IL 60115

Evans Public Library, 215 S. 5th St., Vandalia, IL 62471

Freeport Public Library, 314 W. Stephenson St., Freeport, IL 61032

Gail Borden Public Library, 200 North Grove Avenue, Elgin, IL 60120

Galena Historical Museum (Jo Daviess County), 211 S. Bench St., Galena, IL 61036

Galena Public Library, Galena, IL 61036

Galesburg Public Library, Galesburg, IL 61401

Glenview Public Library, 1930 Glenview Rd., Glenview, IL 60025

Illinois State Archives, Archives Bldg., Springfield, IL 62706

Illinois State Historical Library, Old State Capitol, Springfield, IL 62706

John Mosser Public Library, 106 W. Meek St., Abingdon, IL 61410

LaGrange Public Library, 10 W. Cossitt, LaGrange, IL 60525

Lake County, Illinois Genealogical Society, Cook Memorial Library, 413 N. Milwaukee Ave., Libertyville, IL 60048

Little Rock Township Public Library Genealogical Group. For information send SASE to Genealogy, Little Rock TWP. Library, N. Center Street, Plano, IL 60545

Lyons Public Library, 4209 Joliet Ave., Lyons, IL 60534

Madison County Historical Museum and Library, 715 N. Main St., Edwardsville, IL 62025

Mattoon Public Library, Charleston Avenue and 17th St., Mattoon, IL 61938

Newberry Library, 60 West Walton Street, Chicago, IL 60610

Peoria Public Library, 107 N.E. Monroe St., Peoria, IL 61602

Randolph County Genealogical Society Library, 600 State St., Room 306, Chester, IL 62233

Rock Island Public Library, Rock Island, IL 61201

Rockford Public Library, 215 N. Wyman St., Rockford, IL 61101

Schuyler County Historical Museum and Genealogical Center, Madison and Congress (or) Box 96, Rushville, IL 62681

Shawnee Library System, Rural Route 2, Box 136A, Carterville, IL 62918

Staunton Public Library, George and Santina Sawyer Genealogy Room, 306 W. Main, Staunton, IL 62088 Direct all correspondence concerning this collection to Macoupin County Genealogical Society, P. O. Box 95, Staunton, IL 62088

Three Rivers Public Library District-Local History Collection, P. O. Box 300, Channahon, IL 60410

University of Illinois Library, Urbana, IL 61801

Urbana Free Library, 201 So. Race St., Urbana, IL 61801

Vogel Genealogical Research Library, 305 1st Street, Box 132, Holcomb, IL 61043

Warren County Library, 60 West Side Square, Monmouth, IL 61462

Winnetka Public Library, 768 Oak St., Winnetka, IL 60093

Withers Public Library, 202 East Washington, Bloomington, IL 61701

Zion Benton Public Library, 2400 Gabriel Avenue, Zion, IL 60099

Blackhawk Genealogical Society, P. O. Box 3913, Rock Island, IL 61204-3913

Bloomington-Normal Genealogical Society, P. O. Box 488, Normal, IL 61761-0488

Bond County Genealogical Society, P. O. Box 172, Greenville, IL 62246

Bureau County Genealogical Society, P. O. Box 402, Princeton, IL 61356-0402

Carroll County Genealogical Society, P. O. Box 347, Savanna, IL 61074

Cass County Historical Society, P. O. Box 11, Virginia, IL 62691

Champaign County Genealogical Society, Urbana Free Library - Archives Room, 201 S. Race, Urbana, IL 61801

Chicago Genealogical Society, P. O. Box 1160, Chicago, IL 60690

Chicago Historical Society, North Ave. and Clark St., Chicago, IL 60614

Christian County Genealogical Society, P. O. Box 174, Taylorville, IL 62568

Clay County Genealogical Society, Box 94, Louisville, IL 62858

Clinton County Historical Society, 1091 Franklin Street, Carlyle, IL 62231

Coles County, Illinois Genealogical Society, P. O. Box 225, Charleston, IL 61920

Cumberland and Coles County of Illinois Genealogical Society, Rt. 1, Box 141, Toledo, IL 62468

Cumberland County Historical and Genealogical Society of Illinois, Greenup, IL 62428

Daughter of the Union Veterans of the Civil War 1861-65, 503 S. Walnut, Springfield, IL 62704

Decatur Genealogical Society, P. O. Box 1548, Decatur, IL 62525-1548

Des Plaines Historical Society, 789 Pearson St., Des Plaines, IL 60016

DeWitt County Genealogical Society, Box 329, Clinton, IL 61727

Douglas County Illinois Genealogical Society, P. O. Box 113, Tuscola, IL 61953

Dundee Township Historical Society, 426 Highland Avenue, Dundee, IL 60118

Dunton Genealogical Society, 500 North Dunton, Arlington Heights, IL 60004

Du Page County Genealogical Society, P. O. Box 133, Lomard, IL 60148

Edgar County Genealogical Society, P. O. Box 304, Driskell, Paris, IL 61944

Edwards County Historical Society, P. O. Box 205, Albion, IL 62806

Effingham County Genealogical Society, P. O. Box 1166, Effingham, IL 62401

Elgin Genealogical Society, P. O. Box 1418, Elgin, IL 60121-0818

Fayette County Genealogical Society, Box 177, Vandalia, IL 62471

Fellowship of Brethren Genealogists, 1451 Dundee Ave., Elgin, IL 60120

Forest Park Historical Society, Forest Park Library, 7555 Jackson Avenue, Forest Park, IL 60130

Fort La Motte Genealogical and Historical Society, LaMotte Township Library, Palestine, IL 62451

Fox Valley Genealogical Society, 705 N. Brainard Street, Naperville, IL 60563

Frankfort Area Genealogy Society, P. O. Box 463, West Frankfort, IL 62896

Freeburg Historical and Genealogical Society, Box 69, Freeburg, IL 62243

Fulton County Historical and Genealogical Society, 45 N. Park Drive, Canton, IL 61520

Genealogical Committee of the Stephenson County Historical Society, 110 Coates Pl., Freeport, IL 61032

Genealogical Forum of Elmhurst, Illinois, 120 E. Park, Elmhurst, IL 60126

Genealogical Society of DeKalb County, Illinois, P. O. Box 295, Sycamore, IL 60178

Genealogy Society of Southern Illinois, Route 2, Carterville, IL 62918

Great River Genealogical Society, Quincy Public Library, Quincy, IL 62302

Greater Harvard Area Historical Society, 301 Hart Blvd., P. O. Box 505, Harvard, IL 60033

Greene County Historical and Genealogical Society, P. O. Box 137, Carrollton, IL 62016

Hancock County Historical Society, Carthage, IL 62361

Henry County Genealogical Society, P. O. Box 346, Kewanee, IL 61443

Henry Historical and Genealogical Society, 610 North St., Henry, IL 61537

Illiana Genealogical and Historical Society, P. O. Box 207, Danville, IL 61834

Illiana Jewish Genealogical Society, 3033 Bob-O-Link Road, Flossmoor, IL 60422

Illinois Mennonite Historical and Genealogical Society, P. O. Box 819, Metamora, IL 61548

Illinois State Genealogical Society, P. O. Box 10195, Springfield, IL 62791

Iroquois County Genealogical Society, Old Courthouse Museum, 103 West Cherry St., Watseka, IL 60970

Jackson County Historical Society, Box 7, Murphysboro, IL 62966

Jacksonville Area Genealogical and Historical Society, P. O. Box 21, Jacksonville, IL 62651

Jasper County Genealogical and Historical Society, Newton Public Library, Newton, IL 62448

Jewish Genealogical Society of Illinois, 818 Mansfield Court, Schaumburg, IL 60194

Kane County Genealogical Society, P. O. Box 504, Geneva, IL 60134

Kankakee Valley Genealogical Society, 304 S. Indiana Ave., Kankakee, IL 60901

Kendall County Genealogical Society, P. O. Box 1086, Oswego, IL 60543

Kishwaukee Genealogists (Boone and Winnebago Counties), P. O. Box 5503, Rockford, IL 61125-0503

Knox County Illinois Genealogical Society, P. O. Box 13, Galesburg, IL 61402-0013

LaHarpe Historical and Genealogical Society, Box 289, LaHarpe, IL 61450

Lake County, Illinois Genealogical Society, Cook Memorial Library, 413 N. Milwaukee Ave., Libertyville, IL 60048

LaSalle County Genealogy Guild, Box 534, Ottawa, IL 61350

Lawrence County Genealogical Society, R , Box 44, Bridgeport, IL 62417

Lewis and Clark Genealogical Society, P. O. Box 485, Godfrey, IL 62035

Lexington Genealogical and Historical Society, 318 W. Main St., Lexington, IL 61753

Logan County Genealogical Society, P. O. Box 283, Lincoln, IL 62656

Macoupin County Genealogical Society, P. O. Box 95, Staunton, IL 62088

Madison County Genealogical Society, P. O. Box 631, Edwardsville, IL 62025-0631

Marion County Genealogical and Historical Society, P. O. Box 342, Salem, IL 62881

Marissa Historical and Genealogical Society, P. O. Box 27, Marissa, IL 62257

Marshall County Historical Society, 566 N. High St., Lacon, IL 61540

Mascoutah Historical Society, Mascoutah, IL 62258

Mason County Genealogical Society, P. O. Box 246, Havana, IL 62644

Mason County LDS Genealogical Project, R 1, Box 193, Havana, IL 62644

McDonough County Genealogical Society, P. O. Box 202, Macomb, IL 61455

McHenry County Illinois Genealogical Society, McHenry Library, P. O. Box 184, Crystal Lake, IL 60014-0184

McLean County Genealogical Society, P. O. Box 488, Normal, IL 61761

Mercer County Historical Society, Aledo, IL 61231

Mercer County Historical Society, Genealogical Division, Aledo, IL 61231

Montgomery County Genealogical Society, P. O. Box 212, Litchfield, IL 62056

Moultrie County Historical and Genealogical Society, P. O. Box MM, Sullivan, IL 61951

Mt. Vernon Genealogical Society, Mt. Vernon Public Library, 101 S. 7th, Mt. Vernon, IL 62864

National Archives-Great Lakes Region 7358 South Pulaski Road, Chicago, IL 60629

North Central Illinois Genealogical Society, P. O. Box 4635, Rockford, IL 61110-4635

North Suburban Genealogical Society, Winnetka Public Library, 768 Oak Street, Winnetka, IL 60093

Northwest Suburban Council of Genealogists, P. O. Box AC, Mt. Prospect, IL 60056

Odell Historical and Genealogical Society, P. O. Box 82, Odell, IL 60460

Ogle County Illinois Genealogical Society, P. O. Box 251, Oregon, IL 61061

Ogle County Historical Society, 6th and Franklin Streets, Oregon, IL 61061

Palatines to America, Illinois Chapter, P. O. Box 3884, Quincy, IL 62305

Peoria Genealogical Society, P. O. Box 1489, Peoria, IL 61655

Peoria Historical Society, 942 N.E. Glen Oak Ave., Peoria, IL 61600

Piatt County Historical and Genealogical Society, P. O. Box 111, Monticello, IL 61856

Pike and Calhoun Counties Genealogical Society, Box 104, Pleasant Hill, IL 62366

Polish Genealogical Society, 984 Milwaukee Ave., Chicago, IL 60622

Putnam County Historical Society, P. O. Box 74, Hennepin, IL 61327

Randolph County Genealogical Society, 600 State St., Room 306, Chester, IL 62233

Richfield County, Illinois Genealogical Society, Box 202, Olney, IL 62450

Richland County Genealogical and Historical Society, Box 202, Olney, IL 62450

Rock Island County Historical Society, P. O. Box 632, Moline, IL 61265

Saline County Genealogical Society, P. O. Box 4, Harrisburg, IL 62946

Sangamon County Genealogical Society, P. O. Box 1829, Springfield, IL 62705

Schuyler-Brown Historical and Genealogical Society, P. O. Box 96, Rushville, IL 62681

Shelby County Historical and Genealogical Society, 151 South Washington, Shelbyville, IL 62565

South Suburban Genealogical and Historical Society, P. O. Box 96, South Holland, IL 60473

Stark County Historical Society, West Jefferson, Toulon, IL 61483

St. Clair County, Illinois Genealogical Society, P. O. Box 431, Bellevile, IL 62222

Stephenson County Genealogy Society, P. O. Box 514, Freeport, IL 61032

Stephenson County Historical Society, 110 Coates Place, Freeport, IL 61032

Sterling-Rock Falls Historical Society, 1005 E. 3rd St., P. O. Box 65, Sterling, IL 61081

Swedish American Historical Society, 5125 No. Spaulding Avenue, Chicago, IL 60625

Tazewell County Genealogical Society, P. O. Box 312, Pekin, IL 61554

Thornton Township Historical Society, Genealogical Section, 154 East 154th St., Harvey, IL 60426

Tinley Moraine Genealogists, 16801 80th Ave., Tinley Park, IL 60477

Tree Climbers Society, 2906 Dove St., Rolling Meadows, IL 60008

Tri-County Genealogical Society, P. O. Box 355, Augusta, IL 62311

Union County Genealogical / Historical Research Committee, 101 East Spring St., Anna, IL 62906

Warren County Genealogical Society, P. O. Box 240, Monmouth, IL 61462 Waverly Genealogical and Historical Society, Waverly, IL 62692.

Whiteside County Genealogists, Box 145, Sterling, IL 61081.

Will-Grundy Counties Genealogical Society, P. O. Box 24, Wilmington, IL 60481.

Winnebago and Boone Counties Genealogical Society, P. O. Box 10166, Rockford, IL 61131-0166.

Zion Genealogical Society, Zion Benton Public Library, 2400 Gabriel Avenue, Zion, IL 60099.

Printed Census Records and Mortality Schedules

Federal Census 1820, 1830, 1840, 1850, 1860, 1870, 1880, 1890 (part of McDonough County only), 1900, 1910

Federal Mortality Schedules 1850, 1860, 1870, 1880

State/Territorial Census 1810, 1818, 1820, 1825, 1835, 1845, 1855, 1865

Valuable Printed Sources

Atlases, Maps, and Gazetteers

Adams, James N. *Illinois Place Names*. Springfield, Illinois: Illinois State Historical Society, 1968.

Atlas of the State of Illinois. Knightstown, Indiana: Mayhill Publications, 1972 reprint.

Illinois Sesquicentennial Commission. *Illinois Guide and Gazetteer*. Chicago: Rand McNally, 1969.

Bibliographies

Byrd, Cecil K. *A Bibliography of Illinois Imprints*. Chicago: University of Chicago Press, 1966.

Irons, Victoria, and Patricia C. Brennan. *Descriptive Inventory of the Archives of the State of Illinois*. Springfield, Illinois: Illinois State Archives, 1978.

Newspapers in the Illinois State Historical Library. Springfield, Illinois: Illinois State Historical Library, 1979.

Sinko, Peggy Tuck. *Guide to Local and Family History at the Newberry Library*. Salt Lake City: Ancestry, 1987.

Turnbaugh, Roy C. *A Guide to County Records in the Illinois Regional Archives*. Springfield, Illinois: The Illinois State Archives, 1983.

Genealogical Research Guides

Bowers, Doris R. *Directory of Illinois Genealogical Societies*. Springfield, Illinois: Illinois State Genealogical Society, 1980.

Kozub, Mary Lou. *Searching in Illinois: A Reference Guide to Public and Private Records*. Costa Mesa, California: ISC Publications, 1984.

Volkel, Lowell M. and Marjorie Smith. *How to Research a Family with Illinois Roots*. Thomson, Illinois: Heritage House, 1977.

Wolf, Joseph C. *A Reference Guide for Genealogical and Historical Research in Illinois*. Detroit: Detroit Society for Genealogical Research, 1963.

Histories

Bateman, Newton. *Historical Encyclopedia of Illinois*. Chicago: Munsell Publishing Co., 1925.

Smith, George W. *History of Illinois and Her People*. Chicago: American Historical Society, 1927.

ILLINOIS COUNTY DATA
State Map on Page M-12

Name	Map Index	Date Created	Parent County or Territory From Which Organized
*† **Adams**	E1	1825	Pike
Adams County, 521 Vermont St, Quincy, IL 62301-2934 . . . . (217)223-6300			
(Co Clk has b & d rec from 1878, m rec from 1825; Clk Cir Ct has div, pro & civ ct rec)			
* **Alexander**	I4	1819	Johnson
Alexander County, 2000 Washington Ave, Cairo, IL 62914-1717 . . . . (618)734-3947			
(Co Clk has b, d rec from 1878, m Ind rec from 1819; Clk Cir Ct has div, pro, civ ct rec)			
* **Bond**	G3	1817	Madison
Bond County, PO Box 407, Greenville, IL 62246-0407 . . . . (618)664-0449			
(Co Clk has b, d rec from 1877, m rec from 1817, Ind rec from 1870 discharge rec; Clk Cir Ct has div, pro, civ ct rec)			
* **Boone**	A4	1837	Winnebago
Boone County, 601 N Main St, Belvidere, IL 61008-2600 . . . . (815)544-3103			
(Co Clk has b, m, d rec from 1877, Ind rec from 1843; Clk Cir Ct has div, pro, civ ct rec)			
*† **Brown**	E2	1839	Schuyler
Brown County, 21 W Court St, Mount Sterling, IL 62353-1241 . . . . (217)773-3421			
(Co Clk has b, m, d & Ind rec; Clk Cir Ct has div, pro & civ ct rec)			

Name	Map Index	Date Created	Parent County or Territory From Which Organized

* **Bureau**   C3   1837   Putnam
  Bureau County, County Courthouse, Princeton, IL 61356 .... (815)875-2014
  (Co Clk has m, d rec from 1880, m rec from 1838, lnd rec from 1837, bur permits from 1971)

* **Calhoun**   F2   1825   Pike
  Calhoun County, County Rd, Hardin, IL 62047 .... (618)576-2351
  (Co Clk has b & d rec from 1877, m & lnd rec from 1825)

*† **Carroll**   B3   1839   Jo Daviess
  Carroll County, Rt 78 & Rapp Rd, Mount Carroll, IL 61053 .... (815)244-9171
  (Co Clk has b & d rec from 1877, m rec from 1839 & lnd rec)

* **Cass**   E2   1837   Morgan
  Cass County, County Courthouse, Virginia, IL 62691 .... (217)452-7217
  (Co Clk has b rec from 1860, m rec from 1837, d rec from 1878, lnd rec; Cir Clk has div, pro & civ ct rec)

*† **Champaign**   D5   1833   Vermillion
  Champaign County, 204 E Elm St, Urbana, IL 61801-3324 .... (217)384-3720
  (Co Clk has b & d rec from 1878, m rec from 1833)

* **Christian**   E4   1839   Sangamon, Shelby
  Christian County, 600 N Main St, Taylorville, IL 62568-1599 .... (217)824-4969
  (formerly Dane) (Co Clk has b & d rec from 1878, m rec from 1840, lnd rec from 1856; Clk Cir Ct has div, pro, & civ ct rec from 1875)

*† **Clark**   F6   1819   Crawford
  Clark County, 501 Archer Ave, Marshall, IL 62441-1275 .... (217)826-8311
  (Co Clk has b, d rec from 1877, m rec from 1819, lnd rec from 1818; Local Register has bur rec; Clk Cir Ct has div, pro, civ ct rec)

* **Clay**   G5   1824   Wayne, Lawrence, Fayette
  Clay County, County Courthouse, Louisville, IL 62858 .... (618)665-3626
  (Co Clk has b, d & bur rec from 1878, m rec from 1824, lnd rec from 1825, mil dischrg, entry bks; Clk Cir Ct has div, pro & civ ct rec)

* **Clinton**   G3   1824   Washington, Bond, Fayette, Crawford
  Clinton County, 850 Fairfax County Courthouse, Carlyle, IL 62231 .... (618)594-2464
  (Co Clk has b, d rec from 1877, m rec from 1825, lnd rec from 1818; Clk Cir Ct has div, pro, civ ct rec)

* **Coles**   F5   1830   Clark, Edgar
  Coles County, PO Box 207, Charleston, IL 61920-0207 .... (217)348-0501
  (Co Clk has b, d rec from 1878, m, lnd rec from 1830; Bur Vit Statistics Springfield has b, m, d rec from 1916)

* **Cook**   B5   1831   Putnam
  Cook County, 118 N Clark St Suite 567, Chicago, IL 60602-1311 .... (312)443-6398
  (Co Clk has b, m, d & bur rec from 1871)

* **Crawford**   F6   1816   Edwards
  Crawford County, Douglas St, Robinson, IL 62454-2146 .... (618)546-1212
  (Co Clk has b & d rec from 1877, m rec from 1817, lnd rec from 1816, bur rec from 1975; Clk Cir Ct has div, pro & civ ct rec; phys cert, old school rec and tax rec are available)

*† **Cumberland**   F5   1843   Coles
  Cumberland County, Courthouse Sq, Toledo, IL 62468 .... (217)849-2631
  (Co Clk has b, m, d, bur & lnd rec from 1885; Clk Cir Ct has div, pro & civ ct rec from 1885)

  Dane   1839   Name changed in 1840 to Christian County

* **DeKalb**   B4   1837   Kane
  DeKalb County, 110 E Sycamore St, Sycamore, IL 60178-1497 .... (815)895-9161
  (Co Clk has b, d rec 1878-1916 not complete, from 1916 complete, m, lnd rec from 1837, naturalization rec from 1850, poll bk recs from 1858-1872, War Patient rec 1845-1856; Clk Cir Ct has div, civ ct rec from 1850, pro rec from 1859. DeKalb Co Gen Soc has person who will research this county's records for a small fee; cem rec are available for all of county)

*† **DeWitt**   D4   1839   Macon, McLean
  DeWitt County, 201 W Washington St, Clinton, IL 61727-1639 .... (217)935-2119
  (Co Clk has b, d & bur rec from 1877, m & lnd rec from 1839; Clk Cir Ct has div, pro & civ ct rec from 1839)

*† **Douglas**   E5   1859   Coles
  Douglas County, 401 S Center St, Tuscola, IL 61953-1603 .... (217)253-2411
  (Co Clk has b, m, d & lnd rec from 1859; Clk Cir Ct has div, pro & civ ct rec)

* **Du Page**   B5   1839   Cook
  Du Page County, 421 N County Farm Rd, Wheaton, IL 60187-3978 .... (708)682-7035
  [FHL has some m & cem rec]

* **Edgar**   E6   1823   Clark
  Edgar County, County Courthouse, Paris, IL 61944 .... (217)465-4151
  [FHL has some b, m, d, cem, lnd, nat, pro rec]

* **Edwards**   G5   1814   Madison, Gallatin
  Edwards County, 50 E Main St, Albion, IL 62806-1262 .... (618)445-2115
  (Co Clk has b, d rec from 1877, m, lnd rec from 1815; Clk Cir Ct has div, pro, civ ct rec)

*† **Effingham**   F4   1831   Fayette, Crawford
  Effingham County, PO Box 628, Effingham, IL 62401-0628 .... (217)342-6535
  (Co Clk has b, d rec from 1878 [very incomplete prior to 1916], m rec from 1834, lnd rec from 1833; Clk Cir Ct has div, pro, civ ct rec)

Name	Map Index	Date Created	Parent County or Territory From Which Organized

*† **Fayette** F4 1821 Bond, Wayne, Clark, Jefferson
Fayette County, 221 S 7th St, Vandalia, IL 62471-2755 .... (618)283-5000
(Co Clk has b, d rec from 1877, m, Ind rec from 1821; Clk Cir Ct has div, pro, civ ct rec)

* **Ford** D5 1859 Clark
Ford County, 200 W State St Rm 101, Paxton, IL 60957-1145 .... (217)379-2721
(Co Clk has b & d rec from 1878, m & Ind rec from 1859; Clk Cir Ct has div, pro & civ ct rec)

*† **Franklin** H4 1818 White, Gallatin
Franklin County, Public Sq, Benton, IL 62812-2264 .... (618)438-3221
(Co Clk has b & d rec from 1877, m rec from 1836, pro & civ ct rec from 1838)

* **Fulton** D2 1823 Pike
Fulton County, 100 N Main St, Lewistown, IL 61542-1445 .... (309)547-3041
(Co Clk has b & d rec from 1878, m rec from 1824, Ind rec from 1823; Clk Cir Ct has div, pro & civ ct rec)

* **Gallatin** H5 1812 Randolph
Gallatin County, PO Box K, Shawneetown, IL 62984-0550 .... (618)269-3025
(Co Clk has b, d rec from 1878, m rec from 1830, Ind rec from 1800; Clk Cir Ct has pro rec from 1860)

* **Greene** F2 1821 Madison
Greene County, 519 N Main St, Carrollton, IL 62016-1033 .... (217)942-5443
(Co Clk has b & d rec from 1877, m rec from 1821, Ind rec from 1821, & mil rec from 1862)

* **Grundy** C5 1841 LaSalle
Grundy County, 111 E Washington St, Morris, IL 60450-2268 .... (815)942-9024
(Co Clk has b rec from 1877, d rec from 1878, m, Ind rec from 1841, bur rec from 1976; Clk Cir Ct has div, pro civ ct rec from 1841)

* **Hamilton** H4 1821 White
Hamilton County, Public Sq, McLeansboro, IL 62859-1489 .... (618)643-2721
(Co Clk has b, m, d, bur, div & pro rec from 1821)

* **Hancock** D1 1825 Pike, Unorg. Terr
Hancock County, Courthouse Sq, Carthage, IL 62321-1359 .... (217)357-3911
[FHL has some b, m, cem, civ ct, pro, Ind, nat, tax rec]

* **Hardin** I5 1839 Pope
Hardin County, Main St, Elizabethtown, IL 62931 .... (618)287-2251
(Co Clk has b, m, d & bur rec from 1884, Ind rec from 1880; Clk Cir Ct has div, pro & civ ct rec from 1880)

* **Henderson** C2 1841 Warren
Henderson County, PO Box 308, Oquawka, IL 61469-0308 .... (309)867-2911
(Co Clk has b, m, d rec from 1878, Ind rec from 1841; Clk Cir Ct has div, pro, civ ct rec from 1841)

* **Henry** C2 1825 Fulton
Henry County, 100 S Main, Cambridge, IL 61238 .... (309)937-2426
(Co Clk has incomplete b & d rec from 1877, m rec from 1837, Ind rec from 1835; Clk Cir Ct has div, pro & civ ct rec from 1880, naturalization rec 1870-1940)

* **Iroquois** D5 1833 Vermillion
Iroquois County, 550 S 10th, Watseka, IL 60970-1810 .... (815)432-6960
(Co Clk has b & d rec from 1878, m rec from 1868, Ind rec from 1835; Clk Cir Ct has div & civ ct rec from 1855, pro rec from 1865; Old Courthouse Museum in Watseka may have some records)

*† **Jackson** H3 1816 Randolph, Johnson
Jackson County, 1001 Walnut St, Murphysboro, IL 62966-2177 .... (618)684-2151
(Co Clk has b, d & bur rec from 1872, m rec from 1842, & Ind rec; Clk Cir Ct has div, pro & civ ct rec)

* **Jasper** F5 1831 Clay, Crawford
Jasper County, 100 W Jourdan St, Newton, IL 62448-1973 .... (618)783-3124
(Co Clk has b & d rec from 1877, m & Ind rec from 1835; Clk Cir Ct has div, pro & civ ct rec)

* **Jefferson** G4 1819 Edwards, White
Jefferson County, County Courthouse Rm 105, Mount Vernon, IL 62864-4086 .... (618)244-8020
(Co Clk has b rec from 1878, d rec from 1877, m & Ind rec from 1819)

* **Jersey** F2 1839 Greene
Jersey County, 201 W Pearl St, Jerseyville, IL 62052-1675 .... (618)498-5571
(Co Clk has b & d rec from 1878, m & Ind rec from 1839, div rec from 1840, pro rec from 1850 & civ ct rec from 1845)

*† **Jo Daviess** A3 1827 Henry, Mercer, Putnam
Jo Daviess County, 330 N Bench St, Galena, IL 61036-1828 .... (815)777-0161
(Co Clk has b rec from 1877, a few before this date, m rec from 1830, d rec from 1877; d rec state place of bur; Cir Clk has pro rec from 1830, div & civ ct rec from 1850, & Ind rec from 1828)

* **Johnson** I4 1812 Randolph
Johnson County, PO Box 96, Vienna, IL 62995-0096 .... (618)658-3611
(Co Clk has b, d rec from 1878, m rec from 1834, Ind rec from 1815; Clk Cir Ct has div, pro, civ ct rec)

* **Kane** B5 1836 LaSalle
Kane County, 100 S 3rd St, Geneva, IL 60134-2722 .... (708)232-3400
(Co Clk has b, d rec from 1878, m rec from 1836; Clk Cir Ct has div, pro, civ ct rec)

* **Kankakee** C5 1853 Iroquois, Will
Kankakee County, 450 E Court St, Kankakee, IL 60901-3997 .... (815)937-2990
(Co Clk has b, d rec from 1878, m rec from 1853, div, pro, civ ct, Ind rec)

Name	Map Index	Date Created	Parent County or Territory From Which Organized

* **Kendall** B5 1841 LaSalle, Kane
  Kendall County, 110 W Ridge St, Yorkville, IL 60560-1432 ....(708)553-4104
  (Co Clk has b & d rec from 1878, m & lnd rec from 1841; Clk Cir Ct has div, pro & civ ct rec)

*† **Knox** C2 1825 Fulton
  Knox County, 200 S Cherry St, Galesburg, IL 61401-4991 ....(309)343-3121
  (Co Clk has b & d rec from 1878, m rec from 1830)

* **Lake** A5 1839 McHenry
  Lake County, 18 N County St, Waukegan, IL 60085-4339 ....(708)360-6600
  (Co Clk has b rec from 1871, m rec from 1839 & d rec from 1877; Clk Cir Ct has div, pro, civ ct rec; Rcdr Deeds has lnd rec)

* **LaSalle** C4 1831 Putnam, Vermillion
  LaSalle County, 707 E Etna Rd, Ottawa, IL 61350-1033 ....(815)434-8202
  (Co Clk has b & d rec from 1877, m from 1832; Clk Cir Ct has div & civ ct rec; Pro Office has pro rec; Rec of Deeds has lnd rec)

* **Lawrence** G6 1821 Crawford, Edwards
  Lawrence County, County Courthouse, Lawrenceville, IL 62439 ....(618)943-2346
  (Co Clk has b rec from 1877, d rec from 1878, m, lnd rec from 1821; City Clks has bur rec; Clk Cir Ct has div, pro, civ ct rec; Co Clk has cem book)

* **Lee** B4 1839 Ogle
  Lee County, Galena & 3rd Sts, Dixon, IL 61021 ....(815)288-3309
  (Co Clk has b rec from 1878, m rec from 1839, d rec from 1877, lnd rec from 1852; Clk Cir Ct has div, pro & civ ct rec)

*† **Livingston** C4 1837 LaSalle, McLean
  Livingston County, 112 W Madison St, Pontiac, IL 61764-1871 ....(815)844-5166
  (Co Clk has b rec from 1878, a few from 1856-1877, d rec from 1878, m & lnd rec from 1837, bur rec from 1878, mil dischrg from 1861; Clk Cir Ct has div, pro & civ ct rec)

*† **Logan** E3 1839 Sangamon
  Logan County, 601 Broadway St, Lincoln, IL 62656-2732 ....(217)732-4148
  (Co Clk has b, d rec from 1879, m rec from 1859, lnd rec from 1849; Clk Cir Ct has div, pro, civ ct rec; City Clk has bur rec)

*† **Macon** E4 1829 Shelby
  Macon County, 253 E Wood St Rm 52, Decatur, IL 62523-1488 ....(217)424-1305
  (Co Clk has b rec from 1850, m rec from 1829, d rec from 1877, bur rec from 1 Jan 1964; Clk Cir Ct has div, pro, civ ct rec)

*† **Macoupin** F3 1829 Madison, Greene
  Macoupin County, County Courthouse, Carlinville, IL 62626 ....(217)854-3214
  (Co Clk has b & d rec from 1877, m & lnd rec from 1829; Clk Cir Ct has div, pro & civ ct rec)

* **Madison** G3 1812 St. Clair
  Madison County, 155 N Main St, Edwardsville, IL 62025-1999 ....(618)692-6290
  (Co Clk has b rec from 1860, m rec from 1913 & d rec from 1878; Clk Cir Ct has div, pro & civ ct rec)

* **Marion** G4 1823 Fayette, Jefferson
  Marion County, Broadway & Main St, Salem, IL 62881 ....(618)548-3400
  (Co Clk has b rec from 1878, m rec from 1821, d rec from 1877 & lnd rec from 1823; Clk Cir Ct has div & civ ct rec from 1858, pro rec from 1840)

* **Marshall** C3 1839 Putnam
  Marshall County, 122 N Prairie St, Lacon, IL 61540-1216 ....(309)246-6325
  (Co Clk has a few b, d rec from 1877, m rec from 1840, lnd rec; Clk Cir Ct has div, pro, civ ct rec)

* **Mason** D3 1841 Tazewell, Menard
  Mason County, County Courthouse, Havana, IL 62644 ....(309)543-6661
  (Co Clk has b, d rec from 1877, m, lnd rec from 1841; City Clk has bur rec; Clk Cir Ct has div, pro, civ ct rec)

* **Massac** I4 1843 Pope, Johnson
  Massac County, PO Box 429, Metropolis, IL 62960-0429 ....(618)524-5213
  (Co Clk has b rec from 1864, m rec from 1854, d rec from 1878, bur rec from 1977, lnd rec from 1843)

* **McDonough** D2 1826 Schuyler
  McDonough County, County Courthouse, Macomb, IL 61455 ....(309)833-2474
  (Co Clk has b, d rec from 1877, m rec from 1830, lnd rec from 1812; City Clk has bur rec; Clk Cir Ct has div, pro, civ ct rec)

* **McHenry** A5 1836 Cook
  McHenry County, 2200 N Seminary Ave, Woodstock, IL 60098-2621 ....(815)338-2040
  (Co Clk has b & d rec from 1877, m rec from 1837; Rcdr Deeds has mil ser rec, deeds & lnd rec from 1841; Clk Cir Ct has div & civ ct rec from 1836, & pro rec from 1840)

* **McLean** D4 1830 Tazewell, Unorg. Terr
  McLean County, 104 W Front St, Bloomington, IL 61701-5091 ....(309)888-5001
  (Co Clk has b rec from 1860, m from 1830 & d rec from 1878; Clk Cir Ct has div, pro & civ ct rec; Co Rcdr has lnd rec)

*† **Menard** E3 1839 Sangamon
  Menard County, PO Box 456, Petersburg, IL 62675-0456 ....(217)632-2415
  (Co Clk has b & d rec from 1877, m & lnd rec from 1839; Clk Cir Ct has div, pro & civ ct rec from 1839)

* **Mercer** C2 1825 Unorg. Terr., Pike
  Mercer County, College Ave & SW 3rd St, Aledo, IL 61231 ....(309)582-7021
  (Co Clk has b & d rec from 1877, m & lnd rec from 1835 & bur rec from 1916; Clk Cir Ct has div, pro & civ ct rec)

Name	Map Index	Date Created	Parent County or Territory From Which Organized
* **Monroe**	H2	1816	Randolph, St. Clair

Monroe County, 100 S Main St, Waterloo, IL 62298-1399 .... (618)939-8681
(Co Clk has b rec from 1850, d & bur rec from 1900, m & Ind rec from 1816; Clk Cir Ct has pro rec from 1845, civ ct rec from 1843, and div rec)

| *† **Montgomery** | F3 | 1821 | Bond, Madison |

Montgomery County, 1 Courthouse Sq, Hillsboro, IL 62049-1137 .... (217)532-9530
(Co Clk has b, d rec from Dec. 1877, m, Ind rec from 1821; Clk Cir Ct has div, pro, civ ct rec)

| *† **Morgan** | E3 | 1823 | Sangamon |

Morgan County, 300 W State St, Jacksonville, IL 62650-2063 .... (217)245-4619
(Co Clk has b, d, bur rec from 1878, m rec from 1827, div rec from 1831, pro rec from 1836, civ ct rec from 1828)

| *† **Moultrie** | E4 | 1843 | Shelby, Macon |

Moultrie County, Courthouse, Sullivan, IL 61951 .... (217)728-4389
(Co Clk has b rec from 1859, m, Ind rec from 1840, d rec from 1877, bur rec from 1961; Clk Cir Ct has div, pro, civ ct rec)

| *† **Ogle** | B4 | 1836 | Jo Daviess |

Ogle County, PO Box 357, Oregon, IL 61061-0357 .... (815)732-3201
(Co Clk has b rec from 1860, d rec from 1878, m & Ind rec from 1837; Clk Cir Ct has div, pro & civ ct rec)

| *† **Peoria** | D3 | 1825 | Fulton |

Peoria County, 324 Main St Rm 101, Peoria, IL 61602-1319 .... (309)672-6059
(Co Clk has b & d rec from 1877, m rec from 1825; Clk Cir Ct has div, pro & civ ct rec; Rec of Deeds has Ind rec; census taken of Peoria twp in 1888 & 1899)

| * **Perry** | H3 | 1827 | Randolph, Jackson |

Perry County, Town Sq, Pinckneyville, IL 62274 .... (618)357-5116
(Co Clk has incom b rec from 1879, com from 1916 to present, m rec incom from 1827, d rec from 1879; Cir Clk has div, pro & civ ct rec from 1827)

| *† **Piatt** | E4 | 1841 | DeWitt, Macon |

Piatt County, 101 W Washington St, Monticello, IL 61856-1650 .... (217)762-9487
(Co Clk has b, d rec from 1877, m rec from 1841, Ind rec from 1852; Clk Cir Ct has div, pro, civ ct rec from 1841)

| *† **Pike** | E2 | 1821 | Madison, Bond, Clark |

Pike County, Rt 36, Pittsfield, IL 62363 .... (217)285-6812
(Co Clk has b, d rec from 1877, m rec from 1827, Ind rec from 1821; Clk Cir Ct has div, pro & civ ct rec)

| * **Pope** | I4 | 1816 | Gallatin, Johnson |

Pope County, PO Box 216, Golconda, IL 62938-0216 .... (618)683-4466
(Co Clk has b rec from 1877, some earlier from 1862, d rec from 1878, m & Ind rec from 1816, pro rec 1816-1950, 1845 and 1865 state census, mil dischrg from 1865, militia roll from 1861-62; Clk Cir Ct has pro rec from 1950, civ ct rec from 1816, div & naturalization rec)

| * **Pulaski** | I4 | 1843 | Johnson |

Pulaski County, PO Box 218, Mound City, IL 62963-0218 .... (618)748-9360
(Co Clk has b rec from 1866, m rec from 1861, d rec from 1882, bur rec from 1950, tax rec from 1851; Cir Clk has div, pro & civ ct rec)

| * **Putnam** | C4 | 1825 | Fulton |

Putnam County, 4th St, Hennepin, IL 61327 .... (815)925-7129
(Co Clk has b & d rec from 1878, m, pro & civ ct rec from 1831)

| * **Randolph** | H3 | 1795 | NW Territory, St. Clair |

Randolph County, 1 Taylor St, Chester, IL 62233 .... (618)826-2510
(Co Clk has b rec from 1857, d rec from 1877, m rec from 1804, Ind rec from 1724, & bur rec; Cir Clk has pro & civ ct rec from 1809)

| * **Richland** | G5 | 1841 | Clay, Lawrence |

Richland County, Main St, Olney, IL 62450 .... (618)392-3111
(Co Clk has b & d rec from 1878, m rec from 1841; Clk Cir Ct has div, pro & civ ct rec)

| *† **Rock Island** | C2 | 1831 | Jo Daviess |

Rock Island County, 1504 3rd Ave, Rock Island, IL 61201-8646 .... (309)786-4451
(Co Clk has b, d rec from 1877, m rec from 1833, tax collector rec from 1870, Supervisor's rec from July 1833; Co Rcdr has Ind rec; Clk Cir Ct has div, pro, civ ct rec; Local registrar has bur rec)

| *† **Saint Clair** | G3 | 1790 | NW Territory |

Saint Clair County, 10 Public Sq, Belleville, IL 62220-1698 .... (618)277-6600
(Co Clk has b, m, d & bur rec)

| *† **Saline** | H4 | 1847 | Gallatin |

Saline County, 10 E Poplar St, Harrisburg, IL 62946-1553 .... (618)253-8197
(Co Clk has b rec from 1877, d rec from 1878, m & Ind rec from 1848; Clk Cir Ct has div, pro & civ ct rec; City Clk has bur rec)

| *† **Sangamon** | E3 | 1821 | NW Territory |

Sangamon County, 800 E Monroe St, Springfield, IL 62701-1979 .... (217)753-6600
(Co Clk has b & d rec from 1877, m rec from 1821)

| * **Schuyler** | D2 | 1825 | Pike, Fulton |

Schuyler County, PO Box 190, Rushville, IL 62681-0190 .... (217)322-4734
(Co Clk has b & d rec from 1877, m rec from 1825, & Ind rec; Clk Cir Ct has div, pro, civ ct rec; Schuyler Co Jail Museum gen lib has m rec from 1825, b & d rec, obits from 1856, tax, school, mil, census, cem rec, fam rec & pub genealogies)

Name	Map Index	Date Created	Parent County or Territory From Which Organized

*† **Scott**   E2   1839   Morgan
Scott County, 101 E Market St, Winchester, IL 62694-1258 . . . . (217)742-3178
(Co Clk has b rec from 1860, d rec from 1877, m Ind rec from 1839, Clk Cir Ct has div, pro, civ ct rec)

*† **Shelby**   F4   1827   Fayette
Shelby County, 324 E Main St, Shelbyville, IL 62565-1694 . . . . (217)774-4421
(Co Clk has b rec from 1848, m rec from 1827, d rec from 1878, Ind rec from 1833; Clk Cir Ct has pro rec)

* **Stark**   C3   1839   Knox, Putnam
Stark County, 130 W Main St, Toulon, IL 61483 . . . . (309)286-5911
(Co Clk has b rec from 1855, m rec from 1839 & d rec from 1878; Clk Cir Ct has div, pro & civ ct rec)

*† **Stephenson**   A3   1837   Jo Daviess, Winnebago
Stephenson County, 15 N Galena Ave, Freeport, IL 61032-4390 . . . . (815)235-8289
(Co Clk has m & d rec from 1878, m rec from 1837, pro & civ ct rec from 1894 & Ind rec from 1837)

* **Tazewell**   D3   1827   Sangamon
Tazewell County, 4th & Court Sts, Pekin, IL 61554 . . . . (309)477-2264
(Co Clk has b & d rec from 1878, m rec from 1827; Cir Clk has bur, div, pro & civ ct rec; Rec of Deeds has Ind rec)

* **Union**   I4   1818   Johnson
Union County, 311 W Market St, Jonesboro, IL 62952 . . . . (618)833-5711
(Co Clk has b rec from 1862, d rec from 1877, m, Ind rec from 1818)

*† **Vermilion**   D6   1826   Unorg. Terr., Edgar
Vermilion County, 7 N Vermilion St, Danville, IL 61832-5806 . . . . (217)431-2555
(Co Clk has b rec from 1858, m rec from 1826, d rec from 1877 & bur rec from 1900)

* **Wabash**   G5   1824   Edwards
Wabash County, 4th & Market St, Mount Carmel, IL 62863-1582 . . . . (618)262-4561
(Co Clk has b & d rec from 1877, m & Ind rec from 1857, pro & civ ct rec 1857-1965, cem & naturalization rec; Clk Cir Ct has div rec)

* **Warren**   C2   1825   Pike
Warren County, Public Sq, Monmouth, IL 61462 . . . . (309)734-8592
(Co Clk has b, d rec from 1875, m rec from 1830; Clk Cir Ct has pro, civ ct rec from 1825)

* **Washington**   G3   1818   St. Clair
Washington County, Saint Louis St, Nashville, IL 62263-1599 . . . . (618)327-8314
(Co Clk has b, d, bur rec from 1877, m rec from 1832, Ind rec from 1818; Clk Cir Ct has div, pro, civ ct rec)

* **Wayne**   G5   1819   Edwards
Wayne County, 300 E Main St, Fairfield, IL 62837-2013 . . . . (618)842-5182
(Co Clk has b, m, d, bur rec from 1886, Ind rec; Clk Cir Ct has pro, div, civ ct rec)

* **White**   H5   1815   Gallatin
White County, Main St, Carmi, IL 62821 . . . . (618)382-7211
(Co Clk has b, d rec from 1870, m, Ind rec from 1816, pro rec from 1850)

* **Whiteside**   B3   1836   Jo Daviess, Henry
Whiteside County, 200 E Knox St, Morrison, IL 61270-2819 . . . . (815)772-7201
(Co Clk has b, d rec from 1878, m rec from 1839, CW rec 1861-1865, tax rec from 1840; Clk Cir Ct has div, pro, civ ct rec; Co Rcdr has Ind rec)

* **Will**   C5   1836   Cook, DuPage
Will County, 302 N Chicago St, Joliet, IL 60431-1059 . . . . (815)740-4615
(Co Clk has b, d rec from 1877, m rec from 1836; Clk Cir Ct has div, pro, civ ct rec; Co Rcdr has Ind rec)

* **Williamson**   H4   1839   Franklin
Williamson County, 200 W Jefferson St, Marion, IL 62959-2494 . . . . (618)997-1301
(Co Clk has b rec from 1876, m rec from 1839, d rec from 1877, & Ind rec; City Clk has bur rec; Clk Cir Ct has div, pro & civ ct rec)

* **Winnebago**   A4   1836   Jo Daviess
Winnebago County, 400 W State St, Rockford, IL 61101-1276 . . . . (815)987-3050
(Co Clk has b, m, d, & bur rec from 1850)

* **Woodford**   D4   1841   Tazewell, McLean
Woodford County, PO Box 38, Eureka, IL 61530-0038 . . . . (309)467-2822
(Co Clk has b, d rec from 1871, m rec from 1841; Co Rcdr has Ind rec from 1832; Clk Cir Ct has div, pro, civ ct rec)

* At least one county history has been published about this county.
† Inventory of county archives was made by the Historical Records Survey. (See Introduction)

INDIANA

CAPITAL · INDIANAPOLIS — TERRITORY 1800 — STATE 1816 (19th)
State Map on Page M-13

The French explorer, La Salle, first entered Indiana in 1679. Fur traders were about the only white men in the area for the next half century. Between 1700 and 1735, the French built Fort Miami, near Fort Wayne; Fort Ouiatenon, on the Wabash River; and Vincennes, on the lower Wabash to protect their trading interests. Only Vincennes became a permanent settlement. In 1763, the area became British, but Indian uprisings made settlement difficult. During the Revolutionary War, George Rogers Clark captured Vincennes from the British and helped to end the Indian troubles. With the end of the war, Clarksville, opposite Louisville, Kentucky, was settled in 1784. Following establishment of the Northwest Territory, land was opened to Revolutionary War veterans and others.

Indiana Territory was organized in 1800. Michigan Territory was taken from it in 1805 and Illinois Territory in 1809. The last Indian resistance was finally overcome at the battle of Tippecanoe in 1811. Statehood was granted in 1816. The first counties to be settled were Knox, Harrison, Switzerland, and Clark. Most of the settlers in these counties came from Virginia, Kentucky, and the Carolinas. A group of Swiss settled in the southeast part of the state. Many Germans and Irish came to Indiana around 1830. New Englanders flocked to the state around 1850, settling in the northern counties. Quakers left Tennessee and the Carolinas to establish themselves in Wayne and Randolph Counties away from slavery. Factory growth in the Calumet area attracted many central Europeans to the northwest part of Indiana. Indiana remained in the Union during the Civil War and furnished about 196,000 soldiers to the cause.

Indiana State Board of Health, Division of Vital Statistics, P.O. Box 64-1964, 1330 West Michigan Street, Indianapolis, IN 46206-1964 (to verify current fees, call 317-633-0274), has birth records from October 1907, although general compliance did not occur until 1917. Death records date from 1900. Prior to then, birth and death records are located in the local health office of each county, generally beginning about 1882. Marriage records prior to 1958 are in the county clerk's office where the license was issued. Divorces were granted by the state legislature from 1817 to 1851. Since 1853, the court of common pleas in each county has divorce jurisdiction. Only Marion and St. Joseph's Counties presently have probate courts. The other counties have their records with the clerk of the circuit court or the county clerk. Early probate records are in the court of common pleas, circuit courts, or probate courts (generally between 1829 and 1853). Land records are kept by the county recorder. The earliest land records, from 1789 to 1837, have been published and indexed. Land records prior to 1807 were handled in Cincinnati, Ohio. State or territorial censuses were taken in some areas in 1807, 1810, and 1820. A few fragments of county and state censuses exist for 1853, 1856, 1857, and 1877. These are available at the Indiana State Library, 140 North Senate Avenue, Indianapolis, IN 46204.

Genealogical Archives, Libraries and Societies

Allen County Public Library, P. O. Box 2270, Fort Wayne, IN 46801

American Legion National Headquarters Library, 700 N. Pennsylvania St., Indianapolis, IN 46204

Anderson Public Library, 111 E. 12th Street, Anderson, In 46016

Bloomfield Carnegie Public Library, S. Franklin St., Bloomfield, IN 47424

Danville Public Library, 101 S. Indiana St., Danville, IN 46122

Eckhart Public Library, 603 S. Jackson St., Auburn, IN 46706

Frankfort Community Public Library, 208 W. Clinton St., Frankfort, IN 46401

Genealogy Division, Indiana State Library, 140 No. Senate Avenue, Indianapolis, IN 46204

Goshen College Historical Library, Goshen, IN 46526

Guilford Township Historical Collection, Plainfield Public Library, 1120 Stafford Road, Plainfield, IN 46163

Huntington Public Library, 44 East Park Drive, Huntington, IN 46750

Indiana Historical Society Library, William Henry Smith Memorial Library, 140 N. Senate Ave., Indianapolis, IN 46204

Indiana State Library, 140 N. Senate Avenue, Indianapolis, IN 46204

Lewis Historical Collections Library, Vincennes, IN 47591

Logansport Public Library, 616 E. Broadway, Logansport, IN 46947

Madison-Jefferson County Public Library, Madison, 420 W. Main St., Madison, IN 47250

Marion Public Library, 600 S. Washington St., Marion, IN 46952

Marshall County Historical Center, 317 W. Monroe St., Plymouth, IN 46563

Michigan City Public Library, 100 East Fourth Street, Michigan City, IN 46360

Middletown Public Library, Box 36, 554 Locust St., Middletown, IN 47356

Monroe County Library, c / o Bobbie Taylor, Public Library, 303 E. Kirkwood Ave., Bloomington, IN 47401

New Albany Public Library, New Albany, IN 47150

Noblesville Public Library, 16 S. 10th St., Noblesville, IN 46060

Paoli Public Library, NE Court, Paoli, IN 47454

Plymouth Public Library, 201 N. Center St., Plymouth, IN 46563

Porter County Public Library, 103 Jefferson St., Valparsaiso, IN 46383

Public Library of Fort Wayne and Allen County, 900 Webster, Fort Wayne, IN 46802

Pulaski County Public Library, 121 S. Riverside Dr., Winamac, IN 46996

Rockville Public Library, 106 N. Market St., Rockville, IN 47872

South Bend Public Library, 122 W. Wayne, South Bend, IN 46601

Tipton County Public Library, Genealogical Local History, 127 East Madison St., Tipton, IN 46072

Valparaiso Public Library, 103 Jefferson St., Valparaiso, IN 46383

Vigo County Public Library, One Library Square, Terre Haute, IN 47807

Warsaw Public Library, 315 E. Center St., Warsaw, IN 46580

Willard Library of Evansville, 21 1st Avenue, Evansville, IN 47710

Worthington Public Library, Worthington, IN 47471

Adams County Historical Society, 141 South 2nd Street, Decatur, IN 46733

Allen County Genealogical Society of Indiana, P. O. Box 12003, Fort Wayne, IN 46862

Bartholomew County Genealogical Society, P. O. Box 2455, Columbus, IN 47202

Bartholomew County Historical Society, 524 Third Street, Columbus, IN 47201

Benton County Historical Society, 602 East 7th Street, Fowler, IN 47944

Blackford County Historical Society, P. O. Box 1, Hartford City, IN 47348

Boone County Historical Society, P. O. Box 141, Lebanon, IN 46052

Brown County Genealogical Society, P. O. Box 1202, Nashville, IN 47448

Brown County Historical Society, Inc., P. O. Box 668, Nashville, IN 47448

Carrol County Historical Society, P. O. Box 277, Delphi, IN 46923

Cass County Genealogical Society, P. O. Box 373, Logansport, IN 46947

Clark County Historical Society, P. O. Box 606, Jeffersonville, IN 47130

Clay County Genealogical Society of Indiana, P. O. Box 56, Center Point, IN 47840

Clinton County Historical Society, 609 North Columbia Street, Frankfort, IN 47130

DeKalb County Historical Society, Box 66, Auburn, IN 46706

Delaware County Historical Alliance, P. O. Box 1266, Muncie, IN 47308

Elkhart County Genealogical Society, 1812 Jeanwood Drive, Elkhart, IN 46514

Family Tree and Crests, 6233 Carollton Avenue, Indianapolis, IN 46220

Fountain County Historical Society, Box 148, Kingman, IN 47952

Fulton County Historical Society, 7th & Pontiac, Rochester, IN 46975

Genealogy Section, Kosciusko County Historical Society, P. O. Box 1071, Warsaw, IN 46580

Gibson Historical Society, P. O. Box 516, Princeton, IN 47670

Greene County Historical Society, P. O. Box 29, Lyons, IN 47443

Hamilton County Historical Society, P. O. Box 397, Noblesville, IN 46060

Hancock County Historical Society, Inc., P. O. Box 375, Greenfield, IN 46140-0375

Harrison County Historical Society, 117 West Beaver Street, Corydon, IN 47112

Hendricks County Genealogical Society, 101 South Indiana Street, Danville, IN 46122

Hendricks County Historical Society, P. O. Box 128, Danville, IN 46122

Henry County Historical Society, 606 South 14th St., New Castle, IN 47362

Howard County Genealogical Society, Kokomo Public Library, 220 N. Union, Kokomo, IN 46901

Illiana Genealogical and Historical Society, P. O. Box 207, Danville, IL 61832

Illiana Jewish Genealogical Society, 3033 Bob-O-Link Road, Flossmoor, IL 60422

Indiana Genealogical Society, P. O. Box 10507, Anderson, IN 46852

Indiana Historical Society, 315 W. Ohio Street, Indianapolis, IN 46202

Indiana Society, Sons of the American Revolution, 5401 Central Ave., Indianapolis, IN 46220

Jackson County Genealogical Society, Second and Walnut Streets, Seymour, IN 47274

Jasper County Historical Society, Augusta Street, Rensselaer, IN 47971

Jay County Historical Society, Box 1282, Portland, IN 47371

Johnson County Historical Society, 150 West Madison Street, Franklin, IN 46131

Kosciusko County Historical Society, P. O. Box 1071, Warsaw, IN 46580

LaGrange County Historical Society, Inc., R. R. 1, LaGrange, IN 46761

La Porte County Genealogical Society, 904 Indiana Ave., La Porte, IN 46350

La Porte County Historical Society, La Porte County Complex, La Porte, IN 46350

Madison County Historical Society, Inc., P. O. Box 523, Anderson, IN 46015

Marion-Adams Genealogical Society, 308 Main St., Sheridan, IN 46069

Marion County Historical Society, 140 N. Senate, Indianapolis, In 46204

Marshall County Genealogical Society, 317 W. Monroe, Plymouth, IN 46563

Martin County Historical Society, Inc., P. O. Box 84, Shoals, IN 46504

Miami County Genealogical Society, P. O. Box 542, Peru, IN 46970

Monroe County Genealogical Society, Old Library, East 6th Street & Washington, Bloomington, IN 47401

Montgomery County Historical Society, Crawfordsville District Public Library, 222 So. Washington St., Crawfordsville, IN 47933

Newton County Historical Society, Box 103, Kentland, IN 47951

Noble County Genealogical Society, 109 North York Street, Albion, IN 46701

North Central Indiana Genealogical Society, 2300 Canterbury Drive, Kokomo, IN 46901

Northern Indiana Historical Society, 112 So. Lafayette Blvd., South Bend, IN 44601

Northwest Indiana Genealogical Society, Valparaiso Public Library, 103 Jefferson St., Valparaiso, IN 46383

Northwest Territory Genealogical Society, Lewis Historical Library, Vincennes University, Vincennes, IN 47591

Ohio County Historical Society, 218 South Walnut Street, Rising Sun, IN 47040

Orange County Genealogical Society, P. O. Box 344, Paoli, IN 47454

Perry County Historical Society, Rome, IN 47574

Pike County Historical Society, R. R. 2, Petersburg, IN 47567

Posey County Historical Society, P. O. Box 171, Mt. Vernon, IN 47620

Pulaski County Genealogical Society, R. R. 4, Box 121, Winamac, IN 46996

Randolph County Genealogical Society, R. R. 3, Winchester, IN 47394

Randolph County Historical Society, Route 3, Box 60A, Winchester, IN 47394

Ripley County Historical Society, Inc., P. O. Box 224, Versailles, IN 47042

Rush County Historical Society, 614 N. Jackson Street, Rushville, IN 46173

Scott County Historical Society, P. O. Box 245, Scottsburg, IN 47170

Shelby County Historical Society, Box 74, Shelbyville, IN 46176

South Bend Area Genealogical Society, P. O. Box 1222, South Bend, IN 46624

Southern Indiana Genealogical Society, P. O. Box 665, New Albany, IN 47150

Spencer County Historical Society, Walnut Street, Rockport, IN 47635

Sullivan County Historical Society, P. O. Box 326, Sullivan, IN 47882

Tippecanoe County Area Genealogical Society, 909 South Street, Lafayette, IN 47901

Tri-State Genealogical Society, Willard Library, 21 First Avenue, Evansville, IN 47710

Union County Historical Society, 6 East Seminary Street, Liberty, IN 47353

Vigo County Historical Society, 1411 So. 6th St., Terre Haute, IN 47802

Wabash County Historical Society, Wabash County Museum, 89 West Hill Street, Wabash, IN 46992

Wabash Valley Genealogical Society, P. O. Box 85, Terre Haute, IN 47808

Warren County Historical Society, P. O. Box 176, Williamsport, IN 47993

Washington County Historical Society, 307 East Market Street, Salem, IN 47904

Wayne County Genealogical Society, 200 Salisbury Road N 6, Richmond, IN 47374

Wayne County Historical Society, 1150 North A Street, Richmond, IN 47374

Wells County Historical Society, P. O. Box 143, Bluffton, IN 46714

White County Genealogy Society, 609 South Maple St., Monticello, IN 47960

Printed Census Records and Mortality Schedules

Federal Census 1820, 1830, 1840, 1850, 1860, 1870, 1880, 1900, 1910
State/Territorial Census 1853, 1859, 1866, 1871
Voters 1809
Revolutionary War Pensioners 1835

Valuable Printed Sources

Atlases, Maps, and Gazetteers

Baker, Ronald L. and Marvin Carmony. *Indiana Place Names*. Bloomington, Indiana: Indiana University Press, 1975

Chamberlain, E. *The Indiana Gazetteer, or Topographical Dictionary of the State of Indiana*. Indianapolis: E. Chamberlain, 1849.

New Topographical Atlas and Gazetteer of Indiana, 1871. New York: George H. Adams & Co., 1871. 1975 reprint by Unigraphic Inc., Evansville, Indiana.

Bibliographies

Cammack, Eleanor. *Indiana Methodism: A Bibliography of Printed and Archival Holdings in the Archives of DePauw University*. Greencastle, Indiana: DePauw University, 1964.

Thompson, Donald E. *Preliminary Checklist of Archives and Manuscripts in Indiana Repositories*. Indianapolis: Indiana Historical Society, 1980.

Waters, Margaret R. *Revolutionary Soldiers Buried in Indiana*. Baltimore: Genealogical Publishing Co., 1970.

Genealogical Research Guides

Carty, Mickey Dimon. *Searching in Indiana: A Reference Guide to Public and Private Records*. Costa Mesa, California: ISC Publications, 1985.

Harter, Stuart. *Indiana Genealogy and Local History Sources Index*. Ft. Wayne, Indiana: Stuart Harter, 1985.

Miller, Carolynne L. *Aids for Genealogical Searching in Indiana*. Detroit: Detroit Society for Genealogical Research, 1978.

Newhard, Malinda E. E. *A Guide to Genealogical Research in Indiana*. Harlan, Indiana: Malinda E. E. Newhard, 1979.

Histories

Dunn, Jacob Piatt. *Indiana and Indianans*. Chicago: American Historical Society, 1919.

Haymond, William S. *An Illustrated History of the State of Indiana*. Indianapolis: S. L. Marrow & Co., 1879.

INDIANA COUNTY DATA
State Map on Page M-13

Name	Map Index	Date Created	Parent County or Territory From Which Organized

* **Adams**   C6   1835   Allen, Randolph
Adams County, 112 S 2nd St, Decatur, IN 46733-1694 . . . . (219)724-2600
(Co Clk has m, div, pro & civ ct rec)

*† **Allen**   C6   1824   Unorg. Terr., Randolph
Allen County, 1 E Main St, Fort Wayne, IN 46802-1887 . . . . (219)428-7124
(Co Clk has m rec from 1824, div, pro, civ ct rec from 1823; Rcdr Office has Ind rec; Co Board of Hlth has b, d & bur rec)

* **Bartholomew**   F5   1821   Unorg. Terr., Jackson, Delaware
Bartholomew County, PO Box 924, Columbus, IN 47202-0924 . . . . (812)379-1600
(Co Hlth Office has b, d rec; Co Clk has m rec from 1821, ct rec, pro, wills from 1821; Co Rcdr has Ind rec; Co Clk has cem rec
recorded by the DAR, and some naturalization rec)

* **Benton**   D3   1840   Jasper
Benton County, 700 E 5th St, Fowler, IN 47944-1556 . . . . (317)884-0930
(Co Hlth has b & d rec from 1880; Co Rcdr has Ind rec; Hist Soc has historical rec; Clk Cir Ct has m rec from 1841, pro rec from
1852, div rec from 1857, civ ct rec from 1957)

*† **Blackford**   D6   1838   Jay
Blackford County, 110 W Washington St, Hartford City, IN 47348-2251 . . . . (317)348-3213
(Co Clk has m, div, pro & civ ct rec from 1839; City & Co Hlth Officers have b & d rec; Co Rcdr has Ind rec; Co Coroner has bur rec)

*† **Boone**   E4   1830   Hendricks, Marion
Boone County, 1 Courthouse Sq Rm 212, Lebanon, IN 46052-2150 . . . . (317)482-3510
(Co Clk has m rec from 1831, div, pro & civ ct rec from 1830; Co Hlth Dept has b & d rec; Co Rcdr has Ind rec)

* **Brown**   F4   1836   Monroe, Bartholomew, Jackson
Brown County, Van Buren & Main Sts, Nashville, IN 47448 . . . . (812)988-4796
(Co Hlth Dept has b & d rec from 1882; Co Clk has m, pro & civ ct rec from 1836, div rec from 1850, ct ordered b rec from 1942;
Co Rcdr has Ind rec from 1874; Some rec lost in 1873 fire)

* **Carroll**   D4   1828   Unorg. Terr
Carroll County, County Courthouse, Delphi, IN 46923 . . . . (317)564-4485
(Co Clk has m, div, pro & civ ct rec from 1828; Co Hlth Officer has b, d & bur rec from 1882; Co Rcdr has Ind rec from 1828; Pub
Lib in Delphi has newsp from 1841; Co Hist Soc has bur rec)

* **Cass**   C4   1829   Carroll
Cass County, 200 Court Pk, Logansport, IN 46947-3114 . . . . (219)753-7700
(Co Hlth has b & d rec; Co Clk has m & pro rec from 1892, div & civ ct rec from 1894; Co Aud has Ind rec)

* **Clark**   G5   1801   Knox
Clark County, City Court Bldg 501 E Court Ave, Jeffersonville, IN 47130 . . . . (812)285-6200

*† **Clay**   F3   1825   Owen, Putnam, Vigo, Sullivan
Clay County, 1206 E National Ave, Brazil, IN 47834-2797 . . . . (812)448-8727
(Co Hlth Dept has b, d rec; Co Clk has m, div, pro, civ ct rec from 1851; Co Rcdr has Ind from 1825, some bur rec; some
naturalization rec available)

* **Clinton**   D4   1830   Tippecanoe
Clinton County, 50 N Jackson St, Frankfort, IN 46041-1993 . . . . (317)659-1891
(Co Hlth has b & d rec; Co Clk has m & will rec from 1830, div, pro & civ ct rec from 1888; Co Rcdr has Ind rec)

* **Crawford**   H4   1818   Orange, Harrison, Perry
Crawford County, PO Box 375, English, IN 47118-0375 . . . . (812)338-2565
(Co Clk has m rec from 1818, div, pro, civ ct rec from 1860; Co Hlth Dept has b & d rec; Co Rcdr has Ind rec)

* **Daviess**   G3   1817   Knox
Daviess County, County Courthouse, Washington, IN 47501 . . . . (812)254-1090
(Co Clk has m, div, pro & civ ct rec from 1817)

* **De Kalb**   B6   1835   Allen, Lagrange
De Kalb County, 100 Main St, Auburn, IN 46706 . . . . (219)925-2362
(Co Hlth has b & d rec; Co Clk has m & civ ct rec from 1837, pro rec from 1855, school rec from 1903 to 1932; Co Rcdr has Ind
rec)

* **Dearborn**   F6   1803   Clark
Dearborn County, 215-B W High St, Lawrenceburg, IN 47025-1909 . . . . (812)537-1040
(Clk Cir Ct has m rec, lic 1826, application 1905, div, pro & civ ct rec; Hlth Officer has b & d rec; Co Rcdr has Ind rec)

* **Decatur**   F6   1822   Unorg. Terr
Decatur County, 150 Courthouse Sq Suite 5, Greensburg, IN 47240-2091 . . . . (812)663-2546
(Co Clk has m rec from 1822, div, pro & civ ct rec; Brd of Hlth has b & d rec)

*† **Delaware**   D6   1827   Randolph
Delaware County, PO Box 1089, Muncie, IN 47308-1089 . . . . (317)747-7726
(Co Clk has m, div, pro & civ ct rec from 1827)

* **Dubois**   H3   1818   Pike
Dubois County, Main St, Jasper, IN 47546 . . . . (812)482-1633
(Co Clk has m, div, pro, civ ct rec from 1839; Co Rcdr has Ind rec; Co Hlth Dept has b & d rec)

Name	Map Index	Date Created	Parent County or Territory From Which Organized

* **Elkhart**   B5   1830   Allen, Cass
Elkhart County, 117 N 2nd St, Goshen, IN 46526-3297 .... (219)534-3541
(Co Hlth has b & d rec; Co Clk has m, div, pro & civ ct rec from 1830; Co Rcdr has Ind rec)

* **Fayette**   E6   1819   Wayne, Franklin
Fayette County, 401 N Central Ave, Connersville, IN 47331-1997 .... (317)825-1813
(Co Clk has m, div, pro & civ ct rec from 1819, naturalization rec from 1858)

* **Floyd**   H5   1819   Harrison, Clarke
Floyd County, 211 W 1st St, New Albany, IN 47150-3501 .... (812)948-5411
(Co Hlth has b & d rec; Co Clk has m rec from 1813, div & civ ct rec from 1863, pro rec from 1819)

* **Fountain**   D3   1826   Montgomery, Parke
Fountain County, County Courthouse, Covington, IN 47932-1293 .... (317)793-2192
(Co Hlth has b, d rec from 1885; Co Clk has m rec from 1827, div, pro & civ ct rec from 1830; Co Rcdr has Ind rec from 1828)

* **Franklin**   F6   1811   Clark, Dearborn, Jefferson
Franklin County, 459 Main St, Brookville, IN 47012-1405 .... (317)647-5111
(Co Hlth Dept has b, d rec from 1882; Co Clk has m, div, pro, civ ct rec from 1811, declaration of intent 1826-1925, rec of apprentices 1831-54; Pub Lib has cem rec; Co Rcdr has Ind rec from 1803, soldier's discharge rec from 1866)

*† **Fulton**   C4   1835   Allen, Cass, St. Joseph
Fulton County, 815 Main St, Rochester, IN 46975-1546 .... (219)223-2911
(Co Clk has m, div, pro & civ ct rec from 1836; Co Hlth has b & d rec; Co Rcdr has Ind rec)

* **Gibson**   H2   1813   Knox
Gibson County, Courthouse Sq, Princeton, IN 47670-1542 .... (812)385-8260
(Co Hlth has b & d rec; Co Clk has m rec from 1813, div, pro & civ ct rec from 1820)

* **Grant**   D5   1831   Delaware, Madison, Cass
Grant County, County Courthouse, Marion, IN 46952 .... (317)668-8121
(Co Hlth has b & d rec; Co Clk has m, div, pro & civ ct rec from 1831; Co Aud has Ind rec)

*† **Greene**   F3   1821   Daviess, Sullivan
Greene County, Main & Washington Sts, Bloomfield, IN 47424 .... (812)384-8532
(Co Hlth has b rec from 1885, d rec from 1893; Co Clk has m rec from 1821, div, pro & civ ct rec from 1820; Co Aud has Ind rec from 1824; Co Clk has naturalization rec 1854-1906, ct appt b rec 1941-1978)

* **Hamilton**   E5   1823   Unorg. Terr., Marion
Hamilton County, Public Sq, Noblesville, IN 46060-1697 .... (317)773-6110
(Co Hlth has b & d rec; Co Clk has m, div, pro & civ ct rec from 1833; Co Rcdr has Ind rec)

* **Hancock**   E5   1828   Madison
Hancock County, 9 E Main St, Greenfield, IN 46140-2320 .... (317)462-1106
(Co Clk has m, div, pro, wills, civ ct rec from 1828; Co Rcdr has Ind rec; Co Hlth Dept has b & d rec from 1882)

* **Harrison**   H4   1808   Knox, Clark
Harrison County, 300 N Capitol Ave, Corydon, IN 47112-1139 .... (812)738-8241
(Co Hlth Dept has b, d rec from 1882; Co Clk has m, pro, civ ct rec from 1809, div rec from 1815, Ind rec from 1807)

* **Hendricks**   E4   1824   Unorg. Terr., Putnam
Hendricks County, County Courthouse, Danville, IN 46122-1993 .... (317)745-9207
(Co Hlth has b rec from 1882 to 1920, d rec from 1882; Co Clk has m, div, pro & civ ct rec from 1823; Co Aud has Ind rec)

* **Henry**   E6   1822   Unorg. Terr.
Henry County, Broad St, New Castle, IN 47362 .... (317)529-4705
(Co Hlth Dept has b & d rec from 1882; Co Clk has m, div, pro & civ ct rec from 1822; Co Rcdr has Ind rec from 1823, & cem deeds from 1925)

*† **Howard**   D4   1844   Carroll, Cass, Miami, Grant, Hamilton (Originally Richardville Co)
Howard County, Main & Sycamore, Kokomo, IN 46901-4543 .... (317)456-2204
(Co Clk has m, div, pro & civ ct rec from 1844, Co Rcdr has Ind rec; Co Hlth Dept has b, d & bur rec)

* **Huntington**   C5   1832   Allen, Grant
Huntington County, N Jefferson St, Huntington, IN 46750 .... (219)356-3122
(Co Hlth has b & d rec from 1882; Co Clk has m rec from 1847, civ ct rec from 1840, pro & div rec from 1850; Co Rcdr has Ind rec from 1834)

* **Jackson**   G5   1816   Washington, Clark, Jefferson
Jackson County, PO Box 122, Brownstown, IN 47220-0122 .... (812)358-6116
(Co Hlth has b & d rec; Co Clk has m, div, pro & civ ct rec from 1816; Co Aud has Ind rec)

* **Jasper**   C3   1835   White, Warren
Jasper County, Courthouse Sq, Rensselaer, IN 47978 .... (219)866-4933
(Courthouse burned in 1862, all rec destroyed. Co Hlth Dept has b rec; Co Clk has m, div rec from 1865, d rec from 1882, pro, civ ct rec from 1864)

*† **Jay**   D6   1835   Randolph, Delaware
Jay County, Court St, Portland, IN 47371 .... (219)726-4951
(Co Hlth has b & d rec from 1882; Co Clk has m rec from 1843, div rec from 1882, pro rec from 1836, civ ct rec from 1837; Co Aud has Ind rec from 1836)

* **Jefferson**   G6   1811   Dearborn, Clark
Jefferson County, 300 E Main St, Madison, IN 47250-3537 .... (812)265-8900
(Co Hlth has b, d & bur rec; Co Clk has m, div, pro & civ ct rec; Co Rcdr has Ind rec)

Name	Map Index	Date Created	Parent County or Territory From Which Organized
* **Jennings**	F5	1817	Jefferson, Jackson

Jennings County, County Courthouse, Vernon, IN 47282 .... (812)346-5977
[FHL has some b, m, cem, lnd, pro, nat rec]

* **Johnson**	F5	1823	Unorg. Terr.

Johnson County, 5 E Jefferson St, Franklin, IN 46131 .... (317)736-5000
(Co Hlth has b, d & bur rec from 1882; Co Clk has m, div, pro & civ ct rec from 1830; Co Rcdr has lnd rec)

* **Knox**	G3	1790	Northwest Territory

Knox County, 7th & Broadway, Vincennes, IN 47591 .... (812)885-2521
(Co Clk has m rec from 1807, div rec, also pro rec from 1806 & civ ct rec from 1790; Co Hlth Dept has b & d rec, lnd rec at Co Records Bldg)

* **Kosciusko**	B5	1835	Elkhart, Cass

Kosciusko County, 100 W Center St, Warsaw, IN 46580-2846 .... (219)267-4444
(Co Hlth Dept has b & d rec from 1882; Co Clk has m, div, pro & civ ct rec from 1836; Co Rcdr has lnd rec; Twp Trustees have bur rec)

* **Lagrange**	B6	1832	Elkhart, Allen

Lagrange County, 114 W Michigan St, Lagrange, IN 46761-1853 .... (219)463-2183
(Co Hlth has b & d rec from 1882; Co Clk has m, div, pro & civ ct rec from 1832; Co Rcdr has lnd rec from 1832)

* **Lake**	B3	1836	Porter, Newton

Lake County, 2293 N Main St, Crown Point, IN 46307-1896 .... (219)755-3440
(Co Hlth has b & d rec; Clk Cir Ct has m, div, pro & civ ct rec from 1837; Co Rcdr has lnd rec)

*† **LaPorte**	B4	1832	St. Joseph

LaPorte County, Courthouse Sq, La Porte, IN 46350 .... (219)326-6808
(Co Clk has m rec from 1832, div, pro & civ ct rec from 1834; Co Rcdr has lnd rec; Co Hlth Dept has b, d & bur rec)

* **Lawrence**	G4	1818	Orange

Lawrence County, Bedford Sq, Bedford, IN 47421 .... (812)275-7543
(Co Hlth has b & d rec; Co Clk has m, div & civ ct rec from 1818, pro rec from 1820; Co Rcdr has lnd rec)

* **Madison**	D5	1823	Unorg. Terr, Marion

Madison County, 16 E 9th St, Anderson, IN 46016-1576 .... (317)641-9480
(Co Hlth Dept has b rec from 1891, d rec from 1895; local cem have bur rec; Co Clk has m rec from 1884, div, pro, civ ct rec from 1880; Co Auditor has lnd rec from 1867; Co Board of Hlth has school rec 1904-32)

*† **Marion**	E5	1822	Unorg. Terr

Marion County, 200 E Washington St, Indianapolis, IN 46204-3353 .... (317)236-3200
[FHL has some m, cem, civ ct, lnd, nat, pro rec]

*† **Marshall**	B4	1835	St. Joseph, Elkhart

Marshall County, 211 W Madison St, Plymouth, IN 46563-1762 .... (219)936-8922
(Co Hlth has b, d & bur rec from 1882; Co Clk has m, div, pro & civ ct rec from 1836; Co Rcdr has lnd rec)

* **Martin**	G4	1820	Daviess, Dubois

Martin County, PO Box 170, Shoals, IN 47581-0170 .... (812)247-3651
(Co Hlth has b & d rec; Co Clk has m & pro rec from 1820, div & civ ct rec from 1842; Co Rcdr has lnd rec)

* **Miami**	C5	1832	Cass

Miami County, 21 Court St, Peru, IN 46970-2266 .... (317)472-3901
(Co Hlth has b, d & bur rec; Co Clk has m, div, pro & civ ct rec from 1843)

*† **Monroe**	F4	1818	Orange

Monroe County, PO Box 547, Bloomington, IN 47402-0547 .... (812)333-3600
(Co Hlth has b, d & bur rec from 1882; Co Clk has m & civ ct rec from 1818, div rec from 1870 & pro from 1831; Co Rcdr has lnd rec)

* **Montgomery**	E3	1823	Parke, Putnam

Montgomery County, 100 E Main St, Crawfordsville, IN 47933-1715 .... (317)364-6400
(Co Hlth Dept has b, d rec from 1882; Co Clk has m, div, pro, civ ct rec from 1823; Co Rcdr has lnd rec from 1823; Crawfordsville Publ Lib has cem rec from 1823; Co Clk has partial list of naturalization rec)

*† **Morgan**	F4	1822	Unorg. Terr

Morgan County, PO Box 1556, Martinsville, IN 46151-0556 .... (317)342-1025
[FHL has some m, cem, lnd, pro rec]

* **Newton**	C3	1859	Jasper

Newton County, Courthouse Sq, Kentland, IN 47951 .... (219)474-6081
(Co Hlth Dept has b, d rec; Town Hall has bur rec; Co Clk has m rec from 1850, div, civ ct rec from 1878, pro rec from 1861, incomplete immigration rec)

* **Noble**	B6	1835	Elkhart, Lagrange, Allen

Noble County, 101 N Orange St, Albion, IN 46701-1097 .... (219)636-2736
(Co Hlth Dept has b, d rec; Co Clk has m, div, pro, civ ct rec from 1859; Co Auditor has lnd rec; City Clk has bur rec)

* **Ohio**	G6	1844	Dearborn

Ohio County, Main St, Rising Sun, IN 47040 .... (812)438-2062
(Co Clk has m, div, pro, civ ct rec from 1844)

* **Orange**	G4	1816	Washington, Knox, Gibson

Orange County, Court St, Paoli, IN 47454 .... (812)723-2649
(Co Hlth has b rec from 1882, d & bur rec; Co Clk has m, div, pro & civ ct rec from 1816; Co Rcdr has lnd rec from 1816)

Name	Map Index	Date Created	Parent County or Territory From Which Organized

* **Owen**   F4   1819   Daviess, Sullivan
Owen County, County Courthouse, Spencer, IN 47460 .... (812)829-2325
(Co Hlth Dept has b, d rec from 1882; Co Clk has m, civ ct rc from 1819, div rec from 1832, pro rec from 1833; Co Rcdr has Ind rec from 1819)

* **Parke**   E3   1821   Unorg. Terr, Vigo
Parke County, County Courthouse, Rockville, IN 47872 .... (317)569-5132
(Co Hlth Dept has b, d rec; Co Clk has m, div, pro, civ ct rec from 1833, early naturalization rec, not indexed, hard to find; Co rcdr has Ind rec)

* **Perry**   H4   1814   Warrick, Gibson
Perry County, 8th St, Cannelton, IN 47520 .... (812)547-3741
(Co Hlth Dept has b, d rec from 1890; Co Clk has m, div, pro, civ ct rec from 1813; Co Rcdr has Ind rec from 1813)

* **Pike**   H3   1817   Gibson, Perry
Pike County, Main St, Petersburg, IN 47567 .... (812)354-6025
(Co Hlth Dept has b, d rec; Co Clk has m, div, pro, civ ct rec from 1817; Co Rcdr has Ind rec)

* **Porter**   B3   1835   St. Joseph
Porter County, 16 E Lincolnway, Valparaiso, IN 46383-5698 .... (219)465-3400
(Co Hlth Dept has b, d rec; Co Clk has m, div, pro, civ ct rec from 1836; Co Auditor has Ind rec)

*† **Posey**   H2   1814   Warrick, Knox, Gibson
Posey County, County Courthouse, Mount Vernon, IN 47620 .... (812)838-1306
(Co Hlth Dept has b, d rec from 1882; Co Clk has m, div, pro, civ ct rec from 1815; Co Rcdr has Ind rec)

* **Pulaski**   C4   1835   Cass, St. Joseph
Pulaski County, 112 E Main St, Winamac, IN 46996-1344 .... (219)946-3313
(Co Clk has m, div, pro, civ ct rec from 1839; Co Rcdr has b, d rec from 1882, Ind rec)

* **Putnam**   E3   1822   Unorg. Terr., Vigo, Owen
Putnam County, PO Box 546, Greencastle, IN 46135-0546 .... (317)653-2648
(Co Hlth Dept has b, d rec; Co Clk has m rec from 1822, div, pro rec from 1825, civ ct rec from 1828; Co Rcdr has Ind rec)

* **Randolph**   D6   1818   Wayne
Randolph County, County Courthouse 3rd Fl, Winchester, IN 47394 .... (317)584-7070
(Co Hlth has b & d rec; Co Clk has m, div, pro & civ ct rec; Co Rcdr has Ind rec from 1818 & newspapers from 1876)

Richardville (see Howard)

* **Ripley**   F6   1816   Dearborn, Jefferson
Ripley County, PO Box 177, Versailles, IN 47042 .... (812)689-6115
(Co Hlth Dept has b, d rec; Co Clk has m, div, pro, civ ct rec from 1818; Co Rcdr has Ind rec)

* **Rush**   E6   1822   Unorg. Terr
Rush County, PO Box 429, Rushville, IN 46173-0429 .... (317)932-2086
(Co Hlth has b, d & bur rec from 1882; Co Clk has m, div, pro, civ ct rec from 1822; Co Rcdr has Ind rec)

*† **Saint Joseph**   B4   1830   Cass
Saint Joseph County, 227 W Jefferson Blvd, South Bend, IN 46601-1830 .... (219)284-9534
(Co Hlth has b, d & bur rec; Co Clk has m, div, pro & civ ct rec; Co Asr has Ind rec)

* **Scott**   G5   1820   Clark, Jefferson, Jennings
Scott County, 1 E McClain Ave, Scottsburg, IN 47170-1848 .... (812)752-4769
(Co Hlth Dept has b, d rec; Co Clk has m, div, pro, civ ct rec from 1820; Co Rcdr has Ind rec)

*† **Shelby**   F5   1822   Unorg. Terr
Shelby County, 315 S Harrison St, Shelbyville, IN 46176-2161 .... (317)392-6320
(Co Hlth has b, d & bur rec; Co Clk has m, div, pro & civ ct rec; Co Aud has Ind rec)

* **Spencer**   H3   1818   Warrick, Perry
Spencer County, 541 Main St, Rockport, IN 47635-1478 .... (812)649-6027
(Co Hlth Dept has b rec from 1882, d rec from 1830; Cem trustees have bur rec; Co Clk has m rec from 1818, div, civ ct rec from 1883, pro rec from 1848; Co Rcdr has Ind rec)

* **Starke**   B4   1835   St. Joseph
Starke County, Washington St, Knox, IN 46534 .... (219)772-9128
(Co Clk has m, div, pro, civ ct rec from 1850; Co Auditor has Ind rec from 1850; Co Hlth Dept has b & d rec)

* **Steuben**   B6   1835   LaGrange
Steuben County, SE Public Sq, Angola, IN 46703-1926 .... (219)665-9364
(Co Hlth Dept has b, d rec; Co Clk has m, div, pro, civ ct rec from 1837, Ind rec from middle 1800s)

* **Sullivan**   F3   1817   Knox
Sullivan County, County Courthouse, Sullivan, IN 47882 .... (812)268-4657
(Co Clk has m, div, pro & civ ct rec from 1850)

* **Switzerland**   G6   1814   Dearborn, Jefferson
Switzerland County, County Courthouse, Vevay, IN 47043 .... (812)427-3175
(Co Hlth has b, d & bur rec; Co Clk has m, div, civ ct, pro rec from 1814; Co Rcdr has Ind rec)

*† **Tippecanoe**   D3   1826   Unorg. Terr, Parke
Tippecanoe County, 20 N 3rd St, Lafayette, IN 47901-1222 .... (317)423-9215
(Clk Cir Ct has m rec from 1830, d rec, also div rec from 1850, pro & civ ct rec from 1832 & naturalization rec)

*† **Tipton**   D5   1844   Hamilton, Cass, Miami
Tipton County, County Courthouse, Tipton, IN 46072 .... (317)675-2795
(Co Clk has m rec from 1844, div, pro & civ ct rec from 1850)

Name	Map Index	Date Created	Parent County or Territory From Which Organized

* **Union** E6 1821 Wayne, Franklin, Fayette
  Union County, 26 W Union St Rm 105, Liberty, IN 47353-1350 .... (317)458-6121
  (Clk Cir Ct has m, div, pro & civ ct rec from 1821; Co Hlth has b rec from 1882, d rec from 1907)

*† **Vanderburgh** H3 1818 Gibson, Posey, Warrick
  Vanderburgh County, PO Box 3356, Evansville, IN 47732-3356 .... (812)426-5160
  (Co Hlth Dept has b, d, bur rec; Co Clk has m, civ ct rec from 1835, div, pro rec from 1850; Co Assessor has Ind rec)

* **Vermillion** E3 1824 Parke
  Vermillion County, PO Box 8, Newport, IN 47966-0008 .... (317)492-3500
  (Co Hlth Dept has b, d rec from 1882; Co Clk has m, div, pro, civ ct rec from 1824; Co Rcdr has Ind rec)

* **Vigo** F3 1818 Sullivan
  Vigo County, 3rd & Wabash, Terre Haute, IN 47807 .... (812)238-8211
  (Co Clk has m, pro & civ ct rec from 1818, div rec from 1825)

* **Wabash** C5 1832 Cass, Grant
  Wabash County, 1 W Hill St, Wabash, IN 46992-3151 .... (219)563-0661
  (Co Clk has m, div, pro & civ ct rec from 1835; Co Hlth Dept has b & d rec; Co Rcdr & Museum has bur rec)

* **Warren** D3 1827 Fountain
  Warren County, N Monroe St, Williamsport, IN 47993 .... (317)762-3510
  (Fountain-Warren Co Hlth Dept [210 S Perry St, Attica 47918] has b & d rec from 1882; Co Clk has m & div rec from 1827, pro rec from 1829, civ ct rec from 1828; Co Rcdr has Ind rec from 1827)

*† **Warrick** H3 1813 Knox
  Warrick County, County Courthouse, Boonville, IN 47601-1596 .... (812)897-6120
  (Co Hlth has b, d & bur rec; Co Clk has m rec from 1819, div, civ ct, pro rec from 1813; Co Rcdr has Ind rec)

* **Washington** G5 1814 Clark, Harrison, Jefferson
  Washington County, County Courthouse, Salem, IN 47167-2086 .... (812)883-5748
  (Co Hlth has b & d rec from 1882; Co Clk has m, div, pro & civ ct rec from 1814, wills from 1813, newspapers from 1891; Co Rcdr has Ind rec; Co Hist Soc has many family rec)

* **Wayne** E6 1811 Clark, Dearborn
  Wayne County, 401 E Main St, Richmond, IN 47374-4289 .... (317)973-9200
  (Co Clk has m rec from 1810, div & civ ct rec from 1873, pro rec from 1818; City-Co Hlth Officer has b, d & bur rec)

*† **Wells** C6 1835 Allen, Delaware, Randolph
  Wells County, 102 W Market St, Bluffton, IN 46714-2050 .... (219)824-2320
  (Co Hlth Dept has b, d rec; Co Clk has m, div, civ ct rec from 1837, pro rec from 1838; Co Rcdr has Ind rec)

* **White** C4 1834 Carroll
  White County, PO Box 350, Monticello, IN 47960-0350 .... (219)583-7032
  (Co Clk has m, div pro & civ ct rec from 1834; Co Rcdr has Ind rec; Co Hlth Dept has b, d & bur rec)

* **Whitley** C5 1835 Elkhart, Allen
  Whitley County, 302 S Chauncey St Courthouse Sq, Columbia City, IN 46725-2402 .... (219)248-3102
  (Co Hlth Dept has b, d rec from 1882; Co Clk has m rec from 1836, div, civ ct rec from 1853, pro rec; Co Rcdr has Ind rec)

* At least one county history has been published about this county.
† Inventory of county archives was made by the Historical Records Survey. (See Introduction)

IOWA

CAPITAL · DES MOINES — TERRITORY 1838 — STATE 1846 (29th)
State Map on Page M-14

Apart from its discovery by Marquette and Joliet and the occasional fur trapper, Iowa was unknown to the white man until Julien Dubuque came in 1788. Through the permission of the Fox Indians, Dubuque established a mining settlement near the present-day city that bears his name. With the Louisiana Purchase in 1803, the United States acquired the territory and built Fort Madison and Fort Armstrong. Dubuque was abandoned following its founder's death in 1810. Little further settlement occurred until the Fox and Sauk tribes were forced to cede over nearly 9,000 square miles of Iowa territory in 1833. With the opening of this land, settlers flocked to the area. The first settlers came from the eastern and southern states, the majority of whom originally came from the British Isles.

Iowa was part of the Territory of Indiana immediately after its purchase, then part of the Territory of Louisiana. From 1812 to 1821, Iowa was part of the Missouri Territory. When Missouri became a state in 1821, Iowa was left without government and remained so until 1834. In 1838, Iowa became a territory, following two years each as a part of the Michigan and Wisconsin Territories. In 1846, Iowa became a state with Iowa City as its capital. Des Moines became the capital in 1857.

Immediately prior to and after statehood, thousands of immigrants flocked to Iowa. The principal groups were Scandinavians, to the central and western sections; Hollanders, to the south central section; Germans, along the

Mississippi River; Scottish and Welsh, to the mining towns of the southern counties; and Czechs to the east central section. Iowa sided with the Union in the Civil War, sending over 76,000 men to serve in the Union army.

Some counties began keeping birth and death records as early as 1870, although it was not required until 1880. General compliance did not occur until 1924. Delayed registration of births also took place by 1940. These files are kept by the clerk of the district court. The Division of Vital Records, Iowa State Department of Health, Lucas State Office Building, Des Moines, IA 50319 (to verify current fees, call 515-281-5871), has birth, marriage, and death records where taken after July 1, 1880. Copies of records are available only to immediate family members, so relationship and reason for seeking information must be stated when writing. Statewide indexes by year are available. The birth index begins July 1, 1880, the marriage index begins July 1, 1916, and the death index, January 1891. Parentage is not listed on any death record until July 1904.

Early marriage records, some as early as 1850, may be obtained from county clerks. Many of these records have also been transcribed and published. Early divorce proceedings are located in the district courts. Transcribed copies were sent to the state beginning in 1906. Additional information may be obtained from the State Historical Society of Iowa, East 12th and Grand Avenue, Des Moines, IA 50319. Probate courts were created when Iowa became a territory. These were eventually discontinued and probate matters assigned to the district court. Copies of wills and probates can be obtained from the district court clerk. Territorial censuses were taken in 1836, 1838, 1844, and 1846, however, copies exist for only a few counties. State censuses were taken in 1847, 1849, 1851, 1852, 1853, 1854, 1856, 1885, 1895, 1905, 1915, and 1925. A few town censuses were also taken in the 1880's and 1890's.

Genealogical Archives, Libraries and Societies

Burlington Public Library, 501 N. Fourth St., Burlington, IA 52601

Charlotte Brett Memorial Collection of Genealogical Books and Magazines, Spencer Public Library, 21 E. 3rd Street, Spencer, Iowa 51301

Eisenhower, Mamie Doud, Birthplace, Museum and Library, 709 Carroll St (P. O. Box 55), Boone, IA 50036

Ericson Public Library, 702 Greene St., Boone, IA 50036

Family History Department, Donnellson Public Library, Donnellson, IA 52625

Gibson Memorial Library, 310 North Maple, Creston, IA 50801

Glenwood Public Library, Glenwood, IA 51534

Iowa Genealogical Society Library, P. O. Box 7735, Des Moines, IA 50320

Iowa Historical and Genealogical Library, Iowa Dept. of History and Archives, East 12th St. and Grand Ave., Des Moines, IA 50319

LeMars Public Library, 46 First St., S.W., LeMars, IA 51031

Marshalltown Public Library, 36 N. Center St., Marshalltown, IA 50158

Mason City Public Library, Mason City, IA 50401

Museum of History and Science, Park Avenue at South St., Waterloo, IA 50701

Norwegian-American Historical Museum, Decorah, IA 52101

Public Library, S. Market and Second St., Oskaloosa, IA 52577

Public Library, Sixth & Jackson Sts., Sioux City, IA 51101

Sherry Foresman Library, R 1, Box 23, Menlo, IA 50164

Spencer Public Library, 21 East Third St., Spencer, IA 51301

Urbandale Public Library, 7305 Aurora Ave., Urbandale, IA 50322

Adair County Anquestors Genealogical Society, R 1, Box 23, Menlo, IA 50164

Adams County Genealogical Society, P. O. Box 117, Prescott, IA 50859

American-Schleswig-Holstein Heritage Society, P. O. Box 21, Le Claire, IA 52753

Appanoose County Iowa Genealogy Society, Apt. 402, 1009 Shamrock Lane, Centerville, IA 52544

Benton County Historical Society, 612 First Avenue, Vinton, IA 52349-1705

Boone County Genealogical Society, Box 453, Boone, IA 50036

Boone County Historical Society, P. O. Box 1, Boone, IA 50036

Botna Valley Genealogical Society, P. O. Box 633, Oakland, IA 51560

Bremer County Genealogical Society, Route 1, Box 132, Plainfield, IA 50666

Buena Vista Genealogical Society, 501 Lake Ave., Storm Lake, IA 50588

Buena Vista County Historical Society, Box 882, Storm Lake, IA 50588

Carroll County, Iowa Genealogical Society, P. O. Box 21, Carroll, IA 51401

Cass County Iowa Genealogical Society, 706 Hazel Street, Atlantic, IA 50022

Cedar County Genealogcial Society, 409 Sycamore St., Tipton, IA 52772-1649

Cedar County Historical Society, 409 Sycamore St., Tipton, IA 52772-1649

Central Community Historical Society, R. R. 2, Box 98, DeWitt, IA 52742

Central Iowa Genealogical Society, Box 945, Marshalltown, IA 50158

Cherokee County Historical Society, P. O. Box 247, Cleghorn, IA 51014

Chickasaw County Genealogical Society, P. O. Box 434, New Hampton, IA 50659

Clayton County Genealogical Society, Box 846, Elkader, IA 52043

Crawford County Genealogical Society, P. O. Box 26, Vail, IA 51465

Delaware County Genealogical Society, 200 E. Main St., Manchester, IA 52057

Des Moines County Genealogical Society, P. O. Box 493, Burlington, IA 52601

Dubuque County-Key City Genealogical Society, P. O. Box 13, Dubuque, IA 52004-0013

Federation of Genealogical Societies, P. O. Box 220, Davenport, IA 52805

Franklin County Genealogical Society of Hampton, Iowa, RR 1, P. O. Box 119, Geneva, IA 50633

Fremont County Historical Society, Sidney, IA 51652

Gateway Genealogical Society, 618 14th Ave., Camanche, IA 52730

Greater Sioux County Genealogical Society, Sioux Center Public Library, 327 First Ave., N.E., Sioux Center, IA 51250

Greene County Iowa Genealogical Society, P. O. Box 133, Jefferson, IA 50129

Grundy County Genealogical Society, 708 West St. Reinbeck, IA 50669-1365

Guthrie County Genealogical Society, P. O. Box 96, Jamaica, IA 50128

Hancock County Genealogical Society, Box 81, Klemme, IA 50449

Hardin County, Iowa Genealogical Society, P. O. Box 252, Eldora, IA 50627

Harrison County, Iowa Genealogical Society, Rt. 2 Box 135, Woodbine, IA 51579

Henry County Genealogical Society, P. O. Box 81, Mt. Pleasant, IA 52641

Iowa City Genealogical Society, Box 822, Iowa City, IA 52244

Iowa County Historical Society, Ladora, IA 52251

Iowa Department, Daughters of Union Veterans, R 1, Box 23, Menlo, IA 50164

Iowa Genealogical Society, P. O. Box 7735, Des Moines, IA 50322

Iowa Lakes Genealogical Society, Box 91, Everly, IA 51338

Iowa Society, Sons of the American Revolution, 227 Clinton St., Boone, IA 50036

Jackson County Genealogical Chapter, Box 1065, Maquoketa, IA 52060

Jasper County Genealogical Society, P. O. Box 163, Newton, IA 50208

Jefferson County Genealogical Society, Route 1, Fairfield, IA 52556

Johnson County Historical Society, P. O. Box 5081, Coralville, IA 51141

Jones County Genealogical Society, P. O. Box 174, Anomosa, IA 52205

Lee County Genealogical Society of Iowa, P. O. Box 303, Keokuk, IA 52632

Linn County Heritage Society, P. O. Box 175, Cedar Rapids, IA 52406

Madison County Genealogy Society, P. O. Box 26, Winterset, IA 50273-0026

Marion County Genealogical Society, P. O. Box 385, Knoxville, IA 50138

Mid-America Genealogical Society, P. O. Box 316, Davenport, IA 52801

Mills County Genealogical Society, Glenwood Public Library, 109 N. Vine St., Glenwood, IA 51534

Monroe County Genealogical Society, Albia Public Library, 203 Benton Ave. E., Albia, IA 52531

Nishnabotna Genealogical Society, Rt. 2, Box 129, Harlan, IA 51537

North Central Iowa Genealogical Society, P. O. Box 237, Mason City, IA 50401

Northeast Iowa Genealogical Society, Grout Museum of History and Science, 503 South Street, Waterloo, IA 50701

Northwest Iowa Genealogical Society, LeMars Public Library, 46 First St., S.W., LeMars, IA 51031

Old Fort Genealogical Society, P. O. Box #1, Fort Madison, IA 52627

Page County Genealogical Society, Rural Route 2, Box 236, Shenandoah, IA 51610

Palo Alto County Genealogical Society, 207 N. Wallace St., Emmetsburg, IA 50536

Pioneer Sons and Daughters Genealogical Society, P. O. Box 2103, Des Moines, IA 50310

Poweshiek County Historical & Genealogical Society, P. O. Box 280, 206 North Mill St., Montezuma, IA 50171

Ringgold County Genealogical Society, 204 W. Jefferson, Mount Ayr, IA 50854

Sac County Genealogical Society, P. O. Box 234, Lytton, IA 50561

Scott County Iowa Genealogical Society, P. O. Box 3132, Davenport, IA 52808

State Historical Society of Iowa, 600 E. Locust, Des Moines, IA 50319

State Historical Society of Iowa, 402 Iowa Ave., Iowa City, IA 52240

Story County Chapter of the Iowa Genealogical Society, c / o Chamber of Commerce, 205 Clark Ave., Ames, IA 50010

Tama County Tracers Genealogical Society, 200 North Broadway, P. O. Box 84, Toledo, IA 52342

Taylor County Genealogical Society, RR 3, Bedford, IA 50833

Tree Stumpers, Rt. 1, Box 65, Meriden, IA 51037

Union County Genealogical Society, Gibson Memorial Library, 310 North Maple, Creston, IA 50801

Wapello County Genealogical Society, P. O. Box 163, Ottumwa, IA 52501

Warren County Genealogical Society, Rt. 2, 802 Kennedy St., Indianola, IA 50125

Washington County Genealogical Society, P. O. Box 446, Washington, IA 52353

Wayne County Genealogical Society, 304 North Franklin, Corydon, IA 50060

Webster County Genealogical Society, P. O. Box 1584, Fort Dodge, IA 50501

Woodbury County Genealogical Society, P. O. Box 624, Sioux City, IA 51102

Wright County Genealogical Searchers, P. O. Box 225, Clarion, IA 50525

Printed Census Records and Mortality Schedules

Federal Census 1840, 1850, 1860, 1870, 1880, 1900, 1910
Federal Mortality Schedules 1850, 1860, 1870, 1880
State/Territorial Census 1836, 1840-1849, 1851, 1852, 1854, 1856, 1885, 1895, 1905, 1915, 1925
Sac and Fox Indian Census 1847

Valuable Printed Sources

Atlases, Maps, and Gazetteers

Alphabetical Listings of Iowa Post Offices, 1833-1970. Iowa Postal History Society, n.d.

Hair, James T. *Iowa State Gazetteer*. Chicago: Bailey & Hair, 1865.

Bibliographies

A Bibliography of Iowa Newspapers, 1836-1976. Iowa City: State Historical Society of Iowa, 1979.

Cheever, L. O. *Newspaper Collection of the State Historical Society of Iowa*. Iowa City: State Historical Society of Iowa, 1969.

Peterson, Becki. *Iowa County Records Manual*. Iowa City: State Historical Society of Iowa, 1987.

Histories

Morford, Charles. *Biographical Index to the County Histories of Iowa*. Baltimore: Gateway Press, 1979.

Petersen, William J. *Iowa History Reference Guide*. Iowa City: State Historical Society of Iowa, 1952.

IOWA COUNTY DATA
State Map on Page M-14

Name	Map Index	Date Created	Parent County or Territory From Which Organized
* **Adair**	D2	1851	Cass

Adair County, PO Box L, Greenfield, IA 50849-1290 .... (515)743-2445
(Clk Dis Ct has b & d rec from 1880, m rec from 1870, div, pro & civ ct rec from 1852)

| * **Adams** | C2 | 1851 | Taylor |

Adams County, Davis & 9th, Corning, IA 50841 .... (515)322-4711
(Clk Dis Ct has b & d rec from 1880, m rec from 1853, div rec 1910, pro & civ ct rec from 1860; Co Rcdr has Ind rec)

| * **Allamakee** | G6 | 1847 | Clayton |

Allamakee County, PO Box 248, Waukon, IA 52172-0248 .... (319)568-3318
(Co Clk has b & d rec from 1880, m rec from 1848, pro & civ ct rec from 1852, div rec & a bur book; Co Rcdr has old newsprs; Co census taken 1 Jun 1880)

| * **Appanoose** | F1 | 1843 | Davis |

Appanoose County, County Courthouse, Centerville, IA 52544 .... (515)856-6101
(Clk Dis Ct has b & d rec from 1880, m rec from 1846, div, pro & civ ct rec from 1847, naturalization rec 1868-1953; Co Rcdr has Ind & mill dischrg from 1850; census taken 1856, 1885, 1895)

| * **Audubon** | C3 | 1851 | Cass, Black Hawk |

Audubon County, County Courthouse, Audubon, IA 50025 .... (712)563-4275
(Clk Dis Ct has b, d & bur rec from 1880, m rec from 1856, div from 1867, civ ct rec from 1861, & pro rec from 1855; Co Rec has Ind rec)

| * **Benton** | G3 | 1837 | Indian Land Purchase |

Benton County, 100 E 4th St, Vinton, IA 52349-1771 .... (319)472-2766
(Clk Dis Ct has b, d, bur rec from 1880, m rec from 1852, div rec from 1900, pro rec from 1872, civ ct rec from 1850, & Ind rec from 1846)

| * **Black Hawk** | F4 | 1843 | Delaware |

Black Hawk County, 316 E 5th St, Waterloo, IA 50703-4712 .... (319)291-2500
(Clk Dis Ct has m rec from 1854, div & pro rec from 1880, b & d rec from 1880 & 1935)

| * **Boone** | D3 | 1846 | Polk |

Boone County, County Courthouse, Boone, IA 50036 .... (515)432-6291
(Clk Dis Ct has b & d rec from 1880, m & pro rec from 1850, div rec from 1900, civ ct rec from 1851, school rec 1889-1925, & naturalization rec 1867-1916; Co Rcdr has Ind rec)

| * **Bremer** | F5 | 1851 | Winnebago, Indian Reserve |

Bremer County, 415 E Bremer Ave, Waverly, IA 50677-3536 .... (319)352-5040
[FHL has some m, cem, civ ct, Ind, nat, pro, tax rec]

| * **Buchanan** | G4 | 1837 | Delaware |

Buchanan County, 210 5th Ave NE, Independence, IA 50644-1959 .... (319)334-2196
(Clk Dis Ct has b, d rec from 1880, m rec from 1848, div, pro, civ ct rec from 1845)

| * **Buena Vista** | C5 | 1851 | Sac, Clay |

Buena Vista County, PO Box 1186, Storm Lake, IA 50588-1186 .... (712)749-2546
(Clk Dis Ct has b, m, d, pro rec from 1880, div & civ ct rec from 1877)

| **Buncombe** (changed to Lyon, 1862) | | | |

| * **Butler** | F5 | 1851 | Buchanan, Black Hawk |

Butler County, PO Box 325, Allison, IA 50602-0307 .... (319)267-2487
(Clk Dis Ct has b, d, div, pro, civ ct rec from 1880, m rec from 1854, old cir ct rec from 1870)

Name	Map Index	Date Created	Parent County or Territory From Which Organized

* **Calhoun**   C4   1855   Formerly Fox County
Calhoun County, PO Box 273, Rockwell City, IA 50579-0273 .... (712)297-8122
(Clk Dis Ct has b, d, pro rec from 1880; m rec from 1863; bur rec from 1900; div rec from 1906 & civ ct rec from 1872)

*† **Carroll**   C3   1851   Guthrie
Carroll County, PO Box 867, Carroll, IA 51401-0867 .... (712)792-4327
(Clk Dis Ct has b & d rec from 1880, m rec from 1868, div rec from 1923, pro rec from 1858, civ ct rec from 1871, naturalization rec from 1873, tax roll 1934, & census rec 1875, 1880, 1885, 1895; Co Rcdr has Ind rec)

* **Cass**   C2   1851   Pottawattamie
Cass County, 7th St Courthouse, Atlantic, IA 50022 .... (712)243-2105
(Clk Dis Ct has b & d rec from 1880, m rec from 1877, div rec from 1906, pro rec from 1870, dis ct rec from 1865)

* **Cedar**   H3   1837   Wisconsin Territory
Cedar County, 400 Cedar St, Tipton, IA 52772-1752 .... (319)886-2101
(Clk Dis Ct has b, d, bur rec from 1880, m, pro, civ ct rec from 1839, div rec from 1850; Co Rcdr has Ind rec)

* **Cerro Gordo**   E5   1851   Floyd
Cerro Gordo County, 220 N Washington Ave, Mason City, IA 50401-3254 .... (515)421-3074
[FHL has some m & cem rec, 1856 census]

*† **Cherokee**   B5   1851   Crawford
Cherokee County, PO Box F, Cherokee, IA 51012 .... (712)225-2706
(Clk Dis Ct has b & d rec from 1880, m rec from 1872, div, pro, civ ct rec, some cem rec)

* **Chickasaw**   F5   1851   Fayette
Chickasaw County, Prospect St, New Hampton, IA 50659 .... (515)394-2106
(Clk Dis Ct has b, div, civ ct rec from 1880, m rec from 1853, pro rec from 1857, d rec 1880-1919 & from 1941; Co Rcdr has Ind rec)

* **Clarke**   E2   1846   Lucas
Clarke County, 117 1/2 S Main St, Osceola, IA 50213-1299 .... (515)342-2213
(Clk Dis Ct has b & d rec from 1880, m rec from 1850, pro & civ ct rec 1865, div rec from 1905; Co Rcdr has Ind rec)

* **Clay**   C5   1851   Indian Lands
Clay County, 215 W 4th St, Spencer, IA 51301-3822 .... (712)262-4335
(Clk Dis Ct has b & d rec from 1880, m rec from 1866, pro rec from 1871, div rec from 1906, civ ct rec from 1869; Co Aud has Ind rec)

* **Clayton**   G5   1837   Dubuque
Clayton County, 111 High St, Elkader, IA 52043 .... (319)245-2204
(Clk Dis Ct has b rec from 1880, m rec from 1848, d rec from 1880-1921 and from 1941 to present, div rec from 1880, pro, civ ct rec from 1840, naturalization rec from 1858; Co Rcdr has Ind rec from 1839)

* **Clinton**   I3   1837   Dubuque
Clinton County, PO Box 157, Clinton, IA 52732-0157 .... (319)243-6210
(Clk Dis Ct has b & d rec 1880-1935 & from 1941, m & pro from 1840, div & civ ct rec from mid 1800s; Co Rcdr has Ind rec from 1840)

* **Crawford**   C3   1851   Shelby
Crawford County, PO Box 546, Denison, IA 51442-0546 .... (712)263-2242
(Clk Dis Ct has b & d rec from 1880, m rec from 1855, div rec from 1906, pro rec from 1869, civ ct rec from 1866 & some naturalization rec; Co Rcdr has Ind rec from 1859)

*† **Dallas**   D3   1846   Polk
Dallas County, 801 Court St, Adel, IA 50003-1478 .... (515)993-4789
(Clk Dis Ct has b & d rec from 1880, m rec from 1850, div rec from 1881, pro rec from 1863 & civ ct rec from 1860; Co Rcdr has Ind rec)

* **Davis**   F1   1843   Van Buren
Davis County, Courthouse Sq, Bloomfield, IA 52537-1600 .... (515)664-2011
(Clk Dis Ct has b & d rec from 1880, m rec from 1844, div, pro & civ ct rec from 1830)

* **Decatur**   E1   1846   Appanoose
Decatur County, 207 N Main St, Leon, IA 50144-1647 .... (515)446-4331
(Courthouse burned in 1874; Co Clk has b, d, div, pro rec from 1880; m rec from 1874, Ind rec from 1874, and some mil dischrg rec and cem rec)

* **Delaware**   H4   1837   Dubuque
Delaware County, PO Box 527, Manchester, IA 52057-0527 .... (319)927-4942
(Clk Dis Ct has b, d rec from 1880, m, div, civ ct rec from 1851, pro rec from 1849; Co Rcdr has Ind rec)

* **Des Moines**   H1   1834   Wisconsin Territory
Des Moines County, PO Box 158, Burlington, IA 52601-0158 .... (319)753-8272
(Clk Dis Ct has b rec from 1880, m, div, pro, civ ct rec from 1835, d rec from 1880 to 1921 and then from 1941, naturalization from 1840)

* **Dickinson**   C6   1851   Kossuth
Dickinson County, 18th & Hill County Courthouse, Spirit Lake, IA 51360 .... (712)336-1138
(Clk Dis Ct has b, m, d, bur, div, pro, civ ct rec from 1880; Co Rcdr has Ind rec)

*† **Dubuque**   H4   1834   Michigan Territory
Dubuque County, 720 Central Ave, Dubuque, IA 52001-7079 .... (319)589-4418
(Clk Dis Ct has b & d rec from 1880, m rec from 1840, div from 1900, pro from 1835 & civ ct rec from 1836; Co Rcdr has Ind rec from 1836)

Name	Map Index	Date Created	Parent County or Territory From Which Organized

* **Emmet**   C6   1851   Kossuth, Dickinson
Emmet County, 609 1st Ave N, Estherville, IA 51334 .... (712)362-3325
(Clk Dis Ct has b rec from 1883, m & d rec from 1890, div from 1915, pro rec from 1885)

* **Fayette**   G5   1837   Clayton
Fayette County, Vine St, West Union, IA 52175 .... (319)422-6061
(Clk Dis Ct has b & d rec from 1880, m rec from 1851, div from 1897, pro from 1869, civ ct from 1852; Co Rcdr has Ind rec from 1855)

* **Floyd**   F5   1851   Chickasaw
Floyd County, 101 S Main St, Charles City, IA 50616-2756 .... (515)228-7111
(Clk Dis Ct has b & d rec from 1880, m & div rec from 1860, pro & civ ct rec from 1854)

Fox (see Calhoun)

* **Franklin**   E5   1851   Chickasaw
Franklin County, 12 1st Ave NW, Hampton, IA 50441 .... (515)456-5626
(Clk Cir Ct has b, d rec from 1880, m rec from 1855, pro rec from 1864, div, civ ct rec from 1869; Co Rcdr has Ind rec)

* **Fremont**   B1   1847   Pottawattamie
Fremont County, Courthouse Sq, Sidney, IA 51652-0549 .... (712)374-2232
(Clk Dis Ct has b, d rec from 1880, except 1935-41, limited m rec from 1848, div, pro, civ ct rec; Co Rcdr has Ind rec)

* **Greene**   D3   1851   Dallas
Greene County, County Courthouse, Jefferson, IA 50129-2294 .... (515)386-2516
(Clk Dis Ct has b, d, div & civ ct rec from 1880, m & pro rec from 1854; Co Rcdr has Ind rec)

* **Grundy**   F4   1851   Black Hawk
Grundy County, 700 G Ave, Grundy Center, IA 50638-1440 .... (319)824-5229
(Clk Dis Ct has b, div, civ ct rec from 1880, m rec from 1856, d rec from 1881, pro rec from 1870; Co Rcdr has Ind rec)

* **Guthrie**   D3   1851   Jackson
Guthrie County, 200 N 5th St, Guthrie Center, IA 50115-1331 .... (515)747-3415
(Clk Dis Ct has b, d rec from 1880, m rec from 1852, div rec from 1883, pro rec from 1881, civ ct rec from 1916)

* **Hamilton**   E4   1856   Webster
Hamilton County, County Courthouse, Webster City, IA 50595-3158 .... (515)832-1771
(Clk Dis Ct has b, m, d, div, pro, civ ct rec from 1880) (Once known as Yell County)

* **Hancock**   E5   1851   Wright
Hancock County, 855 State St, Garner, IA 50438-1645 .... (515)923-2532
(Clk Dis Ct has b, m, d, bur, div rec from 1880, pro, civ ct rec from 1856)

* **Hardin**   E4   1851   Black Hawk
Hardin County, Edgington Ave, Eldora, IA 50627-1741 .... (515)858-3461
(Clk Dis Ct has b, d rec from 1880, m rec from 1864, div rec from 1889, pro, civ ct, Ind rec from 1853)

* **Harrison**   B3   1851   Pottawattamie
Harrison County, 113 N 2nd Ave, Logan, IA 51546-1331 .... (712)644-2665
(Clk Dis Ct has b & d rec from 1880, m & div rec from 1853, pro rec from 1869, civ ct rec from 1850 & some bur rec)

* **Henry**   G2   1836   Wisconsin Territory
Henry County, 100 E Washington St, Mount Pleasant, IA 52641-1931 .... (319)385-8480
(Clk Dis Ct has b rec from 1880, m, d, div, pro, civ ct & adoption rec from 1836, naturalization rec from 1841; Co Rcdr has Ind rec from 1836)

* **Howard**   F6   1851   Chickasaw, Floyd
Howard County, 218 N Elm St, Cresco, IA 52136-1522 .... (319)547-2661
(Clk Dis Ct has b, m, d, rec from 1880, div & civ ct rec from 1876, pro rec from 1877; Co Rcdr has Ind rec from 1855)

* **Humboldt**   D5   1851   Webster
Humboldt County, County Courthouse, Dakota City, IA 50529-9999 .... (515)332-1806
(Clk Dis Ct has b rec from 1880, m rec from 1858, d rec from 1895, div rec from 1890, pro rec from 1873 & civ ct rec from 1892)

*† **Ida**   C4   1851   Cherokee
Ida County, 401 Moorehead St, Ida Grove, IA 51445-1429 .... (712)364-2628
(Clk Dis Ct has b, m, d, div, pro, civ ct rec from 1880; Co Rcdr has Ind rec)

* **Iowa**   G3   1843   Washington
Iowa County, Court Ave, Marengo, IA 52301 .... (319)642-3914
(Clk Dis Ct has b & d rec from 1880, m rec from 1846, pro rec from 1850, civ ct rec from 1900, div rec from 1901)

* **Jackson**   I4   1837   Wisconsin Territory
Jackson County, 201 W Platt St, Maquoketa, IA 52060-2243 .... (319)652-4946
(Clk Dis Ct has b & d rec from 1880, m rec from 1850, div rec from 1906, pro rec from 1869 & civ ct rec from 1858)

*† **Jasper**   E3   1846   Mahaska
Jasper County, 100 1st St, Newton, IA 50208 .... (515)792-3255
(Clk Dis Ct has b, d rec from 1880, m rec from 1849, pro rec from 1882, civ ct rec from 1857, div rec)

* **Jefferson**   G2   1839   Indian Land Purchase
Jefferson County, PO Box 984, Fairfield, IA 52556-0984 .... (515)472-3454
(Clk Dis Ct has b, d, div & civ ct rec 1880, m rec 1839 & pro rec 1850; Co Rcdr has Ind rec)

* **Johnson**   G3   1837   Des Moines
Johnson County, 417 S Clinton St, Iowa City, IA 52240-4108 .... (319)356-6060
(Clk Dis Ct has b & d rec from 1880, m rec from 1839, pro rec from 1840, div & civ ct rec; Co Aud has Ind rec)

Name	Map Index	Date Created	Parent County or Territory From Which Organized

* **Jones**   H4   1837   Wisconsin Territory
Jones County, High St, Anamosa, IA 52205 .... (319)462-4341
(Clk Dis Ct has b & d rec from 1880, m & pro rec from 1840, div rec from 1895, & civ ct rec; Co Rcdr has Ind rec & mil discharge rec from 1864)

* **Keokuk**   G2   1837   Washington
Keokuk County, Courthouse Sq, Sigourney, IA 52591-1499 .... (515)622-2210
(Clk Dis Ct has b, d rec from 1880, m, div, pro, civ ct rec from 1845; Co Rcdr has Ind rec)

Kishkekosh (changed to Monroe, 1846)

* **Kossuth**   D6   1851   Webster
Kossuth County, 114 W State St, Algona, IA 50511-2613 .... (515)295-3240
(Clk Dis Ct has b rec from 1880 to 1935 and from 1941 to present, m rec from 1857, d bur rec from 1880, pro rec from 1877, div, civ ct rec)

* **Lee**   G1   1836   Des Moines
Lee County, PO Box 1443, Fort Madison, IA 52627-1443 .... (319)372-3523
(Clk Dis Ct, Keokuk, has b rec from 1880; Clk Dis Ct, Ft. Madison, has b, d rec 1880-1921, 1941 to present, pro rec from 1838; Clk Dis Ct, Keokuk, has m, pro rec from 1873, d rec from 1867, div rec from 1906, civ ct rec from 1898; Co Rcdr has Ind rec)

* **Linn**   G3   1837   Wisconsin Territory
Linn County, 50 3rd Ave Bridge, Cedar Rapids, IA 52401-1704 .... (319)398-3411
(Clk Dis Ct has b rec from 1880-1934, 1941 to present; d rec from 1880-1919, 1941 to present, m rec from 1840, div, pro, civ ct rec from 1860)

* **Louisa**   H2   1836   Des Moines
Louisa County, 117 S Main St, Wapello, IA 52653-1547 .... (319)523-4541
(Clk Dis Ct has b, d rec from 1880, m rec from 1842, div, pro, civ ct rec)

* **Lucas**   E2   1846   Monroe
Lucas County, County Courthouse, Chariton, IA 50049 .... (515)774-4421
(Clk Dis Ct has b & d rec from 1880, m rec from 1849, div rec from 1900, pro rec from 1850 & civ ct rec from 1900)

* **Lyon**   B6   1851   Woodbury
Lyon County, 206 S 2nd Ave, Rock Rapids, IA 51246-1597 .... (712)472-2623
(Clk Dis Ct has b, m, d, div, pro, civ ct, Ind rec from 1880)

* **Madison**   D2   1846   Polk
Madison County, PO Box 152, Winterset, IA 50273-0152 .... (515)462-4451
(Clk Dis Ct has b, d rec from 1880, m rec from 1855, bur rec from 1849, div, civ ct rec from 1861, pro rec from 1852; Co Rcdr has Ind rec)

* **Mahaska**   F2   1843   Fox, Sac Indian Purchase
Mahaska County, PO Box 30, Oskaloosa, IA 52577-0030 .... (515)673-7786
(Clk Dis Ct has b & d rec from 1880, m, div, pro & civ ct rec from 1844)

* **Marion**   E2   1845   Washington
Marion County, PO Box 497, Knoxville, IA 50138-0497 .... (515)828-2207
(Clk Dis Ct has b, d rec from 1880, m rec from 1846, div, pro rec from 1845)

* **Marshall**   F4   1846   Jasper
Marshall County, 17 E Main St, Marshalltown, IA 50158-4906 .... (515)754-6373
(Clk Dis Ct has b & d rec from 1880, m, pro, civ ct & div rec from 1850, & crim ct rec)

* **Mills**   B2   1851   Pottawattamie
Mills County, 418 Sharp St, Glenwood, IA 51534-1756 .... (712)527-4880
(Clk Dis Ct has incom b rec 1880, d & div rec 1880, pro & civ ct rec 1851)

* **Mitchell**   F6   1851   Chickasaw
Mitchell County, County Courthouse, Osage, IA 50461 .... (515)732-3726
(Clk Dis Ct has m rec from 1860, b, d, div, pro & civ ct rec from 1880; Co Rcdr has Ind rec)

* **Monona**   B3   1851   Harrison
Monona County, 610 Iowa Ave, Onawa, IA 51040-1699 .... (712)423-2491
(Clk Dis Ct has b rec from 1880, m rec from 1857, d rec from 1880, bur rec from 1950, div rec from 1856, pro rec from 1858 & civ ct rec from 1856)

* **Monroe**   F2   1843   Wapello (formerly Kishkekosh)
Monroe County, County Courthouse, Albia, IA 52531 .... (515)932-5212
(Clk Dis Ct has b & d rec from 1880, m, div, pro & civ ct rec from 1845; Co Rcdr has Ind & mil dischrg rec)

*† **Montgomery**   C2   1851   Polk
Montgomery County, 105 Coolbaugh St, Red Oak, IA 51566 .... (712)623-4986
(Clk Dis Ct has b & d rec from 1880, m rec from 1856, div rec from 1873, pro rec from 1860 & civ ct rec from 1873; Co Rcdr has Ind rec)

* **Muscatine**   H3   1836   Des Moines
Muscatine County, PO Box 327, Muscatine, IA 52761-0327 .... (319)263-6511
(Clk Dis Ct has b & d rec from 1880, m rec from 1837, div & civ ct rec from 1861 & pro rec from 1866)

* **O'Brien**   B5   1851   Cherokee
O'Brien County, 155 S Hayes, Primghar, IA 51245 .... (712)757-3255
(Clk Dis Ct has b, m, div, pro & civ ct rec from 1880, some d & bur rec)

Name	Map Index	Date Created	Parent County or Territory From Which Organized

* **Osceola** B6 1851 Woodbury
Osceola County, 614 5th Ave, Sibley, IA 51249-1704 .... (712)754-3595
(Clk Dis Ct has b, m, d, div, pro, civ ct rec from 1880)

* **Page** C1 1847 Pottawattamie
Page County, 112 E Main St, Clarinda, IA 51632-2197 .... (712)542-3214
[FHL has some m, cem, pro rec]

* **Palo Alto** C5 1858 Kossuth
Palo Alto County, 11th & Broadway, Emmetsburg, IA 50536 .... (712)852-3603
(Clk Dis Ct has b rec from 1880 to 1904, m rec from 1880, some d rec from 1880, div pro & civ ct rec)

* **Plymouth** A5 1851 Woodbury
Plymouth County, 3rd Ave & 2nd St SE, Le Mars, IA 51031 .... (712)546-6100
(Clk Dis Ct has b, d, div & pro rec from 1880, m rec from 1869, civ ct rec from 1869; Co Rcdr has Ind rec)

* **Pocahontas** C5 1851 Humboldt, Greene
Pocahontas County, Court Sq County Courthouse, Pocahontas, IA 50574 .... (712)335-4208
(Clk Dis Ct has b & d rec from 1880, m rec from 1881, div & civ ct rec from 1860, pro rec from 1872; Co Rcdr has Ind rec)

*† **Polk** E3 1846 Indian Lands
Polk County, 500 Mulberry St, Des Moines, IA 50309-4238 .... (515)286-3772
(Clk Ct has b & d rec from 1941, m rec from 1846, pro rec from 1855, civ ct rec from 1850, div rec from 1870, & naturalization rec 1870-1928)

* **Pottawattamie** B2 1848 Indian Lands
Pottawattamie County, 227 S 6th St, Council Bluffs, IA 51501-4209 .... (712)328-5604
(Clk Ct has b & d rec 1880-1921, & from 1941, m rec from 1840, div rec from 1907, pro rec from 1898)

* **Poweshiek** F3 1843 Mesquakie Indian Lands
Poweshiek County, 302 E Main St, Montezuma, IA 50171 .... (515)623-5644
(Clk Dis Ct has b, d, div & civ ct rec from 1880, m, pro rec from 1860; Co Rcdr has Ind rec)

* **Ringgold** D1 1847 Taylor
Ringgold County, County Courthouse, Mount Ayr, IA 50854 .... (515)464-3234
(Clk Dis Ct has b, m, d, div, pro, civ ct rec from 1880; Co Rcdr has Ind rec)

*† **Sac** C4 1851 Greene
Sac County, PO Box 368, Sac City, IA 50583-0368 .... (712)662-7791
(Clk Dis Ct has b, m, bur, div, pro, civ ct rec from 1888; Co Rcdr has Ind rec from 1856; Courthouse burned 1888, some charred rec recovered)

* **Scott** I3 1837 Wisconsin Territory
Scott County, 416 W 4th St, Davenport, IA 52801-1187 .... (319)326-8647
(Clk Dis Ct has b, d & bur rec from 1880, m rec from 1837, div & pro rec from 1838 & civ ct rec from 1851)

* **Shelby** C3 1853 Cass
Shelby County, PO Box 431, Harlan, IA 51537-0431 .... (712)755-5543
(Clk Ct has b, m, d, div, pro & civ ct rec from 1880, pro rec are limited from 1853, newspapers are available at Public Library)

* **Sioux** B5 1851 Plymouth
Sioux County, 210 Central Ave SW, Orange City, IA 51041-1751 .... (712)737-2286
(Clk Dis Ct has b, d rec from 1880, m, pro, civ ct rec from 1870, div rec from 1908)

Slaughter (changed to Washington, 1939)

* **Story** E3 1846 Jasper, Polk, Boone
Story County, 900 6th St, Nevada, IA 50201-2004 .... (515)382-6581
(Clk Dis Ct has b & d rec from 1880, m, div, pro, civ ct crim rec from 1854)

* **Tama** F4 1843 Boone, Benton
Tama County, County Courthouse, Toledo, IA 52342 .... (515)484-3721
(Clk Dis Ct has b & d rec from 1880, m rec from 1853, div rec from 1908, pro rec from 1895 & civ ct rec from 1859)

*† **Taylor** C1 1847 Page
Taylor County, County Courthouse, Bedford, IA 50833 .... (712)523-2095
(Clk Dis Ct has b, d & bur rec from 1880, m rec from 1854, div rec from 1858, pro rec from 1863, civ ct rec from 1858; Co Rcdr has Ind rec)

* **Union** D2 1851 Clarke
Union County, 300 N Pine St, Creston, IA 50801-2430 .... (515)782-7315
(Clk Dis Ct has b, d, div, pro & civ ct rec from 1880, m rec from 1856; Co Asr has Ind rec)

* **Van Buren** G1 1836 Des Moines
Van Buren County, PO Box 475, Keosauqua, IA 52565-0475 .... (319)293-3129
(Clk Dis Ct has b & d rec from 1880, m, div, pro & civ ct rec from 1837)

Wahkaw (changed to Woodbury, 1853)

* **Wapello** F2 1843 Indian Lands
Wapello County, 4th & Court Sts, Ottumwa, IA 52501-2599 .... (515)683-0060
[FHL has some b, m, d, cem, civ ct, Ind, nat, pro rec]

* **Warren** E2 1846 Polk
Warren County, PO Box 379, Indianola, IA 50125-0379 .... (515)961-1033
(Clk Dis Ct has b, d, div, pro, civ ct rec from 1880, m rec from 1850)

Name	Map Index	Date Created	Parent County or Territory From Which Organized
* **Washington**	G2	1837	Wisconsin Territory (formerly Slaughter)

Washington County, PO Box 391, Washington, IA 52353-0391 .... (319)653-7741
(Clk Dis Ct has b & d rec from 1880, m rec from 1844, div, pro & civ ct rec from 1836 & some unindexed naturalization rec; Co Rcdr has Ind rec)

| * **Wayne** | E1 | 1846 | Appanoose |

Wayne County, PO Box 424, Corydon, IA 50060-0424 .... (515)872-2264
(Clk Dis Ct has b & d rec from 1880, m rec from 1851, div rec from 1906, pro rec from 1891, civ ct rec from 1875 & cir rec from 1860)

| * **Webster** | D4 | 1851 | Yell, Risley (now known as Hamilton) |

Webster County, 701 Central Ave, Fort Dodge, IA 51501-3813 .... (515)576-7115
(Clk Dis Ct has b rec from 1876, m rec from 1853, d rec from 1860, div rec from 1870, pro rec from 1855 & civ ct rec 1860; Co Aud has Ind rec)

| * **Winnebago** | E6 | 1857 | Kossuth |

Winnebago County, 126 S Clark St, Forest City, IA 50436-1793 .... (515)582-4520
(Clk Ct has b & d rec from 1880, m, div, pro & civ ct rec from 1865; Co Regstr has bur rec)

| * **Winneshiek** | G6 | 1847 | Indian Lands |

Winneshiek County, 201 W Main St, Decorah, IA 52101-1775 .... (319)382-2469
(Clk Dis Ct has b & d rec from 1880, m rec from 1851, div rec from 1855, pro rec from 1853 & civ ct rec from 1855)

| *† **Woodbury** | B4 | 1851 | Indian Lands (formerly Wahkaw) |

Woodbury County, 101 Court St, Sioux City, IA 51101-1909 .... (712)279-6616
(Clk Dis Ct has b, d rec from 1880, some m rec from 1854, m rec from 1880, div rec from 1857, pro rec from 1868, civ ct rec from 1850, adoption rec from 1920, mental rec from 1871)

| * **Worth** | E6 | 1851 | Mitchell |

Worth County, 1000 Central Ave, Northwood, IA 50459-1523 .... (515)324-2840
(Clk Dis Ct has b rec from 1880 incom, m rec from 1858, d rec from 1880 to 1919, div rec from 1879, pro & civ ct rec from 1857 & naturalization rec; Co Aud has Ind rec)

| * **Wright** | E5 | 1851 | Webster |

Wright County, PO Box 306, Clarion, IA 50525-0306 .... (515)532-3113
(Clk Dis Ct has b, d & pro rec from 1880, m rec from 1860, div & civ ct rec from 1873, naturalization rec 1857-1929; Co Rcdr has Ind rec; City Clerks and libraries have bur rec)

Yell (Now known as Hamilton County)

* At least one county history has been published about this county.
† Inventory of county archives was made by the Historical Records Survey. (See Introduction)

KANSAS

CAPITAL · TOPEKA — TERRITORY 1854 — STATE 1861 (34th)
State Map on Page M-15

Kansas was part of the Louisiana Purchase in 1803. Government expeditions to the area reported it to be a desert, starting the myth of the Great American Desert. As the land was deemed unfit for white habitation, Indians from the East were moved into the area to live. Hostilities between the whites and the Indians increased when the Santa Fe Trail traversed the state beginning in 1821. To protect travelers, forts were established along the trail, beginning with Fort Leavenworth in 1827. Later, the Oregon Trail crossed northeastern Kansas.

Kansas remained unorganized territory until 1854 when the Kansas-Nebraska Act created the Kansas and Nebraska territories. Kansas had the same boundaries as today except that its western boundary was the "summit of the Rocky Mountains". The Kansas-Nebraska Act also stipulated that the people of a territory would decide by majority vote whether Kansas would be a free or slave state. This act stimulated migration to Kansas as both pro and antislavery forces tried to gain the upper hand. The violence that marked the years from 1854 to statehood in 1861 led to the term "Bleeding Kansas". Kansas ultimately voted to be a free state. The population in 1861 was 110,000, consisting primarily of Southerners and New Englanders, along with others from Illinois, Indiana, Ohio, and Kentucky.

During the Civil War, Kansas had over 20,000 Union soldiers. Its men suffered the highest mortality rate of any state in the Union. Many of the remaining Indian tribes in the state agreed to leave the state by 1867 and move to Oklahoma. The few which refused to go fought against the inhabitants until 1878. A post-Civil War boom occurred due to the Homestead Act and railroad growth. Many Civil War veterans took up homesteads in the state and other settlers came from Germany, Russia, Sweden, England, and Mexico.

A few counties began keeping birth and death records in 1885. These may be obtained from the county clerk, Some cities also have birth and death records from 1910 to 1940. The Bureau of Registration and Health Statistics, Kansas State Department of Health, 6700 South Topeka Avenue, Topeka, KS 66620 (to verify current fees, call 913-296-1400), has birth and death records since July 1, 1911, marriages since May 1, 1913, and divorces since July 1, 1951. County clerks and probate court clerks have also kept marriage records. Divorces prior to 1951 are on file with the district court. After July 1951, probate judges handle probate matters, wills, and in most counties have civil court records. Real estate records are kept by the county recorder and county assessor. State and territorial censuses exist for 1855, 1865, 1875, 1885, 1895, 1905, 1915, and 1925. All censuses are available at the Kansas State Historical Society, 120 West Tenth, Topeka, KS 66612-1291. Some counties have voter censuses for 1856, 1857, and 1859.

Genealogical Archives, Libraries and Societies

Arkansas City Public Library, 213 W. 5th Ave., Arkansas City, KS 67705

Garden City Public Library, 210 N. 7th, Garden City, KS 67846

Johnson County Library, 8700 Shawnee Mission Parkway, Merriam, KS 66202

Lyon County Historical Museum, 118 East 6th Street, Emporia, KS 66801

Mennonite Library and Archives, Bethel College, 300 E. 27th St., North Newton, KS 67117

Pittsburg Public Library, 211 West 4th St., Pittsburg, KS 66762

Public Library, Independence, KS 67301

Public Library, Sixth & Minnesota Sts., Kansas City, KS 66101

Topeka Genealogical Society Library, 2717 S.E. Indiana Street, Topeka, KS 66605 Direct mail to P. O. Box 4048, Topeka, KS 66604-0048

Topeka Public Library, 1515 West 10th, Topeka, KS 66604

Western Kansas Archives, Forsyth, Library, Hay, Kansas 67601

Wichita City Library, 220 So. Main St., Wichita, KS 67202

Allen County Genealogical Society, Iola Public Library, Iola, KS 66749

Barton County Genealogical Society, Box 425, Great Bend, KS 67530

Bluestem Genealogical Society, 117 North Main, Eureka, KS 67045

Blue Valley Genealogical Society, P. O. Box 53, Marysville, KS 66508

Branches and Twigs Genealogical Society, Route 1, Kingman, KS 67068

Chanute Genealogy Society, 1000 South Allen Street, Chanute, KS 66720

Cherokee County Genealogical Society of Southeast Kansas, Columbus Public Library, 205 North Kansas, Columbus, KS 66725

Cloud County Genealogical Society, Rt. 3, Concordia, KS 66901

Cowley County Genealogical Society, P. O. Box 102, Arkansas City, KS 67005

Crawford County Genealogical Society, Pittsburg Public Library, 211 West 4th St., Pittsburg, KS 66762

Decatur County Genealogical Society, 307 North Rodehaver, Oberlin, KS 67749

Douglas County Genealogical Society, P. O. Box 3664, Lawrence, KS 66046-0664

Douglas County Historical Society, Watkins Community Museum, 1047 Massachusetts St., Lawrence, KS 66044

East Central Kansas Genealogical Society, P. O. Box 101, Garnett, KS 66032

Finney County Genealogical Society, P. O. Box 592, Garden City, KS 67846

Flint Hills Genealogy Society, P. O. Box 555, Emporia, KS 66801

Fort Hays Kansas Genealogical Society, Forsyth Library, FHS University, Hays, KS 67601

Harper County Genealogical Society, Harper Public Library, 10th and Oak, Harper, KS 67058

Heritage Genealogical Society, P. O. Box 73, Neodesha, KS 66757

Historical Society of the Downs Carnegie Library, South Morgan Avenue, Downs, KS 67437

Hodgeman County Genealogical Society, P. O. Box 441, Jetmore, KS 67854

Jefferson County Genealogical Society, Box 174, Oskaloosa, KS 66066

Johnson County Genealogical Society, Inc., P. O. Box 8057, Shawnee Mission, KS 66208

Kansas Council of Genealogical Societies, Inc., P. O. Box 3858, Topeka, KS 66604-6858

Kansas Genealogical Society, Inc., P. O. Box 103, Dodge City, KS 67801

Kansas Society, DAR, 1000 West 55th Street South, Wichita, KS 67217

Kansas State Historical Society, Memorial Bldg., Topeka, KS 66603

LaBette Genealogical Society, Box 826, Parsons, KS 67357

Leavenworth County Genealogical Society, Inc., P. O. Box 362, Leavenworth, KS 66048

Liberal Area Genealogical Society, P. O. Box 1094, Liberal, KS 67905-1094

Linn County Historical Society, Box 137, Pleasanton, KS 66075

Lyon County Historical Society, 118 E. 6th Street, Emporia, KS 66801

Miami County Genealogical Society, P. O. Box 123, Paola, KS 66071

Midwest Historical and Genealogical Society, Inc., Box 1, Wichita, KS 67201

Montgomery County Genealogical Society, Box 444, Coffeyville, KS 67337

Morris County Genealogical Society, Box 42-A, Rt. 2, White City, KS 66872

North Central Kansas Genealogical Society, Box 251, Cawker City, KS 67430

Northwest Kansas Genealogical & Historical Society, 700 W. 3rd, Oakley, KS 67748

Norton County Genealogical Society, 101 E. Lincoln, Norton, KS 67654

Old Fort Genealogical Society of Southeast Kansas, 201 S. National Ave., Fort Scott, KS 66701

Osborne County Genealogical and Historical Society, Osborne Public Library, Osborne, KS 67473

Osage County Genealogical Society, c / o Lyndon Carnegie Library, P. O. Box 563, 126 E. 6, Lyndon, KS 66451

Osage County Historical Society, P. O. Box 361, Lyndon, KS 66451

Phillips County Genealogical Society, Box 114, Phillipsburg, KS 67661

Rawlins County Genealogical Society, P. O. Box 203, Atwood, KS 67730

Reno County Genealogical Society, P. O. Box 5, Hutchinson, KS 67501

Republic County Genealogical Society, Rt. 1, Belleville, KS 66935

Riley County Genealogical Society, 2005 Claflin Road, Manhattan, KS 66502

Santa Fe Trail Genealogical Society, P. O. Box 1048, Syracuse, KS 67878

Sherman County Historical and Genealogical Society, P. O. Box 684, Goodland, KS 67735

Smoky Valley Genealogical Society and Library, Inc., 211 West Iron, Suite 205, Salina, KS 67401-2613

St. Marys Historical Society, 710 Alma Street, St. Marys, KS 66536

Stafford County Historical and Genealogical Society, 201 South Park, Stafford, KS 67578

Stevens County Genealogical Society, HC 01, Box 12, Hugoton, KS 67951

Topeka Kansas Genealogical Society, P. O. Box 4048, Topeka, KS 66604-0048

University of Kansas, Lawrence, KS 66044

Wichita Genealogical Society, P. O. Box 3705, Wichita, KS 67201-3705

Woodson County Genealogical Society, 410 North State Street, Yates Center, KS 66783

Printed Census Records and Mortality Schedules

Federal Census 1860, 1870, 1880, 1900, 1910
Federal Mortality Schedules 1860, 1870, 1880
State/Territorial Census 1855, 1856, 1857, 1858, 1859, 1865, 1875, 1885, 1895, 1905, 1915, 1925

Valuable Printed Sources

Atlases, Maps, and Gazetteers

Baughman, Robert W. *Kansas in Maps*. Topeka: Kansas State Historical Society.

————. *Kansas Post Offices, May 29, 1828 - August 3, 1961*. Topeka: Kansas State Historical Society, 1961.

Rydjord, John. *Kansas Place Names*. Norman, Oklahoma: University of Oklahoma Press, 1972.

Bibliographies

Anderson, Aileen. *Kansas Newspapers: A Directory of Newspaper Holdings in Kansas*. Topeka: Kansas Library Network Board, 1984.

Barry, Louise. *Comprehensive Index 1875-1930 to Collections, Biennial Reports and Publications of the Kansas State Historical Society*. Topeka: Kansas State Historical Society, 1959.

Directory of Historical and Genealogical Societies in Kansas. Topeka: Kansas State Historical Society, 1989.

Histories

Bright, John D. *Kansas: The First Century*. New York: Lewis Historical Publishing Co., 1957.

Socolofsky, Homer E. and Huber Self. *Historical Atlas of Kansas*. Norman, Oklahoma: University of Oklahoma Press, 1972.

KANSAS COUNTY DATA
State Map on Page M-15

Name	Map Index	Date Created	Parent County or Territory From Which Organized
* **Allen**	B5	1855	Original county
Allen County, 1 N Washington St, Iola, KS 66749-2841 .... (316)365-7491			
(City Clk has b, d & bur rec; Pro Judge has m & pro rec; Clk Dis Ct has div & civ ct rec; Reg Deeds has Ind rec)			
* **Anderson**	B5	1855	Original county
Anderson County, 100 E 4th Ave, Garnett, KS 66032-1595 .... (913)448-6841			
(State Dept Vit Statistics has b, d rec from 1900; Clk Dis Ct has m, div, pro, civ ct rec from 1857; Co Appraiser has Ind rec from 1900; individual twns have bur rec)			
Arapahoe (Disorganized) (1870 census missing) (Inc. some of Colo)			
* **Atchison**	B3	1855	Original county
Atchison County, 5th & Parallel, Atchison, KS 66002 .... (913)367-1653			
(Co Clk has b rec from 1891-1906, d rec from 1891-1911; City Clk has b, d rec from 1911; Clk Dis Ct has div rec; Magistrate Ct has pro rec; Reg of Deeds has Ind rec)			

Name	Map Index	Date Created	Parent County or Territory From Which Organized

Barber E6 1867 Harper
Barber County, 120 E Washington Ave, Medicine Lodge, KS 67104-1421 .... (316)886-3961

* **Barton** F4 1867 Ellsworth
Barton County, PO Box 1089, Great Bend, KS 67530-1089 .... (316)792-7391
(Co Clk has b & d rec 1892-1911, m, div, pro, civ ct & Ind rec from 1872, & some cem rec)

Billings (see Norton)

* **Bourbon** A5 1855 Original county
Bourbon County, 210 S National Ave, Fort Scott, KS 66701-1328 .... (316)223-3800
(Clk Ct has div rec from 1870; Pro Judge has m, pro rec from 1870, civ ct rec from 1963; Bur Vit Statistics, Topeka has b, d rec from 1911)

Breckenridge (see Lyon)

* **Brown** B2 1855 Original county
Brown County, Courthouse Sq, Hiawatha, KS 66434 .... (913)742-2581
(Clk Dis Ct has div, pro, civ ct rec from 1800s, m rec; Reg of Deeds has Ind rec from 1857)

Buffalo (see Gray County)

* **Butler** C5 1855 Original county
Butler County, 200 W Central Ave, El Dorado, KS 67042-2101 .... (316)321-1960
(Co Clk has b & d rec 1887-1912, & Ind rec from 1887; Dis Ct has m, div, pro & civ ct rec; City Bldg 220 E 1st, El Dorado 67042 has bur rec)

Calhoun   1855 Name changed to Jackson after Civil War

* **Chase** C5 1859 Butler
Chase County, PO Box 547, Cottonwood Falls, KS 66845-0547 .... (316)273-6423
(Co Clk has b rec from 1886 to 1911, d rec from 1886 to 1910)

Chautauqua C6 1875 Howard
Chautauqua County, 215 N Chautauqua St, Sedan, KS 67361-1397 .... (316)725-3370
(Pro Judge has m & pro rec; City Clk has d & bur rec; Clk Dis Ct has div & civ ct rec; Reg Deeds has Ind rec)

* **Cherokee** A6 1855 Unorg. Terr
Cherokee County, PO Box 14, Columbus, KS 66725-0014 .... (316)429-2042
[FHL has some b, m, d, cem, pro, Ind, nat rec]

* **Cheyenne** I2 1875 Kirwin Land District
Cheyenne County, PO Box 985, Saint Francis, KS 67756-0985 .... (913)332-2401
(City Clerk has b, d & bur rec; Clk Dis Ct has m, pro, div, civ ct rec from 1886; Reg of Deeds has Ind rec; Hist Soc has census & school rec)

* **Clark** G6 1885 Ford
Clark County, PO Box 886, Ashland, KS 67831-0886 .... (316)635-2813
(Co Clk has b rec from 1904-1910; City Clk has b, bur rec from 1910; Pro Judge has m, pro rec; Clk Dis Ct has div, civ ct rec; Reg Deeds has Ind rec)

* **Clay** D3 1857 Original county
Clay County, PO Box 98, Clay Center, KS 67432-0098 .... (913)632-2552
(Co Clk has b, m, d rec 1885-1911; Clk Dis Ct has div, pro, civ ct rec; Reg Deeds has Ind rec)

* **Cloud** D3 1860 Formerly Shirley County
Cloud County, 811 Washington St, Concordia, KS 66901-3415 .... (913)243-4319
(Co Clk has b, m & d rec from 1885 to 1910; Clk Dis Ct has div rec; Pro Judge has pro & civ ct rec; Reg Deeds has Ind rec)

* **Coffey** B5 1855 Original county
Coffey County, 6th & Neosho, Burlington, KS 66839 .... (316)364-2191
(Clk Dis Ct has b & d rec 1892-1910, m rec from 1855, div, pro, civ ct rec from 1857; Reg of Deeds has Ind rec from 1857; Hist Soc & Public Libr have cem books)

* **Comanche** F6 1867 Kiowa
Comanche County, PO Box 397, Coldwater, KS 67029-0397 .... (316)582-2361
(Co Clk has b, d rec from 1891-1911; Magistrate Judge has m rec from 1891-1912, pro, civ ct rec; Clk Dis Ct has div rec; Reg Deeds has Ind rec)

* **Cowley** C6 1867 Formerly Hunter
Cowley County, 311 E 9th Ave, Winfield, KS 67156-2864 .... (316)221-4066
(City Clk has b rec; Pro Ct has m, div, pro rec from 1870, & d rec; Clk Dis Ct has civ ct rec; Appraisers Office has Ind rec)

* **Crawford** A6 1867 Bourbon
Crawford County, County Courthouse, Girard, KS 66743 .... (316)724-6115
(Co Clk has b rec from 1887 to 1911; Board of Health has b rec from 1911 to present; Co Clk has d rec from 1887 to 1908; Pro Ct has m & pro rec; Clk Dis Ct has div & civ ct rec)

Davis   1871 Riley (see Geary)

* **Decatur** G2 1875 Norton
Decatur County, 194 S Penn Ave, Oberlin, KS 67749-2243 .... (913)475-2132
(Pro Judge has m, div & mil rec from 1880, pro rec from 1900, civ ct rec from 1937 & Ind rec; b & d rec from 1885 & bur rec from 1913 are sent to Topeka, Kansas by the City Clk)

* **Dickinson** D4 1855 Original county
Dickinson County, PO Box 248, Abilene, KS 67410-0248 .... (913)263-3774
(Co Clk has incom b rec from 1892, m rec & d rec from 1892)

Name	Map Index	Date Created	Parent County or Territory From Which Organized

* **Doniphan**   B2   1855   Original county
  Doniphan County, Main St, Troy, KS 66087 .... (913)985-3513
  (Clk Dis Ct has b & d rec from 1898-1910, m, div, pro & civ ct rec from 1856; Reg of Deeds has Ind rec from 1858; A yearly county census is taken)

  Dorn (See Nesho)

* **Douglas**   B4   1855   Original county
  Douglas County, 111 E 11th St, Lawrence, KS 66044-2990 .... (913)841-7700
  (Co Clk has Ind rec; Dis Ct Offices have m, civ ct & crim ct rec; Reg of Deeds has Ind rec)

* **Edwards**   F5   1874   Kiowa
  Edwards County, 312 Massachusetts Ave, Kinsley, KS 67547-1099 .... (316)659-3121
  (Pro Judge has m, div, pro & civ ct rec from 1874; Reg Deeds has Ind rec from 1874)

* **Elk**   C6   1875   Howard
  Elk County, PO Box 606, Howard, KS 67349-0606 .... (316)374-2490
  (Clk Dis Ct has b & d rec 1885-1911, m & pro rec from 1875, div & civ ct rec from 1906, & Ind rec from 1871; Cthouse burned in 1906)

* **Ellis**   F4   1867   Unorg. Terr
  Ellis County, 1204 Fort St, Hays, KS 67601-3899 .... (913)625-6558
  (Co Clk has b, m, d, div, immi, naturalization rec from 1868, pro rec from 1867, civ ct rec from 1951, Ind rec from 1871, co school rec from 1896; individual cem have bur rec)

* **Ellsworth**   E4   1867   Saline
  Ellsworth County, PO Box 396, Ellsworth, KS 67439-0396 .... (913)472-4161
  (Pro Judge has m & pro rec; City Clk has d & bur rec; Clk Dis Ct has div rec; Co Ct has civ ct rec; Reg Deeds has Ind rec)

* **Finney**   H5   1883   Arapahoe, Foote, Sequoyah
  Finney County, PO Box M, Garden City, KS 67846-0450 .... (316)276-3051
  (Pro Judge has m, pro rec from 1885; Clk Dis Ct has div, civ ct rec from 1885; formerly Sequoyah Co, Sequoyah Co has rec in Ford Co; Garfield Co is now part of Finney Co and Finney Co has the rec of Garfield Co)

  Foote (See Gray)

* **Ford**   G6   1873   Unorg. Terr
  Ford County, Central & Spruce Sts, Dodge City, KS 67801-4482 .... (316)227-3184
  (City Clk has b, d & bur rec; Pro Judge has m, pro & civ ct rec; Clk Dis Ct has div rec; Co Clk has Ind rec)

*† **Franklin**   B4   1855   Original county
  Franklin County, 3rd & Main Sts, Ottawa, KS 66067 .... (913)242-1471
  [FHL has some m, cem, civ ct, pro, Ind, nat rec]

  Garfield (annexed to Finney, 1893)

* **Geary**   C4   1855   Davis Co 1875 to 1888, Riley
  Geary County, 8th & Franklin, Junction City, KS 66441 .... (913)238-3912
  (Pro Ct has m, pro rec from 1860; Clk Dis Ct has div rec from 1860; Co Ct has civ ct rec from 1937; City Ct records b, d rec and then sends data to Bur Vit Statistics, Topeka; Reg Deeds has Ind rec from 1858)

  Godfrey (Changed to Seward 1861)

*† **Gove**   G4   1868   Unorg. Terr
  Gove County, PO Box 128, Gove, KS 67736-0128 .... (913)938-2300
  [FHL has some cem rec]

*† **Graham**   G3   1867   Rooks
  Graham County, 410 N Pomeroy St, Hill City, KS 67642-1645 .... (913)674-3453
  (Pro Judge has m & pro rec; Clk Dis Ct has div & civ ct rec; Reg Deeds has Ind rec)

* **Grant**   H6   1873   Finney, Kearney
  Grant County, 108 S Glenn St, Ulysses, KS 67880-2551 .... (316)356-1335
  (Pro Judge has m rec; Clk Dis Ct has div, pro & civ ct rec; Reg of Deeds has Ind rec; local census taken every year, state census taken in 1988; City Clk has cem rec)

*† **Gray**   G6   1887   Finney, Ford
  Gray County, PO Box 487, Cimarron, KS 67835-0487 .... (316)855-3618
  (Pro Judge has m rec from 1887, pro rec from 1885; Clk Dis Ct has div rec from 1887; Reg Deeds has Ind rec from 1887) (Gray Co has been named Foote, Buffalo & Sequoia before it became Gray Co. Co Clk has tax rolls census of 1889 to present, also dis school rec of pupils with various information; Reg Deeds has deeds from 1886, mtg rec are available from 1887)

* **Greeley**   I4   1873   Hamilton
  Greeley County, PO Box 277, Tribune, KS 67879-0277 .... (316)376-4256
  (City Clk has b rec; Pro Judge has m & pro rec; Co Ct has civ ct rec; Reg Deeds has Ind rec)

*† **Greenwood**   C5   1855   Original county
  Greenwood County, 311 N Main St, Eureka, KS 67045-1321 .... (316)583-7421
  (Pro Judge has m & pro rec; Clk Dis Ct has div rec; Reg Deeds has Ind rec)

* **Hamilton**   I5   1873   Unorg. Terr
  Hamilton County, N Main St, Syracuse, KS 67878 .... (316)384-5629
  (Pro Judge has m & pro rec from 1886; City Clk has d & bur rec; Clk Dis Ct has div rec; Co Clk has Ind rec from 1884)

* **Harper**   E6   1867   Kingman
  Harper County, County Courthouse, Anthony, KS 67003-2799 .... (316)842-5555
  (Pro Judge has m & pro rec; Clk Dis Ct has div & civ ct rec; Reg Deeds has Ind rec)

Name	Map Index	Date Created	Parent County or Territory From Which Organized
* **Harvey**	D5	1872	McPherson, Sedgwick, Marion

Harvey County, PO Box 687, Newton, KS 67114-0687 .... (316)283-6900
(Pro Ct has m rec from 1800s; Dis Ct has div, pro, civ rec from 1872; Reg of deeds has lnd rec from 1800s)

| * **Haskell** | H6 | 1887 | Finney |

Haskell County, PO Box 518, Sublette, KS 67877-0518 .... (316)675-2263
(Dept of Legal Stat has b & d rec; Pro Judge has m & pro rec; Dis Ct has div rec)

| * **Hodgeman** | G5 | 1879 | Indian Lands (Est. 1868) |

Hodgeman County, PO Box 247, Jetmore, KS 67854-0247 .... (316)357-6421
(City Clk has b, d & bur rec from 1911; Pro Judge has m & pro rec from 1887; Clk Dis Ct has div & civ ct rec from 1887; Reg of Deeds has lnd rec from 1879)

| **Howard** | | 1875 | Taken to form Elk & Chautauqua |

Hunter (See Cowley)

| * **Jackson** | B3 | 1855 | (see Calhoun) |

Jackson County, Courthouse Sq, Holton, KS 66436-1791 .... (913)364-2891
(Co Clk has b, d rec 1903-1911; Pro Judge has m rec from 1867, pro rec from 1857, civ ct rec from 1900; Clk Dis Ct has div rec; Reg Deeds has lnd rec from 1858)

| * **Jefferson** | B3 | 1855 | Original county |

Jefferson County, PO Box 321, Oskaloosa, KS 66066-0321 .... (913)863-2272
(Pro Judge has m & pro rec; Clk Dis Ct has div rec; Reg Deeds has lnd rec)

| † **Jewell** | E2 | 1867 | Mitchell |

Jewell County, 307 N Commercial St, Mankato, KS 66956-2025 .... (913)378-3121
(Clk Dis Ct has m, div, pro, civ ct rec from 1871, some naturalization rec; Yearly census by Appraisers Office)

| *† **Johnson** | A4 | 1855 | Original county |

Johnson County, Santa Fe & Kansas Aves, Olathe, KS 66061-3195 .... (913)782-5000
(Clk Dis Ct has div & civ ct rec from 1861; Pro Ct has m & pro rec; State Dept of Health, Division of Vital Stat has b & d rec; bur rec are kept by Registration Dis)

| * **Kearny** | H5 | 1873 | Finney |

Kearny County, 305 N Main St, Lakin, KS 67860 .... (316)355-6422
(Co Clk has b, m & d rec 1900-1910; Clk Dis Ct has div & civ ct rec from 1894, pro rec from 1895; Reg of Deeds has lnd rec from 1894; Co Clk & Co Hist Soc have newsprs)

| * **Kingman** | E6 | 1886 | Unorg. Terr |

Kingman County, 130 N Spruce St, Kingman, KS 67068-1647 .... (316)532-2521
(Clk Dis Ct has m rec 1875-1915, 1917 to present, div, pro, civ ct rec from 1878; Reg of Deeds has lnd rec from 1890 & d rec; Kingman City Clerk has b rec)

| * **Kiowa** | F6 | 1886 | Comanche, Edwards |

Kiowa County, 211 E Florida Ave, Greensburg, KS 67054-2294 .... (316)723-3366
(In 1875 Kiowa Co disappeared from map & terr was divided between Edwards & Comanche Cos. Kiowa reappeared in 1886 being formed from parts of Edwards & Comanche) Clk Dis Ct has m rec; Reg of Deeds has lnd rec from 1886 and school rec 1881-1965)

| * **Labette** | B6 | 1867 | Neosho |

Labette County, PO Box 387, Oswego, KS 67356-0387 .... (316)795-2138
(Co Clk has b rec from 1885-1896, & d rec 1885-1889; Pro Judge has m & pro rec from 1870; Clk Dis Ct has div & civ ct rec from 1870; Reg of Deeds has lnd rec from 1875; A yearly county census taken 1915-1979)

| * **Lane** | G4 | 1877 | Finney |

Lane County, 144 South Ln, Dighton, KS 67839 .... (316)397-5356
(Bur Vit Statistics, Topeka, has b, d rec; Magistrate Court has m, div, pro, civ ct rec; Reg Deeds has lnd rec; City of Dighton has bur rec)

| * **Leavenworth** | B3 | 1855 | Original county |

Leavenworth County, S 4th & Walnut St, Leavenworth, KS 66048-2781 .... (913)682-7611
[FHL has some cem rec]

| * **Lincoln** | E3 | 1867 | Ellsworth |

Lincoln County, 216 E Lincoln Ave, Lincoln, KS 67455-2097 .... (913)524-4757
(Co Clk has m, d, pro & div rec from 1870)

| * **Linn** | A5 | 1855 | Original county |

Linn County, PO Box B, Mound City, KS 66056-0601 .... (913)795-2660
(Co Clk has m, bur, div, pro, civ ct & lnd rec)

| * **Logan** | H4 | 1881 | Wallace (changed from St. John 1887) |

Logan County, 710 W 2nd St, Oakley, KS 67748-1233 .... (913)672-4244
(City Clk has b, d & bur rec; Pro Judge has m & pro rec; Clk Dis Ct has div & civ ct rec; Co Clk has lnd rec from 1885)

Lykins (See Miami)

| * **Lyon** | C4 | 1857 | Madison (see Breckenridge) |

Lyon County, 402 Commercial St, Emporia, KS 66801-4000 .... (316)342-4950
(Clk Dis Ct has m rec from 1861, div rec from 1860, pro rec from 1859, civ ct rec from 1858; Reg of Deeds has lnd rec from 1856; Emporia City Clk has b & d rec)

| **Madison** | | 1860 | Divided to Morris & Lyon Counties |

Name	Map Index	Date Created	Parent County or Territory From Which Organized

Marion   D5   1855   Chase
Marion County, S 3rd St Courthouse Sq, Marion, KS 66861 .... (316)382-2185
(Co Clk has b & d rec 1885-1911; Clk Dis Ct has m rec from 1800s, div, pro & civ ct rec; Reg of Deeds has school rec 1873-1964 & Ind rec)

* **Marshall**   C2   1855   Original county
Marshall County, 1201 Broadway, Marysville, KS 66508-1844 .... (913)562-5361
(Co Clk has b rec 1885-1911, d rec 1889-1911; Clk Dis Ct has m, div, pro, civ ct rec; Reg Deeds has Ind rec)

McGhee See Cherokee

* **McPherson**   D5   1867   Unorg. Terr
McPherson County, Kansas & Maple Sts, McPherson, KS 67460 .... (316)241-3656
(Co Clk has b rec 1888-1911, m rec from 1888, d & bur rec 1888-1909; Clk Dis Ct has div & civ ct rec from 1873, m & pro rec from 1870)

* **Meade**   G6   1885   Unorg. Terr
Meade County, 200 N Fowler St, Meade, KS 67864 .... (316)873-2581
(Pro Judge has b, m, pro & civ ct rec; City Clk has bur rec; Clk Dis Ct has div rec; Reg Deeds has Ind rec)

* **Miami**   A4   1855   Formerly Lykins
Miami County, 120 S Pearl St, Paola, KS 66071-1774 .... (913)294-3976
[FHL has some b, m, d, cem, civ ct, pro, nat rec]

Mitchell   E3   1867   Kirwin Land District
Mitchell County, PO Box 190, Beloit, KS 67420-0190 .... (913)738-3652
(Pro Judge has m & pro rec; Clk Dis Ct has div rec; Reg Deeds has Ind rec)

*† **Montgomery**   B6   1867   Labette
Montgomery County, PO Box 446, Independence, KS 67301-0446 .... (316)331-4840
(Co Clk has b, d rec 1886-1911; Pro Ct has m, pro rec from 1870; Clk Dis Ct has div, civ ct rec from 1870; Reg Deeds has Ind rec from 1870)

† **Morris**   C4   1855   Madison (formerly Wise)
Morris County, 501 W Main St, Council Grove, KS 66846-1701 .... (316)767-5518
(Pro Judge has m & pro rec; City Clk has bur & d rec; Clk Dis Ct has div & civ ct rec; Reg Deeds has Ind rec)

* **Morton**   I6   1881   Stanton
Morton County, PO Box 1116, Elkhart, KS 67950-1116 .... (316)697-2157
(Co Clk has m rec from 1887, div & civ ct rec from 1900, Ind rec from 1887)

Nemaha   C2   1855   Original county
Nemaha County, 607 Nemaha St, Seneca, KS 66538-1761 .... (913)336-2146
(Co Clk b, m & d rec 1885-1911; Clk Dis Ct has m, pro, civ ct rec from 1857)

Neosho   1855   Original County
(originally Dorn - name changed 1861)

* **Ness**   G4   1867   Hodgeman
Ness County, 202 W Sycamore St, Ness City, KS 67560-1558 .... (913)798-2401
(Pro Judge has m, pro rec; Clk Ct has div rec; City Clk has civ ct rec; Reg Deeds has Ind rec; State Bur Vit Statistics has b, d rec)

* **Norton**   G2   1867   Unorg. Terr. (changed to Billings 1873, back to Norton 1874)
Norton County, PO Box 70, Norton, KS 67654-0070 .... (913)877-2363
(Clk Dis Ct has m & div rec; Pro Ct has pro & civ ct rec; Reg of Deeds has Ind rec from 1874 & some cem rec; City Clks have b & d rec)

*† **Osage**   B4   1855   Formerly Weller
Osage County, PO Box 226, Lyndon, KS 66451-0226 .... (913)828-4812
(Co Clk has b rec from 1886 to 1921, m rec from 1885 to 1911, d rec from 1885 to 1909; Clk Dis Ct has div rec from 1863; Co Ct has civ ct rec from 1929; Reg Deeds has Ind rec from 1858)

* **Osborne**   F3   1867   Mitchell
Osborne County, 423 W Main St, Osborne, KS 67473-2302 .... (913)346-2431
(Pro Judge has m, pro, civ ct rec, div rec from 1872; Reg Deeds has Ind rec)

Otoe   1860   Butler

† **Ottawa**   D3   1860   Saline
Ottawa County, 307 N Concord St, Minneapolis, KS 67467-2140 .... (913)392-2279
(Co Clk has m, div & pro rec; City Officers have b rec from 1911, d rec)

* **Pawnee**   F5   1860   Rush, Stafford
Pawnee County, 715 Broadway, Larned, KS 67550-3098 .... (316)285-3721
(Clk Dis Ct has m rec from 1873, div, pro, civ ct & naturalization rec; Reg of Deeds has Ind rec; City Clk has b & d rec 1897-1911, & bur rec from 1886; a census taken in 1886)

*† **Phillips**   F2   1867   Kirwin Land District
Phillips County, 3rd & State Sts, Phillipsburg, KS 67661 .... (913)543-5513
(Pro Judge has m & pro rec; City Clk has d & bur rec; Clk Dis Ct has div & civ ct rec; Co Clk has Ind rec)

* **Pottawatomie**   C3   1857   Riley, Calhoun
Pottawatomie County, PO Box 187, Westmoreland, KS 66549-0187 .... (913)457-3314
(Co Clk has b, m, d rec 1885-1910; Unified Ct System has div, pro, civ ct rec; Reg Deeds has Ind rec)

* **Pratt**   F6   1867   Stafford
Pratt County, 300 S Ninnescah St, Pratt, KS 67124-2733 .... (316)672-7761
(Co Clk has b rec from 1887 to 1900)

Name	Map Index	Date Created	Parent County or Territory From Which Organized

* **Rawlins** H2 1873 Kirwin Land District
  Rawlins County, 607 Main St, Atwood, KS 67730-1896 .... (913)626-3351

* **Reno** E5 1867 Sedgwick, McPherson
  Reno County, 206 W 1st Ave, Hutchinson, KS 67501-5245 .... (316)665-2931
  (Co Clk has b & d rec 1890-1910; Clk Dis Ct has div rec; Pro Judge has pro rec)

* **Republic** D2 1860 Washington, Cloud
  Republic County, County Courthouse, Belleville, KS 66935 .... (913)527-5691

* **Rice** E4 1867 Reno
  Rice County, 101 W Commercial St, Lyons, KS 67554-2727 .... (316)257-2232
  (Clk Dis Ct has m rec from 1872, div, pro & civ ct rec; Reg of Deed has Ind rec from 1871; City Clk has b rec 1895-1910, and bur rec)

Richardson (changed to Wabaunsee, 1859)

* **Riley** C3 1855 Unorg. Terr., Wabaunsee
  Riley County, 110 Courthouse Plaza, Manhattan, KS 66502-6018 .... (913)537-0700
  (Co Clk has b, d rec 1885-1886, 1892-1909; City Clk has b, d rec from 1910; Pro Ct has pro rec; Reg Deeds has Ind rec; City cems have bur rec)

* **Rooks** F3 1867 Kirwin Land District
  Rooks County, 115 N Walnut St, Stockton, KS 67669-1663 .... (913)425-6391
  (Clk Dis Ct has b & d rec 1888-1905, m & div rec from 1888, pro rec from 1881, & civ ct rec; Reg of Deeds has Ind rec)

* **Rush** F4 1867 Unorg. Terr
  Rush County, PO Box 220, La Crosse, KS 67548-0220 .... (913)222-2726
  (City Clk has b, d & bur rec; Pro Judge has m from 1876, pro & civ ct rec; Clk Dis Ct has div; Reg Deeds has Ind rec)

Russell F4 1867 Ellsworth
  Russell County, PO Box 113, Russell, KS 67665-0113 .... (913)483-4641
  (Co Clk has m, pro & civ ct rec from 1876, also div rec)

* **Saline** D4 1860 Original county
  Saline County, 300 W Ash St, Salina, KS 67401-2396 .... (913)827-1961
  (Pro Judge has m & pro rec; Reg Deeds has Ind rec)

* **Scott** H4 1873 Finney
  Scott County, 303 Court St, Scott City, KS 67871-1122 .... (316)872-2420
  (City Clk has b & d rec; Pro Judge has m & pro rec; Co Clk has bur rec; Clk Ct has div & civ ct rec)

* **Sedgwick** D5 1867 Butler
  Sedgwick County, 525 N Main St, Wichita, KS 67203-3703 .... (316)383-7166
  (Dis Pro Ct has m & pro rec from 1870; Dis Civ Ct has civ ct rec; Community Hlth Dept (1900 E 9th, Wichita KS 67214) has b & d rec; Co Clk has Ind rec from 1887)

Sequoyah (See Gray & Finney)

*† **Seward** H6 1855 Indian Lands
  Seward County, 415 N Washington Ave, Liberal, KS 67901-3497 .... (316)624-0211
  (City Clk has b, d & bur rec; Pro Judge has m & pro rec; Clk Dis Ct has div & civ ct rec; Reg Deeds has Ind rec; Co Clk has newspapers from 1873)

*† **Shawnee** B4 1855 Original county
  Shawnee County, 200 SE 7th St, Topeka, KS 66603-3922 .... (913)291-4040
  (Co Clk has b, m & d rec 1894-1911; Pro Ct has m rec 1856-1906; Clk Dis Ct has div, pro, civ ct rec; Reg of Deeds has Ind rec from 1855)

* **Sheridan** G3 1873 Unorg. Terr
  Sheridan County, PO Box 899, Hoxie, KS 67740-0899 .... (913)675-3361
  (Co Clk has incomp b & d rec 1887-1910; Clk Dis Ct has m, div, pro & civ ct rec; Reg of Deeds has Ind rec)

Sherman I3 1873 Kirwin Land District
  Sherman County, 813 Broadway, Goodland, KS 67735-3056 .... (913)899-7581
  (Co Clk has newspaper files from 1898, school & census rec; City Clk has b & d rec; Pro Judge has m & pro rec from 1886; Clk Dis Ct has div & civ ct rec from 1887; City Clk has Ind rec from 1888)

Shirley (see Cloud)

Smith F2 1867 Unorg. Terr
  Smith County, 218 S Grant St, Smith Center, KS 66967-2798 .... (913)282-6533
  (Pro Judge has m & pro rec from 1875; Clk Dis Ct has div & civ ct rec from 1875; Co Clk has Ind rec from 1872)

St. John (see Logan)

Stafford F5 1867 Unorg. Terr
  Stafford County, 209 N Broadway St, Saint John, KS 67576-2042 .... (316)549-3509

Stanton I6 1873 Reorganized
  Stanton County, PO Box 190, Johnson, KS 67855-0190 .... (316)492-2140
  (City Clk has b & bur rec; Pro Judge has m & pro rec; Clk Dis Ct has div & civ ct rec)

Stevens H6 1873 Indian Lands
  Stevens County, 200 E 6th St, Hugoton, KS 67951-2652 .... (316)544-2541
  [FHL has some cem rec]

Name	Map Index	Date Created	Parent County or Territory From Which Organized
* **Sumner**	D6	1867	Cowley

Sumner County, 500 N Washington Ave, Wellington, KS 67152-4096 .... (316)326-3395
(Pro Judge has m & pro rec; Clk Dis Ct has div rec; Co Clk has Ind rec)

| * **Thomas** | H3 | 1873 | Kirwin Land District |

Thomas County, 300 N Court Ave, Colby, KS 67701-2439 .... (913)462-2561
(Pro Judge has m, pro & civ ct rec; City Clk has d rec; Clk Dis Ct has div rec; Reg Deeds has Ind rec)

| * **Trego** | G4 | 1867 | Ellis |

Trego County, 216 N Main St, WaKeeney, KS 67672-2189 .... (913)743-5773
(Pro Judge has m & pro rec; Clk Dis Ct has div & civ ct rec)

| * **Wabaunsee** | C4 | 1855 | Riley, Morris (formerly Richardson) |

Wabaunsee County, PO Box 278, Alma, KS 66401-0278 .... (913)765-3414
(Co Clk has b, m, d rec 1892-1910; Dis Ct has div, pro, civ ct rec)

| **Wallace** | I4 | 1868 | Indian Lands (see Logan) |

Wallace County, 313 Main St, Sharon Springs, KS 67758-9998 .... (913)852-4282
(Co Clk has b, m, d rec 1895-1911; Clk Dis Ct has div rec; Pro Judge has pro, civ ct rec; Reg Deeds has Ind rec)

| * **Washington** | D2 | 1855 | Original county |

Washington County, 214 C St, Washington, KS 66968-1928 .... (913)325-2974
(Co Clk has b, m & d rec 1887-1911; Clk Dis Ct has m rec from 1868, div, pro, civ ct rec from 1873, naturalization rec 1870-1938; Reg of Deeds has Ind rec)

Weller (see Osage)

| * **Wichita** | H4 | 1873 | Indian Lands |

Wichita County, PO Box 279, Leoti, KS 67861-0279 .... (316)375-2731
(Pro Judge has m & pro rec from 1887, civ ct rec; City Clk has d & bur rec from 1887; Clk Dis Ct has div rec from 1887; Reg Deeds has Ind rec from 1885)

| * **Wilson** | B6 | 1855 | Original county |

Wilson County, 615 Madison St, Fredonia, KS 66736-1383 .... (316)378-2186
(Pro Judge has m, pro & civ ct rec; Clk Dis Ct has div rec; Reg Deeds has Ind rec)

Wise (see Morris)

| **Woodson** | B5 | 1855 | Original county |

Woodson County, 105 W Rutledge St, Yates Center, KS 66783-1237 .... (316)625-2179
(Co Clk has b rec from 1885 to 1911, m rec from 1860, div rec from 1863, pro rec from 1863, civ ct rec from 1934 & Ind rec from 1861)

| * **Wyandotte** | A4 | 1859 | Original county |

Wyandotte County, 710 N 7th St, Kansas City, KS 66101-3087 .... (913)573-2800
(City Clk has b & d rec; Pro Judge has m & pro rec; Clk Dis Ct has div rec; Reg Deeds has Ind rec)

* At least one county history has been published about this county.

† Inventory of county archives was made by the Historical Records Survey. (See Introduction)

KENTUCKY

CAPITAL · FRANKFORT — STATE 1792 (15th)
State Map on Page M-16

Long before any white man had explored Kentucky, the entire area was claimed by Virginia as part of Augusta County. As early as 1750, Dr. Thomas Walker explored the eastern part of Kentucky. Daniel Boone followed in 1767. The first permanent settlement took place at Harrodsburg in 1774. The next year, Colonel Richard Henderson of North Carolina formed the Transylvania Company. He purchased almost half of Kentucky from Indian tribes, comprising all of the land between the Kentucky River in the central part of the state and the Cumberland River in the extreme western part. Daniel Boone settled Boonesboro in 1775 as well. In 1776, the Kentucky area was taken away from Fincastle County, Virginia and became Kentucky County, Virginia. In 1780, Kentucky County was divided into three counties; Fayette, Jefferson, and Lincoln; which were in turn divided into nine counties within a decade.

This early period of settlement was one of much bloodshed and danger as the Indians tried to keep their lands. The courageous early settlers came mainly from Maryland, North Carolina, Pennsylvania, Tennessee, and Virginia, and were of German, English, Irish, and Scottish descent. Statehood came to Kentucky on 1 June 1792. After the Louisiana Purchase in 1803, migration and settlement in Kentucky increased. Immigrants from Russia, Italy, Poland, and Austria came to the area. The War of 1812 involved many Kentucky men. Although neutral in the Civil War, Kentucky had over 75,000 of its men in the Union forces and 35,000 to 60,000 in the Confederate forces. The extreme western tip of Kentucky is sometimes referred to as the Jackson Purchase Region since it was purchased in 1818 from the Chickasaw Indians during Andrew Jackson's presidency. It includes Calloway, Marshall, McCracken, Graves, Fulton, Hickman, Carlisle, and Ballard counties.

Kentucky began registering births and deaths on 1 January 1911. They are kept at the Office of Vital Statistics, Department of Health Services, 275 East Main Street, Frankfort, KY 40621. Also located there are the following births and deaths prior to 1911:

1 - City of Louisville - birth records from 1898, death records from 1866
2 - City of Lexington - birth records from 1906, death records from 1898
3 - City of Covington - birth records from 1896, death records from 1880
4 - City of Newport - birth records from 1890, death records from 1880

To verify current fees, call 502-564-4212.

Records of births and deaths from some counties as early as 1851 are in the Kentucky Historical Society, 300 West Broadway, P.O. Box H, Frankfort, KY 40621. Counties, in most cases, have marriage records from within a few years of their organization. Statewide collection of marriage and divorce records dates only from June 1, 1958. Divorces prior to 1849 were granted by the state legislature. From 1849 to 1959, divorces were usually recorded by the circuit court and were often interfiled with other court matters. County clerks keep wills and other probate records. Copies are also available at the Department of Libraries and Archives, Public Records Division, 300 Coffee Tree Road, P.O. Box 537, Frankfort, KY 40602-0537 and the Kentucky Historical Society. Naturalization records are filed in the district courts in Bowling Green, Catlettsburg, Covington, Frankfort, London, Louisville, Owensboro, and Paducah. The office of the Clerk of the Circuit Court also has these records. Many counties administered school censuses between 1870 and 1932 (mostly 1895 to 1910), which list all members of the family.

Genealogical Archives, Libraries and Societies

Adair County Public Library, 307 Greensburg Street, Columbia, KY 42728

Ashland Public Library, 1740 Central Ave., Ashland, KY 41101

Boyd County Public Library, 1740 Central Ave., Ashland, KY 41101

Breckinridge County Public Library (Special Collections), Hardinsburg, KY 40143

Forrest C. Pogue Library, Murray State University, Murray, KY 42071

Fulton Public Library, 312 Main Street, Fulton, KY 42050

Gallatin Public Library, Box 258, Warsaw, KY 41095

George Coon Public Library, Box 230, 114 S. Harrison St., Princeton, KY 42445

Greenup County Public Library, 203 Harrison St., Greenup, KY 41144

Henderson Public Library, 101 South Main St., Henderson, KY 42420

John Fox Memorial Library, D. A. Shrine, Duncan Tavern St., Paris, KY 40361

John L. Street Memorial Library, Rt. 6, Box 278A, Cadiz, KY 42211

Kenton County Public Library, 5th and Scott, Covington, KY 41011 (Very good Kentucky collection of genealogical aids).

Kentucky Historical Society Library, 300 W. Broadway, P. O. Box H, Frankfort, KY 40621

Kentucky Library, Western Kentucky University, Bowling Green, KY 42101

Kentucky State Library and Archives, Public Records Division, 300 Coffee Tree Road, P. O. Box 537, Frankfort, KY 40602-0537

Laurel County Public Library, 116 E. 4th St., London, KY 40741

Leslie County Public Library, P. O. Box 498, Hyden, KY 41749

Lexington Public Library, 2nd and Market Streets, Lexington, KY 40507

Louisville Free Public Library, 4th and York Sts., Louisville, KY 40203

Margaret I. King Library, University of Kentucky, Lexington, KY 40506

Morganfield Public Library, Morganfield, KY 42437

Owensboro-Daviess County Public Library, Kentucky Room: Local History and Genealogy, 450 Griffith Ave., Owensboro, KY 42301

Perry County Public Library, High Street, Hazard, KY 41701

Pikeville Public Library, 210 Pike Ave., Pikeville, KY 41501

Public Library, 109 S. Main St., Winchester, KY 40391

Wayne County Public Library, 159 South Main Street, Monticello, KY 42633

Adair County Genealogical Society, P. O. Box 613, Columbia, KY 42728

Ancestral Trails Historical Society, P. O. Box 573, Vine Grove, KY 40175

Bell County Historical Society, Box 1344, Middlesboro, KY 40965

Bicentennial Heritage Corp., P. O. Box 356, Liberty, KY 42539

Breathitt County Genealogical Society, c / o Breathitt County Public Library, 1024 College Ave., Jackson, KY 41339

Bullitt County Genealogical Society, P. O. Box 960, Shepherdsville, KY 40165

Butler County Historical / Genealogical Society, Box 146, Morgantown, KY 42261

Christian County Genealogical Society, 1101 Bethel St., Hopkinsville, KY 42240

Clay County Genealogical and Historical Society, Inc., P. O. Box 394, Manchester, KY 40962

Corbin Genealogy Society, P. O. Box 353, Corbin, KY 40701

Eastern Kentucky Genealogical Society, Box 1544, Ashland, KY 41101

Fayette County, Kentucky Genealogical Society, P. O. Box 8113, Lexington, KY 40533

Filson Club, 1310 So. Third St., Louisville, KY 40208

Fulton County Genealogical Society, P. O. Box 31, Fulton, KY 42050

Garrard County Historical Society, 128 Redwood, Richmond, KY 40475

Genealogical Society of Hancock County, Old Courthouse, Hawesville, KY 42348

Grayson County Historical Society, Leitchfield, KY 42754

Green County Historical Society, P. O. Box 276, Greensburg, KY 42743

Harlan County Genealogical Society, P. O. Box 1498, Harlan, KY 40831

Harlan Heritage Seekers, P. O. Box 853, Harlan, KY 40831

Harrodsburg Historical Society, Genealogical Committee, Box 316, Harrodsburg, KY 40330

Hart County Historical Society, P. O. Box 606, Munfordville, KY 42765

Hickman County Historical Society, Rt. 3, Box 255, Clinton, KY 42031

Hopkins County Genealogical Society, P. O. Box 51, Madisonville, KY 42431

Jewish Genealogical Society of Louisville, Annette & Milton Russman, 3304 Furman Blvd., Louisville, KY 40220

Johnson County Historical / Genealogical Society, P. O. Box 788, Paintsville, KY 41240

Kentucky Genealogical Society, P. O. Box 153, Frankfort, KY 40602

Kentucky Historical Society, P. O. Box H, Frankfort, KY 40602-2108

Knox County Historical Society, Inc., P. O. Box 528, Barbourville, KY 40906

KYOWVA Genealogical Society, P. O. Box 1254, Huntington, WV 25715

Lewis County Historical Society, P. O. Box 212, Vanceburg, KY 41179

Louisville Genealogical Society, P. O. Box 5164, Louisville, KY 40205

Lyon County Historical Society, P. O. Box 894, Eddyville, KY 42038

Magoffin County Historical Society, P. O. Box 222, Salyersville, KY 41465

Marshall County, Kentucky Genealogical Society, P. O. Box 373, Benton, KY 42025

Mason County Genealogical Society, P. O. Box 266, Maysville, KY 41056

McCracken County Genealogical Society, 4640 Buckner Lane, Paducah, KY 42001

Metcalfe County Historical Society, Rt. 1, Box 371, Summer Shade, KY 42166

Muhlenberg County Genealogical Society, Public Library, Broad St., Central City, KY 42330

National Society of the Sons of the American Revolution, National Headquarters, 1000 South Fourth Street, Louisville, KY 40203

Nelson County Genealogical Roundtable, P. O. Box 409, Bardstown, KY 40004

Perry County Genealogical and Historical Society, Inc., HC 32, Box 550, Vicco, KY 41773

Pike County Historical Society, P. O. Box 752, Pikeville, KY 41501

Pulaski County Historical Society, Public Library Building, Somerset, KY 42501

Rockcastle County Historical Society, P. O. Box 930, Mt. Vernon, KY 40456

Rowan County Historical Society, 236 Allen Ave., Morehead, KY 40351

Scott County Genealogical Society, Scott County Public Library, East Main, Georgetown, KY 40324

Southern Historical Association, University of Kentucky, Lexington, KY 40506

South Central Kentucky Historical / Genealogical Society, P. O. Box 80, Glasgow, KY 42141

Southern Kentucky Genealogical Society, P. O. Box 1905, Bowling Green, KY 42101

Vanlear Historical Society, P. O. Box 12, Vanlear, KY 41265

West-Central Kentucky Family Research Association P. O. Box 1932, Owensboro, KY 42302

Printed Census Records and Mortality Schedules

Federal Census 1810, 1820, 1830, 1840, 1850, 1860, 1870, 1880, 1900, 1910
Federal Mortality Schedules 1850, 1860, 1870, 1880
Tax Lists 1790, 1800
Union Veterans and Widows 1890
Non-resident Tax Lists 1794-1805
School Census 1870-1932

Valuable Printed Sources

Atlases, Maps, and Gazetteers

Field, Thomas P. *A Guide to Kentucky Place Names*. Lexington, Kentucky: University of Kentucky, 1961.

Murphy, Thelma M. *Kentucky Post Offices, 1794-1819*. Indianapolis, 1975.

Sames, James W. III. *Index of Kentucky and Virginia Maps, 1562-1900*. Frankfort, Kentucky: Kentucky Historical Society, 1976.

Bibliographies

Coleman, J. Winston Jr. *A Bibliography of Kentucky History*. Lexington, Kentucky: University of Kentucky Press, 1949.

Duff, Jeffrey Michael. *Inventory of Kentucky Birth, Marriage, and Death Records, 1852-1910*. Frankfort, Kentucky: Department for Libraries and Archives, 1982.

Hathaway, Beverly W. *Inventory of County Records of Kentucky*. West Jordan, Utah: Allstates Research Co., 1974.

Teague, Barbara. *Guide to Kentucky Archival and Manuscript Collections*. Frankfort, Kentucky: Kentucky Department for Libraries and Archives, 1988.

Genealogical Research Guides

Elliott, Wendy L. *Guide to Kentucky Genealogical Research*. Bountiful, Utah: American Genealogical Lending Library, 1987.

Hathaway, Beverly W. *Kentucky Genealogical Research Sources*. West Jordan, Utah: Allstates Research Co., 1974.

McCay, Betty L. *Sources for Genealogical Searching in Kentucky*. Indianapolis: Betty L. McCay, 1969.

Histories

Collins, Richard H. *History of Kentucky*. Frankfort, Kentucky: Kentucky Historical Society, 1966.

KENTUCKY COUNTY DATA
State Map on Page M-16

Name	Map Index	Date Created	Parent County or Territory From Which Organized	
* **Adair**	E3	1802	Green	
Adair County, 500 Public Sq, Columbia, KY 42728-1451				(502)384-2801
(Co Clk has m & Ind rec from 1802)				
* **Allen**	D2	1815	Barren, Warren	
Allen County, PO Box 336, Scottsville, KY 42164-0336				(502)237-3706
(Co Clk has m & pro rec from 1902; Cir Ct Clk has div rec from 1902)				
*† **Anderson**	F4	1827	Franklin, Mercer, Washington	
Anderson County, 151 S Main St, Lawrenceburg, KY 40342-1192				(502)839-3041
(Co Clk has m, pro & Ind rec from 1827, school rec; Clk Cir Ct has civ ct rec 1857)				
Ballard	A3	1842	Hickman, McCracken	
Ballard County, PO Box 145, Wickliffe, KY 42087-0145				(502)335-5168
(Co Clk has m, Ind rec from 1880; Clk Cir Ct has div, pro rec; Courthouse burned 1880)				
* **Barren**	E3	1799	Green, Warren	
Barren County, County Courthouse 1st Fl, Glasgow, KY 42141-2812				(502)651-3783
(Co Clk has m & Ind rec; Clk Cir Ct has pro, div & civ ct rec)				
* **Bath**	G4	1811	Montgomery	
Bath County, Main St, Owingsville, KY 40360				(606)674-2613
(Co Clk has m, pro & Ind rec from 1811)				
* **Bell**	G2	1867	Knox, Harlan	
Bell County, County Courthouse, Pineville, KY 40977				(606)337-6143
(Co Clk has m & Ind rec)				
* **Boone**	F6	1799	Campbell	
Boone County, 2950 E Washington Sq, Burlington, KY 41005				(606)334-2108
(Co Clk has m & pro rec from 1799)				
* **Bourbon**	G5	1786	Fayette	
Bourbon County, Main St, Paris, KY 40361				(606)987-2430
(Co Clk has m & pro rec from 1786; Clk Cir Ct has civ ct rec from 1786 & div rec)				
Boyd	H5	1860	Carter, Lawrence, Greenup	
Boyd County, 2800 Louisa St, Catlettsburg, KY 41129-1610				(606)739-5116
(Co Clk has m & Ind rec from 1860; Clk Cir Ct has div, pro & civ ct rec)				
* **Boyle**	F4	1842	Mercer, Lincoln	
Boyle County, Main St, Danville, KY 40422				(606)238-1100
(Co Clk has m, Ind, wills & civ ct rec from 1842; Clk Cir Ct has div & pro rec)				
* **Bracken**	G5	1797	Campbell, Mason	
Bracken County, Locus St, Brooksville, KY 41004				(606)735-2952
(Co Clk has m, pro & Ind rec from 1797)				
Breathitt	H3	1839	Clay, Estill, Perry	
Breathitt County, 1127 Main St, Jackson, KY 41339-1194				(606)666-3810
(Co Clk has m, pro & Ind rec from 1875; Clk Cir Ct has div & civ ct rec)				
*† **Breckinridge**	D4	1800	Hardin	
Breckinridge County, PO Box 227, Hardinsburg, KY 40143-0227				(502)756-2269
(Co Clk has m rec from 1852, some b & d rec from 1852 to 1875, Ind & div rec from 1800; Clk Cir Ct has pro rec from 1890, civ ct rec)				
* **Bullitt**	E4	1797	Jefferson, Nelson	
Bullitt County, Buckman St, Shepherdsville, KY 40165				(502)543-2262
(Co Clk has m rec from 1796, pro, Ind rec; Clk Cir Ct has div, civ ct rec)				
* **Butler**	D3	1810	Logan, Ohio	
Butler County, PO Box 448, Morgantown, KY 42261-0448				(502)526-5676
(Co Clk has m & Ind rec from 1810; Clk Cir Ct has div & civ ct rec)				

Name	Map Index	Date Created	Parent County or Territory From Which Organized

* **Caldwell**   C3   1809   Livingston
Caldwell County, 100 E Market St Rm 3, Princeton, KY   42445-1675 .... (502)365-6754
(Co Clk has m, pro, Ind rec, wills, court orders, guardians, inventories, and settlements from 1809; Clk Cir Ct has div, civ ct rec)

* **Calloway**   B2   1821   Hickman
Calloway County, 101 S 5th St, Murray, KY   42071-2583 .... (502)753-2920
(Co Clk has m, pro, Ind, service discharges, minister bonds, election rec; Clk Cir Ct has div rec)

* **Campbell**   G5   1795   Harrison, Mason, Scott
Campbell County, PO Box 340, Newport, KY   41071 .... (606)292-3838
(Co Clk has m, pro & Ind rec from1785)

*† **Carlisle**   A2   1886   Ballard
Carlisle County, Court St, Bardwell, KY   42023 .... (502)628-5451
(Co Clk has m, pro & Ind rec)

Carroll   F5   1838   Gallatin, Henry, Trimble
Carroll County, Court St County Courthouse, Carrollton, KY   41008 .... (502)732-2446
(Co Clk has m, wills & Ind rec from 1838; Clk Cir Ct has pro, div & civ ct rec)

* **Carter**   H5   1838   Greenup, Lawrence
Carter County, Courthouse Rm 232, Grayson, KY   41143 .... (606)474-5188
(Co Clk has b & d rec from 1911 to 1954, m rec from 1838; Cir Ct Clk has div, pro & civ ct rec)

* **Casey**   F3   1807   Lincoln
Casey County, PO Box 310, Liberty, KY   42539-0310 .... (606)787-6471
(Co Health Dept has b, d rec; Co Clk has m, pro, Ind rec from 1806; Clk Cir Ct has pro rec from 1978, Clk Cir Ct has div, civ ct rec)

* **Christian**   C2   1797   Logan
Christian County, 511 S Main St, Hopkinsville, KY   42240-2300 .... (502)887-4105
(Co Clk has m, pro, Ind rec, wills from 1797; Clk Cir Ct has pro rec from 1978, div, civ ct rec)

* **Clark**   G4   1793   Bourbon, Fayette
Clark County, 34 S Main St Rm 103, Winchester, KY   40391-2600 .... (606)745-0200
(Clk Ct has m & pro rec from 1793, deeds, will, settlements & mtgs from 1793; Clk Cir Ct has div & civ ct rec)

Clay   G3   1807   Madison, Floyd, Knox
Clay County, PO Box 463, Manchester, KY   40962-0463 .... (606)598-3663
(Co Clk has m, Ind rec from 1807, pro rec, wills; Clk Cir Ct has div rec)

* **Clinton**   F2   1836   Wayne, Cumberland
Clinton County, County Courthouse, Albany, KY   42602 .... (606)387-5234
(Co Clk has m, deeds, mtgs, wills from 1865)

* **Crittenden**   B3   1842   Livingston
Crittenden County, 107 S Main St, Marion, KY   42064-1500 .... (502)965-5251
(Co Clk has m, pro, Ind, civ ct rec, election returns from 1842; Clk Cir Ct has div rec)

* **Cumberland**   E2   1799   Green
Cumberland County, PO Box 275, Burkesville, KY   42717-0275 .... (502)864-3726
(Co Clk has some m rec from 1882 to 1923 & from 1927, pro rec from 1815, Ind rec from 1799; Clk Cir Ct has pro rec from 1968, div and civ ct rec)

* **Daviess**   D4   1815   Ohio
Daviess County, PO Box 389, Owensboro, KY   42302-0389 .... (502)685-8434
(Co Clk has m & Ind rec from 1815, pro rec; Clk Cir Ct has div & civ ct rec)

* **Edmonson**   D3   1825   Grayson, Hart, Warren
Edmonson County, Main & Cross St, Brownsville, KY   42210 .... (502)597-2819
(Co Clk has m rec from 1840)

* **Elliott**   H4   1869   Carter, Lawrence, Morgan
Elliott County, PO Box 225, Sandy Hook, KY   41171-0225 .... (606)738-5421
(Co Clk has m rec from 1934, pro rec from 1957, Ind rec from 1869; Clk Cir Ct has div rec from 1957 & civ ct rec; Co Health Center has b & d rec)

* **Estill**   G4   1808   Clark, Madison
Estill County, 130 Main St, Irvine, KY   40336-1098 .... (606)723-5156
(Co Clk has m, bur, pro & Ind rec from 1808, Clk Cir Ct has div and civ ct rec)

*† **Fayette**   F4   1780   Kentucky Co Virginia
Fayette County, 162 E Main St, Lexington, KY   40507-1363 .... (606)253-3344
(Co Clk has m rec from 1795, pro rec & Ind rec from 1794; Clk Cir Ct has div & civ ct rec)

* **Fleming**   G5   1798   Mason
Fleming County, Court Sq, Flemingsburg, KY   41041-1399 .... (606)845-7571
(Co Clk has m, pro & Ind rec from 1798)

* **Floyd**   H4   1800   Fleming, Mason, Montgomery
Floyd County, 3rd Ave, Prestonburg, KY   41653 .... (606)886-9193
(Co Clk has m & Ind rec from 1800)

* **Franklin**   F4   1795   Woodford, Mercer, Shelby
Franklin County, PO Box 338, Frankfort, KY   40602-0338 .... (502)875-8702
(Co Clk has m, pro, Ind & civ ct rec from 1795, Confederate Pension Applications; Clk Cir Ct has div rec)

Name	Map Index	Date Created	Parent County or Territory From Which Organized

* **Fulton**   A2   1845   Hickman
Fulton County, Moulton & Wellington Sts, Hickman, KY 42050 .... (502)236-2727
(Co Clk has m, pro & lnd rec from 1845; Clk Cir Ct has div & civ ct rec)

* **Gallatin**   F5   1799   Franklin, Shelby
Gallatin County, PO Box 616, Warsaw, KY 41095-0616 .... (606)567-5411
(Co Clk has m, pro & lnd rec from 1799; Clk Cir Ct has div & civ ct rec)

* **Garrard**   F4   1797   Madison, Lincoln, Mercer
Garrard County, Public Sq, Lancaster, KY 40444 .... (606)792-3531
[FHL has some m, cem, civ ct, pro, lnd, tax rec]

* **Grant**   F5   1820   Pendleton
Grant County, PO Box 469, Williamstown, KY 41097-0469 .... (606)824-3321
(Co Clk has m, pro & lnd rec from 1820)

  Graves   B2   1824   Hickman
Graves County, Courthouse, Mayfield, KY 42066 .... (502)247-3626
(Co Clk has m, pro, civ ct, lnd rec from 1888; Clk Cir Ct has div rec)

* **Grayson**   D3   1810   Hardin, Ohio
Grayson County, 100 Court Sq, Leitchfield, KY 42754 .... (502)259-3201
(Co Clk has m & lnd rec from 1896; Clk Cir Ct has pro, div & civ ct rec)

* **Green**   E3   1793   Lincoln, Nelson
Green County, 203 W Court St, Greensburg, KY 42743-1522 .... (502)932-4024
(Co Clk has m & lnd rec, wills, civ ct rec from 1793, pro rec to 1978; Clk Cir Ct has div rec; Co Health Office has b & d rec)

* **Greenup**   H5   1804   Mason
Greenup County, 301 Main St, Greenup, KY 41144-1055 .... (606)473-7455
(Co Clk has m rec 1803, pro rec 1837, b & d rec from 1911 to 1949; Clk Cir Ct has div & civ ct rec 1803)

  Hancock   D4   1829   Daviess, Ohio, Breckinridge
Hancock County, County Administration Bldg, Hawesville, KY 42348 .... (502)927-6117
(Co Clk has m, pro & lnd rec from 1829; Clk Cir Ct has div & civ ct rec)

* **Hardin**   E4   1793   Nelson
Hardin County, 14 Public Sq, Elizabethtown, KY 42701-1437 .... (502)765-2171
(Co Clk has m & lnd rec; will not make rec searches)

* **Harlan**   H2   1819   Knox
Harlan County, PO Box 956, Harlan, KY 40831-0956 .... (606)573-2600
(Co Clk has m & lnd rec from 1820; Clk Cir Ct has div & civ ct rec)

* **Harrison**   G5   1794   Bourbon, Scott
Harrison County, 190 W Pike St, Cynthiana, KY 41031-1426 .... (606)234-2232
(Co Clk has m, pro & lnd rec from 1794; Clk Cir Ct has div & civ ct rec)

* **Hart**   E3   1819   Hardin, Barren, possibly Green
Hart County, PO Box 277, Munfordville, KY 42765 .... (502)524-2751

* **Henderson**   C4   1799   Christian
Henderson County, 232 1st St, Henderson, KY 42420-3146 .... (502)827-5671
(Co Clk has b & d rec 1911 to 1949, m rec from 1806, lnd rec from 1797, wills from 1800, other pro rec 1942 to 1978; Dis Clk has pro rec from 1979; Cir Ct Clk has div & civ ct rec)

* **Henry**   F5   1799   Shelby
Henry County, PO Box 202, New Castle, KY 40050-0202 .... (502)845-2891
(Co Clk has m rec from 1799, pro, lnd & civ ct rec; Clk Cir Ct has div rec)

* **Hickman**   A2   1821   Caldwell, Livingston
Hickman County, Courthouse Sq, Clinton, KY 42031-1295 .... (502)653-4369
(Co Clk has m, pro & lnd rec from 1822, b & d rec from 1854; Clk Cir Ct has div & civ ct rec)

* **Hopkins**   C3   1807   Henderson
Hopkins County, Main & Center, Madisonville, KY 42431-2064 .... (502)821-8294
(Co Clk has m, pro, civ ct rec & lnd rec)

  Jackson   G3   1858   Rockcastle, Owsley, Madison, Clay, Estill, Laurel
Jackson County, PO Box 700, McKee, KY 40447 .... (606)287-7800
(Co Clk has b, m, d & lnd rec)

* **Jefferson**   E4   1780   Kentucky Co Virginia
Jefferson County, 527 W Jefferson St, Louisville, KY 40202-2814 .... (502)625-5000
(Co Clk has m & pro rec from 1781; Clk Cir Ct has div rec from 1850; Archivist has civ ct rec from 1780)

*† **Jessamine**   F4   1799   Fayette
Jessamine County, PO Box 38, Nicholasville, KY 40356-0036 .... (606)885-4161
(Co Clk has m, pro, deeds & mtgs from 1799; Cir Ct Clk has div rec)

* **Johnson**   H4   1843   Floyd, Morgan, Lawrence
Johnson County, Court St, Paintsville, KY 41240 .... (606)789-2550
[FHL has some m, cem, civ ct, lnd, pro, tax rec]

* **Kenton**   F6   1840   Campbell
Kenton County, 3rd & Court St 1st Fl, Covington, KY 41012 .... (606)491-0702
(Co Clk has m & lnd rec from 1860, pro rec from 1860 to 1977; Clk Cir Ct has div & civ ct rec

Name	Map Index	Date Created	Parent County or Territory From Which Organized
Knott	H3	1884	Perry, Breathitt, Floyd, Letcher

Knott County, PO Box 446, Hindman, KY 41822-0446 .... (606)785-5651
(Co Clk has m, civ ct rec & Ind rec from 1886)

† **Knox**   G2   1800   Lincoln
Knox County, PO Box 105, Barbourville, KY 40906-0105 .... (606)546-3568
(Co Clk has m & Ind rec)

Larue   E3   1843   Hardin
Larue County, County Courthouse, Hodgenville, KY 42748 .... (502)358-3544
(Co Clk has m, Ind rec from 1843, pro rec from 1843 to 1979; Clk Cir Ct has div rec, pro rec from 1979)

† **Laurel**   G3   1826   Whitley, Clay, Knox, Rockcastle
Laurel County, County Courthouse, London, KY 40741 .... (606)864-5158

Lawrence   H4   1822   Floyd, Greenup
Lawrence County, 122 S Main Cross St, Louisa, KY 41230-1393 .... (606)638-4108
(Co Clk has m & Ind rec from 1822, pro rec from 1822 to 1977; Clk Cir Ct has div rec)

Lee   G4   1870   Owsley, Breathitt, Wolfe, Estill
Lee County, PO Box 551, Beattyville, KY 41311 .... (606)464-2596
(Co Clk has m, pro, Ind rec from 1870; Clk Cir Ct has div, civ ct rec)

Leslie   H3   1878   Clay, Harlan, Perry
Leslie County, PO Box 916, Hyden, KY 41749 .... (606)672-2193
(Co Clk has m, pro, & Ind rec; Clk Cir Ct has div & civ ct rec)

* **Letcher**   H3   1842   Perry, Harlan
Letcher County, PO Box 58, Whitesburg, KY 41858-0058 .... (606)633-2432
(Co Clk has m & Ind rec from 1842 & pro rec)

* **Lewis**   H5   1807   Mason
Lewis County, 2nd St, Vanceburg, KY 41179 .... (606)796-3062
(Co Clk has m & Ind rec from 1807, pro rec from 1806 & civ ct rec)

Lincoln   F3   1780   Kentucky Co Virginia
Lincoln County, County Courthouse, Stanford, KY 40484 .... (606)365-2601
(Co Clk has m, div, pro, civ ct rec from 1792)

* **Livingston**   B3   1798   Christian
Livingston County, PO Box 400, Smithland, KY 42081-0400 .... (502)928-2162
(Co Clk has m rec from 1799, pro & Ind rec from 1800; Clk Cir Ct has div & ct rec; rec through 1865 have been microfilmed)

* **Logan**   D2   1792   Lincoln
Logan County, 426 E 4th St, Russellville, KY 42276-1897 .... (502)726-6061
(Co Clk has m, pro, Ind & order bks; rec from 1792, survey bks from 1792 to 1860)

Lyon   B3   1854   Caldwell
Lyon County, PO Box 350, Eddyville, KY 42038-0350 .... (502)388-2331
(Co Clk has b rec from 1912 to 1932, m & Ind rec from 1854; Clk Cir Ct has div rec)

* **Madison**   G4   1786   Lincoln
Madison County, 101 W Main St, Richmond, KY 40475-1415 .... (606)624-4703
(Co Clk has m & Ind rec from 1787, pro rec from 1850 to 1977; Dis Ct has pro rec from 1978; Clk Cir Ct has div & civ ct rec)

Magoffin   H4   1860   Floyd, Johnson, Morgan
Magoffin County, Court St, Salyersville, KY 41465 .... (606)349-2216
(Co Clk has m rec from 1860)

Marion   E4   1834   Washington
Marion County, Main St, Lebanon, KY 40033 .... (502)692-2651
(Co Health Dept has b & d rec; Co Clk has m & Ind rec from 1863, pro rec from 1863 to 1978; Clk Cir Ct has pro rec from 1979, div & civ ct rec)

* **Marshall**   B2   1842   Callaway
Marshall County, 1101 Main St, Benton, KY 42025-1498 .... (502)527-3323
(Co Clk has m & Ind rec from 1848)

Martin   H4   1870   Lawrence, Floyd, Pike, Johnson
Martin County, Main St, Inez, KY 41224 .... (606)298-2810
(Co Clk has b rec from 1903 to 1949, m rec from 1883, d rec from 1911 to 1949; Cir Clk has div, pro & civ ct rec)

* **Mason**   G5   1789   Bourbon
Mason County, PO Box 234, Maysville, KY 41056-0234 .... (606)564-3341
(Co Clk has m, pro & Ind rec from 1789; Clk Cir Ct has div rec from 1929 & civ ct rec from 1792)

McCracken   B3   1825   Hickman
McCracken County, Washington & 7th Sts, Paducah, KY 42003 .... (502)444-4700
(Co Clk has m, pro & Ind rec from 1825)

† **McCreary**   F2   1912   Wayne, Pulaski, Whitley
McCreary County, Main St, Whitley City, KY 42653 .... (606)376-2411
(Co Clk has m rec from 1912, 1923 to 1927 burned, also Ind rec)

McLean   C4   1854   Muhlenberg, Daviess, Ohio
McLean County, PO Box 57, Calhoun, KY 42327-0057 .... (502)273-3082
(Co Clk has m, pro, Ind rec from 1854, m bonds bef 1907 were burned, but Co Clk has the index for these rec)

Name	Map Index	Date Created	Parent County or Territory From Which Organized

† **Meade** D4 1824 Hardin, Breckinridge
Meade County, PO Box 614, Brandenburg, KY 40108-0614 .... (502)422-2152
(Co Clk has m rec from 1967, some m, Ind rec & wills from 1824, recent tax rec; Clk Cir Ct has div & pro rec)

Menifee G4 1869 Powell, Wolfe, Bath, Morgan, Montgomery
Menifee County, County Courthouse, Frenchburg, KY 40322 .... (606)768-3512
(Co Clk has m rec from 1869; Clk Cir Ct has div rec from 1869)

* **Mercer** F4 1786 Lincoln
Mercer County, 224 S Main St, Harrodsburg, KY 40330-1696 .... (606)734-6310
(Co Clk has m, pro, Ind rec from 1786; Clk Cir Ct has div rec; Co Judge has civ ct rec)

* **Metcalfe** E3 1860 Monroe, Adair, Barren, Cumberland, Green
Metcalfe County, PO Box 850, Edmonton, KY 42129 .... (502)432-4821
(Co Clk has m & Ind rec)

* **Monroe** E2 1820 Barren, Cumberland
Monroe County, PO Box 335, Tompkinsville, KY 42167-0335 .... (502)487-5471
(Co Clk has m, pro & Ind rec from 1863; Clk Cir Ct has div & civ ct rec)

* **Montgomery** G4 1797 Clark
Montgomery County, Court St, Mount Sterling, KY 40353 .... (606)498-8700
(Co Health Dept has b & d rec; Co Clk has m rec from 1864, Ind rec, pro rec from 1797; Clk Cir Ct has div & civ ct rec)

Morgan H4 1823 Floyd, Bath
Morgan County, 505 Prestonsburg St, West Liberty, KY 41472-1162 .... (606)743-3897
(Co Clk has b rec from 1911 to 1949, m, pro & Ind rec)

* **Muhlenberg** C3 1799 Christian, Logan
Muhlenberg County, PO Box 272, Greenville, KY 42345-0272 .... (502)338-1441
(Co Clk has m & Ind rec; Clk Cir Ct has pro & div rec)

* **Nelson** E4 1785 Jefferson
Nelson County, 113 E Stephen Foster Ave, Bardstown, KY 40004-1546 .... (502)348-1800
(Co Clk has m & pro rec from 1784)

* **Nicholas** G5 1800 Bourbon, Mason
Nicholas County, PO Box 329, Carlisle, KY 40311-0329 .... (606)289-5591
(Co Clk has m, pro & Ind rec from 1800; Clk Cir Ct has div & civ rec)

* **Ohio** D3 1799 Hardin
Ohio County, PO Box 85, Hartford, KY 42347-0085 .... (502)298-3673
(Co Health Dept has d rec from 1911; Co Clk has m & Ind rec from 1799, pro rec from 1801; veterans discharge rec from 1861; Clk Cir Ct has div rec, pro rec from 1978

Oldham F5 1824 Henry, Shelby, Jefferson
Oldham County, 100 Main St, La Grange, KY 40031 .... (502)222-9311
(Co Clk has m, pro & Ind rec from 1824; Clk Cir Ct has div & civ ct rec)

Owen F5 1819 Scott, Franklin, Gallatin, Pendleton
Owen County, County Courthouse, Owenton, KY 40359 .... (502)484-3405
(Co Clk has b & d rec from 1911 to 1949, m, pro & Ind rec from 1819; Clk Cir Ct has div & civ ct rec at State Archives - Frankfort)

Owsley G3 1843 Clay, Estill, Breathitt
Owsley County, 154 Main St, Booneville, KY 41314 .... (606)593-5735
(Co Clk has m, pro & Ind rec from 1929; Clk Cir Ct has div & civ ct rec; Co Judge has pro rec)

* **Pendleton** G5 1799 Bracken, Campbell
Pendleton County, County Courthouse Sq, Falmouth, KY 41040 .... (606)654-4321
(Co Clk has m rec from 1799, pro rec from 1800 & Ind rec; Clk Cir Ct has div & civ ct rec)

* **Perry** H3 1821 Clay, Floyd
Perry County, PO Box 150, Hazard, KY 41702 .... (606)436-4614
(Co Clk has m, Ind rec from 1821, Clk Cir Ct has div rec; Clk Dis Ct has pro, civ ct, wills)

Pike I3 1822 Floyd
Pike County, PO Box 631, Pikeville, KY 41501-0631 .... (606)432-6240
(Co Clk has b & d rec from 1911 to 1949, m & Ind rec from 1824, pro rec from 1822 & school rec from 1895 to 1934)

Powell G4 1852 Clark, Estill, Montgomery
Powell County, Court St, Stanton, KY 40380 .... (606)663-4390
(Co Clk has m & Ind rec from 1865; Clk Cir Ct has div, pro & civ ct rec)

* **Pulaski** F3 1799 Green, Lincoln
Pulaski County, PO Box 724, Somerset, KY 42501-0724 .... (606)679-2042
(Co Clk has m, pro & Ind rec from 1799; Clk Cir Ct has div & cir ct rec)

Robertson G5 1867 Nicholas, Bracken, Mason, Fleming, Harrison
Robertson County, PO Box 95, Mount Olivet, KY 41064 .... (606)724-5212
(Co Clk has m & Ind rec from 1881, school census rec from 1895; Clk Cir Ct has pro, div & civ ct rec from 1867)

Rockcastle G3 1810 Pulaski, Lincoln, Madison
Rockcastle County, PO Box 365, Mount Vernon, KY 40456-0365 .... (606)256-2831
(Co Clk has m & Ind rec from 1873; Clk Cir Ct has div rec from 1873, pro & civ ct rec)

Rowan G4 1856 Fleming, Morgan
Rowan County, E Main St 2nd Fl, Morehead, KY 40351 .... (606)784-5212
(Co Clk has m, pro & Ind rec from 1890; Clk Cir Ct has div rec; Co Judge has civ ct rec)

Name	Map Index	Date Created	Parent County or Territory From Which Organized
Russell	F3	1826	Cumberland, Adair, Wayne, Pulaski

    Russell County, PO Box 579, Jamestown, KY 42629-0579 .... (502)343-2125
    (Co Clk has m, pro, civ ct & Ind rec from 1826; Clk Cir Ct has div rec)

* **Scott**   F5   1792   Woodford
    Scott County, 101 E Main St, Georgetown, KY 40324-1794 .... (502)863-7875
    (Co Clk has m rec from 1837, pro & Ind rec from 1837, some earlier; Clk Cir Ct has div & civ ct rec)

* **Shelby**   F4   1792   Jefferson
    Shelby County, 501 Main St, Shelbyville, KY 40065-1133 .... (502)663-1220
    (Co Clk has b rec from 1911 to 1948, also m & pro rec)

Simpson   D2   1819   Allen, Logan, Warren
    Simpson County, PO Box 268, Franklin, KY 42134-0268 .... (502)586-8161
    (Co Clk has m rec from 1892)

Spencer   E4   1824   Shelby, Bullitt, Nelson
    Spencer County, Main St, Taylorsville, KY 40071 .... (502)477-8121
    (Co Clk has m rec from 1852, pro & Ind rec from 1824; Clk Cir Ct has div & civ ct rec)

* **Taylor**   E3   1848   Green
    Taylor County, Court & Broadway, Campbellsville, KY 42718 .... (502)465-6677
    [FHL has some m, cem, civ ct, Ind, pro, tax rec]

* **Todd**   C2   1820   Christian, Logan
    Todd County, PO Box 157, Elkton, KY 42220-0157 .... (502)265-2363
    (Co Clk has m, div, pro, civ ct, Ind rec, wills, inventory & appr rec)

Trigg   C2   1820   Christian, Caldwell
    Trigg County, PO Box 1310, Cadiz, KY 42211-0609 .... (502)522-6661
    (Co Health Dept has b, d rec; Co Clk has m, Ind rec from 1820, pro rec 1820-1977; Clk Cir Ct has div, civ ct rec)

Trimble   F5   1837   Henry, Oldham, Gallatin
    Trimble County, Main St & Hwy 42, Bedford, KY 40006 .... (502)255-7174
    (Co Clk has b rec from 1911 to 1950, m rec from 1865, Ind rec from 1800)

* **Union**   C4   1811   Henderson
    Union County, PO Box 119, Morganfield, KY 42437 .... (502)389-1334
    (Co Clk has m, pro & Ind rec from 1811)

* **Warren**   D3   1797   Logan
    Warren County, 429 E 10th St, Bowling Green, KY 42101-2250 .... (502)843-4146
    (Co Clk has b, m & Ind rec from 1797, pro rec from 1797 to 1978, Veterans discharges from 1917)

* **Washington**   F4   1792   Nelson
    Washington County, PO Box 446, Springfield, KY 40069-0446 .... (606)336-3471
    (Co Clk has m & Ind rec from 1792, pro rec from 1792 to 1978, school census from 1898 to 1917; Clk Cir Ct has div rec, civ ct
    rec from 1792, pro rec from 1978; Board of Ed has school census from 1922)

* **Wayne**   F2   1801   Pulaski, Cumberland
    Wayne County, PO Box 565, Monticello, KY 42633 .... (606)348-6661
    (Co Clk has m, Ind rec from 1800, pro rec 1800 to 1978)

Webster   C3   1860   Hopkins, Union, Henderson
    Webster County, PO Box 155, Dixon, KY 42409-0155 .... (502)639-5042
    (Co Clk has m, Ind rec from 1860, Ind rec from 1860, pro rec from 1860 to 1977; Clk Cir Ct has div, civ ct rec, pro reg after 1978)

Whitley   G2   1818   Knox
    Whitley County, Main St, Williamsburg, KY 40769 .... (606)549-6002
    (Co Clk has b rec from 1915 to 1949, m & pro rec from 1865 & Ind rec from 1818)

* **Wolfe**   H4   1860   Owsley, Breathitt, Powell, Morgan
    Wolfe County, PO Box 400, Campton, KY 41301-0400 .... (606)668-3515
    (Co Clk has m rec from 1913, Ind rec from 1860; Clk Cir Ct has div, pro, civ ct rec)

* **Woodford**   F4   1789   Fayette
    Woodford County, County Courthouse, Versailles, KY 40383 .... (606)873-3421
    (Co Clk has m, pro & Ind rec from 1789; Clk Cir Ct has div & civ ct rec)

* At least one county history has been published about this county.
† Inventory of county archives was made by the Historical Records Survey. (See Introduction)

LOUISIANA

CAPITAL · BATON ROUGE — TERRITORY 1805 — STATE 1812 (18th)
State Map on Page M-17

    Although discovered early in the 1500's, Louisiana was not settled until 1714, when the French settled Natchitoches on the Red River. The first organized migration from France occurred between 1717 and 1722 under the control of the Compagnie des Indes and a Scottish entrepreneur, John Law. New Orleans was founded in 1718 by Jean Baptiste Le Moyne, sieur de Bienville, sometimes called the "father of Louisiana", and became the capital in 1722. Other early settlers came from German-speaking areas of Europe, while some were brought from Africa to serve as slaves.

In 1755, the British expelled the French settlers of Acadia, and later, Nova Scotia. As many as 5,000 of these French Acadians, who became known as Cajuns, settled in Louisiana. Descendants of the older French and Spanish settlers became known as Creoles. In 1763, Spain was given all of Louisiana east of the Mississippi, except the area around New Orleans. Taking control of the area in 1769, the Spanish began keeping records in earnest. During the Revolutionary War, some British sympathizers moved into the area to avoid the conflict. In 1800, Spain ceded Louisiana to the French, although they continued to administer the area until about 1803.

The Louisiana Purchase in 1803 made Louisiana part of the United States. The next year, Louisiana was divided into two sections, the District of Louisiana north of the 33rd parallel, and the Territory of Orleans south of the 33rd parallel. Immediately thereafter, large numbers of Americans from south of the Ohio River moved into the area. In 1805, Louisiana was divided into twelve counties, but smaller civil divisions called parishes gradually took over the functions of the counties. By 1807, the Territory of Orleans consisted of nineteen parishes, which followed the boundaries of the old Spanish ecclesiastical parishes. Parishes in Louisiana serve the same function as counties do in other states.

Spanish west Florida, between the Mississippi and Pearl rivers and including Baton Rouge, was occupied by English-speaking settlers in 1810. When Louisiana was admitted to the Union in 1812, this area was included as part of the state. Baton Rouge became the capital in 1849. Louisiana seceded from the Union in 1861. In May 1862, Union naval forces occupied New Orleans, cutting off nearly all trade which caused severe hardships throughout the state. A military government was established and the courts reorganized. Louisiana furnished over 77,000 soldiers to the Confederacy and 5,000 to the Union. In 1867, Louisiana became part of the Fifth Military District under General Philip Henry Sheridan. Louisiana was readmitted to the Union in 1868.

The Department of Health and Human Resources, P.O. Box 60630, New Orleans, LA 70160, has records of births and deaths since 1914. Delayed registration of births since 1939 are also available. To verify current fees, call 504-568-5175.

Colonial marriages were recorded in the judicial records of the French Superior Council and the Spanish Cabildo. Originals are kept at the Louisiana Historical Center Library and State Museum, 400 Esplanade Avenue, New Orleans, LA 70116 (mailing address: 751 Chartres Street, New Orleans, LA 70116) and the royal notaries, Custodian of Notarial Records, 421 Loyola Avenue, Room B-4, New Orleans, LA 70112. No statewide registration of marriages exists. All marriage records are kept by the parishes. For information about wills, deeds, divorces, or civil court records write the clerk of each parish. Various military and local censuses were taken between 1699 and 1805. A special census of New Orleans was taken in 1805. Most of these censuses have been published.

Genealogical Archives, Libraries and Societies

Alexandria Historical and Genealogical Library, 503 Washington, Alexandria, LA 71301

Baton Rouge, Diocese of, Archives Dept., P. O. Box 2028, Baton Rouge, LA 70821

Centroplex Library, 120 St. Louis St., Baton Rouge, LA 70821

East Ascension Genealogical and Historical Society Genealogy Library, Ascension Parish Library, Gonzales, LA 70707-1006

East Baton Rouge Parish Library, Centroplex Branch, P. O. Box 1471, Baton Rouge, LA 70821

Hill Memorial Library, Louisiana State University, Baton Rouge, LA 70803

Howard Tilton Library, The Map and Genealogy Room, Tulane University, New Orleans, LA 70118

Lincoln Parish Library, Box 637, 509 W. Alabama, Ruston, LA 71270

Louisiana State Library, State Capitol Ground, Baton Rouge, LA 70804

New Orleans Public Library, 219 Loyola Ave., New Orleans, LA 70112

Ouachita Parish Public Library, 1800 Stubbs Ave., Monroe, LA 71201

Rapides Parish Library, 411 Washington St., Alexandria, LA 71301

Shreve Memorial Library, Genealogy Department, 424 Texas St., P. O. Box 21523, Shreveport, LA 71120

Tangipahoa Parish Library, P. O. Box 578, Amite, LA 70422

Allen Genealogical and Historical Society, P. O. Box 789, Kinder, LA 70648

Ark-La-Tex Genealogical Association, P. O. Box 4462, Shreveport, LA 71134-0462

Baton Rouge, Diocese of, Archives Dept., P. O. Box 2028, Baton Rouge, LA 70821

Baton Rouge Genealogical and Historical Society, P. O. Box 80565 SE Station, Baton Rouge, LA 70898

Central Louisiana Genealogical Society, P. O. Box 12206, Alexandria, LA 71315-2006

Christmas History of Louisiana, 7024 Morgan Rd., Greenwell Springs, LA 70739

East Ascension Genealogical and Historical Society, P. O. Box 1006, Gonzales, LA 70707-1006

Evangeline Genealogical & Historical Society, P. O. Box 664, Ville Platte, LA 70586

Feliciana (East) History Committee, P. O. Box 8341, Clinton, LA 70722

Feliciana (West) Historical Society, P. O. Box 338, St. Francisville, LA 70775

Genealogical Research Society of New Orleans, P. O. Box 51791, New Orleans, LA 70150

Genealogy West, 5644 Abbey Dr., New Orleans, LA 70131-3808

Jefferson Genealogical Society, P. O. Box 961, Metairie, LA 70004

Jennings, Louisiana Genealogical Society, 136 Greenwood Drive, Jennings, LA 70546

Lafayette Genealogical Society, 105 Gill Drive, Lafayette, LA 70507

Lafourche Heritage Society, 412 Menard St., Thibodaux, LA 70301

Louisiana-Daughters of the American Revolution, 2564 Donald Drive, Baton Rouge, LA 70809

Louisiana Genealogical and Historical Society, P. O. Box 3454, Baton Rouge, LA 70821

Louisiana Society, Sons of the American Revolution, 3059 Belmont Ave., Baton Rouge, LA 70808

Genealogical Research Society of New Orleans, P. O. Box 71791, New Orleans, LA 70150

Natchitoches Genealogical and Historical Assoc., P. O. Box 1349, Natchitoches, LA 71458-1349

North Louisiana Genealogical Society, P. O. Box 324, Ruston, LA 71270

Plaquemines Parish Genealogical Society, 203 Highway 23, South Buras, LA 70041

Southwest Louisiana Genealogical Society, P. O. Box 5652, Lake Charles, LA 70606-5652

St. Bernard Genealogical Society, Inc., P. O. Box 271, Chalmette, LA 70044

St. Tammany Genealogical Society, Rt. 4, Box 332, Covington, LA 70433

Terrebonne Genealogical Society, P. O. Box 295, Sta. 2, Houma, LA 70360

Vermilion Genealogical Society, P. O. Box 117, Abbeville, LA 70511-0117

Printed Census Records and Mortality Schedules

Federal Census 1810, 1820, 1830, 1840, 1850, 1860, 1870, 1880, 1900, 1910
Federal Mortality Schedules 1850, 1860, 1870, 1880
Union Veterans and Widows 1890
French Colonial Census 1699-1732
State/Territorial Census 1706, 1721, 1726
Free Colored Residents 1804
Residents 1814, 1820, 1821

Valuable Printed Sources

Bibliographies

Hebert, Donald J. *A Guide to Church Records in Louisiana*. Eunice, Louisiana: Donald J. Hebert, 1975.

————. *South Louisiana Records: Lafourche-Terrebonne*. Cecilia, Louisiana: Donald J. Hebert, 1978.

————. *Southwest Louisiana Records*. Eunice, Louisiana: Donald J. Hebert, 1976.

Resources in Louisiana Libraries. Baton Rouge: Louisiana State Library, 1971.

Genealogical Research Guides

Boling, Yvette Guillot. *A Guide to Printed Sources for Genealogical and Historical Research in the Louisiana Parishes*. Jefferson, Louisiana: Yvette Guillot Boling, 1985.

Genealogical Sources

Conrad, Glenn R. *First Families of Louisiana*. Baton Rouge: Claitor's Publishing Division, 1970.

Histories

Cummings, Light Townsend and Glenn Jeansonne. *A Guide to the History of Louisiana*. Westport, Connecticut: Greenwood Press, 1982.

Fortier, Alcee. *A History of Louisiana*. New York: Manzi, Joyant & Co.

Gayarre, Charles. *History of Louisiana*. New Orleans: Pelican Publishers.

LOUISIANA PARISH DATA
State Map on Page M-17

Name	Map Index	Date Created	Parent Parish or Territory From Which Organized
* **Acadia**	F6	1886	St. Landry

Acadia Parish, PO Box 922, Crowley, LA 70527-0922 .... (318)788-8881
(Par Clk has m, div, pro & civ ct rec from 1886)

Name	Map Index	Date Created	Parent Parish or Territory From Which Organized

† **Allen**   F6   1912   Calcasieu
Allen Parish, PO Box G, Oberlin, LA 70655-2007 . . . . (318)639-4396
(Par Clk has m, div, pro & civ ct rec from 1913)

* **Ascension**   D6   1807   St. James
Ascension Parish, Houmas St, Donaldsonville, LA 70346 . . . . (504)473-9866
(Par Clk has m rec from 1763, div, pro & civ ct rec from 1800 & Ind rec from 1770)

*† **Assumption**   D7   1807   Original Parish
Assumption Parish, Martin Luther King Dr & Hwy 1, Napoleonville, LA 70390 . . . . (504)369-7435
(Par Clk has m rec from 1800, pro rec from 1841, Ind rec from 1788, div & civ ct rec from 1868)

Attakapas (Original parish discontinued)

* **Avoyelles**   E5   1807   Original Parish - reorg. 1873
Avoyelles Parish, 301 N Main St, Marksville, LA 71351-2493 . . . . (318)253-7523
(Par Clk has m, Ind rec from 1808, div, pro, civ ct rec from 1856)

Baton Rouge (see East Baton Rouge)

*† **Beauregard**   G5   1913   Calcasieu
Beauregard Parish, PO Box 310, De Ridder, LA 70634-0310 . . . . (318)463-7019
(Par Clk has m, div, pro, civ ct & Ind rec from 1913)

* **Bienville**   G3   1848   Claiborne
Bienville Parish, 300 Courthouse Sq, Arcadia, LA 71001 . . . . (318)263-2123
(Par Clk has m, div, pro & civ ct rec from 1848)

† **Bossier**   H2   1843   Claiborne
Bossier Parish, PO Box 369, Benton, LA 71006-0369 . . . . (318)965-2336
(Par Clk has m, div, pro, civ ct, Ind & inquest rec from 1843)

Caddo   H2   1838   Natchitoches
Caddo Parish, 501 Texas St, Shreveport, LA 71101-5476 . . . . (318)226-6911
(Par Clk has m, div, pro, civ ct, mtg & conveyance rec from 1835)

*† **Calcasieu**   G6   1840   St. Landry
Calcasieu Parish, PO Box 1030, Lake Charles, LA 70602-1030 . . . . (318)437-3550
(Par Clk has m, div, pro, civ ct & Ind rec from 1910)

* **Caldwell**   E3   1838   Catahoula, Ouachita
Caldwell Parish, Main St, Columbia, LA 71418 . . . . (318)649-2681
(Par Clk has m, div, pro, civ ct & Ind rec from 1838)

* **Cameron**   G7   1870   Calcasieu, Vermillion
Cameron Parish, PO Box 549, Cameron, LA 70631-0549 . . . . (318)775-5316
(Par Clk has m, div, pro, civ ct & Ind rec from 1870, veterans discharges from 1918; area churches & funeral homes have bur rec)

Carroll (See East & West Carroll)

Catahoula   E4   1808
Catahoula Parish, PO Box 198, Harrisonburg, LA 71340-0198 . . . . (318)744-5497
(Par Clk has m, pro, Ind rec from early 1800s, div, civ ct rec from early 1900s)

* **Claiborne**   G2   1828   Natchitoches
Claiborne Parish, Courthouse Sq, Homer, LA 71040 . . . . (318)927-9601
(Par Clk has m, div, pro, civ ct, Ind rec from 1850; Courthouse burned 1849)

Concordia   E4   1805   Avoyelles
Concordia Parish, PO Box 790, Vidalia, LA 71373-0790 . . . . (318)336-4204
(Par Clk has m rec from 1840, div, pro, civ ct & Ind rec from 1850)

* **DeSoto**   G3   1843   Natchitoches, Caddo
DeSoto Parish, Parish Courthouse, Mansfield, LA 71052 . . . . (318)872-0738
(Par Clk has m & Ind rec from 1843, div, pro & civ ct rec)

* **East Baton Rouge**   D6   1810   Original parish
East Baton Rouge Parish, 222 Saint Louis St, Baton Rouge, LA 70802-5817 . . . . (504)389-3000
(Par Clk has m rec from 1840, div, pro, civ ct, Ind rec from 1782)

* **East Carroll**   D2   1877   Carroll
East Carroll Parish, 400 1st St, Lake Providence, LA 71254-2616 . . . . (318)559-2256
[FHL has some m, Ind, pro rec]

* **East Feliciana**   D5   1824   Seceded from Feliciana
East Feliciana Parish, PO Box 595, Clinton, LA 70722-0595 . . . . (504)683-5145
(Par Clk has m, div, pro, civ ct, Ind, slave sales, contracts, mtgs, sheriffs sales & donations rec from 1824)

* **Evangeline**   F5   1911   St. Landry
Evangeline Parish, Court St 2nd Fl, Ville Platte, LA 70586 . . . . (318)363-5651
(Par Clk has m, div, pro, civ ct, Ind rec from 1911)

Feliciana (see East Feliciana)

Franklin   E3   1843   Catahoula, Ouachita, Madison
Franklin Parish, 210 Main St, Winnsboro, LA 71295-2750 . . . . (318)435-9429
(Par Clk has m, div, pro, civ ct & Ind rec from 1843)

Name	Map Index	Date Created	Parent Parish or Territory From Which Organized

*† Grant   F4   1869   Rapides, Winn
Grant Parish, Main St, Colfax, LA 71417 .... (318)627-3157
(Par Clk has m, div, pro, civ ct & Ind rec from 1878)

* Iberia   E7   1868   St. Martin, St. Mary
Iberia Parish, 300 Iberia St Suite 400, New Iberia, LA 70560-4543 .... (318)365-8246
(Par Clk has m, div, pro, civ ct & Ind rec from 1868)

* Iberville   D6   1807   Assumption, Ascension
Iberville Parish, PO Box 423, Plaquemine, LA 70765-0423 .... (504)687-5160
(Par Clk has m & Ind rec from 1770, div, pro, civ ct rec from 1807)

Jackson   F3   1845   Claiborne, Ouachita, Union
Jackson Parish, PO Box 737, Jonesboro, LA 71251-0737 .... (318)259-2424
[FHL has some m, Ind, pro rec]

*† Jefferson   C7   1825   Orleans
Jefferson Parish, 2nd & Derbigny, Gretna, LA 70053-3299 .... (504)364-2800
(Par Clk has m rec from 1863, div, pro & civ ct rec from 1825, Ind rec from 1827)

* Jefferson Davis   F6   1913   Calcasieu
Jefferson Davis Parish, PO Box 1409, Jennings, LA 70546-1409 .... (318)824-4792
(Par Clk has m, div, pro, civ ct, Ind rec from 1913, a few transcribed rec from Calcasieu Parish; Courthouse burned 1910)

*† Lafayette   E6   1823   St. Martin
Lafayette Parish, PO Box 4508, Lafayette, LA 70502-4508 .... (318)233-6220
(Par Clk has m, div, pro, civ ct & Ind rec from 1823)

*† Lafourche   C7   1807
Lafourche Parish, 209 Green St, Thibodaux, LA 70301-3021 .... (504)446-8427
(Par Clk has b, m, div, pro, civ ct & Ind rec from 1808)

* LaSalle   F4   1910   Catahoula
LaSalle Parish, PO Box 57, Jena, LA 71342-0057 .... (318)992-2101
(Par Clk has m, div, pro, civ ct & Ind rec from 1910)

* Lincoln   F2   1873   Bienville, Jackson, Union, Clairborne
Lincoln Parish, 100 W Texas Ave, Ruston, LA 71270-4463 .... (318)255-3663
(Par Clk has m, div, pro & civ ct rec from 1873)

* Livingston   D6   1832   Baton Rouge, Ascension
Livingston Parish, PO Box 427, Livingston, LA 70754-0427 .... (504)686-2266
(Par Clk has m, div, pro, civ ct & Ind rec from 1875)

Madison   D3   1838   Concordia
Madison Parish, 100 N Cedar St, Tallulah, LA 71282-3840 .... (318)574-0655
(Par Clk has m rec from 1866, div rec from 1839, pro rec from 1850, civ ct rec from 1882, deeds from 1839 & mtg from 1865)

*† Morehouse   E2   1844   Ouachita
Morehouse Parish, 125 E Madison St, Bastrop, LA 71221 .... (318)281-4132
(Par Clk has m, div, pro & civ ct rec from 1870, Ind rec & mtg rec from 1844, cem abstract from 1867 to 1957)

† Natchitoches   G4   1807   Original Parish
Natchitoches Parish, PO Box 799, Natchitoches, LA 71458-0799 .... (318)352-2714
(Clk Ct has m rec from 1780, also div, pro & civ ct rec)

Opelousas (see Saint Landry)

*† Orleans   C4   1807   Original Parish
Orleans Parish, 1300 Perdido St, New Orleans, LA 70112-2112 .... (504)565-6580
(Clk Civ Dis Ct has div, pro & civ ct rec from 1805; Reg of Conveyances has Ind rec from 1832; Pub Lib has voter registration rec from 1895 to 1941, city directories from 1805, precinct bks from 1895 to 1952)

*† Ouachita   E2   1807   Original Parish
Ouachita Parish, 300 Saint John St, Monroe, LA 71201-7398 .... (318)323-5188
(Par Clk has m, div, pro, civ ct & Ind rec from 1805)

† Plaquemines   B7   1807   Orleans
Plaquemines Parish, Hwy 39, Pointe a la Hache, LA 70082-9999 .... (504)333-4343
(Par Clk has m rec from 1809, div, pro, civ ct & Ind rec from 1800)

* Pointe Coupee   E6   1807   Feliciana, Avoyelles
Pointe Coupee County, PO Box 86, New Roads, LA 70760-0086 .... (504)638-9596
(Clk Ct has m rec from 1735, div rec from 1800, pro, civ ct, conveyances & mtg from 1780)

* Rapides   F5   1807   Original Parish
Rapides Parish, 700 Murray St, Alexandria, LA 71301-8023 .... (318)473-8153
(Par Clk has m, div, pro, civ ct & Ind rec from 1864)

Red River   G3   1871   Caddo, Bossier, Bienville, Natchitoches, DeSoto
Red River Parish, 615 E Carroll St, Coushatta, LA 71019-8537 .... (318)932-5719
(Clk Ct has m & pro rec from 1871, div & civ ct rec from 1904)

Richland   E3   1868   Ouachita, Carroll, Franklin, Morehouse
Richland Parish, 108 Courthouse Sq, Rayville, LA 71269-2647 .... (318)728-2061
(Par Clk has m, div, pro, civ ct, Ind rec from 1869)

Name	Map Index	Date Created	Parent Parish or Territory From Which Organized

*† Sabine   G4   1843   Natchitoches
Sabine Parish, PO Box 419, Many, LA 71449-0419 .... (318)256-6223
(Par Clk has m, div, pro, civ ct & lnd rec from 1843)

† Saint Bernard   B7   1807   Original Parish
Saint Bernard Parish, 8201 W Judge Perez Dr, Chalmette, LA 70043-1696 .... (504)277-6371
[FHL has some m, civ ct, lnd rec]

† Saint Charles   C7   1807   Original Parish
Saint Charles Parish, PO Box 302, Hahnville, LA 70057-0302 .... (504)783-6246
[FHL has some m, civ ct, lnd, pro rec]

Saint Helena   D5   1810   Livingston
Saint Helena Parish, Court Sq, Greensburg, LA 70441 .... (504)222-4514
(Par Clk has rec from 1804, Co employees do not have time to chk rec)

* Saint James   D7   1807   Original Parish
Saint James Parish, PO Box 106, Convent, LA 70723-0063 .... (504)562-7431
(Par Clk has m rec from 1846, div, pro & civ ct rec from 1809)

* Saint John the Baptist   C6   1807   Original Parish
Saint John the Baptist Parish, 1801 W Airline Hwy, La Place, LA 70068-3336 .... (504)652-9569
(Par Clk has m, div, pro, civ ct & lnd rec)

* Saint Landry   E6   1807   Avoyelles, Rapides
Saint Landry Parish, Court & Landry Sts, Opelousas, LA 70570 .... (318)942-5606
(Par Clk has m rec from 1808, div rec from 1813, pro rec from 1809 & civ ct rec from 1813)

* Saint Martin   E6   1807   Original Parish
Saint Martin Parish, County Courthouse, Saint Martinville, LA 70582 .... (318)394-2210
[FHL has some m, civ ct, lnd, pro, tax rec]

* Saint Mary   E7   1811   Assumption
Saint Mary Parish, 500 Main St Rm 5, Franklin, LA 70538-6198 .... (318)828-4100
(Par Clk has m, div, pro, civ ct & lnd rec from 1800)

* Saint Tammany   C6   1810   St. Helena, Orleans
Saint Tammany Parish, PO Box 1090, Covington, LA 70434-1090 .... (504)898-2430
(Par Clk has m, div, pro, civ ct rec from 1812, lnd rec from 1810, mark & brand bks from 1816, early road dis listing persons
working on pub road from 1816, tax rec from 1880, vet discharge papers WWI, WWII & others)

* Tangipahoa   C6   1869   Livingston, St. Tammany, St. Helena, Washington
Tangipahoa Parish, PO Box 215, Amite, LA 70422-0215 .... (504)748-3211
(Par Clk has m, div, pro, civ ct & lnd rec, also conveyance, will, donation rec from 1869)

Tensas   E3   1843   Concordia
Tensas Parish, Courthouse Sq, Saint Joseph, LA 71366 .... (318)766-3921
(Par Clk has m, div, pro & civ ct rec from 1843)

*† Terrebonne   D7   1822   La Fourche
Terrebonne Parish, 301 Goode St, Houma, LA 70360-4513 .... (504)868-5050

* Union   F2   1839   Ouachita
Union Parish, Main & Bayou Sts 1st Fl, Farmerville, LA 71241 .... (318)368-3055
(Par Clk has m, div & pro rec from 1839 & civ ct rec)

* Vermilion   F7   1844   Lafayette
Vermilion Parish, PO Box 790, Abbeville, LA 70511-0790 .... (318)898-4310
(Par Clk has m, div, pro, civ ct & lnd rec from 1885)

* Vernon   G5   1871   Natchitoches, Rapides, Sabine
Vernon Parish, 201 3rd St, Leesville, LA 71496 .... (318)238-1384
(Par Clk Ct has m rec from 1890, div, pro & civ ct rec from 1871)

*† Washington   C5   1819   St. Tammany
Washington Parish, Washington & Main St, Franklinton, LA 70438 .... (504)839-4663
(Par Clk Ct has m, div, pro, civ ct & lnd rec from 1897)

* Webster   G2   1871   Claiborne, Bienville, Bossier
Webster Parish, PO Box 370, Minden, LA 71058-0370 .... (318)371-0366
(Par Clk has m, div, pro, civ ct & lnd rec from 1871)

West Baton Rouge   D6   1807   Baton Rouge
West Baton Rouge Parish, PO Box 757, Port Allen, LA 70767-0757 .... (504)383-4755
[FHL has some m, lnd, pro rec]

West Carroll   E2   1877   Carroll
West Carroll Parish, PO Box 630, Oak Grove, LA 71263-0630 .... (318)428-3390
(Par Clk has m rec from 1877, div, pro, civ ct & lnd rec from 1833)

* West Feliciana   D5   1824   Feliciana
West Feliciana Parish, Royal & Prosperity, Saint Francisville, LA 70775 .... (504)635-3864
(Par Clk has m rec from 1879, div, pro & civ ct rec from 1900, lnd rec from 1811)

Name	Map Index	Date Created	Parent Parish or Territory From Which Organized
† **Winn**	F3	1851	Natchitoches, Catahoula, Rapides

Winn Parish, PO Box 951, Winnfield, LA 71483-0951 .... (318)628-5824
(Par Clk has m, div, pro, civ ct & lnd rec from 1886)

* At least one county history has been published about this county.
† Inventory of county archives was made by the Historical Records Survey. (See Introduction)

MAINE

CAPITAL · AUGUSTA — STATE 1820 (23rd)
State Map on Page M-18

Vikings and other explorers may have sighted the coast of Maine as early as 1000 AD. The first explorers known to have definitely explored this coast were John and Sebastian Cabot in 1498. Over the next century, English, Portuguese, French, and Spanish expeditions visited the area. Attempts at settlement were made between 1607 and 1625, but all proved unsuccessful. In 1625, the first permanent settlement was made at Permaquid by the English. Other settlements followed rapidly including York, Saco, Biddeford, Cape Elizabeth, Falmouth (present-day Portland), and Scarboro. Two members of the Plymouth Colony, Sir Ferdinando Gorges and Captain John Mason, were granted the land between the Merrimack and Kennebec rivers in 1622. In 1629, they divided their lands, with Gorges taking the present state of Maine and Mason, New Hampshire. France likewise claimed the area. Indians sided with the French, which resulted in the French and Indian Wars from about 1632 until 1759.

Massachusetts purchased the province of Maine from Gorges' heirs in 1677 and set up a government in the area. After the death of King Charles in 1685, Massachusetts lost all of its legal standings, forcing landholders to resecure their land at high fees. These land titles were recorded in Boston, but Maine also kept a special land office at York. The area was called the Province of Maine of the Massachusetts Bay Colony until 1779, when it became the District of Maine. Following the Revolution, in which Maine suffered more damage than any other New England area, settlement increased rapidly. The biggest deterrent to settlement was the difficulty of travel in the area, as roads were extremely poor. During the War of 1812, several Maine cities were captured by the British and the eastern part of Maine came under British control. Desires for separation from Massachusetts intensified, resulting in statehood in 1820 as part of the Missouri Compromise.

The Aroostook War in the 1830's brought about 10,000 troops into the area in 1838-1839, although no actual fighting occurred. The War ended in 1842, when a treaty settled the boundary between Maine and New Brunswick. During the Civil War, Maine supplied over 70,000 men to the Union armies. Early settlers were mainly English, Scotch-Irish, and Huguenots. From 1740 to 1800, some German families came to Waldoboro. About 15 percent of the current population descends from two early French groups. The Acadians came from Nova Scotia to the Saint John Valley after 1763 and French Canadians came from Quebec after the Civil War. Artisans from England, Scotland, and Scandinavia came to work in the factories and shipyards during the nineteenth century. About 1870, a large number of Swedes settled in the northeast corner of Maine, organizing such cities as New Sweden, Stockholm, Jemtland, and Linneus.

Very early in their history, Maine towns began keeping records of births, deaths, and marriages, which continued until state registration began in 1892. These records were kept by selectmen or town clerks. Many of these records have been printed, while the remainder are available for searching in city offices. Town histories have also been published for the large majority of Maine cities and usually contain genealogical information about early settlers. State records are kept at the Division of Vital Statistics, Department of Human Services, State House, Station 11, Augusta, ME 04330. Records from prior to 1892 are kept at the Maine State Archives Building, State House Station 84, Augusta, ME 04333. To verify current fees, call 207-289-3181.

Adoption decrees are at the Probate or Superior Court where the adoption was granted, but are sealed after August 8, 1953. Land records are in the sixteen offices of court clerks. The sixteen registrars of probate have settlements of estates. War service records, including grave registrations, are at the office of the Adjutant General in Augusta. Since Maine was part of Massachusetts until 1820, soldiers may be listed in Massachusetts military records. Lists of many pension and bounty records have also been published. In 1827, a state census was taken, but returns exist for only a few areas, including Portland, Bangor, and unincorporated areas. These returns are available at the Maine State Archives. The returns for Eliot are at the Maine Historical Society, 435 Congress Street, Portland, ME 04101.

Genealogical Archives, Libraries and Societies

Auburn Public Library, Court & Spring Sts., Auburn, ME 04210

Bangor Public Library, 145 Harlow St., Bangor, ME 04401

Bath, Patten Free Library, Maine History and Genealogy Room, 33 Summer St., Bath, ME 04530

Kennebunk Free Library, 112 Main Street, Kennebunk, ME 04043

Maine State Library, State House, Augusta, ME 04330

Walker Memorial Library, P. O. Box 1279, Westbrook, ME 04098 Att: Karen L. Sherman Crocker.

Bethel Historical Society, P. O. Box 12, Bethel, ME 04217

Camden Historical Society, 80 Mechanic St., Camden, ME 04843

Cherryfield - Narraguagus Historical Society, P. O. Box 96, Cherryfield, ME 04622

Maine Genealogical Society, P. O. Box 221, Farmington, ME 04938

Maine Historical Society, 485 Congress St., Portland, ME 04111

Maine Society, Sons of the American Revolution, 117 Falmouth Road, Falmouth, ME 04105

Old York Historical Society, P. O. Box 312, York, ME 03909

Sunrise Research Institute, P. O. Box 156, Whitneyville, ME 04692

Printed Census Records and Mortality Schedules

Federal Census 1790, 1800, 1810, 1820, 1830, 1840, 1850, 1860, 1870, 1880, 1900, 1910
Union Veterans and Widows 1890
Residents 1652, 1674, 1703, 1711
Muster Rolls 1775, 1776, 1779
Voters 1787
Federal Assessment 1798

Valuable Printed Sources

Atlases, Maps, and Gazetteers

Chadbourne, Ava Harriet. *Maine Place Names and the Peopling of Its Towns*. Portland, Maine: The Bond Wheelwright Co., 1955.

Denis, Michael. *Maine Towns and Counties: What was What, Where and When*. Oakland, Maine: Danbury House, 1988.

Rutherford, Phillip R. *The Dictionary of Maine Place Names*. Freeport, Maine: The Bond Wheelwright Co., 1970.

Varney, George Jones. *A Gazetteer of the State of Maine*. Boston: B. B. Russell, 1881.

Bibliographies

Frost, John E. *Maine Genealogy: A Bibliographic Guide*. Portland, Maine: Maine Historical Society, 1977.

Jordan, William B. *Maine in the Civil War: A Bibliographic Guide*. Portland, Maine: Maine Historical Society, 1976.

Public Record Repositories in Maine. Augusta, Maine: Maine State Archives, 1976.

Genealogical Research Guides

New England Library Association. *Genealogist's Handbook for New England Research*. Lynnfield, Massachusetts: Bibliography Committee, 1980.

Wright, Norman Edgar. *Genealogy in America, Volume 1: Massachusetts, Connecticut, and Maine*. Salt Lake City, Deseret Book, 1968.

Genealogical Sources

Flagg, Charles Alcott. *An Alphabetical Index of Revolutionary Pensioners Living in Maine*. Baltimore: Genealogical Publishing Co., 1967.

Sargent, William M. *Maine Wills, 1670-1760*. Portland, Maine: Brown, Thurston & Co., 1887.

Histories

Hatch, Louis Clint. *Maine: A History*. New York: American Historical Society, 1919.

MAINE COUNTY DATA
State Map on Page M-18

Name	Map Index	Date Created	Parent County or Territory From Which Organized

* Androscoggin   G2   1854   Cumberland, Oxford, Kennebec
Androscoggin County, 2 Turner, Auburn, ME 04210-5978 .... (207)784-8390
(Clk Sup Ct has div, civ ct rec from 1854; City Clk has m, b, d, bur rec; Reg of Pro has pro rec)

Towns Organized Before 1800: Durham 1789, Greene 1788, Lewiston 1795, Lisbon 1799, Livermore 1795, Turner 1786

* Aroostook   B4   1839   Washington
Aroostook County, PO Box 803, Houlton, ME 04730-0787 .... (207)532-7317
(Co Clk has div & civ ct rec from 1839; Twn Clks keep b, m, d & bur rec; Pro Ct has pro rec)

* Cumberland   H2   1760   York
Cumberland County, 142 Federal St, Portland, ME 04101-4151 .... (207)871-8380
(Co Clk has d, pro & lnd rec from 1760; City or Twn Clks have b, m, d & bur rec)

Towns Organized Before 1800: Bridgton 1794, Brunswick 1739, Cape Elizabeth 1765, Falmouth 1718, Freeport 1789, Gorham 1764, Gray 1778, Harpswell 1758, New Gloucester 1774, North Yarmouth 1732, Otisfield 1798, Portland 1786, Scarborough 1658, Standish 1785, Windham 1762

* Franklin   F2   1838   Cumberland
Franklin County, 38 Main St, Farmington, ME 04938-1818 .... (207)778-6614
(Twn Clk, Farmington has b rec, m, d & bur rec; Clk Sup Ct has div rec from 1852 & civ ct rec; Reg Deeds has lnd rec; Pro Judge has pro rec)

Towns Organized Before 1800: Farmington 1794, Jay 1795, New Sharon 1794

* Hancock   F5   1789   Lincoln
Hancock County, 60 State St, Ellsworth, ME 04605-1926 .... (207)667-9542
(Twn Clks have b, m & d rec; Sup Ct has div & civ ct rec; Co Pro Office has pro rec; Reg of Deeds has lnd rec; Co Clk has m rec from 1789 to 1891)

Towns Organized Before 1800: Bar Harbor 1796, Blue Hill 1789, Bucksport 1792, Castine 1796, Deer Isle 1789, Gouldsboro 1789, Mount Desert 1789, Penobscot 1787, Sedgwick 1789, Sullivan 1789, Trenton 1789

* Kennebec   G3   1799   Lincoln
Kennebec County, 95 State St, Augusta, ME 04330-5611 .... (207)622-0971
[FHL has some m, cem, lnd, pro rec]

Towns Organized Before 1800: Augusta 1797, Belgrade 1796, China 1796, Clinton 1795, Fayette 1795, Hallowell 1771, Litchfield 1795, Monmouth 1792, Mount Vernon 1792, Pittsdon 1779, Readfield 1791, Sidney 1792, Vassalboro 1771, Wayne 1798, Winslow 1771, Winthrop 1771

* Knox   G4   1860   Lincoln, Waldo
Knox County, PO Box 885, Rockland, ME 04841-0885 .... (207)594-0420
(Twn Clks have b, m & d rec; Sup Ct has div & civ ct rec; Pro Ct has pro rec from 1860; Reg of Deeds has lnd rec from 1860)

Towns Organized Before 1800: Camden 1791, Cushing 1789, Thomaston 1777, Union 1786, Vinalhaven 1789, Warren 1776

* Lincoln   G3   1760   York
Lincoln County, High St County Courthouse, Wiscasset, ME 04578 .... (207)882-6311
(Clk Cts has m, pro, lnd rec from 1860, civ ct rec from 1861; Clk Sup Ct has pro rec from 1760)

Towns Organized Before 1800: Alno 1794, Boothbay 1764, Bristol 1765, Dresden 1794, Newcastle 1753, Nobleboro 1788, Waldoboro 1773, Wiscasset 1760

* Oxford   F1   1805   York, Cumberland
Oxford County, PO Box 179, South Paris, ME 04281-0179 .... (207)743-6359
(Twn Clks have b, m, d rec; Clk Cts has m rec from 1877 to 1897, div rec from 1930, pro, lnd rec from 1805, civ ct rec from 1930)

Towns Organized Before 1800: Bethel 1796, Buckfield 1793, Buxton 1772, Fryeburg 1777, Hartford 1798, Hebron 1792, Norway 1797, Paris 1793, Sumner 1798, Waterford 1797

* Penobscot   D4   1816   Hancock
Penobscot County, 97 Hammond St, Bangor, ME 04401-4922 .... (207)942-8535
(Clk Cts has div rec from 1900 & civ ct rec from 1821)

Towns Organized Before 1800: Hampden 1794, Orrington 1788

* Piscataquis   D3   1838   Penobscot, Somerset
Piscataquis County, 51 E Main St, Dover-Foxcroft, ME 04426-1306 .... (207)564-2161
(Twn Clks have b, m & d rec; Sup Ct has div & civ ct rec; Pro Ct has pro rec; Reg of Deeds has lnd rec)

* Sagadahoc   G3   1854   Lincoln
Sagadahoc County, PO Box 246, Bath, ME 04530-0246 .... (207)443-8200
(Twn Clks have b, m & d rec; Dist Ct has div rec; Sup Ct has civ ct rec; Reg of Probates has pro rec from 1854; Reg of Deeds has lnd rec from 1854)

Towns Organized Before 1800: Bath 1781, Bowdoin 1788, Bowdoinham 1762, Georgetown 1716, Topsham 1764, Woolwich 1759

* Somerset   E2   1809   Kennebec
Somerset County, County Courthouse, Skowhegan, ME 04976 .... (207)474-9861
(Clk Cts has some m rec from 1800s, pro rec from 1809)

Towns Organized Before 1800: Canaan 1788, Cornville 1798, Fairfield 1788, Norridgewock 1788, Starks 1795

Name	Map Index	Date Created	Parent County or Territory From Which Organized
* Waldo	G4	1827	Hancock, Lincoln, Kennebec

Waldo County, 73 Church St, Belfast, ME 04915-1705 .... (207)338-3282
(Co Clk has m rec from 1828 to 1887 not indexed, also has div & Sup Ct rec from 1828; Twn or City Clks have b, m, d & bur rec; Pro Ct has pro rec)

Towns Organized Before 1800: Belfast 1773, Frankfort 1789, Northport 1796, Prospect 1794

| * Washington | E6 | 1789 | Lincoln |

Washington County, PO Box 297, Machias, ME 04654-0297 .... (207)255-3127
(Twn Clks have b, m, d, bur rec; Clk Cts has div, civ ct rec from 1931, pro rec from 1785, Ind rec from 1783, naturalizations from 1854; div, civ ct rec prior to 1931 are in the custody of Maine State Archives, Augusta, Maine)

Towns Organized Before 1800: Addison 1797, Columbia 1796, Eastport 1798, Harrington 1797, Machias 1784, Steuben 1795

| * York(shire) | H1 | 1652 | Original county reorg. 1658 |

York(shire) County, Court St, Alfred, ME 04002 .... (207)324-1571
(Twn Clks have b, m, d & bur rec; Clk Cts has div & civ ct rec; Reg of Probates has d & pro rec from 1637; Reg of Deeds has Ind rec from 1636)

Towns Organized Before 1800: Berwick 1713, Biddeford 1718, Cornish 1794, Hollis 1798, Kennebunkport 1653, Kittery 1652, Lebanon 1767, Limington 1792, Lyman 1778, Newfield 1794, Parsonfield 1785, Saco 1762, Sanford 1768, Shapleigh 1785, Waterboro 1787, Wells 1653, York 1652

* At least one county history has been published about this county.
† Inventory of county archives was made by the Historical Records Survey. (See Introduction)

MARYLAND

CAPITAL · ANNAPOLIS — STATE 1788 (7th)
State Map on Page M-19

In 1524, Giovanni de Verrazano, an Italian navigator who sailed for the French government, became the first European to set foot on Maryland soil. In 1608, Captain John Smith explored the area and made maps of it. The first settlement took place on Kent Island, where William Claiborne set up a trading post. Several years later, in 1632, George Calvert, Lord Baltimore, secured from Charles I the land on both sides of Chesapeake Bay north of Virginia to the 40th parallel. Lord Baltimore, however, died before the charter could be signed. His son, Cecilius Calvert, the second Lord Baltimore, received the grant in his place and began efforts to colonize the area as a haven for persecuted Catholics and those of other religions. The first emigrants left in 1634 and were comprised of twenty Catholics and about 200 Protestants. They purchased land from the Indians and settled St. Mary's. The colony experienced great growth, partly due to the passage of the Act Concerning Religion, which outlawed any intolerance of any person professing a belief in Christ. Among the groups attracted by this religious freedom were a large group of Puritans, who settled Anne Arundel County. Meanwhile, conflicts between Claiborne's group and those controlled by Lord Baltimore led to almost continuous warfare. Not until Claiborne's death in 1677 did hostilities cease.

Settlements during the first century of Maryland's colonization were confined to areas by rivers, streams, and bays, as water provided practically the only efficient means of transportation. Baltimore was founded in 1729 and soon became a major port and commercial center. The Appalachian section of Maryland was not settled until about 1740, when English, Scottish, and Scotch-Irish migrated from St. Mary's, Charles, and Prince George's Counties. Not long afterward, Germans from Pennsylvania also came into the area. The influx of settlers was so great, that by 1748 Frederick County was organized in the northwest section of Maryland. Many Acadians driven from Nova Scotia came to Baltimore in 1755. Race riots in Santo Domingo brought about a thousand more French to Baltimore in 1793. Canal diggers from Ireland swelled Baltimore's population between 1817 and 1847. They became farmers and miners in the Appalachians. Baltimore also provided refuge to thousands of Germans who fled their country after the Revolution of 1848.

Maryland adopted a Declaration of Rights in 1776 as well as a state constitution. In 1788, Maryland ratified the Constitution and became the seventh state in the Union. The British ravaged Chesapeake Bay during the War of 1812, but were unable to take Baltimore. Their failed attempt to capture Fort McHenry was the inspiration for Francis Scott Key to write "The Star Spangled Banner". The National Road was completed from Cumberland to Wheeling in 1818. During the Civil War, soldiers from Maryland fought for both sides. Over 46,000 men fought for the Union, while more than 5,000 fought for the Confederacy.

Civil registration of births and deaths began in 1898, except for Baltimore City, where records began in 1875. These are available at the Division of Vital Records, 201 West Preston, P.O. Box 13146, Baltimore, MD 21203. Only the individual himself, a parent, or an authorized representative has access to these records if the event occured within the last 100 years. The Maryland State Archives, Hall of Records, 350 Rowe Boulevard, Annapolis, MD 21401, also has many birth and death records. A few counties also have pre-1720 births and deaths in county land records. To verify current fees, call 301-225-5988.

Marriage banns and registers have been kept by the clergy since 1640. County clerks have been required to issue marriage licenses since 1777, and to issue ministers' returns since 1865. These records are kept by the circuit court clerk of each county and in the State Archives. The earliest land records, 1633-1683, were headrights distributed by the Calvert family. The names of the persons receiving these have been published. Land bounties for military service in the Revolutionary War and original land records since 1643 are in the Maryland State Archives. Wills were kept by the county registrar of wills from as early as 1634. These are also at the State Archives. A colonial census was taken in 1776 for most counties. A list of males over 18 who did and did not take oaths of fidelity in 1778 has been published. No state censuses were taken for Maryland, but there is an 1868 police census for some city wards of Baltimore.

Genealogical Archives, Libraries and Societies

Dorchester County Public Library, 305 Gay St., Cambridge, MD 21613

Enoch Pratt Free Library, 400 Cathedral St., Baltimore, MD 21201

George Peabody Library of the Johns Hopkins University, 17 E. Mt. Vernon Place, Baltimore, MD 21202

Hall of Records Commission, College Ave. & St. John Sts., Annapolis, MD 21401

Maryland State Library, Court of Appeals Bldg., 361 Rowe Blvd. Annapolis, MD 21401

Washington, D.C. Temple Branch Genealogical Library, P. O. Box 49, 1000 Stoneybrook Drive, Kensington, MD 20895

Worcester Room, c / o The Worcester County Library, 307 North Washington Street, Snow Hill, MD 21863

Allegany County Historical Society, 218 Washington St., Cumberland, MD 21502

Anne Arundel Genealogical Society, P. O. Box 221, Pasadena, MD 21122

Baltimore County Historical Society, Agriculture Bldg., 9811 Van Buren Lane, Cockeysville, MD 21030

Calvert County Genealogical Committee, Calvert County Historical Society, P.O. Box 358, Prince Frederick, MD 20678

Calvert County Genealogy Society, P. O. Box 9, Sunderland, MD 20689

Calvert County Historical Society, P. O. Box 358, Prince Frederick, MD 20678

Caroline County Historical Society, Preston, MD 21655

Carroll County Genealogical Society, 50 East Main Street, Westminster, MD 21157

Catonsville Historical Society and Genealogical Section, P. O. Box 9311, Catonsville, MD 21228

Charles County Historical Society, Route 3, Box 65, LaPlata, MD 20646

Dorchester County Historical Society, Meredith House, 904 LaGrange St., Cambridge, MD 21613

Dundalk Patapsco Neck Historical Society, P. O. Box 9235, Dundalk, MD 21222

Emmitsburg Historical Society, Emmitsburg, MD 21727

Frederick County Genealogical Society, P. O. Box 234, Frederick, MD 21770

Garrett County Historical Society, County Courthouse, Oakland, MD 21550

Genealogical Club of the Montgomery County Historical Society, 103 W. Montgomery Ave., Rockville, MD 20850

Genealogical Society of Allegany County, P. O. Box 3103, LaVale, MD 21502

Genealogical Society of Cecil County, Box 11, Charlestown, MD 21914

Harford County Historical Society, 324 Kenmore Ave., (The Hayes House), Bel Air, MD 21014

Heritage Genealogical Society, P. O. Box 113, Lineboro, MD 21088-0113

Historical Society of Carroll County, 210 East Main Street, Westminster, MD 21157

Historical Society of Cecil County, 135 East Main St., Elkton, MD 21921

Historical Society of Frederick Co., Inc., 24 E. Church St., Frederick, MD 21701

Howard County Genealogical Society, Box 274, Columbia, MD 21045

Jewish Historical Society of Maryland, 15 Lloyd St., Baltimore, MD 21202

Kent County Historical Society, Church Alley, Chestertown, MD 21620

Lower Del-Mar-Va Genealogical Society, P. O. Box 3602, Salisbury, MD 21801

Maryland Genealogical Society, 201 W. Monument St., Baltimore, MD 21201

Maryland Historical Society, 201 W. Monument St., Baltimore, MD 21201

Maryland Society, Sons of the American Revolution, 7977 Timmons Road, Union Bridge, MD 21791

Mid-Atlantic Germanic Society, 12111 Mt. Albert Road, Ellicott City, MD 21043

Middletown Valley Historical Society, Rt. 3, Box 187, Middletown, MD 21769

Montgomery County Historical Society, 103 W. Montgomery Ave., (Beall-Dawson House), Rockville, MD 20850

National Archives-New England Region, 380 Trapelo Rd., Waltham, MA 02154

National Archives Microfilm Rental Program, Box 30, Annapolis Junction, MD 20701

National Capital Buckeye Chapter of the Ohio Genealogical Society, P. O. Box 105, Bladensburg, MD 20710-0105

Old Bohemia Historical Society, Warwick, MD 21912

Prince George's County Genealogical Society, Box 819, Bowie, MD 20718-0819

Prince George's County Historical Society, Montpelier Mansion, Laurel, MD 20810

Queene Anne's County Historical Society, Wright's Chance, Commerce Street, Centreville, MD 21617

Society for the History of Germans in Maryland, P. O. Box 22585, Baltimore, MD 22585

Saint Mary's County Genealogical Society, General Delivery, Callaway, MD 20620

St. Mary's County Historical Society, Leonardtown, MD 20650

Somerset County Historical Society, Treackle Mansion, Princess Anne, MD 21853

Talbot County Historical Society, 29 S. Washington St., Easton, MD 21601

Unitarian and Universalist Genealogical Society, 10605 Lakespring Way, Cockeysville, MD 21030

United Methodist Historical Society, Inc., Lovely Lane United Methodist Church, 2200 St. Paul St., Baltimore, MD 21218

Upper Shore Genealogical Society of Maryland, Box 275, Easton, MD 21601

Washington County Historical Society, The Miller House, 135 W. Washington St., Hagerstown, MD 21740

Printed Census Records and Mortality Schedules

Federal Census 1790, 1800, 1810, 1820, 1830 (except Montgomery, Prince George's, St. Mary's, Queen Annes, and Somerset counties), 1840, 1850, 1860, 1870, 1880, 1900, 1910
Union Veterans and Widows 1890
Freemen 1637, 1641, 1642
Residents 1638, 1683, 1710, 1748, 1758
Rate List 1642
Tobacco Assessment 1681, 1682, 1684, 1686, 1688
List of Rebels 1747
State/Territorial Census 1776, 1783, 1798
Oaths of Fidelity 1777-1778

Valuable Printed Sources

Atlases, Maps, and Gazetteers

Gannett, Henry. *A Gazetteer of Maryland and Delaware*. Baltimore: Genealogical Publishing Co., 1976.

Gazetteer of Maryland. Baltimore: Maryland State Planning Commission, 1941.

Bibliographies

Hartsook, Elisabeth and Gust Skordas. *Land Office and Prerogative Court Records of Colonial Maryland*. Baltimore: Genealogical Publishing Co., 1968.

Hofstetter, Eleanor O. and Marcella S. Eustis. *Newspapers in Maryland Libraries: A Union List*. Baltimore: Maryland State Department of Education, 1977.

Passano, Eleanor Phillips. *An Index of the Source Records of Maryland: Genealogical, Biographical, Historical*. Baltimore: Genealogical Publishing Co., 1967.

Pedley, Avril J. M. *The Manuscript Collections of the Maryland Historical Society*. Baltimore: Maryland Historical Society, 1968.

Pritchett, Morgan H. and Susan R. Woodcock. *The Eastern Shore of Maryland: An Annotated Bibliography*. Queenstown, Maryland.

Sullivan, Larry E., et al. *Guide to the Research Collections of the Maryland Historical Society*. Baltimore: Maryland Historical Society, 1981.

Genealogical Research Guides

Heisey, John W. *Maryland Research Guide*. Indianapolis: Heritage House, 1986.

Meyer, Mary K. *Genealogical Research in Maryland: A Guide*. Baltimore: Maryland Historical Society, 1983.

Genealogical Sources

A Name Index to the Baltimore City Tax Records, 1798-1808, of the Baltimore City Archives. Baltimore: Baltimore City Archives, 1981.

Barnes, Robert. *Maryland Marriages, 1634-1777*. Baltimore: Genealogical Publishing Co., 1975.

Brumbaugh, Gaius Marcus and Margaret Roberts Hodges. *Revolutionary Records of Maryland*. Baltimore: Genealogical Publishing Co., 1967.

Cotton, Jane Baldwin. *Maryland Calendar of Wills*. Baltimore: Genealogical Publishing Co., 1968.

Magruder, James M. *Index of Maryland Colonial Wills*. Baltimore: Genealogical Publishing Co., 1967.

————. *Magruder's Maryland Colonial Abstracts: Wills, Accounts, and Inventories, 1772-1777*. Baltimore: Genealogical Publishing Co., 1972.

Muster Rolls and Other Records of Service of Maryland Troops in the American Revolution. Baltimore: Genealogical Publishing Co., 1972.

Histories

Scarf, J. Thomas. *History of Maryland from the Earliest Period to the Present Day*. Hatboro, Pennsylvania: Tradition Press, 1967 reprint.

MARYLAND COUNTY DATA
State Map on Page M-19

Name	Map Index	Date Created	Parent County or Territory From Which Organized
*† **Allegany**	G2	1789	Washington

Allegany County, 3 Pershing St, Cumberland, MD 21502-3043 . . . . (301)777-5911
(Clk Cir Ct has m, div, civ ct, Ind rec from 1791, naturalization rec from 1821 to 1973; Reg of Wills has pro rec)

| *† **Anne Arundel** | D4 | 1650 | Original county |

Anne Arundel County, 44 Calvert St, Annapolis, MD 21401-1986 . . . . (301)222-1821
(Clk Cir Ct has m rec from 1905, div & civ ct rec from 1870, Ind rec from 1851; Reg of Wills has pro rec; Hall of Rec has m rec from 1770 to 1904, also earlier rec of civ ct & Ind rec)

| * **Baltimore** | D3 | 1659 | Original county |

Baltimore County, 400 Washington Ave, Towson, MD 21204-4606 . . . . (301)887-3196
(Clk Cir Ct has m, div, civ ct & Ind rec from 1851; Reg of Wills has pro rec)

| **Baltimore City** | C3 | 1729 | Baltimore |

Baltimore City, 100 N Holliday St, Baltimore, MD 21202-3417 . . . . (301)396-3100
(City Health has b, d & bur rec; Com Pleas Ct has m rec; Clk Cir Ct has div rec, trust estates, adoptions & change of name from 1853; Reg of Wills has pro rec)

| * **Calvert** | D5 | 1654 | Original county (formerly Patuxent) |

Calvert County, 175 Main St, Prince Frederick, MD 20678-9302 . . . . (301)535-1600
(Clk Cir Ct has m, div, civ ct & Ind rec from 1882; Reg of Wills has pro rec from 1882; Courthouse burned 1882, most rec destroyed; earlier rec available State Hall of Rec)

| * **Caroline** | B4 | 1773 | Dorchester, Queen Annes |

Caroline County, PO Box 207, Denton, MD 21629-0207 . . . . (301)479-0660
(Clk Cir Ct has m, div, civ ct & Ind rec from 1774; Reg of Wills has d & pro rec)

| *† **Carroll** | E2 | 1837 | Baltimore, Frederick |

Carroll County, 225 N Center St, Westminster, MD 21157-5194 . . . . (301)876-2085
(Clk Cir Ct has m rec 1837-1900 not indexed, from 1900 indexed, div, civ ct, Ind rec from 1837)

| * **Cecil** | C2 | 1674 | Kent |

Cecil County, E Main St, Elkton, MD 21921 . . . . (301)398-0200
(Clk Cir Ct has m rec from 1777, div & civ rec, Ind rec from 1674; Reg of Wills, Courthouse has pro rec; Clk Ct has indices from 1674)

| * **Charles** | D5 | 1658 | Original county |

Charles County, PO Box B, La Plata, MD 20646-0167 . . . . (301)645-0550
(Clk Cir Ct has m rec from 1865, div & civ ct rec from 1796, Ind rec from 1658 at Hall of Rec, Annapolis, MD; Reg of Wills has pro rec)

| * **Dorchester** | B5 | 1668 | Original county |

Dorchester County, PO Box 26, Cambridge, MD 21613-0026 . . . . (301)228-1700
(Clk Cir Ct has m rec from 1780, div rec from 1821, civ ct rec from 1860, Ind rec from 1669, plat rec from 1912, equity dock rec from 1821 & corporation rec from 1858)

| * **Frederick** | E3 | 1748 | Prince Georges |

Frederick County, 12 E Church St, Frederick, MD 21701-5402 . . . . (301)694-1100
(Clk Cir Ct has b, d rec 1865-1870, m rec from 1778, div rec from 1807, civ ct, Ind rec from 1847; Reg of Wills has pro rec)

| *† **Garrett** | I2 | 1872 | Allegany |

Garrett County, 203 S 4th St, Oakland, MD 21550-1535 . . . . (301)334-8970
(Clk Cir Ct has m, div, civ ct, Ind rec from 1872; Reg of Wills has pro rec)

| * **Harford** | C2 | 1773 | Baltimore |

Harford County, 220 S Main St, Bel Air, MD 21014-3833 . . . . (301)838-6000
(Co Health has b & d rec; Clk Ct has m & Ind rec from 1773, div & civ ct rec from 1803)

Name	Map Index	Date Created	Parent County or Territory From Which Organized
*† **Howard**	D3	1851	Baltimore, Anne Arundel

Howard County, 3430 Courthouse Dr, Ellicott City, MD 21043-4300 .... (301)992-2025
(Clk Cir Ct has m, div, civ ct & lnd rec; Reg of Wills has pro rec)

| * **Kent** | C3 | 1642 | Original county |

Kent County, 230 N Cross St, Chestertown, MD 21620-1512 .... (301)778-4600
(Clk Cir Ct has m rec from 1796, div rec from 1867, civ ct rec from early 1800s & lnd rec from 1656)

| *† **Montgomery** | E3 | 1776 | Frederick |

Montgomery County, 100 Maryland Ave Courthouse 2nd Fl, Rockville, MD 20850 .... (301)217-1000
(Clk Cir Ct has m rec from 1799, div, civ ct & lnd rec from 1776) (1830 census missing)

| * **Prince Georges** | D4 | 1695 | Charles, Calvert |

Prince George's County, 7911 Anchor St, Landover, MD 20785-4804 .... (301)350-9700
(many rec with Clk Cir Ct before 1785 - deeds complete - no fires) (1830 census missing)

| * **Queen Annes** | C4 | 1706 | Talbot |

Queen Annes County, 208 N Commerce St, Centreville, MD 21617-1015 .... (301)758-0322
(1830 census missing)(Clk Cts has m, div, civ ct & lnd rec; Orphan's Ct has pro rec)

| * **Saint Marys** | D6 | 1637 | Original county |

Saint Marys County, PO Box 653, Leonardtown, MD 20650-0653 .... (301)475-5621
(1830 census missing)

| * **Somerset** | B6 | 1666 | Original county |

Somerset County, 21 Prince William St, Princess Anne, MD 21853 .... (301)651-0320
(1830 census missing)(Clk Cir Ct has m, div, civ ct & lnd rec from 1666; Reg of Wills has pro rec)

| * **Talbot** | C5 | 1662 | Kent |

Talbot County, Washington St, Easton, MD 21601 .... (301)822-2401
(Clk Cir Ct has m rec from 1794, div rec from 1908, civ ct rec from 1818 & lnd rec from 1662; Reg of Wills has pro rec)

| *† **Washington** | F2 | 1776 | Frederick |

Washington County, 95 W Washington St, Hagerstown, MD 21740-4831 .... (301)791-3000
(Clk Cir Ct has m rec from 1799, div, pro, civ ct & lnd rec; other rec may be found at Washington Co Free Library, Hagerstown, MD)

| *† **Wicomico** | B6 | 1867 | Somerset, Worcester |

Wicomico County, PO Box 198, Salisbury, MD 21803-0198 .... (301)543-6551
(Clk Cir Ct has m, div, civ ct & lnd rec from 1867, crim rec, equity ct rec, naturalization & juvenile ct rec)

| * **Worcester** | A6 | 1742 | Somerset |

Worcester County, 1 W Market St, Snow Hill, MD 21863-1073 .... (301)632-1194
(Clk Cir Ct has m rec from 1866, div rec from 1900, civ ct rec from 1916; Reg of Wills has pro rec)

* At least one county history has been published about this county.
† Inventory of county archives was made by the Historical Records Survey. (See Introduction)

MASSACHUSETTS

CAPITAL - BOSTON — STATE 1788 (6th)
State Map on Page M-7

The first settlement in Massachusetts was at Plymouth in 1620. It was there that the Pilgrims from the Mayflower settled. The Puritans followed within a decade, setting up the towns of Salem in 1628 under John Endecott and Boston in 1630 under John Winthrop. The Massachusetts Bay Colony, founded in 1630, provided for a large amount of self-government. Within the next decade, more than 20,000 immigrants, almost entirely British, came to Massachusetts. Religious intolerance in Massachusetts led many to settle elsewhere, such as Rhode Island, Connecticut, New Hampshire, and Maine. In 1691, Plymouth Colony was joined to the Massachusetts Bay Colony, along with parts of Maine and Nova Scotia.

Massachusetts played a prominent role in the Revolutionary War from the Boston Tea Party to Lexington and Concord and the Battle of Bunker Hill. A state constitution was adopted in 1780 and Massachusetts became the sixth state to ratify the Constitution, with the proviso that the Bill of Rights be added.

In 1786, the Ohio Land Company was formed which led many Massachusetts residents to migrate to Ohio. New immigrants, primarily from England, continued to come to Massachusetts for at least two centuries. Maine was finally separated from Massachusetts in 1819 and became a state in 1820. In the 1830's, factories began to be built and the demand for workers stimulated renewed immigration. Around mid-century, emigrants from Ireland, Germany, and France came to escape disasters and political turmoil in their countries. A few years later, Italians, Russians, Poles, and Portuguese came to work in the factories, mills, and fisheries. During the Civil War, Massachusetts furnished 146,000 men to the Union forces.

Vital statistics have been kept throughout Massachusetts since the earliest days. These records have also been published by each town to assist the researcher. Statewide registration began in 1841. These records are available at the Massachusetts State Archives, Columbia Point, 220 Morrissey Boulevard, Boston, MA 02125. A search of town records can yield additional information not found on state records. Vital records after 1890 are available from the Registrar of Vital Statistics, 150 Tremont Street Room B-3, Boston, MA 02108. To verify current fees, call 617-727-0110.

To obtain copies, it is necessary to state your relationship to the person and the reason for wanting the record. Divorce records from 1738 to 1888 are filed in the county court, the governor's council records, the superior court, or the supreme judicial court. After 1888, divorce proceedings were usually filed at the county probate court and superior court. Records of wills, deeds, and land transactions are in the county offices. Tax records, some of which have been published, were kept by city or county assessors. All war service records after the Revolutionary War are at the office of the Adjutant General, 100 Cambridge Street, Boston, MA 02202. Naturalization records were filed in the various county and district courts. These were copied and indexed in the 1930's by the WPA for the years 1791 to 1906. The copies and index are at the National Archives, Boston Branch, 380 Trapelo Road, Waltham, MA 02154. For records after 1906, contact the National Archives, Boston Branch or Immigration and Naturalization Service, U. S. Department of Justice, JFK Federal Building, Government Center, Boston, MA 02203. State censuses were taken in 1855 and 1865. The originals are at the Massachusetts State Archives.

Genealogical Archives, Libraries and Societies

(Every town library in Massachusetts has books of vital statistics from adjoining communities and numerous biographies and histories about early residents).

American Antiquarian Society Library, 185 Salisbury St., Worcester, MA 01609

Attleboro Public Library, 74 N. Main Street, Attleboro, MA 02703

Berkshire Athenaeum, 1 Wendell Avenue, Pittsfield, MA 01201

Boston Public Library, P. O. Box 286, Boston, MA 02117

Brockton Public Library, 304 Main St., Brockton, MA 02401

Clarke Wright Fuller Memorial Library, P. O. Box 2571, Holyoke, MA 01041

Eastham Public Library, Box 338, Samoset Rd., Eastham, MA 02642

Essex Institute, 132 Essex St., Salem, MA 01970

Forbes Library, 20 West St., Northampton, MA 01060

Greenfield Public Library, 402 Main St., Greenfield, MA 01301

Haverhill Public Library, 99 Main St., Haverhill, MA 01830

Jones Library, 43 Amity St., Amherst, MA 01002

Lynn Public Library, 5 N. Common St., Lynn, MA 01902

Lynnfield Public Library, 18 Summer Street, Lynnfield, MA 01940 (Good genealogical reference room).

Massachusetts State Library, Beacon Hill, Boston, MA 02155

New Bedford Massachusetts City Library, Pleasant St., New Bedford, MA 02740

Springfield City Library, 220 State Street, Springfield, MA 01103

Sturgis Library, Main St., Barnstable, MA 02630

Swansea Free Public Library, 69 Main St., Swansea, MA 02777

Yarmouth Library, 297 Main St., Yarmouth Port, MA 02675

American Jewish Historical Society, 2 Thornton Rd., Waltham, MA 02154

American-Portuguese Genealogical Society, P. O. Box 644, Taunton, MA 02780

Berkshire Family History Association, P. O. Box 1437, Pittsfield, MA 01201

Bristol County Chapter, Massachusetts Society of Genealogists, 459 Madison St., Fall River, MA 02720

Congregational Christian Historical Society, 14 Beacon St., Boston, MA 02108

Danvers Historical Society, Danvers, MA 01923

Dedham Historical Society, 612 High St., Dedham, MA 02026

Essex Institute, 132 Essex St., Salem, MA 01970

General Society of Mayflower Descendants, Box 3297, Plymouth, MA 02361

Hampden Chapter, Massachusetts Society of Genealogists, Inc., 25 Edison Drive, Ludlow, MA 01056

Harwich Historical Society, P. O. Box 17, Harwich, MA 02645

Irish Ancestral Research Assn., Box 619, Sudbury, MA 01776

Jewish Genealogical Society of Boston, 1501 Beacon St. #501, Brookline, MA 02146

Massachusetts Historical Society, 1154 Boylston St., Boston, MA 02215

Massachusetts Society of Mayflower Descendants, 101 Newbury St., Boston, MA 02116

Massachusetts Society, Sons of the American Revolution, 21 Milton Road, Brookline, MA 02146

Medford Historical Society, 10 Governors Ave., Medford, MA 02155

Middleborough Historical Association, Inc., Jackson St., Middleboro, MA 02346

Middlesex Chapter, Massachusetts Society of Genealogists, 244 Flanders Road, Westboro, MA 01581

National Headquarters, General Society of Mayflower Descendants, 4 Willow St., Plymouth, MA 02361

New England Historic Genealogical Society, 101 Newbury St., Boston, MA 02116

Old Colony Historical Society, 66 Church Green, Taunton, MA 02780

Peabody Historical Society, 35 Washington St., Peabody, MA 01960

Plymouth Colony Genealogists, 60 Sheridan St., Brockton, MA 02402

Western Massachusetts Genealogical Society, P. O. Box 206, Forest Park Station, Springfield, MA 01108

Winchester Historical Society, 1 Copley Street, Winchester, MA 01890

Printed Census Records and Mortality Schedules

Federal Census 1790, 1800, 1810, 1820, 1830, 1840, 1850, 1860, 1870, 1880, 1900, 1910
Federal Mortality Schedules 1850, 1860, 1870, 1880
Union Veterans and Widows 1890
Freemen 1630-1691
Militia List 1675
Soldiers in the French and Indian War 1754-1763
State/Territorial Census 1779, 1855, 1865
U.S. Direct Tax List 1798

Valuable Printed Sources

Atlases, Maps, and Gazetteers

Denis, Michael J. *Massachusetts Towns and Counties: What was What, Where and When*. Oakland, Maine: Danbury House, 1984.

Gannett, Henry. *A Geographic Dictionary of Massachusetts*. Baltimore: Genealogical Publishing Co., 1978.

Guzzi, Paul. *Historical Data Relating to Counties, Cities, and Towns in Massachusetts*. Boston: Commonwealth of Massachusetts, 1975.

Massachusetts Gazetteer. Wilmington, Delaware: American Historical Publications, 1985.

Nason, Elias. *A Gazetteer of the State of Massachusetts*. Boston: B. B. Russell, 1874.

Bibliographies

Haskell, John D. Jr. *Massachusetts: A Bibliography of Its History*. Boston: G. K. Hall & Co., 1976.

Holbrook, Jay Mack. *Bibliography of Massachusetts Vital Records: An Inventory of the Original Birth, Marriage, and Death Volumes*. Oxford, Massachusetts: Holbrook Research Institute, 1986.

Genealogical Research Guides

Genealogist's Handbook for New England Research. Lynnfield, Massachusetts: New England Library Association, 1980.

Wright, Norman E. *Genealogy in America, Volume 1: Massachusetts, Connecticut, and Maine*. Salt Lake City: Deseret Book, 1968.

Genealogical Sources

Bailey, Frederic W. *Early Massachusetts Marriages*. Baltimore: Genealogical Publishing Co., 1968 reprint.

Jones, E. Alfred. *The Loyalists of Massachusetts and Their Memorials, Petitions, and Claims*. Baltimore: Genealogical Publishing Co., 1969 reprint. *Lists of Persons Whose Names Have Been Changed in Massachusetts, 1780-1892*. Boston: Wright & Potter Printing Co., 1893.

Massachusetts Soldiers and Sailors of the Revolutionary War. Boston: Wright & Potter Printing Co., 1908.

Histories

Hutchinson, Thomas. *The History of the Colony and Province of Massachusetts Bay*. Cambridge, Massachusetts: Harvard University Press, 1936.

Kaufman, Martin, et al. *A Guide to the History of Massachusetts*. New York: Greenwood Press, 1988.

MASSACHUSETTS COUNTY DATA
State Map on Page M-7

Name	Map Index	Date Created	Parent County or Territory From Which Organized
* **Barnstable**	F7	1685	New Plymouth Colony

Barnstable County, Rt 6-A, Barnstable, MA 02630 .... (508)362-2511
(Clk Cir Ct has div & civ ct rec from 1828)

Towns Organized Before 1800: Barnstable 1638, Chatham 1712, Dennis 1793, Eastham 1646, Falmouth 1694, Harwich 1694, Mashpee 1763, Orleans 1797, Provincetown 1727, Truro 1709, Wellfleet 1763, Yarmouth 1639

Name	Map Index	Date Created	Parent County or Territory From Which Organized

* **Berkshire**   E2   1760   Hampshire
Berkshire County, 76 East St, Pittsfield, MA 01201-5304 . . . . (413)448-8424
(Clk Cts has div rec from 1761 to 1922, civ ct rec from 1761; Pro Judge has div rec from 1922 & pro rec from 1761)

Towns Organized Before 1800: Adams 1778, Alford 1773, Becket 1765, Cheshire 1793, Clarksburg 1798, Dalton 1784, Egremont 1760, Great Barrington 1761, Hancock 1776, Lanesborough 1765, Lee 1777, Lenox 1767, Mount Washington 1779, New Ashford 1781, New Marlborough 1759, Otis 1773, Peru 1771, Pittsfield 1761, Richmond 1765, Standisfield 1762, Savoy 1797, Sheffield 1733, Stockbridge 1739, Tyringham 1762, Washington 1777, West Stockbridge 1774, Williamstown 1765

* **Bristol**   F6   1685   New Plymouth Colony
Bristol County, 9 Court St, Taunton, MA 02780-3223 . . . . (508)823-6588
(Clk Cts has civ ct rec from 1796, also naturalization rec; bur rec are at cem; b, m, d rec are at city offices; Pro Ct has div rec from 1921, also pro rec)

Towns Organized Before 1800: Attleboro 1694, Berkley 1735, Dartmouth 1652, Dighton 1712, Easton 1725, Freetown 1683, Mansfield 1770, New Bedford 1787, Norton 1710, Raynham 1731, Rehoboth 1645, Sandwich 1638, Somerset 1790, Swansea 1667, Taunton 1639, Westport 1787

* **Dukes**   G7   1695   (Martha's Vineyard)
Dukes County, PO Box 190, Edgartown, MA 02539 . . . . (508)627-5535
(Clk Cts has div rec & sup ct rec from 1859; Pro Ct has pro rec; Twn Clks have b, m, d & bur rec)

Towns Organized Before 1800: Chilmark 1694, Edgartown 1671, Tisbury 1671

*† **Essex**   D6   1643   Original county
Essex County, 36 Federal St, Salem, MA 01970-3437 . . . . (508)741-0200
[FHL has some b, m, d, civ ct, pro, lnd rec]

Towns Organized Before 1800: Amesbury 1668, Andover 1646, Beverly 1668, Boxford 1694, Danvers 1752, Hamilton 1793, Haverhill 1641, Ipswich 1634, Lynn 1635, Lynnfield 1782, Manchester 1645, Marblehead 1633, Methuen 1725, Middleton 1728, Newbury 1635, Newburyport 1764, Rowley 1639, Salem 1630, Salisbury 1639, Topsfield 1648, Wenham 1643

* **Franklin**   D3   1811   Hampshire
Franklin County, 425 Main St, Greenfield, MA 01301-3313 . . . . (413)774-4015
(Clk Cts has div rec from 1811 in concurrent jurisdiction with pro ct; Clk Cts has civ ct rec from 1811 in concurrent jurisdiction with Dis Ct & Sup Judicial Ct; Reg Pro has pro rec; Reg Deeds has lnd rec)

Towns Organized Before 1800: Ashfield 1765, Bernardston 1762, Buckland 1779, Charlemont 1765, Colrain 1761, Conway 1767, Deerfield 1677, Gil 1793, Greenfield 1753, Hawley 1792, Heath 1785, Leverett 1774, Leyden 1784, Montague 1754, New Salem 1753, Northfield 1714, Orange 1783, Rowe 1785, Shelburne 1768, Shutesbury 1761, Sunderland 1714, Warwick 1763, Wendell 1781, Whately 1771, Williamsburg 1771

* **Hampden**   E3   1812   Hampshire
Hampden County, 50 State St, Springfield, MA 01103-2002 . . . . (413)781-8100
(Clk Cts has most div rec from 1812 to 1932 & civ ct rec)

Towns Organized Before 1800: Blandford 1741, Brimfield 1714, Chester 1765, Granville 1754, Holland 1783, Longmeadow 1783, Monson 1760, Montgomery 1780, Palmer 1752, Southwick 1770, Springfield 1641, Wales 1762, West Springfield 1774, Westfield 1669, Wilbraham 1763

* **Hampshire**   E3   1662   Middlesex
Hampshire County, 99 Main St, Northampton, MA 01060-3119 . . . . (413)584-0557
(City Clks have b, m & d rec; Sup Ct or Pro Ct has div rec; Pro Ct has pro rec; Sup Ct has civ ct rec; Co Planner has lnd rec from 1632)

Towns Organized Before 1800: Amherst 1759, Belchertown 1761, Chesterfield 1762, Cummington 1779, Easthampton 1785, Goshen 1781, Granby 1768, Hadley 1661, Middlefield 1783, Northampton 1656, Pelham 1743, Plainfield 1785, Russell 1792, South Hadley 1753, Southampton 1753, Ware 1761, Westhampton 1778, Worthington 1768

* **Middlesex**   D5   1643   Original county
Middlesex County, 40 Thorndike St, East Cambridge, MA 02141-1755 . . . . (617)494-4003
(Clk Cts has b rec 1632-1745, m rec 1651-1793, d rec 1651-1689, div rec from 1888, civ ct rec from 1648; Rcdr Deeds, PO Box 68, E Cambridge, Mass. 02141 has lnd rec for Southern Dis; Reg Deeds, 360 Gorham St, Lowell, Mass. 01852 has lnd rec for Northern Dis; Lnd rec 1 July 1855 for nothern part of Co are at Lowell, Mass., lnd rec from 1639 to 1 July 1855 for all of Co and then up to the present are at E. Cambridge)

Towns Organized Before 1800: Acton 1735, Ashby 1767, Bedford 1729, Billerica 1655, Boxborough 1783, Burlington 1799, Cambridge 1631, Carlisle 1780, Chelmsford 1655, Concord 1635, Dracut 1702, Dunstable 1673, Framingham 1675, Groton 1655, Holliston 1724, Hopkinton 1715, Lexington 1713, Lincoln 1754, Littleton 1715, Malden 1649, Marlborough 1660, Medford 1630, Natick 1650, Newton 1691, Pepperell 1753, Reading 1644, Sherborn 1674, Shirley 1753, Stoneham 1725, Stow 1683, Sudbury 1639, Tewksbury 1734, Townsend 1732, Tyngsboro 1789, Waltham 1738, Watertown 1630, Wayland 1780, Westford 1729, Weston 1713, Wilmington 1730, Woburn 1642

* **Nantucket**   G7   1695   Original county
Nantucket County, Town & County Bldg, Nantucket, MA 02554 . . . . (508)228-7229
(Reg Pro has div rec 1922 to 1979, pro rec; Twn Clks have b, m, d, bur rec; Clks Cts has civ ct rec from 1721; Reg Deeds has lnd rec)

Towns Organized Before 1800: Nantucket 1687

Name	Map Index	Date Created	Parent County or Territory From Which Organized

* **Norfolk**   E6   1793   Suffolk

Norfolk County, 650 High St, Dedham, MA 02026-1855 . . . . (617)326-1600

(Pro Judge has div & pro rec; Clk Cts has civ ct rec from 1928; Reg Deeds has Ind rec)(Originally part of the northeastern section of Mass and some twns at present part of NH, The old rec are now at Salem in Essex Co which originally included most of Norfolk Co)

Towns Organized Before 1800: Bellingham 1719, Braintree 1640, Brookline 1705, Canton 1797, Cohasset 1770, Dedham 1636, Dover 1784, Franklin 1778, Medfield 1650, Milton 1662, Needham 1711, Quincy 1792, Randolph 1793, Sharon 1765, Walpole 1724, Weymouth 1635, Wrentham 1673

* **Plymouth**   E6   1685   New Plymouth Colony

Plymouth County, PO Box 3535, Plymouth, MA 02361-3535 . . . . (508)747-1350

(Clk Ct has civ ct rec from 1700 also div rec concurrent with Reg of Pro)

Towns Organized Before 1800: Abinton 1712, Bridgewater 1656, Carver 1790, Duxbury 1637, Halifax 1734, Hanover 1727, Hingham 1635, Hull 1644, Kingston 1726, Marshfield 1640, Middleborough 1669, Pembroke 1712, Plymouth 1620, Plympton 1707, Rochester 1686, Scituate 1633, Wareham 1739

* **Suffolk**   E6   1643   Original county

Suffolk County, 55 Pemberton Sq Government Ctr, Boston, MA 02108-1701 . . . . (617)235-8000

(Reg of b, d, m, Boston, Mass.; Clk Cts has div rec; Reg Pro has pro rec & civ ct rec; Reg Deeds has Ind rec; part of 1800 census missing)

Towns Organized Before 1800: Boston 1630, Chelsea 1739, Dorchester 1630, Roxbury 1630

* **Worcester**   E4   1731   Suffolk, Middlesex

Worcester County, 2 Main St, Worcester, MA 01608-1116 . . . . (508)756-2441

[FHL has some m, civ ct, Ind, pro rec]

Towns Organized Before 1800: Ashburnham 1765, Athol 1762, Auburn 1778, Barre 1753, Berlin 1784, Bolton 1738, Boylston 1786, Brookfield 1673, Charlton 1754, Douglas 1746, Fitchburg 1764, Gardner 1785, Grafton 1735, Greenwich 1754, Hardwick 1739, Harvard 1732, Hubbardston 1767, Lancaster 1653, Leicester 1714, Leominster 1740, Lunenburg 1728, Mendon 1667, Milford 1780, New Braintree 1751, Northborough 1766, Northbridge 1772, Oakham 1762, Oxford 1693, Paxton 1765, Petersham 1754, Phillipston 1786, Princeton 1759, Royalston 1765, Rutland 1714, Shrewsbury 1720, Southborough 1727, Spencer 1753, Sterling 1781, Sutton 1714, Templeton 1762, Upton 1735, Uxbridge 1727, Warren 1742, Westborough 1717, Westminster 1759, Winchendon 1764, Worcester 1684

* At least one county history has been published about this county.
† Inventory of county archives was made by the Historical Records Survey. (See Introduction)

MICHIGAN

CAPITAL · LANSING — TERRITORY 1805 — STATE 1837 (26th)
State Map on Page M-20

French explorers in their search for furs and the Northwest Passage first discovered Michigan in the early 17th century. The first permanent settlement was made by Jacques Marquette at Sault Ste. Marie in 1668. In 1701, Antoine de la Mother Cadillac established Fort Pontchartrain, later named Detroit. The French used the area only for fur trading, so that when the British gained control in 1763 there were still only a few white settlers in the area. The Indians, led by Pontiac, rebelled against the British and laid seige to Detroit for five months but ultimately were defeated. In 1774, Michigan became part of the Quebec Territory. The area was used by the British in the Revolutionary War as the base of operations for their attacks on Kentucky. Michigan became part of the United States by the Treaty of Paris in 1783, but the British retained control of the forts at Detroit and Michilimackinac. Michigan became part of the Northwest Territory in 1787. General Anthony Wayne occupied Fort Detroit in 1796 and Jay's Treaty was signed, giving the United States control of all of Michigan.

In 1800, Michigan became part of the Indiana Territory and then became a territory itself in 1805. During the War of 1812, General Hull, who commanded the U.S. forces in Michigan, attempted to invade Canada, failed and ultimately surrendered Detroit to the British. Only after Admiral Perry's victory in 1813 were the Americans again able to take Detroit. The first public land sales took place in 1818. Work on the Erie Canal started the same year and steamship travel was established between Buffalo and Detroit, which greatly increased settlement of the area. Treaties with the Indians in 1819 and 1821 further opened up the area to settlement. Transportation into the area was greatly facilitated by the opening of the Erie Canal in 1825, construction of a road through the Kalamazoo Valley in 1829, and the completion of the Chicago Road in 1835. In 1835, Michigan lost land along its southern border to Ohio and gained the upper peninsula. Two years later Michigan became the twenty-sixth state.

By 1840, nearly half of the land in the southern peninsula was cultivated by settlers from New York, New England, and Germany. The next fifty years saw tens of thousands of immigrants arrive to work in the lumber and mining camps. They came from Canada, Ireland, Finland, Norway, Sweden, Wales, Poland, Italy, and England, especially from the Cornwall area. Religious refugees from Holland also made their way to Michigan, settling around Grand Rapids and the western coast. During the Civil War, more than 87,000 men served in the Union forces from Michigan.

County registration of births and deaths began in 1867 and gained general compliance by 1915. These are available from county clerks, along with delayed registration of birth for many counties. The state also has copies available from the Office of the State Registrar, Michigan Department of Health, P.O. Box 30035, Lansing, MI 48909. To verify current fees, call 517-335-8655.

Vital records prior to 1867 were handled by the Clerk of the Circuit Court. Most counties kept marriage records from their creation. Starting in 1805, marriages were required to be registered with the clerk of the local district court. Divorces were first recorded in the supreme court, then later by the clerk of the circuit, chancery, or county court. The records are available from the county court. Wayne county began keeping probate records in 1797, while other counties began about 1817. These records are kept by the clerk of the probate court. The circuit and district courts handled naturalizations, but the records are held by the county clerks.

The first land office opened in Detroit in 1818. The Registrar of Deeds handles all land matters for each county. The earliest land records are private land claims granted by France and England. These records are at the National Archives, Chicago Branch, 7538 South Pulaski Road, Chicago, IL 60629. Claims for 1790 to 1837 have been transcribed, indexed, and published. The Michigan State Archives, Department of State, 3405 North Logan Street, Lansing, MI 48198, also has many land and tax records. More than twenty early territorial censuses were taken in various areas of Michigan from 1810 to 1830 and are available in published form. Other territorial and state enumerations were made between 1827 and 1904.

Genealogical Archives, Libraries and Societies

Bay City Branch Library, 708 Center Avenue, Bay City, MI 48706

Burton Historical Collection of the Detroit Public Library, 5201 Woodward Avenue, Detroit, MI 48202 (The oldest local history and genealogy collection in the state).

Central Michigan University Library, Mt. Pleasant, MI 48858 (good genealogical collection)

Detroit Society for Genealogical Research, Detroit Public Library, 5201 Woodward Ave., Detroit, MI 48202

Flint Public Library, 1026 E. Kearsley, Flint, MI 48502

Friends of the Mitchell Public Library Research Committee, 22 North Manning St., Hillsdale, MI 49242

Grand Rapids Public Library, 111 Library St., N.E., Grand Rapids, MI 49502

Herrick Public Library, 300 River Ave., Holland, MI 49423

Jackson Public Library, 244 W. Michigan Ave., Jackson, MI 49201

Library of Michigan, 717 W. Allegan, P. O. Box 30007, Lansing, MI 48909

Mason County Genealogical, Historical Resource Center, c / o Rose Hawley Museum, 305 E. Filer Street, Ludington, MI 49431 (Good genealogical collection).

Mt. Clemens Public Library, 150 Cass Ave., Mt. Clemens, MI 48403

Ogemaw District Library, 107 West Main Box 427, Rose City, MI 48654

Orion Township Public Library, 845 S. Lapeer Road, Lake Orion, MI 48035 (Fine genealogical collection).

Polish Archives, St. Mary's College, Orchard Lake, MI 48033

Sage Branch Library, 100 East Midland Street, Bay City, MI 48706

South Side Branch Library, 311 Lafayette Street, Bay City, MI 48706

Sturgis Public Library, N. Nottawa at West St., Sturgis, MI 49091

Webster Memorial Library, 200 Phelps St., Decatur, MI 49045

Westland Michigan Genealogical Library, P. O. Box 70, Westland, MI 48185

White Pine Library Cooperative, 1840 N. Michigan, Suite 114, Saginaw, MI 48602-5590

Ypsilanti Historical Society Museum, 220 North Huron Street, Ypsilanti, MI 48197

Albion Historical Society, Gardner House Museum, 509 S. Superior St., Albion, MI 49224

Bay County Genealogical Society, P. O. Box 27, Essexville, MI 48732

Branch County Genealogical Society, P. O. Box 443, Coldwater, MI 49036

Branch County Historical Society, P. O. Box 107, Coldwater, MI 49036

Calhoun County Genealogical Society, c / o Albion Public Library, 501 S. Superior Street, Albion, MI 49224

Cheboygan County Genealogical Society, P. O. Box 51, Cheboygan, MI 49721

Clinton County: The Genealogists of the Historical Society, P. O. Box 23, St. Johns, MI 48879

Dearborn Genealogical Society, P. O. Box 1112, Dearborn, MI 48121-1112

Detroit Society for Genealogical Research, Detroit Public Library, 5201 Woodward Ave., Detroit, MI 48202

Dickinson County Genealogical Society, 401 Iron Mountain Street, Iron Mountain, MI 49801

Downriver Genealogical Society, 1394 Cleophus, Box 476, Lincoln Park, MI 48146

Eaton County Genealogical Society, 100 Lawrence Ave., Charlotte, MI 48813

Farmington Genealogical Society, 23500 Liberty, Farmington, MI 48024

Flat River Historical Society, P. O. Box 188, Greenville, MI 48838

Flint Genealogical Society, P. O. Box 1217, Flint, MI 48501

Four Flags Area Genealogical Society, P. O. Box 414, Niles, MI 49120

French-Canadian Heritage Society of Michigan, Library of Michigan, P. O. Box 30007, Lansing, MI 48909

Gaylord Fact-Finders Genealogical Society, Rt. 2, Box 2033A, Grayling, MI 49738

Genealogical Association of Southwestern Michigan, Box 573, St. Joseph, MI 49085

Genealogical Society of Flemish Americans, 18740 Thirteen Mile Road, Roseville, MI 48066

Genealogical Society of Monroe County, Michigan, P. O. Box 1428, Monroe, MI 48161

Genealogical Society of Washtenaw County, Michigan, Inc., P. O. Box 7155, Ann Arbor, MI 48107

Grand Haven Genealogical Society, Loutit Library, 407 Columbus, Grand Haven, MI 49417

Grand Traverse Genealogical Society, 430 S. Airport Road East, Traverse City, MI 49684

Gratiot County Historical and Genealogical Society, P. O. Box 73, Ithaca, MI 48847

Huron Shores Genealogical Society, 1909 Bobwhite, Oscoda, MI 48750

Huron Valley Genealogical Society, 1100 Atlantic, Milford, MI 48042

Holland Genealogical Society, Herrick Public Library, 300 River Ave., Holland, MI 49423

Jackson County Genealogical Society, c / o Jackson District Library, 244 W. Michigan Avenue, Jackson, MI 49201

Jewish Genealogical Society of Michigan, 4987 Bantry Drive, West Bloomfield, MI 48322

Jewish Historical Society of Michigan, Genealogical Branch, 3345 Buckingham Trail, West Bloomfield, MI 48033

Kalamazoo Valley Genealogical Society, P. O. Box 405, Comstock, MI 49041

Kalkaska Genealogical Society, P. O. Box 353, Kalkaska, MI 49646

Kinseekers, 5697 Old Maple Trail, Grawn, MI 49637

Lapeer County Genealogical Society, City Branch Library, 921 W. Nepressing Street, Lapeer, MI 48446

Livingston County Genealogical Society, P. O. Box 1073, Howell, MI 48844-1073

Livonia Historical Society, 38125 Eight Mile Rd., Livonia, MI 48152

Lyon Township Genealogical Society, Lyon Township Public Library, 27025 Milford Road, New Hudson, MI 48165

Macomb County Genealogy Group, Mount Clemens Public Library, 150 Cass Ave., Mount Clemens, MI 48043

Marquette County Genealogical Society, Peter White Public Library, 217 N. Front St., Marquette, MI 49855

Mason County Genealogical Society, P. O. Box 352, Ludington, MI 49431

Mason County Historical Society, 1687 S. Lake Shore Drive, Ludington, MI 49431

Michigan Chapter, Ohio Genealogical Society, 34233 Shawnee, Westland, MI 48185

Michigan Genealogical Council, Liaison Office, Library of Michigan, 717 W. Allegan, Lansing, MI 48909

Michigan Historical Comm., 505 State Office Bldg., Lansing, MI 48913

Michigan Society, Sons of the American Revolution, 2031 L'Anse, St. Clair Shore, MI 48081

Midland County Historical Society, Midland Center for the Arts, 1801 W. St. Andrews Dr., Midland, MI 48640

Midland Genealogical Society, Grace A. Dow Library, 1710 W. St. Andrews Dr., Midland, MI 48640

Mid-Michigan Genealogical Society, Library of Michigan, Box 30007, 717 W. Allegan St., Lansing, MI 48909

Muskegon County Genealogical Society, Hackley Library, 316 W. Webster Avenue, Muskegon, MI 49440

Northeast Michigan Genealogical Society, c / o Jesse Besser Museum, 491 Johnson Street, Alpena, MI 49707

Northville Genealogical Society, 42164 Gladwin Dr., Northville, MI 48167

Northwest Oakland County Historical Society, 306 South Saginaw St., Holly, MI 48442

Northwestern Michigan College, Mark Osterlin Library, 1704 East Front Street, Traverse City, MI 49684

Oakland County Genealogical Society, P. O. Box 1094, Birmingham, MI 48012

Ogemaw Genealogical and Historical Society, c / o West Branch Public Library, West Branch, MI 48661

Polish Genealogical Society of Michigan, c / o Burton Historical Collection, 5201 Woodward Avenue, Detroit, MI 48202

Pontiac Area Historical and Genealogical Society, P. O. Box 901, Pontiac, MI 48056

Reed City Area Genealogical Society, Reed City Public Library, 410 W. Upton Ave., Reed City, MI 49677

Rockwood Area Historical Society, P. O. Box 68, Rockwood, MI 48173

Rose City Area Historical Society, Inc., Ogemaw District Library, 107 West Main Box 427, Rose City, MI 48654

Roseville Historical & Genealogical Society, Roseville Public Library, 29777 Gratiot Ave., Roseville, MI 48066

Saginaw Genealogical Society, Saginaw Public Library, 505 Janes Ave., Saginaw, MI 48507

Shiawassee County Genealogical Society, P. O. Box 841, Owosso, MI 48867

Sterling Heights Genealogical and Historical Society, P. O. Box 1154, Sterling Heights, MI 48311-1154

Three Rivers Genealogy Club, 13724 Spence Road, Three Rivers, MI 49093

Van Buren Regional Genealogical Society, Webster Memorial Library, 200 North Phelps St., Decatur, MI 49045

Western Michigan Genealogical Society, Grand Rapids Public Library, Library Plaza, Grand Rapids, MI 49503

Western Wayne County Genealogical Society, P. O. Box 63, Livonia, MI 48152

Ypsilanti Historical Society Museum, 220 North Huron Street, Ypsilanti, MI 48197

Printed Census Records and Mortality Schedules

Federal Census 1820, 1830, 1840, 1850, 1860, 1870, 1880, 1900, 1910
Federal Mortality Schedules 1850, 1860, 1870, 1880
Union Veterans and Widows 1890
Territorial Tax List 1805

Residents 1831
State/Territorial Census 1884, 1894, 1904

Valuable Printed Sources

Atlases, Maps, and Gazetteers

Blois, John T. *Gazetteer of the State of Michigan*. Detroit: S. L. Rood & Co., 1839.

Romig, Walter. *Michigan Place Names*. Gross Pointe, Michigan: Walter Romig, 1972.

Welch, Richard. *County Evolution in Michigan, 1790-1897*. Lansing, Michigan: Michigan State Library, 1972.

Bibliographies

Michigan County Histories: A Bibliography. Lansing, Michigan: Michigan State Library, 1978.

Michigan Newspapers on Microfilm. Lansing, Michigan: Michigan State Library, 1975.

Russell, Donna Valley. *Michigan Censuses, 1710-1830, Under the French, British, and Americans*. Detroit: Detroit Public Library, 1982.

Sourcebook of Michigan Census, County Histories, and Vital Records. Lansing, Michigan: Library of Michigan, 1986.

Warner, Robert M. and Ida C. Brown. *Guide to Manuscripts in the Michigan Historical Collections of the University of Michigan*. Ann Arbor: University of Michigan, 1963.

Genealogical Research Guides

Anderson, Alloa and Polly Bender. *Genealogy in Michigan: What, When, Where*. Ann Arbor: Alloa Anderson, 1978.

McGinnis, Carol. *Michigan Genealogy: Sources and Resources*. Baltimore: Genealogical Publishing Co., 1987.

Michigan Cemetery Compendium. Spring Arbor, Michigan: HAR-AL Inc., 1979.

Genealogical Sources

Genealogy of the French Families of the Detroit River Region. Detroit: Detroit Society for Genealogical Research, 1976.

Records of Service of Michigan Volunteers in the Civil War. Lansing, Michigan: State of Michigan, 1915.

Histories

Moore, Charles. *History of Michigan*. Chicago: Lewis Publishing Co., 1915.

MICHIGAN COUNTY DATA
State Map on Page M-20

Name	Map Index	Date Created	Parent County or Territory From Which Organized
Aishcum (Changed to Lake, 1843)			
* **Alcona**	E6	1840	Alpena, Cheboygan
Alcona County, 106 5th St, Harrisville, MI 48740 .... (517)724-5374			
(Co Clk has b, m, d, div, pro, civ ct rec from 1870, also bur rec from 1940)			
*† **Alger**	C3	1885	Schoolcraft
Alger County, 101 Court St, Munising, MI 49862-1196 .... (906)387-2076			
(Co Clk has b, d & lnd rec from 1884, m rec from 1887, div & civ ct rec from 1885; Pro Ct has pro rec)			
* **Allegan**	G4	1831	Kalamazoo
Allegan County, 113 Chestnut St, Allegan, MI 49010-1362 .... (616)673-8471			
(Co Clk has b & d rec from 1867, m rec from 1836, div, civ ct & lnd rec from 1835, naturalization rec from 1850)			
*† **Alpena**	D6	1840	Cheboygan
Alpena County, 720 W Chisholm St, Alpena, MI 49707-2453 .... (517)356-0115			
(Co Clk has b rec from 1869, m, d, div & civ ct rec from 1871; Pro Judge has pro rec; Reg Deeds has lnd rec)			
Anamickee (changed to Alpena, 1843)			
Antrim	D4	1840	Grand Traverse
Antrim County, PO Box 520, Bellaire, MI 49615-0520 .... (616)533-8607			
(Co Clk has b, m, d, div & civ ct rec from 1867; Pro Judge has pro rec from 1863; Reg Deeds has lnd rec)			
Arenac	E6	1883	Bay, Saginaw
Arenac County, PO Box 747, Standish, MI 48658-0747 .... (517)846-4626			
(Co Clk has b, m, d, div, civ ct rec from 1883, bur rec from 1952)			

Name	Map Index	Date Created	Parent County or Territory From Which Organized

† **Baraga**   C2   1875   Houghton
Baraga County, 12 S 3rd St, L'Anse, MI 49946-1090 .... (906)524-6183
(Co Clk has b, m, d, div, civ ct & Ind rec from 1875 & bur rec from 1950)

* **Barry**   G4   1829   St. Joseph, Kalamazoo
Barry County, 220 W State St, Hastings, MI 49058-1849 .... (616)948-4810
(Co Clk has b, d rec from 1867, m rec from 1839, div rec from 1869, civ ct rec from 1845; Pro Ct has pro rec; Reg Deeds has Ind rec)

*† **Bay**   F5   1857   Saginaw, Midland
Bay County, 515 Center Ave, Bay City, MI 48708-5941 .... (517)892-3528
(Co Clk has b rec from 1868, m rec from 1857, d rec from 1867, div rec from 1883; civ ct rec from 1965; Pro Ct has pro rec; Reg Deeds has Ind rec)

* **Benzie**   E4   1863   Grand Traverse, Leelanau
Benzie County, 224 Court Pl, Beulah, MI 49617 .... (616)882-9671
(Co Clk has b & d rec from 1868, m & civ ct rec from 1869, div & pro rec from 1870, naturalization rec from 1871, bur rec from 1934)

* **Berrien**   H4   1829   Cass
Berrien County, 811 Port St, Saint Joseph, MI 49085-1114 .... (616)983-7111
(Co Clk has b & d rec from 1867, m rec from 1831, div & civ ct rec from 1834; Pro Ct has pro rec; Land Description Office has Ind rec)

* **Branch**   H5   1829   St. Joseph, Lenawee
Branch County, 31 Division St, Coldwater, MI 49036-1904 .... (517)279-8411
(Co Clk has b, d rec from 1867, m rec from 1833, div, civ ct rec from 1848; City and Township Clks have bur rec; Pro Ct has pro rec; Reg Deeds has Ind rec)

*† **Calhoun**   G5   1829   St. Joseph, Kalamazoo
Calhoun County, 315 W Green St, Marshall, MI 49068-1585 .... (616)781-0700
(Co Clk has b, d, m rec from 1867, bur rec 1952-1978, div, civ ct rec from 1867, naturalization rec from 1918, military discharge rec from 1919, election rec from 1972; Pro Ct has pro rec)

* **Cass**   H4   1829   Lenawee
Cass County, 120 N Broadway St, Cassopolis, MI 49031-1302 .... (616)445-8621
(Co Clk has b & d rec from 1867, m rec from 1837, div & civ ct rec from 1830)

Charlevoix   D4   1869   Emmet
Charlevoix County, 301 State St County Bldg, Charlevoix, MI 49720 .... (616)547-7200
(Co Clk has b rec from 1867, m & d rec from 1868, div & civ ct rec from 1869, pro rec from 1881 & Ind rec from 1869)

*† **Cheboygan**   D5   1840   Mackinac
Cheboygan County, 870 S Main St, Cheboygan, MI 49721-2220 .... (616)627-8808
(Co Clk has b, m, d rec from 1867, div, civ ct rec from 1884; Reg of Pro has pro rec from 1854; Reg of Deeds has Ind rec from 1854)

Cheonoquet (changed to Montmorency, 1843)

Chippewa   C5   1826   Mackinac
Chippewa County, 319 Court St, Sault Sainte Marie, MI 49783-2183 .... (906)635-6300
(Co Clk has b rec from 1869, m rec from 1868, d rec from 1870, div rec from 1891, civ ct rec; Pro Ct has pro rec; Reg Deeds has Ind rec)

Clare   E5   1840   Isabella, Midland, Mecosta
Clare County, PO Box 438, Harrison, MI 48625-0438 .... (517)539-7131
(Co Clk has b, m, d, bur, div, civ ct & Ind rec)

* **Clinton**   F5   1818   Shiawssee, Kent
Clinton County, 100 E State St, Saint Johns, MI 48879-1571 .... (517)224-5100
(Co Clk has b, d rec from 1867, m rec from 1840, div rec from 1839, civ ct rec)

Crawford   E5   1818   Cheboygan, Antrim, Kalkaska
Crawford County, 200 W Michigan Ave, Grayling, MI 49738-1745 .... (517)348-2841
(Co Clk has b rec from 1879, m, d & div rec from 1878, civ ct rec from 1881, pro rec from 1879, Ind rec from 1863)

Delta   C3   1843   Mackinac
Delta County, 310 Ludington St, Escanaba, MI 49829-4057 .... (906)786-1763
(Co Clk has b, m, d, div, civ ct, pro & Ind rec from 1867)

Des Moines   1834   Disorganized

* **Dickinson**   C2   1891   Marquette, Menominee
Dickinson County, PO Box 609, Iron Mountain, MI 49801-0609 .... (906)774-0988
(Co Clk has b, m, d, div & civ ct rec, naturalization, articles of incorporation & crim rec from 1891; Pro Ct has pro rec; Reg Deeds has Ind rec)

* **Eaton**   G5   1837   St. Joseph, Kalamazoo, Calhoun
Eaton County, 1045 Independence Dr, Charlotte, MI 48813-1095 .... (517)543-7500
(Co Clk has b & d rec from 1867, m rec from 1838, div & civ ct rec 1847; Pro Judge has pro rec)

* **Emmet**   D5   1853   Mackinac
Emmet County, 200 Division St, Petoskey, MI 49770-2444 .... (616)348-1744
(Co Clk has b, m, d & civ ct rec from 1867, div rec from 1875)

Name	Map Index	Date Created	Parent County or Territory From Which Organized

*† Genesee F6 1835 Lapeer
Genesee County, 900 S Saginaw St Rm 202, Flint, MI 48502 .... (313)257-3283
(Co Clk has b, d rec from 1867, m rec from 1835, div rec from 1890, civ ct, crim rec from 1835; Pro Judge has pro rec; Cem custodians have bur rec)

Gladwin E5 1875 Saginaw, Midland
Gladwin County, 401 W Cedar Ave, Gladwin, MI 48624-2023 .... (517)426-7351
(Co Clk has b, m, d, bur, div & civ ct rec from 1880; Pro Ct has pro rec; Reg Deeds has lnd rec)

Gogebic C1 1881 Ontonagon
Gogebic County, 200 N Moore St, Bessemer, MI 49911-1052 .... (906)663-4518
(Co Clk has b, m, d, div, civ ct & naturalization rec from 1887; Pro Ct has pro rec; Reg Deeds has lnd rec)

* Grand Traverse E4 1851 Mackinac
Grand Traverse County, 400 Boardman Ave, Traverse City, MI 49684-2577 .... (616)922-4700
(Co Clk has b, d rec from 1867, m rec from 1853, div, civ ct rec from 1882; Townships have bur rec; Title Companies have lnd rec)

* Gratiot F5 1855 Saginaw, Clinton
Gratiot County, 214 E Center St, Ithaca, MI 48847-1446 .... (517)875-5215
(Co Clk has b, d, div & civ ct rec from 1867, m rec from 1855)

* Hillsdale H5 1835 Lenawee
Hillsdale County, 29 N Howell St County Courthouse, Hillsdale, MI 49242-1865 .... (517)437-3391
(Co Clk has b & d rec from 1867, m rec from 1835, div & civ ct rec from 1845; Pro Ct has pro rec; Reg Deeds has lnd rec)

Houghton B1 1845 Marquette, Schoolcraft, Ontonagon
Houghton County, 401 E Houghton Ave, Houghton, MI 49931-2016 .... (906)482-1150
(Co Clk has b & d rec from 1867, m rec from 1855, div & civ ct rec from 1853, lnd rec from 1847, naturalization rec from 1848, inquests from 1890, military rec-few CW, 1 bk WWI, many bks WWII; Pro Judge has pro rec)

* Huron F6 1840 Saginaw, St. Clair, Sanilac
Huron County, 250 E Huron Ave, Bad Axe, MI 48413-1317 .... (517)269-9942
Co Clk has b, m, d, div & civ ct rec from 1867; Pro Judge has pro rec; Reg Deeds has lnd rec)

* Ingham G5 1838 Washtenaw, Jackson, Eaton
Ingham County, PO Box 179, Mason, MI 48854-0179 .... (517)676-0240
(Co Clk has b & d rec from 1867, m rec from 1838, div & civ ct rec from 1839; bur rec are with Twnship & City Clks; Pro Ct has pro rec)

* Ionia G5 1831 Kent
Ionia County, Main St, Ionia, MI 48846 .... (616)527-5322
(Co Clk has b & d rec from 1867, m rec from 1837, div & civ ct rec from 1890)

*† Iosco E6 1857 Saginaw, Cheboygan
Iosco County, PO Box 838, Tawas City, MI 48764-0838 .... (517)362-3497
(Co Clk has b rec from 1867, m rec from 1862, d rec from 1868, bur rec 1961-1978, div, civ ct rec from 1859, naturalization rec from 1894 to 1903, declaration of intention 1859-1906)

*† Iron C2 1885 Marquette, Menominee
Iron County, 2 S 6th St, Crystal Falls, MI 49920-1413 .... (906)875-3221
(Co Clk has b, m, d, div, civ ct rec from 1895; Pro Ct has pro rec; Reg Deeds has lnd rec; Townships and cities have bur rec)

* Isabella F5 1831 Saginaw, Midland
Isabella County, 200 N Main St, Mount Pleasant, MI 48858-2321 .... (517)772-0911
(Co Clk has b, m, d, div & civ ct rec from 1880)

Isle Royal 1875 Disorganized 1897
(attached 1885 to Houghton, 1897 to Keweenaw where rec now are held)

*† Jackson G5 1832 Washtenaw
Jackson County, 120 W Michigan Ave, Jackson, MI 49201-1315 .... (517)788-4265
(Co Clk has b & d rec from 1867, m rec from 1830s, div rec from 1800s, immigration rec; Pro Ct has pro rec; Clk Dis Ct has civ ct rec; Reg Deeds has lnd rec)

* Kalamazoo G4 1829 St. Joseph
Kalamazoo County, 201 W Kalamazoo Ave, Kalamazoo, MI 49007 .... (616)383-8840
(Co Clk has b & d rec from 1867, m rec from 1831, div & civ ct rec from 1800s; Pro Judge has pro rec; Reg Deeds has lnd rec)

* Kalkaska E4 1870 Grand Traverse, Antrim
Kalkaska County, 605 N Birch St, Kalkaska, MI 49646 .... (616)258-3300
(Co Clk has b, m, d, div & civ ct rec from 1871 & bur rec; Pro Judge has pro rec; Reg Deeds has lnd rec)

Kanotin (changed to Iosco, 1843)

Kautawaubet (changed to Wexford, 1843)

Kaykakee (changed to Clare, 1843)

* Kent F4 1836 Kalamazoo
Kent County, 300 Monroe Ave NW, Grand Rapids, MI 49503 .... (616)774-3548
(Co Clk has b & d rec from 1867, m rec from 1845, bur rec from 1959; Clk Cir Ct has div & civ ct rec from 1867; Pro Ct has pro rec; Reg Deeds has lnd rec)

Keweenaw B2 1861 Houghton
Keweenaw County, 4th St County Courthouse, Eagle River, MI 49924-9999 .... (906)337-2229
(Co Clk has b, m & d rec from 1867, div & civ ct rec, lnd rec from 1848; Pro Ct has pro rec)

Name	Map Index	Date Created	Parent County or Territory From Which Organized

Lake   E4   1870   Oceana, Mason, Newaygo
Lake County, 800 10th St, Baldwin, MI 49304 . . . . (616)745-4641
(Co Clk has b, d rec from 1870, m, Ind rec from 1872, civ ct rec from 1871; Pro Ct has pro rec; Township Clks have bur rec)

* **Lapeer**   F6   1835   Oakland
Lapeer County, 255 Clay St, Lapeer, MI 48446-2298 . . . . (313)667-0356
(Co Clk has b & d rec from 1868, m, div & civ ct rec from 1835)

* **Leelanau**   E4   1840   Grand Traverse
Leelanau County, PO Box 467, Leland, MI 49654-0467 . . . . (616)256-9824
(Co Clk has b, m & d rec from 1867, div rec from 1870 & civ ct rec; Pro Judge has pro rec)

* **Lenawee**   H6   1822   Wayne
Lenawee County, 425 N Main St, Adrian, MI 49221-2198 . . . . (517)263-8831
(Co Clk has b, m & d rec from 1867, div & civ ct rec from 1870; Courthouse burned 1852)

* **Livingston**   G6   1836   Shiawassee, Washtenaw
Livingston County, 200 E Grand River Ave, Howell, MI 48843-2267 . . . . (517)546-0500
(Co Clk has b, d, div, civ ct rec from 1867, m rec from 1836; Pro Judge has pro rec; Reg Deeds has Ind rec)

* **Luce**   C4   1887   Chippewa, Mackinac
Luce County, E Court St, Newberry, MI 49868 . . . . (906)293-5521
(Co Clk has b, m, d, div, civ ct, Ind rec from 1887; Pro Judge has pro rec)

* **Mackinac**   C4   1818   Wayne and the French
Mackinac County, 100 Marley St, Saint Ignace, MI 49781 . . . . (906)643-7300
(This county first called Michilimackinac, changed in 1849 to Mackinac. Co Clk has b & d rec from 1873, m rec from 1867, div & civ ct rec from 1808)

* **Macomb**   G7   1818   Wayne
Macomb County, 40 N Gratiot Ave, Mount Clemens, MI 48043-5688 . . . . (313)469-5100
(Co Clk has b, d, bur rec from 1867, m rec from 1848, div rec from 1847, Ind rec; Pro Ct has pro rec)

* **Manistee**   E4   1855   Mackinac, Ottawa, Oceana, Grand Traverse
Manistee County, 415 3rd St, Manistee, MI 49660-1606 . . . . (616)723-3331
(Co Clk has b & d rec from 1867, m & div rec from 1856, civ ct rec from 1855; Pro Ct has pro rec; Reg Deeds has Ind rec)

Manitou   1855   Disbanded 1895

*† **Marquette**   C2   1851   Chippewa, Houghton
Marquette County, 234 W Baraga Ave, Marquette, MI 49855-4751 . . . . (906)228-1501
(Co Clk has b & d rec from 1867, m rec from 1851, div & civ ct rec from 1852

* **Mason**   E4   1840   Ottawa, Oceana
Mason County, 300 E Ludington Ave, Ludington, MI 49431-2121 . . . . (616)843-8202
(Co Clk has b, m, d, div, civ ct rec from 1867; City Clks have bur rec; Pro Ct has pro rec; Reg Deeds has Ind rec)

* **Mecosta**   F4   1840   Newaygo
Mecosta County, 400 Elm St, Big Rapids, MI 49307-1849 . . . . (616)592-0783
(Co Clk has b & d rec from 1867, m rec from 1859, div & civ ct rec from 1860, naturalization rec; Pro Ct has pro rec from 1864; Reg Deeds has Ind rec from 1859)

Meegisee (Changed to Antrim, 1843)

* **Menominee**   D2   1863   Marquette
Menominee County, 839 10th Ave, Menominee, MI 49858-3000 . . . . (906)863-9968
(Co Clk has b, m, d, div, civ ct rec from 1861; Pro Judge has pro rec; Reg Deeds has Ind rec)

Michilimackinac (changed to Mackinac, 1849)

* **Midland**   F5   1850   Saginaw
Midland County, 220 W Ellsworth St, Midland, MI 48640-5180 . . . . (517)832-6739
(Co Clk has b rec from 1869, m rec from 1868, d rec from 1867, div & civ ct rec from 1916; Pro Ct has pro rec; Reg Deeds has Ind rec)

Mikenauk (changed to Roscommon, 1843)

* **Missaukee**   E4   1840   Antrim, Grand Traverse
Missaukee County, PO Box J, Lake City, MI 49651 . . . . (616)839-4967
(Co Clk has b, m, d, bur, div, civ ct & Ind rec from 1871; Pro Judge has pro rec, some rec destroyed by fire 1944)

* **Monroe**   H6   1817   Wayne
Monroe County, 106 E 1st St, Monroe, MI 48161-2143 . . . . (313)243-7081
(Co Clk has b rec from 1874, m rec from 1818, d rec from 1867, div & civ ct rec to 1945; Pro Ct has pro rec; Reg Deeds has Ind rec)

* **Montcalm**   F4   1831   Ionia
Montcalm County, 211 W Main St, Stanton, MI 48888 . . . . (517)831-5226
(Co Clk has b & d rec from 1867, m rec from 1858, div & civ ct rec from 1865; Pro Ct has pro rec; Reg Deeds has Ind rec)

Montmorency   D5   1881   Cheboygan, Alpena
Montmorency County, County Courthouse, Atlanta, MI 49709 . . . . (517)785-4794
(most rec lost in fire 1942, still has vital rec others start 1943)

*† **Muskegon**   F4   1859   Ottawa
Muskegon County, 990 Terrace St, Muskegon, MI 49442-3398 . . . . (616)724-6221
(Co Clk has b, m, d, div & civ ct rec from 1859; Pro Ct has pro rec; Reg Deeds has Ind rec)

Neewago (changed to Alcoma, 1843)

Name	Map Index	Date Created	Parent County or Territory From Which Organized

* **Newaygo**   F4   1840   Kent, Muskegon, Oceana
Newaygo County, PO Box 293, White Cloud, MI 49349-0293 . . . . (616)689-7235
(Co Clk has b, d, civ ct rec from 1867, m rec from 1851, div rec from 1854)

Notipekago (Changed to Mason, 1843)

* **Oakland**   G6   1819   Wayne
Oakland County, 1200 N Telegraph Rd, Pontiac, MI 48341-1045 . . . . (313)858-1000
(Co Clk has b & d rec from 1867, m rec from 1827, naturalization rec from 1827)

* **Oceana**   F4   1831   Ottawa
Oceana County, PO Box 153, Hart, MI 49420 . . . . (616)873-4328
(Co Clk has b & m rec from 1867, d rec from 1868; Clk Cir Ct has div & civ ct rec; Pro Ct has pro rec; Reg Deeds has lnd rec)

Ogemaw   E5   1880   Saginaw, Bay
Ogemaw County, PO Box 8, West Branch, MI 48661-0008 . . . . (517)345-0215
(Co Clk has b rec from 1879, m, d, civ ct rec from 1876, div rec from 1877; Pro Ct has pro rec; Reg Deeds has lnd rec)

Okkuddo (changed to Otsego, 1843)

* **Ontonagon**   C1   1848   Chippewa, Houghton
Ontonagon County, 725 Greenland Rd, Ontonagon, MI 49953-1492 . . . . (906)884-4255
(Co Clk has b, d rec from 1868, m rec from 1861, div, civ ct rec from 1854, lnd rec from 1850; Pro Ct has pro rec; Cem associations have bur rec)

* **Osceola**   E4   1840   Mason, Newaygo, Mecosta
Osceola County, 301 W Upton Ave, Reed City, MI 49677-1149 . . . . (616)832-5818
(Co Clk has b & m rec from 1869, d & div rec from 1870, civ ct rec from 1963 & bur rec; Pro Judge has pro rec; Treas. has lnd rec)

Oscoda   E5   1840   Cheboygan, Alpena, Alcona
Oscoda County, 311 Morenci, Mio, MI 48647 . . . . (517)826-3241
(Co Clk has b, m, d, bur, div & civ ct rec from 1881, lnd rec from 1850; Pro Judge has pro rec)

Otsego   D5   1875   Mackinac, Alpena, Cheboygan, Antrim
Otsego County, 225 W Main St, Gaylord, MI 49735-1348 . . . . (517)732-6484
(Co Clk has b, m, d, div, civ ct, lnd rec from 1875)

* **Ottawa**   F4   1837   Kent
Ottawa County, 414 Washington St, Grand Haven, MI 49417-1473 . . . . (616)846-8310
(Co Clk has b & d rec from 1867, m & civ ct rec from 1847 & div rec from 1863)

Presque Isle   D5   1840   Mackinac
Presque Isle County, 151 E Huron Ave, Rogers City, MI 49779-1316 . . . . (517)734-3288
(Co Clk has b & d rec from 1871, m rec from 1842 & div rec from 1900)

Reshkauko (changed to Charlevoix, 1843)

Roscommon   E5   1875   Cheboygan, Midland
Roscommon County, PO Box 98, Roscommon, MI 48653-0098 . . . . (517)275-5923
(Co Clk has b & d rec from 1874, m, div, pro, civ ct & lnd rec from 1875)

* **Saginaw**   F5   1835   Oakland
Saginaw County, 111 S Michigan Ave, Saginaw, MI 48602-2086 . . . . (517)790-5251
(Co Clk has b & m rec from 1867, d rec from 1868, div rec from 1886, civ ct rec from 1843; Pro Ct has pro rec; Equalization Dept has lnd rec)

* **Saint Clair**   F7   1822   Wayne
Saint Clair County, 201 McMorran Blvd, Port Huron, MI 48060-4006 . . . . (313)985-2031
(Co Clk has b rec from 1867, m rec from 1834, d rec from 1868, div, civ ct rec from 1849)

* **Saint Joseph**   H4   1829   Wayne
Saint Joseph County, PO Box 189, Centreville, MI 49032-0189 . . . . (616)467-6361
(Co Clk has b & d rec from 1867, m rec from 1832, div & civ ct rec from 1900, naturalization rec; Pro Ct has pro rec; Reg Deeds has lnd rec)

* **Sanilac**   F6   1848   Oakland, St. Clair, Lapeer
Sanilac County, 60 W Sanilac Rd, Sandusky, MI 48471-1094 . . . . (313)648-3212
(Co Clk has b rec from 1860, d rec from 1867, m rec from 1849, div & civ ct rec from 1854; Pro Ct has pro rec; Reg Deeds has lnd rec)

* **Schoolcraft**   C3   1848   Chippewa, Houghton, Marquette
Schoolcraft County, 300 Walnut St, Manistique, MI 49854-1491 . . . . (906)341-5532
(Co Clk has b, m, d, div, civ ct, lnd rec from 1870; Pro Ct has pro rec from 1870)

Shawano (changed to Crawford, 1843)

* **Shiawassee**   F5   1822   Oakland, Genesee
Shiawassee County, 208 N Shiawassee St, Corunna, MI 48817-1494 . . . . (517)743-2279
(Co Clk has b, m & d rec from 1867, div & civ ct rec from 1848; Pro Judge has pro rec; Reg Deeds has lnd rec; fire destroyed many rec 1867)

Tonedagana (changed to Emmet, 1843)

* **Tuscola**   F6   1840   Saginaw
Tuscola County, 440 N State St, Caro, MI 48723-1555 . . . . (517)673-5999
(Co Clk has b & d rec from 1866, div rec from 1884, civ ct rec from 1887 & m rec from 1851)

Unwattin (changed to Osceola, 1843)

Name	Map Index	Date Created	Parent County or Territory From Which Organized

* **Van Buren** G4 1829 Cass
Van Buren County, 212 Paw Paw St, Paw Paw, MI 49079-1492 .... (616)657-5581
(Co Clk has b & d rec from 1867, m rec from 1836, div & civ ct rec from 1837; Pro Ct has pro rec; Reg Deeds has lnd rec)

Wabassee (changed to Kalkaska, 1843)

* **Washtenaw** G6 1826 Wayne
Washtenaw County, PO Box 8645, Ann Arbor, MI 48107-8645 .... (313)994-2400
(Co Clk has b, m & d rec from 1867, div, civ ct & lnd rec, naturalization & supervisors rec from 1835)

* **Wayne** G6 1815 Original county
Wayne County, 600 Randolph St, Detroit, MI 48226-2831 .... (313)224-0471
[FHL has some b, m, d, cem, lnd, nat, pro rec)

* **Wexford** E4 1840 Manistee
Wexford County, 437 E Division St, Cadillac, MI 49601-1905 .... (616)779-9450
(Co Clk has b rec from 1868, m, d, div, civ ct rec from 1869)

* At least one county history has been published about this county.
† Inventory of county archives was made by the Historical Records Survey. (See Introduction)

MINNESOTA

CAPITAL · ST. PAUL — TERRITORY 1849 — STATE 1858 (23rd)
State Map Page M-21

French fur traders and missionaries were the first white men to enter Minnesota. Among the early explorers was Daniel Greysolon, Sieur Du Lhut (Duluth) who built a fort on the shores of Lake Superior and claimed the region for France. Father Louis Hennepin explored the upper Mississippi River in 1680, discovering the Falls of St. Anthony, where Minneapolis is today. Eastern Minnesota was given to the British in 1763 and fur trading was taken over by the Northwest Company. This area became part of the United States in 1783 and part of the Northwest Territory in 1787. The land west of the Mississippi River became part of the United States with the Louisiana Purchase in 1803. Zebulon Pike was sent to explore the area and set up Fort Anthony, later called Fort Snelling, at the junction of the Minnesota and Mississippi rivers. Fort Snelling became the first large settlement, located near present-day St. Paul, and by 1823, steamboats were coming up the Mississippi to the fort. The American Fur Company took over the fur trading industry in 1815, finally ending British control of the area.

In 1836, Minnesota was part of the Wisconsin Territory. The next year, the Sioux and Chippewa Indians sold their claim to the St. Croix Valley, opening the area to lumbering. Real settlement of the area began in earnest with settlers from the eastern United States coming to the eastern part of the state. In 1849, Minnesota became a territory. Further treaties with the Indians between 1851 and 1855 opened up western Minnesota to settlement. With completion of the railroad to the Mississippi River, and settlement in 1854, immigration greatly increased. An 1862 Sioux rebellion, in which more than 500 settlers were killed, resulted in the last of the Indian's claims being relinquished.

During the Civil War, Minnesota furnished about 24,000 men to the Union. After the war Minnesota boomed due to its timber, mines, mills, and agriculture. Homesteaders moved into the western and southwestern sections primarily from Germany, Sweden, and Norway. Poland, Lithuania, and the Balkan States furnished much of the labor for the packing plants around the Twin Cities at the turn of the century. Other ethnic groups to come to the state include Danes, Canadians, English, Finns, and Russians.

State registration of births began in 1900 and deaths in 1908. These records are available from the Minnesota Department of Health, Section of Vital Statistics, P.O. Box 9441, 717 Delaware Street S.E., Minneapolis, MN 55440. To verify current fees, call 612-623-5121.

Records prior to 1900 are in the offices of the District Court clerks. Marriage registration began within a decade of a county's formation. The administrator's office of each county's district court has both marriage and divorce records, except for Hennepin County which are at the State Department of Health. Probate records are at the Probate Court clerk's office. The first general land office was established in Wisconsin in 1848, but was transferred to Stillwater, Minnesota in 1849. These early books and township plats are at the Land Bureau, 658 Cedar Street, St. Paul, MN 55101. The National Archives, Chicago Branch, 7358 South Pulaski Road, Chicago, IL 60629, has land entry case files. Mortgages and deeds are kept by the registrar of deeds in each county. Minnesota was included in the Wisconsin and Iowa Territorial censuses in 1836 and 1840. Minnesota Territorial censuses exist for 1849, 1850, 1855, and 1857. State censuses were taken in 1865, 1875, 1885, and 1905.

Genealogical Archives, Libraries and Societies

Folke Bernadette Memorial Library, Gustavus Adolphus College, St. Peter, MN 56082

Heart O'Lakes Genealogical Library, 714 Summit Ave., Detroit Lakes, MN 56501

Minneapolis Public Library, 300 Nicolet Ave., Minneapolis, MN 55401

Public Library, 90 West 4th, St. Paul, MN 55102

Rochester Public Library, Broadway at First Street, S.E., Rochester, MN 55901

Rolvaag Memorial Library, St. Olaf College, Northfield, MN 55057

University of Minnesota Library, Minneapolis, MN 55455

Ylvisaker Library, Concordia College, Moorhead, MN 56560

American Swedish Institute, 2600 Park Ave., Minneapolis, MN 55407

Anoka County Genealogical Society, 1900 Third Ave., Anoka, MN 55303

Association for Certification of Minnesota Genealogists, Inc., 330 South Park, Mora, MN 55051

Benton County Historical Society, Box 312, Sauk Rapids, MN 56379

Blue Earth County Historical Society, 606 South Broad Street, Mankato, MN 56001

Brown County Historical Society, New Ulm, MN 56073

Crow Wing County Minnesota Genealogical Society, 2103 Graydon Ave., Brainerd, MN 56401

Dakota County Genealogical Society, P. O. Box 74, South St. Paul, MN 55075

Dodge County Genealogical Society, Box 683, Dodge Center, MN 55927

Douglas County Genealogical Society, P. O. Box 505, Alexandria, MN 56308

Fillmore County Historical Society, County Courthouse, Preston, MN 55965

Freeborn County Genealogical Society, P. O. Box 403, Albert Lee, MN 56007

Genealogy Guild of Wilkin County Minnesota and Richland County, North Dakota, Leach Public Library, Wahpeton, N D 58075

Genealogical Society of Carlton County, P. O. Box 204, Cloquet, MN 55720

Heart of Lakes Genealogical Society, 1324 Jackson Ave., Detroit Lakes, MN 56501

Heritage Searchers of Kandiyohi County, 610 NE Hwy 71, Willmar, MN 56201

Itasca County Genealogical Club, P. O. Box 130, Bovey, MN 55709

Minnesota Genealogical Society, P. O. Box 16069, St. Paul, MN 55116-0069

Minnesota Gen. Soc., English Interest GP., 9009 Northwood Circle, New Hope, MN 55427

Minnesota Historical Society, 690 Cedar St., St. Paul, MN 55101

Minnesota Society, Sons of the American Revolution, 2546 Cedar Ave., Minneapolis, MN 55404

Mower County Genealogical Society, P. O. Box 145, Austin, MN 55912

Nicollet County Historical Society and Museum, P. O. Box 153, St. Peter, MN 56082

Nobles County Historical Society, c / o 219 11th Ave., Worthington, MN 56187

Northfield / Rice County Genealogical Society, 408 Division Street, Northfield, MN 55057

Northwest Territory French and Canadian Heritage Institute, P. O. Box 26372, St. Louis Park, MN 55426

Norwegian-American Historical Association, Northfield, MN 55057

Olmsted County Genealogical Society, P. O. Box 6411, Rochester, MN 55903

Olmsted County Historical Society, Box 6411, Rochester, MN 55903

Otter Tail County Genealogical Society, 1110 Lincoln Ave. W., Fergus Falls, MN 56537

Pipestone County Genealogical Society, 113 South Hiawatha, Pipestone, MN 56164

Prairieland Genealogical Society, Southwest Historical Center, Southwest State University, Marshall, MN 56358

Range Genealogical Society, P. O. Box 388, Chisholm, MN 55768

Renville County Genealogical Society, Box 331, Renville, MN 56284

Rice County Genealogical Society, 408 Division St., Northfield, MN 55057

South Central Genealogical Society, 110 North Park St., Fairmont, MN 56031

St. Cloud Area Genealogists, Inc., P. O. Box 213, St. Cloud, MN 56302-0213

Stearns County Historical Society, Box 702, St. Cloud, MN 56301

Swift County Historical Society, Box 39, Benson, MN 56215

Twin Ports Genealogical Society, P. O. Box 16895, Duluth, MN 55816-0895

Verndale Historical Society, Verndale, MN 56481

Waseca Area Genealogy Society, Inc., P. O. Box 314, Waseca, MN 56093

White Bear Lake Genealogical Society, P. O. Box 10555, White Bear Lake, MN 55110

Winona County Genealogical Roundtable, P. O. Box 363, Winona, MN 55987

Wright County Genealogical Society, 911 2nd Avenue South, Buffalo, MN 55313

Printed Census Records and Mortality Schedules

Federal Census 1850, 1860, 1870, 1880, 1890 (part of Wright County only), 1900, 1910
Union Veterans and Widows 1890
State/Territorial Census 1836, 1849, 1857, 1865, 1875, 1885, 1895, 1905

Valuable Printed Sources

Atlases, Maps, and Gazetteers

Illustrated Historical Atlas of the State of Minnesota. Chicago: A. T. Andreas, 1874.

Upham, Warren. *Minnesota Geographic Names: Their Origin and Historic Significance*. St. Paul: Minnesota Historical Society, 1969.

Bibliographies

Genealogical Resources of the Minnesota Historical Society: A Guide. St. Paul: Minnesota Historical Society, 1989.

Hage, George S. *Newspapers on the Minnesota Frontier, 1849-1860*. St. Paul: Minnesota Historical Society, 1967.

Kirkeby, Lucille L. *Holdings of Genealogical Value in Minnesota's County Museums*. Brainerd, Minnesota: Lucille L. Kirkeby, 1986.

Treude, Mai. *Windows to the Past: A Bibliography of Minnesota County Atlases*. Minneapolis: University of Minnesota, 1980.

Genealogical Research Guides

Pope, Wiley R. and Alissa L. Wiener. *Tracing Your Ancestors in Minnesota: A Guide to the Sources*. St. Paul: Minnesota Family Trees, 1980.

Porter, Robert B. *How to Trace Your Minnesota Ancestors*. Center City, Minnesota: Porter Publishing Co., 1985.

Genealogical Sources

Lareau, Paul J. and Elmer Courteau. *French-Canadian Families of the North Central States: A Genealogical Dictionary*. St. Paul: Northwest Territory French and Canadian Heritage Institute, 1981.

Histories

Brook, Michael. *Reference Guide to Minnesota History*. St. Paul: Minesota Historical Society, 1974.

Burnquist, Joseph A. *Minnesota and Its People*. Chicago: S. J. Clark, 1924.

Follwell, William Watts. *A History of Minnesota*. St. Paul: Minnesota Historical Society, 1921.

MINNESOTA COUNTY DATA
State Map on Page M-21

Name	Map Index	Date Created	Parent County or Territory From Which Organized
† **Aitkin**	D4	1857	Cass, Itasca

Aitkin County, 209 2nd St NW, Aitkin, MN 56431-1297 .... (218)927-2102
(Clk Dis Ct has b rec from 1883, m rec from 1885, d rec from 1887, div rec from 1886, pro, civ ct rec, naturalization rec from 1885; Co Rcdr has Ind rec)

Andy Johnson (changed from Toombs 1858 & to Wilkin 1868)

*† **Anoka**	E5	1857	Ramsey

Anoka County, 325 E Main St, Anoka, MN 55303-2479 .... (612)421-4760
(Clk Dis Ct has b & d rec from 1870, m rec from 1865, div, civ ct & Ind rec from 1866; Pro Judge has pro rec)

* **Becker**	C3	1858	Indian Lands

Becker County, PO Box 787, Detroit Lakes, MN 56501-0787 .... (218)847-7659
(Co Rcdr has b, m & d rec from 1871, div, pro & civ ct rec from 1940)

*† **Beltrami**	B3	1897	Unorg. Terr

Beltrami County, 619 Beltrami Ave NW, Bemidji, MN 56601-3041 .... (218)759-4109
(Beltrami was attached to Becker County for many years for record purposes. Ct Administrator has b, m, d, div, pro & civ ct rec from 1896, Ind rec from 1969; Hist Soc has Ind rec prior to 1969)

† **Benton**	E4	1849	Original county

Benton County, 531 Dewey St, Foley, MN 56329 .... (612)968-6254
(Co Rcdr has b, m, d & Ind rec; Clk Dis Ct has div & civ ct rec from 1951, pro rec from 1887; State Archives has div & civ ct rec before 1951)

*† **Big Stone**	E2	1862	Pierce

Big Stone County, 20 2nd St SE, Ortonville, MN 56278-1544 .... (612)839-2537
(Clk Dis Ct has b, m, d rec from 1881, div, civ ct rec from 1885; Ct Judge has pro rec; Co Rcdr has Ind rec)

*† **Blue Earth**	G4	1853	Unorg. Terr

Blue Earth County, 204 S 5th St, Mankato, MN 56001-4585 .... (507)625-3031
(Clk Dist Ct has b, d rec from 1870, m rec from 1865, div, civ ct rec from 1854, pro rec from 1858; Reg Deeds has Ind rec)

Breckenridge (See Clay, Toombs & Wilkin)

Name	Map Index	Date Created	Parent County or Territory From Which Organized
* **Brown**	G3	1855	Nicollett, Blue Earth

Brown County, Center & State Sts, New Ulm, MN 56073 . . . . (507)359-7900
(Co Rcdr has b & d rec from 1870, m rec from 1857, Ind rec; Clk Dis Ct has div & pro rec from 1856, civ ct rec from 1885, MN Hist Soc has naturalization rec)

Buchanan (Discontinued)

| * **Carlton** | D5 | 1857 | Pine, St. Louis |

Carlton County, 30 Maple St, Carlton, MN 55718 . . . . (218)384-4281
(Clk Dis Ct has b, m, d, bur, div, pro, civ ct, Ind rec & naturalization rec from 1872)

| * **Carver** | F4 | 1855 | Hennepin |

Carver County, 600 E 4th St, Chaska, MN 55318-2183 . . . . (612)448-3435
(Clk Dis Ct has b, m & d rec from 1870, div, pro & civ ct rec from 1856; Co Rcdr has Ind rec)

| *† **Cass** | C4 | 1851 | Original county |

Cass County, Hwy 371, Walker, MN 56484 . . . . (218)547-3300
(Clk Dis Ct has b, d rec from 1896, m rec from 1897, div rec from 1899, civ ct rec from 1898, pro rec; Co Rcdr has Ind rec; City or township clks have bur rec)

| *† **Chippewa** | F3 | 1862 | Pierce |

Chippewa County, 11th St & Hwy 7, Montevideo, MN 56265 . . . . (612)269-7774
(Clk Dis Ct has b, m, d, div, pro, civ ct rec from 1870; Co Rcdr has Ind rec from 1870; City Clks have bur rec)

| * **Chisago** | E5 | 1851 | Washington |

Chisago County, County Courthouse, Center City, MN 55012 . . . . (612)257-1300
(Clk Dis Ct has b & d rec from 1870, m rec from 1852, civ ct rec from 1880 & div rec; Pro Judge has pro rec; Reg Deeds has Ind rec)

| * **Clay** | C2 | 1858 | Formerly Breckenridge (changed 1862) |

Clay County, 807 11th St N, Moorhead, MN 56560-1500 . . . . (218)299-5002
(Ct Administrator has b, m, d, div, pro & civ ct rec from 1872)

| * **Clearwater** | C3 | 1902 | Beltrami |

Clearwater County, 213 N Main Ave, Bagley, MN 56621 . . . . (218)694-6520
(Clk Dis Ct has b, m, d, div, pro & civ ct rec from 1903; Co Rcdr has Ind rec)

| **Cook** | B7 | 1874 | Lake |

Cook County, PO Box 1048, Grand Marais, MN 55604-0117 . . . . (218)387-2524
(Clk Dis Ct has b rec from 1879, m, d, div, civ ct rec from 1901; Co Rcdr has Ind rec)

| * **Cottonwood** | G3 | 1857 | Brown |

Cottonwood County, 900 3rd Ave, Windom, MN 56101-1699 . . . . (507)831-1905
(Clk Dis Ct has b, m, d, div & civ ct rec from 1871)

| * **Crow Wing** | D4 | 1857 | Cass, Aitkin |

Crow Wing County, 326 Laurel St, Brainerd, MN 56401-3523 . . . . (218)828-3970

| *† **Dakota** | F5 | 1849 | Original county |

Dakota County, 1560 Hwy 55 W, Hastings, MN 55033-2392 . . . . (612)438-4295
(Clk Dis Ct has b & d rec from 1870, m rec from 1857, div & civ ct rec from 1853)

| *† **Dodge** | G5 | 1855 | Olmsted |

Dodge County, PO Box 38, Mantorville, MN 55955-0038 . . . . (507)635-6230
(Clk Dis Ct has b, d, div, civ ct rec from 1870, m rec from 1865, pro rec from 1858, school rec from 1917)

Doty (see St. Louis & Lake)

| *† **Douglas** | E3 | 1858 | Todd |

Douglas County, 305 8th Ave W, Alexandria, MN 56308-1758 . . . . (612)762-2381
(Co Rcdr has b, m, d & Ind rec; Ct Administrator has div, pro & civ ct rec; attached to Stearns until 1866)

| **Faribault** | G4 | 1855 | Blue Earth |

Faribault County, N Main St, Blue Earth, MN 56013 . . . . (507)526-5145
(Ct Administrator has b, m, d & pro rec from 1870, civ ct rec from 1950, naturalization rec; Reg Deed has Ind rec)

| *† **Fillmore** | G6 | 1853 | Wabasha |

Fillmore County, Fillmore St, Preston, MN 55965 . . . . (507)765-2144
(Ct Administrator has b & d rec from 1870, m rec from 1865, div & civ ct rec from 1885, pro rec from 1858; Co Rcdr has Ind rec; State census 1865-1895)

| *† **Freeborn** | G5 | 1857 | Wabasha |

Freeborn County, 411 S Broadway Ave, Albert Lea, MN 56007-4506 . . . . (507)377-5153
(Clk Dis Ct has b & d rec from 1870, m & civ ct, crim rec from 1857; Co Rcdr has Ind rec from 1854; Pro office has pro rec from 1866)

| *† **Goodhue** | F5 | 1853 | Wabasha |

Goodhue County, 509 5th St W Rm 310, Red Wing, MN 55066-2525 . . . . (612)388-8261
(Ct Administrator has b & d rec from 1870, m & pro rec from 1854, div & civ ct rec from 1951; MN Hist Soc has div & civ ct rec from 1854 to 1950; State census to 1925)

| *† **Grant** | E2 | 1868 | Stearns |

Grant County, County Courthouse, Elbow Lake, MN 56531 . . . . (218)685-4520
(Clk Dis Ct has b & d rec from 1877, m rec from 1869, div & civ ct rec from 1883; Pro Judge has pro rec; Reg Deeds has Ind rec)

| * **Hennepin** | F5 | 1852 | Dakota |

Hennepin County, 300 S 6th St, Minneapolis, MN 55487-0001 . . . . (612)348-7574
(Clk Dis Ct has b & d rec from 1870, m, div & civ ct rec from 1853)

Name	Map Index	Date Created	Parent County or Territory From Which Organized

*† **Houston**   G6   1854   Fillmore
Houston County, 304 S Marshall St, Caledonia, MN 55921-1324 .... (507)724-5211
(Clk Dis Ct has b & d rec from 1870, m rec from 1854, civ ct rec from 1856 & div rec; Pro Judge has pro rec; Reg Deeds has Ind rec)

† **Hubbard**   C3   1883   Cass
Hubbard County, 301 Court St, Park Rapids, MN 56470-1421 .... (218)732-3196
(Co Rcdr has b, d & Ind rec; License Center has m rec; Clk Dis Ct has div, pro & civ ct rec)

* **Isanti**   E5   1857   Anoka
Isanti County, 237 2nd Ave SW, Cambridge, MN 55008-1536 .... (612)689-3859
(Clk Dis Ct has b rec from 1869, m rec from 1871, d rec from 1873, bur rec 1900-1908, 1941-1979, div, civ ct rec from 1872, pro rec from 1892; Co Rcdr has Ind rec)

* **Itasca**   C4   1849   Original county
Itasca County, Courthouse, Grand Rapids, MN 55744-2600 .... (218)327-2941
(Clk Dis Ct has b, m, d & pro rec, div & civ ct rec from 1950; MN Hist Soc has div & civ ct rec to 1950 & naturalization rec)

*† **Jackson**   G3   1857   Unorg. Terr
Jackson County, 413 4th St, Jackson, MN 56143-1529 .... (507)847-4400
(Ct Administrator has b, d, div, pro & civ ct rec from 1870, m rec from 1868; Co Rcdr has Ind rec from 1870)

Johnson (see Wilkin)

*† **Kanabec**   E5   1858   Pine
Kanabec County, 18 Vine St N, Mora, MN 55051-1351 .... (612)679-1022
(Clk Dis Ct has b, d rec from 1883, m, div, civ ct rec from 1882, pro rec from 1891; Co Rcdr has Ind rec; Mora City Hall has bur rec)

* **Kandiyohi**   E3   1858   Meeker
Kandiyohi County, 515 Becker Ave SW, Willmar, MN 56201-3281 .... (612)231-6202
(Clk Dis Ct has b, m, d, div, civ ct rec from 1870)

* **Kittson**   A2   1862   Unorg. Terr., formerly Pembina
Kittson County, 410 S 5th St, Hallock, MN 56728 .... (218)843-3632
(Clk Dis Ct has b, m, d, div, pro & civ ct rec from 1880s, Co Rcdr has Ind rec; MN Hist Soc has naturalization rec)

* **Koochiching**   B4   1906   Itasca
Koochiching County, 4th St & 6th Ave, International Falls, MN 56649 .... (218)283-6261
(Clk Dis Ct has b, m, d, div, civ ct, pro rec from 1907)

* **Lac qui Parle**   F2   1871   Brown, Redwood
Lac qui Parle County, 600 6th St, Madison, MN 56256-1233 .... (612)598-3536
[FHL has some cem rec]

* **Lake**   C6   1856   Formerly Doty
Lake County, 601 3rd Ave, Two Harbors, MN 55616 .... (218)834-8300
(Clk Dis Ct has b rec from 1898, m & d rec from 1891, div & civ ct rec from 1892; City Clk has bur rec; Pro Judge has pro rec)

* **Lake of the Woods**   A3   1922   Beltrami
Lake of the Woods County, 206 SE 8th Ave, Baudette, MN 56623 .... (218)634-2836
(Clk Dis Ct has b, m, d, div, pro, civ ct rec from 1923)

* **Le Sueur**   F4   1853   Unorg. Terr
Le Sueur County, 88 South Pk, Le Center, MN 56057 .... (612)357-2251
(Clk Dis Ct has b & d rec from 1870, m rec from 1854, div & civ ct rec from 1880, some school rec from 1920 to 1945; Pro Judge has pro rec from 1855; Reg Deeds has Ind rec from 1850)

*† **Lincoln**   F2   1866   Lyon
Lincoln County, N Rebecca, Ivanhoe, MN 56142 .... (507)694-1529
(Clk Dis Ct has b & m rec from 1879, d & civ ct rec from 1880, div rec from 1891; Pro Judge has pro rec from 1877; Reg Deeds has Ind rec from 1873)

* **Lyon**   F2   1868   Redwood
Lyon County, 607 Main St W, Marshall, MN 56258-3021 .... (507)537-6727
(Clk Dis Ct has b, d rec from 1874, m rec from 1872, div, pro, civ ct rec from 1880; Co Rcdr has Ind rec)

Mahnomen   C3   1906   Becker, Norman
Mahnomen County, PO Box 379, Mahnomen, MN 56557-0379 .... (218)935-5669
(Clk Dis Ct has b, m, d, div & civ ct rec from 1908)

Mankahta (Discontinued)

† **Marshall**   B2   1879   Kittson
Marshall County, 208 E Colbin Ave, Warren, MN 56762 .... (218)745-4851
(Clk Dis Ct has b & d rec from 1884, m rec from 1880, div rec from 1900 & civ ct rec from 1898; Co Rcdr has Ind rec)

*† **Martin**   G4   1857   Faribault, Brown
Martin County, 201 Lake Ave, Fairmont, MN 56031-1845 .... (507)238-3214
(Co Rcdr has b rec from 1874, m rec from 1864, d rec from 1879 & Ind rec; Ct Administrator has div, pro & civ ct rec)

* **McLeod**   F4   1856   Carver
McLeod County, 830 11th St E, Glencoe, MN 55336-2216 .... (612)864-5551
(Ct Administrator has b & d rec from 1870, m, div, pro & civ ct rec from 1865)

*† **Meeker**   E4   1856   Wright, Stearns
Meeker County, 325 N Sibley Ave, Litchfield, MN 55355-2155 .... (612)693-2458
(Clk Dis Ct has b, m, d, div, civ ct rec from 1870, pro rec from 1858, school rec, naturalization rec from 1884; Co Rcdr has Ind rec)

Name	Map Index	Date Created	Parent County or Territory From Which Organized
*† **Mille Lacs**	E4	1857	Kanabec

Mille Lacs County, 635 2nd St SE, Milaca, MN 56353-1305 .... (612)983-2561

Monongalia (Discontinued)

*† **Morrison**	E4	1856	Benton, Stearns

Morrison County, County Courthouse, Little Falls, MN 56345 .... (612)632-2941
(Ct Administrator has b & d rec from 1870, m rec from 1860, div & civ ct rec from 1950; State Archives has div & civ ct rec to 1950; Co Rcdr has Ind rec)

* **Mower**	G5	1855	Fillmore, Freeborn

Mower County, 201 1st St NE, Austin, MN 55912-3475 .... (507)437-9535
(Clk Dis Ct has b, d rec from 1870, m rec from 1865, div, civ ct rec from 1900, pro rec from 1856; Co Rcdr has Ind rec)

† **Murray**	G2	1857	Lyon

Murray County, 2500 28th St, Slayton, MN 56172 .... (507)836-6148
(Clk Dis Ct has b, m, d, div, pro & civ ct rec; Co Rcdr has Ind rec)

*† **Nicollet**	F4	1853	Unorg. Terr

Nicollet County, 501 S Minnesota Ave, Saint Peter, MN 56082-2533 .... (507)931-6800
(Clk Dis Ct has b, d rec from 1870, m rec from 1856, div, pro, civ ct rec from 1853; Co Rcdr has Ind rec)

*† **Nobles**	G2	1857	Jackson

Nobles County, 10th St, Worthington, MN 56187 .... (507)372-8263
(Clk Dis Ct has b, m & d rec from 1872, div rec from 1882 & civ ct rec from 1874; Pro Judge has pro rec)

* **Norman**	C2	1881	Polk

Norman County, 16 3rd Ave E, Ada, MN 56510-1362 .... (218)784-2101
(Clk Dis Ct has b & d rec from 1881, m rec from 1882, some div rec & civ ct rec; Pro Judge has pro rec)

*† **Olmsted**	G6	1855	Unorg. Terr

Olmsted County, 515 2nd St SW, Rochester, MN 55902-3124 .... (507)285-8115
(Clk Dis Ct has incomplete b, d rec from 1871, m rec from 1855, div rec from 1860, civ ct rec from 1858; Coroner and Dept of Health have bur rec; Co Ct has pro rec)

*† **Otter Tail**	D3	1858	Pembina, Cass

Otter Tail County, Junius Ave County Courthouse, Fergus Falls, MN 56537 .... (218)739-2271
(Clk Dis Ct has b, d rec from 1870, m rec from 1869, div rec from 1897, pro, civ ct rec from 1872)

Pembina (changed to Kittson, 1878)

Pennington	B2	1910	Red Lake

Pennington County, PO Box 619, Thief River Falls, MN 56701 .... (218)681-2407
(Clk Dis Ct has b, m, d, div, pro, civ ct rec from 1910; Co Rcdr has Ind rec)

Pierce (Disorganized)

* **Pine**	D5	1856	Unorg. Lands

Pine County, County Courthouse, Pine City, MN 55063 .... (612)629-6781
(Clk Dis Ct has b rec from 1874, d rec from 1879, m, div & civ ct rec from 1871; Pro Judge has pro rec; Reg Deeds has Ind rec)

*† **Pipestone**	G2	1857	Murray

Pipestone County, 408 S Hiawatha Ave, Pipestone, MN 56164-1562 .... (507)825-4494
(Clk Dis Ct has b, m, d, div, pro, civ ct rec from 1877; Co Rcdr has Ind rec)

* **Polk**	C2	1858	Indian Lands

Polk County, 612 N Broadway, Crookston, MN 56716-1452 .... (218)281-5408
(Ct Administrator has b, m, d, pro & civ ct rec from 1875; Co Rcdr has Ind rec)

* **Pope**	E3	1862	Pierce

Pope County, 130 Minnesota Ave E, Glenwood, MN 56334-1628 .... (612)634-5301
(Clk Dis Ct has b, m, d rec from 1870, div, civ ct rec from 1880, pro rec from 1867)

* **Ramsey**	F5	1849	Original county

Ramsey County, 15 Kellogg Blvd W Rm 286, Saint Paul, MN 55102-1690 .... (612)298-5980
(Clk Dis Ct has b & d rec from 1870, m rec from 1850, div & civ ct rec from 1900, pro rec from 1849; Hist Soc has civ ct rec from 1858 to 1899 & Ind rec)

Red Lake	B2	1896	Polk

Red Lake County, 100 Langavin St, Red Lake Falls, MN 56750 .... (218)253-2598
(Ct Administrator has b, m, d, div, pro & civ ct rec from 1897, school rec from 1900 to 1955; Co Rcdr has Ind rec)

*† **Redwood**	F3	1862	Brown

Redwood County, PO Box 130, Redwood Falls, MN 56283-0130 .... (507)637-8325
(Ct Administrator has b, m & d rec from 1865, div rec from 1871, pro rec from 1877, civ ct rec from 1867; Co Rcdr has Ind rec)

*† **Renville**	F3	1855	Unorg. Terr

Renville County, 500 DePue Ave E, Olivia, MN 56277-1334 .... (612)523-2080
(Clk Dis Ct has b, m, d rec from 1870 div, pro, civ ct rec; Co Rcdr has Ind rec)

*† **Rice**	F5	1853	Original county

Rice County, 218 3rd St NW, Faribault, MN 55021-5146 .... (507)334-2281
(Clk Dis Ct has b, d, div, pro, civ ct rec from 1870; m rec from 1856, bur rec; Co Rcdr has Ind rec)

*† **Rock**	G2	1857	Nobles as Unorg. Co. Brown

Rock County, PO Box 245, Luverne, MN 56156-0245 .... (507)283-9501
(Clk Dis Ct has b, m, d, div & civ ct rec from 1872)

Name	Map Index	Date Created	Parent County or Territory From Which Organized

* **Roseau**   A3   1894   Kittson
Roseau County, 216 Center St W, Roseau, MN 56751-1498 .... (218)463-2541
(Clk Dis Ct has b, m, d, div & civ ct rec from 1895; Pro Judge has pro rec from 1895; Reg Deeds has Ind rec)

* **Saint Louis**   C5   1856   Doty (now Lake)
Saint Louis County, 100 N 5th Ave W, Duluth, MN 55802-1202 .... (218)726-2380
(Clk Dis Ct has b, d, m rec from 1870, bur permits from 1938, div, civ ct rec from 1859, Ind rec from 1859; Co Ct has pro rec; Branch courthouses also at Virginia and Hibbing, MN)

† **Scott**   F4   1853   Dakota
Scott County, 428 Holmes St S Rm 212, Shakopee, MN 55379-1348 .... (612)445-7750

*† **Sherburne**   E4   1856   Benton
Sherburne County, 13880 Hwy 10, Elk River, MN 55330-4601 .... (612)441-3844
(Ct Administrator has b & d rec from 1870, m rec from 1858, div rec from 1884, pro rec from 1893, civ ct rec from 1877; Co Rcdr has Ind rec)

* **Sibley**   F4   1853   Unorg. Terr
Sibley County, 400 Court St, Gaylord, MN 55334 .... (612)237-2427
(Ct Administrator has b, d & div rec from 1860, m rec from 1856, pro & civ ct rec from 1870; Co Rcdr has Ind rec from 1855)

*† **Stearns**   E4   1855   Indian Lands
Stearns County, PO Box 1378, Saint Cloud, MN 56302-1378 .... (612)259-3620
(Ct Administrator has div, pro & civ ct rec from 1870; Co Rcdr has Ind rec; License Center has b, m & d rec)

* **Steele**   G5   1855   Unorg. Terr., Dodge
Steele County, 111 E Main St, Owatonna, MN 55060-3052 .... (507)451-8040
(Clk Dis Ct has b & d rec from 1870, m rec from 1855, div, pro & civ ct rec from 1858; Co Rcdr has Ind rec from 1858)

* **Stevens**   E2   1862   Pierce, Big Stone
Stevens County, PO Box 530, Morris, MN 56267-0530 .... (612)589-4764
(Clk Dis Ct has b, d rec from 1872, m rec from 1869, div, civ ct rec from 1873, pro rec from 1901; Co Rcdr has Ind rec from 1871; cem sexton has bur rec)

Superior (changed to Saint Louis, 1855)

* **Swift**   E2   1870   Chippewa, Unorg. Lands
Swift County, PO Box 110, Benson, MN 56215-0110 .... (612)843-2744
(Clk Dis Ct has b rec from 1870, m, div, civ ct rec from 1871, d rec from 1872, pro rec; Co Rcdr has Ind rec)

* **Todd**   D3   1855   Stearns
Todd County, 215 1st Ave S, Long Prairie, MN 56347-1351 .... (612)732-4431
(Clk Dis Ct has div rec from 1880, civ ct rec from 1874, pro rec; Co Rcdr has b & d rec from 1870, m rec from 1867, land rec, school census from 1914)

Toombs (changed to Andy Johnson Co, 1858; changed to Wilkin Co, 1868)

*† **Traverse**   E2   1862   Toombs
Traverse County, County Courthouse, Wheaton, MN 56296 .... (612)563-4242
(Clk Dis Ct has b, m, d, div, pro, civ ct & Ind rec from 1881)

*† **Wabasha**   F6   1849   Original county
Wabasha County, 625 Jefferson Ave, Wabasha, MN 55981-1577 .... (612)565-2648
(Ct Administrator has b & d rec from 1870, m rec from 1868, div & civ ct rec)

* **Wadena**   D3   1858   Cass, Todd
Wadena County, Jefferson St, Wadena, MN 56482 .... (218)631-2895
(Clk Dis Ct has b, m & d rec from 1873, div & civ ct rec from 1881)

Wahnata (Disorganized)

* **Waseca**   G4   1857   Steele
Waseca County, 307 N State St, Waseca, MN 56093-2992 .... (507)835-0617
(Clk Dis Ct has b, d, pro & civ ct rec from 1870, m & div rec from 1858)

*† **Washington**   F5   1849   Original county
Washington County, 14900 61st St N, Stillwater, MN 55082-6161 .... (612)439-3220
(Clk Dis Ct has b, d rec from 1870, m rec from 1845, div, civ ct rec from 1847, pro rec from 1850)

* **Watonwan**   G4   1860   Brown
Watonwan County, PO Box 518, Saint James, MN 56081-0518 .... (507)375-3341
(Clk Dis Ct has b, m & d rec from 1863, div & civ ct rec from 1865; Pro Judge has pro rec; Reg Deeds has Ind rec)

Wilkin   D2   1858   Cass, Toombs, Johnson
Wilkin County, 5th St S, Breckenridge, MN 56520 .... (218)643-4972
(Clk Dis Ct has b rec from 1874, m & div rec from 1890, d rec from 1875, civ ct rec from 1858; Pro Judge has pro rec)

* **Winona**   G6   1854   Unorg. Terr
Winona County, 171 W 3rd St, Winona, MN 55987-3192 .... (507)457-6320
(Clk Dis Ct has b & d rec from 1870, m, div & civ ct rec from 1854, pro rec from 1871, school rec from 1909 to 1939)

*† **Wright**   E4   1855   Hennepin
Wright County, 10 2nd St NW, Buffalo, MN 55313-1165 .... (612)682-3900
(Clk Dis Ct has b & d rec from 1871, m rec from 1866, div & civ ct rec from 1870; Pro Judge has pro rec; Reg Deeds has Ind rec)

Name	Map Index	Date Created	Parent County or Territory From Which Organized
*† **Yellow Medicine**	F2	1871	Redwood

Yellow Medicine County, 415 9th Ave, Granite Falls, MN 56241-1367 .... (612)564-3325
(Clk Dis Ct has b, m rec from 1872, d, div, pro, civ ct rec, naturalization rec from 1872; Co Rcdr has Ind rec)

* At least one county history has been published about this county.
† Inventory of county archives was made by the Historical Records Survey. (See Introduction)

MISSISSIPPI

CAPITAL · JACKSON — TERRITORY 1798 — STATE 1817 (20th)
State Map on Page M-22

Spaniards, including Hernando de Soto, first explored this area between 1539 and 1542. The French, led by Marquette and Joliet, explored the area in 1673 and claimed the Mississippi Valley for France in 1682. They established a settlement at Biloxi in 1699 and at Fort Rosalie (now Natchez) in 1716. The British gained control of Mississippi in 1763. Grants of land near Natchez, given to retired English military officers, resulted in migration of Protestants to the formerly Catholic region. During the Revolutionary War, the Natchez District remained loyal to England. Many Tories from the colonies moved into the area at this time. Between 1779 and 1781, Spain took control of the Natchez District. In 1783, Spain gained western Florida, which included part of Mississippi.

The Georgia legislature authorized the Yazoo land sales between 1789 and 1794, bringing hundreds of settlers into the area. Mississippi was made a territory in 1798, with Natchez as the capital. Georgia abandoned claims to the northern portion in 1802 and Spain relinquished the Gulf Coast region during the War of 1812. Thousands of settlers soon entered the area from the eastern and northern states. In 1817, the eastern part of the territory was severed and became the Alabama Territory. Later the same year, Mississippi became the 20th state. Another land boom occurred in 1837, when the last of the Indian lands were opened up to settlement. Mississippi's white population in 1850 was mostly of British extraction, with a few small colonies of Greeks and Italians.

In 1861, Mississippi seceded from the Union. Estimates suggest that over 112,000 men served in the Confederate forces, while just over 500 fought for the Union. Mississippi was readmitted to the Union in 1870.

A few counties kept birth and death records from as early as 1879. State registration of births and deaths began in November 1912. General compliance was not reached until 1921. Records are available from Vital Records, State Board of Health, P.O. Box 1700, Jackson, MS 39215. To verify current fees, call 601-354-6606.

The Mississippi Department of Archives and History, 100 South State Street, P.O. Box 571, Jackson, MS 39205, has early censuses and tax rolls, newspaper files, microfilms of the Federal Censuses, records of Mississippi's Confederate soldiers, and some birth and death records. Wills, deeds, and probate files are held by the chancery clerks or probate courts in each county. Some early land records have been published. Federal land case files are at the National Archives, Atlanta Branch, 1557 St. Joseph Avenue, East Point, GA 30334. Territorial and state censuses were frequently taken between 1792 and 1866 for various counties. Published indexes are available for many of them.

Genealogical Archives, Libraries and Societies

Attala County Library, 328 Goodman St., Kosciusko, MS 39090

Batesville Public Library, 106 College Street, Batesville, MS 38606

Biloxi Public Library, P. O. Box 467, Biloxi, MS 39533

Columbus Public Library, 314 N. 7th St., Columbus, MS 39701

Dept. of Archives and History, Archives History Bldg., Capitol Green, Jackson, MS 39205

Evans Memorial Library, Aberdeen, MS 39730

Greenwood-Leflore Public Library, 408 W. Washington, Greenwood, MS 38930

Gulfport-Harrison County Public Library, Box 4018, 14th St. & 21st Ave., Gulfport, MS 39501

Historical Trails Library, Route 1, Box 373, Philadelphia, MS 39350

Jackson-George Regional Library System, headquarters in Pascagoula City Library, 3214 Pascagoula Street, P. O. Box 937, Pascagoula, MS 39567

Jennie Stephens Smith Library, Box 846, Court Ave. & Main St., New Albany, MS 38652

Lafayette County-Oxford Public Library, 401 Bramlett Blvd., Oxford, MS 38655

Lauren Rogers Memorial Library and Museum, P. O. Box 1108, 5th at 7th St., Laurel, MS 39440

L. W. Anderson Genealogical Library, P. O. Box 1647, Gulfport, MS 39502

Marks-Quitman County Library, 315 E. Main, Marks, MS 38646

McCain Library & Archives, University of Southern Mississippi, Southern Station, Box 5148, Hattiesburg, MS 39406-5148

Meridian Public Library, 2517 7th St., Meridian, MS 39301

Northeast Regional Library, 1023 Fillmore, Corinth, MS 38834

Public Library, 341 Main St., Greenville, MS 38701

Public Library, Vicksburg, MS 39180

Union County, Library, P. O. Box 22, New Albany, MS 38652

University of Mississippi Library, University, MS 38652

Aberdeen Genealogical Society, Mrs. William Nickles, Pres., Aberdeen, MS 39730

Chickasaw County Historical and Genealogical Society, 101 Tindall Circle, Houston, MS 38851

Genealogical Society of DeSoto County, Mississippi, P. O. Box 303, Hernando, MS 38632

Historical and Genealogical Society of Panola County, 105 Church Street, Batesville, MS 38606

Itawamba County Historical Society, P. O. Box 7G, Mantachie, MS 38855

Jackson County Genealogical Society, P. O. Box 984, Pascagoula, MS 39567

Mississippi Coast Genealogical and Historical Society, P. O. Box 513, Biloxi, MS 39530.

Mississippi Dept. of Archives and History, P. O. Box 571, Jackson, MS 39205

Mississippi Genealogical Society, P. O. Box 5301, Jackson, MS 39216

Mississippi Society, Sons of the American Revolution, 529 Pawnee Way, Madison, MS 39110

Northeast Mississippi Historical and Genealogical Society, P. O. Box 434, Tupelo, MS 38801.

Ocean Springs Genealogy Society, P. O. Box 1055, Ocean Springs, MS 39564

Rankin County Historical Society, P. O. Box 841, Brandon, MS 39042

Skipwith Historical and Genealogical Society, Inc., P. O. Box 1382, Oxford, MS 38655

South Mississippi Genealogical Society, Southern Station, Box 5148, Hattiesburg, MS 39406-5148

Tate County Mississippi Genealogical and Historical Society, P. O. Box 974, Senatobia, MS 38668

Vicksburg Genealogical Sociey, Inc., 104 Evelyn St., Vicksburg, MS 39180

West Chickasaw County Genealogy and Historical Society, P. O. Box 42, Houston, MS 38851

Printed Census Records and Mortality Schedules

Federal Census 1820, 1830 (except Pike County), 1840, 1850, 1860 (except Hancock, Washington, and Tallahatchie counties), 1870, 1880, 1900, 1910

Union Veterans and Widows 1890

State/Territorial Census 1810, 1816, 1822-1825, 1837, 1841, 1845, 1853, 1866

Valuable Printed Sources

Atlases, Maps, and Gazetteers

Mississippi Maps, 1816-1873. Jackson, Mississippi: Mississippi Historical Society, 1974.

Oakley, Bruce C. *A Postal History of Mississippi's Stampless Period, 1799-1860.* Baldwyn, Mississippi: Magnolia Publishers, 1969.

Bibliographies

Survey of Records in Mississippi Court Houses. Jackson, Mississippi: Mississippi Genealogical Society, 1967.

Genealogical Research Guides

Wright, Norman Edgar. *North American Genealogical Sources: Southern States.* Provo, Utah: Brigham Young University Press, 1968.

Genealogical Sources

King, J. Estelle Stewart. *Mississippi Court Records, 1799-1835.* Baltimore: Genealogical Publishing Co., 1969.

Rowland, Mrs. Dunbar. *Mississippi Territory in the War of 1812.* Baltimore: Genealogical Publishing Co., 1968.

MISSISSIPPI COUNTY DATA
State Map on Page M-22

Name	Map Index	Date Created	Parent County or Territory From Which Organized
* **Adams**	G1	1799	Natchez District
Adams County, 1 Court St, Natchez, MS 39120-2011 .... (601)446-6684			
[FHL has some m, cem, civ ct, pro, lnd rec]			
* **Alcorn**	B5	1870	Tippah, Tishomingo
Alcorn County, PO Box 112, Corinth, MS 38834-0112 .... (601)286-7700			
(Clk Chan Ct has div rec from 1913 & chan ct rec; Clk Cir Ct has civ ct rec from 1860)			

Name	Map Index	Date Created	Parent County or Territory From Which Organized

*† Amite   G2   1809   Wilkinson
Amite County, PO Box 680, Liberty, MS 39645 .... (601)657-8022
[FHL has some m, cem, civ ct, Ind, pro rec]

* Attala   D4   1833   Choctaw Cession
Attala County, W Washington St, Kosciusko, MS 39090 .... (601)289-2921
(Clk Cir Ct has m rec; Clk Chan Ct has div, pro, Ind & old newspapers)

Bainbridge (created from Covington in 1823, discontinued in 1824)

Benton   B4   1870   Marshall, Tippah
Benton County, Main St, Ashland, MS 38603 .... (601)224-6611
(Chan Clk has div, pro, deeds & wills from 1871)

* Bolivar   C2   1836   Choctaw Cession
Bolivar County, 401 S Court St, Cleveland, MS 38732-2696 .... (601)843-2071
(Clk Cir Ct, Cleveland Miss has m & civ ct rec; Clk Chan Ct has div, pro & Ind rec) (Clk Cir Ct, Rosedale Miss has m rec from 1866, civ ct rec from 1870; Clk Chan Ct has div, pro & Ind rec) (Chan & Cir Clks office in both Courthouses. Rosedale rec go back about 20 years further than Cleveland, it being the older of the two towns)

* Calhoun   C4   1852   Lafayette, Yalobusha
Calhoun County, PO Box 8, Pittsboro, MS 38951-0008 .... (601)983-3117
(Courthouse burned in 1922) (Clk Chan Ct has m, div, pro, civ ct & Ind rec from 1922, Ind abstracts from 1852)

* Carroll   D3   1833   Choctaw Cession
Carroll County, PO Box 291, Carrollton, MS 38917-0291 .... (601)237-9283
(Co Clk has m, div, pro, civ ct & Ind rec from 1870)

* Chickasaw   C5   1836   Chickasaw Cession, 1832
Chickasaw County, County Courthouse, Houston, MS 38851 .... (601)456-2513
(Clk Cir Ct, Houston has m, div, pro, civ ct rec & all Ind rec for Co) (Clk Cir Ct, Okolona has m rec from 1877 & civ ct rec; Clk Chan Ct has div & pro rec from 1886)

* Choctaw   D4   1833   Chickasaw Cession of 1832
Choctaw County, 112 Quinn St, Ackerman, MS 39735 .... (601)285-6329
(Clk Cir Ct has m, div, pro, civ ct, Ind rec from 1881)

* Claiborne   F2   1802   Jefferson
Claiborne County, PO Box 449, Port Gibson, MS 39150-0449 .... (601)437-5841
(Chan Clk has m rec from 1816, div rec from 1856, pro & civ ct rec from 1802)

* Clarke   F5   1812   Washington
Clarke County, PO Box M, Quitman, MS 39355-1013 .... (601)776-2126
(Chan Clk has div & pro rec from 1875)

* Clay   C5   1871   Chickasaw, Lowndes, Monroe, Oktibbeha (formerly Colfax)
Clay County, PO Box 815, West Point, MS 39773-0815 .... (601)494-3124
(Clk Cir Ct has m, civ ct rec; Clk Chan Ct has div, pro, Ind rec from 1872)

* Coahoma   C2   1836   Chickasaw Cession, 1836
Coahoma County, 115 1st St, Clarksdale, MS 38614-4227 .... (601)624-3001
(Clk Cir Ct has m, civ ct rec from 1848; crim ct rec, voter rec from 1949; Clk Chan Ct has div, pro, Ind rec)

Colfax   1871   Name changed to Clay, 1876

* Copiah   F3   1823   Hinds
Copiah County, PO Box 507, Hazlehurst, MS 39083-0507 .... (601)894-3021
(Clk Chan Ct has div rec from 1840, pro & Ind rec from 1825, confederate veterans rec; Clk Cir Ct has m rec from 1825 & civ ct rec)

Covington   G4   1819   Lawrence, Wayne
Covington County, PO Box 1679, Collins, MS 39428-1679 .... (601)765-4242
(Clk Chan Ct has m, div & pro rec from 1900, civ ct rec & Ind rec from 1860)

De Soto   B3   1836   Indian Lands
De Soto County, 2535 Hwy 51 S Courthouse Sq, Hernando, MS 38632-2134 .... (601)429-5011
(Clk Chan Ct has div, pro & Ind rec)

† Forrest   G4   1906   Perry
Forrest County, 629 Main St, Hattiesburg, MS 39401-3453 .... (601)582-3213
[FHL has some m, cem, Ind, pro rec]

Franklin   G2   1809   Adams
Franklin County, PO Box 297, Meadville, MS 39653-0297 .... (601)384-2330
[FHL has some m, cem, civ ct, Ind, pro rec]

* George   H5   1910   Greene, Jackson
George County, Courthouse Sq, Lucedale, MS 39452 .... (601)947-7506
(Clk Cir Ct has m rec & civ ct rec from 1911; Clk Chan Ct has div, pro & Ind rec from 1911)

Greene   G5   1811   Amite, Franklin, Wayne
Greene County, PO Box 610, Leakesville, MS 39451-0610 .... (601)394-2377
[FHL has some m, cem, Ind, pro rec]

† Grenada   C3   1870   Carroll, Yalobusha, Choctaw, Talahatchie, Webster, Montgomery
Grenada County, PO Box 1208, Grenada, MS 38901-1208 .... (601)226-1821
(Clk Cir Ct has m rec, div, pro rec from 1870, Ind rec from 1835)

Name	Map Index	Date Created	Parent County or Territory From Which Organized
* **Hancock**	I4	1812	Mobile District

Hancock County, 242 Main St, Bay Saint Louis, MS 39520-3595 .... (601)467-5404
(Clk Cir Ct has m & civ ct rec; Clk Chan Ct has div, pro & Ind rec)

Harrison   I5   1841   Hancock, Jackson
Harrison County, 1801 23rd Ave, Gulfport, MS 39501-2983 .... (601)865-4001
(Clk Cir Ct has m rec from 1841 & civ ct rec; Clk Chan Ct has div, pro & Ind rec)

* **Hinds**   F3   1821   Choctaw Cession, 1820
Hinds County, PO Box 686, Jackson, MS 39205-0686 .... (601)968-6501
(Clk Cir Ct has m rec from 1823, civ ct rec from 1930; Clk Chan Ct has div, pro, Ind rec)

Holmes   D3   1833   Yazoo
Holmes County, PO Box 239, Lexington, MS 39095-0239 .... (601)834-2508
(Chan Clk has div & pro rec from 1894, also deeds, wills from 1833 & bur rec; Clk Cir Ct has m, civ ct rec)

† **Humphreys**   D2   1918   Holmes, Washington, Yazoo, Sunflower
Humphreys County, PO Box 547, Belzoni, MS 39038-0547 .... (601)247-1740
(Clk Cir Ct has b & m rec; Clk Chan Ct has div, pro & Ind rec from 1918)

Issaquena   E2   1844   Washington
Issaquena County, PO Box 27, Mayersville, MS 39113-0027 .... (601)873-2761
(Clk Chan Ct has m rec from 1866, div, pro, civ ct & Ind rec from 1850)

Itawamba   B5   1836   Chickasaw Cession, 1832
Itawamba County, 201 W Main St, Fulton, MS 38843-1153 .... (601)862-3421
(Clk Chan Ct has m, div, pro, civ ct & Ind rec)

* **Jackson**   H5   1812   Mobile District
Jackson County, 3109 Canty St, Pascaqoula, MS 39567-4209 .... (601)769-3131
(Clk Chan Ct has div & pro rec from 1875, also justice of the peace dockets & licenses of physicians & dentists from 1875; Clk Cir Ct has m rec from 1875)

* **Jasper**   F4   1833   Indian Lands
Jasper County, Court St, Bay Springs, MS 39422 .... (601)764-3368
(Co Clk has div, pro & civ ct rec from 1906; Cir Clk has m rec)

* **Jefferson**   F2   1799   Natchez, originally Pickering
Jefferson County, 307 Main St, Fayette, MS 39069 .... (601)786-3021
(Clk Chan Ct has m rec from 1798, div rec from 1860, pro & Ind rec from 1798)

Jefferson Davis   G3   1906   Covington, Lawrence
Jefferson Davis County, PO Box 1137, Prentiss, MS 39474-1137 .... (601)792-4204

Jones   G4   1826   Covington, Wayne
Jones County, PO Box 1468, Laurel, MS 39441-1468 .... (601)428-0527
(Clk Cir Ct has m rec from 1882 & civ ct rec from 1907; Clk Chan Ct at Laurel & Ellisville, Miss has div & Ind rec)

* **Kemper**   E5   1833   Choctaw Cession, 1832
Kemper County, PO Box 188, De Kalb, MS 39328-0188 .... (601)743-2460
(Clk Cir Ct has m rec from 1912; Clk Chan Ct has div, pro, civ ct & Ind rec from 1912)

* **Lafayette**   B4   1836   Chickasaw Cession
Lafayette County, PO Box 1240, Oxford, MS 38655-1240 .... (601)234-7563
(Chan Clk has m, div, pro & civ ct rec)

*† **Lamar**   G4   1904   Marion, Pearl River
Lamar County, PO Box 247, Purvis, MS 39475-0247 .... (601)794-8504
(Clk Cir Ct has m rec; Clk Chan Ct has div, pro & Ind rec from 1900s; JP has civ ct rec)

* **Lauderdale**   E5   1833   Choctaw Cession
Lauderdale County, 500 Constitution Ave, Meridian, MS 39301-5160 .... (601)482-9714
(Clk Chan Ct has div, pro & Ind rec; Co Health has b & d rec; Clk Cir Ct has m & civ ct rec)

Lawrence   G3   1814   Marion
Lawrence County, PO Box 40, Monticello, MS 39654-0040 .... (601)587-7162
(Clk Cir Ct has m & civ ct rec; Clk Chan Ct has div, pro & Ind rec from 1815)

* **Leake**   E4   1833   Choctaw Cession
Leake County, Court Sq, Carthage, MS 39051 .... (601)267-7372
(Clk Chan Ct has m rec, div, pro rec from 1871, civ ct rec, Ind rec from 1833, wills from 1840, mil discharge rec from 1918)

Lee   B5   1866   Itawamba, Pontotoc
Lee County, 300 W Main St, Tupelo, MS 38801-3920 .... (601)841-9100
(Clk Chan Ct has div, pro & Ind rec; Clk Cir Ct has m rec; Justice Ct has civ ct rec)

* **Leflore**   D3   1871   Carroll, Sunflower, Tallahatchie
Leflore County, 315 W Market St, Greenwood, MS 38930-4330 .... (601)453-1041
(Clk Cir Ct has m & civ ct rec; Clk Chan Ct has div & pro rec from 1871 & Ind rec from 1834)

Lincoln   G3   1870   Franklin, Lawrence, Copiah, Pike, Amite
Lincoln County, 300 S 1st St, Brookhaven, MS 39601-3321 .... (601)835-3411
(Clk Chan Ct has div, pro & civ ct rec from 1893; Clk Dis Ct has m rec from 1893)

* **Lowndes**   D5   1830   Monroe
Lowndes County, PO Box 1364, Columbus, MS 39703-1364 .... (601)329-5880
(m, div, pro, civ ct, Ind rec from 1830 to 1900 are at the Lowndes Co Dept of Archives and History, also Bible rec, manuscripts, cen rec. All recs for this county are complete from 1830 to date)

Name	Map Index	Date Created	Parent County or Territory From Which Organized

* **Madison**   E3   1828   Yazoo
Madison County, PO Box 404, Canton, MS   39046-0404 .... (601)859-1177
(Clk Chan Ct has m, div, pro, civ ct & lnd rec from 1828)

* **Marion**   G3   1811   Amite, Wayne, Franklin
Marion County, 502 Broad St Suite 2, Columbia, MS   39429-3037 .... (601)736-2691
(Clk Chan Ct has m, div, pro, civ ct & lnd rec)

Marshall   B4   1836   Chickasaw Cession, 1832
Marshall County, PO Box 219, Holly Springs, MS   38635-0219 .... (601)252-4431
(Clk Chan Ct has div, pro & deeds from 1836)

* **Monroe**   C5   1821   Chickasaw Cession, 1821
Monroe County, PO Box 578, Aberdeen, MS   39730-0578 .... (601)369-8143
(Clk Cir Ct has m & civ ct rec; Clk Chan Ct has div rec, pro & lnd rec from 1821)

Montgomery   D4   1871   Carroll, Choctaw
Montgomery County, PO Box 71, Winona, MS   38967-0071 .... (601)283-2333
(Clk Chan Ct has div, pro, civ ct, lnd rec from 1871; Clk Cir Ct has m rec)

Neshoba   E4   1833   Chocktaw Cession, 1830
Neshoba County, PO Box 67, Philadelphia, MS   39350-0067 .... (601)656-3581
(Clk Chan Ct has div, pro rec from 1890; Clk Cir Ct has m rec from 1912)

* **Newton**   E4   1836   Neshoba
Newton County, PO Box 68, Decatur, MS   39327-0068 .... (601)635-2367
(Clk Chan Ct has div, pro, civ ct, wills & deed rec from 1876; Clk Cir Ct has m rec)

Noxubee   D5   1833   Choctaw Cession, 1830
Noxubee County, PO Box 147, Macon, MS   39341-0147 .... (601)726-4243
(Clk Cir Ct has m & civ ct rec from 1834; Clk Chan Ct has div, pro & lnd rec from 1834)

* **Oktibbeha**   D5   1833   Choctaw Cession, 1830
Oktibbeha County, 101 E Main St, Starkville, MS   39759-2955 .... (601)323-5834
(Clk Chan Ct has div, pro & civ ct rec from 1880, lnd rec from 1834; Clk Cir Ct has m rec)

* **Panola**   B3   1836   Chickasaw Cession, 1832
Panola County, 151 Public Sq, Batesville, MS   38606-2220 .... (601)563-6205
(Clk Chan Ct has div & pro rec from 1836; Clk Cir Ct has m rec from 1885, civ ct rec from 1836)

*† **Pearl River**   H4   1890   Hancock, Marion
Pearl River County, PO Box 431, Poplarville, MS   39470-0431 .... (601)795-2237
(Clk Chan Ct has div, pro & civ ct rec from 1890; Clk Cir Ct has m rec)

Perry   G5   1820   Greene
Perry County, PO Box 198, New Augusta, MS   39462-0198 .... (601)964-8398
(Clk Chan Ct has div, pro, civ ct & lnd rec from 1878; Clk Cir Ct has m rec from 1877)

Pickering (changed to Jefferson, 1802)

* **Pike**   G3   1815   Marion
Pike County, PO Box 309, Magnolia, MS   39652-0309 .... (601)783-3362
(Clk Chan Ct has div, pro, civ ct, lnd rec from 1882; Clk Cir Ct has m rec)

* **Pontotoc**   C5   1836   Chickasaw Cession, 1832
Pontotoc County, PO Box 209, Pontotoc, MS   38863-0209 .... (601)489-3900
(Clk Cir Ct has m rec from 1836 to 1840 missing, also m rec from July 1867 through all of 1870s are missing; Clk Chan Ct has pro, civ ct, lnd rec from 1836, div rec)

* **Prentiss**   B5   1870   Tishomingo
Prentiss County, PO Box 477, Booneville, MS   38829-0477 .... (601)728-8151
(Clk Chan Ct has div, pro & civ ct rec from 1870, lnd rec from 1836; Clk Cir Ct has m rec)

Quitman   C3   1877   Panola, Coahoma
Quitman County, PO Box 100, Marks, MS   38646-0100 .... (601)326-2661
(Clk Chan Ct has div & pro rec from 1877; Clk Cir Ct has m & civ ct rec)

* **Rankin**   F3   1828   Hinds
Rankin County, 221 N Timber St, Brandon, MS   39042-3198 .... (601)825-2217
(Clk Chan Ct has div, pro & lnd rec from 1829)

Scott   E4   1833   Choctaw Cession, 1832
Scott County, PO Box 630, Forest, MS   39074-0630 .... (601)469-1922
(Clk Chan Ct has div, civ ct rec from 1900, pro, deeds, deeds of trust from 1835, also lnd & chattel, old church & cem plots rec; Clk Cir Ct has m rec)

Sharkey   E2   1876   Warren, Washington, Issaquena
Sharkey County, County Courthouse, Rolling Fork, MS   39159 .... (601)873-2755
[FHL has some m, civ ct, lnd, pro rec]

* **Simpson**   F3   1824   Choctaw Cession, 1820
Simpson County, 109 W Pine Ave, Mendenhall, MS   39114-3597 .... (601)847-2626
(Clk Cir Ct has m & civ ct rec; Clk Chan Ct has div rec from 1880, some pro & lnd rec)

* **Smith**   F4   1833   Choctaw Cession, 1820
Smith County, Main St, Raleigh, MS   39153 .... (601)782-4751
(Clk Cir Ct has m rec from 1912; Clk Chan Ct has div, pro, civ ct & lnd rec from 1892)

Name	Map Index	Date Created	Parent County or Territory From Which Organized
Stone	H5	1916	Harrison

Stone County, PO Box 7, Wiggins, MS   39577-0007 .... (601)928-5266
(Clk Chan Ct has div, pro, Ind rec, veteran's mil discharges from 1916; Clk Cir Ct has m, civ ct rec)

Sumner (changed to Webster, 1882)

* **Sunflower**	C2	1844	Bolivar

Sunflower County, 2nd St, Indianola, MS   38751 .... (601)887-4703
(Clk Chan Ct has m, div, pro, civ ct, Ind rec from 1871)

Tallahatchie	C3	1833	Choctaw Cession, 1820

Tallahatchie County, PO Box H, Charleston, MS   38921-0330 .... (601)647-5551
(Clk Cir Ct has m rec from 1909; Clk Chan Ct has div & pro rec from 1909 & Ind rec from 1858)

* **Tate**	B3	1873	Marshall, Tunica, DeSoto

Tate County, 201 S Ward St, Senatobia, MS   38668-2616 .... (601)562-5661
(Clk Cir Ct has m rec from 1873; Clk Chan Ct has div, pro, civ ct & Ind rec from 1873)

*† **Tippah**	B5	1836	Chickasaw Cession, 1832

Tippah County, PO Box 99, Ripley, MS   38663-0099 .... (601)837-7374
(Clk Chan Ct or Clk Cir Ct has m rec from 1856, also div, pro & civ ct rec from 1856)

* **Tishomingo**	B6	1836	Chickasaw Cession, 1832

Tishomingo County, 1008 Hwy 25 S, Iuka, MS   38852-1020 .... (601)423-7010
(Clk Chan Ct has div, pro, civ ct & Ind rec; Clk Cir Ct has m rec)

† **Tunica**	B3	1836	Chickasaw Cession, 1832

Tunica County, PO Box 217, Tunica, MS   38676-0217 .... (601)363-2451
(Clk Chan Ct has div, pro, civ ct & Ind rec; Clk Cir Ct has m rec)

* **Union**	B5	1870	Pontotoc, Tippah

Union County, 109 Main St, New Albany, MS   38652 .... (601)534-1900
(Clk Chan Ct has div, pro & civ ct rec; Clk Cir Ct has m rec)

† **Walthall**	G3	1910	Marion, Pike

Walthall County, PO Box 351, Tylertown, MS   39667-0351 .... (601)876-4947
(Clk Cir Ct has m rec from 1914; Clk Chan Ct has div, pro, civ ct, Ind rec from 1914)

* **Warren**	F2	1809	Natchez District

Warren County, PO Box 351, Vicksburg, MS   39181-0351 .... (601)636-4415
(Clk Chan Ct has div, pro, civ ct & Ind rec; Clk Cir Ct has m rec)

* **Washington**	D2	1827	Warren, Yazoo

Washington County, PO Box 309, Greenville, MS   38702-0309 .... (601)332-1595
(Clk Cir Ct has m rec from 1858, civ ct rec from 1890; Clk Chan Ct has div rec from 1856, pro, Ind rec from 1831)

* **Wayne**	G5	1809	Washington

Wayne County, Azalea Dr, Waynesboro, MS   39367 .... (601)735-2873
(Clk Chan Ct has m, bur, div, pro, civ ct & Ind rec)

* **Webster**	D4	1874	Montgomery, Chickasaw, Choctaw, Oktibbeha

Webster County, Main St, Walthall, MS   39771-9999 .... (601)258-4131
(Originally Summer, named changed 1882) (Clk Cir Ct has m, civ ct rec; Clk Chan Ct has div, pro, Ind rec from 1800)

Wilkinson	G1	1802	Adams

Wilkinson County, PO Box 516, Woodville, MS   39669-0516 .... (601)888-4381
(Clk Chan Ct has m, div, pro, civ ct & Ind rec)

* **Winston**	D5	1833	Choctaw Cession, 1830

Winston County, 115 S Court Ave, Louisville, MS   39339-2935 .... (601)773-3631
[FHL has some m, cem, civ ct, Ind, pro rec]

* **Yalobusha**	C4	1833	Choctaw Cession, 1830

Yalobusha County, PO Box 664, Water Valley, MS   38965-0664 .... (601)473-2091
(Clk Cir Ct, Coffeyville has m rec; Clk Chan Ct has div, pro, civ ct & Ind rec) (Clk Chan Ct, Water Valley has div, pro, civ ct & Ind rec)

* **Yazoo**	E3	1823	Hinds

Yazoo County, PO Box 68, Yazoo City, MS   39194-0068 .... (601)746-2661
(Clk Chan Ct has m rec from 1845; div, pro, civ ct & Ind rec from 1823, newspapers)

* At least one county history has been published about this county.

† Inventory of county archives was made by the Historical Records Survey. (See Introduction)

MISSOURI

CAPITAL · JEFFERSON CITY — TERRITORY 1812 — STATE 1821 (24th)
State Map on Page M-23

In 1541, De Soto became the first white man to view Missouri. The French explorers Marquette and Joliet followed in 1673 and discovered the Missouri River. Robert Cavelier, Sieur de la Salle, claimed the entire Mississippi River Valley for France in 1682. In 1700, the first settlement was made by the French near the Des Peres River, south of St. Louis, but lasted for only a short time. The first permanent settlement was in 1735, when French lead miners established Ste. Genevieve. France ceded the area to Spain in 1763. Unaware of the cession, the French founded St. Louis the following year. The first American settlement was in 1787 in Ste. Genevieve County. After 1795, Americans mainly from Kentucky, Tennessee, Virginia, and the Carolinas came for the free land Spain was offering. In 1800, Spain returned the region to France. Four years later the majority of the 10,000 residents were American. The Louisiana Purchase in 1803 made Missouri part of the United States. Two years later Missouri became part of the Territory of Louisiana. Missouri became a territory in 1812. Indian raids continued until about 1815, when treaties were signed and settlement increased. When Missouri became a state in 1821, there were about 57,000 white settlers. European immigrants came into the state from Ireland, England, Poland, Switzerland, Bohemia, and Italy to mix with the Americans and descendants of the early French settlers. Mormon immigrants settled in western Missouri in 1831, but were expulsed in 1839. The Platte Purchase of 1837 added six northwestern counties to the state. Missouri was the start of many migrations to the West as both the Santa Fe and Oregon Trails began at Independence, Missouri. Even with all these migrations, Missouri was the fifth most populous state at the end of the Civil War.

In 1861, the legislature considered secession but voted against it. After the start of the Civil War, the governor repudiated Lincoln's call for troops and called up the state militia to fight for the Confederacy. Federal troops defeated the militia, forcing the governor and legislature to flee to the south. A provisional government was installed until the state government was reorganized in 1864. An estimated 40,000 men fought for the Confederacy, while about 109,000 fought for the Union. Numerous battles were fought in the state, which became one of the important battlegrounds of the war.

County clerks were required to register births and deaths from 1883 to 1893. Records still extant can be obtained from the county clerk or the Missouri State Archives, 1001 Industrial Drive, P.O. Box 778, Jefferson City, MO 65102. State registration of births and deaths began in 1863, but did not reach full compliance until 1911. The records after 1910 can be obtained from the Bureau of Vital Records, P.O. Box 570, Jefferson City, MO 65102. To verify current fees for birth records, call 314-751-6387. 573

Some marriages from 1825 to the present may be obtained at the office of the Recorder of Deeds in each county. Some of the earliest land claims and grants have been published. Records of the local land offices are in the Missouri State Archives. Tract book, plat maps, and land patents are at the BLM Eastern States Office, 350 South Pickett Street, Alexandria, VA 22304. Divorce proceedings were filed with a court of common pleas, a circuit court, or the state legislature. Most can be obtained from the circuit court clerk. Unfortunately, many of the county courthouses in Missouri, along with their records, have been burned. The State Historical Society of Missouri, 1020 Lowry, Columbia, MO 65201, has other records which may be of help to researchers. A few Spanish censuses were taken as early as 1772. Portions of Missouri were included in the 1810 census of Louisiana Territory. Missouri Territory took censuses in 1814, 1817, 1819, and 1820, but the latter was destroyed. Incomplete censuses exist for 1821 and at four-year intervals from 1825 to 1863, and in 1876. Copies are at the State Historical Society of Missouri and the Missouri State Archives, as well as some county offices.

Genealogical Archives, Libraries and Societies

Adair County Public Library, Library Lane, Kirksville, MO 63501

Boonslick Regional Library, (serving Boonville, Cooper and Pettis Counties), Sedalia, MO 63501

Cape Girardeau County Genealogical Library, Riverside Regional Library, Box 389, Union St., Jackson, MO 63755

City-County Library, 403 South Jefferson, Neosho, MO 64850

Clay County Archives, P. O. Box 99, Liberty, MO 64068

Clay County Museum Assn. Library, 14 North Main Street, Liberty, MO 64086

Cole County Museum, 109 Madison, Jefferson City, MO 65101

Genealogy Friends of the Library, c / o Phyllis Chancellor Holley, 507 W. Hickory, Neosho, MO 64850

Heritage Library, Johnson County Historical Society, 135 E. Pine St., Warrensburg, MO 64093

Joplin Public Library, 4th and Main Streets, Joplin, MO 64801

Kansas City Public Library, 311 East 12th St., Kansas City, MO 64106

Kent Library, Southeast Missouri Stake College, Cape Girardeau, MO 63701

Keytesville Library, 110 Bridge Street, Keytesville, MO 65261

Maryville Public Library, Genealogy Division, 5th & Main, Maryville, MO 64468

Mercer County Library, 601 Grant, Princeton, MO 64673

Mid-Continent Public Library, Genealogy & Local History Dept., 317 W. 24 Hwy., Independence, MO 64050

Missouri State Library, 308 East High Street, Jefferson City, MO 65101

Newton County Museum Library, 121 N. Washington, P. O. Box 675, Neosho, MO 64850

Records and Archives, Office of Sec. of State Capitol Bldg., Jefferson, MO 65101

Riverside Regional Library, P. O. Box 389, Jackson, MO 63755

St. Louis Public Library, 1301 Olive St., St. Louis, MO 63103

Shelbina Carnegie Public Library, Box 247, 102 N. Center St., Shelbina, MO 63468

Springfield Public Library, Reference Dept. and Shepard Room, 397 E. Central St., Springfield, MO 65801

Adair County Historical Society and Library, 308 S. Franklin St., Kirksville, MO 63501

American Family Records Association, 311 East 12th Street, Kansas City, MO 64106

Andrew County Historical Society, Box 12, Savannah, MO 64485

Audrain County Area Genealogical Society, 305 West Jackson St., Mexico, MO 65265

Audrain County Historical Society, P. O. Box 3, Mexico, MO 65265

Boone County Historical Society, 2205 Ridgemont Court, Columbia, MO 65203

Camden County, Missouri Historical Society, Linn Creek, MO 65052

Cape Girardeau County Missouri Genealogical Society, 204 S. Union Ave., Jackson, MO 63755

Carthage, Missouri Genealogical Society, Rt. 3, Carthage, MO 64836

Cass County Historical Society, 400 E. Mechanic, Harrisonville, MO 64701

Concordia Historical Institute, 301 DeMun Ave., St. Louis, MO 63105

Dallas County Historical Society, P. O. Box 594, Buffalo, MO 65622

Daughters of Union Veterans of the Civil War, 1861-1865, Missouri Department, 8521 Eulalie Ave., Brentwood, MO 63144

DeKalb County Historical Society, P. O. Box 477, Maysville, MO 64469

Excelsior Springs Genealogical Society, P. O. Box 601, Excelsior Springs, MO 64024

Family Tree Climbers, Box 422, Lawson, MO 64062

Four Rivers Genealogical Society, 314 W. Main St., P. O. Box 146, Washington, MO 63090

Genealogical Society of Butler County, Missouri, Inc., P. O. Box 426, Poplar Bluff, MO 63901

Genealogical Society of Central Missouri, P. O. Box 26, Columbia, MO 65205

Genealogical Society of Liberty, P. O. Box 442, Liberty, MO 64068

Genealogy Friends of the Library, P. O. Box 314, Neosho, MO 64850

Genealogy Society of Pulaski County Missouri, P. O. Box 226, Crocker, MO 65452

Genealogy Study Group of the Newton County Historical Society, P. O. Box 675, Neosho, MO 64850

Graham Historical Society, 417 South Walnut, Maryville, MO 64468

Grundy County Genealogical Society, 1715 East 8th St., Trenton, MO 64683

Harrison County Genealogical Society, P. O. Box 65, Bethany, MO 64424

Heart of America Genealogical Society, Public Library, 311 East 12th St., Kansas City, MO 64106

Historical Society of Maries County, Missouri, P. O. Box 289, Vienna, MO 65582

Jackson County Genealogical Society, Box 2145, Independence, MO 64055

Joplin Genealogical Society, P. O. Box 152, Joplin, MO 64802

Kimmswick Historical Society, P. O. Box 41, Kimmswick, MO 63053

Laclede County Genealogical Society, P. O. 350, Lebanon, MO 65536

Lawrence County, Historical Society, P. O. Box 406, Mt. Vernon, MO 65712

Lewis County Historical Society, Inc., 614 Clark Street, Canton, MO 63435

Lincoln County Missouri Genealogical Society, P. O. Box 192, Hawk Point, MO 63349

Linn County, Missouri Genealogy Researchers, 771 Tomahawk, Brookfield, MO 64628

Livingston County, Missouri Genealogical Society, 450 Locust St., Chillicothe, MO 64601

Mari-Osa Heritage Society, P. O. Box 257, Westphalia, MO 65085

Mercer County Genealogical Society, Princeton, MO 64673

Mid-Missouri Genealogical Society, Inc., P. O. Box 715, Jefferson, MO 65102

Mine Au Breton Historical Society Rt. 1, Box 3154, Potosi, MO 63664

Mississippi County Genealogical Society, P. O. Box 5, Charleston, MO 63834

Missouri Baptist Historical Society, William Jewell College Library, Liberty, MO 64068

Missouri Genealogical Society, P. O. Box 382, St. Joseph, MO 64502

Missouri Historical Society, Jefferson Memorial Bldg., Forest Park, St. Louis, MO 63112

Missouri State Genealogical Association, P. O. Box 833, Columbia, MO 65205-0833

Missouri Territorial Pioneers, 3929 Milton Drive, Independence, MO 64055

Moniteau County Missouri Historical Society, California, MO 65018

Morgan County Missouri Historical Society, P. O. Box 177, Versailles, MO 65084

National Archives-Central Plains Region, 2306 East Bannister Rd., Kansas City, MO 64131

Newton County Historical Society, P. O. Box 675, Neosho, MO 64850

Nodaway County Genealogical Society, P. O. Box 214, Maryville, MO 64468

Northwest Missouri Genealogical Society, P. O. Box 382, St. Joseph, MO 64502

Old Mines Area Historical Society, Route 1, Box 300Z, Cadet, Old Mines, MO 63630

Oregon County Genealogical Society, Courthouse, Alton, MO 65606

Ozark County Genealogical and Historical Society, 16 Harlin Hts., Gainesville, MO 65655

Ozarks Genealogical Society, P. O. Box 3494 Dept. GH 1089, Springfield, MO 65804

Phelps County Genealogical Society, Box 571, Rolla, MO 65401

Pike County Genealogical Society, P. O. Box 364, Bowling Green, MO 63334

Platte County Missouri Genealogical Society, P. O. Box 103, Platte City, MO 64079

Randolph County Historical Society, Box 116, Moberly, MO 65270

Ray County Genealogical Association, 809 West Royle, Richmond, MO 64085

Ray County Historical Society, Box 2, Richmond, MO 64085

Reynolds County, Missouri Genealogy and Hisotrical Society, P. O. Box 281, Ellington, MO 63638

St. Charles County Genealogical Society, P. O. Box 715, St. Charles, MO 63301

St. Louis Genealogical Society, 9011 Manchester Rd., Suite 3, St. Louis, MO 63144

Santa Fe Trail Researchers Genealogical Society, Route 1, Franklin, MO 65250

Scotland County Historical Society, P. O. Box 263, Memphis, MO 63555

South-Central Missouri Genealogical Society, 939 Nichols Dr., West Plains, MO 65775

South Vernon Genealogical Society, R-2, Box 280, Sheldon, MO 64784

Southwest Missouri Genealogical Society, 939 Nichols Drive, West Plains, MO 65775

State Historical Society of Missouri, Hitt and Lowry Sts., Columbia, MO 65201

Texas County Missouri Genealogical & Historical Society, Box 12, Houston, MO 65483

Thrailkill Genealogical Society, 2018 Gentry Street, North, Kansas City, MO 64116

Union Cemetery Historical Society, 2727 Main St., Suite 120, Kansas City, MO 64108

Vernon County Genealogical Society, Nevada Public Library, 225 West Austin, Nevada, MO 64772

Vernon County Historical Society, 231 No. Main Street, Nevada, MO 64772

West Central Missouri Genealogical Society, 705 Broad Street, Warrensburg, MO 64093

White River Valley Historical Society, Box 565, Point Lookout, MO 65726

Printed Census Records and Mortality Schedules

Federal Census 1830, 1840, 1850, 1860, 1870, 1880, 1900, 1910
Union Veterans and Widows 1890
State/Territorial Census 1876

Valuable Printed Sources

Atlases, Maps, and Gazetteers

Beck, Lewis Caleb. *A Gazetteer of the States of Illinois and Missouri*. New York: Arno Press, 1975 reprint.

Campbell, Robert Allen. *Campbell's Gazetteer of Missouri*. St. Louis: R. A. Campbell, 1875.

Ramsay, Robert Lee. *Our Storehouse of Missouri Place Names*. Columbia, Missouri: University of Missouri, 1952.

Bibliographies

Williams, Betty H. *A Genealogical Tour Through the Courthouses and Libraries of Missouri*. Warrensburg, Missouri: Betty H. Williams, 1972.

Williams, Jacqueline Hogan and Betty Harvey Williams. *Resources for Genealogical Research in Missouri*. Warrensburg, Missouri: Jacqueline Hogan Williams, 1969.

Genealogical Research Guides

Parkin, Robert E. *Guide to Tracing Your Family Tree in Missouri*. St. Louis: Genealogical Research and Publishing, 1979.

Genealogical Sources

Ellsberry, Elizabeth Prather. *Bible Records of Missouri*. Chillicothe, Missouri: Elizabeth Prather Ellsberry, 1963.

Histories

Conrad, Howard L. *Encyclopedia of the History of Missouri*. St. Louis: Southern History Co., 1901.

History of Southeast Missouri. Chicago: Goodspeed Publishing Co., 1888.

Williams, Walter. *A History of Norhtwest Missouri*. Chicago: Lewis Publishing Co., 1915.

MISSOURI COUNTY DATA
State Map on Page M-23

Name	Map Index	Date Created	Parent County or Territory From Which Organized
* **Adair**	E2	1841	Macon

Adair County, County Courthouse, Kirksville, MO 63501 . . . . (816)665-3350
(Co Rcdr has m & Ind rec from 1840; Clk Cir Ct has div & civ ct rec; Pro Clk has pro rec; Co Clk has school enumeration rec)

Allen (changed to Atchison, 1845)

* **Andrew**	G2	1841	Platte Purchase

Andrew County, PO Box 206, Savannah, MO 64485-0206 . . . . (816)324-3624
(Co Clk has b & d rec from 1883 to 1893; Clk Cir Ct has m, div & civ ct rec from 1841; Ind & mil ser rec; Pro Judge has pro rec from 1841)

Arkansas		1813	New Madrid

(abolished 1819 when Terr of Arkansas was formed)

Ashley (changed to Texas, 1845)

Name	Map Index	Date Created	Parent County or Territory From Which Organized

* **Atchison** H2 1843 Holt
Atchison County, PO Box J, Rock Port, MO 64482-0410 . . . . (816)744-2707
(part of Platte Purchase; attached to Holt Co until 1854; lost 10-mile strip to Iowa, 1848)(Co Rcdr has m, d & Ind rec; Clk Cir Ct has d, div & civ ct rec; Co Clk has b rec from 1883 to 1893; Pro Judge has pro rec)

* **Audrain** D3 1831 Monroe
Audrain County, County Courthouse, Mexico, MO 65265 . . . . (314)581-8211
(created in 1831, but remained attached to Callaway, Monroe & Ralls Cos until 1836. In 1842 gained an addtional 31 sq miles from Monroe Co)(Co Clk has b rec from 1883 to 1886; Rcdr Deeds has m & Ind rec; Clk Cir Ct has div & civ ct rec; Pro Judge has pro rec)

* **Barry** F7 1835 Greene
Barry County, County Courthouse, Cassville, MO 65625 . . . . (417)847-2561
(error in survey, rectified in 1876, established the western line 2 1/2 miles east of previous boundary; in 1872 many rec in Cir Clks office were destroyed by fire)(Rcdr Deeds has m & Ind rec; Clk Cir Ct has div & civ ct rec; Pro Judge has pro rec)

* **Barton** G6 1855 Jasper
Barton County, County Courthouse, Lamar, MO 64759 . . . . (417)682-3529
(Courthouse burned in 1860. Co Clk has b rec from 1883 to 1897; d rec from 1883 to 1899; Rcdr Deeds has div, Ind rec; Pro Ct has pro rec; Magistrate Ct, division 2, has civ ct rec)

* **Bates** G5 1841 Cass, Van Buren, Jackson
Bates County, County Courthouse, Butler, MO 64730 . . . . (816)679-3371
(Feb 22, 1855, the three southern tiers of twnships in Cass Co were added to Bates; Courthouse burned in 1861; some rec prior to 1861) (Co Clk has b & d rec from 1883 to 1887; Co Rcdr has m rec from 1860 & Ind rec from 1840; Clk Cir Ct has div rec from 1860; Pro Judge has pro rec)

* **Benton** F5 1835 Pettis, St. Clair
Benton County, PO Box 1238, Warsaw, MO 65355-1238 . . . . (816)438-7326
(Benton remained unorganized until Jan 1837, in 1845, 24 sq miles of northwest part of Benton became parts of Pettis, and Hickory Co was created, reducing Benton to its present size. Co Clk has b, d rec from 1883, m rec from 1839; Clk Cir Ct has div, civ ct rec; Pro Ct has pro rec; Rcdr of Deeds has Ind rec)

* **Bollinger** B6 1851 Cape Girardeau, Stoddard, Wayne
Bollinger County, PO Box 46, Marble Hill, MO 63764-0046 . . . . (314)238-2126
(In 1866 courthouse destroyed by fire, in 1884 courthouse burned while occupied only by the Co Clks office)(Co Clk has b, d rec from 1882 to 1892; Clk Cir Ct and Rcdr has m, div, Ind rec; Cir Judge has pro rec)

* **Boone** E4 1820 Howard
Boone County, 8th & Walnut, Columbia, MO 65201 . . . . (314)874-7574
(Co Clk has m, div, pro, civ ct & Ind rec from 1821)

* **Buchanan** G3 1838 Platte Purchase
Buchanan County, 5th & Jules Sts, Sainte Joseph, MO 64501 . . . . (816)271-1411
(Rcdr Deeds has m rec; Clk Cir Ct has div rec; Pro Judge has pro rec; Mag Ct has civ ct rec; Co Asr has Ind rec)

* **Butler** C7 1849 Wayne
Butler County, County Courthouse, Poplar Bluff, MO 63901 . . . . (314)785-8201
[FHL has some m, cem, civ ct, Ind, pro rec, 1876 census]

* **Caldwell** F3 1836 Ray
Caldwell County, PO Box 67, Kingston, MO 64650-0067 . . . . (816)586-2571
(April 19, 1860 courthouse destroyed by fire, all recs destroyed except those of the pro ct; Nov. 28, 1896 courthouse destroyed by fire)(Rcdr Office has m, Ind rec; Clk Cir Ct has div rec; Division two Cir Ct has pro rec; Division one Cir Ct has civ ct rec)

* **Callaway** D4 1820 Montgomery
Callaway County, 5 E 5th St, Fulton, MO 65251-1700 . . . . (314)642-0730
(Co Clk has b & d rec from 1883 to 1888; Co Rcdr has m & Ind rec; Clk Cir Ct has div rec; Pro Judge has pro rec)

* **Camden** E5 1841 Benton, Pulaski
Camden County, 1 Court Cir, Camdenton, MO 65020 . . . . (314)346-4440
(organized as Kinderhook, renamed Feb 23, 1843; line between Camden & Miller changed in 1845)(Co Rcdr has m & div rec from 1902; Pro Judge has pro rec from 1902; Clk Cir Ct has civ ct rec from 1902; Tompkins Abstract Office has Ind rec; Courthouse burned 1902)

Cape Girardeau B6 1812 Original District
Cape Girardeau County, 1 Barton Sq, Jackson, MO 63755-1866 . . . . (314)243-3547
(present size of county since Mar 5, 1849, courthouse burned in 1870)(Co Clk has b, d rec 1883 to 1893, Ind rec 1821 to 1859; Co Rcdr has m rec; Clk Cir Ct has div, civ ct rec; Pro Judge has pro rec)

* **Carroll** F3 1833 Ray
Carroll County, County Courthouse, Carrollton, MO 64633 . . . . (816)542-0615
(Co Clk has b rec 1883 to 1895, d rec 1883 to 1890; Clk Cir Ct has div, civ ct rec from 1833, naturalization rec 1843 to 1919; Rcdr Deeds has m rec, Ind rec from 1833; Pro Office has pro rec)

* **Carter** C7 1859 Ripley, Shannon
Carter County, PO Box 517, Van Buren, MO 63965-0517 . . . . (314)323-4527
[FHL has some m, cem, civ ct, Ind, pro rec]

*† **Cass** G4 1835 Jackson
Cass County, County Courthouse, Harrisonville, MO 64701 . . . . (816)884-5100
(Organized as Van Buren, renamed Feb. 19, 1849; three southern tiers of townships relinquished to Bates Co Feb 22, 1855; Co Clk has b rec from 1861 to 1896, civ ct rec from 1843; Rcdr Deeds has m, div & Ind rec; Associate Division has pro rec)

Name	Map Index	Date Created	Parent County or Territory From Which Organized

* **Cedar**   F6   1845   Dade, St Clair
Cedar County, PO Box 126, Stockton, MO   65785-0126 .... (417)276-3514
(Co Clk has m, div & Ind rec from 1845, pro & civ ct rec)

* **Chariton**   E3   1820   Howard
Chariton County, County Courthouse, Keytesville, MO   65261 .... (816)288-3273
(Courthouse burned Sept 20, 1864, only a few rec lost)(Co Clk has b rec from 1883 to 1887, m & div rec from 1821, pro rec from 1876, Ind rec from 1827 & wills from 1865)

* **Christian**   F7   1859   Greene, Taney, Webster
Christian County, PO Box 549, Ozark, MO   65721-0549 .... (417)485-6360
(Sources differ on date organized, some say Mar 8, 1859, others say Mar 8, 1860; Co seat, Ozark, selected May 1859; Courthouse burned 1865. Cir Clk and Rcdr has m, div, civ ct, Ind rec; Pro Office has pro rec)

* **Clark**   D2   1836   Lewis
Clark County, 111 E Court St, Kahoka, MO   63445-1268 .... (816)727-3283
(Co Clk has m, div, pro, civ ct & Ind rec from 1836)

Clark (old)   1818   Arkansas
(never organized; abolished in 1819 when terr of Arkansas was created)

* **Clay**   G3   1822   Ray
Clay County, Administration Bldg Courthouse Sq, Liberty, MO   64086 .... (816)792-7733
(Rcdr Deeds has m & Ind rec; Clk Cir Ct has div & civ ct rec from 1822; Pro Ct has pro rec)

* **Clinton**   G3   1833   Clay
Clinton County, PO Box 245, Plattsburg, MO   64477-0245 .... (816)539-3713
(Co Clk has m, div, civ ct, Ind rec from 1833, service rec from WWI; Pro Judge has pro rec)

*† **Cole**   E4   1820   Cooper
Cole County, 301 E High St, Jefferson City, MO   65101-3212 .... (314)634-9110
(Clk Cir Ct has div & civ ct rec from 1821; Pro Judge has pro rec from 1821; Rcdr Deeds has m rec from 1821)

* **Cooper**   E4   1818   Howard
Cooper County, PO Box 123, Boonville, MO   65233-0123 .... (816)882-2114
(Co Clk has b & d rec from 1883 to 1893, bur rec; Cir Clk & Rcdr has m, div, civ ct rec & naturalization rec from 1819, Ind rec from 1812; Associate Cir Ct has pro rec from 1828)

* **Crawford**   D5   1829   Gasconade
Crawford County, 201 Main St, Steelville, MO   65565 .... (314)775-2376
(1829-1835 Co Ct rec lost; Courthouse burned Feb 15, 1873; Courthouse burned Jan 5, 1884)(Co Clk has m, div, civ ct & Ind rec from 1832; Pro Judge has pro rec from 1889)

* **Dade**   F6   1841   Greene
Dade County, County Courthouse, Greenfield, MO   65661 .... (417)637-2724
(lost 10-mile strip on northern boundary to Cedar Co & 9-mile strip on southern boundary to Lawrence Co, reducing it to its present limits, Mar 28, 1845; Courthouse burned in 1863, but rec had been removed to safety)(Co Rcdr has m rec from 1867 & Ind rec; Clk Cir Ct has div rec from 1867; Pro Judge has pro & civ ct rec)

*† **Dallas**   E6   1841   Polk
Dallas County, PO Box 436, Buffalo, MO   65622-0436 .... (417)345-2632
(organized 1842 as Niangua Co; in 1844 boundaries slightly changed & name changed to Dallas; Courthouse burned Oct 18, 1863; second courthouse burned Jul 30, 1864 & rec destroyed; the replaced rec were burned Sept 3, 1867)(Co Rcdr has b, m, d, bur, div, pro, civ ct & Ind rec)

* **Daviess**   G2   1836   Ray
Daviess County, County Courthouse, Gallatin, MO   64640 .... (816)663-2641
[FHL has some b, m, d, cem, civ ct, Ind, pro rec]

* **DeKalb**   G2   1845   Clinton
DeKalb County, PO Box 248, Maysville, MO   64469-0248 .... (816)449-5402
(In 1878 courthouse burned, many rec being destroyed, but rec of cir clks office were preserved along with a few papers of other offices; Co Rcdr has m & div rec; Co Clk has b rec from 1880 to 1902; Pro Judge has pro rec)

* **Dent**   D6   1851   Crawford, Shannon
Dent County, County Courthouse, Salem, MO   65560 .... (314)729-4144
(Courthouse burned in 1864, destroying some of the ct rec)(Clk Cir Ct has m, div & civ ct rec; Clk Mag Ct has pro rec; Co Rcdr has Ind rec)

Dodge   1851   Putnam
(discontinued in 1853; had lost terr when Iowa boundary was established, bringing its area below the constitutional limit of 400 sq miles; its terr was added to Putnam Co)

* **Douglas**   E7   1857   Ozark, Taney
Douglas County, 203 SE 2nd Ave, Ava, MO   65608 .... (417)683-4714
(terr increased in 1864 by addition of portions of Taney & Webster Cos)(Clk Cir Ct & Rcdr have m, div & civ ct rec; Pro & Mag Judge have pro rec)

* **Dunklin**   B7   1845   Stoddard
Dunklin County, PO Box 188, Kennett, MO   63857-0188 .... (314)888-2796
(In 1853 a strip one mile wide was taken from Stoddard and added to northern boundary of Dunklin Co)(Courthouse burned in 1872, all rec lost)(Rcdr Deeds has m, Ind rec; Clk Cir Ct has div, civ ct rec; Pro Judge has pro rec)

Name	Map Index	Date Created	Parent County or Territory From Which Organized

* **Franklin**   C5   1818   St. Louis
Franklin County, PO Box 311, Union, MO 63084-0311 .... (314)583-6355
(boundaries not accurately defined until 1845; Co Clk has b rec from 1883 to 1892, d rec from 1883 to 1887; Rcdr Deeds has m & Ind rec; Clk Cir Ct has div rec; Pro Judge has pro rec)

* **Gasconade**   D5   1820   Franklin
Gasconade County, PO Box 295, Hermann, MO 65041-0295 .... (314)486-5427
(In 1869 relinquished 36 sq miles to Crawford Co)(Co Clk has b rec 1867 to 1897, d rec 1883 to 1901)

* **Gentry**   G2   1841   Clinton
Gentry County, County Courthouse, Albany, MO 64402-1499 .... (816)726-3618
(Organization completed 1843; courthouse burned 1885) (Co Clk has b, d rec 1883 to 1893, m rec from 1885; Clk Cir Ct has m, div, civ ct, Ind rec from 1885; Cir Ct Division II has pro rec from 1885)

* **Greene**   F6   1833   Crawford
Greene County, 940 Boonville Ave, Springfield, MO 65802 .... (417)868-4055
(Courthouse burned 1861; Archives & Rec Center, 1126 Boonville, Springfield, MO has Assessor, Collector, Cir Ct, Co Clk, Pro Ct & Sheriff & Treasurer rec Ind & personal tax rec 1833 to 1930, nat rec; Rcdr Deeds has m & Ind rec)

* **Grundy**   F2   1841   Livingston
Grundy County, 700 Main St, Trenton, MO 64683-2063 .... (816)359-6305
(Co Clk has b, d rec 1881 to 1890; Co Rcdr has m, div, Ind rec; Pro Office has pro rec)

* **Harrison**   G2   1845   Daviess
Harrison County, PO Box 27, Bethany, MO 64424-0027 .... (816)425-6424
(Jan 1874 Courthouse burned; Ind bks, ct rec, pro rec & most of the co rec were saved; tax bks were destroyed; Co Clk has some b rec from 1883 to 1893; Clk Cir Ct has m & div rec from 1858 & civ ct rec from 1845; Pro Judge has pro rec from 1853)

Hempstead   1818   Arkansas
(abolished 1819 when terr of Arkansas was created)

*† **Henry**   F5   1834   Lafayette
Henry County, Main & Franklin Sts, Clinton, MO 64735-2199 .... (816)885-6963
(originally Rives Co; name changed Oct 15, 1841; Co Rcdr has m & Ind rec from 1830, mil dis; Co Clk has div & civ ct rec; Associate Cir Ct has pro rec; b & bur rec in Henry Co Museum)

* **Hickory**   F5   1845   Benton, Polk
Hickory County, Main & Polk Sts, Hermitage, MO 65668 .... (417)745-6450
(Courthouse burned 1852 and 1881; many rec destroyed; Co Clk has b rec 1883 to 1898; Clk Cir Ct has m rec 1872, div rec 1858 & civ ct rec 1858; Pro Judge has pro rec from 1845)

* **Holt**   H2   1841   Platte Purchase
Holt County, 102 Nodaway St, Oregon, MO 64473-9643 .... (816)446-3303
(Co Clk has incomplete b & d rec from 1883 to 1893, m rec from 1841, div & Ind rec from 1841; Clk Cir Ct has civ ct rec from 1841; Pro Judge has pro rec from 1849)(Courthouse burned 30 Jan 1965, most rec undamaged)

* **Howard**   E4   1816   St. Charles, St. Louis
Howard County, PO Box 551, Fayette, MO 65248-0551 .... (816)248-2284
(Courthouse burned 1887; rec were saved & some date to 1816)

Howell   D7   1857   Oregon, Ozark
Howell County, County Courthouse Sq, West Plains, MO 65775 .... (417)256-2591
(Courthouse destroyed during CW; Co Clk has b rec from 1883 to 1895, d rec from 1883 to 1893; Cir Clk & Rcdr Deeds has m, div, civ ct & Ind rec; Associate Cir Ct has pro rec)

* **Iron**   C6   1857   Dent, Madison, Reynolds, St. Francis, Washington, Wayne
Iron County, 250 S Main St, Ironton, MO 63650-1308 .... (314)546-2912
(Co Clk has b rec from 1883 to 1885, m, div, pro & Ind rec)

* **Jackson**   G4   1826   Lafayette
Jackson County, 415 E 12th St, Kansas City, MO 64106-2706 .... (816)881-3333
(nearly all its terr was acquired from Osage & Kansas Indians, June 2, 1825)(Dept of Rcds has m & Ind rec; Ct Administrator has div & civ ct rec; Pro Judge has pro rec)

*† **Jasper**   G6   1841   Newton
Jasper County, County Courthouse, Carthage, MO 64836-1696 .... (417)358-0416
(Courthouse destroyed in 1863; rec had been removed were returned in 1865; Courthouse burned in 1883; no mention of fate of rec)(Co Clk has b rec from 1883 to 1900 & d rec from 1883 to 1891; Rcdr Deeds has m rec; Pro Judge has pro rec & civ ct rec)

* **Jefferson**   C5   1818   Ste. Genevieve, St. Louis
Jefferson County, PO Box 100, Hillsboro, MO 63050-0100 .... (314)789-3911
[FHL has some m, cem, civ ct, Ind, pro rec]

*† **Johnson**   F4   1834   Lafayette
Johnson County, County Courthouse, Warrensburg, MO 64093-1794 .... (816)747-6161
(Co Rcdr has m, Ind rec; Clk Cir Ct has div rec; Pro Judge has pro, civ ct rec; Co Clk has b, d rec 1883 to 1893)

Kinderhook   1841   Benton, Pulaski
(renamed Camden Feb 23, 1843)

* **Knox**   E2   1845   Scotland
Knox County, 305 E Lafayette St, Edina, MO 63537 .... (816)397-2184
(Co Rcdr has m, div & Ind rec; Associate Cir Judge has pro & civ ct rec; Hist Soc in Courthouse has b & d rec from 1883 to 1890)

Name	Map Index	Date Created	Parent County or Territory From Which Organized

* **Laclede**　　E6　　1849　　Camden, Pulaski, Wright
Laclede County, 2nd & Adam Sts, Lebanon, MO　65536 . . . . (417)532-5471
(Co Rcdr has m rec; Clk Cir Ct has div & civ ct rec; Pro Judge has pro rec; Co Asr has Ind rec)

* **Lafayette**　　F4　　1820　　Cooper
Lafayette County, Main Sts, Lexington, MO　64067 . . . . (816)259-4315
(Originally called Lillard, changed Feb. 16, 1825. Co Rcdr has m, div, pro, civ ct, Ind rec from 1821)

* **Lawrence**　　F6　　1845　　Barry, Dade
Lawrence County, PO Box 309, Mount Vernon, MO　65712-0309 . . . . (417)466-2638
(Rcdr Deeds has m & Ind rec from 1846; Clk Cir Ct has div & civ ct rec from 1846; Pro Judge has pro rec from 1846; Rcdr Deeds has Ind rec from 1846)

Lawrence (old)　　　　1815　　New Madrid
(abolished 1818)

* **Lewis**　　D2　　1833　　Marion
Lewis County, 100 E Lafayette St, Monticello, MO　63457 . . . . (314)767-5205
(Clk Cir Ct has m, div & Ind rec; Pro Judge has pro & civ ct rec)

Lillard　　　　1820　　Cooper
(Changed to Lafayette Feb 16, 1825)

* **Lincoln**　　C4　　1818　　St. Charles
Lincoln County, 201 Main St, Troy, MO　63379-1194 . . . . (314)528-4415
(Co Rcdr has m rec from 1825; Pro Judge has pro rec from 1823; Co Rcdr has d & bur rec; Clk Cir Ct has div rec)

*† **Linn**　　E3　　1837　　Chariton
Linn County, County Courthouse, Linneus, MO　64653 . . . . (816)895-5417
(Co Clk has incomplete b, d rec 1883 to 1888; Co Rcdr has m, Ind rec from 1842; local funeral homes have bur rec; Clk Cir Ct has div rec from 1837; Pro Office has pro rec from 1840)

* **Livingston**　　F3　　1837　　Carroll
Livingston County, County Courthouse, Chillicothe, MO　64601 . . . . (816)646-2293
[FHL has some m, cem, civ ct, Ind, nat, pro rec]

*† **Macon**　　E3　　1837　　Randolph
Macon County, PO Box 96, Macon, MO　63552-0096 . . . . (816)385-2913
(Co Clk has b, d rec 1883 to 1893; Co Rcdr has m, Ind rec; Clk Cir Ct has div rec; Cir Ct Division II has pro rec)

* **Madison**　　C6　　1818　　Cape Girardeau, Ste. Genevieve
Madison County, 1 Courthouse Sq, Fredericktown, MO　63645-1137 . . . . (314)783-2176
(Co Clk has b rec from 1883 to 1900, d rec from 1883 to 1892; Clk Cir Ct has m, div & civ ct rec; Clk Mag Ct has pro rec; Co Asr has Ind rec)

* **Maries**　　D5　　1855　　Osage, Pulaski
Maries County, PO Box 167, Vienna, MO　65582-0167 . . . . (314)422-3388
(In 1859 and 1868 small tracts of land were exchanged with Phelps Co, Courthouse burned Nov. 6, 1868 nearly all rec destroyed)(Clk Cir Ct has m rec from 1873, div, civ ct rec from 1866, Ind rec from 1855, school rec from 1911; Pro Division has pro rec from 1880)

*† **Marion**　　D3　　1822　　Ralls
Marion County, County Courthouse, Palmyra, MO　63461 . . . . (314)769-2549
(Clk Cir Ct has m, div, civ ct & Ind rec from 1827, veteran dis rec; Pro Ct has pro rec)

*† **McDonald**　　G7　　1849　　Newton
McDonald County, PO Box 665, Pineville, MO　64856-0665 . . . . (417)223-4717
(In 1876 an error in survey was corrected, establishing a new eastern line which annexed a 2 1/2 mile strip previously included in Barry Co; in 1863 Courthouse & rec were burned)(Rcdr Deeds has m rec; Clk Cir Ct has div, civ ct & Ind rec; Pro Judge has pro rec)

* **Mercer**　　F2　　1845　　Grundy
Mercer County, County Courthouse, Princeton, MO　64673 . . . . (816)748-3425
(Courthouse burned 24 Mar, 1898, nearly all rec of the Cir Clk & Rcdr, Treas and Sheriff rec were destroyed or badly damaged, rec in office of Pro Judge and Co Clk were saved, but many were badly damaged; Co Clk has b rec 1883 to 1894, d rec 1883 to 1891; Clk Cir Ct has m, div, pro, civ ct, Ind rec; Cir Ct Div 2 has pro rec; local register has bur rec)

* **Miller**　　E5　　1837　　Cole
Miller County, Courthouse Sq, Tuscumbia, MO　65082 . . . . (314)369-2731
(line between Camden or Miller changed 1845; terr from Morgan annexed 1860; minor changes in 1868)(Co Clk has b rec from 1883 to 1891; Co Rcdr has m & div rec; Pro Judge has pro rec; Clk Cir Ct has civ ct rec)

* **Mississippi**　　B7　　1845　　Scott
Mississippi County, PO Box 304, Charleston, MO　63834-0304 . . . . (314)683-2146
(Clk Cir Ct has m, div & civ ct rec; Pro Judge has pro rec; Co Rcdr has Ind rec)

* **Moniteau**　　E4　　1845　　Cole, Morgan
Moniteau County, 200 E Main St, California, MO　65018-1675 . . . . (314)796-4661
[FHL has some m, cem, civ ct, Ind, pro rec]

* **Monroe**　　D3　　1831　　Ralls
Monroe County, 300 N Main St, Paris, MO　65275-1399 . . . . (816)327-5817
(Clk Cir Ct has m, div & civ ct rec; Pro Judge has pro rec; Co Asr has Ind rec)

Name	Map Index	Date Created	Parent County or Territory From Which Organized

* **Montgomery** D4 1818 St. Charles
Montgomery County, 211 E 3rd St, Montgomery City, MO 63361-1956 .... (314)564-3357
(Co rec burned 1864; Clk Cir Ct has m rec from 1864, div & civ ct rec from 1886; Pro Judge has pro rec from 1890; Mag Ct has rec from 1947)

* **Morgan** E5 1833 Cooper
Morgan County, 100 E Newton St, Versailles, MO 65084-1298 .... (314)378-5436
(Courthouse burned 1887; rec were saved)

* **New Madrid** B7 1812 Original district
New Madrid County, PO Box 68, New Madrid, MO 63869-0068 .... (314)748-2524
(Rcdr Deeds has m rec; Clk Cir Ct has div & civ ct rec; Pro Clk has pro rec)

* **Newton** G7 1838 Barry
Newton County, Main & Wood Sts County Courthouse Sq, Neosho, MO 64850 .... (417)451-4540
(In 1846 a strip two miles wide was detached from Newton & attached to Jasper; Courthouse burned 1862; no mention of fate of rec)(Co Clk has m, div, pro, civ ct & Ind rec)

Niangua 1842 Polk
(boundaries slightly changed & name changed to Dallas Dec 10, 1844)

* **Nodaway** G2 1841 Andrew
Nodaway County, PO Box 218, Maryville, MO 64468-0218 .... (816)582-2251
(Clk Cir Ct has m & div rec from 1845; Pro Ct Clk has pro rec)

* **Oregon** D7 1845 Ripley
Oregon County, PO Box 324, Alton, MO 65606-0324 .... (417)778-7475
(Courthouse burned during CW; rec were removed and most of them saved)(Clk Cir Ct has m, div & civ ct rec; Pro Judge has pro rec; Rcdr Deeds has Ind rec)

* **Osage** D4 1841 Gasconade
Osage County, Main St, Linn, MO 65051 .... (314)897-2139
(Mar 1, 1855 boundaries between Osage & Pulaski defined. Nov 15, 1880, Courthouse burned; fireproof vaults saved rec)

* **Ozark** E7 1841 Taney (changed to Decatur 1843, back to Ozark, 1845)
Ozark County, PO Box 416, Gainesville, MO 65655-0416 .... (417)679-3516
(Clk Cir Ct has m, div & civ ct rec; Co Clk has Co Comm minutes)

* **Pemiscot** B7 1851 New Madrid
Pemiscot County, Ward Ave, Caruthersville, MO 63830 .... (314)333-4203
(Courthouse & contents burned 1883)(Rcdr Deeds has m & Ind rec from 1883; Clk Cir Ct has div & civ ct rec from 1890; Pro Judge has pro rec; Rcdr Deeds has Ind rec from 1883)

* **Perry** B6 1820 Ste. Genevieve
Perry County, 15 W Sainte Marie St, Perryville, MO 63775-1399 .... (314)547-4242
[FHL has some m, civ ct, pro, Ind, nat rec]

*† **Pettis** F4 1833 Cooper, Saline
Pettis County, 415 S Ohio Ave, Sedalia, MO 65301-4496 .... (816)826-5395
[FHL has some m, cem, civ ct, pro, Ind rec]

Phelps D5 1857 Crawford, Pulaski, Maries
Phelps County, 3rd & Rolla Sts, Rolla, MO 65401 .... (314)364-1891
(Co Clk has m, div, civ ct, Ind rec from 1857, pro rec)

*† **Pike** C3 1818 St. Charles
Pike County, 115 W Main St, Bowling Green, MO 63334-1693 .... (314)324-2412
(Courthouse burned 1864; no mention of fate of rec)

* **Platte** G3 1838 Platte Purchase
Platte County, PO Box 30CH, Platte City, MO 64079 .... (816)431-2232
(attached to Clay for civil & mil purpose from Dec 1836 to Dec 31, 1838)(Co Clk has b rec from 1883 to 1887, d rec from 1883 to 1888; Rcdr Deeds has m & Ind rec; Clk Cir Ct has div rec; Pro Judge has pro & civ ct rec)

* **Polk** F6 1835 Greene
Polk County, County Courthouse Rm 12, Bolivar, MO 65613 .... (417)326-4031
(Co Rcdr has m rec from 1835 & Ind rec from 1836; Clk Cir Ct has div & civ ct rec 1857; Pro Judge has pro rec from 1947)

* **Pulaski** E5 1833 Crawford
Pulaski County, Waynesville Sq, Waynesville, MO 65583 .... (314)774-6609
(Co Clk has m, div, pro & civ ct rec from 1903)

Pulaski (old) 1818 Franklin
(organization not perfected & much of its terr became Gasconade in 1820; abolished 1819 when terr of Arkansas was created)

* **Putnam** F2 1843 Linn
Putnam County, County Courthouse, Unionville, MO 63565 .... (816)947-2674
(when Iowa boundary was established, the areas of both Putnam & Dodge were below the constitutional limit; Dodge disorganized in 1853 & its terr was regained by Putnam)(Clk Cir Ct has b rec from 1878 to 1903, m rec from 1854, div rec from 1855, civ ct rec from 1855 & Ind rec from 1848; Pro Judge has pro rec from 1848)

* **Ralls** D3 1820 Pike
Ralls County, Main St, New London, MO 63459 .... (314)985-7111
(Co Clk has b & d rec from 1883 to 1886; Clk Cir Ct & Rcdr Deeds has m, div, civ ct & Ind rec from 1821; Pro Judge has pro rec)

Name	Map Index	Date Created	Parent County or Territory From Which Organized

* **Randolph** E3 1829 Chariton
Randolph County, S Main St, Huntsville, MO 65259 .... (816)277-4717
(a few rec lost when Courthouse burned 1880)(Co Rcdr has m rec; Clk Cir Ct has div rec)

* **Ray** F3 1820 Howard
Ray County, PO Box 536, Richmond, MO 64085-0536 .... (816)776-3184
(Rec of interest to genealogists obtainable from Ray Co Historical Society, Richmond, Mo. 64085, write for rates)(Co Clk has b, d rec 1883 to 1884; Rcdr of Deeds has m, Ind rec; Clk Cir Ct has div, civ ct rec; Pro Judge has pro rec)

*† **Reynolds** C6 1845 Shannon
Reynolds County, Courthouse Sq, Centerville, MO 63633 .... (314)648-2494
(Courthouse burned 1872, all rec lost; Co Clk has b rec from 1883, m, div, pro & civ ct rec from 1872)

*† **Ripley** C7 1833 Wayne
Ripley County, County Courthouse, Doniphan, MO 63935 .... (314)996-3215
[FHL has some m, cem, civ ct, Ind, pro rec]

  Rives   1834 Lafayette
(name changed to Henry Oct 15, 1841)

* **Saint Charles** C4 1812 Original district
Saint Charles County, 3rd & Jefferson Sts, Saint Charles, MO 63301 .... (314)949-3080
[FHL has some m, cem, civ ct, Ind, pro rec, 1852 census]

* **Saint Clair** F5 1841 Rives (later Henry)
Saint Clair County, PO Box 405, Osceola, MO 64776-0405 .... (417)646-2315
(Co Clk has b & d rec from 1883 to 1887; Rcdrs Office has m rec from 1855 & Ind rec from 1867; Clk Cir Ct has div & pro rec)

  Saint Francois C5 1821 Jefferson, Ste. Genevieve, Washington
Saint Francois County, County Courthouse Sq, Farmington, MO 63640 .... (314)756-5411
(Co Rcdr has m & Ind rec; Clk Cir Ct has div rec; Associate Cir Ct has pro rec)

* **Sainte Genevieve** C5 1812 Original District
Sainte Genevieve County, 55 S 3rd St, Sainte Genevieve, MO 63670-1601 .... (314)883-5589
(Co Clk has b, d rec 1883 to 1892; Cir Clk-Rcdr has m, div, civ ct, Ind rec; Cir Ct Judge has pro rec; various churches in Co have bur rec)

* **Saline** F4 1820 Cooper, Howard
Saline County, County Courthouse, Marshall, MO 65340 .... (816)886-3331
(Courthouse burned 186? but rec were saved)

* **Schuyler** E2 1845 Adair
Schuyler County, PO Box 187, Lancaster, MO 63548-0187 .... (816)457-3842
(Co Clk has b & d rec from 1883 to 1893; Clk Cir Ct has m & div rec; Pro Judge & Mag Cts have pro & civ ct rec)

* **Scotland** E2 1841 Lewis
Scotland County, County Courthouse, Memphis, MO 63555 .... (816)465-7027
(Co Clk has b & d rec from 1883 to 1889; Clk Cir Ct has m, div, civ ct & Ind rec from 1841; Pro Judge has pro rec from 1841)

* **Scott** B7 1821 New Madrid
Scott County, PO Box 188, Benton, MO 63736-0188 .... (314)545-3549
(Rcdr Deeds has m & Ind rec; Clk Cir Ct has div & civ ct rec; Pro Judge has pro rec)

* **Shannon** D6 1841 Ripley, Washington
Shannon County, County Courthouse, Eminence, MO 65466 .... (314)226-3414
(Courthouse destroyed during CW; Co Clk has m rec from 1881, div, pro, civ ct & Ind rec from 1872; Courthouse burned 1863, 1871, 1938, Rcdr Office Burned 1893; some Ind rec in Ironton, MO prior to 1872)

*† **Shelby** D3 1835 Marion
Shelby County, 1 Courthouse Sq, Shelbyville, MO 63469 .... (314)633-2181
(Rcdr Deeds has m & Ind rec; Clk Cir Ct has div rec; Pro Ct has pro rec; Clk Mag Ct has civ ct rec)

* **St. Louis** C4 1812 Original district
St. Louis County, 41 S Central Ave, Clayton, MO 63105-1719 .... (314)889-2016
(Co Clk has b rec from 1877 to 1910)(Rcdr Deeds has m & Ind rec; Clk Cir Ct has div & civ ct rec; Co Clk has inc of cities, twns, etc, proceedings of Co Ct since 1887, old & new road files)

  St. Louis City C4 1764

* **Stoddard** B7 1835 Cape Girardeau
Stoddard County, PO Box H, Bloomfield, MO 63825-0209 .... (314)568-3339
(Courthouse burned 1864 but rec had been removed to safety; Co Clk has b rec from 1883 to 1886; Rcdr Deeds has m rec; Clk Cir Ct has div rec; Pro Judge has pro rec; Clk Mag Ct has civ ct rec; Co Clk has mil service rec)

  Stone F7 1851 Taney
Stone County, PO Box 45, Galena, MO 65656-0045 .... (417)357-6127
(Co Clk has m, Ind rec from 1851, pro civ ct rec from 1800, discharge rec from 1918)

* **Sullivan** F2 1843 Linn
Sullivan County, 2nd St, Milan, MO 63556 .... (816)265-3786
(Rcdr Deeds has b rec from 1867 to 1895 inc, m rec from 1845 & d rec from 1883 to 1896, Ind rec from 1845; Clk Cir Ct has div & civ ct rec from 1845; Pro Judge has pro rec from 1845)

Name	Map Index	Date Created	Parent County or Territory From Which Organized
* **Taney**	F7	1837	Greene

Taney County, PO Box 156, Forsyth, MO 65653-0156 . . . . (417)546-2241
(Clk Cir Ct has m, div, civ ct & Ind rec; Pro Judge has pro rec; Co Clk has voter registration rec from 1961; Courthouse burned 1885)

| * **Texas** | D6 | 1845 | Shannon, Wright (formerly Ashley, changed to Texas 1845) |

Texas County, 210 N Grand Ave, Houston, MO 65483-1226 . . . . (417)967-2112
(Rcdr Deeds has m rec from 1855 & Ind rec from 1845; Clk Cir Ct has div & civ ct rec from 1855; Associate Cir Ct has pro rec from 1850)

| **Van Buren** | | 1835 | Jackson |

(name changed to Cass Feb 19, 1849)

| * **Vernon** | G5 | 1851 | Bates |

Vernon County, 102 W Cherry, Nevada, MO 64772-3368 . . . . (417)667-3157
(Vernon created Feb. 15, 1851, but act was declared unconstitutional since its territory was exactly that of Bates; legally created Feb. 27, 1855; reorganized Oct. 17, 1865 after total suspension of civil order during CW; Courthouse destroyed during that period, but clk had taken the rec with him when he joined the army and all rec were later recovered except one deed book. Co Clk has b, d rec 1883 to 1904; Rcdr of Deeds has m, Ind rec; Clk Cir Ct has div, civ ct rec; Pro Ct has pro rec; Co Hist Soc has bur rec)

| * **Warren** | D4 | 1833 | Montgomery |

Warren County, 105 S Market St, Warrenton, MO 63383-1903 . . . . (314)456-3331
[FHL has some b, m, d, cem, civ ct, Ind, nat, pro rec]

| * **Washington** | C5 | 1813 | Ste. Genevieve |

Washington County, 102 N Missouri St, Potosi, MO 63664-1744 . . . . (314)438-4901
(Co Clk has b rec 1883 to 1891, d rec 1883 to 1886, 1875 to present; Clk Cir Ct has m, div, civ ct, Ind rec from 1825; Pro Office has pro rec from 1814; Funeral homes have bur rec)

| * **Wayne** | C6 | 1818 | Cape Girardeau |

Wayne County, County Courthouse, Greenville, MO 63944 . . . . (314)224-3221
(Courthouse burned with all the rec 1854, burned again in 1892)(Co Clk has b & d rec from 1914 to 1940; Clk Cir Ct & Rcdr has m, div & Ind rec; Associate Cir Ct has pro rec)

| * **Webster** | E6 | 1855 | Greene, Wright |

Webster County, County Courthouse, Marshfield, MO 65706 . . . . (417)468-2223
(Courthouse burned 1863 but rec were saved with the exception of tax rolls & election returns) (Co Clk has b rec from 1883 to 1893, d rec from 1883 to 1887; Co Rcdr has m & Ind rec; Clk Cir Ct has div & civ ct rec; Pro Judge has pro rec)

| * **Worth** | G2 | 1861 | Gentry |

Worth County, County Courthouse, Grant City, MO 64456 . . . . (816)564-2219
(Co Clk has b & d rec from 1883 to 1893, m, div, pro, civ ct & Ind rec from 1861)

| * **Wright** | E6 | 1841 | Pulaski |

Wright County, PO Box 98, Hartville, MO 65667-0098 . . . . (417)741-6661
(1864 Courthouse burned, destroying many rec; 1897 Courthouse destroyed with all its rec)(Clk Cir Ct has m, div & civ ct rec; Pro Judge has pro rec; Co Rcdr has Ind rec)

* At least one county history has been published about this county.

† Inventory of county archives was made by the Historical Records Survey. (See Introduction)

MONTANA

CAPITAL · HELENA — TERRITORY 1864 — STATE 1889 (41st)
State Map on Page M-24

At least sixteen tribes of Indians roamed over the Montana region when the first explorers came to the area. Fur traders were the only whites in the area before 1800. Obtaining the area in the Louisiana Purchase, President Jefferson sent Lewis and Clark to explore the new territory. They reached Montana in 1805. Trading posts remained the only settlements until the establishment of Fort Benton, which became the first permanent settlement in 1846. Steamboats first reached Fort Benton in 1859, but the first real influx of people came in 1862 when gold was discovered southeast of Butte. Copper, silver, and other minerals were discovered about twenty years later, which opened up mines and brought Irish, German, Austrian, Polish, and Czech workers to the area.

The western part of Montana became part of the United States in 1846 through the Oregon Treaty. In 1860, this portion was made into Missoula County, Washington Territory. By 1864, all of Montana was included in the Idaho Territory. In 1864, Montana became an organized territory, and the 41st state in 1889.

Some counties began recording births and deaths as early as 1864. Statewide registration began in 1907, reaching general compliance by 1920. These records are available at the Bureau of Records and Statistics, State Department of Health, Helena, MT 59601. To verify current fees, call 406-444-2614.

Marriage and divorce records were kept by the counties. Probate records from 1864 to 1889 were kept by the counties, and since then by the district courts. Naturalization records are in county and district courts. The earliest land records are at the National Archives, Denver Branch, Building 48, Denver Federal Center, Denver, CO 80225. Records of patents on homesteads are at county offices. The BLM, 222 North 32nd Street, Box 30157, Billings, MT 59107, has tract books, township plats, and pre-1908 patent records. In 1860, western Montana was part of Washington Territory, and eastern Montana was part of the unorganized area of Nebraska Territory. Federal censuses for Montana Territory are available for 1870 and 1880. Indexes have been published for all of these. Mortality schedules for the 1870 and 1880 censuses are at the Montana Historical Society, 225 North Roberts Street, Helena, MT 59620.

Genealogical Archives, Libraries and Societies

Cascade County Historical Museum and Archives, 1400 First Avenue North, Great Falls, MT 59401-3299

Havre-Hill County Library, P. O. Box 1151, Havre, MT 59501

Mansfield Library, University of Montana, Missoula, MT 59812

Miles City Public Library, 1 South 10th, Miles City, MT 59301

Montana State Library, 930 East Lyndale Avenue, Helena, MT 59601

Montana State University Library, Bozeman, MT 59717

Parmly Billings Library, 510 N. Broadway, Billings, MT 59101

Public Library, 106 W. Broadway St., Butte, MT 59701

Public Library, Great Falls, MT 59401

Public Library, Pine and Pattee Sts., Missoula, MT 59801

State University Library, Missoula, MT 59801

Big Horn County Genealogical Society, Rt. 1, Box 1166, Hardin, MT 59034

Broken Mountains Genealogical Society, Box 261, Chester, MT 59522

Carbon County Historical Society, Box 476, Red Lodge, MT 59068

Central Montana Genealogy Society, 701 W. Main Street, Lewistown, MT 59457

Flathead Valley Genealogical Society, 134 Lawrence Lane, Kalispell, MT 59901

Fort Assiniboine Genealogical Society, P. O. Box 321, Havre, MT 59501

Gallatin Genealogy Society, P. O. Box 1783, Bozeman, MT 59715

Great Falls Genealogy Society, Paris Gibson Square, 1400 First Avenue North, Great Falls, MT 59401

Lewis and Clark County Genealogical Society, P. O. Box 5313, Helena, MT 59604

Lewistown Genealogy Society, Inc., 701 West Main, Lewistown, MT 59457

Miles City Genealogical Society, Miles City Public Library, 1 South 10th, Miles City, MT 59301

Mineral County Historical Society, Box 533, Superior, MT 59872

Montana Historical Society, 225 N. Roberts St., Helena, MT 59620

Montana Society, Sons of the American Revolution, Pres., Roy L. Johnson, 408 S. Black, Bozeman, MT 59715

Montana State Genealogical Society, P.O. Box 555, Chester, MT 59522

Park County Genealogy Society, Park County Public Library, 228 West Callender St., Livingston, MT 59047

Powell County Genealogical Society, 912 Missouri Ave., Deer Lodge, MT 59722

Root Diggers Genealogical Society, P. O. Box 249, Glasgow, MT 59230

Western Montana Genealogical Society, P. O. Box 2714, Missoula, MT 59806-2714

Yellowstone Genealogy Forum, Parmly Billings Library, 510 N. Broadway, Billings, MT 59101

Printed Census Records and Mortality Schedules

Federal Census 1860 (eastern part with Nebraska, western part with Washington), 1870, 1880, 1900, 1910
Federal Mortality Schedules 1870, 1880
Union Veterans and Widows 1890
Poll List 1864

Valuable Printed Sources

Atlases, Maps, and Gazetteers

Cheney, Roberta Carkeek. *Names on the Face of Montana*. Missoula, Montana: University of Montana Publications in History, 1971.

Bibliographies

John, Henry. *Bibliography of Montana Local Histories*. Montana Library Association, 1977.

Genealogical Research Guides

Richards, Dennis. *Montana's Genealogical and Local History Records*. Detroit: Gale Research Co., 1981.

Genealogical Sources

Parpart, Paulette K. and Donald E. Spritzer. *The Montana Historical and Genealogical Data Index*. Montana Library Association, 1987.

Histories

Burlingame, Merrill C. and K. Ross Toole. *A History of Montana*. New York: Lewis Historical Publishing Co., 1957.

Miller, Joaquin. *An Illustrated History of the State of Montana*. Chicago: Lewis Publishing Co., 1894.

MONTANA COUNTY DATA
State Map on Page M-24

Name	Map Index	Date Created	Parent County or Territory From Which Organized
† **Beaverhead**	C2	1865	Original county

Beaverhead County, 2 S Pacific Cluster 3, Dillon, MT 59725 . . . . (406)683-5245
(Co Clk has b rec from 1902, d rec from 1901, lnd, mining, lease, mtg rec from 1864 & voting rec; Clk Dis Ct has div, pro & civ ct rec)

Big Horn	G3	1913	Rosebud, Yellowstone

Big Horn County, 121 3rd St W, Hardin, MT 59034-1905 . . . . (406)665-3520
(Co Clk has b, d, naturalization & lnd rec from 1913; Clk Dis Ct has m, div, pro & civ ct rec)

* **Blaine**	F6	1912	Chouteau, Hill

Blaine County, PO Box 278, Chinook, MT 59523-0278 . . . . (406)357-3250
(Co Clk has b, d & lnd rec from 1912; Clk Dis Ct has m, div, pro & civ ct rec)

Broadwater	D3	1897	Jefferson, Meagher

Broadwater County, PO Box 489, Townsend, MT 59644-0489 . . . . (406)266-3443
(Co Clk has b & d rec from 1907; Clk Ct has m, div, pro & civ ct rec)

*† **Carbon**	F2	1895	Park, Yellowstone

Carbon County, PO Box 887, Red Lodge, MT 59068-0887 . . . . (406)446-1595
(Co Clk has b rec from 1878, d rec from 1903, m, div, pro, civ ct & lnd rec from 1895)

* **Carter**	I3	1917	Custer

Carter County, Courthouse Park St, Ekalaka, MT 59324 . . . . (406)775-8749
(Co Clk b, d & lnd rec from 1917; Clk Cts has m, div, pro & civ ct rec)

* **Cascade**	D5	1887	Chouteau, Meagher

Cascade County, 415 2nd Ave N, Great Falls, MT 59401-2536 . . . . (406)761-6700
(Co Clk & Rcdr has b, d & lnd rec from 1897, mil service rec from 1918; Clk Cts has m, div, pro & civ ct rec)

Chouteau	E5	1865	Original county

Chouteau County, 1308 Franklin, Fort Benton, MT 59442 . . . . (406)622-5151
(Co Clk has b & d rec from 1895, bur rec & lnd rec from 1878; Clk Cts has m rec from 1888, div & civ ct rec from 1879 & pro rec from 1892)

* **Custer**	H3	1865	Original county

Custer County, 1010 Main St, Miles City, MT 59301-3419 . . . . (406)232-7800
(Co Clk has b, d rec from 1907, lnd rec from 1909; Clk Dis Ct has m, div, pro rec; J P has civ ct rec; cem associations have bur rec)

* **Daniels**	H6	1920	Valley, Sheridan

Daniels County, PO Box 247, Scobey, MT 59263-0247 . . . . (406)487-5561
(Co Clk has b, d, lnd rec from 1820; Clk of Ct has m, div, pro, civ ct rec from 1920; funeral home has bur rec)

* **Dawson**	I5	1860	Original county

Dawson County, 207 W Bell St, Glendive, MT 59330-1694 . . . . (406)365-3562
(Co Clk has b & d rec from 1895, lnd rec from 1882; Clk Cts has m, div & civ ct rec from 1882, pro rec from 1889)

* **Deer Lodge**	C3	1865	Original county

Deer Lodge County, 800 S Main St, Anaconda, MT 59711-2999 . . . . (406)563-8421

* **Fallon**	I4	1913	Custer

Fallon County, 10 W Fallon Ave, Baker, MT 59313 . . . . (406)778-2883
(Clk & Rcdr has b rec from 1884, d rec from 1919, lnd rec; Clk Cts has m rec from 1913, div, pro & civ ct rec)

*† **Fergus**	F5	1885	Meagher

Fergus County, 712 W Main St, Lewistown, MT 59457-2562 . . . . (406)538-5119
(Co Clk has b & d rec; Clk Cts has m, div, pro & civ ct rec; Co Asr has lnd rec)

† **Flathead**	B6	1893	Missoula

Flathead County, 800 S Main St, Kalispell, MT 59901-5400 . . . . (406)752-5300
(Co Clk & Rcdr has b & d rec from 1882, lnd rec from 1884, bur rec from 1893; Clk Dis Ct has m, div, pro & civ ct rec from 1893)

* **Gallatin**	D3	1865	Original county

Gallatin County, 311 W Main St Rm 204, Bozeman, MT 59715-4576 . . . . (406)585-1430
(Co Clk has b, d & lnd rec; Clk Dis Ct has m, div & pro rec)

Garfield	G5	1919	Valley, McCone

Garfield County, PO Box 7, Jordan, MT 59337-0007 . . . . (406)557-2760
(Co Clk has b rec from 1919)

* **Glacier**	C6	1919	Teton

Glacier County, 502 E Main St, Cut Bank, MT 59427-3025 . . . . (406)873-5063
(Co Clk has b, d & lnd rec from 1919; Clk Cts has m, div, pro & civ ct rec)

Name	Map Index	Date Created	Parent County or Territory From Which Organized
* **Golden Valley**	F3	1920	Musselshell

Golden Valley County, PO Box 10, Ryegate, MT 59074-0010 .... (406)568-2231
(Co Clk & Rcdr has b, d & Ind rec; Clk Cts has m, div, pro & civ ct rec)

| **Granite** | B4 | 1893 | Deer Lodge |

Granite County, Sampson & Kearney Sts, Philipsburg, MT 59858 .... (406)859-3771
(Co Clk & Rcdr have b & d rec from 1882, Ind rec from 1884, bur rec from 1893; Clk Cts has m, div, pro & civ ct rec)

| * **Hill** | E6 | 1912 | Chouteau |

Hill County, 315 4th St County Courthouse, Havre, MT 59501-3999 .... (406)265-5481
(Co Clk & Rcdr has b & d rec from 1907 & Ind rec from 1865; Clk Cts has m, div, pro & civ ct rec)

| **Jefferson** | D3 | 1866 | Original county |

Jefferson County, PO Box H, Boulder, MT 59632-0249 .... (406)225-4251
(Co Clk has b & d rec from 1907 & Ind rec from 1865; Clk Dis Ct has m, div, pro & civ ct rec)

| **Judith Basin** | E4 | 1920 | Fergus, Cascade |

Judith Basin County, Courthouse, Stanford, MT 59479 .... (406)566-2250
(Co Clk & Rcdr has b, d & Ind rec from 1920; Clk Cts has m, div, pro & civ ct rec)

| † **Lake** | B5 | 1923 | Flathead, Missoula |

Lake County, 106 4th Ave E, Polson, MT 59860-2125 .... (406)883-6211
(Co Clk has b, d, bur, Ind rec from 1923; Clk Cts has m, div, pro, civ ct rec from 1923)

| **Lewis & Clark** | C4 | 1865 | Original county |

Lewis & Clark County, 316 N Park Ave, Helena, MT 59624 .... (406)443-1010
(Co Clk has b rec from 1907, d rec from 1895 & Ind rec from 1865; Clk Dis Ct has m, div, pro & civ ct rec)

| **Liberty** | D6 | 1920 | Chouteau, Hill |

Liberty County, 101 1st St E, Chester, MT 59522 .... (406)759-5365
(Co Clk has b, d, Ind rec from 1920; Clk Dis Ct has m rec from 1920, div, pro, civ ct rec)

| *† **Lincoln** | A6 | 1909 | Flathead |

Lincoln County, 512 California Ave, Libby, MT 59923 .... (406)293-7781
(Co Clk has b, d & Ind rec from 1909; Clk Dis Ct has m, div, pro & civ ct rec; Co Clk also has some transcribed b & d rec prior to 1909)

| *† **Madison** | D2 | 1865 | Original county |

Madison County, 110 W Wallace St, Virginia City, MT 59755 .... (406)843-5392
(Co Clk & Rcdr has b & d rec from 1909, Ind rec from 1864; Clk Cts has m rec from 1887, div, pro & civ ct rec from 1865)

| **McCone** | H5 | 1919 | Dawson, Richland |

McCone County, 206 2nd Ave, Circle, MT 59215 .... (406)485-3505
(Co Clk & Rcdr has b, d, bur & Ind rec from 1919; Clk Cts has m, div, pro & civ ct rec)

| * **Meagher** | D4 | 1867 | Original county |

Meagher County, 15 W Main St, White Sulphur Springs, MT 59645 .... (406)547-3612
(Co Clk & Rcdr has b & d rec from 1896, bur rec from 1884 & Ind rec from 1866; Clk Cts has m & pro rec from 1866, div & civ ct rec from 1867 & naturalization rec from 1867)

| † **Mineral** | A5 | 1914 | Missoula |

Mineral County, 300 River St, Superior, MT 59872 .... (406)822-4541
(Co Clk & Rcdr has b, d, bur & Ind rec from 1914; Clk Dis Ct has m, div, pro & civ ct rec from 1914)

| *† **Missoula** | B4 | 1865 | Original county |

Missoula County, 200 W Broadway St, Missoula, MT 59802-4292 .... (406)721-5700
(Co Clk has b & d rec from 1895 & Ind rec; Clk Cts has m, div, pro & civ ct rec)

| **Musselshell** | F4 | 1911 | Fergus, Yellowstone |

Musselshell County, 506 Main St, Roundup, MT 59072-2498 .... (406)323-1104
(Co Clk has b, d & Ind rec from 1911; Clk Cts has m, div, pro & civ ct rec)

| *† **Park** | E2 | 1887 | Gallatin |

Park County, 414 E Callender St, Livingston, MT 59047-2799 .... (406)222-6120
(Co Clk has b, d & Ind rec from 1907; Clk Dis Ct has m, div, pro & civ ct rec)

| * **Petroleum** | F4 | 1924 | Fergus, Garfield |

Petroleum County, 201 E Main, Winnett, MT 59087 .... (406)429-5311
(Director of Rec has b, m, d, bur, div, pro, civ ct & Ind rec from 1925)

| **Phillips** | G6 | 1915 | Valley |

Phillips County, County Courthouse, Malta, MT 59538 .... (406)654-2429
(Co Clk has b, d & Ind rec; Clk Cts has m, div, pro & civ ct rec)

| **Pondera** | C6 | 1919 | Chouteau |

Pondera County, 20 4th Ave SW, Conrad, MT 59425-2340 .... (406)278-7681
(Co Clk has b, d & Ind rec from 1919; Clk Cts has m, div, pro & civ ct rec)

| * **Powder River** | H3 | 1919 | Custer |

Powder River County, Courthouse Sq, Broadus, MT 59317 .... (406)436-2657
(Co Clk has b, d rec from 1919, Ind rec from 1890s, election rec from 1919; Clk Dist Ct has m, div rec from 1919, pro, civ ct, crim rec from 1882)

| **Powell** | C4 | 1901 | Missoula |

Powell County, 409 Missouri Ave, Deer Lodge, MT 59722-1084 .... (406)846-3680
(Co Clk has b, d & Ind rec from 1907; Clk Cts has m, div, pro & civ ct rec from 1901)

Name	Map Index	Date Created	Parent County or Territory From Which Organized

Prairie   H4   1915   Custer
Prairie County, County Courthouse, Terry, MT 59349 .... (406)637-5575
(Co Clk has b, d & Ind rec from 1915; Clk Cts has m, div, pro & civ ct rec from 1915)

*† **Ravalli**   B3   1893   Missoula
Ravalli County, S 2nd & Bedford Sts, Hamilton, MT 59894 .... (406)363-1900
(Co Clk & Rcdr has b & d rec from 1911, Ind rec from 1871, voter reg from 1937; Clk Cts has m, div & civ ct rec from 1893, pro rec from 1888)

Richland   I5   1914   Dawson
Richland County, 201 W Main St, Sidney, MT 59270-4035 .... (406)482-1706
(Co Clk has b rec from 1910, d & Ind rec from 1914; Clk Dis Ct has m, div, pro & civ ct rec)

Roosevelt   H6   1919   Valley, Richland
Roosevelt County, 400 2nd Ave S, Wolf Point, MT 59201-1600 .... (406)653-1590
(Co Clk & Rcdr has b, d & Ind rec from 1919; Clk Dis Ct has m, div, pro & civ ct rec from 1919)

* **Rosebud**   H3   1901   Custer
Rosebud County, PO Box 47, Forsyth, MT 59327-0047 .... (406)356-2251
(Co Clk has b & d rec from 1900; Clk Dis Ct has m, div, pro & civ ct rec)

*† **Sanders**   A5   1905   Missoula
Sanders County, Main St, Thompson Falls, MT 59873 .... (406)827-4392
(Co Clk & Rcdr has b, m, div, pro, civ ct & Ind rec from 1906, d rec from 1907 & sale of twn lots of Thompson Falls from 1895 to 1955)

* **Sheridan**   I6   1913   Custer
Sheridan County, 100 W Laurel Ave, Plentywood, MT 59254-1699 .... (406)765-2310
(Co Clk has b, d, bur & Ind rec from 1913; Clk Cts has m, div, pro & civ ct rec from 1913)

† **Silver Bow**   C3   1881   Deer Lodge
Silver Bow County, 155 W Granite St, Butte, MT 59701-9215 .... (406)723-8262
(May 2, 1977 the city of Butte and county of Silver Bow were unified to form the Butte-Silver Bow government. Co Clk & Rcdr has b, d rec from 1890, Ind rec from 1881, mil discharge rec from 1932; Clk Cts has m, div, pro, civ ct rec)

*† **Stillwater**   E2   1913   Sweet Grass, Yellowstone, Carbon
Stillwater County, PO Box 147, Columbus, MT 59019-0147 .... (406)322-4546
(Co Clk has b, d & Ind rec from 1913; Clk Dis Ct has m, div, pro & civ ct rec)

*† **Sweet Grass**   E3   1895   Meagher, Park, Yellowstone
Sweet Grass County, PO Box 460, Big Timber, MT 59011-0460 .... (406)932-5152
(Co Clk & Rcdr has b rec from 1907, d & bur rec from 1900, Ind rec from 1895; Clk Dis Ct has m, div, pro & civ ct rec from 1895)

* **Teton**   C5   1893   Chouteau
Teton County, PO Box 610, Choteau, MT 59422 .... (406)466-2151
(Co Clk has b, d & bur rec from 1899; Clk Dis Ct has m, div, pro & civ ct rec)

*† **Toole**   D6   1914   Teton
Toole County, 226 1st St S, Shelby, MT 59474-1920 .... (406)434-5121
(Co Clk & Rcdr has b, d & bur rec from 1914 & Ind rec from 1890; Clk Cts has m rec from 1914, div, pro & civ ct rec)

* **Treasure**   G3   1918   Rosebud
Treasure County, PO Box 392, Hysham, MT 59038-0392 .... (406)342-5547
(Co Clk & Rcdr has b, d & Ind rec from 1919; Clk Dis Ct has m, div, pro & civ ct rec)

* **Valley**   G6   1893   Dawson
Valley County, PO Box 311, Glasgow, MT 59203-0311 .... (406)228-8221
(Co Clk & Rcdr has b, d & Ind rec from early 1900s; Clk Cts has m, div, pro & civ ct rec)

Wheatland   E4   1917   Meagher, Sweet Grass
Wheatland County, PO Box C, Harlowton, MT 59036-0903 .... (406)632-4891
(Co Clk & Rcdr has b rec from 1917, d, bur & Ind rec; Clk Cts has m, div, pro & civ ct rec)

Wibaux   I4   1914   Dawson
Wibaux County, 200 S Wibaux, Wibaux, MT 59353 .... (406)795-2410
(Co Clk & Rcdr has b, d & bur rec from 1914, Ind rec from 1884; Clk Dis Ct has m, div, pro & civ ct rec from 1914)

* **Yellowstone**   F3   1883   Gallatin, Meagher, Custer, Carbon
Yellowstone County, PO Box 35001, Billings, MT 59107-5001 .... (406)256-2785
(Co Clk has b, d & Ind rec from 1883)

* At least one county history has been published about this county.
† Inventory of county archives was made by the Historical Records Survey. (See Introduction)

NEBRASKA

CAPITAL · LINCOLN — TERRITORY 1854 — STATE 1867 (37th)
State Map on Page M-25

In 1714, the first European to enter the Nebraska area appears to have been Etienne Veniard de Bourgmond, a French adventurer. His report about the area used the term Nebraska for the first time. Six years later a Spanish soldier, Pedro de Villasur, led an expedition into Nebraska but was massacred by Pawnee Indians. Fur traders were the only whites in the area until after the Louisiana Purchase in 1803. After 1803, a number of expeditions explored the area, some of which reported Nebraska to be a vast wasteland. The first permanent settlement was Bellevue, established in 1823. Other forts and trading posts were established, especially along the Oregon and Mormon trails.

In 1834, Nebraska was placed under the supervision of Arkansas, Michigan, and Missouri and termed Indian country from which all whites were excluded. Later, Nebraska was part of the territories of Indiana, Louisiana, and Missouri. Most of the Indian tribes had ceded their land to the United States by 1854 when Nebraska became a territory. It included all the territory between 40 and 49 degrees north latitude and between the Missouri River and the crest of the Rocky Mountains, meaning that parts of Colorado, Montana, North and South Dakota, and Wyoming were then part of Nebraska. In 1861, the Colorado and Dakota Territories were created and in 1863 the formation of the Idaho Territory reduced Nebraska to nearly its present size.

Early settlers were mainly stragglers from the California Gold Rush and the Oregon migration. Some of the thousands who traveled the Oregon, California, and Mormon Trails either stopped their migration in Nebraska or returned to Nebraska upon seeing the Rocky Mountains. During the 1850's, many Germans settled in Nebraska. Two decades later, a large group of Germans from Russia settled Lancaster and nearby counties. After the passage of the Homestead Act, many Scandinavians came to the area. Today most Nebraskans are of German, Czech, Swedish, or Russian descent.

During the Civil War, Nebraska sided with the Union and supplied over 3,000 men to its forces. The first railroad to the Pacific Coast was begun at Omaha in 1865 and completed four years later. Nebraska was admitted to the Union in 1867 as the 37th state. Many Civil War veterans came to Nebraska to secure cheap land and brought about the state's largest population growth.

Statewide registration of births and deaths began in 1905 and was generally complied with by 1920. These records are available from the Bureau of Vital Statistics, State Department of Health, 301 Centennial Mall South, P.O. Box 95007, Lincoln, NE 68509. Relationship to the individual and the reason for the request must accompany all requests for copies of records, along with written permission from the individual if the birth or marriage occurred within the last 50 years. To verify current fees, call 402-471-2871.

Marriage records were kept by the counties following their organization. Probate records are kept by the County Judge in most counties. Territorial and state censuses exist for parts of Nebraska for 1854, 1855, 1856, 1860, 1865, and 1869. Some have been transcribed, indexed, and published. For existing records contact the Nebraska State Historical Society, Department of Reference Services, 1500 "R" Street, P. O. Box 82554, Lincoln, NE 68501. A detailed census of German immigrants from Russia living in Lincoln was taken from 1913 to 1914.

Genealogical Archives, Libraries and Societies

Alliance Public Library, 202 West 4th St., Alliance, NE 69301

Bayard Public Library, Bayard, NE 69334

Big Springs Public Library, Big Springs, NE 69122

Bridgeport Public Library, Bridgeport, NE 69336

Broadwater Public Library, Broadwater, NE 69125

Chadron Public Library, Chadron, NE 69337

Chappell Public Library, Chappell, NE 69129

Columbus Public Library, Columbus, NE 68601

Cravath Memorial Library, Hay Spring, NE 69347

Crawford Public Library, Crawford, NE 69339

Dalton Public Library, Dalton, NE 69131

Gering Public Library, Gering, NE 69341

Gordon Public Library, Gordon, NE 69343

Grand Island Public Library, 211 S. Washington, Grand Island, NE 68801

Hemingford Public Library, Hemingford, NE 69348

Kearney Public Library, Kearney, NE 68847

Kimball Public Library, Kimball, NE 69145

Lewellen Public Library, Lewellen, NE 69147

Lexington Public Library, Box 778, Lexington, NE 68850

Lisco Library, Lisco, NE 69148

Lue R. Spencer D. A. R. Genealogical Library, c / o Edith Abbott Memorial Library, Second and Washington Streets, Grand Island, NE 68801

Lyman Public Library, Lyman, NE 69352

Minatare Public Library, Minatare, NE 69356

Morrill Public Library, Morrill, NE 69358

Nancy Fawcett Memorial Library, Lodgepole, NE 69149

Nebraska D. A. R. Library, 202 West 4th St., Alliance, NE 69301

Nebraska State Law Library, Third Floor, Nebraska State Capitol Bldg., 1445 K, Lincoln, NE 68508

Nemaha Valley Museum, Inc., P. O. Box 25, Auburn, NE 68305

Norfolk Public Library, North 4th Street, Norfolk, NE 68701

Omaha Public Library, 215 South 15th St., Omaha, NE 68102

Oshkosh Public Library, Oshkosh, NE 69154

Phelps County Museum Library, Holdrege Area Genealogy, Box 164, Holdrege, NE 68949

Potter Public Library, Box 317, Potter, NE 69156

Public Library, 136 South 14th St., Lincoln, NE 68508

Quivey Memorial Library, Mitchell, NE 69357

Rushville Public Library, Rushville, NE 69360

Scottsbluff Public Library, Scottsbluff, NE 69361

University of Nebraska Library, Lincoln, NE 68503

Wayne Public Library, 410 Main St., Wayne, NE 68787

Adams County Genealogical Society, P. O. Box 424, Hastings, NE 68901

American Historical Society of Germans from Russia, 631 D St., Lincoln, NE 68502

Cairo Roots, Rt. 1, Box 42, Cairo, NE 68824

Chase County Genealogical Society, P. O. Box 303, Imperial, NE 69033

Cherry County Genealogical Society, Box 380, Valentine, NE 69201

Cheyenne County Genealogical Society, Box 802, Sidney, NE 69162

Dawson County Genealogical Society, 514 E. 8th St., Cozad, NE 69130

Dawson County Historical Society, P. O. Box 369, Lexington, NE 68850

Eastern Nebraska Genealogical Society, P. O. Box 541, Fremont, NE 68025

Fillmore Heritage Genealogical Society, Rt. 2, Box 28, Exeter, NE 68351

Fort Kearny Genealogical Society, Box 22, Kearney, NE 68847

Frontier County Genealogical Society, Box 507, Curtis, NE 69025

Furnas County Genealogical Society, P. O. Box 166, Beaver City, NE 68926

Gage County Historical Society, Box 793, Beatrice, NE 68310

Genealogical Seekers, 871 West 6th, Wahoo, NE 68066

Greater Omaha Genealogical Society, P. O. Box 4011, Omaha, NE 68104

Greater York Area Genealogical Society, Kilgore Memorial Library, 6th and Nebraska, York, NE 68467

Holdrege Area Genealogy Club, RR1, Box 29, Bertrand, NE 68927

Holt County Historical Society, P. O. Box 376, O'Neill, NE 68763

Hooker County Genealogical Society, Box 280, Mullen, NE 69152

Lexington Genealogy Society, Box 778, Lexington, NE 68850

Lincoln-Lancaster County Genealogy Society, P. O. Box 30055, Lincoln, NE 68503-0055

Nebraska Society, Sons of the American Revolution, 6731 Sumner St., Lincoln, NE 68506

Nebraska State Genealogical Society, P. O. Box 5608, Lincoln, NE 68505

North Platte Genealogical Society, P. O. Box 1452, North Platte, NE 69101

Northeastern Nebraska Genealogical Society P. O. Box 249, Lyons, NE 68038

Northern Antelope County Genealogical Society, Box 267, Orchard, NE 68764

Northwest Genealogical Society, P. O. Box 6, Alliance, NE 69301-006

Perkins County Genealogical Society, Box 418, Grant, NE 69140

Plains Genealogical Society, Kimball Public Library, 208 South Walnut Street, Kimball, NE 69145

Platte Valley Kinseekers, P. O. Box 153, Columbus, NE 68601

Prairie Pioneer Genealogical Society, Box 1122, Grand Island, NE 68802

Ravenna Genealogical Society 105 Alba Street, Ravenna, NE 68869

Seward County Genealogical Society, RR 1, Box 198, Beaver Crossing, NE 68313

South Central Genealogical Society, Rt. 2, Box 57, Minden, NE 68959

Southeast Nebraska Genealogical Society, P. O. Box 562, Beatrice, NE 68301

Southwest Nebraska Genealogical Society, Box 156, McCook, NE 69001

Thayer County Genealogical Society, Box 388, Belvidere, NE 68315

Thomas County Genealogical Society, Box 136, Thedford, NE 69166

Tri-State Corners Genealogical Society, Lydia Bruun Woods Memorial Library, 120 E. 18th St., Falls City, NE 68355

Valley County Genealogical Society, 619 S. 10th, Ord, NE 68862

Washington County Genealogical Society, Blair Public Library, Blair, NE 68008

Printed Census Records and Mortality Schedules

Federal Census 1860, 1870, 1880, 1900, 1910
Federal Mortality Schedules 1860, 1870, 1880
Union Veterans and Widows 1890
State/Territorial Census 1854, 1855, 1856, 1865-1884, 1885

Valuable Printed Sources

Atlases, Maps, and Gazetteers

Fitzpatrick, Lilian L. *Nebraska Place Names*. Lincoln, Nebraska: University of Nebraska Press, 1967.

Nimmo, Sylvia. *Maps Showing the County Boundaries of Nebraska, 1854-1925*. Papillion, Nebraska: Sylvia Nimmo.

Bibliographies

Diffendahl, Anne P. *A Guide to the Newspaper Collection of the State Archives*. Lincoln, Nebraska: Nebraska State Historical Society, 1977.

Nimmo, Sylvia and Mary Cutler. *Nebraska Local History and Genealogy Reference Guide: A Bibliography of County Research Materials in Selected Repositories*. Papillion, Nebraska: Sylvia Nimmo, 1987.

Genealogical Research Guides

Cox, E. Evelyn. *Ancestree Climbing in the Midwest*. Ellensburg, Washington: E. Evelyn Cox, 1977.

McCallson, Ilene. "Research in Nebraska," in the July-August 1977 issue of *The Genealogical Helper*. Logan, Utah: Everton Publishers.

Genealogical Sources

Luebke, Frederick C. *Immigrants and Politics: The Germans of Nebraska, 1880-1900*. Lincoln, Nebraska: University of Nebraska Press.

Histories

Andreas, A. T. *History of the State of Nebraska*. Evansville, Indiana: Unigraphic Inc., 1975 reprint.

Morton, J. Sterling. *Illustrated History of Nebraska*. Lincoln, Nebraska: Jacob North & Co., 1907.

NEBRASKA COUNTY DATA
State Map on Page M-25

Name	Map Index	Date Created	Parent County or Territory From Which Organized
* **Adams**	D6	1867	Clay

Adams County, 4th & Denver Sts, Hastings, NE 68901 .... (402)461-7107
(Co Judge has m & pro rec; Clk Dis Ct has div & Ind rec)

| * **Antelope** | C3 | 1871 | Pierce |

Antelope County, 501 Main St, Neligh, NE 68756-1424 .... (402)887-4410

| * **Arthur** | G4 | 1887 | Unorg. Terr |

Arthur County, Main St, Arthur, NE 69121 .... (308)764-2203
(Arthur County was formed in 1887, but it did not become a county until 1913. Before 1913, records were kept at McPherson County)(Co Clk has Ind rec from 1913, Co Ct has m, pro, civ ct rec from 1913; Clk Dis Ct has div rec from 1913; Co Cem Sexton has bur rec; Co Supt of Schools has school cen from 1913)

| * **Banner** | I4 | 1888 | Cheyenne |

Banner County, State St, Harrisburg, NE 69345 .... (308)436-5265
(Co Clk has b rec from 1920, Ind rec from 1890; Co Ct has m, pro, civ ct rec from 1890; Dept of Health has bur, div rec)

Blackbird (See Thurston)

| * **Blaine** | E4 | 1885 | Custer |

Blaine County, Lincoln Ave, Brewster, NE 68821 .... (308)547-2222
(Co Judge has pro & civ ct rec; Co Clk has div & Ind rec from 1887)

| * **Boone** | C4 | 1871 | Platte |

Boone County, 222 S 4th St, Albion, NE 68620-1247 .... (402)395-2055
(Co Clk has m rec from 1932, div, pro & civ ct rec; Rcdr Deeds has Ind rec; State Archives, 1500 "R" Street, Lincoln, NE 68508 has m rec to 1932)

| * **Box Butte** | H3 | 1887 | Unorg. Terr |

Box Butte County, 5th & Box Butte Sts, Alliance, NE 69301 .... (308)762-6565
(Co Clk has m & Ind rec; Co Judge has pro & civ ct rec; Clk Dis Ct has div rec)

| * **Boyd** | D2 | 1891 | Holt |

Boyd County, County Courthouse, Butte, NE 68722 .... (402)775-2391
(Co Clk has b, d rec from 1917, div, civ ct, Ind rec from 1897; Co Judge has m rec, civ ct rec from 1894)

| * **Brown** | E3 | 1883 | Unorg. Terr |

Brown County, 148 W 4th St, Ainsworth, NE 69210-1696 .... (402)387-2705
(attached to Holt Co Nebr prior to 1883) (Co Supt of schools has school census rec from 1883; Co Clk has m & Ind rec from 1883, naturalization rec from 1884 to 1922, mil dis rec from 1919; Co Judge has pro rec; Clk Dis Ct has div & civ ct rec)

| * **Buffalo** | D5 | 1855 | Original county |

Buffalo County, 16th & Central Ave, Kearney, NE 68848 .... (308)236-1226
(Co Clk has m rec from 1872; Co Judge has pro & civ ct rec from 1872; Clk Dis Ct has div rec; Reg Deeds has Ind rec)

| * **Burt** | B4 | 1854 | Original county |

Burt County, 111 N 13th St, Tekamah, NE 68061-1043 .... (402)374-1955
(Co Clk has m & Ind rec; Co Judge has pro & civ ct rec; Clk Dis Ct has div rec)

| * **Butler** | B5 | 1856 | Unorg. Terr |

Butler County, 451 5th St, David City, NE 68632 .... (402)367-3091
(Co Clk has Ind rec from 1869; Co Ct has m, pro rec; Dis Ct has div, civ ct rec)

Calhoun (Changed to Saunders 8 Jan 1862)

| * **Cass** | B5 | 1854 | Original county |

Cass County, 4th & Main Sts, Plattsmouth, NE 68048 .... (402)296-2164
(Co Clk has m rec from 1855; Co Ct has pro & civ ct rec from 1854; Cem Board has bur rec; Clk Dis Ct has div rec from 1855; Co Surveyor has Ind rec from 1857; Reg Deeds has deeds & mtgs)

| * **Cedar** | C3 | 1857 | Original county |

Cedar County, 101 S Broadway Ave, Hartington, NE 68739 .... (402)254-7411
(Co Clk has m & Ind rec; Co Judge has pro & civ ct rec; Clk Dis Ct has div rec)

Name	Map Index	Date Created	Parent County or Territory From Which Organized

* **Chase**   G6   1873   Unorg. Terr
Chase County, 921 Broadway, Imperial, NE   69033 . . . . (308)882-5266
(Co Judge has m, pro & civ ct rec from 1886; Clk Dis Ct has div rec from 1886; Co Clk has Ind rec from 1886)

* **Cherry**   F3   1883   Unorg. Terr
Cherry County, PO Box 120, Valentine, NE   69201-0120 . . . . (402)376-2771
(Co Clk has m & Ind rec; Co Ct has pro & civ ct rec; Clk Dis Ct has div rec)

* **Cheyenne**   H5   1867   Unorg. Terr
Cheyenne County, 1000 10th Ave, Sidney, NE   69162-1612 . . . . (308)254-2141
(Co Clk has m & Ind rec; Co Ct has pro rec; Clk Dis Ct has div rec)

* **Clay**   C6   1855   Original county
Clay County, 111 W Fairfield St, Clay Center, NE   68933-1436 . . . . (402)762-3463
(Co Clk has Ind rec from 1871 & m rec; Co Ct has pro & civ ct rec; Clk Dis Ct has div rec)

* **Colfax**   B4   1869   Dodge
Colfax County, 411 E 11th St, Schuyler, NE   68661-1940 . . . . (402)352-3434
(Co Judge has m rec from 1869, pro rec from 1886 & civ ct rec from 1885; Clk Dis Ct has div rec from 1881; Co Clk has Ind rec from 1860)

* **Cuming**   B4   1855   Burt
Cuming County, PO Box 290, West Point, NE   68788-0290 . . . . (402)372-2144
(Co Judge has m, pro rec from 1866, civ ct rec from 1960, school cen; Clk Dis Ct has div rec from 1869)

* **Custer**   E4   1877   Unorg. Terr
Custer County, 431 S 10th Ave, Broken Bow, NE   68822-2099 . . . . (308)872-5701
(Co Clk has b rec from 1910, d rec from 1915, obituaries from 1877, pioneer biographical data; Custer Co Hist Soc has many other rec; Co Judge has m rec from 1878, pro & civ ct rec from 1887; Clk Dis Ct has div rec from 1881; Reg Deeds has Ind rec from 1880)

* **Dakota**   B3   1855   Original county
Dakota County, PO Box 38, Dakota City, NE   68731-0038 . . . . (402)987-2126
(Co Clk has m & Ind rec; Co Judge has pro rec from 1864, civ ct rec from 1872; Clk Dis Ct has div rec from 1866)

* **Dawes**   H3   1885   Sioux
Dawes County, 451 Main St, Chadron, NE   69337-2649 . . . . (308)432-2863
(Co Clk has Ind rec from 1880; Co Judge has m, pro rec; Clk Dis Ct has div rec)

* **Dawson**   E5   1860   Buffalo
Dawson County, 7th & Washington Sts, Lexington, NE   68850 . . . . (308)324-2127
(Co Clk has m rec from 1873; Co Ct has pro & civ ct rec; Clk Dis Ct has div rec; Reg Deeds has Ind rec)

* **Deuel**   H5   1888   Cheyenne
Deuel County, 3rd & Vincent, Chappell, NE   69129 . . . . (308)874-3308
(Co Judge has m & pro rec; Co Clk has bur, div & Ind rec, dis ct rec from 1890)

* **Dixon**   B3   1856   Original county
Dixon County, 302 3rd St, Ponca, NE   68770 . . . . (402)755-2881
(Co Clk has b, d & bur rec from 1919 but they are not public & Ind rec from 1871)

* **Dodge**   B4   1854   Original county
Dodge County, 435 N Park Ave, Fremont, NE   68025-4967 . . . . (402)727-2765
(Co Clk has m rec; Co Judge has pro rec; Clk Dis Ct has div rec; Reg Deeds has Ind rec)

* **Douglas**   B5   1854   Original county
Douglas County, 1819 Farnam St, Omaha, NE   68183-0001 . . . . (402)444-7000
(Co Judge has m & pro rec; Clk Dis Ct has div rec; Co Clk has mil service discharges)

Dundy   G6   1873   Unorg. Terr
Dundy County, Chief St, Benkelman, NE   69021 . . . . (308)423-2058
(Co Clk has b rec from 1907, d rec from 1904, also bur, div & civ ct rec; Co Judge has pro rec)

Emmet (Changed from L'eau Qui Court 18 Feb 1867. Changed to Knox 21 Feb 1873)

* **Fillmore**   C6   1856   Unorg. Terr
Fillmore County, 900 G St, Geneva, NE   68361-2005 . . . . (402)759-4931
(Co Clk has m & Ind rec from 1872, delayed b, physicians rec; Co Ct has pro & civ ct rec; Clk Dis Ct has div rec; Co Supt of Schools has school census)

Forney (changed to Nemaha)

* **Franklin**   D6   1867   Kearney
Franklin County, 405 15th Ave, Franklin, NE   68939-1309 . . . . (308)425-6202
(Co Clk has m rec from 1872, div & Ind rec)

* **Frontier**   F6   1872   Unorg. Terr
Frontier County, 1 Wellington St, Stockville, NE   69042-0040 . . . . (308)367-8641
(Co Judge has m & pro rec; Co Clk has div & Ind rec; Supt Schools has school census)

* **Furnas**   E6   1873   Unorg. Terr
Furnas County, PO Box 387, Beaver City, NE   68926-0387 . . . . (308)268-4145
(Co Judge has m, pro & civ ct rec; Clk Dis Ct has div rec; Co Clk has Ind rec from 1873)

* **Gage**   B6   1855   Original county
Gage County, PO Box 429, Beatrice, NE   68310-0429 . . . . (402)228-3355
(Co Judge has m, pro rec from 1860; Clk Dis Ct has div rec)

Name	Map Index	Date Created	Parent County or Territory From Which Organized

* **Garden** G4 1887 Cheyenne, Deuel
Garden County, Main St, Oshkosh, NE 69154 .... (308)772-3924
(Co Clk has m & Ind rec; Co Judge has pro & civ ct rec; Clk Dis Ct has div rec)

* **Garfield** D4 1884 Wheeler
Garfield County, PO Box 218, Burwell, NE 68823-0218 .... (308)346-4161
(Co Judge has m, div & pro rec)

*† **Gosper** E6 1873 Unorg. Terr
Gosper County, PO Box 136, Elwood, NE 68937-0136 .... (308)785-2611
(Co Judge has m & pro rec from 1891, civ ct rec from 1920; Co Clk has div rec from 1880 & Ind rec)

Grant G4 1887 Unorg. Terr
Grant County, PO Box 139, Hyannis, NE 69350-0139 .... (308)458-2488
(Co Clk has m & Ind rec from 1888, div rec from 1892; Co Judge has pro & civ ct rec)

*† **Greeley** D4 1871 Boone
Greeley County, 28th & Kildare Sts, Greeley, NE 68842 .... (308)428-3625
(Co Clk has m & Ind rec; Co Judge has pro rec; Clk Dis Ct has div & civ ct rec)

Greene (Changed to Seward 3 Jan 1862)

* **Hall** D5 1858 Original county
Hall County, 121 S Pine St, Grand Island, NE 68801 .... (308)381-5080
(Co Clk has m rec from 1869; Co Judge has pro rec; Clk Dis Ct has div & civ ct rec; Reg Deeds has Ind rec)

* **Hamilton** C5 1867 York
Hamilton County, County Courthouse, Aurora, NE 68818-2097 .... (402)694-3443
(Co Clk has m & Ind rec from 1870; Co Judge has pro & civ ct rec; Clk Dis Ct has div rec)

* **Harlan** E6 1871 Unorg. Terr
Harlan County, PO Box 379, Alma, NE 68920-0379 .... (308)928-2173
(Co Clk has m & Ind rec; Co Judge has pro & civ ct rec; Clk Dis Ct has div rec; Reg Deeds has Ind rec)

Harrison (Never org co in southwest corner of state. With Lincoln in 1870 cen.)

* **Hayes** F6 1877 Unorg. Terr
Hayes County, Troth St, Hayes Center, NE 69032 .... (308)286-3413
(Co Clk has d, bur & Ind rec)

Hitchcock F6 1873 Unorg. Terr
Hitchcock County, 229 E 'D' St, Trenton, NE 69044 .... (308)334-5646
(Co Clk has m, Ind, div & civ ct rec; Co Judge has pro rec)

* **Holt** D3 1860 Knox (see West)
Holt County, PO Box 329, O'Neill, NE 68763-0329 .... (402)336-1762
(Co Clk has m rec from 1878; Co Judge has pro & civ ct rec from 1882; Reg Deeds has Ind rec from 1879; Clk Dis Ct has div rec from 1879)

* **Hooker** F4 1889 Unorg. Terr
Hooker County, PO Box 184, Mullen, NE 69152-0184 .... (308)546-2244
(Co Clk has b & d rec from 1919 & Ind rec from 1889; Co Judge has m & pro rec)

*† **Howard** D5 1871 Hall
Howard County, 612 Indian St, Saint Paul, NE 68873-1642 .... (308)754-4343
(Co Judge has m, pro, civ ct, Ind rec from 1872, div rec from 1873, naturalization papers from 1872)

Izard (changed to Stanton)

Jackson (Never org co in southwest corner of state. With Lincoln in 1870 cen.)

* **Jefferson** B6 1856 Gage
Jefferson County, 411 4th St, Fairbury, NE 68352-2536 .... (402)729-2323
(Co Clk has m rec; Co Judge has pro & civ ct rec; Clk Dis Ct has div rec; Reg Deeds has Ind rec)

* **Johnson** B6 1855 Original county
Johnson County, PO Box 416, Tecumseh, NE 68450-0416 .... (402)335-3246
(Co Clk has m & Ind rec from 1858; Co Judge has pro & civ ct rec; Clk Dis Ct has div rec from 1858)

Jones 1856 Gage (changed to Jefferson, 1864)

* **Kearney** D6 1860 Original county
Kearney County, PO Box 339, Minden, NE 68959-0339 .... (308)832-1155
(Co Clk has m rec from 1872 & Ind rec; Co Judge has pro & civ ct rec; Clk Dis Ct has div rec)

Keith G5 1873 Lincoln
Keith County, PO Box 149, Ogallala, NE 69153-0149 .... (308)284-4726
(Co Clk has b, d & Ind rec; Co Judge has m rec; Clk Dis Ct has div, pro & civ ct rec)

* **Keya Paha** E2 1884 Brown, Rock
Keya Paha County, PO Box 349, Springview, NE 68778-0349 .... (402)497-3791
(Co Clk has m, div, pro, civ ct & Ind rec from 1886, school census)

Kimball I5 1888 Cheyenne
Kimball County, 114 E 3rd St, Kimball, NE 69145-1456 .... (308)235-2241
(Co Clk has div & pro rec; Co Judge has m, civ ct rec)

Name	Map Index	Date Created	Parent County or Territory From Which Organized

* **Knox** C3 1857 Emmet
  Knox County, Main, Center, NE 68724 .... (402)288-4282
  (Co Clk has m rec; Co Judge has pro & civ ct rec; Clk Dis Ct has div rec; Reg Deeds has lnd rec)

  L'Eau Qui Court 1857 Emmett (changed to Knox, 1873)

* **Lancaster** B5 1856 Original county
  Lancaster County, 555 S 10th St, Lincoln, NE 68508-2803 .... (402)471-7481
  [FHL has some m & cem rec]

* **Lincoln** F5 1860 Unorg. Terr. (see Shorter)
  Lincoln County, County Sq, North Platte, NE 69101 .... (308)534-4350
  (Co Judge has m, div, pro & civ ct rec; Reg Deeds has lnd rec)

* **Logan** F4 1885 Custer
  Logan County, PO Box 8, Stapleton, NE 69163-0008 .... (308)636-2311
  (Co Judge has m, div, pro, civ ct rec from 1885, partial bur rec; Co Clk has lnd rec)

*† **Loup** E4 1855 Unorg. Terr
  Loup County, 4th St, Taylor, NE 68879 .... (308)942-3135
  (Co Judge has m & pro rec; Co Clk has div, civ ct & lnd rec from 1887)

  Lyon (Never org co in southwest corner of state. With Lincoln in 1870 cen.)

* **Madison** C4 1856 Platte
  Madison County, PO Box 290, Madison, NE 68748-0290 .... (402)454-3311
  (Co Clk has m & lnd rec from 1868, pro rec from 1863, div & civ ct rec from 1907)

  McPherson F4 1887 Lincoln, Keith, Logan
  McPherson County, PO Box 122, Tryon, NE 69167-0122 .... (308)587-2363
  (Co Clk has m, div & lnd rec; Co Judge has pro & civ ct rec)

*† **Merrick** C5 1858 Original county
  Merrick County, PO Box 27, Central City, NE 68826-0027 .... (308)946-2881
  (Co Clk has b & d rec; Co Judge has m, div, pro & civ ct rec; Reg Deeds has lnd rec from 1873)

  Monroe (Never org co in southwest corner of state. With Lincoln in 1870 cen.)

* **Morrill** H4 1908 Cheyenne
  Morrill County, PO Box 610, Bridgeport, NE 69336-0610 .... (308)262-0860
  (Co Clk has b, d & bur rec from 1917 & lnd rec from 1909; Co Judge has m & pro rec)

* **Nance** C4 1879 Merrick
  Nance County, PO Box 338, Fullerton, NE 68638-0338 .... (308)536-2331
  (Co Clk has m rec from 1890, lnd rec from 1879; Co Judge has pro rec; Clk Dis Ct has div & civ ct rec from 1882)

* **Nemaha** A6 1854 Original county
  Nemaha County, 1824 N St, Auburn, NE 68305-2341 .... (402)274-4213
  (Co Clk has m from 1856, lnd rec from 1855; Co Judge has div, pro & civ ct rec)

* **Nuckolls** C6 1860 Clay
  Nuckolls County, 150 S Main St, Nelson, NE 68961 .... (409)225-4361
  (Co Judge has m & pro rec; Clk Dis Ct has div & civ ct rec; Co Clk has lnd rec from 1900 obtained only with description of lnd in question)

* **Otoe** A5 1854 Original county
  Otoe County, PO Box 249, Nebraska City, NE 68410-0249 .... (402)873-3586
  (Co Clk has m, div & civ ct rec; Co Judge has pro rec; Reg Deeds has lnd rec)

* **Pawnee** B6 1855 Original county
  Pawnee County, County Courthouse, Pawnee City, NE 68420 .... (402)852-2962
  (Co Clk has m rec from 1858, lnd, div & civ ct rec; Co Judge has pro rec)

* **Perkins** G5 1887 Keith
  Perkins County, PO Box 156, Grant, NE 69140-0156 .... (308)352-4643
  (Co Clk has m, div, civ ct & lnd rec; Co Judge has pro rec)

* **Phelps** E6 1873 Unorg. Terr
  Phelps County, 715 5th Ave, Holdrege, NE 68949-2256 .... (308)995-4469
  (Co Clk has m & lnd rec; Co Judge has pro rec; Clk Dis Ct has div rec)

* **Pierce** C3 1856 Madison
  Pierce County, 111 W Court St, Pierce, NE 68767-1224 .... (402)329-4225
  (Co Clk has m & lnd rec; Co Judge has pro & civ ct rec; Clk Dis Ct has div rec; Co Supt of Schools has school attendance rec)

* **Platte** C4 1856 Original county
  Platte County, 2610 14th St, Columbus, NE 68601-4929 .... (402)563-4904
  (Co Judge has m & pro rec; Clk Dis Ct has div & civ ct rec; Co Asr has lnd rec)

* **Polk** C5 1856 Original county
  Polk County, County Courthouse, Osceola, NE 68651 .... (402)747-5431
  (Co Judge has m & pro rec; Co Clk has lnd rec)

* **Red Willow** F6 1873 Frontier
  Red Willow County, 500 Norris Ave, McCook, NE 69001-2006 .... (308)345-1552
  (Co Judge has m, pro & civ ct rec; Clk Dis Ct has div rec; Co Clk has lnd rec abt 1870)

Name	Map Index	Date Created	Parent County or Territory From Which Organized

* **Richardson**   A6   1854   Original county
   Richardson County, 1701 Stone St, Falls City, NE 68355-2026 .... (402)245-2911
   (Co Clk has b, d rec from 1918; Co Judge has m rec from 1800s, pro, civ ct rec; Reg Deeds has Ind rec; local cemeteries have bur rec; Clk Dis Ct has div rec)

   Rock   E3   1857   Brown
   Rock County, 400 State St, Bassett, NE 68714 .... (402)684-3933
   (Co Judge has m rec; Co Clk has div rec from 1889, pro, civ ct, Ind rec from 1889)

* **Saline**   B6   1855   Gage, Lancaster
   Saline County, 215 Court St, Wilber, NE 68465 .... (402)821-2374
   (Co Clk has b, d from 1976, Ind rec from 1886; Co Ct has m rec from 1886, pro rec from 1870; Clk Dis Ct has div, civ ct rec from 1886)

* **Sarpy**   B5   1857   Original county
   Sarpy County, 1208 Golden Gate Dr, Omaha, NE 68046-2838 .... (402)339-3225
   (Co Judge has m & pro rec; Co Clk has Ind rec)

* **Saunders**   B5   1856   Sarpy, Douglas
   Saunders County, Chestnut St Courthouse, Wahoo, NE 68066 .... (402)443-8101
   (Co Clk has m, bur, div, pro, civ ct & Ind rec)

* **Scotts Bluff**   I4   1881   Cheyenne
   Scotts Bluff County, 1825 10th St, Gering, NE 69341-2444 .... (308)436-6600
   (Co Clk has m rec; Co Judge has div, pro & civ ct rec)

*† **Seward**   C5   1855   Greene
   Seward County, County Courthouse, Seward, NE 68434 .... (402)643-2883
   (Co Clk has m rec & Ind rec from 1866; Co Ct has pro rec from 1869; Clk Dis Ct has div rec from 1868, civ ct rec from 1869)

* **Sheridan**   H3   1885   Sioux
   Sheridan County, 301 E 2nd St, Rushville, NE 69360 .... (308)327-2633
   (Co Judge has m, pro & civ ct rec; Clk Dis Ct has div rec)

* **Sherman**   D5   1871   Buffalo
   Sherman County, PO Box 456, Loup City, NE 68853-0456 .... (308)745-1513
   (Co Clk has m rec from 1883, div & civ ct rec from 1882, Ind rec from 1873, naturalization rec from 1882 to 1920; Co Clk Magistrate has pro rec)

   Shorter (Changed to Lincoln 11 Dec 1861)

* **Sioux**   I3   1877   Unorg. Terr
   Sioux County, Main St, Harrison, NE 69346 .... (308)668-2443
   (Co Clk has Ind rec; Co Judge has m, pro & civ ct rec; Clk Dis Ct has div rec)

* **Stanton**   B4   1855   Dodge (formerly Izard)
   Stanton County, 804 Ivy St, Stanton, NE 68779 .... (402)439-2222
   (Co Clk has m rec from 1869, Ind rec from 1868, div rec from 1875; Co Judge has pro rec; Clk Dis Ct has civ ct rec)

   Taylor (Never org co in southwest corner of state. With Lincoln in 1870 cen.)

* **Thayer**   C6   1871   Jefferson
   Thayer County, 235 N 4th St, Hebron, NE 68370-1549 .... (402)768-6126
   (Co Judge has m, pro & civ ct rec; Clk Dis Ct has div rec; Co Clk has Ind rec)

* **Thomas**   F4   1887   Blaine
   Thomas County, PO Box 226, Thedford, NE 69166-0226 .... (308)645-2261
   (Co Clk has m from 1887, Ind rec; Clk Dis Ct has div & civ ct rec; Co Judge has pro rec)

   Thurston   B3   1865   Burt
   Thurston County, 106 S 5th St, Pender, NE 68047 .... (402)385-2343
   (Co Judge has m & pro rec from 1889; Clk Dis Ct has div & civ ct rec from 1889; Co Clk has Ind rec from 1885)(Thurston Co was orginally an Indian res & prior to organization was called Blackbird. From 1884 to 1889 it was administered by Dakota Co according to Co Clk)

* **Valley**   D4   1871   Unorg. Terr
   Valley County, 125 S 15th St, Ord, NE 68862 .... (308)728-3700
   (Co Judge has m & pro rec; Clk Dis Ct has div & civ ct rec; Co Clk has Ind rec from 1883)

* **Washington**   B4   1854   Original county
   Washington County, PO Box 466, Blair, NE 68008-0466 .... (402)426-6822
   (Co Clk has b, d, bur & Ind rec; Judge's Office has m, pro & civ ct rec; Clk Dis Ct has div rec)

* **Wayne**   B3   1871   Thurston
   Wayne County, 510 N Pearl St, Wayne, NE 68787-1939 .... (402)375-2288
   (Co Judge has m, pro & civ ct rec from 1871; Clk Dis Ct has div rec; Co Clk has Ind rec from 1870)

*† **Webster**   D6   1867   Unorg. Terr
   Webster County, 621 N Cedar St, Red Cloud, NE 68970-2397 .... (402)746-2716
   (Co Clk has m, Ind, div, pro & civ ct rec from 1871, naturalization rec from 1874)

   West (changed to Holt 9 Jan 1862)

* **Wheeler**   D4   1877   Boone
   Wheeler County, County Courthouse, Bartlett, NE 68622 .... (308)654-3235
   (Co Clk has civ ct, Ind rec)

Name	Map Index	Date Created	Parent County or Territory From Which Organized
* **York**	C5	1855	Original county

York County, 510 Lincoln Ave, York, NE 68467-2945 . . . . (402)362-7759
(Co Clk has m & lnd rec; Co Judge has pro & civ ct rec; Clk Dis Ct has div rec)

* At least one county history has been published about this county.

† Inventory of county archives was made by the Historical Records Survey. (See Introduction)

NEVADA

CAPITAL · CARSON CITY — TERRITORY 1861 — STATE 1864 (36th)
State Map on Page M-26

The first whites to enter Nevada did so in the 1820's. Among those to explore the area were Jedediah Smith, Peter Ogden, Kit Carson, and later John C. Fremont. In 1821, Mexico gained its independence from Spain and claimed Nevada as part of its territory. During the 1840's, numerous wagon trains crossed Nevada on their way to California. In 1848, Nevada, along with other western states, became part of the United States. The first non-Indian settlement was made at Mormon Station (Genoa) in 1849. The following year, most of Nevada became part of the Utah Territory. In 1853 and 1856, residents of the Carson River Valley petitioned to become part of California Territory because Utah was not protecting them. Discovery of gold in 1859 at the Comstock Lode brought thousands to Nevada. People from England, Italy, Scandinavia, Germany, France, and Mexico came to the area to join the migrating Americans in the search for gold and silver. Nevada became a territory in 1861 and achieved statehood just two years later.

During the Civil War, Nevada had over 1,000 men serve in the Union forces. After the Civil War, Nevada's borders were enlarged slightly, taking away from both Utah and Arizona. During the decade of the 1880's, the Comstock Lode declined and with it the population of the state. Discoveries of silver at Tonopah, gold at Goldfield and copper at Ely led to new booms which lasted until World War I. Gambling was legalized in 1931 which brought a new boom to Nevada.

Birth and death records from 1867 to June 30, 1911, and marriage records, deeds, and land records from 1864 are in each county recorder's office. Birth and death files from July 1, 1911 are at the Nevada State Department of Health, Division of Vital Statistics, 505 East King Street, Room 102, Carson City, NV 89710. To verify current fees, call 702-885-4480.

Probate actions before 1861 were recorded in the Utah Territorial Courts, whose records are at the Nevada State Library and Archives, Division of Archives and Records, 101 South Fall Street, Carson City, NV 90710. Probate records after 1864 are in the district courts. Federal census records for 1850 and 1860 are with the Utah Territory Census. Copies of an 1862 territorial census are at the Nevada State Library and Archives.

Genealogical Archives, Libraries and Societies

Las Vegas Public Library, 400 E. Mesquite Ave., Las Vegas, NV 89101

Nevada State Historical Society Library, P. O. Box 1192, Reno, NV 89501

University of Nevada Library, Reno, NV 89507

Washoe County Library, Reno, NV 89507

Churchill County Historical and Genealogical Society, c / o Churchill County Museum, 1050 South Main St., Fallon, NV 89406

Clark County, Nevada Genealogical Society, P. O. Box 1929, Las Vegas, NV 89125-1929

Humboldt County Genealogical Society, Humboldt County Library, 85 East 5th St., Winnemucca, NV 89445

Jewish Genealogical Society of Las Vegas, P. O. Box 29342, Las Vegas, NV 89126

Nevada Society, Sons of the American Revolution, 309 Duke Circle, Las Vegas, NV 89107

Nevada State Genealogical Society, P. O. Box 20666, Reno, NV 89515

Northeastern Nevada Genealogical Society, P. O. Box 1903, Elko, NV 89801

Printed Census Records and Mortality Schedules

Federal Census 1860 (with Utah), 1870, 1880, 1900, 1910
Union Veterans and Widows 1890
State/Territorial Census 1872
Inhabitants 1875

Valuable Printed Sources

Atlases, Maps, and Gazetteers

Carlson, Helen S. *Nevada Place Names: A Geographical Dictionary*. Reno: University of Nevada Press, 1974.

Bibliographies

Lee, Joyce C. *Genealogical Prospecting in Nevada: A Guide to Nevada Directories*. Nevada Library Association, 1984.

Lingenfelter, Richard E. *The Newspapers of Nevada, 1858-1958: A History and Bibliography*. San Francisco: John Howell Books, 1964.

Genealogical Research Guides

Spiros, Joyce V. Hawley. *Genealogical Guide to Arizona and Nevada*. Gallup, New Mexico: Verlene Publishing, 1983.

Histories

Nevada, The Silver State. Carson City: Western States Historical Publishers, 1970.

NEVADA COUNTY DATA
State Map on Page M-26

Name	Map Index	Date Created	Parent County or Territory From Which Organized
Carson (discontinued)			
Churchill	D2	1861	Original county
Churchill County, 10 W Williams Ave, Fallon, NV 89406-2940 .... (702)423-6028			
(Co Clk has m, div, pro & civ ct rec from 1905)			
* **Clark**	G5	1909	Lincoln
Clark County, 200 S 3rd St, Las Vegas, NV 89155-0001 .... (702)455-3156			
(Co Clk has m, div, pro & civ ct rec from 1909; Co Rcdr has lnd rec)			
† **Douglas**	E1	1861	Original county
Douglas County, PO Box 218, Minden, NV 89423-0218 .... (702)782-9821			
(Co Clk has m, div, pro & civ ct rec)			
*† **Elko**	B5	1869	Lander
Elko County, 571 Idaho St, Elko, NV 89801-3787 .... (702)738-5398			
(Co Clk has m applications, div, pro, civ ct rec from 1876; Co Rcdr has b, d, bur, lnd rec)			
* **Esmeralda**	F3	1861	Original county
Esmeralda County, PO Box 547, Goldfield, NV 89013-0547 .... (702)485-6367			
(Co Clk has b rec from 1900, m, d, bur rec from 1898, div rec from 1908, civ ct rec from 1907)			
*† **Eureka**	D4	1873	Lander
Eureka County, PO Box 677, Eureka, NV 89316-0677 .... (702)237-5262			
(Co Rcdr has b, m, d, bur rec; Co Clk has div, pro, civ ct rec from 1874)			
Humboldt	B2	1861	Original county
Humboldt County, Bridge & 5th Sts, Winnemucca, NV 89445-3199 .... (709)623-6343			
(Co Clk has m from 1881, div & civ ct rec from 1863, pro rec from 1900, naturalization rec from 1864, inquests 1862; Co Rcdr has lnd rec; see 1860 Utah cen)			
Lander	D3	1862	Original county
Lander County, 315 S Humboldt, Battle Mountain, NV 89820-1982 .... (702)635-5738			
(Co Clk has m rec from 1867, div rec, pro & civ ct rec from 1865; Aud has some b rec)			
* **Lincoln**	F5	1866	Nye
Lincoln County, 1 Main St, Pioche, NV 89043 .... (702)962-5390			
(Co Clk has m, div, pro, civ ct & lnd rec from 1873)			
Lyon	D1	1861	Original county
Lyon County, 31 S Main St, Yerington, NV 89447-2532 .... (702)463-3341			
(Co Rcdr has m & lnd rec from 1862; Co Clk has div, pro & civ ct rec from 1890)			
† **Mineral**	E2	1911	Esmeralda
Mineral County, PO Box 1450, Hawthorne, NV 89415-1450 .... (702)945-2446			
(Co Clk has m applications, div, pro & civ ct rec from 1911; Co Rcdr has lnd rec)			
*† **Nye**	F4	1864	Esmeralda
Nye County, PO Box 1031, Tonopah, NV 89049-1031 .... (702)482-8127			
(Co Clk has m, div, pro & civ ct rec from 1860; Co Rcdr has lnd rec)			
* **Ormsby**	D1	1861	Original county
Ormsby County, Carson City, NV 89701			
(Co Clk has m, div, pro & civ ct rec)			
Pahute (Discontinued)			

Name	Map Index	Date Created	Parent County or Territory From Which Organized

* **Pershing**   C2   1919   Humboldt
    Pershing County, PO Box 820, Lovelock, NV 89419-0820 .... (702)273-2208
    (Co Clk has m, div, pro & civ ct rec from 1919)

   Roop (Discontinued)

   St. Mary's (Discontinued)

* **Storey**   D1   1861   Original county
    Storey County, PO Box D, Virginia City, NV 89440-0139 .... (702)847-0968
    (Co Rcdr has b, m & d rec from 1875; Co Clk has div & civ ct rec from 1861, pro rec from 1875)

*† **Washoe**   C1   1861   Original county
    Washoe County, PO Box 11130, Reno, NV 89520-0027 .... (702)328-3110
    (Dis Health Dept has b, d, bur rec from 1900; Co Clk-Rcdr has m rec from 1871; Co Clk has div, pro, civ ct rec from 1862; Co Rcdr has lnd rec from 1862)

* **White Pine**   D5   1869   Lincoln
    White Pine County, PO Box 1002, Ely, NV 89301-1002 .... (702)289-8841
    (Co Clk has m from 1885, div, pro & civ ct rec from 1907, naturalization rec; Co Rcdr has lnd rec from 1885)

                * At least one county history has been published about this county.
          † Inventory of county archives was made by the Historical Records Survey. (See Introduction)

NEW HAMPSHIRE

CAPITAL · CONCORD — STATE 1788 (9th)
State Map on Page M-27

    The first Europeans to see New Hampshire were Martin Pring in 1603, Samuel de Champlain in 1605, and Captain John Smith in 1614. In 1622, the King of England granted all of the land between the Merrimac and Kennebec Rivers to Ferdinando Gorges and John Mason. The first settlement occurred three years later at Little Harbor (present-day Rye). Dover was settled about the same time and Strawberry Bank (later Portsmouth), Exeter, and Hampton were all settled by 1638. In 1629, New Hampshire was separated from Maine and in 1641 was made part of the Massachusetts Colony. It remained so until 1679, when it became a Royal British Province. Seven years later it became part of the Dominion of New England, which lasted three years. Three years of independence followed until a royal government was established in 1692. From 1699 to 1741, New Hampshire was governed by the royal governor of Massachusetts. Victories over the Indians in 1759 opened New Hampshire to increased settlement. As the population grew, boundary disagreements and land disputes grew more heated. Finally in 1764, the Connecticut River was declared the western boundary.

    New Hampshire supported the Revolution, especially following the punitive measures imposed on New England by England. In 1788, New Hampshire was the ninth state to ratify the Constitution. Many settlers heading west from Massachusetts and Connecticut stopped for a time in New Hampshire and Vermont. During the first two hundred years of its history, most settlers were English. The next 75 years saw tens of thousands come from Scandinavia, Greece, Italy, and France.

    In 1819 the Toleration Act was passed prohibiting taxing to support any church. In 1842, the boundary between New Hampshire and Quebec was settled. During the Civil War, just under 34,000 men from New Hampshire served in the Union Army. Following the war, industry, transportation, and communications expanded. The textile, leather, and shoe industries brought renewed immigration from French Canadians and others.

    Vital statistics were kept by towns from their organization, although they are not complete. Until 1883, less than half of the vital records were recorded and even those that were recorded gave little information regarding parents or birthplaces. After 1901, the records are more complete and informative. Copies of state records are available from the Bureau of Vital Records and Health Statistics, Health and Welfare Building, Hazen Drive, Concord, NH 03301. Be sure to state your relationship and reason for requesting the information. To verify current fees, call 603-271-4654.

    Probate records were kept by a provincial Registry of Probate until 1771 when probate courts were created. Clerks of probate courts in each county are in charge of wills. The state office in Concord has charge of the census records. Tax records are generally found in the town clerk's office and some may be found in the New Hampshire Division of Records Management and Archives, 71 South Fruit Street, Concord, NH 03301. Almost all towns have published town histories which contain much genealogical information about early settlers.

Genealogical Archives, Libraries and Societies

Archive Center of the Historical Society of Cheshire County, 246 Main St., Keene, NH 03431 (603) 352-1895

Baker Memorial Library, Dartmouth College, Hanover, NH 03755

City Library, Carpenter Memorial Bldg., 405 Pine St., Manchester, NH 03104

Dartmouth College Archives, Baker Library, Hanover, NH 03755

Dover Public Library, 73 Locust St., Dover, NH 03820

Exeter Public Library, 86 Front St., Exeter, NH 03833 Has genealogy and local history room.

Keene Public Library, Wright Room, 60 Winter St., Keene, NH 03431

New Hampshire State Library, 20 Park St., Concord, NH 03303

Piscataqua Pioneers "Special Collection", Dimond Library, University of New Hampshire, 3rd Floor, Durham, NH 03824

Portsmouth Athenaeum, 9 Market St., Portsmouth, NH 03801

Acadian Genealogical and Historical Association, P. O. Box 668, Manchester, NH 03105

American-Canadian Genealogical Society, P. O. Box 668 Manchester, NH 03105

Carroll County Chapter, NHSOG, P. O. Box 250, Freedom, NH 03836

Historical Society of Chesire County, P. O. Box 803, Keene, NH 03431

Merrimack Valley Society of Genealogists, Rt. 1, Contoocook, NH 03229

New Hampshire Historical Society, Library, 30 Park St., Concord, NH 03301

New Hampshire Society of Genealogists, P. O. Box 633, Exeter, NH 03833

New Hampshire Society, Sons of the American Revolution, Kona Farm Road, Box 141, Moultonboro, NH 03226

North Country Genealogical Society, P. O. Box 618, Littleton, NH 03561

Rockingham Society of Genealogists, P. O. Box 81, Exeter, NH 03833-0081

Printed Census Records and Mortality Schedules

Federal Census 1790, 1800 (except parts of Rockingham and Strafford counties), 1810, 1820 (except Grafton County), 1830, 1840, 1850, 1860, 1870, 1880, 1900, 1910

Union Veterans and Widows 1890

Residents 1735, 1776

Valuable Printed Sources

Atlases, Maps, and Gazetteers

Farmer, John and Jacob B. Moore. *A Gazetteer of the State of New Hampshire*. Concord, New Hampshire: J. B. Moore, 1823.

Hayward, John. *A Gazetteer of New Hampshire*. Boston: J. P. Jewett, 1849.

Town and City Atlas of the State of New Hampshire. Boston: D. H. Hurd & Co., 1892.

Bibliographies

Cobb, David A. *New Hampshire Maps to 1900: An Annotated Checklist*. Hanover, New Hampshire: New Hampshire Historical Society, 1981.

Haskell, John D. Jr. *New Hampshire: A Bibliography of Its History*. Boston: G. K. Hall & Co., 1979.

Genealogical Research Guides

Denis, Michael J. *New Hampshire Towns and Counties*. Oakland, Maine: Danbury House, 1986.

Genealogist's Handbook for New England Research. Lynnfield, Massachusetts: New England Library Association, 1980.

Towle, Laird C. and Ann N. Brown. *New Hampshire Genealogical Research Guide*. Bowie, Maryland: Heritage Books, 1983.

Genealogical Sources

Noyes, Sybil. *Genealogical Dictionary of Maine and New Hampshire*. Baltimore: Genealogical Publishing Co., 1976 reprint.

Stearns, Ezra S. *Genealogical and Family History of the State of New Hampshire*. New York: Lewis Publishing Co., 1908.

Histories

Squires, James Duane. *The Granite State of the United States: A History of New Hampshire from 1623 to the Present*. New York: American Historical Co., 1956.

NEW HAMPSHIRE COUNTY DATA
State Map on Page M-27

Name	Map Index	Date Created	Parent County or Territory From Which Organized

*† Belknap E5 1840 Strafford, Merrimac
Belknap County, 64 Court St, Laconia, NH 03246-3679 .... (603)524-3570
(Twn or City Clks have b, m & d rec; Clk Sup Ct has div & civ ct rec; Pro Judge has pro rec from 1841; Reg Deeds has Ind rec from 1841)

Towns Organized Before 1800: Alton 1796, Barnstead 1727, Centre Harbor 1797, Gilmanton 1727, Meredith 1768, New Hampton 1777, Sanbornton 1770

*† Carroll E5 1840 Strafford
Carroll County, Rt 171, Ossipee, NH 03864 .... (603)539-7751
(Clk Ct has div & civ ct rec from 1859; Twn Clk of each twn has b, m, d & bur rec; Pro Judge has pro rec)

Towns Organized Before 1800: Albany 1766, Brookfield 1794, Chatham 1767, Conway 1765, Eaton 1766, Effingham 1788, Moultonborough 1777, Ossippee 1785, Sandwich 1768, Tamworth 1766, Tuftonborough 1795, Wakefield 1774, Wolfeborough 1770

*† Cheshire F4 1769 Original county
Cheshire County, 33 West St, Keene, NH 03431-3355 .... (603)352-8215
(Twn or City Clks have b, m, d & bur rec; Co Clk has div & civ ct rec; Reg Pro has pro rec; Reg Deeds has Ind rec)

Towns Organized Before 1800: Alstead 1763, Chesterfield 1752, Dublin 1771, Fitzwilliam 1773, Gilsum 1763, Hinsdale 1753, Jaffrey 1773, Keene 1753, Marlborough 1776, Marlow 1761, Nelson 1774, Richmond 1752, Rindge 1768, Stoddard 1774, Sullivan 1787, Surry 1769, Swanzey 1753, Walpole 1752, Winchester 1753

*† Coos C5 1803 Grafton
Coos County, PO Box 309, Lancaster, NH 03584-0309 .... (603)788-4900
(Twn or City Clks have b, m, d & bur rec; Clk Sup Ct has div & civ ct rec from 1887; Reg Pro has pro rec; Reg Deeds has Ind rec)

Towns Organized Before 1800: Bartlett 1790, Cambridge 1773, Colebrook 1790, Columbia 1797, Dalton 1784, Dummer 1773, Jefferson 1796, Kilkenny 1774, Lancaster 1763, Millsfield 1774, Northumberland 1779, Stratford 1773, Stewartstown 1799, Success 1773, Whitefield 1774

*† Grafton E5 1769 Original county
Grafton County, PO Box 108, Woodsville, NH 03785-0108 .... (603)787-6941
(1820 census missing? Clk Ct has div & civ ct rec; Pro Judge has pro rec)

Towns Organized Before 1800: Alexandria 1782, Bath 1761, Benton 1764, Bethlehem 1799, Bridgewater 1788, Campton 1761, Canaan 1761, Danbury 1795, Dorchester 1761, Enfield 1761, Franconia 1764, Grafton 1778, Groton 1796, Hanover 1761, Haverhill 1763, Hebron 1792, Hill 1778, Holderness 1761, Landaff 1764, Lebanon 1761, Lisbon 1768, Lincoln 1764, Littleton 1784, Lyman 1761, Lyme 1761, Orange 1780, Orford 1761, Plymouth 1763, Rumney 1761, Thornton 1781, Warren 1763, Wentworth 1766, Woodstock 1786

* Hillsborough F5 1769 Original county
Hillsborough County, 19 Temple St, Nashua, NH 03060-3472 .... (603)882-9471
(Co Clk has div & pro rec from 1771)

Towns Organized Before 1800: Amherst 1760, Antrim 1777, Bedford 1780, Brookline 1769, Deering 1774, Francestown 1772, Goffstown 1761, Greenfield 1791, Hancock 1779, Hillsborough 1772, Hollis 1746, Hudson 1746, Litchfield 1749, Lyndeborough 1764, Manchester 1751, Mason 1768, Merrimac 1745, Milford 1794, Nashua 1746, New Ipswich 1762, New Boston 1763, Pelham 1746, Peterborough 1760, Sharon 1791, Temple 1769, Weare 1764, Wilton 1762, Windsor 1798

*† Merrimack F5 1823 Rockingham, Hillsboro
Merrimack County, 163 N Main St, Concord, NH 03301-5001 .... (603)228-0331
(Co Clk has div rec from 1840, civ ct rec from 1823; Twn or City Clk has b, m, d & bur rec; Pro Judge has pro rec from 1823; Reg Deeds has Ind rec from 1823)

Towns Organized Before 1800: Andover 1779, Bradford 1787, Bow 1727, Boscawen 1760, Canterbury 1727, Chichester 1727, Concord 1765, Dunbarton 1765, Epsom 1727, Henniker 1768, Hopkinton 1765, Loudon 1773, Newbury 1778, New London 1779, Northfield 1780, Pembroke 1759, Pittsfield 1782, Salisbury 1768, Sutton 1784, Warner 1774

* Rockingham F6 1769 Original county
Rockingham County, North Rd, Brentwood, NH 03042 .... (603)679-2256
(Clk Cts has div & civ ct rec from 1769; Twn or City Clk has b, m, d & bur rec; Reg Pro has pro rec from 1770; Reg Deeds has Ind rec from 1643)

Towns Organized Before 1800: Atkinson 1767, Brentwood 1742, Candia 1763, Chester 1722, Danville 1760, Deerfield 1766, East Kingston 1738, Epping 1741, Exeter 1638, Gosport 1715, Greenland 1704, Hampstead 1749, Hampton 1638, Hampton Falls 1712, Kensington 1737, Kingston 1694, Londonderry 1722, New Castle 1692, Newington 1764, New Market 1727, Newtown 1749, North Hampton 1742, Northwood 1773, Nottingham 1722, Plaistow 1749, Poplin 1764, Portsmouth 1653, Raymond 1765, Rye 1726, Salem 1750, Sandown 1756, Seabrook 1763, South Hampton 1742, Stratham 1716, Windham 1742

* Strafford F6 1769 Original county
Strafford County, County Farm Rd, Dover, NH 03820 .... (603)742-3065
(Twn or City Clk has b, m, d, bur & civ ct rec; Clk Sup Ct has div rec; Reg Pro has pro rec; Reg Deeds has Ind rec from 1773)

Towns Organized Before 1800: Barrington 1722, Dover 1623, Durham 1732, Farmington 1798, Lee 1766, Madbury 1755, Middleton 1778, New Durham 1762, Rochester 1722, Somersworth 1754

Name	Map Index	Date Created	Parent County or Territory From Which Organized
* **Sullivan**	F4	1827	Cheshire

Sullivan County, PO Box 45, Newport, NH 03773-0045 . . . . (603)863-3450
(Twn or City Clks have b, m, d & bur rec; Clk Sup Ct has div & civ ct rec from 1827; Reg Pro has pro rec; Reg Deeds has lnd rec; other rec of interest to genealogists at Richards Library, Newport, NH)

Towns Organized Before 1800: Acworth 1766, Charlestown 1753, Claremont 1764, Cornish 1763, Croydon 1763, Goshen 1791, Grantham 1761, Langdon 1787, Lempster 1761, Newport 1761, Plainfield 1761, Springfield 1794, Unity 1764, Washington 1776, Wendell 1731

* At least one county history has been published about this county.
† Inventory of county archives was made by the Historical Records Survey. (See Introduction)

NEW JERSEY

CAPITAL · TRENTON — STATE 1787 (3rd)
State Map on Page M-28

In 1524, Verrazano became the first European to stand on New Jersey soil. Henry Hudson laid claim in 1609 to the area for the Dutch, who then set up trading posts at present-day Jersey City and Camden in the 1620's. The Swedes tried to settle the area as well, but were dominated by the Dutch in 1655. Less than a decade later, in 1664, the British captured the entire area. That same year Lord John Berkeley and Sir George Carteret were granted the land between the Delaware and Hudson rivers. They opened the land to settlers who came in large numbers. Among those early settlers were British emigrants, Puritans from Connecticut who established Newark, Scotch-Irish Presbyterians who settled the eastern counties, and Quakers who settled in the Delaware River Valley. The new settlers were diverse in religion but united in opposition to the tax and monetary policies of the proprietors. In 1682, Carteret's heirs sold east Jersey to William Penn. In 1702, New Jersey was put under a royal governor, which they shared with New York until 1738. In 1738, New Jersey had a governor and a legislature of its own. Many important battles of the Revolutionary War took place in New Jersey. Residents supported both sides in the war. New Jersey was the third state to ratify the Constitution and was one of the major forces behind the rights of small states and equal representation in the Senate. The 1790 Census showed New Jersey with a population of 184,139, most of whom were English, Dutch, or Swedish.

Research conditions are not as favorable in New Jersey as in some other states. Since there was no law requiring a record to be kept of births and deaths until 1878, the family Bible is about the only source for this information. The State Registrar's Office, State of New Jersey, Department of Health, John Fitch Plaza, P.O. Box 1540, Trenton, NJ 08625, has birth, death, and marriage records from 1878. Earlier records are kept in the Bureau of Archives and History, Department of Education, State Street, Trenton, NJ. Marriage licenses are issued in cities by the registrar of vital statistics or the city clerk. Divorce records are kept in the Superior Court, Chancery Division, at the State House in Trenton. Naturalization proceedings are kept at the federal circuit and district courts and the State Supreme Court. To verify current fees, call 609-292-4087.

Records of deeds from 1664 to 1703 are in the New Jersey Archives, Vol. XXI; from 1664 to 1790 in the Secretary of State's Office; and from 1790 to the present in the county clerk's offices. The Secretary of State in Trenton has the original of wills and probate matters and early guardianship and orphans' courts proceedings. Copies of wills and administrations of estates beginning in 1804 are at county courthouses. Wills and administrations of estates from 1682 to 1805 have been abstracted and published in the State Archives. An index of New Jersey wills has also been published. A 1793 military census has been published and helps to make up for the destroyed 1790 Census.

Genealogical Archives, Libraries and Societies

Atlantic City Free Public Library, Illinois and Pacific Aves., Atlantic City, NJ 08401

Burlington County Library, Woodlane Rd., Mt. Holly, NJ 08060

Gardiner A. Sage (Theological) Library, 21 Seminary Place, New Brunswick, NJ 08901

Gloucester County Historical Society Library, 17 Hunter St., Woodbury, NJ 08096

Joint Free Public Library of Morristown and Morris Township, Box 267M, 1 Miller Rd., Morristown, NJ 07960

Morris County Free Library, 30 East Hanover Ave., Whippany, NJ 07981

New Jersey State Library, Jerseyana and Genealogy, 185 West State Street, Trenton, NJ 08625-0520

Princeton University Library, Princeton, NJ 08540

Rutgers University Library, New Brunswick, NJ 08903

Strickler Research Library, c / o Ocean County Historical Society, 26 Hadley Ave., Toms River, NJ 08754

Westfield Memorial Library, 425 East Broad St., Westfield, NJ 07090

Association of Jewish Genealogical Societies, 1485 Teaneck Road, Teaneck, NJ 07666

Atlantic County Historical Society, P. O. Box 301, Somers Point, NJ 08244

Camden County Historical Society, Euclid Ave. and Park Blvd., Camden, NJ 08103

Cape May Historical Society, Courthouse, Cape May, NJ 08204

Cumberland County Historical Society, P. O. Box 16, Greenwich, NJ 08323

Descendants of Founders of New Jersey, 850-A Thornhill Court, Lakewood, NJ 08701

Genealogical Society of Bergen County, New Jersey, P. O. Box 432, Midland Park, NJ 07432

Genealogical Society of New Jersey, P. O. Box 1291, New Brunswick, NJ 08903

Genealogical Society of Westfield, Westfield Memorial Library, 425 East Broad St., Westfield, NJ 07090

Genealogy Club of the Metuchen-Edison Regional Historical Society, P. O. Box 61, Metuchen, NJ 08840

Glassboro State College, Glassboro, NJ 08028 Historical Society of Boonton Township, RD 2, Box 152, Boonton, NJ 07005

Hunterdon County Historical Society, Hiram E. Deats Memorial Library, 114 Main Street, Felmington, NJ 08822

Jewish Genealogical Society of North Jersey, 1 Bedford Road, Pompton Lakes, NJ 07442

Metuchen / Edison Genealogy Club, 48 Elliot Place, Edison, NJ 08817

Monmouth County Genealogy Club, Monmouth County Historical Association, 70 Court St., Freehold, NJ 07728

Morris Area Genealogy Society, P. O. Box 105, Convent Station, NJ 07961

National Archives-Northeast Region, Building 22-Ocean Terminal, Bayonne, NJ 07002

Neptune Township Historical Society, 25 Neptune Blvd., Neptune, NJ 07753

New Jersey Historical Society, 230 Broadway, Newark, NJ 07104

Ocean County Genealogical Society, 135 Nautilus Drive, Manahawkin, NJ 08058-2452

Ocean County Historical Society, 26 Hadley Avenue, Toms River, NJ 08753

Passaic County, New Jersey Genealogy Club, c / o 430 Mt. Pleasant Ave., West Paterson, NJ 07424

Passaic County Historical Society, Lambert Castle Garret Mt. Reservation, Paterson, NJ 07509

Salem County New Jersey Historical Society, 81-83 Market St., Salem, NJ 08079

Vineland Historical and Antiquarian Society, Box 35, Vineland, NJ 08360

Printed Census Records and Mortality Schedules

Federal Census 1830, 1840, 1850, 1860, 1870, 1880, 1890 (part of Hudson County only), 1900, 1910
Federal Mortality Schedules 1850, 1860, 1870, 1880
Union Veterans and Widows 1890
Quit Rents 1682, 1684-1685, 1696
Freeholders 1755
Militia Census 1793
State/Territorial Census 1885, 1895, 1905, 1915

Valuable Printed Sources

Atlases, Maps, and Gazetteers
Gannett, Henry. *A Geographic Dictionary of New Jersey*. Baltimore: Genealogical Publishing Co., 1978 reprint.

Bibliographies
Barker, Bette Marie, et al. *Guide to Family History Sources in the New Jersey State Archives*. Trenton, New Jersey: New Jersey Department of Archives and Records Management, 1987.

Genealogical Research Guides
Stryker-Rodda, Kenn. *New Jersey: Digging for Ancestors in the Garden State*. Detroit: Detroit Society for Genealogical Research, 1978.

Genealogical Sources
New Jersey Index of Wills. Baltimore: Genealogical Publishing Co., 1969 reprint.

Office of the [New Jersey] Adjutant General. *Records of Officers and Men of New Jersey in Wars, 1791-1815*. Trenton, New Jersey: State Gazette Publishing Co., 1909.

Histories
Chambers, Theodore F. *The Early Germans of New Jersey: Their History, Churches, and Genealogies*. Baltimore: Genealogical Publishing Co., 1969 reprint.

Kull, Irving. *New Jersey: A History*. New York: American Historical Society, 1930.

NEW JERSEY COUNTY DATA

State Map on Page M-28

Name	Map Index	Date Created	Parent County or Territory From Which Organized

* Atlantic   F4   1837   Gloucester
Atlantic County, 2 Main St W, Mays Landing, NJ 08330-1800 .... (609)625-4011
(Co Clk has div rec from 1949, civ ct, lnd & cem rec from 1837; Co Surr has pro rec)

*† Bergen   B5   1683   Prov East Jersey
Bergen County, 21 Main St, Hackensack, NJ 07601-7000 .... (201)646-2500
(Co Clk has div rec from 1955, civ ct & lnd rec)

* Burlington   E4   1694   Original county
Burlington County, 49 Rancocas Rd, Mount Holly, NJ 08060-1384 .... (609)265-5000
(Co Clk has div rec from 1966, pro & lnd rec from 1785 & civ ct rec from 1880)

* Camden   E4   1844   Gloucester
Camden County, 5th & Mickle Blvd, Camden, NJ 08103-4000 .... (609)757-8457
[FHL has some cem, lnd, pro, tax rec]

* Cape May   G4   1692   Cumberland
Cape May County, 7 N Main St, Cape May Court House, NJ 08210-2117 .... (609)465-7111
(Settled 1682; Co Clk has m from 1795 to 1878, civ ct rec from 1797, lnd rec from 1690, physicians & midwives rec from 1894, newspapers from 1858; Co Surr has pro rec)

* Cumberland   F3   1748   Salem
Cumberland County, Broad & Fayette St, Bridgeton, NJ 08302-2552 .... (609)451-8000
(Co Clk has div rec, also civ ct rec from 1903 & lnd rec from 1787; Co Surr has pro rec)

* Essex   B5   1683   Prov East Jersey
Essex County, 469 King Blvd, Newark, NJ 07102 .... (201)621-4916
(Co Clk has m rec from 1795 to 1879, div, civ ct rec from 1948, naturalizations from 1779-1929; City Clks have b, d rec; Co Surr has pro rec; Reg Deeds has lnd rec)

* Gloucester   E3   1686   Original county
Gloucester County, 1 N Broad St, Woodbury, NJ 08096-4611 .... (609)853-3237
(Co Clk has civ ct & lnd rec from about 1787; Surr Ct has pro rec; Clk Sup Ct has div rec; Courthouse burned 1786; early rec preserved at Surveyor General's Office, Burlington & Sec of State Office, Trenton)

* Hudson   B5   1840   Bergen
Hudson County, 595 Newark Ave, Jersey City, NJ 07306-2301 .... (201)795-6000

* Hunterdon   C4   1714   Burlington
Hunterdon County, 71 Main St, Flemington, NJ 08822-1412 .... (908)782-4300
(Co Clk has m rec from 1795 to 1875, civ ct rec from 1714, deeds & mtg from 1716; Surr Ct has pro rec; Sup Ct has div rec)

* Mercer   D4   1838   Somerset, Middlesex, Hunterdon, Burlington
Mercer County, PO Box 8068, Trenton, NJ 08650-0068 .... (609)989-6517
(Co Surr has pro rec; Co Clk has civ ct & lnd rec from 1838, also judgements, tax maps, business name rec & corporation rec)

* Middlesex   D5   1683   Prov East Jersey
Middlesex County, 1 John F Kennedy Sq, New Brunswick, NJ 08901-2149 .... (908)745-3000
(Co Clk has m, div, civ ct & lnd rec)

* Monmouth   D5   1683   Prov East Jersey
Monmouth County, Main St Hall of Records, Freehold, NJ 07728 .... (908)431-7387
(Co Clk has m rec from 1795 to 1892 & lnd rec from 1667)

*† Morris   C4   1739   Hunterdon
Morris County, PO Box 900, Morristown, NJ 07963-0900 .... (201)285-6040
(Co Clk has m from 1795 to 1881, civ ct rec from 1739 to 1978, lnd rec from 1785, slave rec from 1804 to 1820, naturalization rec from 1816, veteran dis rec from 1945; Co Surr has pro rec; Clk Sup Ct has div rec)

*† Ocean   E5   1850   Monmouth
Ocean County, PO Box CN 2191, Toms River, NJ 08754 .... (908)244-2121
(Co Clk has pro & civ rec from 1850)

*† Passaic   B5   1837   Bergen, Essex
Passaic County, 77 Hamilton St, Paterson, NJ 07505-2097 .... (201)881-4120
(Co Clk has div rec from 1947, civ ct rec from 1900, also lnd rec)

* Salem   F3   1694   Original county
Salem County, 92 Market St, Salem, NJ 08079-1913 .... (609)935-7510
(Co Clk has m rec 1795-1956, civ ct rec from 1875, lnd rec from 1786; Co Surr has pro rec; City Clks have b, d, bur rec)

* Somerset   C4   1688   Middlesex
Somerset County, PO Box 3000, Somerville, NJ 08876-1262 .... (908)231-7000
(Co Clk has civ ct rec from 1777 & lnd rec from 1785)

Name	Map Index	Date Created	Parent County or Territory From Which Organized
*† **Sussex**	B4	1753	Morris

Sussex County, PO Box 709, Newton, NJ 07860-0709 . . . . (201)579-0200
(Co Clk has slave b rec, m rec 1795-1878, civ ct rec from 1753, lnd rec from 1800, crim rec from 1753, naturalizations, road returns from 1780, jury lists from 1805)

| * **Union** | C5 | 1857 | Essex |

Union County, 2 Broad St, Elizabeth, NJ 07201-2204 . . . . (908)527-4966
(Clk Sup Ct has div rec from 1848, civ ct rec; Surrogate has pro rec from 1857; Reg Deeds has lnd rec)

| * **Warren** | C4 | 1824 | Sussex |

Warren County, Rt 519 Wayne Dumont Jr Administration Bldg, Belvidere, NJ 07823 . . . . (908)475-5361
(Municipal Clks have b, d rec; Co Clk has m, lnd rec from 1825, div, civ ct rec; Surr office has pro rec)

* At least one county history has been published about this county.

† Inventory of county archives was made by the Historical Records Survey. (See Introduction)

NEW MEXICO

CAPITAL · SANTA FE — TERRITORY 1850 — STATE 1912 (47th)
State Map on Page M-29

The first white men to set foot in New Mexico were Alva Nunez Cabeza de Vaca and his three companions in 1536. They had been shipwrecked off the coast of Texas in 1528, and wandered through the Southwest for eight years. During this time, they heard tales of the Seven Cities of Cibola with the gold-studded houses. On returning to Mexico they related these tales and inspired others to explore the area. Among those who followed was Francisco Coronado in 1540. He found only Indian villages, and treated the Indians with such hostility that from then on the Indians hated the Spaniards and caused nothing but trouble.

In 1598, San Juan was founded as the first permanent Spanish settlement in New Mexico. Santa Fe was founded about 1610 and became the capital. Hostilities with the Indians continued for centuries, but became especially fierce around 1680. Pueblo Indians captured Santa Fe and forced the Spaniards to El Paso. The Spanish regained control in 1692-93, but suffered continued raids for the remainder of their control. In 1706, Albuquerque was founded.

Mexico gained its independence from Spain in 1821 and claimed New Mexico as one of its provinces. The same year, the Santa Fe Trail was opened and trade commenced between the United States and Mexico. During the Mexican War, General Stephen Kearny occupied New Mexico and declared it part of the United States. New Mexico officially became part of the United States in 1848. Two years later, the New Mexico Territory was formed comprising the present state of Arizona and part of Colorado in addition to New Mexico. The Colorado portion was taken away in 1861, and the Arizona section made into its own territory in 1863. The Gadsden Purchase in 1854 added the Gila Valley in Catron and Grant Counties.

During the Civil War, New Mexico was invaded by Confederate forces. They were defeated by Union forces in 1862 and forced to withdraw. New Mexico furnished about 6,000 men to the Union forces. The coming of the railroad stimulated settlement in eastern and southern New Mexico along with economic development. In June 1906, Congress passed a bill providing for the admission of Arizona and New Mexico as one state on the condition that the majority of voters in each state approved it. A majority of New Mexican voters approved statehood, but the Arizona voters did not, so both remained as territories. New Mexico finally became a state in 1912.

Birth and death records from as early as 1880, along with delayed birth certificates from 1867 are at the Vital Statistics Bureau, New Mexico Health Services, P.O. Box 968, Santa Fe, NM 87504. Registration was required after 1920. Copies are available only to the registrant, family members, or by court order. To verify current fees, call 505-827-2338.

County clerks have records of marriages, wills, property deeds, and administrations. Private land grants were recorded by the county clerk. The first land grants were given by Spain and Mexico. These records, along with records of public land distributed while New Mexico was a territory, are located at the BLM, New Mexico State Office, Federal Building, Box 1449, Santa Fe, NM 87501. Many of these records have also been microfilmed. Spanish and Mexican colonial censuses exist for 1750, 1790, 1802, 1816, 1822, 1823, 1827, 1830, and 1845, although they are not complete. They are available at the New Mexico Records Center and Archives, University of New Mexico Library, Special Collections, Albuquerque, NM 87131, and have been transcribed, indexed, and published.

Genealogical Archives, Libraries and Societies

Deming Public Library, Deming, NM 88030

History Library Museum of New Mexico, Palace of the Governors, Santa Fe, NM 87501

Lovington Public Library, 103 North First Street, Lovington, NM 88260

New Mexico State Library Commission, 301 Don Gasper, Santa Fe, NM 87501

Portales Public Library, 218 S. Ave. B, Portales, NM 88130

Public Library, 423 East Central Ave., Albuquerque, NM 87101

Roswell Public Library, 301 North Pennsylvania Ave., Roswell, NM 88201

University of New Mexico Library, Albuquerque, NM 87131

Artesia Genealogical Society, P. O. Box 803, Artesia, NM 88210

Chaves County Genealogical Society, P. O. Box 51, Roswell, NM 88201

Eddy County Genealogical Society, P. O. Box 461, Carlsbad, NM 88220

New Mexico Jewish Historical Society, 1428 Miracerros South, Santa Fe, NM 87501

Genealogy Club of the Albuquerque Public Library, 423 Central Ave. NE, Albuquerque, NM 87102

Lea County Genealogical Society, P. O. Box 1044, Lovington, NM 88260

Los Alamos Family History Society, 433 Estante Way, Los Alamos, NM 87544

Los Alamos Genealogical Society, 2161-B 36th St., Los Alamos, NM 87544

New Mexico Genealogical Society, P. O. Box 8283, Albuquerque, NM 87198-8330

New Mexico Society, Sons of the American Revolution, 12429 Chelwood Court N.W., Albuquerque, NM 87112

Roswell Genealogical Society, 2604 N. Kentucky, Roswell, NM 88201

Sierra County Genealogical Society, Truth or Consequences Public Library, P.O. Box 311, Truth or Consequences, NM 87901

Southern New Mexico Genealogical Society, P. O. Box 2563, Las Cruces, NM 88004

Southeastern New Mexico Genealogical Society, P. O. Box 5725, Hobbs, NM 88240

Southeastern New Mexico Genealogical Research Library, Will Rogers Community Center, Room 115, 200 East Park St., Hobbs, NM 88240

Totah Tracers Genealogical Society, #975, Hwy. 64 W., Bloomfield, NM 87413

Printed Census Records and Mortality Schedules

Federal Census 1850, 1860, 1870, 1880, 1900, 1910
Union Veterans and Widows 1890
Spanish/Mexican Census 1790, 1823, 1845
State/Territorial Census 1885

Valuable Printed Sources

Atlases, Maps, and Gazetteers

Beck, Warren A. and Ynez D. Haase. *Historical Atlas of New Mexico*. Norman, Oklahoma: University of Oklahoma Press, 1969.

Pearce. T. M. *New Mexico Place Names: A Geographical Dictionary*. Albuquerque: University of New Mexico Press, 1965.

Bibliographies

Grove, Pearce S., et al. *New Mexico Newspapers: A Comprehensive Guide to Bibliographic Entries and Locations*. Albuquerque: University of New Mexico Press, 1975.

Genealogical Research Guides

Spiros, Joyce V. Hawley. *Handy Genealogical Guide to New Mexico*. Gallup, New Mexico: Verlene Publishing, 1981.

Genealogical Sources

Chavez, Fray Angelico. *Origins of New Mexico Families in the Spanish Colonial Period*. Santa Fe: Historical Society of New Mexico, 1954.

Histories

Beck, Warren. *New Mexico: A History of Four Centuries*. Norman, Oklahoma: University of Oklahoma Press, 1962.

Tyler, Daniel. *Sources for New Mexican History*. Santa Fe: Museum of New Mexico Press, 1984.

NEW MEXICO COUNTY DATA
State Map on Page M-29

Name	Map Index	Date Created	Parent County or Territory From Which Organized
† **Bernalillo**	E3	1852	Original county

Bernalillo County, 1 Civic Plaza 10th Fl, Albuquerque, NM 87102 . . . . (505)768-4000
(Co Clk has m from 1885, pro rec from 1895, lnd rec from 1888; Clk Dis Ct has div & civ ct rec)

Catron	F2	1921	Socorro

Catron County, PO Box 507, Reserve, NM 87830-0507 . . . . (505)533-6423
(Co Clk has b, m, pro & lnd rec from 1921; Clk Dis Ct has div & civ ct rec)

* **Chaves**	F5	1887	Lincoln

Chaves County, 401 N Main St, Roswell, NM 88201-4726 . . . . (505)624-6614
(Co Clk has m rec from 1891, pro & lnd rec, voter reg from 1930, mil dis from 1919; Clk Dis Ct has div & civ ct rec)

Cibola	E2	1981	Valencia

Cibola County, 515 W High Ave, Grants, NM 87020-2526 . . . . (505)287-9431
(Co Clk has rec from 1981)

† **Colfax**	C5	1869	Taos

Colfax County, PO Box 1498, Raton, NM 87740-1498 . . . . (505)445-9661
(Co Clk has m rec from 1890, pro rec from 1903 & lnd rec from 1864; Clk Dis Ct has div & civ ct rec)

* **Curry**	E6	1909	Quay, Roosevelt

Curry County, 700 N Main St, Clovis, NM 88101-6664 . . . . (505)763-5591
(Co Clk has m rec from 1905, informal pro rec from 1909, lnd rec from 1903; Dis Ct has div rec and formal pro rec)

De Baca	E5	1917	Chaves, Guadalupe, Roosevelt

De Baca County, PO Box 347, Fort Sumner, NM 88119-0347 . . . . (505)355-2601
(Co Clk has m, pro & lnd rec from 1917; Clk Dis Ct has div rec; Magistrate Judge has civ ct rec)

† **Dona Ana**	G3	1852	Original county

Dona Ana County, 251 W Amador Ave, Las Cruces, NM 88005-2800 . . . . (505)525-6659
(Co Clk has m & pro rec from 1870, lnd rec from 1801, liens from 1905, mtgs from 1873; Clk Dis Ct has div & civ ct rec)

*† **Eddy**	G5	1889	Lincoln

Eddy County, PO Box 1139, Carlsbad, NM 88221-1139 . . . . (505)887-9511
(Co Clk has m, pro, lnd rec & newspapers from 1891; Clk Dis Ct has div & civ ct rec)

*† **Grant**	G2	1868	Dona Ana

Grant County, PO Box 898, Silver City, NM 88062-0898 . . . . (505)538-9581
(Co Clk has m rec from 1872, pro rec from 1884, lnd rec from 1871, newspaper rec from 1900; Dis Ct Clk has div rec; Municipal Ct has civ ct rec)

Guadalupe	E5	1891	Lincoln, San Miguel

Guadalupe County, 420 Park Ave, Santa Rosa, NM 88435 . . . . (505)472-3791
(Co Clk has m from 1895, pro rec from 1894 & lnd rec from 1893)

Harding	D6	1921	Mora, Union

Harding County, PO Box 1002, Mosquero, NM 87733-1002 . . . . (505)673-2301
(Co Clk has m, div, pro, civ ct & lnd rec from 1921)

*† **Hidalgo**	H2	1919	Grant

Hidalgo County, 300 S Shakespeare St, Lordsburg, NM 88045-1939 . . . . (505)542-9213
(Co Clk has m, pro & lnd rec from 1920; Clk Dis Ct has div & civ ct rec)

* **Lea**	G6	1917	Chaves, Eddy

Lea County, PO Box 4C, Lovington, NM 88260 . . . . (505)396-8521
(Co Clk has m & pro rec from 1917, also lnd rec)

* **Lincoln**	F4	1869	Socorro, Dona Ana

Lincoln County, 300 Central Ave, Carrizozo, NM 88301 . . . . (505)648-2331
(Co Clk has m rec from 1882, pro rec from 1880, newspapers from 1890)

Los Alamos	D4	1949	Sandoval, Santa Fe

Los Alamos County, 2300 Trinity Dr, Los Alamos, NM 87544-3051 . . . . (505)662-8010
(Co Clk has m, pro & lnd rec from 1949 & bur rec from 1961; Clk Dis Ct has div & civ ct rec)

*† **Luna**	G3	1901	Dona Ana, Grant

Luna County, 700 S Silver Ave, Deming, NM 88030-4173 . . . . (505)546-6501
(Co Clk has m, pro & lnd rec from 1901, Deming newspapers from 1901)

* **McKinley**	D2	1899	Bernalillo, Valencia, San Juan, Rio Arriba

McKinley County, 200 W Hill Ave, Gallup, NM 87301-6309 . . . . (505)722-3869
(Co Clk has b rec from 1907 to 1958, m, pro & lnd rec from 1901, also voters reg; Clk Dis Ct has div rec)

† **Mora**	C5	1860	Taos

Mora County, Hwy 518, Mora, NM 87732 . . . . (505)387-5279
(Co Clk has m & pro rec from 1891, lnd rec from 1920; Clk Dis Ct has div & civ ct rec)

† **Otero**	G4	1899	Dona Ana, Lincoln, Socorro

Otero County, PO Box 1749, Alamogordo, NM 88311-1749 . . . . (505)437-7427
(Co Clk has m, pro & lnd rec from 1899, voters reg certif from 1939; Clk Dis Ct has div & civ ct rec from 1899)

Name	Map Index	Date Created	Parent County or Territory From Which Organized

Quay   E6   1903   Guadalupe
Quay County, 300 S 3rd St, Tucumcari, NM 88401-2870 .... (505)461-2112
(Co Clk has m & Ind rec from 1893, pro rec; Clk Dis Ct has div & civ ct rec)

Rio Arriba   C3   1852   Original county
Rio Arriba County, County Courthouse, Tierra Amarilla, NM 87575 .... (505)588-7255
(Co Clk has m & pro rec from 1852)

* **Roosevelt**   F6   1903   Chaves, Guadalupe
Roosevelt County, County Courthouse, Portales, NM 88130 .... (505)356-8562
(Co Clk has m, pro, Ind rec from 1903, discharges from 1919, newspapers published in county; Dis Ct Clk has div, civ ct rec)

* **San Juan**   C2   1887   Rio Arriba
San Juan County, PO Box 550, Aztec, NM 87410-0550 .... (505)334-9471
(Co Clk has m, Ind rec from 1887, pro rec from 1899; Dis Ct Clk has div, civ ct rec; city cem associations have bur rec)

† **San Miguel**   D5   1852   Original county
San Miguel County, County Courthouse, Las Vegas, NM 87701 .... (505)425-9331
(Co Clk has m rec from 1880, pro rec from 1939, Ind rec from 1800; Clk Dis Ct has div, civ ct rec from 1882)

* **Sandoval**   D3   1903   Bernalillo
Sandoval County, PO Box 40, Bernalillo, NM 87004-3000 .... (505)867-2209

Santa Ana   1844   Original county (abolished by 1880)

*† **Santa Fe**   D4   1852   Original county
Santa Fe County, PO Box 1985, Santa Fe, NM 87504-1985 .... (505)984-5080
(Co Clk has m rec from 1900, pro rec from 1894 & Ind rec from 1848)

* **Sierra**   G3   1884   Socorro
Sierra County, 300 Date St, Truth or Consequences, NM 87901-2362 .... (505)894-6215
(Co Clk has m & Ind rec from 1884, pro rec, mil dis rec from 1945; Clk Dis Ct has div & civ ct rec)

* **Socorro**   F3   1852   Original county
Socorro County, 131 Court St, Socorro, NM 87801-4505 .... (505)835-0589
(Co Clk has m from 1885, pro rec from 1912, Ind rec from 1859, b & d rec from 1907 to 1941)

*† **Taos**   C5   1852   Original county
Taos County, PO Box 676, Taos, NM 87571-0676 .... (505)758-8836
(Co Clk has b, m, d, bur & pro rec from 1846)

* **Torrance**   E4   1903   Lincoln, San Miguel, Socorro, Santa Fe, Valencia
Torrance County, 9th & Allen, Estancia, NM 87016 .... (505)384-2221
(Courthouse burned in 1910)(Co Clk has m, informal pro, Ind rec from 1911; Clk Dis Ct has div, civ ct rec)

† **Union**   C6   1893   Colfax, Mora, San Miguel
Union County, 200 Court St, Clayton, NM 88415-3116 .... (505)374-9491
(Co Clk has m from 1894, pro, civ ct & Ind rec; Clk Dis Ct has div rec)

† **Valencia**   E4   1852   Original county
Valencia County, PO Box 1119, Los Lunas, NM 87031-1119 .... (505)865-9681
(Co Clk has m rec from 1865, pro rec from 1900; Clk Dis Ct has div & civ ct rec)

* At least one county history has been published about this county.
† Inventory of county archives was made by the Historical Records Survey. (See Introduction)

NEW YORK

CAPITAL · ALBANY — STATE 1788 (11th)
State Map on Page M-30

Giovanni da Verrazano is recognized as the discoverer of New York as he entered New York Harbor in 1524. The next explorers to come to New York were Samuel de Champlain in 1603 and 1609, and Henry Hudson came in 1609. Hudson, employed by the Dutch, returned favorable reports about the area, resulting in the formation of the Dutch West Indies Company in 1621. Although its main goal was trade, the company also established settlements at Fort Orange (Albany) in 1624, and New Amsterdam the next year on Manhattan Island. The Dutch induced settlers from Scandinavia, Great Britain, and Germany to emigrate to the area, and some Puritans migrated from Massachusetts and Connecticut about 1640. The English also established settlements in the area, notably on Long Island and northeast of New Amsterdam. In 1664, Charles II granted all the land from the Connecticut River to Delaware Bay, including all of New Netherland, to his brother James. Colonel Richard Nicolls was appointed governor and ordered to take control of the area from the Dutch. This he did in 1664 when the settlers refused to fight. New York grew slowly due to the hostility of the French who came from Canada and the Iroquois. About 1740, many people from Connecticut settled in Long Island, Dutchess, Westchester, and Orange counties. The end of the

French and Indian War and a treaty with the Indians ceding all their lands east of Rome opened up Central New York to settlement.

Prior to the Revolutionary War, settlers lived on Long Island, on the banks of the Hudson River, along the Mohawk River (mainly Palatine Germans), and in the extreme southeastern part of the state. Nearly one-third of the battles in the Revolutionary War were fought in New York, including Ethan Allen's victory at Fort Ticonderoga and the victory at Saratoga. New York became the eleventh state to ratify the Constitution. The state grew rapidly and by 1820 New York City became the nation's largest city. During the Civil War, New York supplied 448,000 troops to the Union cause. Growth during the next half century came from the Irish, who settled New York City and along the Erie Canal; Germans, who settled upstate in Rochester and Buffalo; and eastern, southern, and central Europeans, who came to work in the factories in Buffalo, Rochester, Schenectady, and New York City. Predominating nationalities include Italian, Russian, German, Polish, Irish, Austrian, English, Hungarian, Swedish, Norwegian, Czech, Greek, French, Finnish, and Danish.

New York law forbids issuance of any birth record for genealogical research unless it has been on file for at least 75 years. Marriage and death records must have been on file for at least 50 years. The Bureau of Vital Records, State Department of Health, Empire State Plaza Tower Building, Albany, NY 12237, has birth, death, and marriage records since 1880, except for the five boroughs of New York City. Marriage records are also kept here from 1847 to 1865. The Municipal Archives, Archives Division of the Department of Records and Information Center, 52 Chambers Street, New York, NY 10007, has birth, death, and marriage records to 1898 for all five boroughs. Individual county offices also have birth and death records for the boroughs. Birth, death, and marriage records for Albany, Buffalo, and Yonkers from 1914 are with the registrars of each city. Other cities and towns generally have birth, death, and marriage records from 1880. To verify current fees in New York City, call 212-619-4530. To verify current fees in New York State, call 518-474-3075.

A number of old church, cemetery, and marriage records are in the New York State Library, Department of Education, Manuscripts and History Section, Albany, NY. They also have some published genealogies, local histories, and the federal censuses of New York State from 1800 to 1870. The New York State Archives, Cultural Education Center, Empire State Plaza, Albany, NY 12230, has vital records mostly from before 1880 scattered among local government records. An inventory of these records is available upon request from the Archives. Marriage bonds, 1753-1783, were extensively damaged in a 1911 fire but have been largely restored.

State censuses were conducted in 1855, 1865, 1875, 1885, 1892, 1905, 1915, and 1925. These censuses show the names and ages of each member of every household and sometimes the county of birth. Most county offices have copies of the returns for their county. The New York State Archives also has the statewide census returns for 1915 and 1925 along with all the earlier state censuses for Albany County. Military service, pension, and land grant records for soldiers who served in the Revolution and the War of 1812 are available through the Archives.

Genealogical Archives, Libraries and Societies

Adriance Memorial Library, 93 Market St., Poughkeepsie, NY 12601

Blauvelt Free Library, 86 S. Western Hwy, Blauvelt, NY 10913

Buffalo and Erie County Public Library, Lafayette Square, Buffalo, NY 14203

Columbia University, Journalism Library, New York, NY 10027

East Hampton Free Library, 159 Main St., East Hampton, NY 11937

Flower Memorial Library, Genealogical Committee, Watertown, NY 13601

Franklin County Historical and Museum Society, 51 Milwaukee Street, Malone, NY 12953

Genesee County Library, Department of History, 131 West Main Street, Batavia, NY 14020

Geneva Free Library, 244 Main St., Geneva, NY 14456

Goshen Library and Historical Society, Main Street, Goshen NY 10924

Guernsey Memorial Library, 3 Court Street, Norwich, NY 13815

Hamilton Public Library, 13 Broad Street, Hamilton, NY 13346

John Lont Research Center, P. O. Box 732, Adams Basin, NY 14410

John M. Olin Library, Cornell University, Ithaca, NY 14853

Johnstown Public Library, 38 S. Market St., Johnstown, NY 12095

Margaret Reaney Memorial Library and Museum, 19 Kingsbury Ave., St. Johnsville, NY 13452 Phone (518) 568-7822 (Specializing in the Palatine Germans of the Mohawk Valley.)

Moore Memorial Library, 59 Genessee Street, Green, NY 13778

Newburgh Free Library, 124 Grand Street, Newburgh, NY 12550

New City Library, 220 North Main Street, New City, NY 10956

New York Public Library, 5th Ave. and 42nd Sts., New York, NY 10016

New York State Library, Albany, NY 12224

New York - Ulster County, Elting Library, Historical and Genealogical Department, 93 Main Street, New Paltz, NY 12561

Ogdensburg Public Library, 312 Washington Street, Ogdensburg, NY 13669

Oneida Library, 220 Broad St., Oneida, NY 13421

Onondaga County Public Library, Local History and Special Collections, 447 South Salina Street, Syracuse, NY 13202-2494

Patterson Library, 40 S. Portage St., Westfield, NY 14757

Port Chester Public Library, 1 Haseco Ave., Port Chester, NY 10573

Queens Borough Public Library, 89-11 Merrick Blvd., Jamaica, NY 11432

Richmond Memorial Library, 19 Ross Street, Batavia, NY 14020

Rochester Public Library, Local History Division, 115 South Avenue, Rochester, NY 14604

Roswell P. Flower Genealogy Library, 229 Washington St., Watertown, NY 13601

Steele Memorial Library, One Library Plaza, Elmira, NY 14901

Tioga County Historical Society, Museum and Genealogical Committee, 110-112 Front St., Owego, NY 13827

Utica Public Library, 303 Genesee St., Utica, NY 13501

Adirondack Genealogical-Historical Society, 100 Main Street, Saranac Lake, NY 12983

Albany Jewish Genealogical Society, Rabbi Don Cashman, P. O. Box 3850, Albany, NY 12203

Bethlehem Historical Association, Clapper Road, Selkirk, NY 12158

Brooklyn Historical Society, 128 Pierrepont St., Brooklyn, NY 11201

Broome County, The Southern Tier Genealogy Club, P. O. Box 680, Vestal, NY 13851-0680

Capital District Genealogical Society, P. O. Box 2175, Empire State Plaza Station, Albany, NY 12220

Cayuga-Owasco Lakes Historical Society, Box 241, Moravia, NY 13118

Central New York Genealogical Society, Box 104, Colvin Station, Syracuse, NY 13205

Chautauqua County New York Genealogical Society, P. O. Box 404, Fredonia, NY 14063

Chemung County Historical Society, 415 East Water St., Elmira, NY 14901

Colonial Dames of America, 421 East 61st St., New York, NY 10021

Cortland Historical Society, 25 Homer Ave., Cortland, NY 13045

Creole-American Genealogical Society, Inc., P. O. Box 2666, Church St. Station, New York City, NY 10008

DeWitt Historical Society, 116 N. Cayuga St., Ithaca, NY 14850

Dutchess County Genealogical Society, P. O. Box 708, Poughkeepsie, NY 12602

Dutchess County Historical Society, P. O. Box 88, Poughkeepsie, NY 12602

Empire State Society, Sons of the American Revolution, 13 Garden Ave., Massapequa, NY 11758

Essex County Historical Society, Adirondack Center Museum, Court St., Elizabethtown, NY 12932

Finger Lakes Genealogical Society, P. O. Box 47, Seneca Falls, NY 13148

Genealogical Conference of New York, Inc., Interlaken, NY 14847-0299

Genealogy Workshop, Brooklyn Historical Society, 128 Pierrepont St., Brooklyn, NY 11201

General Society of Colonial Wars, 122 East 58th St., New York, NY 10022

Goshen Library and Historical Society, Main Street, Goshen NY 10924

Holland Society, 122 E. 58th St., New York, NY 10022

Historical Society of Middletown and Walkill Precinct, Inc., 25 East Ave., Middletown, NY 10940

Huguenot Historical Society, 14 Forest Glen Rd., New Paltz, NY 12561

Institute for Jewish Research, 1048 Fifth Ave., New York, NY 10028

Jefferson County Historical Society, 228 Washington St., Watertown, NY 13601

Jewish Genealogical Society, Inc., P. O. Box 6398, New York, NY 10128

Jewish Genealogical Society of Capital District, 55 Sycamore Street, Albany, NY 12208

Jewish Genealogical Society of Greater Buffalo, 174 Peppertree Drive, #7, Amherst, NY 14228

Jewish Genealogical Society of Long Island, 37 West Cliff Drive, Dix Hills, NY 11746

Kodak Genealogical Club, c / o Kodak Park Activities Association, Eastman Kodak Company, Rochester, NY 14650

Lee Baeck Institute, German-Jewish families, 129 East 73 St., New York, NY 10021

Livingston-Steuben County Genealogical Society, 9297 Shaw Road, Nunda, NY 14517

Madison County Historical Society, 435 Main Street, P. O. Box 415, Cottage Lawn Historic House, Oneida, NY 13421

Minisink Valley Historical Society, Port Jervis, NY 12771

National Society of Colonial Dames of America in the State of New York, Library, 215 East 71st St., New York, NY 10021

New York Genealogical and Biographical Society, 122 East 58th St., New York, NY 10022-1939

New York Historical Association, 170 Central Park, West, New York, NY 10024

New York State Historical Association, Fenimore House, Lake Rd., Cooperstown, NY 13326

Northern New York American-Canadian Genealogical Society, P. O. Box 1256, Plattsburgh, NY 12901

Nyando Roots Genealogical Society, P. O. Box 175, Massena, NY 13662

Oneida County Genealogical Club, Oneida County Historical Society, 318 Genesee St., Utica, NY 13502

Onondaga Historical Association, 311 Montgomery St., Syracuse, NY 13202

Ontario County Genealogical Society, 55 North Main St., Canandaigua, NY 14424

Ontario County Historical Society, 55 North Main St., Canandaigua, NY 14424

Orange County Genealogical Society, Old Court House, 101 Main Street, Goshen, NY 10924

Rochester Genealogical Society, P. O. Box 92533, Rochester, NY 14692

Saint Lawrence Valley Genealogical Society, P. O. Box 86, Potsdam, NY 13676-0086

Schenectady County Historical Society, 32 Washington Avenue, Schenectady, NY 12305

Schuyler County Historical Society and Library, 108 North Catherine Street, Rt. 14, Montour Falls, NY 14865

Southhold Historical Society, Southhold, Long Island, NY 11971

Staten Island Historical Society, Richmondtown, Staten Island, NY 10301

Steuben County Historical Society, P. O. Box 349, Bath, NY 14810

Suffolk County Historical Society, Riverhead, Long Island, NY 11901

Tioga County Historical Society, 110-112 Front St., Owego, NY 13827

Town of Dayton Historical Society, P. O. Box 15, Dayton, NY 14041

Twin Tiers Genealogical Society, P. O. Box 763, Elmira, NY 14902

Ulster County Genealogical Society, P. O. Box 333, Hurley, NY 12443

Wayne County Historical Society, 21 Butternut Street, Lyons, NY 14489

Westchester County Genealogical Society, P. O. Box 518, White Plains, NY 10603

Westchester County Historical Society, 75 Grasslands Road, Valhalla, NY 10595

Western New York Genealogical Society, P. O. Box 338, Hamburg, NY 14075

Yates County Genealogical and Historical Society, 200 Main St., Penn Yan, NY 14527

Printed Census Records and Mortality Schedules

Federal Census 1790, 1800, 1810, 1820, 1830, 1840, 1850, 1860, 1870, 1880, 1890 (parts of Westchester and Suffolk counties only), 1900, 1910
Union Veterans and Widows 1890
State/Territorial Census 1663-1772, 1814, 1835, 1845, 1855, 1865, 1875, 1892, 1905, 1915, 1925
Loyalists 1782

Valuable Printed Sources

Atlases, Maps, and Gazetteers

French, John Homer. *Gazetteer of the State of New York*. Syracuse, New York: R. P. Smith, 1860.

Spafford, Horatio Gates. *Gazetteer of the State of New York, 1824*. Heart of the Lakes Publishing, 1981.

Bibliographies

Bielinski, Stefan. *A Guide to the Revolutionary War Manuscripts in the New York State Library*. Albany, New York: New York State American Revolutionary Bicentennial Commission, 1976.

Guide to Records in the New York State Archives. Albany, New York: New York State Archives, 1983.

Lopez, Manuel D. *New York: A Guide to Information and Reference Sources*. Metuchen, New Jersey: Scarecrow Press, 1980.

Mercer, Paul. *Bibliographies and Lists of New York State Newspapers: An Annotated Guide*. Albany, New York: New York State Library, 1984.

New York Public Library. *Dictionary Catalog of the Local History and Genealogy Division*. Boston: G. K. Hall & Co., 1967.

Genealogical Research Guides

Bailey, Rosalie Fellows. *Guide to Genealogical and Biographical Sources for New York City (Manhattan), 1783-1898*. New York: Rosalie Fellows Bailey, 1954.

Wright, Norman Edgar. *North American Genealogical Sources: Mid Atlantic States and Canada*. Provo, Utah: Brigham Young University Press, 1968.

Yates, Melinda. *Gateway to America: Genealogical Research in the New York State Library*. Albany, New York: New York State Library, 1982.

Genealogical Sources

Culbertson, Judi and Tom Randall. *Permanent New Yorkers: A Biographical Guide to the Cemeteries of New York*. Chelsea, Vermont: Chelsea Green, 1987.

Place, Frank II. *Index of Personal Names in J. H. French's Gazetteer of the State of New York*. Cortland, New York: Cortland County Historical Society, 1962.

Histories

Flick, A. C. *The History of the State of New York*. Port Washington, New York: Ira J. Friedman, 1962.

NEW YORK COUNTY DATA
State Map on Page M-30

Name	Map Index	Date Created	Parent County or Territory From Which Organized
*† **Albany**	G3	1683	Original county

Albany County, 16 Eagle St, Albany, NY 12207-1019 .... (518)445-7644
(Hall of Rec has m rec from 1870 to 1936, lnd rec from 1652, tax rolls from 1850, city directories from 1830, naturalization rec from 1827 to 1978; Co Clk has div & civ ct rec; Surr Ct has pro rec)

Name	Map Index	Date Created	Parent County or Territory From Which Organized

* **Allegany**   C2   1806   Genesee
Allegany County, Court St, Belmont, NY 14813 . . . . (716)268-7612
(Co Clk has m rec from 1908 to 1935, div & civ ct rec, also Ind rec from 1807)

* **Bronx**   H1   1912   New York
Bronx County, 851 Grand Concourse Rm 118, Bronx, NY 10451-2937 . . . . (212)590-3644
(Co Clk has m, div, sup civ ct rec from 1914)

*† **Broome**   E3   1806   Tioga
Broome County, 44 Hawley St, Binghamton, NY 13901-3722 . . . . (607)778-2451
(Co Clk has m rec from 1908 to 1935, mil rolls from 1808, naturalization rec from 1860, div rec, civ ct rec, Ind rec & state census;
Surr Ct has pro rec from 1806; Twn & City Clks have b, m, d & bur rec from 1880)

*† **Cattaraugus**   C2   1808   Genesee
Cattaraugus County, 303 Court St, Little Valley, NY 14755-1028 . . . . (716)938-9111
(Co Clk has div & Ind rec from 1808, civ ct rec from 1850 & naturalization rec; Twn & City Clks have b, m & d rec; Surr Ct has pro
rec)

* **Cayuga**   E3   1799   Onondaga
Cayuga County, 160 Genesee St, Auburn, NY 13021-3421 . . . . (315)253-1011
(Co Clk has pro, civ ct rec from 1799, Ind rec from 1794, DAR county cem rec 1790-1960; Twn or City Clks have b, m, rec)

  Charlotte   1772   Albany (renamed Washington, 1784)

  Chautauqua   B2   1808   Genesee
Chautauqua County, Gerace Office Bldg, Mayville, NY 14757 . . . . (716)753-4211
(Co Clk has m rec from 1908, div, civ ct, Ind rec from 1811; Surr Ct has pro rec; Twn or City Clks have b, m, d, bur rec)

*† **Chemung**   E2   1836   Tioga
Chemung County, 425 Pennsylvania Ave, Elmira, NY 14904-1762 . . . . (607)737-2811
(Co Clk has m rec from 1908 to 1936, div, civ ct & Ind rec; Surr Ct has pro rec; Twn Clks have m rec)

* **Chenango**   F3   1798   Herkimer, Tioga
Chenango County, 5 Court St, Norwich, NY 13815-1676 . . . . (607)335-4500
(Co Clk has m, div, civ ct & Ind rec; Surr Ct has pro rec; Twn Clks have b, m & d rec)

* **Clinton**   G6   1788   Washington
Clinton County, 137 Margaret St, Plattsburgh, NY 12901-2933 . . . . (518)565-4700
(Co Clk has div rec from 1869 & Ind rec from 1778, state census; Surr Ct has pro rec; Twn & City Clks have b, m, d & civ ct rec)

* **Columbia**   G3   1786   Albany
Columbia County, Allen & Union Sts, Hudson, NY 12534 . . . . (518)828-3339
(Co Clk has m rec from 1908 to 1934, civ ct rec from 1825, Ind rec from 1790, naturalization rec from 1853; Surr Ct has pro rec
from 1787; Twn Clks have b, m & d rec)

* **Cortland**   E3   1808   Ononodaga
Cortland County, 60 Central Ave, Cortland, NY 13045-2718 . . . . (607)753-5052
(Co Clk has m rec from 1910 to 1935, div rec, civ ct rec from 1808, Ind rec from 1808; Surr Ct has pro rec; Twn & City Clks have
b, m, d rec)

* **Delaware**   F2   1797   Ulster, Otsego
Delaware County, 4 Court St, Delhi, NY 13753-1081 . . . . (607)746-2123
(Co Clk has m rec from 1908 to 1931, div, civ ct & Ind rec from 1797, state census from 1855, naturalization rec from 1810 to
1955; Surr Ct has pro rec; Twn Clks have b, m, d & bur rec)

* **Dutchess**   G2   1683   Original county
Dutchess County, 22 Market St, Poughkeepsie, NY 12601-3233 . . . . (914)431-2020
(Co Clk has m rec from 1908 to 1935, div & civ ct rec from 1847, Ind rec from 1718, state census; Surr Ct has pro rec; Twn & City
Clks have b, m & d rec; Co Archives has tax rolls from 1854 to 1954, colonial ct rec from 1730 to 1799)

* **Erie**   C3   1821   Niagara
Erie County, 95 Franklin St, Buffalo, NY 14202-3968 . . . . (716)858-6392
(Co Clk has m rec from 1820 to 1935, div & civ ct rec from 1809 & Ind rec from 1810)

* **Essex**   G5   1799   Clinton
Essex County, Court St, Elizabethtown, NY 12932 . . . . (518)873-6301
(Co Clk has m rec from 1908 to 1936, div rec from 1936, pro, civ ct & Ind rec from 1799, state census; Twn & City Clks have b,
m, d & bur rec)

* **Franklin**   G5   1808   Clinton
Franklin County, 63 W Main St, Malone, NY 12953-1817 . . . . (518)483-6767
(Co Clk has m rec from 1908 to 1935, some div rec from 1808 & civ ct rec from 1808; Surr Ct has pro rec; various twns hold b, m
& d rec)

* **Fulton**   G4   1838   Montgomery
Fulton County, 223 W Main St, Johnstown, NY 12095-2309 . . . . (518)762-0540
(Co Clk has m rec from 1900 to 1926)

* **Genesee**   C3   1802   Ontario
Genesee County, Main & Court Sts, Batavia, NY 14020-3199 . . . . (716)344-2550
(Co Clk has m rec from 1908 to 1934, div, civ ct & Ind rec from 1802, state census; Surr Ct has pro rec; Twn & City Clks have b,
m, d & bur rec)

* **Greene**   G2   1800   Ulster, Albany
Greene County, Main St, Catskill, NY 12414-1396 . . . . (518)943-2050
(Co Clk has m rec from 1900 to 1935, div, civ ct & Ind rec from 1800; Surr Ct has pro rec; Twn Clks have b, m & d rec)

Name	Map Index	Date Created	Parent County or Territory From Which Organized

* **Hamilton**   G4   1816   Montgomery
Hamilton County, Rt 8, Lake Pleasant, NY   12108 .... (518)548-7111
(Co Clk has div, civ ct & Ind rec; Surr Ct has pro rec; Twn & City Clks have b, m, d & bur rec)

* **Herkimer**   F4   1791   Montgomery
Herkimer County, 109 Mary St, Herkimer, NY   13350-1921 .... (315)867-1002
(Co Clk has m rec from 1908 to 1934, div & civ ct rec)

* **Jefferson**   E5   1805   Oneida
Jefferson County, 175 Arsenal St, Watertown, NY   13601-2522 .... (315)785-3090
(Co Clk has m rec from 1908 to 1933, civ ct rec from 1847, Ind & div rec, state census & many other rec; Surr Ct has pro rec)

* **Kings**   G1   1683   Original county
Kings County, 360 Adams St, Brooklyn, NY   11201-3712 .... (212)566-5292
(Dept of Health, Brooklyn Borough Office, 295 Flatbush Ave Extension, Brooklyn, NY 11201 has b, d & bur rec; City Clk, Mun. Bldg, Brooklyn, NY 11201 has m rec; Co Clk, Sup Ct Bldg, 360 Adams St, Brooklyn, NY 11201 has div rec; Surr Ct. Sup Ct Bldg, 360 Adams St, Brooklyn, NY 11201 has pro rec; Clk Civ Ct, 120 Schermerhorn St, Brooklyn, NY 11201 has civ ct rec; Co Reg, Municipal Bldg, Joralemon & Court Sts, Brooklyn, NY 11201 has Ind rec)

* **Lewis**   F4   1805   Oneida
Lewis County, 7660 N State St, Lowville, NY   13367-1328 .... (315)376-5333
(Co Clk has incomplete m & d rec from 1847, div & civ ct rec from 1907, Ind rec from 1805, naturalization rec 1808-1906, military rolls from 1862-1866; Surr Ct has pro rec)

* **Livingston**   C3   1821   Genesee, Ontario
Livingston County, 2 Court St, Geneseo, NY   14454 .... (716)243-2500
(Co Clk has div, civ ct, Ind rec from 1821)

* **Madison**   F3   1806   Chenango
Madison County, N Court St, Wampsville, NY   13163-9999 .... (315)366-2011
(Co Clk has m rec from 1905 to 1934, div rec from 1900, civ ct rec from 1889 & Ind rec from 1806; Surr Ct has pro rec; Twn Clks have b, m, d, & bur rec)

* **Monroe**   D4   1821   Genesee, Ontario
Monroe County, 39 W Main St, Rochester, NY   14614-1408 .... (716)428-5151
(Co Clk has m rec from 1908 to 1935, div & civ ct rec from 1860, Ind rec from 1821, naturalization rec from 1822; Surr Ct has pro rec; Twn Clks have m & bur rec; Co Health Dept, 111 Westfall Rd, Rochester, NY 14620 has b & d rec; Co Historian, 39 Main St. W., Rochester, NY has state census)

* **Montgomery**   G3   1772   Albany (as Tryon to 1784)
Montgomery County, Broadway, Fonda, NY   12068 .... (518)853-3431
(Co Clk has m rec from 1908 to 1935, div & civ ct rec from 1795, Ind rec from 1772, state census, naturalization rec from 1850, survey maps; Surr Ct has pro rec; Twn & City Clks have b, m, d & bur rec)

* **Nassau**   H1   1898   Queens
Nassau County, 240 Old Country Rd, Mineola, NY   11501-4248 .... (516)535-2663
(Co Clk has m rec from 1907 to 1935, div, civ ct, Ind, business names from 1899; Surr Ct has pro rec; Twn Clks have b, m, d rec)

* **New York**   G1   1683   Original county
New York County, 60 Centre St, New York, NY   10007-1402 .... (212)374-8742
(Co Clk has div rec from 1754, naturalization rec from 1794 to 1924, state census)

* **Niagara**   C4   1808   Genesee
Niagara County, PO Box 461, Lockport, NY   14095-0461 .... (716)439-6100
(Co Clk has m rec from 1908 to 1935; div rec from 1850, civ ct, Ind rec; Surr Ct has pro rec; Twn and City Clks have b, m, d, bur rec)

* **Oneida**   F4   1798   Herkimer (see Jefferson)
Oneida County, 800 Park Ave, Utica, NY   13501-2220 .... (315)798-5700
(Co Clk has div rec, also Ind rec from 1791; Surr Ct has pro rec; Twn Clks have b, m, d & bur rec)

* **Onondaga**   E3   1794   Herkimer
Onondaga County, 421 Montgomery St, Syracuse, NY   13202-2984 .... (315)435-2070
(Co Clk & Twn Clks have m rec from 1908 to 1935; Co Clk has div rec from 1849, civ ct rec from 1799 & Ind rec from 1794; Surr Ct has pro rec; Co Clk has census rec from 1850 to 1925)

* **Ontario**   D3   1789   Montgomery
Ontario County, 27 N Main St, Canandaigua, NY   14424-1447 .... (716)396-4376
(Rcds Management Officer has m rec from 1908 to 1933, div rec from 1887, pro, civ ct & Ind rec from 1789, Revolutionary War service rec from 1820 to 1832, military rosters from 1862 to 1920, state census, co maps from 1798, naturalization rec from 1803 to 1954; Twn & City Clks have b & d rec)

* **Orange**   G1   1683   Original county
Orange County, 255-275 Main St, Goshen, NY   10924 .... (914)294-5151
(Co Clk has m rec from 1908 to 1933, div & civ ct rec from 1852, Ind rec from 1703 & census rec)

* **Orleans**   C4   1824   Genesee
Orleans County, Courthouse Sq, Albion, NY   14411 .... (716)589-4457
(Co Clk has div & civ ct rec from 1880, Ind rec from 1826, state census; Surr Ct has pro rec; Twn & City Clks have b, m & d rec)

* **Oswego**   E4   1816   Oneida, Onondaga
Oswego County, 46 E Bridge St, Oswego, NY   13126-2123 .... (315)349-3400
(Co Clk has m rec from 1907 to 1935)

Name	Map Index	Date Created	Parent County or Territory From Which Organized

* **Otsego**   F3   1791   Montgomery
Otsego County, 197 Main St, Cooperstown, NY 13326-1129 .... (607)547-4276
(Co Clk has m rec 1908 to 1936, div rec from 1900, civ ct rec from 1891, Ind rec from 1791; Surr Ct has pro rec; Twn & City Clks have b, m, d rec)

* **Putnam**   G1   1812   Dutchess
Putnam County, 2 County Ctr, Carmel, NY 10512 .... (914)225-3641
(Co Clk has div rec from 1880, pro rec, civ ct rec from 1820, Ind rec from 1814; Twn Clks have b, m, d & bur rec)

* **Queens**   G1   1683   Original county
Queens County, 88-11 Sutphin Blvd, Jamaica, NY 11435-3716 .... (718)520-3137
(Co Clk has state census, div rec, naturalization rec to 1941, military discharges; Surr Ct has pro rec; City Reg has Ind rec; Supreme Civ Ct has civ ct rec)

* **Rensselaer**   G3   1791   Albany
Rensselaer County, 1600 7th Ave, Troy, NY 12180-3409 .... (518)270-2700
(Co Clk has m rec 1908 to 1930s, div, civ ct, Ind rec from 1791, naturalization rec from 1830; maps)

* **Richmond**   G1   1683   Original county
Richmond County, 18 Richmond Terr, Staten Island, NY 10301-1935 .... (718)390-5386
[FHL has some b, m, d, cem, civ ct, pro, Ind, nat rec, 1855, 1865, 1875, 1915, 1925 censuses]

* **Rockland**   G1   1798   Orange
Rockland County, 11 New Hempstead Rd, New City, NY 10956-3636 .... (914)638-5100
(Co Clk has m rec from 1908 to 1935, also div & civ ct rec)

* **Saint Lawrence**   F5   1802   Clinton, Herkimer, Montgomery
Saint Lawrence County, 48 Court St, Canton, NY 13617-9987 .... (315)379-2000
(Co Clk has div, civ ct & Ind rec from 1802; Surr Ct has pro rec; Twn Clks have b, m & d rec)

* **Saratoga**   G4   1791   Albany
Saratoga County, 40 McMasters St, Ballston Spa, NY 12020-1999 .... (518)885-5381
(Co Clk has m rec from 1908 to 1935, div & civ ct rec from 1791)

* **Schenectady**   G3   1809   Albany
Schenectady County, 620 State St, Schenectady, NY 12305-2113 .... (518)382-3220
(Co Clk has m rec from 1908 to 1930, div, civ ct rec from 1858, Ind rec from 1630, maps from 1630, city directories, 1892, 1909, 1913 to 1968; Surr Ct has pro rec)

* **Schoharie**   G3   1795   Albany, Otsego
Schoharie County, PO Box 549, Schoharie, NY 12157-0549 .... (518)295-8316
(Co Clk has div, civ ct & Ind rec; Surr Ct has pro rec; Twn Clks have b, m & d rec)

* **Schuyler**   D3   1854   Tompkins, Steuben, Chemung
Schuyler County, 105 9th St, Watkins Glen, NY 14891-1496 .... (607)535-2132
(Co Clk has div, civ ct & Ind rec from 1854, state census; Surr Ct has pro rec; Twn Clks have b, m, d & bur rec)

* **Seneca**   D3   1804   Cayuga
Seneca County, 1 DiPronio Dr, Waterloo, NY 13165-1681 .... (315)539-5655
(Co Seat is Waterloo, ct is held at Ovid in addition to being held at Waterloo, no rec kept at Ovid; Co Clk has div & civ ct rec from 1900, Ind rec from 1804; Surr Ct has pro rec; Twn & City Clks have b, m, d & bur rec)

* **Steuben**   D2   1796   Ontario
Steuben County, 3 Pulteney Sq, Bath, NY 14810-1573 .... (607)776-9631
(Co Clk has m rec from 1908 to 1936, div, civ ct rec, Ind rec from 1796, Surr Ct has pro rec; Twn & City Clks have b, m, d rec; Co Clk has state cen rec, div & civ ct rec from 1840, Ind rec from 1796; Surr Ct has pro rec; Twn & City Clks have b, m & d rec)

* **Suffolk**   H1   1683   Original county
Suffolk County, County Ctr, Riverhead, NY 11901 .... (516)548-3888
(Co Clk has b, d rec 1847 to 1849; m rec 1847 to 1849, 1908 to 1935, civ ct rec from 1725, Ind rec from 1666, session court min 1669 to 1687, jury lists 1820 to 1872; Surr Ct has pro rec; Twn & City Clks have b, m, d, bur rec)

* **Sullivan**   G2   1809   Ulster
Sullivan County, 100 North St, Monticello, NY 12701-1160 .... (914)794-3000
(Co Clk has m rec from 1908 to 1933, div rec from 1885 & Ind rec from 1809; Surr Ct has pro & civ ct rec; Twn Clks have b, m & d rec)

* **Tioga**   E2   1791   Montgomery
Tioga County, 16 Court St, Owego, NY 13827-1515 .... (607)687-3133
(Co Clk has m rec from 1902 to 1926, div, sup ct, co ct rec & Ind rec from 1791; Twn Clks have b, m & d rec)

* **Tompkins**   E3   1817   Cayuga, Seneca
Tompkins County, 320 N Tioga St, Ithaca, NY 14850-4284 .... (607)274-5434
(Co Clk has m rec from 1908 to 1934; div, civ ct, Ind rec from 1817; Surr Ct has pro rec from 1817; Tompkins Co Health Dept has b, d rec)

* **Tryon**   1772   Albany (renamed Montgomery 1784)

* **Ulster**   G2   1683   Original county
Ulster County, 285 Wall St, Kingston, NY 12401-3817 .... (914)339-5680
(Co Clk has m rec 1908 to 1925, div, civ ct rec from 1793, Ind rec from 1685, also state cen rec; Twn Clks have b, m, d rec; Surr Ct has pro rec)

Name	Map Index	Date Created	Parent County or Territory From Which Organized

* **Warren**   G4   1813   Washington
  Warren County, Rt 9, Lake George, NY 12845 .... (518)761-6429
  (Co Clk has div rec from 1918, civ ct & Ind rec from 1813, military rec from 1862, naturalization rec from 1856, state census; Surr Ct has pro rec; Twn & City Clks have b, m & d rec)

* **Washington**   H4   1772   Albany (see Charlotte)
  Washington County, Upper Broadway, Fort Edward, NY 12828 .... (518)747-3374
  (Co Clk has div rec from1918, civ rec from 1878, civ ct rec from 1773, Ind rec from 1762, naturalization rec from 1794, state census, appointments & commissions from 1788 to 1906; Surr Ct has pro rec from 1787 to 1900; Twn Clks have b, m, d & bur rec)

* **Wayne**   D4   1823   Ontario, Seneca
  Wayne County, 26 Church St, Lyons, NY 14489-1134 .... (315)946-5400
  (Co Clk has div, civ ct, Ind rec, maps, crim ct rec, misc rec from 1823; Surr Ct has pro rec; Co Historian has bur rec; Twn Clks have b, m, d rec)

* **Westchester**   G1   1683   Original county
  Westchester County, 110 Grove St, White Plains, NY 10601-2504 .... (914)285-2000
  (Co Clk has pro rec from 1896, div & civ ct rec; Co Archives has pro rec to 1895, Ind rec, naturalization rec from 1808, military discharges, maps from 1776; Twn Clks have b, m & d rec)

* **Wyoming**   C3   1841   Genesee
  Wyoming County, 143 N Main St, Warsaw, NY 14569-1123 .... (716)786-8810
  (Co Clk has div, civ ct & Ind rec from 1841, state census; Surr Ct has pro rec; Twn Clks have b, m & d rec)

* **Yates**   D3   1823   Ontario, Steuben
  Yates County, 110 Court St Rm 198, Penn Yan, NY 14527-1130 .... (315)536-4011
  (Co Clk has m rec from 1908 to 1933, div & civ ct rec, Ind rec from 1788, state census; Surr Ct has pro rec; Twn Clks have b, m & d rec)

* At least one county history has been published about this county.

† Inventory of county archives was made by the Historical Records Survey. (See Introduction)

NORTH CAROLINA

CAPITAL · RALEIGH — STATE 1789 (12th)
State Map on Page M-31

Sir Walter Raleigh received a grant from Queen Elizabeth in 1584, which he used to colonize North Carolina. His first expedition in 1584 brought glowing reports of Roanoke Island. These reports led to attempts to establish a permanent colony in 1585. Internal and external problems led the settlers to return to England the following year with Sir Francis Drake. In 1587, another group was sent, headed by John White. He returned to England later in the year in a desperate attempt for supplies. It took him three years to return, at which time the settlement had vanished with only carvings on trees as evidence of inhabitance.

The first permanent settlement was started in 1653, when groups from Virginia occupied the section north of the Albemarle Sound. North Carolina was first differentiated from South Carolina in 1691, but continued to be ruled by governors from South Carolina until 1711. From 1706 to 1725, towns near the coast were founded by French Huguenot, German, and Swiss settlers. Between 1730 and 1770, with the heaviest influx around 1746, Scottish Highlanders came to North Carolina. Large groups of Scotch-Irish left Pennsylvania via the Shenandoah Valley to settle in Virginia. Many continued on to North Carolina. They settled mostly in the western section of the state around present-day Iredell County and numbered 20,000 in just a few years. By 1760, Germans in Forsyth and Guilford counties numbered 15,000. A colony of English speaking Quakers from Virginia, Pennsylvania, and Nantucket settled in Rockingham, Guilford, and Chatham Counties.

On achieving statehood, North Carolina ceded Tennessee to the United States. By 1850, a quarter of native North Carolinians had left the state to live in other states or territories. North Carolina seceded from the Union in 1861. It provided the most troops of any state to the Confederacy, an estimated 125,000. North Carolina also had the most casualties, over 40,000 killed. Union forces received over 3,000 soldiers from North Carolina. North Carolina was readmitted to the Union in 1868. Between 1862 and 1907, twenty-four counties in southern and western North Carolina lost many records to fire or war.

Nearly all useful genealogical county records up to about 1910 are in the North Carolina State Archives, 109 East Jones Street, Raleigh, NC 27611. Counties where births and deaths occurred kept a duplicate copy of the information sent to the state. After 1741, prior to marriage, one had the choice of publishing banns or buying a license which required posting of a bond. Surviving marriage bonds, except for Granville and Davie counties, are in the North Carolina State Archives. They contain the names of the groom, the bride, the other bondsman, and the witness. None of the parish registers containing records of births, deaths, and marriages prior to 1820 have survived. Although many early land grants have been lost, there are still many at the Land Office, Secretary of State, Administration Building, Raleigh, NC 27603. They are also on microfilm at the State Archives. Many of these records have been transcribed and indexed by the Alvaretta Kenan Register in the book *State Censuses of North Carolina, 1784-1787*, published by Genealogical Publishing Company, 1973. In 1784, the U.S. Continental Congress demanded a list of inhabitants. The lists which have survived have been indexed and published.

The Department of Human Resources, Division of Health Services, Vital Records Branch, Box 2091, Raleigh, NC 27602 has birth records from October 1913, death records from 1 January 1930, and marriage records from January 1962. Death records from 1913 through 1929 are available from the Archives and Records Section, State Records Center, 215 North Blount Street, Raleigh, NC 27602. To verify current fees, call 919-733-3526.

Genealogical Archives, Libraries and Societies

Burke County Public Library, 204 South King St., Morganton, NC 28655

Davidson County Public Library, 224 S. Main St., Lexington, NC 27292

Division of Archives and Reports, Office of Archives and History, State Dept. of Art, Culture and History, 109 E. Jones St., Raleigh, NC 27611

North Carolina State Library, 109 E. Jones St., Raleigh, NC 27611

Pack Memorial Public Library, 67 Haywood St., Asheville, NC 28801

Public Library of Charlotte and Mecklenburg County, 310 No. Tyron St., Charlotte, NC 28202

Richard H. Thornton, Memorial Library, Box 339, Main & Spring Sts., Oxford, NC 27565

Robeson County Public Library, Box 1346, 101 N. Chestnut St., Lumberton, NC 28358

Rowan Public Library, 201 W. Fisher St., Box 1009, Salisbury, NC 28144

Sandhill Regional Library, Box 548, 1104 E. Broad Ave., Rockingham, NC 28379

Thomas Hackney Braswell Memorial Library, 334 Falls Rd., Rocky Mount, NC 27801

Union County Public Library, 316 E. Windsor, Monroe, NC 28110

Alamance County, North Carolina Genealogical Society, P. O. Box 3052, Burlington, NC 27215-3052

Albemarle Genealogical Society, P. O. Box 87, Currituck, NC 27929

Alleghany Historical-Genealogical Society, Box 817, Sparta, NC 28675

Beaufort County Genealogical Society, P. O. Box 1089, Washington, NC 27889-1089

Broad River Genealogical Society, P. O. Box 2261, Shelby, NC 28151-2261

Burke County Genealogical Society, P. O. Box 661, Morganton, NC 28655

Caldwell County Genealogical Society, Box 2476, Lenoir, NC 28645

Carolinas Genealogical Society, 605 Craig St., Monroe, NC 28110

Cary Historical Society, P. O. Box 134, Cary, NC 27511

Catawba County Genealogical Society, P. O. Box 2406, Hickory, NC 28603

Cumberland County Genealogical Society, P. O. Box 53299, Fayetteville, NC 28305

Durham-Orange Genealogical Society, 2117 Faucette Ave., Durham, NC 27704

Eastern North Carolina Genealogical Society, P. O. Box 395, New Bern, NC 28560

Forsyth County Genealogical Society, Box 5715, Winston-Salem, NC 27113

Genealogical Society of Davidson County, P. O. Box 1665, Lexington, NC 27292

Genealogical Society of Iredell County, P. O. Box 946, Statesville, NC 28677

Genealogical Society of the Original Wilkes County, N. Wilkesboro, NC 28659

Genealogical Society of Rowan County, P. O. Box 4305, Salisbury, NC 28144

Guilford County Genealogical Society, P. O. Box 9693, Greensboro, NC 27429-0693

Henderson County Genealogical & Historical Society, 432 N. Main Street, Hendersonville, NC 28739

Historic Foundation of the Presbyterian and Reformed Churches, Montreat, NC 28757

Jewish Genealogy Society of Raleigh, 8701 Sleepy Creek Dr., Raleigh, NC 27612

Johnston County Genealogical Society, Public Library of Johnston County and Smithfield, Smithfield, NC 27577

Mecklenburg, North Carolina Genealogical Society, P. O. Box 32453, Charlotte, NC 28232

Moore County Genealogical Society, P. O. Box 56, Carthage, NC 28327

North Carolina Genealogical Society, P. O. Box 1492, Raleigh, NC 27602

North Carolina Society, Sons of the American Revolution, Pres., Rev. Walser H. Allen, Jr., 2221 Oleander Dr., Wilmington, NC 28403

North Carolina Society of County and Local Historians, 1209 Hill St., Greensboro, NC 27408

Old Buncombe County Genealogical Society, P. O. Box 2122, Asheville, NC 28802

Old Dobbs County Genealogical Society, P. O. Box 617, Goldsboro, NC 27530

Olde Mecklenburg Genealogical Society, P. O. Box 32453, Charlotte, NC 28232

Old New Hanover County Genealogical Society, P. O. Box 2536, Wilmington, NC 28402

Old Tryon County Genealogical Society, Box 938, Forest City, NC 28043

Onslow County Genealogical Society, P. O. Box 1739, Jacksonville, NC 28541-1739

Polk County North Carolina Genealogical Society, 485 Hunting Country Road, Tryon, NC 28782

Randolph County Genealogical Society, Randolph County Public Library, 201 Worth St., Asheboro, NC 27203

Rockingham County Historical Society, P. O. Box 84, Wentworth, NC 27375

Society of Loyalist Descendants (American Revolution), P. O. Box 848, Desk 120, Rockingham, NC 28379

Society of Richmond County Descendants, P. O. Box 848, Desk 120, Rockingham, NC 28379

Southport Historical Society, 501 N. Atlantic Ave., Southport, NC 28461

Southwestern North Carolina Genealogical Society, 101 Blumenthal, Murphy, NC 28906

Stanley County Genealogical Society, Box 31, Albemarle, NC 28001

Surry County Genealogical Society, Box 997, Dobson, NC 27017

Swain County, North Carolina, Genealogical and Historical Society, P. O. Box 267, Bryson City, NC 28713

University of North Carolina, Drawer 870, Chapel Hill, NC 27514

VA-NC Piedmont Genealogical Society, P. O. Box 2272, Danville, VA 24541

Wake County Genealogical Society, P. O. Box 17713, Raleigh, NC 27619

Wayne County Historical Association, P. O. Box 665, Goldsboro, NC 27530

Wilkes Genealogical Society, Inc., P. O. Box 1629, North Wilkesboro, NC 28659

Yadkin County Historical Society, P. O. Box 1250, Yadkinville, NC 27055

Printed Census Records and Mortality Schedules

Federal Census 1790 (supplemented by tax lists for Caswell, Granville, and Orange counties), 1800, 1810 (except Craven, Greene, New Hanover, and Wake counties), 1820 (except Currituck, Franklin, Martin, Montgomery, Randolph, and Wake counties), 1830, 1840, 1850, 1860, 1870, 1880, 1890 (parts of Gaston and Cleveland counties only), 1900, 1910

Federal Mortality Schedules 1850, 1860, 1870, 1880

Union Veterans and Widows 1890

Residents 1701

Colonial Census 1741-1752

State/Territorial Census 1784-1787

Valuable Printed Sources

Atlases, Maps, and Gazetteers

Clay, James W., et al. *North Carolina Atlas*. Chapel Hill: University of North Carolina Press, 1975.

Corbitt, David LeRoy. *The Formation of the North Carolina Counties, 1663-1943*. Raleigh: State Department of Archives and History, 1975.

Powell, William S. *The North Carolina Gazetteer*. Chapel Hill: University of North Carolina Press, 1968.

Bibliographies

Archival and Manuscript Repositories in North Carolina: A Directory. Raleigh: Society of North Carolina Archivists, 1987.

Davis, Richard C. and Linda Angle Miller. *Guide to the Cataloged Collections in the Manuscript Department of the William R. Perkins Library, Duke University*. Santa Barbara: Clio Books, 1980.

Guide to Research Materials in the North Carolina State Archives, Section B: County Records. Raleigh: North Carolina Department of Cultural Resources, 1988.

Jones, Roger C. *North Carolina Newspapers on Microfilm: Titles Available from the Division of Archives and History*. Raleigh: State Department of Archives and History, 1984.

Genealogical Research Guides

Leary, Helen F. M. and Maurice R. Stirewalt. *North Carolina Research: Genealogy and Local History*. Raleigh: North Carolina Genealogical Society, 1980.

Schweitzer, George K. *North Carolina Genealogical Research*. Knoxville, Tennessee: George K. Schweitzer, 1984.

Genealogical Sources

Grimes, J. Bryan. *Abstracts of North Carolina Wills, 1690-1760*. Baltimore: Genealogical Publishing Co., 1975.

Hofmann, Margaret M. *Province of North Carolina, 1663-1729, Abstracts of Land Patents*. Weldon, North Carolina: Noanoke News Co., 1979.

Manarin, Louis H. and W. T. Jordan Jr. *North Carolina Troops, 1861-1865: A Roster*. Raleigh: State Department of Archives and History, 1966.

Olds, Fred A. *An Abstract of North Carolina Wills, 1760-1800*. Baltimore: Genealogical Publishing Co., 1968.

Powell, William S. *Dictionary of North Carolina Biography*. Chapel Hill: Southern Historical Collection, 1979.

Histories

Lefler, Hugh Talmage and Alfred Ray Newsome. *The History of a Southern State: North Carolina*. Chapel Hill: University of North Carolina Press, 1973.

NORTH CAROLINA COUNTY DATA
State Map on Page M-31

Name	Map Index	Date Created	Parent County or Territory From Which Organized
*† **Alamance**	D4	1849	Orange

Alamance County, 124 W Elm St, Graham, NC 27253-2802 . . . . (919)228-1312
(Clk Sup Ct has div, pro & civ rec from 1849; Reg of Deeds has b, m & d rec)

| **Albemarle** | | 1663 | 1 of 3 original cos. discontinued in 1739 |
| * **Alexander** | F4 | 1847 | Iredell, Caldwell & Wilkes |

Alexander County, 100 1st St SW, Taylorsville, NC 28681-2592 . . . . (704)632-2215
(Reg Deeds has b, m, d & bur rec, Ind rec; Clk Sup Ct has div, pro & civ ct rec from 1865)

| * **Alleghany** | F3 | 1859 | Ashe |

Alleghany County, Main St, Sparta, NC 28675 . . . . (919)372-8949
(Clk Sup Ct has b & d rec from 1914, m rec from 1868, also div rec, pro rec from 1883, civ ct rec from 1869 & Ind rec from 1860)

| * **Anson** | E5 | 1750 | Bladen |

Anson County, N Green St, Wadesboro, NC 28170 . . . . (704)694-2796
(Reg Deeds has b rec from 1913, m rec from 1869, d rec & Ind rec; Clk Sup Ct has div rec from 1868, pro rec from 1750 & civ ct rec from 1770; Courthouse burned 1868)

| **Archdale** | | 1705 | Changed to Beaufort 1712 |
| * **Ashe** | G3 | 1799 | Wilkes |

Ashe County, Court St, Jefferson, NC 28640 . . . . (919)246-8841
(Clk has b & d rec from 1913, m rec from 1853, div, pro & civ ct rec from 1800)

| * **Avery** | G4 | 1911 | Caldwell, Mitchell, Watauga |

Avery County, Main St, Newland, NC 28657 . . . . (704)733-5186
(Clk Sup Ct has div, pro, civ ct & Ind rec from 1911)

| **Bath** | | 1696 | Discontinued in 1739 |
| * **Beaufort** | B4 | 1712 | Bath (formerly Archdale) |

Beaufort County, 112 W 2nd St, Washington, NC 27889-4940 . . . . (919)946-7721
[FHL has some m, cem, civ ct, Ind, pro, tax rec]

| * **Bertie** | B4 | 1722 | Chowan |

Bertie County, 106 W Dundee St, Windsor, NC 27983-1208 . . . . (919)794-5300
(Reg Deeds has b, m & d rec; Clk Sup Ct has div & civ ct rec from 1869 & pro rec from 1763)

| * **Bladen** | D6 | 1734 | New Hanover, Bath |

Bladen County, Courthouse Dr, Elizabethtown, NC 28337 . . . . (919)862-3438
(Reg Deeds has b & d rec from 1914, m rec from 1893 & Ind rec from 1734; Clk Sup Ct has div & civ ct rec from 1893 & pro rec from 1734; Courthouse burned 1800-1893)

| * **Brunswick** | C7 | 1764 | New Hanover, Bladen |

Brunswick County, PO Box 249, Bolivia, NC 28422-0249 . . . . (919)253-4331
(Reg of Deeds has b, m, d & bur rec; Clk Sup Ct has div rec from 1900, pro rec & wills from 1858, civ ct rec from 1882)

| * **Buncombe** | H4 | 1791 | Burke, Rutherford |

Buncombe County, 60 Courthouse Plaza, Asheville, NC 28801-3519 . . . . (704)251-6007
(Courthouse burned 1830-35; Reg Deeds has b, m, d, bur & Ind rec; Clk Sup Ct has div & pro rec from 1832 & civ ct rec)

| * **Burke** | G4 | 1777 | Rowan |

Burke County, PO Box 796, Morganton, NC 28655 . . . . (704)438-5540
(Reg Deeds has b & d rec from 1913, m, Ind rec & service discharges from 1865; Clk Sup Ct has div, pro & civ ct rec from 1865)

| **Bute** | | 1764 | Discontinued in 1779 |
| * **Cabarrus** | F5 | 1792 | Mecklenburg |

Cabarrus County, PO Box 70, Concord, NC 28026-0070 . . . . (704)786-4137
(Courthouse burned 1874; Reg deeds has b & d rec from 1913, m & Ind rec from 1792, military discharges from 1919; Clk Sup Ct has div, pro & civ ct rec)

| * **Caldwell** | G4 | 1841 | Burke, Wilkes |

Caldwell County, PO Box 1376, Lenoir, NC 28645 . . . . (704)758-0161
(Reg Deeds has b, m, d & Ind rec; Clk Sup Ct has div, civ ct & pro rec from 1841)

| * **Camden** | A3 | 1777 | Pasquotank |

Camden County, Hwy 343, Camden, NC 27921 . . . . (919)338-0066
(Clk Sup Ct has div & civ ct rec from 1896, pro rec from 1912)

| * **Carteret** | B5 | 1722 | Craven |

Carteret County, Courthouse Sq, Beaufort, NC 28516 . . . . (919)728-8500
(Reg Deeds has b, m, d & Ind rec; Clk Sup Ct has div, pro & civ ct rec)

Name	Map Index	Date Created	Parent County or Territory From Which Organized

* **Caswell** D3 1777 Orange
  Caswell County, E Church St & North Ave, Yanceyville, NC 27379 .... (919)694-4193
  (Clk Sup Ct has div, pro & civ ct rec)
* **Catawba** F4 1842 Lincoln
  Catawba County, PO Box 389, Newton, NC 28658-0389 .... (704)464-7880
  (Clk Sup Ct has div, pro & civ ct rec from 1843)
* **Chatham** D4 1770 Orange
  Chatham County, Courthouse Sq, Pittsboro, NC 27312 .... (919)542-3240
  (Reg Deeds has b & d rec from 1913, m & Ind rec from 1771; Clk Sup Ct has div rec from 1913, pro rec from 1771 & civ ct rec from 1869)
* **Cherokee** I5 1839 Macon
  Cherokee County, 201 Peachtree St, Murphy, NC 28906-2994 .... (704)837-5527
  (Clk Sup Ct has div, pro & civ ct rec)
* **Chowan** B4 1670 Albemarle
  Chowan County, S Broad St, Edenton, NC 27932 .... (919)482-2323
  [FHL has some b, m, d, cem, civ ct, Ind, pro rec]
* **Clay** I5 1861 Cherokee
  Clay County, PO Box 118, Hayesville, NC 28904-0118 .... (704)389-6301
  (Reg Deeds has b, m, d, pro & Ind rec)
* **Cleveland** G5 1841 Rutherford, Lincoln
  Cleveland County, PO Box 1210, Shelby, NC 28150 .... (704)484-4800
  (Reg Deeds has b & d rec from 1914, m rec from 1851, Ind rec from 1841; Clk Sup Ct has div rec from 1921, pro rec from 1843 & civ ct rec from 1914)
*† **Columbus** D6 1808 Bladen, Brunswick
  Columbus County, 111 Washington St, Whiteville, NC 28472-3323 .... (919)642-5700
  (Reg Deeds has b & d rec from 1913, m rec from 1867; Clk Sup Ct has div & civ rec from 1868, pro rec from 1817)
*† **Craven** B5 1712 Prec. Bath Co
  Craven County, 302 Broad St, New Bern, NC 28560-4903 .... (919)633-3126
  (1810 census missing) (Reg Deeds has b & d rec from 1914, m & pro rec from 1780, civ ct rec from 1915 & Ind rec from 1710; City Clk has bur rec from 1800; Clk Sup Ct has div rec from 1915)
* **Cumberland** D5 1754 Bladen
  Cumberland County, 113 Dick St, Fayetteville, NC 28301-5725 .... (919)486-1351
  (Reg Deeds has b, m, d & bur rec; Clk Sup Ct has div rec from 1930, pro rec from 1850 & civ ct rec from 1900)
* **Currituck** A3 1670 Albemarle
  Currituck County, PO Box 39, Currituck, NC 27929-0039 .... (919)232-2075
  (1820 census missing; Courthouse burned 1842) (Reg Deeds has b, m, d & Ind rec; Clk Sup Ct has div, pro & civ ct rec)
* **Dare** A4 1870 Currituck, Tyrell, Hyde
  Dare County, Budleigh St, Manteo, NC 27954 .... (919)473-1101
  (Reg Deeds has b & d rec from 1913, m rec from 1870; Clk Sup Ct has div, pro & civ ct rec from 1870)
* **Davidson** E4 1822 Rowan
  Davidson County, PO Box 1067, Lexington, NC 27292 .... (704)249-7011
  (Reg Deeds has b, m, d, bur & Ind rec from 1823; Clk Sup Ct has div, pro & civ ct rec from 1823)
* **Davie** F4 1836 Rowan
  Davie County, 123 S Main St, Mocksville, NC 27028-2424 .... (704)634-5513
  (Reg Deeds has b, m, d, bur & Ind rec; Clk Sup Ct has div & civ ct rec from 1834, pro rec from 1837)
  Dobbs   1758 Johnston, (discontinued 1791)
* **Duplin** C5 1750 New Hanover
  Duplin County, Courthouse Plaza, Kenansville, NC 28349 .... (919)296-1240
  (Reg Deeds has b, d rec from 1913, m rec from 1749, maps, deeds, Ind grants and deeds of trust from 1749, corporations, assumed names and partnerships from 1899; Clk Sup Ct has wills, Ind division rec)
* **Durham** D4 1881 Orange, Wake
  Durham County, 201 E Main St, Durham, NC 27701-3641 .... (919)560-0025
  (Co Health Dept has b, d & bur rec; Reg Deeds has m & Ind rec; Clk Sup Ct has div, pro & civ ct rec from 1881)
* **Edgecombe** C4 1741 Bertie
  Edgecombe County, 301 Saint Andrews St, Tarboro, NC 27886-5111 .... (919)823-6161
  [FHL has some m, div, cem, civ ct, Ind, pro, tax rec]
* **Forsyth** E4 1849 Stokes
  Forsyth County, Hall of Justice Rm 700, Winston-Salem, NC 27101 .... (919)727-2071
  (Reg Deeds has b, m, d & Ind rec; Clk Sup Ct has div, pro & civ ct rec from 1849)
* **Franklin** C4 1779 Bute
  Franklin County, 215 E Nash St, Louisburg, NC 27549-2545 .... (919)496-5994
  (1820 census missing) (Reg Deeds has b & d rec from 1913, m rec from 1869, Ind rec from 1779 & pro rec; Clk Sup Ct has div rec)
* **Gaston** F5 1846 Lincoln
  Gaston County, 151 South St, Gastonia, NC 28052-4128 .... (704)868-5800
  (Reg Deeds has b, m & d rec from 1913, Ind rec from 1847; Clk Sup Ct has div rec)

Name	Map Index	Date Created	Parent County or Territory From Which Organized

* Gates   B3   1779   Chowan, Hertford, Perquimans
Gates County, PO Box 141, Gatesville, NC 27938-0141 .... (919)357-1240
(Reg Deeds has b, m, d, bur & Ind rec; Clk Sup Ct has div, pro & civ ct rec from 1780)

Glasgow   1791   (Discontinued 1799)

Graham   I5   1872   Cherokee
Graham County, PO Box 575, Robbinsville, NC 28771-0575 .... (704)479-3361
(Reg Deeds has b, d rec from 1913, m, Ind rec from 1873; Clk Sup Ct has div, civ ct, pro rec from 1872)

* Granville   D3   1746   Edgecombe, Orig. Glasgow
Granville County, 141 Williamsboro St, Oxford, NC 27565-3318 .... (919)693-5240
(Clk Sup Ct has div, pro & Ind rec)

* Greene   C5   1799   Dobbs or Glasgow
Greene County, 2nd & Greene, Snow Hill, NC 28580-0675 .... (919)747-3505
(Courthouse burned in 1876) (Reg deeds has b, m, d, bur, Ind rec from 1876; Clk Sup Ct has div, civ ct, pro rec from 1876)

* Guilford   E4   1770   Rowan, Orange
Guilford County, 301 Market St, Greensboro, NC 27402 .... (919)373-3778
(Reg Deeds has b, m, d, bur & Ind rec; Clk Sup Ct has div rec from 1974, pro rec from 1929 & civ ct rec from 1974) (Courthouse burned 1872, many older rec still available)

* Halifax   C3   1758   Edgecombe
Halifax County, King St, Halifax, NC 27839 .... (919)583-1131
(Reg Deeds has b & d rec from 1913, m rec from 1867, div, pro & spec proceedings from 1868, civ ct rec from 1893, Ind rec from 1729 & mil dis from 1918)

* Harnett   D5   1855   Cumberland
Harnett County, 729 S Main St, Lillington, NC 27546 .... (919)893-7500
(Reg Deeds has b, m, d & Ind rec; Clk Sup Ct has div, pro & civ ct rec from 1920, rec from 1855 to 1920 were destroyed in a fire)

* Haywood   H4   1808   Buncombe
Haywood County, County Courthouse Annex, Waynesville, NC 28786 .... (704)452-6625
[FHL has some b, m, cem, civ ct, Ind, pro, tax rec, 1849 Catawba Indian census]

* Henderson   H5   1838   Buncombe
Henderson County, 100 N King St, Hendersonville, NC 28792-5053 .... (704)697-4808
(Reg Deeds has b & d rec from 1914, m rec from 1800, Ind rec from 1837; Clk Sup Ct has div, pro & civ ct rec from 1841)

* Hertford   B3   1759   Bertie, Chowan, Northampton, Gates
Hertford County, King St, Winton, NC 27986 .... (919)358-7845
(Reg Deeds has b, d & bur rec from 1913, m rec from 1884, Ind rec from 1866; Clk Sup Ct has div & civ ct rec from 1883, pro rec from 1869; Courthouse burned 1832-1862)

* Hoke   D5   1911   Cumberland, Robeson
Hoke County, 227 N Main St, Raeford, NC 28376-0266 .... (919)875-8751
(Reg Deeds has b, m, d & Ind rec from 1911; Clk Sup Ct has div, pro & civ ct rec from 1911)

* Hyde   A4   1712   Wickham, Pres. Bath Co
Hyde County, 264 Business Hwy, Swan Quarter, NC 27885 .... (919)926-5711
(Reg Deeds has b, d, bur rec from 1913, m rec from 1850, Ind rec from 1736, marr bonds from 1735 to 1867, delayed birth cert from late 1800s; Clk Sup Ct has div, civ ct rec from 1868, pro rec from 1774)

* Iredell   D4   1788   Rowan
Iredell County, PO Box 788, Statesville, NC 28677-0788 .... (704)878-3000
(Reg Deeds has b, m, d, bur, Ind rec; Clk Sup Ct has div rec from 1820, pro, civ ct rec from 1788) (Courthouse burned in 1854)

* Jackson   H5   1851   Haywood, Macon
Jackson County, 50 Keener St Suite 102, Sylva, NC 28779 .... (704)586-4312
(Reg Deeds has b, m, d, bur, & Ind rec; Clk Sup Ct has div, pro, civ ct & rec of estates from 1851)

* Johnston   C4   1746   Craven
Johnston County, 207 E Johnston St, Smithfield, NC 27577-4515 .... (919)989-5100
[FHL has some b, m, cem, civ ct, Ind, pro, tax rec]

* Jones   B5   1778   Craven
Jones County, PO Box 266, Trenton, NC 28585-0266 .... (919)448-7571
(Reg Deeds has b, d, rec from 1913, m rec from 1850, Ind rec from 1779; Clk Sup Ct has div rec from 1869, pro rec from 1779, civ ct rec) (Courthouse burned in 1862)

* Lee   D5   1907   Chatham, Moore
Lee County, PO Box 1968, Sanford, NC 27331-1968 .... (919)774-8403
(Reg Deeds has b, d & Ind rec; Clk Sup Ct has m, div, pro & civ ct rec from 1907)

* Lenoir   C5   1791   Dobbs
Lenoir County, PO Box 3289, Kinston, NC 28502-3289 .... (919)523-2417
(Clk Sup Ct has div, pro & civ ct rec from 1880; Courthouse burned 1878)

* Lincoln   F5   1778   Tryon
Lincoln County, 115 W Main St, Lincolnton, NC 28092-2643 .... (704)732-3361
(Reg Deeds has b, m, d, bur & Ind rec; Clk Sup Ct has div & civ ct rec from 1920, pro rec from 1869)

* Macon   I5   1828   Haywood
Macon County, 5 W Main St, Franklin, NC 28734-3005 .... (704)524-6421
[FHL has some m rec]

Name	Map Index	Date Created	Parent County or Territory From Which Organized

* **Madison** H4 1851 Buncombe, Yancey
Madison County, PO Box 684, Marshall, NC 28753-0684 .... (704)649-2531
(Reg Deeds has b, m, d, bur, Ind rec; Clk Sup Ct has div, pro, civ ct rec from 1851)

* **Martin** B4 1774 Halifax, Tyrell
Martin County, PO Box 668, Williamston, NC 27892-0668 .... (919)792-1901
(Courthouse burned in 1884; 1820 cen missing; Reg Deeds has b, m, d & Ind rec; Clk Sup Ct has div & civ ct rec from 1800s, pro rec from 1700s)

McDowell G4 1842 Burke, Rutherford
McDowell County, 10 E Court St, Marion, NC 28752-4041 .... (704)652-7121
(Reg Deeds has b, m, d & Ind rec; Clk Sup Ct has div, pro & civ ct rec from 1842)

* **Mecklenburg** F5 1762 Anson
Mecklenburg County, 600 E 4th St, Charlotte, NC 28202-2835 .... (704)336-2040
(Reg Deeds has b & d rec from 1913, m rec from 1850 & Ind rec from 1763; Clk Sup Ct has div, pro & civ ct rec from 1930)

Mitchell G4 1861 Burke, Caldwell, McDowell, Watauga, Yancey
Mitchell County, Crimson Laurel Way Adminstration Bldg, Bakersville, NC 28705 .... (704)688-2434
(Clk Sup Ct has div & pro rec from 1861, civ ct rec from 1912)

* **Montgomery** E5 1779 Anson
Montgomery County, PO Box 637, Troy, NC 27371-0637 .... (919)572-2575
(Courthouse burned 1835; 1820 census missing) (Reg Deeds has b, m, d, bur, pro & Ind rec; Clk Sup Ct has div & civ ct rec from 1842)

*† **Moore** E5 1784 Cumberland
Moore County, PO Box 936, Carthage, NC 28327-0936 .... (919)947-2396
(Courthouse burned in 1889) (Reg Deeds has b & d rec from 1913, m & Ind rec from 1889, Ind grants from 1784; Clk Sup Ct has div, pro & civ ct rec)

*† **Nash** C4 1777 Edgecombe
Nash County, County Courthouse, Rm 104, Nashville, NC 27856 .... (919)459-4141
(Reg Deeds has b & d rec from 1913, m rec from 1872; Clk Sup Ct has div & civ ct rec from 1876, pro & Ind rec from 1869; oldest wills in Dept of Archives, Raleigh, N.C.)

* **New Hanover** C6 1729 Craven
New Hanover County, 320 Chestnut St Suite 502, Wilmington, NC 28401-4090 .... (919)341-7184
(Courthouse burned 1798, 1819 & 1840; 1810 cen missing; Reg of Deeds has b, m & d rec; Clk Sup Ct has div, pro & civ ct rec)

* **Northampton** B3 1741 Bertie
Northampton County, Jefferson St, Jackson, NC 27845 .... (919)534-2501
(Reg Deeds has b, m, d & Ind rec; Clk Sup Ct has div rec from 1800, pro & civ ct rec from 1761)

* **Onslow** B6 1734 Preceding Bath
Onslow County, 521 Mill Ave, Jacksonville, NC 28540-4258 .... (919)347-4717
(Reg Deeds has b, d rec from 1914, m rec from 1893, Ind rec from 1734; Clk Sup Ct has div, pro, civ ct rec from 1915, prior rec in Dept Archives and History, Raleigh, NC 27602)

* **Orange** D4 1752 Bladen, Granville, Johnston
Orange County, 106 E Margaret Ln, Hillsborough, NC 27278-2546 .... (919)732-8181
(Courthouse burned 1789; Reg Deeds has b & d rec from 1913, m & Ind rec from 1754, div rec from 1869, pro rec from 1756 & civ rec from 1865)

* **Pamlico** B5 1872 Beaufort, Craven
Pamlico County, PO Box 776, Bayboro, NC 28515-0776 .... (919)745-3133
(Reg Deeds has b rec from 1913, m, d & Ind rec from 1872; Clk Sup Ct has div, pro & civ ct rec from 1872)

* **Pasquotank** A3 1670 Prec. Albemarle
Pasquotank County, PO Box 39, Elizabeth City, NC 27907-0039 .... (919)335-0865
(Courthouse burned 1862; Clk Sup Ct has div, pro & civ ct rec; Reg Deeds has b & d rec from 1913, m rec from 1867, Ind rec from 1700's)

* **Pender** C6 1875 New Hanover
Pender County, PO Box 5, Burgaw, NC 28425-0005 .... (919)259-1200
(Reg Deeds has b, m, d & Ind rec; Clk Sup Ct has div, pro & civ ct rec)

* **Perquimans** A3 1670 Prec. Albemarle
Perquimans County, PO Box 45, Hertford, NC 27944-0045 .... (919)426-8484
(Perquimans Co was known as Berkeley Precinct from 1671 to 1681)

* **Person** D3 1791 Caswell
Person County, County Courthouse, Roxboro, NC 27573 .... (919)597-7228
(Reg Deeds has b, m, d & Ind rec; Clk Sup Ct has div, pro & civ ct rec from 1791)

* **Pitt** B4 1760 Beaufort
Pitt County, 1717 W 5th St, Greenville, NC 27834-1698 .... (919)830-6302
(Courthouse burned 1857; Reg Deeds has b & d rec from 1913, m rec from 1866, real estate rec from 1762; Clk Sup Ct has div, pro, civ ct & Ind rec from 1885)

* **Polk** G5 1855 Henderson, Rutherford
Polk County, PO Box 308, Columbus, NC 28722-0308 .... (704)894-3301
(Clk Sup Ct has div rec from 1932, pro, civ ct rec from 1872)

Name	Map Index	Date Created	Parent County or Territory From Which Organized

* **Randolph**   E4   1779   Guilford
    Randolph County, 145 Worth St, Asheboro, NC 27203-5509 .... (919)629-2131
    (1820 cen missing; Reg Deeds has b & d rec from 1913, m rec from 1800, Ind rec; Clk Sup Ct div & civ ct rec, pro rec from 1786)

* **Richmond**   E5   1779   Anson
    Richmond County, Rockingham, NC 28379 ....
    (Reg Deeds has b & d rec from 1913, m rec from 1870, Ind rec from 1784; Clk Sup Ct has div rec from 1913, pro rec from 1782)

* **Robeson**   D6   1787   Bladen
    Robeson County, 500 N Elm St, Lumberton, NC 28358-5595 .... (919)671-3000
    (Reg Deeds has b rec from 1913, m rec from 1787, d rec from 1915, Ind rec from 1799; Clk Sup Ct has div, civ ct rec from 1920, pro rec from 1868)

* **Rockingham**   E3   1785   Guilford
    Rockingham County, PO Box 26, Wentworth, NC 27375-0026 .... (919)342-8700
    (Courthouse burned 1906; Reg of Deeds has m rec from 1868, deeds from 1787, b & d rec from 1913; Clk Sup Ct has wills from 1804; N.C. Hist Com has m rec from 1741 to 1868)

* **Rowan**   F4   1753   Anson
    Rowan County, 202 N Main St, Salisbury, NC 28144-4346 .... (704)636-0361
    (Reg Deeds has b, m, d & Ind rec; Clk Sup Ct has div rec from 1881, pro & civ ct rec)

* **Rutherford**   G5   1779   Burke, Tryon
    Rutherford County, PO Box 630, Rutherfordton, NC 28139-0630 .... (704)286-9136
    (Clk Sup Ct has b rec from 1917, d rec from 1913, m, div, pro, civ ct & Ind rec from 1779, tax lists & voter registration; Courthouse burned in 1857)

* **Sampson**   C5   1784   Duplin, New Hanover
    Sampson County, 313 Rowan Rd, Clinton, NC 28328-4700 .... (919)592-6308
    (Courthouse burned 1921)

  Scotland   E5   1899   Richmond
    Scotland County, 1405 West Blvd, Laurinburg, NC 28352 .... (919)277-0470
    (Reg Deeds has b rec from 1913, m, d, bur rec from 1899; Clk Sup Ct has div, pro & civ ct rec from 1899)

* **Stanley**   E5   1841   Montgomery
    Stanley County, 201 S 2nd St, Albemarle, NC 28001-5747 .... (704)983-7204
    [FHL has some m, cem, civ ct, Ind, pro rec]

* **Stokes**   E3   1789   Surry
    Stokes County, Hwy 89, Danbury, NC 27016 .... (919)593-2811
    [FHL has some b, m, d, cem, div, civ ct, Ind, pro, tax rec]

* **Surry**   F3   1770   Rowan
    Surry County, PO Box 345, Dobson, NC 27017-0345 .... (919)386-8131
    (Reg Deeds has b, m, d, bur, Ind rec; Clk Sup Ct has div, civ ct rec, pro rec from 1771)

* **Swain**   I4   1871   Jackson, Macon
    Swain County, Mitchell St, Bryson, NC 28713 .... (704)488-9273
    (Reg Deeds has b & d rec 1913, m rec 1907; Clk Sup Ct has div & civ rec from 1900)

* **Transylvania**   H5   1861   Henderson, Jackson
    Transylvania County, 28 E Main St, Brevard, NC 28712-3738 .... (704)884-3100
    (Clk Sup Ct has div, pro & civ ct rec)

  Tryon   1768   Discontinued 1779 (see Lincoln)

  Tyrrell   A4   1729   Bertie, Chowan, Currituck, Pasquotank
    Tyrrell County, Water St, Columbia, NC 27925 .... (919)796-1371
    (Reg Deeds has b & d rec from 1913, m rec from 1862; Clk Sup Ct has div rec, pro, wills from 1730 & civ ct rec from 1900)

* **Union**   F5   1842   Anson, Mecklenburg
    Union County, 500 N Main St, Monroe, NC 28112-4730 .... (704)283-3500
    (Reg Deeds has b, m, d & bur rec; Clk Sup Ct has div, rec, pro & civ ct rec from 1843)

* **Vance**   C3   1881   Franklin, Granville, Warren
    Vance County, 122 Young St, Henderson, NC 27536-4268 .... (919)492-2141
    (Clk Sup Ct has div, pro, civ ct rec)

* **Wake**   D4   1770   Cumberland, Johnston, Orange
    Wake County, 336 Fayetteville Mall, Raleigh, NC 27602 .... (919)856-6000
    (1810 & 1820 cen missing)

* **Warren**   C3   1779   Bute, Discontinued 1779
    Warren County, PO Box 709, Warrenton, NC 27589-0709 .... (919)257-3261
    (Reg Deeds has b & d rec from 1913, m & Ind rec from 1764; Clk Sup Ct has div & pro rec from 1764, civ ct rec from 1968)

* **Washington**   A4   1799   Tyrell
    Washington County, 120 Adams St, Plymouth, NC 27962-1308 .... (919)793-5823
    (Reg Deeds has b & d rec from 1913, m rec from 1851, Ind rec from 1799; Clk Sup Ct has div rec from 1871, pro & civ ct rec from 1873) (Courthouse burned 1862-1869-1873)

* **Watauga**   G3   1849   Ashe, Caldwell, Wilkes, Yancey
    Watauga County, 403 W King St, Boone, NC 28607-3531 .... (704)264-1300
    (Reg Deeds has b & d rec from 1914, m rec from 1872; Clk Sup Ct has div, pro & civ ct rec from 1872)

Name	Map Index	Date Created	Parent County or Territory From Which Organized
* Wayne	C5	1779	Craven, Dobbs

Wayne County, 215 S William St, Goldsboro, NC 27530-4824 .... (919)731-1400
(Reg Deeds has b, m, d, bur & Ind rec; Clk Sup Ct has div, pro & civ ct rec)

| * Wilkes | F4 | 1777 | Surry |

Wilkes County, 110 North St, Wilkesboro, NC 28697 .... (919)651-7300
(Reg Deeds has b & d rec from 1913, m & Ind rec from 1778; Clk Sup Ct has div, pro & civ ct rec)

| Wilson | C4 | 1855 | Edgecombe, Johnston, Nash, Wayne |

Wilson County, PO Box 1728, Wilson, NC 27894-1728 .... (919)237-3913
(Reg Deeds has b, m, d & Ind rec; Clk Sup Ct has div & civ ct rec from 1868, pro rec from 1855)

| * Yadkin | F4 | 1850 | Surry |

Yadkin County, PO Box 146, Yadkinville, NC 27055-0146 .... (919)679-4200
(Reg Deeds has b, d rec from 1913, m, Ind rec from 1850; Clk Sup Ct has div, civ ct rec; pro rec from 1850)

| *† Yancey | G4 | 1833 | Buncombe, Burke |

Yancey County, County Courthouse, Burnsville, NC 28714 .... (704)682-3971
(Reg Deeds has b, m, d, bur rec; Clk Sup Ct has div rec from 1875, pro, Ind rec from 1870, civ ct rec from 1870. Dept Archives and History in Raleigh, NC has older rec)

* At least one county history has been published about this county.
† Inventory of county archives was made by the Historical Records Survey. (See Introduction)

NORTH DAKOTA

CAPITAL · BISMARCK — TERRITORY 1861 — STATE 1889 (39th)

State Map on Page M-32

The first white man to visit North Dakota was the French explorer, Pierre Gaultier de Varennes, who reached Indian villages on the Missouri River in 1738. The French laid claim to the area in 1682, but permitted British fur trading. The Louisiana Purchase in 1803 gave the southwestern half of North Dakota to the United States. Lewis and Clark explored the area the following year.

The first permanent white settlement was made by Scottish pioneers from Canada in 1812 at Pembina. As Indians were driven westward, settlers came into the eastern regions of the state to farm. The Dakota Territory was organized in 1861 and included the two Dakotas, Montana, and Wyoming. The first Homestead Act offered free land to settlers, but the Civil War and Indian wars delayed settlement. During the Civil War, about 200 men fought for the Union forces. In 1864, the Montana Territory was created, which took the Wyoming and Montana areas from the Dakota Territory.

As railroads reached completion, settlement in North Dakota began in earnest. In 1871, railroads reached the Red River from St. Paul and Duluth. Dreams of acres of fertile land drew thousands of northern and middle Europeans to North Dakota. Norwegians led the immigration, but large numbers of Swedes, Danes, Icelanders, Czechs, Poles, and Dutch also came. FrenchCanadians came from Canada. Germans settled around Bismarck and the south central counties, which is evident from the names of the cities in the area, such as Leipzig, Strassburg and Danzig. The Dakota Territory was divided into North and South Dakota about 1873. In 1889, North Dakota became the thirty-ninth state in the Union.

Registration of births and deaths was required from 1893 to 1895 and after 1899. General compliance with the law was not reached until about 1923. Copies of these records are available from the Division of Vital Records, State Department of Health, First Floor Judicial Wing, Bismarck, ND 58505. To verify current fees, call 701-224-2360.

Marriage certificates and licenses are filed in the office of the county judge. Since July 1, 1925, copies of licenses and marriage certificates have been forwarded to the State Registrar, who can issue certified copies. District Court Clerks have charge of civil court, divorce, and probate records. North Dakota was included in the 1836 Wisconsin, 1840 Iowa, 1850 Minnesota, and 1860-1880 Dakota Territorial censuses. Original patents and copies of township plats are available from the BLM, 222 North 32nd Street, Box 30157, Billings, MT 59107. Records of the local land offices are at the State Historical Society of North Dakota, North Dakota Heritage Center, Bismarck, ND 58505. The county registrars of deeds have deeds and land titles dating from the time land became available for private purchase.

Genealogical Archives, Libraries and Societies

Minot Public Library, 516 Second Avenue, S.W., Minot, ND 58701

Public Library, Fargo, ND 58102

Public Library, Grand Forks, ND 58201

Public Library, Minot, ND 58701

Red River Valley Genealogical Society Library, Human Services Bldg., 15 Broadway, Suite 512, Fargo, ND 58016

State Library, Bismarck, ND 58501

University of North Dakota Library, Grand Forks, ND 58201

Bismarck-Mandan Historical and Genealogical Society, Box 485, Bismarck, ND 58501

Genealogy Guild of Wilkin County, Minnesota and Richland County, North Dakota, c / o Leach Public Library, Wahpeton, ND 58075

Germans from Russia Heritage Society, 1008 E. Central Ave., Bismarck, ND 58501

Medora Centennial Commission, Box 212, Medora, ND 58645

McLean County Genealogical Society, P. O. Box 51, Garrison, ND 58540

Mouse River Loop Genealogical Society, Box 1391, Minot, ND 58702-1391

Red River Valley Genealogy Society, P. O. Box 9284, Fargo, ND 58106

State Historical Society of North Dakota, Liberty Memorial Bldg., Bismarck, ND 58501

Printed Census Records and Mortality Schedules

Federal Census 1860, 1870, 1880, 1900, 1910
Union Veterans and Widows 1890
State/Territorial Census 1836, 1885

Valuable Printed Sources

Atlases, Maps, and Gazetteers

Northwestern Gazetteer: Minnesota, North and South Dakota and Montana Gazetteer and Business Directory. St. Paul: Polk, 1914.

Williams, Mary Ann Barnes. *Origins of North Dakota Place Names*. Washburn, North Dakota, 1966.

Bibliographies

Bye, John E. *Guide to Manuscripts and Archives*. Fargo, North Dakota: North Dakota Insititute for Regional Studies, 1985.

Genealogical Research Guides

Oihus, Colleen A. *Guide to Genealogical / Family History Sources*. Grand Forks, North Dakota: University of North Dakota, 1986.

Histories

Lounsberry, Clement A. *North Dakota History and People*. Washington, DC: Liberty Press, 1919.

Rath, George. *The Black Sea Germans in the Dakotas*. Peru, Nebraska: George Rath, 1977.

NORTH DAKOTA COUNTY DATA
State Map on Page M-32

Name	Map Index	Date Created	Parent County or Territory From Which Organized
* **Adams**	C2	1907	Stark, comprising part of old Hettinger
			Adams County, County Courthouse, Hettinger, ND 58639 .... (701)567-2460
			(Clk Dis Ct has m, div, pro, civ ct, Ind rec from 1907; State Dept Health has b & d rec)
Allred (see McKenzie)			
* **Barnes**	H3	1875	Cass (Burbank, disorganized)
			Barnes County, PO Box 774, Valley City, ND 58072-0774 .... (701)845-8512
			(Clk Dis Ct has b, d, bur & civ ct rec; Co Judge has m & pro rec)
* **Benson**	F5	1883	Ramsey
			Benson County, 311 B Ave S, Minnewaukan, ND 58351 .... (701)473-5340
			(Clk Dis Ct has b rec from late 1890s, m rec from late 1800s, d, div, pro, civ ct rec from 1895, bur rec from 1900; Reg Deeds has Ind rec)
Billings	B3	1879	Unorg. Terr
			Billings County, PO Box 138, Medora, ND 58645-0138 .... (701)623-4491
			(Clk Dis Ct has m rec from 1893, bur rec from 1922, div rec, pro rec from 1895, civ ct rec from 1890 & Ind rec from 1886)

Name	Map Index	Date Created	Parent County or Territory From Which Organized

* **Bottineau**   E6   1873   Unorg. Terr
Bottineau County, 315 W 5th St, Bottineau, ND 58318-1214 .... (701)228-3983
(Clk Dis Ct has b, d, bur rec from 1943, m rec from 1887, div, pro, civ ct rec from 1889, naturalization rec from 1884; Reg Deeds has Ind rec)

Bowman   B2   1883   Billings
Bowman County, 104 W 1st, Bowman, ND 58623 .... (701)523-3450
(Clk Dis Ct has m rec from 1907, div rec, pro & civ ct rec from 1908, Ind rec from 1896 & bur rec)

Buffalo (See Burleigh, Kidder, Logan, McHenry, Rolette & Sheridan)

Buford (See Williams)

Burbank (disorganized & transferred to Trail & Griggs)

* **Burke**   C6   1910   Ward
Burke County, PO Box 219, Bowbells, ND 58721-0219 .... (701)377-2718
(Clk Dis Ct has b rec from 1905, m, d, bur, div, pro, civ ct rec from 1910, Ind rec from 1900, homestead patents from 1903)

* **Burleigh**   E3   1873   Buffalo (discontinued)
Burleigh County, 514 E Thayer Ave, Bismarck, ND 58501-4413 .... (701)222-6702
(Clk Dis Ct has m & pro rec from 1898, civ ct rec from 1876, bur rec from 1950s)

* **Cass**   H3   1873   Original county
Cass County, 207 9th St S, Fargo, ND 58103-1833 .... (701)241-5660
(Clk Dis Ct has div & civ ct rec from 1885)

Cavalier   G6   1873   Pembina
Cavalier County, 901 3rd St, Langdon, ND 58249-2457 .... (701)256-2124
(Clk Dis Ct has m, pro & civ ct rec from 1881, div rec from 1888, Reg Deeds has Ind rec)

Church (See Sheridan)

De Smet (See Pierce)

* **Dickey**   G2   1881   La Moure
Dickey County, 309 N 2nd St, Ellendale, ND 58436 .... (701)349-3560
(Clk Dis Ct has b & d rec from 1943, m & pro rec from 1883, bur rec from 1932, div rec from 1885, pro rec from 1883 & civ ct rec from 1884)

* **Divide**   B6   1910   Williams
Divide County, 300 N Main St, Crosby, ND 58730 .... (701)965-6351
(Clk Dis Ct has b, d & bur rec also civ ct rec from 1910; Co Judge has m rec from 1910 & pro rec; Reg Deeds has Ind rec)

* **Dunn**   C3   1908   Stark, Mercer
Dunn County, County Courthouse, Manning, ND 58642 .... (701)573-4447
(Clk Dis Ct has m rec from 1908, bur rec from 1943, div, pro & civ ct rec)

Dunn, old (formed from part of Howard (discontinued) in 1883 & annexed to Stark in 1897)

Eddy   G4   1885   Foster
Eddy County, 524 Central Ave, New Rockford, ND 58356-1698 .... (701)947-2434

* **Emmons**   E2   1879   Unorg. Terr
Emmons County, PO Box 87, Linton, ND 58552-0087 .... (701)254-4701
(Clk Dis Ct has b rec from 1889, m rec from 1888, d, bur, div &civ ct rec from 1890, pro rec from 1884 & naturalization rec from 1886; Reg Deeds has Ind rec)

Flanery (See Williams)

Foster   G4   1873   Pembina
Foster County, 1000 5th St N, Carrington, ND 58421-1113 .... (701)652-2491
(Clk Dis Ct has b & d rec from 1900, m, div, pro & civ ct rec 1884; Reg Deeds has Ind rec)

† **Golden Valley**   B3   1912   Billings
Golden Valley County, PO Box 596, Beach, ND 58621-0596 .... (701)872-4352
(Clk Dis Ct has b, m, d, bur, div, pro, civ ct, ind rec from 1912)

* **Grand Forks**   H5   1873   Pembina
Grand Forks County, PO Box 1477, Grand Forks, ND 58206-1477 .... (701)780-8238
(Clk Dis Ct has b rec from 1903, d rec from 1908, div rec from 1878, bur & civ ct rec, adoption rec & change of name; Co Judge has m rec from 1887, pro rec from 1880)

Grant   D2   1916   Morton
Grant County, County Courthouse, Carson, ND 58529 .... (701)622-3615
(Clk Dis Ct has b rec from 1945, m, d, bur, div, pro & civ ct rec from 1916; Reg of Deeds has Ind rec)

Griggs   G4   1881   Foster, Burbank, Traill
Griggs County, PO Box 326, Cooperstown, ND 58425-0326 .... (701)797-2772
(Clk Dis Ct has b rec from 1901, m, pro rec from 1883, d rec from 1901, div, civ ct rec from 1887; Reg Deeds has Ind rec from 1880)

Gringras   Buffalo & Dakota Terr. (Named changed to Wells, 1881)

Hettinger   C2   1883   Stark
Hettinger County, 336 Pacific Ave, Mott, ND 58646 .... (701)824-2545
(Clk Dis Ct has b, d, bur rec from 1943, m, div, pro, civ ct rec from 1907; Reg Deeds has Ind rec)

Hettinger, old (See Adams)

Howard (See Dunn, Old)

Name	Map Index	Date Created	Parent County or Territory From Which Organized
* **Kidder**	F3	1873	Buffalo

Kidder County, PO Box 110, Steele, ND 58482-0110 .... (701)475-2672
(Clk Dis Ct has b, d & bur rec from 1943, div, civ ct rec from 1885; Co Judge has m rec from 1887, pro rec from 1883; Reg Deeds has lnd rec from 1881)

La Moure   G2   1873   Pembina
La Moure County, 202 4th Ave NE, La Moure, ND 58458 .... (701)883-5193
(Clk Dis Ct has b, m, d, bur, div, pro & civ ct rec from 1881)

Logan   F2   1873   Buffalo
Logan County, 301 Main St, Napoleon, ND 58561 .... (701)754-2504
(Clk Dis Ct has b & d rec from 1893, m, div, civ ct rec from 1890, pro rec from 1898, bur rec from 1926; Reg Deeds has lnd rec from 1884)

McHenry   E5   1873   Buffalo
McHenry County, 407 Main St S, Towner, ND 58788 .... (701)537-5729
(Clk Dis Ct has m rec from 1903, div, pro & civ ct rec from 1900; Reg Deeds has lnd rec)

* **McIntosh**   F2   1883   Logan
McIntosh County, 112 NE 1st St, Ashley, ND 58413 .... (701)288-3450
[FHL has some cem rec]

* **McKenzie**   B4   1905   Billings, Stark (comprising the unorganized cos of Allred, Old McKenzie & Wallace)
McKenzie County, PO Box 523, Watford, ND 58854-0523 .... (701)842-3451
(Clk Dis Ct has b, d rec from 1943, m, div, pro, civ ct rec from 1905, bur rec; Reg Deeds has lnd rec)

McKenzie, old   1883   Howard (annexed to Billings, 1897)

* **McLean**   D4   1883   Stevens
McLean County, 712 5th Ave, Washburn, ND 58577 .... (701)462-8541
(Clk Dis Ct has m rec from 1887, bur rec from 1920, div, civ ct rec from 1891, pro rec from 1900; Reg Deeds has lnd rec; Division Vital Statistics, Bismarck, has b, d rec)

† **Mercer**   D3   1875   Original county
Mercer County, PO Box 39, Stanton, ND 58571-0039 .... (701)745-3262
(Clk Dis Ct has b, d, bur rec from 1942, m rec from 1894, div, civ ct rec from 1906, pro rec from 1898; Reg Deeds has lnd rec; State Arch has nat rec)

*† **Morton**   D3   1873   Original county
Morton County, 210 2nd Ave NW, Mandan, ND 58554-3158 .... (701)667-3355
(Clk Dis Ct has b rec from 1883, m rec from 1888, d rec from 1873, bur rec from 1943, div, pro rec from 1900s, civ ct rec from late 1800s; Reg Deeds has lnd rec from late 1800s)

* **Mountrail**   C5   1909   Ward
Mountrail County, PO Box 69, Stanley, ND 58784-0069 .... (701)628-2915
(Old Mountrail formed 1873, annexed to Ward in 1891. Clk Dis Ct has b rec, m, d, div, pro, civ ct, citizenship rec from 1909, incomplete bur rec)

Nelson   G5   1883   Foster, Grand Forks
Nelson County, PO Box 565, Lakota, ND 58344-0565 .... (701)247-2462
(Clk Dis Ct has b, d, bur rec from 1940, m, pro, lnd rec from 1880, div, civ ct rec)

Oliver   D3   1885   Mercer
Oliver County, PO Box 166, Center, ND 58530-0166 .... (701)794-8748
(Clk Dis Ct has m rec from 1915, also d rec; Co Judge has pro & civ ct rec; Reg Deeds has lnd rec)

* **Pembina**   H6   1867   Indian Lands
Pembina County, PO Box 357, Cavalier, ND 58220-0357 .... (701)265-4275
(Clk Dis Ct has b & d rec from 1893, a few m rec from 1872, bur rec from 1943, div rec from 1883, pro rec from 1875 & civ ct rec from 1883)

* **Pierce**   F5   1887   De Smet
Pierce County, 240 2nd St SE, Rugby, ND 58368-1830 .... (701)776-6161
(Clk Dis Ct has b, d, bur rec from 1943, m rec from 1888, div, civ ct rec from 1900, pro rec from 1898; Reg Deeds has lnd rec)

* **Ramsey**   G5   1873   Pembina
Ramsey County, 6th & 4th St, Devils Lake, ND 58301 .... (701)662-7069
(Clk Dis Ct has b, d & bur rec from 1890, div & civ ct rec; Co Judge has m & pro rec; Reg Deeds has lnd rec)

* **Ransom**   H2   1873   Pembina
(Clk Dis Ct has b & d rec from 1943, m from 1882, div, pro & civ ct rec)

* **Renville**   D6   1910   Ward (See Renville, old)
Renville County, PO Box 68, Mohall, ND 58761-0068 .... (701)756-6398
(Clk Dis Ct has b & d rec from abt 1940, m, bur, div, pro, civ ct & lnd rec from 1910)

Renville, old (Formed 1873 from part of Buffalo Co, Dakota Terr; part taken to form Ward in 1885 & parts annexed to Bottineau & Ward in 1894)

* **Richland**   I2   1873   Original county
Richland County, PO Box 966, Wahpeton, ND 58074-0936 .... (701)642-7818
(Clk Dis Ct has b & d rec from 1900, div & civ ct rec from 1883, some bur rec; Co Judge has m rec from 1890, pro rec from 1876; Reg Deeds has lnd rec)

* **Rolette**   F6   1873   Buffalo
Rolette County, PO Box 460, Rolla, ND 58367-0460 .... (701)477-3816
(Clk Dis Ct has b, d & bur rec from 1943, m, div, civ ct rec from 1887, pro rec from 1896)

Name	Map Index	Date Created	Parent County or Territory From Which Organized

Sargent H2 1883 Ransom
Sargent County, PO Box 98, Forman, ND 58032-0098 . . . . (701)724-3355
(Clk Dis Ct has b, d rec from 1943, m rec from 1886, bur rec from 1948, pro rec from 1883, div, civ ct rec)

* **Sheridan** E4 1909 McLean (See Sheridan, old)
Sheridan County, PO Box 636, McClusky, ND 58463-0636 . . . . (701)363-2207
(Co Clk has b, d rec from 1943, m, div, pro, civ ct, Ind rec from 1909, bur rec)

Sheridan, Old (formed 1873 from part of Buffalo Co, Dakota Terr; part taken to form part of Church in 1887; annexed to McLean in 1891)

Sioux D2 1915 Standing Rock Reservation
Sioux County, PO Box L, Fort Yates, ND 58538-0529 . . . . (701)854-3853
(Clk Dis Ct has m rec from 1916, bur, div, pro, civ ct & Ind rec)

Slope B2 1915 Billings
Slope County, PO Box JJ, Amidon, ND 58620-0449 . . . . (701)879-6275
(Clk Dis Ct has m, d, bur, div, pro, civ ct rec from 1915, Ind rec; Division Vital Statistics, Bismark has b rec)

* **Stark** C3 1879 Unorg. Terr
Stark County, PO Box 130, Dickinson, ND 58602-0130 . . . . (701)264-7636
(Clk Dis Ct has b & d rec from 1898, bur rec, div & civ ct rec from 1887 & naturalization rec from 1887 to 1963)

Steele H4 1883 Grand Forks, Griggs
Steele County, County Courthouse, Finley, ND 58230 . . . . (701)524-2790
(Clk Dis Ct has b & d rec from 1894 to 1896, 1900 to 1901, div & civ ct rec from 1886; Co Judge has m rec from 1883, pro rec
from 1886)

* **Stutsman** G3 1873 Pembina
Stutsman County, 511 2nd Ave SE, Jamestown, ND 58401-4210 . . . . (701)252-9037
(Clk Dis Ct has b, d, bur, div, civ ct rec; Reg Deeds has Ind red; Co Judge has m & pro rec)

* **Towner** F6 1883 Rolette, Cavalier
Towner County, PO Box 517, Cando, ND 58324-0517 . . . . (701)968-3424
(Clk Dis Ct has m rec from 1888, div rec from 1890, pro rec from 1886, civ ct rec from 1889, Ind rec from 1884 & bur rec)

* **Traill** H4 1875 Grand Forks, Burbank, Cass
Traill County, County Courthouse, Hillsboro, ND 58045 . . . . (701)436-4454
(Clk Dis Ct has b rec from 1910, m rec from 1887, d rec from 1907, bur rec from 1915, div rec from 1890 & pro rec from 1882)

Wallace (See McKenzie)

* **Walsh** H5 1881 Grand Forks
Walsh County, 600 Cooper Ave, Grafton, ND 58237-1542 . . . . (701)352-2851
(Clk Dis Ct has m rec from 1884, div, pro, civ ct rec from 1881; State Vit Rec has b & d rec from 1881)

* **Ward** D5 1885 Renville
Ward County, 3rd St SE, Minot, ND 58701-6498 . . . . (701)857-6460
(Clk Dis Ct has b, d, bur rec & div from 1900; Co Judge has m & pro rec; Reg Deeds has Ind rec)

* **Wells** F4 1873 Sheridan (formerly Gingras)
Wells County, PO Box 596, Fessenden, ND 58438-0596 . . . . (701)547-3122
(Clk Dis Ct has b, m, d, bur, div, pro & civ ct rec)

*† **Williams** B5 1890 Buford, Flannery
Williams County, 205 E Broadway, Williston, ND 58801-6123 . . . . (701)572-1700
(Clk Dis Ct has b, d, bur, div, civ ct rec from early 1900s; Reg Deeds has Ind rec; Co Ct has m & pro rec)

* At least one county history has been published about this county.
† Inventory of county archives was made by the Historical Records Survey. (See Introduction)

OHIO

CAPITAL · COLUMBUS — TERRITORY 1799 — STATE 1803 (17th)
State Map on Page M-33

French traders utilized the western part of Ohio and the English settled in the eastern part of the state in the early 1700's. English expansion toward the West brought the two into conflict by the 1740's. The French and Indian War finally resolved these, with the English obtaining the area. However, settlement of this region was discouraged, due in part to the hostile Indians in the area. Americans in their search for space and fertile, inexpensive land came to the area despite British desires to the contrary. Conflicts between the Indians, who sided with the British, and the Americans were the result. The treaty ending the Revolutionay War ceded the area to the United States.

Following acquisition of the new territory, the eastern seaboard states simply extended their borders to include the new area. The establishment of the Northwest Territory put an end to this practice in 1787. The following year, the first permanent settlement was made at Marietta by the Ohio Company of New England. The company, formed by Puritans from Massachusetts and Connecticut, purchased about a million acres of land in southeast Ohio. About 1800, the Virginia Bounty consisting of over four million acres between the Scioto and Little Miami rivers was set aside for settlers from Virginia and Kentucky. The Chillicothe section in Ross County attracted many settlers from Kentucky and Tennessee. Mid-state on the eastern border, Germans, Scotch-Irish, and Quakers crossed the Ohio River from Pennsylvania to settle. Another group of settlers from New Jersey traveled down the Ohio River and settled the area between the Little and Big Miami rivers. Here, along with Scotch-Irish and Dutch settlers, they cultivated some 300,000 acres in the southwestern corner of Ohio and established Cincinnati.

The Indian problem continued until 1794, when General Anthony Wayne drove them from the state. With the Indians gone, the Western Reserve in the northeast corner along Lake Erie was opened to settlers. It contained four million acres. Connecticut emigrants were the main settlers in this area. In future Erie and Huron counties to the west, Connecticut refugees who had been burned out by the British during the Revolutionary War began to settle. The area became known as the "Fire Lands" for this reason. A "Refugee Tract" (comprising approximately Franklin, Licking, and Perry counties) was set aside east of the Scioto River for Canadians who had aided the Americans in the Revolutionary War and who had lost their lands in Canada as a punishment.

Ohio became a territory in 1799. The next year, the Indiana Territory was formed which reduced Ohio to its present size. Ohio was granted statehood in 1803. Steamboat travel brought many settlers up the Ohio River and down Lake Erie. The completion of canals, roads, and railroads opened up the northeastern part of the state after 1815, while the opening of the Erie Canal in 1825 increased settlement from the Northeast. During the Civil War, Ohio had some 313,000 men serve in the Union forces.

A few counties have birth and death records from as early as 1840. Individual counties were required to keep these records in 1867. After 1908, birth and death records are at the Division of Vital Statistics, Ohio Department of Health, 65 South Front Street, Columbus, OH 43216. To verify current fees, call 614-466-2531.

Probate courts have marriage records. A statewide index to marriages since 1949 is at the Division of Vital Statistics. Divorce records were kept by the state Supreme Court until 1852, and then by the Court of Common Pleas in each county. The county recorder has land records for each county. Early records of land grants, bounty land, and land purchases are at the Ohio Land Office, Auditor of State, 88 East Broad Street, Columbus, OH 43215. Most records of the Western Reserve are at the Connecticut Secretary of State's office. Virginia bounty land warrants are at the Virginia State Library, 11th Street at Capitol Square, Richmond, VA 23219. Town or county censuses were taken between 1798 and 1911 in some counties.

Genealogical Archives, Libraries and Societies

Akron Public Library, 55 South Main St., Akron, OH 44309

American Jewish Archives, Clifton Ave., Cincinnati, OH 45220

Carnegie Library, 520 Sycamore St., Greensville, OH 45331

Carnegie Public Library, 127 S. North St., Washington Court House, OH 43160

Champaign County Library, 160 W. Market St., Urbana, OH 43078 Ph. (513) 653-3811

Chillicothe and Ross County Public Library, 140 S. Paint St., Chillicothe, OH 45601

Cincinnati Public Library, 800 Vine St., Cincinnati, OH 45202

Cleveland Public Library, 325 Superior Ave., Cleveland, OH 44114

Dayton and Montgomery Counties Public Library, 215 East Third St., Dayton, OH 45406

Fairfield County District Library, 219 N. Broad St., Lancaster, Ohio 43130

Geauga West Library, 13455 Chillicothe Rd., Chesterland, OH 44026

Glendover Warren County Museum, Lebanon, OH 45036

Granville Public Library, 217 E. Broadway, Granville, OH 43023

Greene County Room, Greene County District Library, 76 E. Market St., Xenia, OH 45385

Guernsey County District Public Library, 800 Steubenville Ave., Cambridge, OH 43725

Harrison County Genealogical Chapter Library, 45507 Unionvale Road, Cadiz, OH 43907

Hayes Presidential Center Library, 1337 Hayes Avenue, Fremont, OH 43420

Johnson - St. Paris Library, East Main St., St. Paris, OH 43072 Ph: (513) 663-4349

Lakewood Public Library, 15425 Detroit Avenue, Lakewood, OH 44107

Lorain Public Library, 351 6th St., Lorain, OH 44052

Mennonite Historical Library, Bluffton College, Bluffton, OH 45817 (Large collection of genealogical materials relating particularly to Mennonites and Amish.)

Middletown Public Library, 1320 1st Ave., Middletown, OH 45042

Milan Public Library, P. O. Box 1550, Milan, OH 44846

Morley Library, 184 Phelps St., Painesville, OH 44077

Norwalk Public Library, 46 W. Main St., Norwalk, OH 44857

Ohio Historical Society Library, 1985 Velma Avenue, Columbus, OH 43211

Ohio State Library, 65 South Front St., Columbus, OH 43215

Portsmouth Public Library, 1220 Gallia St., Portsmouth, OH 45662

Public Library of Cincinnati and Hamilton County, Eighth and Vine Sts., Cincinnati, OH 45202-2071

Public Library of Columbus and Franklin County, 96 S. Grant Ave., Columbus, OH 43215

Public Library of Youngstown and Mahoning County, 305 Wick Ave., Youngstown, OH 44503

Sidney Public Library, 230 E. North St., Sidney, OH 45365

Stark County District Library, 715 Market Avenue, North Canton, OH 44702

Toledo Public Library, Local Historical and Genealogical Department, 325 Michigan St., Toledo, OH 43624

Tri-County Lineage Research Society (Hancock, Seneca, Wood), Kaubisch Library, Fostoria, OH 44830

University of Cincinnati Library, Cincinnati, OH 45221

Warder Public Library, 137 E. High Street, Springfield, OH 45502

Warren-Trumbull County Public Library, 444 Mahoning Ave., N.W., Warren, OH 44483-4692

Wayne County Public Library, 304 N. Market St., Wooster, OH 44691

Adams County Genealogical Society, P. O. Box 231, West Union, OH 45693

Allen County Historical Society, Elizabeth M. MacDonall Memorial Library, 620 West Market Street, Lima, OH 45801

Allen County Chapter, OGS, 620 West Market Street, Lima, OH 45801

Alliance Chapter, OGS, P. O. Box 3630, Alliance, OH 44601

Ashland County Chapter, Ohio Genealogical Society, P. O. Box 681, Ashland, OH 44805

Ashtabula County Genealogical Society, Henderson Library, 54 E. Jefferson Street, Jefferson, OH 44047

Athens County Chapter, OGS, 65 N. Court St., Athens, OH 45701

Auglaize County Chapter, OGS, P. O. Box 2021, Wapakoneta, OH 45895

Belmont County Chapter, OGS, 361 South Chestnut St., Barnesville, OH 43713

Brecksville-Cayahoga Chapter, OGS, P. O. Box 41114, Brecksville, OH 44141

Brown County Chapter, OGS, Box 83, Georgetown, OH 45121

Butler County Chapter, OGS, Box 2011, Middletown, OH 45042

Carroll County Chapter, OGS, 59 Third St. NE, Carrollton, OH 44615

Champaign County, Genealogical Society of OGS, P. O. Box 680, Urbana, OH 43078

Champaign County Historical Society, 809 E. Lawn Ave., Urbana, OH 43078

Cincinnati Historical Society, Eden Park, Cincinnati, OH 45202

Clark County Chapter, OGS, P. O. Box 1412, Springfield, OH 45501

Clermont County Chapter, OGS, P. O. Box 394, Batavia, OH 45103

Columbiana County Chapter, OGS, P. O. Box 861, Salem, OH 44460

Coshocton County Chapter, OGS, P. O. Box 117, Coshocton, OH 43812

Cuyahoga County-Brecksville Chapter, P. O. Box 41114, Brecksville, OH 44141

Cuyahoga County-Greater Cleveland Chapter, P. O. Box 40254, Cleveland, OH 44140

Cuyahoga-East County Chapter, OGS, P. O. Box 24182, Lyndhurst, OH 44124

Cuyahoga Southwest Chapter, OGS, 18631 Howe Road, Strongsville, OH 44136

Cuyahoga West Chapter, OGS, P. O. Box 26196, Fairview Park, OH 44126-0196

Darke County Chapter, OGS, P. O. Box 908, Greenville, OH 45331

Darke County Historical Society, 205 North Broadway, Greenville, OH 45331

Defiance County Chapter, OGS, P. O. Box 675, Defiance, OH 43512

Delaware County Chapter, OGS, P. O. Box 317, Delaware, OH 43015

Erie County Chapter, OGS, P. O. Box 1301, Sandusky, OH 44870

Fairfield County Chapter, OGS, P. O. Box 1470, Lancaster, OH 43130-0570

Fayette County Genealogical Society, P. O. Box 342, Washington Court House, OH 43160

Firelands Historical Society, 4 Case Avenue, Norwalk, OH 44857

Firelands Kinologists, 150 Coleman Court, New London, OH 44851

Florida Chapter, OGS, 2625 Johnson Point, Leesburg, FL 32748

Franklin County Genealogical Society, P. O. Box 2503, Columbus, OH 43216

Franklin County Historical Society, 280 E. Broad St., Columbus, OH 43215

Fulton County Chapter, OGS, 305 Chestnut St., Swanton, OH 43558

Gallia County Historical Society, P. O. Box 295, Gallipolis, OH 45631

Greater Cleveland Genealogical Society, P. O. Box 9639, Cleveland, OH 44140

Greene County Chapter, OGS, P. O. Box 706, Xenia, OH 45385

Greene County Room, Greene County District Library, 76 E. Market St., Xenia, OH 45385

Guernsey County Chapter, OGS, Box 472, Cambridge, OH 43725

Hamilton County Chapter, OGS, P. O. Box 15851, Cincinnati, OH 45215

Hancock County Chapter, OGS, P. O. Box 672, Findlay, OH 45840-0672

Hardin County Chapter, OGS, P. O. Box 520, Kenton, OH 43326

Hardin County Historical Society, P. O. Box 503, Kenton, OH 43326

Harrison County Genealogical Society, 45507 Unionvale Road, Cadiz, OH 43907

Harrison County Genealogical Society, Chapter of O.G.S., 45507 Unionvale Road, Cadiz, OH 43907

Highland County Historical Society, 151 E. Main St., Hillsboro, OH 45133

Holmes County Chapter, OGS, P. O. Box 136, Millersburg, OH 44654

Huron County Chapter OGS, P. O. Box 923, Norwalk, OH 44857

Indiana I Chapter, OGS, Rt. 5, Logansport, IN 46947

International Society for British Genealogy and Family History, P. O. Box 20425, Cleveland, OH 44120

Jackson County Chapter, OGS, Box 807, Jackson, OH 45640

Jefferson County Chapter, OGS, 109 Meadow Road, Wintersville, OH 43952

Jefferson County Historical Association, Box 4268, Steubenville, OH 43952

Jewish Genealogical Society of Cleveland, 996 Eastlawn Dr., Highland Heights, OH 44143

Jewish Genealogical Society of Dayton, P. O. Box 338, Dayton, OH 45406

Johnstown Genealogy Society, P. O. Box 345, Johnstown, OH 43031

Knox County Chapter, OGS, Box 1098, Mt. Vernon, OH 43050

KYOWVA Genealogical Society, P. O. Box 1254, Huntington, WV 25715

Lake County Chapter, OGS, Morley Public Library, 184 Phelps St., Painsville, OH 44077

Lawrence County Chapter, OGS, P. O. Box 945, Ironton, OH 45638

Licking County Chapter, OGS, P. O. Box 4037, Newark, OH 43055

Logan County Genealogical Society, Box 36, Bellefontaine, OH 43311

Lorain County Chapter, OGS, P. O. Box 865, Elyria, OH 44036-0865

Lorain County Historical Society, 509 Washington Ave., Elyria, OH 44035

Lucas County Chapter, OGS, Toledo-Lucas County Public Library, c / o Local History and Genealogy Dept., 325 North Michigan Street, Toledo, OH 43624

Madison County Chapter, OGS, P. O. Box 102, London, OH 43140

Mahoning County Chapter, OGS, 3430 Rebecca Dr., Canfield, OH 44406

Marion Area Genealogical Society, P. O. Box 844, Marion, OH 43302

Marion County Chapter, OGS, P. O. Box 844, Marion, OH 43302

Medina County Genealogical Society, P. O. Box 804, Medina, OH 44256-0804

Meigs County Chapter, OGS, P. O. Box 346, Pomeroy, OH 45769

Mercer County Chapter, OGS, Box 437, Celina, OH 45822

Miami County Historical Society of Ohio, P. O. Box 305, Troy, OH 45373

Miami Valley Genealogical Society, P. O. Box 1364, Dayton, OH 45401

Michigan Chapter, Ohio Gen. Society, 34233 Shawnee, Westland, MI 48185

Monroe County Chapter, OGS, P. O. Box 641, Woodsfield, OH 43793

Monroe County Historical Society, P. O. Box 538, Woodsfield, OH 43793

Montgomery County Chapter of the Ohio Genealogical Society, P. O. Box 1584, Dayton, OH 45401

Morgan County Chapter, OGS, P. O. Box 418, McConnelsville, OH 43756

Morrow County Chapter, OGS, P. O. Box 401, Mount Gilead, OH 43338

Muskingum County Chapter, OGS, P. O. Box 3066, Zanesville, OH 43701

Noble County Chapter, OGS, P. O. Box 444, Caldwell, OH 43724

Northwestern Ohio Genealogical Society, P. O. Box 17066, Toledo, OH 43615

Ohio Commandery of the Military Order of the Loyal Legion of the U.S., Rt. 1 Box 172, Marshallville, OH 44645

Ohio Dept. - Sons of Union Veterans of the Civil War, 616 West Summit St., Alliance, OH 44601

Ohio Dept. Ladies of the Grand Army of the Republic, Rt. 1, Box 172, Marshallville, OH 44645

Ohio Genealogical Society, P. O. Box 2625, Mansfield, OH 44906

Ohio Society Sons of the American Revolution, 2170 Brookridge Drive, Dayton, OH 45431

Ottawa County Chapter, OGS, P. O. Box 193, Port Clinton, OH 43452

Palatines to America, P. O. Box 101G4, Capitol Univ., Columbus, OH 43209

Perry County Chapter, OGS, P. O. Box 275, Junction City, OH 43748

Pike County Chapter, OGS, P. O. Box 224, Waverly, OH 45690

Portage County Chapter, OGS, 6252 N. Spring St., Ravenna, OH 44266

Richland County Chapter, OGS, P. O. Box 3154, Lexington, OH 44904

Ross County Chapter, OGS, P. O. Box 395, Chillicothe, OH 45601

Sandusky County Historical Society, 1337 Hayes Ave., Fremont, OH 43420

Sandusky County Kin Hunters, 1337 Hayes Ave., Fremont, OH 43420

Scioto County Chapter, OGS, P. O. Box 812, Portsmouth, OH 45662

Seneca County Chapter, OGS, P. O. Box 841, Tiffin, OH 44883

Shelby Genealogical Society, 65 Marvin Avenue, Shelby, OH 44875

Society of the War of 1812 in the State of Ohio, 34465 Crew Road, Pomeroy, OH 45769

Southern California Chapter, OGS, P. O. Box 5057, Los Alamitos, CA 90721-5057

Southern Ohio Genealogical Society, P. O. Box 414, 229 Crestview Dr., Hillsboro, OH 45133

Southwest Butler County Genealogical Society, c / o Soldiers, Sailors & Pioneers Monument, So. Monument Ave., Hamilton, OH 45011

Stark County Chapter, OGS, 7300 Woodcrest NE, North Canton, OH 44721

Stark County Historical Society, 749 Hazlett Ave., N.W., Canton, OH 44708

Summit County Chapter, OGS, P. O. Box 2232, Akron, OH 44309

Tri-County Lineage Research Society Kaubisch Library, Fostoria, OH 44830

Trumbull County Chapter, OGS, Box 309, Warren, OH 44483

Twinsburg Historical Society, Twinsburg, OH 44087

Tuscarawas County Chapter, OGS, P. O. Box 141, New Philadelphia, OH 44663

Union County Chapter, OGS, P. O. Box 438, Marysville, OH 43040

Van Wert County Chapter, OGS, P. O. Box 485, Van Wert, OH 45891

Vinton County Historical and Genealogical Society, P. O. Box 141, McArthur, OH 45641

Warren County Chapter, OGS, 300 East Silver St., Lebanon, OH 45036

Washington County Chapter, OGS, P. O. Box 2174, Marietta, OH 45750

Wayne County Chapter, OGS, 546 East Bowman Street, Wooster, OH 44691

Wayne County Historical Society, 546 E. Bowman Street, Wooster, OH 44691

Wellington Genealogical Workshop, P. O. Box 224, Wellington, OH 44090

West Augusta Historical and Genealogical Society, 1510 Prairie Dr., Belpre, OH 45714

Western Reserve Historical Society, 10825 East Blvd., Cleveland, OH 44106

Williams County Chapter, OGS, P. O. Box 293, Bryan, OH 43506

Wood County Chapter, OGS, P. O. Box 722, Bowling Green, OH 43402

Wyandot County Chapter, OGS, P. O. Box 414, Upper Sandusky, OH 43351

Printed Census Records and Mortality Schedules

Federal Census 1820, 1830, 1840, 1850, 1860, 1870, 1880, 1890 (parts of Hamilton and Clinton counties only), 1900, 1910

Federal Mortality Schedules 1850, 1860, 1880

Union Veterans and Widows 1890

State/Territorial Census 1887-1907

Valuable Printed Sources

Atlases, Maps, and Gazetteers

Brown, Lloyd Arnold. *Early Maps of the Ohio Valley: A Selection of Maps, Plans and Views Made by Indians and Colonials from 1673 to 1783*. Pittsburgh, Pennsylvania: University of Pittsburgh Press, 1959.

Kilbourn, John. *The Ohio Gazetteer*. Columbus, Ohio: John Kilbourn, 1826.

Bibliographies

Adams, Marilyn. *Southeastern Ohio Local and Family History Sources in Print*. Atlanta: Heritage Research, 1979.

Ohio Local and Family History Sources in Print. Clarkston, Georgia: Heritage Research, 1984.

Guide to Local Government Records at the Ohio University Library. Athens, Ohio: Ohio University Library, 1986.

Gutgesell, Stephen. *Guide to Ohio Newspapers, 1793-1973: Union Bibliography of Ohio Newspapers Available in Ohio Libraries*. Columbus, Ohio: Ohio Historical Soceity, 1976.

Harter. Stuart. *Ohio Genealogy and Local History Sources Index*. Ft. Wayne, Indiana: CompuGen Systems, 1986.

Ohio County Government Microfilm: Microfilm Available from the Ohio Historical Society. Columbus, Ohio: Ohio Historical Society, 1987.

Pike, Kermit J. *Guide to Major Manuscript Collections in the Library of the Western Reserve Historical Society*. Cleveland: Western Reserve Historical Society, 1987.

Genealogical Research Guides

Bell, Carol Willsey. *Ohio Genealogical Guide*. Youngstown, Ohio: Bell Books, 1987.

Douthit, Ruth Long. *Ohio Resources for Genealogists with some References for Genealogical Searching in Ohio*. Detroit: Detroit Society for Genealogical Research, 1971.

Khouw, Petta. *County by County in Ohio Genealogy*. Columbus, Ohio: State Library of Ohio, 1978.

McCay, Betty L. *Sources for Genealogical Searching in Ohio*. Indianapolis: Betty L. McCay, 1973.

Genealogical Sources

Flavell, Carol Willsey. *Ohio Genealogical Periodical Index: A County Guide*. Youngstown, Ohio: Carol Willsey Flavell, 1979.

Smith, Clifford N. *The Federal Land Series*. Chicago: American Library Association, 1978.

Histories

Biographical Encyclopedia of Ohio. Cincinnati: Galaxy Publishing, 1875.

Randall, Emilius O. *History of Ohio*. New York: Century History Co., 1912.

Phillips, W. Louis. *Jurisdictional Histories for Ohio's 88 Counties*. W. Louis Phillips, 1983.

OHIO COUNTY DATA
State Map on Page M-33

Name	Map Index	Date Created	Parent County or Territory From Which Organized
*† **Adams**	F7	1797	Hamilton

Adams County, 110 W Main St, West Union, OH 45693-1347 .... (513)544-2344
(Courthouse burned in 1910, some rec saved, some as early as 1796, others to 1799; rec of several adjacent cos prior to their formation included;Pro Ct has b & d rec 1888 to 1893, m rec 1803 to 1853 & from 1910, pro rec 1849 to 1860 & from 1910; Board of Health has b & d rec from 1908; Clk Ct has div & civ ct rec from 1910; Co Rcdr has lnd rec from 1797)

*† **Allen**	G4	1820	Shelby

Allen County, 301 N Main St, Lima, OH 45801-4456 .... (419)228-3700
(Pro Ct has b & d rec 1867, m rec 1831; Clk Cts has div & civ ct rec 1831; Co Museum has nat rec 1851 to 1929)

*† **Ashland**	D3	1846	Wayne, Richland, Huron, Lorain

Ashland County, 110 W 2nd St, Ashland, OH 44805-2101 .... (419)289-0000
(Clk Cts has div & civ ct rec from 1846)

* **Ashtabula**	B2	1808	Trumbull, Geauga

Ashtabula County, 25 W Jefferson St, Jefferson, OH 44047-1092 .... (216)576-9090
(Pro Ct has b & d rec 1867 to 1908, m rec from 1811, pro rec from 1800's; Health Dept has b & d rec from 1909; Clk Cts has div rec from 1811, civ ct rec from 1800's; Co Rcdr has lnd rec from 1800)

*† **Athens**	D6	1805	Washington

Athens County, Court & Washington Sts, Athens, OH 45701 .... (614)592-3242
(Pro Judge has b,m & pro rec; Clk Cts has div & civ rec from 1800; Rcdr has lnd rec)

Name	Map Index	Date Created	Parent County or Territory From Which Organized

* Auglaize   G4   1848   Allen, Mercer, Darke, Hardin, Logan, Shelby, Van Wert
Auglaize County, 36 E Auglaize St, Wapakoneta, OH 45895-1505 .... (419)738-7896
(Pro Judge has b, m, d & pro rec; Clk Cts has div & civ ct rec from 1848; Co Rcdr has Ind rec)

*† Belmont   C5   1801   Jefferson, Washington
Belmont County, 100 W Main St, Saint Clairsville, OH 43950-1225 .... (614)695-2121
(Clk Cts has div & civ ct rec from 1820; Pro Ct has b, m, d & pro rec; Co Health Dept has bur rec)

*† Brown   F7   1818   Adams, Clermont
Brown County, Danny L Pride Courthouse, Georgetown, OH 45121 .... (513)378-3100
(Pro Judge has b, m & pro rec from 1800s; Co Health has d rec from 1800s; Clk Cts has div & civ ct rec from 1800s; Co Rcdr has Ind rec)

* Butler   G6   1803   Hamilton
Butler County, 130 High St, Hamilton, OH 45011-2756 .... (513)887-3000
(Co Health has b & d rec; Pro Judge has m & pro rec; Clk Cts has div & civ ct rec; Co Aud Ind rec)

* Carroll   C4   1833   Columbiana, Stark, Harrison, Jefferson, Tuscarawas
Carroll County, 119 Public Sq, Carrollton, OH 44615-1448 .... (216)627-2250
(Clk Cts has div & civ ct rec from 1833; Pro Ct has b & d rec 1867 to 1909, m & pro rec from 1833; Co Rcdr has Ind rec from 1833; Board of Health has b & d rec from 1909)

* Champaign   F5   1805   Greene, Franklin
Champaign County, Main & Court St, Urbana, OH 43078 .... (513)653-5896
(Pro Judge has b, m & pro rec; Co Health has d rec; Co Aud has bur rec; Clk Cts has d & civ ct rec; Co Rcdr has Ind rec)

* Clark   F5   1818   Champaign, Madison, Greene
Clark County, 101 N Limestone St, Springfield, OH 45502-1123 .... (513)328-2458
(Clark Co Hist Soc., Memorial Hall, Springfield, Ohio 45502 may assist you in your work, also Warder Public Lib., Springfield)

* Clermont   G7   1800   Hamilton
Clermont County, 76 S Riverside Dr, Batavia, OH 45103-2635 .... (513)732-7300
(Clk Cts has div rec from 1861 & civ ct rec from 1803)

* Clinton   F6   1810   Highland, Warren
Clinton County, 46 S South St, Wilmington, OH 45177-2214 .... (513)382-2103
(Pro Ct has b, d rec bef 1908; Co Health Office has b, d rec aft 1908; Pro Ct has b, d rec from 1867 to 1908; Pro Judge has m, pro rec from 1810; Clk Cts has div, civ ct rec from 1810; Co Rcdr has Ind rec from 1810)

*† Columbiana   B4   1803   Jefferson, Washington
Columbiana County, 105 S Market St, Lisbon, OH 44432-1255 .... (216)424-9511
(Clk Cts has div & civ ct rec)

* Coshocton   D5   1810   Muskingum, Tuscarawas
Coshocton County, 349 1/2 Main St, Coshocton, OH 43812-1510 .... (614)622-1753
(Pro Ct has b, m, pro rec; City Health Board has d rec; County Trustees have bur rec; Clk Cts has div, civ ct rec; Co Rcdr has Ind rec)

* Crawford   E4   1820   Delaware
Crawford County, 112 E Mansfield St, Bucyrus, OH 44820-2389 .... (419)562-5876
(Co Health Dept has b, d rec for Crestline, Ohio and the Rural Routes of Crawford Co 1908 to present; Bucyrus City Health Dept has same rec for City of Bucyrus; Gallon City Health Dept has same rec for City of Gallon; Pro Judge has b, d rec 1867 to 1908, m, pro rec from 1831; Co Rcdr has Ind rec; Clk Cts has div, civ ct rec from 1834)

*† Cuyahoga   C2   1808   Geauga
Cuyahoga County, 1200 Ontario St, Cleveland, OH 44113-1604 .... (216)443-7950
(Pro Ct has b rec 1859 to 1901, d rec 1868 to 1908; Western Reserve Hist Soc has m rec 1810 to 1941, tax rec 1819 to 1869; M Lic Bureau has m rec from 1810; Co Cthouse has nat rec 1818 to 1906, pro rec from 1810; Clk Cts has div rec 1837 to 1925; Co Admin Bldg has Ind rec 1810 to 1971)

* Darke   G5   1809   Miami
Darke County, 4th & Broadway, Greenville, OH 45331 .... (513)547-7370
(Pro Judge has b, d rec from 1867 to 1908, m rec from 1817; Clk Cts has div, civ ct rec from 1820; Co Rcdr has Ind rec from 1816, bur rec (veterans graves) from 1832)

* Defiance   G3   1845   Williams, Henry, Paulding
Defiance County, 500 Court St, Defiance, OH 43512-2157 .... (419)782-4761
(Clk Cts has div & civ ct rec from 1845; General Health Dis has d & bur rec; Pro Judge has b & m rec from 1845)

* Delaware   E5   1808   Franklin
Delaware County, 91 N Sandusky St, Delaware, OH 43015-1797 .... (614)369-8761
(Chan Ct has div & civ ct rec from 1825; Pro Ct has b, m, d, pro rec)

* Erie   E3   1838   Huron, Sandusky
Erie County, 323 Columbus Ave, Sandusky, OH 44870-2695 .... (419)627-7705
(Co Health has b rec from 1908, d & bur rec; Pro Judge has m & pro rec; Clk Cts has div & civ ct rec from 1870; Co Rcdr has Ind rec)

* Fairfield   E6   1800   Ross, Washington
Fairfield County, 224 E Main St, Lancaster, OH 43130-3842 .... (614)687-7030
(Pro Judge has b rec from 1803 to 1907, m, d, pro rec; Clk Cts has div rec from 1860, civ ct rec from 1800; Co Rcdr has Ind rec from 1803)

Name	Map Index	Date Created	Parent County or Territory From Which Organized

*† Fayette F6 1810 Ross, Highland
Fayette County, 110 E Court St, Washington Court House, OH 43160-1355 .... (614)335-7020
(Clk Cts has div rec from 1853 & civ ct rec from 1828)

*† Franklin E5 1803 Ross
Franklin County, 410 S High St, Columbus, OH 43215 .... (614)462-3322
(Pro Ct has b, d rec prior to 1908, m, pro rec; Bureau Vital Statistics has b, d rec after 1908; Clk Cts has div, civ ct rec from 1803; Co Auditor has Ind rec)

* Fulton G2 1850 Lucas, Henry, Williams
Fulton County, 210 S Fulton St Rm B-10, Wauseon, OH 43567-1355 .... (419)337-9255
(Clk Cts has div & civ ct rec; Pro Ct has b, m, d rec)

* Gallia D7 1803 Washington, Adams
Gallia County, 18 Locust St, Gallipolis, OH 45631-1251 .... (614)446-4374
(Pro Judge has b, m, d & pro rec; Co Health has bur rec; Clk Cts has div & civ ct rec from 1850; Co Rcdr has Ind rec)

*† Geauga C2 1806 Trumbull
Geauga County, 231 Main St, Chardon, OH 44024-1243 .... (216)285-2222
(Pro Judge has b, m, d & pro rec; Co Health has bur rec; Clk Cts has div & civ ct rec from 1806; Co Rcdr has Ind rec)

* Greene F6 1803 Hamilton, Ross
Greene County, 45 N Detroit St, Xenia, OH 45385-3199 .... (513)376-5000
(Pro Judge has b rec from 1869 to 1908, pro & m rec 1803; Clk Cts has div, civ ct & crim rec 1802; Co Rcdr has deeds & plat maps 1803; Aud has tax rec 1803; Health Dept has b rec from 1908)

* Guernsey C5 1810 Belmont, Muskingum
Guernsey County, 836 Steubenville Ave, Cambridge, OH 43725-2335 .... (614)432-2505
(Clk Cts has div rec from 1850, civ ct rec from 1810; Pro Judge has b, m & pro rec; City-Co Health Dept has d rec)

*† Hamilton G7 1790 Original county
Hamilton County, 1000 Main St, Cincinnati, OH 45202-1217 .... (513)632-6500
(Pro Judge has m, bur & pro rec; Co Health has d rec; Clk Cts has div & civ ct rec from 1900; Co Rcdr has Ind rec)

*† Hancock F3 1820 Logan
Hancock County, 300 S Main St, Findlay, OH 45840-3345 .... (419)424-7037
[FHL has some b, m, d, cem, civ ct, Ind, pro, tax rec]

* Hardin F4 1820 Logan
Hardin County, Public Sq, Kenton, OH 43326-9700 .... (419)674-2205
(Clk Cts has div & civ ct rec from 1864; Health Dept has b & d rec; Pro Ct has m & d rec; Co Rcdr has Ind rec)

* Harrison C5 1813 Jefferson, Tuscarawas
Harrison County, 100 W Market St, Cadiz, OH 43907-1132 .... (614)942-8861
(Clk Cts has div, civ ct rec from 1813; Pro Judge has b rec to 1917, m, pro rec; Health Office has b rec from 1917, d, bur rec)

* Henry G3 1820 Shelby
Henry County, PO Box 546, Napoleon, OH 43545-0546 .... (419)592-4876
(Pro Judge has b, d rec from 1867 to 1908, m, pro rec from 1847; Clk Cts has div & civ ct rec from 1880; Co Rcdr has Ind rec from 1835)

* Highland F7 1805 Ross, Adams, Clermont
Highland County, 114 Governor Foraker Pl, Hillsboro, OH 45133-1055 .... (513)393-1911
(Pro Ct has m & d rec 1867 to 1909, b rec to 1905; Health Dept has b, m, d rec from 1909; Clk Cts has div & civ ct rec from 1832, some nat & adoption rec; Co Rcdr has Ind rec)

* Hocking D6 1818 Athens, Ross, Fairfield
Hocking County, 1 E Main St, Logan, OH 43138-1207 .... (614)385-5195
(Pro Judge has b, m & pro rec; Co Health has d rec; Clk Cts has div & civ ct rec from 1873; Co Rcdr has Ind rec)

* Holmes D4 1824 Coshocton, Wayne, Tuscarawas
Holmes County, E Jackson St, Millersburg, OH 44654-1349 .... (216)674-0286
(Pro Judge has b, d & pro rec; Clk Cts has div & civ ct rec from 1825; Co Rcdr has Ind rec)

* Huron E3 1815 Portage, Cuyahoga
Huron County, 2 E Main St, Norwalk, OH 44857 .... (419)668-3092
(Pro Judge has b, d rec from 1867 to 1908, m rec from 1815, estate and guardianship rec from 1815, naturalizations from 1859 to 1900; Health Dept has b, d rec from 1908 to present except for city of Bellevue, Ohio, those rec are in its Health Dept; Co Clk has common pleas ct rec from 1815, div and naturalizations to 1859; Co Rcdr has Ind and mortgage rec from 1808, Connecticut Fire Sufferers rec 1792 to 1808, mil discharge rec from 1865; Co Auditor has tax rec from 1820; Co Hist Lib has Infirmary rec from 1848 to 1900, tax rec from 1815 to 1825, Co Comissioners Journals from 1815, Ind Partition rec from 1815 to 1920, co militia lists 1864 & 1865, indigent soldier bur rec 1880 to 1920)

*† Jackson E7 1816 Scioto, Gallia, Athens, Ross
Jackson County, 226 Main St, Jackson, OH 45640 .... (614)286-3301
(Pro Judge has b, m & pro rec; Co Health has d & bur rec; Clk Cts has div & civ ct rec; Co Rcdr has Ind rec)

* Jefferson B4 1797 Washington
Jefferson County, 301 Market St, Steubenville, OH 43952-2149 .... (614)283-4111
(Pro Judge has m, pro, naturalization rec; Clk Cts has div, civ ct rec from 1797, Co Rcdr has Ind rec from 1797; Board of Health, Steubenville, has b, d rec)

Name	Map Index	Date Created	Parent County or Territory From Which Organized

*† Knox   D4   1808   Fairfield
Knox County, 106 E High St, Mount Vernon, OH   43050-3453 .... (614)397-2727
(Co Health has b rec from 1908, d & bur rec; Pro Judge has m rec from 1803 & pro rec; Clk Cts has div & civ ct rec from 1810; Co Rcdr has Ind rec)

*† Lake   C2   1840   Geauga, Cuyahoga
Lake County, 105 Main St, Painesville, OH   44077-3414 .... (216)357-2500
(Clk Cts has civ ct rec from 1840)

* Lawrence   E7   1815   Gallia, Scioto
Lawrence County, 5th & Park Ave, Ironton, OH   45638 .... (614)533-4355
(Pro Ct has b rec 1864 to 1908, m rec from 1900, d rec 1868 to 1933, pro rec from 1817; Health Dept has b & d rec from 1908; Clk Cts has civ ct rec from 1817, div rec from 1819; Co Rcdr has Ind rec from 1817)

* Licking   D5   1808   Fairfield
Licking County, 20 S 2nd St, Newark, OH   43055-5663 .... (614)349-6000
(Pro Judge has b, m & pro rec; Co Health has d rec; Clk Cts has div rec from 1876 & civ ct rec from 1872; Co Rcdr has Ind rec)

* Logan   F4   1818   Champaign
Logan County, Main & E Columbus 2nd Fl, Bellefontaine, OH   43311 .... (513)599-7275
(Pro Judge has b, m & pro rec; Clk Cts has div & civ ct rec from 1818; Co Rcdr has Ind rec)

*† Lorain   D3   1822   Huron, Cuyahoga, Medina
Lorain County, PO Box 749, Elyria, OH   44036-0749 .... (216)329-5536
(Pro Judge has b, m & pro rec; Clk Cts has div rec from 1850 & civ ct rec from 1824; Co Rcdr has Ind rec; the Elyria Public Lib & Lorain Co Hist Soc both have some bks of this locality of genealogical interest)

*† Lucas   F2   1835   Wood, Sandusky, Henry
Lucas County, 1 Government Ctr Suite 800, Toledo, OH   43604-2202 .... (419)245-4000
(Clk Cts has div, civ ct rec from 1850; Pro Judge has b rec from 1865 to 1908, pro rec; Pro Judge has d rec aft 1935)

*† Madison   F5   1810   Franklin
Madison County, County Courthouse, London, OH   43140 .... (614)852-2972
(Co Health has b & d rec; Pro Judge has m & pro rec; Clk Cts has div rec from 1800s & civ ct rec; Co Rcdr has Ind rec)

* Mahoning   B3   1846   Columbiana, Trumbull
Mahoning County, 120 Market St, Youngstown, OH   44503-1710 .... (216)740-2104
(Co Health has b & d rec; Pro Judge has m & pro rec; Clk Cts has div & civ ct rec; Co Aud has Ind rec)

* Marion   E4   1820   Delaware
Marion County, 114 N Main St, Marion, OH   43302-3030 .... (614)387-5871
(Pro Judge has b, m & pro rec; Co Health has d rec; Clk Cts has div & civ ct rec; Co Rcdr has Ind rec)

* Medina   D3   1812   Portage
Medina County, 93 Public Sq, Medina, OH   44256-2292 .... (216)723-3641
(Pro Ct has b & d rec to 1909, m & pro rec; Health Dept has b & d rec from 1909; Clk Cts has div & civ ct rec from 1818; Co Rcdr has Ind rec)

* Meigs   D7   1819   Gallia, Athens
Meigs County, 2nd St, Pomeroy, OH   45769 .... (614)992-2895
(Pro Judge has b, m, d rec; Clk Cts has div, civ ct rec from 1819; Co Rcdr has Ind rec)

* Mercer   G4   1820   Darke
Mercer County, 101 N Main St, Celina, OH   45822-1794 .... (419)586-3178
(Pro Judge has b & d rec from 1867 to 1908, m rec from 1830, pro rec from 1829; Clk Cts has div & civ ct rec from 1824)

* Miami   G5   1807   Montgomery
Miami County, 201 W Main St, Troy, OH   45373-3263 .... (513)332-6800
(Clk Cts has div & civ ct rec from 1807; Pro Judge has m, d & pro rec; Co Health has b rec)

* Monroe   C6   1813   Belmont, Washington, Guernsey
Monroe County, PO Box 574, Woodsfield, OH   43793-0574 .... (614)472-5181
(Clk Cts has div, civ ct rec from early 1800s)

*† Montgomery   G6   1803   Hamilton, Wayne Co., Michigan
Montgomery County, 451 W 3rd St, Dayton, OH   45422-0002 .... (513)225-4000
(Clk Cts has div & civ ct rec)

* Morgan   D6   1817   Washington, Guernsey, Muskingum
Morgan County, 19 E Main St, McConnelsville, OH   43756-1198 .... (614)962-4752

* Morrow   E4   1848   Knox, Marion, Delaware, Richland
Morrow County, 48 E High St, Mount Gilead, OH   43338-1430 .... (419)947-2085
(Co Health has b rec; Pro Judge has m, d & pro rec; Clk Cts has div & civ ct rec from 1800; Co Rcdr has Ind rec)

* Muskingum   D5   1804   Washington, Fairfield
Muskingum County, PO Box 268, Zanesville, OH   43702-0268 .... (614)455-7104
(Pro Ct has b & d rec 1867 to 1909, m & pro rec from 1851; Health Dept has b & d rec from 1909; Clk Common Pleas Ct has div & civ ct rec from 1804, Supreme Ct rec 1805 to 1852; Co Rcdr has Ind rec from 1804)

* Noble   C5   1851   Monroe, Washington, Morgan, Guernsey
Noble County, County Courthouse, Caldwell, OH   43724 .... (614)732-2969
(Clk Cts has div, civ ct rec from 1851)

Name	Map Index	Date Created	Parent County or Territory From Which Organized
* **Ottawa**	E2	1840	Erie, Sandusky, Lucas

Ottawa County, 315 Madison St Rm 103, Port Clinton, OH 43452-1936 .... (419)734-6700
(Co Health Dept has b, d, bur rec; Pro Judge has m, pro rec; Clk Cts has div, civ ct rec, crim rec, from 1840; naturalizations from 1905 to 1929; Co Rcdr has lnd rec)

* **Paulding**	G3	1820	Darke

Paulding County, County Courthouse, Paulding, OH 45879 .... (419)399-8210
(Co Health has b & d rec; Pro Judge has m & pro rec; Clk Cts has div rec; Co Judge has civ ct rec; Co Rcdr has lnd rec)

* **Perry**	D6	1818	Washington, Fairfield, Muskingum

Perry County, 121 W Brown St, New Lexington, OH 43764-1241 .... (614)342-2045
(Pro Ct has b, d rec from 1867, m rec from 1818)

* **Pickaway**	E6	1810	Ross, Fairfield, Franklin

Pickaway County, 207 S Court St, Circleville, OH 43113-1601 .... (614)474-6093
[FHL has some b, m, d, cem, civ ct, lnd, pro, tax rec]

*† **Pike**	E7	1815	Ross, Scioto, Adams

Pike County, 100 E 2nd St, Waverly, OH 45690-1399 .... (614)947-2715
(Pro Judge has b, m & pro rec; Clk Cts has div & civ ct rec from 1815; Co Rcdr has lnd rec)

* **Portage**	C3	1808	Trumbull

Portage County, PO Box 1035, Ravenna, OH 44266 .... (216)297-3644
(Mayor's Office has b, d & bur rec; Pro Judge has m & pro rec; Clk Cts has div & civ ct rec from 1820; Co Treas has lnd rec)

* **Preble**	G6	1808	Montgomery, Butler

Preble County, 100 Main St, Eaton, OH 45320 .... (513)456-8160
(Pro Judge has b & d rec from 1867, pro rec from 1800 & m rec from 1808; Clk Cts has div & civ ct rec from 1850; Co Rcdr has lnd rec from 1804)

* **Putnam**	G3	1820	Shelby

Putnam County, 245 E Main St, Ottawa, OH 45875-1968 .... (419)523-3656
(Clk Cts has div & civ ct rec from 1834)

* **Richland**	D4	1808	Fairfield

Richland County, 50 Park Ave E, Mansfield, OH 44902-1888 .... (419)755-5501
(Clk Cts has div & civ ct rec from 1815)

*† **Ross**	E6	1798	Adams, Washington

Ross County, N Paint St, Chillicothe, OH 45601 .... (614)773-5115
(Pro Judge has b, m, d & pro rec; Clk Cts has div from late 1800s & civ ct rec; Co Rcdr has lnd rec)

* **Sandusky**	E3	1820	Huron

Sandusky County, 100 N Park Ave, Fremont, OH 43420-2473 .... (419)334-6100
(Co Health has b, d & bur rec; Pro Judge has m & pro rec; Clk Cts has div rec from 1820 & civ ct rec; Co Rcdr has lnd rec from 1822)

*† **Scioto**	E7	1803	Adams

Scioto County, 602 7th St, Portsmouth, OH 45662-3948 .... (614)353-5111
(Clk Cts has div & civ ct rec from 1817)

*† **Seneca**	E3	1820	Huron

Seneca County, 81 Jefferson St, Tiffin, OH 44883-2354 .... (419)447-4550
(Pro Judge has b, m & pro rec; Co Health has d rec; Clk Cts has div & civ ct rec from 1826; Co Rcdr has lnd rec)

* **Shelby**	G5	1819	Miami

Shelby County, 129 E Court St, Sidney, OH 45365-3095 .... (513)498-7226
(Clk Cts has civ ct rec from 1819; Pro Judge has b, m, d, estates, guardianships, trusteeships from 1825; Co Rcdr has lnd rec from 1819)

*† **Stark**	C4	1808	Columbiana

Stark County, 209 Tuscarawas St W, Canton, OH 44702-2219 .... (216)438-0800
(Health Dept has b rec; Pro Ct has m & pro rec; Clk Cts has civ ct rec; Family Ct has div rec; Co Rcdr has lnd rec)

*† **Summit**	C3	1840	Portage, Medina, Stark

Summit County, 175 S Main St, Akron, OH 44308-1306 .... (216)379-2512
[FHL has some b, m, d, cem, civ ct, lnd, nat, pro, tax rec]

*† **Trumbull**	B3	1800	Jefferson, Wayne Co. Michigan

Trumbull County, 160 High St NW, Warren, OH 44481-1005 .... (216)841-0562
(Clk Cts has div, civ ct & citizenship rec from 1800)

* **Tuscarawas**	C4	1808	Muskingum

Tuscarawas County, Public Sq, New Philadelphia, OH 44663 .... (216)364-8811
(Pro Judge has b, m, d, pro rec; Clk Cts has div, civ ct rec from 1808, immigration & naturalization rec from 1907; Co Rcdr has lnd rec)

* **Union**	F4	1820	Franklin, Madison, Logan, Delaware

Union County, 5th & Court St, Marysville, OH 43040 .... (513)642-2841

* **Van Wert**	G4	1820	Darke

Van Wert County, 121 E Main St 2nd Fl, Van Wert, OH 45891-1795 .... (419)238-6159
(Clk Cts has div & civ ct rec; Pro Judge has b & d rec 1867 to 1908, m rec from 1840, pro rec frm 1837; Board of Health has b & d rec from 1908; Co Rcdr has lnd rec from 1823)

Name	Map Index	Date Created	Parent County or Territory From Which Organized
* Vinton	E7	1850	Gallia, Athens, Ross, Jackson, Hocking

Vinton County, Vinton County Courthouse, McArthur, OH   45651-1296 .... (614)596-4571
(Pro Judge has b, d rec from 1867 to 1950, m rec from 1850, pro rec from 1867; Co Health Dept has b rec aft 1950; Clk Cts has div, civ ct, Ind rec from 1850)

| * Warren | G6 | 1803 | Hamilton |

Warren County, 320 E Silver St, Lebanon, OH   45036-2361 .... (513)932-4040
(Pro Judge has b & d rec from 1867, m & pro rec from 1803; Clk Cts has div & civ ct rec; Co Rcdr has Ind rec)

| *† Washington | C6 | 1788 | Original county |

Washington County, 205 Putnam St, Marietta, OH   45740-3017 .... (614)373-6623
(Pro Judge has b, d rec from 1867, m, pro rec from 1789; Clk Cts has div, civ ct rec from 1795; Co Rcdr has Ind rec)

| * Wayne | D4 | 1808 | Columbiana |

Wayne County, 107 W Liberty St, Wooster, OH   44691-4850 .... (216)263-3124
(the original Wayne Co was established 15 Aug 1796, this co disappeared from Ohio in 1803 when Ohio became a State; it ultimately became Wayne Co Michigan; the present Wayne Co Ohio was established 13 Feb 1808)(Pro Ct has b & d rec 1867 to 1908, m rec from 1813, pro rec from 1812; Board of Health has b & d rec from 1908; Clk Common Pleas Ct has div & civ ct rec from 1812; Co Rcdr has Ind rec from 1812)

| * Williams | G2 | 1820 | Darke |

Williams County, County Courthouse Sq 4th Fl, Bryan, OH   43506 .... (419)636-2059
(Clk Cts has div & civ ct rec)

| * Wood | F3 | 1820 | Logan |

Wood County, 1 Courthouse Sq, Bowling Green, OH   43402-2473 .... (419)354-9280
(Clk Cts has div rec from 1851, also civ ct rec; Pro Judge has b rec to 1908, m & d rec; Health Dept has b rec from 1908)

| * Wyandot | E4 | 1845 | Marion, Crawford, Hardin, Hancock |

Wyandot County, County Courthouse, Upper Sandusky, OH   43351 .... (419)294-1432
(Co Health has b rec from 1845 to 1908; Pro Judge has m rec from 1845, d rec from 1845 to 1908, bur rec from 1845 to 1908 & pro rec from 1845; Clk Cts has div & civ ct rec from 1845; Co Rcdr has Ind rec from 1845)

* At least one county history has been published about this county.
† Inventory of county archives was made by the Historical Records Survey. (See Introduction)

OKLAHOMA

CAPITAL · OKLAHOMA CITY — TERRITORY 1890 — STATE 1907 (46th)
State Map on Page M-34

In 1541, Coronado became the first white man to enter Oklahoma. French traders passed through the area in the 16th and 17th centuries, but no settlements were made. The United States acquired the area in the Louisiana Purchase in 1803. Oklahoma then became part of the Indiana Territory, except for the Panhandle which remained under Spanish control. Oklahoma became part of the Missouri Territory in 1812. In 1817, the federal government began sending Indians to the area from Alabama, Georgia, Florida, and Mississippi. The state was divided among the five nations: Creek, Cherokee, Chickasaw, Choctaw, and Seminole. Most of Oklahoma became part of the Arkansas Territory in 1819, while the Panhandle became part of Mexico following its independence from Spain in 1821.

The western part of the Louisiana Purchase, including the Arkansas Territory, was designated as Indian Territory in 1830. When the United States annexed the Republic of Texas, the Panhandle of Oklahoma (which became "No Man's Land") was included as it was unattached to any territory. During the Civil War, the five Indian nations sided with the Confederacy. About 3,500 Indians helped the Confederates, mostly through the Confederate Indian Brigade and the Indian Home Guard. The Indians suffered horribly during the war as both life and property were wantonly destroyed. The peace treaties forced them to surrender land in western Oklahoma and grant rights-of-way to the railraods. The central part of the state was designated as "Unassigned Lands". By 1872, railroads crossed the area and hordes of settlers arrived. Soldiers drove them away, but these settlers along with the railroad companies petitioned Congress to open up these areas. As a result, the government purchased the "Unassigned Lands" and "No Man's Land" from the Indians in 1889.

Oklahoma was unique in its use of land runs. During a land run, an entire district would be opened to settlement on a given day on a first-come basis. The first run in 1889 attracted about 50,000 people. Farmers from Illinois, Iowa, and Kansas chose the western and northwestern sections of the state, while those from Arkansas, Missouri, and Texas chose the southern and eastern parts of the state. The territorial government was established in 1890, with Guthrie as its capital. Absorption of reservations opened more territory for settlement in the years that followed. The 1893 land run in the northwest section of the state attracted nearly 100,000 new settlers. The first oil boom occurred in 1897 at Bartlesville, bringing thousands more new settlers. More absorption of reservations occurred until only the eastern part of the state remained as Indian Territory. In 1906, the Oklahoma and Indian territories were combined, allowing Oklahoma to be admitted to the Union the following year. The capital was moved to Oklahoma City in 1910.

Some counties kept birth and death records as early as 1891, although they are quite incomplete. These are kept at the county courthouses. Statewide registration began in 1908, with general compliance by 1930. They are available from the Registrar of Vital Statistics, State Department of Health, 1000 Northeast Tenth Street, P.O. Box 53551, Oklahoma City, OK 73152. To verify current fees, call 405-271-4040.

County clerks have all marriage, court, and land records. Local land office records are at the Oklahoma Department of Libraries, State Archives Division, 200 N. E. 18th Street, Oklahoma City, OK 73105. The National Archives, Kansas City Branch, 2306 East Bannister Road, Kansas City, KS 64131, and Fort Worth Branch, 501 West Felix Street, P.O. Box 6216, Fort Worth, TX 76115, have the land entry case files, the original tract books and the township plats of the general land office. The patents and copies of the tract books and township plats are at the BLM, New Mexico State Office, Federal Building, Box 1449, Santa Fe, NM 87501.

Genealogical Archives, Libraries and Societies

American Heritage Library, P. O. Box 176, Davis, OK 73030

Atoka County Library, 205 East 1st, Atoka, OK 74525

Carnegie Public Library, Fifth and B St., Lawton, OK 73501

Cherokee City-County Public Library, 602 S. Grand Ave., Cherokee, OK 73728

Chickasha Public Library, 527 Iowa Avenue, Chicakasha, OK 73018

Cushing Public Library, Box 551, 215 N. Steele, Cushing, OK 74203

Lawton Public Library, 110 S.W. Fourth St., Lawton, OK 73501

Metropolitan Library System, 131 Dean McGee Ave., Oklahoma City, OK 73102

Muldrow Public Library, City Hall Building, Main Street, Muldrow, OK 74948

Oklahoma Department of Libraries, 200 NE 18, Oklahoma City, OK 73105

Oklahoma Department of Libraries, Legislative Reference Division, 109 Capitol, Oklahoma City, OK 73105

Ponca City Library, 515 East Grand, Ponca City, OK 74601

Public Library, Muskogee, OK 74401

Public Library, 220 So. Cheyenne, Tulsa, OK 74103

Sapulpa Public Library, 27 W. Dewey, Sapulpa, OK 74066

Stanley Tubbs Memorial Library, 101 East Cherokee, Sallisaw, OK 74955

State D.A.R. Library, Historical Bldg., Oklahoma City, OK 73105

Tulsa Central Library, 400 Civic Center, Tulsa, OK 74103

University of Oklahoma Library, Norman, OK 73069

Vinita Public Library, Maurice Haynes Memorial Building, 211 W. Illinois, Vinita, OK 74301

Weatherford Public Library, 219 East Franklin, Weatherford, OK 73096 (genealogy collection).

Abraham Coryelle Chapter, D.A.R., Mrs. Floyd Sloan, RR 3, Vinita, OK 74301

Arbuckle Historical Society, 201 S. 4th, Davis, OK 73030

Atoka County Genealogical Society, P. O. Box 83, Atoka, OK 74525

Bartlesville Genealogical Society, Bartlesville Public Library, Sixth and Johnstone, Bartlesville, OK 74003

Broken Arrow, Oklahoma Genealogical Society, P. O. Box 1244, Broken Arrow, OK 74036

Bryan County Heritage Society, P. O. Box 153, Calera, OK 74730

Canadian County Genealogical Society, P. O. Box 866, El Reno, OK 73036

Cleveland County Genealogical Society, P. O. Box 6176, Norman, OK 73070

Coal County Historical and Genealogical Society, Box 322, Coalgate, OK 74538

Craig County Oklahoma Genealogical Society, P. O. Box 484, Uinita, OK 74301

Delaware County, Oklahoma Historical Society, Rt. 1, Box 467, Grove, OK 74344

Federation of Oklahoma Genealogical Societies, P. O. Box 26151, Oklahoma City, OK 73126

Fort Gibson Genealogical and Historical Society, P. O. Box 416, Fort Gibson, OK 74434.

Garfield County Genealogists, Inc., P. O. Box 1106, Enid, OK 73702

Grady County Genealogical Society, P. O. Box 792, Chickasha, OK 73023

Grant County Historical Society, Box 127, Medford, OK 73759

Haskell County Genealogy Society, 408 N.E. 6th Street, Stigler, OK 74462

Logan County Genealogical Society, P. O. Box 1419, Guthrie, OK 73044

Love County Historical Society, P. O. Box 134, Marietta, OK 73448

Major County Genealogical Society, Box 24, Rt. 2, Okeene, OK 73763

Mayes County Genealogical Society, P. O. Box 924, Chouteau, OK 74337

McClain County, Oklahoma Historical and Genealogical Society, 203 Washington Street, Purcell, OK 73080

McCurtian County Genealogy Society, P. O. Box 1832, Idabel, OK 74745

Muldrow Genealogical Society, P. O. Box 1253, Muldrow, OK 74948

Muskogee County Genealogical Society, 801 W. Okmulgee, Muskogee, OK 74401

Noble County Genealogy Society, 601 12th Street, Perry, OK 73077

Northwest Oklahoma Genealogical Society, P. O. Box 834, Woodward, OK 73801

Oklahoma Genealogical Society, P. O. Box 12986, Oklahoma City, OK 73157

Oklahoma Historical Society, Historical Bldg., Oklahoma City, OK 73105

Oklahoma Society, Sons of the American Revolution, P. O. Box 715, Sapulpa, OK 74066

Okmulgee County Genealogical Society, P. O. Box 805, Okmulgee, OK 74447

Ottawa County Genealogical Society, Box 1383, Miami, OK 74354

Pawhuska, Oklahoma Genealogical Society, P. O. Box 807, Pawhuska, OK 74056

Payne County Genealogical Society, Stillwater Public Library, 206 W. 6th, Stillwater, OK 74074

Pocahontas Trails Genealogical Society Rt. 2, Box 40, Mangum, OK 73554

Pioneer Genealogical Society, P. O. Box 1965, Ponca City, OK 74602

Pittsburg County Genealogical and Historical Society, Inc., 113 East Carl Albert Parkway, McAlester, OK 74501

Pontotoc County Historical and Genealogical Society, 221 West 16th St., Ada, OK 74820

Poteau Valley Genealogical Society, P. O. Box 1031, Poteau, OK 74953

Pushmataha County Historical Society, P. O. Box 285, Antlers, OK 74523

Sons and Daughters of the Cherokee Strip Pioneers, P. O. Box 465, Enid, OK 73702

Southwest Oklahoma Genealogical Society, P. O. Box 148, Lawton, OK 73502

Sequoyah Genealogical Society, P. O. Box 1112, Sallisaw, OK 74955

Tex-Ok Panhandle Genealogical Society, 1613 Grinnell, Perryton, TX 79070

Three Forks Genealogical Society, 102-1/2 South State Street, Wagoner, OK 74467

Tulsa Genealogical Society, P. O. Box 585, Tulsa, Ok 74101

Western Plains Weatherford Genealogical Society, P. O. Box 1672, Weatherford, OK 73096

Western Trail Genealogical Society, Box 70, Altus, OK 73522

Woods County Genealogists, P. O. Box 234, Alva, OK 73717

Printed Census Records and Mortality Schedules

Federal Census 1860 (with Arkansas), 1900, 1910

State/Territorial Census 1890 (Logan, Oklahoma, Cleveland, Canadian, Kingfisher, Payne, and Beaver counties only)

Union Veterans and Widows 1890

Valuable Printed Sources

Atlases, Maps, and Gazetteers

Morris, John W. and Edwin C. McReynolds. *Historical Atlas of Oklahoma*. Norman, Oklahoma: University of Oklahoma Press, 1976.

————. *Ghost Towns of Oklahoma*. Norman, Oklahoma: University of Oklahoma Press, 1978.

Shirk, George H. *Oklahoma Place Names*. Norman, Oklahoma: University of Oklahoma Press, 1974.

Bibliographies

Blessing, Patrick Joseph. *Oklahoma: Records and Archives*. Tulsa: University of Tulsa Publications in American Social History, 1978.

Gibson, A. M. *A Guide to Regional Manuscript Collections in the University of Oklahoma Library*. Norman, Oklahoma: University of Oklahoma Press, 1960.

Genealogical Research Guides

Brown, Jean C. *Oklahoma Research: The Twin Territories*. Sapulpa, Oklahoma: Jean C. Brown, 1975.

Elliott, Wendy L. *Research in Oklahoma*. Bountiful, Utah: American Genealogical Lending Library, 1987.

Mooney, Thomas G. *Exploring Your Cherokee Ancestry: A Basic Genealogical Research Guide*. Tahlequah, Oklahoma: Cherokee National Historical Society, 1987.

Genealogical Sources

Parsons, B. S. *1832 Census of the Creek Indians*. Genealogical Publications, 1978.

Histories

Gibson, Arrell Morgan. *Oklahoma: A History of Five Centuries*. Norman, Oklahoma: University of Oklahoma Press, 1988.

Hall, Ted Byron. *Oklahoma Indian Territory*. Ft. Worth, Texas: American Reference Publishers, 1971.

Litton, Gaston. *History of Oklahoma at the Golden Anniversary of Statehood*. New York: Lewis Historical Publishing Co., 1957.

McReynolds, Edwin C. *Oklahoma: A History of the Sooner State*. Norman, Oklahoma: University of Oklahoma Press, 1964.

OKLAHOMA COUNTY DATA
State Map on Page M-34

Name	Map Index	Date Created	Parent County or Territory From Which Organized

* **Adair**   I4   1907   Cherokee Lands
Adair County, PO Box 169, Stilwell, OK 74960-0169 .... (918)696-7198
(Clk Cts has m, div, pro & civ ct rec from 1907; Co Asr has Ind rec)

* **Alfalfa**   F6   1907   Woods
Alfalfa County, 300 S Grand Ave County Courthouse, Cherokee, OK 73728-8000 .... (405)596-2392
(State Vit Rec has b & d rec; Ct Clk has m, div, pro, civ ct, Ind rec)

*† **Atoka**   H2   1907   Choctaw Lands
Atoka County, 201 E Court St, Atoka, OK 74525-2056 .... (405)889-2643
(Clk Cts has m rec from 1897, div, pro & civ ct rec from 1913; Co Clk has Ind rec)

* **Beaver**   D6   1890   Original county (Public Lands)
Beaver County, 111 W 2nd St, Beaver, OK 73932 .... (405)625-3151
(Clk Cts has m, div & civ ct rec from 1890, pro rec from 1891)

*† **Beckham**   D4   1907   Roger Mills
Beckham County, PO Box 67, Sayre, OK 73662-0067 .... (405)928-2457
[FHL has some m & cem rec]

* **Blaine**   F4   1892   Original county
Blaine County, 212 N Weigle Ave, Watonga, OK 73772-3893 .... (405)623-5890
(Clk Ct has m, div, pro, civ ct rec from 1892; Co Clk has Ind rec from 1892; Dept Vital Statistics, Oklahoma City, has b, d rec)

* **Bryan**   H2   1907   Choctaw Lands
Bryan County, 402 W Evergreen St, Durant, OK 74701-4703 .... (405)924-2201
(Co Clk has m, div, Ind rec from 1907, pro & civ ct rec; State Vit Rec has b & d rec)

* **Caddo**   F4   1901   Original Lands
Caddo County, PO Box 1427, Anadarko, OK 73005-1427 .... (405)247-3105
(Clk Ct has m, div, pro & civ ct rec from 1902)

* **Canadian**   F4   1889   Original county (Wichita-Caddo Lands)
Canadian County, 301 N Choctaw Ave, El Reno, OK 73036-2407 .... (405)262-1070
(Clk Ct has Ind rec; State Vit Rec has b & d rec, m rec from 1890, div, pro & civ ct rec from 1900, voting rec 1909)

* **Carter**   G2   1907   Chickasaw Lands
Carter County, 1st & B St SW, Ardmore, OK 73401 .... (405)223-8162
[FHL has some m, cem, nat rec]

*† **Cherokee**   I4   1907   Cherokee Lands
Cherokee County, 213 W Delaware St, Tahlequah, OK 74464-3639 .... (918)456-3171
(Clk Ct has m, div & civ ct rec from 1907; Co Clk has Ind rec)

Choctaw   I2   1907   Choctaw Lands
Choctaw County, County Courthouse, Hugo, OK 74743 .... (405)326-5331
(Clk Ct has m, div, pro & civ ct rec from 1907; Co Clk has Ind rec)

*† **Cimarron**   A6   1907   Beaver
Cimarron County, PO Box 145, Boise City, OK 73933-0145 .... (405)544-2251
(Clk Ct has m, div, pro, civ ct rec from 1908; Co Clk has Ind rec from 1908; Dept Vital Statistics, Oklahoma City, has b, d rec)

* **Cleveland**   G3   1889   Unassigned Lands
Cleveland County, 201 S Jones Ave, Norman, OK 73069-6046 .... (405)366-0201
(Ct Clk has m, div, pro, civ ct rec; Co Clk has Ind rec from 1889, some discharge rec, physicians' licenses, final receipts, fed & state tax liens, judgements; State Vit Rec has b & d rec)

* **Coal**   H3   1907   Choctaw Lands
Coal County, 3 N Main St, Coalgate, OK 74538-2832 .... (405)927-3122
(Clk Ct has m, div, pro & civ ct rec from 1907; Co Clk has Ind rec)

* **Comanche**   E3   1901   Kiowa, Comanche, Apache Lands
Comanche County, PO Box 9026, Lawton, OK 73501 .... (405)353-3717
(Clk Ct has m, div, pro, civ ct, Ind rec from 1901; State Vit Rec has b & d rec)

* **Cotton**   F2   1912   Comanche
Cotton County, 301 N Broadway St, Walters, OK 73572-1271 .... (405)875-3026
(Co Clk has b rec 1912 to 1945, d & Ind rec, surveys, school census; Ct Clk has m, div, pro, civ ct rec)

* **Craig**   I6   1907   Cherokee Lands
Craig County, 301 W Canadian Ave, Vinita, OK 74301-3640 .... (918)256-2507
(Clk Ct has m rec from 1902, div, pro & civ ct rec from 1907; Co Clk has Ind rec)

Creek   H4   1907   Creek Lands
Creek County, PO Box 129, Sapulpa, OK 74067-0129 .... (918)224-0278
(Clk Ct has m rec from 1907, div, pro & civ ct rec; Co Clk has Ind rec from 1907; Dis Ct in Bristow has m & div rec; Co Ct Clk in Drumright has m & div rec)

* **Custer**   E4   1890   Cheyenne, Arapaho Lands
Custer County, 675 W 'B' St, Arapaho, OK 73620 .... (405)323-4420
(Co Clk has m, div, pro rec from 1899, civ ct rec from 1894, real-estate, deeds, mtgs & releases, army & U.S. service rec from 1892, school cen from 1913 & co reg of electors from 1916; Cem Assn has bur rec fro each city)

Name	Map Index	Date Created	Parent County or Territory From Which Organized

Day 1892 Cheyenne, Arapaho Lands (discontinued 1906)

* **Delaware** I5 1907 Cherokee
Delaware County, Krouse St, Jay, OK 74346 .... (918)253-4432
[FHL has some m, cem, pro rec]

* **Dewey** E5 1892 Original county (Cheyenne, Arapaho Lands)
Dewey County, PO Box 368, Taloga, OK 73667-0368 .... (405)328-5390
(Ct Clk has m, pro, civ ct rec from 1893, div rec from 1894; Co Clk has Ind rec from 1892; State Vit Rec has b & d rec)

* **Ellis** D5 1907 Day, Woodward
Ellis County, 100 S Washington Courthouse Sq, Arnett, OK 73832 .... (405)885-7301
(Clk Ct has m rec from 1892, div rec from 1893, pro rec from 1908 & civ ct rec from 1896; Co Clk has Ind rec from 1898)

* **Garfield** F5 1893 Orginally "O", changed to Garfield 1901 (Cherokee Outlet)
Garfield County, County Courthouse Rm 101, Enid, OK 73701 .... (405)237-0227
(Clk Dis Ct has m, div, pro & civ ct rec from 1893; Reg Deeds has Ind rec from 1893 State Vit Rec has b & d rec)

* **Garvin** G3 1907 Chickasaw Lands
Garvin County, Walnut & Grant, Pauls Valley, OK 73075-3290 .... (405)238-2685
(Clk Ct has m, div, pro & civ ct rec from 1908, Co Clk has Ind rec; State Vit Rec has b rec)

* **Grady** F3 1907 Caddo, Comanche
Grady County, PO Box 459, Chickasha, OK 73023-0459 .... (405)224-5211
(Clk Ct has m, div, civ ct, pro rec from 1907; Co Clk has Ind rec from 1907; State Vit Rec has b & d rec)

* **Grant** F6 1893 Original county (Cherokee Outlet)
Grant County, County Courthouse Rm 104, Medford, OK 73759-1244 .... (405)395-2214
(Clk Ct has m, div, pro & civ ct rec from 1893)

* **Greer** D3 1886 Org. by Texas, to Okla. by court decision
Greer County, Courthouse Sq, Mangum, OK 73554-4260 .... (405)782-2329
(Organized as Greer Co, Texas in 1886; an act of Congress on May 4, 1896 declared it Greer Co, Okla; a fire in 1901 destroyed the co rec; Clk Ct has m, div, pro & civ ct rec from 1901; Co Clk has Ind rec)

Harmon D3 1909 Greer, Jackson
Harmon County, 114 W Hollis County Courthouse, Hollis, OK 73550 .... (405)688-3658
(Clk Ct has m, div, pro & civ ct rec from 1909)

* **Harper** D6 1907 Indian Lands, Woods, Woodward
Harper County, 311 SE 1st, Buffalo, OK 73834 .... (405)735-2012
(Ct Clk has m, div, pro, civ ct rec; Co Clk has Ind rec from 1895, school rec 1912 to 1958; State Vit Rec has b & d rec)

† **Haskell** I3 1908 Choctaw Lands
Haskell County, 202 E Main St, Stigler, OK 74462-2439 .... (918)967-4352
(Clk Ct has m, div, pro & civ ct rec from 1907; Co Clk has Ind rec)

Hughes H3 1907 Creek Lands (Creek & Choctaw Lands)
Hughes County, PO Box 914, Holdenville, OK 74848-0914 .... (405)379-2746
(Clk Ct has m, div, pro & civ ct rec from 1907; Co Clk has Ind rec from 1907; State Vit Rec has b & d rec)

Jackson D3 1907 Greer
Jackson County, 101 W Broadway, Altus, OK 73521-3898 .... (405)482-4420
(Clk Ct has m, div, pro & civ ct rec from 1907; Co Clk has Ind rec)

* **Jefferson** F2 1907 Comanche (Chickasaw)
Jefferson County, 220 N Main St Rm 101, Waurika, OK 73573-2235 .... (405)228-2241
(Clk Ct has m, div, pro & civ ct rec from 1908; Co Clk has Ind rec)

* **Johnston** G2 1907 Chickasaw Lands
Johnston County, PO Box 338, Tishomingo, OK 73460-0338 .... (405)371-3058
(Clk Ct has m, div, pro & civ ct rec from 1907; prior to 1907 these rec are kept by Clk Dis Ct, Ardmore, Okla)

* **Kay** G6 1895 Original county (Cherokee Outlet)
Kay County, PO Box 450, Newkirk, OK 74647-0450 .... (405)362-3116
(Clk Ct has m, div, pro, civ ct rec from 1893; Co Clk has Ind rec from 1893; State Bureau Vital Statistics, Oklahoma City, has b, d rec)

* **Kingfisher** F5 1890 Original county
Kingfisher County, PO Box 118, Kingfisher, OK 73750-0118 .... (405)375-3808
(Co Clk has m rec from 1900, div, pro, civ ct rec from 1896, Ind rec from 1898; State Vit Rec has b & d rec)

* **Kiowa** E3 1901 Original county (Kiowa-Comanche-Apache Lands)
Kiowa County, County Courthouse, Hobart, OK 73651 .... (405)726-5125
(Clk Ct has m, div, pro, civ ct, Ind rec from 1901; City Clk office has bur rec; State Bureau Vital Statistics, Oklahoma City, has b, d rec)

Latimer I3 1902 Choctaw Lands
Latimer County, 109 N Central St, Wilburton, OK 74578-2440 .... (918)465-2021
(Clk Ct has m from 1906, div, pro & civ ct rec)

* **Le Flore** I3 1907 Choctaw Lands
Le Flore County, PO Box 607, Poteau, OK 74953-0607 .... (918)647-2527
(Clk Ct has m rec from 1898, div, pro & civ ct rec from 1907; Co Clk has Ind rec)

*† **Lincoln** G4 1891 Original county (Iowa-Kickapoo-Sac-Fox Lands)
Lincoln County, PO Box 126, Chandler, OK 74834-0126 .... (405)258-1264
(Clk Dis Ct has m, div, pro, civ ct rec from 1900; Co Clk has Ind rec; Dept Vital Statistics, Oklahoma City, has b, d rec)

Name	Map Index	Date Created	Parent County or Territory From Which Organized

* **Logan**   G4   1890   Original county
Logan County, 301 E Harrison Ave, Guthrie, OK 73044-4939 .... (405)282-2124
(Clk Ct has m rec from 1889, div, pro & civ ct rec; Co Clk has Ind rec from 1889)

* **Love**   G2   1907   Chickasaw Lands
Love County, 405 W Main St, Marietta, OK 73448-2837 .... (405)276-3059
(Co Clk has b & d rec from 1958 & Ind rec from 1904; Clk Ct has m, div, pro & civ ct rec)

* **Major**   F5   1907   Woods
Major County, PO Box 379, Fairview, OK 73737-0379 .... (405)227-4732
(Clk Ct has m rec from late 1800's, div, pro & civ ct rec from 1908; Co Clk has Ind rec)

* **Marshall**   G2   1907   Chickasaw Lands
Marshall County, County Courthouse, Madill, OK 73446-2261 .... (405)795-3165
(Clk Ct has m, div, pro & civ ct rec from 1907; Co Clk has Ind rec; Co Supt has school rec; State Vit Rec has b & d rec)

*† **Mayes**   I5   1907   Indian Lands (Cherokee Lands)
Mayes County, PO Box 95, Pryor, OK 74362-0095 .... (918)825-0639
(Clk Ct has m, div, pro & civ ct rec from 1907; Co Clk has Ind rec from 1907; Co Treas has tax rec; Co Asr has assessment rec)

* **McClain**   G3   1907   Chickasaw Lands
McClain County, PO Box 629, Purcell, OK 73080-0629 .... (405)527-3117
(Co Clk has Ind rec; Co Supt has school rec; State Vit Rec has b & d rec)

* **McCurtain**   I2   1907   Choctaw Lands
McCurtain County, 108 N Central Ave, Idabel, OK 74745-3835 .... (405)286-7428
(Clk Ct has m, div, pro & civ ct rec from 1907)

*† **McIntosh**   H4   1907   Indian Lands (Creek Lands)
McIntosh County, 110 N 1st St, Eufaula, OK 74432-2449 .... (918)689-2362
(Co Clk has b & d rec from 1911 to 1918, also Ind rec; Clk Ct has m, div, pro & civ ct rec from 1907)

* **Murray**   G2   1907   Chickasaw Lands
Murray County, PO Box 240, Sulphur, OK 73086-0240 .... (405)622-3777
(Co Clk has Ind rec; Ct Clk has m, div, pro, civ ct rec; State Vit Rec has b & d rec)

*† **Muskogee**   I4   1898   Creek
Muskogee County, PO Box 2307, Muskogee, OK 74402-2307 .... (918)682-9601
(Dept Vital Statistics, Oklahoma City, has b, d rec; Clk Ct has m rec from 1890, div, pro, civ ct rec from 1907, criminal or felony rec from 1940; Co Clk has Ind rec)

* **Noble**   G5   1893   Cherokee Outlet
Noble County, PO Box 409, Perry, OK 73077-0409 .... (405)336-2771
(Clk Ct has m, div, pro & civ ct rec from 1893; Co Clk has Ind rec from 1893; State Vit Rec has b & d rec)

* **Nowata**   I6   1907   Cherokee Lands
Nowata County, 229 N Maple St, Nowata, OK 74048-2654 .... (918)273-0175
(Clk Dis Ct has m, div, pro, civ ct rec from 1907; Co Clk has Ind rec from 1911; Dept Vital Statistics, Oklahoma City, has b, d rec)

O (see Garfield)

Okfuskee   H4   1907   Creek Lands
Okfuskee County, PO Box 26, Okemah, OK 74859-0026 .... (918)623-0939
(Clk Ct has m, div, pro & civ ct rec; Co Clk has Ind rec)

Oklahoma   G4   1890   Original county
Oklahoma County, 321 Park Ave, Oklahoma City, OK 73102-3603 .... (405)236-2727
(Co Clk has m, div, pro & civ ct rec from 1890)

* **Okmulgee**   H4   1907   Creek Lands
Okmulgee County, 314 W 7th St, Okmulgee, OK 74447-5028 .... (918)756-3836
(Clk Ct has m, div, pro & civ ct rec; Co Clk has Ind rec from 1900)

Osage   H5   1907   Osage Indian Lands
Osage County, PO Box 87, Pawhuska, OK 74056-0087 .... (918)287-2615
(Co Clk has Ind rec from 1907)

* **Ottawa**   I6   1907   Cherokee Nation
Ottawa County, County Courthouse, Miami, OK 74354 .... (918)542-9408
(Clk Ct has m, div, pro & civ ct rec; Co Clk has Ind rec from 1890)

Pawnee   G5   1893   Cherokee Outlet
Pawnee County, County Courthouse, Pawnee, OK 74058 .... (918)762-3741
(Clk Ct has m rec from 1893, div & civ ct rec from 1894, pro rec from 1911)

* **Payne**   G5   1890   Original county
Payne County, 606 S Husband St, Stillwater, OK 74074-4044 .... (405)624-9300
(Clk Ct has m, div, pro, civ ct rec from 1894; Co Clk has Ind rec; Dept Vital Statistics, Oklahoma City, has b, d rec)

† **Pittsburg**   H3   1907   Choctaw Lands
Pittsburgh County, 2nd & Carl Albert, McAlester, OK 74501 .... (918)423-6865
(Co Health has b, d & bur rec; Clk Ct has m, div, pro & civ ct rec from 1890; Co Clk has Ind rec from 1890)

* **Pontotoc**   G3   1907   Chickasaw Lands
Pontotoc County, 13th & Broadway, Ada, OK 74820 .... (405)332-1425
(Clk Ct has m, div, pro & civ ct rec from 1907)

Name	Map Index	Date Created	Parent County or Territory From Which Organized
* **Pottawatomie**	G3	1891	Original county (Pottawatomie-Shawnee Lands)

Pottawatomie County, 325 N Broadway St, Shawnee, OK 74801-6938 . . . . (405)273-4305
(Clk Ct has m, div, pro & civ ct rec; Co Clk has Ind rec from 1892)

| *† **Pushmataha** | I2 | 1907 | Choctaw Lands |

Pushmataha County, 203 SW 3rd St, Antlers, OK 74523-3899 . . . . (405)298-2512

| * **Roger Mills** | D4 | 1892 | Cheyenne-Arapaho Lands |

Roger Mills County, PO Box 708, Cheyenne, OK 73628 . . . . (405)497-3365
(Ct Clk has m, pro, civ ct rec from 1800's, div rec from 1900; Co Clk has Ind rec from 1800's; State Vit Rec has b & d rec)

| * **Rogers** | I5 | 1907 | Cherokee Nation (Coo-wee-Scoowee Dist) |

Rogers County, 219 S Missouri Ave, Claremore, OK 74017-7832 . . . . (918)341-0585
(Clk Ct has m, div, pro & civ ct rec from 1907)

| **Seminole** | G3 | 1907 | Seminole Indian Lands |

Seminole County, PO Box 457, Wewoka, OK 74884-0457 . . . . (405)257-2450
(Clk Ct has m, div, pro & civ ct rec from 1907)

| * **Sequoyah** | I4 | 1907 | Cherokee Indian Lands |

Sequoyah County, 120 E Chickasaw Ave Box 8, Sallisaw, OK 74955-4655 . . . . (918)775-5539
(Clk Ct has m, div, pro & civ ct rec from 1907)

| **Stephens** | F3 | 1907 | Comanche County |

Stephens County, County Courthouse, Duncan, OK 73533 . . . . (405)255-4193
[FHL has some cem rec]

| **Texas** | C6 | 1907 | Beaver |

Texas County, 319 N Main St, Guymon, OK 73942-4843 . . . . (405)338-3233
(Clk Ct has m, div, pro, civ ct rec from 1907; Co Clk has Ind rec; Dept Vital Statistics, Oklahoma City, has b, d rec)

| **Tillman** | E3 | 1907 | Comanche Indian Lands |

Tillman County, PO Box 992, Frederick, OK 73542-0992 . . . . (405)335-3421
(Clk Ct has m, div, pro & civ ct rec from 1907; Co Clk has Ind rec from 1907)

| **Tobucksy** (See Pittsburg) | | | |
| * **Tulsa** | H5 | 1905 | Creek Lands |

Tulsa County, 500 S Denver Ave, Tulsa, OK 74103-3835 . . . . (918)596-5000
(Clk Ct has m, div, pro & civ ct rec from 1907)

| * **Wagoner** | I4 | 1908 | Creek Lands |

Wagoner County, 307 E Cherokee St, Wagoner, OK 74467 . . . . (918)485-2141
(Clk Ct has m, div, pro & civ ct rec from 1908)

| * **Washington** | H5 | 1897 | Cherokee Lands |

Washington County, 420 S Johnstone Ave, Bartlesville, OK 74003-6602 . . . . (918)336-0330
(Clk Ct has m, div, pro & civ ct rec from 1907)

| * **Washita** | E4 | 1900 | Cheyenne-Arapaho Lands |

Washita County, PO Box 380, Cordell, OK 73632-0380 . . . . (405)832-2284
(Clk Ct has m, div, pro, civ ct rec from 1900; Dept Vital Statistics, Oklahoma City, has b, d rec)

| * **Woods** | E6 | 1893 | Cherokee Outlet |

Woods County, PO Box 386, Alva, OK 73717 . . . . (405)327-2126
(Co Clk has m rec from 1894, div, civ ct, Ind rec from 1893, pro rec from 1901, school rec)

| **Woodward** | E5 | 1893 | Cherokee Outlet |

Woodward County, 1600 Main St, Woodward, OK 73801-3068 . . . . (405)256-8097
[FHL has some m, cem, nat, pro rec]

* At least one county history has been published about this county.
† Inventory of county archives was made by the Historical Records Survey. (See Introduction)

OREGON

CAPITAL · SALEM — TERRITORY 1848 — STATE 1859 (33rd)
State Map on Page M-35

In 1543, the Oregon coast was sighted by Spanish explorers. Captain James Cook sighted Oregon in 1778, but it was the Americans under Captain Robert Gray in 1792 who sailed up the Columbia River and made the first landing. A few days later, the British sailed further inland and claimed the Columbia and its drainage basin for the British, thereby establishing a rivalry for control of Oregon that lasted until 1846.

Sea otter trade was the basic impetus for settlement in the early years. John Astor's American Fur Company established Fort Astoria on the coast, but due to the War of 1812 sold out to the Northwest Company in 1813. Hudson's Bay Company absorbed the Northwest Company in 1821 and dominated the fur trade for the next two decades. The early fur traders were mainly Canadian, British, and American and they often married Indian women.

Missionaries entered the area in the 1830's, leading to the first substantial migration along the Oregon Trail in 1842. By 1843, Willamette Valley settlers had set up their own government and were demanding that the British leave the area. Most of these early settlers were from Missouri, Ohio, Illinois, Tennessee, Kentucky, and New England. In 1846, the British signed the Treaty of Washington which established the 49th parallel as the international boundary between Canada and the United States.

The Oregon Territory was organized in 1848, comprising present-day Oregon, Washington, Idaho, western Montana, and a corner of Wyoming. Two years later, the Territorial Legislature passed the Donation Land Act of 1850. This act gave 320 acres to every male American over age eighteen already in Oregon. If he were to marry by December 1, 1851, his wife would receive an equal amount of land. Men settling in the area by the end of 1853 were granted 160 acres of land and, if married, an equal amount was allotted to their wives. This act greatly encouraged migration to Oregon. Over the next decade, the population quadrupled, mainly due to settlers from the United States, Germany, Sweden, England, Norway, Russia, Finland, Italy, Denmark, Ireland, Austria, Greece, and Czechoslovakia. Statehood was granted in 1859. During the Civil War, the Union received nearly 2,000 soldiers from Oregon. After the war, Indian uprisings resulted in many battles and eventual relegation of the Indians to reservations. The Union Pacific Railroad was completed in 1869, beginning a thirty-year expansion in population which quadrupled Oregon's population

Birth and death records from 1903 are available from the Oregon State Health Division, Vital Statistics Section, P.O. Box 116, Portland, OR 97207. In making a request, it is necessary to state relationship and reasons for the request as only the immediate family can obtain copies of records. An index to births and deaths from 1903 to 1984 is available from the Oregon State Archives, 1005 Broadway N.E., Salem, OR 97310. To verify current fees, call 503-229-5710.

County clerks have marriage records from the date of organization. Records after 1906 can be obtained from the county or the state. Divorces were granted by the territorial legislature prior to 1853. These records are available at the Oregon State Archives. After 1853, they were recorded in the circuit court of each county. Since 1925, divorce records may also be obtained from the Oregon State Health Division. A probate court handled probate matters in the territorial era. A few early records are at the Oregon State Archives. Since 1859, the probate judge in each county has had jurisdiction over wills. Some records are in the circuit court but most are with the clerk of each county court. The 1850 census for the Oregon Territory is available and has been indexed. Territorial and state censuses also exist for a few counties for many years between 1842 and 1905.

Genealogical Archives, Libraries and Societies

Albany Public Library, Albany, OR 97321

Astoria Public Library, 450 10th St., Astoria, OR 97103

City Library, 100 West 13th Avenue, Eugene, OR 97401

Klamath County Library, 126 South Third Street, Klamath Falls, OR 97601

Lebanon City Library, 626 2nd St., Lebanon, OR 97355

Oregon Historical Society Library, 1230 S.W. Park Ave., Portland, OR 97201

Oregon State Archives, 1005 Broadway N.E., Salem, OR 97301

Oregon State Library, State Library Building, Summer and Court Sts., Salem, OR 97310

Portland Library Association, 801 S.W. Tenth Ave., Portland, OR 97205

Public Library, LaGrande, OR 97850

University of Oregon Library, Eugene, OR 97403

ALSI Historical and Genealogical Society, Inc., P. O. Box 822, Waldport, OR 97394

Blue Mountain Genealogical Society, P. O. Box 1801, Pendleton, OR 97801

Clackamas County Family History Society, Inc., P. O. Box 995, Oregon City, OR 97045

Clatsop County Historical Society, 1618 Exchange St., Astoria, OR 97103

Clatsop County Genealogical Society, Astoria Public Library, 450 10th St., Astoria, OR 97103

Coos Bay Genealogical Forum, P. O. Box 1067, North Bend, OR 97459

Cottage Grove Genealogical Society, P. O. Box 388, Cottage Grove, OR 97424

Deschutes County Historical and Genealogical Society, P. O. Box 5252, Bend, OR 97708

Digger O'Dells Restaurant Gen. Society, 333 East Main St., Medford, OR 97501

Genealogical Forum of Portland, Inc., 1410 S.W. Morrison, Room 812, Portland, OR 97205

Genealogical Heritage Council of Oregon, P. O. Box 628, Ashland, OR 97520-0021

Genealogical Society of Douglas County, Oregon, P. O. Box 579, Roseburg, OR 97470

Grants Pass Genealogical Society, P. O. Box 1834, Grants Pass, OR 97526

Jewish Genealogical Society of Oregon, 7335 SW Linette Way, Beaverton, OR 97007

Juniper Branch of the Family Finders, P. O. Box 652, Madras, OR 97741

Klamath Basin Genealogical Society, 1555 Hope St., Klamath Falls, OR 97603

Lake County Historical Society, 35 South G St., Lakeview, OR 97630

LaPine Genealogy Society, P. O. Box 2081, LaPine, OR 97739

Lebanon Genealogical Society, Labanon Public Library, 626 2nd St., Lebanon, OR 97355

Linn Genealogical Society, P. O. Box 1222, Albany, OR 97321

Mid-Columbia Genealogical Society, The Dalles Public Library, 722 Court Street, The Dalles, OR 97058

Mid-Valley Genealogical Society, P. O. Box 1511, Corvallis, OR 97339

Milton-Freewater Genealogical Club, 127 S.E. 6th St., Milton Freewater, OR 97862

Oregon Genealogical Society, P. O. Box 10306, Eugene, OR 97440-2306

Oregon Society, Sons of the American Revolution, 5190 S.W., Chestnut Ave., Beaverton, OR 97005

Pocahontas Trails Genealogical Society, Oregon Regional Chapter, 537 NE Locust Street, Oakland, OR 97462

Polk County Genealogical Society, 535 S.E. Ash St., Dallas, OR 97338

Portland Library Association, 801 S.W. Tenth Ave., Portland, OR 97205

Port Orford Genealogical Society, Port Orford Public Library, 555 W. 20th St., Port Orford, OR 97465

Rogue Valley Genealogical Society, Suite 204 Franklin Building, 125 South Central Ave., Medford, OR 97501

Siuslaw Genealogical Society, Siuslaw Public Library, P. O. Box A, Florence, OR 97439

Sweet Home Genealogical Society, Sweet Home Library, 13th and Kalmia Sts., Sweet Home, OR 97386

Tillamook County Historical Society Genealogy Study Group, P. O. Box 123, Tillamook, OR 97141

Umatilla County Historical Society, Box 253, Pendleton, OR 97801

Willamette Valley Genealogical Society, P. O. Box 2083, Salem, OR 97308

Woodburn Genealogical Club, 2220 Oregon Court, Woodburn, OR 97071

Yamhill County Genealogical Society, P. O. Box 568, McMinnville, OR 97128

Yaquina Genealogical Society, Toledo Public Library, 173 NW Seventh St., Toledo, OR 97391

Printed Census Records and Mortality Schedules

Federal Census 1850, 1860, 1870, 1880, 1900, 1910
Union Veterans and Widows 1890
State/Territorial Census 1845-1857

Valuable Printed Sources

Atlases, Maps, and Gazetteers

Brown, Erma Skyles. *Oregon Boundary Change Maps, 1843-1916*. Lebanon, Oregon: End of Trail Researchers, 1970.

Historical Oregon: Overland State Routes, Old Military Roads, Indian Battle Grounds, Old Forts, Old Gold Mines. Corvallis, Oregon: Western Guide Publishers, 1972.

McArthur, Lewis A. *Oregon Geographic Names*. Portland, Oregon: Oregon Historical Society, 1965.

Bibliography

Vaughan, Thomas and Priscilla Knuth. *A Bibliography of Pacific Northwest History*. Portland, Oregon: Oregon Historical Society, n.d.

Genealogical Sources

Brandt, Patricia and Nancy Gilford. *Oregon Biography Index*. Corvallis, Oregon: Oregon State University Press, 1976.

Genealogical Material in Oregon Donation Land Claims Abstracted from Applications. Portland, Oregon: Genealogical Forum of Oregon, 1975.

Histories

Carey, Charles Henry. *History of Oregon*. Chicago: Pioneer Historical Publishing Co., 1922.

Hines, H. K. *An Illustrated History of the State of Oregon*. Chicago: Lewis Publishing Co., 1893.

Wojcik, Donna M. *The Brazen Overlanders of 1845*. Portland, Oregon: Donna M. Wojcik, 1976.

OREGON COUNTY DATA
State Map on Page M-35

Name	Map Index	Date Created	Parent County or Territory From Which Organized
* **Baker**	C4	1862	Wasco

Baker County, 1995 3rd St, Baker, OR 97814-3399 .... (503)523-6414
(Co Clk has m, div, pro & civ ct rec from 1862)

Name	Map Index	Date Created	Parent County or Territory From Which Organized

*† **Benton**　　H4　　1847　　Polk
　　Benton County, 180 NW 5th St, Corvallis, OR　97330-4777 . . . . (503)757-6800
　　(Co Clk has b & d rec from 1907, m, div, pro, civ ct & Ind rec from 1850 & mil dis from 1919)

　Champoeg　　　　　　1843　　Orig. Co (Name changed to Marion)

* **Clackamas**　　G3　　1843　　Original county
　　Clackamas County, 906 Main St, Oregon City, OR　97045-1881 . . . . (503)655-8581
　　(Co Clk has m & Ind rec from 1846; State Board of Health has b, d, bur rec; State Archivist has custody of some old county rec)

　Clark (Now part of state of Washington)

*† **Clatsop**　　H2　　1844　　Twality
　　Clatsop County, PO Box 179, Astoria, OR　97103-0179 . . . . (503)325-1000
　　(Co Clk has m, Ind rec from abt 1860, div, civ ct rec from abt 1875, pro rec from abt 1880; Dept of Vital Statistics has b, d rec; City of Astoria has bur rec)

* **Columbia**　　H2　　1854　　Washington
　　Columbia County, County Courthouse, Saint Helens, OR　97051 . . . . (503)397-4322
　　(Co Clk has m, div, pro & civ ct rec from 1854; Co Clk has pro rec from 1880, m rec from 1890; State Vit Rec has b & d rec; Trial Ct Admin has div & civ ct rec from 1860)

*† **Coos**　　I6　　1853　　Umpqua, Jackson
　　Coos County, 250 N Baxter St, Coquille, OR　97423-1894 . . . . (503)396-3121
　　(Co Clk has b & d rec 1906 to 1929, m rec from 1857, Ind rec from 1854, widows' mil pensions 1929 to 1950, some school rec; State Vit Rec has b, delayed b, d rec; State Cts in Coquille has div & pro rec; Imm & Nat in Portland has nat rec 1876 to 1980)

　Crook　　E5　　1882　　Wasco
　　Crook County, 300 E 3rd St, Prineville, OR　97754-1949 . . . . (503)447-6555
　　(Co Clk has b rec from 1907 to 1941, d rec from 1907 to 1939, m rec from 1883, div, pro rec from 1883, civ ct, Ind rec from 1882)

* **Curry**　　I7　　1855　　Coos
　　Curry County, PO Box 746, Gold Beach, OR　97444-0746 . . . . (503)247-7011
　　(Co Clk has m & Ind rec from 1859; State Ct Clk in Gold Beach has pro & civ ct rec; Vital Statistics, Portland, has b, d rec)

* **Deschutes**　　F5　　1916　　Crook
　　Deschutes County, 1130 NW Harriman St, Bend, OR　97701-1947 . . . . (503)388-6570
　　(Co Clk has m & Ind rec from 1916; State Vit Rec has b & d rec)

* **Douglas**　　H6　　1852　　Umpqua 1852 & 1862
　　Douglas County, 1036 SE Douglas Ave, Roseburg, OR　97470-3396 . . . . (503)672-3311
　　(1863 absorbed Umpqua)(Co Clk has m, Ind, ct journals from 1852, mining rec from 1850s, div, pro, dis ct rec 1852 to 1920s; Cir Ct has div, pro, dis ct rec from 1930s; State Dept of Health, Portland, has b, d rec)

* **Gilliam**　　E3　　1885　　Wasco
　　Gilliam County, 221 S Oregon St, Condon, OR　97823 . . . . (503)384-2311
　　(Co Clk has m, div, pro, civ ct, Ind rec from 1885; State Vital Statistics, Portland, has b, d rec; local cem districts have bur rec)

* **Grant**　　D4　　1864　　Wasco, Umatilla
　　Grant County, 200 S Canyon Blvd, Canyon City, OR　97820 . . . . (503)575-0059
　　(Co Clk has m, pro, Ind rec from 1864; State Vit Rec has b & d rec)

* **Harney**　　D6　　1889　　Grant
　　Harney County, 450 N Buena Vista St, Burns, OR　97720-1565 . . . . (503)573-6641
　　(Co Clk has m, pro, Ind, voter reg rec from 1889; State Vit Rec has b & d rec 1924 to 1944)

*† **Hood River**　　F3　　1908　　Wasco
　　Hood River County, 309 State St, Hood River, OR　97031-2037 . . . . (503)386-3970
　　(Co Clk has m, div, pro, civ ct rec from 1908, Ind rec from 1895; Oregon Board of Health, Portland, has b, d rec; cem associations have bur rec)

* **Jackson**　　H7　　1852　　Umpqua
　　Jackson County, 10 S Oakdale, Medford, OR　97501-2952 . . . . (503)776-7231
　　(Co Clk has m rec from 1863, pro rec from 1833, Ind rec from 1853, voter registration from 1952, State Vit Rec has b & d rec)

* **Jefferson**　　F4　　1914　　Crook
　　Jefferson County, 657 C St, Madras, OR　97741-1709 . . . . (503)475-2449
　　(Co Clk has m, div, pro, civ ct, Ind rec from 1914; Vital Statistics, Portland, has b, d rec)

*† **Josephine**　　H7　　1856　　Jackson
　　Josephine County, County Courthouse, Grants Pass, OR　97526 . . . . (503)474-5221
　　(Co Clk has m & Ind rec from 1857, mining rec from 1863; State Vit Rec has b & d rec; Cir Ct has div, pro, civ ct rec)

*† **Klamath**　　F7　　1882　　West part of Lake Co.
　　Klamath County, 316 Main St, Klamath Falls, OR　97601-6385 . . . . (503)883-5134
　　(Co Clk has m rec from 1882, Ind rec from 1880; State Vit Rec has b & d rec; Cir Ct has div, pro, civ ct rec)

　Lake　　E6　　1874　　Jackson, Wasco
　　Lake County, 513 Center St, Lakeview, OR　97630-1579 . . . . (503)947-6006
　　(Co Clk has m, div, pro, civ ct & Ind rec from 1875)

* **Lane**　　G5　　1845　　Linn, Douglas, Benton, Klamath, Deschutes, Lincoln
　　Lane County, 125 E 8th Ave, Eugene, OR　97401-2926 . . . . (503)687-4203
　　(Co Clk has m rec from 1852, Ind rec from 1855, div, pro, civ ct rec from 1853; State Board of Health, Portland, has b, d rec)

　Lewis (Now part of state of Washington)

Name	Map Index	Date Created	Parent County or Territory From Which Organized
* **Lincoln**	H4	1893	Benton, Polk

Lincoln County, 225 W Olive St, Newport, OR 97365-3811 .... (503)265-6611
(Co Clk has b & d rec 1907 to 1916, m rec from 1905, Ind rec from 1893, voter reg from 1920, mil dis from 1945; Dis Ct has div, pro, civ ct rec; Bureau Vital Statistics, Portland, has b, d rec)

| *† **Linn** | G4 | 1847 | Champoeg |

Linn County, PO Box 100, Albany, OR 97321-0031 .... (503)967-3825
(Co Clk has m rec from 1850, div, pro & civ ct rec from 1854, mil enum of 1905)

| * **Malheur** | C6 | 1887 | Baker |

Malheur County, PO Box 4, Vale, OR 97918-0004 .... (503)473-5151
(Co Clk has m, pro, Ind rec from 1887)

| * **Marion** | G4 | 1843 | Orig Co. (name changed from Champoeg) |

Marion County, 100 High St NE, Salem, OR 97301-3665 .... (503)588-5212
(Co Clk has m rec from 1849, Ind rec from 1850; State Vit Rec has b & d rec from 1903; Dis Ct has div, pro, civ ct rec; State Arch has will rec 1853 to 1951, nat rec 1849 to 1975, assessment rolls 1857 to 1925)

| *† **Morrow** | E3 | 1885 | Umatilla |

Morrow County, PO Box 338, Heppner, OR 97836-0338 .... (503)676-9061
(Co Clk has m, pro, div & civ ct rec from 1885)

| *† **Multnomah** | G3 | 1854 | Washington, Clackamas |

Multnomah County, 1021 SW 4th Ave, Portland, OR 97204-1123 .... (503)248-3511
(Co Clk has div, civ ct & Ind rec from 1854)

| * **Polk** | H4 | 1845 | Yamhill |

Polk County, 850 Main St Rm 201, Dallas, OR 97338-3116 .... (503)623-9217
(Co Clk has m, pro & Ind rec; Clks office cannot make searches, will assist otherwise)

| * **Sherman** | E3 | 1889 | Wasco |

Sherman County, PO Box 365, Moro, OR 97039-0365 .... (503)565-3606
(Co Clk has m & pro rec from 1889, b rec from 1904 to 1939, d rec from 1905 to 1952 & civ ct rec from 1894)

| *† **Tillamook** | H3 | 1853 | Clatsop, Polk, Yamhill |

Tillamook County, 201 Laurel Ave, Tillamook, OR 97141-2381 .... (503)842-3402
(Co Clk has m rec from 1862, div, pro & civ ct rec from 1860)

Twality (Changed to Washington 1849)

| *† **Umatilla** | D2 | 1862 | Wasco |

Umatilla County, 216 SE 4th St, Pendleton, OR 97801-2590 .... (503)276-7111
(Co Clk has m, div, pro, civ ct & Ind rec from 1862)

| **Umpqua** | | 1851 | Benton, Linn (absorbed by Douglas 1863) |

| * **Union** | C3 | 1864 | Baker |

Union County, 1106 K Ave, LaGrande, OR 97850-2131 .... (503)963-1001
(Co Clk has m & Ind rec from 1875, imm rec 1900 to 1975; State Vit Rec has b & d rec from 1903; Clk Cir Ct has div, pro, civ ct rec from 1854)

| * **Wallowa** | B2 | 1887 | Union |

Wallowa County, 101 S River St Rm 202, Enterprise, OR 97828-1300 .... (503)426-3586
[FHL has some cem rec]

| *† **Wasco** | F3 | 1854 | Clackamas, Marion, Linn, Lane, Douglas, Jackson |

Wasco County, 5th & Washington, The Dalles, OR 97058 .... (503)296-2207
(Co Clk has m & Ind rec from 1854; State Vit Rec has b & d rec from 1903; Clk Cir Ct has div, pro, civ ct rec from 1854)

| † **Washington** | H3 | 1843 | Orig Co. (formerly Twality) |

Washington County, 155 N 1st Ave, Hillsboro, OR 97124-3070 .... (503)648-8681
(Co Clk has m & Ind rec from 1850; State Vit Rec has b & d rec; Ct Services Dept has div, pro, civ ct rec)

| **Wheeler** | E4 | 1899 | Crook, Gilliam, Grant |

Wheeler County, PO Box 327, Fossil, OR 97830-0327 .... (503)763-2400
(Co Clk has pro rec from 1899, Ind rec; State Vit Rec has b, m, d rec; Clk Cir Ct has div & civ ct rec)

| * **Yamhill** | H3 | 1843 | Original county |

Yamhill County, 535 E 5th St, McMinnville, OR 97128-4593 .... (503)472-9371
(Co Clk has m rec from 1881, Ind rec from 1853; State Vit Rec has b & d rec)

* At least one county history has been published about this county.
† Inventory of county archives was made by the Historical Records Survey. (See Introduction)

PENNSYLVANIA

CAPITAL · HARRISBURG — STATE 1787 (2nd)
State Map on Page M-36

The Swedes made the first permanent white settlement in Pennsylvania in 1643 and built the first log cabins in America. These settlers remained here to become the nucleus for William Penn's colony despite being conquered by the Dutch and the English. In 1681, King Charles II granted William Penn a charter which made Penn proprietor and governor of Pennsylvania. He first visited the colony in 1682 and set up a General Assembly at Chester. Penn named his capital Philadelphia, and before allowing settlers into any area, bought the land from the Indians. On Penn's second visit (1699-1701), he granted the Charter of Privileges, which made the legislature independent of the executive and virtually in control of the colony.

Penn established the colony as a refuge for those who were persecuted for their religious beliefs. The persecuted from throughout Europe came, including Quakers from England, Scotland, Ireland, and Wales; Palatines from the Rhine Valley; Anabaptists (Mennonites) from Germany and Switzerland; Dunkards (members of the Church of the Brethren) from Germany in 1721; Roman Catholics from England in 1732; Moravians via Georgia in 1740; Welsh, Swiss, and Scotch-Irish between 1700 and 1728; and the Pennsylvania Dutch (who were Germans) around 1740. Indian relations remained peaceable until the French arrived in 1753 and stirred up the Indians, leading to the French and Indian War and Pontiac's War which ended in 1764.

Philadelphia played an important role during the Revolution and in the drafting of the Constitution. Pennsylvania was among the greatest contributors of men, money, and supplies to the Revolutionary War and was the site of many of the important battles, such as Washington's crossing of the Delaware, the battles of Brandywine and Germantown, and the winter camp at Valley Forge. In 1787, Pennsylvania was the second state to ratify the Constitution. Philadelphia served as the capital of the United States from 1790 to 1800.

Boundary disputes were nearly constant until 1800. The boundary with Maryland was settled by the Mason and Dixon survey, 1763-1767. The Pennamite War between 1769 and 1775 was fought between settlers from Connecticut and Pennsylvania over the Wyoming Valley. This was finally settled in 1782 by the Decree of Trenton, which gave the land to Pennsylvania, and Connecticut finally yielded in 1784. Southwestern Pennsylvania was also claimed by Virginia, but this dispute was settled in 1785. In 1792, Pennsylvania bought the Erie triangle to gain a port on Lake Erie.

Tens of thousands of settlers came in the early 1800's to work in mines and industry. These came from Italy, Poland, Russia, Austria, Germany, Czechoslovakia, England, Ireland, Hungary, Sweden, Greece, France, Norway, Denmark, and Finland. By 1811, steamboats began traveling from Pittsburgh to New Orleans. The railroad canal line extended from Philadelphia to Pittsburgh by 1834. With these improvements more immigrants came, so that by 1840 there was no longer a frontier in Pennsylvania. Pennsylvania had the first anti-slavery society in 1775. It is no wonder that the state was so pro-Union. Nearly 400,000 men served for the Union, and the battle of Gettysburg was fought on Pennsylvania soil.

Statewide registration of births and deaths began in January 1906. Copies are available from the Division of Vital Statistics, State Department of Health, 101 South Mercer Street, P.O. Box 1528, New Castle, PA 16103. To verify current fees, call 412-656-3100.

Records prior to 1906 were kept (by the registrar of wills) in individual counties or cities, some as early as 1852. Individual counties or cities also kept marriage records, some from the early 1800's, though most from 1885. Original Oaths of Allegiance, 1727 to 1794, are at the Bureau of Archives and History, P.O. Box 1026, Harrisburg, PA 17108. Most later immigrants filed for naturalization in a county court. The state land office, established in 1682, is now the Bureau of Land Records. The Bureau of Archives and History, P.O. Box 1026, Harrisburg, PA 17108, sells warrantee township maps which show the original land grants within present township boundaries, as well as names and other information for the original warrantee and patentee. Records about the Wyoming Valley prior to 1782 are kept in Hartford, Connecticut.

Genealogical Archives, Libraries and Societies

Altoona Public Library, "The Pennsylvania Room," 1600 Fifth Ave., Altoona, PA 16602

Bloomsburg Public Library, 225 Market St., Bloomsburg, PA 17815

Buhl-Henderson Community Library, 11 Sharpsville Ave., Sharon, PA 16146

Carnegie Free Library, 1301 7th Ave., Beaver Falls, PA 15010

Carnegie Library, Pennsylvania Room, 4400 Forbes Ave., Pittsburgh, PA 15213

Centre County Library and Historical Museum, 203 N. Allegheny St., Bellefonte, PA 16823

Chester County Archives and Records Service, 117 West Gay Street, West Chester, PA 19380

Citizens Library, 55 South College Street, Washington, PA 15301

Coyle Free Library, 102 N. Main St., Chambersburg, PA 17201

Easton Area Public Library, 6th & Church Sts., Easton, PA 18042

Erie City and County Library, 3 S. Perry Square, Erie, PA 10511

Fackenthal Library, Franklin and Marshall College, Lancaster, PA 17602

Ford City Public Library, 1136 4th Ave., Ford City, PA 16226

Free Library of Philadelphia, Logan Square, Philadelphia, PA 19141

Green Free Library, 134 Main St., Wellsboro, PA 16901

Historical Society of Evangelical and Reformed Church Archives and Libraries, College Ave. and James St., Lancaster, PA 17604

James V. Brown Library, 19 East 4th St., Williamsport, PA 17701

Lutheran Historical Society Library, Gettysburg, PA 17325

Lutheran Theological Seminary Library, Mt. Airy, Philadelphia, PA 19119

Mennonite Library and Archives of Eastern Pennsylvania, 1000 Forty Foot Road, Lansdale, PA 19446

Methodist Historical Center, 326 New St., Philadelphia, PA 19106

Mt. Lebanon Public Library, 16 Castle Shannon Blvd., Pittsburgh, PA 15228

Muncy Historical Society and Museum of History, 131 So., Main St., Muncy, PA 17756

Myerstown Community Library, Box 242, 199 N. College St., Myerstown, PA 17067

New Castle Public Library, 207 E. North St., New Castle, PA 16101

Oil City Library, 2 Central Ave., Oil City, PA 16301

Osterhout Free Public Library, 71 So. Franklin St., Wilkes-Barre, PA 18701

Pennsylvania Historical and Museum Commission Division of Archives and Manuscripts, Box 1026, Harrisburg, PA 17108

Pennsylvania State Library, P. O. Box 1601, Harrisburg, PA 17105-1601

Reading Public Library, Fifth and Franklin Sts., Reading, PA 19607

Resource and Research Center for Beaver County and Local History, Carnegie Free Library, 1301 Seventh Ave., Beaver Falls, PA 15010

Schlow-Memorial Library, 100 E. Beaver Ave., State College, PA 16801

Spruance Library, Mercer Museum, Doylestown, PA 18901

Susquehanna County Free Library, Monument Square, Montrose, PA 18801

University Library, Pennsylvania State University, University Park, PA 16802

University of Pennsylvania Library, Central Bldg., 34th St. below Woodland, Philadelphia, PA 19104

Warren Public Library, Box 489, 205 Market St., Warren, PA 16365

Adams County Pennsylvania Historical Society, P. O. Box 4325, Gettysburg, PA 17325

Allegheny Foothills Historical Society, Boyce Park Adm. Bldg., 675 Old Franklin Rd., Pittsburgh, PA 15239

American Swedish Historical Foundation, 1900 Pattiso Ave., Philadelphia, PA 19145

Armstrong County Historical and Museum Society, Inc., 300 North McKean Street, Kittanning, PA 16201

Beaver County Genealogical Society, 1216 Fourth St. Exit, Vanport, PA 15009

Bedford County Historical Committee, 231 S. Juliana St., Bedford, PA 15522

Berks County Genealogical Society, P. O. Box 14774, Reading, PA 19612

Blair County Genealogical Society, P. O. Box 855, Altoona, PA 16603

Blair County Historical Society, P. O. Box 1083, Altoona, PA 16603

Bradford County Historical Society, 21 Main St., Towanda, PA 18848

Bradford Landmark Society, 45 East Corydon, Bradford, PA 16701

Brownsville Historical Society, Box 24, Brownsville, PA 15417

Bucks County Genealogical Society, P. O. Box 1092, Doylestown, PA 18901

Bucks County Historical Society, Pine and Ashland St., Doylestown, PA 18901

Cambria County Historical Society, West High St., Ebensburg, PA 15931

Cameron County Historical Society, 139 E. Fourth St., Emporium, PA 15834

Capital Area Genealogical Society, P. O. Box 4502, Harrisburg, PA 17111-4502

Central Pennsylvania Genealogical Pioneers, Northumberland, PA 17857

Centre County Genealogical Society, P. O. Box 1135, State College, PA 16804

Centre County Historical Society, 1001 E. College Ave., State College, PA 16801

Chester County Historical Society, 225 N. High St., West Chester, PA 19380

Clarion County Historical Society, Courthouse, Clarion, PA 16214

Clearfield County Historical Society, 104 East Pine St., Clearfield, PA 16830

Clinton County Historical Society, East Water St., Lock Haven, PA 15370

Cocalico Valley Historical Society, 249 W. Main St., Ephrata, PA 17522

Columbia County Historical Society, Box 197, Orangeville, PA 17859

Connellsville Area Historical Society, Connellsville, PA 15425

Cornerstone Genealogical Society, P. O. Box 547, Waynesburg, PA 15370

Crawford County Genealogical Society, 848 North Main Street, Meadville, PA 16335

Cumberland County Historical Society, P. O. Box 626, Carlisle, PA 17013

Delaware County Historical Society, Box 1036 Widener College, Chester, PA 19013

Elizabeth Township Historical Society, 5811 Smithfield St., Boston, PA 15135

Elk County Genealogical Society, P. O. Box 142, Johnsonburg, PA 15845

Elk County Historical Society, County Courthouse, Ridgway, PA 15853

Erie County Historical Society, 117 State St., Erie, PA 16501

Erie Society for Genealogical Research, P. O. Box 1403, Erie, PA 16512

Evangelical and Reformed Historical Society, Philip Schaff Library, Lancaster Theological Seminary, 555 W. James St., Lancaster, PA 17603

Forest County Historical Society, c / o Courthouse, Tionesta, PA 16353

Friends Historical Association, Haverford College, Haverford, PA 19041

Fulton County Historical Society, Box 115, McConnellsburg, PA 17233

Genealogical Society of Pennsylvania, 1300 Locust St., Philadelphia, PA 19107

Genealogical Society of Southwestern Pennsylvania, P. O. Box 894, Washington, PA 15301

Greene County Historical Society, Rd 2, Waynesburg, PA 15370

Heritage Society of Pennsylvania, P. O. Box 146, Laughlintown, PA 15655

Historic Schaefferstown, Inc., Box 1776, Schaefferstown, PA 17088

Historical Society of Dauphin County, 219 S. Front St., Harrisburg, PA 17104

Historical and Genealogical Society of Indiana County, Pennsylvania, 6th and Wayne Ave., Indiana, PA 15701

Historical and Genealogical Society of Jefferson County, Box 51, Brookville, PA 15825

Historical and Genealogical Society of Somerset County, Inc., Box 533, Somerset, PA 15501

Historical Society of Berks County, 940 Centre Ave., Reading, PA 19605

Historical Society of Evangelical and Reformed Church Archives and Libraries, College Ave. and James St., Lancaster, PA 17604

Historical Society of Green Tree, 10 West Manilla Ave., Pittsburgh, PA 15220

Historical Society of McKean County, Courthouse, Smethport, PA 16749

Historical Society of Montgomery County, 1654 DeKalb St., Norristown, PA 19401

Historical Society of Pennsylvania, 1300 Locust St., Philadelphia, PA 19107

Historical Society of Perry County, Headquarters and Museum, 129 North Second St., Newport, PA 17074

Historical Society of Schuylkill County, 14 N. Third St., Pottsville, PA 17901

Historical Society of Western Pennsylvania, 4338 Bigelow Blvd., Pittsburgh, PA 15213

Historical Society of York County, 250 East Market St., York, PA 17403

Homestead Penn. Historical Society, 1110 Silvan Ave., Homestead, PA 15120

Huntingdon County Historical Society, P. O. Box 305, Huntingdon, PA 16652

Indiana County Historical & Genealogical Society, South Sixth & Wayne, Indiana, PA 15701

Jewish Genealogical Society of Philadelphia, 332 Harrison Ave., Elkins Park, PA 19117

Jewish Genealogical Society of Pittsburgh, 2131 Fifth Ave., Pittsburgh, PA 15219

Juniata County Historical Society, Star Route, Mifflintown, PA 17059

Kittochtinny Historical Society, Chambersburg, PA 17201

Lackawanna County Historical Society, 232 Monroe Ave., Scranton, PA 18510

Lancaster County Historical Society, 230 N. President Ave. Lancaster, PA 17603

Lancaster Mennonite Historical Society, 2215 Millstream Road, Lancaster, PA 17602-1499

Lawrence County Historical Society, 2nd Floor, Box 1745, Public Library, New Castle, PA 16103

Lebanon County Historical Society, 924 Cumberland St., Lebanon, PA 17042

Lehigh County Historical Society, P. O. Box 1548, Allentown, PA 18105

Ligonier Valley Historical Society, Star Route East, Ligonier, PA 15658

Lycoming County Genealogical Society, P. O. Box 3625, Williamsport, PA 17701

Lycoming County Historical Society and Museum, 858 West 4th St., Williamsport, PA 17701

Masontown Historical Society, Box 769, Masontown, PA 15461

McKean County Genealogical Society, Box 335, Bradford, PA 16701

McKean County Historical Society, Courthouse, Smethport, PA 16749

Mercer County Genealogical Society, Box 812, Sharon, PA 16146

Mercer County Historical Society, 119 S. Pitt St., Mercer, PA 16137

Mifflin County Historical Society, 17 North Main St., Lewistown, PA 17044

Monroe County Historical Society, 9th and Main St., Stroudsburg, PA 18360

Montgomery County Historical Society, 1654 Dekalb St., Norristown, PA 19401

Montour County Historical Society, 1 Bloom St., Danville, PA 17821

Muncy Historical Society and Museum of History, 131 So., Main St., Muncy, PA 17756

National Archives-Mid-Atlantic Region 5000 Wissahickon Ave., Philadelphia, PA 19144

Northampton County Historical and Genealogical Society, 101 So. 4th St., Easton, PA 18042

Northumberland County Historical Society, 1150 N. Front St., Sunbury, PA 17801

Oil City Heritage Society, P. O. Box 962, Oil Creek Station, Oil City, PA 16301

Old York Road Genealogical Society, 1030 Old York Road, Abington, PA 19001

Pennsylvania Genealogical Society, 1300 Locust St., Philadelphia, PA 19107

Pennsylvania German Society, Box 97, Breinigsville, PA 18031

Pennsylvania Society, Sons of the American Revolution, R. D. 1, Box 422, Monongahela, PA 15063

Perry County Historical Society, 129 N 2nd St., Newport, PA 17074

Perry Historian Genealogical Society, P. O. Box 73, Newport, PA 17074

Pike County Historical Society, c / o Milford Comm. House, Milford, PA 18337

Pioneer Historical Society of Bedford County, Box 421, Bedford, PA 15522

Potter County Historical Society, 308 N. Main St., Coudersport, PA 16915

Presbyterian Historical Society, 425 Lombard St., Philadelphia, PA 19147

Schuylkill County Historical Society, 14 N. 3rd St., Pottsville, PA 17901

Scottish Historic and Research Society of the Delaware Valley, Inc., 102 St. Paul's Road, Ardmore, PA 19003

Sewickley Valley Historical Society, 200 Broad, Sewickley, PA 15143

Slippery Rock Heritage Association, Box 501, Slippery Rock, PA 16057

Slovenian Genealogical Society, 609 Gale Rd. Camp Hill, PA 17011

Snyder County Historical Society, 30 East Market St., P. O. Box 276, Middleburg, PA 17842

Sommerset County Historical & Genealogical Society, Rd 2 Box 238, Somerset, PA 15501

South Central Pennsylvania Genealogical Society, P. O. Box 1824, York, PA 17405

Southwestern Pennsylvania Genealogical Society, Box 894, Washington, PA 15301

St. Marys and Benzinger Township Historical Society, Genealogical Dept., 319 Erie Ave., St. Marys, PA 15857

Sullivan County Historical Society, Courthouse Square, LaPorte, PA 18626

Susquehanna Depot Historical Society, Inc., P. O. Box 161, Susquehanna, PA 18847

Susquehanna County Historical Society, Montrose, PA 18801

Tarentum Genealogical Society, Community Library of Allegheny Valley, 315 East Sixth Avenue, Tarentum, PA 15084

Tioga County Historical Society, 120 Main St., Box 724, Wellsboro, PA 16901

Tulpehocken Settlement Historical Society, Box 53, Womelsdorf, PA 19567

Tuscarora Township Historical Society, Bradford County, R.D. 2, Box 105-C, Laceyville, PA 18623

Union County Historical Society, Courthouse, Lewisburg, PA 17837

Venango County Genealogical Club, P. O. Box 811, Oil City, PA 16301

Venango County Historical Society, P. O. Box 101, 301 South Park Street, Franklin, PA 16323

Warren County Genealogical Society, 6 Main St., North Warren, PA 16365

Warren County Historical Society, 210 Fourth Ave., Box 427, Warren, PA 16365

Washington County Historical Society and Library, LeMoyne House, 49 East Maiden St., Washington, PA 15301

Wattsburg Area Historical Society, P. O. Box 240, Wattsburg, PA 16442-0240

Wayne County Historical Society, 810 Main St, Box 446, Honesdale, PA 18431

Western Pennsylvania Genealogical Society, 4338 Bigelow Blvd., Pittsburgh, PA 15213

Westmoreland, Historical Society of, 151 Old Salem Rd., Greensburg, PA 15601

Windber - Johnstown Genealogical Society, 85 Colgate Ave., Johnstown, PA 15905

Wyoming County Historical Society, P. O. Box 309, Tunkhannock, PA 18657

Wyoming Historical and Genealogical Society, 69 S. Franklin St., Wilkes-Barre, PA 18701

Printed Census Records and Mortality Schedules

Federal Census 1790, 1800, 1810, 1820, 1830, 1840, 1850, 1860, 1870, 1880, 1900, 1910
Federal Mortality Schedules 1850, 1860, 1870, 1880
Union Veterans and Widows 1890
U.S. Direct Tax 1798

Valuable Printed Sources

Atlases, Maps, and Gazetteers

Espenshade, A. Howry. *Pennsylvania Place Names*. Baltimore: Genealogical Publishing Co., 1970 reprint.

Gordon, Thomas. *A Gazetteer of the State of Pennsylvania*. New Orleans: Polyanthos, 1975 reprint.

Bibliographies

Dructor, Robert M. *A Guide to Genealogical Sources at the Pennsylvania State Archives*. Harrisburg, Pennsylvania: Pennsylvania Historical and Museum Commission, 1980.

Fortna, Nancy L. P. and Frank M. Suran. *Guide to County and Municipal Records on Microfilm in the Pennsylvania State Archives*. Harrisburg, Pennsylvania: Pennsylvania Historical and Museum Commission, 1982.

Harriss, Helen L. *Pennsylvania Genealogical Resources Directory*. Pittsburgh, Pennsylvania: Helen L. Harriss, 1985.

Molitor, Albert J. *Genealogical Sources, Southeastern Pennsylvania*. Abington, Pennsylvania: Old York Road Genealogical Society, 1980.

Salisbury, Ruth. *Pennsylvania Newspapers: A Bibliography and Union List*. Pennsylvania Library Association, 1969.

Wall, Carol. *Bibliography of Pennsylvania History: A Supplement*. Harrisburg, Pennsylvania: Pennsylvania Historical and Museum Commission, 1976.

Wilkinson, Norman B. *Bibliography of Pennsylvania History*. Harrisburg, Pennsylvania: Pennsylvania Historical and Museum Commission, 1957.

Genealogical Research Guides

Bell, Raymond Martin. *Searching in Western Pennsylvania*. Detroit: Detroit Society for Genealogical Research, 1977.

Hoenstine, Floyd G. *Guide to Genealogical Searching in Pennsylvania*. Hollidaysburg, Pennsylvania: Floyd G. Hoenstine, 1978.

Pennsylvania Line: A Research Guide to Pennsylvania Genealogy and Local History. Laughlintown, Pennsylvania: Southwest Pennsylvania Genealogical Services, 1983.

Weikel, Sally A. *Genealogical Research in Published Pennsylvania Archives*. Harrisburg, Pennsylvania: State Library of Pennsylvania, 1974.

Genealogical Sources

Jordan, Wilfred. *Colonial and Revolutionary Families of Pennsylvania*. New York: Lewis Historical Publishing Co., 1934.

Myers, Albert Cook. *Immigration of the Irish Quakers into Pennsylvania*. Baltimore: Genealogical Publishing Co., 1969.

Rupp, Israel Daniel. *Thirty Thousand Names of German, Swiss, Dutch, French and Other Immigrants in Pennsylvania from 1727 to 1776*. Baltimore: Genealogical Publishing Co., 1965 reprint.

Strassburger, Ralph Beaver. *Pennsylvania German Pioneers*. Baltimore: Genealogical Publishing Co., 1966 reprint.

Histories

Donehoo, George P. *Pennsylvania: A History*. Chicago: Lewis Historical Publishing Co., 1926.

Shenk, Hiram H. *Encyclopedia of Pennsylvania*. Harrisburg, Pennsylvania: National Historical Association, 1932.

PENNSYLVANIA COUNTY DATA
State Map on Page M-36

Name	Map Index	Date Created	Parent County or Territory From Which Organized
*† **Adams**	F2	1800	York

Adams County, 111 Baltimore St, Gettysburg, PA 17325-2312 . . . . (717)334-6781
(Clk of Ct has b, d rec from 1852 to 1855, 1893 to 1905, m rec rec 1852 to 1855, 1856 to present; Prothonotary Office has div, civ ct rec from 1800; Co Rcdr has pro, lnd rec from 1800)

* **Allegheny**	B3	1788	Westmoreland, Washington

Allegheny County, 436 Grant St, Pittsburgh, PA 15219-2403 . . . . (412)355-5313
(Reg Wills has m rec; Prothonotary's Office, 1st floor, City Co Bldg has div rec; Clk Ct has pro & civ ct rec; Rcdr Deeds has lnd rec)

* **Armstrong**	C4	1800	Allegheny, Lycoming, Westmoreland

Armstrong County, Market St, Kittanning, PA 16201 . . . . (412)543-2500
(Co Reg & Rcdr has b, d & bur rec from 1893 to 1905, m rec from 1895, pro, deeds, petitions & plan of lots from 1805; Div Vit Rec in Newcastle has b rec from 1906; Prothonotary has pro & lnd rec from 1805)

*† **Beaver**	B4	1800	Allegheny, Washington

Beaver County, 3rd & Turnpike St, Beaver, PA 15009 . . . . (412)728-5700
(Co Clk has b rec from 1893 to 1907, m rec from 1885, d rec from 1834, bur rec from 1852 to 1855 & 1893 to 1907, div rec from 1805, pro rec from 1800 & civ ct rec from 1797)

* **Bedford**	D2	1771	Cumberland

Bedford County, 230 S Juliana St, Bedford, PA 15522-1716 . . . . (814)623-4836
(Prothonotary has b rec from 1852 to 1854, & from 1893 to 1906, m rec from 1852 to 1854 and from 1885, d rec from 1852 to 1854, & from 1893 to 1906, div rec from 1804, pro rec from 1771, civ ct rec from 1771 & warrants from 1771)

*† **Berks**	G3	1752	Bucks, Lancaster, Philadelphia

Berks County, 33 N 6th St, Reading, PA 19601-3540 . . . . (215)378-8000
(Co Clk has b, d rec from 1894 to 1905, m rec from 1885, pro rec from 1752; Prothonotary Office has div, civ ct rec; Rcdr of Deeds has lnd rec)

*† **Blair**	D3	1846	Huntingdon, Bedford

Blair County, 423 Allegheny St, Hollidaysburg, PA 16648-2022 . . . . (814)695-5541
(Prothonotary has div, pro, civ ct rec from 1846, nat rec from 1848, m rec from 1885, b & d rec 1893 to 1905)

*† **Bradford**	G6	1812	Luzerne, Lycoming

Bradford County, 301 Main St, Towanda, PA 18848-1884 . . . . (717)265-5700
(name changed from Ontario in 1812)(Clk Orph Ct has b & d rec 1892 to 1906, m rec from 1885; Co Clk has div rec from 1878, civ ct rec from 1850; Reg Wills has pro rec from 1812; Rcdr Deeds has lnd rec from 1812)

* **Bucks**	H3	1682	Original county

Bucks County, Main & Court Sts, Doylestown, PA 18901 . . . . (215)348-6000
(Orph Ct has b & d rec 1893 to 1906, m rec from 1885; Prothonotary has div rec from 1878, civ ct rec from 1682; Reg Wills has pro rec from 1684)

* **Butler**	B4	1800	Allegheny

Butler County, Main St, Butler, PA 16001 . . . . (412)285-4731
(Co Clk has b, d rec from 1893 to 1906, m rec from 1885, div rec from 1805; Orphan's Ct has pro rec from 1804; Prothonotary Office has civ ct, lnd rec from 1804; Co Clk has naturalization rec from 1804)

*† **Cambria**	D3	1804	Somerset, Bedford, Huntingdon

Cambria County, 200 S Center St, Edensburg, PA 15931-1936 . . . . (814)472-5440
(Co Clk has b & d from 1893 to 1906, m rec from 1885, div rec from 1866, pro rec from 1819, civ ct rec from 1849 & lnd rec from 1846)

Name	Map Index	Date Created	Parent County or Territory From Which Organized
* **Cameron**	D5	1860	Clinton, Elk, McKean, Potter

Cameron County, 20 E 5th St, Emporium, PA 15834-1469 . . . . (814)486-2315
(Co Clk has b & d rec from 1860 to 1905, m div, pro, civ ct & Ind rec from 1860)

* **Carbon**	H4	1842	Northampton, Monroe

Carbon County, Broadway Lock Box 129, Jim Thorpe, PA 18229-0129 . . . . (717)325-3611
(Co Clk has b rec from 1894 to 1905, d rec from 1890 to 1904, m rec from 1885, pro rec from 1843; Prothonotary has div rec; Clk Cts has civ ct rec; Rcdr Deeds has Ind rec)

* **Centre**	E4	1800	Lycoming, Mifflin, Northumberland

Centre County, County Courthouse, Bellefonte, PA 16823-3005 . . . . (814)355-6700
(Co Clk has b, d rec from 1893 to 1905, m rec from 1885; Prothonotary has div rec from 1890, civ ct rec from 1800, nat rec from 1800; Reg of Wills has pro rec from 1800; Rcdr of Deeds has Ind rec from 1801)

* **Chester**	H2	1682	Original county

Chester County, Market & High Sts, West Chester, PA 19380 . . . . (215)344-6000
(Co Arch has b & d rec 1852 to 1855 & 1893 to 1906, m rec 1852 to 1855 & 1885 to 1930, div rec 1804 to 1828, pro rec 1714 to 1923, civ ct rec 1714 to 1900, Ind rec 1716 to 1905, criminal ct rec 1681 to 1900, tax rec 1715 to 1939, poorhouse rec 1798 to 1937)

* **Clarion**	C5	1839	Venango, Armstrong

Clarion County, 421 Main St, Clarion, PA 16214-1028 . . . . (814)226-4000
(Register and Rcdr has b, d rec from 1893 to 1906, m rec from 1885, pro, Ind rec from 1840; Prothonotary Clk has div rec from 1880, civ ct rec from 1874)

* **Clearfield**	D4	1804	Northumberland, Lycoming

Clearfield County, N 2nd & Market Sts, Clearfield, PA 16830 . . . . (814)765-2641
(Co Reg & Rcdr has b & d rec from 1893 to 1905 & m rec from 1885; Prothonotary has d & civ ct rec from 1828; Co Rcdr has pro rec from 1875; Co Comm has Ind rec)

* **Clinton**	E5	1839	Lycoming, Centre

Clinton County, County Courthouse, Lock Haven, PA 17745 . . . . (717)893-4000
(Co Clk has b, m, d, div, pro, civ ct & Ind rec)

* **Columbia**	G4	1813	Northumberland

Columbia County, PO Box 380, Bloomsburg, PA 17815-0380 . . . . (717)784-1991
(Co Clk has b & d rec from 1893 to 1905, m rec from 1888, civ ct rec from 1814 & div rec)

* **Crawford**	B6	1800	Allegheny

Crawford County, 360 Center St, Meadville, PA 16335 . . . . (814)336-1151
(Co Clk has b, d & bur rec from 1893 to 1905, m rec from 1885, div rec, pro, civ ct & Ind rec from 1800)

* **Cumberland**	F3	1750	Lancaster

Cumberland County, Hanover & High Sts, Carlisle, PA 17013 . . . . (717)240-6100
(Reg Wills has b & d rec from 1894 to 1905, m rec from 1885 & pro rec from 1750; Prothonotary has div & civ ct rec from 1751; Rcdr Deeds has Ind rec from 1751)

* **Dauphin**	F3	1785	Lancaster

Dauphin County, Front & Market Sts, Harrisburg, PA 17101-2012 . . . . (717)255-2741
(Co Clk has b & d rec 1893 to 1906, m rec from 1885, pro rec from 1795; Prothonotary has div & civ ct rec; Rcdr Deeds has Ind rec; Clk Orph Ct has rec from 1795)

*† **Delaware**	H2	1789	Chester

Delaware County, W Front St, Media, PA 19063 . . . . (215)891-4000
(Co Clk has b, d rec from 1893 to 1906, m rec from 1885, div rec from 1927, pro rec from 1790, civ ct rec from 1897, Ind rec from 1789, administration rec from 1790, Orphan Ct rec from 1865, delayed b rec from 1875 to 1900)

* **Elk**	D5	1843	Jefferson, McKean, Clearfield

Elk County, Main St, Ridgway, PA 15853 . . . . (814)776-1161
(Reg & Rcdr has b & d rec 1893 to 1906, m rec from 1895, pro rec from 1847, Ind rec from 1861; Prothonotary has div & civ ct rec from 1843)

*† **Erie**	B6	1800	Allegheny

Erie County, 140 W 6th St, Erie, PA 16501-1002 . . . . (814)451-6000
(Co Clk has b, d rec from 1893 to 1906, m rec from 1885; Prothonotary has div, civ ct rec from 1823; Reg Wills has pro rec from 1823; Co Rcdr has Ind rec from 1823; Courthouse burned 1823-all rec destroyed)

*† **Fayette**	B2	1783	Westmoreland

Fayette County, 61 E Main St, Uniontown, PA 15401-3514 . . . . (412)430-1201
(Clk Orph Ct has b & d rec from 1893 to 1905, m rec from 1885 & pro rec from 1784; Prothonotary has div rec also civ ct rec from 1784 ; Rcdr Deeds has Ind rec from 1784)

*† **Forest**	C5	1848	Jefferson, Venango

Forest County, 526 Elm St, Tionesta, PA 16353 . . . . (814)755-3537
(Co Reg & Rcdr has b rec from 1893 to 1906, m, div & Ind rec)

* **Franklin**	E2	1784	Cumberland

Franklin County, 157 Lincoln Way E, Chambersburg, PA 17201-2211 . . . . (717)264-4125
(Co Clk has b, d rec from 1894 to 1906, m rec from 1885, div rec from 1884, pro, Ind rec from 1785)

* **Fulton**	D2	1850	Bedford

Fulton County, N 2nd St, McConnellsburg, PA 17233 . . . . (717)485-4212
(Clk Orphan Ct has b, d rec from 1895 to 1905, m rec from 1885, Orphan rec from 1850; Prothonotary has div, civ ct rec from 1850; Reg Will has pro rec from 1850; Rcdr Deeds has Ind rec from 1850)

Name	Map Index	Date Created	Parent County or Territory From Which Organized

*† **Greene**   B2   1796   Washington
     Greene County, 93 E High St County Office Bldg, Waynesburg, PA 15370-1888 .... (412)852-1171
     (Co Clk has b & d rec from 1893 to 1915, m rec from 1885; Prothonotary has div rec from 1816 & civ ct rec from 1797; Co Reg
     has pro rec from 1796; Rcdr Deeds has Ind rec from 1796)

* **Huntingdon**   E3   1787   Bedford
     Huntingdon County, 223 Penn St, Huntingdon, PA 16652-1443 .... (814)643-3091
     (Co Clk has b rec from 1894 to 1906, m rec from 1885, d rec from 1894 to 1905, div pro & civ ct rec from 1787)

* **Indiana**   C3   1803   Westmoreland, Lycoming
     Indiana County, 825 Philadelphia St, Indiana, PA 15701-3934 .... (412)465-3800
     (Co Orphan Ct has b, d rec from 1893 to 1906, m rec from 1884, pro rec from 1894, Ind rec from 1803; Prothonotary Ct has div
     rec from 1879, civ ct rec from 1894)

* **Jefferson**   C5   1804   Lycoming
     Jefferson County, 200 Main St, Brookville, PA 15825-1236 .... (814)849-8031
     (Co Clk has b rec 1892 to 1906, d & bur rec 1893 to 1906, m rec from 1885, Ind rec from 1828, pro rec from 1832; Bureau Vit
     Rec in Newcastle has b & d rec from 1906)

* **Juniata**   E3   1831   Mifflin
     Juniata County, PO Box 68, Mifflintown, PA 17059-0068 .... (717)436-8991
     (Co Clk has b & d rec 1893 to 1907, m rec from 1885, div rec from 1900, pro, civ ct Ind rec from 1831, nat rec early 1800s to
     1930)

* **Lackawanna**   H5   1878   Luzerne
     Lackawanna County, PO Box 133, Scranton, PA 18503 .... (717)963-6723
     (Co Comm Office has m, div, pro & civ ct rec from 1878)

*† **Lancaster**   G2   1729   Chester
     Lancaster County, 50 N Duke St, Lancaster, PA 17602-2805 .... (717)299-8300
     (Reg Wills has b rec from 1893 to 1905, m rec from 1885, d, div, pro, civ ct & Ind rec from 1729; Prothonotary Ct has rec of
     Common Pleas, div rec; Clk Orphans Ct has orphan rec; Rcdr Deeds has Ind rec from 1729; Ct Common Pleas has d rec from
     1894 to 1927)

*† **Lawrence**   B4   1850   Beaver, Mercer
     Lawrence County, 433 Court St, New Castle, PA 16101-3599 .... (412)658-2541
     (Co Clk has b, d, bur rec 1893 to 1905, m rec from 1893, div & civ ct rec from 1855; Reg & Rcdr has pro & Ind rec)

* **Lebanon**   G3   1813   Dauphin, Lancaster
     Lebanon County, 400 S 8th St, Lebanon, PA 17042-6794 .... (717)274-2801
     (Clk Orph Ct has b rec from 1893 to 1906, m rec from 1885; Prothonotary has div rec from 1888; Reg Wills has pro rec from
     1813)

*† **Lehigh**   H3   1812   Northampton
     Lehigh County, 455 Hamilton St, Allentown, PA 18101-1614 .... (215)820-3000
     (Clk Orphan Ct has b rec from 1895 to 1905, d rec from 1893 to 1904, m rec from 1885; Prothonotary Ct has div, civ ct rec from
     1812; Reg of Wills has pro rec from 1812; Rcdr of Deeds has deed rec from 1812)

*† **Luzerne**   G4   1786   Northumberland
     Luzerne County, 211 N River St, Wilkes-Barre, PA 18704-5038 .... (717)825-1500
     (Reg Wills has b, d & bur rec from 1893 to 1906, m rec from 1885, pro rec from 1786; Prothonotary has div & civ ct rec; Rcdr
     Deeds has Ind rec)

* **Lycoming**   F5   1795   Northumberland
     Lycoming County, 48 W 3rd St, Williamsport, PA 17701-6536 .... (717)327-2200
     (Co Clk has b rec from 1893 to 1905, d rec from 1893 to 1898, m rec from 1885, pro rec from 1850, Ind rec from 1795;
     Prothonotary Ct has div, civ ct rec from 1795; The James V. Brown Library, 19 E. Fourth St., Williamsport, PA is the major source
     of Lycoming Co genealogical information)

* **McKean**   D6   1804   Lycoming
     McKean County, 500 W Main St, Smethport, PA 16749-1144 .... (814)887-5571
     [FHL has some b, m, d, cem, civ ct, Ind, nat, pro rec]

* **Mercer**   B5   1800   Allegheny
     Mercer County, 138 S Diamond St, Mercer, PA 16137-1284 .... (412)662-3800
     (Co Clk has b & d rec from 1893 to 1905, m rec from 1885, pro rec from 1800; Prothonotary Officer has div & civ ct rec)

* **Mifflin**   E3   1789   Cumberland, Northumberland
     Mifflin County, 20 N Wayne St, Lewistown, PA 17044-1770 .... (717)248-6733
     (Co Clk has b rec from 1893 to 1905, m rec from 1885, pro & Ind rec from 1789; Prothonotary has pro & civ ct rec)

* **Monroe**   H4   1836   Pike, Northampton
     Monroe County, County Courthouse Sq, Stroudsburg, PA 18360 .... (717)424-5100
     (Co Clk has b rec 1892 to 1905, m rec from 1885, civ ct rec from 1845, div rec from 1900)

* **Montgomery**   H3   1784   Philadelphia
     Montgomery County, Swede & Airy Sts, Norristown, PA 19404 .... (215)278-3000
     (Clk Orph Ct has b & d rec from 1893 to 1915, m rec from 1885; Rcdr Deeds has Ind rec from 1784; Prothonotary has div & civ ct
     rec from 1784; Reg Wills has pro rec from 1784; Rcdr Deeds has Ind rec from 1784)

* **Montour**   F4   1850   Columbia
     Montour County, 29 Mill St, Danville, PA 17821-1945 .... (717)271-3012
     (Prothonotary & Clk Cts has b & d rec from 1893 to 1905, m rec from 1885, div, civ ct rec from 1850)

Name	Map Index	Date Created	Parent County or Territory From Which Organized

* **Northampton**   H4   1752   Bucks
Northampton County, 7th & Washington Sts, Easton, PA 18042-7411 .... (215)559-3000
(Clk Orphan Ct has b rec from 1893 to 1936, m rec from 1885; Prothonotary Office has div, civ ct rec; Reg Wills has pro rec; Rcdr Deeds has Ind rec)

* **Northumberland**   F4   1772   Lancaster, Berks, Cumberland
Northumberland County, 2nd & Market Sts, Sunbury, PA 17801 .... (717)988-4100
(Reg and Rcdr has b, d rec from 1893 to 1905, m rec from 1885, pro, Ind rec from 1772; Prothonotary Office has div, civ ct rec)

Ontario (See Bradford)

* **Perry**   E3   1820   Cumberland
Perry County, PO Box 37, New Bloomfield, PA 17068-0037 .... (717)582-2131
(Co Clk has b rec from 1893 to 1918, m rec from 1870 & Ind rec from 1820)

* **Philadelphia**   H3   1682   Original county
Philadelphia County, Broad & Market Sts, Philadelphia, PA 19107 .... (215)686-1776
(Clk Orph Ct has m rec; Prothonotary has div & civ ct rec from 1874; Reg Wills has pro rec; Dept Rec has Ind rec)

* **Pike**   I5   1814   Wayne
Pike County, 506 Broad St, Milford, PA 18337-1511 .... (717)296-7613
(Clk Comm has b & d rec from 1885 to 1905, m rec from 1885, div, pro, civ ct & Ind rec from 1814)

* **Potter**   E5   1804   Lycoming
Potter County, 227 N Main St, Coudersport, PA 16915-1686 .... (814)274-8290
(Prothonotary has b, d & bur rec from 1893 to 1905, m rec from 1885, div rec from 1885)

* **Schuylkill**   G3   1811   Berks, Northampton
Schuylkill County, N 2nd St & Laurel Blvd, Pottsville, PA 17901-2528 .... (717)622-5570
(Clk Comm has b & d rec from 1893 to 1905, m rec from 1885, div rec from 1878, pro, civ ct & Ind rec from 1811)

* **Snyder**   F4   1855   Union
Snyder County, 11 W Market St, Middleburg, PA 17842-1018 .... (717)837-4207
(Clk Cts has b, d & bur rec from 1893 to 1905, m from 1885, div, civ ct rec from 1855; Co Reg & Rcdr has pro & Ind rec; Susquehanna Univ Lib in Selinsgrove has local census rec)

* **Somerset**   C2   1795   Bedford
Somerset County, 111 E Union St, Somerset, PA 15501-1416 .... (814)445-5154
(Reg Wills has b, d rec from 1893 to 1906, m rec from 1885, pro rec from 1795; Rcdr Deeds has Ind rec from 1795, mil dis rec from 1865; Prothonotary has div & civ ct rec from 1795, nat rec 1795 to 1955)

* **Sullivan**   G5   1847   Lycoming
Sullivan County, Main & Muncy, Laporte, PA 18626 .... (717)946-5201
(Clk Orph Ct has b & d rec from 1893 to 1905, m rec from 1885; Prothonotary has div rec from 1847, civ ct rec from 1847; Reg Wills has pro rec 1847)

* **Susquehanna**   H6   1810   Luzerne
Susquehanna County, County Courthouse, Montrose, PA 18801 .... (717)278-4600
(Co Clk has div & civ ct rec from 1812)

* **Tioga**   F6   1804   Lycoming
Tioga County, 116-118 Main St, Wellsboro, PA 16901 .... (717)724-1906
(Reg & Rcdr has b & d rec 1893 to 1906, m rec from 1885, pro & Ind rec from 1806; Prothonotary has civ ct rec from 1813, div rec)

* **Union**   F4   1813   Northumberland
Union County, 103 S 2nd St, Lewisburg, PA 17837-1996 .... (717)524-4461
(Prothonotary has b rec 1893 to 1905, m rec from 1885, d rec from 1898, div & civ ct rec from 1813; Reg & Rcdr has pro & Ind rec from 1813)

* **Venango**   B5   1800   Allegheny, Lycoming
Venango County, Liberty & 12th Sts, Franklin, PA 16323-1295 .... (814)437-6871
(Clk Cts & Rcdr Deeds has Ind rec from 1806, div & civ ct rec, b & d rec from 1893 to 1905, m rec from 1885, pro rec from 1806)

*† **Warren**   C6   1800   Allegheny, Lycoming
Warren County, 204 4th Ave, Warren, PA 16365-2399 .... (814)723-7550
(Reg and Rcdr has b, d rec from 1893 to 1906, m rec from 1885, pro, Ind rec from 1819; Prothonotary Office has div, civ ct rec)

*† **Washington**   B3   1781   Westmoreland
Washington County, 100 W Beau St, Washington, PA 15301-4432 .... (412)228-6700
(Chief Clk has b & d rec from 1893 to 1906, m rec from 1885, bur, civ ct & Ind rec from 1850, div & pro rec from 1843)

*† **Wayne**   H5   1796   Northampton
Wayne County, 925 Court St, Honesdale, PA 18431-1922 .... (717)253-5970
(Prothonotary has b & d rec from 1893 to 1906, m rec from 1885, div rec from 1900 & civ ct rec from 1798; Co Reg & Rcdr has pro & Ind rec from 1798)

*† **Westmoreland**   C3   1773   Bedford
Westmoreland County, Main St, Greensburg, PA 15601-2405 .... (412)830-3000
(Co Clk has b rec from 1893 to 1905, m rec from 1893 & pro rec from 1800; Prothonotary has div rec; Clk Cts has civ ct rec; Reg Deeds has Ind rec)

* **Wyoming**   G5   1842   Luzerne
Wyoming County, Court House Sq, Tunkhannock, PA 18657-1228 .... (717)836-3200
(Clk Cts has b, d rec from 1893 to 1905, m rec from 1885, div, pro, civ ct, Ind rec from 1842)

Name	Map Index	Date Created	Parent County or Territory From Which Organized
* **York**	F2	1749	Lancaster

York County, 28 E Market St, York, PA 17401-1501 .... (717)771-9675
(Co Clk has b, d rec from 1893 to 1907, m rec from 1885, div, civ ct, lnd rec from 1749)

* At least one county history has been published about this county.
† Inventory of county archives was made by the Historical Records Survey. (See Introduction)

RHODE ISLAND

CAPITAL · PROVIDENCE — STATE 1790 (13th)
State Map on Page M-7

Giovanni da Verrazano was the first proven white to visit Rhode Island. In 1524, he visited Block Island, the site of present-day Newport. The first white settler was the Reverend William Blackstone, who came from Boston to Cumberland in 1634. Two years later, Roger Williams established the first permanent settlement at Providence and bought all the land he settled from the Indians. Banned from the Massachusetts Bay Colony because of his religious and political views, Williams helped other refugees from the colony to settle in Rhode Island. Among these were Anne Hutchinson, John Clarke, and William Coddington, who with Williams, helped to buy the island of Aquidneck and founded Portsmouth. The next year, internal dissension led to the founding of Newport at the other end of the island. In 1642, Samuel Gorton settled Warwick. These four settlements united and sent Roger Williams to England to obtain a charter. The grant he obtained from Parliament in 1644 permitted them to choose their own form of government. In 1647, the four settlements created a government under the name of Providence Plantations. In 1663, King Charles II granted "Rhode Island and Providence Plantations" a new charter which guaranteed religious freedom and democratic government.

Early settlers included Quakers and refugees from Massachusetts. The towns of Bristol, Little Compton, Tiverton, and Warren from Massachusetts became part of Rhode Island in 1747. Newport became a shipping center due to the triangular trade between the West Indies and Africa. Rum was taken to Africa in exchange for slaves. These slaves were taken to the West Indies in exchange for molasses, which was taken to Newport to be made into rum. Border disputes arose between Rhode Island, Massachusetts, and Connecticut. Rhode Island was the first colony to declare independence from England, doing so in May 1776. Newport was occupied for nearly three years by the British during the Revolutionary War. Rhode Island was the last to accept the Constitution, fearful of a strong central government and high taxes.

Slavery was gradually abolished starting in 1784. The decline in trade, agriculture (due to more fertile lands opening in the west), and whaling led to the growth of factories in the state. Thousands of foreign laborers entered the state to fill the new jobs. They were of all nationalities, but especially Italian, English, Irish, Polish, Russian, Swedish, German, and Austrian. In 1843, the Freeman's Constitution was adopted, which entitled anyone born in the United States instead of just land owners to vote. During the Civil War, about 23,000 men served in the Union armed forces. In 1862, Rhode Island gained the town of East Providence and part of the town of Pawtucket from Massachusetts and gave Fall River to Massachusetts.

Town clerks have kept records of births, marriages, and deaths since the 1630's, but they are more complete after 1700. Statewide registration began in January 1853 with general compliance by 1915. These records are at the Rhode Island Department of Health, Division of Vital Statistics, Cannon Building, Room 101, 75 Davis Street, Providence, RI 02908. To verify current fees, call 401-277-2811.

Early divorce records were recorded in the supreme court records. Divorce records before 1962 are at the Providence Archives, Phillips Memorial Library, River Avenue and Eaton Street, Providence, RI 02918. Colonial censuses and lists exist for 1747 to 1754, 1774, and 1782. State censuses were taken at ten-year intervals from 1865 to 1935, but the 1895 census is missing. Originals are at the Rhode Island State Archives, State House, Room 43, Providence, RI 02903. The Rhode Island Historical Society Library, 121 Hope Street, Providence, RI 02903, has one of the largest collections of early records in New England.

Genealogical Archives, Libraries and Societies

East Greenwich Free Library, 82 Pierce St., East Greenwich, RI 02818

John Hay Library, Brown University, Providence, RI 02912
Providence Public Library, 229 Washington St., Providence, RI 02903

Rhode Island Historical Society Library, 121 Hope St., Providence, RI 02903

Rhode Island State Archives, 314 State House, Providence, RI 02900

Rhode Island State Library, 82 Smith, State House, Providence, RI 02903

Westerley Public Library, Box 356, Broad St., Westerly, RI 02891

Newport Historical Society, 82 Touro St., Newport, RI 02840

Rhode Island Genealogical Society, 13 Countryside Drive, Cumberland, RI 02864

Rhode Island Mayflower Descendants, 128 Massasoit, Warwick, RI 02888

Rhode Island Society, Sons of the American Revolution, P. O. Box 137, East Greenwich, RI 02818

Rhode Island State Historical Society, 52 Power St., Providence, RI 02906

Printed Census Records and Mortality Schedules

Federal Census 1790, 1800, 1810, 1820, 1830, 1840, 1850, 1860, 1870, 1880, 1900, 1910
Union Veterans and Widows 1890
State/Territorial Census 1747, 1770, 1774, 1777, 1779, 1782, 1865, 1875, 1885, 1895, 1905, 1915, 1925, 1935

Valuable Printed Sources

Atlases, Maps, and Gazetteers

Beers, Daniel G. *Atlas of the State of Rhode Island and Providence Plantations*. Philadelphia: Daniel G. Beers, 1870.

Gannett, Henry. *A Geographic Dictionary of Connecticut and Rhode Island*. Baltimore: Genealogcial Publishing Co., 1978 reprint.

Wright, Marion I. *Rhode Island Atlas*. Providence, Rhode Island: Rhode Island Publications Society, 1980.

Genealogical Research Guides

Sperry, Kip. *Rhode Island Sources for Family Historians and Genealogists*. Logan, Utah: Everton Publishers, 1986.

Rubincam, Milton. *Genealogical Research: Methods and Sources*. Washington, DC: American Society of Genealogists, 1980.

Genealogical Sources

Arnold, James N. *Vital Records of Rhode Island, 1636-1850*. Providence, Rhode Island: Narragansett Historical Publishing Co., 1911.

Austin, John Osborne. *The Genealogical Dictionary of Rhode Island*. Baltimore: Genealogical Publishing Co., 1978 reprint.

Beaman, Alder G. *Rhode Island Vital Records, New Series*. Princeton, Massachusetts: Alder G. Beaman, 1976.

MacGunnigle, Bruce C. *Rhode Island Freemen, 1747-1755: A Census of Registered Voters*. Baltimore: Genealogical Publishing Co., 1977.

Smith, Joseph C. *Civil and Military List of Rhode Island, 1647-1850*. Providence, Rhode Island, 1901.

Histories

McLoughlin, William G. *Rhode Island: A Bicentennial History*. New York: W. W. Norton & Co., 1978.

Monahan, Clifford P. *Rhode Island: A Students' Guide to Localized History*. New York: Teachers College Press, Columbia University, 1974.

RHODE ISLAND COUNTY DATA
State Map on Page M-7

Name	Map Index	Date Created	Parent County or Territory From Which Organized
* **Bristol**	F6	1747	Newport

    Bristol County, 516 Main St, Warren, RI 02885-4369 . . . . (401)245-7977
    (There is no Co Clk in Bristol Co, the twns of Bristol, Warren & Barrington have b, m, d, bur & pro rec; Providence RI has div rec; 5th Dis Ct Warren has civ ct rec)(four twns in Bristol Co)
    Towns Organized Before 1800: Barrington 1717, Bristol 1681, Warren 1746-7

Name	Map Index	Date Created	Parent County or Territory From Which Organized

* **Kent**　　　　F5　　　1750　　　Providence
Kent County, 222 Quaker Ln, West Warwick, RI 02893-2144 . . . . (401)822-1311
(Twn Clk, E. Greenwich has b, m, d & lnd rec from 1677, bur & pro rec; contact City or Twn Clk in each of 5 twns in Kent Co to get rec)

Towns Organized Before 1800: Coventry 1741, East Greenwich 1677, Warwick 1642-3, West Greenwich 1741

* **Newport**　　F5　　　1703　　　Original county
Newport County, 8 Washington Sq, Newport, RI 02840-7199 . . . . (401)841-8330
(Newport County was incorporated June 22, 1703 as Rhode Island County; June 16, 1729, incorporated as Newport County and included then Newport, Portsmouth, Jamestown and New Shoreham. 1746-47 eastern boundary adjusted under decree of the King of England incorporating Tiverton and Little Compton into County. June 16, 1743, Town of Middletown was taken from the Town of Newport and became part of County. On September 17, 1963, New Shoreham joined Washington County. Land area is 104.9 sq. mi. 5 towns and 1 city in Newport County. City of Newport settled in 1639. Line between Newport and Portsmouth established Sept 14, 1640. Incorporated as a city June 1, 1784. City Charter repealed Mar 27, 1787. City incorporated the second time May 6, 1853 and the Charter accepted May 20, 1853. A new City Charter was drawn up under the provisions of the Home Rule Amendment to the State Constitution providing for Council-Manager form of government approved by the voters Nov 4, 1952 and enacted Nov 1, 1953. City Clk Office, Newport has b rec from 1670, m rec from 1693, d rec from 1697; local cem offices have bur rec; Fam & Sup Cts have div rec; Pro Ct has pro rec from 1784; Dis Ct has civ ct rec; Rcdr Deeds has lnd rec from 1780; Newport His Soc, 82 Touro St, Newport, RI has early ch rec, lnd rec, pro rec, and cen reports of City of Newport 1820, 1840, 1880)

Towns Organized Before 1800: Jamestown 1678, Little Compton 1746-7, Middletown 1743, New Shoreham 1672, Portsmouth 1638, Tiverton 1746-7

* **Providence**　　F5　　　1703　　　Original county
Providence County, 250 Benefit St, Providence, RI 02903-2700 . . . . (401)277-3220
(City Clk of Providence reports as follows: Family Ct has div rec; Pro Judge has pro rec; Municipal Ct has civ ct rec; Rcdr Deeds has lnd rec)(22 twns in Providence Co)

Towns Organized Before 1800: Cranston 1754, Cumberland 1746-7, Foster 1781, Glocester 1730-1, Johnston 1759, North Providence 1765, Providence 1636, Scituate 1730-1, Smithfield 1730-1

* **Washington**　　F5　　　1729　　　Newport (Formerly Naragannset)
Washington County, 4800 Tower Hill Rd, Wakefield, RI 02879-2239 . . . . (401)782-4121
(Town Clk, South Kingston, Town Hall, Wakefield, RI 02879 has b, m, d, pro, lnd rec from 1723, bur rec of Rhode Island incorporated 1723. Twenty towns in Washington Co)

Towns Organized Before 1800: Charlestown 1738, Exeter 1742-3, Hopkinton 1757, North Kingstown 1641, Richmond 1747, South Kingstown (Pettaquamscutt) 1657-8, Westerly 1669

* At least one county history has been published about this county.
† Inventory of county archives was made by the Historical Records Survey. (See Introduction)

SOUTH CAROLINA

CAPITAL - COLUMBIA — STATE 1788 (8th)
State Map on Page M-37

Both the Spanish and French attempted to settle South Carolina from its discovery in 1521 until 1663, but they failed. In 1663, King Charles II granted the territory between the 31st and 36th parallels from ocean to ocean to eight noblemen. The first permanent settlement, called Charles Town, was situated on the Ashley River. It was settled by a group of English people from England and from Barbados. A group of Dutch from New York came after a few months, and were later joined by others direct from Holland. Ten years later, the town was moved to the present site of Charleston. Other early settlers include Quakers in 1675; Huguenots in 1680; dissenters from the Episcopal Church in Somerset in 1683; Irish in 1675; and Scotch Presbyterians in 1684 who settled at Port Royal. In 1729, Carolina was divided into North and South Carolina and in 1732, part of South Carolina became Georgia. In 1730, the colonial government provided incentives for landowners in new townships, so settlers gathered along the banks of the Santee and the Edisto Rivers. From 1732 to 1763, a number of families came from England, Scotland, Ireland, Wales, Switzerland, and Germany into the central section of South Carolina. The "Up Country" or western half of the state, was first settled between 1745 and 1760 by immigrants from the Rhine area of Germany, the Northern American colonies, and the Ulster section of Ireland.

Battles with Spanish, French, Indians, and pirates occupied the settlers prior to the Revolutionary War. A treaty in 1760 ended the Cherokee War and opened up more land for settlement. With the offer of tax-free land for a decade, Scotch-Irish immigrants and settlers from other colonies swelled the western lands. South Carolina entered the Union in 1788 as the eighth state. Overseas immigration dwindled about 1815 and virtually ceased between 1830 and 1840. Political refugees from Germany immigrated to South Carolina in 1848.

South Carolina was the first state to secede from the Union in 1860. The first shots were fired by South Carolina troops on Fort Sumter on April 12, 1861. The state was devastated by General William Tecumseh Sherman during the war. An estimated 63,000 men served in the Confederate forces from South Carolina. Readmission to the Union came in 1868. After the Civil War, agriculture declined and employment shifted to the textile industry.

In 1769, nine judicial districts were established —Charleston, Georgetown, Beaufort, Orangeburg, Ninety-Six, Camden, and Cheraws. Records were kept at Charleston until 1780. In 1790, the capital was moved from Charleston to Columbia, although some functions remained at Charleston until after the Civil War. In 1795, Pinckney and Washington districts were created and three years later the nine districts were divided into twenty-four in the following manner:

Ninety-Six District: Abbeville, Edgefield, Newberry, Laurens, and Spartanburg (all formed in 1795)
Washington District: Pendleton and Greenville
Pinckney District: Union and York
Camden District: Chester, Lancaster, Fairfield, Kershaw, and Sumter
Cheraws District: Chesterfield, Darlington, and Marlborough
Georgetown District: Georgetown and Marion
Charleston District: Charleston and Colleton
Orangeburg District: Orangeburg and Barnwell
Districts were changed to counties in 1868.

Birth and death records from 1915 to the present are in the Office of Vital Records and Public Health Statistics, 2600 Bull Street, Columbia, SC 29201, and from the county clerks. City of Charleston birth records are available since 1877 at the City Health Department. Death records for the city are also available from 1821. Marriage records from July 1, 1950, are at the Office of Vital Records. To verify current fees, call 803-734-4830.

Marriage records from about July 1910, plus some in the early 1800's, are at the office of the Probate Judge in each county. Before statewide registration, the ordinary of the province could issue a marriage license or banns could be published in a church. Some marriage settlements from the 1760's to the 1800's are at the South Carolina Department of Archives and History, 1430 Senate Street, P.O. Box 11669, Capitol Station, Columbia, SC 29211. Divorce was illegal in South Carolina until 1949. Proceedings are kept by the county court, but there are restrictions on availability. Before 1732, the secretary of the province kept probate records. After that, they were kept by the courts of ordinary and probate courts in each county. No colonial censuses remain. State censuses exist for 1829 (Fairfield and Laurens districts) and 1839 (Kershaw District) along with the 1869 population returns and 1875 agricultural and population returns. These are all kept at the South Carolina Department of Archives and History.

Genealogical Archives, Libraries and Societies

Abbeville-Greenwood Regional Library, N. Main St., Greenwood, SC 29646

Calhoun County Museum, Archives Library, 303 Butler Street, St. Matthews, SC 29135

Camden Archives and Museum, 1314 Broad Street, Camden, SC 29020

Free Library, 404 King St., Charleston, SC 29407

Greenville County Library, 300 College St., Greenville, SC 29601

Laurens County Library, 321 S. Harper St., Laurens, SC 29360

Public Library, Rock Hill, SC 29730

Public Library, So. Pine St., Spartanburg, SC 29302

Richland County Public Library, 1400 Sumter St., Columbia, SC 29201

Rock Hill Public Library, Box 32, 325 S. Oakland Ave., Rock Hill, SC 29730

South Carolina Archives Dept., 1430 Senate St., Columbia, SC 29201

South Carolina State Library, 1500 Senate St., Columbia, SC 29201

Bluffton Historical Preservation Society, Inc., P. O. Box 742, Bluffton, SC 29910

Charleston Chapter, South Carolina Genealogical Society, 1300 N. Edgewater, Charleston, SC 29407

Chester County Genealogical Society, P. O. Box 336, Richburg, SC 29729

Columbia Chapter, South Carolina Genealogical Society, P. O. Box 11353, Columbia, SC 29211

Huguenot Society of South Carolina, 21 Queen Street, Charleston, SC 29401

Laurens County "Chapter", 108 Woodvale, Fountain Inn, SC 29644

Lexington County, South Carolina Genealogical Association, P. O. Box 1442, Lexington, SC 29072

Old Darlington District Chapter, South Carolina Genealogical Society, 201 Green St., Hartsville, SC 29550

Orangeburg German-Swiss Genealogical Society, P. O. Box 20266, Charleston, SC 29413

Pee Dee Chapter, South Carolina Genealogical Society, P. O. Box 236, Latta, SC 29565

Pinckney District Chapter, South Carolina Genealogical Society, P. O. Box 5281, Spartanburg, SC 29304

Piedmont Historical Society, P. O. Box 8096, Spartanburg, SC 29305

South Carolina Historical Society, P. O. Box 5401, Spartanburg, SC 29304

South Carolina Society, Sons of the American Revolution, P. O. Box 2413, Spartanburg, SC 29303

University of South Carolina Society, Columbia, SC 29208

Printed Census Records and Mortality Schedules

Federal Census 1790, 1800, 1810, 1820 (except Clarendon County), 1830 (except Clarendon County), 1840 (except Clarendon County), 1850 (except Clarendon County), 1860, 1870, 1880, 1900, 1910
Federal Mortality Schedules 1850, 1860, 1870, 1880
Union Veterans and Widows 1890
Residents 1670, 1775, 1776, 1860
Heads of Families 1781
Loyalists 1783

Valuable Printed Sources

Atlases, Maps, and Gazetteers

Neuffer, Claude Henry. *Names in South Carolina*. Columbia, South Carolina: University of South Carolina, 1954.

Bibliographies

Chandler, Marion C. and Earl W. Wade. *The South Carolina Archives: A Temporary Summary Guide*. Columbia, South Carolina: South Carolina Department of Archives and History, 1976.

Cote, Richard. *South Carolina Family and Local History: A Bibliography*. Easley, South Carolina: Southern Historical Press, 1981.

Moore, John Hammond. *Research Material in South Carolina: A Guide*. Columbia, South Carolina: University of South Carolina Press, 1967.

———. *South Carolina Newspapers*. Columbia, South Carolina: University of South Carolina Press, 1988.

Genealogical Research Guides

Frazier, Evelyn McDaniel. *Hunting Your Ancestors in South Carolina*. Jacksonville, Florida: Florentine Press, 1977.

Holcomb, Brent H. *A Guide to South Carolina Genealogical Research and Records*. Oxford, Massachusetts: Brent H. Holcomb, 1986.

McCay, Betty L. *State Outline for South Carolina Sources*. Indianapolis: Betty L. McCay, 1970.

Schweitzer, George K. *South Carolina Genealogical Research*. Knoxville, Tennessee: George K. Schweitzer, 1985.

Genealogical Sources

Holcomb, Brent H. *South Carolina Marriages, 1688-1799*. Baltimore: Genealogical Publishing Co., 1980.

———. *South Carolina Naturalizations, 1783-1850*. Baltimore: Genealogical Publishing Co., 1985.

Houston, Martha Lou. *Indexes to the County Wills of South Carolina*. Baltimore: Genealogical Publishing Co., 1964.

Moore, Carolina T. and Agatha Aimar. *Abstracts of the Wills of the State of South Carolina, 1670-1740*. Columbia, South Carolina: R. L. Bryan Co., 1960.

Revill, Janie. *A Compilation of the Original Lists of Protestant Immigrants to South Carolina, 1763-1773*. Baltimore: Genealogical Publishing Co., 1974 reprint.

Salley, A. S. Jr. *Marriage Notices in the South Carolina Gazette and Its Successors, 1732-1801*. Baltimore: Genealogical Publishing Co., 1965.

Stephenson, Jean. *Scotch-Irish Migration to South Carolina, 1772*. Strasburg, Virginia: Shenandoah Publishing House, 1971.

Histories

McCrady, Edward. *The History of South Carolina*. New York: Paladin Press, 1969.

Ramsey, David. *History of South Carolina*. Newberry, South Carolina: W. J. Duffie, 1858.

SOUTH CAROLINA COUNTY DATA
State Map on Page M-37

Name	Map Index	Date Created	Parent County or Territory From Which Organized
† **Abbeville**	G4	1785	District 96

Abbeville County, PO Box 99, Abbeville, SC 29620-0099 .... (803)459-5074
(Clk Ct has Ind rec from 1873, div & civ ct rec)

Name	Map Index	Date Created	Parent County or Territory From Which Organized

*† Aiken F5 1871 Edgefield, Orangeburg, Barnwell, Lexington
Aiken County, 828 Richland Ave W, Aiken, SC 29801-3834 . . . . (803)642-2013
(Co Health has b & d rec; Pro Judge has m rec from 1911 & pro rec from 1875; Clk Ct has div, civ ct & lnd rec)

† Allendale E6 1919 Barnwell, Hampton
Allendale County, PO Box 126, Allendale, SC 29810-0126 . . . . (803)584-2737
[FHL has some cem rec]

*† Anderson G3 1826 Pendleton District
Anderson County, PO Box 1656, Anderson, SC 29622-1656 . . . . (803)260-4053
(Co Health Dept has b, d, bur rec; Pro Judge has m, pro rec; Clk Ct has div rec from 1949, lnd rec from 1788, civ ct rec)

Bamberg E6 1897 Barnwell
Bamberg County, PO Box 150, Bamberg, SC 29003-0150 . . . . (803)245-3025
(Clk Ct has div & civ ct rec; Pro Judge has pro & m rec; Co Health has b & d rec)

* Barnwell E6 1798 Orangeburg District
Barnwell County, PO Box 723, Barnwell, SC 29812-0723 . . . . (803)259-3485
(Co Clk has civ ct, lnd rec from mid-1700s, div, chancery & equity rec; Pro Judge has m & pro rec)

* Beaufort D7 1769 Original District
Beaufort County, PO Box 1128, Beaufort, SC 29901-1228 . . . . (803)525-7307
(Co Clk has b & d rec from 1915)

* Berkeley C6 1882 Charleston
Berkeley County, 223 N Live Oak Dr, Moncks Corner, SC 29461-3707 . . . . (803)761-8210
(Clk Ct has div & civ ct rec; Pro Judge has m & pro rec; Co Health Dept has b, d & bur rec)

Berkeley   1683 (Discontinued) (Original Co not present Berkeley Co.)

* Calhoun D5 1908 Lexington, Orangeburg
Calhoun County, 302 S Railroad Ave, Saint Matthews, SC 29135-1452 . . . . (803)874-3524
(Co Health has b & d rec from 1915; Pro Judge has m rec from 1911, pro rec from 1908; Clk Ct has civ ct rec from 1908, div rec from 1949; Hist Commission has lnd, Bible, cem & gen col from 1735)

Camden District   Original District (Discontinued)

Carteret District (Name changed to Granville 1700)

* Charleston C6 1769 Original District
Charleston County, PO Box 70219, North Charleston, SC 29415 . . . . (803)723-6724
(Co Health has b & d rec; Pro Judge has m, pro & civ ct rec; Clk Ct has div rec; Co Reg has lnd rec)

Cheraws District   1769 Original District (Discontinued)

*† Cherokee F2 1897 Union, York, Spartanburg
Cherokee County, PO Box 866, Gaffney, SC 29342-0866 . . . . (803)487-2562
(Co Health has b & d rec; Pro Judge has m & pro rec; Clk Ct has div, civ ct & lnd rec)

* Chester E3 1785 Craven, Camden District
Chester County, Main St, Chester, SC 29706 . . . . (803)385-2605
(Pro Judge has pro rec from 1789, m rec from 1911; Clk Ct has deeds from 1785, div & civ ct rec)

* Chesterfield C3 1798 Cheraws District
Chesterfield County, 200 W Main St, Chesterfield, SC 29709-1527 . . . . (803)623-2574
(Clk Ct has b, d, bur, div, pro & civ ct rec; Pro Judge has m rec)

Claremont (See Sumter)

Clarendon D5 1855 Sumter District
Clarendon County, PO Box E, Manning, SC 29102-0136 . . . . (803)435-4444
(Cen schedules missing for 1820, 1830, 1840 & 1850) (Co Health has b, d & bur rec from 1915; Pro Judge has m rec from 1911 & pro rec from 1856; Clk Ct has div rec from 1947, civ ct & lnd rec from 1856)

* Colleton D7 1798 Charleston District
Colleton County, PO Box 620, Walterboro, SC 29488-0620 . . . . (803)549-5791
(Pro Judge has m & pro rec; Clk Ct has div rec, also civ ct & lnd rec from 1864)

Colleton, Old (Discontinued)

Craven, Old (Discontinued)

* Darlington C4 1798 Cheraws District
Darlington County, Courthouse Public Sq, Darlington, SC 29532 . . . . (803)393-3836
(Co Clk has m rec from 1912, div rec from 1950, civ ct rec, lnd rec from 1806)

*† Dillon B3 1910 Marion
Dillon County, PO Box 449, Dillon, SC 29536-0449 . . . . (803)774-1400
(Clk Cts has civ ct rec, deeds, real estate & mtgs from 1910)

* Dorchester D6 1897 Berkeley, Colleton
Dorchester County, PO Box 613, Saint George, SC 29477 . . . . (803)563-2331
(Co Clk has b rec from 1915)

* Edgefield F5 1785 District 96
Edgefield County, PO Box 663, Edgefield, SC 29824-0663 . . . . (803)637-5781
(Co Health has b, d & bur rec; Pro Judge has m & pro rec; Co Clk has lnd, civ ct rec from 1939, div rec from 1942; judgements & crim rec from 1839 & plat rec from 1907; small portion of Aiken Co added to Edgefield 1966)

Name	Map Index	Date Created	Parent County or Territory From Which Organized
* **Fairfield**	E3	1798	Camden District

Fairfield County, 115 S Congress St Drawer 60, Winnsboro, SC   29180-0060 . . . . (803)635-1415
(Co Health has b & d rec; Pro Judge has m & pro rec; Clk Ct has div rec from 1947, civ ct & Ind rec from 1795)

*† **Florence**   C4   1888   Marion, Darlington, Clarendon, Williamsburg
Florence County, 180 N Irby St, Florence, SC   29501-3456 . . . . (803)665-3031
(Co Health has b & d rec; Pro Judge has m & pro rec; Clk Ct has div, civ ct & Ind rec)

* **Georgetown**   B5   1769   Original District
Georgetown County, 715 Prince St, Georgetown, SC   29440-3631 . . . . (803)546-5011
(Co Health Dept has b, d rec; Pro Judge has m rec from 1911, pro rec; Clk Ct has div rec from 1949, civ ct rec, Ind rec from 1866)

Granville District (See Carteret)

* **Greenville**   G2   1798   Washington District
Greenville County, 301 University Ridge Suite 100, Greenville, SC   29601-3665 . . . . (803)240-7105
(Clk Ct has b & d rec from 1915, m rec from 1911, div & pro rec)

* **Greenwood**   F4   1897   Abbeville, Edgefield
Greenwood County, 528 Monument St, Greenwood, SC   29646 . . . . (803)229-6622
(Co Health has b & d rec; Pro Judge has m & pro rec; Clk Ct has div rec from 1937; civ ct & Ind rec from 1897)

* **Hampton**   E7   1878   Beaufort
Hampton County, PO Box 7, Hampton, SC   29924-0007 . . . . (803)943-3668
(Co Health Dept has b, d rec; Clk Ct has civ ct, Ind rec; Pro Judge has m, pro rec)

Horry   B4   1802   Georgetown Dist
Horry County, PO Box 677, Conway, SC   29526-0677 . . . . (803)248-1200
(Co Health has b, d bur rec; Clk Ct has div rec from 1947, civ ct rec; Pro Judge has m & pro rec)

*† **Jasper**   E7   1912   Beaufort, Hampton
Jasper County, PO Box 248, Ridgeland, SC   29936-0248 . . . . (803)726-8832
(Co Health has b & d rec; Pro Judge has m & pro rec; Clk Ct has div, civ ct & Ind rec)

* **Kershaw**   D3   1798   Camden District
Kershaw County, 1121 Broad St, Camden, SC   29020-3638 . . . . (803)425-1527
(Clk Ct has div rec from 1949, civ ct & Ind rec from 1791)

* **Lancaster**   D3   1798   Camden District
Lancaster County, PO Box 1809, Lancaster, SC   29720-1411 . . . . (803)285-1581
(Co Health has b & d rec; Pro Judge has m & pro rec; Clk Ct has div rec from 1958, civ ct rec from 1800 & Ind rec from 1762)

* **Laurens**   F3   1785   District 96
Laurens County, PO Box 445, Laurens, SC   29360-0445 . . . . (803)984-5124
(Co Health has b & d rec; Pro Judge has m & pro rec; Clk Ct has div rec also civ ct rec from 1900 & Ind rec from 1790)

*† **Lee**   D4   1902   Darlington, Sumter, Kershaw
Lee County, PO Box 309, Bishopville, SC   29010 . . . . (803)484-5341
(Co Health has b rec from 1915, d rec from 1902, div & bur rec; Pro Judge has m & pro rec from 1902; Clk Ct has civ ct & Ind rec from 1902)

* **Lexington**   E4   1804   Orangeburg District
Lexington County, 139 E Main St, Lexington, SC   29072-3456 . . . . (803)359-8212
(Co Health has b & d rec; Pro Judge has m & pro rec; Clk Ct has div rec from 1949, Ind rec from 1839 & civ ct rec)

Liberty (Changed to Marion District)

* **Marion**   B4   1798   Georgetown District
Marion County, PO Box 183, Marion, SC   29571-0183 . . . . (803)423-3904
(Co Health has b, d & bur rec; Pro Judge has m & pro rec; Clk Ct has div rec from 1948, civ ct & Ind rec from 1800)

* **Marlboro**   C3   1798   Cheraws District
Marlboro County, PO Box 996, Bennetsville, SC   29512-0996 . . . . (803)479-5613
(Co Clk has b, d, bur, div & civ ct rec; Pro Judge has m & pro rec)

† **McCormick**   G4   1916   Greenwood, Abbeville
McCormick County, PO Box 86, McCormick, SC   29835-0086 . . . . (803)465-2195
(Co Health Dept has b rec from 1912, d rec from 1916; Pro Judge has m, pro rec from 1916; Clk Ct has div, civ ct, Ind rec from 1916; Co Treas has tax rec from 1916)

* **Newberry**   F3   1785   District 96
Newberry County, PO Box 278, Newberry, SC   29108-0278 . . . . (803)321-2110
(Clk Ct has b & d rec from 1915, m rec from 1911, div rec from 1949, pro, civ ct & Ind rec from 1776)

Ninety-Six District   1769   Original District (discontinued)

*† **Oconee**   H2   1868   Pickens
Oconee County, W Main St, Walhalla, SC   29691 . . . . (803)638-4280
(Co Health Dept has b, d rec from 1915; Pro Judge has m rec from 1911, pro rec from 1868; Clk Ct has div rec from 1949, civ ct, Ind rec from 1868)

Orange (Former county in Orangeburg District abt 1800, mostly in present-day Orangeburg County, with parts in present-day counties of Bamberg, Calhoun and Lexington)

* **Orangeburg**   D5   1769   Original District
Orangeburg County, 190 Sunnyside St NE, Orangeburg, SC   29115-5463 . . . . (803)533-1000
(Clk Ct has div rec from 1949, civ ct & Ind rec from 1865; Co Hlth has b, d, bur rec; Pro Judge has m, pro rec)

Name	Map Index	Date Created	Parent County or Territory From Which Organized

Pendleton   1798   Washington District (discontinued 1826)
(See Pickens & Anderson)

*† **Pickens**   G2   1825   Pendleton District
Pickens County, PO Box 215, Pickens, SC   29671-0215 . . . . (803)878-7809
(Clk Ct has b & d rec from 1915, div rec from 1949, civ ct rec from 1868; Pro Judge has m & pro rec)

Pickney District   1793   Original District (discontinued)

*† **Richland**   D4   1799   Kershaw District
Richland County, 1701 Main St, Columbia, SC   29201-2833 . . . . (803)748-4684
(Cen schedules missing for 1800; Pro Judge has m, pro & civ ct rec; Co Aud has lnd rec)

Salem (Former county in Sumter District abt 1800, part of Sumter County abt 1810. Parts lay in the present-day counties of Lee, Sumter, Clarendon and Florence.)

† **Saluda**   F4   1896   Edgefield
Saluda County, 101 S 9th St, Saluda, SC   29138 . . . . (803)445-3303
(Clk Ct has div, civ ct & lnd rec)

* **Spartanburg**   F2   1785   District 96
Spartanburg County, 180 Magnolia St, Spartanburg, SC   29301-2392 . . . . (803)596-2500
(Co Health Dept has b, d rec; Pro Judge has m rec from 1911, pro rec from 1700; Clk Ct has div rec, civ ct rec from 1785; RMC Office has lnd rec)

* **Sumter**   D4   1798   Camden District
Sumter County, 141 N Main St, Sumter, SC   29150-4965 . . . . (803)773-1581
(Co Health Dept has b, d rec; Pro Judge has m rec from 1910, pro rec from 1900; Clk Ct has div, civ ct lnd rec)

* **Union**   F3   1798   District 96
Union County, PO Box G, Union, SC   29379-0200 . . . . (803)429-1630
(Clk Ct has civ ct rec from 1785)

Washington   1793   Original District (discontinued)

* **Williamsburg**   C5   1802   Georgetown District
Williamsburg County, 125 W Main St, Kingstree, SC   29556-3347 . . . . (803)354-6855
(Clk Ct has div rec from 1948, civ ct, lnd & plat rec from 1806; Pro Judge has m rec from 1911, also pro rec)

Winyaw (Formerly a county in Georgetown District, later became Georgetown County)

York   E2   1785   Camden & Pickney District
York County, 2 Congress St, York, SC   29745 . . . . (803)684-8532
(Co Health has b rec from 1915, d & bur rec; Pro Judge has m & pro rec; Clk Ct has div rec from 1942, civ ct & lnd rec form 1786)

* At least one county history has been published about this county.
† Inventory of county archives was made by the Historical Records Survey. (See Introduction)

SOUTH DAKOTA

CAPITAL · PIERRE — TERRITORY 1861 — STATE 1889 (40th)
State Map on Page M-38

French explorers entered South Dakota in 1742, but French interest waned after the French and Indian War. The United States gained the region with the Louisiana Purchase in 1803. Lewis and Clark made their exploration of the area between 1804 and 1806. Only hardy fur traders ventured into the area before 1858. In that year, the Yankton Sioux Indians ceded their claim to southeastern Dakota to the United States. Settlements sprang up at Yankton, Vermillion, and other sites between the Big Sioux and Missouri rivers. In 1861, the Dakotas were made into their own territory, after years in the Missouri, Minnesota, Iowa, Wisconsin, Michigan and Nebraska territories. The Dakota Territory covered all of North and South Dakota, Montana, and northern Wyoming. Montana was taken away in 1864, Wyoming in 1868, and the territory divided into North and South Dakota in 1867.

About 200 men from the Dakota Territory served with the Union during the Civil War. Discovery of gold in the Black Hills in 1875 led to an upswing in settlement. Railroads came into the area between 1878 and 1888 and stimulated the Dakota land boom. South Dakota entered the Union in 1889 and all but three of its 68 counties were formed. Railroads reached the western part of the state during the first decade of the 20th century, bringing thousands of homesteaders to the area. The predominating nationalities in South Dakota are Norwegian, German, Russian, Swedish, Danish, Czech, English, Austrian, Irish, Finnish, Polish, Greek, and Italian.

Records before 1905 exist for some counties in the office of the Registrar of Deeds. Records of births, marriages, divorces, and deaths from 1905 are in the State Department of Health, Health Statistics Program, 523 East Capitol, Pierre, SD 57501. To verify current fees, call 605-773-3355.

Wills and probate matters are kept by the district court clerks. Probate records prior to statehood were kept by the Territorial Probate Court and are available from the Archives Division of the South Dakota State Historical Society, 800 Governors Drive, Pierre, SD 57501. South Dakota was included in the 1836 Wisconsin, 1840 Iowa, 1850 Minnesota (Pembina District), and 1860 to 1880 Dakota territorial censuses. Indexes have been published for some of these censuses. State and territorial censuses for 1885, 1895, 1905, 1915, 1925, 1935, and 1945 are available at the State Historical Society.

Genealogical Archives, Libraries and Societies

Alexander Mitchell Public Library, 519 S. Kline St., Aberdeen, SD 57401

State Historical Society Library, Memorial Bldg., Pierre, SD 57501

University of South Dakota Library, Vermillion, SD 57069

Aberdeen Area Genealogical Society, Box 493, Aberdeen, SD 57402-0493

Brookings Area Genealogical Society, 524 Fourth Street, Brookings, SD 57006

Family Tree Society, Winner, SD 57528

Lake County Genealogical Society, Karl Mundt Library, Dakota State College, Madison, SD 57042

Lyman-Brule Genealogical Society, Box 555, Chamberlain, SD 57325

Mitchell Area Genealogical Society, 1004 W. Birch St., Mitchell, SD 57301

Pierre-Ft. Pierre Genealogical Society, P. O. Box 925, Pierre, SD 57501

Rapid City Society For Genealogical Research, P. O. Box 1495, Rapid City, SD 57701

Sioux Valley Genealogical Society, P. O. Box 655, Sioux Falls, SD 57101

South Dakota Genealogical Society, Box 490, Winner, SD 57580

Tri-State Genealogical Society, 905 5th St., Belle Fourche, SD 57717

Printed Census Records and Mortality Schedules

Federal Census 1860, 1870, 1880, 1890 (part of Union County only), 1900, 1910
Union Veterans and Widows 1890
State/Territorial Census 1836, 1885, 1895, 1905, 1915, 1925, 1935, 1945

Valuable Printed Sources

Atlases, Maps, and Gazetteers

Historic Sites Committee. *Clay County Place Names*. Vermillion, South Dakota: Clay County Historical Society, 1976.

Bibliographies

Directory of Special Libraries and Information Centers: Colorado, South Dakota, Utah, Wyoming. Denver: Rocky Mountain Chapter, Special Libraries Association, 1987.

Histories

Kingsbury, George W. *History of Dakota Territory*. Chicago: S. J. Clarke, 1915.

Schell, Herbert S. *History of South Dakota*. Lincoln, Nebraska: University of Nebraska Press, 1968.

SOUTH DAKOTA COUNTY DATA
State Map on Page M-38

Name	Map Index	Date Created	Parent County or Territory From Which Organized
Armstrong (See Dewey and Ziebach)			
Aurora	G3	1879	Brule

Aurora County, PO Box 366, Plankinton, SD 57368-0366 .... (605)942-7165
(Clk Cts has b & d rec from 1905, m rec from 1883, bur, div, pro & civ ct rec from 1879)

| * **Beadle** | G4 | 1879 | Spink, Clark |

Beadle County, 450 3rd St SW, Huron, SD 57350-1814 .... (605)353-7165
(Clk Cts has div rec from 1884, pro & civ ct rec from 1893, Ind rec; Reg Deeds has b, m, d, bur rec)

| *† **Bennett** | D2 | 1909 | Indian Lands |

Bennett County, PO Box 281, Martin, SD 57551-0281 .... (605)685-6969
(attached to Fall River Co until 1911)(Reg Deeds has Ind rec from 1907, m rec from 1912, b & d rec from 1913, bur rec from 1943; Clk Cts has div, pro, civ ct rec)

| **Bon Homme** | G2 | 1862 | Charles Mix |

Bon Homme County, PO Box 6, Tyndall, SD 57066-0006 .... (605)589-3382
(Clk Cts has b rec from 1905, m rec from 1887, d rec from 1909, bur rec from 1935, pro rec from 1900, civ ct rec from 1878 & div rec)

Name	Map Index	Date Created	Parent County or Territory From Which Organized

Boreman (See Corson)

* **Brookings**   H4   1862   Unorg. Terr
Brookings County, 314 6th Ave, Brookings, SD 57006-2041 .... (605)688-4208
(Clk Cts has b, m, d, bur, div, pro & civ ct rec; Reg Deeds has Ind rec)

* **Brown**   G5   1879   Beadle
Brown County, 101 1st Ave SE, Aberdeen, SD 57401-4203 .... (605)622-2451
(Clk Cts has b, m, d, bur, div, pro & civ ct rec; Reg Deeds has Ind rec)

* **Brule**   F3   1875   Old Buffalo (discontinued)
Brule County, 300 S Courtland St, Chamberlain, SD 57325-1599 .... (605)734-5443
(Reg of Deeds has b, d rec from 1905, bur rec from 1941, Ind rec from 1880; Treasurer has m rec from 1882; Co Clk has div rec from 1885, pro rec from 1880, civ ct rec from 1882, naturalization, citizenship rec from 1880)

*† **Buffalo**   F3   1873   Territorial County
Buffalo County, PO Box 148, Gann Valley, SD 57341-0148 .... (605)293-3234
(Reg Deeds has b, d rec from 1905, bur rec from 1941, Ind rec; Treasurer has m rec from 1887; Co Clk has div rec from 1915, pro, civ ct rec from 1885)

Buffalo, Old (See Brule)

Butte   B4   1883   Harding
Butte County, 839 5th Ave, Belle Fourche, SD 57717-1799 .... (605)892-4485
(Reg Deeds has b, d rec from 1905, bur rec from 1930, Ind rec; Treasurer has m rec from 1890; Clk of Ct has div rec from 1890, pro rec from 1884, civ ct rec from 1892)

Campbell   E6   1873   Buffalo
Campbell County, PO Box 37, Mound City, SD 57646 .... (605)955-3366
(Reg of Deeds has b, d rec from 1905, Ind rec; Treasurer has m rec from 1888; Clk of Ct has div, civ ct rec from 1885, pro rec from 1890; Co Auditor has school rec)

* **Charles Mix**   G2   1862   Original District
Charles Mix County, PO Box 640, Lake Andes, SD 57356-0640 .... (605)487-7131
(Clk Cts has b, m & d rec from 1905, bur rec, div, pro & civ ct rec from 1890)

*† **Clark**   H4   1873   Hanson
Clark County, PO Box 294, Clark, SD 57225 .... (605)532-5851
(Reg Deeds has m rec from 1884, b & d rec from 1905, bur rec from 1941, mil dis rec from 1919, Ind rec; Clk Cts has div pro, civ ct rec)

* **Clay**   H2   1862   Unorg. Terr
Clay County, 211 W Main St, Vermillion, SD 57069-2097 .... (605)624-2281
(Reg Deeds has b, d rec from 1905, m rec from 1880, Ind rec from 1863, bur rec from 1962; Clk Ct has pro rec from 1875, civ ct rec from 1866, div rec from 1889)

* **Codington**   H5   1877   Indian Lands
Codington County, 14 1st Ave Se, Watertown, SD 57201-3611 .... (605)886-8497
(Clk Cts has b, d, bur & div rec from 1905, m rec from 1900, pro rec from 1893 & civ ct rec from 1883)

Cole (See Union)

Corson   D6   1909   Boreman, Dewey
Corson County, PO Box 175, McIntosh, SD 57641-0175 .... (605)273-4201
(Reg Deeds has b, d, Ind rec from 1909; Treasurer has m rec; Clk Ct has div, pro, civ ct rec)

* **Custer**   B3   1875   Indian Lands
Custer County, 420 Mt Rushmore Rd, Custer, SD 57730-1998 .... (605)673-4816
(Clk Cts has b & d rec from 1905, m rec from 1887, div, pro & civ ct rec from 1890)

Davison   G3   1873   Hanson
Davison County, 200 E 4th Ave, Mitchell, SD 57301-2692 .... (605)996-7727
(Reg Deeds has b & d rec from 1905, m, bur, Ind rec; Clk Ct has div, pro, civ ct rec from 1880)

* **Day**   H5   1879   Clark
Day County, 710 W 1st St, Webster, SD 57274-1391 .... (605)345-3771
(Reg Deeds has b, d rec from 1905, Ind rec from 1879 bur rec from 1930; Treasurer has m rec from 1880; Clk Ct has div, civ ct rec from 1885, pro rec from 1898)

Deuel   I4   1862   Brookings
Deuel County, PO Box 125, Clear Lake, SD 57226 .... (605)874-2120
(Reg Deeds has b rec from 1876, d rec from 1905, bur rec from 1941; Treasurer has m rec from 1887; Clk Ct has div, pro rec from 1889, civ ct rec from 1880. Deuel County has 1860-70 federal cen)

* **Dewey**   E5   1910   Indian Reservation, Armstrong (see Rusk)
Dewey County, County Courthouse, Timber Lake, SD 57656 .... (605)865-3672
(Reg Deeds has b, m, d, Ind rec from 1910, bur rec from 1941; Clk ct has pro, civ ct, div rec from 1910)

* **Douglas**   G2   1873   Charles Mix
Douglas County, PO Box 36, Armour, SD 57313 .... (605)724-2585
(Reg Deeds has b & d rec from 1905, Ind rec; Treasurer has m rec from 1884; Clk Cts has civ ct rec from 1884, div & pro rec from 1887)

Edmunds   F5   1873   Buffalo
Edmunds County, 2nd St, Ipswich, SD 57451 .... (605)426-6671
(Reg Deeds has b rec from 1905, d rec from 1887, Ind rec from 1883, bur rec from 1941, m rec from 1887; Clk Ct has div rec from 1887, civ ct, pro rec from 1884)

Name	Map Index	Date Created	Parent County or Territory From Which Organized

* **Fall River**   B2   1883   Custer
Fall River County, 906 N River St, Hot Springs, SD 57747-1387 .... (605)745-5132
(Reg Deeds has Ind rec from 1883, b & d rec from 1905, m rec; Clk Cts has div, pro, civ ct rec from 1890)

*† **Faulk**   F5   1873   Buffalo
Faulk County, PO Box 309, Faulkton, SD 57438-0309 .... (605)598-6224
(Reg Deeds has b rec from 1888, d rec from 1900, Ind rec from 1888, bur rec from 1900; Treasurer has m rec from 1888; Clk Ct has div, civ ct rec from 1900, pro rec from 1888)

* **Grant**   I5   1873   Codington, Deuel
Grant County, 210 E 5th Ave, Milbank, SD 57252-2433 .... (605)432-6711
(Clk Cts has b & d rec from 1905, m rec from 1890, div, pro, civ ct rec from 1897, newspapers from 1880; Reg Deeds has Ind rec)

* **Gregory**   F2   1862   Yankton
Gregory County, PO Box 430, Burke, SD 57523-0430 .... (605)775-2665
(Reg Deeds has m rec from 1898, b, d, Ind, mil dis rec from 1905, bur rec from 1941; Clk Ct has div, pro, civ ct rec from 1899)

*† **Haakon**   D4   1914   Stanley
Haakon County, PO Box 70, Philip, SD 57567-0070 .... (605)859-2627
(Clk Cts has b, m, d, bur, div, pro, civ ct, mental ill, guardian & adoption rec from 1915)

* **Hamlin**   H4   1873   Deuel
Hamlin County, PO Box 256, Hayti, SD 57241-0256 .... (605)783-3751
(Reg Deeds has b, d, bur rec from 1905, Ind rec, m rec from 1879; Clk Ct has div, civ ct rec from 1885, pro rec from 1890, naturalization rec from 1880; school cen from 1903, school rec from 1890)

Hand   F4   1873   Buffalo
Hand County, 415 W 1st Ave, Miller, SD 57362-1346 .... (605)853-3337
(Reg Deeds has b, d rec from 1905, bur, Ind rec; Treasurer has m rec from 1883; Clk Ct has div rec from late 1800s, pro rec from 1880s, civ ct rec from 1889)

Hanson   H3   1871   Buffalo, Deuel
Hanson County, PO Box 127, Alexandria, SD 57311-0127 .... (605)239-4446
(Clk Cts has b, m, d, bur, div, pro & civ ct rec from 1905)

* **Harding**   B5   1909   Unorg. Terr
Harding County, 901 Ramsland St, Buffalo, SD 57720 .... (605)375-3351
(Reg Deeds has b, d, bur, Ind rec from 1909; Treasurer has m rec from 1909; Clk Ct has div, pro, civ ct, school cen rec from 1909)

* **Hughes**   E4   1874   Buffalo
Hughes County, 104 E Capitol Ave, Pierre, SD 57501-2563 .... (605)773-3713
(Clk Cts has div & civ ct rec from 1880, pro rec from 1890; Reg Deeds has b, m, d, bur, Ind rec)

* **Hutchinson**   G2   1862   Unorg. Terr
Hutchinson County, PO Box 7, Olivet, SD 57052-0007 .... (605)387-5335
(Reg Deeds has Ind rec from 1876, m rec from 1887, b & d rec from 1905, bur rec from 1914; Clk Cts has div & civ ct rec from 1883, pro rec from 1899; Co Auditor has school rec from 1924)

* **Hyde**   F4   1873   Buffalo
Hyde County, PO Box 306, Highmore, SD 57345-0306 .... (605)852-2512
(Clk Cts has b & d rec from 1905, m rec from 1887, bur rec from 1936, div & civ ct rec from 1884 & pro rec from 1892)

*† **Jackson**   D3   1915   Stanley
Jackson County, 1 Main St, Kadoka, SD 57543 .... (605)837-2121
(Reg Deeds has b, m, d, bur, div pro, civ ct, Ind rec)

* **Jerauld**   G3   1883   Aurora
Jerauld County, PO Box 435, Wessington Springs, SD 57382-0435 .... (605)539-1202
(Reg Deeds has b, d, bur rec from 1905, m rec from 1890, Ind rec; Clk Cts has pro rec from 1890, cir ct rec from 1889, civ ct rec from 1895, div rec from 1900; Auditor's Office has school censuses)

* **Jones**   E3   1917   Lyman
Jones County, PO Box 448, Murdo, SD 57559-0448 .... (605)669-2361
(Reg Deeds has b, d, Ind rec, m rec; Clk Ct has div, pro, civ ct rec from 1917)

Kingsbury   H4   1873   Hanson
Kingsbury County, 101 2nd St SE, De Smet, SD 57231 .... (605)854-3811
(Clk Cts has b, d & bur rec from 1905, m rec from 1890, div & civ ct rec from 1920, pro rec & naturalization rec)

Lake   H3   1873   Brookings, Hanson
Lake County, 200 E Center County Courthouse, Madison, SD 57042 .... (605)256-5644
(Clk Cts has b & d rec from 1905, m rec from 1874, bur rec from 1941, div & civ ct rec from 1881 & pro rec from 1884)

* **Lawrence**   B4   1875   Unorg. Terr
Lawrence County, , Deadwood, SD 57732 .... (605)578-1941
(Reg Deeds has b rec from 1905, d rec from 1906; Treasurer has m rec from 1887; Clk Ct has div, pro, civ ct rec, real estate rec from 1895; City Auditor has bur rec)

* **Lincoln**   H2   1862   Minnehaha
Lincoln County, 100 E 5th St, Carton, SD 57013-1732 .... (605)987-2581
(Reg Deeds has b, d rec from 1905, bur rec; Treasurer has m rec from 1890; Clk Ct has pro rec from 1890, civ ct, div rec from 1872)

Lugenbeel (See Washabaugh)

Name	Map Index	Date Created	Parent County or Territory From Which Organized

* **Lyman**   F3   1873   Unorg. Terr
Lyman County, County Courthouse, Kennebec, SD 57544 .... (605)869-2247
(Reg Deeds has b rec from 1905, d rec from 1920, bur, Ind rec; Treasurer has m rec from 1905; Clk Ct has div, pro, civ ct rec from 1880)

* **Marshall**   H6   1885   Day
Marshall County, County Courthouse, Britton, SD 57430 .... (605)448-5213
(Reg Deeds has b, d rec from 1905, bur rec, m rec from 1887; Clk Ct has div rec from 1888, pro rec from 1889, civ ct rec)

* **McCook**   H3   1873   Hanson
McCook County, 130 W Essex Ave, Salem, SD 57058-8901 .... (605)425-2781
(Reg Deeds has m rec from 1882, bur rec from 1895, b & d rec from 1905, Ind rec; Clk Cts has civ ct & nat rec from 1880, pro rec from 1881, some school censuses from 1900)

* **McPherson**   F6   1873   Buffalo
McPherson County, County Courthouse, Leola, SD 57456 .... (605)439-3316
(Reg Deeds has b, d rec from 1905, bur rec from 1941, Ind rec; Treasuer has m rec from 1887; Clk Ct has pro from 1893, civ ct rec from 1889, nat rec from 1884, div rec)

* **Meade**   C4   1889   Lawrence
Meade County, PO Box 939, Sturgis, SD 57785-0939 .... (605)347-4411
[FHL has some m & cem rec]

*† **Mellette**   E2   1909   Lyman
Mellette County, S 1st St, White River, SD 57579 .... (605)259-3230
(Reg Deeds has b, d rec from 1912, bur rec from 1913, Ind rec; Treasurer has m rec from 1912; Clk Ct has div, pro, civ ct rec from 1911)

*† **Miner**   H3   1873   Hanson
Miner County, N Main St, Howard, SD 57349 .... (605)772-4612
(Reg Deeds has b, d rec from 1905, bur rec, Ind rec, m rec from 1886; Clk Ct has pro, civ ct rec from 1886, div rec)

* **Minnehaha**   I3   1862   Territorial County
Minnehaha County, 415 N Dakota Ave, Sioux Falls, SD 57102-0136 .... (605)339-6418
(Clk Cts has div, pro & civ ct rec from 1876; Reg Deeds has m rec from 1876, b & d rec from 1905, Ind rec)

* **Moody**   I3   1873   Brookings, Minnehaha
Moody County, 101 E Pipestone Ave, Flandreau, SD 57028-1730 .... (605)997-3181
(Reg Deeds has b, d rec from 1905, bur rec; Treasurer has m rec from 1873; Clk Ct has pro rec from 1890, civ ct rec from 1905, div rec, newspapers since 1880s)

* **Pennington**   B3   1875   Unorg. Terr
Pennington County, PO Box 230, Rapid City, SD 57709-0230 .... (605)394-2575
(Reg Deeds has b, d rec from 1905; Treasurer has m rec from 1887; Clk Ct has div, civ ct rec from 1877, pro rec from 1884)

* **Perkins**   C5   1909   Harding, Butte
Perkins County, PO Box 27, Bison, SD 57620-0027 .... (605)244-5626
(Reg Deeds has b, d, bur, rec from 1909; Treasurer has m rec from 1909; Clk Ct has pro, civ ct, div, naturalization rec from 1909)

* **Potter**   E5   1875   Buffalo
Potter County, 201 S Exene St, Gettysburg, SD 57442-1598 .... (605)765-9472
(Clk Cts has b & d from 1885, civ ct rec from 1884 & adoption rec from 1941; Reg Deeds has Ind rec)

Roberts   H6   1883   Grant
Roberts County, 411 2nd Ave E, Sisseton, SD 57262-1495 .... (605)698-3395
(Clk Cts has b, d, bur rec from 1905, m & div rec from 1890, pro & civ ct rec from 1889)

Rusk (formed as Rusk from unorg terr 1873; name changed to Dewey in 1883, Dewey organized 1910)

* **Sanborn**   G3   1883   Miner
Sanborn County, PO Box 56, Woonsocket, SD 57385-0056 .... (605)796-4515
(Clk Cts has div, pro & civ ct rec from 1905; Reg Deeds has b, m, d, bur, Ind rec)

Shannon   C2   1875   Territorial Co. (Attached to Fall River County)
Shannon County, 906 N River St, Hot Springs, SD 57747-1387 .... (605)745-5131

* **Spink**   G4   1873   Hanson
Spink County, 210 E 7th Ave, Redfield, SD 57469-1299 .... (605)472-1825
(Clk Cts has b & d rec from 1905, m rec from 1887, bur rec from 1941, div & civ ct rec from 1882 & pro rec from 1880)

* **Stanley**   E4   1873   Unorg. Terr
Stanley County, PO Box 595, Fort Pierre, SD 57532-0595 .... (605)223-2673
(Reg Deeds has m rec from 1890, bur rec from 1892, b & d rec from 1905, Ind rec; Clk Cts has div, pro, civ ct rec from 1890)

* **Sully**   E4   1873   Potter
Sully County, Main St, Onida, SD 57564 .... (605)258-2535
(Reg Deeds has b, m, d, bur, Ind rec; Clk Cts has pro & civ ct rec)

Todd   E2   1909   Lugenbeel, Meyer, Tripp, Washabaugh
Todd County, 200 E 3rd St, Winner, SD 57580 .... (605)842-2266
(Though created by legislative act 9 March 1909, Todd has never been fully organized. It was formed from parts of Lugenbeel, Meyer, Tripp & Washabaugh; part of the unorg co of Bennett, comprising part of Rosebud Indian Reservation, annexed in 1911; within the limits of Rosebud Indian Reservation)

* **Tripp**   F2   1873   Unorg. Terr
Tripp County, 200 E 3rd St, Winner, SD 57580-1806 .... (605)842-2266
(Reg Deeds has b, rec from 1909, bur rec from 1941; Treasurer has m rec from 1909; Clk Ct has civ, pro, civ ct rec from 1912)

Name	Map Index	Date Created	Parent County or Territory From Which Organized
* **Turner**	H2	1871	Lincoln

Turner County, PO Box 446, Parker, SD 57053-0446 . . . . (605)297-3115
(Clk Cts has b & d rec from 1905, m rec from 1872, div rec from 1907, pro rec from 1886, civ ct rec from 1900)

| * **Union** | I2 | 1862 | Unorg. Terr |

Union County, PO Box 757, Elk Point, SD 57025-0757 . . . . (605)356-2132
(formerly Cole, named changed 7 Jan 1864)

| * **Walworth** | E5 | 1873 | Buffalo |

Walworth County, PO Box 199, Selby, SD 57472-0199 . . . . (605)649-7878
(Reg Deeds has b, d, bur rec from 1905, Ind rec; Treasurer has m rec from 1889; Clk Ct has div rec from 1889, pro, civ ct rec from 1892, criminal rec)

| † **Washabaugh** | | 1883 | Lugenbeel |

(unorg: formed from part of Lugenbeel; within limits of Pine Ridge Indian Reservation; part taken to form parts of Bennett, Mellette & Todd in 1909 & part comprising part of Rosebud Indian Reservation, annexed to Mellette in 1911)

Washington (unorg; formed from part of Sahnnon in 1883; within limits of Pine Ridge Indian Reservation; part taken to form part of Bennett in 1909)

| * **Yankton** | H2 | 1862 | Unorg. Terr |

Yankton County, 410 Walnut St, Yankton, SD 57078-4313 . . . . (605)668-3438
(Reg Deeds has b, d rec from 1905, bur rec; Treasurer has m rec from 1900; Clk Ct has div, pro, civ ct rec from 1900; Director Assessments has Ind rec)

| * **Ziebach** | D4 | 1911 | Schnasse, Sterling, Armstrong (within limits of Cheyenne River Indian Res) |

Ziebach County, PO Box 68, Dupree, SD 57623-0068 . . . . (605)365-5157
(Reg Deeds has b, m, d, bur, Ind rec from 1911; Clk Cts has div, pro, civ ct rec from 1911)

* At least one county history has been published about this county.
† Inventory of county archives was made by the Historical Records Survey. (See Introduction)

TENNESSEE

CAPITAL · NASHVILLE — STATE 1796 (16th)
State Map on Page M-39

The Spanish first visited Tennessee in the mid-1500's, but they made no attempt to colonize the area. King Charles II included Tennessee in his grant of the Carolinas in 1663 and the first English visited the area a decade later. That same year, Marquette and Joliet landed at the site of the future city of Memphis. In 1682, La Salle built a fort at the mouth of the Hatchie River in west Tennessee. Rivalry between the French and the English continued until the end of the French and Indian War in 1763. After explorations of the area by the likes of Daniel Boone, the first settlers entered the area in 1769 from North Carolina and Virginia. They settled in the Watauga Valley and banded together as the Watauga Association in 1771. By 1772, there were four areas of settlement: north of the Holstein River, near Bristol; along the Watauga River, near Elizabethton; west of the Holstein River, near Rogersville; and along the Nolichucky River, near Erwin. North Carolina formally annexed Tennessee in 1776 as Washington County.

During the Revolutionary War, there were a number of volunteers from the state and some notable battles, including the Battle of Kings Mountain in 1780, which was the turning point of the war in the South. In 1784, North Carolina ceded Tennessee to the United States in order to secure federal protection for the area. When the federal government refused to acknowledge the cession, the people in Tennessee organized the State of Franklin. This lasted but four years and North Carolina regained control of the area in 1789. North Carolina again ceded the area to the United States in 1789, which formed the Southwest Territory in 1790.

Settlement of middle Tennessee began with the founding of Nashville in 1779. The west Tennessee area was the last to be settled. In 1796, Tennessee became a state. Twenty years later, the first steamboat reached Nashville. Early white settlers of Tennessee were predominantly English, but there were many Scotch-Irish, Germans, and Irish as well as some French and Dutch. Most of the Americans came from South Carolina, Virginia, and North Carolina. Many of the Scotch-Irish came through the Shenandoah Valley, while the Germans settled in several of the counties west of Chattanooga.

In 1861, Tennessee seceded from the Union. The Confederacy received about 110,000 soldiers from Tennessee and the Union about 31,000, mostly from east Tennessee. Tennessee was readmitted to the Union in 1866.

Official registration of births and deaths began in 1914. Birth records from 1908 and death records since 1936 are available from the Division of Vital Records, State Department of Health and Environment, Cordell Hunt Building,

Nashville, TN 37219. It is necessary to state relationship to the individual and the reason for the request. Certified copies of records of births and deaths in Nashville, Knoxville, and Chattanooga between 1881 and 1914 are also available at the Division of Vital Records. Certified copies of births and deaths in Memphis are available from the Shelby County Health Department in Memphis. Certified copies of the records of the District School Enumeration Census for 1908-1912 are available from the Division of Vital Records. To verify current fees, call 615-741-1763. Toll-free in Tennessee—1-800-423-1901.

Certificates of marriage prior to July 1, 1945, are available from the county court clerk of each county. Marriage records after 1945 are available from the Division of Vital Records. Some marriage records have been published. Divorce records are usually kept by the circuit court of each county. The counties maintain records of wills, deeds, taxpayer lists, guardianships, and other court proceedings at county courthouses. Some of these records have been transcribed and are in the Tennessee State Library and Archives, 403 Seventh Avenue North, Nashville, TN 37219. No state or territorial censuses were taken by Tennessee, however there was an 1897 census for Memphis.

Genealogical Archives, Libraries and Societies

Blount County Library, 300 E. Church St., Maryville, TN 37801

Carroll County Library, 159 E. Main St., Huntingdon, TN 38344

Chattanooga-Hamilton County Bicentennial Library, Genealogy / Local History Dept., 1001 Broad Street, Chattanooga, TN 37402

Cossitt-Goodwyn Library, 33 So. Front St., Memphis, TN 38103

East Tennessee Historical Center, 500 W. Church Ave., Knoxville, TN 37902

H. B. Stamps Memorial Library, 415 W. Main St., Rogersville, TN 37857

Highland Rim Regional Library Center, 2102 Mercury Blvd., Murfreesboro, TN 37130

Jackson-Madison County Library, 433 East Lafayette, Jackson, TN 38301

Lawson McGhee Library, Public Library of Knox County, 500 W. Church Ave., Knoxville, TN 37902

Magness Memorial Library, McMinnville, TN 37110

McClung Historical Collection, East Tennessee Historical Center, 600 Market St., Knoxville, TN 37902

Memphis Public Library and Information Center, 1850 Peabody, Memphis, TN 38104

Memphis State University Library, Mississippi Valley Collection, Memphis, TN 38104

Morristown-Hamblen Library, 417 W. Main St., Morristown, TN 37814

Public Library of Knox County, McClung Historical Collection, 600 Market St., Knoxville, TN 37902

Public Library of Nashville and Davidson County, 222 8th Ave. No., Nashville, TN 37203

Tennessee Genealogical Library, 3340 Poplar Ave., Memphis, TN 38111

Tennessee State Library and Archives, 403 7th Ave. N., Nashville, TN 37219

Bedford County Historical Society, 624 South Brittain Street, Shelbyville, TN 37160

Blount County Genealogical and Historical Society, P. O. Box 653, Maryville, TN 37803

Bradley County Historical Society, P. O. Box 4845, Cleveland, TN 37320-4845

Claiborne County Historical Society, P. O. Box 32, Tazewell, TN 37879

Coffee County Historical Society, P. O. Box 524, Manchester, TN 37355

Delta Genealogical Society, Rossville Public Library, 504 McFarland Ave., Rossville, GA 30741

East Tennessee Historical Society, 500 W. Church Ave., Knoxville, TN 37902-2505

Fentress County Genealogical Society, P. O. Box 178, Jamestown, TN 38556

Franklin County Historical Society, P. O. Box 130, Winchester, TN 37398

Giles County Historical Society, P. O. Box 693, Pulaski, TN 38478

Greene County Genealogical Society, 1324 Mt. Bethel Road, Greeneville, TN 37743

Hamblen County Genealogical Society, P. O. Box 1213, Morristown, TN 37816-1213

Hancock County Historical & Genealogical Society, P. O. Box 277, Sneedville, TN 37869

Hawkins County Genealogical Society, P. O. Box 439, Rogersville, TN 37857

Holston Territory Genealogical Society, P. O. Box 433, Bristol, VA 24203

Jefferson County Genealogical Society, P. O. Box 267, Jefferson City, TN 37760

Jonesborough Genealogical Society, P. O. Box 314, Jonesborough, TN 37659

Macon County Historical Society, Kay Crowder, Treasurer, Rt. 3, Lafayette, TN 37083

Marshall County, Tennessee Historical Society, 224 3rd Avenue North, Lewisburg, TN 37091

Maury County Tennessee Historical Society, P. O. Box 147, Columbia, TN 38401

Mid-West Tennessee Genealogical Society, P. O. Box 3343, Jackson, TN 38301

Morgan County Genealogical and Historical Society, Rt. 2, Box 992, Wartburg, TN 37887

Obion County Genealogical Society, P. O. Box 241, Union City, TN 38261

Old James County Historical Society, P. O. Box 203, Ooltewah, TN 37363

Pellissippi Genealogical and Historical Society, Clinton Public Library, 118 South Hicks, Clinton, TN 37716

Roane County Genealogical Society, P. O. Box 297, Kingston, TN 37763-0297

Signal Mountain Genealogical Society, Inc., 103 Florida Avenue, Signal Mountain, TN 37377

Tennessee Genealogical Society, P. O. Box 111249, Memphis, TN 38111-1249

Tennessee Society, Sons of the American Revolution, 1712 Natchez Trace, Nashville, TN 37212

Union County Historical Society, Inc., P. O. Box 95, Maynardville, TN 37807

Upper Cumberland Genealogical Association, Putnam Library, 48 East Broad St., Cookeville, TN 38501

Van Buren County Historical Society, P. O. Box 126, Spencer, TN 38585

Watauga Association of Genealogists, Upper East Tennessee, P. O. Box 117, Johnson City, TN 37605-0117

Weakley County Genealogical Society, Box 92, Martin, TN 38237

Printed Census Records and Mortality Schedules

Federal Census 1810 (Rutherford and Grainger counties only), 1820 (Bedford, Davidson, Dickson, Franklin, Giles, Hardin, Hickman, Humphreys, Jackson, Lawrence, Lincoln, Maury, Montgomery, Overton, Perry, Robertson, Rutherford, Shelby, Smith, Stewart, Sumner, Warren, Wayne, White, Williamson, and Wilson counties only), 1830, 1840, 1850, 1860, 1870, 1880, 1900, 1910
Federal Mortality Schedules 1850, 1860, 1880
Union Veterans and Widows 1890
War of 1812 Pensioners 1883

Valuable Printed Sources

Atlases, Maps, and Gazetteers

Fullerton, Ralph O. *Place Names of Tennessee*. Nashville: Department of Conservation, Division of Geology, 1974.

McBride, Robert M. *Eastin Morris Tennessee Gazetteer, 1834 and Matthew Rhea's Map of the State of Tennessee, 1832*. Nashville: Gazetteer Press, 1971.

Bibliographies

Fulcher, Richard Carlton. *Guide to County Records and Genealogical Resources in Tennessee*. Baltimore: Genealogical Publishing Co., 1987.

Guide to Microfilmed Manuscripts in the Tennessee State Library. Nashville: Tennessee State Library and Archives, 1984.

Smith, Sam B. *Tennessee History: A Bibliography*. Knoxville: University of Tennessee Press, 1974.

Tennessee Newspapers: A Cumulative List of Microfilmed Tennesse Newspapers in the Tennessee State Library and Archives. Nashville: Tennessee State Library and Archives, 1978.

Genealogical Research Guides

Elliott, Wendy L. *Research in Tennessee*. Bountiful, Utah: American Genealogical Lending Library, 1987.

Hailey, Naomi M. *A Guide to Genealogical Research in Tennessee*. Evansville, Indiana: Cook & McDowell Publications, 1979.

Hathaway, Beverly West. *Genealogical Research Sources in Tennessee*. West Jordan, Utah: Allstates Research Co., 1972.

McCay, Betty L. *Sources for Searching in Tennessee*. Indianapolis: Betty L. McCay, 1970.

Schweitzer, George K. *Tennessee Genealogical Research*. Knoxville: George K. Schweitzer, 1986.

TENNESSEE COUNTY DATA
State Map on Page M-39

Name	Map Index	Date Created	Parent County or Territory From Which Organized
*† **Anderson**	C4	1801	Knox
Anderson County, 100 N Main St, Clinton, TN 37716-3615 . . . . (615)457-5400			
(Co Clk has m & pro rec)			
*† **Bedford**	E5	1807	Rutherford
Bedford County, 1 Public Sq, Shelbyville, TN 37160-3953 . . . . (615)684-1921			
(Courthouse destroyed by fire and by a tornado in the past. Co Clk has m rec from 1863, pro rec; Clk Cir Ct has div rec)			
* **Benton**	G4	1835	Henry, Humphreys
Benton County, Court Sq, Camden, TN 38320 . . . . (901)584-6053			
(Co Clk has m rec from 1836, pro rec from 1840; Clk Cir Ct has div & civ ct rec; Reg Deeds has Ind rec)			

Name	Map Index	Date Created	Parent County or Territory From Which Organized

* Bledsoe D5 1807 Roane
Bledsoe County, PO Box 212, Pikeville, TN 37367-0212 .... (615)447-2137
(Courthouse burned in 1908. Co Clk has m, pro rec from 1908)

*† Blount C5 1795 Knox
Blount County, 301 Court St, Maryville, TN 37801-4997 .... (615)982-4391
(Co Clk has m & pro rec from 1795; Clk Cir Ct has div rec; Reg Deeds has Ind rec)

*† Bradley D5 1836 Indian Lands
Bradley County, PO Box 46, Cleveland, TN 37364-0046 .... (615)479-9654
(Courthouse destroyed by fire in Nov, 1864. Co Clk has m, rec from 1864; Cir and Sessions Ct has div, civ ct rec; Reg Deeds has Ind rec; Vital Records, Nashville, has b, d rec; Clk & Master has pro rec)

* Campbell C4 1806 Anderson, Claiborne
Campbell County, PO Box 13, Jacksboro, TN 37757-0013 .... (615)562-4985
(Co Clk has m rec from 1838)

* Cannon E5 1836 Coffee, Warren, Wilson
Cannon County, County Courthouse, Woodbury, TN 37190 .... (615)563-4278
(Co Clk has m rec from 1838)

Carroll G4 1821 Western District
Carroll County, PO Box 110, Huntingdon, TN 38344 .... (901)986-8237
(Co Clk has m rec from 1838)

* Carter A4 1796 Washington
Carter County, Main St County Courthouse, Elizabethton, TN 37643 .... (615)542-1814
[FHL has some m, cem, civ ct, Ind, pro, tax rec]

*† Cheatham F4 1856 Davidson, Dickson, Montgomery
Cheatham County, 100 Public Sq, Ashland City, TN 37015-1711 .... (615)792-5179
(Co Clk has m & pro rec from 1865; Clk Cir Ct has div & civ ct rec; Reg Deeds has Ind rec)

* Chester H5 1875 Hardeman, Madison, Henderson, McNairy
Chester County, PO Box 205, Henderson, TN 38340-0205 .... (901)989-2233
(Co Clk has m & pro rec from 1890; Clk Cir Ct has div & civ ct rec)

* Claiborne C4 1801 Grainger, Hawkins
Claiborne County, PO Box 173, Tazewell, TN 37879-0173 .... (615)626-3283
(Co Clk has m rec; Clk Cir Ct has div rec; Reg Deeds has Ind rec)

* Clay E4 1870 Jackson, Overton
Clay County, PO Box 218, Celina, TN 38551-0218 .... (615)243-2249
(Co Clk has b rec from 1909 to 1929, m, pro, civ ct rec from 1871)

* Cocke B4 1797 Jefferson
Cocke County, Court Ave, Newport, TN 37821 .... (615)623-6176
(Co Clk has b, d rec from 1909 to 1911, 1928 to 1930, m, pro rec from 1877; Cir Ct has div, civ ct rec; Reg Deeds has Ind rec; Stokely Memorial Library, Newport, Tenn. has a genealogical section)

* Coffee E5 1836 Franklin, Warren, Bedford
Coffee County, 300 Hillsboro Blvd Box 8, Manchester, TN 37355-2702 .... (615)728-3024
(Co Clk has m rec from 1854, pro rec from 1836; Clk Cir Ct has div & civ ct rec; Reg Deeds has Ind rec)

*† Crockett H4 1845 Lauderdale, Dyer, Madison, Gibson, Haywood
Crockett County, County Courthouse, Alamo, TN 38001 .... (901)696-5452
(Many early cen rec of residents of Crockett County can be found in surrounding counties; Co Clk has m, div, pro, civ ct, Ind rec from 1872, b & d rec from 1925)

* Cumberland D4 1856 Bledsoe, Morgan, Roane
Cumberland County, Main St, Crossville, TN 38555 .... (615)484-8212
(Co Clk has m, pro rec from 1905; Clerk & Master and Cir Ct Clk have div rec)

* Davidson F4 1783 Washington
Davidson County, 700 2nd Ave S, Nashville, TN 37210-2006 .... (615)244-1000
(Co Clk has m rec from 1789, pro rec from 1783; Clk Cir Ct has div & civ ct rec; Reg Deeds has Ind rec)

* Decatur G5 1845 Perry
Decatur County, PO Box 488, Decaturville, TN 38329-0488 .... (901)852-3417
(Co Clk has m rec from 1869)

* DeKalb E4 1837 Cannon, Warren, White
DeKalb County, County Courthouse Rm 205, Smithville, TN 37166 .... (615)597-5177
(Co Clk has m from 1848 & pro rec; Clk Chan Ct has div rec)

* Dickson F4 1803 Montgomery, Robertson
Dickson County, Court Sq, Charlotte, TN 37036-4935 .... (615)789-4171
(Courthouse was destroyed by tornado about 1835, a large number of the rec were destroyed. Co Clk has m rec from 1839, wills, Ind rec from 1803.)

* Dyer H4 1823 Western District
Dyer County, PO Box 1360, Dyersburg, TN 38025-1360 .... (901)286-7814
(Co Clk has m, pro rec from 1850, div, civ ct rec from 1927, funeral rec from 1914 to 1956; Reg Deeds has Ind rec)

* Fayette H5 1824 Shelby, Hardeman
Fayette County, Court Sq County Courthouse, Somerville, TN 38068 .... (901)465-5213
(Co Clk has b, d rec from 1925 to 1939, m rec from 1838, m rec 1918 to 1925 lost in fire; Clk & Master has pro rec)

Name	Map Index	Date Created	Parent County or Territory From Which Organized

* **Fentress**   D4   1823   Morgan, Overton
Fentress County, PO Box C, Jamestown, TN 38556-0200 .... (615)879-8014
(Co Clk has m rec from 1905)

* **Franklin**   E5   1807   Bedford, Warren
Franklin County, Public Sq, Winchester, TN 37398 .... (615)967-2541
(Co Clk has m rec from 1838 & pro rec from 1808)

* **Gibson**   H4   1823   Western District
Gibson County, County Courthouse, Trenton, TN 38382 .... (901)855-7642
(Co Clk has m & pro rec from 1824)

* **Giles**   F5   1809   Maury
Giles County, PO Box 678, Pulaski, TN 38478-0678 .... (615)363-1509
(Bureau Vital Statistics, Nashville, has b, d rec; Co Clk has m rec from 1865, pro rec; Clk and Master Office has div rec; Cir Ct has civ ct rec; Reg Deeds has lnd rec. Courthouse burned during Civil War)

* **Grainger**   C4   1796   Hawkins, Knox
Grainger County, County Courthouse, Rutledge, TN 37861 .... (615)828-3511
[FHL has some b, m, d, cem, civ ct, lnd, pro, tax rec]

* **Greene**   B4   1783   Washington
Greene County, 101 S Main St, Greenville, TN 37743-4932 .... (615)639-5321
(Co Clk has m & pro rec)

* **Grundy**   E5   1844   Coffee, Warren
Grundy County, PO Box 215, Altamont, TN 37301-0215 .... (615)692-3622
(Co Clk has m & pro rec from 1850)

* **Hamblen**   C4   1870   Grainger, Hawkins
Hamblen County, 511 W 2nd North St, Morristown, TN 37814-3964 .... (615)586-1993
(Bureau Vit Statistics, Nashville, has b, d rec; Co Clk has m, pro rec from 1870; Clk and Master has div rec; Cir Ct has civ ct rec; Reg Deeds has lnd rec)

*† **Hamilton**   D5   1819   Rhea
Hamilton County, County Courthouse, Chattanooga, TN 37402 .... (615)757-2185
(Bureau Vit Statistics, Nashville, has b, d rec; Co Clk has m rec from 1857; Cir Ct and Clk and Master has div rec; Pro Division Chancery Ct has pro rec; Civil Division Session Ct and Cir Ct has civ ct rec; Reg Deeds has lnd rec)

* **Hancock**   C4   1844   Claiborne, Hawkins
Hancock County, Main St, Sneedville, TN 37869-9501 .... (615)733-4341
(Co Clk has m, pro rec from 1930)

* **Hardeman**   H5   1823   Western District
Hardeman County, 100 N Main St, Bolivar, TN 38008-2322 .... (901)658-3541
(Bureau Vit Statistics, Nashville, has b, d rec; Co Clk has m, pro rec from 1823, tax lists from 1824; Reg Deeds has lnd rec. Bur rec are published in book, Cem Records of Hardeman County, Tenn., by Davidson, Owens, Boyd, in six vols from cem listings)

* **Hardin**   G5   1819   Western District
Hardin County, 601 Main St, Savannah, TN 38372-2061 .... (901)925-3921
(Co Clk Ct has m rec from 1860, div, pro & civ ct rec, settlements, wills & lnd grants from 1865)

* **Hawkins**   B4   1786   Sullivan
Hawkins County, Main St, Rogersville, TN 37857-3390 .... (615)272-7002
(Co Clk has m rec from 1789 & pro rec; Clk Cir Ct has div & civ ct rec; Reg Deeds has lnd rec)

† **Haywood**   H5   1823   Western District
Haywood County, 1 N Washington St, Brownsville, TN 38012-2561 .... (901)772-2362
(Co Clk has m rec from 1859, div rec from 1941 to 1965 & pro rec from 1826)

* **Henderson**   G5   1821   Western District
Henderson County, Church & Main Sts, Lexington, TN 38351 .... (901)968-2856
(Clk Chan Ct has b rec; Co Clk has m rec from 1893; Clk Cir Ct has div & civ ct rec; Reg Deeds has lnd rec; Courthouse burned 1863 & 1895, some rec saved)

* **Henry**   G4   1821   Western District
Henry County, County Courthouse, Paris, TN 38242-0024 .... (901)642-2412
[FHL has some b, m, d, cem, civ ct, lnd, pro, tax rec]

* **Hickman**   G5   1807   Dickson
Hickman County, Public Sq Rm 8, Centerville, TN 37033 .... (615)729-2621
(Courthouse burned 1865, all rec lost. Bureau Vit Statistics, Nashville, has b, d rec; Co Clk has m, pro rec from 1867; Cir Ct Clk has div rec, civ ct rec; Reg Deeds has lnd rec from 1807)

* **Houston**   G4   1871   Dickson, Stewart
Houston County, PO Box 388, Erin, TN 37061-0388 .... (615)289-3141
(Co Clk has m rec; Clk Cir Ct has div & civ ct rec; Co Ct has pro rec; Reg Deeds has lnd rec)

* **Humphreys**   G4   1809   Stewart, Smith
Humphreys County, 102 Thompson St, Waverly, TN 37185 .... (615)296-7671
(Courthouse burned in 1876 & in 1898, great lack of rec, lnd rec are only thing that is complete; Co Clk has deed rec from 1809, m from 1861, wills & inventories from 1838)

* **Jackson**   E4   1801   Smith
Jackson County, PO Box 346, Gainesboro, TN 38562-0346 .... (615)268-9212
(Co Clk has m & pro rec from 1870)

Name	Map Index	Date Created	Parent County or Territory From Which Organized
* **Jefferson**	C4	1792	Green, Hawkins

Jefferson County, PO Box 710, Dandridge, TN 37725-0710 .... (615)397-2935
(Bureau Vit statistics, Nashville, has b, d rec; Co Clk has m, pro, wills from 1792; Clk and Master has div rec; Cir Ct Clk has civ ct rec; Reg Deeds has Ind rec)

Johnson	A4	1836	Carter

Johnson County, 222 Main St, Mountain City, TN 37683 .... (615)727-9633
(Co Clk has m & pro rec from 1836; Chan Ct has div & civ ct rec)

* **Knox**	C4	1792	Greene, Hawkins

Knox County, 300 W Main Ave, Knoxville, TN 37902-1805 .... (615)521-2385
(Bureau Vit Statistics, Nashville, has b, d rec; Co Arch has pro rec from 1789, m, div, civ ct rec from 1792, tax rec from 1806; Reg Deeds has Ind rec)

* **Lake**	H4	1870	Obion

Lake County, 229 Church St, Tiptonville, TN 38079-1162 .... (901)253-7582
(Co Clk has pro rec from 1870, m rec from 1883; Chancery & Cir Ct have div rec; Reg & Tax Assessor have Ind rec)

* **Lauderdale**	I4	1835	Dyer, Tipton

Lauderdale County, County Courthouse, Ripley, TN 38063 .... (901)635-2561
(Bureau Vit Statistics, Nashville, has b, d rec; Co Clk has m rec from 1838, pro rec; Chancery Ct has div rec; General Sessions Ct has civ ct rec; Reg Deeds has Ind rec)

* **Lawrence**	F5	1817	Hickman, Maury

Lawrence County, PO Box NBU 2, Lawrenceburg, TN 38464 .... (615)762-7700
(Co Health has b rec; Co Clk has m rec from 1818 & pro rec from 1829; Clk Cir Ct has div rec; Reg Deeds has Ind rec)

* **Lewis**	G5	1843	Hickman, Maury, Wayne, Lawrence

Lewis County, County Courthouse, Hohenwald, TN 38462 .... (615)796-3378
(Co Clk has m rec from 1881, pro rec from 1940 & general sessions ct rec; Clk Cir Ct has div rec; Reg Deeds has Ind rec) (this co completely abolished for one year following the CW, for that year rec will be found in Maury, Lawrence, Hickman & Wayne Cos; Guardian bonds & court minutes begin 1846)

* **Lincoln**	F5	1809	Bedford

Lincoln County, PO Box 577, Fayetteville, TN 37334-0577 .... (615)433-2454
(Co Clk has m & pro rec; Clk Cir Ct has div rec; Clk & Master has civ ct rec; Reg Deeds has Ind rec)

*† **Loudon**	C5	1870	Blount, Monroe, Roane, McMinn

Loudon County, Grove St, Loudon, TN 37774 .... (615)458-3314
(Co Clk has m rec from 1870; Clk Cir Ct has div & civ ct rec from 1870; Reg Deeds has Ind rec from 1870)

* **Macon**	E4	1842	Smith, Sumner

Macon County, Public Sq Courthouse, Lafayette, TN 37083 .... (615)666-2333
(Co Clk has b rec from 1908 to 1912, m rec from 1901, pro rec from 1900; Clk Cir Ct has div, civ ct rec; Reg Deeds has Ind rec)

* **Madison**	H5	1821	Western District

Madison County, County Courthouse Rm 105, Jackson, TN 38301 .... (901)423-6022
(Co Clk has m rec from 1838 & pro rec from 1825)

* **Marion**	E5	1817	Indian Lands

Marion County, County Courthouse Sq, Jasper, TN 37347 .... (615)942-2515
(Co Clk has m rec from 1919, pro rec from 1874; Courthouse burned 1822, m rec destroyed)

* **Marshall**	F5	1836	Bedford, Lincoln, Giles, Maury

Marshall County, Public Sq, Lewisburg, TN 37091 .... (615)359-1072
(Co Clk Ct has m rec & pro rec from 1836)

* **Maury**	F5	1807	Williamson

Maury County, PO Box 1615, Columbia, TN 38402-1615 .... (615)381-3690
(Bureau Vit Statistics in Nashville has b & d rec; Co Clk has m rec; Clk & Master has div, pro, civ ct rec; Reg Deeds has Ind rec)

* **McMinn**	D5	1819	Indian Lands

McMinn County, 6 E Madison Ave, Athens, TN 37303-3659 .... (615)745-1281
(Co Clk has m, pro rec, co ct min from 1820, chancery ct rec from 1844)

* **McNairy**	H5	1823	Hardin

McNairy County, County Courthouse, Selmer, TN 38375 .... (901)645-3511
(Co Clk has m rec from 1861, some b, d, cemetery rec, Clk Cir Ct has div rec; Reg Deeds has Ind rec)

* **Meigs**	D5	1836	Hamilton, McMinn, Rhea

Meigs County, Main St, Decatur, TN 37322 .... (615)334-5747
(Co Clk has m & pro from 1836; Clk Cir Ct has div & civ ct rec; Reg Deeds has Ind rec)

* **Monroe**	C5	1819	Roane

Monroe County, 105 College St, Madisonville, TN 37354-1451 .... (615)442-3981
(Co Clk has m rec from 1838, pro rec 1853, wills 1833 & co ct rec 1868)

* **Montgomery**	F4	1796	Tennessee

Montgomery County, PO Box 687, Clarksville, TN 37041-0687 .... (615)648-5711
(Bureau Vit Statistics, Nashville, has b, d rec; Co Clk has m rec from 1838, pro rec from 1797; Clk Cir Ct has div rec; Criminal Ct Clk has civ ct rec; Reg Deeds has Ind rec)

* **Moore**	F5	1871	Bedford, Franklin

Moore County, County Courthouse, Lynchburg, TN 37352 .... (615)759-7346
[FHL has some m, cem, civ ct, Ind, pro, tax rec]

Name	Map Index	Date Created	Parent County or Territory From Which Organized

* **Morgan**   D4   1817   Roane
Morgan County, Main St, Wartburg, TN 37887 .... (615)346-3480
(Co Clk has b rec from 1908 to 1912, m rec from 1862, div, pro rec also Ind rec from 1818)

* **Obion**   H4   1823   Western District
Obion County, County Courthouse, Union City, TN 38261 .... (901)885-3831
(Bureau Vit Statistics, Nashville, has b, d rec; Co Clk has m rec from 1824, pro rec from 1833; Cir and Chancery Ct has div rec; Cir and General Sessions Ct has civ ct rec; Reg Deeds has Ind rec)

* **Overton**   D4   1806   Jackson
Overton County, County Courthouse Annex University St, Livingston, TN 38570 .... (615)823-5630
(Bureau Vit Statistics, Nashville, has b, d rec; Co Clk has m, pro rec from 1867; Cir Ct has div, civ ct rec; Reg Deeds has Ind rec)

* **Perry**   G5   1818   Hickman
Perry County, PO Box 16, Linden, TN 37096-0016 .... (615)589-2216
(Co Clk has b rec from 1908 to 1912-1925 to 1939 & m rec from 1899)

* **Pickett**   D4   1879   Fentress, Overton
Pickett County, County Courthouse, Byrdstown, TN 38549 .... (615)864-3879
(Co Health has b rec; Co Clk has m & pro rec from 1935; Clk & Master & Clk Cir Ct has div rec; Clk Cir Ct has civ ct rec; Reg Deeds has Ind rec)

* **Polk**   D5   1839   Bradley, McMinn
Polk County, PO Box 128, Benton, TN 37307-0158 .... (615)338-4524
[FHL has some m, cem, civ ct, Ind, pro rec]

* **Putnam**   E4   1854   White, Jackson, Overton, Dekalb
Putnam County, County Courthouse, Cookeville, TN 38501 .... (615)526-7106
(Courthouse burned in 1899. Co Clk has b, d rec from 1925 to 1940, partial b, d rec from 1908 to 1912; m rec from 1879, pro rec from 1900, wills from 1876; Chancery Ct as div, civ ct rec from 1900; Reg Deeds has Ind rec from 1854; Cir Ct Clk has Cir Ct Rec from 1900; Pat Franklin, County Historian, Rte. 2, Box 408, Cookeville, Tenn. 38501 has misc co rec)

* **Rhea**   D5   1807   Roane
Rhea County, 301 N Market St, Dayton, TN 37321-1271 .... (615)775-7808
(Co Clk has m rec from 1808)

* **Roane**   D5   1801   Knox, Blount
Roane County, PO Box 546, Kingston, TN 37763-0546 .... (615)376-5556
(Co Clk has m & pro rec from 1801)

* **Robertson**   F4   1796   Tennessee
Robertson County, County Courthouse Rm 101, Springfield, TN 37172 .... (615)384-5895
(State Lib in Nashville has b & d rec from 1925, m rec from 1839, pro rec from 1796, civ ct rec from 1832, div rec from 1844; Reg Deeds has Ind rec from 1796)

*† **Rutherford**   E5   1803   Davidson
Rutherford County, 26 Public Sq, Murfreesboro, TN 37130 .... (615)898-7799
(Co Clk has m & pro rec from 1804)

* **Scott**   D4   1849   Fentress, Morgan, Anderson
Scott County, PO Box 87, Huntsville, TN 37756-0087 .... (615)663-2588
[FHL has some m, d, cem, civ ct, Ind, pro rec]

* **Sequatchie**   E5   1858   Hamilton, Bledsoe, Marion
Sequatchie County, Cherry St, Dunlap, TN 37327 .... (615)949-2522
(Co Clk has b, m, d, pro rec from 1858; Cir Ct Clk has div, civ ct rec; Reg Deeds has Ind rec)

* **Sevier**   C5   1794   Jefferson
Sevier County, 125 Court Ave, Sevierville, TN 37862-3594 .... (615)453-5502
(Co Clk has m rec from 1856 & pro rec from 1900, wills from 1850)

* **Shelby**   I5   1819   Hardin
Shelby County, 160 N Mid-America Mall, Memphis, TN 38103-1800 .... (901)576-4244
(Co Health has b, d & bur rec; Co Clk has m rec from 1820; Clk Cir Ct has div rec; Pro Judge has pro rec; Gen Sessions Ct has civ ct rec; Reg Deeds has Ind rec)

* **Smith**   E4   1799   Sumner
Smith County, 218 Main St, Carthage, TN 37030-1541 .... (615)735-9833
(State Lib & Arch have microfilm rec)

* **Stewart**   G4   1803   Montgomery
Stewart County, Main St, Dover, TN 37058 .... (615)232-7616
(Co Clk has m & pro rec from 1898; Reg Deeds has Ind rec & deeds from 1803; Courthouse burned during CW)

*† **Sullivan**   B4   1779   Washington
Sullivan County, PO Box 530, Blountville, TN 37617-0530 .... (615)323-6428
(Co Clk has m rec from 1863, b rec 1908 to 1912, d rec 1925 to 1938; Clk & Master has pro rec)

* **Sumner**   E4   1786   Davidson
Sumner County, County Courthouse Rm 108, Gallatin, TN 37066 .... (615)452-4063
(Co Clk has m & pro rec)

    Tennessee   1788   (Co. surrendered name when state became Tennessee 1796)

Name	Map Index	Date Created	Parent County or Territory From Which Organized

*† Tipton I5 1823 Western District
   Tipton County, PO Box 528, Covington, TN 38019-0528 .... (901)476-0207
   (Co Clk has m rec from 1840; Genl Sessions Ct has div rec from 1823, civ ct rec; Chancery Ct has pro rec from 1823; Reg Deeds
   has Ind rec; State has b, d, bur rec)

* Trousdale E4 1870 Macon, Smith, Wilson
   Trousdale County, Main St & Court Sq, Hartsville, TN 37074 .... (615)374-2906
   (Co Clk has m, pro rec from 1906; Clk Cir Ct has div, civ ct rec; Reg Deeds has Ind rec)

* Unicoi B4 1875 Carter, Washington
   Unicoi County, County Courthouse PO Box 340, Erwin, TN 37650-0340 .... (615)743-3381
   (Co Clk has m, pro rec from 1875; Clk Cir Ct and Chan Ct has div, civ ct rec; Reg Deeds has Ind rec from 1875)

* Union C4 1850 Anderson, Campbell, Claiborne, Grainger, Knox
   Union County, PO Box 395, Maynardville, TN 37807-0395 .... (615)992-8043
   (Co Clk has m & pro rec; Co Asr has Ind rec)

* Van Buren E5 1840 Bledsoe, Warren, White
   Van Buren County, Courthouse Sq, Spencer, TN 38585 .... (615)946-2121
   (Co Clk has b rec from 1925 to 1938, d rec from 1926 to 1938, m & pro rec from 1840; Clk & Master has div rec from 1840; Gen
   Sessions Ct has civ ct rec from 1840; Reg Deeds has Ind rec from 1840)

* Warren E5 1807 White
   Warren County, PO Box 231, McMinnville, TN 37110-0231 .... (615)473-2623
   (Co Clk has m rec from 1852, d rec from 1925, pro rec from 1827; Cir Ct Clk has div, civ ct rec; Reg Deeds has Ind rec)

Washington B4 1777 Covered present state. Many counties from section.
   Washington County, PO BOx 218, Jonesborough, TN 37659-0218 .... (615)753-1621
   (This co also embraced parts of present N.C. Cos) (Co Clk has b rec from 1908 to 1912 & from 1925 to 1938, m rec from 1787,
   pro rec from 1780 & wills from 1779)

* Wayne 1785 (Abolished 1788)
   (This Wayne Co created under the state of Franklin. Included present Carter Co & part of Johnson Co)

* Wayne 1817 Hickman
   Wayne County, PO Box 206, Waynesboro, TN 38485-0206 .... (615)722-3653
   (Co Clk has m rec from 1857 & pro rec from 1848)

* Weakley H4 1823 Western District
   Weakley County, County Courthouse, Dresden, TN 38225 .... (901)364-2285
   (Co Clk has m rec from 1840, pro rec & wills from 1828; Clk Cir Ct has div rec)

* White E4 1806 Overton, Jackson, Smith
   White County, County Courthouse Rm 205, Sparta, TN 38583 .... (615)836-3203
   (Co Clk has m rec from 1838, about two dozen before that from 1809, wills, settlements, deeds & inventories from 1806)

* Williamson F4 1799 Davidson
   Williamson County, 1320 W Main St, Franklin, TN 37064-3700 .... (615)790-5712
   (Co Clk has m rec from 1800, tax, wills, minutes, deeds from 1799)

*† Wilson E4 1799 Sumner
   Wilson County, PO Box 918, Lebanon, TN 37088-0918 .... (615)444-0314
   (Co Clk has m rec from 1802, pro rec from 1800; Clk and Master and Cir Ct Clk has div rec; Reg Deeds has Ind rec)

* At least one county history has been published about this county.

† Inventory of county archives was made by the Historical Records Survey. (See Introduction)

TEXAS

CAPITAL - AUSTIN — STATE 1845 (28th)
State Map on Page M-40

Following a shipwreck in 1528, Alvar Nunez Cabeza de Vaca and others wandered across Texas and the Southwest for eight years. On returning to Mexico, the tales they told of the Seven Cities of Cibola inspired other explorers to search for the golden cities. In so doing, they crossed parts of the state but had no interest in settling the area. The French also came to the area around 1685, but their attempt at settlement failed. Seeing a threat from the French, the Spanish sent missionaries into Texas to found missions. Their goal was to convert the Indians and to civilize the frontier. The first permanent settlement began in 1682 near El Paso. By 1820, there were still only a few thousand white settlers in all of Texas.

Texas became part of Mexico in 1821, when Mexico achieved independence from Spain. Stephen Austin reached an agreement with Mexico that same year to bring American settlers into the area. The first colony was started in 1821 on the lower Brazos. Former residents of Alabama, Louisiana, Mississippi, and Tennessee came to the area, so that by 1832 there were over 20,000 Americans in Texas. In 1835, the Battle of Gonzales began the revolution against Mexico. The Texans quickly took San Antonio, but Santa Anna recaptured it and destroyed the small force at the Alamo. Sam Houston led the Texas army to victory over the Mexicans in 1836.

The Republic of Texas lasted from 1836 to 1845. The United States annexed Texas in 1845, making Texas the 28th state. The following year, Mexico declared war on the United States in an effort to reclaim Texas and other territory. Over 6,000 Texans fought against Mexico during the war. Mexico was defeated and gave up its claim to Texas. In 1850, Texas gave up its claims to Colorado, Wyoming, Kansas, and Oklahoma. In 1861, Texas seceded from the Union. During the Civil War, some 60,000 Texans fought for the Confederacy and only about 1,200 for the Union. Texas was readmitted to the Union in 1870. During the 1870's, most Indians were moved to the Indian Territory in Oklahoma.

Statewide registration of births and deaths began in 1903. These records are available from the Bureau of Vital Statistics, Texas Department of Health, 1100 West 49th Street, Austin, TX 78756. To verify current fees, call 512-458-7380.

Cities also have had requirements to register births and deaths at various times, which have been forwarded to the state and county clerks. Marriage records have been forwarded to the Bureau of Vital Statistics only since 1966. Records prior to that time are available from the county clerk. Prior to 1836, only Catholic Churches could perform marriages, so some Protestant marriages will be found in Catholic records. Reports of divorce or annulment began to be filed with the Bureau of Vital Statistics in 1968. Prior to then, the district clerk of each county kept these records. Probate records have been kept by probate clerks in each county. Naturalization records have generally been filed with the district court clerk. After September 1906, the National Archives, Fort Worth Branch, 501 Felix Street, P.O. Box 6216, Fort Worth, TX 76115, has naturalization records. Several censuses were taken in Texas prior to statehood, including municipality censuses and some mission and military district censuses between 1792 and 1836. Many have been published. Available mission censuses have been translated and are available on microfilm at the University of Texas, Institute of Texas Cultures, San Antonio, TX 78713. School censuses were taken in 1854 and 1855 by some counties and are available at the Texas State Archives, P.O. Box 12927, Austin, TX 78711.

Genealogical Archives, Libraries and Societies

Amarillo Public Library, 300 East 4th, P. O. Box 2171, Amarillo, TX 79189

Arlington Public Library, 101 E. Abram, Arlington, TX 76010

Bay City Public Library, 1900 5th St., Bay City, TX 77414

Beaumont Public Library, Box 3827, 800 Pearl St., Beaumont, TX 77704

Belton City Library, 301 E. 1st Avenue, Belton, TX 76513

Bryan Public Library, 201 E. 26th St., Bryan, TX 77801

Catholic Archives of Texas, 1600 Congress Ave., Austin, TX 78801

Chaparral Genealogical Library and Society, P. O. Box 606, Tomball, TX 77375

City-College Library, 1825 May St., Brownsville, TX 78520

Clayton Library, Center for Genealogical Research, 5300 Caroline, Houston, TX 77004

Corsicana Public Library, 100 N. 12 St., Corsicana, TX 75110

Dallas Public Library, Genealogy Section, 1515 Young St., Dallas, TX 75201

Denison Library Genealogy Group, 1531 W. Main, Denison, TX 75020

Ector County Library, 622 N. Lee, Odessa, TX 79760

El Paso Genealogical Library, 3651 Douglas, El Paso, TX 79903

El Paso Public Library, Document Genealogy Dept., 501 N. Oregon St., El Paso, TX 79901

El Progreso Memorial Library, 129 W. Nopal, Uvalde, TX 78801

Euless Public Library, 201 N. Ector Drive, Euless, TX 76039

Fort Belknap Archives (Young County), Box 27, Rt. 1, Newcastle, TX 76372

Fort Worth Public Library, 300 Taylor Street, Fort Worth, TX 76102

Genealogical Research Library, 4524 Edmondson Ave., Dallas, TX 75205

Grand Prairie Memorial Library, 901 Conover, Grand Prairie, TX 75051

Harlingen Public Library, 504 E. Tyler Ave., Harlingen, TX 78550

Hood County Library, 222 N. Travis, Granbury, TX 76048 (Collection includes papers of Judge Henry Davis plus other good Hood County genealogical materials).

Houston Metropolitan Research Center, 500 McKinney St., Houston, TX 77002

Houston Public Library, 500 McKinney Ave., Houston, TX 77002

Huntsville Public Library, 1214 14th St., Huntsville, TX 77340

Kurth Memorial Library, 101 Calder Square, Lufkin, TX 75901

La Retama Public Library, 505 N. Mesquite St., Corpus Christi, TX 78401

Learning Resource Center, Western Texas College, Snyder, TX 79549

Lubbock City-County Library, 1306 9th St., Lubbock, TX 79401

Luling Public Library, 215 South Pecan Ave., Luling, TX 78648

McLennan County Library, 1717 Austin Ave., Waco, TX 76701

Mesquite Public Library, 300 Grubb Dr., Mesquite, TX 75149

Mirabeau B. Lamar Library, University of Texas, Austin, TX 78712

Montgomery County Library, Box 579, San Jacinto and Phillips, Conroe, TX 77301

Moore Memorial Library, 1701 9th Avenue North, Texas City, TX 77590

Mt. Pleasant Municipal Library, Box 1285, 213 N. Madison, Mt. Pleasant, TX 75455

Ora McMullen Room, Kurth Memorial Library, 101 Calder Square, Lufkin, TX 75901

Pilot Point Community Library, 105 South Jefferson St., Pilot Point, TX 76258

Public Library, Longview, TX 75601

Quitman Public Library, 202 E. Goode Street, P. O. Box 77, Quitman, TX 75783

Rosenberg Library, 2310 Sealy, Galveston, TX 77550

San Antonio Public Library, 203 S. St. Mary's St., San Antonio, TX 78205

San Augustine Public Library, 413 E. Columbia, San Augustine, TX 75972

Scarborough Library of Genealogy, History and Biography of South and Southwest, c / o McMurry College Library, McMurry Station, Abilene, TX 79605

Scurry County Library, 1916 23rd St., Snyder, TX 79549

Sherman Public Library, Local History and Genealogy Dept., 421 N. Travis, Sherman, TX 75090

Southwest Genealogical Society and Library, 412 W. College St. A, Carthage, TX 75633-1406

Temple Public Library, 101 North Main Street, Temple, TX 76501

Texarkana Public Library, 901 State Line Ave., Texarkana, TX-AR 75501

Texas State Library, 1201 Brazos St., Box 12927 Capitol St., Austin, TX 78711

Tyrell Public Library, 695 Pearl St., Beaumont, TX 77701

Waco Public Library, 1717 Austin Ave., Waco, TX 76701

Walworth Harrison Public Library, Genealogy Room, 3716 Lee Street, Greenville, TX 75401

Weatherford Public Library, 1214 Charles St., Weatherford, TX 76086

Amarillo Genealogical Society, Amarillo Public Library, 300 East 4th, P. O. Box 2171, Amarillo, TX 79189

Anderson County Genealogical Society, P. O. Box 2045, Palestine, TX 75802

Archer County Historical Commission, Rt. 1, Windthorst, TX 76389

Ark-La-Tex Genealogical Association, Inc., P. O. Box 4462, Shreveport, LA 71104

Arlington Genealogical Society Arlington Public Library, 101 E. Anram St., Arlington, TX 76010

Armstrong County Historical Assoc., Rt. 1, Box 233, Claude, TX 79019

Athens Genealogical Organization, Henderson Public Library, 121 Prairieville St., Athens, TX 75751

Austin Genealogical Society, P. O. Box 1507, Austin, TX 78767-1507

Austin County Historical Commission, 206 S. Masonic St., Bellville, TX 77418

Bandera Chapter, DAR, Rt. 1, Box 2, Bandera, TX 78003

Bay Area Heritage Society P. O. Box 4161, Baytown, TX 77520

Beaumont Heritage Society, 2985 French Road, Beaumont, TX 77706

Bellville Historical Society, P. O. Box 67, Bellville, TX 77418

Big Bend Genealogical Society, P. O. Box 56, Alpine, TX 79830

Boerne Area Historical Society, Box 178, Boerne, TX 78006

Borden County Historical Commission, Box 23, Gail, TX 79738

Bosque Valley Heritage Society, Box 168, Valley Mills, TX 76689

Brazos Genealogical Association, P. O. Box 5493, Bryan, TX 77805-5493

Brazosport Genealogical Society, P. O. Box 813, Lake Jackson, TX 77566

Brooks County Historical Commission, 604 W. Blucher, Falfurrias, TX 78355

Brown County Historical Society, P. O. Box 146, Brownwood, TX 76801

Burkburnett Genealogical Society, Burkburnett Library, 215 East Fourth St., Burkburnett, TX 76354

Burnet County Genealogical Society, Herman Brown Free Library, 100 East Washington Street, Burnet, TX 78611

CAGE: Cleveland Area Genealogical Enterprises, Austin Memorial Library, 220 S. Bonham, Cleveland, TX 77327

Calhoun County Genealogical Society, P. O. Box 1150, Port Lavaca, TX 77979

Cass County Genealogical Society, P. O. Box 541, Atlanta, TX 75551

Castro County Genealogical Society, P. O. Box 911, Dimmitt, TX 79027

Central Texas Genealogical Society, Waco McLennan County Library, 1717 Austin Ave., Waco, TX 76701

Chambers County Heritage Society, P. O. Box 870, Mont Belvieu, TX 77580

Chaparral Genealogical Library and Society, P. O. Box 606, Tomball, TX 77375

Cherokee County Genealogical Society, P. O. Box 1332, Jacksonville, TX 75766

Childress Genealogical Society, 117 Ave. B., N.E., Childress, TX 79201

Clan McLaren Society of North America, Ltd., 5843 Royal Crest Dr., Dallas, TX 75230

Clear Lake Area Historical Society, P. O. Box 24, Seabrook, TX 77586

Coastal Bend Genealogical Society, P. O. Box 2711, Corpus Christi, TX 78403

Collin County Genealogical Society, P. O. Box 864752, Plano, TX 75086

Comal County Family Historians, P. O. Box 583, New Braunfels, TX 78130

Cooke County Heritage Society, P. O. Box 150, Gainesville, TX 76240

Coryell County Genealogical Society, Gatesville Public Library, 811 Main Street, Gatesville, TX 76528

Cottle County Genealogical Society, Box 1005, Paducah, TX 79248

Crockett County Historical Society, P. O. Drawer B, Ozona, TX 76943

Cross Timbers Genealogical Society, Inc., P. O. Box 197, Gainsville, TX 76240

Cypress Basin Genealogical and Historical Society, P. O. Box 403, Mt. Pleasant, TX 75455

Czech Heritage Society of Texas, 9174 Westview, Houston, TX 77055

Dallas County East Genealogical Society, 7637 Mary Dan Drive, Dallas, TX 75217-4603

Dallas Genealogical Society, P. O. Box 12648, Dallas, TX 75225

Deaf Smith County Genealogical Society, 211 E. 4th St., Hereford, TX 79045

Denton County Genealogical Society, P. O. Box 23322, TWU Station, Denton, TX 76204

Donley County Genealogical Society, Box 116, Clarendon, TX 79226

Duncanville Texas Genealogical Society, 622 West Camp Wisdom Road, Duncanville, TX 75116

East End Historical Assoc., P. O. Box 2424, Galveston, TX 77550

East Texas Genealogical Society, P. O. Box 6967, Tyler, TX 75711

Ellis County Genealogical Society, Box 385, Waxahachie, TX 75165

El Paso Genealogical Society, El Paso Main Public Library, 501 N. Oregon Street, El Paso, TX 79901

Forney Heritage Society, 98 FM 2757, Forney, TX 75126

Fort Bend County Genealogical Society, P. O. Box 274, Richmond, TX 77469

Fort Brown Genealogical Society, 608 E. Adams, Brownsville, TX 78520

Fort Clark Historical Society P. O. Box 1061, Brackettville, TX 78832

Fort Worth Genealogical Society, P. O. Box 9767, Fort Worth, TX 76147-2767

Freestone County Genealogical Society, P. O. Box 14, Fairfield, TX 75840

Galveston County Genealogical Society, 2310 Sealy, c / o Rosenberg Library, Galveston, TX 77550

Genealogical and Historical Society of Caldwell County, 215 South Pecan Ave., Luling, TX 78648

Genealogical Society of the Big Spring, Howard County Library, Big Spring, TX 79720

Genealogical Society of Kendall County, P. O. Box 623, Boerne, TX 78006

Genealogical Society of Northeast Texas, 2400 Clarksville St., PJC Box 187, Paris, TX 75460

German-Texas Heritage Society, Rt. 2, Box 239A, Buda, TX 78610

Gillespie County Historical Society, P. O. Box 542, Longview, TX 75606

Grand Prairie Genealogical Society, P. O. Box 532026, Grand Prairie, TX 75053

Grayson County, Texas Genealogical Society, 421 N. Travis, Sherman, TX 75090

Gregg County Historical and Genealogical Society, P. O. Box 542, Longview, TX 75606

Grimes County Heritage Assoc., 1215 East Washington Ave., Navasota, TX 77868

Guadalupe Victoria Chapter, DAR, Mrs. A. N. Leatherwood, Regent, 607 Avenue D., Victoria, TX 77901

Guadalupe County Genealogical Society, 707 East College St., Sequin, TX 78155

Gulf Coast Ancestry Researchers P. O. Box 157, Wallisville, TX 77597

Harris County Genealogical Society, P. O. Box 391, Pasadena, TX 77501

Harrison County Historical Society, Old Courthouse Museum, Peter Whetstone Square, Marshall, TX 75670

Heart of Texas Genealogical Society, P. O. Box 133, Rochelle, TX 76872

Hemphill County Historical and Genealogical Society, Rt. 2, Canadian, TX 79014

Henderson County Historical Society, P. O. Box 943, Athens, TX 75751

Heritage Assoc. of San Marcos P. O. Box 1806, San Marcos, TX 78666

Heritage Society of Washington County, P. O. Box 1123, Brenham, TX 77833

High Plains Genealogical Society, Unger Memorial Library, 825 Austin, Plainview, TX 79072

Hill County Genealogical Society, P. O. Box 72, Brandon, TX 76628

Hill Country Genealogical Society, Prairie Mt. Rt., Llano, TX 78643

Hillsboro Heritage League, P. O. Box 2, Hillsboro, TX 76645

Hispanic Genealogical Society, 2932 Barksdale, Houston, TX 77093

Hood County Genealogical Society, P. O. Box 1623, Granbury, TX 76048

Hopkins County Genealogical Society, P. O. Box 624, Sulphur Springs, TX 75482

Houston Area Genealogical Association, 2507 Tannehill, Houston, TX 77008-3052

Houston Genealogical Forum, P. O. Box 271469, Houston, TX 77277-1469

Humble Genealogy Society, P. O. Box 2723, Humble, TX 77338

Hunt County Genealogical Society, P. O. Box 398, Greenville, TX 75401

Hutchinson County Genealogical Society, Hutchinson County Library, 625 Weatherly St., Borger, TX 79007

Jewish Genealogical Society of Houston, P. O. Box 980126, Houston, TX 77098

Johnson County Genealogical Society, P. O. Box 10246, Cleburne, TX 76033-5246

Karnes County Historical Society, Box 162, Karnes City, TX 78118

Kaufman County Genealogical Society, Box 337, Terrell, TX 75160

Kent County Genealogical and Historical Society, Box 414, Jayton, TX 79528

Kerrville Genealogical Society of Kerrville 505 Water St., Kerrville, TX 78028

Lake Cities Historical Society, P. O. Box 1222, Lake Dallas, TX 75065

Lake Jackson Historical Assoc., P. O. Box 242, Lake Jackson, TX 77566

Lamesa Area Genealogical Society, Box 1264, Lamesa, TX 79331

Lee County Genealogical Society, Rt. 1, Box 8-D, Ledbetter, TX 78946

Leon County Genealogical Society, P. O. Box 500, Centerville, TX 75833

Liberty County Historical Commission, P. O. Box 23, Liberty, TX 77575

Limestone County Genealogical Society, 350 E. Rusk St., Mexia, TX 76667

Lubbock Heritage Society, P. O. Box 5443, Lubbock, TX 79417

Lufkin Genealogical & Historical Society, 1008 Reen, Lufkin, TX 75901

Madison County Genealogical Society, Box 26, Madisonville, TX 77864

Matagorda County Genealogical Society, P. O. Box 264, Bay City, TX 77404-0264

McAllen Genealogical Society, c / o McAllen Memorial Library, 601 N. Main St., McAllen, TX 78501

Mesquite Historical and Genealogical Society, P. O. Box 165, Mesquite, TX 75185-0165

Methodist Historical Society, Fondren Library, Southern Methodist University, Dallas, TX 75222

Mid-Cities Genealogical Society, P. O. Box 407, Bedford, TX 76095-0407

Midland Genealogical Society, Box 1191, Midland, TX 79702

Montgomery County Genealogical & Historical Society, Inc., P. O. Box 751, Conroe, TX 77305-0751

Nacogdoches Genealogical Society, P. O. Box 4634, Nacogdoches, TX 75962

National Archives-Southeast Region, 501 West Felix Street, P. O. Box 6216, Fort Worth, TX 76115

Navarro County Genealogical Society, P. O. Box 2278, Corsicana, TX 75151

New Boston Genealogical Society, P. O. Box 404, New Boston, TX 75570

Newton County Historical Commission, Box 56, Burkeville, TX 75932

Nolan County Genealogical Assoc., County-City Library, P. O. Box 780, Sweetwater, TX 79556

North Texas Genealogical and Historical Association, Box 4602, Wichita Falls, TX 76308

Orange County Historical Society, P. O. Box 1345, Orange, TX 77630

Palo Pinto County Historical Assoc., Box 42, Palo Pinto, TX 76072

Pampa Genealogical and Historical Society, 430 N. Summer St., Pampa, TX 79065

Panhandle-Plains Historical Society, Box 967, W. T. Station, Canyon, TX 79016

Parker County Genealogical Society, 1214 Charles St., Weatherford, TX 76086

Pecan Valley Genealogical Society, Brownwood Public Library, 600 Carnegie Blvd., Brownwood, TX 76801

Permian Basin Genealogical Society, 321 West 5th Street, Odessa, TX 79761

Plano Heritage Assoc., 1900 West 15th St., Plano, TX 75075

Polish Genealogical Society of Texas, 218 Beaver Bend, Houston, TX 77037

Polk County Heritage Society, 207 North Beatty St., Livingston, TX 77351

Public Library, Longview, TX 75601

Red River County Texas Genealogical Society, P. O. Drawer D, Clarksville, TX 75426

Refugio County Historical Society, Refugio County Museum, 102 West St., Refugio, TX 78377

Roberts County Historical Commission, Roberts County Museum, Box 306, Miami, TX 79059

Rusk County Historical Commission, P. O. Box 1773, Henderson, TX 75652

Salado Historical Society, P. O. Box 251, Salado, TX 76571

San Angelo Genealogical and Historical Society, Inc., P. O. Box 3453, San Angelo, TX 76901

San Antonio Genealogical and Historical Society, P. O. Box 17461, San Antonio, TX 78217-0461

San Jacinto County Heritage Society, P. O. Box 505, Coldspring, TX 77331

San Marcos / Hays County Genealogical Society, P. O. Box 503, San Marcos, TX 78666

Schleicher County Historical Society, Box 473, Eldorado, TX 76936

Smith County Historical Society, 624 N. Broadway, Tyler, TX 75702

South Plains Genealogical Society, P. O. Box 6607, Lubbock, TX 79493

South Texas Genealogical Society, P. O. Box 754, Beeville, TX 78104

Southeast Texas Genealogical and Historical Society, Tyrrell Historical Library, P. O. Box 3827, Beaumont, TX 77704

Southwest Texas Genealogical Society, P. O. Box 295, Uvalde, TX 78802

Southwest Genealogical Society, San Antonio College Library, 1300 San Pedro Ave., San Antonio, TX 78212

Stephens County Genealogical Society, P. O. Box 350, Breckenridge, TX 76024

Stephens County Historical Assoc., 201 N. Harding, Breckenridge, TX 76024

Taylor Heritage Society, P. O. Box 385, Taylor, TX 76574

Terrell County Historical Commission, P. O.Box 7, Sanderson, TX 79848

Texarkana USA Genealogy Society, P. O. Box 2323, Texarkana, TX 75501

Texas Catholic Historical Society, 3812 Lafayette, Fort Worth, TX 76107

Texas-Oklahoma Panhandle Genealogical Society, 1613 S. Grinnell, Perryton, TX 79070

Texas Society, Sons of the American Revolution, 3342 Dartmoor Dr., Dallas, TX 75229

Texas State Genealogical Society, 3904-J Run of Oaks, Austin, TX 78704

Texas State Historical Association, Box 8011, University Station, Austin, TX 78712

Texas Tent of the Daughters of Union Veterans, 814 Woodrow, Arlington, TX 76012

Texas Wendish Heritage Society, P. O. Box 311, Giddings, TX 78942

Tip O'Texas Genealogical Society, Harlingen Public Library, Harlingen, TX 78550

Tom Green County Historical Preservation League, P. O. Box 1625, San Angelo, TX 76902

Val Verde County Genealogy Society, P. O. Box 442052, Del Rio, TX 78842

Van Zandt County Genealogical Society, P. O. Drawer 716, Canton, TX 75103

Victoria County Genealogical Society, 302 N. Main St., Victoria, TX 77901

Waller County Historical Society, P. O. Box 235, Brookshire, TX 75455

Wallisville Heritage, P. O. Box 16, Wallisville, TX 77597

Ward County Genealogical Society, 400 East Fourth St., Monahans, TX 79756

Webb County Heritage Foundation, P. O. Drawer 29, Laredo, TX 78042

West Bell Genealogical Society, P. O. Box 851, Killeen, TX 76540

West Texas Genealogical Society, P. O. Box 2307, Abilene, TX 79604

Williamson County Genealogical Society, P. O. Box 585, Round Rock, TX 78680

Winkler County Genealogical Society, P. O. Box 1028, Kermit, TX 79745

Wise County Genealogical Society, P. O. Box 126, Rhome, TX 76078

Wise County Historical Society, Box 427, Decatur, TX 76234

Wood County Genealogical Society, P. O. Box 832, Quitman, TX 75783

Yoakum County Historical Commission, Box 960, Plains, TX 79355

Yorktown Historical Society, Yorktown Historical Museum, P. O. Box 884, Yorktown, TX 78164

Zapata County Historical Commission, Box 6305, Zapata, TX 78076

Printed Census Records and Mortality Schedules

Federal Census 1850, 1860, 1870, 1880, 1890 (parts of Ellis, Hood, Rusk, Trinity, and Kaufman counties only), 1900, 1910
Federal Mortality Schedules 1850, 1860, 1870, 1880
Union Veterans and Widows 1890
Residents 1782-1836
State/Territorial Census 1829-1836
School Census 1854-1855

Valuable Printed Sources

Atlases, Maps, and Gazetteers

Bartholomew, Ed. *800 Texas Ghost Towns*. Fort Davis, Texas: Frontier Book Publishers, 1971.

Day, James M. *Maps of Texas, 1527-1900: The Map Collection of the Texas State Archives*. Austin, Texas: Pemberton Press, 1974.

Gannett, Henry. *A Gazetteer of Texas*. Washington, DC: Government Printing Office, 1904.

Pool, William C. *A Historical Atlas of Texas*. Austin, Texas: Encino Press, 1975.

Wheat, Jim. *More Ghost Towns of Texas*. Garland, Texas: Lost and Found, 1980.

————. *Postmasters and Post Offices of Texas, 1846-1930*. Garland, Texas: Lost and Found, 1974.

Bibliographies

Carefoot, Jan. *Guide to Genealogical Resources in the Texas State Archives*. Austin, Texas: Texas State Library, 1984.

Crofford-Gould, Sharry. *Texas Cemetery Inscriptions: A Source Index*. San Antonio: Limited Editions, 1977.

Genealogical Research Guides

Kennedy, Imogene Kinard and J. Leon Kennedy. *Genealogical Records in Texas*. Baltimore: Genealogical Publishing Co., 1987.

Welch, June Rayfield. *The Texas Courthouse Revisited*. Dallas: GLA Press, 1984.

Genealogical Sources

Gracy, Alice Duggan. *Early Texas Birth Records, 1838-1878*. Austin, Texas: Alice Duggan Gracy, 1969.

Miller, Thomas Lloyd. *Bounty and Donation Land Grants of Texas, 1835-1888*. Austin, Texas: University of Texas Press, 1967.

Histories

Brown, John Henry. *History of Texas from 1685-1892*. St. Louis: L. E. Daniell, 1893.

Wharton, Clarence R. *Texas Under Many Flags*. Chicago: American Historical Society, 1930.

Whisenhunt, Donald W. *Chronology of Texas History*. Austin, Texas: Eakin Press, 1982.

TEXAS COUNTY DATA
State Map on Page M-40

Name	Map Index	Date Created	Parent County or Territory From Which Organized
* **Anderson**	E6	1846	Houston

Anderson County, 500 N Church St, Palestine, TX 75801-3024 . . . . (903)723-7432
(Dis Clk has div rec; Co Clk has b & d rec from 1903, m, pro & lnd rec from 1846, also civ ct rec; cities have b & d rec from 1953)

Andrews	D2	1875	Bexar

Andrews County, PO Box 727, Andrews, TX 79714-0727 . . . . (915)524-1426
(Co Clk has b, m & civ ct rec from 1910, pro rec from 1911 & lnd rec from 1884; Dis Clk has div rec)

* **Angelina**	E7	1846	Nacogdoches

Angelina County, 215 E Lufkin Ave, Lufkin, TX 75901-3047 . . . . (409)634-8339
(Co Clk has some b rec from 1875 to 1979, d rec from 1903, m, pro, lnd rec from 1846; Dis Clk has div rec; Co Clk and Dis Clk have civ ct rec from 1920)

Name	Map Index	Date Created	Parent County or Territory From Which Organized

* Aransas   G5   1871   Refugio
Aransas County, 301 N Liveoak St, Rockport, TX 78382-2744 .... (512)729-7430
(Co Clk has b & d rec from 1901, m, pro, civ ct rec & deeds from 1871)

* Archer   D4   1858   Fannin
Archer County, PO Box 815, Archer City, TX 76351-0815 .... (817)574-4615
(Co Clk has b rec from 1880, m, d, bur, div, pro, civ ct, Ind rec)

* Armstrong   C3   1876   Bexar
Armstrong County, PO Box 189, Claude, TX 79019 .... (806)226-2081
(Co Clk has b & d rec from 1903, m & pro rec from 1890, civ ct rec from 1898 & deeds from 1883; Clk Cir Ct has div rec)

* Atascosa   G4   1856   Bexar
Atascosa County, Circle Dr, Jourdanton, TX 78026 .... (512)769-2511
(Co Clk has b rec from 1890, d rec from 1903, m, pro & Ind rec from 1856, civ ct rec from 1860; Dis Clk has div rec)

* Austin   F6   1837   Old Mexican Municipality
Austin County, 1 E Main St, Bellville, TX 77418-1598 .... (409)865-5911
(Co Clk has b, d rec from 1903, m rec from 1824, pro rec from 1835, civ ct rec from 1877 and Ind rec from 1828, naturalization rec from 1896, declaration rec from 1876; State has delayed b cert)

* Bailey   C2   1876   Bexar
Bailey County, 300 S 1st St, Muleshoe, TX 79347-3621 .... (806)272-3044
(Co Clk has b, m, pro & civ ct rec from 1918, Ind rec from 1882; Dis Clk has div rec; Ellis Funeral Home in Muleshoe has bur rec)

*† Bandera   F4   1856   Uvalde, Bexar
Bandera County, 500 Main St, Bandera, TX 78003 .... (512)796-3332
(Co Clk has b & d rec from 1904, m, div, pro, civ ct & Ind rec from 1856, also cattle brands from 1856)

*† Bastrop   F5   1836   Old Mexican Municipality
Bastrop County, 803 Pine St, Bastrop, TX 78602-3841 .... (512)321-4443
(Co Clk has b & d rec from 1903, m rec from 1860, pro rec from 1850, civ ct rec from 1890, Ind rec from 1837; Dis Clk has div & civ ct rec)

Baylor   D4   1858   Fannin
Baylor County, PO Box 689, Seymour, TX 76380-0689 .... (817)888-3322
(Co Clk has b & d rec from 1903, m rec from 1879, div rec from 1881, pro & civ ct rec from 1880)

* Bee   G5   1857   Goliad, Refugio, Live Oak, San Patricio
Bee County, 105 W Corpus Christi St, Beeville, TX 78102-5684 .... (512)358-3664
(Co Clk has b & d rec from 1903, m, pro & Ind rec from 1858, civ ct rec from 1876; Dis Clk has div rec)

* Bell   E5   1850   Milam
Bell County, Main & Central Sts, Belton, TX 76513 .... (817)939-3521
(Co Clk has b & d rec from 1903, m, pro, civ ct & Ind rec from 1850)

Bexar   F4   1836   Old Mexican Municipality (established 1718)
Bexar County, 100 Dolorosa St Rm 1120-A, San Antonio, TX 78205-3002 .... (512)220-2011
(Co Clk has b rec from 1838, m rec from 1837, d rec from 1903, pro rec from 1843, Ind rec from 1700's, Spanish church rec from 1737 to 1859, minutes of Spanish City Council from 1815 to 1820)

* Blanco   F4   1858   Gillespie, Comal, Burnet, Hays
Blanco County, PO Box 65, Johnson City, TX 78636-0117 .... (512)868-7357
(Co Clk has b, d rec from 1903, m, div, pro, civ ct, Ind rec from 1876)

* Borden   D3   1876   Bexar
Borden County, 101 Main St, Gail, TX 79738 .... (915)856-4312
(Co Clk has b & d rec from 1903, m, div & civ ct rec from 1891, pro rec from 1894)

Bosque   E5   1854   McLennan, Milam
Bosque County, Morgan & Main Sts, Meridian, TX 76665 .... (817)435-2201
(Co Clk has b, d rec from 1902, m, pro, Ind rec from 1854, civ ct rec; Dis Clk has div rec)

Bowie   D7   1840   Red River
Bowie County, PO Box 248, New Boston, TX 75570-0248 .... (903)628-2571
(Co Clk has b, m, d, pro, civ ct rec & deeds from 1889)

* Brazoria   G6   1836   Old Mexican Municipality
Brazoria County, 111 E Locust St, Angleton, TX 77515-4622 .... (409)849-5711
(Co Clk has b rec from 1901, d rec from 1903, m rec from 1829, Co Clk has pro rec from 1837, civ ct rec from 1896, Ind rec from 1826, mil rec from 1919, crim, delayed b certificates, election rec from 1800's)

* Brazos   F6   1841   Washington, Robertson
Brazos County, 300 E 26th St, Bryan, TX 77803-5359 .... (409)775-7400
(originally Navasota Co - changed to Brazos 1842; Co Clk has m rec from 1841, b & d rec from 1900, pro rec from 1844, civ ct rec from 1959, some civ ct rec earlier)

Brewster   F1   1887   Presidio
Brewster County, 201 W Ave, Alpine, TX 79830 .... (915)837-3366
(Co Clk has b & d rec from 1903, m, div, pro & civ ct rec from 1887)

* Briscoe   C3   1876   Bexar
Briscoe County, 415 Main St, Silverton, TX 79257 .... (806)823-2131
(Co Clk has b & d rec 1903 to 1916 & 1927 to present, Silverton Cem Assoc has bur rec)

Name	Map Index	Date Created	Parent County or Territory From Which Organized

Brooks   H5   1911   Starr, Zapata, Hidalgo
Brooks County, County Courthouse, Falfurrias, TX 78355 . . . . (512)325-5604
(Co Clk hsa b, m, d, pro & civ ct rec from 1911)

*† **Brown**   E4   1856   Travis, Comanche
Brown County, 200 S Broadway St, Brownwood, TX 76801-3136 . . . . (915)643-2594
(Co Clk has cattle brands from 1880; Dis Clk has div rec; Co Clk has b rec from 1900, d rec from 1903, civ ct & Ind rec)

Buchanan (Changed to Stephens 1861)

* **Burleson**   F5   1846   Milam, Washington
Burleson County, 205 W Buck St, Caldwell, TX 77836-1798 . . . . (409)567-4326
(Co Clk has b, d rec from 1903, m, pro, civ ct, Ind rec from 1845; Dis Clk has div rec from 1845)

* **Burnet**   E5   1852   Travis, Bell, Williamson
Burnet County, 220 S Pierce St, Burnet, TX 78611-3136 . . . . (512)756-5420
(Co Clk has b, d rec from 1903, m, bur, pro, Ind rec from 1852, civ ct rec from 1876; Dis Clk has div rec)

*† **Caldwell**   F5   1848   Gonzales
Caldwell County, Main St, Lockhart, TX 78644 . . . . (512)398-2428
(Co Clk has b & d rec from 1903, m & Ind rec from 1848 & civ ct rec; Dis Clk has div rec)

† **Calhoun**   G6   1846   Victoria, Matagorda, Jackson
Calhoun County, 211 S Ann St, Port Lavaca, TX 77979-4249 . . . . (512)553-4411
(Co Clk has b & d rec from 1903, m & deeds from 1846, pro rec from 1849, civ ct rec from 1850, crim rec from 1909 & discharge rec from 1919)

* **Callahan**   D4   1858   Bexar, Travis, Bosque
Callahan County, 400 Market St, Baird, TX 79504-5305 . . . . (915)854-1217
(Co Clk has b, d rec from 1903, m, pro, Ind rec from 1877; Dis Clk has div, civ ct rec)

* **Cameron**   H5   1848   Nueces
Cameron County, 964 E Harrison St, Brownsville, TX 78520-7123 . . . . (512)544-0815
(Co Clk has b rec from 1800, d rec from 1900, pro rec from 1850, civ ct rec from 1964, Ind rec from 1845, marks & brands, mil dis & comm ct rec from 1848, also assumed names)

* **Camp**   D6   1874   Upshur
Camp County, 126 Church St, Pittsburg, TX 75686 . . . . (903)856-2731
(Co Clk has b, d rec from 1903, m, pro, civ ct rec from 1874, Ind rec from 1854, marks and brands from 1874)

Carson   C3   1876   Bexar
Carson County, 501 Main St, Panhandle, TX 79068 . . . . (806)537-3873
(Co Clk has b, d rec from 1903, m rec from 1888, div rec from 1902, pro rec from 1907, Ind rec from 1883)

Cass   D7   1846   Bowie
Cass County, PO Box 468, Linden, TX 75563-0468 . . . . (903)756-5071
(Name changed to Davis 1861, renamed Cass 1871) (Co Clk has b, d rec from 1903, m rec from 1847, pro rec from 1846, Ind rec from 1846; Dis Clk has div, civ ct rec)

Castro   C2   1876   Bexar
Castro County, 100 E Bedford St, Dimmitt, TX 79027-2643 . . . . (806)647-3338
(Co Clk has b, m, d, div, pro, civ ct & Ind rec)

* **Chambers**   F6   1858   Jefferson, Liberty
Chambers County, 404 Washington, Anahuac, TX 77514 . . . . (409)267-3471
(Co Clk has b rec from 1903, d rec from 1908, m, pro, civ ct, Ind rec from 1875, div rec from 1910)

* **Cherokee**   E6   1846   Nacogdoches
Cherokee County, 6th St, Rusk, TX 75785 . . . . (903)683-2350
(Co Clk has civ ct & div rec; Co Clk has b & d rec from 1903, m, pro & civ ct rec from 1846)

* **Childress**   C3   1876   Bexar, Youngland District
Childress County, 100 Ave 'E' NW, Childress, TX 79201-3755 . . . . (817)937-6143
(Co Clk has b & d rec from 1903, m rec from 1893, div & civ ct rec from 1900, pro rec from 1894, Ind rec from 1895)

Clay   D4   1857   Cooke
Clay County, 100 N Bridge St, Henrietta, TX 76365-2858 . . . . (817)538-4631
(Co Clk has b, d rec from 1903, m rec from 1874, pro, Ind rec from 1873, civ ct rec from 1876)

* **Cochran**   D2   1876   Bexar
Cochran County, 100 N Main St, Morton, TX 79346-2558 . . . . (806)266-5450
(Co Clk has b, d, div, pro & civ ct rec from 1926, m rec from 1924, Ind rec from 1884, cattle brands from 1921)

* **Coke**   E3   1889   Tom Green
Coke County, 13 E 7th St, Robert Lee, TX 76945 . . . . (915)453-2631
(Co Clk has b, d rec from 1903, m, div, pro, civ ct rec from 1891, Ind rec from 1875)

* **Coleman**   E4   1858   Travis, Brown
Coleman County, PO Box 591, Coleman, TX 76834-0591 . . . . (915)625-2889
[FHL has some m, cem, nat, pro rec]

* **Collin**   D5   1846   Fannin
Collin County, 210 S McDonald St, McKinney, TX 75069-5655 . . . . (214)548-4100
(Co Clk has b & d rec from 1903, civ ct rec to 1970, co ct at law rec from 1976, m, pro rec; Dis Clk has div & Ind rec)

* **Collingsworth**   C3   1876   Bexar, Youngland District
Collingsworth County, County Courthouse, Wellington, TX 79095 . . . . (806)447-2408
(Co Clk has b rec from 1891, m rec from 1890, d rec from 1892, div & civ ct rec from 1903)

Name	Map Index	Date Created	Parent County or Territory From Which Organized

Colorado   F5   1837   Old Mexican Municipality
Colorado County, 400 Spring St, Columbus, TX 78934-2456 .... (409)732-2155
(Co Clk has b & d rec from 1903, m & pro rec from 1837; Dis Clk has div & civ ct rec)

* **Comal**   F4   1846   Bexar, Gonzales, Travis
Comal County, 100 Main Plaza, New Braunfels, TX 78130-5140 .... (512)620-5501
(Co Clk has b rec 1903 to 1910 & 1930 to 1950, m rec from 1846, d rec from 1903, pro, Ind, nat, civ ct rec from 1846, mil dis rec from 1919)

* **Comanche**   E4   1856   Bosque, Coryell
Comanche County, County Courthouse, Comanche, TX 76442 .... (915)356-2655
(Co Clk has b, d & bur rec from 1903, m rec from 1856, pro rec from 1897, civ ct rec from 1934 & Ind rec from 1859)

* **Concho**   E3   1858   Bexar
Concho County, PO Box 98, Paint Rock, TX 76866-0098 .... (915)732-4322
(Co Clk has b rec from 1800, m, pro, Ind rec from 1879, bur rec from 1883, d rec from 1903, div & civ ct rec from 1907)

* **Cooke**   D5   1848   Fannin
Cooke County, Dixon St County Courthouse, Gainesville, TX 76240 .... (817)668-5420
(Co Clk has b, d rec from 1903, m, pro, civ ct, Ind rec from 1850; Dis Clk has div rec)

* **Coryell**   E5   1854   Bell
Coryell County, PO Box 237, Gatesville, TX 76528-0237 .... (817)865-5016
(Co Clk has b & d rec from 1903, m, pro, civ ct & Ind rec from 1854)

* **Cottle**   C3   1876   Fannin
Cottle County, PO Box 717, Paducah, TX 78248-0717 .... (806)492-3823
(Co Clk has b, m, d, bur, div, pro, civ ct & Ind rec from 1892)

Crane   E2   1887   Tom Green
Crane County, PO Box 578, Crane, TX 79731-0578 .... (915)558-3581
(Co Clk has b rec from 1928, m, d, div, pro, civ ct & Ind rec from 1927 & bur rec from 1953)

Crockett   F3   1875   Bexar
Crockett County, 907 Ave D, Ozona, TX 76943 .... (915)392-2022
(Co Clk has b, d rec from 1903, div, pro, civ ct rec from 1892, bur rec after Jan. 1, 1980)

* **Crosby**   D3   1876   Bexar District
Crosby County, PO Box 218, Crosbyton, TX 79322-0218 .... (806)675-2334
(Co Clk has b, d rec from 1903, m, pro & civ ct rec from 1887, Ind rec from 1886; Dis Clk has div rec)

Culberson   E1   1911   El Paso
Culberson County, PO Box 158, Van Horn, TX 79855-0158 .... (915)283-2058
(Co Clk has b, m, d, div, pro, civ ct, Ind rec from 1911, bur rec from 1972)

* **Dallam**   B2   1876   Bexar
Dallam County, 101 E 5th St, Dalhart, TX 79022-2728 .... (806)249-4751
(Co Clk has b, d rec from 1903, m, civ ct rec from 1891, div rec from 1892, pro rec from 1900, Ind rec from 1876)

* **Dallas**   D5   1846   Nacogdoches, Robertson
Dallas County, 500 Main St, Dallas, TX 75202-3513 .... (214)653-7131
(Co Clk has b & d rec from 1903, m rec from 1846, pro & civ ct rec; Dis Ct has div rec)

Davis (Changed to Cass 1871)

* **Dawson**   D2   1876   Bexar
Dawson County, N 1st & Main Sts, Lamesa, TX 79331 .... (806)872-3778
(Co Clk has b, m, d, bur, pro, Ind rec from 1905, civ ct rec from 1920; Dis Clk has div rec)

* **Deaf Smith**   C2   1876   Bexar
Deaf Smith County, 243 E 3rd County Courthouse, Hereford, TX 79045 .... (806)364-1746
(Co Clk has b, d rec from 1903, m, pro, civ ct rec from 1891, Ind rec from 1882, brand rec, discharge rec from 1919; funeral homes have bur rec; Dis Clk has div rec, doctor recs from 1903)

* **Delta**   D6   1870   Hopkins, Lamar
Delta County, PO Box 455, Cooper, TX 75432-0455 .... (903)395-4110
(Co Clk has b, pro & civ ct rec from 1903, m rec from 1870, d rec from 1916 & Ind rec)

*† **Denton**   D5   1846   Fannin
Denton County, 401 W Hickory St, Denton, TX 76201-9030 .... (817)565-8500
(Co Clk has b, d & bur rec from 1903, m, pro, civ ct & Ind rec from 1876; Dis Clk has div rec from 1876; Courthouse burned 1875, a few prior rec saved)

† **DeWitt**   G5   1846   Goliad, Gonzales, Victoria
DeWitt County, 307 N Gonzales St, Cuero, TX 77954-2870 .... (512)275-3724
(Co Clk has b & d rec from 1903, m, pro, civ ct, Ind rec & cattle brands from 1846, CW muster roll for home guard groups from 1861)

Dickens   D3   1876   Bexar
Dickens County, PO Box 120, Dickens, TX 79229-0120 .... (806)623-5531
(Co Clk has b, m, d, bur, div, pro, civ ct & Ind rec from 1891)

* **Dimmit**   G3   1858   Uvalde, Bexar, Maverick, Webb
Dimmit County, 103 N 5th St, Carrizo Springs, TX 78834-3198 .... (512)876-3569
(Co Clk has b & d rec from 1903, m & div ct rec from 1881, pro rec from 1882 & Ind rec; Dis Clk has div rec)

Name	Map Index	Date Created	Parent County or Territory From Which Organized

* **Donley**   C3   1881   Jack
Donley County, PO Box U, Clarendon, TX 79226-2020 .... (806)874-3436
(Co Clk has b rec from 1877, m & Ind rec & brands from 1882, d rec from 1903, pro rec from 1923, mil dis rec from 1919)

   Duval   H5   1858   Live Oak, Starr, Neuces
Duval County, 400 E Gravis St, San Diego, TX 78384-1816 .... (512)279-3322
(Co Clk has b & d rec from 1903, m, pro & Ind rec from 1877, also civ ct rec)

* **Eastland**   D4   1858   Bosque, Coryell, Travis
Eastland County, PO Box 110, Eastland, TX 76448-0110 .... (817)629-8622
(Co Clk has b, d rec from 1903 to 1930, 1940 to 1950, m, pro, Ind rec from 1873; Dis Ct has div rec from 1903)

   Ector   E2   1887   Tom Green
Ector County, 300 N Grant Ave, Odessa, TX 79761-5162 .... (915)335-3045
(Co Clk has b, m, d, bur, pro, civ ct, Ind rec from 1896; Dis Clk has div rec)

* **Edwards**   F3   1858   Bexar
Edwards County, PO Box 184, Rocksprings, TX 78880-0184 .... (512)683-2235
(Co Clk has b & d rec from 1903, m, div, pro, civ ct rec & deeds from 1884)

* **El Paso**   E1   1850   Bexar
El Paso County, 500 E San Antonio Ave, El Paso, TX 79901-2421 .... (915)546-2071
(Co Clk has b, d & bur rec from 1903, m rec from 1880, pro, civ ct & Ind rec, also mil dis rec from 1919)

* **Ellis**   E5   1849   Navarro
Ellis County, PO Box 250, Waxahachie, TX 75165-0250 .... (214)937-8620
[FHL has some m, d, cem, civ ct, Ind, nat, pro rec]

   Encinal (Discontinued)

* **Erath**   E5   1856   Bosque, Coryell
Erath County, County Courthouse Sq, Stephenville, TX 76401-4219 .... (817)965-1482
(Co Clk has b, d rec from 1903, m rec from 1869, pro rec from 1876, Ind rec from 1867)

* **Falls**   E5   1850   Limestone, Milam
Falls County, PO Box 458, Marlin, TX 76661-0458 .... (817)883-2061
(Co Clk has b, d rec from 1903, m rec from 1854, pro, Ind rec)

* **Fannin**   D6   1837   Red River
Fannin County, County Courthouse, Bonham, TX 75418 .... (903)583-7486
(Co Clk has b rec from 1903, a few from 1874 to 1876, d rec from 1903, m rec from 1852, pro, Ind, civ ct rec from 1838)

*† **Fayette**   F5   1837   Bastrop, Colorado
Fayette County, 151 N Washington St, La Grange, TX 78945-2657 .... (409)968-3251
(Co Clk has b, d rec from 1903, m, pro, Ind rec from 1838; Dis Clk has div rec from 1838)

* **Fisher**   D3   1876   Bexar
Fisher County, PO Box 368, Roby, TX 79543-0368 .... (915)776-2401
(Co Clk has b, d & m rec from 1903, Ind rec from 1886, pro & civ ct rec from 1920)

* **Floyd**   C3   1876   Bexar
Floyd County, 100 Main St, Floydada, TX 79235 .... (806)983-3236
(Co Clk has b, m, d, pro, civ ct rec from 1903, Ind rec from 1876; Dis Clk has div rec)

* **Foard**   D4   1891   Hardman, Knox, King, Cottle
Foard County, PO Box 539, Crowell, TX 79227-0539 .... (817)684-1365
(Co Clk has b & d rec from 1903, m, div, pro, civ ct & Ind rec from 1891)

* **Fort Bend**   F6   1837   Austin
Fort Bend County, PO Box 520, Richmond, TX 77469 .... (713)342-3411
(Co Clk has b, d rec from 1903, m, Ind rec from 1838, pro rec from 1836 civ ct rec from 1876)

* **Franklin**   D6   1875   Titus
Franklin County, Dallas & Kaufman Sts, Mount Vernon, TX 75457 .... (903)537-4252
(Co Clk has div rec from 1884, b, d rec from 1903, m, pro rec from 1875, Ind rec from 1846)

* **Freestone**   E6   1850   Limestone
Freestone County, Main & Mount Sts, Fairfield, TX 75840-1594 .... (903)389-2635
(Co Clk has b, d rec from 1903, Ind rec from 1851, m & pro rec from 1853, civ ct rec)

* **Frio**   G4   1858   Atascosa, Bexar, Uvalde
Frio County, PO Box X, Pearsall, TX 78061-1423 .... (512)334-2214
(Co Clk has b, d rec from 1903, m rec from 1876, pro rec from 1874, civ ct rec from 1907, Ind rec from 1871)

* **Gaines**   D2   1876   Bexar
Gaines County, 100 S Main St, Seminole, TX 79360-4342 .... (915)758-3521
(Co Clk has b, m, d, bur, pro & civ ct rec from 1905)

* **Galveston**   F6   1838   Brazoria
Galveston County, 722 Moody Ave, Galveston, TX 77550-2317 .... (409)766-2210
(Co Clk has b & d rec from 1903 to 1910 - 1941 to 1951, m, pro & Ind rec from 1838, civ ct rec from 1875)

* **Garza**   D3   1876   Bexar
Garza County, County Courthouse, Post, TX 79356-3241 .... (806)495-3535
(Co Clk has b, m, d, div, pro & civ ct rec from 1907)

*† **Gillespie**   F4   1848   Bexar
Gillespie County, PO Box 351, Fredericksburg, TX 78624 .... (512)997-6515
(Co Clk has b, m, pro rec from 1850, d rec from 1902, Ind rec from 1848, civ ct rec from 1954; Dis Clk has div rec)

Name	Map Index	Date Created	Parent County or Territory From Which Organized

* **Glasscock**   E3   1887   Tom Green
Glasscock County, PO Box 190, Garden City, TX 79739-0190 . . . . (915)354-2371
(Co Clk has b, d rec from 1903, m, civ ct rec from 1893, pro rec from 1895, Ind rec from 1883; Dis Clk has div rec; Co Judge has recent bur rec)

* **Goliad**   G5   1836   Old Mexican Municipality
Goliad County, PO Box 5, Goliad, TX 77963-0005 . . . . (512)645-3294
(Co Clk has b & d rec from 1903, m, pro, civ ct & Ind rec from 1870 & div rec)

* **Gonzales**   F5   1836   Old Mexican Municipality
Gonzales County, 414 Saint Joseph St, Gonzales, TX 78629-4069 . . . . (512)672-2801
(Co Clk has b, d rec from 1903, m, pro, Ind rec, brands from 1829; Dis Clk has div rec)

* **Gray**   C3   1876   Bexar
Gray County, 205 N Russell St, Pampa, TX 79065-6441 . . . . (806)669-8004
(Co Clk has b rec from 1903, m, d, pro, civ ct rec from 1902, bur rec from 1930, Ind rec from 1887, discharge rec from 1919, marks and brands from 1902; Dis Clk has div rec)

* **Grayson**   D5   1846   Fannin
Grayson County, Houston & Lamar Sts, Sherman, TX 75090 . . . . (903)868-9515
(Co Clk has b & d rec from 1900, m, pro, civ ct & Ind rec from 1846; Dis Clk has div rec)

*† **Gregg**   D6   1873   Rusk, Upshur
Gregg County, PO Box 3049, Longview, TX 75606-3049 . . . . (903)758-6181
(Co Clk has b, m, civ ct, Ind rec from 1873, d rec from 1900, pro rec)

* **Grimes**   F6   1846   Montgomery
Grimes County, Main St, Anderson, TX 77830 . . . . (409)873-2662
(Co Clk has b, d & civ ct rec from 1903, m & pro rec from 1848 & Ind rec from 1843)

*† **Guadalupe**   F5   1846   Bexar, Gonzales
Guadalupe County, 101 E Court St, Sequin, TX 78155-5700 . . . . (512)379-4188
(Co Clk has b, d & bur rec from 1935, m & pro rec from 1838, also civ ct & Ind rec; Dis Clk has div rec)

* **Hale**   C2   1876   Bexar
Hale County, 500 Broadway, Plainview, TX 79072 . . . . (806)293-8481
(Bur Vit Statistics has b, d rec; Co Clk has m rec from 1888, pro rec from 1889, Ind rec from 1888; Dis Clk has div, civ ct rec)

* **Hall**   C3   1876   Bexar, Young
Hall County, County Courthouse, Memphis, TX 79245-3343 . . . . (806)259-2511
(Co Clk has b, m, d, div, pro, civ ct, Ind rec from 1890)

Hamilton   E4   1842   Bosque, Comanche, Lampasas, Coryell
Hamilton County, County Courthouse, Hamilton, TX 76531-1859 . . . . (817)386-3518
(Co Clk has incomplete b, d rec from 1903, m rec from 1885, div rec from 1875, pro rec from 1870)

* **Hansford**   B3   1876   Bexar, Young
Hansford County, 1 NW Court, Spearman, TX 79081-3499 . . . . (806)659-2666
(Co Clk has Ind rec from 1875, b, m, d, div, pro, civ ct rec from 1900)

* **Hardeman**   C4   1858   Fannin
Hardeman County, PO Box 30, Quanah, TX 79252-0030 . . . . (817)663-2901
(Co Clk has b & d rec from 1903, m rec from 1885, pro & civ ct rec from 1886, deeds from 1871; Dis Clk has div rec)

Hardin   F7   1858   Jefferson, Liberty
Hardin County, Hwy 326 & Courthouse Sq, Kountze, TX 77625 . . . . (409)246-5185
(Co Clk has b rec from 1892, m, d & Ind rec from 1859, pro rec from 1888; Dis Clk has div rec)

* **Harris**   F6   1836   Formerly Harrisburg Municipality (Original county)
Harris County, 1001 Preston St, Houston, TX 77002-1816 . . . . (713)221-5000
[FHL has some m, d, cem, civ ct, Ind, nat, pro rec]

* **Harrison**   D7   1839   Shelby
Harrison County, Houston & Wellington Sts, Marshall, TX 75670 . . . . (903)935-4858
(Co Clk has b rec from 1903, m rec from 1850, d rec from 1917, pro & Ind rec from 1840, civ ct rec from 1900)

* **Hartley**   B2   1876   Bexar, Young
Hartley County, PO Box T, Channing, TX 79018-0400 . . . . (806)235-3582
(Co Clk has b rec from 1904, m rec from 1891, d rec from 1910, div, pro, civ ct, Ind rec)

* **Haskell**   D4   1858   Fannin, Milam
Haskell County, PO Box 725, Haskell, TX 79521-0725 . . . . (817)864-2451
(Co Clk has b & d rec from 1903, m, pro, civ ct & Ind rec from 1885)

*† **Hays**   F5   1848   Travis
Hays County, County Courthouse, San Marcos, TX 78666 . . . . (512)396-2601
(Co Clk has pro rec from 1839, b rec from 1865, m, civ & criminal ct, pro, Ind rec from 1848, mil rec from 1919; Dis Clk has div rec from 1897)

Hemphill   B3   1876   Bexar, Young
Hemphill County, PO Box 867, Canadian, TX 79014-0867 . . . . (806)323-6212
(Co Clk has b rec from 1876, d rec from 1910, m, div, pro rec from 1887, civ ct, Ind rec, brands and/or cattle registration rec from 1887)

* **Henderson**   E6   1846   Houston, Nacogdoches
Henderson County, Courthouse Sq, Athens, TX 75751 . . . . (903)675-6140
(Co Clk has b & d rec from 1903, m rec from 1880, pro rec from 1860, civ ct rec from 1910 & Ind rec from 1846)

Name	Map Index	Date Created	Parent County or Territory From Which Organized

* **Hidalgo**   H5   1852   Cameron
Hidalgo County, 100 N Closner St, Edinburg, TX 78539-3563 .... (512)383-2751
(Co Clk has b, m, d, pro, civ ct & Ind rec; Dis Clk has div rec)

* **Hill**   E5   1853   Navarro
Hill County, PO Box 398, Hillsboro, TX 76645-0398 .... (817)582-2161
(Courthouse burned sometime between 1874 and 1878. Co Clk has b, d rec from 1903, m, pro, Ind rec from 1853, some bur rec
from 1853; Dis Clk has div rec)

* **Hockley**   D2   1876   Bexar, Young
Hockley County, 800 Houston St Courthouse, Box 13, Levelland, TX 79336 .... (806)894-3185
(Co Clk has b, m, d, pro, civ ct & Ind rec from 1921; attached to Lubbock from 1891 to 1921)

*† **Hood**   E5   1865   Johnson
Hood County, 101 Pearl St, Granbury, TX 76048-2498 .... (817)579-3222
(Co Clk has b & d rec from 1903, m, div, pro, civ ct & Ind rec from 1875; Hood Public Library in Granbury, Texas has many Hood
County rec of the late Judge Henry Davis)

* **Hopkins**   D6   1846   Lamar, Nacogdoches
Hopkins County, PO Box 288, Sulphur Springs, TX 75482-0288 .... (903)885-3929
(Co Clk has b & d rec from 1903, m, pro, civ ct & Ind rec from 1846; Dis Clk has div rec)

* **Houston**   E6   1837   Nacogdoches
Houston County, PO Box 370, Crockett, TX 75835-0370 .... (409)544-3256
(Co Clk has b, m, d rec from 1903, pro, civ ct, Ind rec from 1882; Dis Clk has div rec from 1920; Co Hist Commission has bur rec,
fam histories, community histories from 1800, county history from 1687)

* **Howard**   E3   1876   Bexar, Young
Howard County, 300 Main St, Big Spring, TX 79720-2521 .... (915)263-7247
(Co Clk has b & d rec from 1903, m rec from 1882, pro rec from 1884 & deeds; Dis Clk has div rec also civ ct rec from 1883)

Hudspeth   E1   1917   El Paso
Hudspeth County, PO Box A, Sierra Blanca, TX 79851-0058 .... (915)369-2301
(Co Clk has b, m, d, div, pro, civ ct rec from 1917 & Ind rec from 1836)

* **Hunt**   D6   1846   Fannin, Nacogdoches
Hunt County, 2500 Lee St, Greenville, TX 75401-4246 .... (903)455-6460
(Co Clk has b & d rec from 1903, m rec from 1846, Ind rec from 1843, civ ct rec from 1967; Dis Clk has div rec, pro rec 1896)

* **Hutchinson**   B3   1876   Bexar District
Hutchinson County, PO Box F, Stinnett, TX 79083-0526 .... (806)878-2829
(Co Clk has m, pro, civ ct, Ind rec from 1901; b rec from 1876, d rec; Dis Clk has div rec)

Irion   E3   1889   Tom Green
Irion County, County Courthouse, Mertzon, TX 76941 .... (915)835-2421
(Co Clk has b, d, bur, div, pro & civ ct rec from 1903, m rec from 1889)

* **Jack**   D4   1856   Cooke
Jack County, 100 N Main St, Jacksboro, TX 76056-1746 .... (817)567-2111
(Co Clk has b & d rec from 1903, pro rec from 1857 & Ind rec from 1860, also m & civ ct rec; Dis Clk has div rec)

*† **Jackson**   G5   1836   Old Mexican Municipality
Jackson County, 115 W Main St, Edna, TX 77957-2733 .... (512)782-3563
(Co Clk has b & d rec from 1903, m, pro, Ind rec from 1836, civ ct rec from 1910; Dis Clk has div rec)

* **Jasper**   E7   1836   Old Mexican Municipality
Jasper County, Main & Lamar St, Jasper, TX 75951 .... (409)384-2632
(Co Clk has m, pro, Ind rec from 1849, b rec from 1874, d rec from 1903, civ ct rec from 1911, cem rec; Dis Clk has div rec)

Jeff Davis   E1   1887   Presidio
Jeff Davis County, PO Box 398, Fort Davis, TX 79734-0398 .... (915)426-3251
(Co Clk has d rec from 1904, m rec from 1883, Ind rec from 1890, div rec from 1946, m, div, pro, civ ct & Ind rec from 1887)

* **Jefferson**   F7   1836   Old Mexican Municipality
Jefferson County, 1149 Pearl St, Beaumont, TX 77701-3619 .... (409)835-8475
(Co Clk has b, d rec from 1903, m, pro, civ ct, Ind rec from 1836; Dis Clk has div rec)

Jim Hogg   H4   1913   Brooks, Duval
Jim Hogg County, PO Box 729, Hebbronville, TX 78361-0729 .... (512)527-4031

* **Jim Wells**   H5   1911   Nueces
Jim Wells County, PO Box 1459, Alice, TX 78333-1459 .... (512)668-5702
(Co Clk has b, d, m, pro, civ ct rec from 1911, Ind rec from 1848; Dis Clk has div rec)

* **Johnson**   E5   1854   Ellis, Hill, Navarro
Johnson County, PO Box 662, Cleburne, TX 76033-0662 .... (817)641-4421
(Co Clk has m, Ind, pro rec from 1854, b, d rec from 1903, wills from 1897; Dist Ct has div rec)

* **Jones**   D3   1858   Bexar, Bosque
Jones County, PO Box 552, Anson, TX 79501-0552 .... (915)823-3762
(Co Clk has b & d rec from 1903, m rec & deeds from 1881, pro rec from 1882; Dis Clk has div & civ ct rec)

* **Karnes**   G5   1854   Bexar
Karnes County, 101 N Panna Maria St, Karnes City, TX 78118-2959 .... (512)780-3938
(Co Clk has b & d rec from 1900, m rec from 1875, pro rec from 1870, Ind rec from 1854, civ ct rec from 1900; Dis Clk has div rec
from 1858)

Name	Map Index	Date Created	Parent County or Territory From Which Organized

* **Kaufman**   D6   1848   Henderson
  Kaufman County, Washington St, Kaufman, TX 75142 .... (214)932-4331
  (Co Clk has b & d rec from 1903, m & pro rec from 1850)

* **Kendall**   F4   1862   Kerr, Blanco
  Kendall County, 204 E San Antonio St, Boerne, TX 78006-2050 .... (512)249-9343
  [FHL has some m, cem, civ ct, Ind, nat, pro rec]

  Kenedy   H5   1921   Willacy, Hidalgo, Cameron
  Kenedy County, PO Box 7, Sarita, TX 78385-0007 .... (512)294-5220
  (Co Clk has b rec from 1926, m rec from 1923, d rec from 1929, div, civ ct rec from 1914, pro, Ind rec)

* **Kent**   D3   1876   Bexar, Young
  Kent County, Main St, Jayton, TX 79528 .... (806)237-3881
  (Co Clk has b rec from 1903, also m, d, bur, div, pro & civ ct rec from 1893)

* **Kerr**   F4   1856   Bexar
  Kerr County, 700 Main St, Kerrville, TX 78028-5323 .... (512)257-6181
  (Co Clk has b, d rec from 1903, m, pro, Ind, civ ct rec from 1856; Dis Clk has div rec)

* **Kimble**   F4   1858   Bexar
  Kimble County, 501 Main St, Junction, TX 76849-4763 .... (915)446-3353
  (Co Clk has b, d rec from 1903, m, div, pro, civ ct & Ind rec from 1884)

* **King**   D3   1876   Bexar
  King County, County Courthouse, Guthrie, TX 79236-9999 .... (806)596-4412
  (Co Clk has b, div, civ ct rec from 1914, m rec from 1891, d rec from 1925, pro rec from 1915 & Ind rec from 1878)

* **Kinney**   F3   1850   Bexar
  Kinney County, Ann & James Sts, Brackettville, TX 78832 .... (512)563-2521
  (Co Clk has b, d rec from 1903, m rec from 1872, div, pro, civ ct, Ind rec from 1873; St. Mary's Catholic Church, Brackettville, Tex. has bur rec)

* **Kleberg**   H5   1913   Nueces
  Kleberg County, PO Box 1327, Kingsville, TX 78364-1327 .... (512)592-6448
  (Co Clk has b, m, d, pro, civ ct & Ind rec from 1913; Dis Clk has div rec)

* **Knox**   D4   1858   Young, Bexar
  Knox County, PO Box 196, Benjamin, TX 79505-0196 .... (817)454-2441
  (Co Clk has b rec from 1905, m rec from 1886, d rec from 1917, div rec from 1900's, pro, civ ct, Ind rec from 1887)

* **Lamar**   D6   1840   Red River
  Lamar County, 119 N Main St, Paris, TX 75460-4265 .... (903)737-2420
  (Co Clk has b & d rec from 1903, m, pro, civ ct & Ind rec from 1843; Dis Clk has div rec)

* **Lamb**   C2   1876   Bexar
  Lamb County, 100 6th St, Littlefield, TX 79339-3367 .... (806)385-5173
  (Co Clk has b, m, d, pro rec from 1920, Ind rec from 1915, also civ ct rec)

* **Lampasas**   E4   1856   Bell, Travis
  Lampasas County, PO Box 231, Lampasas, TX 76550-0231 .... (512)556-8271
  (Co Clk has b rec from 1895, d rec from 1910, m rec from 1879, pro rec from 1876, civ ct rec from 1899 & Ind rec from 1872)

* **LaSalle**   G4   1858   Bexar, Webb
  LaSalle County, PO Box 340, Cotulla, TX 78014-0340 .... (512)879-2421
  (Co Clk has b, d, m, div, pro, civ ct, Ind; marks and brand rec from 1881)

* **Lavaca**   F5   1846   Colorado, Victoria, Jackson, Gonzales
  Lavaca County, PO Box 326, Hallettsville, TX 77964-0326 .... (512)798-3612
  (Co Clk has b, d rec from 1903, m, pro, civ ct rec from 1860, Ind rec from 1846)

* **Lee**   F5   1874   Bastrop, Burleston, Washington, Fayette
  Lee County, Main & Hempstead Sts, Giddings, TX 78942 .... (409)542-3684
  (Co Clk has b & d rec from 1903, m, pro, civ ct & Ind rec from 1874; Dis Clk has div rec)

* **Leon**   E6   1846   Robertson
  Leon County, PO Box 98, Centerville, TX 75833-0098 .... (903)536-2352
  (Co Clk has b & d rec from 1903, m rec from 1885, pro rec from 1846, also civ ct & Ind rec)

* **Liberty**   F6   1836   Old Spanish Municipality
  Liberty County, 1923 Sam Houston St, Liberty, TX 77575-4899 .... (409)336-8071
  (Courthouse burned 11 Dec. 1874, rec destroyed. Co Clk has b, d rec from 1903, m rec from 1875, pro, civ ct, Ind rec from 1874; Dis Clk has div rec)

* **Limestone**   E5   1846   Robertson
  Limestone County, PO Box 350, Groesbeck, TX 76642-0350 .... (817)729-5504
  (Co Clk has b & d rec from 1903, pro & civ ct rec from 1900, mil dis rec from 1918, m & Ind rec from 1873; Dis Clk has div rec)

* **Lipscomb**   B3   1876   Bexar
  Lipscomb County, PO Box 175, Lipscomb, TX 79056-0175 .... (806)862-3091
  (Co Clk has b, m, d, div, pro, civ ct, Ind rec from 1887)

* **Live Oak**   G5   1856   Nueces, San Patricio
  Live Oak County, PO Box 280, George West, TX 78022-0280 .... (512)449-2733
  (Co Clk has b & d rec from 1903, m & Ind rec from 1856, pro rec from 1857 & civ ct rec; Dis Clk has div rec)

Name	Map Index	Date Created	Parent County or Territory From Which Organized

* **Llano**   F4   1856   Bexar
Llano County, 801 Ford St, Llano, TX 78643-1997 .... (915)247-4455
(Co Clk has b & d rec from 1903, pro rec from 1856, m & Ind rec from 1880, div & civ ct rec from 1890, some early bur rec)

* **Loving**   E1   1887   Tom Green
Loving County, Hwy 302, Mentone, TX 79754-9999 .... (915)377-2441
(Co Clk has b, m, d, div, pro, civ ct rec from 1931, Ind rec from 1920; Reorg 1931, having been attached to Reeves Co for judicial purposes)

  Lubbock   D2   1876   Bexar, Crosby
Lubbock County, 904 Broadway St, Lubbock, TX 79401-3420 .... (806)741-8089
(Co Clk has b & d rec from 1903, m rec from 1891, pro & civ ct rec from 1904; at one time attached to Crosby)

* **Lynn**   D2   1876   Bexar
Lynn County, PO Box 937, Tahoka, TX 79373-0937 .... (806)998-4750
(Co Clk has b, m, d, bur & civ ct rec from 1903, pro rec from 1905 & Ind rec from 1879)

* **Madison**   E6   1854   Leon, Grimes, Walker
Madison County, 101 W Main St, Madisonville, TX 77864-1901 .... (409)348-2639
(Co Clk has m, pro, Ind rec from 1873, b & d rec from 1903, some bur rec)

*† **Marion**   D7   1860   Cass
Marion County, PO Box F, Jefferson, TX 75657-0420 .... (903)665-3971
(Co Clk has b, d rec from 1903, m, pro, Ind rec from 1860)

* **Martin**   D2   1876   Bexar
Martin County, PO Box 906, Stanton, TX 79782-0906 .... (915)756-3412
(Co Clk has b & d rec from 1910, m, civ ct, div & pro rec from 1885)

* **Mason**   F4   1858   Gillespie
Mason County, Westmoreland St & Post Hill, Mason, TX 76856 .... (915)347-5253
(Co Clk has b, d & bur rec from 1903, m, div, pro, civ ct rec from 1877 & Ind rec from 1850)

* **Matagorda**   G6   1836   Old Mexican Municipality
Matagorda County, 1700 7th St, Bay City, TX 77414-5034 .... (409)244-7680
[FHL has some m, cem, civ ct, Ind, pro rec]

  Maverick   G3   1856   Kenedy
Maverick County, PO Box 4050, Eagle Pass, TX 78853-4050 .... (512)773-2829
(Co Clk has b & d rec from 1903, m rec from 1871, pro & civ ct rec)

* **McCulloch**   E4   1856   Bexar
McCulloch County, County Courthouse, Brady, TX 76825 .... (915)597-2355
(Co Clk has b, d, pro & co ct rec from 1903, m & Ind rec from 1879; Dis Clk has div rec)

* **McLennan**   E5   1850   Milam
McLennan County, 5th & Washington New Records Bldg, Waco, TX 76701 .... (817)757-5000
(Co Clk has b & d rec from 1929, m, pro, civ ct & Ind rec from 1850; Dis Clk has div rec)

* **McMullen**   G4   1858   Bexar, Live Oak, Atascosa
McMullen County, River & Elm Sts, Tilden, TX 78072 .... (512)274-3215
(Co Clk has m, pro, civ ct, Ind rec from 1850, b & d rec from 1903)

* **Medina**   F4   1848   Bexar
Medina County, County Courthouse, Hondo, TX 78861 .... (512)426-5381
(Co Clk has b, d rec from 1903, m, pro, Ind rec from 1848, civ ct rec from 1876)

* **Menard**   E3   1858   Bexar
Menard County, PO Box 1028, Menard, TX 76859-1028 .... (915)396-4682
(Co Clk has b & civ ct rec from 1900, m rec from 1878, d rec from 1917, div rec from 1889, pro & Ind rec from 1880)

* **Midland**   E2   1885   Tom Green
Midland County, 200 W Wall St, Midland, TX 79701-4512 .... (915)688-1000
(Co Clk has b & d rec from 1917, m & Ind rec from 1885, pro rec from 1911, brands from 1885; Dis Clk has div & civ ct rec)

*† **Milam**   F5   1836   Old Mexican Municipality
Milam County, 100 S Fannin Ave, Cameron, TX 76520-4216 .... (817)697-6596
(Co Clk has m rec from 1873, pro, civ ct, Ind rec, brands from 1874, b & d rec from 1903, school censuses 1909 to 1970, mil dis from 1919)

*† **Mills**   E4   1887   Comanche, Brown, Hamilton, Lampasas
Mills County, PO Box 646, Goldthwaite, TX 76844-0646 .... (915)648-2711
(Co Clk has b & d rec from 1903, m, div, pro, civ ct & Ind rec from 1887)

* **Mitchell**   D3   1876   Bexar
Mitchell County, 301 Oak St, Colorado City, TX 79512-6225 .... (915)728-3481
(Co Clk has b, m, d, pro & civ ct rec)

* **Montague**   D5   1857   Cooke
Montague County, PO Box 77, Montague, TX 76251-0077 .... (817)894-2461
(Co Clk has b & d rec from 1903, m, pro & civ ct rec from 1873)

* **Montgomery**   F6   1837   Washington
Montgomery County, 300 N Main St, Conroe, TX 77301-2898 .... (409)539-7885
(Co Clk has m, pro, Ind rec from 1838, b, d, bur rec from 1903, civ ct rec from 1929; Dis Clk has div rec from 1914)

Name	Map Index	Date Created	Parent County or Territory From Which Organized

* **Moore**   B2   1876   Bexar
  Moore County, PO Box 396, Dumas, TX 79029-0396 .... (806)935-6164
  (Co Clk has b, d, bur, pro, civ ct rec from 1901, Ind rec from 1877, m rec from 1894; Dis Clk has div rec)

  Morris   D6   1875   Titus
  Morris County, 500 Broadnax St, Daingerfield, TX 75638-1315 .... (903)645-3911
  (Co Clk has Ind rec from 1849, m & pro rec from 1875, b & d rec from 1903, some delayed b rec; Dis Clk has div & civ ct rec)

* **Motley**   C3   1876   Bexar
  Motley County, Main St, Matador, TX 79244 .... (806)347-2621
  (Co Clk has b & d rec from 1903, m, div, pro, civ ct rec from 1891, also Ind rec from 1891 & a few prior)

* **Nacogdoches**   E7   1836   Old Mexican Municipality
  Nacogdoches County, 101 W Main St, Nacogdoches, TX 75961-5119 .... (409)560-7733
  (Co Clk has b, d rec from 1903, m rec from 1824, pro rec from 1845, Ind rec from 1833, civ ct rec; Dis Clk has div rec)

* **Navarro**   E6   1846   Robertson
  Navarro County, 300 W 3rd Ave, Corsicana, TX 75110-4694 .... (903)654-3035
  (Co Clk has b & d rec from 1903, m rec from 1846, pro & Ind rec from 1850 & civ ct rec; Dis Clk has div rec)

  Navasota (Name changed to Brazos in 1842)

  Newton   E7   1846   Jasper
  Newton County, Courthouse Sq Hwy 190, Newton, TX 75966 .... (409)379-5341
  (Co Clk has b & d rec from 1903, m rec from 1846, pro rec from 1870, also civ ct rec)

* **Nolan**   D3   1881   Young, Bexar
  Nolan County, 102 E 3rd St, Sweetwater, TX 79556-4511 .... (915)235-2462
  (Co Clk has pro rec from 1884, m rec from 1881, Ind rec from 1889, b, d, civ ct rec from 1900; Dis Clk has div rec; Co Justice of Peace has bur rec)

* **Nueces**   G5   1846   San Patricio
  Nueces County, 901 Leopard St, Corpus Christi, TX 78401-3606 .... (512)888-0580
  [FHL has some m, cem, civ ct, Ind, nat, pro, tax rec]

* **Ochiltree**   B3   1876   Bexar
  Ochiltree County, 511 S Main St, Perryton, TX 79070-3154 .... (806)435-8105
  (Co Clk has b rec from 1903, d rec from 1904, m & civ ct rec from 1889, pro rec from 1906, Ind rec from 1890, bur rec from 1902; Dis Clk has div rec from 1891)

* **Oldham**   B2   1876   Bexar
  Oldham County, PO Box 469, Vega, TX 79092-0469 .... (806)267-2667
  (Co Clk has b rec from 1917, d rec from 1918, m & div rec from 1881, bur & pro rec from 1887, civ ct rec from 1911, Ind rec from 1878)

† **Orange**   F7   1852   Jefferson
  Orange County, PO Box 1536, Orange, TX 77631-1536 .... (409)883-7740
  (Co Clk has b & d rec from 1903, m, pro, civ ct, Ind rec from 1852;Dis Clk has div rec; State Lib in Liberty has school rec from 1925)

* **Palo Pinto**   D4   1856   Navarro, Bosque
  Palo Pinto County, PO Box 8, Palo Pinto, TX 76072-0008 .... (817)659-3651
  (Co Clk has b & d rec from 1903, m & Ind rec from 1857, pro & civ ct rec from 1860; Dis Clk has div rec from 1900)

* **Panola**   E7   1846   Harrison, Shelby
  Panola County, Sabine & Sycamore Sts Rm 201, Carthage, TX 75633 .... (903)693-0302
  (Co Clk has b & d rec from 1903, m rec from 1846, pro, civ ct & Ind rec)

* **Parker**   D5   1855   Bosque, Navarro
  Parker County, PO Box 819, Weatherford, TX 76086-0819 .... (817)594-7461
  (Co Clk has b, d rec from 1903, m, pro, Ind rec from 1874, civ ct rec; Dis Clk has div rec; Library, Weatherford, has bur rec)

* **Parmer**   C2   1876   Bexar
  Parmer County, 401 3rd St, Farwell, TX 79325 .... (806)481-3691
  (Co Clk has b, m, d, pro, civ ct, Ind rec from 1908; Dis Clk has div rec from 1908)

* **Pecos**   E2   1871   Presidio
  Pecos County, 103 W Callaghan St, Fort Stockton, TX 79735-7101 .... (915)336-7555
  [FHL has some m & cem rec]

* **Polk**   E6   1846   Liberty
  Polk County, 101 W Church St, Livingston, TX 77351-3201 .... (409)327-8398
  (Co Clk has b, d rec from 1903, m, pro Ind rec from 1846, civ ct rec, Conf. State Army and Navy Roster 1861-1865, comm ct and tax assessments; Dis Clk has div rec)

* **Potter**   B3   1876   Bexar
  Potter County, 511 S Taylor St, Amarillo, TX 79101-2432 .... (806)379-2250
  (Co Clk has b, d rec from 1903 to 1910, from 1941 to 1951, m rec from 1888, pro rec from 1896, civ ct rec from 1889, Ind rec from 1878; Dis Clk has div rec)

* **Presidio**   F1   1850   Bexar
  Presidio County, 320 N Highland St, Marfa, TX 79843 .... (915)729-4812
  (Co Clk has b rec from 1900, m, d, bur, div, pro, civ ct & Ind rec from 1886; Dis Clk has div rec)

* **Rains**   D6   1870   Hopkins, Hunt, Wood
  Rains County, PO Box 187, Emory, TX 75440-0187 .... (903)473-2461
  (Co Clk has b rec from 1902, d rec from 1903, m, div, Ind rec from 1880 & pro rec from 1894)

Name	Map Index	Date Created	Parent County or Territory From Which Organized

* **Randall**   C3   1876   Bexar
Randall County, 401 15th St, Canyon, TX 79015-3838 .... (806)655-7001
(Co Clk has m, pro, civ ct & Ind rec; Dis Clk has div rec)

* **Reagan**   E3   1903   Tom Green
Reagan County, PO Box 100, Big Lake, TX 76932-0100 .... (915)884-2442
(Co Clk has b, m, d, div, pro, civ ct & Ind rec from 1903, some rec from 1883 transferred from Tom Green Co)

   Real   F4   1913   Bandera, Kerr, Edwards
Real County, PO Box 656, Leakey, TX 78873-0656 .... (512)232-5202
(Co Clk has b, m, d, div, pro & civ ct rec from 1913)

* **Red River**   D6   1836   Old Mexican Municipality
Red River County, 400 N Walnut St, Clarksville, TX 75426-3041 .... (903)427-2401
(Co Clk has b, d rec from 1903, m rec from 1845, pro, Ind rec from 1835, brand rec from 1843; Dis Clk has div, civ ct rec)

* **Reeves**   E1   1883   Pecos
Reeves County, PO Box 867, Pecos, TX 79772-0867 .... (915)445-5467
(Co Clk has b & d rec from 1903, m, pro, co ct & Ind rec from 1885, also some deferred b rec from the 1800's)

* **Refugio**   G5   1836   Old Mexican Municipality
Refugio County, PO Box 704, Refugio, TX 78377-0704 .... (512)526-2233
(Co Clk has b & d rec from 1903, m rec from 1851, pro rec from 1840, co ct rec form 1881, Ind rec from 1835)

* **Roberts**   B3   1876   Bexar
Roberts County, Kiowa & Commercial Sts, Miami, TX 79059 .... (806)868-2341
(Co Clk has b & d rec from 1903, m, div, pro, civ ct, Ind rec from 1889, bur rec from 1900)

*† **Robertson**   E5   1837   Milam
Robertson County, Center St, Franklin, TX 77856 .... (409)828-4130
(Co Clk has b & d rec from 1903, m & pro rec from 1837 & Ind rec; Dis Clk has div & civ ct rec)

*† **Rockwall**   D5   1873   Kaufman
Rockwall County, Hwy 66 & Goliad, Rockwall, TX 75087 .... (214)722-5141
(Co Clk has b, m, d rec from 1875, Ind rec from 1890, pro rec from 1877, civ ct rec)

* **Runnels**   E3   1858   Bexar, Travis
Runnels County, Hutchings & Broadway, Ballinger, TX 76821 .... (915)365-2720
(Co Clk has b, d, civ ct rec from 1903, m, pro, Ind rec from 1880, cattle brands 1971 to date, soldiers discharge rec from 1918, school cen 1925 to 1970; Dis Clk has div rec)

* **Rusk**   E7   1843   Nacogdoches
Rusk County, 115 N Main St, Henderson, TX 75625-3198 .... (903)657-0330
(Co Clk has b & d rec from 1903, m, pro, civ ct & Ind rec from 1844)

*† **Sabine**   E7   1836   Old Mexican Municipality
Sabine County, Oak St, Hemphill, TX 75948 .... (409)787-3786
(Co Clk has b & d rec from 1903, m rec from 1880, Ind rec from 1875, pro rec; Dis Clk has div, civ ct rec)

* **San Augustine**   E7   1836   Old Mexican Municipality
San Augustine County, 106 Courthouse, San Augustine, TX 75972-1335 .... (409)275-2452
(Co Clk has pro rec from 1828, Ind rec from 1833, m rec from 1837, d rec from 1903, b rec from 1905; Dis Clk has div, civ ct rec from 1837)

   San Jacinto   F6   1870   Liberty, Polk, Montgomery, Walker
San Jacinto County, Church & Bird Sts, Coldspring, TX 77331 .... (409)653-2324
(Co Clk has b rec from 1903, d rec from 1905, m, div, pro, civ ct, Ind rec from 1870)

* **San Patricio**   G5   1836   Old Mexican Municipality
San Patricio County, PO Box 578, Sinton, TX 78387-0578 .... (512)364-2490
(Co Clk has b rec from 1893, d rec from 1903, m rec from 1858, pro rec from 1847, civ ct rec from 1876 & Ind rec from 1848)

* **San Saba**   E4   1856   Bexar
San Saba County, 518 E Wallace St, San Saba, TX 76877-3611 .... (915)372-3635
(Co Clk has b, d rec from 1903, m, div, civ ct, Ind rec from 1856, pro rec from 1890)

* **Schleicher**   E3   1887   Crockett
Schleicher County, Hwy 277, Eldorado, TX 76936 .... (915)853-2833
(Co Clk has b, d rec from 1903, m, div, pro, civ ct rec from 1901, Ind rec from 1889)

* **Scurry**   D3   1876   Bexar
Scurry County, County Courthouse, Snyder, TX 79549 .... (915)573-5332
(Co Clk has b, d rec from 1903, m, Ind rec from 1884, pro & civ ct rec from 1900; Dis Clk has div rec)

   Shackelford   D4   1858   Bosque
Shackelford County, PO Box 247, Albany, TX 76430-0247 .... (915)762-2232
(Co Clk has b rec from 1903, m, Ind rec from 1874, d, pro rec from 1875, civ ct rec from 1899, div rec)

* **Shelby**   E7   1836   Old Mexican Municipality
Shelby County, Courthouse, Center, TX 75935-3945 .... (409)598-6361
(Co Clk has b, m, pro, civ ct & Ind rec from 1882, d & bur rec from 1903; Dis Clk has div rec)

* **Sherman**   B2   1876   Bexar
Sherman County, 701 N 3rd St, Stratford, TX 79084 .... (806)396-2371
(Co Clk has b, d, pro, civ ct rec from 1903, m, Ind rec from 1901, bur rec from 1895, div rec from 1914, Commission's Court Minutes from 1889, Crim rec from 1891, Cattle and Ranch Brands Register 1892)

Name	Map Index	Date Created	Parent County or Territory From Which Organized

* **Smith** E6 1846 Nacogdoches
Smith County, PO Box 1018, Tyler, TX 75710-1018 .... (903)595-4861
(Co Clk has b & d rec from 1903, m rec from 1848, pro rec from 1847, civ ct rec & deeds rec from 1846)

*† **Somervell** E5 1875 Hood, Johnson
Somervell County, PO Box 1098, Glen Rose, TX 76043-1098 .... (817)897-4427
(Co Clk has b & d rec from 1903, m rec from 1885, div, civ ct rec from 1898, pro & Ind rec from 1875)

* **Starr** H4 1848 Nueces
Starr County, Britton Ave, Rio Grande City, TX 78582 .... (512)487-2954
(Co Clk has Ind rec from 1848, pro rec from 1853, m rec from 1858, b rec from 1880, d rec from 1903, civ ct rec from 1932, marks and brands from 1874, Intentions to become citizens 1883 to 1898, soldier's discharge rec from 1919)

* **Stephens** D4 1858 Bosque
Stephens County, County Courthouse, Breckenridge, TX 76024 .... (817)559-3700
(Co Clk has b, d rec from 1903, m rec from 1876, pro rec from 1886, Ind rec from 1858; Dis Clk has div, civ ct rec. Originally Buchanan, changed to Stephens County 1861)

* **Sterling** E3 1891 Tom Green
Sterling County, PO Box 55, Sterling City, TX 76951-0055 .... (915)378-5191
(Co Clk has b & d rec from 1903, m rec from 1913, div, pro, civ ct & Ind rec from 1891)

* **Stonewall** D3 1876 Bexar
Stonewall County, PO Box P, Aspermont, TX 79502-0914 .... (817)989-2272
(Co Clk has b, m, d, div, civ ct & Ind rec from ca 1900)

Sutton F3 1890 Crockett
Sutton County, 300 E Oak St Suite 3, Sonora, TX 76950-3106 .... (915)387-3815
(Co Clk has b, d rec from 1903, m, div, pro, civ ct, Ind rec from Dec. 1890)

* **Swisher** C3 1876 Bexar, Young
Swisher County, County Courthouse, Tulia, TX 79088-2247 .... (806)995-3294
(Co Clk has b rec from 1904, m, d, bur rec from 1900, div rec from 1905, pro & civ ct rec from 1890, Ind rec from 1888)

* **Tarrant** D5 1849 Navarro
Tarrant County, 100 W Weatherford, Fort Worth, TX 76196-0001 .... (817)334-1195
(Co Clk has b, m, Ind, pro rec from 1876, d rec from 1903; Dis Clk has div & civ ct rec)(1860 cen missing)

Taylor E4 1858 Bexar, Travis
Taylor County, 300 Oak St, Abilene, TX 79602-1521 .... (915)677-1711
[FHL has some m rec]

* **Terrell** F2 1905 Pecos
Terrell County, PO Box 410, Sanderson, TX 79848-0410 .... (915)345-2391

* **Terry** D2 1876 Bexar (attached to Martin from 1889)
Terry County, 5th & Main, Brownfield, TX 79316 .... (806)637-8551
(Co Clk has b & d rec from 1941, m rec from 1904, pro, civ ct, Ind rec & marks & brands from 1904)

Throckmorton D4 1858 Fannin
Throckmorton County, PO Box 309, Throckmorton, TX 76083-0309 .... (817)849-2501
(Co Clk has b rec from 1903, m, d, div, pro rec from 1879, also civ ct & Ind rec)(1870 cen missing)

* **Titus** D6 1846 Red River, Bowie
Titus County, Courthouse Sq, Mount Pleasant, TX 75455 .... (903)572-8891
(Co Clk has b, m, d, bur, pro, civ ct, Ind rec from 1895; Dis Clk has div rec from 1895)

Tom Green E3 1874 Bexar
Tom Green County, 112 W Beauregard Ave, San Angelo, TX 76903-5850 .... (915)653-2385
(Co Clk has b & d rec from 1903, m, pro, civ ct re, from 1875, Ind rec from 1860, cattle brands from 1875)

* **Travis** F5 1840 Bastrop
Travis County, 1000 Guadalupe St, Austin, TX 78701-2336 .... (512)473-9000
(Co Clk has b & d rec from 1903, m, pro, civ ct & Ind rec from 1840)

* **Trinity** E6 1850 Houston
Trinity County, Hwys 94 & 287, Groveton, TX 75845 .... (409)642-1208
(Courthouse burned 1876, some deeds refiled. Co Clk has b rec from 1911, d rec from 1919, m, Ind rec from 1876, div rec from 1920, pro, civ ct rec; County Judge has school rec)

* **Tyler** E7 1846 Liberty
Tyler County, 100 Courthouse, Woodville, TX 75979-5245 .... (409)283-2281
(Co Clk has b rec from 1838, m rec from 1849, d, bur rec from 1903, pro rec from 1845, Ind rec from 1846; Dis Clk has div, civ ct rec)

* **Upshur** D6 1846 Harrison, Nacogdoches
Upshur County, Hwy 154 & Simpson St, Gilmer, TX 75644-2198 .... (903)843-3083
(Co Clk has Ind rec from 1845, pro rec from 1853, civ ct rec from 1871, m rec from 1873, b & d rec from 1903; Dis Clk has div rec)

* **Upton** E2 1867 Tom Green
Upton County, PO Box 465, Rankin, TX 79778-0465 .... (915)693-2861
(Co Clk has b, m, d, div, & civ ct rec from 1910, pro rec from 1910)

*† **Uvalde** F4 1850 Bexar
Uvalde County, PO Box 284, Uvalde, TX 78802-0284 .... (512)278-6614
(Co Clk has b, m, d, pro, civ ct, Ind rec from 1856; Dis Clk has div rec)

Name	Map Index	Date Created	Parent County or Territory From Which Organized

Val Verde   F3   1885   Crockett, Kinney, Pecos
Val Verde County, 400 Pecan St, Del Rio, TX 78840-5140 .... (512)774-3611
(Co Clk has b, d rec from 1903, pro, civ ct, Ind rec from 1885, m rec; Dis Clk has div rec)

* **Van Zandt**   D6   1848   Henderson
Van Zandt County, PO Box 515, Canton, TX 75103-0515 .... (903)567-6503
(Co Clk has b, d rec from 1903, m, pro, Ind rec from 1848; Dis Clk has div rec)

* **Victoria**   G5   1836   Old Mexican Municipality
Victoria County, 115 N Bridge St, Victoria, TX 77901-6544 .... (512)575-4558
(Co Clk has b, d rec from 1903, m, pro, Ind rec from 1838, civ ct rec from 1867; Dis Clk has div rec)

* **Walker**   E6   1846   Montgomery
Walker County, 1100 University Ave, Huntsville, TX 77340-4631 .... (409)291-9500
(Co Clk has m, Ind, commissioners' ct rec from 1846, b, d, pro rec; Dis Clk has div rec)

* **Waller**   F6   1873   Austin, Grimes
Waller County, 836 Austin St, Hempstead, TX 77445-4667 .... (409)826-3357
(Co Clk has b, d rec from 1903, m, pro, civ ct, Ind rec from 1873)

* **Ward**   E2   1887   Tom Green
Ward County, County Courthouse, Monahans, TX 79756 .... (915)943-3294
(Co Clk has b, d, m, pro, civ ct, Ind rec from 1892; Dis Clk has div rec; City funeral homes have bur rec)

* **Washington**   F5   1836   Texas Municipality
Washington County, 105 E Main St, Brenham, TX 77833 .... (409)836-4300
(Co Clk has b, d rec from 1903, m rec from 1837, pro, Ind rec; Dis Clk has div rec)

Webb   H4   1848   Bexar
Webb County, 1000 Houston St, Laredo, TX 78040-8023 .... (512)721-2221
(Co Clk has b & d rec from 1856, m rec from 1850 & pro rec from 1870)

* **Wharton**   G6   1846   Matagorda, Jackson
Wharton County, 101 Milam St, Wharton, TX 77488 .... (409)532-2381
(Co Clk has b & d rec from 1903, m rec from 1857, pro rec from 1849 & Ind rec from 1846)

* **Wheeler**   C3   1876   Bexar, Young
Wheeler County, PO Box 465, Wheeler, TX 79096-0465 .... (806)826-5544
(Co Clk has b & d rec from 1906, m, pro, civ ct & Ind rec from 1879; Dis Clk has div rec)

* **Wichita**   C4   1858   Youngland District
Wichita County, 900 7th St, Wichita Falls, TX 76301 .... (817)766-8100
(Co Clk has limited b rec from 1890, limited d rec from 1900, m, pro & Ind rec from 1882; Dis Clk has div & civ rec)

* **Wilbarger**   C4   1858   Bexar
Wilbarger County, 1700 Wilbarger St, Vernon, TX 76384-4742 .... (817)552-5486
(Co Clk has b, m, d, pro, civ ct, Ind rec from 1900; City Sec has bur rec; Dis Clk has div rec)

Willacy   H5   1911   Hidalgo, Cameron
Willacy County, Hidalgo & 3rd St Courthouse, Raymondville, TX 78580 .... (512)689-2710
(Co Clk has b, m, d, pro, civ ct rec from 1921, Ind rec from 1891)

* **Williamson**   F5   1848   Milam
Williamson County, PO Box 18, Georgetown, TX 78627-0018 .... (512)869-4315
(Co Clk has b & d rec from 1903, m, pro, civ ct & Ind rec from 1848; Dis Clk has div rec)

† **Wilson**   G5   1860   Bexar, Karnes
Wilson County, 1420 3rd St, Floresville, TX 78114-2200 .... (512)393-2845
(Co Clk has b & d rec from 1903, m rec from 1860, pro rec from 1862 & co ct rec from 1876)

* **Winkler**   E2   1887   Tom Green
Winkler County, 100 E Winkler St, Kermit, TX 79745-4236 .... (915)586-3401
(Co Clk has b rec from 1919, d, pro rec from 1912, m, co ct rec from 1911, Ind rec from 1887; Dis Clk has div rec)

* **Wise**   D5   1856   Cooke
Wise County, PO Box 359, Decatur, TX 76234-0359 .... (817)627-3351
(Co Clk has b, d rec from 1903, m rec from 1881, pro rec from 1882, Ind rec from 1852, civ ct rec)

* **Wood**   D6   1850   Van Zandt
Wood County, PO Box 338, Quitman, TX 75783-0338 .... (903)763-2711
(Co Clk has b, d rec from 1903, m, pro, Ind rec from 1879, civ ct rec; Dis Clk has div rec)

* **Yoakum**   D2   1876   Bexar (attached to Martin from 1904 to 1907)
Yoakum County, PO Box 309, Plains, TX 79355 .... (806)456-2721
(Co Clk has b rec from 1878, m & d rec from 1908, pro rec from 1907, civ ct rec from 1930 & Ind rec from 1898; Dis Clk has div rec)

* **Young**   D4   1856   Bosque, Fannin
Young County, PO Box 218, Graham, TX 76046-0218 .... (817)549-8432
(Co Clk has b & d rec from 1903, m, pro, civ ct, deeds, comm ct min & old brands from 1856; Dis Clk has div rec)

* **Zapata**   H4   1858   Starr, Webb
Zapata County, 7th Ave & Hidalgo, Zapata, TX 78076 .... (512)765-9915
[FHL has some m, civ ct, Ind, nat, pro rec]

Name	Map Index	Date Created	Parent County or Territory From Which Organized
Zavala	G3	1858	Uvalde, Maverick

Zavala County, County Courthouse, Crystal City, TX 78839 .... (512)374-2331
(Co Clk has b, m, d, pro & civ ct rec from 1884, Ind rec; Dis Clk has div rec, also some copied rec from parent cos)

* At least one county history has been published about this county.
† Inventory of county archives was made by the Historical Records Survey. (See Introduction)

UTAH

CAPITAL · SALT LAKE CITY — TERRITORY 1850 — STATE 1896 (45th)
State Map on Page M-41

The first documented white men to enter Utah were Father Silvestre Escalante and Father Francisco Dominguez in 1776. Between 1811 and 1840, fur trappers entered Utah and prepared the way for future settlers. The first permanent settlers were the Mormons, who entered the Salt Lake Valley on July 24, 1847, led by Brigham Young. They had been forced out of their homes in Nauvoo, Illinois and crossed the plains to this desert. New groups arrived several times each month, so that by 1850, there were 11,380 residents. Most of the early settlers came from New England, Ohio, Illinois, Missouri, and Canada. Most of the Europeans were English, Germans, Danes, Swedes, Norwegians, Swiss, Hollanders, Welsh, and Scottish. Despite warnings from Jim Bridger that corn could never grow in Utah, the Mormons were able to irrigate the land and develop a healthy agriculture.

With the end of the Mexican War, Utah became a part of the United States. The Mormons created the State of Deseret in 1849 and petitioned Congress for admission to the Union. Deseret included parts of California, Oregon, Idaho, Wyoming, Nevada, Arizona, New Mexico, and Utah. Congress denied the petition, but did create the Territory of Utah in 1850, which included parts of Nevada, Wyoming, Colorado, and Utah. With the creation of the territories of Nevada and Colorado in 1861 and Wyoming in 1868, Utah reached it present size.

In the decade following their arrival in Utah, the Mormon settlers founded some 100 towns in Utah, Nevada, Idaho, California, and Wyoming. Between 1856 and 1860, another 8,000 immigrants came to Utah in handcart companies. The Utah War of 1857-58, when United States troops were sent to suppress a rebellion which never existed, was peaceably settled. Federal troops, however, remained in Utah after the war until 1861. Another wave of Mormon settlement occurred between 1858 and 1868, which established communities in southern Utah, southern Idaho, southeastern Nevada and northern Arizona. The first transcontinental railroad was completed at Promontory Point in Utah in 1869.

A series of acts passed by Congress were aimed at the Mormons and their practice of polygamy. Additionally, these acts abolished womens' suffrage and certain civil rights so that prosecution of polygamists would be easier. As a result of these laws, many Mormons fled the area to Sonora and Chihuahua, Mexico and to Alberta, Canada. Mormon Church President Wilford Woodruff made a proclamation known as the Manifesto in 1890 which discontinued the practice of polygamy. With this roadblock to statehood removed, Utah became a state in 1896.

State registration of births and deaths began in 1905 and are available at the Bureau of Vital Records, Utah State Department of Health, 288 North 1460 West, P.O. Box 16700, Salt Lake City, UT 84116-0700. To verify current fees, call 801-538-6105.

Most counties began keeping ledger entries of births and deaths in 1898. Salt Lake City, Ogden, and Logan also have some birth and death records. Most marriage records since 1887 are at the county clerk's office or the Utah State Archives, Archives Building, State Capitol, Salt Lake City UT 84114. An 1856 territorial census is at the Historical Department of the LDS Church, 50 East North Temple, Salt Lake City, UT 84150. The Family History Library of The Church of Jesus Christ of Latter-day Saints, 35 North West Temple, Salt Lake City, UT 84150, has perhaps the largest collection of genealogical resources, records, books, microfilm, and microfiche in the entire world. These resources are also available through Family History Centers (branches) located throughout the world.

Genealogical Archives, Libraries and Societies

Brigham Carnegie Library, 26 E. Forest, Brigham City, UT 84302

Brigham Young University Library, Provo, UT 84602

Cedar City Public Library, Cedar City, UT 84720

Dixie Genealogical Library, St. George, UT 84770

Everton's Genealogical Library, 3223 S. Main, Nibley, UT 84321

Family History Library of The Church of Jesus Christ of Latter-day Saints, 35 North West Temple, Salt Lake City, UT 84150

L. D. S. Branch Library, 4385 Harold B. Lee Library, B. Y. U., Provo, UT 84602

Logan Public Library, 255 N. Main, Logan, UT 84321

Ogden Public Library, Ogden, UT 84402

Public Library, Manti, UT 84642

Public Library, Springville, UT 84663

Temple Area Genealogical Library, Manti, UT 84642

University of Utah Library, Salt Lake City, UT 84112

Utah State Historical Society Library, 300 Rio Grande, Salt Lake City, UT 84101

Utah State University Library, Logan, UT 84321

Genealogical Society of Utah, 35 North West Temple, Salt Lake City, UT 84150

German Genealogical Society, 544 E. Wilmington Ave., Salt Lake City, UT 84106

Jewish Genealogical Society of Salt Lake City, 3510 Fleetwood Drive, Salt Lake City, UT 84109

St. George Genealogy Club, P. O. Box 184, St. George, UT 84770

Utah Genealogical Association, P. O. Box 1144, Salt Lake City, UT 84110

Utah Society, Sons of the American Revolution, 5539 Capital Reef Dr., West Jordan, UT 84084

Printed Census Records and Mortality Schedules

Federal Census 1850, 1860, 1870, 1880, 1900, 1910
Federal Mortality Schedules 1870
Union Veterans and Widows 1890
State/Territorial Census 1851, 1856

Valuable Printed Sources

Atlases, Maps, and Gazetteers

Gannett, Henry. *Gazetteer of Utah*. Washington, DC: Government Printing Office, 1900.

Leigh, Rufus Wood. *Five Hundred Utah Place Names*. Salt Lake City: Deseret News Press, 1961.

Origins of Utah Place Names. Salt Lake City: Utah Writers' Project, 1940.

Bibliographies

Flake, Chad J. *A Mormon Bibliography, 1830-1930*. Salt Lake City: University of Utah Press, 1978.

Holley, Robert P., et al. *Utah's Newspapers: Traces of Her Past*. Salt Lake City: University of Utah Press, 1984.

Genealogical Research Guides

Chaston, Gloria D. and Laureen R. Jaussi. *Genealogical Records of Utah*. Salt Lake City: Deseret Book Co., 1974.

Guide to Official Records of Genealogical Value in the State of Utah. Salt Lake City: Utah State Archives and Records Service, 1980.

Genealogical Sources

Esshan, Frank. *Pioneers and Prominent Men of Utah*. Salt Lake City: Utah Pioneers Book Publishing Co., 1913.

Special Collections Department, Merrill Library. *Name Index to the Library of Congress Collection of Mormon Diaries*. Logan, Utah: Utah State University Press, 1971.

Sperry, Kip. *A Guide to Indexes of Mormon Works, Mormon Collections and Utah Collections*. Salt Lake City: Historical Department, The Church of Jesus Christ of Latter-day Saints, 1974.

Histories

Whitney. Orson F. *History of Utah*. Salt Lake City: George Q. Cannon & Sons, 1892.

UTAH COUNTY DATA
State Map on Page M-41

Name	Map Index	Date Created	Parent County or Territory From Which Organized
* **Beaver**	F3	1856	Iron, Millard
Beaver County, PO Box 392, Beaver, UT 84713-0392 .... (801)438-2352			
(Co Clk has b rec from 1897 to 1905, m rec from 1887, d rec from 1900 to 1905, div rec from 1871, pro rec from 1872, civ ct rec from 1856; Beaver City Office has bur rec)			
*† **Box Elder**	C3	1856	Unorganized Territory
Box Elder County, 1 S Main St, Brigham City, UT 84302-2599 .... (801)734-2031			
(Co Clk has b & d rec from 1898 to 1905, m rec from 1887, div, pro, civ ct & lnd rec from 1856)			
* **Cache**	B4	1856	Unorg. Terr
Cache County, 170 N Main St, Logan, UT 84321-4541 .... (801)752-3542			
(Co Clk has m rec from 1888; Clk Dis Ct has div, pro & civ ct rec; Co Rcdr has lnd rec)			

Name	Map Index	Date Created	Parent County or Territory From Which Organized

*† Carbon   E5   1894   Emery
Carbon County, 120 E Main St, Price, UT 84501-3057 .... (801)637-4700
(Co Clk has m rec; Clk Dis Ct has div, pro & civ ct rec; Co Rcdr has Ind rec)

*† Daggett   C6   1917   Uintah
Daggett County, PO Box 218, Manila, UT 84046-0218 .... (801)784-3154
(Co Clk has m, bur, div, pro, civ ct & Ind rec from 1918)

* Davis   C4   1850   Salt Lake
Davis County, PO Box 618, Farmington, UT 84025-0618 .... (801)451-3214
(Co Clk has m rec; Clk Dis Ct has div, pro & civ ct rec)

* Duchesne   D5   1913   Wasatch
Duchesne County, PO Box 270, Duchesne, UT 84021-0270 .... (801)738-2435
(Co Clk has m, div, pro & civ ct rec from 1915; Co Rcdr has Ind rec from 1915)

*† Emery   F5   1880   Sanpete, Sevier
Emery County, PO Box 907, Castle Dale, UT 84513-0907 .... (801)381-2465
(Co Clk has m, div, pro & civ ct rec; Co Rcdr has Ind rec)

* Garfield   G4   1864   Iron, Sevier, Kane
Garfield County, PO Box 77, Panguitch, UT 84759-0077 .... (801)676-8826
(Co Clk has m rec from 1890, div, pro & civ ct rec from 1896; Co Rcdr has Ind rec from 1882, d rec from 1896 to 1905) (Garfield Co boundaries were set up in 1864 but there were no officials and they did not function as a co until Mar 1882)

† Grand   E6   1890   Emery, Uintah
Grand County, 125 E Center St, Moab, UT 84532-2449 .... (801)259-5645
(Co Clk has m & pro rec from 1890, div & civ ct rec from 1896, Ind rec)

Great Salt Lake (see Salt Lake)

* Iron   G3   1852   Unorg. Terr
Iron County, PO Box 429, Parowan, UT 84761-0429 .... (801)477-3375
(Co Clk has m rec from 1887; Clk Dis Ct has div, pro & civ ct rec; Co Rcdr has Ind rec)

* Juab   E3   1852   Original county
Juab County, 160 N Main St, Nephi, UT 84648-1412 .... (801)623-0271
(Co Clk has b, m, d, div, pro, civ ct & Ind rec from 1898)

* Kane   G4   1864   Washington, Unorg. Terr
Kane County, 76 N Main St, Kanab, UT 84741-3219 .... (801)644-2551
(Co Clk has m, div, pro & civ ct rec; Co Rcdr has Ind rec)

* Millard   E3   1851   Juab
Millard County, PO Box 226, Fillmore, UT 84631-0226 .... (801)743-6223
(Co Clk has m rec from 1887, div, pro & civ ct rec from 1896; Co Rcdr has Ind rec)

*† Morgan   C4   1862   Davis, Summit
Morgan County, 48th W Young St, Morgan, UT 84050 .... (801)829-6811
(Co Clk has m rec from 1888, div & civ ct rec from 1896, pro rec from 1869; Co Rcdr has Ind rec)

Piute   F4   1866   Sevier
Piute County, 21 N Main, Junction, UT 84740 .... (801)577-2840
(Co Clk has b & d rec from 1898, m rec from 1887, div, pro & civ ct rec from 1872)

* Rich   C5   1864   Formerly Richland
Rich County, PO Box 218, Randolph, UT 84064-0218 .... (801)793-2415
(Co Clk has m rec from 1888, div, pro & civ ct rec from 1872; Co Rcdr has Ind rec)

* Salt Lake   D4   1849   Orig. Co. (Great Salt Lake Co)
Salt Lake County, 2001 State St Rm S2200, Salt Lake City, UT 84190-0001 .... (801)468-3531
(Co Clk has m rec from 1887, div & civ ct rec from 1896, pro rec from 1852; Co Rcdr has Ind rec)

* San Juan   G6   1880   Kane
San Juan County, PO Box 338, Monticello, UT 84535-0338 .... (801)587-2231
(Co Clk has m rec from Nov 1888, div rec from 1891, pro rec from 1888 & civ ct rec from 1891)

*† Sanpete   E4   1852   Original county
Sanpete County, 160 N Main St, Manti, UT 84642-1266 .... (801)835-2131
(Co Clk has b rec from 1897 to 1905, d rec from 1898 to 1905, m rec from 1888, div, pro & civ ct rec from 1878 & Ind rec from 1870)

* Sevier   F4   1864   Sanpete
Sevier County, 250 N Main St, Richfield, UT 84701-2158 .... (801)896-9262
(Co Clk has limited b, d rec from 1898 to 1906, m, Ind rec from 1888, div rec from 1889, pro, civ ct rec from 1896, Ind rec from 1888)

* Summit   D5   1854   Salt Lake
Summit County, PO Box 128, Coalville, UT 84017-0128 .... (801)336-4451
(Co Clk has b rec from 1898 to 1905, d rec from 1898 to 1901, m rec from 1888, div, pro & civ ct rec from 1896; Co Rcdr has Ind rec)

*† Tooele   D3   1852   Original county
Tooele County, 47 S Main St, Tooele, UT 84074-2194 .... (801)882-5550
(Co Clk has b & d rec from 1897 to 1905, m rec from 1887; Clk Dis Ct has div, pro & civ ct rec; Co Rcdr has Ind rec)

Name	Map Index	Date Created	Parent County or Territory From Which Organized

*† **Uintah**   D6   1880   Wasatch
     Uintah County, 152 E 100 North, Vernal, UT   84078 .... (801)781-0770
     (Co Clk has m, div, pro & civ ct rec; Co Rcdr has lnd rec)

*† **Utah**   D4   1852   Original county
     Utah County, 51 S University Ave, Provo, UT   84601-4424 .... (801)373-5510
     (Co Clk has m rec from 1887, div & pro rec from 1859, civ ct rec from 1885; Co Rcdr has lnd rec)

*† **Wasatch**   D5   1862   Summit
     Wasatch County, 25 N Main St, Heber City, UT   84032-1827 .... (801)654-3211
     (Co Clk has b & d rec from 1898 to 1905, m rec from 1879, div & civ ct rec from 1898, pro rec from 1897, lnd rec from 1862)

* **Washington**   G2   1852   Unorg. Terr
     Washington County, 197 E Tabernacle St, Saint George, UT   84770-3473 .... (801)634-5702
     (Co Clk has m rec from 1887, div rec from 1878, pro & civ ct rec from 1874; Co Rcdr has lnd rec)

* **Wayne**   F5   1892   Piute
     Wayne County, 18 S Main, Loa, UT   84747 .... (801)836-2731
     (Co Clk has some b, d rec from 1898 to 1927, m, div, civ ct, pro rec from 1898; Co Rcdr has lnd rec from 1898)

*† **Weber**   C4   1852   Original county
     Weber County, 2549 Washington Blvd, Ogden, UT   84401-3111 .... (801)399-8481
     (Co Clk has m rec from 1887; Clk Dis Ct has div, pro & civ ct rec; Co Rcdr has lnd rec)

                * At least one county history has been published about this county.
            † Inventory of county archives was made by the Historical Records Survey. (See Introduction)

VERMONT

CAPITAL · MONTPELIER — STATE 1791 (14th)
State Map on Page M-27

The earliest European to explore Vermont was Samuel de Champlain, who discovered Lake Champlain in 1609. The French and English disputed the area for years. The French built forts at Isle La Motte in 1666, Crown Point in 1730, and Ticonderoga in 1755. The first permanent settlement made by the English was Fort Dummer in 1724, later named Brattleboro. When France finally gave up its claim to the area following the French and Indian War in 1763, there were fewer than 300 settlers in Vermont.

With the defeat of the French, settlement began in earnest. New Hampshire granted land for 129 towns in Vermont between 1749 and 1764. New York's claim to the area was validated by King George III, resulting in a nullification of all grants made by New Hampshire. Although some grantees obtained new grants from New York, the others banded together under Ethan Allen to form the Green Mountain Boys. They resisted New York's efforts to evict those who did not receive New York grants. The Revolutionary War prevented major conflicts between the Green Mountain Boys and New York. However, Ethan Allen and his men did fight for the colonies, capturing forts Ticonderoga and Crown Point from the British.

In 1776, Vermont held a convention and declared its independence from New York. The next year a constitution was approved making Vermont an independent republic. Vermont remained a republic until statehood was granted in 1791. The settlers in Vermont carried on substantial trade with Canada, most of it avoiding British revenue officers. The War of 1812 severely restricted this smuggling, hence Vermont was very antiwar. When the war ended, many Vermonters left the state to farm better lands in Ohio and few New Englanders came to replace them.

The Champlain Canal opened in 1823, connecting Vermont with New York City. In 1825, the Erie Canal opened, carrying Vermont settlers to Ohio and other western areas. Irish laborers came to work on Vermont railroads, the first of which opened in 1848. During the Civil War, Vermont supplied over 34,000 men to the Union armies.

Most of the early white settlers came from the New England colonies. Other large groups of immigrants came from Ireland in the mid-1800's and French Canada later in the century. Farmers from Finland came into the Markham Mountain region in southwestern Windsor County and the Equinox Mountain section of northern Bennington County. Welsh came to the midwest section of Rutland County to work in the slate quarries. Scottish and Italian stone cutters came to the quarries southeast of Montpelier. Russians, Poles, Czechs, Austrians, and Swedes came to the granite quarries of Rutland County. About half of the foreign-born population in Vermont came from Canada.

Town clerks have kept birth, marriage, and death records since 1760. Many of these records have been indexed for the entire state. The Vital Records Office, Public Records Division, State Administration Building, 6 Baldwin Street, Montpelier, VT 05602, will search these indexes for a fee. This office also has divorce records from 1861 to

1968. For birth, marriage, and death records since 1955 and divorce records since 1968, contact the Division of Vital Statistics, 60 Main Street, P.O. Box 70, Burlington, VT 05402. To verify current fees, call 802-863-7275.

The Vermont Historical Society Library, Pavillion Building, 109 State Street, Montpelier, VT 05602, has the largest genealogical collection in the state. Portions of some colonial censuses are available and have been published. Many colonial land records are at the Vermont State Archives, Division of State Papers, Office of Secretary of State, 109 S Street, Montpelier, VT 05602. Later land transactions have been kept by the town clerks. Naturalization records have been filed primarily in county and district courts.

Genealogical Archives, Libraries and Societies

Bennington Museum, West Main St., Bennington, VT 05201.

Billings Library, Burlington, VT 05401

Brooks Memorial Library, 224 Main Street, Brattleboro, VT 05301

Fletcher Free Library, 235 College St., Burlington, VT 05401

Genealogical Library, Bennington Museum, Bennington, VT 05201

Public Library, Court St., Rutland, VT 05701

University of Vermont Library, Burlington, VT 05401

The Russell Collection, c / o The Dorothy Canfield Library, Main St., Arlington, VT 05250.

Vermont Department of Libraries, Law and Documents Unit, 111 State Street, Montpelier, VT 05602

Vermont Historical Society Library, Pavillion Bldg., 109 State St., Montpelier, VT 05602

Burlington, Vermont Genealogical Group, 36 Franklin Square, Burlington, VT 05401

Genealogical Society of Vermont, Westminster West, RFD 3, Putney, VT 05346

Vermont Genealogical Society, P. O. Box 422, Pittsford, VT 05763

Vermont Historical Society, Pavilion Office Building, 109 State Street, Montpelier, VT 05602

Vermont Society, Sons of the American Revolution, RFD Box 18, Norwich, VT 05055

Printed Census Records and Mortality Schedules

Federal Census 1790, 1800, 1810, 1820, 1830, 1840, 1850, 1860, 1870, 1880, 1900, 1910
Federal Mortality Schedules 1870
Union Veterans and Widows 1890

Valuable Printed Sources

Atlases, Maps, and Gazetteers

Hemenway, Abby M. *Vermont Historical Gazetteer*. Burlington, Vermont: Abby M. Hemenway, 1891.

Swift, Esther Munroe. *Vermont Place Names*. Brattleboro, Vermont: Stephen Greene Press, 1977.

The Vermont Atlas and Gazetteer. Yarmouth, Maine: David DeLorme & Co., 1978.

Bibliographies

A Guide to Vermont's Repositories. Vermont State Archives, 1986.

Gilman, Marcus Davis. *The Bibliography of Vermont*. Burlington, Vermont: Free Press Association, 1897.

Genealogical Research Guides

Genealogist's Handbook for New England Research. Lynnfield, Massachusetts: New England Library Association, 1980.

Rubincam, Milton, *Genealogical Research Methods and Sources*. Washington, DC: American Society of Genealogists, 1972.

Genealogical Sources

Clark, Byron. *A List of Pensioners of the War of 1812*. Baltimore: Genealogical Publishing Co., 1969 reprint.

Dewey, William T. and Byron N. Clark. *Vermont Marriages: Montpelier, Burlington, and Berlin*. Baltimore: Genealogical Publishing Co., 1967 reprint.

Goodrich, John E. *Rolls of Soldiers in the Revolutionary War, 1775-1783*. Rutland, Vermont: Tuttle Co., 1904.

Histories

Barden, Merritt Clarke. *Vermont: Once No Man's Land*. Rutland, Vermont: Tuttle Co., 1928.

Morrissey, Charles T. *Vermont: A Bicentennial History*. New York: W. W. Norton, 1981.

VERMONT COUNTY DATA
State Map on Page M-27

Name	Map Index	Date Created	Parent County or Territory From Which Organized

* **Addison**   D3   1785   Rutland
  Addison County, 5 Court St, Middlebury, VT   05753-1405 . . . . (802)388-4237
  (Twn Clk has b, m, d & bur rec; Co Clk has div & civ ct rec from 1797; Pro Judge has pro rec)

  Towns Organized Before 1800: Addison 1761, Bridport 1761, Cornwall 1761, Ferrisburgh 1762, Leicester 1761, Lincoln 1780, Middlebury 1761, Monkton 1762, New Haven 1761, Orwell 1763, Panton 1761, Ripton 1781, Salisbury 1761, Shoreham 1761, Starksboro 1780, Vergennes 1788, Waltham 1796, Weybridge 1761, Whiting 1763

* **Bennington**   F3   1779   Original county
  Bennington County, 207 South St, Bennington, VT   05201-2247 . . . . (802)447-2700
  (Bennington Twn Clk has b, m, d & bur rec; Co Clk has div rec from 1899, civ ct rec from 1861; Pro Judge has pro rec; Twn Clk, Glastenbury has b rec from 1868 to 1928, d rec from 1883 to 1895, m rec from 1869 to 1927 & lnd rec from 1833 - Glastenbury is an unorg twn or gore, while all rec should be here, some may be found in Shaftsbury Twn Clk office)

  Towns Organized Before 1800: Arlington 1761, Bennington 1749, Dorset 1761, Glastenbury 1761, Landgrove 1780, Manchester 1761, Peru 1761, Pownal 1760, Rupert 1761, Sandgate 1761, Shaftsbury 1761, Sunderland 1761, Winhall 1761

* **Caledonia**   D4   1792   Newly Organized Terr
  Caledonia County, PO Box 404, Saint Johnsbury, VT   05819-0404 . . . . (802)748-6600
  (Twn Clk has b, m, d, bur & lnd rec; Co Clk has div & civ ct rec from 1797; Pro Judge has pro rec)

  Towns Organized Before 1800: Barnet 1763, Burke 1782, Cabot 1780, Danville 1786, Groton 1789, Hardwick 1781, Lyndon 1780, Peacham 1763, Ryegate 1763, Sheffield 1793, St. Johnsbury 1785, Sutton 1782, Walden 1781, Waterford 1780, Wheelock 1785

* **Chittenden**   D3   1787   Original county
  Chittenden County, 175 Main St, Burlington, VT   05401-8310 . . . . (802)863-3467
  (Twn Clk has b, m, d, bur, pro & lnd rec; Co Clk has div rec from 1829 & civ ct rec from 1798)

  Towns Organized Before 1800: Bolton 1763, Burlington 1763, Charlotte 1762, Colchester 1763, Essex 1763, Hinesburg 1762, Huntington 1763, Jericho 1763, Milton 1763, Richmond 1794, Shelburne 1763, St. George 1763, Underhill 1763, Williston 1763

* **Essex**   C5   1792   Unorg. Terr
  Essex County, PO Box 75, Guildhall, VT   05905-0075 . . . . (802)676-3910
  (Co Clk has b & d rec from 1884, m rec & bur rec very few div, co ct rec from 1800, lnd rec from 1762; Pro Judge has pro rec from 1800; Unorg twns & gores of Essex Co consist of: Averill, Avery's Gore, Ferdinand, Lewis, Warren's Gore, Warner's Grant)

  Towns Organized Before 1800: Bloomfield 1762, Brunswick 1761, Canaan 1782, Concord 1780, Guildhall 1761, Lunenburg 1763, Maidstone 1761, Victory 1781

* **Franklin**   C3   1792   Chittenden
  Franklin County, PO Box 808, Saint Albans, VT   05478-0808 . . . . (802)524-3863
  (Co Clk has d & civ ct rec from 1900; Twn Clk has b, m, d, bur & lnd rec; Pro Judge has pro rec)

  Towns Organized Before 1800: Bakersfield 1791, Berkshire 1781, Enosburg 1780, Fairfax 1763, Fairfield 1763, Fletcher 1781, Franklin 1789, Georgia 1763, Highgate 1763, Montgomery 1789, Richford 1780, Sheldon 1763, Swanton 1763, St. Albans 1763

  Grand Isle   C3   1802   Franklin
  Grand Isle County, Rt 2, North Hero, VT   05474 . . . . (802)372-8350
  [FHL has some cem & pro rec]

  Towns Organized Before 1800: Alburg 1781, Grand Isle 1779, Isles La Motte 1779, North Hero 1779, South Hero 1779

* **Lamoille**   D4   1835   Chittenden, Orleans, Franklin
  Lamoille County, PO Box 303, Hyde Park, VT   05655-0303 . . . . (802)888-2207
  (Co Clk has div & civ ct rec from 1837; Twn Clks have b, m, d, bur & lnd rec; Pro Judge has pro rec)

  Towns Organized Before 1800: Cambridge 1781, Elmore 1781, Hyde Park 1781, Johnson 1792, Morristown 1763, Stowe 1763, Wolcott 1781

* **Orange**   E4   1781   Original county
  Orange County, PO Box 95, Chelsea, VT   05038-0095 . . . . (802)685-4610
  (Twn Clk, Chelsea has b, m, d, bur & lnd rec; Co Clk has div & civ ct rec from 1781 & lnd rec from 1771; Pro Judge has pro rec from 1771)

  Towns Organized Before 1800: Bradford 1770, Braintree 1781, Brookfield 1781, Chelsea 1781, Corinth 1764, Fairlee 1761, Newbury 1763, Orange 1781, Randolph 1781, Strafford 1761, Thetford 1761, Topsham 1763, Turnbridge 1761, Vershire 1781, Washington 1781, West Fairlee 1779, Williamstown 1781

* **Orleans**   C4   1792   Original county
  Orleans County, PO Box 787, Newport, VT   05855-0787 . . . . (802)334-2711
  (Town or City Clks have b, m, d, and lnd rec; Dist Pro Ct has pro rec; Co Clk has div, civ ct rec from 1800)

  Towns Organized Before 1800: Barton 1789, Craftsbury 1781, Derby 1779, Glover 1783, Greensboro 1781, Holland 1779, Jay 1792, Westfield 1780

* **Rutland**   E3   1781   Original county
  Rutland County, 83 Center St, Rutland, VT   05701-4039 . . . . (802)775-4394
  (Secretary of State Office, Montpelier, has b, d, m rec from 1760 to 1955, div rec from 1760 to 1968; Twn Clk has lnd rec except old rec from 1779 to 1826, which are filed in the Co Clk's Office; Co Clk has civ ct rec; Pro Ct has pro rec located in Rutland and

also in Fair Haven, Vt.)

Towns Organized Before 1800: Benson 1780, Brandon 1761, Castleton 1761, Chittenden 1780, Clarendon 1761, Danby 1761, Fairhaven 1779, Hubbardton 1764, Ira 1781, Mendon 1781, Middletown Springs 1784, Mt. Holly 1792, Mt. Tabor 1761, Pawlet 1761, Pittsford 1761, Poultney 1761, Rutland 1761, Sherburn 1761, Shrewsbury 1761, Sudbury 1763, Wallingford 1761, Wells 1761, West Haven 1792

* **Washington**   D4   1810   Addison, Orange
Washington County, PO Box 426, Montpelier, VT 05602-0426 . . . . (802)223-2091
(Incorporated as Jefferson Co in 1810, nm changed to Washington in 1814; Secretary of State, Montpelier, has b, d, m rec; Co Clk has div, civ ct rec; Pro Ct has pro rec; City or Town Clk has lnd rec)

Towns Organized Before 1800: Barre 1781, Berlin 1763, Calais 1781, Duxbury 1763, Marshfield 1782, Middlesex 1763, Montpelier 1781, Moretown 1763, Northfield 1781, Plainfield 1797, Roxbury 1781, Waitsfield 1782, Warren 1780, Waterbury 1763, Worcester 1763

* **Windham**   F4   1781   Bennington
Windham County, PO Box 207, Newfane, VT 05345-0207 . . . . (802)365-7979
(Twn Clk has b, m, d, bur & lnd rec; Co Clk has div & civ ct rec from 1825; Pro Judge has pro rec)

Towns Organized Before 1800: Athens 1780, Brattleboro 1753, Brookline 1794, Grafton 1754, Guilford 1754, Halifax 1750, Jamaica 1780, Londonderry 1780, Marlboro 1751, Newfane 1753, Putney 1753, Rockingham 1752, Townshend 1753, Woodbury 1781, Westminster 1752, Whitingham 1770, Wilmington 1751, Windham 1795

* **Windsor**   E4   1781   Original county
Windsor County, 12 The Green, Woodstock, VT 05091-1212 . . . . (802)457-2121
(Co Clk has div & civ ct rec from 1782; Twn Clk has b, m, d, bur & lnd rec; Pro Judge has pro rec)

Towns Organized Before 1800: Andover 1761, Baltimore 1793, Barnard 1761, Bethel 1779, Bridgewater 1761, Cavendish 1761, Chester 1754, Hartford 1761, Hartland 1761, Ludlow 1761, Norwich 1761, Plymouth 1761, Pomfret 1761, Reading 1761, Royalton 1769, Sharon 1761, Springfield 1761, Stockbridge 1761, Westhersfield 1761, Weston 1799, Windsor 1761, Woodstock 1761

* At least one county history has been published about this county.
† Inventory of county archives was made by the Historical Records Survey. (See Introduction)

VIRGINIA

CAPITAL - RICHMOND — STATE 1788 (10th)
State Map on Page M-42

James I granted a charter to the Virginia Company in 1606 to colonize Virginia. The first ships left in 1607 and formed the first permanent English settlement in the New World at Jamestown. Captain John Smith provided the strong leadership needed by the fledgling settlement. Through several harsh winters, the colony struggled to stay alive. New supplies and immigrants came each year, with the most crucial being in 1610, when the 65 surviving settlers were about to give up and return to England. In 1612, John Rolfe cultured the first commercial tobacco and later married Pocahontas. In 1618, the Virginia Company granted land to all free settlers and allowed a general assembly to be held. An Indian massacre in 1622 and internal disputes in the colony led James I to revoke the Virginia Company's charter and to make Virginia a royal colony in 1624.

Immigrants arrived nearly every month. By 1700, Virginia had 80,000 persons in the Tidewater area. Settlers began scattering over the coastal plain and the Piedmont Plateau before 1700. Between 1710 and 1740, passes were discovered across the Blue Ridge mountains into the Shenandoah Valley. Emigrants from Pennsylvania and New Jersey began to enter the valley. As early as 1730, there was a heavy immigration of Scotch-Irish, Germans, and Welsh from Pennsylvania into Virginia, most of whom settled in the upper valleys. They brought with them their religions- Presbyterian, Baptist, and Quaker. Methodist churches were established around 1800. By the mid-18th century, Virginia had grown to over 280,000 people.

Between 1750 and 1784, land grants made to the Ohio Company encouraged exploration beyond the Alleghenies. The new area, southeast of the Ohio River, was organized by Virginia in 1775 as the District of West Augusta, though much was ceded to Pennsylvania in 1779. In the 1770's the Wilderness Road across the Cumberland Gap opened up Kentucky. Kentucky County, which would later become the state of Kentucky, was organized in 1776. Virginia was prominent in the Revolutionary War due to its great leaders — Thomas Jefferson, George Washington, Patrick Henry, George Mason, and Richard Henry Lee. Little fighting occurred on Virginian soil until the final years of the war and the final surrender at Yorktown.

In 1784, Virginia ceded its claims north of the Ohio River to the United States. Virginia entered the Union in 1788. Virginia seceded from the Union in 1861. Robert E. Lee was placed in command of the Confederate troops for Virginia, with Richmond as the capital of the Confederacy. The northwestern counties of the state refused to join in the secession and were admitted to the Union in 1863 as the state of West Virginia. Virginia was the central battlefield for the Civil War, with the first major battle at Bull Run (Manassas) and the final surrender at Appomattox. An estimated 155,000 men from Virginia fought for the Confederacy. Virginia was readmitted to the Union in 1870. Foreign-born citizens include Russians, English, Germans, Italians, Greeks, Polish, Czechs, Irish, Austrians, and Hungarians.

Until 1786, the Anglican Church was the state church of Virginia. In accordance with English law, the church kept parish registers of vital statistics. Unfortunately, most of these are no longer in existence. Those that do exist have been photocopied and are in the Virginia State Library, 11th Street at Capitol Square, Richmond, VA 23219. Most have also been transcribed and published. In 1704, all Virginia landowners except those in Lancaster, Northumberland, Westmoreland, Richmond, and Stafford Counties had to pay a Quit Rent to the king for every fifty acres. A Quit Rent list was made in 1704 for all who paid. Statewide registration of vital statistics began in 1912 and is at the Division of Vital Records and Health Services, P.O. Box 1000, Richmond, VA 23208. To verify current fees, call 804-786-6228.

The Archives Division of the Virginia State Library has copies of all existing Virginia birth and death records prior to 1896 and marriage records 1853-1935. Beginning in 1660, a couple could marry by posting a bond with civil authorities or publishing banns at church. Reporting was required after 1780, but was sometimes done before that. Probate records are at the county level with the general court and at the county and circuit superior court. Independent cities have probates at the circuit court clerk's office. Lists of residents are available for some colonial years. Lists for 1624 and 1779 have been published.

Genealogical Archives, Libraries and Societies

Alderman Library, University of Virginia, Charlottesville, VA 22903

Alexandria Library, 717 Queen St., Alexandria, VA 22314

Blue Ridge Regional Library, 310 E. Church St., Martinsville, VA 24112

Bristol Public Library, 701 Goode St., Bristol, VA 24201

College of William and Mary Library, Williamsburg, VA 23185

Commonwealth of Virginia, Virginia State Library, 1101 Capitol, Richmond, VA 23219

Culpeper Town and County Library, Main and Mason Sts., Culpeper, VA 22701

Danville Public Library, 511 Patton St., Danville, VA 24541

E. Lee Trinkle Library, University of Virginia, Mary Washington College, Fredricksburg, VA 22402

Fairfax County Public Library, Virginia Room, 3915 Chain Bridge Road, Fairfax, VA 22030

Hampton Public Library, 4205 Victoria Blvd., Hampton, VA 23669

Jefferson / Madison Regional Library, 201 E. Market St., Charlottesville, VA 22903

Jones Memorial Library, 2311 Memorial Ave., Lynchburg, VA 24501

Kirn Norfolk Public Library, 301 E. City Hall Ave., Norfolk, VA 23510

Library of the Albemarle County Historical Society, 220 Court Square, Charlottesville, VA 22903

Mary Ball Washington Museum and Library, Inc. P. O. Box 97, Lancaster, VA 22503-0097

Menno Simons Historical Library / Archives, Eastern Mennonite College, Harrisonburg, VA 22801

Page Public Library, 100 Zerkel St., Luray, VA 22835

Petersburg Public Library, 137 S. Sycamore St., Petersburg, VA 23803

Radford Public Library, Recreation Building, Radford, VA 24141

Roanoke City Public Library, Virginia Room, 706 S. Jefferson St., Roanoke, VA 24016

Rockingham Public Library, 45 Newman Ave., Harrisonburg, VA 22801

Shenandoah County Library, Rt. 1, Box 1-B, Edinburg, VA 22824

Southside Regional Library, P. O. Box 10, Boydton, VA 23917

Virginia Historical Library, P. O. Box 7311, Richmond, VA 23211

Virginia State Library, 11th St. at Capitol Square, Richmond, VA 23219-3491

Waynesboro Public Library, 600 South Waynes Avenue, Waynesboro, VA 22980

Albemarle County Historical Society, 220 Court Square, Charlottesville, VA 22901

Augusta County Virginia Historical Society, P. O. Box 686, Staunton, VA 24401

Bath County Historical Society, Inc., P. O. Box 212, Warm Springs, VA 24484

Bedford Historical Society, Inc. P. O. Box 602, Bedford, VA 24523

Central Virginia Genealogical Association, 303 Farm Lane, Charlottesville, VA 22901

Chesterfield Historical Society of Virginia, P. O. Box 40, Chesterfield, VA 23832

Claiborne County Historical Society, Rt. 1, Box 589, Jonesville, VA 24263

Clark County Historical Association, Berryville, VA 22611

Culpeper Historical Society, Inc., P. O. Box 785, Culpeper, VA 22701

Cumberland County Historical Society, Box 88, Cumberland, VA 23040

Ft. Eustis Historical and Archaelogical Assn., P. O. Box 4408, Ft. Eustis, VA 23604

Fairfax Genealogical Society, P. O. Box 2344, Merrifield, VA 22116-2344

Fairfax Historical Society, P. O. Box 415, Fairfax, VA 22030

Genealogical Research Institute of Virginia, P. O. Box 29178, Richmond, VA 23229

Genealogical Society of Page County, Virginia, Page Public Library, 100 Zerkel St., Luray, VA 22835

Goochland County Historical Society, Goochland, VA 23063

Greene County Historical Society, P. O. Box 185, Stanardsville, VA 22973

Harrisonburg-Rockingham Historical Society, 301 South Main Street, Harrisonburg, VA 22801

Historical Society of Washington County, Virginia, Box 484, Abingdon, VA 24210

Holston Territory Genealogical Society, P. O. Box 433, Bristol, VA 24203

King George County Historical Society, P. O. Box 424, King George, VA 22485

King and Queen Historical Society, Newtown, VA 23126

Library of the Albemarle County Historical Society, 220 Court Square, Charlottesville, VA 22903

Lower Del-Mar-Va Genealogical Society, Wicomico County Library, Salisbury, MD 21801

Mathews County Historical Society, P. O. Box 885, Mathews, VA 23109

National Genealogical Society, 4527 Seventeenth Street North, Arlington, VA 22207-2363

New River Historical Society, Box 711, Radford, VA 24141

Norfolk County Historical Society, Chesapeake Public Library, 300 Cedar Road, Chesapeake, VA 23320

Norfolk Genealogical Society, 560 W. Olney Rd., Norfolk, VA 23507

Northern Neck Historical Society, Westmoreland County, Montross, VA 22520

Pittsylvania Historical Society, P. O. Box 846, Chatham, VA 24531

Prince William County Genealogical Society, P. O. Box 2019, Manassas, VA 22110-0812

Roanoke Valley Historical Society, P. O. Box 1904, Roanoke, VA 24008

Rockingham County Historical Society, 301 South Main Street, Harrisonburg, VA 22801

Shenandoah County Historical Society, The Shenandoah County Library, Rt. 1, Box 1-B, Edinburg, VA 22824

Southwestern Virginia Genealogical Society, P. O. Box 12485, Roanoke, VA 24026

Southwest Virginia Historical Society, Wise, VA 24293

Tidewater Genealogical Society, P. O. Box 76, Hampton, VA 23669

Virginia Beach Genealogical Society, P. O. Box 62901, Virginia Beach, VA 23462

Virginia Genealogical Society, P. O. Box 7469, Richmond, VA 23221

VA-NC Piedmont Genealogical Society, P. O. Box 2272, Danville, VA 24541

Virginia Society, Sons of the American Revolution, 7214 Regent Dr., Alexandria, VA 22307

Winchester-Frederick County Historical Society, P. O. Box 97, Winchester, VA 22601

Printed Census Records and Mortality Schedules

Federal Census 1810 (except Grayson, Greenbriar, Halifax, Hardy, Henry, James City, King William, Louisa, Mecklenburg, Nansemond, Northampton, Orange, Patrick, Pittsylvania, Russell, and Tazewell counties), 1820, 1830, 1840, 1850, 1860, 1870, 1880, 1900, 1910
Federal Mortality Schedules 1850, 1860, 1870, 1880
Union Veterans and Widows 1890
Residents 1623, 1624, 1625, 1626, 1774-1775, 1779
Slaveholders 1625
Heads of Families 1782-1785
Taxpayers 1782-1787
Pensioners 1785, 1787, 1840

Valuable Printed Sources

Atlases, Maps, and Gazetteers

Crumrine, Boyd. *The Boundary Controversy Between Pennsylvania and Virginia, 1748-1785*. Pittsburgh, Pennsylvania, 1902.

Doran, Michael F. *Atlas of County Boundary Changes in Virginia, 1634-1895*. Athens, Georgia: Iberian Publishing Co., 1987.

Gannett, Henry. *A Gazetteer of Virginia and West Virginia*. Baltimore: Genealogical Publishing Co., 1975.

Hansen, Raus McDill. *Virginia Place Names: Derivations and Historical Uses*. Verona, Virginia: McClure Press, 1969.

Hiden, Matha W. *How Justice Grew: Virginia Counties*. Williamsburg, Virginia: Jamestown 350th Anniversary Corp., 1957.

Martin, Joseph. *A New and Comprehensive Gazetteer of Virginia and the District of Columbia*. Charlottesville, Virginia: Joseph Martin, 1835.

Sames, James W. III. *Kentucky and Virginia Maps, 1562 to 1900*. Frankfort, Kentucky: Kentucky Historical Society, 1976.

Sanchez-Saavedra, Eugene Michael. *A Description of the Country: Virginia's Cartographers and Their Maps, 1607-1881*. Richmond, Virginia: Virginia State Library, 1975.

Bibliographies

Brown, Stuart E. *Virginia Genealogies: A Trial List of Printed Books and Pamphlets*. Berryville, Virginia: Virginia Book Co., 1967.

Critz, Lalla Campbell. *Magazine of Bibliographies: Featuring the Shenandoah Valley*. Fort Worth, Texas: Magazine of Bibliographies, 1972.

Duncan, Richard R. *Theses and Dissertations on Virginia History: A Bibliography*. Richmond, Virginia: Virginia State Library, 1986.

Stewart, Robert Armistead. *Index to Printed Virginia Genealogies, Including Key and Bibliography*. Baltimore: Genealogical Publishing Co., 1970.

Vogt, John and T. William Kethley Jr. *Marriage Records in the Virginia State Library: A Researcher's Guide*. Athens, Georgia: Iberian Press, 1984.

Genealogical Research Guides

Clay, Robert Young. *Virginia Genealogical Resources*. Detroit: Detroit Society for Genealogical Research, 1980.

McCay, Betty L. *Sources for Genealogical Searching in Virginia and West Virginia*. Indianapolis: Betty L. McCay, 1971.

Stone, Kathryn Crossley. *Research Aids for the Colonial Period: Emphasis Virginia: Dictionary Encyclopedia for Genealogical Research*. Boulder, Colorado: Empire Printing, 1976.

Genealogical Sources

Genealogies of Virginia Families: A Consolidation of Family History Articles from The Virginia Magazine of History and Biography. Baltimore: Genealogical Publishing Co., 1981.

Greer, George Cabell. *Early Virginia Immigrants, 1623-1666*. Lynn Research Genealogical Microfiche, 1990 reprint.

Swem, Earl Gregg. *Virginia Historical Index*. Gloucester, Massachusetts: Peter Smith, 1965.

Histories

Andrews, Matthew Page. *Virginia the Old Dominion*. Richmond, Virginia: Dietz Press, 1949.

Boogher, William Fletcher. *Gleanings of Virginia History*. Baltimore: Genealogical Publishing Co., 1965 reprint.

Bruce, Philip Alexander. *Virginia: Rebirth of the Old Dominion*. New York: Lewis Publishing Co., 1929.

VIRGINIA COUNTY DATA
State Map on Page M-42

Name	Map Index	Date Created	Parent County or Territory From Which Organized
Accawmack (see Northampton)			
* **Accomack**	I4	1634	Northampton
Accomack County, County Courthouse, Accomac, VA 23301 .... (804)787-5776			
(Clk Cir Ct has m rec from 1784, div rec from 1850, pro, civ ct & lnd rec from 1663)			
* **Albemarle**	F4	1744	Goochland, Louisa
Albemarle County, 401 McIntire Rd, Charlottesville, VA 22901-4579 .... (804)296-5841			
(Clk Cir Ct has m rec from 1870, lnd rec from 1748, div, pro & civ ct rec)			
* **Alexandria**	G6		Fairfax (became part of District of Columbia)
Alexandria Ind City, 301 King St, Alexandria, VA 22314-3211 .... (703)838-4550			
(See Dis of Columbia for cen rec of 1800-40; 1920 changed to Arlington)(Alex. Health Center has b, d & bur rec; Clk Cir Ct has m & div rec from 1870, pro, civ ct & lnd rec from 1783)			
* **Alleghany**	D3	1822	Bath, Botetourt, Monroe
Alleghany County, 266 W Main St, Covington, VA 24426-1550 .... (703)962-3906			
(Clk Cir Ct has m rec from 1845, div, pro, civ ct & lnd rec from 1822)			
*† **Amelia**	G3	1734	Brunswick, Prince George
Amelia County, PO Box A, Amelia Court House, VA 23002-0066 .... (804)561-3039			
(Clk Cir Ct has m, div, pro, civ ct & lnd rec from 1734)			
* **Amherst**	E3	1761	Albemarle
Amherst County, 100 E Court St, Amherst, VA 24521-2702 .... (804)929-9321			
(Clk Cir Ct has m, div, pro, civ ct & lnd rec from 1761)			
* **Appomattox**	F3	1845	Buckingham, Campbell, Charlotte, Prince Edwards
Appomattox County, PO Box 672, Appomattox, VA 24522 .... (804)352-5275			
(Clk Cir Ct has m, div & pro rec from 1892, civ ct & lnd rec)			

Name	Map Index	Date Created	Parent County or Territory From Which Organized

* Arlington   G6   1847   Fairfax
    Arlington County, 2100 Clarendon Blvd, Arlington, VA 22201-5445 . . . . (703)358-3000
    [FHL has some m, cem, civ ct, lnd, pro, tax rec]

* Augusta   E4   1738   Orange
    Augusta County, 6 E Johnson St, Staunton, VA 24401-4303 . . . . (703)885-8931
    (Clk Cir Ct has b & d rec from 1853 to 1896, m rec from 1785, pro rec, deeds, original survey bks from 1745, personal prop tax
    rec from 1800 to 1851, lnd tax rec from 1786 & ct of claims rec from 1782 to 1785)

    Barbour (See W. Va.)

* Bath   E4   1790   Augusta, Botetourt, Greenbrier
    Bath County, PO Box 180, Warm Springs, VA 24484-0180 . . . . (703)839-2361
    (Clk Cir Ct has b rec from 1854 to 1880, d rec from 1854 to 1870, div, pro, law & chan rec from 1791)

    Bedford   E3   Ind. City
    Bedford Ind City, 215 E Main St, Bedford, VA 24523-2012 . . . . (703)586-7102

* Bedford   E3   1753   Albemarle, Lunenburg
    Bedford County, 129 E Main St, Bedford, VA 24523-2034 . . . . (703)586-7601
    (Clk Cir Ct has b rec from 1853 to 1897 & 1912 to 1918, d rec from 1853 to 1918, m, div, pro, civ ct & lnd rec from 1754)

    Berkeley (See W. Va)

* Bland   C2   1861   Giles, Tazewell, Wythe
    Bland County, PO Box 295, Bland, VA 24315-0295 . . . . (703)688-4562
    (Clk Cir Ct has m, pro & lnd rec from 1861, div rec from 1900)

    Boone (See W. Va.)

* Botetourt   E3   1769   Augusta
    Botetourt County, 1 W Main St Box 1, Fincastle, VA 24090-3006 . . . . (703)473-8220
    (Clk Cir Ct has b & d rec from 1853 to 1870, m, div, pro & civ ct rec from 1770)

    Braxton (See W. Va.)

    Bristol   B1   Ind. City
    Bristol Ind City, 497 Cumberland St, Bristol, VA 24201-4394 . . . . (703)466-2221
    (Clk Co Ct has m, div, pro, civ ct & lnd rec from 1890)

    Brooke (See W. Va.)

*† Brunswick   G2   1720   Prince George, Isle of Wight, Surry
    Brunswick County, 102 Tobacco St, Lawrenceville, VA 23868-1824 . . . . (804)848-3107
    (Clk Cir Ct has m, div, pro rec from 1732, lnd rec from 1900)

* Buchanan   B2   1858   Russell, Tazewell
    Buchanan County, PO Box 950, Grundy, VA 24614-0950 . . . . (703)935-6500
    (Clk Cir Ct has m, div, pro, civ ct & lnd rec from 1885; Courthouse burned 1885)

* Buckingham   F3   1758   Albemarle, Appomattox
    Buckingham County, PO Box 252, Buckingham, VA 23921-0252 . . . . (804)969-4242
    (Clk Cir Ct has b & d rec from 1896, m, div & pro rec from 1869)

    Buena Vista   E3   Ind. City
    Buena Vista Ind City, 2039 Sycamore Ave, Buena Vista, VA 24416-3133 . . . . (703)261-6121
    (Clk Cir Ct has m, div, pro, civ ct, lnd, service discharge, and company charters rec from 1892)

    Cabell (See W. Va.)

    Calhoun (See W. Va.)

* Campbell   F3   1781   Bedford
    Campbell County, PO Box 7, Rustburg, VA 24588-0007 . . . . (804)332-5161
    (Clk Cir Ct has b & d rec from 1912 to 1918, m, div, pro & deeds from 1782, civ ct & lnd rec, deeds of conveyances from 1782)

* Caroline   G4   1727   Essex, King and Queen, King William
    Caroline County, PO Box 309, Bowling Green, VA 22427-0309 . . . . (804)633-5800
    (Clk Cir Ct has m rec from 1787 to 1853, lnd rec from 1836, also div, pro & civ ct rec)

* Carroll   D1   1842   Grayson, Patrick
    Carroll County, PO Box 515, Hillsville, VA 24343-0515 . . . . (703)728-3331
    (Clk Cir Ct has b rec from 1842 to 1896, m, div, pro, lnd rec from 1842)

    Charles River (See York)(Changed to York 1642)

* Charles City   H3   1634   Original Shire
    Charles City County, PO Box 128, Charles City, VA 23030-0128 . . . . (804)829-2401

* Charlotte   F3   1764   Lunenburg
    Charlotte County, PO Box 38, Charlotte Court House, VA 23923-0038 . . . . (804)542-5147
    (Co Clk has b, d rec from 1853 to 1870, m, pro, civ ct, lnd rec from 1765, and div rec)

    Charlottesville   F4   Ind. City
    Charlottesville Ind City, 605 E Main St, Charlottesville, VA 22901-5397 . . . . (804)971-3101

* Chesapeake   I3   Ind. City
    Chesapeake Ind City, 306 Cedar Rd, Chesapeake, VA 23320-5514 . . . . (804)547-6166
    (Clk Cir Ct, P.O. Box 15205, has b & d rec from 1853 to 1870, m rec from 1706, div rec from 1800, pro & lnd rec from 1637)

*† Chesterfield   G3   1749   Henrico
    Chesterfield County, 9901 Lori Rd, Chesterfield, VA 23832-6626 . . . . (804)748-1200
    (Clk Cir Ct has m rec from 1771, lnd rec from 1749, also div, pro & civ ct rec)

Name	Map Index	Date Created	Parent County or Territory From Which Organized

* **Clarke**   F6   1836   Frederick
    Clarke County, 102 N Church St, Berryville, VA 22611-1110 .... (703)955-1309
    (Clk Cir Ct has m, div, pro, civ ct & lnd rec from 1836)

Clay (See W. Va.)

Clifton Forge   E3   Ind. City
    Clifton Forge Ind City, PO Box 631, Clifton Forge, VA 24422-0631 .... (703)863-5091
    (City Clk has m, div, lnd rec from 1906, also pro rec)

Colonial Heights   G3   1920   Ind. City
    Colonial Heights Ind City, 1507 Boulevard, Colonial Heights, VA 23834-3049 .... (804)520-9265
    (Clk Cir Ct has m, div, pro, civ ct, lnd rec from 1961; Clk Cir Ct., Chesterfield Co, has div, pro, civ ct, land rec prior to 1961)

Covington   D3   Ind. City
    Covington Ind City, 158 N Court Ave, Covington, VA 24426-1534 .... (703)965-6300

* **Craig**   D2   1860   Botetourt, Giles, Roanoke, Monroe, Alleghany, Montgomery
    Craig County, PO Box 185, New Castle, VA 24127-0185 .... (703)864-6141
    (Clk Cir Ct has b rec from 1864 to 1896, m, div, pro, civ ct rec & deeds from 1851)

* **Culpeper**   F5   1748   Orange
    Culpeper County, 135 W Cameron St, Culpeper, VA 22701 .... (703)825-3035
    (Clk Cir Ct has lnd, pro rec from 1749, m rec from 1781, b rec from 1864 to 1896 and from 1912 to 1917, d rec from 1864 to
    1896, Chancery and Civ Ct rec from 1831; Town Clk has bur rec)

* **Cumberland**   F3   1855   Goochland
    Cumberland County, County Courthouse, Cumberland, VA 23040 .... (804)492-4280
    (Clk Cir Ct has m, div, pro & civ ct rec from 1749, b & d rec from 1853 to 1870)

Danville   F2   Ind. City
    Danville Ind City, 212 Lynn St, Danville, VA 24541-1208 .... (804)799-5171

* **Dickenson**   B2   1880   Buchanan, Russell, Wise
    Dickenson County, PO Box 190, Clintwood, VA 24228-0190 .... (703)926-1616
    (Co Health has b, d & bur rec; Clk Cir Ct has m, div, civ ct & lnd rec from 1880, also wills & mil dis)

*† **Dinwiddie**   G3   1752   Prince George
    Dinwiddie County, PO Box 280, Dinwiddie, VA 23841-0280 .... (804)469-4533
    (Clk Cir Ct has b, d rec from 1865 to 1896, m, pro, civ ct, lnd rec from 1833, div rec from 1870)

Doddridge (See W. Va.)

Dunmore (See Shenandoah)

Elizabeth City (see Hampton)

Emporia   G2   Ind. City
    Emporia Ind City, 201 N Main St, Emporia, VA 23847-1605 .... (804)634-3332

* **Essex**   H4   1692   Old Rappahannock
    Essex County, PO Box 445, Tappahannock, VA 22560 .... (804)443-3541
    (Clk Cir Ct has m rec from 1814, div & lnd rec from 1865, pro rec from 1656 & civ ct rec from 1692)

Fairfax   G6   Ind. City
    Fairfax Ind City, 10455 Armstrong St, Fairfax, VA 22030-3630 .... (703)385-7855

* **Fairfax**   G6   1742   Prince William, Loudoun
    Fairfax County, 4110 Chain Bridge Rd, Fairfax, VA 22030-4041 .... (703)246-2000
    (Clk Cir Ct has b rec from 1853 to 1912, m rec from 1853, div rec from 1850, pro, civ ct & lnd rec from 1742)

* **Falls Church**   G6   1950   Ind. City
    Falls Church Ind City, 300 Park Ave, Falls Church, VA 22046-3332 .... (703)241-5014
    (Fairfax Co Clk Cir Ct has b, m, div, pro, civ ct & lnd rec)

* **Fauquier**   F5   1759   Prince William
    Fauquier County, 40 Culpeper St, Warrenton, VA 22186-3298 .... (703)347-8600
    (Clk Cir Ct has b, d rec from 1853 to 1896 and from 1912 to 1917, m pro, lnd rec from 1759, div rec from 1925, civ ct rec from
    1937)

Fayette (See W. Va.)

Fincastle   Botetourt (discontinued 1777)

* **Floyd**   D2   1831   Montgomery, Franklin
    Floyd County, 100 E Main St Rm 200, Floyd, VA 24091-2100 .... (703)745-4158
    (Clk Cir Ct has b & d rec from 1852 to 1872, m, div, pro, civ ct & lnd rec from 1831)

* **Fluvanna**   F4   1777   Albemarle
    Fluvanna County, PO Box 299, Palmyra, VA 22963 .... (804)589-3138
    (Clk Cir Ct has b, d rec from 1853 to 1896, m, div, pro, civ ct, lnd rec from 1777, some bur rec)

Fort Monroe   Ind. City
    (City Clk has m, div, pro rec & deeds from 1865)

Franklin   H2   Ind. City
    Franklin Ind City, 207 2nd Ave W, Franklin, VA 23851-1713 .... (804)562-8500
    (Southampton Co Clk Cir Ct has div, pro, civ ct & lnd rec)

* **Franklin**   E2   1785   Bedford, Henry, Patrick
    Franklin County, Main St, Rocky Mount, VA 24151-1392 .... (703)483-3065
    [FHL has some m, cem, civ ct, lnd, pro, tax rec]

Name	Map Index	Date Created	Parent County or Territory From Which Organized

* **Frederick**   F6   1738   Orange, Augusta
    Frederick County, 9 Court Sq, Winchester, VA 22601-4736 .... (703)665-5666
    (Nine square miles of Fredrick County annexed to city of Winchester)(Clk Cir Ct has b rec from 1853 to 1912, m rec from 1782, d rec from 1853 to 1896, div rec from 1870, pro, lnd rec from 1743)

Fredericksburg   G5   Ind. City
    Fredericksburg Ind City, PO Box 7447, Fredericksburg, VA 22404-7447 .... (703)372-1010

Galax   C1   Ind. City
    Galax Ind City, 123 Main St N, Galax, VA 24333-2907 .... (703)236-3441
    (Galax, Va 24333 is on the line between Grayson & Carroll Cos, contact both cos for their rec of Galax)

* **Giles**   D2   1806   Montgomery, Monroe, Tazewell, Craig, Mercer, Wythe
    Giles County, PO Box 502, Pearisburg, VA 24134-0502 .... (703)921-1722
    (Clk Cir Ct has m rec from 1806, b & d rec from 1858 to 1896, div, pro, civ ct & lnd rec)

Gilmer (See W. Va.)

* **Gloucester**   H4   1651   York
    Gloucester County, PO Box 329, Gloucester, VA 23061-0329 .... (804)693-4042
    (Clk Cir Ct has b rec from 1863 to 1890 and from 1912 to 1916, m rec from 1853, d rec from 1865 to 1890, div, pro, civ ct, land rec from 1865)

* **Goochland**   G4   1727   Henrico
    Goochland County, 2938 River Rd W, Goochland, VA 23063-3229 .... (804)556-5300
    (Clk Cir Ct has m & pro rec from 1730, div & civ ct rec from 1800, lnd rec from 1862)

* **Grayson**   C1   1792   Wythe, Patrick
    Grayson County, 129 Davis St, Independence, VA 24348 .... (703)773-2231
    (Clk Cir Ct has m, div, pro, civ ct, lnd rec from 1793)

Greenbrier (See W. Va.)

Greene   F4   1838   Orange
    Greene County, Court Sq, Stanardsville, VA 22973 .... (804)985-5299
    (Clk Cir Ct has b rec from 1853 to 1896 & 1912 to 1919, d rec from 1838 to 1860, m, div, pro, civ ct & lnd rec from 1838)

* **Greensville**   G2   1781   Brunswick, Sussex
    Greensville County, 337 S Main St, Emporia, VA 23847-2027 .... (804)348-4215
    (Clk Cir Ct has m rec, div, pro, civ ct & lnd rec from 1781)

* **Halifax**   F2   1752   Lunenburg
    Halifax County, Main St Courthouse Sq, Halifax, VA 24558-0786 .... (804)476-2141
    (Clk Cir Ct has m, pro & deeds from 1752)

Hampshire (See W. Va.)

* **Hampton**   H3   1952   Ind. City
    Hampton Ind City, 22 Lincoln St, Hampton, VA 23669 .... (804)727-6000
    (Formerly Elizabeth City)

Hancock (See W. Va.)

* **Hanover**   G4   1720   New Kent
    Hanover County, PO Box 470, Hanover, VA 23069-0470 .... (804)537-6000
    (Clk Cir Ct has m, div, pro, civ ct rec from 1865)

Hardy (See W. Va.)

Harrison (See W. Va.)

* **Harrisonburg**   E5   Ind. City
    Harrisonburg Ind City, 345 S Main St, Harrisonburg, VA 22801-3638 .... (703)434-6776
    (City Clk has b & d rec from 1862 to 1894, m, civ ct & lnd rec from 1778, pro rec from 1803)

* **Henrico**   G4   1634   Original Shire
    Henrico County, 4301 E Parham Rd, Richmond, VA 23229 .... (804)672-4000
    (Clk Cir Ct has m, pro, lnd rec from 1781, also div & civ ct rec)

* **Henry**   E1   1776   Pittsylvania, Patrick
    Henry County, PO Box 1049, Martinsville, VA 24114-1049 .... (703)638-3961
    (Clk Cir Ct has m & lnd rec from 1777, div rec from 1909, also pro rec)

* **Highland**   E4   1847   Bath, Pendleton
    Highland County, Main St, Monterey, VA 24465 .... (703)468-2447
    (Clk Cir Ct has b rec from 1850 to 1898, m, div & lnd rec from 1850, pro rec from 1860, civ ct rec from 1937)

* **Hopewell**   H3   Ind. City
    Hopewell Ind City, 300 N Main St, Hopewell, VA 23860-2740 .... (804)541-2243
    (Clk Cir Ct has m, div, pro & lnd rec; Clk Dis Ct has civ ct rec)

Illinois   1778   (Discontinued 1784)

*† **Isle of Wight**   H3   1634   Original Shire
    Isle of Wight County, Hwy 258 County Courthouse, Isle of Wight, VA 23397-9999 .... (804)357-3191
    (Clk Cir Ct has b rec from 1853 to 1876, d rec from 1853 to 1874, m rec from 1772, div rec from 1853, pro rec from 1647, civ ct rec from 1746)

Jackson (See W. Va.)

Name	Map Index	Date Created	Parent County or Territory From Which Organized

James City H3 1634 Original Shire
James City County, 321-45 Court St W, Williamsburg, VA 23185 .... (804)229-2552
(Clk Cir Ct has b rec from 1865 to 1883, d rec from 1864 to 1884, m, div, pro, civ ct & Ind rec from 1865)

Jefferson (See W. Va.)

Kanawah (See W. Va.)

Kentucky (Discontinued 1780)

* **King & Queen** H4 1691 New Kent
King & Queen County, County Courthouse, King & Queen Courthouse, VA 23085 .... (804)785-2460
(Clk Cir Ct has b, d rec from 1865 to 1898, m, div rec from 1864, pro, civ ct rec from 1865, Ind rec from 1782)

* **King George** G5 1720 Richmond, Westmoreland
King George County, PO Box 105, King George, VA 22485-0105 .... (703)775-3322
(Clk Cir Ct has m rec from 1786, div, civ ct, Ind, pro, wills from 1721)

* **King William** G4 1700 King and Queen
King William County, PO Box 215, King William, VA 23086-0215 .... (804)769-4927
(Clk Cir Ct has m, div, pro, civ ct rec from 1885; fire 1855 burned most rec; some rec back to 1702 have been photocopied)

* **Lancaster** H4 1651 Northumberland, York
Lancaster County, PO Box 125, Lancaster, VA 22503-0125 .... (804)462-5611
(Co Health has b rec; Clk Cir Ct has m rec from 1715, d rec & wills from 1652, div rec from 1800, pro rec from 1700, civ ct rec from 1910 & Ind rec from 1652)

* **Lee** A1 1792 Russell, Scott
Lee County, PO Box 326, Jonesville, VA 24263-0326 .... (703)346-7763
(Clk Cir Ct has b & d rec from 1853 to 1877, m rec 1830, div rec 1832, pro rec 1800, civ ct rec & deeds from 1793)

Lewis (See W. Va.)

Lexington E3 Ind. City
Lexington Ind City, PO Box 922, Lexington, VA 24450-0922 .... (703)463-7133

Lincoln (See W. Va.)

Logan (See W. Va.)

* **Loudoun** F6 1757 Fairfax
Loudoun County, 18 N King St, Leesburg, VA 22075-2818 .... (703)777-0200
(Clk Cir Ct has b rec from 1853 to 1859, 1864 to 1866 & 1869 to 1879, d rec from 1853 to 1866, m rec from 1793, div, pro & Ind rec from 1757, civ ct rec from 1858, tithables from 1758 to 1786)

* **Louisa** F4 1742 Hanover
Louisa County, PO Box 160, Louisa, VA 23093-0160 .... (703)967-0401
(Clk Cir Ct has b rec from 1867 to 1896, m, div, pro rec from 1742)

Lower Norfolk 1637 New Norfolk
(See Princess Anne and Norfolk)

* **Lunenburg** G2 1746 Brunswick
Lunenburg County, County Courthouse, Lunenburg, VA 23952 .... (804)696-2230
(Clk Cir Ct has m, div, pro, civ ct & Ind rec from 1746)

* **Lynchburg** F3 1852 Ind. City
Lynchburg Ind City, 900 Church St, Lynchburg, VA 24504-1620 .... (804)847-1443
(Clk Cir Ct has b, d rec from 1853 to 1868, m, div, pro, civ ct, Ind rec from 1805, slave register, mil discharge rec from WW1, mil rec from CW, criminal rec, business charters from 1805)

* **Madison** F4 1792 Culpeper
Madison County, PO Box 220, Madison, VA 22727-0220 .... (703)948-6102
(Clk Cir Ct has m rec also div, pro, civ ct & Ind rec from 1793)

Manassas Park G6 Ind. City
Manassas Park Ind City, 1 Park Center Pl, Manassas Park, VA 22111-1800 .... (703)335-8800

Marion (See W. Va.)

Marshall (See W. Va.)

Martinsville E1 1940 Ind City
Martinsville Ind City, PO Box 1112, Martinsville, VA 24114-1112 .... (703)638-3971
(Clk Cir Ct has m, div, pro, civ ct & Ind rec from 1942)

Mason (See W. Va.)

* **Mathews** H4 1790 Gloucester
Mathews County, PO Box 463, Mathews, VA 23109-0463 .... (804)725-2550
(Clk Cir Ct has m, div, pro, civ ct & Ind rec from 1865)

McDowell (See W. Va.)

* **Mecklenburg** F2 1764 Lunenburg
Mecklenburg County, Washington St, Boydton, VA 23917 .... (804)738-6191
[FHL has some m, cem, civ ct, Ind, pro, tax rec]

Mercer (See W. Va.)

*† **Middlesex** H4 1673 Lancaster
Middlesex County, Rts 17 & 33, Saluda, VA 23149 .... (804)758-5317
(Clk Cir Ct has b rec from 1840, m rec from 1840, pro, civ ct, Ind rec from 1673)

Monongalia (See W. Va.)

Name	Map Index	Date Created	Parent County or Territory From Which Organized

Monroe (See W. Va.)

* **Montgomery** D2 1776 Fincastle, Botetourt, Pulaski
Montgomery County, 1 E Main St, Christiansburg, VA 24073-3027 .... (703)382-5700
(Clk Cir Ct has b, d rec from 1853 to 1871, m, div, pro, civ ct, Ind rec from 1773)

Morgan (See W. Va.)

* **Nansemond** 1637 Upper Norfolk
(Nansemond County and Suffolk City merged January 1, 1974. Clk Cir Ct has m, pro, civ ct, Ind rec from 1866)

* **Nelson** F3 1807 Amherst
Nelson County, PO Box 55, Lovingston, VA 22949-0055 .... (804)263-4245
(Clk Cir Ct has m, div, pro, civ ct & Ind rec from 1808)

* **New Kent** H4 1654 York(Pt. James City)
New Kent County, PO Box 98, New Kent, VA 23124-0098 .... (804)966-9601
(Clk Cir Ct has b, d rec from 1865 to 1888, m, div, pro, civ ct, Ind rec from 1865)

Newport News H3 Ind. City
Newport News Ind City, 2400 Washington Ave, Newport News, VA 23607-4300 .... (804)247-8411

Nicholas (See W. Va.)

* **Norfolk** H3 1636 Lower Norfolk (changed to Chesapeake City 1963)
Norfolk Ind City, 810 Union St, Norfolk, VA 23510-2717 .... (804)441-2471

Northampton I4 1634 Original Shire (prior to 1642 was called Accawmack)
Northampton County, Business Rt 13, Eastville, VA 23347-9999 .... (804)678-5126
(Clk Cir Ct has m rec from 1706, pro, civ ct & Ind rec from 1632, div rec from 1904)

Northumberland H4 1648 Indian Dist. of Chickacoan
Northumberland County, PO Box 217, Heathsville, VA 22473-0217 .... (804)580-3700
(Clk Cir Ct has m, div, pro, civ ct, Ind rec)

Norton B1 Ind. City
Norton Ind City, PO Box 618, Norton, VA 24273-0618 .... (703)679-1160
(all rec with Wise Co)

* **Nottoway** G3 1788 Amelia
Nottoway County, Hwy 625, Nottoway, VA 23955-9999 .... (804)645-9043
(Clk Cir Ct has m, div rec from 1865, pro, civ ct, Ind rec from 1789)

Ohio (See W. Va.)

* **Orange** F4 1734 Spotsylvania
Orange County, 109-A W Main St, Orange, VA 22960-1524 .... (703)672-3313
(Clk Cir Ct has b rec from 1860 to 1895, m rec 1757, pro, civ ct & deeds from 1734)

* **Page** F5 1831 Rockingham, Shenandoah
Page County, 108 S Court St, Luray, VA 22835-1289 .... (703)743-4142
(Clk Cir Ct has m, div, pro, civ ct & Ind rec from 1831)

* **Patrick** D1 1790 Henry
Patrick County, PO Box 148, Stuart, VA 24171-0148 .... (703)694-7213
(Clk Cir Ct has b & d rec from 1853 to 1896, m, div, pro, civ ct & Ind rec from 1791)

Pendleton (See W. Va.)

* **Petersburg** G3 Ind City
Petersburg Ind City, Courthouse Hill, Petersburg, VA 23803 .... (804)733-2367
(City Clk has b rec from 1853 to 1896, d rec from 1853, m, div, pro & Ind rec from 1784)

* **Pittsylvania** E2 1766 Halifax
Pittsylvania County, 1 S Main St, Chatham, VA 24531-9702 .... (804)432-2041
(Clk Cir Ct has m, div, pro, civ ct, accounts current & inventories of estates from 1767)

Pleasants (See W. Va.)

Pocahontas (See W. Va.)

Poquoson H3 Ind. City
Poquoson Ind City, 830 Poquoson Ave, Poquoson, VA 23662-1797 .... (804)868-7151

* **Portsmouth** I3 Ind. City
Portsmouth Ind City, PO Box 820, Portsmouth, VA 23705-0820 .... (804)393-8746
(Clk Cir Ct has b, d rec from 1858 to 1896, m, div, pro, civ ct, Ind rec from 1848; Portsmouth Pub Health Dept., P.O. Box 250, Portsmouth, Va 23705 has b, d, bur rec. Territory taken from Norfolk County and annexed to Portsmouth County in 1848, 1960 and 1968)

*† **Powhatan** G4 1777 Cumberland, Chesterfield
Powhatan County, 3834 Old Buckingham Rd, Powhatan, VA 23139-7019 .... (804)598-5600
(Clk Cir Ct has m, div, pro, civ ct & Ind rec from 1777)

Preston (See W. Va.)

* **Prince Edward** F3 1752 Amelia
Prince Edward County, PO Box 304, Farmville, VA 23901-0304 .... (804)392-5145
(Clk Cir Ct has b rec from 1853 to 1896, d rec from 1853 to 1869, m, div, pro, civ ct & deeds rec also guardian bk from 1754)

Name	Map Index	Date Created	Parent County or Territory From Which Organized

*† **Prince George**   H3   1700   Charles City
Prince George County, 6400 Courthouse Rd, Prince George, VA 23875-2527 .... (804)733-2600
(Clk Cir Ct has partial b rec from 1865 to 1896, m, div, pro rec from 1865 & civ ct rec from 1945)

* **Prince William**   G5   1727   King George, Stafford
Prince William County, 9311 Lee Ave, Manassas, VA 22110-5598 .... (703)335-6045
(Clk Cir Ct has m rec from 1856, div & civ ct rec from 1823, pro rec from 1734 & lnd rec from 1731)

Princess Anne   1691   Lower Norfolk
(Clk Cir Ct has b rec from 1889 to 1895, m rec 1853, div rec 1814, pro rec 1783, civ ct rec 1937 & min bks 1691. Now part of Ind. City of Virginia Beach)

* **Pulaski**   D2   1839   Montgomery, Wythe
Pulaski County, 45 3rd St NW, Pulaski, VA 24301-5007 .... (703)980-8888
(Clk Cir Ct has m rec from 1882, div, pro, civ ct rec from 1839)

Putnam (See W. Va.)

Radford   D2   Ind City
Radford Ind City, 619 2nd St, Radford, VA 24141-1431 .... (703)731-3603
(Clk Cir Ct has m, div, pro, civ ct & lnd rec from 1892)

Raleigh (See W. Va.)

Randolph (See W. Va.)

* **Rappahannock**   F5   1833   Culpeper
Rappahannock County, PO Box 517, Washington, VA 22747-0517 .... (703)675-3621
(Clk Cir Ct has m, div, pro & civ ct rec from 1833, lnd rec from 1838 & some personal property rec from 1834)

Rappahannock, Old (Abolished 1692)

* **Richmond**   G4   1782   Ind. City
Richmond Ind City, 900 E Broad St, Richmond, VA 23219-6115 .... (804)780-7970
(Dept of Health, Bureau of Vit Rec Madison Building, Richmond, VA 23219 has div rec from 1870 to 1954; Chan Ct for the City of Richmond, City Hall, Richmond, VA 23219 has pro rec; Civ Ct for the city or Richmond, VA 23219 has civ ct rec; Clk Cir Ct has lnd rec for New Kent Co from 1863 to 1865; Chan Ct has lnd rec from the City of Richmond, City Hall, Richmond VA 23219)

* **Richmond**   H4   1692   Rappahannock(old)
Richmond County, 10 Court St, Warsaw, VA 22572 .... (804)333-3781
(Clk Cir Ct has b & d rec from 1853 to 1895, m rec from 1853, div, pro, deeds & wills from 1693)

Ritchie (See W. Va.)

Roane (See W. Va.)

* **Roanoke**   D2   1882   Botetourt, Montgomery
P.O. Box 2610, Roanoke, VA 24010 ....
(Clk Cir Ct has m, div, pro, civ ct & lnd rec from 1838)

* **Roanoke**   Ind. City
Roanoke Ind City, 315 Church Ave SW, Roanoke, VA 24016-5007 .... (703)981-2324
(Clk Cts has b rec from 1884 to 1896, m, div, pro, civ ct & lnd rec from 1884;

* **Rockbridge**   E3   1778   Augusta, Botetourt
Rockbridge County, 2 S Main St, Lexington, VA 24450-2546 .... (703)463-2232
(Clk Cir Ct has b rec from 1853 to 1896, d rec from 1853 to 1870, m, div, pro, civ ct, lnd rec from 1778)

* **Rockingham**   E5   1778   Augusta
Rockingham County, Circuit Ct, Harrisonburg, VA 22801 .... (703)434-4455
(Clk Cir Ct has b rec from 1862 to 1894, d rec from 1890 to 1894, m, pro, civ ct, lnd rec from 1778, div rec from 1833. Some rec burned in 1864)

* **Russell**   B1   1785   Washington
Russell County, PO Box 435, Lebanon, VA 24266 .... (703)889-8023
(Clk Cir Ct has m rec from 1853, div & civ ct rec from 1786, pro rec from 1803 & lnd rec from 1787)

Salem   E3   Ind. City
Salem Ind City, 114 N Broad St, Salem, VA 24153-3734 .... (703)375-3016

* **Scott**   B1   1814   Lee, Russell, Washington
Scott County, 104 E Jackson St, Gate City, VA 24251-3417 .... (703)386-7341
(Clk Cir Ct has b rec from 1853 to 1895, d rec from 1853 to 1892, m, div, pro, civ ct & lnd rec from 1815)

* **Shenandoah**   F5   1772   Frederick (Dunmore 'til 1778)
Shenandoah County, 112 S Main St, Woodstock, VA 22664-1423 .... (703)459-3791
(Clk Cir Ct has m, div, pro, civ ct & lnd rec from 1772)

* **Smyth**   C1   1832   Washington, Wythe
Smyth County, PO Box 1025, Marion, VA 24354-1025 .... (703)783-7186
(Clk Cir Ct has m, div, pro & civ ct rec from 1832)

South Boston   F2   Ind. City
South Boston Ind City, 455 Ferry St, South Boston, VA 24592-3237 .... (804)572-3621

*† **Southampton**   H2   1749   Isle of Wight, Nansemond
Southampton County, County Courthouse, Courtland, VA 23837 .... (804)653-2200
[FHL has some, m, civ ct, lnd, pro rec]

* **Spotsylvania**   G5   1720   Essex, King and Queen, King William
Spotsylvania County, PO Box 99, Spotslyvania, VA 22553-0099 .... (703)582-7010
(Clk Cir Ct has m rec from 1722, b rec from 1864 to 1895 & 1911 to 1915, d rec from 1911 to 1915, civ rec from 1724, pro rec from 1722, lnd rec from 1856, pension rec from 1898 to 1926, coroners inquests from 1879 to 1912)

Name	Map Index	Date Created	Parent County or Territory From Which Organized

* **Stafford**   G5   1664   Westmoreland
Stafford County, PO Box 339, Stafford, VA 22554-0339 .... (703)659-8603
(Clk Cir Ct has m rec from 1854, div & civ ct rec 1664, pro & deeds 1699)

* **Staunton**   F4   Ind. City
Staunton Ind City, 113 E Beverley St, Staunton, VA 24401-4390 .... (703)885-1251
(Clk Cir Ct has b rec from 1853 to 1896, d rec from 1853 to 1892, m, div, pro, civ ct, Ind rec from 1802)

* **Suffolk**   H3   Ind. City
Suffolk Ind City, 441 Market St, Suffolk, VA 23434-5237 .... (804)934-3111
(City Ct has m, div, pro, Ind rec from 1866.)(See Nansemond County)

* **Surry**   H3   1652   James City
Surry County, Hwy 10 & School St, Surry, VA 23883 .... (804)294-5271
(Clk Cir Ct has b & d rec from 1853 to 1896, m rec from 1768, pro & Ind rec from 1652, civ ct rec from 1671, orph accounts
intermittent from 1744, guardian accounts intermittent from 1865, fiduciary accounts from 1831 & div rec)

* **Sussex**   H3   1752   Surry
Sussex County, Rt 735, Sussex, VA 23884-9999 .... (804)246-5511
(Clk Cir Ct has b, m, pro, civ ct & Ind rec from 1754)

Taylor (See W. Va.)

* **Tazewell**   C2   1799   Russell, Wythe
Tazewell County, 315 School St, Tazewell, VA 24651-1398 .... (703)988-7541
(Clk Cir Ct has b, d rec from 1853 to 1870, m, pro, law, Ind rec from 1800, chancery rec from 1832)

Tucker (See W. Va.)

Tyler (See W. Va.)

Upper Norfolk   New Norfolk (see Nansemond)

Upshur (See W. Va.)

* **Virginia Beach**   I3   1963   Ind City
Virginia Beach Ind City, Municipal Ctr, Virginia Beach, VA 23456-9099 .... (804)427-4242
(Clk Cir Ct has b & d rec from 1864 to 1894, m rec from 1749, m rec from 1822 to 1852 were destroyed in fire, div rec fromm
1814, pro, civ ct & Ind rec from 1691)

Warren   F5   1836   Frederick, Shenandoah
Warren County, 22 S Royal Ave, Front Royal, VA 22630-3202 .... (703)636-9973
(Clk Cir Ct has m, div, pro, civ ct & Ind rec from 1836)

Warrosquoyacke   1634   (Changed to Isle of Wight 1637)

Warwick (see Warwick River)

Warwick River   1634   Orig. Shire
Warwick River County, , , VA ....
(Changed to Warwick 1642-3, merged with City of Warwick 1952)

* **Washington**   B1   1776   Fincastle, Montgomery
Washington County, 216 Park St, Abingdon, VA 24210-3312 .... (703)628-8733
(In 1974 nine square miles of Washington County were annexed to the city of Bristol, which is an independent City with its own
Clk's office and rec. Clk Cir Ct has m, div, pro, civ ct, Ind rec from 1777)

Wayne (See W. Va.)

Waynesboro   F4   1948   Ind. City
Waynesboro Ind City, 250 S Wayne Ave, Waynesboro, VA 22980-4622 .... (703)942-6600
(Clk Cir Ct has m, div, pro civ ct & Ind rec from 1948)

Webster (See W. Va.)

* **Westmoreland**   H5   1653   Northumberland
Westmoreland County, Polk St, Montross, VA 22520 .... (804)493-8911
(Clk Cir Ct has b & d rec from 1855 to 1895, m rec from 1786, div rec from 1850, pro, civ ct & Ind rec from 1653)

Wetzel (See W. Va.)

* **Williamsburg**   H3   Ind. City
Williamsburg Ind City, 401 Lafayette St, Williamsburg, VA 23185-3617 .... (804)220-6100
(Clk Cir Ct has m, div, pro, Ind rec from 1865, District Ct rec from 1953)

Winchester   F6
Winchester Ind City, 5 N Kent St, Winchester, VA 22601-5037 .... (703)667-5770

Wirt (See W. Va.)

* **Wise**   B1   1856   Lee, Russell, Scott
Wise County, 108 Main St, Wise, VA 24293 .... (703)328-2321
(Clk Cir Ct has m & div rec from 1856)

Wood (See W. Va.)

Wyoming (See W. Va.)

* **Wythe**   C2   1789   Montgomery(Pt. Grayson)
Wythe County, 225 S 4th St, Wytheville, VA 24382-2502 .... (703)228-6644
(Clk Cir Ct has m, div, pro, civ ct & Ind rec from 1790)

Yohogania   1776   (Discontinued 1786)

Name	Map Index	Date Created	Parent County or Territory From Which Organized
* **York**	H3	1634	Formerly Charles River

York County, PO Box 532, Yorktown, VA 23690-0532 . . . . (804)898-0200

* At least one county history has been published about this county.
† Inventory of county archives was made by the Historical Records Survey. (See Introduction)

WASHINGTON

CAPITAL · OLYMPIA — TERRITORY 1853 — STATE 1889 (42nd)
State Map on Page M-43

In 1775, Spaniards became the first white men to touch Washington soil. American fur traders came between 1789 and 1792, claiming much of the Northwest for America. The British explored Puget Sound in 1792, claiming the whole area for England. The first settlement of the area was at Astoria, a trading post established by John Jacob Astor. The British, however, controlled the area for the most part until the 1840's. Spain withdrew its claim in 1819. In 1836, Marcus Whitman established the second settlement near Walla Walla. Once Whitman and other missionaries had come, other settlers soon followed. The Willamette Valley and Columbia Valley were the main points of settlement. In 1846, the present boundary was established between the United States and Canada as Britain withdrew its claim to the area.

The Oregon Territory was created in 1848, including the present states of Oregon, Washington, Idaho, and parts of Montana and Wyoming. Settlers went farther north in 1849 to obtain food and lumber for the California gold fields. The Oregon Donation Act of 1850 guaranteed from 160 to 640 acres of land to those who settled and cultivated land before 1855. Some 30,000 settlers came as a result of this act, which prompted Congress to organize the Washington Territory in 1853. During the Civil War, Washington supplied nearly a thousand men to the Union forces. Prospectors entered the area in 1860, when gold was discovered near Walla Walla. The Idaho Territory was created in 1863 from parts of eastern Washington Territory. In 1888, the transcontinental railroads reached Washington, bringing with them a new influx of settlers. Washington became the forty-second state in 1889. Seattle was its largest city and the chief supply point for the Alaskan gold rush.

During its peak growth years, settlers from Wisconsin, Minnesota, and other western states came by the thousands. Canadian farmers came to obtain good land at a low price. Most of the newcomers were Canadian, Swedish, Norwegian, English, German, Finnish, Italian, Russian, Danish, and Scottish.

Since 1907, the State Department of Health, Vital Records, P.O. Box 9709, ET-11, Olympia, WA 98504, has birth and death records for the state. To verify current fees, call 206-753-5396. Toll-free, out of state 1-800-551-0562, or in state 1-800-331-0680.

Records prior to that are in the offices of the County Auditors, and usually go back to 1891. City health departments in Seattle, Spokane, Bellingham, and Tacoma also have birth and death records. County Auditors also have marriage and land records. County clerks have wills and probate records. Territorial and state censuses exist for a few counties for various years prior to 1892. These partial censuses are available at the Washington State Library, Capitol Campus, AJ-11, Olympia, WA 98504.

Genealogical Archives, Libraries and Societies

Burlington Public Library, 900 Fairhaven St., Burlington, WA 98233

Clark County Museum, 1511 Main, Vancouver, WA 98668

Everett Public Library, 2702 Hoyt Avenue, Everett, WA 98201

Ft. Vancouver Regional Library, 1007 E. Mill Plain Blvd., Vancouver, WA 98660

Mid-Columbia Library, 405 South Dayton, Kennewick, WA 99336

Neill Public Library, N. 210 Grand Avenue, Pullman, WA 99163

Olympia Timberland Library, 8th and Franklin, Olympia, WA 98501

Public Library, P. O. Box 1197, Bellingham, WA 98225

Public Library, 4th Ave. and Madison, Seattle, WA 98104 (Since 1955, the general genealogical collection of the State Library has been in this library).

Public Library, 1120 So. Tacoma Ave., Tacoma, WA 98402

Regional Public Library, 7th and Franklin St., Olympia, WA 98501

Seattle Public Library, 4th Ave. and Madison, Seattle, WA 98101

Spokane Public Library, West 916 Main Ave., Spokane, WA 99201 (Genealogy Room, maintained with Eastern Washington Genealogical Society, Northwest Room, marterials pertain to the Pacific Northwest),

Stillaguamish Valley Genealogical Society & Library of North Snohomish County, P. O. Box 34, Arlington, WA 98223

University of Washington Library, Seattle, WA 98105

Washington State Historical Society Library, State Historical Bldg., 315 North Stadium Way, Tacoma, WA 98403

Washington State Library, State Library Bldg., Olympia, WA 98501

Washington State University Library, Holland Library, Pullman, WA 99164-5610

Whitman County Library, S. 192 Main Street, Colfax, WA 99111

Chehalis Valley Historical Society, 268-11 Oak Meadows Rd., Oakville, WA 98568

Chelan Valley Genealogical Society, P. O. Box "Y", Chelan, WA 98816

Clallam County Genealogical Society, Genealogy Library, Clallam County Museum, 223 East Fourth Street, Port Angeles, WA 98362

Clark County Genealogical Society, P. O. Box 2728, 1511 Main St., Vancouver, WA 98668

Douglas County Genealogical Society, P. O. Box 580, Waterville, WA 98858

Eastern Washington Genealogical Society, P. O. Box 1826, Spokane, WA 99201.

Eastside Genealogical Society, P. O. Box 374, Bellevue, WA 98009

Ellensburg, Washington Genealogical Group, 507 E. Tacoma Street, Ellensburg, WA 98926

Ft. Vancouver Historical Society, Box 1834, Vancouver, WA 98663

Genealogical Society of Pierce County, P. O. Box 98634, Tacoma, WA 98498-0634

Grant County Genealogical Society, Ephrata Public Library, 339 1st Avenue, SW, Ephrata, WA 98823

Grays Harbor Genealogy Society, P. O. Box 867, Cosmopolis, WA 98537

Jefferson County Genealogical Society, 210 Madison, Port Townsend, WA 98368

Kitsap County Genealogical Society, c / o 4305 Lakeview Drive, S.E., Port Orchard, WA 98366

Kittitas County Genealogical Society, Kittitas County Museum, 114 E. 3rd Street, Ellensburg, WA 98926

Lower Columbia Genealogical Society, P. O. Box 472, Longview, WA 98632

Maple Valley Historical Society, P. O. Box 123, Maple Valley, WA 98038

Metis Genealogical Society, Chapter of the Eastern Washington Genealogical Society, N. 6206 Washington, Spokane, WA 99208

North Central Washington Genealogical Society, P. O. Box 613, Wenatchee, WA 98801

Northeast Washington Genealogical Society, Colville Public Library, 195 S. Oak, Colville, WA 99114

Okanogan County Genealogical Society, Route 1, Box 323, Omake, WA 98841

Olympia Genealogical Society, Olympia Public Library, 8th and Franklin, Olympia, WA 98501

Pacific County Genealogical Society, P. O. Box 843, Ocean Park, WA 98640

Puget Sound Genealogical Society, P. O. Box 601, Tracyton, WA 98393-0601

Seattle Genealogical Society, P. O. Box 1708, Seattle, WA 98111

Skagit Valley Genealogical Society, P. O. Box 715, Conway, WA 98238

Sno-Isle Genealogical Society, P. O. Box 63, Edmonds, WA 98020

Southeastern Lincoln County Historical Society, Sprague, WA 99032

South King County Genealogical Society, P. O. Box 3174, Kent, WA 98032

State Capitol Historical Association, 211 W. 21st Ave., Olympia, WA 98501

Stillaguamish Valley Genealogical Society of North Snohomish County, P. O. Box 34, Arlington, WA 98223

Tacoma-Pierce County Genealogical Society, P. O. Box 1952, Tacoma, WA 98401

Tonasket Genealogical Society, P. O. Box 84, Tonasket, WA 98855

Tri-City Genealogical Society, P. O. Box 1410, Richland, WA 99352-1410

Walla Walla Valley Genealogical Society, P. O. Box 115, Walla Walla, WA 99362

Washington Society, Sons of the American Revolution, 12233 9th Ave., NW., Seattle, WA 98177

Washington State Genealogical Society, Box 1422, Olympia, WA 98507

Washington State Historical Society Library, State Historical Bldg., 315 North Stadium Way, Tacoma, WA 98403

Whatcom Genealogical Society, P. O. Box 1493, Bellingham, WA 98227-1493

Whitman County Genealogical Society, P. O. Box 393, Pullman, WA 99163

Willapa Harbor Genealogical Society, Raymond Public Library, 507 Duryea St., Raymond, WA 98577

Yakima Valley Genealogical Society, P. O. Box 445, Yakima, WA 98907

Printed Census Records and Mortality Schedules

Federal Census 1860 (except Benton, Columbia, San Juan, and Snohomish counties), 1870 (except Benton and Columbia counties), 1880, 1900, 1910
Federal Mortality Schedules 1860, 1870, 1880
Union Veterans and Widows 1890
State/Territorial Census 1872-1888

Valuable Printed Sources

Atlases, Maps, and Gazetteers

Abbott, Newton Carl, et al. *The Evolution of Washington Counties*. Yakima: Yakima Valley Genealogical Society and Klickitat County Historical Society, 1978.

Meany, Edmond S. *Origin of Washington Geographic Names*. Detroit: Gale Research Co., 1968 reprint.

Phillips, James W. *Washington State Place Names*. Seattle: University of Washington Press, 1971.

Bibliographies

Genealogical Resources in Washington State: A Guide to Genealogical Records held at Repositories, Government Agencies, and Archives. Olympia, Washington: Division of Archives and Records Management, 1983.

Histories

Avery, Mary Williamson. *Washington: A History of the Evergreen State.* Seattle: University of Washington Press, 1967.

Hawthorne, Julian. *History of Washington.* New York: American Historical Publishing Co., 1893.

Hines. H. K. *An Illustrated History of the State of Washington.* Chicago: Lewis Publishing Co., 1893.

Stewart, Edgar I. *Washington, Northwest Frontier.* New York: Lewis Historical Publishing Co., 1957.

WASHINGTON COUNTY DATA
State Map on Page M-43

Name	Map Index	Date Created	Parent County or Territory From Which Organized
*† **Adams**	C4	1883	Whitman

Adams County, 210 W Broadway Ave, Ritzville, WA 99169-1860 . . . . (509)659-0090
(Co Aud has b & d rec to 1907, also m rec; Co Clk has div & pro rec; Co Asr has Ind rec)

*† **Asotin**	A6	1883	Garfield

Asotin County, PO Box 159, Asotin, WA 99402-0159 . . . . (509)243-4181
(Co Aud has b & m rec from 1891, d rec from 1891 to 1907; Co Clk has div & pro rec; Co Asr has Ind rec from 1891)

*† **Benton**	D6	1905	Yakima, Klickitat

Benton County, PO Box 190, Prosser, WA 99350-0190 . . . . (509)786-5600
(Co Aud has b rec from 1905 to 1907, m rec from 1905; Co Clk has div, pro & civ ct rec; Co Asr has Ind rec)

Chehalis			Original Co. (now Grays Harbor, changed 1915)

*† **Chelan**	E3	1899	Kittitas, Okanogan

Chelan County, PO Box 3025, Wenatchee, WA 98807-3025 . . . . (509)664-5380
(Co Aud has b & d rec from 1900 to 1907, m rec from 1900; City Clk has bur rec; Chelan Co Clk has div, pro & civ ct rec)

* **Clallam**	H3	1854	Jefferson

Clallam County, 223 E 4th St, Port Angeles, WA 98362-3025 . . . . (206)452-7831
[FHL has 1889 census]

* **Clark**	G6	1844	Original county (formerly Vancouver Co, changed 1849)

Clark County, PO Box 5000, Vancouver, WA 98668 . . . . (206)699-2292
(Co Aud has b, d rec from 1890 to 1906, m rec from 1890, Ind rec from 1850; Co Clk has div, pro, civ rec from 1890)

* **Columbia**	B6	1875	Walla Walla

Columbia County, 341 E Main St, Dayton, WA 99328-1361 . . . . (509)382-4542
(Co Clk has div, pro & civ ct rec from 1891; Co Aud has b rec from 1891 to 1907, m rec from 1876, d rec from 1907, Ind rec from 1864)

*† **Cowlitz**	G6	1854	Lewis

Cowlitz County, 312 SW 1st Ave, Kelso, WA 98626-1798 . . . . (206)577-3016
(Co Aud has m rec from 1867, d rec from 1891 to 1907, Ind rec; Co Clk has div, pro & civ ct rec from 1874, naturalization and adoption rec from 1869)

* **Douglas**	D3	1883	Lincoln

Douglas County, PO Box 516, Waterville, WA 98858-0516 . . . . (509)745-8529
(Co Aud has b rec to 1907, bur rec to 1909, Ind rec to 1925, m, d, div, pro & civ ct rec, also mining claims from 1890)

* **Ferry**	C2	1899	Stevens

Ferry County, PO Box 302, Republic, WA 99166-0302 . . . . (509)775-3161
(Co Clk has div, pro & civ ct rec from 1899)

* **Franklin**	C5	1883	Whitman

Franklin County, 1016 N 4th Ave, Pasco, WA 99301-3706 . . . . (509)545-3525
(Co Aud has b, d & bur rec from 1891 to 1910, m rec from 1891, Ind rec; Co Clk has div, pro & civ ct rec from 1891)

*† **Garfield**	A5	1881	Columbia

Garfield County, PO Box 915, Pomeroy, WA 99347-0915 . . . . (509)843-3731
(Co Aud has b & d rec from 1891 to 1907, m rec from 1891, bur rec from 1891 to 1918; Co Clk has div, pro & civ ct rec from 1882; Co Aud has Ind rec from 1891)

Grant	D4	1909	Douglas

Grant County, PO Box 37, Ephrata, WA 98823-0037 . . . . (509)754-2011
(Co Aud has m & Ind rec from 1909; Co Clk has div, pro & civ ct rec)

* **Grays Harbor**	H4	1854	Organized as Chehalis, changed 1915

Grays Harbor County, PO Box 711, Montesano, WA 98563-0590 . . . . (206)249-3842
(Co Aud has b, d rec from 1891 to 1907, m rec from 1891, Ind rec from 1855; Co Clk has div, pro, civ ct rec from 1860)

Island	G2	1853	Original county

Island County, PO Box 5000, Coupeville, WA 98239-5000 . . . . (206)679-7359
(Co Aud has b & d rec from 1870 to 1907, m rec from 1855 & Ind rec from 1853; Co Clk has div, pro & civ ct rec)

Name	Map Index	Date Created	Parent County or Territory From Which Organized

* Jefferson H3 1852 Original county
Jefferson County, PO Box 1220, Port Townsend, WA 98368-0920 .... (206)385-9125
(Co Aud has b & d rec from 1891 to 1907, m rec from 1853; Co Clk has div rec from 1886 & pro rec from 1891)

*† King F4 1852 Original county
King County, 516 3rd Ave, Seattle, WA 98104 .... (206)344-4040
(Rec & Elections Div, Rec Section has b, m, d & Ind rec from 1853; Clk Sup Ct has div, pro & civ ct rec)

* Kitsap G3 1857 King
Kitsap County, 614 Division St, Port Orchard, WA 98366-4676 .... (206)876-7164
(Co Aud has b rec from 1891 to 1907, d rec from 1892 to 1907, also m rec from 1892; Co Clk has div & civ rec from 1888, pro & adoption rec from 1861 & Ind rec from 1857)

* Kittitas E4 1883 Yakima
Kittitas County, 205 W 5th Ave, Ellensburg, WA 98926-2887 .... (509)962-7531
(Co Aud has b, d rec from 1891 to 1907, m rec from 1884, Ind rec from 1882; Co Clk has div, pro, civ ct rec from 1890's)

* Klickitat E6 1859 Walla Walla
Klickitat County, 205 S Columbus Ave Rm 204, Goldendale, WA 98620-9294 .... (509)773-5744
(Co Clk has div, pro, civ ct rec; Co Aud has m rec)

*† Lewis G5 1845 Original county
Lewis County, 351 NW North St, Chehalis, WA 98532-1926 .... (206)748-9121
(Co Aud has b & d rec from 1891 to 1907, m rec from 1850; Co Clk has div, pro & civ ct rec from abt 1870)

*† Lincoln C3 1883 Spokane
Lincoln County, PO Box 369, Davenport, WA 99122-0369 .... (509)725-1401
(Co Aud has b, d rec from 1891 to 1907, m, Ind rec from 1891; Co Clk has div, pro, civ ct rec)

Mason H4 1854 Thurston
Mason County, PO Box 186, Shelton, WA 98584-0186 .... (206)427-9670
(Co Aud has m rec from 1892, d rec from 1891 to 1906, Ind rec from 1850's; Co Clk has div, pro & civ ct rec)

* Okanogan D2 1888 Stevens
Okanogan County, PO Box 72, Okanogan, WA 98840-0072 .... (509)422-3650
(Co Aud has b, d rec from 1891 to 1908, m rec from 1891, Ind rec from 1891, patents from 1892 and mines from 1888; Co Clk has div, pro, civ ct rec from 1896)

* Pacific H5 1851 Original county
Pacific County, PO Box 67, South Bend, WA 98586-0067 .... (206)875-9300
(Co Aud has b & d rec from 1891 to 1905, m rec from 1868; Co Clk has div, pro & civ ct rec; Co Asr has Ind rec)

*† Pend Oreille A2 1911 Stevens
Pend Oreille County, PO Box 5000, Newport, WA 99156-5000 .... (509)447-2435
(Co Aud has b, m & Ind rec from 1911; Co Clk has div pro & civ ct rec from 1911)

* Pierce F4 1852 Original county
Pierce County, 930 Tacoma Ave S, Tacoma, WA 98402-2108 .... (206)591-7455
(Co Aud has m & Ind rec; Co Clk has div, pro, criminal & civ ct rec from 1890, adoptions)

* San Juan G2 1873 Whatcom
San Juan County, PO Box 1249, Friday Harbor, WA 98250-1249 .... (206)378-2163
(Co Clk has div, pro & civ ct rec; Co Aud has b rec from 1892 to 1907, d rec from 1890 to 1907 & m rec from 1878)

Sawamish (See Mason)

*† Skagit F2 1883 Whatcom
Skagit County, PO Box 837, Mount Vernon, WA 98273-0837 .... (206)336-9440
(Co Aud has b & d rec from 1891 to 1907, m rec from 1884, Ind rec from 1872; Co Clk has div, pro & civ ct rec from 1870)

Skamania F6 1854 Clark
Skamania County, PO Box 790, Stevenson, WA 98648-0790 .... (509)427-5141
(Co Aud has Ind rec; Co Clk has m, div, pro & civ ct rec from 1856)

*† Snohomish F3 1861 Island
Snohomish County, 3000 Rockefeller Ave Rm 246, Everett, WA 98201-4046 .... (206)388-3466
(Co Aud has b, d rec from 1891 to 1907, m rec from 1891; Co Clk has div, pro, civ ct rec)

*† Spokane A3 1858 Walla Walla, Stevens
Spokane County, 1116 W Broadway Ave, Spokane, WA 99260-0001 .... (509)456-2211
(Spokane Co was organized in 1858 from Walla Walla, then disorganized & reorganized in 1879 from Stevens Co)(Co Aud has b & d rec from 1890 to 1907, m rec from 1890 & Ind rec; Co Clk has div, pro & civ ct rec)

*† Stevens B2 1863 Walla Walla
Stevens County, PO Box 191, Colville, WA 99114-0191 .... (509)684-3751
(Co Aud has b & d rec from 1891 to 1907, m rec from 1861, Ind rec from 1883; Co Clk has div, pro & civ ct rec from 1889)

* Thurston G5 1852 Original county
Thurston County, 2000 Lakeridge Dr SW, Olympia, WA 98502-6042 .... (206)754-3800
(Co Aud has b & d rec from 1891 to 1907, m rec from 1891; Co Clk has div, pro & civ ct rec)

Vancouver (Changed to Clark in 1849)

Wahkiakum H5 1854 Lewis
Wahkiakum County, PO Box 116, Cathlamet, WA 98612-0116 .... (206)795-3558
(Co Aud has b rec from 1891 to 1907, m rec from 1891; Co Clk has bur, div, pro, civ ct rec & Ind rec from 1868)

Name	Map Index	Date Created	Name Created	Parent County or Territory From Which Organized
* **Walla Walla**	C6	1854		Original county

Walla Walla County, PO Box 836, Walla Walla, WA 99362-0259 .... (509)527-3221
(Co Clk has div, pro & civ ct rec from 1860)

| * **Whatcom** | F1 | 1854 | | Original county |

Whatcom County, PO Box 1144, Bellingham, WA 98227-1144 .... (206)676-6777
(Co Aud has b, d rec from 1891 to 1907, m rec from 1869, Ind rec; Co Clk has div, pro, civ ct rec)

| * **Whitman** | A4 | 1871 | | Stevens |

Whitman County, 400 N Main St, Colfax, WA 99111-2031 .... (509)397-4622
(Co Aud has b & d rec from 1891 to 1907, m & Ind rec from 1873; Co Clk has div & civ ct rec from 1864, pro rec from 1870, naturalization rec from 1880 to 1937)

| *† **Yakima** | E5 | 1865 | | Walla Walla |

Yakima County, 2nd & B Sts, Yakima, WA 98901 .... (509)575-4120
(Co Aud has b & d rec from 1891 to 1907, m rec from 1880 & Ind rec; Co Clk has div, pro & civ ct rec from 1890)

* At least one county history has been published about this county.
† Inventory of county archives was made by the Historical Records Survey. (See Introduction)

WEST VIRGINIA

CAPITAL · CHARLESTON — STATE 1863 (35th)
State Map on Page M-44

Fur traders entered western Virginia by the mid-1600's, with the first expedition across the Blue Ridge and Allegheny mountains occurring in 1671. In 1712, Baron de Graffenreid visited the eastern Panhandle to find land for Swiss families. The first settlements were made by Welsh, German, and Scotch-Irish from Pennsylvania by 1734. Other early settlers came from Maryland to settle in Berkeley and Jefferson counties. In 1775, the west Augusta District was established by Virginia, which included all of present West Virginia and part of western Pennsylvania. Most of the northern part of the county was ceded to Pennsylvania in 1779 in exchange for Pennsylvania relinquishing its claims to the rest of the county.

When Virginia seceded from the Union in 1861, western counties objected. Fifty western counties united to form "The Restored Government of Virginia" and petitioned Congress for re-admittance to the Union. The state of West Virginia was admitted to the Union in 1863, after Union victories in the area cleared out the Confederates. During the Civil War, West Virginia had about 32,000 soldiers in the Union army and 9,000 in the Confederate army. In the 1870's industrial expansion in West Virginia attracted black immigrants from the southern states and European immigrants, especially Italians, Poles, Hungarians, Austrians, English, Germans, Greeks, Russians, and Czechs.

Statewide registration of births and deaths began in 1917. Records are at the Division of Vital Statistics, State Department of Health, State Office Building No. 3, Charleston, WV 25305. To verify current fees, call 304-348-2931.

Although most state records were destroyed in a 1921 fire, most counties have records from 1853. Some counties also have marriage records from 1870. Divorce records are kept by the county clerk of the circuit court. Probate records have been kept by the county courts and are found in deed books and court order books. Naturalization proceedings were recorded in the minutes and dockets of the courts until 1906, since any court could naturalize immigrants. After 1929, only federal courts handled naturalizations. State censuses were taken in some counties between 1782 and 1785, and have been published along with tax records.

Genealogical Archives, Libraries and Societies

Cabell County Public Library, 900-5th Ave., Huntington, WV 25701

Division of Archives and History, Cultural Center, Capitol Complex, Charleston, WV 25305

Huntington Public Library, Huntington, WV 25701

Morgantown Public Library, 373 Spruce St., Morgantown, WV 26505

West Virginia and Regional History Collection, Colson Hall, West Virginia University Library, Morgantown, WV 26506

Berkelely County Genealogical-Historical Society, P. O. Box 1624, Martinsburg, WV 25401

Boone County West Virginia Genealogical Society, P. O. Box 295, Madison, WV 25130

Brooke County Genealogical-Historical Society, 1200 Pleasant Ave. Wellsburg, WV 26070

Cabell-Wayne County Historical Society, Box 9412, Huntington, WV 25704

Doddridge County Historical Society, Box 23, West Union, WV 26456

Genealogy Society of Fayette & Raleigh Counties, Inc., P. O. Box 68, Oak Hill, WV 25901-0068

Gilmer County Historical Society, 706 Mineral Road, Glenville, WV 26351

Grant County Genealogical-Historical Society, Lahmansville, WV 26731

Hacker's Creek Pioneer Descendants, 321 Highland Avenue, SW, Massillon, OH 44646

Hancock County Genealogical-Historical Society, 103 Bell St., Weirton, WV 26067

Hardy County Genealogical-Historical Society, Moorefield, WV 26836

Jackson County Historical Society, P. O. Box 22, Ripley, WV 25271

Kanawha Valley Genealogical Society, P. O. Box 8555, South Charleston, WV 25303

KYOWVA Genealogical Society, P. O. Box 1254, Huntington, WV 25715

Lewis County Genealogical-Historical Society, 252 Main Avenue, Weston, WV 26452

Lincoln County Genealogical Society, P. O. Box 92, Griffithsville, WV 25521

Logan County Genealogical Society, P. O. Box 1959, Logan, WV 25601

Marion County Genealogical Club, Inc., Marion County Library, Monroe Street, Fairmont, WV 26554

Mason County Genealogical-Historical Society, Henderson, WV 25106

Mercer County Genealogical-Historical Society, Athens, WV 24712

Mineral County Genealogical-Historical Society, 107 Orchard Street, Keyser, WV 26726

Mingo County Genealogical Society, Box 2581, Williamson, WV 25661

Monroe County Historical Society, P. O. Box 465, Union, WV 24983

Morgan County Historical and Genealogical Society, Box 52, Berkeley Springs, WV 25411

Pendleton County Historical Society, Main Street, Franklin, WV 26807

Ritchie County Historical Society, 200 S. Church St., Harrisville, WV 26362

Tyler County Historical Society, Box 317, Middlebourne, WV 26149

Upshur County, West Virginia Historical Society, P. O. Box 753, Buckhannon, WV 26201

West Augusta Historical & Genealogical Society, 2515 10th Avenue, Parkersburg, WV 26101

West Virginia Genealogy Society, Inc., P. O. Box 172, Elkview, WV 25071

West Virginia Historical Society, Cultural Center, Capitol Complex, Charleston, WV 25305

West Virginia, Sons of the American Revolution, 132 N. Court St., Lewisburg, WV 24901

Wetzel County Genealogical Society, P. O. Box 464, New Martinsville, WV 26155-0464

Wheeling Area Genealogical Society, 2237 Marshall Ave., Wheeling, WV 26003

Wyoming County Genealogical Society, P. O. Box 1456, Pineville, WV 24874

Printed Census Records and Mortality Schedules

Federal Census 1870, 1880, 1900, 1910
Union Veterans and Widows 1890

Valuable Printed Sources

Atlases, Maps, and Gazetteers

Gannett, Henry. *A Gazetteer of Virginia and West Virginia*. Baltimore: Genealogical Publishing Co., 1975.

Kenny, Hamill. *West Virginia Place Names*. Piedmont, West Virginia: Place Name Press, 1945.

New Descriptive Atlas of West Virginia. Clarksburg, West Virginia: Clarksburg Publishing Co., 1933.

Bibliographies

Forbes, Harold M. *West Virginia Genealogy: A Bibliography and Guide to Research*. Morgantown, West Virginia: West Virginia University Press, 1981.

Hess, James W. *Guide to Manuscripts and Archives in the West Virginia Collection*. Morgantown, West Virginia: West Virginia University Library, 1974.

Mertins, Barbara. *Newspapers in the University of West Virginia Library*. Morgantown, West Virginia: West Virginia University Library, 1973.

Shetler, Charles. *Guide to the Study of West Virginia History*. Morgantown, West Virginia: West Virginia University Library, 1960.

Stewart, Robert Armistead. *Index to Printed Virginia Genealogies*. Baltimore: Genealogical Publishing Co., 1970 reprint.

Swem, Earl Gregg. *Virginia Historical Index*. Gloucester, Massachusetts: Peter Smith, 1965.

Genealogical Research Guides

Elliott, Wendy L. *Guide to Genealogical Research in West Virginia Records*. Bountiful, Utah: American Genealogical Lending Library, 1987.

McCay, Betty L. *Genealogical Searching in Virginia and West Virginia*. Indianapolis: Betty L. McCay, 1971.

Genealogical Sources

Crozier, William Armstrong. *A Key to Southern Pedigrees*. Baltimore: Genealogical Publishing Co., 1953.

Johnston, Ross B. *West Virginia Estate Settlements, 1753-1850*. Fort Worth, Texas: American Reference Publishers, 1969.

———. *West Virginians in the American Revolution*. Parkersburg, West Virginia: West Augusta Historical and Genealogical Society, 1959.

Lewis, Virgil A. *The Soldiery of West Virginia*. Baltimore: Genealogical Publishing Co., 1967 reprint.

Reddy, Anne Waller. *West Virginia Revolutionary Ancestors*. Baltimore: Genealogical Publishing Co., 1963 reprint.

Sims, Edgar Barr. *Index to Land Grants in West Virginia*. Charlestown, West Virginia: Auditor's Office, 1952.

Histories

Ambler, Charles Henry. *West Virginia, the Mountain State*. New York: Prentice-Hall, 1940.

Callahan, James Morton. *History of West Virginia, Old and New*. Chicago: American Historical Society, 1923.

Sims, Edgar Barr. *Making a State*. Charlestown, West Virginia: State of West Virginia, 1956.

WEST VIRGINIA COUNTY DATA
State Map on Page M-44

Name	Map Index	Date Created	Parent County or Territory From Which Organized	
* **Barbour**	F4	1843	Harrison, Lewis, Randolph	
			Barbour County, PO Box 310, Philippi, WV 26416-0310	(304)457-2232
			(Co Clk has b, m, d & pro rec from 1843, Ind rec from 1845; Clk Cir Ct has div & civ ct rec)	
* **Berkeley**	I5	1772	Frederick, VA	
			Berkeley County, 119 W King St, Martinsburg, WV 25401-3209	(304)267-3000
			(Co Clk has b & d rec from 1865, m rec from 1781, pro rec from 1772 & Ind rec from 1880; Clk Cir Ct has div rec)	
* **Boone**	C1	1847	Kanawha, Cabell, Logan	
			Boone County, 200 State St, Madison, WV 25130-1152	(304)369-3925
			(Co Clk has b, m, d, pro, Ind rec from 1865; Cir Clk has div, civ ct rec)	
* **Braxton**	E3	1836	Kanawha, Lewis, Nicholas	
			Braxton County, PO Box 486, Sutton, WV 26601-0486	(304)765-2833
			(Co Clk has b, m & d indexes from 1853 to 1886, pro & Ind rec; Clk Cir Ct has div & civ ct rec)	
* **Brooke**	E6	1796	Ohio	
			Brooke County, Main & 7th Sts, Wellsburg, WV 26070	(304)737-3661
			(Co Clk has b & d rec from 1853, m, pro & Ind rec from 1797; Clk Cir Ct has div & civ ct rec)	
* **Cabell**	B2	1809	Kanawha	
			Cabell County, 8th St & 4th Ave, Huntington, WV 25701	(304)526-8625
			(Co Clk has b & d rec from 1853, m rec from 1809 & Ind rec from 1808; Clk Cir Ct has div & civ ct rec from 1809)	
* **Calhoun**	D3	1856	Gilmer	
			Calhoun County, Main St, Grantsville, WV 26147	(304)354-6725
			(Co Clk has b, m, d, pro, Ind rec from 1856)	
* **Clay**	D2	1858	Braxton, Nicholas	
			Clay County, Main St, Clay, WV 25043	(304)587-4259
			(Co Clk has b, m, d & pro rec from 1858)	
* **Doddridge**	E4	1845	Harrison, Tyler, Ritchie, Lewis	
			Doddridge County, 118 E Court St, West Union, WV 26456-1262	(304)873-2631
			(Co Clk has b & d rec from 1853, m, pro & Ind rec from 1845; Clk Cir Ct has civ ct rec)	
* **Fayette**	D2	1831	Kanawha, Greenbrier, Logan	
			Fayette County, Court St, Fayetteville, WV 25840-1298	(304)574-1200
			(Co Clk has b, d rec from 1866, m, pro, Ind rec from 1831; Cir Clk has div, civ ct rec)	
*† **Gilmer**	D3	1845	Lewis, Kanawha	
			Gilmer County, 10 Howard St, Glenville, WV 26351-1246	(304)462-7641
			(Co Clk has b, d & civ ct rec from 1853, m, pro & Ind rec from 1845)	
*† **Grant**	G4	1866	Hardy	
			Grant County, 5 Highland Ave, Petersburg, WV 26847-1705	(304)257-4422
			(Co Clk has b, m, d, div, pro, civ ct & Ind rec from 1866)	
* **Greenbrier**	E1	1777	Montgomery	
			Greenbrier County, PO Box 506, Lewisburg, WV 24901-0506	(304)645-2373
			(Co Clk has b, d rec from 1853, m rec from 1781, pro, Ind rec from 1780, Court Order rec)	
* **Hampshire**	H4	1753	Frederick, VA	
			Hampshire County, Main St, Romney, WV 26757-1696	(304)822-5112
			(Co Clk has b, m, d rec from 1865, pro rec from 1780, inc chan rec from 1831 & Ind rec)	

Name	Map Index	Date Created	Parent County or Territory From Which Organized

* **Hancock**   E7   1848   Brooke
Hancock County, PO Box 367, New Cumberland, WV 26047-0367 .... (304)564-3311
(Co Clk has b, m, d, pro & Ind rec from 1848; Clk Cir Ct has div rec)

* **Hardy**   G4   1785   Hampshire
Hardy County, Washington St, Moorefield, WV 26836 .... (304)538-2929
(Co Clk has b, m, d & bur rec from 1853, pro & Ind rec from 1786, civ ct rec from 1960 & div rec)

* **Harrison**   E4   1784   Monongalia
Harrison County, 301 W Main St, Clarksburg, WV 26301-2909 .... (304)624-8611
(Co Clk has b & d rec from 1853, m & survey rec from 1784, pro rec from 1788 & Ind rec from 1786)

* **Jackson**   C3   1831   Kanawha, Mason, Wood
Jackson County, Court St, Ripley, WV 25271 .... (304)372-2011
(Co Clk has b, d, pro rec from 1853, m, Ind rec from 1831; Cir Clk has div rec, civ ct rec from 1831)

* **Jefferson**   I5   1801   Berkeley
Jefferson County, George & Washington Sts, Charles Town, WV 25414 .... (304)725-9761
(Co Clk has b, d rec from 1853 (except CW years), m, pro, wills, Ind rec from 1801)

* **Kanawha**   C2   1788   Greenbrier, Montgomery
Kanawha County, PO Box 3627, Charleston, WV 25336 .... (304)357-0101
(Co Clk has b, d rec from 1853, m rec from 1824, pro rec from 1831, Ind rec from 1790)

* **Lewis**   E4   1816   Harrison
Lewis County, 110 Center Ave, Weston, WV 26452 .... (304)269-8215
(Co Clk has b, d rec from 1853, m, pro, Ind rec from 1816, sale bills, appr. wills; Clk Cir Ct has div rec)

*† **Lincoln**   C2   1867   Boone, Cabell, Kanawha
Lincoln County, 8000 Court Ave, Hamlin, WV 25523-1419 .... (304)824-3336
(Co Clk has b, m, d, pro & Ind rec from 1909)

* **Logan**   C1   1824   Kanawha, Cabell, Giles
Logan County, Main & Stratton Sts, Logan, WV 25601 .... (304)752-2000
(Co Clk has b, m & d rec from 1872, pro & Ind rec)

*† **Marion**   E5   1842   Harrison, Monongalia
Marion County, 211 Adams St, Fairmont, WV 26554-2876 .... (304)367-5440
(Co Clk has b, m, & d rec from 1872, pro & Ind rec)

* **Marshall**   E5   1835   Ohio
Marshall County, 7th St, Moundsville, WV 26041 .... (304)845-1220
(Co Clk has b & d rec from 1853, m & deeds rec from 1835, pro rec from 1850; Cir Clk has div & civ ct rec)

* **Mason**   C3   1804   Kanawha
Mason County, 6th & Main, Point Pleasant, WV 25550 .... (304)675-1997
[FHL has some b, m, d, cem, civ ct, Ind, pro, tax rec]

* **McDowell**   C1   1858   Tazewell Co, VA
McDowell County, PO Box 447, Welch, WV 24801-0447 .... (304)436-6587
(Co Clk has b rec from 1872, m rec from 1861, d rec from 1894, pro rec from 1897; Cir Clk has div rec)(County seat was first Perryville, changed to Welch in 1892)

* **Mercer**   D1   1837   Giles, VA & Tazewell, VA
Mercer County, County Courthouse Sq, Princeton, WV 24740 .... (304)425-9571
(Co Clk has b, m & d rec from 1853, pro & Ind rec from 1837; Clk Cir Ct has div & civ ct rec from 1837)

*† **Mineral**   H4   1866   Hampshire
Mineral County, 150 Armstrong St, Keyser, WV 26726-3505 .... (304)788-3924
(Co Clk has b, m, d, pro, Ind rec, wills & deeds from 1866)

* **Mingo**   B1   1895   Logan
Mingo County, PO Box 1197, Williamson, WV 25661-1197 .... (304)235-1638
(Co Clk has b, m, d & Ind rec from 1895, bur rec from 1959; Clk Cir Ct has div, pro & civ ct rec)

* **Monongalia**   F5   1776   Dist of Augusta
Monongalia County, 243 High St, Morgantown, WV 26505-5434 .... (304)291-7230
(Co Clk has b & d rec from 1853, m rec from 1796, pro rec from early 1800's, Ind rec from 1843, civ ct rec from 1924 to 1971; Clk Cir Ct has div & civ ct rec)

* **Monroe**   E1   1799   Greenbrier
Monroe County, Main St, Union, WV 24983 .... (304)772-3096
(Co Clk has b & d rec from 1853, m & Ind rec from 1799 & pro rec)

* **Morgan**   H5   1820   Berkeley, Hampshire
Morgan County, 202 Fairfax St, Berkeley Springs, WV 25411-1501 .... (304)258-2774
(Co Clk has b, m, d & pro rec from 1865, Ind rec from 1820; Clk Cir Ct has div & civ ct rec)

* **Nicholas**   D2   1818   Greenbrier, Kanawha
Nicholas County, 700 Main St, Summersville, WV 26651-1444 .... (304)872-3630
(Co Clk has b rec from 1855, m & Ind rec from 1812, d rec from 1890, pro rec from 1880; Clk Cir Ct has div & civ ct rec)

* **Ohio**   E6   1776   Dist. of Augusta
Ohio County, 205 City County Bldg, Wheeling, WV 26003 .... (304)234-3656
(Co Clk has b, d rec from 1853, m rec from 1793, pro rec from 1777, Ind rec from 1778; Clk Cir Ct has div, civ ct rec from 1884)

Name	Map Index	Date Created	Parent County or Territory From Which Organized

*† **Pendleton**   G3   1787   Augusta, VA, Hardy, VA, Rockingham, VA, Bath, VA
Pendleton County, PO Box 89, Franklin, WV   26807-0089 . . . . (304)358-2505
(Co Clk has b & d rec from 1853, m rec from 1800, pro & Ind rec from 1789)

* **Pleasants**   D4   1851   Ritchie, Tyler, Wood
Pleasants County, County Courthouse, Saint Marys, WV   26170 . . . . (304)684-7542
(Co Clk has b, m, d & pro rec from 1853, Ind rec from 1851; Clk Cir Ct has div & civ ct rec)

*† **Pocahontas**   F2   1821   Pendleton, Randolph, Bath (all Virginia)
Pocahontas County, 900C 10th Ave, Marlinton, WV   24954-1310 . . . . (304)799-4549
(Co Clk has b rec from 1853, d rec from 1854, m, pro & Ind rec from 1822; Clk Cir Ct has div & civ ct rec)

* **Preston**   F5   1818   Monongalia
Preston County, 101 W Main St, Kingwood, WV   26537-1121 . . . . (304)329-0070
(Co Clk has b, m, d, pro & Ind rec from 1869; Clk Cir Ct has div & civ ct rec)

† **Putnam**   C3   1848   Kanawha, Mason, Cabell
Putnam County, County Courthouse, Winfield, WV   25213 . . . . (304)586-0202
(Co Clk has b rec from 1848, d rec from 1853, m & pro rec from 1849, Ind rec from 1841; Clk Cir Ct has div & civ ct rec)

* **Raleigh**   D1   1850   Fayette
Raleigh County, 215 Main St County Courthouse, Beckley, WV   25801 . . . . (304)255-9123
(Co Clk has b, m, d, pro & Ind rec from 1850; Clk Cir Ct has div, crim & cir ct rec)

*† **Randolph**   F3   1787   Harrison
Randolph County, 2 Randolph Ave, Elkins, WV   26241-4063 . . . . (304)636-0543
(Co Clk has b rec from 1856, m, pro, wills from 1787 & d rec from 1853)

*† **Ritchie**   D4   1843   Harrison, Lewis, Wood
Ritchie County, 115 E Main St, Harrisville, WV   26362-1271 . . . . (304)643-2163
(Co Clk has b & d rec from 1853, m & pro rec from 1843, Ind rec from 1844 & fiduciary rec from 1863)

*† **Roane**   D3   1856   Kanawha, Jackson, Gilmer
Roane County, 200 Main St, Spencer, WV   25276-1497 . . . . (304)927-2860
(Co Clk has b, m, d, pro, Ind rec from 1856)

* **Summers**   D1   1871   Greenbrier, Monroe, Mercer
Summers County, Ballengee St, Hinton, WV   25951 . . . . (304)466-3770
(Co Clk has b, m, d, pro, Ind rec from 1871; Cir Ct Clk has div, civ ct rec)

*† **Taylor**   F4   1844   Barbour, Harrison, Marion, Preston
Taylor County, 214 W Main St, Grafton, WV   26354-1387 . . . . (304)265-1401
(Co Clk has b, m, d, pro, Ind rec from 1853, Cir Ct Clk has div, civ ct rec)

* **Tucker**   F4   1856   Randolph
Tucker County, 1st & Walnut Sts, Parsons, WV   26287 . . . . (304)478-2414
(Co Clk has b, m, d, pro, Ind rec, deeds & agreements; Clk Cir Ct has div & civ ct rec)

* **Tyler**   E5   1814   Ohio
Tyler County, PO Box 66, Middlebourne, WV   26149-0066 . . . . (304)758-2102
(Co Clk has b, m & d rec from 1853, incomplete m rec from 1815, pro & Ind rec from 1815; Clk Cir Ct has div & civ ct rec)

* **Upshur**   E3   1851   Randolph, Barbour, Lewis
Upshur County, Main St, Buckhannon, WV   26201 . . . . (304)472-1068
(Co Clk has b, m, d, Ind rec from 1853; Cir Ct Clk has div, pro, civ ct rec)

* **Wayne**   B2   1842   Cabell
Wayne County, Hendricks St, Wayne, WV   25570 . . . . (304)272-5101
(Co Clk has b & d rec from 1853 & m rec from 1854)

* **Webster**   E3   1860   Braxton, Nicholas
Webster County, PO Box 32, Webster Springs, WV   26288-0032 . . . . (304)847-2508
(Co Clk has b, m, d, bur, pro & Ind rec from 1887)

* **Wetzel**   E5   1846   Tyler
Wetzel County, PO Box 156, New Martinsville, WV   26155-0156 . . . . (304)455-1390
(Co Clk has b, m, d, pro & Ind rec from 1846; Clk Cir Ct has div rec)

* **Wirt**   D4   1848   Wood, Jackson
Wirt County, PO Box 53, Elizabeth, WV   26143-0053 . . . . (304)275-4271
(Co Clk has b & d rec from 1870, m rec from 1854, pro & Ind rec from 1848; Clk Cir Ct has div rec)

* **Wood**   D4   1798   Harrison
Wood County, PO Box 1474, Parkersburg, WV   26102-1474 . . . . (304)424-1850
(Co Clk has b & d rec from 1853, m & pro rec from 1800, Ind rec from 1798, military discharges from 1919; Clk Cir Ct has div & civ ct rec)

Wyoming   C1   1850   Logan
Wyoming County, Bank St, Pineville, WV   24874 . . . . (304)732-8000
(Co Clk has b, m, d, pro, Ind, bond bk, co court order bks, fiduciary rec from 1850; Clk Cir Ct has div, civ ct rec)

* At least one county history has been published about this county.
† Inventory of county archives was made by the Historical Records Survey. (See Introduction)

WISCONSIN

CAPITAL · MADISON — TERRITORY 1836 — STATE 1847 (30th)
State Map on Page M-45

Jean Nicolet, a French explorer, first explored Wisconsin in 1634. Many other Frenchmen explored the area in the next few decades, leading to the first trading post at La Baye in 1648. The French gave up their claim to the area following the French and Indian War in 1763. A few settlers came to the area as early as 1766. Wisconsin became part of the United States in 1783 and part of the Northwest Territory in 1787. The British effectively controlled the area until after the War of 1812. Following inclusion in the Indiana Territory in 1800 and the Illinois Territory in 1809, Wisconsin became part of the Michigan Territory in 1818.

The first large-scale immigration took place in the 1820's, due to a lead-mining boom in the mines of southern Wisconsin. Following several Indian wars which eliminated Indian threats, settlers flocked to the southeastern areas of the state along Lake Michigan. The cities of Milwaukee, Racine, and Kenosha were settled during the 1830's. In 1836, Congress created the Wisconsin Territory, which included lands west of the Mississippi River to the Missouri River. The creation of the Iowa Territory in 1838 took away much of the western portion.

In the 1840's many families arrived from Germany and New York. The biggest influx of people came about 1848 when the last Indian lands were relinquished and Wisconsin became a state. They came from the northern European countries, doubling the population between 1850 and 1860. In the Civil War, Wisconsin provided about 90,000 men to the Union. The leading nationalities in Wisconsin are German (by nearly three to one), Polish, Norwegian, Russian, Austrian, Swedish, Czech, Italian, Danish, Hungarian, English, Finnish, Greek, Irish, and French.

A few counties began keeping birth and death records in the 1850's. Statewide registration began in 1907. Both pre- and post- 1907 records are at the State Historical Society of Wisconsin, 816 State Street, Madison, WI 53706. To obtain copies write to the Center for Health Statistics, P.O. Box 309, Madison, WI 53701, and state the reason for the request. To verify current fees, call 608-266-1371.

Wills, deeds, land grants, and taxpayer lists are available in county courthouses. War service records are available from the Office of the Adjutant General, Madison, WI 53702. Residents of Wisconsin were included in the territorial censuses of Indiana in 1820, Michigan in 1830, and Wisconsin in 1849. Special censuses were taken by the territory or state in 1836, 1838, 1840, 1842, 1846, 1847, 1855, 1865, 1875, 1885, 1895, and 1905.

Genealogical Archives, Libraries and Societies

Beaver Dam Community Library, 311 S. Spring Street, Beaver Dam, WI 53916

Brown County Library, Local History and Genealogy Dept., 515 Pine Street, Green Bay, WI 54301

Fond du Lac Public Library, 32 Sheboygan Street, Fond du Lac, WI 54935

LaCrosse Public Library, Archives and Local History, 800 Main Street, LaCrosse, WI 54601

Local History and Genealogical Library, Racine County Historical Society and Museum, Inc., 701 South Main Street, Racine, WI 53403 Mailing address: P. O. Box 1527, Racine, WI 53401

Marathon County Historical Museum, 403 McIndoe, Wausau, WI 54401

Marathon County Public Library, 400 First St., Wausau, WI 54401

Milwaukee Public Library, 814 West Wisconsin Ave., Milwaukee, WI 53202

Monroe County, Wisconsin Local History Room and Research Library, Rt. 2, Box 21, Sparta, WI 54656

Northland College - Dexter Library Area Research Center, 1411 Ellis Ave., Ashland, WI 54806

Oshkosh Public Library, 106 Washington Ave., Oshkosh, WI 54901

Sheboygan County Historical Research Center, 504 Broadway, Sheboygan Falls, WI 53085

University Archives - Parkside Library, University of Wisconsin, Kenosha, WI 53141

University of Wisconsin / Eau Clair, William D. McIntyre Library, Eau Claire, WI 54701

University of Wisconsin / LaCrosse, Murphy Library, 1631 Pine St., La Crosse, WI 54601

University of Wisconsin / Green Bay, 7th Floor, Library Learning Center, Green Bay, WI 54301

University of Wisconsin / Platteville, Karrmann Library, 725 West Main St., Platteville, WI 53818

University of Wisconsin / River Falls, Davee Library, 120 Cascade Ave., River Falls, WI 54022

University of Wisconsin / Stevens Point, Learning Resources Center, Stevens Point, WI 54481

University of Wisconsin / Stout, Robert L. Pierce Library, Menomonie, WI 54751

University of Wisconsin / Superior, Jim Dan Hill Library, Superior, WI 54880

University of Wisconsin / Whitewater, Anderson Library, West Main St., Whitewater, WI 53190

University of Wisconsin, Milwaukee Library, P. O. Box 604, Milwaukee, WI 53211

Village of North Fond du Lac Public Library, 719 Wisconsin Ave., North Fond du Lac, WI 54935

Ashland County, Wisconsin, Ashland Historical Society, Att: Genealogy Dept., P. O. Box 433, Ashland, WI 54806

Bay Area Genealogical Society, P. O. Box 283, Green Bay, WI 54305

Bayfield County, Wisconsin, Genealogical Society, Rt. 1, Box 139, Mason, WI 54856

Chippewa County Genealogical Society, 1427 Hilltop Blvd., Chippewa Falls, WI 54729-1920

Fond du Lac County Genealogical Society, Spillman Library, 719 Wisconsin Avenue, North Fond du Lac, WI 54935

Fond du Lac County Historical Society, P. O. Box 1284, Fond du Lac, WI 54935

Fox Valley Genealogical Society, P. O. Box 1592, Appleton, WI 54913-1592

French-Canadian / Acadian Genealogists of Wisconsin, 4527 South Oakwood Terrace, New Berlin, WI 53151

Genealogical Research Society of Eau Claire, Chippewa Valley Museum, P. O. Box 1204, Eau Claire, WI 54702

Grant County, Wisconsin Genealogical Society, 955 Williams Street, Platteville, WI 53818

Heart O'Wisconsin Genealogical Society, MacMillan Memorial Library, 490 East Grand Avenue, Wisconsin Rapids, WI 54494

Jewish Genealogical Society of Milwaukee, 9280 N. Fairway Dr., Milwaukee, WI 53217

Kenosha County Genealogical Society, 4902-52nd St., Kenosha, WI 53142

Lafayette County Genealogical Workshop, P. O. Box 443, Shullsburg, WI 53586

LaCrosse Area Genealogical Society, P. O. Box 1782, LaCrosse, WI 54601

Manitowoc County Genealogical Society, P. O. Box 345, Manitowoc, WI 54220

Marathon County Genealogical Society, P. O. Box 1518, Wausau, WI 54402-1518

Marshfield Area Genealogy Group, P. O. Box 337, Marshfield, WI 54449

Menomonee Falls Historical Society, Box 91, Menomonee Falls, WI 53051

Milwaukee County Genealogical Society, P. O. Box 27326, Milwaukee, WI 53227

Milwaukee County Historical Society, 910 North 3rd Street, Milwaukee, WI 53203

Monroe, Juneau, Jackson County Wisconsin Genealogy Workshop, Rt. 3, Box 253, Black River Falls, WI 54615

Northern Wisconsin Genealogists, P. O. Box 321, Shawano, WI 54166

Northwoods Genealogical Society, P. O. Box 1132, Rhinelander, WI 54501

Oconomowoc Genealogical Club of Waukesha County, 733 E. Sherman Ave., Oconomowoc, WI 53066

Polish Genealogical Society of Wisconsin, P. O. Box 37476, Milwaukee, WI 53237

Pommerscher Verein Freistadt Rundschreiben (Pomeranian Society of Freistadt), P. O. Box 204, Germantown, WI 53022

Plymouth Genealogical Society, Plymouth Public Library, 317 E. Main, Plymouth, WI 53073

Rock County Genealogical Society, P. O. Box 711, Janesville, WI 53547

Saint Croix Valley Genealogical Society, Box 396, River Falls, WI 54022

State Historical Society of Wisconsin, University of Wisconsin, 816 State St., Madison, WI 53706

Stevens Point Area Genealogical Society, Charles M. White Library, 1325 Church St., Stevens Point, WI 54481

Twin Ports Genealogical Society, P. O. Box 16895, Duluth, MN 55816-0895

Washburn County Genealogical Society, P. O. Box 366, Shell Lake, WI 54871

Watertown Genealogical Society, P. O. Box 91, Watertown, WI 53094-0091

Waukesha County Genealogical Society, P. O. Box 1541, Waukesha, WI 53187-1541

White Pine Genealogical Society, P. O. Box 512, Marienette, WI 54143

Winnebagoland Genealogical Society, Oshkosh Public Library, 106 Washington Ave., Oshkosh, WI 54901-4985

Wisconsin Society, Sons of the American Revolution, 3230 Meachem Road, Racine, WI 53405

Wisconsin State Genealogical Society, Inc., 2109 20th Avenue, Monroe, WI 53566

Wisconsin State Old Cemetery Society, 9955 W. St. Martens Rd., Franklin, WI 53132

Printed Census Records and Mortality Schedules

Federal Census 1820 (with Michigan), 1830 (with Michigan), 1840, 1850, 1860, 1870, 1880, 1900, 1910
Union Veterans and Widows 1890
State/Territorial Census 1836, 1838, 1842, 1846, 1847, 1855, 1865, 1875, 1885, 1895, 1905

Valuable Printed Sources

Atlases, Maps, and Gazetteers

Fox, Michael J. *Maps and Atlases Showing Land Ownership in Wisconsin*. Madison, Wisconsin: State Historical Society of Wisconsin, 1978.

Gard, Robert E. *The Romance of Wisconsin Place Names*. New York: October House, 1968.

Hunt, John Warren. *Wisconsin Gazetteer*. Madison, Wisconsin: B. Brown, 1853.

Robinson, Arthur Howard. *The Atlas of Wisconsin: General Maps and Gazetteer*. Madison, Wisconsin: University of Wisconsin Press, 1974.

Bibliographies

Collections of the State Historical Society of Wisconsin, 1855-1917. Madison, Wisconsin: State Historical Society of Wisconsin.

Gleason, Margaret. *Printed Resources for Genealogical Searching in Wisconsin: A Selected Bibliography*. Detroit: Detroit Society for Genealogical Research, 1964.

Oehlerts, Donald E. *Guide to Wisconsin Newspapers, 1833-1957*. Madison, Wisconsin: State Historical Society of Wisconsin, 1958.

Schlinkert, Leroy. *Subject Bibliography of Wisconsin History*. Madison, Wisconsin: State Historical Society of Wisconsin, 1947.

Genealogical Research Guides

Ryan, Carol Ward. *Searching for Your Ancestors in the Wisconsin Libraries*. Green Bay: Carol Ward Ryan, 1988.

Wilson, Victoria. *Wisconsin Genealogical Addresses*. Milwaukee: Victoria Wilson, 1978.

Genealogical Sources

Patterson, Betty. *Some Pioneer Families of Wisconsin: An Index*. Madison, Wisconsin: Wisconsin State Genealogical Society, 1977.

Histories

Current, Richard Nelson. *Wisconsin: A Bicentennial History*. New York: W. W. Norton & Co., 1977.

Nesbit, Robert Carrington. *Wisconsin: A History*. Madison, Wisconsin: University of Wisconsin Press, 1973.

Paul, Justus F. and Barbara Potts Paul. *The Badger State: A Documentary History of Wisconsin*. Grand Rapids: William B. Eerdmans, 1979.

Peck, George Wilbur. *Wisconsin: Comprising Sketches of Counties, Towns, Events, Institutions and Persons Arranged in Cyclopedic Form*. Madison, Wisconsin: Western Historical Association, 1906.

Usher, Ellis Baker. *Wisconsin: Its Story and Biography, 1848-1913*. Chicago: Lewis Publishing Co., 1914.

WISCONSIN COUNTY DATA
State Map on Page M-45

Name	Map Index	Date Created	Parent County or Territory From Which Organized
Adams	E5	1848	Portage
Adams County, PO Box 278, Friendship, WI 53934-0278 .... (608)339-4200			
(Reg Deeds has b rec from 1860, m rec from 1859, d rec from 1873, Ind rec from 1853; Clk Ct has div & civ ct rec; Reg Pro has pro rec)			
* **Ashland**	C4	1860	Unorg. Terr
Ashland County, 201 2nd St W, Ashland, WI 54806-1652 .... (715)682-7000			
(Reg Deeds has b rec from 1863, m rec from 1879, d rec from 1877; Clk Cir Ct has div & civ ct rec from 1873; Reg in Pro has pro rec from 1890; Reg Deeds has Ind rec from 1860)			
Bad Ax (See Vernon)			
*† **Barron**	D3	1859	Formerly Dallas (changed 1869) & Polk
Barron County, 330 E La Salle Ave, Barron, WI 54812-1591 .... (715)537-6200			
[FHL has some m, cem, nat rec, 1905 census]			
Bayfield	B4	1845	Ashland, Orig. La Pointe(changed 1866)
Bayfield County, 117 E 5th St, Washburn, WI 54891-9464 .... (715)373-6100			
(Reg Deeds has b, m, d rec, also Ind rec from 1850; Clk Cir Ct has div rec from 1889, pro rec from 1870 & civ ct rec from 1888)			
* **Brown**	E7	1818	Territorial county
Brown County, PO Box 1600, Green Bay, WI 54305-5600 .... (414)436-3250			
(Reg Deeds has b rec from 1746, m rec from 1821 & d rec from 1834; Clk Ct has div & civ ct rec from 1832; Reg Pro has pro rec from 1828; see Mich for 1820-30 censuses)			
*† **Buffalo**	E3	1853	Trempealeau
Buffalo County, 407 N 2nd St, Alma, WI 54610-9673 .... (608)685-4940			
(Reg Deeds has b, m, d & bur rec; Clk Cir Ct has div & civ ct rec; Reg in Pro has pro rec)			
* **Burnett**	C3	1856	Polk
Burnett County, 7410 County Rd K Box 115, Siren, WI 54872-9043 .... (715)349-2147			
(Reg Deeds has b, m, d rec from 1861, Ind rec from 1856, service discharge rec from 1919, school rec from 1912; Clk Ct has div rec, civ ct rec from 1856; Reg Pro has pro rec from 1856)			

Name	Map Index	Date Created	Parent County or Territory From Which Organized

* **Calumet** E6 1836 Territorial county
Calumet County, 206 Court St, Chilton, WI 53014-1198 . . . . (414)849-2361
(Reg Deeds has b rec from 1851, m rec from 1846 & d rec from 1866; Clk Cir Ct has div rec from 1880 & civ ct rec from 1877; Reg in Pro has pro rec from 1868; Reg Deeds has Ind rec from 1840)

*† **Chippewa** D4 1845 Crawford
Chippewa County, 711 N Bridge St, Chippewa Falls, WI 54729-1876 . . . . (715)723-1831
(Reg Deeds has b rec from 1858, m rec from 1860, d rec from 1870, Ind rec from 1856, naturalization rec from 1895 to 1955, 1905 state census; Reg Pro has pro rec)

*† **Clark** E4 1853 Crawford
Clark County, 517 Court St, Neillsville, WI 54456-1992 . . . . (715)743-3241
(Co Clk has b rec from 1858, m rec from 1860, d rec from 1870, Ind rec from 1856, naturalization rec from 1895 to 1955, 1905 state census; Reg Pro has pro rec from 1854)

* **Columbia** F5 1846 Portage
Columbia County, PO Box 177, Portage, WI 53901-0177 . . . . (608)742-2191
(Reg Deeds has Ind, b, m, d & bur rec; Clk Cir Ct has div & civ ct rec; Reg in Pro has pro rec)

* **Crawford** F4 1818 Territorial county
Crawford County, 220 N Beaumont Rd, Prairie du Chien, WI 53821-1405 . . . . (608)326-0200
(Co Clk has b rec from 1866, m rec 1820, d & bur rec 1880, div & civ ct rec 1848, pro rec 1819; see Mich. for 1820-30 cen)

Dallas (Changed to Barron)

* **Dane** G5 1836 Territorial county
Dane County, 210 Martin Luther King Jr Blvd Rm 12, Madison, WI 53709-0001 . . . . (608)266-4121
(Reg Deeds has b, m, d rec from 1904; Clk Ct has div, civ ct rec from 1848, pro rec from 1935)

* **Dodge** F6 1836 Territorial county
Dodge County, County Courthouse, Juneau, WI 53039 . . . . (414)386-4411
(Reg Deeds has b, m, d & Ind rec from 1877; Clk Ct has div & civ ct rec; Reg Pro has pro rec from 1854)

* **Door** E7 1851 Brown
Door County, 138 S 4th Ave, Sturgeon Bay, WI 54235-2204 . . . . (414)743-5511
(Reg Deeds has b, m, d & Ind rec from 1850; Clk Ct has div rec from 1900 & civ ct rec from 1860; Reg Pro has pro rec from 1863)

*† **Douglas** B3 1854 Unorg. Terr
Douglas County, 1313 Belknap St, Superior, WI 54880-2769 . . . . (715)394-0341
(Reg Deeds has b, m & d rec from 1878; Clk Ct has div, pro & civ ct rec from 1878; Co Treas has prop owners rec from 1854)

*† **Dunn** D3 1854 Chippewa
Dunn County, 800 Wilson Ave, Menomonie, WI 54751-2785 . . . . (715)232-1677
(Reg Deeds has b, m & d rec from abt 1860)

*† **Eau Claire** E4 1856 Chippewa
Eau Claire County, 721 Oxford Ave, Eau Claire, WI 54703-5481 . . . . (715)839-5106
(Reg Deeds has b, m, d, Ind rec from 1856; Clk Ct has div ct rec from 1856, civ ct rec from 1929)

* **Florence** C6 1882 Marinette, Oconto
Florence County, PO Box 410, Florence, WI 54121-0410 . . . . (715)528-3201
(Reg Deeds has b, m, d & Ind rec; Clk Cir Ct has div, pro & civ ct rec)

* **Fond du Lac** F6 1836 Territorial county
Fond du Lac County, 160 S Macy St, Fond du Lac, WI 54935-4241 . . . . (414)929-3000
(Reg Deeds has b rec from 1847, m rec from 1849 & d rec from 1868)

Forest C6 1885 Langlade, Oconto
Forest County, County Courthouse, Crandon, WI 54520 . . . . (715)478-2422
(Reg Deeds has b, m, d & Ind rec from 1885; Clk Ct has div & civ ct rec; Reg Pro has pro rec)

Gates (see Rusk)

*† **Grant** G4 1836 Territorial county
Grant County, 130 W Maple St, Lancaster, WI 53813-1625 . . . . (608)723-2675
(Reg Deeds has b, m, d & Ind rec; Clk Cir Ct has div & civ ct rec; Reg in Pro has pro rec)

* **Green** G5 1836 Territorial county
Green County, County Courthouse, Monroe, WI 53566-2098 . . . . (608)328-9430
(Reg Deeds has b rec from 1907, m rec from 1846, d rec from 1878; Clk Cir Ct has div & civ ct rec; Co Judge has pro rec)

Green Lake F6 1858 Marquette District
Green Lake County, 570 South St, Green Lake, WI 54941-9720 . . . . (414)294-4060
(Reg Deeds has b & d rec from 1876, m & Ind rec from 1852, veterans discharges from 1945; Clk Cts has div & civ ct rec; Reg Pro has pro rec)

* **Iowa** G5 1829 Territorial county
Iowa County, 222 N Iowa St, Dodgeville, WI 53533-1557 . . . . (608)935-5445
(Reg Deeds has b & d rec from 1866, m rec from 1852, Ind rec from 1835; Clk Cir Ct has div rec from 1860 & civ ct rec from 1809; Reg Pro has pro rec from 1890; see Mich for 1830 census)

Iron C4 1893 Ashland, Oneida
Iron County, 300 Taconite St, Hurley, WI 54534-1546 . . . . (715)561-3375
(Reg Deeds has b, m, d & Ind rec from 1893; Clk Cts has div & civ ct rec; Reg Pro has pro rec)

Name	Map Index	Date Created	Parent County or Territory From Which Organized

† **Jackson**   E4   1853   LaCrosse
Jackson County, 307 Main St, Black River Falls, WI 54615-1756 .... (715)284-0208
(Reg Deeds has b, m, d, bur & Ind rec; Clk Ct has div & civ ct rec; Reg Pro has pro rec)

* **Jefferson**   G6   1837   Milwaukee
Jefferson County, 320 S Main St, Jefferson, WI 53549-1718 .... (414)674-2500
(Reg Deeds has b & m rec from 1850, d rec from 1840 & Ind rec from 1838; Clk Cir Ct has div rec from 1851 & civ ct rec from 1843; Reg in Pro has pro rec from 1840)

* **Juneau**   F5   1856   Adams
Juneau County, 220 E State St, Mauston, WI 53948-1345 .... (608)847-9300
(Reg Deeds has b, m & d rec from 1880, Ind rec from 1854; Clk Ct has div & civ ct rec; Reg Pro has pro rec)

* **Kenosha**   G7   1850   Racine
Kenosha County, 912 56th St, Kenosha, WI 53140-3747 .... (414)656-6400
(Co Clk has m rec from 1900)

* **Kewaunee**   E7   1852   Manitowoc
Kewaunee County, 613 Dodge St, Kewaunee, WI 54216 .... (414)388-4410
(Reg Deeds has b & Ind rec from 1873, m & d rec from 1874; Reg in Pro has pro rec from 1867)

*† **La Crosse**   F4   1851   Unorg. Terr
La Crosse County, 400 4th St N, La Crosse, WI 54601-3200 .... (608)785-9581
(Reg Deeds has b, m, d & Ind rec from 1851; Clk Cir Ct has div & civ ct rec; Reg in Pro has pro rec from 1851)

La Pointe (See Bayfield)

* **Lafayette**   G5   1846   Iowa
Lafayette County, 626 Main St, Darlington, WI 53530-1396 .... (608)776-4850
(Reg Deeds has b rec from 1860, m rec from 1847, d rec from 1877, Ind rec from 1840; Clk Ct has div & civ ct rec; Reg Pro has pro rec)

* **Langlade**   D5   1880   Lincoln, Oconto(formerly New, changed 1880)
Langlade County, 800 Clermont St, Antigo, WI 54409-1985 .... (715)627-6200
(Reg Deeds has b & d rec; Co Clk has m rec from 1918; Clk Cir Ct has div & civ ct rec; Reg in Pro has pro rec; Co Asr has Ind rec)

Lincoln   D5   1874   Marathon
Lincoln County, 1110 E Main St, Merrill, WI 54452-2554 .... (715)536-0312
[FHL has some m & cem rec, 1905 census]

* **Manitowoc**   E7   1836   Territorial county
Manitowoc County, 1010 S 8th St, Manitowoc, WI 54220-5392 .... (414)683-4000
(Reg Deeds has b, m, d & Ind rec; Clk Cir Ct has div, pro & civ ct rec)

*† **Marathon**   D5   1850   Portage
Marathon County, 500 Forest St, Wausau, WI 54401-5568 .... (715)847-5500
(Reg Deeds has b, m & d rec from 1900, Ind rec from 1850; Clk Cir Ct has div & civ ct rec from 1900; Co Ct has pro rec from 1900)

* **Marinette**   D7   1879   Oconto
Marinette County, 1926 Hall Ave, Marinette, WI 54143-1728 .... (715)735-3371
(Reg Deeds has b, m, d & Ind rec from 1879; Clk Cir Ct has div & civ ct rec from 1879; Reg in Pro has pro rec from 1879)

Marquette   F5   1836   Marquette District
Marquette County, 77 W Park St, Montello, WI 53949 .... (608)297-9114
(Reg Deeds has b rec from 1876, m, d rec from 1869, Ind rec; Clk Cir Ct has div, civ ct rec from 1878, naturalization rec from 1868 to 1936; Reg Pro has pro rec from 1890)

Menominee   D6   1961   Menominee Indian Reservation
Menominee County, County Courthouse, Keshena, WI 54135 .... (715)799-3311
(Co Clk has b, m, d & Ind rec)

* **Milwaukee**   G7   1834   Territorial county
Milwaukee County, 910 N 9th St, Milwaukee, WI 53233-1417 .... (414)278-4067
(Co Clk has m rec from 1834)

Monroe   F4   La Crosse
Monroe County, 112 S Court St, Sparta, WI 54656-1764 .... (608)269-8705

New (see Langlade)

Oconto   D6   1851   Unorg. Terr
Oconto County, 300 Washington St, Oconto, WI 54153-1621 .... (414)834-5322
(Reg Deeds has b, m, d & bur rec; Clk Cts has div & civ ct rec; Reg in Pro has pro rec; Oconto Hist Soc has hist rec)

*† **Oneida**   C5   1885   Lincoln
Oneida County, PO Box 400, Rhinelander, WI 54501-0400 .... (715)369-6144
(Reg Deeds has b, m, d & Ind rec; Clk Cir Ct has div & civ ct rec; Reg in Pro has pro rec)

* **Outagamie**   E6   1851   Brown
Outagamie County, 410 S Walnut St, Appleton, WI 54911-5936 .... (414)832-5077
(Reg Deeds has b, m & d rec from 1852; Clk Cts has div & civ ct rec from 1855; Reg in Pro has pro rec from 1855)

* **Ozaukee**   F7   1853   Milwaukee
Ozaukee County, 121 W Main St, Port Washington, WI 53074-1813 .... (414)377-6400
(Reg Deeds has b, m, d & Ind rec from 1853; Clk Cir Ct has div, pro & civ ct rec; Co Treas has tax rolls from 1851)

Name	Map Index	Date Created	Parent County or Territory From Which Organized

*† Pepin   E3   1858   Dunn
Pepin County, 740 7th Ave W, Durand, WI 54736-1628 .... (715)672-8857
(Reg Deeds has b, m, d & Ind rec; Clk Cir Ct has div & civ ct rec; Reg in Pro has pro rec)

* Pierce   E3   1853   Saint Croix
Pierce County, PO Box 119, Ellsworth, WI 54011-0119 .... (715)273-3531
(Co Clk has b & d rec from 1876, m rec from 1855, div rec from 1875, pro rec from 1878 & civ ct rec from 1869)

*† Polk   D3   1853   Saint Croix
Polk County, 914 1st Ave N, Balsam Lake, WI 54810 .... (715)485-3161
(Reg Deeds has b rec from 1858, m rec from 1861, d rec from 1866 & Ind rec; Clk Ct has div & civ ct rec ; Reg Pro has pro rec)

* Portage   E5   1836   Territorial county
Portage County, 1516 Church St, Stevens Point, WI 54481-3598 .... (715)346-1351
(Reg Deeds has b rec from 1863, m rec from 1772, d rec from 1856; Clk Cir Ct has div, civ ct rec from 1844; Co Judge has pro rec from 1890)

Price   C4   1879   Chippewa, Lincoln
Price County, 100 N Lake Ave, Phillips, WI 54555-1221 .... (715)339-3325
(Reg Deeds has b & m rec from 1880, d rec from 1884, Ind rec from 1867; Clk Cir Ct has div & civ ct rec from 1882; Reg in Pro has pro rec from 1879; Co Clk has m applications)

* Racine   G7   1836   Territorial county
Racine County, 730 Wisconsin Ave, Racine, WI 53403-1274 .... (414)636-3121
(Reg Deeds has b rec from 1876, m rec from 1837, d rec from 1853, Ind rec from 1837, veterans rec from 1918; Fam Ct has div rec from 1940; Pro Ct has pro rec from 1846; Clk Cts has civ ct rec from 1970)

* Richland   F4   1842   Iowa
Richland County, Seminary & Central Sts, Richland Center, WI 53581 .... (608)647-2197
(Reg Deeds has b, d rec from 1870, m, Ind rec from 1850; Clk Ct has div, civ ct rec from 1860; Reg Pro has pro rec from 1851; City Clks have bur rec)

* Rock   G6   1836   Territorial county
Rock County, 51 S Main St, Janesville, WI 53545-3978 .... (608)755-2160
(Reg Deeds has b, m & d rec from 1849, Ind rec from 1839)

*† Rusk   D4   1901   Chippewa(name changed from Gates 1905)
Rusk County, 311 Miner Ave E, Ladysmith, WI 54848-1862 .... (715)532-2100
(Reg Deeds has b, m, d & Ind rec from 1872; Co Ct has div, pro & civ ct rec)

*† Saint Croix   D3   1840   Territorial county
Saint Croix County, 911 4th St, Hudson, WI 54016-1656 .... (715)386-4600
(Reg Deeds has b, m, d & Ind rec; Clk Cir Ct has div & civ ct rec; Reg in Pro has pro rec)

* Sauk   F5   1840   Territorial county
Sauk County, 515 Oak St, Baraboo, WI 53913-2416 .... (608)356-5581
(Reg Deeds has b rec from 1860, m rec from 1850, d rec from 1870; Clk Cir Ct has div rec; Reg in Pro has pro rec)

* Sawyer   C4   1883   Ashland, Chippewa
Sawyer County, PO Box 273, Hayward, WI 54843-0273 .... (715)634-4866
(Reg Deeds has b, m, d, bur, div, pro & civ ct rec)

*† Shawano   D6   1853   Oconto
Shawano County, 311 N Main St, Shawano, WI 54166-2198 .... (715)526-9150
[FHL has some m & cem rec, 1905 census]

*† Sheboygan   F7   1836   Territorial county
Sheboygan County, 615 N 6th St, Sheboygan, WI 53081-4612 .... (414)459-3003
(Reg Deeds has b, m, d & Ind rec from 1872; Co Ct has div, ct & naturalization rec from 1850; Reg Pro has pro rec from 1850)

*† Taylor   D4   1875   Clark, Lincoln, Marathon, Chippewa
Taylor County, 224 S 2nd St, Medford, WI 54451-1899 .... (715)748-3131
(Reg Deeds has b, m, d, Ind rec from 1875; Clk Ct has div, civ ct rec from 1875; Judge's Office has pro rec)

*† Trempealeau   E4   1854   Crawford, LaCrosse
Trempealeau County, PO Box 67, Whitehall, WI 54773-0067 .... (715)538-2311
(Reg Deeds has b, m, d & bur rec; Clk Cir Ct has div & civ ct rec; Reg in Pro has pro rec)

*† Vernon   F4   1851   Richland, Crawford(formerly Bad Ax, changed 1862)
Vernon County, W Decker, Viroqua, WI 54665 .... (608)637-3569
(Reg Deeds has b, m, d & Ind rec; Clk Cir Ct has div & civ ct rec; Reg in Pro has pro rec)

* Vilas   C5   1893   Oneida
Vilas County, PO Box 369, Eagle River, WI 54521-0369 .... (715)479-3600
[FHL has some m rec, 1905 census]

* Walworth   G6   1836   Territorial county
Walworth County, PO Box 1001, Elkhorn, WI 53121-1001 .... (414)741-4241
(Reg Deeds has b, rec from 1845, m, Ind rec from 1839, d rec from 1872, bur rec from 1969, div, civ ct rec from 1850, pro rec from 1800's)

* Washburn   C3   1883   Burnett
Washburn County, 110 W 4th Ave, Shell Lake, WI 54871 .... (715)468-7808
(Reg Deeds has b, m, d & Ind rec from 1883; Clk Cts has div, pro & civ ct rec from 1883)

Name	Map Index	Date Created	Parent County or Territory From Which Organized
* **Washington**	F6	1836	Territorial county

Washington County, 432 E Washington St, West Bend, WI 53095-2500 .... (414)338-4301
(Co Clk has b, m & d rec from 1850, div & civ ct rec from 1849; Reg in Pro has pro rec from 1851)

| * **Waukesha** | G6 | 1846 | Milwaukee |

Waukesha County, 515 W Moreland Blvd, Waukesha, WI 53188-2428 .... (414)548-7010
(Reg Deeds has b rec from 1860, m rec from 1846, d rec from 1879; Clk Cts has div rec from 1847, civ ct rec from 1962; Reg in Pro has pro rec from 1846; Co Clk has m applications from 1899)

| * **Waupaca** | E6 | 1851 | Brown, Winnebago |

Waupaca County, 811 Harding St, Waupaca, WI 54981-1588 .... (715)258-6200
(Reg Deeds has b, m, d, Ind rec from 1852; Clk Ct has div rec from 1907, civ ct rec from 1880; Cir Ct has pro rec from 1857)

| *† **Waushara** | E5 | 1851 | Marquette |

Waushara County, 209 S Saint Marie St, Wautoma, WI 54982 .... (414)787-4631
(Reg Deeds has b & d rec from 1876, m & Ind rec from 1852; Clk Ct has div rec; Reg Pro has pro rec)

| * **Winnebago** | E6 | 1838 | Territorial county |

Winnebago County, 415 Jackson St, Oshkosh, WI 54901-4751 .... (414)235-2500
(Reg Deeds has b & Ind rec from 1861, m rec from 1870 & d rec)

| * **Wood** | E5 | 1856 | Portage |

Wood County, 400 Market St, Wisconsin Rapids, WI 54494-4825 .... (715)421-8460
(Reg Deeds has b, m & d rec from 1875; Clk Cts has div & civ ct rec from 1875; Reg in Pro has pro rec from 1875)

* At least one county history has been published about this county.
† Inventory of county archives was made by the Historical Records Survey. (See Introduction)

WYOMING

CAPITAL · CHEYENNE — TERRITORY 1868 — STATE 1890 (44th)
State Map on Page M-46

Before 1800, only a few fur traders and explorers entered the Wyoming region. After the Louisiana Purchase, Lewis and Clark and others explored the area. The American and Rocky Mountain Fur Companies explored the area extensively over the next three decades and opened the Overland Trail. In 1834, Fort Laramie became the first permanent settlement in Wyoming. In 1849, it became a supply depot on the Oregon Trail, with up to 50,000 individuals going through the fort in 1850 alone. The second settlement in the state was at Fort Bridger in 1842.

When the Dakota Territory was established in 1861, Wyoming was included in it. Laramie County was organized in 1867 and included all of the present state of Wyoming. Between 1867 and 1869, the transcontinental Union Pacific Railway was built through southern Wyoming, bringing the towns of Laramie, Cheyenne, Rawlins, Rock Springs, Green River, and Evanston into existence. Wyoming Territory was created in 1868 with its six or seven thousand inhabitants. Yellowstone Park was established in 1872. With the removal of the Arapaho and Cheyenne Indians to reservations and the defeat of the Sioux in 1877, northern Wyoming was opened to cattle grazing. A cattle boom followed, which reached its peak in the 1880's.

In 1890, Wyoming became a state. The Carey Act of 1894 provided for the reclamation and homesteading of desert land, which stimulated new settlements in northern Wyoming. Mormons established towns in the Big Horn Basin. By 1940, Wyoming's foreign-born residents came from England, Germany, Sweden, Russia, Italy, Austria, Greece, Denmark, Norway, Ireland, Poland, Finland, Czechoslovakia, France, and Hungary.

Birth and death records from 1909 and marriage records from 1 May 1941 are at the Vital Records Section, Division of Health and Medical Services, Hathaway Building, Cheyenne, WY 82002. To verify current fees, call 307-777-7591.

Earlier records are with the county courts. Prior to statehood, probate records were kept by the territorial probate court. After statehood they were kept by the district court in each county, as were naturalization and land records. A state census exists for 1905, and is available at the Wyoming State Archives, Museums and Historical Department, Barrett Building, 2301 Central, Cheyenne, WY 82002.

Genealogical Archives, Libraries and Societies

Cheyenne Genealogical Society, Laramie County Library, Central Ave., Cheyenne, WY 82001

Fremont County Genealogical Society, Riverton Branch Library, 1330 W. Park Ave., Riverton, WY 82501

Converse County Genealogical Society, 119 N. 9th St., Douglas, WY 82633

Laramie Peekers Genealogy Society of Platte County, Wyoming, 1108 21st St., Wheatland, WY 82201

Natrona County Genealogical Society, P. O. Box 9244, Casper, WY 82601

Park County Genealogy Society, P. O. Box 3056, Cody, WY 82414

Powell Valley Genealogical Club, P. O. Box 184, Powell, WY 82435

Sheridan Society for Genealogical Research, Inc., 1704 Big Horn Ave., Sheridan, WY 82801

Sublette County Genealogy Society, P. O. Box 1186, Pinedale, WY 82941

Wyoming Society, Sons of the American Revolution, 1040 S. Thurmond, Sheridan, WY 82801

Printed Census Records and Mortality Schedules

Federal Census 1860 (with Nebraska), 1870, 1880, 1900, 1910
Union Veterans and Widows 1890

Valuable Printed Sources

Atlases, Maps, and Gazetteers

Urbanek, Mae. *Wyoming Place Names*. Boulder, Colorado: Johnson Publishing Co., 1967.

Bibliographies

Directory of Special Libraries and Information Centers, Colorado, South Dakota, Utah, Wyoming. Denver: Rocky Mountain Chapter, Special Libraries Association, 1987.

Homsher, Lola. *Guide to Wyoming Newspapers, 1867-1967*. Cheyenne: Wyoming State Library, 1971.

Genealogical Research Guides

Spiros, Joyce V. Hawley. *Genealogical Guide to Wyoming*. Gallup, New Mexico: Verlene Publishing, 1982.

Genealogical Sources

Beach, Cora M. *Women of Wyoming*. Casper, Wyoming: S. E. Boyer & Co., 1927.

Progressive Men of the State of Wyoming. Chicago: A. W. Bowen & Co., 1903.

Histories

Chamblin, Thomas S. *The Historical Encyclopedia of Wyoming*. Dallas: Taylor Publishing, 1970.

Coutant, C. G. *The History of Wyoming*. Laramie: Chaplin, Spafford & Mathison, 1899.

Larson, T. A. *History of Wyoming*. Lincoln, Nebraska: University of Nebraska Press, 1965.

Murray, Robert A. *Military Posts of Wyoming*. Fort Collins, Colorado: Old Army Press, 1974.

WYOMING COUNTY DATA
State Map on Page M-46

Name	Map Index	Date Created	Parent County or Territory From Which Organized
* **Albany**	G1	1868	Original county

Albany County, County Courthouse, Laramie, WY 82070 . . . . (307)721-2541
(Co Clk has m rec from 1869, Ind rec from 1865; Clk Ct has div, pro, civ ct, nat rec from 1869; State Vit Rec has b & d rec from 1909)

* **Big Horn**	D6	1890	Fremont, Johnson

Big Horn County, PO Box 31, Basin, WY 82410-0031 . . . . (307)568-2357
(Co Clk has m & Ind rec from 1896; Clk Dis Ct has div, pro, civ ct rec from 1896)

* **Campbell**	G5	1911	Crook, Weston

Campbell County, 500 S Gillette Ave Suite 220, Gillette, WY 82716-4208 . . . . (307)682-7285
(Co Clk has m & Ind rec from 1912, election rec, auto titles & chattels; Clk Ct has div, pro, civ ct rec; State Vit Rec has b & d rec)

* **Carbon**	E2	1868	Original county

Carbon County, PO Box 6, Rawlins, WY 82301-0006 . . . . (307)328-2668
(Co Clk has m rec from 1876, Ind rec from 1880; for 1860 cen see Nebr; Dis Ct has div, pro, civ ct rec; State Vit Rec has b & d rec)

Carter (changed to Sweetwater 13 Dec 1869)

* **Converse**	G3	1888	Laramie, Albany

Converse County, PO Box 990, Douglas, WY 82633-0990 . . . . (307)358-2061
(Co Clk has m, Ind, mil discharge, tax rec from 1888, poll rec from 1930; Clk Ct has div, pro, civ ct rec from 1888; State Vit Rec has b & d rec)

* **Crook**	H6	1885	Pease

Crook County, PO Box 37, Sundance, WY 82729-0037 . . . . (307)283-1323
(Co Clk has m, Ind rec from 1855; Clk Ct has div, pro, civ ct rec; Bur Vital Statistics, Cheyenne, has b, d rec)

Name	Map Index	Date Created	Parent County or Territory From Which Organized

Fremont　　D3　　1884　　Sweetwater
　　Fremont County, PO Box CC, Lander, WY　82520-0900 .... (307)332-2405
　　[FHL has some m, d, cem, civ ct, Ind rec]

*† **Goshen**　　H2　　1911　　Platte, Laramie
　　Goshen County, PO Box 160, Torrington, WY　82240-0160 .... (307)532-4051
　　(Co Clk has m & Ind rec; Clk Dis Ct has div, pro & civ ct rec)

* **Hot Springs**　　D4　　1911　　Fremont
　　Hot Springs County, Arapahoe St, Thermopolis, WY　82443-2299 .... (307)864-3515
　　(Co Clk has m rec from 1913 & Ind rec; Clk Dis Ct has div, pro & civ ct rec)(Ind rec transcribed from Fremont Co)

Johnson　　F5　　1875　　Pease
　　Johnson County, 76 N Main St, Buffalo, WY　82834-1847 .... (307)684-7272
　　(Co Clk has m & Ind rec; Clk Dis Ct has div, pro & civ ct rec)(Originally Pease Co)

*† **Laramie**　　H1　　1867　　Original county
　　Laramie County, 19th St & Cary Ave, Cheyenne, WY　82001 .... (307)638-4296
　　(Co Clk has m rec from 1868; for 1860 cen see Nebr)

* **Lincoln**　　B2　　1913　　Uinta
　　Lincoln County, PO Box 670, Kemmerer, WY　83101-0670 .... (307)877-9056
　　(Co Clk has m rec from 1913 & Ind rec; Clk Dis Ct has div & pro rec from 1913 & civ ct rec)

* **Natrona**　　E3　　1888　　Carbon
　　Natrona County, 200 N Center St Rm 157, Casper, WY　82601-1991 .... (307)235-9206
　　(Co Clk has m & Ind rec from 1888, soldier's discharge, power of attorneys, notary & commissions tax license-state & fed; Clk Dis Ct has div, pro & civ ct rec)

Niobrara　　H3　　1911　　Converse
　　Niobrara County, PO Box 420, Lusk, WY　82225-0420 .... (307)334-2211
　　(Co Clk has m & Ind rec from 1888; Clk Dis Ct has div, pro & civ ct rec)

*† **Park**　　C5　　1909　　Big Horn
　　Park County, 1002 Sheridan Ave, Cody, WY　82414-3590 .... (307)587-5548
　　(Co Clk has m, Ind rec from 1911; Clk Ct has div, pro, civ ct rec; Bur Vital Statistics, Cheyenne, has b, d rec)

Pease (changed to Johnson 13 Dec. 1879)

*† **Platte**　　H2　　1913　　Laramie
　　Platte County, PO Box 728, Wheatland, WY　82201-0728 .... (307)322-3555
　　(Co Clk has m & Ind rec from 1890; Clk Dis Ct has div, pro & civ ct rec)

* **Sheridan**　　E6　　1888　　Johnson
　　Sheridan County, 224 S Main St Suite B2, Sheridan, WY　82801-4855 .... (307)674-6822
　　(Co Clk has m & Ind rec from 1888; Clk Dis Ct has div, pro & civ ct rec)

Sublette　　C3　　1921　　Fremont
　　Sublette County, PO Box 250, Pinedale, WY　82941-0250 .... (307)367-4372
　　(Co Clk has m rec from 1923, Ind rec from 1910; Clk Dis Ct has div, pro, civ ct rec from 1923; State Vit Rec has b & d rec)

† **Sweetwater**　　C2　　1867　　Original county (formerly Carter, changed 1869)
　　Sweetwater County, 50 W Flaming Gorge Way, Green River, WY　82935-4212 .... (307)875-2611
　　(Co Clk has m rec from 1864 & Ind rec from 1876; Clk Dis Ct has div, pro & civ ct rec; for 1860 cen see Nebr)

* **Teton**　　B4　　1921　　Lincoln
　　Teton County, PO Box 1727, Jackson, WY　83001-1727 .... (307)733-4430
　　(Co Clk has m, div, pro & civ ct rec)

* **Uinta**　　B1　　1869　　Original county
　　Uinta County, 225 9th St, Evanston, WY　82930-3415 .... (307)789-2471
　　(for 1860 cen see Nebr)(Co Clk has m rec; Clk Dis Ct has div & pro rec)

* **Washakie**　　E5　　1911　　Big Horn, Johnson
　　Washakie County, 10th St & Big Horn Ave, Worland, WY　82401 .... (307)347-6491
　　(Co Clk has m & Ind rec; Clk Dis Ct has div, pro & civ ct rec)

* **Weston**　　H5　　1890　　Crook
　　Weston County, 1 W Main St, Newcastle, WY　82701-2106 .... (307)746-4744
　　(Co Clk has m rec from 1890, Ind rec from 1886; Clk Dis Ct has div, pro, civ ct rec from 1890; State Vit Rec has b & d rec)

* At least one county history has been published about this county.
† Inventory of county archives was made by the Historical Records Survey. (See Introduction)

COUNTY INDEX

Bath, Kentucky, 97
Bath, North Carolina, 182
Bath, Virginia, 266
Baton Rouge, Louisiana, 105
Baxter, Arkansas, 17
Bay, Florida, 42
Bay, Michigan, 123
Bayfield, Wisconsin, 284
Baylor, Texas, 244
Beadle, South Dakota, 227
Bear Lake, Idaho, 59
Beaufort, North Carolina, 182
Beaufort, South Carolina, 224
Beauregard, Louisiana, 105
Beaver, Oklahoma, 203
Beaver, Pennsylvania, 215
Beaver, Utah, 257
Beaverhead, Montana, 151
Becker, Minnesota, 129
Beckham, Oklahoma, 203
Bedford, Pennsylvania, 215
Bedford, Tennessee, 233
Bedford, Virginia, 266
Bedford, Virginia, 266
Bee, Texas, 244
Belknap, New Hampshire, 165
Bell, Kentucky, 97
Bell, Texas, 244
Belmont, Ohio, 196
Beltrami, Minnesota, 129
Ben Hill, Georgia, 48
Benewah, Idaho, 59
Bennett, South Dakota, 227
Bennington, Vermont, 261
Benson, North Dakota, 188
Bent, Colorado, 30
Benton, Alabama, 7
Benton, Arkansas, 17
Benton, Florida, 42
Benton, Indiana, 74
Benton, Iowa, 81
Benton, Minnesota, 129
Benton, Mississippi, 136
Benton, Missouri, 143
Benton, Oregon, 209
Benton, Tennessee, 233
Benton, Washington, 275
Benzie, Michigan, 123
Bergen, New Jersey, 168
Berkeley, South Carolina, 224
Berkeley, Virginia, 266
Berkeley, West Virginia, 279
Berks, Pennsylvania, 215
Berkshire, Massachusetts, 118
Bernalillo, New Mexico, 171
Berrien, Georgia, 48
Berrien, Michigan, 123
Bertie, North Carolina, 182

Bethel, Alaska, 11
Bexar, Texas, 244
Bibb, Alabama, 7
Bibb, Georgia, 48
Bienville, Louisiana, 105
Big Horn, Montana, 151
Big Horn, Wyoming, 289
Big Stone, Minnesota, 129
Billings, Kansas, 89
Billings, North Dakota, 188
Bingham, Idaho, 59
Black Hawk, Iowa, 81
Blackbird, Nebraska, 156
Blackford, Indiana, 74
Bladen, North Carolina, 182
Blaine, Idaho, 59
Blaine, Montana, 151
Blaine, Nebraska, 156
Blaine, Oklahoma, 203
Blair, Pennsylvania, 215
Blanco, Texas, 244
Bland, Virginia, 266
Bleckley, Georgia, 48
Bledsoe, Tennessee, 234
Blount, Alabama, 7
Blount, Tennessee, 234
Blue Earth, Minnesota, 129
Boise, Idaho, 59
Bolivar, Mississippi, 136
Bollinger, Missouri, 143
Bon Homme, South Dakota, 227
Bond, Illinois, 65
Bonner, Idaho, 59
Bonneville, Idaho, 59
Boone, Arkansas, 17
Boone, Illinois, 65
Boone, Indiana, 74
Boone, Iowa, 81
Boone, Kentucky, 97
Boone, Missouri, 143
Boone, Nebraska, 156
Boone, Virginia, 266
Boone, West Virginia, 279
Borden, Texas, 244
Boreman, South Dakota, 228
Bosque, Texas, 244
Bossier, Louisiana, 105
Botetourt, Virginia, 266
Bottineau, North Dakota, 189
Boulder, Colorado, 30
Boundary, Idaho, 59
Bourbon, Kansas, 89
Bourbon, Kentucky, 97
Bowie, Texas, 244
Bowman, North Dakota, 189
Box Butte, Nebraska, 156
Box Elder, Utah, 257
Boyd, Kentucky, 97

Boyd, Nebraska, 156
Boyle, Kentucky, 97
Bracken, Kentucky, 97
Bradford, Florida, 42
Bradford, Pennsylvania, 215
Bradley, Arkansas, 17
Bradley, Tennessee, 234
Branch, Michigan, 123
Branciforte, California, 25
Brantley, Georgia, 48
Braxton, Virginia, 266
Braxton, West Virginia, 279
Brazoria, Texas, 244
Brazos, Texas, 244
Breathitt, Kentucky, 97
Breckenridge, Kansas, 89
Breckenridge, Minnesota, 129
Breckinridge, Kentucky, 97
Bremer, Iowa, 81
Brevard, Florida, 42
Brewster, Texas, 244
Briscoe, Texas, 244
Bristol Bay, Alaska, 11
Bristol, Massachusetts, 118
Bristol, Rhode Island, 220
Bristol, Virginia, 266
Broadwater, Montana, 151
Bronx, New York, 176
Brooke, Virginia, 266
Brooke, West Virginia, 279
Brookings, South Dakota, 228
Brooks, Georgia, 48
Brooks, Texas, 245
Broome, New York, 176
Broward, Florida, 42
Brown, Illinois, 65
Brown, Indiana, 74
Brown, Kansas, 89
Brown, Minnesota, 130
Brown, Nebraska, 156
Brown, Ohio, 196
Brown, South Dakota, 228
Brown, Texas, 245
Brown, Wisconsin, 284
Brule, South Dakota, 228
Brunswick, North Carolina, 182
Brunswick, Virginia, 266
Bryan, Georgia, 49
Bryan, Oklahoma, 203
Buchanan, Iowa, 81
Buchanan, Minnesota, 130
Buchanan, Missouri, 143
Buchanan, Texas, 245
Buchanan, Virginia, 266
Buckingham, Virginia, 266
Bucks, Pennsylvania, 215
Buena Vista, Iowa, 81
Buena Vista, Virginia, 266

Chase, Kansas, 89
Chase, Nebraska, 157
Chatham, Georgia, 49
Chatham, North Carolina, 183
Chattahoochee, Georgia, 49
Chattooga, Georgia, 49
Chautauqua, Kansas, 89
Chautauqua, New York, 176
Chaves, New Mexico, 171
Cheatham, Tennessee, 234
Cheboygan, Michigan, 123
Chehalis, Washington, 275
Chelan, Washington, 275
Chemung, New York, 176
Chenango, New York, 176
Cheonoquet, Michigan, 123
Cheraws Dist., South Carolina, 224
Cherokee, Alabama, 7
Cherokee, Georgia, 49
Cherokee, Iowa, 82
Cherokee, Kansas, 89
Cherokee, North Carolina, 183
Cherokee, Oklahoma, 203
Cherokee, South Carolina, 224
Cherokee, Texas, 245
Cherry, Nebraska, 157
Chesapeake, Virginia, 266
Cheshire, New Hampshire, 165
Chester, Pennsylvania, 216
Chester, South Carolina, 224
Chester, Tennessee, 234
Chesterfield, South Carolina, 224
Chesterfield, Virginia, 266
Cheyenne, Colorado, 30
Cheyenne, Kansas, 89
Cheyenne, Nebraska, 157
Chickasaw, Iowa, 82
Chickasaw, Mississippi, 136
Chicot, Arkansas, 17
Childress, Texas, 245
Chilton, Alabama, 7
Chippewa, Michigan, 123
Chippewa, Minnesota, 130
Chippewa, Wisconsin, 285
Chisago, Minnesota, 130
Chittenden, Vermont, 261
Choctaw, Alabama, 7
Choctaw, Mississippi, 136
Choctaw, Oklahoma, 203
Chouteau, Montana, 151
Chowan, North Carolina, 183
Christian, Illinois, 66
Christian, Kentucky, 98
Christian, Missouri, 144
Church, North Dakota, 189
Churchill, Nevada, 162
Cibola, New Mexico, 171
Cimarron, Oklahoma, 203

Citrus, Florida, 42
Clackamas, Oregon, 209
Claiborne, Louisiana, 105
Claiborne, Mississippi, 136
Claiborne, Tennessee, 234
Clallam, Washington, 275
Clare, Michigan, 123
Claremont, South Carolina, 224
Clarendon, South Carolina, 224
Clarion, Pennsylvania, 216
Clark (old), Missouri, 144
Clark, Arkansas, 17
Clark, Idaho, 60
Clark, Illinois, 66
Clark, Indiana, 74
Clark, Kansas, 89
Clark, Kentucky, 98
Clark, Missouri, 144
Clark, Nevada, 162
Clark, Ohio, 196
Clark, Oregon, 209
Clark, South Dakota, 228
Clark, Washington, 275
Clark, Wisconsin, 285
Clarke, Alabama, 7
Clarke, Georgia, 49
Clarke, Iowa, 82
Clarke, Mississippi, 136
Clarke, Virginia, 267
Clatsop, Oregon, 209
Clay, Alabama, 7
Clay, Arkansas, 17
Clay, Florida, 42
Clay, Georgia, 49
Clay, Illinois, 66
Clay, Indiana, 74
Clay, Iowa, 82
Clay, Kansas, 89
Clay, Kentucky, 98
Clay, Minnesota, 130
Clay, Mississippi, 136
Clay, Missouri, 144
Clay, Nebraska, 157
Clay, North Carolina, 183
Clay, South Dakota, 228
Clay, Tennessee, 234
Clay, Texas, 245
Clay, Virginia, 267
Clay, West Virginia, 279
Clayton, Georgia, 49
Clayton, Iowa, 82
Clear Creek, Colorado, 30
Clearfield, Pennsylvania, 216
Clearwater, Idaho, 60
Clearwater, Minnesota, 130
Cleburne, Alabama, 7
Cleburne, Arkansas, 17
Clermont, Ohio, 196

Cleveland, Arkansas, 17
Cleveland, North Carolina, 183
Cleveland, Oklahoma, 203
Clifton Forge, Virginia, 267
Clinch, Georgia, 49
Clinton, Illinois, 66
Clinton, Indiana, 74
Clinton, Iowa, 82
Clinton, Kentucky, 98
Clinton, Michigan, 123
Clinton, Missouri, 144
Clinton, New York, 176
Clinton, Ohio, 196
Clinton, Pennsylvania, 216
Cloud, Kansas, 89
Coahoma, Mississippi, 136
Coal, Oklahoma, 203
Cobb, Georgia, 49
Cochise, Arizona, 14
Cochran, Texas, 245
Cocke, Tennessee, 234
Coconino, Arizona, 14
Codington, South Dakota, 228
Coffee, Alabama, 7
Coffee, Georgia, 50
Coffee, Tennessee, 234
Coffey, Kansas, 89
Coke, Texas, 245
Colbert, Alabama, 8
Cole, Missouri, 144
Cole, South Dakota, 228
Coleman, Texas, 245
Coles, Illinois, 66
Colfax, Mississippi, 136
Colfax, Nebraska, 157
Colfax, New Mexico, 171
Colleton, Old, South Carolina, 224
Colleton, South Carolina, 224
Collier, Florida, 42
Collin, Texas, 245
Collingsworth, Texas, 245
Colonial Heights, Virginia, 267
Colorado, Texas, 246
Colquitt, Georgia, 50
Columbia, Arkansas, 17
Columbia, Florida, 42
Columbia, Georgia, 50
Columbia, New York, 176
Columbia, Oregon, 209
Columbia, Pennsylvania, 216
Columbia, Washington, 275
Columbia, Wisconsin, 285
Columbiana, Ohio, 196
Columbus, North Carolina, 183
Colusa, California, 25
Comal, Texas, 246
Comanche, Kansas, 89
Comanche, Oklahoma, 203

Dickson, Tennessee, 234
Dillingham, Alaska, 11
Dillon, South Carolina, 224
Dimmit, Texas, 246
Dinwiddie, Virginia, 267
Divide, North Dakota, 189
Dixie, Florida, 43
Dixon, Nebraska, 157
Dobbs, North Carolina, 183
Doddridge, Virginia, 267
Doddridge, West Virginia, 279
Dodge, Georgia, 50
Dodge, Minnesota, 130
Dodge, Missouri, 144
Dodge, Nebraska, 157
Dodge, Wisconsin, 285
Dolores, Colorado, 30
Dona Ana, New Mexico, 171
Doniphan, Kansas, 90
Donley, Texas, 247
Dooly, Georgia, 50
Door, Wisconsin, 285
Dorchester, Maryland, 114
Dorchester, South Carolina, 224
Dorn, Kansas, 90
Dorsey, Arkansas, 18
Doty, Minnesota, 130
Dougherty, Georgia, 50
Douglas, Colorado, 30
Douglas, Georgia, 50
Douglas, Illinois, 66
Douglas, Kansas, 90
Douglas, Minnesota, 130
Douglas, Missouri, 144
Douglas, Nebraska, 157
Douglas, Nevada, 162
Douglas, Oregon, 209
Douglas, South Dakota, 228
Douglas, Washington, 275
Douglas, Wisconsin, 285
Drew, Arkansas, 18
Du Page, Illinois, 66
Dubois, Indiana, 74
Dubuque, Iowa, 82
Duchesne, Utah, 258
Dukes, Massachusetts, 118
Dundy, Nebraska, 157
Dunklin, Missouri, 144
Dunmore, Virginia, 267
Dunn, North Dakota, 189
Dunn, old, North Dakota, 189
Dunn, Wisconsin, 285
Duplin, North Carolina, 183
Durham, North Carolina, 183
Dutchess, New York, 176
Duval, Florida, 43
Duval, Texas, 247
Dyer, Tennessee, 234

Eagle, Colorado, 30
Early, Georgia, 50
East Baton Rouge, Louisiana, 105
East Carroll, Louisiana, 105
East Feliciana, Louisiana, 105
Eastland, Texas, 247
Eaton, Michigan, 123
Eau Claire, Wisconsin, 285
Echols, Georgia, 50
Ector, Texas, 247
Eddy, New Mexico, 171
Eddy, North Dakota, 189
Edgar, Illinois, 66
Edgecombe, North Carolina, 183
Edgefield, South Carolina, 224
Edmonson, Kentucky, 98
Edmunds, South Dakota, 228
Edwards, Illinois, 66
Edwards, Kansas, 90
Edwards, Texas, 247
Effingham, Georgia, 50
Effingham, Illinois, 66
El Dorado, California, 25
El Paso, Colorado, 30
El Paso, Texas, 247
Elbert, Colorado, 30
Elbert, Georgia, 50
Elizabeth City, Virginia, 267
Elk, Kansas, 90
Elk, Pennsylvania, 216
Elkhart, Indiana, 75
Elko, Nevada, 162
Elliott, Kentucky, 98
Ellis, Kansas, 90
Ellis, Oklahoma, 204
Ellis, Texas, 247
Ellsworth, Kansas, 90
Elmore, Alabama, 8
Elmore, Idaho, 60
Emanuel, Georgia, 50
Emery, Utah, 258
Emmet, Iowa, 83
Emmet, Michigan, 123
Emmet, Nebraska, 157
Emmons, North Dakota, 189
Emporia, Virginia, 267
Encinal, Texas, 247
Erath, Texas, 247
Erie, New York, 176
Erie, Ohio, 196
Erie, Pennsylvania, 216
Escambia, Alabama, 8
Escambia, Florida, 43
Esmeralda, Nevada, 162
Essex, Massachusetts, 118
Essex, New Jersey, 168
Essex, New York, 176
Essex, Vermont, 261

Essex, Virginia, 267
Estill, Kentucky, 98
Etowah, Alabama, 8
Eureka, Nevada, 162
Evangeline, Louisiana, 105
Evans, Georgia, 50
Fairbanks, Alaska, 11
Fairfax, Virginia, 267
Fairfax, Virginia, 267
Fairfield, Connecticut, 35
Fairfield, Ohio, 196
Fairfield, South Carolina, 225
Fall River, South Dakota, 229
Fallon, Montana, 151
Falls Church, Virginia, 267
Falls, Texas, 247
Fannin, Georgia, 51
Fannin, Texas, 247
Faribault, Minnesota, 130
Faulk, South Dakota, 229
Faulkner, Arkansas, 18
Fauquier, Virginia, 267
Fayette, Alabama, 8
Fayette, Georgia, 51
Fayette, Illinois, 67
Fayette, Indiana, 75
Fayette, Iowa, 83
Fayette, Kentucky, 98
Fayette, Ohio, 197
Fayette, Pennsylvania, 216
Fayette, Tennessee, 234
Fayette, Texas, 247
Fayette, Virginia, 267
Fayette, West Virginia, 279
Feliciana, Louisiana, 105
Fentress, Tennessee, 235
Fergus, Montana, 151
Ferry, Washington, 275
Fillmore, Minnesota, 130
Fillmore, Nebraska, 157
Fincastle, Virginia, 267
Finney, Kansas, 90
Fisher, Texas, 247
Flagler, Florida, 43
Flanery, North Dakota, 189
Flathead, Montana, 151
Fleming, Kentucky, 98
Florence, South Carolina, 225
Florence, Wisconsin, 285
Floyd, Georgia, 51
Floyd, Indiana, 75
Floyd, Iowa, 83
Floyd, Kentucky, 98
Floyd, Texas, 247
Floyd, Virginia, 267
Fluvanna, Virginia, 267
Foard, Texas, 247
Fond du Lac, Wisconsin, 285

Green, Wisconsin, 285
Greenbrier, Virginia, 268
Greenbrier, West Virginia, 279
Greene, Alabama, 8
Greene, Arkansas, 18
Greene, Georgia, 51
Greene, Illinois, 67
Greene, Indiana, 75
Greene, Iowa, 83
Greene, Mississippi, 136
Greene, Missouri, 145
Greene, Nebraska, 158
Greene, New York, 176
Greene, North Carolina, 184
Greene, Ohio, 197
Greene, Pennsylvania, 217
Greene, Tennessee, 235
Greene, Virginia, 268
Greenlee, Arizona, 14
Greensville, Virginia, 268
Greenup, Kentucky, 99
Greenville, South Carolina, 225
Greenwood, Colorado, 31
Greenwood, Kansas, 90
Greenwood, South Carolina, 225
Greer, Oklahoma, 204
Gregg, Texas, 248
Gregory, South Dakota, 229
Grenada, Mississippi, 136
Griggs, North Dakota, 189
Grimes, Texas, 248
Gringras, North Dakota, 189
Grundy, Illinois, 67
Grundy, Iowa, 83
Grundy, Missouri, 145
Grundy, Tennessee, 235
Guadalupe, Colorado, 31
Guadalupe, New Mexico, 171
Guadalupe, Texas, 248
Guernsey, Ohio, 197
Guilford, North Carolina, 184
Gulf, Florida, 43
Gunnison, Colorado, 31
Guthrie, Iowa, 83
Gwinnett, Georgia, 51
Haakon, South Dakota, 229
Habersham, Georgia, 51
Haines, Alaska, 11
Hale, Alabama, 8
Hale, Texas, 248
Halifax, North Carolina, 184
Halifax, Virginia, 268
Hall, Georgia, 51
Hall, Nebraska, 158
Hall, Texas, 248
Hamblen, Tennessee, 235
Hamilton, Florida, 43
Hamilton, Illinois, 67

Hamilton, Indiana, 75
Hamilton, Iowa, 83
Hamilton, Kansas, 90
Hamilton, Nebraska, 158
Hamilton, New York, 177
Hamilton, Ohio, 197
Hamilton, Tennessee, 235
Hamilton, Texas, 248
Hamlin, South Dakota, 229
Hampden, Massachusetts, 118
Hampshire, Massachusetts, 118
Hampshire, Virginia, 268
Hampshire, West Virginia, 279
Hampton, South Carolina, 225
Hampton, Virginia, 268
Hancock, Alabama, 8
Hancock, Georgia, 51
Hancock, Illinois, 67
Hancock, Indiana, 75
Hancock, Iowa, 83
Hancock, Kentucky, 99
Hancock, Maine, 110
Hancock, Mississippi, 137
Hancock, Ohio, 197
Hancock, Tennessee, 235
Hancock, Virginia, 268
Hancock, West Virginia, 280
Hand, South Dakota, 229
Hanover, Virginia, 268
Hansford, Texas, 248
Hanson, South Dakota, 229
Haralson, Georgia, 51
Hardee, Florida, 43
Hardeman, Tennessee, 235
Hardeman, Texas, 248
Hardin, Illinois, 67
Hardin, Iowa, 83
Hardin, Kentucky, 99
Hardin, Ohio, 197
Hardin, Tennessee, 235
Hardin, Texas, 248
Harding, New Mexico, 171
Harding, South Dakota, 229
Hardy, Virginia, 268
Hardy, West Virginia, 280
Harford, Maryland, 114
Harlan, Kentucky, 99
Harlan, Nebraska, 158
Harmon, Oklahoma, 204
Harnett, North Carolina, 184
Harney, Oregon, 209
Harper, Kansas, 90
Harper, Oklahoma, 204
Harris, Georgia, 51
Harris, Texas, 248
Harrison, Indiana, 75
Harrison, Iowa, 83
Harrison, Kentucky, 99

Harrison, Mississippi, 137
Harrison, Missouri, 145
Harrison, Nebraska, 158
Harrison, Ohio, 197
Harrison, Texas, 248
Harrison, Virginia, 268
Harrison, West Virginia, 280
Harrisonburg, Virginia, 268
Hart, Georgia, 51
Hart, Kentucky, 99
Hartford, Connecticut, 35
Hartley, Texas, 248
Harvey, Kansas, 91
Haskell, Kansas, 91
Haskell, Oklahoma, 204
Haskell, Texas, 248
Hawaii, Hawaii, 57
Hawkins, Tennessee, 235
Hayes, Nebraska, 158
Hays, Texas, 248
Haywood, North Carolina, 184
Haywood, Tennessee, 235
Heard, Georgia, 51
Hemphill, Texas, 248
Hempstead, Arkansas, 18
Hempstead, Missouri, 145
Henderson, Illinois, 67
Henderson, Kentucky, 99
Henderson, North Carolina, 184
Henderson, Tennessee, 235
Henderson, Texas, 248
Hendricks, Indiana, 75
Hendry, Florida, 43
Hennepin, Minnesota, 130
Henrico, Virginia, 268
Henry, Alabama, 8
Henry, Georgia, 51
Henry, Illinois, 67
Henry, Indiana, 75
Henry, Iowa, 83
Henry, Kentucky, 99
Henry, Missouri, 145
Henry, Ohio, 197
Henry, Tennessee, 235
Henry, Virginia, 268
Herkimer, New York, 177
Hernando, Florida, 43
Hertford, North Carolina, 184
Hettinger, North Dakota, 189
Hettinger, old, North Dakota, 189
Hickman, Kentucky, 99
Hickman, Tennessee, 235
Hickory, Missouri, 145
Hidalgo, New Mexico, 171
Hidalgo, Texas, 249
Highland, Ohio, 197
Highland, Virginia, 268
Highlands, Florida, 43

Jim Wells, Texas, 249
Jo Daviess, Illinois, 67
Johnson, Arkansas, 19
Johnson, Georgia, 52
Johnson, Illinois, 67
Johnson, Indiana, 76
Johnson, Iowa, 83
Johnson, Kansas, 91
Johnson, Kentucky, 99
Johnson, Minnesota, 131
Johnson, Missouri, 145
Johnson, Nebraska, 158
Johnson, Tennessee, 236
Johnson, Texas, 249
Johnson, Wyoming, 290
Johnston, North Carolina, 184
Johnston, Oklahoma, 204
Jones, Alabama, 9
Jones, Georgia, 52
Jones, Iowa, 84
Jones, Mississippi, 137
Jones, Nebraska, 158
Jones, North Carolina, 184
Jones, South Dakota, 229
Jones, Texas, 249
Josephine, Oregon, 209
Juab, Utah, 258
Judith Basin, Montana, 152
Juneau, Alaska, 11
Juneau, Wisconsin, 286
Juniata, Pennsylvania, 217
Kalamazoo, Michigan, 124
Kalkaska, Michigan, 124
Kanabec, Minnesota, 131
Kanawah, Virginia, 269
Kanawha, West Virginia, 280
Kandiyohi, Minnesota, 131
Kane, Illinois, 67
Kane, Utah, 258
Kankakee, Illinois, 67
Kanotin, Michigan, 124
Karnes, Texas, 249
Kauai, Hawaii, 57
Kaufman, Texas, 250
Kautawaubet, Michigan, 124
Kay, Oklahoma, 204
Kaykakee, Michigan, 124
Kearney, Nebraska, 158
Kearny, Kansas, 91
Keith, Nebraska, 158
Kemper, Mississippi, 137
Kenai Peninsula, Alaska, 12
Kendall, Illinois, 68
Kendall, Texas, 250
Kenedy, Texas, 250
Kennebec, Maine, 110
Kenosha, Wisconsin, 286
Kent, Delaware, 37

Kent, Maryland, 115
Kent, Michigan, 124
Kent, Rhode Island, 221
Kent, Texas, 250
Kenton, Kentucky, 99
Kentucky, Virginia, 269
Keokuk, Iowa, 84
Kern, California, 25
Kerr, Texas, 250
Kershaw, South Carolina, 225
Ketchikan, Alaska, 12
Kewaunee, Wisconsin, 286
Keweenaw, Michigan, 124
Keya Paha, Nebraska, 158
Kidder, North Dakota, 190
Kimball, Nebraska, 158
Kimble, Texas, 250
Kinchafoonee, Georgia, 52
Kinderhook, Missouri, 145
King & Queen, Virginia, 269
King George, Virginia, 269
King William, Virginia, 269
King, Texas, 250
King, Washington, 276
Kingfisher, Oklahoma, 204
Kingman, Kansas, 91
Kings, California, 25
Kings, New York, 177
Kingsbury, South Dakota, 229
Kinney, Texas, 250
Kiowa, Colorado, 31
Kiowa, Kansas, 91
Kiowa, Oklahoma, 204
Kishkekosh, Iowa, 84
Kit Carson, Colorado, 31
Kitsap, Washington, 276
Kittitas, Washington, 276
Kittson, Minnesota, 131
Klamath, Oregon, 209
Kleberg, Texas, 250
Klickitat, Washington, 276
Knott, Kentucky, 100
Knox, Illinois, 68
Knox, Indiana, 76
Knox, Kentucky, 100
Knox, Maine, 110
Knox, Missouri, 145
Knox, Nebraska, 159
Knox, Ohio, 198
Knox, Tennessee, 236
Knox, Texas, 250
Kodiak, Alaska, 12
Koochiching, Minnesota, 131
Kootenai, Idaho, 60
Kosciusko, Indiana, 76
Kossuth, Iowa, 84
L'Eau Qui Court, Nebraska, 159
La Crosse, Wisconsin, 286

La Moure, North Dakota, 190
La Paz, Arizona, 14
La Plata, Colorado, 31
La Pointe, Wisconsin, 286
Labette, Kansas, 91
Lac qui Parle, Minnesota, 131
Lackawanna, Pennsylvania, 217
Laclede, Missouri, 146
Lafayette, Arkansas, 19
Lafayette, Florida, 44
Lafayette, Louisiana, 106
Lafayette, Mississippi, 137
Lafayette, Missouri, 146
Lafayette, Wisconsin, 286
Lafourche, Louisiana, 106
Lagrange, Indiana, 76
Lake of the Woods, Minnesota, 131
Lake, California, 25
Lake, Colorado, 31
Lake, Florida, 44
Lake, Illinois, 68
Lake, Indiana, 76
Lake, Michigan, 125
Lake, Minnesota, 131
Lake, Montana, 152
Lake, Ohio, 198
Lake, Oregon, 209
Lake, South Dakota, 229
Lake, Tennessee, 236
Lamar, Alabama, 9
Lamar, Georgia, 52
Lamar, Mississippi, 137
Lamar, Texas, 250
Lamb, Texas, 250
Lamoille, Vermont, 261
Lampasas, Texas, 250
Lancaster, Nebraska, 159
Lancaster, Pennsylvania, 217
Lancaster, South Carolina, 225
Lancaster, Virginia, 269
Lander, Nevada, 162
Lane, Kansas, 91
Lane, Oregon, 209
Langlade, Wisconsin, 286
Lanier, Georgia, 52
Lapeer, Michigan, 125
LaPorte, Indiana, 76
Laramie, Wyoming, 290
Larimer, Colorado, 31
Larue, Kentucky, 100
Las Animas, Colorado, 31
LaSalle, Illinois, 68
LaSalle, Louisiana, 106
LaSalle, Texas, 250
Lassen, California, 25
Latah, Idaho, 60
Latimer, Oklahoma, 204
Lauderdale, Alabama, 9

Madison, Kansas, 91
Madison, Kentucky, 100
Madison, Louisiana, 106
Madison, Mississippi, 138
Madison, Missouri, 146
Madison, Montana, 152
Madison, Nebraska, 159
Madison, New York, 177
Madison, North Carolina, 185
Madison, Ohio, 198
Madison, Tennessee, 236
Madison, Texas, 251
Madison, Virginia, 269
Magoffin, Kentucky, 100
Mahaska, Iowa, 84
Mahnomen, Minnesota, 131
Mahoning, Ohio, 198
Major, Oklahoma, 205
Malheur, Oregon, 210
Manassas Park, Virginia, 269
Manatee, Florida, 44
Manistee, Michigan, 125
Manitou, Michigan, 125
Manitowoc, Wisconsin, 286
Mankahta, Minnesota, 131
Marathon, Wisconsin, 286
Marengo, Alabama, 9
Maricopa, Arizona, 14
Maries, Missouri, 146
Marin, California, 26
Marinette, Wisconsin, 286
Marion, Alabama, 9
Marion, Arkansas, 19
Marion, Florida, 44
Marion, Georgia, 53
Marion, Illinois, 68
Marion, Indiana, 76
Marion, Iowa, 84
Marion, Kansas, 92
Marion, Kentucky, 100
Marion, Mississippi, 138
Marion, Missouri, 146
Marion, Ohio, 198
Marion, Oregon, 210
Marion, South Carolina, 225
Marion, Tennessee, 236
Marion, Texas, 251
Marion, Virginia, 269
Marion, West Virginia, 280
Mariposa, California, 26
Marlboro, South Carolina, 225
Marquette, Michigan, 125
Marquette, Wisconsin, 286
Marshall, Alabama, 9
Marshall, Illinois, 68
Marshall, Indiana, 76
Marshall, Iowa, 84
Marshall, Kansas, 92

Marshall, Kentucky, 100
Marshall, Minnesota, 131
Marshall, Mississippi, 138
Marshall, Oklahoma, 205
Marshall, South Dakota, 230
Marshall, Tennessee, 236
Marshall, Virginia, 269
Marshall, West Virginia, 280
Martin, Florida, 44
Martin, Indiana, 76
Martin, Kentucky, 100
Martin, Minnesota, 131
Martin, North Carolina, 185
Martin, Texas, 251
Martinsville, Virginia, 269
Mason, Illinois, 68
Mason, Kentucky, 100
Mason, Michigan, 125
Mason, Texas, 251
Mason, Virginia, 269
Mason, Washington, 276
Mason, West Virginia, 280
Massac, Illinois, 68
Matagorda, Texas, 251
Matanuska-Susitna, Alaska, 12
Mathews, Virginia, 269
Maui, Hawaii, 57
Maury, Tennessee, 236
Maverick, Texas, 251
Mayes, Oklahoma, 205
McClain, Oklahoma, 205
McCone, Montana, 152
McCook, South Dakota, 230
McCormick, South Carolina, 225
McCracken, Kentucky, 100
McCreary, Kentucky, 100
McCulloch, Texas, 251
McCurtain, Oklahoma, 205
McDonald, Missouri, 146
McDonough, Illinois, 68
McDowell, North Carolina, 185
McDowell, Virginia, 269
McDowell, West Virginia, 280
McDuffie, Georgia, 53
McGhee, Kansas, 92
McHenry, Illinois, 68
McHenry, North Dakota, 190
McIntosh, Georgia, 53
McIntosh, North Dakota, 190
McIntosh, Oklahoma, 205
McKean, Pennsylvania, 217
McKenzie, North Dakota, 190
McKenzie, old, North Dakota, 190
McKinley, New Mexico, 171
McLean, Illinois, 68
McLean, Kentucky, 100
McLean, North Dakota, 190
McLennan, Texas, 251

McLeod, Minnesota, 131
McMinn, Tennessee, 236
McMullen, Texas, 251
McNairy, Tennessee, 236
McPherson, Kansas, 92
McPherson, Nebraska, 159
McPherson, South Dakota, 230
Meade, Kansas, 92
Meade, Kentucky, 101
Meade, South Dakota, 230
Meagher, Montana, 152
Mecklenburg, North Carolina, 185
Mecklenburg, Virginia, 269
Mecosta, Michigan, 125
Medina, Ohio, 198
Medina, Texas, 251
Meegisee, Michigan, 125
Meeker, Minnesota, 131
Meigs, Ohio, 198
Meigs, Tennessee, 236
Mellette, South Dakota, 230
Menard, Illinois, 68
Menard, Texas, 251
Mendocino, California, 26
Menifee, Kentucky, 101
Menominee, Michigan, 125
Menominee, Wisconsin, 286
Merced, California, 26
Mercer, Illinois, 68
Mercer, Kentucky, 101
Mercer, Missouri, 146
Mercer, New Jersey, 168
Mercer, North Dakota, 190
Mercer, Ohio, 198
Mercer, Pennsylvania, 217
Mercer, Virginia, 269
Mercer, West Virginia, 280
Meriwether, Georgia, 53
Merrick, Nebraska, 159
Merrimack, New Hampshire, 165
Mesa, Colorado, 31
Metcalfe, Kentucky, 101
Miami, Indiana, 76
Miami, Kansas, 92
Miami, Ohio, 198
Michilimackinac, Michigan, 125
Middlesex, Connecticut, 35
Middlesex, Massachusetts, 118
Middlesex, New Jersey, 168
Middlesex, Virginia, 269
Midland, Michigan, 125
Midland, Texas, 251
Mifflin, Pennsylvania, 217
Mikenauk, Michigan, 125
Milam, Texas, 251
Millard, Utah, 258
Mille Lacs, Minnesota, 132
Miller, Arkansas, 19

Noble, Ohio, 198
Noble, Oklahoma, 205
Nobles, Minnesota, 132
Nodaway, Missouri, 147
Nolan, Texas, 252
Nome, Alaska, 12
Norfolk, Massachusetts, 119
Norfolk, Virginia, 270
Norman, Minnesota, 132
North Slope, Alaska, 12
North Star, Alaska, 12
Northampton, North Carolina, 185
Northampton, Pennsylvania, 218
Northampton, Virginia, 270
Northumberland, Pennsylvania, 218
Northumberland, Virginia, 270
Northwest Arctic, Alaska, 12
Norton, Kansas, 92
Norton, Virginia, 270
Notipekago, Michigan, 126
Nottoway, Virginia, 270
Nowata, Oklahoma, 205
Noxubee, Mississippi, 138
Nuckolls, Nebraska, 159
Nueces, Texas, 252
Nye, Nevada, 162
O'Brien, Iowa, 84
O, Oklahoma, 205
Oakland, Michigan, 126
Obion, Tennessee, 237
Ocean, New Jersey, 168
Oceana, Michigan, 126
Ochiltree, Texas, 252
Oconee, Georgia, 53
Oconee, South Carolina, 225
Oconto, Wisconsin, 286
Ogemaw, Michigan, 126
Ogle, Illinois, 69
Oglethorpe, Georgia, 53
Ohio, Indiana, 76
Ohio, Kentucky, 101
Ohio, Virginia, 270
Ohio, West Virginia, 280
Okaloosa, Florida, 44
Okanogan, Washington, 276
Okeechobee, Florida, 44
Okfuskee, Oklahoma, 205
Okkuddo, Michigan, 126
Oklahoma, Oklahoma, 205
Okmulgee, Oklahoma, 205
Oktibbeha, Mississippi, 138
Oldham, Kentucky, 101
Oldham, Texas, 252
Oliver, North Dakota, 190
Olmsted, Minnesota, 132
Oneida, Idaho, 61
Oneida, New York, 177
Oneida, Wisconsin, 286

Onondaga, New York, 177
Onslow, North Carolina, 185
Ontario, New York, 177
Ontario, Pennsylvania, 218
Ontonagon, Michigan, 126
Opelousas, Louisiana, 106
Orange, California, 26
Orange, Florida, 44
Orange, Indiana, 76
Orange, New York, 177
Orange, North Carolina, 185
Orange, South Carolina, 225
Orange, Texas, 252
Orange, Vermont, 261
Orange, Virginia, 270
Orangeburg, South Carolina, 225
Oregon, Missouri, 147
Orleans, Louisiana, 106
Orleans, New York, 177
Orleans, Vermont, 261
Ormsby, Nevada, 162
Osage, Kansas, 92
Osage, Missouri, 147
Osage, Oklahoma, 205
Osborne, Kansas, 92
Osceola, Florida, 44
Osceola, Iowa, 85
Osceola, Michigan, 126
Oscoda, Michigan, 126
Oswego, New York, 177
Otero, Colorado, 32
Otero, New Mexico, 171
Otoe, Kansas, 92
Otoe, Nebraska, 159
Otsego, Michigan, 126
Otsego, New York, 178
Ottawa, Kansas, 92
Ottawa, Michigan, 126
Ottawa, Ohio, 199
Ottawa, Oklahoma, 205
Otter Tail, Minnesota, 132
Ouachita, Arkansas, 19
Ouachita, Louisiana, 106
Ouray, Colorado, 32
Outagamie, Wisconsin, 286
Outer Ketchikan, Alaska, 12
Overton, Tennessee, 237
Owen, Indiana, 77
Owen, Kentucky, 101
Owsley, Kentucky, 101
Owyhee, Idaho, 61
Oxford, Maine, 110
Ozark, Missouri, 147
Ozaukee, Wisconsin, 286
Pacific, Washington, 276
Page, Iowa, 85
Page, Virginia, 270
Pahute, Nevada, 162

Palm Beach, Florida, 44
Palo Alto, Iowa, 85
Palo Pinto, Texas, 252
Pamlico, North Carolina, 185
Panola, Mississippi, 138
Panola, Texas, 252
Park, Colorado, 32
Park, Montana, 152
Park, Wyoming, 290
Parke, Indiana, 77
Parker, Texas, 252
Parmer, Texas, 252
Pasco, Florida, 44
Pasquotank, North Carolina, 185
Passaic, New Jersey, 168
Patrick, Virginia, 270
Paulding, Georgia, 53
Paulding, Ohio, 199
Pawnee, Kansas, 92
Pawnee, Nebraska, 159
Pawnee, Oklahoma, 205
Payette, Idaho, 61
Payne, Oklahoma, 205
Peach, Georgia, 53
Pearl River, Mississippi, 138
Pease, Wyoming, 290
Pecos, Texas, 252
Pembina, Minnesota, 132
Pembina, North Dakota, 190
Pemiscot, Missouri, 147
Pend Oreille, Washington, 276
Pender, North Carolina, 185
Pendleton, Kentucky, 101
Pendleton, South Carolina, 226
Pendleton, Virginia, 270
Pendleton, West Virginia, 281
Pennington, Minnesota, 132
Pennington, South Dakota, 230
Penobscot, Maine, 110
Peoria, Illinois, 69
Pepin, Wisconsin, 287
Perkins, Nebraska, 159
Perkins, South Dakota, 230
Perquimans, North Carolina, 185
Perry, Alabama, 9
Perry, Arkansas, 19
Perry, Illinois, 69
Perry, Indiana, 77
Perry, Kentucky, 101
Perry, Mississippi, 138
Perry, Missouri, 147
Perry, Ohio, 199
Perry, Pennsylvania, 218
Perry, Tennessee, 237
Pershing, Nevada, 163
Person, North Carolina, 185
Petersburg, Virginia, 270
Petroleum, Montana, 152

Sumner, Mississippi, 139
Sumner, Tennessee, 237
Sumter, Alabama, 10
Sumter, Florida, 45
Sumter, Georgia, 54
Sumter, South Carolina, 226
Sunflower, Mississippi, 139
Superior, Minnesota, 133
Surry, North Carolina, 186
Surry, Virginia, 272
Susquehanna, Pennsylvania, 218
Sussex, Delaware, 38
Sussex, New Jersey, 169
Sussex, Virginia, 272
Sutter, California, 27
Sutton, Texas, 254
Suwannee, Florida, 45
Swain, North Carolina, 186
Sweet Grass, Montana, 153
Sweetwater, Wyoming, 290
Swift, Minnesota, 133
Swisher, Texas, 254
Switzerland, Indiana, 77
Talbot, Georgia, 54
Talbot, Maryland, 115
Taliaferro, Georgia, 54
Talladega, Alabama, 10
Tallahatchie, Mississippi, 139
Tallapoosa, Alabama, 10
Tama, Iowa, 85
Taney, Missouri, 149
Tangipahoa, Louisiana, 107
Taos, New Mexico, 172
Tarrant, Texas, 254
Tate, Mississippi, 139
Tattnall, Georgia, 54
Taylor, Florida, 45
Taylor, Georgia, 54
Taylor, Iowa, 85
Taylor, Kentucky, 102
Taylor, Nebraska, 160
Taylor, Texas, 254
Taylor, Virginia, 272
Taylor, West Virginia, 281
Taylor, Wisconsin, 287
Tazewell, Illinois, 70
Tazewell, Virginia, 272
Tehama, California, 27
Telfair, Georgia, 54
Teller, Colorado, 32
Tennessee, Tennessee, 237
Tensas, Louisiana, 107
Terrebonne, Louisiana, 107
Terrell, Georgia, 54
Terrell, Texas, 254
Terry, Texas, 254
Teton, Idaho, 61
Teton, Montana, 153

Teton, Wyoming, 290
Texas, Missouri, 149
Texas, Oklahoma, 206
Thayer, Nebraska, 160
Thomas, Georgia, 54
Thomas, Kansas, 94
Thomas, Nebraska, 160
Throckmorton, Texas, 254
Thurston, Nebraska, 160
Thurston, Washington, 276
Tift, Georgia, 54
Tillamook, Oregon, 210
Tillman, Oklahoma, 206
Tioga, New York, 178
Tioga, Pennsylvania, 218
Tippah, Mississippi, 139
Tippecanoe, Indiana, 77
Tipton, Indiana, 77
Tipton, Tennessee, 238
Tishomingo, Mississippi, 139
Titus, Texas, 254
Tobucksy, Oklahoma, 206
Todd, Kentucky, 102
Todd, Minnesota, 133
Todd, South Dakota, 230
Tolland, Connecticut, 36
Tom Green, Texas, 254
Tompkins, New York, 178
Tonedagana, Michigan, 126
Tooele, Utah, 258
Toole, Montana, 153
Toombs, Georgia, 55
Toombs, Minnesota, 133
Torrance, New Mexico, 172
Towner, North Dakota, 191
Towns, Georgia, 55
Traill, North Dakota, 191
Transylvania, North Carolina, 186
Traverse, Minnesota, 133
Travis, Texas, 254
Treasure, Montana, 153
Trego, Kansas, 94
Trempealeau, Wisconsin, 287
Treutlen, Georgia, 55
Trigg, Kentucky, 102
Trimble, Kentucky, 102
Trinity, California, 27
Trinity, Texas, 254
Tripp, South Dakota, 230
Troup, Georgia, 55
Trousdale, Tennessee, 238
Trumbull, Ohio, 199
Tryon, New York, 178
Tryon, North Carolina, 186
Tucker, Virginia, 272
Tucker, West Virginia, 281
Tulare, California, 27
Tulsa, Oklahoma, 206

Tunica, Mississippi, 139
Tuolumne, California, 27
Turner, Georgia, 55
Turner, South Dakota, 231
Tuscaloosa, Alabama, 10
Tuscarawas, Ohio, 199
Tuscola, Michigan, 126
Twality, Oregon, 210
Twiggs, Georgia, 55
Twin Falls, Idaho, 61
Tyler, Texas, 254
Tyler, Virginia, 272
Tyler, West Virginia, 281
Tyrrell, North Carolina, 186
Uinta, Wyoming, 290
Uintah, Utah, 259
Ulster, New York, 178
Umatilla, Oregon, 210
Umpqua, Oregon, 210
Uncompahgre, Colorado, 32
Unicoi, Tennessee, 238
Union, Arkansas, 20
Union, Florida, 45
Union, Georgia, 55
Union, Illinois, 70
Union, Indiana, 78
Union, Iowa, 85
Union, Kentucky, 102
Union, Louisiana, 107
Union, Mississippi, 139
Union, New Jersey, 169
Union, New Mexico, 172
Union, North Carolina, 186
Union, Ohio, 199
Union, Oregon, 210
Union, Pennsylvania, 218
Union, South Carolina, 226
Union, South Dakota, 231
Union, Tennessee, 238
Unwattin, Michigan, 126
Upper Norfolk, Virginia, 272
Upshur, Texas, 254
Upshur, Virginia, 272
Upshur, West Virginia, 281
Upson, Georgia, 55
Upton, Texas, 254
Utah, Utah, 259
Uvalde, Texas, 254
Val Verde, Texas, 255
Valdez Cordova, Alaska, 12
Valencia, New Mexico, 172
Valley, Idaho, 61
Valley, Montana, 153
Valley, Nebraska, 160
Van Buren, Arkansas, 20
Van Buren, Iowa, 85
Van Buren, Michigan, 127
Van Buren, Missouri, 149

White, Tennessee, 238
Whiteside, Illinois, 70
Whitfield, Georgia, 55
Whitley, Indiana, 78
Whitley, Kentucky, 102
Whitman, Washington, 277
Wibaux, Montana, 153
Wichita, Kansas, 94
Wichita, Texas, 255
Wicomico, Maryland, 115
Wilbarger, Texas, 255
Wilcox, Alabama, 10
Wilcox, Georgia, 55
Wilkes, Georgia, 55
Wilkes, North Carolina, 187
Wilkin, Minnesota, 133
Wilkinson, Georgia, 55
Wilkinson, Mississippi, 139
Will, Illinois, 70
Willacy, Texas, 255
Williams, North Dakota, 191
Williams, Ohio, 200
Williamsburg, South Carolina, 226
Williamsburg, Virginia, 272
Williamson, Illinois, 70
Williamson, Tennessee, 238
Williamson, Texas, 255
Wilson, Kansas, 94
Wilson, North Carolina, 187
Wilson, Tennessee, 238
Wilson, Texas, 255
Winchester, Virginia, 272
Windham, Connecticut, 36
Windham, Vermont, 262
Windsor, Vermont, 262
Winkler, Texas, 255

Winn, Louisiana, 108
Winnebago, Illinois, 70
Winnebago, Iowa, 86
Winnebago, Wisconsin, 288
Winneshiek, Iowa, 86
Winona, Minnesota, 133
Winston, Alabama, 10
Winston, Mississippi, 139
Winyaw, South Carolina, 226
Wirt, Virginia, 272
Wirt, West Virginia, 281
Wise, Kansas, 94
Wise, Texas, 255
Wise, Virginia, 272
Wolfe, Kentucky, 102
Wood, Ohio, 200
Wood, Texas, 255
Wood, Virginia, 272
Wood, West Virginia, 281
Wood, Wisconsin, 288
Woodbury, Iowa, 86
Woodford, Illinois, 70
Woodford, Kentucky, 102
Woodruff, Arkansas, 20
Woods, Oklahoma, 206
Woodson, Kansas, 94
Woodward, Oklahoma, 206
Worcester, Maryland, 115
Worcester, Massachusetts, 119
Worth, Georgia, 56
Worth, Iowa, 86
Worth, Missouri, 149
Wrangell-Petersburg, Alaska, 12
Wright, Iowa, 86
Wright, Minnesota, 133
Wright, Missouri, 149

Wyandot, Ohio, 200
Wyandotte, Kansas, 94
Wyoming, New York, 179
Wyoming, Pennsylvania, 218
Wyoming, Virginia, 272
Wyoming, West Virginia, 281
Wythe, Virginia, 272
Yadkin, North Carolina, 187
Yakima, Washington, 277
Yalobusha, Mississippi, 139
Yamhill, Oregon, 210
Yancey, North Carolina, 187
Yankton, South Dakota, 231
Yates, New York, 179
Yavapai, Arizona, 14
Yazoo, Mississippi, 139
Yell, Arkansas, 21
Yell, Iowa, 86
Yellow Medicine, Minnesota, 134
Yellowstone, Montana, 153
Yoakum, Texas, 255
Yohogania, Virginia, 272
Yolo, California, 27
York(shire), Maine, 111
York, Nebraska, 161
York, Pennsylvania, 219
York, South Carolina, 226
York, Virginia, 273
Young, Texas, 255
Yuba, California, 27
Yukon-Kuyokukuk, Alaska, 12
Yuma, Arizona, 14
Yuma, Colorado, 33
Zapata, Texas, 255
Zavala, Texas, 256
Ziebach, South Dakota, 231

MIGRATION TRAILS

COAST PATH: Coastal road from Boston to Plymouth, Massachusetts, traveling in a south by southeast direction. Approximately 35 miles. **Map page M48.**
Massachusetts: Suffolk, Norfolk, Plymouth

KENNEBUNK ROAD: Coastal road from Boston, Massachusetts through Kennebunk and Portland to Augusta, Maine traveling in a north by northeast direction. Approximately 180 miles. **Map page M48.**
Massachusetts: Suffolk, Middlesex, Essex
New Hampshire: Rockingham
Maine: York, Cumberland, Sagadahoc,. Kennebec

BAY ROAD: From Boston to Taunton and New Bedford, Massachusetts traveling in a south direction. Approximately 60 miles. **Map page M48.**
Massachusetts: Suffolk, Norfolk, Bristol

OLD CONNECTICUT PATH: From Boston traveling in a west by southwest direction to Springfield, where it splits. One branch goes straight south to Hartford, Connecticut. The other goes to Albany, New York traveling in a west by northwest direction. Approximately 290 miles. **Map page M48.**
Massachusetts: Suffolk, Middlesex, Worcester, Hampden, Hampshire, Berkshire
Connecticut: Hartford
New York: Columbia, Rensselaer, Albany

OLD ROEBUCK ROAD: From Boston, Massachusetts to Providence, Rhode Island traveling in a south by southwest direction. Approximately 60 miles. **Map page M48.**
Massachusetts: Suffolk, Norfolk, Bristol
Rhode Island: Providence

BOSTON POST ROAD: From Boston, Massachusetts to New York City. There are at least two different routes. One follows the Old Connecticut Path to Hartford, Connecticut continuing south to New Haven, then west by southwest through Bridgeport and Stamford, Connecticut to New York City. The other follows the Old Roebuck Road to Providence, Rhode Island, then continuing south by southwest, then following the coastal line across Connecticut to New Haven, west by southwest through Bridgeport and Stamford to New York City. Approximately 275 miles. **Map page M48.**

Route 1
Massachusetts: Suffolk, Middlesex, Worcester, Hampden
Connecticut: Hartford, Middlesex, New Haven, Fairfield
New York: Westchester, Bronx, New York, Kings, Queens

Route 2
Massachusetts: Suffolk, Norfolk, Bristol
Rhode Island: Providence, Kent, Washington
Connecticut: New London, Middlesex, New Haven, Fairfield
New York: Westchester, Bronx, New York, Kings, Queens

HUDSON RIVER PATH: From New York City to Albany, New York traveling in a north direction. Approximately 156 miles. **Map page M48.**
New York: (East side of Hudson River) Kings, Queens, New York, Bronx, Westchester, Putnam, Dutchess, Columbia, Rensselaer, Albany, (West side of Hudson River), Rockland, Orange, Ulster, Greene, Albany
New Jersey: (West side of Hudson River) Hudson, Bergen

LAKE CHAMPLAIN TRAIL: A continuation north of the Hudson River Path from Albany, New York to the St. Lawrence River in Canada. Approximately 200 miles. **Map page M48.**
New York: Albany, Saratoga, Warren, Essex, Clinton
Canada: Quebec

CATSKILL ROAD: West from Springfield, Massachusetts to the Hudson River, then to Wattle's Ferry on the Susquehanna River. Approximately 90 miles. **Map page M48.**
Massachusetts: Hampden, Berkshire
New York: Columbia, Greene

GREENWOOD ROAD: From Hartford, Connecticut to Albany, New York traveling in a northwest direction. Approximately 70 miles. **Map page M48.**
Connecticut: Hartford, Litchfield
Massachusetts: Berkshire
New York: Columbia, Rensselaer, Albany

MOHAWK or IROQUOIS TRAIL: West by northwest from Albany, New York along the Mohawk River to Utica and Rome, diverging with a branch to Fort Oswego on Lake Ontario. Approximately 190 miles. **Map page M48.**
New York: Albany, Schenectady, Herkimer, Oneida, Oswego

GREAT GENESEE ROAD: West from Utica, New York to the Genesee River and on to Fort Niagara, New York. Approximately 195 miles. **Map page M48.**
New York: Oneida, Madison, Onondaga, Cayuga, Wayne, Monroe, Genesee, Niagara

LAKE TRAIL or LAKE SHORE PATH: West by southwest from Buffalo, New York along the shore of Lake Erie to Cleveland, Ohio, continuing west to Sandusky County, Ohio, where it joins and becomes part of the Great Trail or Great Path . Approximately 260 miles. **Map page M50.**
New York: Erie, Chautauqua
Pennsylvania: Erie
Ohio: Ashtabula, Lake, Cuyahoga, Lorain, Erie, Sandusky,

FORBIDDEN PATH or CATSKILL TURNPIKE: West from Albany, New York across the state to Lake Erie, New York. Approximately 220 miles. **Map page M48.**
New York: Albany, Schoharie, Otsego, Chenango, Cortland, Tompkins, Schuyler, Steuben, Allegany, Cattaraugus, Erie

MINSI PATH: South by southwest from Kingston, New York to Port Jervis, then on the west side of the Delaware River to Philadelphia, Pennsylvania. Approximately 110 miles. **Map page M48.**
New York: Ulster, Sullivan, Orange,
Pennsylvania: Pike, Monroe, Northampton, Bucks, Montgomery, Philadelphia

LEHIGH and LACKAWANNA PATHS: South from the Forbidden Path or Catskill Turnpike in Otsego County, New York, through Scranton, Pennsylvania to Northampton County, where it joins the Minsi Path. Approximately 90 miles. **Map page M48.**
New York: Otsego, Delaware
Pennsylvania: Wayne, Susquehanna, Lackawanna, Monroe, Northampton

TUSCARORA PATH: Southwest from Scranton, Pennsylvania to Bedford, Pennsylvania. Approximately 215 miles. **Map page M48.**
Pennsylvania: Lackawanna, Luzerne, Columbia, Northumberland, Snyder, Mifflin, Huntingdon, Bedford

NEW YORK - PHILADELPHIA POST ROAD: Southwest from New York City to Philadelphia, Pennsylvania. Approximately 106 miles. **Map page M48.**
New York: Kings, Queens, New York
New Jersey: Hudson, Union, Middlesex, Mercer, Burlington
Pennsylvania: Philadelphia

FALL LINE or SOUTHERN ROAD: South by southwest from Philadelphia, Pennsylvania through Baltimore, Maryland; Richmond, Virginia; Raleigh and Fayetteville, North Carolina; Cheraw, Camden, and Columbia, South Carolina; and west from Augusta, Georgia, passing through Macon and Columbus, Georgia to Montgomery, Alabama. Approximately 1,200 miles. **Map page M47.**

Pennsylvania: Delaware, Philadelphia

Delaware: New Castle

Maryland: Cecil, Harford, Baltimore, Anne Arundel, Howard, Prince Georges

Virginia: Arlington, Fairfax, Prince William, Stafford, Spotsylvania, Caroline, Hanover, Richmond, Henrico, Chesterfield, Dinwiddie, Brunswick

North Carolina: Warren, Franklin, Wake, Johnson, Harnett, Cumberland, Hoke, Scotland

South Carolina: Marlboro, Chesterfield, Kershaw, Richland, Lexington, Aiken

Georgia: Richmond, McDuffie, Warren, Hancock, Baldwin, Jones, Bibb, Crawford, Taylor, Talbot, Muscogee

Alabama: Russell, Lee, Macon, Montgomery

FAYETTEVILLE, ELIZABETHTOWN, and WILMINGTON TRAIL of NORTH CAROLINA: Southeast direction from Fayetteville through Elizabethville to Wilmington, North Carolina. Approximately 95 miles. **Map page M49.**

North Carolina: Cumberland, Bladen, Columbus, Brunswick

CAMDEN - CHARLESTON PATH: Southeast direction from Camden, to Charleston, South Carolina. Approximately 150 miles. **Map page M49.**

South Carolina: Kershaw, Sumter, Calhoun, Orangeburg, Dorchester, Charleston

CHARLESTON - SAVANNAH TRAIL: Southwest along the coast from Charleston, South Carolina to Savannah, Georgia. Approximately 120 miles. **Map page M49.**

South Carolina: Charleston, Colleton, Beaufort, Jasper

Georgia: Chatham

RICHMOND - WILLIAMSBURG ROAD: East by southeast from Richmond, Virginia along the James River to Williamsburg, Virginia. Approximately 45 miles. **Map page M49.**

Virginia: Henrico, Charles City, James City

SECONDARY COAST ROAD: South by southwest direction from Peterburg, Virginia along the coast to Charleston, South Carolina. Approximately 475 miles. **Map page M47.**

Virginia: Prince George, Sussex, Southampton, Isle of Wight, Suffolk

North Carolina: Gates, Hertford, Bertie, Martin, Beaufort, Craven, Jones, Onslow, Pender, New Hanover, Brunswick

South Carolina: Horry, Georgetown, Charleston

GREAT INDIAN WARPATH: Southwest direction from Philadelphia, through Lancaster, Pennsylvania; Hagerstown, Maryland; Martinsburg, West Virginia; Harrisonburg and Roanoke, Virginia; to Chattanooga, Tennessee. This great trunk trail has had many names for various sections and branches. Approximately 550 miles. **Map page M47.**

Pennsylvania: Philadelphia, Delaware, Chester, Lancaster, York, Adams

Maryland: Washington

West Virginia: Berkeley

Virginia: Frederick, Shenandoah, Rockingham, Augusta, Rockbridge, Botetourt, Roanoke, Montgomery, Pulaski, Wythe, Smyth, Washington

Tennessee: Sullivan, Washington, Greene, Cocke, Sevier, Blount, Monroe, McMinn, Bradley

PHILADELPHIA WAGON ROAD: West by southwest from Philadelphia through Lancaster, Pennsylvania to Hagerstown, Maryland (part of the Great Indian Warpath into the Shenandoah Valley). Approximately 140 miles. **Map page M49.**

Pennsylvania: Philadelphia, Delaware, Chester, Lancaster, York, Adams

Maryland: Washington

West Virginia: Berkeley

Virginia: Frederick, Shenandoah

GREAT VALLEY ROAD or GREAT WAGON ROAD: Southwest direction from Hagerstown, Maryland through the Shenandoah Valley to Roanoke, Virginia (part of the Great Indian Warpath). Approximately 150 miles. **Map page M49.**

Maryland: Washington

West Virginia: Berkeley

Virginia: Frederick, Shenandoah, Rockingham, Augusta, Rockbridge, Botetourt, Roanoke

GREAT TRADING PATH: Southwest direction from Roanoke, Virginia into northeast Tennessee (part of the Great Indian Warpath). The section from Roanoke to the Cumberland Gap was later part of the Wilderness Road. Approximately 190 miles. **Map page M49.**

Virginia: Roanoke, Montgomery, Pulaski, Wythe, Smyth, Washington

Tennessee: Sullivan, Hawkins, Hancock, Claiborne

SAURA-SAPONI TRAIL: South by southwest direction from Charlottesville, Virginia to the area of Greensboro, North Carolina. Approximately 120 miles. **Map page M49.**

Virginia: Albemarle, Nelson, Amherst, Campbell, Pittsylvania

North Carolina: Caswell, Rockingham, Guilford

OCCANEECHI PATH: Southwest direction from the Bermuda Hundred on the James River near Richmond, Virginia through Salisbury, North Carolina; Camden, South Carolina; to Augusta, Georgia. Approximately 500 miles. **Map page M47.**

Virginia: Prince George, Dinwiddie, Brunswick, Lunenburg, Mecklenburg

North Carolina: Granville, Durham, Orange, Alamance, Guilford, Randolph, Davidson, Rowan, Cabarrus, Mecklenburg

South Carolina: York, Chester, Lancaster, Kershaw, Fairfield, Richland, Lexington, Aiken

Georgia: Columbia, Richmond

RAYSTOWN PATH or FORBE'S ROAD or OLD TRADING PATH: West from Philadelphia, through Harrisburg and Bedford to Pittsburgh, Pennsylvania. Approximately 210 miles. **Map page M48.**

Pennsylvania: Philadelphia, Chester, Delaware, Lancaster, Lebanon, Dauphin, Cumberland, Franklin, Fulton, Bedford, Somerset, Westmoreland, Allegheny

KITTANNING PATH: West by northwest from the Tuscarora Path through Altoona and Kittanning, to the Allegheny River all in Pennsylvania. Approximately 115 miles. **Map page M48.**

Pennsylvania: Mifflin, Huntingdon, Blair, Cambria, Indiana, Armstrong

VENANGO PATH: North from Kittanning, to the Great Shamokin Path, joining together near Corry, Pennsylvania, then turning west to Erie, Pennsylvania. Approximately 110 miles. **Map page M50.**

Pennsylvania: Butler, Venango, Forest, Warren, Erie

GREAT SHAMOKIN PATH: Northwest from New York City through New Jersey to Susquehannah County, Pennsylvania, then west to Lake Erie. Approximately 440 miles. **Map page M48.**

New York: Kings, Queens, New York

New Jersey: Essex, Morris, Sussex

Pennsylvania: Pike, Wayne, Susquehanna, Bradford, Tioga, Potter, McKean, Warren, Erie

MARYLAND ROAD: West from Baltimore, to Cumberland, Maryland. This was the first section of the National Road. Approximately 110 miles. **Map page M49.**

Maryland: Baltimore, Carroll, Frederick, Washington, Allegany

GIST'S TRACE or NEMACOLIN'S PATH: West by northwest from Cumberland, Maryland to Christopher Gist's plantation between the Youghiogheny and Monongahela Rivers in Pennsylvania. Portions would become part of Braddock's Road and the National Road. Approximately 60 miles. **Map page M49.**

Maryland: Allegany, Garrett

Pennsylvania: Somerset, Fayette

BRADDOCK'S ROAD: West by northwest from Cumberland, Maryland along part of Gist's Trace and on to Ft. Duquesne at Pittsburgh, Pennsylvania. Approximately 100 miles. **Map page M49.**

Maryland: Allegany, Garrett

Pennsylvania: Somerset, Fayette, Allegheny

BURD'S ROAD: Northwest from Gist's Plantation to Ft. Burd and Brownsville on the Monongahela River, Pennsylvania. It became a link in the National Road. Approximately 35 miles. **Map page M47.** (Not keyed, part of the National Road)

Pennsylvania: Fayette

CUMBERLAND ROAD: West from Brownsville, Pennsylvania to Ft. Henry at Wheeling, West Virginia. Approximately 50 miles. **Map Page M47.** (Not keyed, part of the National Road)

Pennsylvania: Fayette, Washington

West Virginia: Ohio

THE NATIONAL ROAD: West from Baltimore, Maryland to St. Louis, Missouri, linking the Maryland Road, Gist's Trace, Braddock's Road, Burd's Road, and the Cumberland Road to Wheeling, West Virginia; then continuing through Columbus, Ohio; Indianapolis and Terre Haute, Indiana; Vandalia, Illinois to St. Louis, Missouri. Approximately 755 miles. **Map page M47.**

Maryland: Baltimore, Carroll, Frederick, Washington, Allegany, Garrett

Pennsylvania: Somerset, Fayette, Washington

West Virginia: Ohio

Ohio: Belmont, Guernsey, Muskingum, Licking, Franklin, Madison, Clark, Montgomery, Preble

Indiana: Wayne, Henry, Hancock, Marion, Hendricks, Morgan, Putnam, Clay, Vigo

Illinois: Clark, Cumberland, Jasper, Effingham, Fayette, Bond, Madison

Missouri: St. Louis

GREAT TRAIL or GREAT PATH: From Pittsburgh, Pennsylvania in west by northwest direction to Detroit, Michigan. Approximately 270 miles. **Map page M50.**

Pennsylvania: Allegheny, Beaver, Lawrence

Ohio: Mahoning, Stark, Wayne, Ashland, Huron, Seneca, Sandusky, Ottawa, Lucas

Michigan: Monroe, Wayne

DETROIT - CHICAGO ROAD: From Detroit, Michigan in a west by southwest direction to Chicago, Illinois. Approximately 275 miles. **Map page M50.**

Michigan: Wayne, Monroe, Lenawee, Hillsdale, Branch, St. Joseph, Cass, Berrien

Indiana: LaPorte, Porter, Luke

Illinois: Cook

CHICAGO - DUBUQUE HIGHWAY: West by northwest from Chicago, Illinois to the Mississippi River at Dubuque, Iowa. Approximately 170 miles. **Map page M50.**

Illinois: Cook, DuPage, Kane, McHenry, Boone, Winnebago, Stephenson, Jo Daviess

Iowa: Dubuque

MIHOAUKEE TRAIL: North from Chicago, Illinois along the shore of Lake Michigan to Milwaukee, Wisconsin, then continuing north by northwest to Fond du Lac, Wisconsin. Approximately 110 miles. **Map page M50.**
Illinois: Cook, Lake
Wisconsin: Kenosha, Racine, Milwaukee, Washington, Fond du Lac

PECATONICA TRAIL: From Lake Michigan at Green Bay south by southwest to Madison, Wisconsin, then south to Illinois, then southeast to the Illinois River in Bureau County, Illinois. Approximately 290 miles. **Map page M50.**
Wisconsin: Brown, Calumet, Fond du Lac, Dodge, Columbia, Dane, Rock
Illinois: Winnebago, Stephenson, Ogle, Lee, Bureau

KELLOGG TRAIL: A continuation of the Pecatonica Trail in a southeast direction from the Illinois River in Putnam County, Illinois to Terre Haute, Indiana. Approximately 160 miles. **Map page M50.**
Illinois: Putnam, Marshall, LaSalle, Livingston, Ford, Iroquois, Vermilion
Indiana: Parke, Vigo

OLD CHICAGO ROAD: South by southeast from Chicago, Illinois to Indianapolis, Indiana. Approximately 165 miles. **Map page M50.**
Illinois: Cook
Indiana: Lake, Newton, Benton, Tippecanoe, Clinton, Boone, Marion

LAFAYETTE ROAD: South by southeast from Lafayette, Indiana to the Ohio River in Crawford County, Indiana. Approximately 170 miles. **Map page M50.**
Indiana: Tippecanoe, Montgomery, Putnam, Owen, Monroe, Lawrence, Orange, Crawford

MICHIGAN ROAD: Straight south from South Bend, Indiana to Indianapolis, Indiana. Approximately 140 miles. **Map page M50.**
Indiana: St. Joseph, Marshall, Fulton, Miami, Howard, Tipton, Hamilton, Marion

VINCENNES AND INDIANAPOLIS ROAD: South by southwest from Detroit, Michigan through Defiance, Ohio, Ft. Wayne and Indianapolis to Vincennes, Indiana. Approximately 360 miles. **Map page M50.**
Michigan: Wayne, Monroe
Ohio: Lucas, Wood, Henry, Defiance, Paulding
Indiana: Allen, Wells, Huntington, Grant, Madison, Hamilton, Marion, Morgan, Monroe, Greene, Knox

MIAMI PATH: North from Cincinnati, Ohio through western Ohio to Defiance, Ohio, where the trail joins the Vincennes and Indianapolis Road. Approximately 180 miles. **Map page M50.**
Ohio: Hamilton, Butler, Preble, Drake, Mercer, Van Wert, Paulding, Defiance

TENNESSEE, OHIO AND GREAT LAKES TRAIL: North from Chattanooga, Tennessee to Detroit, Michigan. Approximately 480 miles. **Map page M47.**
Tennessee: Hamilton, Rhea, Roane, Morgan, Fentress, Pickett
Kentucky: Wayne, Russell, Adair, Casey, Boyle, Mercer, Jessamine, Fayette, Bourbon, Nicholas, Robertson, Mason
Ohio: Brown, Highland, Clinton, Green, Clark, Champaign, Logan, Hardin, Hancock, Wood, Lucas
Michigan: Monroe, Wayne

SCIOTO TRAIL: Straight south from Sandusky Bay, on Lake Erie along the Scioto River to Portsmouth on the Ohio River, being the northernmost extension of the Warriors Path. Approximately 220 miles. **Map page M50.**
Ohio: Sandusky, Seneca, Crawford, Marion, Delaware, Franklin, Pickaway, Ross, Pike, Scioto

WARRIORS PATH of KENTUCKY: A continuation of the Scioto Trail in a south direction from the Ohio River at Portsmouth, Ohio, to the Cumberland Gap, Kentucky. Approximately 190 miles. **Map page M51.**

Kentucky: Greenup, Carter, Rowan, Bath, Montgomery, Powell, Estell, Jackson, Laurel, Knox, Bell

ZANE'S TRACE: In a general southwest direction from Wheeling, West Virginia through Chillicothe, Ohio to Maysville, Kentucky. Approximately 255 miles. **Map page M50.**

West Virginia: Ohio

Ohio: Belmont, Guernsey, Muskingum, Perry, Fairfield, Hocking, Ross, Pike, Adams, Brown

Kentucky: Mason

MAYSVILLE TURNPIKE: A continuation of Zane's Trace from Maysville, Kentucky southwest to Elizabethtown, Kentucky. Approximately 165 miles. **Map page M50.**

Kentucky: Mason, Robertson, Nicholas, Bourbon, Fayette, Woodford, Anderson, Washington, Nelson, Hardin

PAMUNKEY - NEW RIVER TRAIL: West from the Pamunkey River north of Richmond, Virginia through Charlottesville and Staunton, Virginia into West Virginia to the New River in Fayette County where it connects with the Kanawha Branch of the Great Indian Warpath. Approximately 135 miles. **Map page M49.**

Virginia: Hanover, Louisa, Albemarle, Augusta, Bath

West Virginia: Greenbriar, Fayette

RICHMOND ROAD or CHESAPEAKE BRANCH of the GREAT INDIAN WARPATH: Beginning at Richmond, Virginia running in a west by southwest direction through Lynchburg and Roanoke, becoming the Great Indian Warpath at Ft. Chissel on the New River. Approximately 135 miles. **Map page M49.**

Virginia: Henrico, Powhatan, Cumberland, Buckingham, Appomattox, Amherst, Bedford, Roanoke, Montgomery

KANAWHA BRANCH of the GREAT INDIAN WARPATH: Starting at Chillicothe, Ohio in a southeast direction crossing the Ohio River at Gallipolis, Ohio and following the Kanawha River past Charlestown, West Virginia, then following the New River of the Chiswets, and joining the main path. Approximately 205 miles. **Map page M49.**

Ohio: Ross, Jackson, Gallia

West Virginia: Mason, Putnam, Kanawha, Fayette, Raleigh, Summers, Mercer

Virginia: Giles, Pulaski

WILDERNESS ROAD: Cleared by Daniel Boone and 30 axmen, followed the Great Indian Warpath on the North Fork of the Holston River on the Virginia-Tennessee border, west to the Cumberland Gap, then taking the Warriors Path into Kentucky. From there continuing northwest through Harrodsburg, on to Louisville, Kentucky. Approximately 180 miles. **Map page M51.**

Tennessee: Sullivan, Hawkins, Hancock, Claiborne

Kentucky: Bell, Knox, Laurel, Rockcastle, Lincoln, Boyle, Mercer, Washington, Nelson, Spencer, Jefferson

BUFFALO TRACE: From Louisville, Kentucky west by northwest across southern Indiana to Vincennes, through Centralia, Illinois, then west by southwest to Kaskaskia, Illinois on the Missouri River. Approximately 320 miles. **Map page M50.**

Kentucky: Jefferson

Indiana: Floyd, Harrison, Washington, Orange, Martin, Daviess, Knox

Illinois: Lawrence, Richland, Clay, Marion, Jefferson, Washington, Perry, Randolph

CHICAGO KASKASKIA ROAD: A road from Lake Michigan, south by southwest, through Peoria and Springfield, Illinois east of St. Louis to Kaskaskia on the Missouri River. Approximately 350 miles. **Map page M50.**

Illinois: Cook, Will, Grundy, Marshall, Woodford, Tazewell, Logan, Sangamon, Montgomery, Bond, Madison, St. Clair, Randolph

JONESBORO ROAD: Starting on the Coast at New Bern, North Carolina running in a northwest direction above Raleigh through Greensboro and Salem to the Catawba River, there joining Rutherford's War Trace to Asheville, then along the Broad River into Tennessee on the Catawba Trail to Knoxville, Tennessee. Approximately 345 miles. **Map page M49.**

North Carolina: Craven, Lenoir, Greene, Wilson, Nash, Wake, Durham, Orange, Alamance, Guilford, Forsyth, Davie, Iredell, Alexander, Catawba, Burke, McDowell, Buncombe, Madison

Tennessee: Cocke, Jefferson, Knox

WILMINGTON, HIGHPOINT and NORTHERN TRAIL: Starting at Wilmington, North Carolina running in a northwest direction to the Greensboro area, then north into Virginia where it joins the Great Indian Warpath near Roanoke, Virginia. Approximately 255 miles. **Map page M49.**

North Carolina: Brunswick, Columbus, Robeson, Scotland, Richmond, Moore, Randolph, Guilford, Rockingham

Virginia: Henry, Franklin, Roanoke

OLD NORTHWESTERN TURNPIKE: From Alexandria (Washington D. C. area) west in the upper counties of Virginia, into two counties in West Virginia, then across Garrett County, Maryland, back into West Virginia to Parkersburg on the Ohio River. Approximately 180 miles. **Map page M49.**

Virginia: Fairfax, Arlington, Loudoun, Clarke, Frederick

West Virginia: Hampshire, Mineral

Maryland: Garrett

West Virginia: Preston, Taylor, Harrison, Doddridge, Ritchie, Wood

NEW RIVER and SOUTHERN TRAIL: Starting at the Yadkin River, it is a continuation of the Catawba and Northern Trail. North across the small part of Virginia into West Virginia, where it connects with the Kanooba Branch of the Great Indian Warpath in Mercer County. Approximately 165 miles. **Map page M49.**

North Carolina: Wilkes, Alleghany

Virginia: Grayson, Carroll, Wythe, Pulaski, Giles

West Virginia: Mercer

CATAWBA and NORTHERN TRAIL: Starting in York County, South Carolina at the point where it intersects the lower Cherokee Traders Path running north along the Catawba River, then cross country to the Yadkin River in North Carolina to join the New River and Southern Trail. Approximately 100 miles. **Map page M49.**

South Carolina: York

North Carolina: Gaston, Lincoln, Catawba, Alexander, Wilkes

OLD CHEROKEE PATH: From Seneca, South Carolina runs north by northeast across North Carolina to the Great Indian Warpath in Virginia. Approximately 150 miles. **Map page M49.**

South Carolina: Oconee, Pickens, Greenville

North Carolina: Polk, Rutherford, McDowell, Burke, Caldwell, Watauga,

Tennessee: Johnson

Virigina: Washington

RUTHERFORD'S WAR TRACE: A continuation of the Jonesboro Road from the Catawba River north of Salisbury, North Carolina in a southwest direction through Asheville to the Little Tennessee River near Franklin, where it joins the Black Fox Trail. Approximately 180 miles. **Map page M49.**

North Carolina: Davie, Rowan, Iredell, Catawba, Burke, McDowell, Buncombe, Haywood, Jackson, Macon, Cherokee

CATAWBA TRAIL: A continuation of the Old South Carolina State Road in a northwest direction across the small part of North Carolina, through the Great Smoky Mountains into the Great Valley of Tennessee, crossing the

Great Indian Warpath and the Holston River at the western tip of Virginia, then to the Cumberland Gap, where it joins the Warrior's Path of Kentucky. Approximately 120 miles. **Map page M51.**

North Carolina: Polk, Henderson, Buncombe, Madison

Tennessee: Cocke, Greene, Hamblen, Grainger, Claiborne, Hancock

Virginia: Lee

CUMBERLAND TRACE: West from Knoxville to Nashville, Tennessee. Approximately 180 miles. **Map page M51.**

Tennessee: Knox, Loudon, Roane, Cumberland, White, Putnam, Smith, Trousdale, Wilson, Davidson

NASHVILLE ROAD: West by northwest from Knoxville, Tennessee to near Monterey, where it joins the Cumberland Trace. Approximately 85 miles. **Map page M51.**

Tennessee: Knox, Anderson, Morgan, Fentress, Overton, Putnam

CUMBERLAND and GREAT LAKES TRAIL: North by northwest from Nashville, Tennessee to near Lexington, Kentucky where it joins the Tennessee, Ohio, and Great Lakes Trail. Approximately 214 miles. **Map page M51.**

Tennessee: Davidson, Sumner, Macon

Kentucky: Monroe, Cumberland, Adair, Casey, Boyle, Mercer,

CUMBERLAND and OHIO FALLS TRAIL: North by northwest from Nashville, Tennessee to Louisville, Kentucky on the Ohio River. Approximately 175 miles. **Map page M51.**

Tennessee: Davidson, Robertson

Kentucky: Logan, Warren, Edmonson, Hart, Hardin, Bullitt, Jefferson

RUSSELLVILLE - SHAWNEETOWN TRAIL: Northwest from Russellville, Kentucky to Shawneetown, Illinois on the Ohio River. Approximately 110 miles. **Map page M51.**

Kentucky: Logan, Todd, Muhlenberg, Hopkins, Webster, Union

Illinois: Gallatin

NASHVILLE - SALINE RIVER TRAIL: Northwest from Nashville, Tennessee through the small part of Kentucky, crossing the Ohio River near Paducah into Illinois, then to Kaskaskia on the Mississippi River. Approximately 200 miles. **Map page M51.**

Tennessee: Davidson, Cheatham, Montgomery

Kentucky: Christian, Trigg, Lyon, Marshall, McCracken

Illinois: Massac, Johnson, Union, Jackson, Randolph

BOLIVAR and MEMPHIS TRAIL: West from Bolivar, Tennessee to Memphis and the Mississippi River. Approximately 60 miles. **Map Page M51.**

Tennessee: Hardeman, Fayette, Shelby

WEST TENNESSEE CHICKASAW TRAIL: South from Bolivar, Tennessee to the junction point with Natchez Trace Trail in Mississippi. Approximately 160 miles. **Map page M51.**

Tennessee: Hardeman,

Mississippi: Tippah, Union, Pontotoc

CISCO and MIDDLE TENNESSEE TRAIL: A continuation of West Tennessee Chickasaw Trail, northeast from Bolivar, Tennessee to the Tennessee River in Benton County Tennessee. Approximately 65 miles. **Map page M51.**

Tennessee: Hardeman, Chester, Henderson, Carroll, Benton

MISSISSIPPI and TENNESSEE RIVER TRAIL: West from the Tennessee River to the Mississippi River. Approximately 90 miles. **Map page M51.**

Tennessee: Benton, Carroll, Gibson, Dyer

LOWER WARPATH or WEST TENNESSEE TRAIL: West from Nashville, Tennessee to the Tennessee River. As the trail continues beyond the Tennessee River, it becomes the Mississippi and Tennessee River Trail. Approximately 60 miles. **Map page M51.**

Tennessee: Davidson, Cheatham, Dickson, Humphreys

CISCA and ST. AUGUSTINE TRAIL or NICKAJACK TRAIL: Northwest from Augusta, Georgia through Athens, Georgia and through Chattanooga to Nashville, Tennessee. Approximately 240 miles. **Map page M47.**

Georgia: Richmond, Columbia, McDuffie, Warren, Taliaferro, Greene, Morgan, Walton, Barrow, Hall, Forsyth, Cherokee, Bartow, Gordon, Whitfield, Catoosa

Tennessee: Hamilton, Marion, Franklin, Coffee, Bedford, Rutherford, Davidson

BLACK FOX TRAIL: Northeast from the Hiwassee River in North Carolina to the Stone River in Tennessee, where it junctions with the Cisca and St. Augustine Trail. Approximately 140 miles. **Map page M51.**

North Carolina: Cherokee

Tennessee: Polk, Bradley, Hamilton, Bledsoe, Van Buren, Warren, Cannon, Rutherford

UNICOI TURNPIKE: Northwest from the trailhead at Tallulah Falls, to the trailhead in North Carolina, intersects with Black Fox Trail and Rutherford War Trace on the Hiwassee River. Approximately 60 miles. **Map page M51.**

Georgia: Rabun, Towns

North Carolina: Clay, Cherokee

AUGUSTA and CHEROKEE TRAIL: Northwest on the west side of the Savannah River from Augusta, Georgia to where it intersects with the Lower Cherokee Traders Path, continues until it joins the trailhead at Tallulah Falls, Georgia with Coosa-Tugaloo Indian Path and Unicoi Turnpike. Approximately 100 miles. **Map page M51.**

Georgia: Richmond, Columbia, Lincoln, Wilkes, Elbert, Hart, Franklin, Stephens, Habersham

FT. CHARLOTTE and CHEROKEE OLD PATH: Northwest from Ft. Charlotte, South Carolina along the east side of the Savannah River where it intersects with the Lower Cherokee Traders Path, continuing on to the trailhead where Coosa-Tugaloo Path and Old Cherokee Path come together. Approximately 70 miles. **Map page M51.**

South Carolina: McCormick, Abbeville, Anderson, Oconee

CHARLESTON - FT. CHARLOTTE TRAIL: West by northwest from Charleston, South Carolina across southeast South Carolina to the Savannah River, where it joins the Ft. Charlotte and Cherokee Old Path. Approximately 105 miles. **Map page M47.**

South Carolina: Charleston, Dorchester, Orangeburg, Aiken, Edgefield, McCormick

FT. MOORE - CHARLESTON TRAIL: West by northwest from Charleston, South Carolina to Augusta, Georgia, where it joins a trailhead junction. Approximately 150 miles. **Map page M49.**

South Carolina: Charleston, Dorchester, Colleton, Bamberg, Barnwell, Aiken

OLD SOUTH CAROLINA STATE ROAD: Northwest from Charleston, South Carolina through Columbia and Greenville to the North Carolina border where it joins the Catawba Trail. Approximately 180 miles. **Map page M47.**

South Carolina: Charleston, Dorchester, Orangeburg, Calhoun, Lexington, Newberry, Laurens, Spartanburg, Greenville

LOWER CHEROKEE TRADERS' PATH: West by southwest from Charlotte, North Carolina across the northern section of South Carolina to the Tugaloo River, where it joins the Tugaloo-Apalachee Bay Trail. Approximately 215 miles. **Map page M51.**

South Carolina: York, Cherokee, Spartanburg, Greenville, Anderson, Oconee

North Carolina: Mecklenburg, Gaston

TUGALOO - APALACHEE BAY TRAIL: South by southwest from the Tugaloo River in Georgia across the Florida panhandle to the Gulf of Mexico. Approximately 310 miles. **Map page M47.**

Georgia: Stephens, Franklin, Madison, Jackson, Clarke, Oconee, Walton, Newton, Butts, Lamar, Upson, Taylor, Schley, Sumter, Lee, Dougherty, Baker, Mitchell, Grady

Florida: Leon, Wakulla

COOSA - TUGALOO INDIAN WARPATH: Northeast from Birmingham, Alabama through eastern Alabama then northern Georgia to the Tugaloo River between Georgia and South Carolina. Approximately 200 miles. **Map page M51.**

Alabama: Jefferson, St. Clair, Etowah, Cherokee

Georgia: Floyd, Bartow, Cherokee, Dawson, Hall, Banks, Stephens

OKFUSKEE TRAIL: North to south trail along the Tallapoosa River in eastern Alabama. Approximately 70 miles. **Map page M52.**

Alabama: Randolph, Cleburne, Cherokee

MIDDLE CREEK TRADING PATH: West by southwest from McCormack, South Carolina across Georgia to eastern Alabama. Approximately 230 miles. **Map page M47.**

South Carolina: McCormack

Georgia: Lincoln, Wilkes, Taliaferro, Greene, Morgan, Jasper, Butts, Spalding, Pike, Meriwether, Troup

Alabama: Chambers

LOWER CREEK TRADING POST: West by southwest from Augusta, Georgia to Macon, Georgia, then west to Birmingham, Alabama; then west by northwest to the Tombigbee River in eastern Mississippi, continuing west by northwest to Oxford, Mississippi. Then west by southwest through Clarksdale to the Mississippi River. Approximately 540 miles. **Map page M47.**

Georgia: Richmond, McDuffie, Warren, Hancock, Baldwin, Jones, Bibb, Monroe, Upson, Meriwether, Troup

Alabama: Randolph, Clay, Talladega, Shelby, Jefferson, Walker, Fayette, Lamar

Mississippi: Monroe, Lee, Pontotoc, Lafayette, Panola, Quitman, Coahoma

AUGUSTA - SAVANNAH TRAIL: South by southeast from Augusta, Georgia along the Savannah River on the Georgia side to Savannah, Georgia. Approximately 125 miles. **Map page M49.**

Georgia: Richmond, Burke, Screven, Effingham, Chatham

SAVANNAH - JACKSONVILLE TRAIL: South from Savannah, Georgia along the Atlantic Coast to Jacksonville, Florida. Approximately 135 miles. **Map page M52.**

Georgia: Chatham, Bryan, Liberty, McIntosh, Glynn, Camden

Florida: Nassau, Duval

JACKSONVILLE - ST. AUGUSTINE TRAIL: From Jacksonville, Florida south along the coastline to St. Augustine. Approximately 40 miles. **Map page M52.**

Florida: Duval, St. Johns

AUGUSTA - ST. AUGUSTINE TRAIL: From Augusta, Georgia south to join the Old Trading Path through several counties, then southeast to St. Augustine, Florida. Approximately 290 miles. **Map page M52.**

Georgia: Richmond, Burke, Jenkins, Candler, Evans, Tattnall, Appling, Bacon, Ware, Clinch, Echols

Florida: Hamilton, Columbia, Union, Bradford, Clay, St. Johns

OLD TRADING PATH: From the Savannah River southwest across Georgia to the Apalachicola River in Florida, then west through the Florida panhandle to Pensacola Bay, Florida. Approximately 335 miles. **Map page M52.**

Georgia: Effingham, Bullock, Evans, Tattnall, Appling, Bacon, Coffee, Atkinson, Berrien, Cook, Colquitt, Grady, Decatur

Florida: Jackson, Washington, Holmes, Walton, Okaloosa, Santa Rosa

ST. AUGUSTINE - FLINT RIVER TRAIL: From St. Augustine, Florida west to a junction with the Jacksonville-Apalachee Bay Trail, past Tallahassee to the Chattahoochee on the Apalachicola River. Approximately 170 miles. **Map page M52.**

Florida: St. Johns, Clay, Bradford, Union, Columbia, Hamilton, Madison, Jefferson, Leon, Gadsden, Jackson

JACKSONVILLE - APALACHEE BAY TRAIL: From Jacksonville, Florida west across Florida to meet the Tugaloo-Apalachee Bay Trail, then south to Apalachee Bay. Approximately 170 miles. **Map page M52.**

Florida: Duval, Baker, Hamilton, Madison, Jefferson, Wakulla

ST. AUGUSTINE - APALACHEE TRAIL: West from St. Augustine, Florida to Alachua, then west by northwest to Tallahassee, Florida. Approximately 205 miles. **Map page M52.**

Florida: St. Johns, Clay, Alachua, Gilchrist, Lafayette, Taylor, Jefferson, Leon

ALACHUA - TAMPA BAY TRAIL: From Alachua, Florida trailhead south to Tampa Bay, Florida. Approximately 140 miles. **Map page M52.**

Florida: Alachua, Marion, Sumter, Hernando, Pasco, Hillsborough, Pinellas

MACON and MONTGOMERY TRAIL: From Montgomery, Alabama east through Columbus then east by northeast to Macon, Georgia. Approximately 120 miles. **Map page M52.**

Alabama: Montgomery, Macon, Russell, Lee

Georgia: Muskogee, Talbot, Taylor, Crawford, Bibb

CHATTANOOGA - WILLSTOWN ROAD: North by northeast from the junction with the Tallapoosa Trail to Chattanooga, Tennessee. Approximately 70 miles. **Map page M52.**

Alabama: Etowah, DeKalb

Georgia: Walker

Tennessee: Hamilton

TALLAPOOSA TRAIL: From Montgomery, Alabama north through Birmingham, then in a north by northeast direction to join the Chattanooga-Willstown Road. Approximately 190 miles. **Map page M52.**

Alabama: Montgomery, Elmore, Autauga, Chilton, Shelby, Jefferson, St. Clair, Etowah

ALABAMA - CHICKASAW TRAIL: From Montgomery, Alabama in a northwest direction to the Tombigbee River in Mississippi. Approximately 170 miles. **Map page M52.**

Alabama: Montgomery, Autauga, Chilton, Bibb, Tuscaloosa, Fayette, Lamar

Mississippi: Monroe

TOMBIGBEE amd ARKANSAS RIVER TRAIL: West from the Tombigbee River in Monroe County, Mississippi across the state to the mouth of the Arkansas River. Approximately 180 miles. **Map page M52.**

Mississippi: Monroe, Chickasaw, Calhoun, Yalobusha, Tallahatchie, Sunflower, Bolivar

NATCHEZ TRACE or CHICKASAW TRAIL: From Natchez, Mississippi north by northeast to Nashville, Tennessee. Approximately 380 miles. **Map page M47.**

Mississippi: Adams, Jefferson, Claiborne, Hinds, Madison, Leake, Winston, Oktibbeha, Clay, Monroe

Alabama: Marion, Franklin, Colbert, Lauderdale

Tennessee: Lawrence, Giles, Maury, Williamson, Davidson

MEMPHIS, PONTOTOC and MOBILE TRAIL: From Memphis, Tennessee south by southeast through Pontotoc, Mississippi, then southwest to Grenada, then south by southeast to Mobile, Alabama. Approximately 360 miles. **Map page M47.**

Tennessee: Shelby

Mississippi: DeSoto, Marshall, Union, Pontotoc, Calhoun, Grenada, Montgomery, Attala, Leake, Neshoba, Newton, Jasper, Clarke, Wayne, Greene

Alabama: Washington, Mobile

GAINE'S TRACE: From the Tombigbee River in Monroe County, Mississippi northeast to the Tennessee River near Decatur, Alabama. Approximately 120 miles. **Map page M51.**

Mississippi: Monroe

Alabama: Lamar, Marion, Winston, Lawrence, Morgan

GREAT SOUTH TRAIL: From Nashville, Tennessee south through Huntsville and Birmingham, Alabama to Mobile, Alabama. Approximately 435 miles. **Map page M47.**

Tennessee: Davidson, Rutherford, Bedford, Lincoln

Alabama: Madison, Morgan, Cullman, Blount, Jefferson, Bibb, Perry, Marengo, Clarke, Washington, Mobile

ALABAMA, CHOCTAW and NATCHEZ TRAIL: From Montgomery, Alabama west through Jackson, Mississippi to Vicksburg, Mississippi. Approximately 290 miles. **Map page M52.**

Alabama: Montgomery, Lowndes, Dallas, Marengo, Choctaw

Mississippi: Lauderdale, Newton, Scott, Rankin, Hinds, Warren

ALABAMA and MOBILE TRAIL: From Montgomery, Alabama southwest to Mobile, Alabama. Approximately 150 miles. **Map page M52.**

Alabama: Montgomery, Lowndes, Butler, Monroe, Clark, Baldwin,

UPPER CREEKS - PENSACOLA TRAIL: From Montgomery, Alabama in a southwestwerly direction around the boundary of the panhandle of Florida, then turning southeast to Pensacola Bay, Florida. Approximately 235 miles. **Map page M52.**

Alabama: Montgomery, Lowndes, Butler, Conecuh, Escambia, Baldwin

Florida: Escambia

NATCHEZ - LOWER CREEKS TRAIL: From Natchez east across lower Mississippi and lower Alabama to Montgomery, Alabama. Approximately 310 miles. **Map page M52.**

Mississippi: Adams, Franklin, Lincoln, Lawrence, Jefferson Davis, Covington, Jones, Wayne

Alabama: Washington, Clark, Monroe

MOBILE and NATCHEZ TRAIL: From Mobile, Alabama across lower Mississippi in a west by northwest direction to Natchez, Mississippi. Approximately 220 miles. **Map page M52.**

Alabama: Mobile

Mississippi: George, Perry, Forest, Lamar, Marion, Walthall, Pike, Amite, Franklin, Adams

CHOCTAW - BAY ST. LOUIS TRAIL: From Meridian, Mississippi south by southwest to Bay St. Louis, Mississippi. Approximately 155 miles. **Map page M52.**

Mississippi: Lauderdale, Clarke, Jasper, Jones, Forest, Lamar, Pearl River, Hancock

JACKSON'S MILITARY ROAD: From Nashville, Tennessee south by southwest through Florence, Alabama to Columbus, Mississippi, joining the Lake Ponchartrain Trail and ending at Lake Ponchartrain, Louisiana. Approximately 445 miles. **Map page M47.**

Tennessee: Davidson, Williamson, Maury, Giles, Lawrence

Alabama: Lauderdale, Colbert, Franklin, Marion

Mississippi: Monroe, Lowndes, Noxubee, Winston, Neshoba, Newton, Jasper, Smith, Covington, Jefferson Davis, Marion, Walthall

Louisiana: Washington, St. Tammany

LAKE PONCHARTRAIN TRAIL: Southeast from Wilkinson, Mississippi to Lake Pontchartrain, then northeast until the trail joins Jackson's Military Road. Approximately 80 miles. **Map page M52.**

Mississippi: Wilkinson

Louisiana: East Feliciana, St. Helena, Livingston, Tangipahoa, St. Tammany, Washington

NATCHEZ - NEW ORLEANS TRAIL: From Natchez, Mississippi south along the Mississippi River, then east to New Orleans, Louisiana. Approximately 125 miles. **Map page M52.**

Mississippi: Adams, Wilkinson

Louisiana: West Feliciana, East Feliciana, East Baton Rouge, Ascension, St. James, St. John the Baptist, St. Charles, Jefferson, Orleans

MAP SECTION

Fifty-six maps are included in this section. Forty-six are of the states, each printed on a single page. Some of the smaller mid-Atlantic and New England states are combined, they are: Connecticut, Massachusetts, and Rhode Island on page M7; New Jersey and Delaware, page M27; and New Hampshire and Vermont are combined on page M41.

These maps will be very valuable for research as they show the counties in each state plus the counties of bordering states. For a thorough search, counties in the state of primary interest along with counties of bordering states should be examined.

The maps are printed in color and county boundaries, county names, rivers, and lakes are shown for each state. You can easily follow the travels of your ancestors as they moved within a state or through many states by studying the county and state boundaries as well as the river courses found on each map.

Six migration trail maps are included in this section showing 122 separate migration trails. These maps are printed in color, and the trails are easily located and followed from beginning to end. Starting on page M47 you will find written descriptions of each of these migration trails. As you study the trails and the written descriptions you can follow the travels of your ancestors from state to state and from county to county. Names of the states and counties each trail passes through are listed.

Hundreds of hours have been expended in accurately showing these migration trails on the maps and describing each of them. Every effort possible has been made for perfection and these maps will be of great help as you follow the travels of your ancestors.

Our special thanks go to Floren and Phyllis Preece for their time and effort in preparing the accurate and thorough migration trail maps and the descriptions of the trails. Without their help these maps could not have been included.

On page M53 is a map showing all of the waterways in the eastern part of the United States during the period 1785–1850. The Cumberland Road is also shown on the map. States, towns and cities in relation to the waterways are depicted. Waterways played an important role in travel routes during this time period.

On page M54 is a map showing the railroads in the United States by 1860. The railroad provided a convenient way of travel during this era. It was sometimes the only way of travel available as settlers moved from one part of the country to another. This map also shows the states, counties, towns and cities — similar to the map showing the waterways.

Two important maps that show the growth of the United States from 1820 to 1860 also appear in this section.

You will find this unique section of maps of great value as you trace the travels of early immigrants as they established residences throughout the country.

The University of Utah, Department of Geography, provided the expertise to place the migration trails, railroads, and waterways in the correct locations on the maps.

MAP SECTION

Table of Contents

State Maps

ALABAMA COUNTY MAP

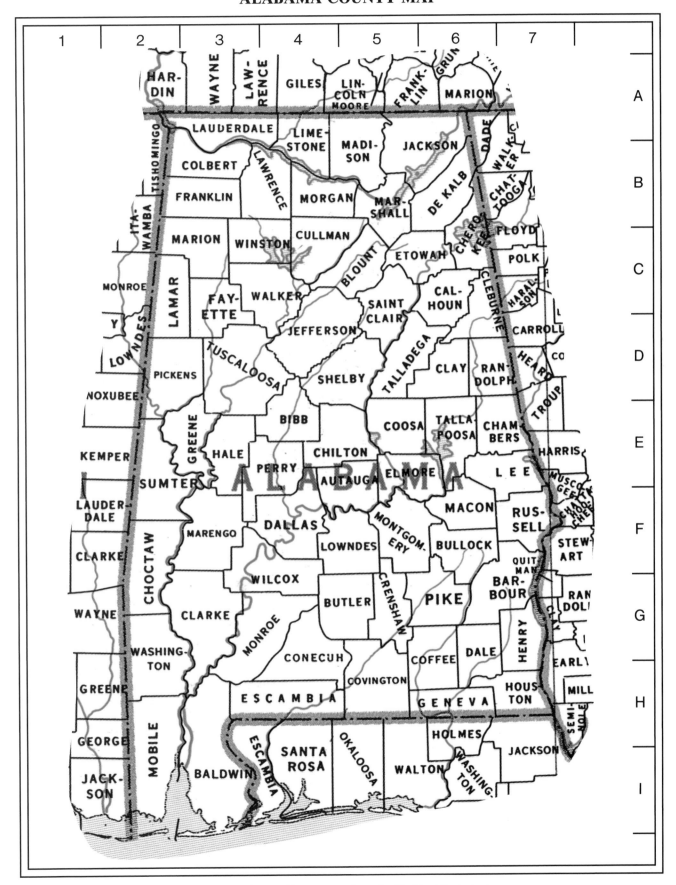

Bordering States: Tennessee, Georgia, Florida, Mississippi

ALASKA COUNTY MAP

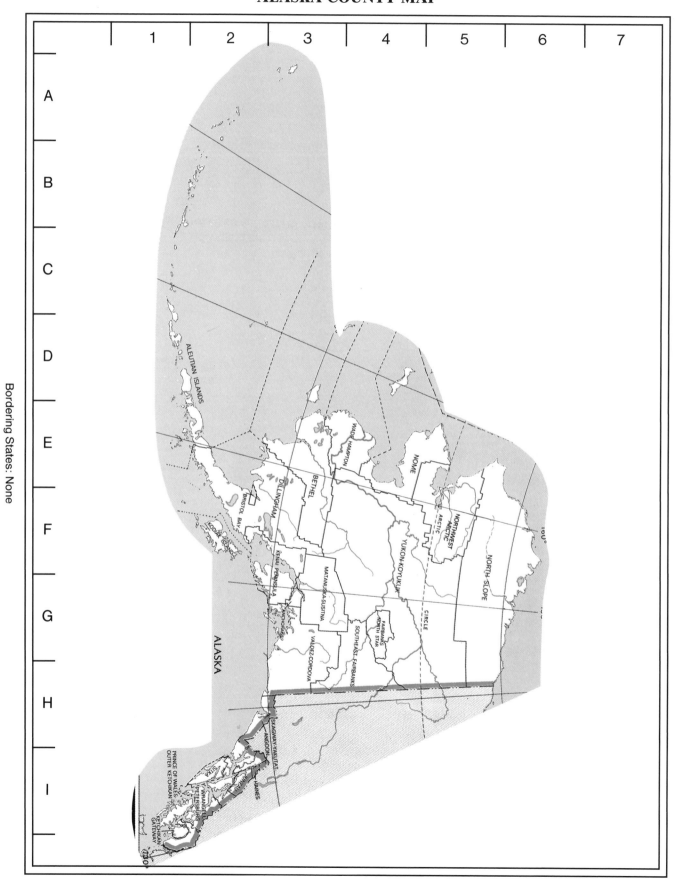

Bordering States: None

ARIZONA COUNTY MAP

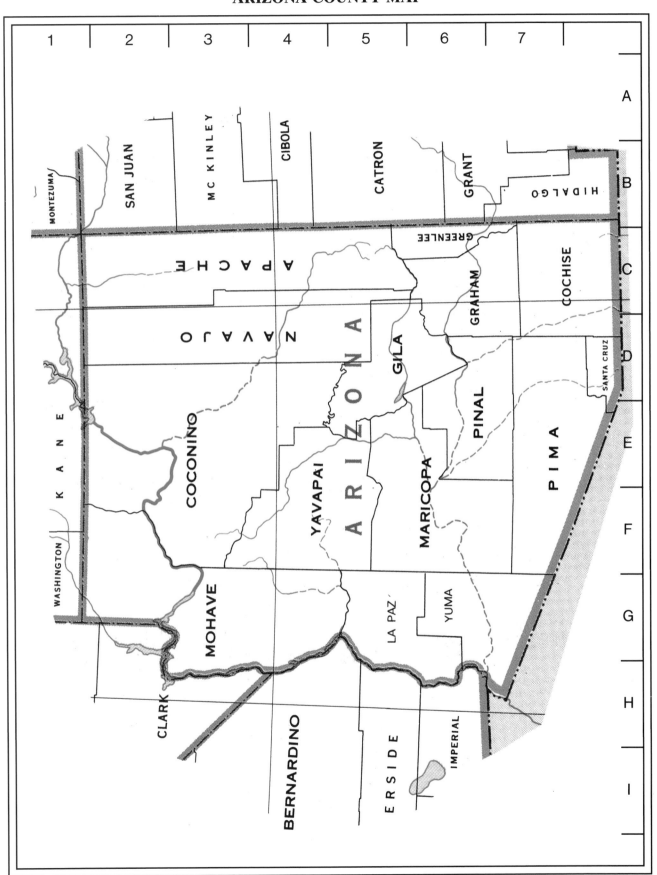

Bordering States: Colorado, New Mexico, California, Nevada, Utah

ARKANSAS COUNTY MAP

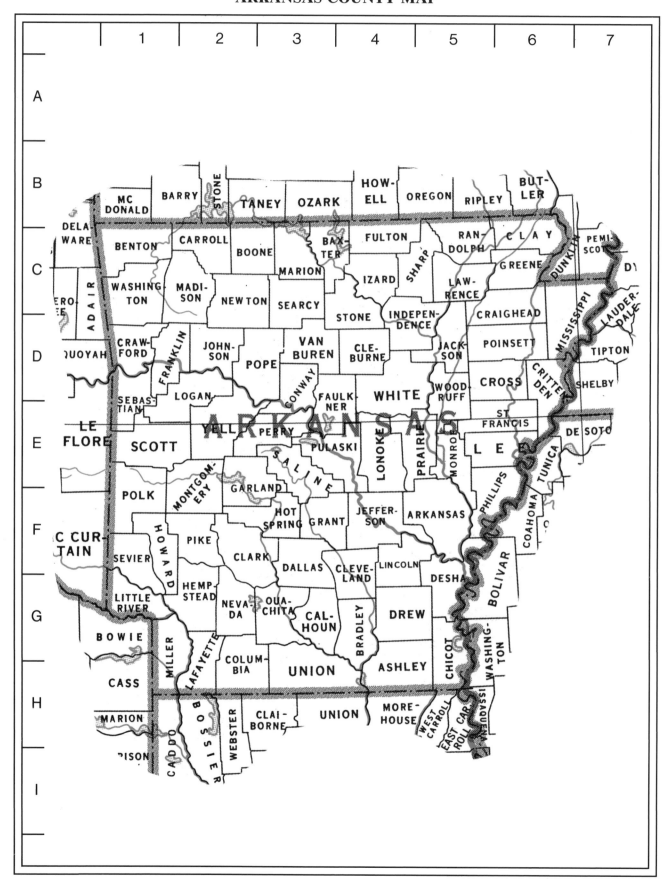

Bordering States: Missouri, Tennessee, Mississippi, Louisiana, Texas, Oklahoma

CALIFORNIA COUNTY MAP

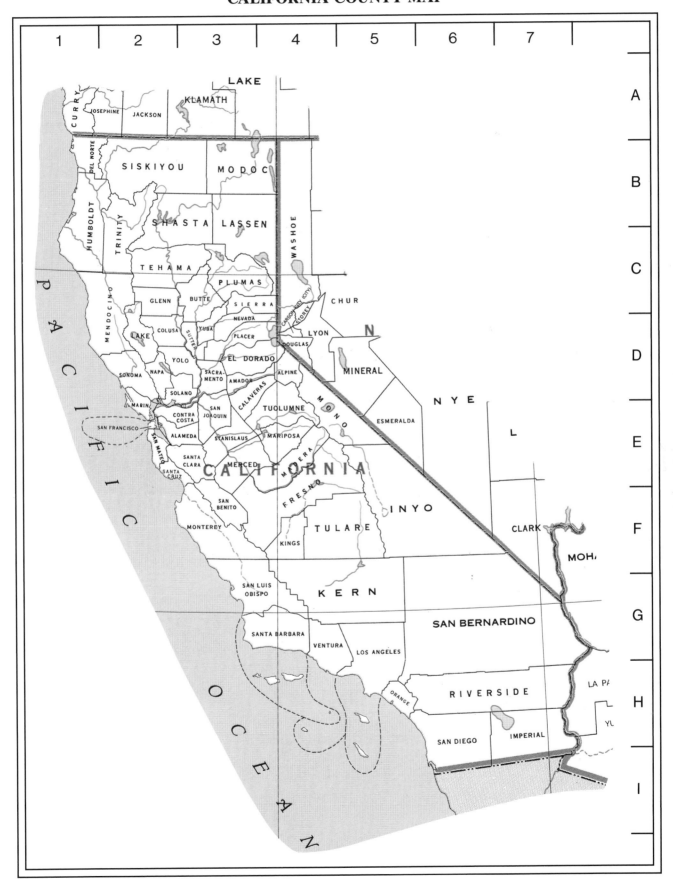

Bordering States: Oregon, Nevada, Arizona

COLORADO COUNTY MAP

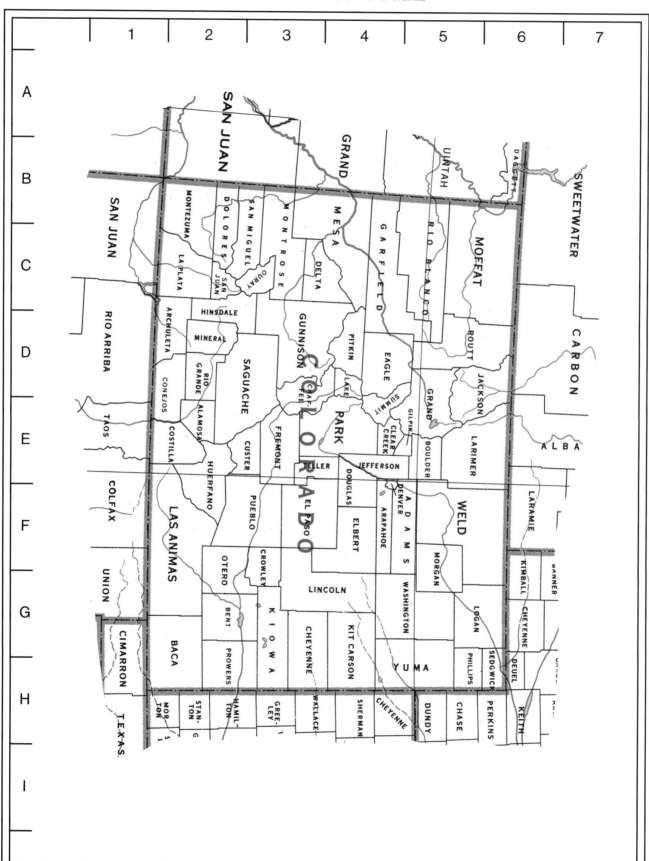

Bordering States: Wyoming, Nebraska, Kansas, Oklahoma, New Mexico, Utah

CONNECTICUT, MASSACHUSETTS, RHODE ISLAND COUNTY MAP

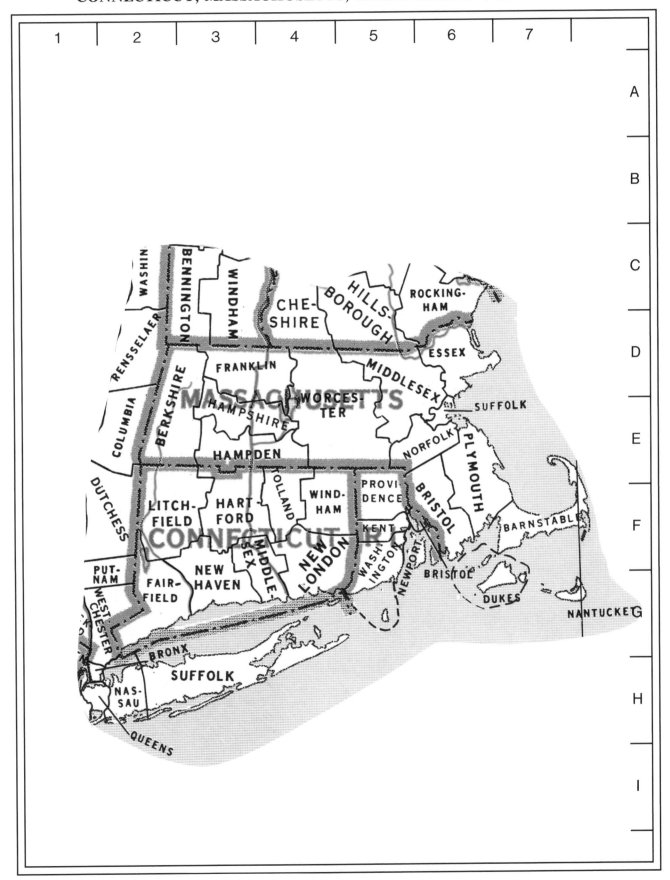

FLORIDA COUNTY MAP

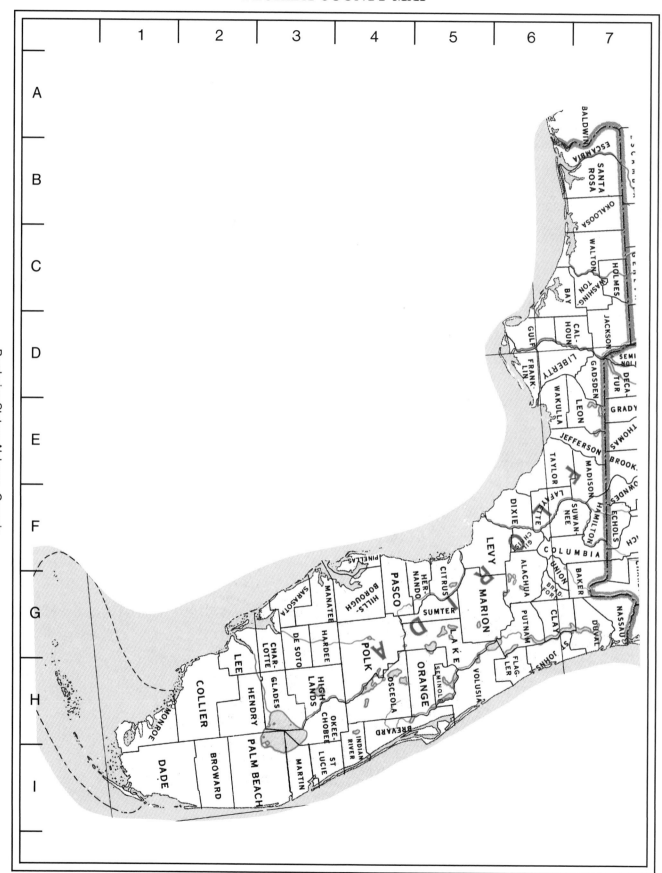

Bordering States: Alabama, Georgia

GEORGIA COUNTY MAP

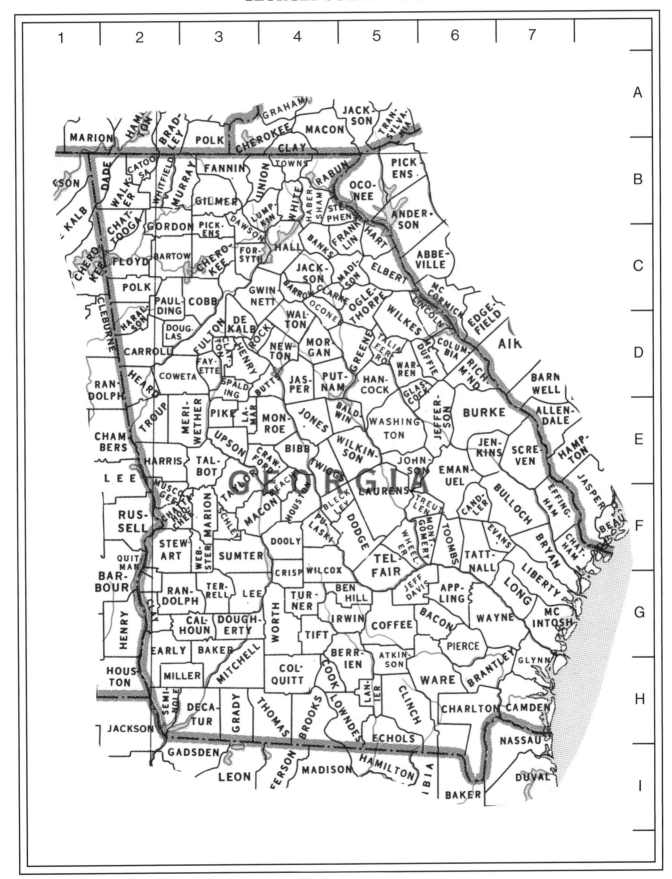

Bordering States: Tennessee, North Carolina, South Carolina, Florida, Alabama

HAWAII COUNTY MAP

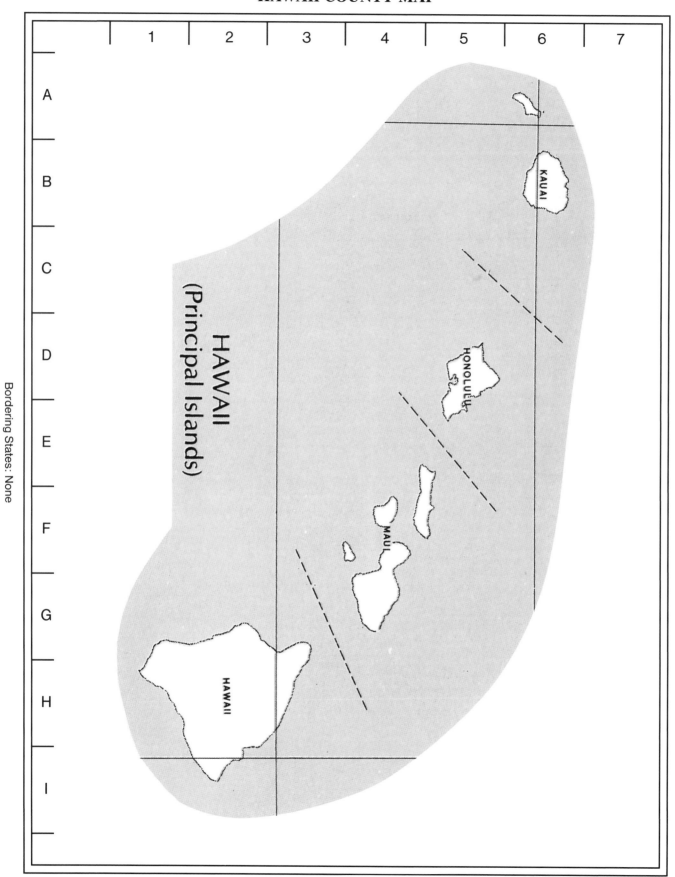

Bordering States: None

HAWAII
(Principal Islands)

KAUAI

HONOLULU

MAUI

HAWAII

IDAHO COUNTY MAP

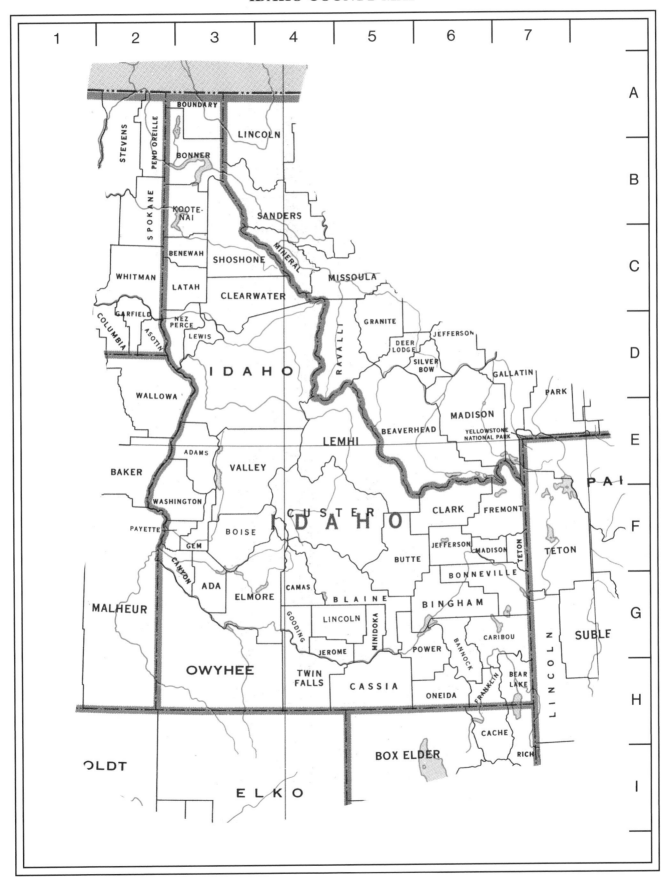

Bordering States: Montana, Wyoming, Utah, Nevada, Oregon, Washington

ILLINOIS COUNTY MAP

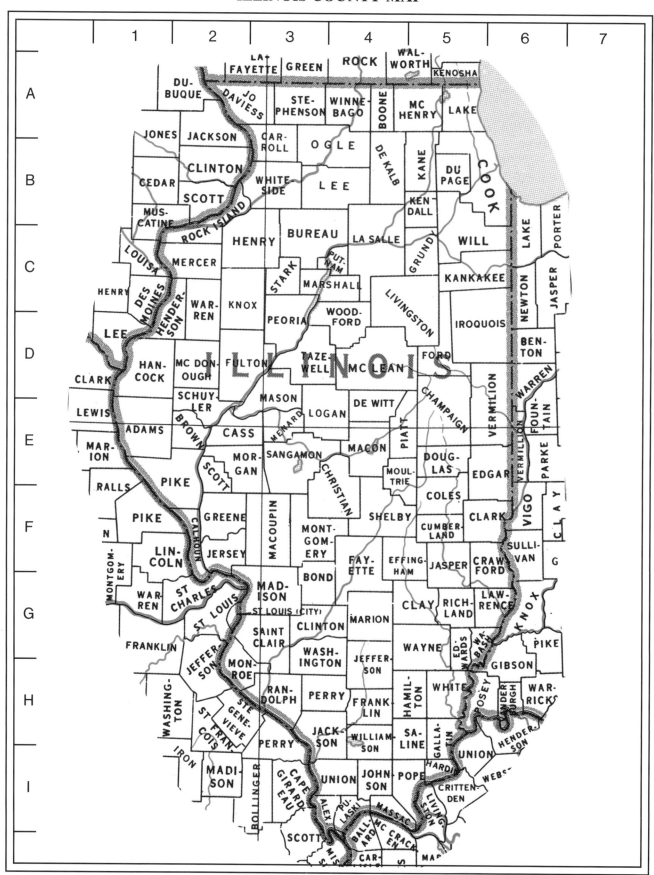

Bordering States: Wisconsin, Indiana, Kentucky, Missouri, Iowa

INDIANA COUNTY MAP

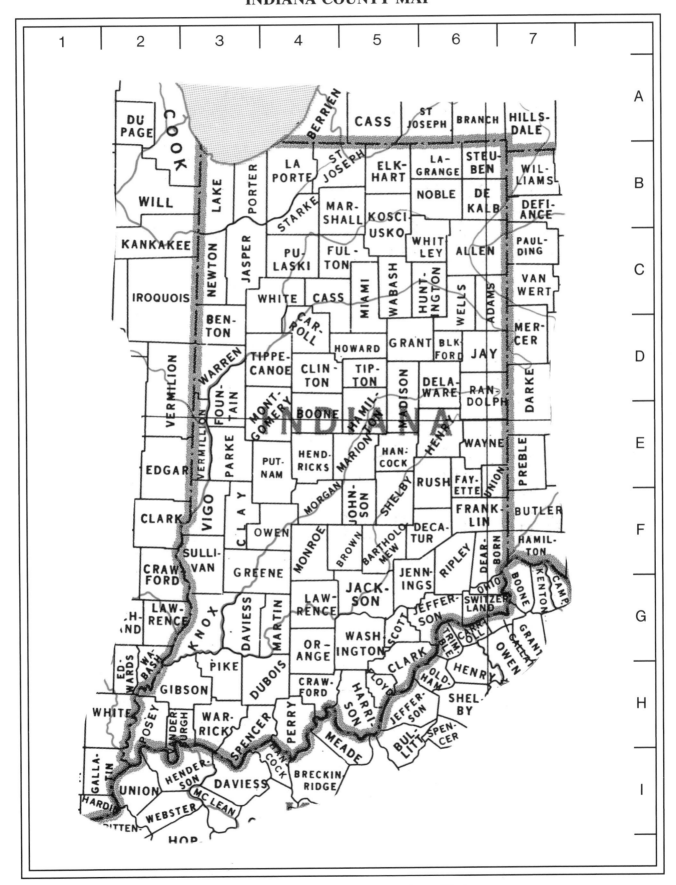

Bordering States: Michigan, Ohio, Kentucky, Illinois

IOWA COUNTY MAP

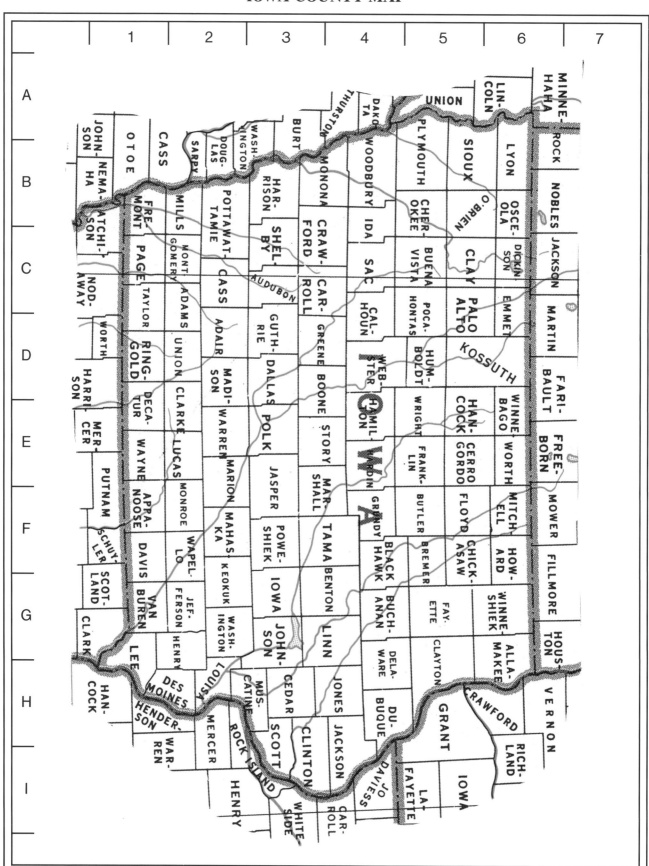

KANSAS COUNTY MAP

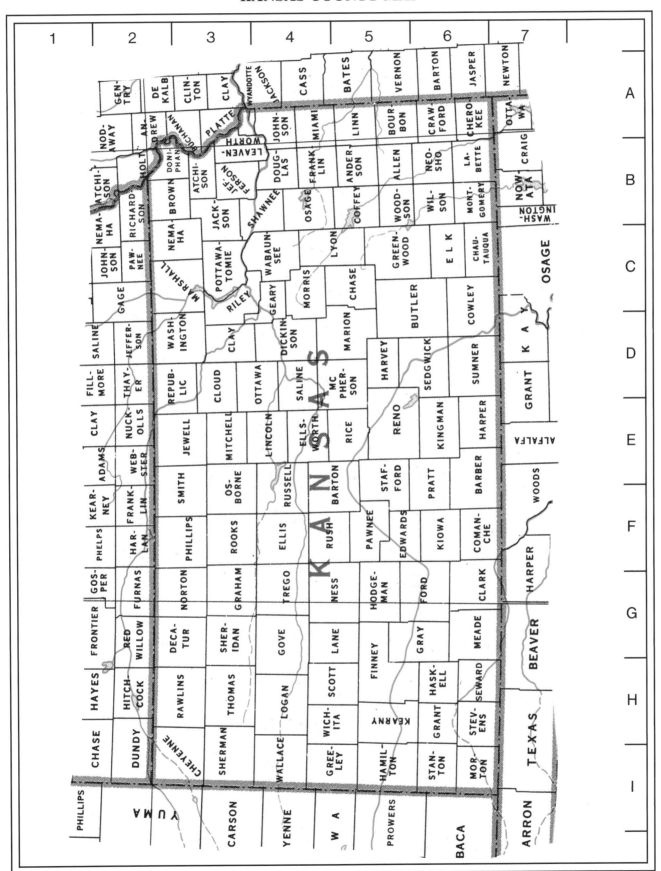

Bordering States: Nebraska, Missouri, Oklahoma, Colorado

Bordering States: Nebraska, Missouri, Oklahoma, Colorado

KENTUCKY COUNTY MAP

Bordering States: Indiana, Ohio, West Virginia, Virginia, Tennessee, Missouri, Illinois

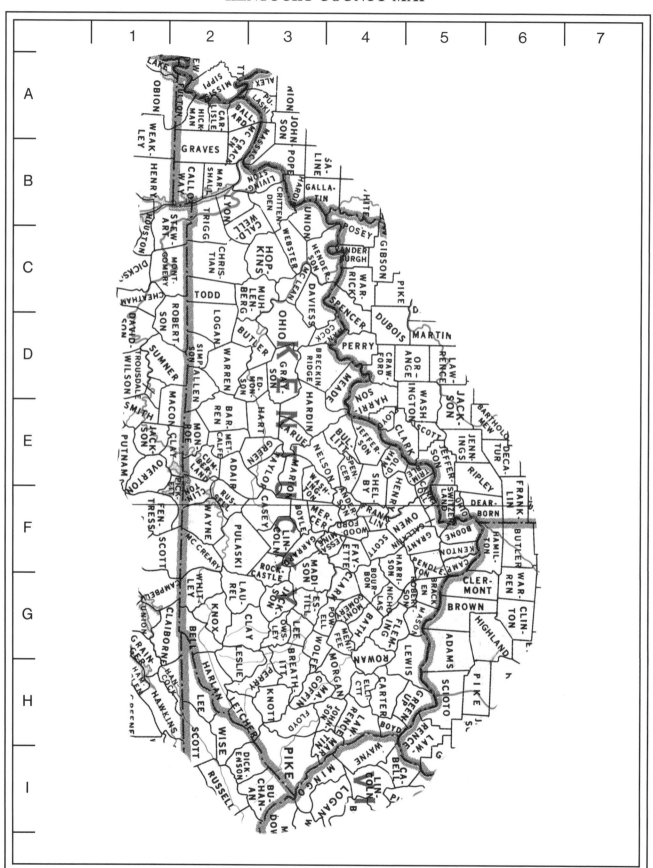

LOUISIANA COUNTY MAP

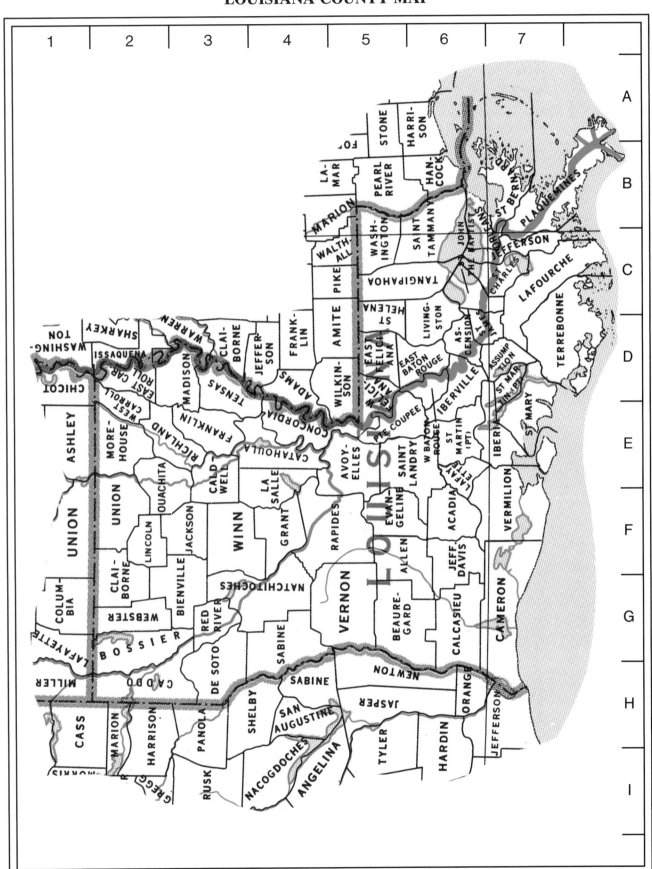

Bordering States: Arkansas, Mississippi, Texas

MAINE COUNTY MAP

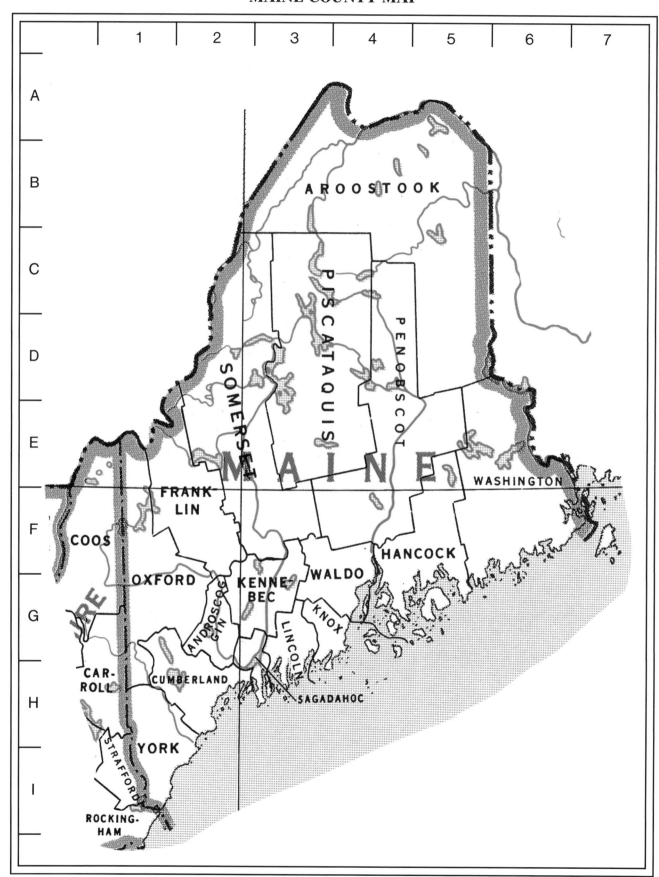

Bordering State: New Hampshire

MARYLAND COUNTY MAP

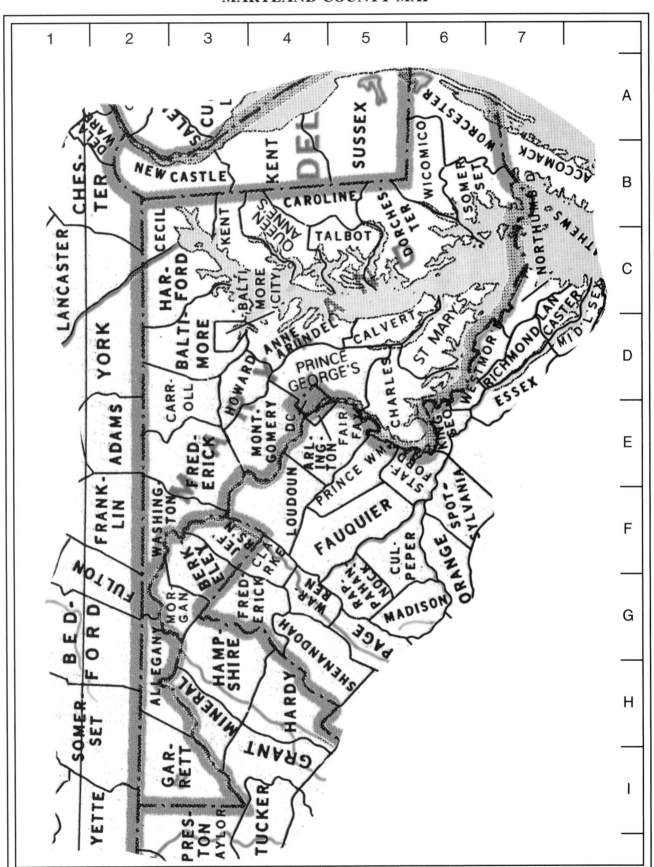

Bordering States: Pennsylvania, Delaware, Virginia, West Virginia

MICHIGAN COUNTY MAP

Bordering States: Ohio, Indiana, Wisconsin

MINNESOTA COUNTY MAP

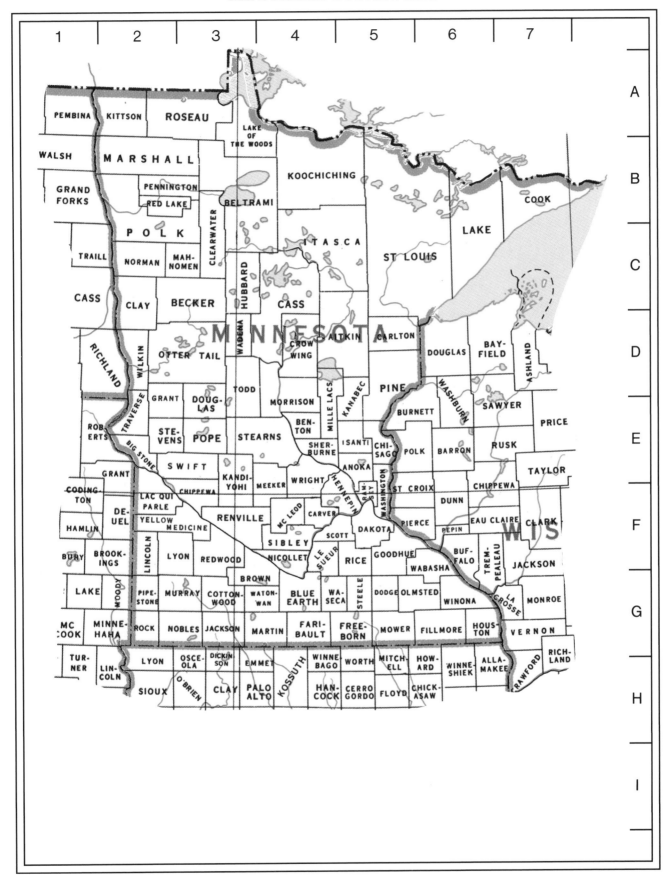

Bordering States: Wisconsin, Iowa, South Dakota, North Dakota

MISSISSIPPI COUNTY MAP

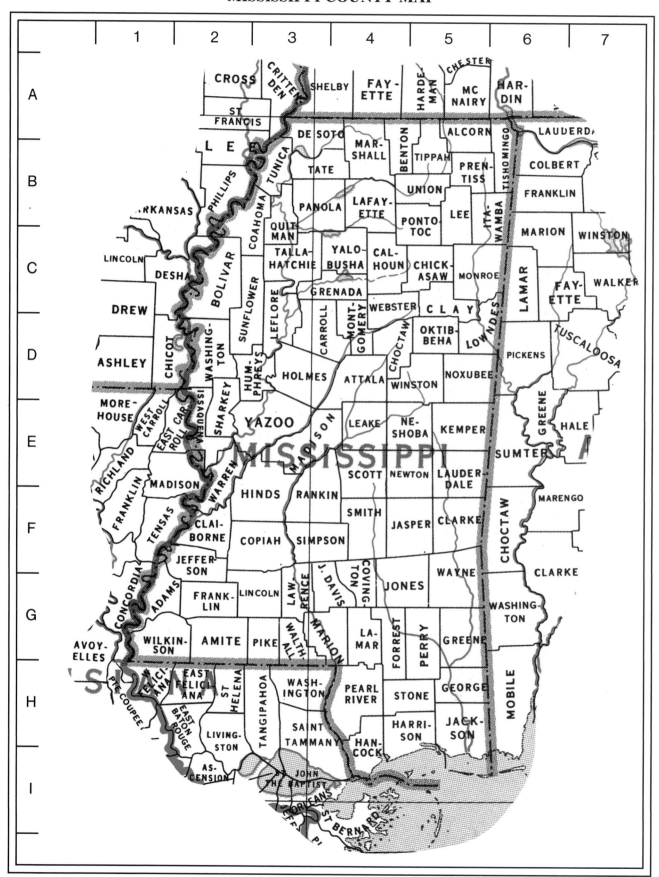

Bordering States: Tennessee, Alabama, Louisiana, Arkansas

MISSOURI COUNTY MAP

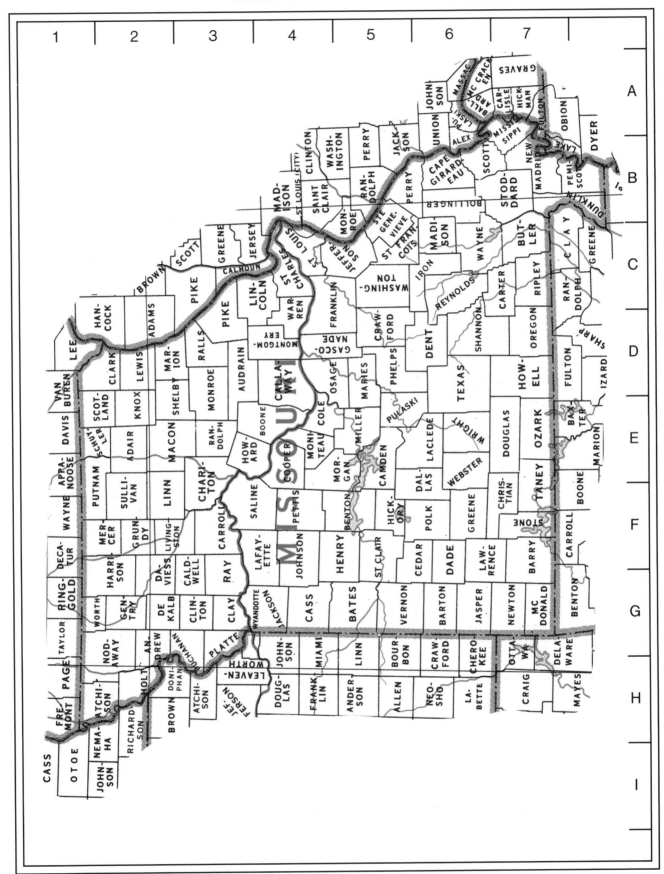

Bordering States: Iowa, Illinois, Kentucy, Tennessee, Arkansas, Oklahoma, Kansas, Nebraska

MONTANA COUNTY MAP

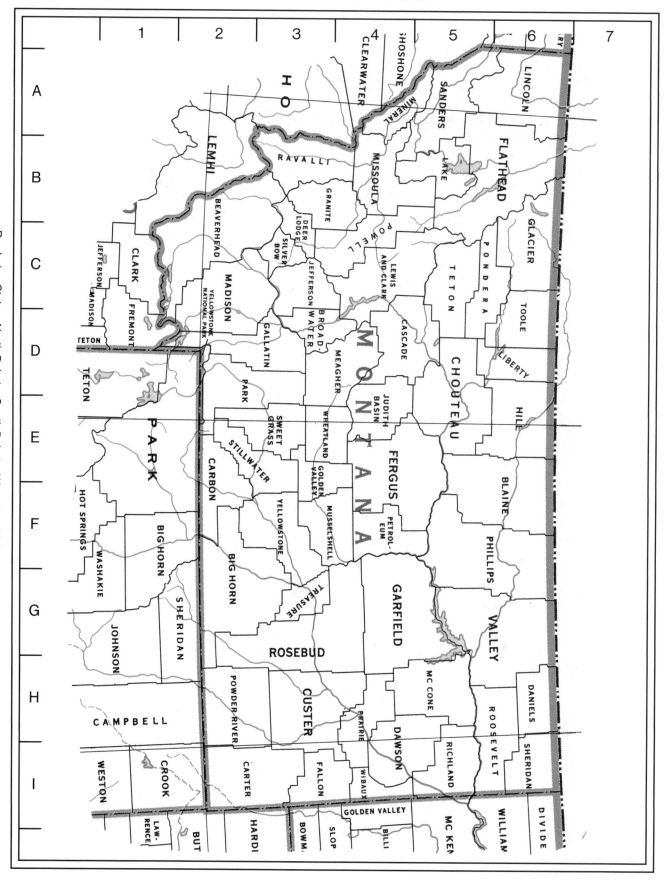

NEBRASKA COUNTY MAP

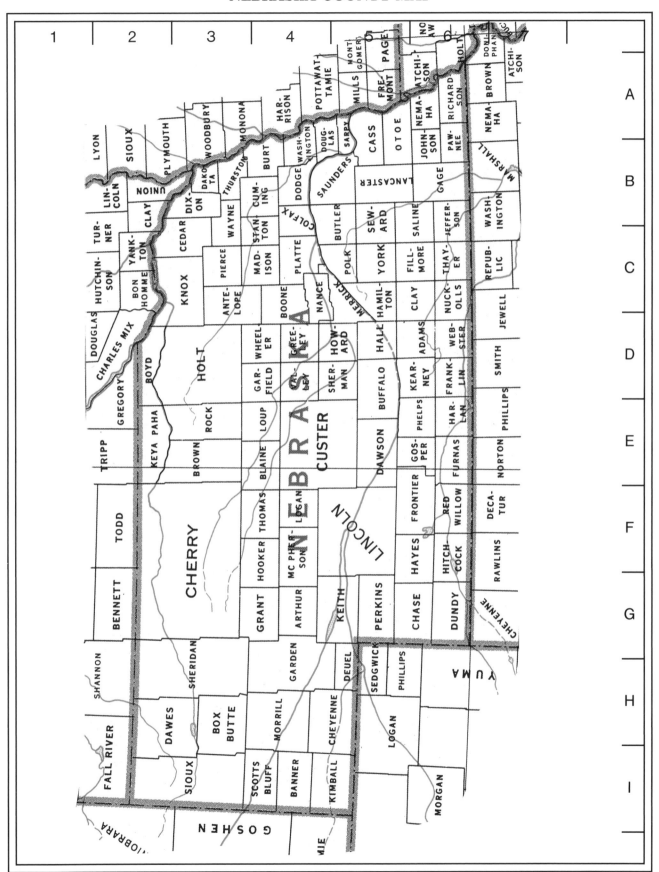

Bordering States: South Dakota, Iowa, Missouri, Kansas, Colorado, Wyoming

NEVADA COUNTY MAP

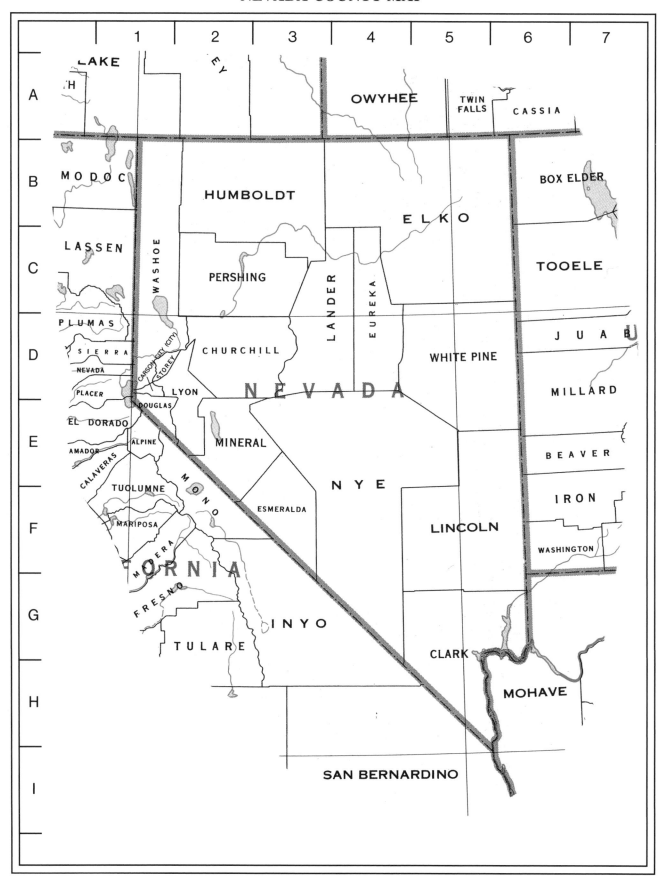

Bordering States: Oregon, Idaho, Utah, Arizona, California

NEW HAMPSHIRE, VERMONT COUNTY MAP

Bordering States: Maine, Massachusetts, New York

NEW JERSEY, DELAWARE COUNTY MAP

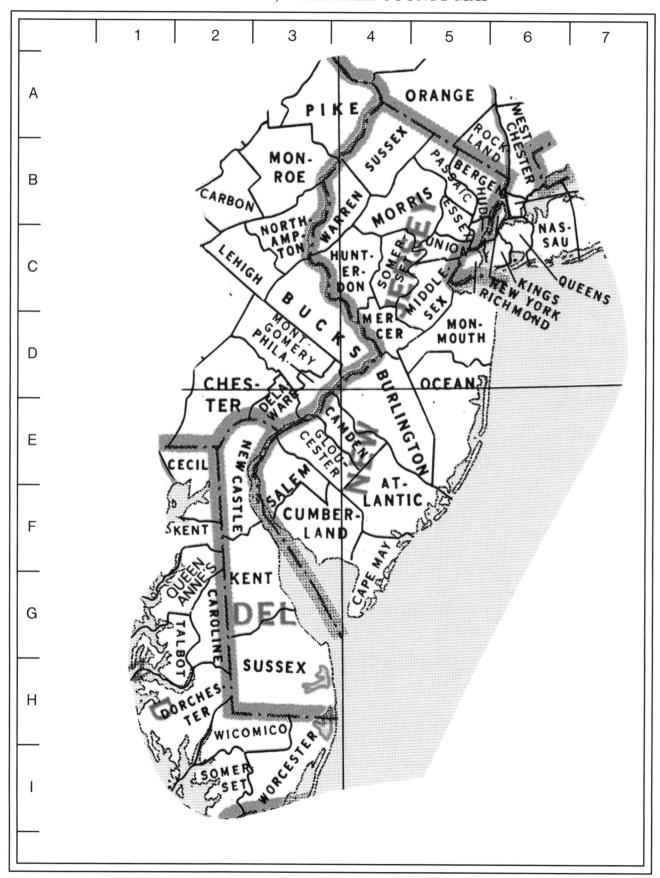

Bordering States: New York, Maryland, Pennsylvania

NEW MEXICO COUNTY MAP

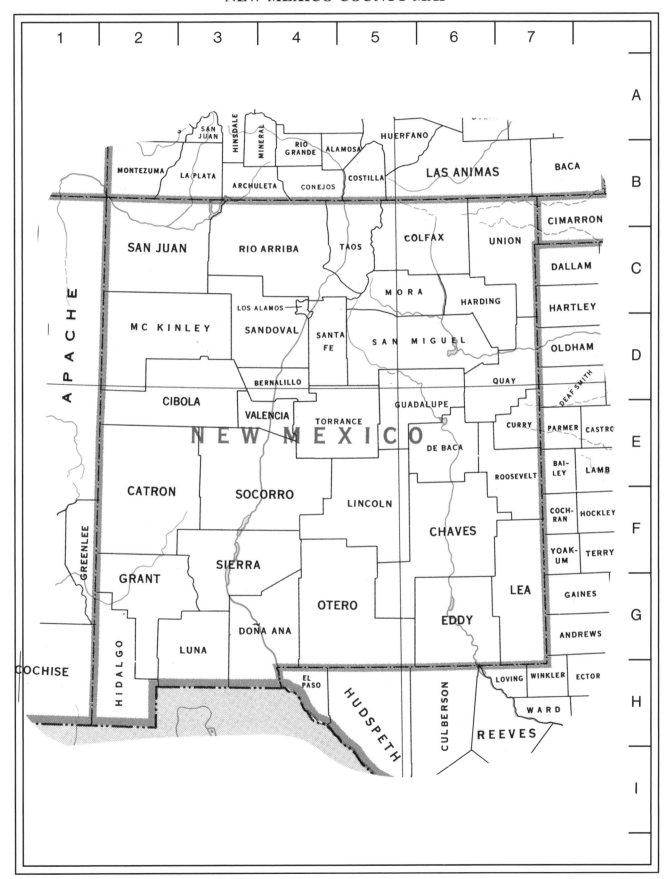

Bordering States: Colorado, Oklahoma, Texas, Arizona, Utah

NEW YORK COUNTY MAP

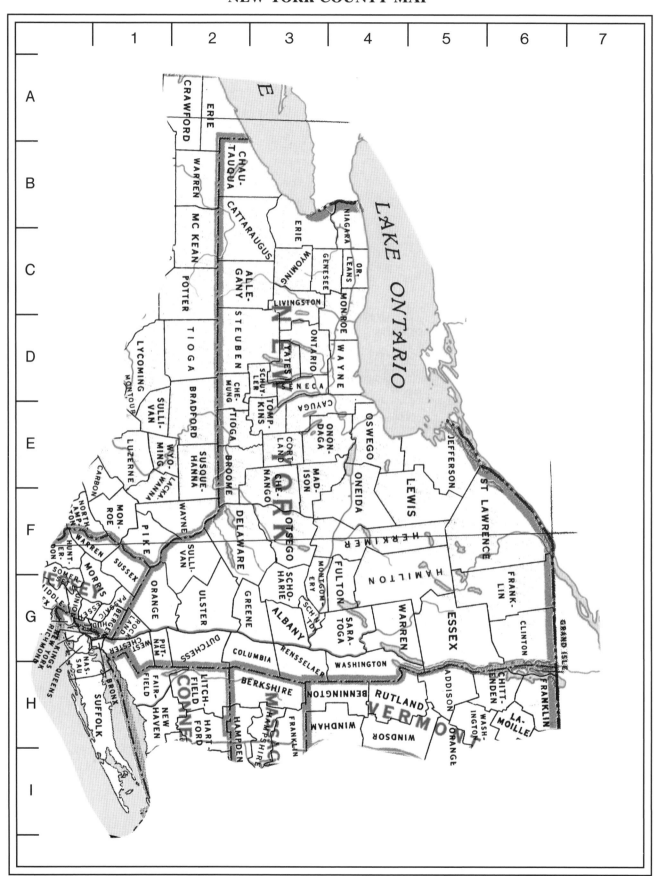

Bordering States: Vermont, Massachusetts, Connecticut, Pennsylvania

NORTH CAROLINA COUNTY MAP

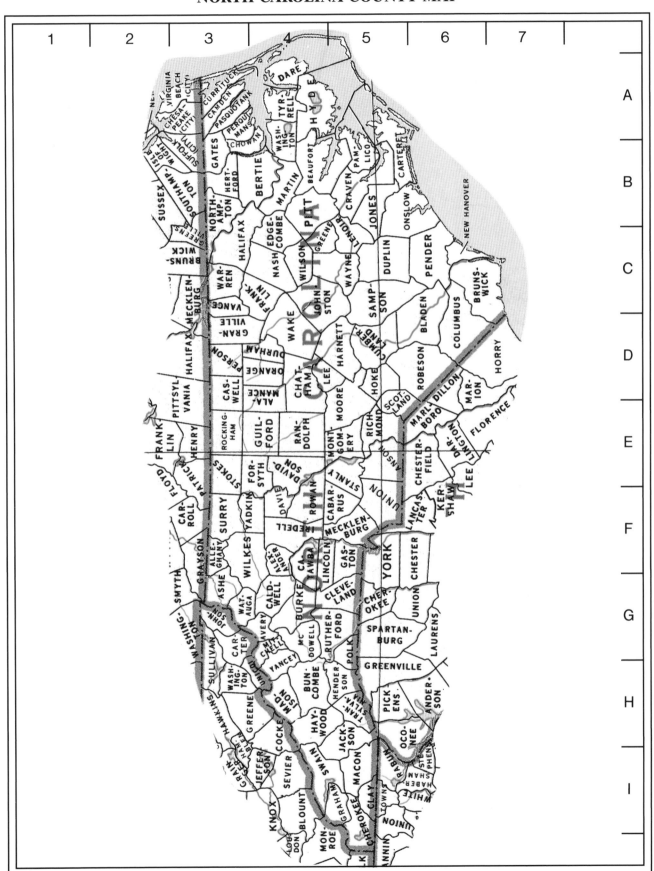

Bordering States: Virginia, South Carolina, Georgia, Tennessee

NORTH DAKOTA COUNTY MAP

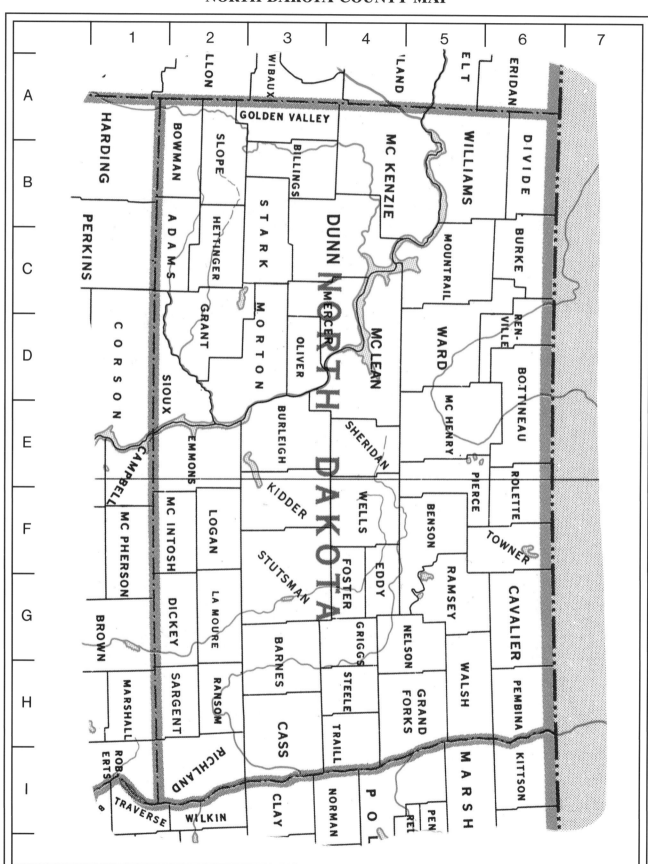

Bordering States: Minnesota, South Dakota, Montana

OHIO COUNTY MAP

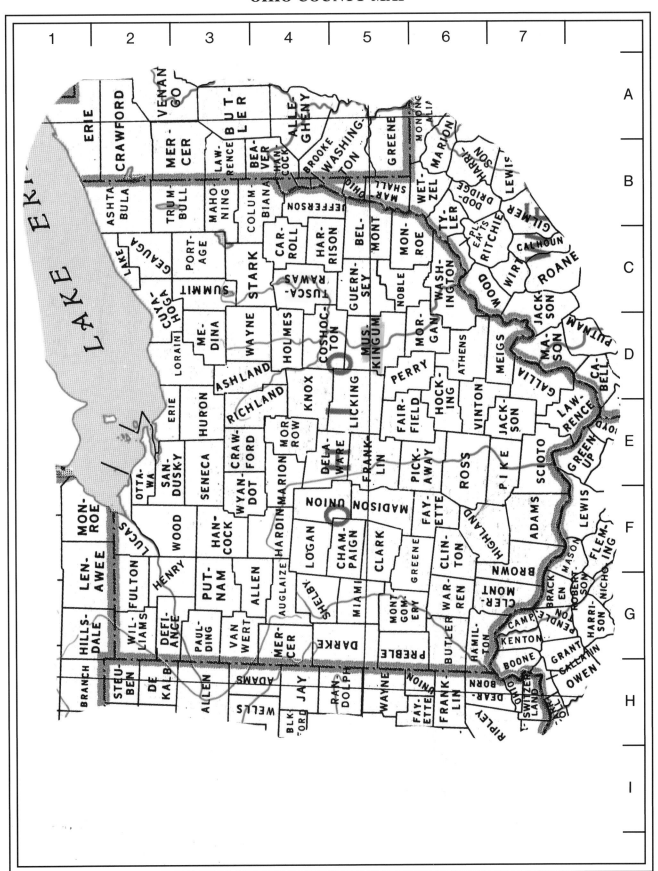

Bordering States: Michigan, Pennsylvania, West Virginia, Kentucky, Indiana

OKLAHOMA COUNTY MAP

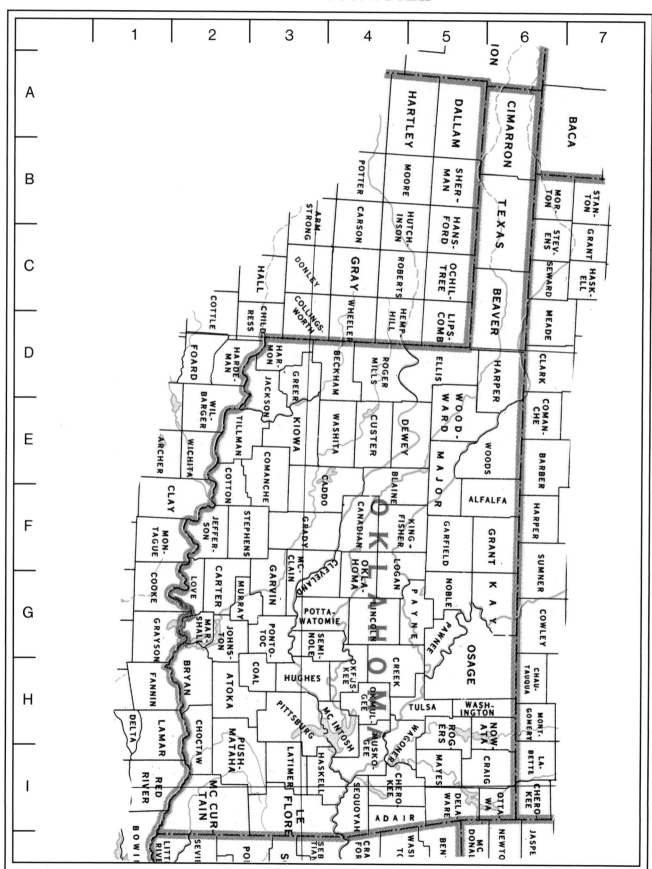

Bordering States: Kansas, Missouri, Arkansas, Texas, New Mexico, Colorado

OREGON COUNTY MAP

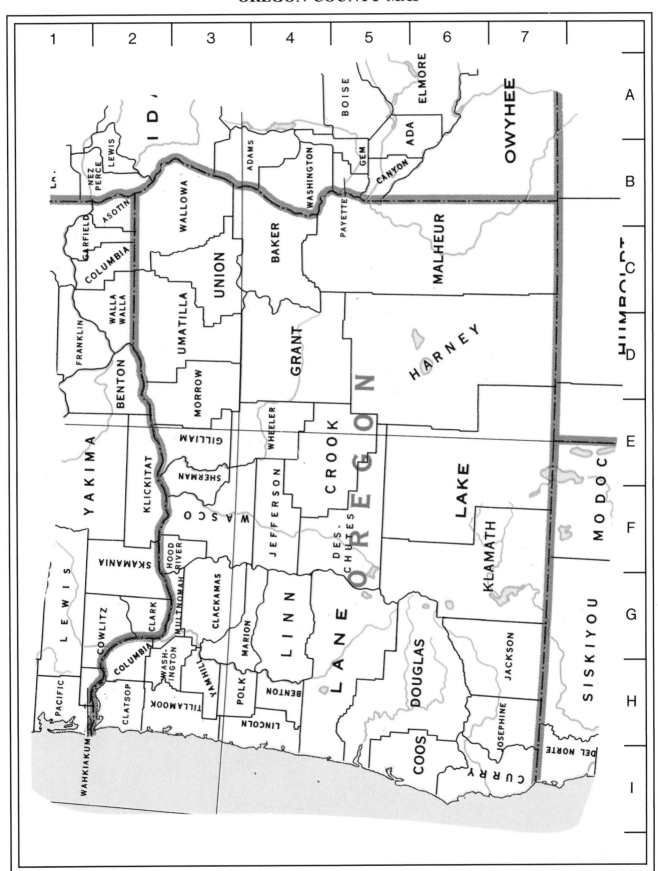

Bordering States: Washington, Idaho, Nevada, California

PENNSYLVANIA COUNTY MAP

Bordering States: New York, New Jersey, Delaware, Maryland, West Virginia, Ohio

SOUTH CAROLINA COUNTY MAP

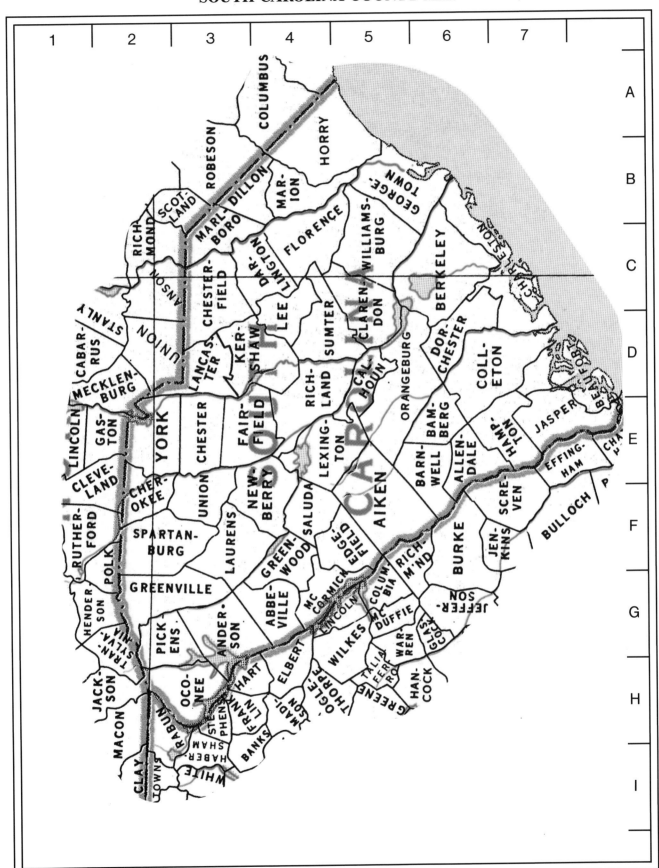

Bordering States: North Carolina, Georgia

SOUTH DAKOTA COUNTY MAP

Bordering States: North Dakota, Minnesota, Iowa, Nebraska, Wyoming, Montana

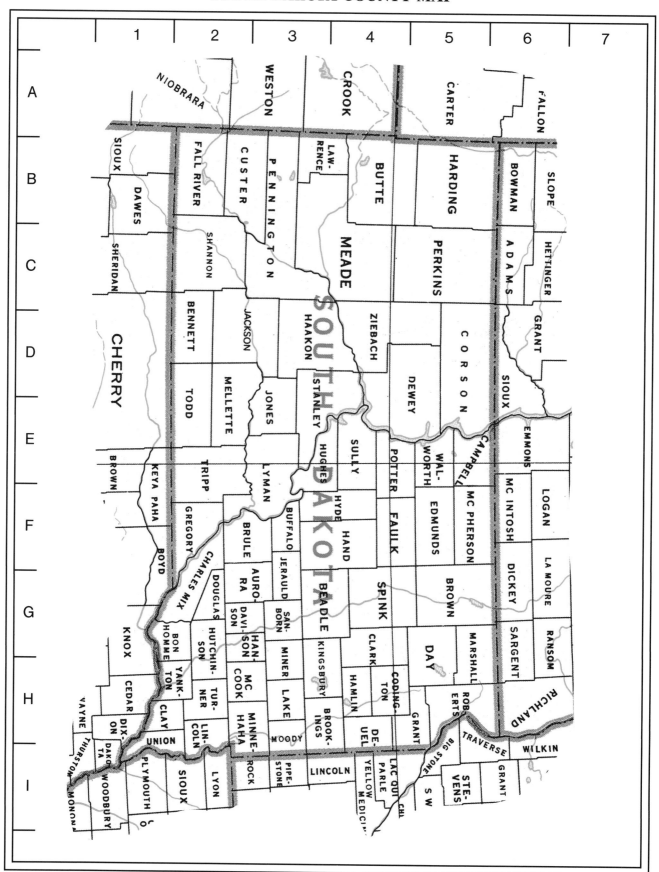

TENNESSEE COUNTY MAP

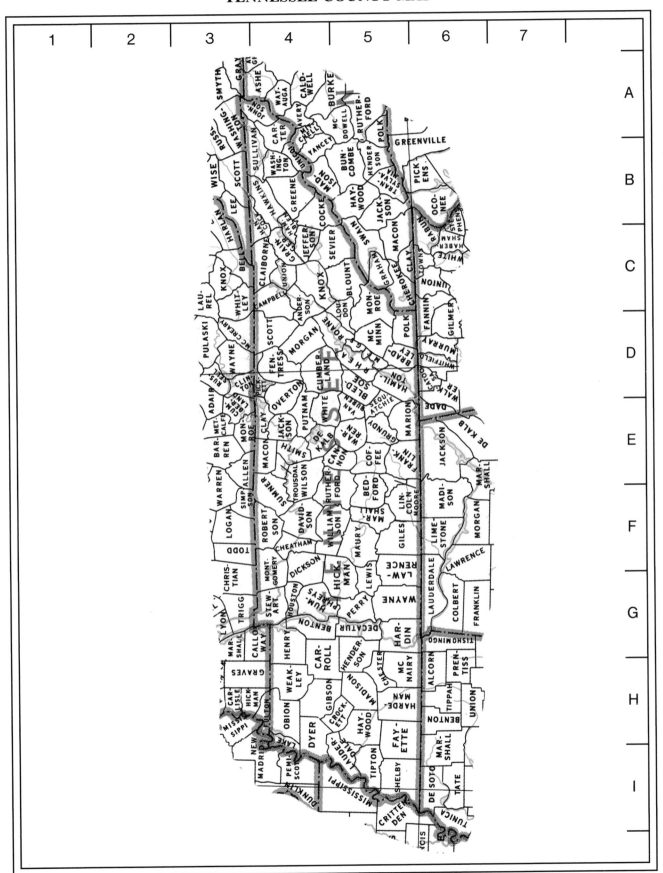

TEXAS COUNTY MAP

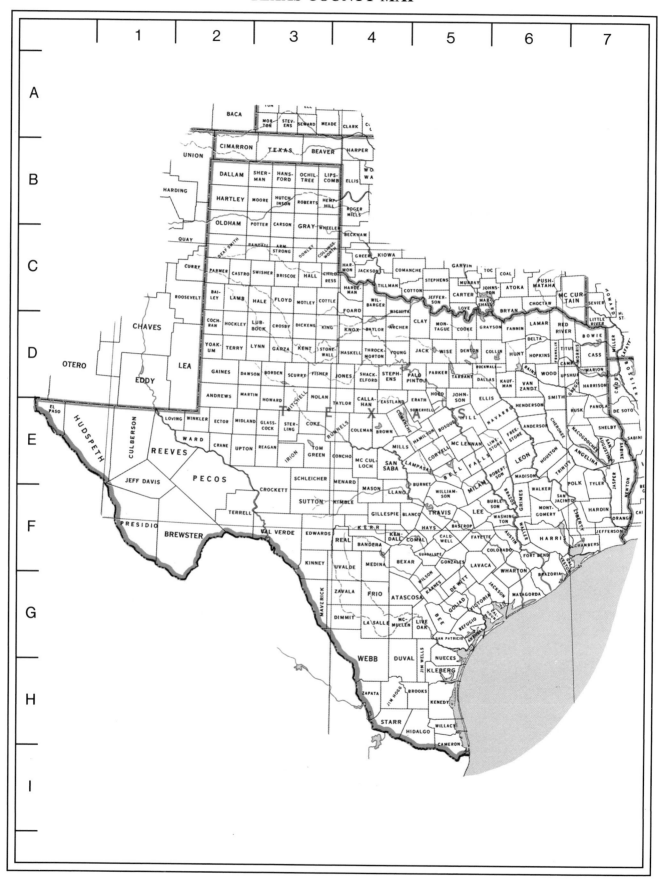

Bordering States: Oklahoma, Arkansas, Louisiana, New Mexico

UTAH COUNTY MAP

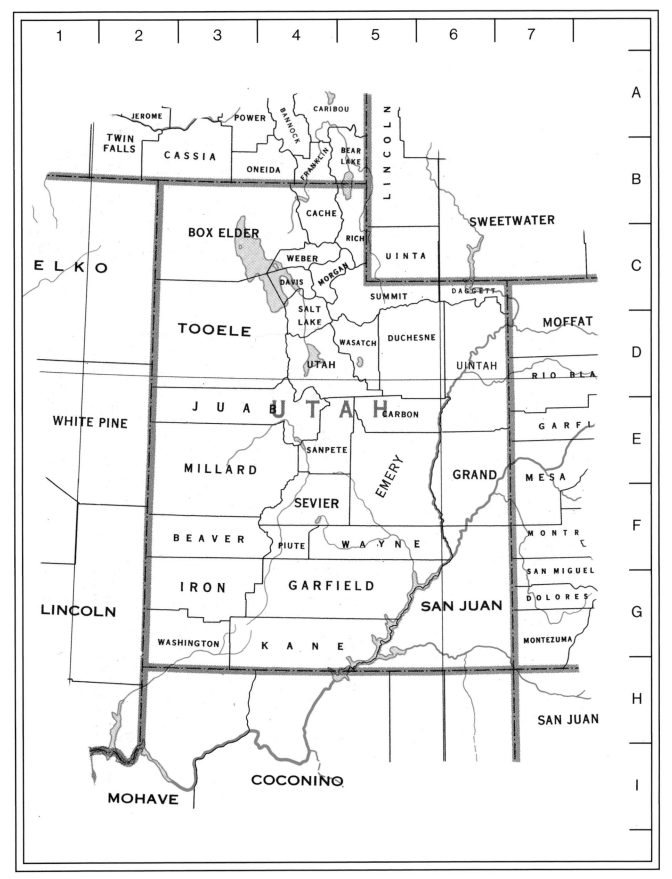

Bordering States: Idaho, Wyoming, Colorado, Arizona, Nevada

Eighth Edition of the Handy Book for Genealogists

VIRGINIA COUNTY MAP

Bordering States: West Virginia, Maryland, North Carolina, Tennessee, Kentucky

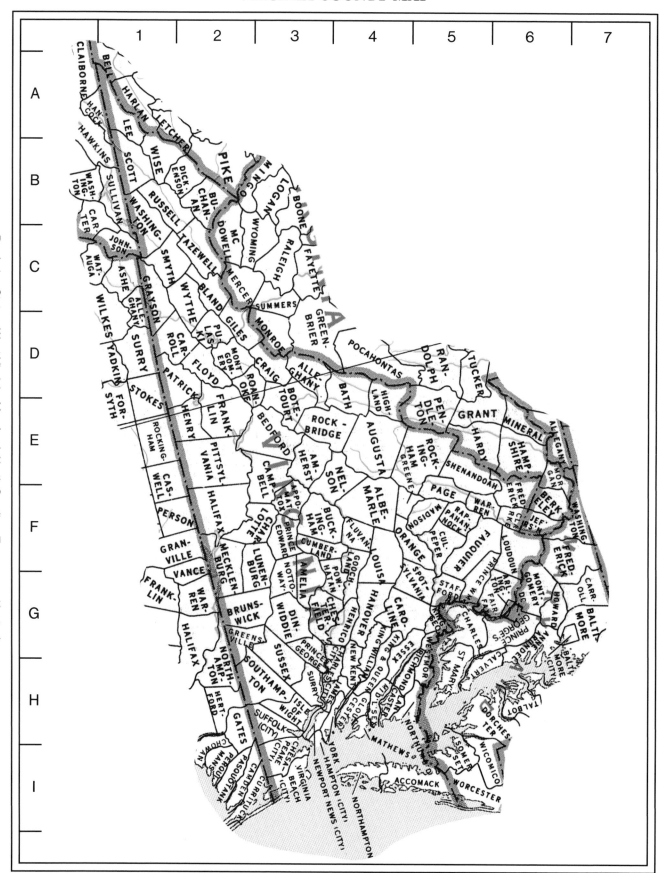

WASHINGTON COUNTY MAP

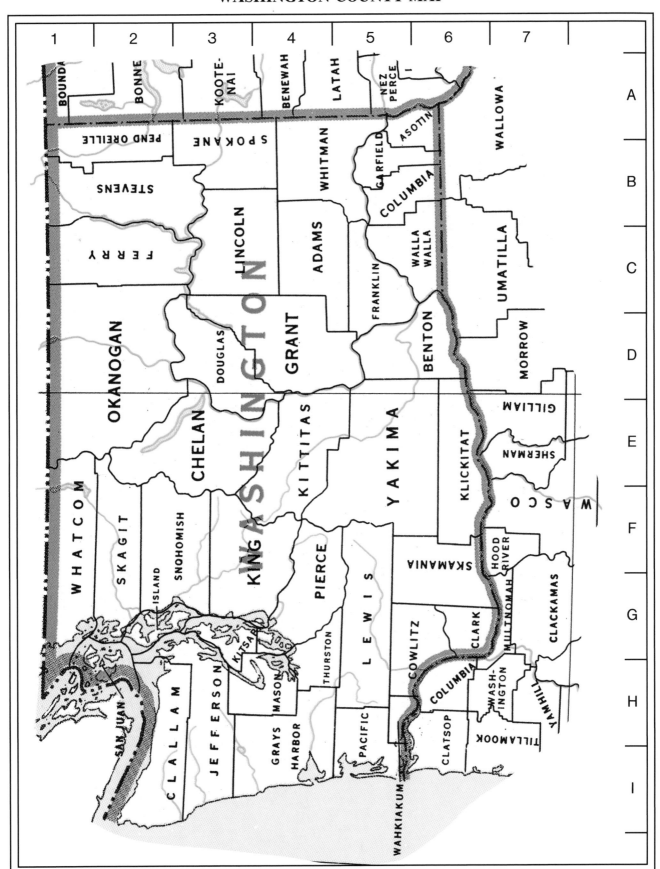

Bordering States: Idaho, Oregon

WEST VIRGINIA COUNTY MAP

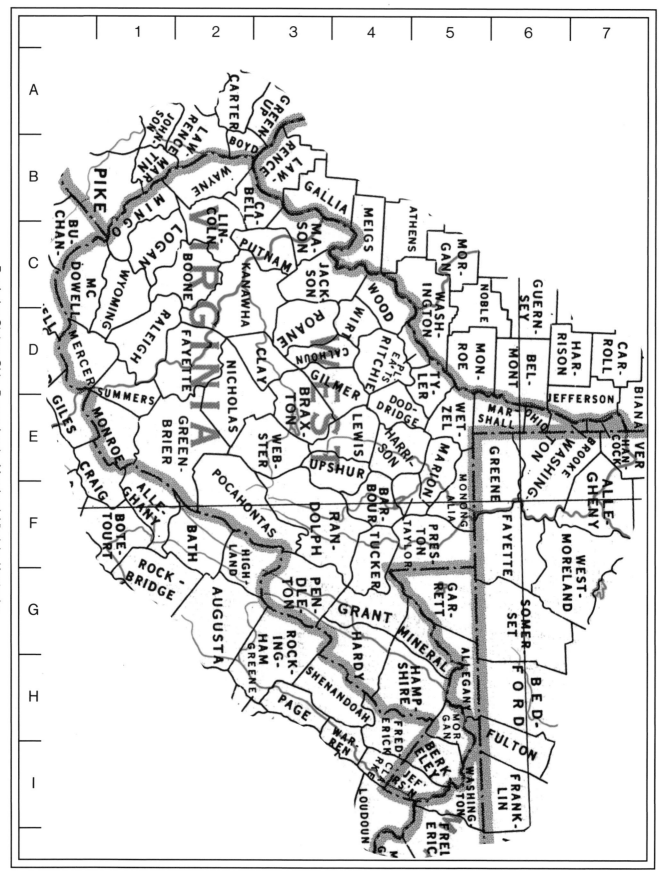

Bordering States: Ohio, Pennsylvania, Maryland, Virginia, Kentucky

WISCONSIN COUNTY MAP

Bordering States: Michigan, Illinois, Iowa, Minnesota

WYOMING COUNTY MAP

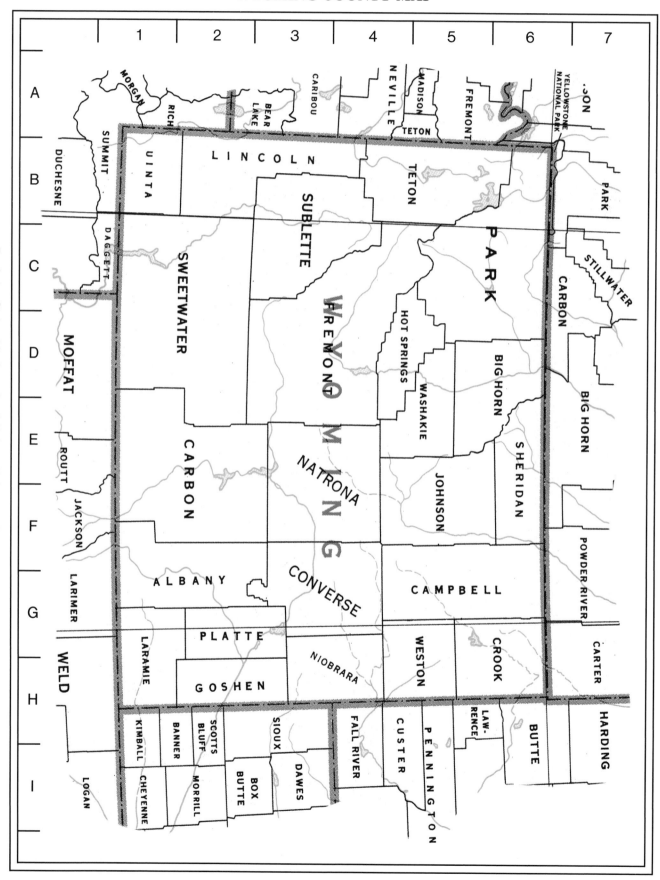

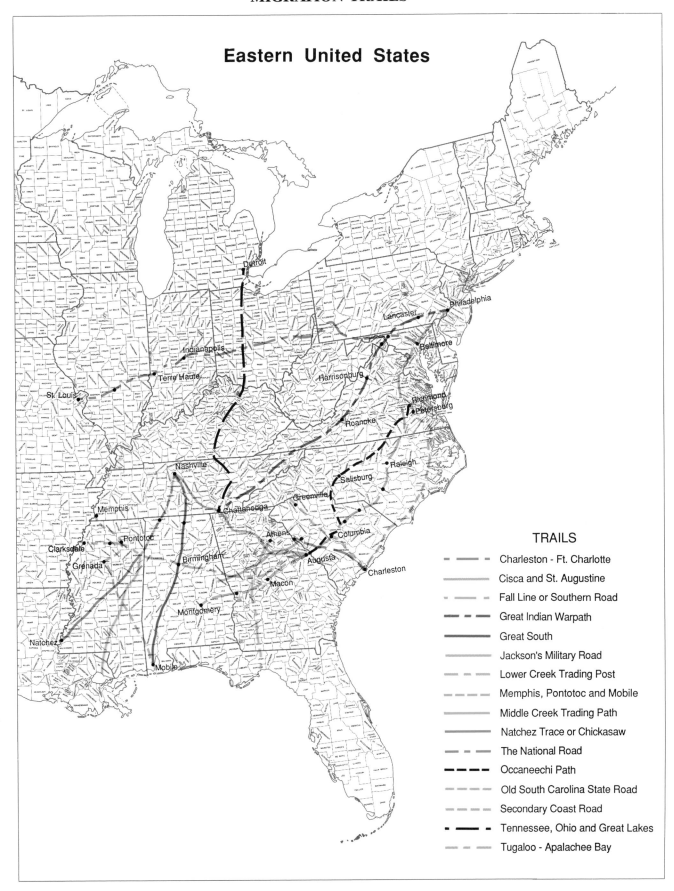

Eastern United States

TRAILS

- – – – – Charleston - Ft. Charlotte
- ———— Cisca and St. Augustine
- – – – – Fall Line or Southern Road
- ▬ ▬ ▬ Great Indian Warpath
- ▬▬▬▬ Great South
- ———— Jackson's Military Road
- – – – – Lower Creek Trading Post
- – – – – Memphis, Pontotoc and Mobile
- ———— Middle Creek Trading Path
- ———— Natchez Trace or Chickasaw
- – ▬ – ▬ The National Road
- ▬ ▬ ▬ Occaneechi Path
- – – – – Old South Carolina State Road
- – – – – Secondary Coast Road
- ▬ ▬ ▬ Tennessee, Ohio and Great Lakes
- – – – – Tugaloo - Apalachee Bay

MIGRATION TRAILS

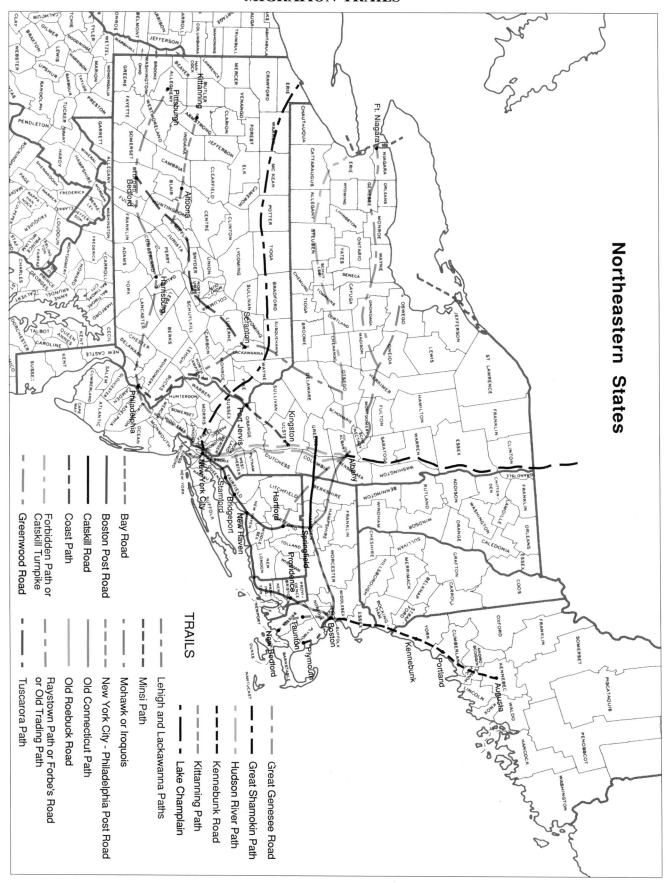

Northeastern States

TRAILS

Bay Road

Boston Post Road

Catskill Road

Coast Path

Forbidden Path or
Catskill Turnpike

Greenwood Road

Lehigh and Lackawanna Paths

Minsi Path

Mohawk or Iroquois

New York City – Philadelphia Post Road

Old Connecticut Path

Old Roebuck Road

Raystown Path or Forbe's Road
or Old Trading Path

Tuscarora Path

Great Genesee Road

Great Shamokin Path

Hudson River Path

Kennebunk Road

Kittanning Path

Lake Champlain

MIGRATION TRAILS

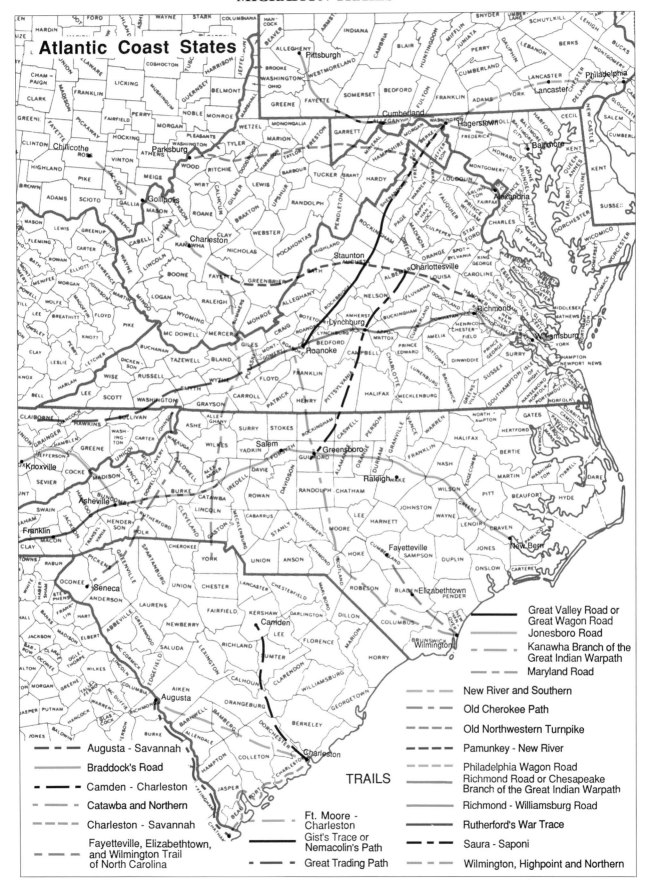

Atlantic Coast States

TRAILS

Great Valley Road or
Great Wagon Road

Jonesboro Road

Kanawha Branch of the
Great Indian Warpath

Maryland Road

New River and Southern

Old Cherokee Path

Old Northwestern Turnpike

Pamunkey - New River

Philadelphia Wagon Road

Richmond Road or Chesapeake
Branch of the Great Indian Warpath

Richmond - Williamsburg Road

Rutherford's War Trace

Saura - Saponi

Wilmington, Highpoint and Northern

Augusta - Savannah

Braddock's Road

Camden - Charleston

Catawba and Northern

Charleston - Savannah

Fayetteville, Elizabethtown,
and Wilmington Trail
of North Carolina

Ft. Moore -
Charleston

Gist's Trace or
Nemacolin's Path

Great Trading Path

MIGRATION TRAILS

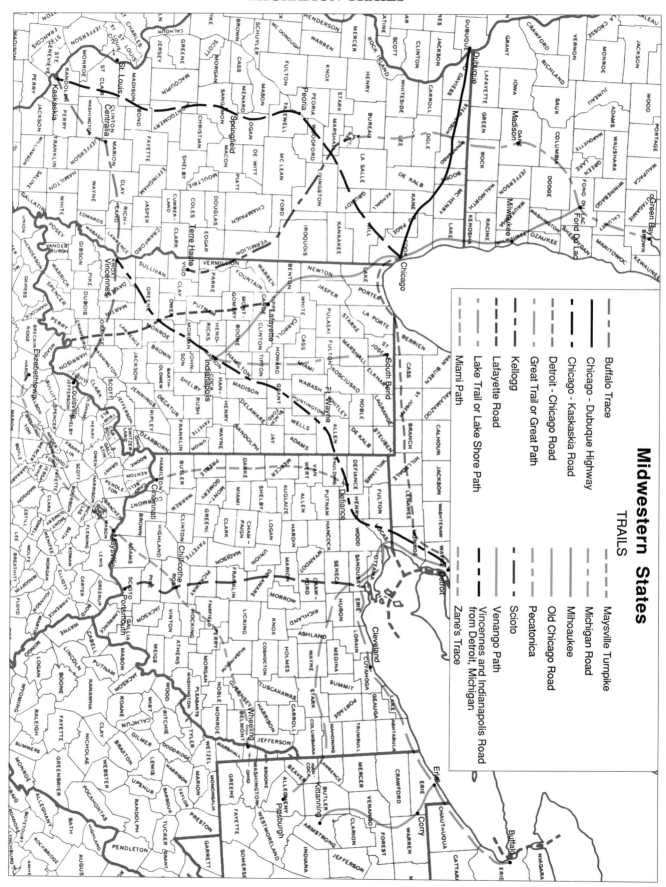

MIGRATION TRAILS

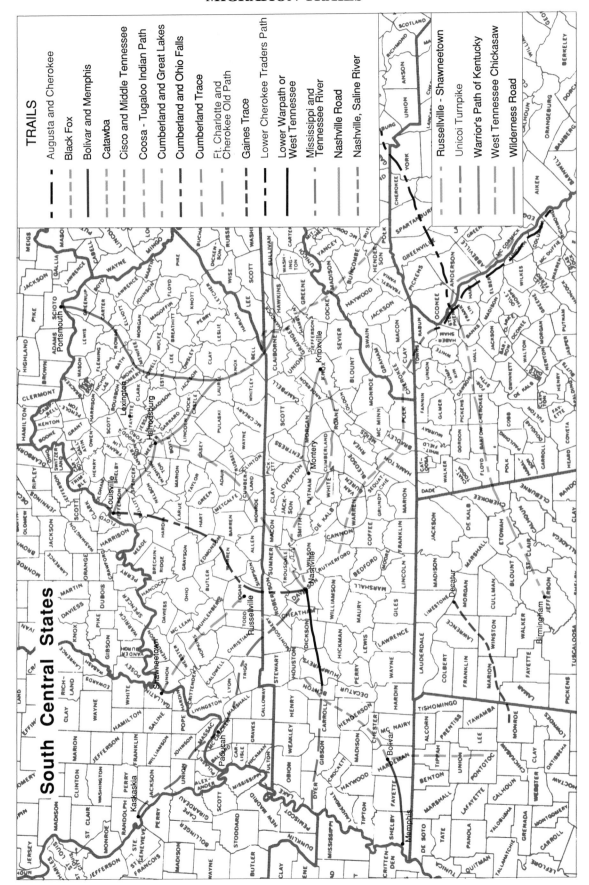

TRAILS

- — · — Augusta and Cherokee
- — · — Black Fox
- ———— Bolivar and Memphis
- Catawba
- — · · — Cisco and Middle Tennessee
- — · — Coosa - Tugaloo Indian Path
- — · — Cumberland and Great Lakes
- — · · — Cumberland and Ohio Falls
- ———— Cumberland Trace
- · · · · · · Ft. Charlotte and Cherokee Old Path
- — · — Gaines Trace
- — · · — Lower Cherokee Traders Path
- ———— Lower Warpath or West Tennessee
- ———— Mississippi and Tennessee River
- ———— Nashville Road
- Nashville, Saline River
- — · — Russellville - Shawneetown
- Unicoi Turnpike
- — · — Warrior's Path of Kentucky
- West Tennessee Chickasaw
- — · — Wilderness Road

South Central States

MIGRATION TRAILS

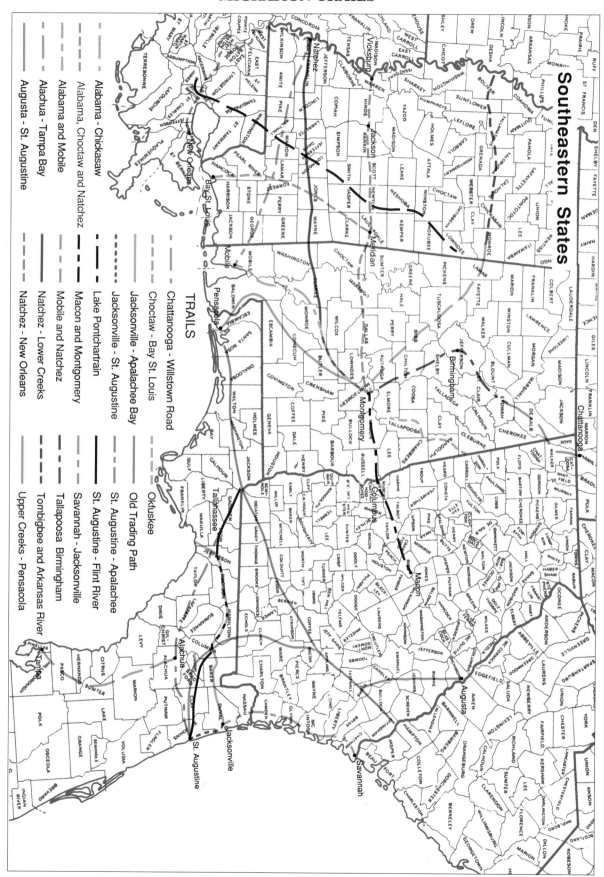

TRAILS

- Alabama - Chickasaw
- Alabama, Choctaw and Natchez
- Alabama and Mobile
- Alachua - Tampa Bay
- Augusta - St. Augustine
- Chattanooga - Willstown Road
- Choctaw - Bay St. Louis
- Jacksonville - Apalachee Bay
- Jacksonville - St. Augustine
- Lake Pontchartrain
- Macon and Montgomery
- Mobile and Natchez
- Natchez - Lower Creeks
- Natchez - New Orleans
- Oktuskee
- Old Trading Path
- St. Augustine - Apalachee
- St. Augustine - Flint River
- Savannah - Jacksonville
- Tallapoosa Birmingham
- Tombigbee and Arkansas River
- Upper Creeks - Pensacola

Southeastern States

CANALS AND THE CUMBERLAND ROAD 1785 - 1850

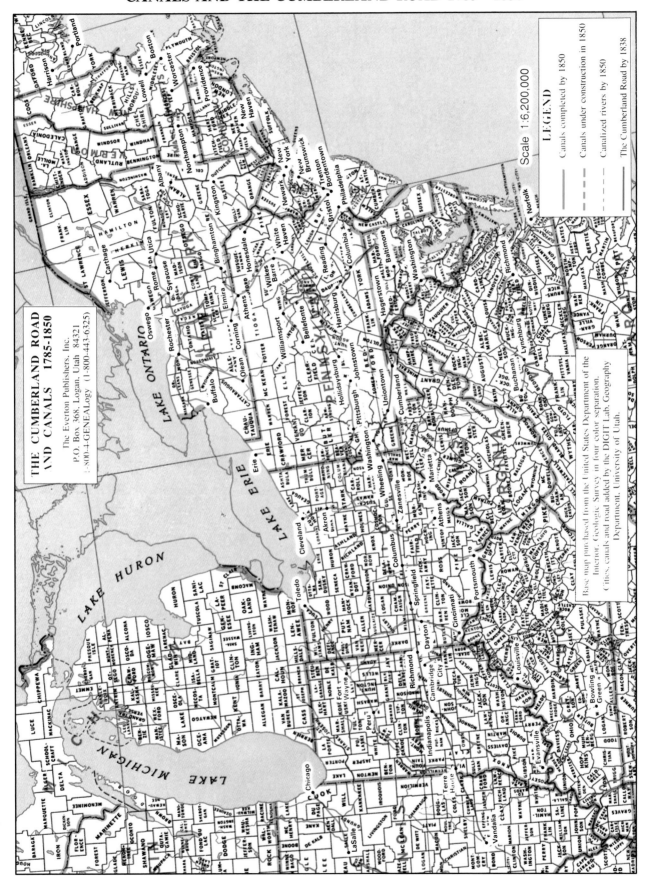

RAILROADS BY 1860

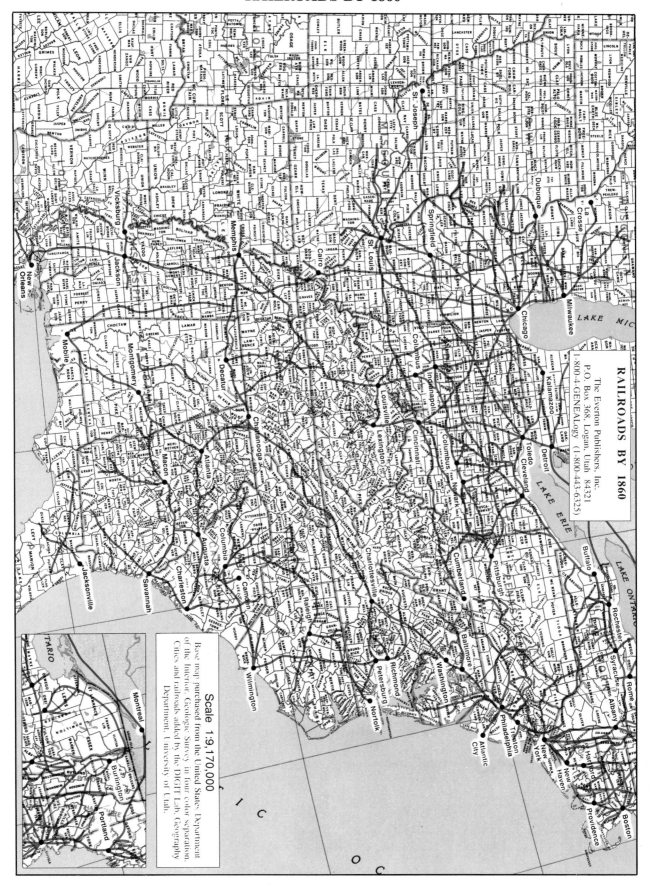

RAILROADS BY 1860

The Everton Publishers, Inc.
P.O. Box 368, Logan, Utah 84321
1-800-4-GENEALogy (1-800-443-6325)

Scale 1:9,170,000

Base map purchased from the United States Department
of the Interior, Geologic Survey in four color separation.
Cities and railroads added by the DIGIT Lab, Geography
Department, University of Utah.

TERRITORIAL GROWTH — 1775 - 1820

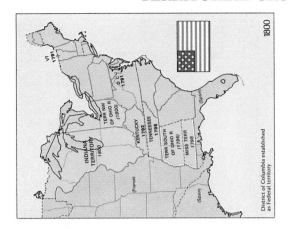

1800

Indiana Territory 1800
TERR. NW OF OHIO R. (1800)
KENTUCKY 1792
TENNESSEE 1796
TERR. SOUTH OF OHIO R. (1790)
MISS. TERR. 1798
VT 1791
(France)
(Spain)

District of Columbia established as Federal territory

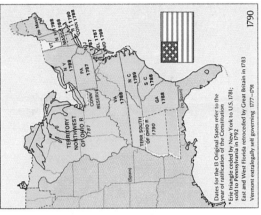

1790

TERRITORY NORTHWEST OF OHIO R. 1787
VT 1791
N.H. 1788
MASS 1788
CONN 1788
N.Y. 1788
PA. 1787
DEL. 1787
MD. 1788
VA. 1788
N.C. 1789
S.C. 1788
GA. 1788
TERR. SOUTH OF OHIO R. 1790
CONN. RESERVE
(to Mass.)
N.J. 1787
R.I. 1790
(Spain)
(to Spain)

Dates for the 13 Original States refer to the year of ratification of the Constitution

* Erie triangle ceded by New York to U.S. 1781; sold to Pennsylvania in 1792

East and West Florida retroceded by Great Britain in 1783

Vermont extralegally self governing 1777–1791

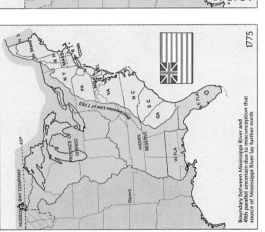

1775

HUDSON'S BAY COMPANY
N.H.
N.Y.
MASS.
CONN.
R.I.
PA.
N.J.
PROVINCE OF QUEBEC
VA.
N.C.
S.C.
GA.
INDIAN RESERVE
W. FLA.
E. FLA.
Proclamation Line of 1763
(to Mass.)
(Spain)

Boundary between Mississippi River and 49th parallel uncertain due to misconception that source of Mississippi River lay further north

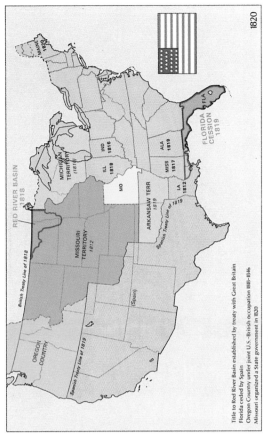

1820

RED RIVER BASIN 1818
MAINE 1820
MICHIGAN TERRITORY (1819)
IND. 1816
ILL. 1818
MO
MISSOURI TERRITORY 1812
ALA 1819
MISS 1817
LA 1812
ARKANSAW TERR. 1819
FLORIDA FLA CESSION 1819
OREGON COUNTRY
British Treaty Line of 1818
Spanish Treaty Line of 1819
Spanish Treaty Line of 1819
(Spain)

Title to Red River Basin established by treaty with Great Britain
Florida ceded by Spain
Oregon Country under joint U.S.–British occupation 1818–1846
Missouri organized a State government in 1820

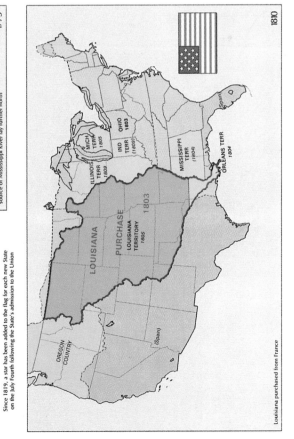

1810

OREGON COUNTRY
LOUISIANA
PURCHASE 1803
LOUISIANA TERRITORY 1805
ILLINOIS TERR. 1809
IND. TERR. (1809)
MICH. TERR. 1805
OHIO 1803
MISSISSIPPI TERR. (1804)
ORLEANS TERR. 1804
(Spain)
(Spain)

Louisiana purchased from France

TERRITORIAL GROWTH

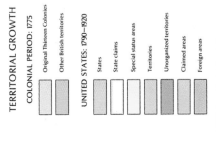

COLONIAL PERIOD: 1775

Original Thirteen Colonies

Other British territories

UNITED STATES: 1790–1920

States

State claims

Special status areas

Territories

Unorganized territories

Claimed areas

Foreign areas

1803 Dates of territorial acquisitions
1805 Dates of initial territorial organization
(1809) Dates of latest change within given time period
1812 Dates of admission to the Union

Since 1819, a star has been added to the flag for each new State on the July Fourth following the State's admission to the Union

TERRITORIAL GROWTH — 1830 – 1860

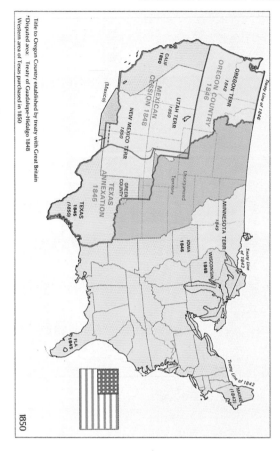

1830

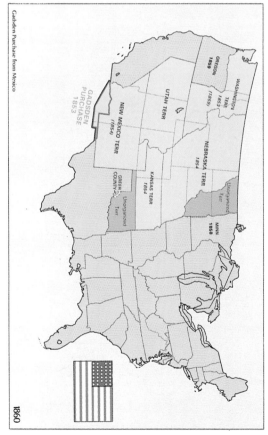

Title to Oregon Country established by treaty with Great Britain
*Disputed area: Treaty of Guadalupe-Hidalgo 1848
Western area of Texas purchased in 1850

1850

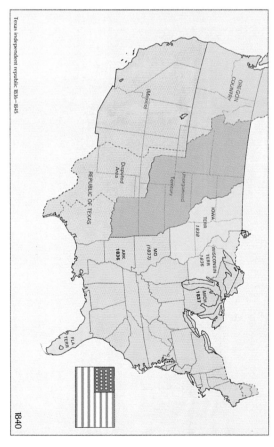

Texas independent republic 1836–1845

1840

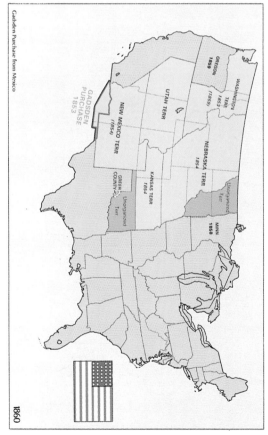

Gadsden Purchase from Mexico

1860